encyclopedia of

# mission and missionaries

## ROUTLEDGE ENCYCLOPEDIAS OF RELIGION AND SOCIETY

David Levinson, *Series Editor*

**The Encyclopedia of Millennialism and Millennial Movements**

Richard A. Landes, *Editor*

**The Encyclopedia of African and African-American Religions**

Stephen D. Glazier, *Editor*

**The Encyclopedia of Fundamentalism**

Brenda E. Brasher, *Editor*

**The Encyclopedia of Religious Freedom**

Catharine Cookson, *Editor*

**The Encyclopedia of Religion and War**

Gabriel Palmer-Fernandez, *Editor*

**The Encyclopedia of Religious Rites, Rituals, and Festivals**

Frank A. Salamone, *Editor*

**The Encyclopedia of Pentecostal and Charismatic Christianity**

Stanley M. Burgess, *Editor*

**The Encyclopedia of Religion, Communication, and Media**

Daniel A. Stout, *Editor*

**The Encyclopedia of Mission and Missionaries**

Jonathan J. Bonk, *Editor*

# encyclopedia of
# mission
# and
# missionaries

**Jonathan J. Bonk,** Editor

*Religion and Society*
A Berkshire Reference Work

# ROUTLEDGE
### New York   London

Published in 2007 by

Routledge
270 Madison Avenue
New York, NY 10016
www.routledge-ny.com

Published in Great Britain by Routledge
2 Park Square
Milton Park, Abingdon
Oxon OX14 4RN
www.routledge.com

A Berkshire Reference Work
Routledge is an imprint of Taylor & Francis Group.

10 9 8 7 6 5 4 3 2 1

**Library of Congress Cataloging-in-Publication Data**

Encyclopedia of mission and missionaries/Jonathan J. Bonk, editor.
    p. cm.—(Routledge encyclopedias of religion and society)
  "A Berkshire Reference work."
  Includes bibliographical references and index.
  ISBN 978-0-415-96948-2 (alk. paper)
  1. Missions—Encyclopedias.   2. Missionaries—
Encyclopedias.   I. Bonk, Jon, 1945–
  BV2040.E48 2007
  266.003—dc22                  2007030597

# Contents

# Editorial Advisory Board

# List of Entries

## List of Entries

# Introduction

Any single volume purporting to be encyclopedic requires an explanation, or at least an excuse. The idea for the *Encyclopedia of Mission and Missionaries*—to take its place among already published volumes in Routledge's Religion and Society series of encyclopedias—was spelled out to me by David Levinson in a letter dated 30 August 2004, excerpted below:

> Our vision for the missions and missionaries volume is to focus on central themes in the missionary enterprise and not cover specific missionaries or missionary organizations, as these are well documented in existing reference works.... We would also like the volume to be interdisciplinary with contributions from missiology, history, and anthropology.

This encyclopedia neither replaces nor replicates any of the numerous dictionaries, encyclopedias, and gazetteers that have been produced on the subject in the major European languages over the past two centuries. Such reference tools are usually geared to religious insiders with an active interest *in* and commitment *to* Christian mission. Rightly perceived as religiously partisan, these immensely useful tools often escape the serious attention of nontheological reference librarians and their clientele. The purpose of this volume, then, is to provide nonspecialists with an overview of a phenomenon without which any attempt to understand, interpret, or assess the major social, economic, and political movements of the past two millennia, and their trajectories into the present, are inadequate, if not futile. For good or for ill, scarcely any human society has been unaffected by Christian mission, whether directly or indirectly.

The ambitious goal of the encyclopedia is attempted by means of a series of wide-ranging essays by reputable scholars, representing disciplines whose scholarly foci naturally intersect with Christian mission history, theory, and practice. The challenge for the editors has been considerable. An editorial judgment has predetermined the length of each contribution by ranking its relative importance in relation to an understanding of the whole field of Christian mission studies. As a rule, the more general the subject, the lengthier the essay. Thus, for example, survey essays on "Africa" or "South America" or "History" are among the lengthier *first tier* articles, as are those, on "Roman Catholic Missions" and "Protestant Missions." Slightly shorter *second tier* entries include major academic disciplines with a highly developed scholarly interest—including publications—in Christian mission, while significantly restricted *third tier* essays include those on research, libraries, bibliography, biography, and so on. *Fourth tier* entries on specific aspects of mission—church planting, family, or money, for example—are generally less than 1,000 words each, and merely try to fill in key gaps. All of these are supplemented by sidebars featuring images and texts that illumine, complement, or otherwise augment the essays.

Headwords have been selected and defined with a view to inviting essays that will range across the entire field of mission studies, pointing beyond themselves to resources that can better satisfy those who wish to pursue research on a given subject. These essays, in turn, have been carefully edited and cross-referenced to ensure a minimum of overlap. Finally, the entire work is thoroughly indexed to ensure access to subthemes and topics addressed or alluded to within the essays. It is only in this sense, then, that this work can be considered encyclopedic.

## Acknowledgements

The bewildering diversity and range of scholarly interest *in* and contributions *to* Christian mission over the past two millennia required the cooperation of a team of scholars with established reputations in missiology, history, anthropology, religion, film and photography, statistics and demographics, and research resources. By helping to determine both the scope and delimitations of the encyclopedia, by suggesting themes and headwords, by proposing contributors and sidebars, and by contributing essays to the present volume, the consulting editors animated and sustained the project from its conception to its completion.

The editorial team, in alphabetical order, includes Dwight Baker, associate director of the Overseas Ministries Study Center in New Haven, Connecticut; Tony Gittins, SVD, Bishop Francis X. Ford, MM, Professor of Missiology at the Catholic Theological Union in Chicago; Rosalind Hackett, distinguished professor in the humanities and professor of religious studies in the Department of Religious Studies at the University of Tennessee, Knoxville; Todd Johnson, director of the Center for the Study of Global Christianity at Gordon-Conwell Theological Seminary in Massachusetts; Lalsangkima Pauchua, from Mizoram, associate professor of the history and theology of mission at Asbury Theological Seminary in Wilmore, Kentucky; Dana Robert, professor of missions and church history at Boston University; Martha Smalley, research services librarian at the Yale Divinity School Library in New Haven, Connecticut; and Jack Thompson, director of the Centre for the Study of Christianity in the Non-Western World at the University of Edinburgh in Scotland.

I am honored, and readers may be reassured, by their association with the enterprise. While they must not be reproached for any of the conspicuous shortcomings inevitable in such a compressed yet ambitious work, without their wise counsel and open-handed assistance, the encyclopedia as it is would have been greatly diminished. Finally, I would be ungrateful indeed were I not also to thank David Levinson, Cassie Lynch, and Scott Eldridge at Berkshire Publishing Group for their tireless work in preparing the volume for Routledge.

JONATHAN J. BONK

Executive director, Overseas Ministries Study Center
Editor, *International Bulletin of Missionary Research*
Project director, *Dictionary of African Christian Biography*

# List of Contributors

**Adeney, Frances S.**
Louisville Presbyterian Theological Seminary
*Sociology*

**Adogame, Afe**
University of Edinburgh
*African Independent Churches*
*Indigenous Religions*

**Ahn, Kyo Seong**
Cambridge University
*Asia, East*

**Akinade, Akintunde E.**
High Point University
*Translation*

**Álvarez, Carmelo**
Christian Theological Seminary
*Caribbean*

**Anderson, Allan H.**
Graduate Institute for Theology and Religion
*Pentecostal and Charismatic Movements*

**Anderson, Gerald H.**
Independent Scholar
*Biography*
*Professional Associations*

**Baker, Dwight P.**
Overseas Ministry Study Center
*Commerce*

**Barrett, David B.**
Independent Scholar
*Statistics*

**Barringer, Terry**
Cambridge University Libraries
*Journals*

**Benson, Linda**
Oakland University
*Asia, Central*

**Bliese, Richard H.**
Luther Theological Seminary
*Liturgy*

**Bonk, Jonathan J.**
Overseas Ministries Study Center
*Money*

**Boshoff, Willem S.**
University of South Africa (UNISA)
*Archaeology*

**Breen, John**
School of Oriental and African Studies
*Shinto*

**Brett, Edward T.**
LaRoche College
*Latin America*

## List of Contributors

**Burrows, William R.**
Orbis Books
*Dialogue*
*Roman Catholic Church*
*Secularism, Atheism*

**Choi, Hyaeweol**
Arizona State University
*Gender*

**Clouse, Robert**
Indiana State University
*Millinarianism*

**Cook, Richard**
Trinity College
*Fundamentalism*

**Covell, Ralph R.**
Denver Seminary
*China*

**Daniel, William**
Emory University
*Internationalism*

**Davies, Noel A.**
Welsh National Centre for Ecumenical Studies
*Ecumenism*

**Deats, Richard**
Independent Scholar
*Pacifism*

**Denis, Philippe**
University of KwaZulu-Natal
*African Traditional Religion*
*Oral History*

**Dries, Angelyn**
St. Louis University
*Missionary Vocation and Service*
*Religious Communities*

**Ebel, Jonathan**
University of Illinois, Urbana-Champaign
*War*

**Escobar, Juan Samuel**
Palmer Theological Seminary
*Revolution*

**Friesen, Randy**
MBMS International
*Short-term Missions*

**Gallman, Andrew**
Houghton College
*Bible Translation*

**Gibbs, Eddie**
Fuller Theological Seminary
*Church Growth Movement*

**Gittins, Anthony**
Catholic Theological Union
*Culture*

**Glazier, Stephen D.**
University of Nebraska, Lincoln
*Racism*

**Gornik, Mark**
City Seminary of New York
*Urban Mission*

**Grafton, David D.**
Evangelical Theological Seminary in Cairo
*Coptic Church*

**Grundmann, Christoffer**
Valparaiso University
*Medicine*
*Sickness and Healing*

**Hartley, Ben**
Palmer Theological Seminary
*Pietism*

**Hayes, Stephen**
Orthodox Society of St. Nicholas of Japan
*Ethiopianism*

**Heim, S. Mark**
Andover Newton Theological School
*Pluralism*

**Hexham, Irving**
University of Calgary
*Jehovah's Witnesses*
*Religious Studies*

**Higgins, Susan**
Milligan College
*Linguistics*

**Hilliard, David**
Flinders University
*Oceania*

**Hofmeyr, J. W.**
University of Pretoria
*Monasticism*

**Hunter III, George**
Asbury Theological Seminary
*Celtic Missions*

**Ingleby, Jonathan**
Redcliffe
*Orientalism*

**Irwin, Eunice**
Asbury Seminary
*Apologetics*

**Jenkins, Paul**
University of Basel
*Photography*

**Johnson, Todd M.**
Center for the Study of Global Christianity
*Martyrdom*
*Missiometrics*

**Jongeneel, Jan A.**
Universiteit Utrecht
*Europe*
*Terminology*

**Kalu, Ogbu**
McCormick Theological Seminary
*Political Economy*

**Kim, Kirsteen**
University of Birmingham
*Theology*

**King, Roberta**
Fuller Theological Seminary
*Music and Ethnomusicology*

**Kollman, Paul V.**
University of Notre Dame
*Slavery*

**Kovacs, Abraham**
Independent Scholar
*Counter Reformation*
*Protestant Churches*

**Kreider, Alan**
Mennonite Biblical Seminary
*Ancient Church*
*Christendom*

**Lewis, Bonnie Sue**
University of Dubuque Theological Seminary
*Native Americans*

**Lodwick, Kathleen**
Pennsylvania State University
*Opium*

**Lutz, Jessie G.**
Independent Scholar
*Conversion*
*Education—Religious, Theological*

**Marten, Michael**
Independent Scholar
*Middle East*

**Maxey, James**
Lutheran School of Theology
*Orality*

**Maxwell, David**
Keele University
*Empire*

**McConnell, Douglas**
School of Intercultural Studies
*Children, Youth, and Missions*
*Sex Trade*

**McGee, Gary B.**
Assemblies of God Theological Seminary
*Miracles*

**Mobley, Kendal P.**
Center for Global Christianity and Mission
*Social Gospel*

## List of Contributors

**Moreau, A. Scott**
Wheaton College Graduate School
*Internet*

**Morgan, David**
Valparaiso University
*Materiality*

**Morrison, Hugh**
University of Waikato
*Parachurch*

**Norris, Frederick**
Emmanuel School of Religion
*Nestorians*

**Ojo, Matthews A.**
Obafemi Awolowo University
*Reverse Mission*

**Oladipo, Caleb**
Baptist Theological Seminary at Richmond
*Paternalism*
*Philosophy*

**Pachuau, Lalsangkima**
Center of Theological Inquiry
*Conciliar Missions*

**Padilla, Rene**
Kairos Foundation
*Liberation Theology*

**Pankratz, James N.**
Conrad Grebel University College
*Militarism*

**Park, Timothy**
Fuller Seminary
*Church Planting*

**Phan, Peter C.**
Georgetown University
*Asian Theology*

**Pierson, Paul E.**
Fuller Theological Seminary
*Central America*
*Development*

**Pongracz, Tricia**
Museum of Biblical Art
*Art*

**Provost-Smith, Patrick**
Harvard Divinity School
*Conquest*

**Ross, Cathy**
Crowther Centre for Mission Education
*Family*

**Roxborogh, John**
Knox College
*Asia, Southeast*
*Technology*

**Rutt, Douglas**
Concordia Theological Seminary
*New Religious Movements*

**Sawatsky, Walter**
Associated Mennonite Biblical Seminary
*Peace Churches*
*Russia*

**Scherer, James**
Lutheran School of Theology at Chicago
*Moratorium*
*Reformation*

**Schmidt, Alvin**
Illinois College
*Civilization*

**Scott, Jamie**
York University
*Fiction*
*Film*

**Seitz, Jonathan**
Princeton Theological Seminary
*Partnership*

**Seton, Rosemary**
University of London, SOAS
*Archives*

**Shea, Paul**
Houghton College
*Environment*
*Sports*

**Shenk, David W.**
Independent Scholar
*Prayer*

**Shenk, Wilbert**
Fuller Theological Seminary
*Enlightenment*
*Mission Methods and Strategy*
*Theory—Catholic, Protestant, Evangelistic*

**Shorter, Aylward**
Missionaries of Africa
*Inculturation*

**Skreslet, Stanley H.**
Union Theological Seminary
*History*

**Smalley, Martha**
Yale Divinity School
*Reference Tools*

**Sogaard, Viggo B.**
Fuller Theological Seminary
*Media and Mass Communications*

**Stackhouse, Max**
Princeton Theological Seminary
*Globalization*
*Human Rights*

**Stamoolis, James J.**
Trinity International University
*Orthodox/Coptic Missions*

**Staples, Russell**
Andrews University
*Millennialism and Adventism*

**Stewart, David**
Luther Seminary
*Liberalism*

**Stuehrenberg, Paul F.**
Yale Divinity School Library
*Libraries*

**Svelmoe, William**
St. Mary's College
*Faith Missions*

**Taylor, William**
WEA Missions Commission
*Training*

**Thomas, Norman**
Independent Scholar
*Bibliography*

**Thompson, Todd**
Emmanuel College, University of Cambridge
*Evangelicalism*

**Vadakumpadan, Paul**
Independent Scholar
*India*

**Van Gelder, Craig**
Luther Seminary
*North America*
*Postmodernism*

**Vogt, Peter**
Moravian Church
*Moravians*

**Walsh, Michael**
Heythrop College
*Crusades*

**Ward, Kevin**
University of Leeds
*Africa*
*Revival*

**Whiteman, Darrell**
E. Stanley Jones School of World Mission and
    Evangelism
*Contextualization, Models of*

**Widmer, Kurt**
Independent Scholar
*Mormonism*

**Witmer, Andrew C.**
University of Virginia
*Criticism*
*Exploration*

**Woodberry, Dudley**
Fuller Theological Seminary
*Islam*

List of Contributors

**Woodberry, Robert D.**
University of Texas at Austin
*Economics*
*Modernity*
*Politics*

**Wright, Christopher**
Langham Partnership International
*Bible*
*Ethics*

**Yates, Timothy**
Independent Scholar
*Mission Conferences*

**Young, Richard**
Princeton Theological Seminary
*Buddhism*

## Africa

Emphasis on the great missionary movement of the nineteenth century sometimes gives the impression that Africa was one of the last continents to be evangelized and that missionary work was largely undertaken by Europeans and North Americans. This seriously misrepresents the state of affairs. Orthodox Christianity flourished in northeast Africa for more than a millennium before the onset of the Western missionary endeavor. The Acts of the Apostles records a story of the conversion of an Ethiopian (or Nubian) official by the evangelist Philip. This comes in the chapter before Paul, the apostle to Europe, is introduced. A flourishing Christian community emerged early in Egypt, in the Greek-speaking metropolis of Alexandria. From there it spread into the countryside of Egypt, where monasticism was born. Monks were to be important as missionaries in other parts of Africa, just as they were to be for the evangelization of other parts of the world. In Nubia (modern Sudan) and Ethiopia, monks from Byzantium and Syria were crucial for the establishment of Christianity. Eventually Christianity died out in Nubia, after a long attrition in the face of Islam. But in Egypt and in Ethiopia Christianity survived: in Egypt as a minority within an Islamic state, in Ethiopia as the core faith of the kingdom. Ethiopia's *abuna* (patriarch) was until the twentieth century an Egyptian monk, but the church itself developed as an autonomous and distinctive form of Orthodox Christianity, based around the Amhara people and culture, but with a missionary impetus, particularly among the Oromo people.

## Catholic Mission

Catholic religious orders became active in Africa during the Middle Ages, associated particularly with Portuguese expansionism, especially in Angola and Mozambique. Unfortunately, Portuguese involvement in the slave trade often undermined the missionary message and made it appear an alien and destructive force. The one area where this was partially overcome was the Congo, where the baptism of the *manikongo* (king) in the late fifteenth century created an African Christian kingdom which was not simply dependent on Portuguese influence and which strenuously tried to mitigate the effects of the slave trade. In the sixteenth century the Congo even produced its own indigenous bishop, Henrique, a son of the king. Italian Capuchin friars were particularly important in serving the church in the Congo in the seventeenth and eighteenth centuries, although by this time the disintegration of the Congo state had made the continued existence of a vibrant Christianity precarious in the extreme.

## Evangelical Mission

The revival of missionary activity in Africa was associated with the abolitionist movement undertaken in the second half of the eighteenth century by evangelical Protestants. The decision of the British in 1806 to abolish the slave trade and to actively prevent other countries from participating in the trade gave a new impetus to African evangelization. Part of this new movement was the desire to foster legitimate trade and to encourage new forms of agriculture and commerce on the African continent that would provide a context in which the Gospel could be preached and have some chance of taking root. This task was seen as reparation for previous European Christian involvement in the trafficking of people and as an affirmation of the common humanity of Africans and Europeans. In West Africa, the establishment of Sierra Leone as a "province of freedom" provided an environment in which freed slaves could build their lives anew as a Christian people. Missions in the evangelical tradition—Baptists, the Anglican Church Missionary Society, and the Methodist Wesleyan Missionary Society—established work in Sierra Leone.

In the 1840s, new converts began to evangelize the Yoruba people of Nigeria, from whom many of the freed slaves were descended. The success of European missionary work in nineteenth-century West Africa was largely due to these "Creoles" (freed slaves) who returned as pioneers of both Christian faith and Christian culture (education, commerce, and health). One of the most famous of these Yoruba evangelists was Samuel Ajayi Crowther, who pioneered work in his native Yoruba and also became a missionary on the Niger among the Igbo peoples and the tribes of the delta region. In 1862 Crowther was made a bishop, the first African Anglican to be accorded this honor. Henry Venn, the leader of the Church Missionary Society (CMS), saw in Crowther the fulfillment of his own vision of the euthanasia of mission—the creation of "self-propagating self-governing, self-financing" local churches.

## South Africa

In South Africa the existence and political importance of white settlers meant that opportunities for black initiative in mission work was more circumscribed. The Dutch Reformed Church (DRC) had at first seen itself primarily as the shepherd of the Afrikaner community, preserving distinctive European Christian values amidst the numerous "pagan" peoples of South Africa. As slave owners, Afrikaners did, however, begin to conceive a responsibility for transmitting the faith to Malay slaves and the indigenous people of the western Cape whose societies were beginning to crumble and who were coming into the orbit of Cape Dutch society as dependent servants and workers. At first the baptized were admitted into the DRC as subsidiary members of Afrikaner households. But as this form of patriarchal Christianity eroded (not least because of the British abolition of slavery in the 1830s), a separate Church for Colored People—the Sending (Mission) Kerk—emerged. This early example of the formal segregation of Christians along racial lines was important in the

development of the apartheid ideology which held sway in South Africa in much of the twentieth century.

Dutch Reformed Church responsibility toward autonomous black African people like the Xhosa and the Zulu developed in the late nineteenth century, partly as a result of an evangelical awakening. Before that time Afrikaners had associated missionary work with the abolitionist humanitarian movement of the London Missionary Society (LMS), whose agents, Johannes van der Kemp and John Philip, were at the forefront of condemning slavery and insisting on the legal equality of black people in South Africa. Under LMS influence, geographically separate communities of freed slaves were established. Later in the nineteenth century, Methodists, Presbyterians, Anglicans, Lutherans, the Paris Evangelical Society, and Roman Catholics established work among the Xhosa, Zulu, and Sotho people. Strong educational institutions, such as Lovedale and Fort Hare University, were created by this missionary endeavor. African Christian communities emerged that had a sense of pride in their Christian identity and education. These can be seen as parallel to the west African Creole communities, but in a situation where it was much more difficult to assert an autonomous black African Christian leadership and culture.

## Protestant and Catholic

The modern Protestant missionary movement was characterized by its distance from government and establishments, its reliance on lay voluntary enthusiasm, and the opportunities it offered for service to people who did not belong to elite social groups in their home countries. Missionary work provided women with unprecedented roles—by the end of the nineteenth century women had become the majority of missionaries (either as wives or as single women with professional skills in health or education or evangelism). The renewal of Catholic missions came in the first half of the nineteenth century, a generation after the Protestant initiative, but it also followed this pattern. No longer was Catholic mission associated with the old Portuguese dominance or with the old traditional mission orders (such as Dominicans, Franciscans, and Jesuits). Rather, in postrevolutionary France, where the Catholic Church was no longer part of the establishment, new mission societies were created, which relied largely on the donations of ordinary peasants and recruited priests specifically trained for missionary work who were often from low-status peasant families. The Society of African Mission, the Holy Ghost Fathers, and the White Fathers were predominantly French societies, though they also tended increasingly to embody an international identity, with recruits from Germany, Holland, and Ireland. Women's orders were also established to work in parallel with the missionary orders of priests and brothers.

## East Africa

The final area of Africa to be the focus of missionary attention was East Africa. David Livingstone began his missionary career with the LMS at Robert Moffat's Tswana station of Kuruman in South Africa. From there he launched his increasingly ambitious journeys into central and eastern Africa, encountering societies that were in turmoil because of the Arab slave trade. Missionary endeavors began to create islands of security for freed slaves: Bagamoyo, Zanzibar, and Frere Town, near Mombasa. But the real breakthrough in East Africa came when missionaries arrived at the court of the Kabaka of Buganda in the Great Lakes region in 1877. There they found a well-established and sophisticated centralized society which had already been attracted to Islam, but which was keen to respond to the new opportunities, material and commercial, intellectual and spiritual, offered by Christianity.

However, the remarkable response of Buganda was complicated by the presence of two rival versions of Christianity: Anglican (CMS) and Catholic (White Fathers). The rivalry was a scandal but also an opportunity. The seriousness with which the competing missionaries advocated their versions of Christianity proved attractive to the young Buganda courtiers who heard their message. It resulted in a bitter war of religion in which the Protestants (as the Anglicans were known) seized political power and also in a strong missionary zeal among Catholic and Protestant converts. This was seen both in the willingness of the Uganda martyrs to die for their faith in 1886 and in the enthusiasm with which they became missionary evangelists to other parts of East Africa. In both its Protestant and Catholic versions, Christianity became indigenous in the local culture and society, not only in Buganda, but also in other interlacustrine states such as Rwanda and Burundi.

## Colonialism

The conflict in Uganda was part and parcel of the colonial scramble for Africa which got seriously underway

The view from a mission in downtown Windhoek, Namibia. *Courtesy of istockphoto.com.*

## Ancestors in West Africa

**The following story told by the Ashanti people of Ghana is a good example of just how pervasive and powerful ancestors can be to some African groups.**

The Earth was regarded as possessing a spirit or power of its own which was helpful if propitiated, and harmful if neglected, but the land was also regarded as belonging to the ancestors. It is from them that the living have inherited the right to use it. The farmer's prayer, when he offered his sacrifice of mashed yam and fowl, began: 'Grandfather . . . you once came and hoed here and then you left it to me.' It was because his ancestor had hoed there that he had inherited the right to farm there.

It was believed not only that the ancestors owned the land, but also that they constantly kept watch and saw to it that it was used.

A farmer cut himself while felling trees on his farm at the village of Gyansoso, near Wenchi, and died shortly after he had been conveyed home. The *bosom* (god) of the village, when consulted, declared that the farmer had died because his ancestors who had farmed there before him were dissatisfied with him. He was a greedy person who did not share his food with his relatives, and had even neglected his sacrifices to the ancestors.

Source: Busia, K. A. (Kofi Abrefa). (1951). *The position of the chief in the modern political system of the Ashanti: a study of the influence of contemporary social change on Ashanti political institutions* (p. 43). London: The Oxford University Press for the International African Institute.

after the Berlin Conference of 1886. Missionaries were ambivalent about the role of colonial powers. For much of the nineteenth century they had often preferred to operate without the protection of European colonial power, especially if they were under the aegis of supportive African rulers. But the fight against the slave trade also drove missions into seeking the support of colonial powers to ensure that their settlements of freedom could survive and prosper. Once the scramble got underway, missions often looked to their home country for support. Thus, many of the areas where French Catholic missions had been established were claimed by France (which, while often anticlerical at home, was not averse to supporting French missions). The Belgian Congo and Portuguese territories were less ambivalent in their support of Catholic missionaries, explicitly privileging them over Protestants.

Protestant missions tended to look to British support—one reason for the creation of Nyasaland was the campaigning for Scottish missions for British rather than Portuguese rule in that area. The assumption of British rule in Uganda was closely connected with the importance of the Anglican mission there. Germany Protestant mission activity in the early part of the century had had little cause to look for German political support. But Bismarck vigorously utilized German (largely Protestant) mission presence in Namibia, Tanzania, Togo, and Cameroon to justify the creation of a German empire in Africa. Lutherans remain to this day a strong presence in those countries, even though German colonial rule collapsed in 1918.

Whether or not missions had welcome colonial rule, they almost universally supported it once it had been established, though not necessarily uncritically. Missionaries often saw themselves as the protectors of peoples whose lives had been seriously affected for the worse by colonial rule, especially in countries with a strong white-settler presence: In Kenya, Zimbabwe, South Africa, and Namibia the struggle against apartheid was, to some extent, spearheaded by missionaries. But the Kikuyu (Kenyan) saying "There is no difference between a settler and a missionary" well expresses the danger of Christian mission being closely identified with colonial values, especially in relation to the sensitive issues of land ownership and cultural imperialism.

## Literacy

Protestant missions had always placed a high value on literacy and on the importance of establishing a school system. They succeeded in the colonial period in encouraging governments to support education without trying to establish a rival secular school system in competition with mission schools. This partnership was particularly successful in British Africa, where J. H. Oldham of the International Missionary Council brokered a system by which the British provided grants-in-aid to mission schools in return for their willingness to subject themselves to a regime of inspection by government education departments. Catholics were initially skeptical of subjecting themselves to such a regime. But in view of the primary importance of the school as an agent of evangelization in Africa, they were persuaded by Monsignor Arthur Hurley, appointed the Vicar-Apostolic to Catholic missions throughout British Africa, to accept government grants: "Collaborate with all your power. . . . neglect your churches in order to perfect your schools." Both Catholics and Protestants developed extensive primary school systems.

Protestants were more likely to develop secondary schools that aimed at producing leaders and administrators in secular society, while Catholic efforts at this level tended to aim at producing well-educated local priests. The result was the creation of a strong Protestant laity, who became the force behind the nationalist movement against colonialism and who provided the bulk of the first generation of politicians and civil servants in the independent Africa of the late 1950s and 1960s. Protestant churches also developed strong traditions of local leadership and ordained ministry, often with minimal levels of education. In contrast, Catholics were less likely to encourage participation in nationalist movements, but they did promote a strong core of highly educated clergy who provided the first, impressive generation of indigenous bishops such as Joseph Kiwanuka of Uganda (who became the first African Catholic bishop of modern times in 1939).

## Independence

With independence, Protestant-ordained missionaries diminished rapidly. Missionary educationalists, doctors, and agriculturalists continued to be recruited, but their overall significance for the life of the churches became small. The former Protestant mission churches were keen to assert their independence. In the 1970s, talk of a "missionary moratorium" became a marker of maturity and autonomy. Yet overall, foreign missionary numbers did not diminish. The number of Catholic missionary personnel remained high and often provided the majority of parish priests, although under an indig-

enous bishop. A new factor was the growing presence of American evangelical missionaries, who sometimes attempted to establish new churches and often worked as evangelistic mobilizers in parachurch organizations. This new phenomenon is connected to, but not entirely explained by, the rapid rise of charismatic Christianity in Africa since the 1980s. Often regarded as an example of a new kind of colonial missionary endeavor, Charismatic Christianity is more accurately seen as an indigenous African form of Christianity with a strong local missionary impetus.

Its origins can be traced to the burgeoning of secondary school education in the aftermath of independence and the rise of a vibrant evangelical movement among a new generation of articulate, well-educated people, conversant in English or French, somewhat impatient with the geriocratic hierarchies of the mission-founded churches but equally impatient with the failure of independent African political leaders to establish peace, security, and economic welfare. Modern African Charismatic Christianity, diverse and often contradictory as it is, has attempted to create a new African missionary movement, aiming to complete what was left unfinished by the first missionary movement: to evangelize those parts of Africa not yet reached, to engage in a spiritual struggle with demonic forces (whether of traditional religion or modern secularism), and to supply an optimism of aspiration and opportunity, of material and spiritual well-being, which modern states and the modern global system have so clearly and lamentably failed to provide for Africa.

## The New Missions

Modern Pentecostal-Charismatic Christianity is not the first or only movement in which African Christians have asserted their stamp on the missionary character of African Christianity. There have been a number of spiritual movements in which African initiatives have been dominant. The establishment of the Ethiopian independent church movement at the end of the nineteenth century in west and south Africa was a claim by Africans to ownership of the Christian movement. In the early twentieth century, prophets such as Wade Harris of West Africa, Isaiah Shembe of Zululand, and Simeon Kimbangu of the Congo, gave rise to a diversity of independent Christian churches that claimed Africa for Christianity in ways which were not mediated primarily by Western norms of worship and education. Within the mission-founded churches, movements like the Balokole (East African Revival) have internalized Christian values and presented them in African dress.

After independence, indigenous, inculturated forms of theology and worship have been presented as vital for making Christianity truly speak in African forms of life.

In 1900 fewer than 10 percent of Africans acknowledged themselves Christian. By 2000 nearly 50 percent did so. Islam also saw impressive gains and by 2000 had been adopted by a similar percentage of Africans. A major missionary question for Africa is how these two religions "of the book" can live together, how each can undertake the missionary calling integral to its very being without conflict, violence, or war. This is particularly acute in places like Nigeria and the Sudan, where Christianity and Islam have become bound up with ethnicity and a confrontational communal identity. The other profound missionary question for Africans is how to relate to the traditional world view. Protestant and Catholics have each tended to characterize themselves as modern and progressive, often relegating a traditional understanding of the spirit world to a bygone era. Charismatic Christians (who are present in Protestant and Catholic churches as well as in the newer Pentecostalism) cannot be so dismissive of the traditional spirit world. They acknowledge it, but do so in order to "defeat" it.

Charismatics see the traditional spirit world as the world of "Satan," which must be confronted and challenged by the spirit world of the Gospel. At times African Christians see this confrontation as part of the challenge presented by the secular and dying churches of the north, from whom they first received the Christian message. This view of reverse mission is one of the most profound changes in the contemporary Christian world. But just as the early European and North American missionaries were fundamentally transformed by their encounter with Africa, the African missionary enterprise will also change as it deepens its awareness of the complexity and ambiguity of preaching the Gospel in the post-Christian north. The idea of African Christianity as the preserver of conservative forms of Christian belief and practice does not reflect the ambiguity of its contemporary presence in Africa, nor is it likely to characterize the impact it will certainly have on the decaying residual Christianity of the north.

In Africa itself, African Christians continue to recognize the urgency of the missionary task in their own society, culture, and environment.

KEVIN WARD

*See also* African Independent Churches; Ancient Church; Civilization; Commerce; Conciliar Missions; Coptic Church; Education—Religious, Theological; Pentecostal and Charismatic Movements; Protestant Churches; Racism; Roman Catholic Church; Slavery

## Further Reading

Hoehler-Fatton, C. (1996). *Women of fire and spirit: Faith and gender in Roho religion in western Kenya.* Oxford, UK: Oxford University Press.

Kenyatta, J. (1962). *Facing Mount Kenya.* London: Vintage. (Original work published 1938)

Kiernan, J. P. (1990). *The production and management of therapeutic power in Zionist Churches within a Zulu City.* Lewiston, NY: The Edwin Mellen Press.

Omoyajowo, J. A. (1982). *Cherubim and seraphim: The history of an African Independent Church.* New York: Nok Publishers.

Peel, J. D. Y. (1968). *Aladura: A religious movement among the Yoruba.* London: Oxford University Press.

Sandgren, D. P. (1989). *Christianity and the Kikuyu: Religious divisions and social conflict.* New York: Peter Lang.

Sundkler, B. G. M. (1961). *Bantu prophets in South Africa.* Oxford, UK: Oxford University Press.

Sundkler, B. G. M. (1976). *Zulu Zion and some Swazi Zionists.* Oxford, UK: Oxford University Press.

Turner, H. W. (1967). *African Independent Church* (Vols. 1–2). Oxford, UK: Clarendon Press.

Turner, H. W. (1979). *Religious innovation in Africa: Collected essays on new religious movements.* Boston: G.K. Hall and Co.

Welbourn, F. B. (1961). *East African rebels: A study of some independent churches.* London.

Welbourn, F. B., & Ogot, B. A. (1966). *A place to feel at home: A study of independent churches in Western Kenya.* London: Oxford University Press.

West, M. (1975). *Bishops and prophets in a black city: African Independent Churches in Soweto.* Johannesburg, South Africa: Philip.

# African Independent Churches

African Independent Churches (AICs) represent one of the most significant developments in the transmission and transformation of Christianity in Africa. Coming on the heels of mission Christianity and the earliest traces of indigenous appropriations in the form of Ethiopian churches and revival movements, AICs emerged in sub-Saharan Africa in the 1920s and 1930s. They included the Aladura churches in West Africa, Zionist churches in South Africa, and the Roho churches in East Africa.

What now constitutes an important element of African Christian demography emerged under similar but distinct historical, religious, cultural, social, economic, and political circumstances. Although the AICs are no longer confined to local boundaries, these local environments produced the remarkable vitality of this religious phenomenon in a way that attracted more scholarly attention than anywhere else on the shores of Africa. Their unprecedented growth, particularly in a colonial milieu, evoked wide-ranging political and socioreligious reactions and propelled them into prominence—the AICs have received considerable scholarly attention since the 1940s.

Each AIC has its own worldview, rituals, organizational structure, and religious dynamic. AICs demonstrate a significant, complex variety in terms of their foundation histories, the charismatic personality of their founders and leaders, their belief patterns and ritual structures, their organizational policies, and their geographical distribution. The categorization of these indigenous religious initiatives as "independent," "separatist," "syncretistic," "protest," "nativistic," "tribal," "neopagan," "spiritist," "sectarian," "nationalist," "hebraic," "cultic," "messianic," or "post-Christian," at different levels of their developmental histories, reveals the ideological, political, and religious orientations, and the social climate, that pervaded both scholarship and the public sphere in the precolonial and colonial eras. Bengt Sundkler, a pioneer scholar who engaged systematic exploration of what became popularized as AICs, published a pivotal monograph in 1948, *Bantu Prophets in South Africa*. In it, he distinguishes two types of South African Independent churches, *Ethiopian* and *Zionist*.

Harold Turner, a pioneer and foremost scholar on African Independent Churches, particulary the Aladura in West Africa, defined AICs in the late 1960s as "churches founded in Africa, by Africans and for Africans." While this provisional definition was very useful at the time, it is no longer tenable because of changing demographic profiles and expanding religious geographies. One backlash of the postcolonial reconstruction of African church historiography was the revisiting of the term "independent." Hitherto, these church members were largely seen as political protest groups, pseudoreligious fanatics, and harbingers of nationalism, groups destined to witness their extinction in postindependence Africa. However, the resilience and dynamism that characterized these churches following the political independence of many African states, coupled with their rapid proliferation and splinter formations, forced a reevaluation of this view. The appropriation of alternative terms such as "African Initiated Churches,"

"African Indigenous Churches," "African Instituted Churches," and "African International Churches" suggests that there is still no scholarly consensus as to how to view AICs.

## Patterns of Historical Emergence

Two similar but distinctive patterns characterize the emergence of AICs in the 1920s and 1930s. AICs represent groups that started under the initiative of African leadership, both within and outside the immediate purview of mission churches. The first pattern concerns groups that emerged from within existing mission churches as "prayer bands," "societies," or "bible study classes" and later transformed themselves into churches. In East Africa these included the Nomiya Luo Mission, which severed itself from the Anglican Church in 1914. There were other Luo "schisms," such as the Church of Christ in Africa, which began as an Anglican revival movement called *Johera* or "People of Love" in 1952, and separated itself in 1957; and Mario Legio of Africa, a split from Roman Catholicism. The Agikuyu spirit churches, the *Arathi* (prophets or seers), emerged in Central Kenya during the upheavals of the 1920s.

Daniel Nkonyane and Elias Mahlangu, both from the Afrikaner missionary Le Roux's Zion Apostolic Church, led different *amaZioni* (Zionist churches): Mahlungu founded the Zion Apostolic Church of South Africa in 1917, and Nkonyane founded the Christian Catholic Apostolic Church in Zion between 1912 and 1920. Large, more recent groups in southern Africa include the Zion Christian Church, the Nazirite Baptist Church, and Shona Independent Churches.

The 1918 influenza is the backdrop of the earliest AICs in West Africa, particularly in Nigeria, which share a penchant for prayer, healing, prophecy, visions, and dreams. AICs such as the Aladura started to emerge among the Yoruba of western Nigeria in the mid-1920s. The earliest was the Cherubim and Seraphim (C&S), which existed for several years as an interdenominational society until its formalization as a church in 1925. The Christ Apostolic Church (CAC) resulted from the fusion of the Precious Stone Society (a prayer group within the Anglican Church), the Nigerian Faith Tabernacle, and the Great Revival event of 1930. The nucleus church that became established in 1924 under the triumvirate of Joseph Babalola, Isaac Akinyele, and David Odubanjo commenced as a prayer group within the Anglican Church. The Church of the Lord -Aladura (CLA) emerged from a mission church tradition following the suspension of Josiah Ositelu in 1930 from the Anglican Church.

The Celestial Church of Christ (CCC) represents the second pattern of the emergence of AICs in that it did not sever itself from any existing mainline church nor did it experience any institutional friction and ejection; rather, it emerged independently through the visionary experience and charismatic initiative of Samuel Bilehou Oschoffa, a carpenter turned prophet, in 1947.

One feature that characterizes the nascent histories of the earlier AICs is their stormy encounter with colonial and mission authorities. Because of their pragmatic approach to existential questions of life, their belief in the primacy of the Bible, and their charismatic leaders, AICs soon acquired local appeal and drew clientele away from existing mission churches. This sudden popularity coupled with religious, political, and socioeconomic considerations put them on a collision course with both colonial and mission-church authorities. At the inception of the Aladura churches in western Nigeria, members of mission churches deflected in droves. In return, mission churches criticized the AICs of having too much rapport with indigenous culture, of syncretism, and of what they perceived as an indiscriminate use of charismatic gifts. The AICs responded by accusing mission churches of practicing ambivalent Christianity and idolatry, and dressing their polity and liturgical content in foreign (Western) garb.

The intimate relationship between the colonial and the church-mission authorities was often detrimental to an emerging AIC. The colonial administration frequently displayed a spiteful posture and warned of the danger that such groups could pose to constituted authority. The radicalization of the Arathi and Roho churches took place as early as 1930, with both groups facing criticism from the mission and colonial authorities, partly owing to their emphasis on millennial deliverance and their vehement opposition to the colonial occupation of their land. The Arathi and Roho churches also opposed the missions' denunciation of polygyny and clitoridectomy; rejected Western money, amenities, clothing, and food; and spoke against Western and local beliefs and practices that they perceived as opposed to the true tenets of the Christian faith. Most of the earliest AICs faced harsh repression, but nearly all survived and gradually acquired legitimacy in the postindependence era.

## Personality and Founder Myths

Virtually all AICs trace their emergence to a charismatic figure who claimed to have had a traumatic religious experience. The reenactment of these "sacred narratives" by members was a common feature of an AIC both during and after the demise of the prophet. Isaiah Shembe, the Zulu prophet who founded the *amaNazaretha* Church in South Africa, was variously known as a prophet, divine healer, a messianic figure, a liberator, and a messenger of God. The CCC emerged in Dahomey (Benin Republic) through the charismatic personality of Oschoffa, a "carpenter-turned-prophet," following a visionary experience that he had while marooned in the forest in search of timber.

The historiography of the *Joroho* (People of the Spirit) centers on the prophetic leadership of Alfayo Odongo Mango. Roho members portray Mango today as a temporal and spiritual liberator who introduced the first truly African church. AIC founders are venerated even after their demise, through annual celebrations of remembrance. At the *Sikukuu*, the anniversary of Mango's death, members ritually dramatize the fire in which he died and sing hymns about the beginning of the Roho religion.

## Religious Worldview

AICs lay claim to the Bible as the wellspring of their epistemology; God, Jesus Christ, the Holy Spirit, and myriad angels are central to their belief systems. They demonstrate a pragmatic approach to Christian life through their prayer rituals, and prayers form the core of their spirituality. Their cosmologies reflect their sociocultural contexts—special emphasis is placed on spiritual healing, prophecy, visions and dreams, trance, and exorcism. Central to their worldview is a belief in the acquisition, retention, and manipulation of spiritual power to conquer the myriad evil forces that populate the world. Members accept indigenous explanations for diseases, illnesses, and misfortunes, but reject the modus operandi of traditional healing. Through prayers and elaborate ritual action, members attract the attention, power, and action of benevolent forces (God, Jesus Christ, the Holy Spirit, and the angelic forces) against the malevolent forces.

Because of the tenacity with which AIC members engage in ritual activities, they are often accused of incorporating indigenous cosmological ideas into Christian thought patterns. However, the AICs draw from these cosmologies in a way that is consistent with the Bible and not antithetical to it. To buttress this view, they vehemently refuse any compromise with traditional religion. Polygyny is tolerated but not encouraged by most AICs. Dietary prohibitions are similar in most

A church in rural Ghana, Africa, a remnant of the missionary wave in Ghana during the 1800s and 1900s. *Courtesy of Scott Rodgers/istockphoto.com.*

AICs—pork, alcoholic beverages, drugs, tobacco, and cigarettes are strictly forbidden.

## Rituals

AICs offer a celebrative religion with a prodigious number of ritual symbols. Music, drumming, and dancing characterize liturgical systems—spiritual songs and hymns, and the use of sacred language as a revelatory medium are central. Esoteric liturgical language is a common feature: It is what the Roho refer to as *Dhoroho* (language of the Spirit). The hymn repertoire of AICs such as the CCC, Roho, and Zionist is believed to be revealed to, or channelled through, the pastor-founder, prophets, or prophetesses under the influence of the "Holy Spirit." Although other AICs, such as the C&S and CLA, use revealed songs, they develop their hymn repertory within the structural guidelines and style of the hymnals of mainline Western churches.

The cosmologies and the praxis of AICs rely heavily on ritual objects, including consecrated water, candles, perfumes, incense, palm fronds, hand bells, staffs, spears, girdles, crosses, and consecrated oil. Important ritual practices include sacred numerology, the invocation of psalms, and the appropriation of esoteric language in prayers and hymns. The *amaZioni* refer to their staff literally as *isiKhali* (a weapon), symbolizing the power to ward off demons and evil forces. *Ida* (palm fronds) in Aladura symbolize the spiritual "sword." Sanctified water is significant for therapeutic and prophylactic functions, and it assumes a potent force as a symbol for purification and for chasing away malicious spirits.

Numerology and color symbolism play crucial parts and vary from one AIC to another. AICs are easily distinguished by the spiritual regalia worn by members, although the color varies from one group to another. The use of white garments (*soutane* or cloth of the spirit) is typical for the *amaZioni* and the CCC, symbolizing the outward purity of members as a projection of inner sanctity. CCC members even walk barefooted so long as the *soutane* is worn. The Arathi are noted for long white robes and white turbans. Other AICs use white garments in addition to colored garments and the barefoot requirement applies only within the church precincts. Some newer Zionist churches wear other colors than white. The red garment of the *emaJerikho* (Church of Jericho) in Swaziland relates to their claim to possess a special power with which to fight malevolent forces. Color symbolism also applies to other concrete objects such as candles. Because ritual symbols help members to focalize the benevolent powers, they are frequently employed and given many symbolic meanings.

## Ritual Space

Sacred space transcends the traditional church building of the mission churches. Mountains, rivers, and groves have been sacralized and transformed for ritual reenactment. Sacred cities are common features of AICs. Shembe established the Zion Centre on a holy mountain, the *Ekuphakameni,* and another sacred village, the *Inhlangakazi,* where both followers and nonadherents flock for pilgrimage, festivals, healing, and the rejuvenation of spiritual power. Ogere, Oshitelu's hometown, represents CLA's holy city and has become the site for commemorating the annual Mount Taborah Festival. Imeko, the hometown of Oschoffa, hosts the "Celestial City" or "New Jerusalem" on earth, but also becomes a pilgrimage site. The Wakkerstroom (Rapid Stream) becomes the "Jordan" of Zulu Zionism and represents the "source of the living waters." The *Joroho* converge annually on Ruwe and Masanda for the *Sikunuu mar Raper* (Celebration of Remembrance) to worship and celebrate the bravery of their martyrs in the 1934 *mach.* The *Joroho* established rites that reinforce the sanctity of Musanda and constructed permanent graves for Roho pioneers in the vicinity.

AICs celebrate rituals of passage—birth, baptism, marriage, anointment, death, and burial—to create renewal in the life cycle. There are also rites associated with major festivals, seasonal changes, individual achievements, and sanctity, in the case of women. Ritual symbolism and reenactment resonate with indigenous worldviews, although recourse is also made to the Bible. Ritual space within the AICs is in flux, and members have unlimited access because prophets and prophetesses are in attendance to diagnose and explain misfortunes and problems, while at the same time predicting, controlling, and procuring spiritual remedies for other members and clients.

## Organizational Structure

AICs vary in their organizational systems, which depend on the extent of their local appeal and the demographic and cultural composition of their membership. The hierarchical structures are usually very complex, with specific functions carved out for prophets, prophetesses, visionaries, dreamers, elders, teachers, and other functionaries. Most founders and leaders demonstrate their charisma through the spiritual and administrative roles they play, and through their father-figure status. The internal organization of AICs also provides a complex hierarchical structure that varies from group to group. The different ranks within the hierarchy are clearly distinguished by their robes and regalia. The role of prophets, prophetesses, visionaries, and dreamers is central in AIC ritual systems because members believe that they explain, predict, and control events. Their ability to prognosticate future events and provide a panacea for existential

problems resembles the functions of diviners and healers in indigenous cosmologies. In both worldviews, the prophet/prophetess and the traditional healer/diviner are pivotal forces for order and rapprochement between the human and the supersensible cosmos.

## Global Significance

Each AIC emerged in a specific cultural milieu and the context largely shaped its worldview. However, as each group started to witness vertical and horizontal growth, it transcended its immediate geo-ethnic and cultural boundaries. The *amaZioni* spread beyond the Zulu to the Shona and the Swazi, as well as to other ethnic groups in South Africa. The Roho and Arathi churches made footprints in the Kikuyu and Luo regions and beyond, to other parts of East Africa. The Aladura, which had its origin in western Nigeria, made inroads into other parts of Nigeria, the west, and central African sub-regions.

There has been a growing internationalization of some AICs through migration and through new evangelistic strategies that bring them into a global context. Since the 1960s, the Aladura churches have planted branches in Europe, America, and other parts of the world.

The appropriation of media technologies, such as the Internet, has become a popular strategy for transmitting religious ideologies and recruiting new members. More than the Roho and the Zionists, the Aladura membership structure is relatively mixed, and the non-Yoruba membership proportion is remarkably high.

AICs have also been involved in local, regional, national, and intercontinental ecumenical networks. In 1957, the Zionists came under a national umbrella, the Zion Churches in South Africa. The Aladura churches are affiliated with national ecumenical bodies such as the Christian Association of Nigeria (CAN) and the Christian Council of Nigeria (CCN) and have founded the Nigerian Association of Aladura Churches (NAAC). At the continental level, most AICs are members of the Organisation of African Independent Churches (OAIC). Through association with worldwide ecumenical movements such as the World Council of Churches (WCC), AICs such as the CLA and the Kimbangu church are increasingly assuming a global outlook.

Afe Adogame

## Further Reading

Adogame, A. (1999). *Celestial church of Christ: The politics of cultural identity in a West African prophetic-charismatic movement.* Frankfurt am Main, Germany: Peter Lang.

Baeta, C.G. (1962). *Prophetism in Ghana*. London: SCM.

Barrett, D. (1968). *Schism and renewal in Africa: An analysis of six thousand contemporary religious movements*. Nairobi, Kenya: East African Publishing House.

Daneel, M. L. (1974). *Old and new in southern Shona independent churches* (Vol. 1). The Hague, Netherlands: Mouton

Daneel, M. L. (1987). *Quest for belonging: Introduction to a study of African Independent Churches*. Gweru: Mambo Press.

Fogelqvist, A. (1986). *The red-dressed Zionists: Symbols of power in a Swazi independent church*. Uppsala: Uppsala Research Reports in Cultural Anthropology.

Githieya, F. K. (1997). *The freedom of the spirit: African indigenous churches in Kenya*. Atlanta, GA: Scholars Press.

Hoehler-Fatton, C. (1996). *Women of fire and spirit: Faith and gender in Roho religion in Western Kenya*. Oxford, UK: Oxford University Press.

Kenyatta, J. (1962). *Facing Mount Kenya*. London: Vintage. (Original work published 1938)

Kiernan, J. P. (1990). *The production and management of therapeutic power in Zionist churches within a Zulu city*. Lewiston, New York: Edwin Mellen Press.

Omoyajowo, J. A. (1982). *Cherubim and seraphim: The history of an African Independent Church*. New York: Nok Publishers.

Oosthuizen, G. C. (1967). *The theology of a South African Messiah*. London: Brill

Oosthuizen, G. C. (1968). *Post-Christianity in Africa: A theological and anthropological study*. London: C. Hurst.

Oosthuizen, G. C., & Hexham, I. (Eds.). (1992). *Empirical studies of African independent/indigenous churches*. Lewiston, New York: Edwin Mellen Press.

Oosthuizen, G. C. (1992). *The healer-prophet in Afro-Christian churches*. Leiden, Netherlands: E.J. Brill.

Peel, J. D. Y. (1968). *Aladura: A religious movement among the Yoruba*. London: Oxford University Press.

Sandgren, D. P. (1989). *Christianity and the Kikuyu: Religious divisions and social conflict*. New York: Peter Lang.

Sundkler, B. G. M. (1961). *Bantu prophets in South Africa*. Oxford, UK: Oxford University Press.

Sundkler, B. G. M. (1976). *Zulu Zion and some Swazi Zionists*. Oxford, UK: Oxford University Press.

Turner, H. W. (1967). *African Independent Church* (Vols. 1–2). Oxford, UK: Clarendon Press.

Turner, H. W. (1979). *Religious innovation in Africa: Collected essays on new religious movements*. Boston: G.K. Hall.

Welbourn, F. B. (1961). *East African rebels: A study of some independent churches*. London: SCM.

Welbourn, F. B., & Ogot, B.A. (1966). *A Place to feel at home: A study of independent churches in western Kenya*. London: Oxford University Press.

West, M. (1975). *Bishops and prophets in a black city: African independent churches in Soweto*. Johannesburg, South Africa: Philip.

# African Traditional Religion

The expression "African traditional religion," which some authors prefer to use in the plural, sometimes leads to confusion. If religion means a set of beliefs and practices relating to a transcendental reality, a definition that applies to the major world religions, justice is not done to traditional African religion, whose purpose is to develop a relationship of trust with the ancestors of the clan or the tribe so as to prevent misfortune, accidents, and disease.

African traditional religion is pragmatic. Devoid of dogmatism, its aim is to ensure health, wealth, and harmony within the group. It is practiced in the homestead under the aegis of the head of the household. By carrying out specified rites, communication with the ancestors is established. Depending on the circumstances and according to a ritual that has been decided upon, an ox, a goat, or a sheep will be slaughtered. Another way of establishing contact with the ancestors is by giving them something to drink (a portion of beer poured into a corner of the room) or something to eat (a portion of the slaughtered animal that has been reduced to ash in the fire). Appropriate words, recited aloud, accompany the different rituals. Members of the family make attempts to enter into contact with the ancestors when they celebrate rites of passage (birth, initiation to adulthood, marriage, and death) or when the cohesion of the family is threatened by war, illness, or internal conflict.

The ancestors accompany their descendants and ensure their protection, but if these do not show respect, misfortune will befall them. The rituals performed to appease the ancestors are an acknowledgment that the intensity of power lies beyond the living and beyond nature. A disease in Africa does not happen accidentally. It is believed to be caused by other human beings or ancestors or evil spirits. The cause is always some person, living or dead.

In the African worldview, ancestors are the ultimate source of power. They are the mysterious that gives or destroys life. Ancestral power represents a spiritual reality beyond the control of ordinary human beings and as such can be a source of dread. Healing is effected by tapping into this font of power. Traditional healers have access to the power of ancestors. They reveal the source of suffering and often locate it in the displeasure of the ancestral spirits. Ancestor veneration is the African way of confronting and living with the mystery of evil and suffering. It is how Africans celebrate and communicate with the mystery of the sacred it their midst.

## Blurred Distinctions

Distinctions that are commonly made in the West, such as those between sacred and profane or religion and medicine, do not always make sense in Africa. African traditional religion is not an institutionalized religion. It has no priests, cult, or doctrine. It is true that certain people have privileged access to the ancestors—in Zulu society, for example, these mediators are called *sangomas* (diviners), *inyangas* (traditional healers), and *abathandazi* (spiritual mediators)—but the training of these experts and their manner of functioning is fundamentally different from that of priests, rabbis, and imams. They owe their skills to their special relationship to the ancestors, not to professional training. To see African traditional religion as a religion in the true sense of the word, it is necessary, as David Chidester suggests, to adopt a wider and more polysemic definition of the word religion.

The term *traditional* is equally problematic. Nothing is less rigid than traditional African religion. Its strength consists precisely in its ability to adapt. It is perpetually being reinvented, to use an expression brought into current usage by Eric Hobsbawm and Terence Ranger. Today's rituals to the ancestors incorporate modern concepts and experiences. It should also be noted that African traditional religion adopts different forms according to regions, whether it be the rituals used to address the ancestors or the way in which a supreme being, who fulfills the function of a super-ancestor, is conceived.

## Christian Faith and African Traditional Religion

Is it possible to embrace the Christian faith without betraying one's African identity? A colonial product, the religion of the missionaries is in essence suspect. Can an authentic Christianity grow in Africa despite its contested origin? This question is hotly debated. Theologians such as John Mbiti, Jean-Marc Éloi, Kwame Bediako, Tinyiko Maluleke, and Buti Tlhagale, to name only a few, have tried to think through the relationship between the Christian faith and the African worldview for more than thirty years. African Christians understand the African worldview because they are part of it. During the day, many people dissociate themselves from African traditional religion, but at night they consult traditional healers and attend the healing sessions of the indigenous churches. They feel ill at ease because they belong to both the traditional and the Christian worlds. Whether they be opposed to the African customs or whether they are attempting to include them in

their religious practice, reference to ancestral religion is unavoidable.

Some Christians maintain that it is impossible to be loyal to both worlds. Christ and the ancestors are two different spiritual authorities. From a Christian point of view, God is the father of both the living and the dead. He is revealed as the decisive reference point—not the ancestors. Christ is the cardinal source of healing power. The living are offered the freedom of the children of God, free from the inordinate fear of the world of the ancestors and free from the evil spirits that roam about in the villages and in the cities.

The challenge facing the churches is to engage directly with the worldview of the people to whom the gospel is preached. The belief in the powerful influence of the ancestors will not be reduced by simply demoting them to a lower rank in the hierarchy of powers. "The new truth," Tlhagale (2006, 16) observes, "has to engage the old truth in its limitedness, otherwise the African soul will have been ripped of its heart and rendered incapable of accepting a new heart. The new truth has to be articulated in such a way that human experience is not deprived of its own culturally determined way of self-expression and yet at the same time it should allow for the transformation and purification of the old truth brought about by the life-giving power of the gospel."

PHILIPPE DENIS

## Further Reading

Bediako, B. (1990). *Jesus in African culture: A Ghanaian perspective*. Accra: Asempa.

Berglund, A.-I. (1976). *Zulu thought-patterns and symbolism*. London: C. Hurst.

Chidester, D. (1996). *Savage systems: Colonialism and comparative religion in South Africa*. Cape Town: University of Cape Town Press.

Denis, P. (2004). African traditional religion and Christian identity in a group of Manyano leaders. *Missionalia, 32*(2), 177–189.

Éloi, J. M. (1988). *My faith as an African*. New York: Orbis.

Harvey, G. (Ed.). (2000). *Indigenous religion: A companion*. London: Cassell.

Hobsbawm, E., & Ranger, T. (Eds.). (1992). *The invention of tradition*. Cambridge, UK: Cambridge University Press.

Maluleke, T. (1996). Black and African theologies in the new world order. A time to drink from our own wells. *Journal of Theology for Southern Africa, 96*, 3–19.

Platvoet, J. G. (1993). African traditional religions in the religious history of mankind. *Journal for the Study of Religion 6*(2), 29–48.

Tlhagale, B. (2006). The Gospel seed on the African soil. *Worldwide: The church in Southern Africa open to the world*, 16(2), 13–16.

# Ancient Church

The scale and pace of the growth of the "ancient church"—the church in the generations after the apostles and before the reign of the emperor Constantine (306–337 CE)—were remarkable. Because it grew with little emphasis upon missions or missionaries, it has been perennially fascinating to practitioners and scholars of mission.

From a handful of messianic believers on Pentecost, the church within the Roman Empire had come to have approximately six million adherents by the early fourth century—one-tenth of the imperial populace, unevenly scattered but primarily urban. This growth took place despite the fact that the church was illegal and there were occasional outbreaks of persecution. (During this period, its growth may have been of comparable speed to that of the church in the Persian Empire, which was tolerated.)

Why did the ancient church in the Roman Empire grow so rapidly despite disincentives? It is not easy to say, because the early Christian sources do not refer to categories of explanation that occur in later Christian missionary expansion texts. For example, the early Christian writers did little to develop a theology of mission: "The scarcity of reflection about mission remains astonishing" (Brox 1982, 211), and the early Christian leaders left almost no records of attempts to mobilize believers for missionary activity. Surviving early Christian prayers rarely pray for the conversion of pagans, and collections of early Christian admonitions do not urge believers to engage in evangelistic outreach.

In the first three centuries, there were only two missionaries whose names we know—Pantaenus of Alexandria, who went to India, and Gregory Thaumaturgus, who returned to his native Pontus as a missionary bishop. Perhaps most astonishing to us, the churches did not grow because their worship was attractive; for reasons of security, from the late first century onwards, the early Christian communities barred non-Christians from their services.

Nevertheless, the ancient church—which theologized little about mission—grew rapidly. Scholars have pointed to six reasons for this. First, mobility: The early Christians traveled as merchants, emigrants, prisoners, and slaves, and they carried their faith with them. The churches in many places looked back to lay founders who invited others to worship in their houses. Second, miracles: The early Christian communities were reputed to be places of spiritual power, in which healings took place and demonic powers were broken. "Those who have been cleansed [of evil spirits] often both believe and join themselves to the church" (Irenaeus, *Against Heresies*, 2.32.4). Third, martyrdoms: These provided the occasion for the secretive Christians to go public, and their exemplary deaths unsettled onlookers and drew some people to seek membership in the church.

Fourth, apologetics: From the second century onwards Christian writers produced "apologies," reasoned justifications of Christian faith and practice. These may have reached few pagans, but their impact on the Christian community's mission was considerable; the apologists reminded believers that their convictions were intellectually robust and that their lifestyle was exemplary. Fifth, schools: In Rome, Alexandria, and elsewhere, Christian teachers began programs of catechesis and Christian formation in which they taught biblical writings and the Christian lifestyle, and showed how they compared to pagan alternatives.

The most important reason for the growth of the ancient church is the sixth, lifestyle: The Christian churches met domestically, in tenements and "houses of the church"; because they did not admit outsiders, the typical Christian was of necessity unobtrusive. As one pagan critic noted, the Christians were "a secret tribe that lurks in darkness and shuns the light, silent in public, chattering in corners" (Minucius Felix, *Octavius*, 8.3). Yet this critic, like many others, found Christians intriguing as well as despicable. They typically called themselves "resident aliens," which denoted a lifestyle that was both myterious and distinctive.

Where did non-Christians encounter the distinctive Christians? They found them in daily life—on the stairways of tenement houses, at workplaces, in the women's quarters of large households, in shops, and on the streets. A non-Christian might learn that a person she respected was a Christian and would be intrigued; she might learn that the Christian communities provided free burial for all their members; she might observe that the Christians did not expose their unwanted infants and that they went to rubbish heaps to recover babies (generally girls) whom pagan parents had discarded; she might hear that the Christians prayed for the healing and spiritual liberation of troubled people; she might be astonished at the social inclusiveness and egalitarianism of the Christian communities; she might "experience the way Christians did business" (Justin, 1 *Apology* 16). Early Christian writings give accounts of people of this sort, those who longed to be free from compulsions and bondages and whose encounter with Christians made them think that they, too, could be free. It should be noted that the early Christian communities, like their corps of reticent evangelists, were disproportionately made up of women.

The Christian witness was rooted in the distinctive lifestyle of believers and the practices of their churches. The church developed an intensive catechetical program to prepare candidates for baptism, which served as their entry to a new world. The catechesis taught biblical narratives, practices, and beliefs to form believers whose lives would not give the lie to Christian witness of this new world. One Christian apologist said, "Beauty of life causes strangers to join the ranks...We do not talk about great things; we live them" (Minucius Felix, *Octavius,* 31.7, 38.5). Only when the candidates' lives "shine with virtue before the Gentiles so that they may imitate them and become Christians" were they baptized and welcomed at the eucharistic table (*Canons of Hippolytus* 19). Thereafter the ancient churches' worship practices and communal life attempted to ensure that ordinary believers would embody the Christian mission by the way they lived.

ALAN KREIDER

*See also* Africa; Coptic Church; Monasticism; Nestorians; Orthodox/Coptic Missions

## Further Reading

Brox, N. (1982). Zur christlichen mission in der spätantike. In K. Kertelge (Ed.), *Mission im Neuen Testament* [Christian mission in late antiquity] (pp. 190–237). Freiburg-im-Breisgau, Germany: Herder.

Fox, R. L. (1986). *Pagans and Christians.* San Francisco: Harper & Row.

Green, M. (2002). *Evangelism in the early church* (Rev. ed.). Grand Rapids, MI: Eerdmans.

Harnack, A. von. (1902). *The mission and expansion of Christianity in the first three centuries* (Vols. 1–2, James Moffatt, Trans.). New York: G.P. Putnam's.

Hinson, E. G. (1981). *The evangelization of the Roman Empire: Identity and adaptability.* Macon, GA: Mercer University Press.

Kreider, A. (1999). *The change of conversion and the origin of Christendom, Christian mission and modern culture.* Harrisburg, PA: Trinity Press.

Kretschmar, G. (1974). Das christliche leben und die mission in der frühen kirche [Christian life and mission in the early Church]. In H. Frohnes & U. W. Knorr (Eds.), *Kirchengeschichte als missionsgeschichte: I, die alte kirche* [Church history as mission history] (pp. 94-128). Munich: Chr. Kaiser Verlag.

MacDonald, M. Y. (2003). Was Celsus Right? The role of women in the expansion of early Christianity. In D. N. Balch & C. Osiek (Eds.), *Early Christian families in context: An interdisciplinary approach* (pp. 157–184). Grand Rapids, MI: Eerdmans.

MacMullen, R. (1984). *Christianizing the Roman empire (A.D. 100–400).* New Haven, CT: Yale University Press.

Stark, R. (1996). *The rise of Christianity: A sociologist reconsiders history.* Princeton, NJ: Princeton University Press.

# Apologetics

Apologetics is the dimension of Christian theology that deals with the relation between Christian and non-Christian thought. It promotes the Christian faith amidst opposing philosophies, ideologies, and religions, and thereby defends the Gospel against theological attacks that undermine its claims. Historically, apologetics emerged and remains recognizable today as a branch of theology dedicated to the defense of the divine origin and authority of Christianity.

The term "apologetics" is derived from the Greek *apologia*: defense, refers to an apology—a verbal or written discourse offering arguments and evidences in support that "give an answer," "account for" or "defend" a position or a person. Far from backing down, admitting guilt or regret regarding some belief, the motive sustaining apologetic work is to make clear the grounds on which faith claims are based. Apologetics seeks to remove the obstacles that hinder faith in unbelievers and to provide reasonable answers to questions that raise doubt in the minds of believers.

## Mission Significance

Apologetics parallels the field of mission. "Apologetes" are trained to state their religious beliefs in terms of another religious system in intercultural, interreligious, or interdisciplinary settings without compromising their distinctiveness. Apologetic work manifests an evangelizing aim in its articulation of the Gospel to win new converts and a "discipling" aim in its careful formulation (or reformulation) of truth to help Christians understand their lives. Apologetic practice is essential within the field of mission known as "contextualization" (by evangelical Protestants) or "inculturation" (by Roman Catholics), in which an attempt is made to accommodate the Gospel message to a culture's theological understanding (theological contextualization), to interpret Christian faith in terms of specific cultural practices (cultural contextualization), and to establish local churches (indigenous church).

## History

Christian apologetics began with the founding of the church. The perennial challenge has been to defend and contend for the faith amidst major historical shifts.

### Apostolic Era

Apostolic witness to the life, death, and resurrection of Christ establishes the central claim of the Christian faith—that Jesus is both Jewish Messiah and universal Lord. The theological arguments of the New Testament writers form the foundation of Christian apologetics. Sermons (Acts), discourses of Jesus (John's gospel), histories (Luke and Acts), gospels (Matthew and John), and epistles (to Hebrews and Romans) convey the Gospel to Jews, Greeks, Romans, and "pagans" in culturally specific ways. The Holy Spirit's witness to the truth of the Gospel came through the miracles that accompanied apostolic preaching as a sign of Jesus' resurrection and his life and power.

### Early Church Era

Greek apologist Justin Martyr argued Christ's divinity by calling him the *logos* and stating that the fullness of wisdom and knowledge dwelled exclusively in him. This claim utilized a concept of pagan Greek philosophers who posited that knowledge was given to humans supernaturally through the *logos*. Latin apologist Augustine defended and restated Christianity's hope in God at the time the Roman Empire fell to barbarians. Apologists of this era (Clement of Alexandria, Tertullian, and Origen) also contributed doctrines that defeated heresies.

### Medieval Era

Theology is absent early in this period. The Roman Church, consumed by its recovery and its expansion in the West, abandoned intellectual engagement with non-Christian religions. Scholastics argued the credibility of Christianity, discussing external proofs or empirical merits of the sources, faith, and reason. In contrast, most Christians held to their beliefs, relying primarily upon faith while allowing reason, following Augustine. Anselm advanced the notion that belief was necessary to

understanding; Abelard proposed that human reason could achieve an inchoate faith, preparing the way for faith; and Thomas Aquinas advocated the distinction between naturally knowable religious truths and supernaturally knowable religious truths, thus allowing that at least some part of God's divine revelation is discovered and established using philosophical argument.

### Reformation Era

In reaction to Roman Catholic doctrines maintaining the church's exclusive proprietary role in the salvation of unbelievers, Protestant reformers (such as Martin Luther, John Calvin, and Huldrych Zwingli) held that faith was neither devised nor controlled through human means. Rather, salvation was solely by divine grace. The logic of this premise made apologetic work unnecessary. In place of ecclesial agency, reformers elevated Scripture as the divine source that produced faith through active belief. The distinctive details of Protestant and Catholic apologetics affected mission presuppositions, approaches, and methods.

### Enlightenment Era

Subsequent to the focus on religious renewal (the Roman Catholic Counter-Reformation and the Protestant Reformation) came political changes (the French Revolution, the abandonment of feudalism, and the development of nation-states) that liberated people's minds, allowing them to understand that knowledge should not be based on dogmas alone. By elevating reason above knowledge, the Enlightenment forced Christian apologetic methods to try to justify God and the Gospel through human thought.

### Modern Era

After the Enlightenment, progress via science and technology seemed unlimited. Natural philosophy (from Enlightenment thinking) generated modern field of studies known as the sciences as well as the philosophy of secular humanism. German theologian Friedrich Schleiermacher posited the necessity of further specializations within theology—apologetics to respond to the defects of other belief systems and polemics to protect Christianity from its own deviations. Karl Barth, rejecting the notion that unbelievers could come to faith through rational processes, disputed the need to separate apologetics from dogmatics on the grounds that faith should be argued from a Christian position and not from a philosophy that would undermine it.

Emil Brunner countered by explaining that society had rejected the supernatural and needed the thought forms within the culture (for a "missionary theology") to prepare unbelievers to understand the Gospel. The evangelical movement arose in reaction to the Protestant liberalism that denied Christianity's supernatural claims. Well-known apologists who employed rational arguments and empirical evidence to reinforce supernatural claims such as the deity of Christ, the Resurrection, the problem of evil, and revelation were C. S. Lewis and Josh McDowell. The Pentecostal movement, which originated in a belief that God could re-empower the church for Christian witness, disavowed trust in apologetic arguments, preferring persuasion through oral testimonies and signs of the Holy Spirit.

The Vatican II Council of Roman Catholics adapted church positions to meet the realities of the modern world, which led to further shifts in apologetic positions. The Council asserted (1) that salvation is possible in other religions, (2) that Christian doctrines should be restated through a new method of "foundational theology" that establishes faith on the basis of the reliability of prior sources (revelation, tradition, biblical inspiration, and the Magesterium), and (3) that mission should be practiced in a way that allows mutual participation (inculturation and dialogue) to facilitate faith. Dialogue, a common apologetic strategy in this era, took many forms, all of which were consistent with doctrinal teachings and mission goals.

### Postmodern Era

Skepticism about human progress undermined the certitudes of modernity and created questions about the proper apologetic postures for Christians. An apologist on the cusp of the modern-postmodern shift was Francis Schaeffer whose writings rescued believers from despair by restoring meaning through a fresh understanding of Christianity as a transcendent faith. Postmodern apologists include John Stackhouse, who proposed a "humble apologetics" (relativizing reason and selectively using evidences) for a pluralist environment, and Brian MacLaren, whose apologetic of "entering the Christian story" as a way of knowing the faith is similar to Michael Polanyi's epistemology of personal knowledge.

## Global Challenges

The globalized situation of today's world affects apologetics. Migrations and multiculturalism have trans-formed populations so that any religious stance or combination is possible with regard to faith: fundamentalist, pluralist, humanist, or simply eclecticist. Apologists are without a task until the truth-claims of these "faiths" become discernible. But will Christianity be capable of doing apologetics beyond the paradigm of its own historic revelation—the prophetic disclosure of monotheism—while maintaining its theological integrity? Until now it has remained primarily a religion of the West because of its connection to Jewish monotheism and Greek philosophy. Religious historian Karen Armstrong points the way forward by pointing back to beginnings, to what Karl Jaspers termed the Axial Age, when in four distinct regions the great world traditions that nourish the spiritual life of people today came into being: Confucianism and Daoism, Hinduism and Buddhism, Greek philosophy, and Jewish monotheism.

Developing an interreligious apologetics that can reach other traditions is urgent for Christian mission, as is greater positive engagement with the other monotheistic faiths, Judaism and Islam. Three theologians with mission perspectives in this area are Amos Yong, who posits the capacity of Pentecostalism to become, under Spirit-directed intuition, an apologetic approach successful in transcending boundaries, changing categories, and starting new conversations; David Clark, whose "dialogical apologetics" transfers discourse to the interpersonal level for effectiveness in postmodern times; and Paul Griffiths, whose principle of the "necessity of interreligious apologetics" (NOIA) insists upon preserving intentional clarity in communication, a judgment of alien religious claims, and the restoration of witness as an aspect of representing faith.

Because of its proven capacity to answer questions of faith in the globalizing world, apologetics remains vital to the Christian mission.

Eunice Irwin

### Further Reading

Armstrong, K. (2006). *The great transformation: The beginnings of our religious traditions*. New York: Knopf.

Clark, D. K. (1993). *Dialogical apologetics: A person-centered approach to Christian defense*. Grand Rapids, MI: Baker.

Dulles, A. C. (1999). *A history of apologetics*. San Francisco: Ignatius.

Griffiths, P. (1991). *An apology for apologetics: A study of the logic of interrelgious dialogue*. Maryknoll, NY: Orbis Books.

Lane, W. (1994). *Reasonable faith: Christian truth and apologetics*. Wheaton, IL: Crossway.

MacLaren, B. (2003). *The story we find ourselves in: Further adventures of a new kind of Christian.* San Francisco: Jossey-Bass.

Polanyi, M. (1958). *Personal knowledge: Towards a post critical philosophy.* London: Routledge.

Sire, J. W. (1995). On being a fool for Christ and an idiot for nobody: Logocentricity and postmodernity. In T. R. Phillips & D. L. Okholm (Eds.), *Christian apologetics in the postmodern world.* Downers Grove, IL: InterVarsity Press.

Stackhouse, J. G., Jr. (2002). *Humble apologetics: Defending the faith today.* Oxford, UK: Oxford University Press.

Yong, A. (2005). *The spirit poured out on all flesh: Pentecostalism and the possibility of global theology.* Grand Rapids, MI: Baker Books.

# Archaeology

Archaeology, the discipline primarily interested in the interpretation of material remains from prehistoric and earlier cultures, is not too often associated with missionary studies. Authors interested in mission history mostly resort to archival documents as primary resources for historiography. The archives of mission societies are indeed rich in information on earlier perceptions, experiences and activities, primarily from the side of the missionaries. Very little is known or documented of the perceptions held by those who were on the receiving end of missionary activities. The effect of the contact between missionaries and the communities among whom they worked is to be found not only in reflections of faith and belief, but also in changing customs, building techniques, dress codes, diet, and other cultural expressions.

The writing of the history of Christian missionary encounters is as old as the early church. The Book of Acts in the New Testament reports on the emergence of a distinct Christian identity from within the bosom of Judaism, in vigorous interaction with Helenistic religions and culture, but also in early intro-Christian conflict. An endless stream of documents followed during the subsequent twenty centuries, recording the spread of Christianity across the globe.

Characteristic of the extension of European commercial influence throughout the world after 1450 CE and the ensuing colonial period is that the church and missionaries were actively involved in the process. During this age of exploration maps were drawn, voyages were recorded, continents and unknown peoples were "discovered," and Christianity was actively promoted: a New World was emerging.

## Mission Archaeology as Historical Archaeology

Archaeology is focused on the study of material remains of earlier (often prehistoric) cultures. The main aim of this endeavor is to construct a picture of those cultures. When the cultures belong to the postprehistoric era, a multidisciplinary field of archaeological investigation emerges. This field, known as historical archaeology, shares a special relationship with the formal disciplines of anthropology and history (Orser and Fagan 1995, 14). The unique contribution of historical archaeology is the tangible reconstruction and interpretation of artifacts (such as household and agricultural utensils and buildings) and ecofacts (such as the remains of diet, hunting, and agriculture) that can not be reconstructed from historical sources. In the process a picture emerges of a world of everyday, often unrecorded, aspects of ancient and more recent life.

One of the fields of historical archaeology that attracted much attention toward the end of the twentieth century is mission archaeology. This designation came into use in 1988, when David Hurst Thomas (1988, 73) drew attention to "the burgeoning field of mission archaeology," with reference to an exponential growth in knowledge of the field of European–Native-American interaction.

An example of this knowledge is to be found in Boyd, Smith, and Griffin (1951). Griffin writes about the information he gathered in 1948 during the excavations of the Franciscan mission site of San Luis, near Tallahassee, Florida. He concludes with reference to the Spanish missions of Apalachee: "The picture which emerges is not one of cloistered gardens, tolling bells, and peaceful, idyllic communities. Rather it is one of crude structures and few tools, of poverty and discord, of war and martyrdom; but is a picture of greater interest than the one painted with the brush of romance, for it is related to reality" (Boyd, Smith, and Griffin 1951, 157–158).

Thomas's study was followed a decade later by a survey of North and Mesoamerican mission and archaeological literature. Elizabeth Graham (1998, 25–62), an archaeologist involved in extensive research in Belize, gave credence to Thomas's words in an article titled "Mission Archaeology." In this article she reflects upon two aspects of Christianity and the cultural imagination, viz. the Native American cultural imagination and the cultural imagination of the Europeans. Graham

The Santa Barbara Mission, California. *Courtesy of S. Greg Panosian/istockphoto.com.*

(1998, 28) surmises that "both lines of inquiry can benefit from archaeological input." In her survey she covers five areas (La Florida, the American Southwest/Mexican Northwest, Texas, California and Yukatan, the Maya Lowland of Belize, and Guatamala and Mexico). In each case the unique characteristics of the research and the region are described. Subsequently the contribution of archaeology to a better understanding of the mission layout and material culture change is considered. In the process Graham documented a massive amount of literature relevant to mission archaeology, often not written for the sake of understanding missions, but as sections of larger archaeological projects (Graham 1998, 55–62).

## Ongoing Archaeological Research

Mission archaeology as a branch of historical archaeology is best developed in the southeast and southwest of the United States. The Spanish Roman Catholic mission endeavors in these early contact areas of colonization influenced subsequent political, societal, ecclesiastical, and military developments comprehensively.

The Franciscan missions that were conducted between 1573 and 1763 in Spanish Florida have been the object of thorough investigation during the twentieth century (Milanich 2004a, 313–327). In the process the known colonial history of the states of Georgia and Florida was extended by at least two centuries to reflect history that preceded the British colony of Colonel James Oglethorpe in the eighteenth century (Milanich 2004a, 314), while the curtain of romantic fantasy about the missionary history was simultaneously drawn away.

The Californian coastal landscape is characterized by names that reflect Franciscan missions between 1769 and 1823. These names include San Rafael, San Francisco, San José, Santa Clara, Santa Cruz, Monterey, Soledad, San Louis Obispo, Santa Barbara, Los Angeles, and San Diego (Lightfoot 2004, 283). Publications, museums, and parks to introduce the interested person to the history of early missions abound and are easily accessible on the Internet. The California Mission Studies Association accommodate on their website (www.ca-missions. org) an extensive variety of links to related sites on individual mission stations, archaeological information, as well as various adobes, presidios, pueblos, and ranchos. Characteristic of these resources is the extent to which archaeological information is incorporated in the historiographical material.

At the annual conference of the Society of American Archaeology in 2004, a session was devoted to mission archaeology. Most of the papers read at the session were subsequently published in *Missionalia* (volume 32[3], 2004), the journal of the Southern African Missiological Society. As could be expected, the papers reflected a concentration of research in the southern United States, Mesoamerica, and northern South America. However, a global flavor was added by papers on missions in the Ulithi Atoll in Micronesia, Baffin Island, Canada, and South Africa. The contributions from outside the United States were characterized by extensive archival and documentary material, with less comparative archaeological material, which reflect the novelty of an archeological approach to mission studies in those regions.

## The Way Forward

Missionaries have been active over hundreds of years in all continents of the world and on numerous islands. The growing interest in historical archaeology and the focus on areas of contact between aboriginal peoples and colonizing Europeans almost automatically focused attention on missionary activities and influence. Often the missionaries were part of the colonial era, and in many cases they were among the first settlers in newly occupied areas. The archaeological record has already started to show that cultural influence did not move in one direction. Missionaries influenced people and they were influenced by them. There are notorious cases of missionaries with a feeling of superiority over the people among whom they worked, but also remarkable cases of humility, identification, and an ability and willingness to learn. The challenge for mission archaeology will be to expose the uniqueness of each missionary encounter in order to reflect the social and cultural realities behind the tangible archaeological finds.

WILLEM BOSHOFF

## Further Reading

Boshoff, W. S. (2004). Global conversions: The archaeology of missionary engagements. *Missionalia, 32*(3), 309–312.

Boshoff, W. S. (2004). The Bakopa of Boleu and the missionaries from Berlin: The brief existence of Gerlachshoop, first mission station of the Berlin Missionary Society in the ZAR. *Missionalia, 32*(3), 445–471.

Boyd, M. F., Smith, H. G., & Griffin, J. W. (1951). *Here they once stood: The tragic end of the Apalachee Missions.* Gainesville: University of Florida Press.

Descantes, C. (2004). The martyrdom of Father Juan Cantova on Ulithi Atoll: The hegemonic struggle between Spanish colonialism and a Micronesian island polity. *Missionalia, 32*(3), 394–418.

Elders, J. (2004). *Revealing the past, informing the future: A guide to archaeology in parishes.* London: Church House Publishing.

Graham, E. (1998). Mission archaeology. *Annual Review of Anthropology, 27,* 25–62.

Insoll, T. (ed) (2001). *Archaeology and world religion.* London: Routledge.

Lightfoot, K. G. (2004). Native negotiations of missionary practices in Alta California. *Missionalia, 32*(3), 380–393.

Lycett, M. T. (2004). Archaeology under the bell: The mission as situated history in seventeenth century New Mexico. *Missionalia, 32*(3), 357–379.

Milanich, J. T. (2004). A century of research on the Franciscan missions of Spanish Florida. *Missionalia, 32*(3), 313–331.

Milanich, J. T. (2004). Archaeological evidence of colonialism: Franciscan Spanish missions in La Florida. *Missionalia, 32*(3), 332–356.

Orser, C. E., Jr., & Fagan, B. M. (1995). *Historical archaeology.* New York, NY: HarperCollins College Publishers.

Tarble, K., & Scaramelli, F. (2004). A brief but critical presence: The archaeology of a Jesuit mission in the middle Orinoco (1730-1747). *Missionalia, 32*(3), 419–444.

Thomas, D. H. (1988). Saints and soldiers at Santa Catalina: Hispanic designs for colonial America. In M. P. Leone & P. B. Potter Jr. (Eds.), *The recovery of meaning: Historical Archaeology in the Eastern United States* (pp. 73–140). Washington, DC: Smithsonian Institution Press.

# Archives

Archives relating to the study of Christian missions are to be found in every continent and country where Christian missionaries obeyed Christ's injunction: "Go ye into all the world, and preach the gospel" (Mark 16:15). The bulk of these materials are to be found in centers based in the sending countries of Europe, North America, and Australasia, but they have also accumulated in the mission fields of Africa, Asia, South America, and the Pacific where they constitute the records of many Christian churches today. The need to keep mission directors and supporters in the home bases fully informed of news from the mission fields, and the solemn and visionary purpose of missionary work, have ensured the survival in many metropolitan centers of vast quantities of letters, reports, personal papers, audio-visual materials, and artifacts, as well as published memoirs, travel books, translations, and other materials, long after the fulfillment of their immediate purpose. These exceptionally rich source materials document in considerable detail the encounter between Western missionaries and the lands to which they were sent.

A typical mission archive in one of the sending countries consists of board and committee minutes, papers concerning financial matters, missionary application papers and letters, journals, and reports sent home from the mission field by the missionaries themselves. Alongside these are the records of publishing and publicity departments, including vast quantities of visual materials, especially photographs. Of the different kinds of documentation, probably the largest, and certainly the one most consulted by researchers, is the writing of the missionaries themselves; these writings contain crucial firsthand accounts of the work of the mission, the difficulties experienced, the nature of the country, the customs and beliefs of the local people, the flora and fauna, and climatic conditions, not to mention the sometimes dramatic events unfolding around them. Complementing these official archives are the private personal papers of individual missionaries. Where these are available they form a valuable resource, particularly when set alongside the official record. Missionaries were often more candid in letters home to family members or in personal diaries than they were in official correspondence with society officials. Many personal collections, which often include photographs, oral recordings, and other visual materials, have been made available for research purposes.

Photographs are regarded as a very important component of a missionary archive. Early nineteenth-century missionary magazines and other publications often contained drawings and engravings as a way of educating their readers and stimulating their support. During the last quarter of the nineteenth century, photographs were increasingly used, first as the basis of engravings and subsequently as photographic reproductions. Scholars are turning to these sources not as mere illustrations but as innovative and fertile ways of interpreting the past. Pioneers of this development have been the curators of the Basel Mission archive, which can be directly accessed at http://www.bmpix.org. An ongoing initiative is the Internet Missionary Photographic Archive (IMPA) based at the University of Southern California, which contains digitized images from missionary society photographic collections in Britain, Europe, and North America. This electronic resource is particularly rich in images taken in China between 1870 and 1950 but also includes photographs taken in Africa, India, the Caribbean, and Oceania. IMPA can be accessed at www.usc.edu/isd/archives/arc/digarchives/mission.

Many mission agencies and churches have deposited their archives in libraries and other institutions that are able to provide adequate storage and research facilities. This has been an important trend in many English-speaking countries where institutions such as the School of Oriental and African Studies in London and Yale Divinity School in the United States have built up extensive missionary collections and have created electronic guides to them. A useful point of entry into British missionary archives is the Mundus Gateway at http://www.mundus.ac.uk. In the United States both the Yale Divinity Library and the Billy Graham Center at Wheaton College maintain useful links to institutions throughout the world that hold primary source material relating to missions and world Christianity. Another useful resource for missionary materials relating to China is the Ricci 21st Century Roundtable Database on the History of Christianity in China, which can be accessed at http://ricci.rt.usfca.edu/archive/index.aspx.

Although many missionary organizations, both Catholic and Protestant, have retained their archives and made their contents available, many others have chosen not to spend resources in this way and do not readily permit access to uncatalogued materials. In some cases, the archives may not have survived. Many European mission archives, for example, were partially or wholly destroyed as a result of the bombing between 1940 and 1945, while others succumbed to the ravages of time and neglect. The scattered nature of missionary resources also makes the researcher's task difficult, especially when, as is quite common, organizations have changed their name. Some laudable attempts have been made to centralize and publicize information, such as the "Africa in German Mission Archives" project based at the University of Leipzig, but a comprehensive guide to, and listing of, surviving missionary archives in all the sending countries remains an unrealized goal. In seeking to supplement the missionary record, the researcher should be aware that information about missionaries, particularly permits for travel and in times of trouble, can be found in the public archives of both the sending and receiving countries.

The documentary legacy is not only relevant to the study of the mission movement but also forms part of the foundation records of churches, hospitals, schools, and colleges that still exist today in the former mission fields. Not all documentation was sent to missionary society headquarters; some important archives were created and kept locally, and these differ in form and content from those sent to mission headquarters. Examples are church rolls and registers (births, baptisms, communion, catechists, marriages, and funerals), minutes of church meetings, papers of church associations and of prominent church leaders, photographs, printed materials, and building plans. But because of a lack of archive awareness and resources, the lack of trained personnel, the lack of a designated archives center, and the lack of good models of record-keeping in societies that depend heavily on oral transmission of their stories, many of these records have not fared well and, unless steps are taken, will not survive.

However, the outlook is not entirely bleak. A number of centers of church and mission records have been established or are being developed. Among those in India, for example, can be noted the United Theological College at Bangalore, the Carey Library at Serampore, and the Library of the College of Vidyajyoti in Delhi, which contains Jesuit records dating back to the sixteenth century. In Southeast Asia, Trinity Theological College is developing a Singapore-Malaysia church history resource center with a number of partners, while in Hong Kong a research center for the history of Christianity in China has been established at Hong Kong Baptist University. In Africa the position is perhaps less clear. South Africa has a number of important archive centers, including the Cory Library at Rhodes University in Grahamstown and the Church of the Province of South Africa at the University of the Witwatersrand.

Missionary research resources, including archival materials, can be found at the Akrofi-Christaller Memorial Centre in Ghana, while another research center is being developed at Owerri in Nigeria.

Much remains to be done, however, particularly with regard to locating, rescuing, filing, and listing documentary materials, collecting and preserving photographs, and organizing oral-archive projects. But a start has been made and surely will continue.

Rosemary Seton

*See also* Bibliography; Libraries; Oral History; Photography; Professional Associations; Reference Tools

## Further Reading:

Basel Mission Picture Archive. (n.d.). Retrieved May 29, 2007, from http://www.bmpix.org

Cory Library for Historical Research. (2007). Retrieved May 29, 2007 from: http://campus.ru.ac.za

Internet Missionary Photographic Archive. (2007). Retrieved May 29, 2007, from usc.edu/isd/archives/arc/digarchives/mission

Mundus: Gateway to Missionary Collections in the United Kingdom. (2007). Retrieved May 29, 2007, from http://www.Mundus.ac.uk

Yale University Divinity School Library. (2007). Retrieved May 29, 2007, from http://www.library.yale.edu/div/

Ricci 21st Century Roundtable. (n.d.). Retrieved May 29, 2007, from http://ricci.rt.usfca.edu/roundtable.html

# Art

Though Asian Christian art is little known outside of the various churches, Christian institutions, and private buyers who favor it, this increasingly well-connected Christian community affords the genre a worldwide audience. Asian Christian art is thus oddly positioned in that it enjoys a limited, yet global appeal. Rooted in the various Christian missionary activities undertaken historically throughout Asia, this network of patrons, gradually cultivated over the course of the twentieth century, continues to make Asian Christian art a vital and viable endeavor.

## Cultivating Asian Christian Art

Though a goal of Christian art may be to appeal to the global community of Christians, the staid, didactic quality of much Christian Asian "art" has long been recognized. The genre's uneven historical development is generally attributed to the role art played in the life of the particular mission in a given region. As Bill Dryness has succinctly noted, "Where there was a measure of ability and sensitivity (as for example with Rossi and Constantini in China) a promising start was made" but that more often than not art that "was introduced (and which inevitably upset local cultural patterns) was not of much intrinsic value; it was something to overcome rather than build upon" (Dryness 1979, 67). Far from an indictment of Christian missions' influence on art, Dryness's characterization serves only to suggest the complex context for the development of Christian Art in Asia.

### Importance of Communicating Message

The limited appeal of didactic biblical illustration is conveyed beautifully by novelist Pearl Buck in a passage from *The Good Earth* (1931). Buck, who was raised in China, where her parents worked as missionaries, describes a seemingly failed encounter between protagonist Wang Lung, a temporarily displaced, illiterate farmer, and a Western missionary in the streets of an unnamed Chinese city early in the twentieth century:

> Wang Lung, although frightened to take anything from his hand, was more frightened to refuse, seeing the man's strange eyes and fearful nose. He took what was thrust at him, then, and when he had courage to look at it after the foreigner had passed it on, he saw on the paper a picture of a man, white-skinned, who hung upon the crosspiece of wood. The man was without clothes except for a bit about his loins, and to all appearances he was dead, since his head drooped upon his shoulder and his eyes were closed above his bearded lips. Wang Lung looked at the pictured man in horror and with increasing interest. There were characters beneath, but of these he could make nothing.

Shaken by the encounter, Wang Lung takes the puzzling image home to his family's grass-mat shack to ponder it with his father and young sons:

> The two boys cried out in delight and horror, "And see the blood streaming out of his side!"
> And the old man said, "Surely this was a very evil man to be thus hung."
> But Wang Lung was fearful of the picture and pondered as to why a foreigner had given it to him, whether or not some brother of this foreigner's had

not been so treated and the other brethren seeking revenge. He avoided, therefore, the street on which he had met the man and after a few days, when the paper was forgotten, O-Lan took it and sewed it into a shoe sole together with other bits of paper she picked up here and there to make the soles firm. (Buck 2005, 131–132)

Stuffed into the sole of a shoe, the frightening image of the crucified Christ was presumably forgotten, its message of redemptive suffering lost. Buck's lyrical prose underscores the difficulty of transmitting theological meaning visually and the consequent irrelevance borne by a message not clearly communicated.

## Importance of Indigenization of Art

Through this missed encounter, Buck aptly illustrated the need—increasingly felt by the "younger churches" and their emissaries as the twentieth century wore on—for the indigenization or accommodation of the Christian message in Asia. Visual art became part of a concerted effort to quite literally illustrate Christianity as a globally relevant, universal faith. Catholic and Protestant missionaries instructed and encouraged local artists to interpret biblical texts visually, using the art forms and cultural norms, signs, and symbols specific to a particular populace. Such a strategy's appeal to those working to establish firmly the Christian church in Asia was

> . . . that it helps to remove the foreign aspect of Christianity. It helps to dissipate the deadly prejudice which regards the church as an alien cult. In these days of excessive nationalism the more our universal faith can be freed from its distinctively Western accessories the less likely it is to be boycotted in some anti-Western trend. (Fleming 1938, 2)

### Role of the Catholic Church

Though indigenization of the Christian message was employed historically by Christian missionaries, Archbishop Celso Costantini, the papal delegate to China from 1922 to 1933, is widely recognized as the movement's twentieth-century champion (Butler 1972, 255; Fleming 1938, 12). Upon his arrival in China in 1922, "holding that it had always been the practice of the Roman Catholic Church to adapt herself to the customs and forms of the countries to which she had carried the faith," the archbishop instructed Catholic missionaries there to embrace a Chinese visual idiom in the service of

art for the church. In 1950 Costantini organized an exhibition on the subject of indigenous art at the Vatican, which "set the seal of official approval on indigenous art in the mission fields" (Butler 1972, 255). The exhibition was also credited with inspiring "a stream of such art, both Catholic and Protestant" (Butler 1972, 257), a current that today includes the works of Jayasuriya, Chinnawong, Darsane, Qi, and Sasongko.

## Developing a Market

Though indigenous art was discussed as a means to inculcate believers abroad, patrons for this art were deliberately cultivated among the Western faithful back home. Early proponents of the movement realized early on that encouraging local artists to produce "indigenized" biblical art, a difficult task to begin with, would be even more so if artists had no market for their work (Lehmann 1969, 36). Missiologist Daniel Johnson Fleming (1877–1969), a vocal proponent of the need for a mission-supported, indigenous artistic strategy, recognized and addressed this issue quite matter of factly. In his early survey of the nascent field, *Each With His Own Brush: Contemporary Art in Asia and Africa* (1938, 10), Fleming identified the

> . . . one obstacle that Western Christians and churches might well help to remove. . . . Obviously indigenous art is needed by the younger churches; but would not homes and churches in the West be enriched by some beautiful originals by an Eastern artist? Such originals are not only available, but their sale in the more wealthy West is almost a matter of life or death for Christian art in several lands.

Introducing the Western faithful to this art became an important concern and was undertaken in all manner of ways. Fleming (whose illustrated survey was itself an example) gave the example of Christmas cards "hand-colored by young women under the supervision of Bishop Shen's mother" at St. Luke's Studio in Nanking, China, which were distributed both locally and abroad (Fleming 1938, 11).

According to Fleming, failure to support such artistic endeavor resulted in dire consequences not merely for the indigenous art movement but for the Christian artist and by extension the communion of the faithful. He cited the example of Chinese Christian artist Hsu Chi Hua:

> . . . who recently died at the early age of twenty-five, was the second artist convert (1932). He was known for his fervor of faith, his forbearance, and his deep

religious disposition. After completing a three-year course in art he attempted to support his mother by his painting. While his pictures found many admirers, there were few purchasers. His lungs became seriously affected; his furniture traveled to the pawnshop; his Christian pictures were brought to the [Catholic University of Peking] to secure money for doctor's bills. However, try as they might, there was no demand. During this last illness he was continually planning whole series of new religious pictures which he longed to execute after his recovery. In him, Chinese Christian art lost a promising exponent. (Fleming 1938, 12–13)

Positioning art as an expression of faith allowed Fleming to argue for much broader implications for artistic patronage: support of this art became support for the Gospel message abroad.

### Appeal to a Western Audience

In *Christian Art in Africa and Asia* (1969, 10) theologian Arno Lehmann (1901–1984) spoke of the genre in terms of an "ecumenical art," for him proof of a "universal church, that crosses the boundaries of nations and races . . . " Lehmann's characterization suggested that the appeal of "exotic" illustrations of the Bible to a Western faithful audience could be twofold: the art's creation implied the successful implantation of the Christian message abroad, while its purchase permitted the patron to support very tangibly the works' continued production and by extension the dissemination of the Gospel message.

By way of surveying the field, Lehmann cited the various outlets for Asian Christian art, which simultaneously introduced a Western audience to indigenous art while cultivating its production. His list included his own book on the subject, first published in 1955; articles and books printed by "the Christian press of various countries and languages"; various books and encyclopedias, filmstrips, and Christmas and New Year's cards (Lehmann 1969, 10). Thus, by 1969, thirty years after Fleming's call for support, indigenous Christian art had begun to be actively disseminated worldwide through a network of Christian presses, missions, missionary societies, and churches.

Lehmann, like Fleming before him, helped to introduce the worldwide Christian community to indigenous Christian art, while offering effective strategies to continue to nurture it. For this, Fleming and Lehmann are regarded by subsequent proponents of Asian Christian art as the movement's pioneers (Takenaka 1975,

12). Their efforts led over time to the development of a broad Christian market spiritually vested in the success of indigenous art.

## Important Publications

In 1975 *Christian Art in Asia*, the most visually comprehensive survey of the field to date, was published. Written by Masao Takenaka, professor of Christian ethics at Doshisha University in Kyoto, Japan, at the behest of the Christian Conference in Asia (formerly the Working Committee of the East Asia Christian Conference), the book took thirteen years to compile. Takenaka visited many of the artists represented. Working from the premise that "Asian Christian art does not need to be invented, but rather the artists need to be discovered," he featured 120 works by 107 artists from 18 countries, suggesting the genre's breadth and vitality (Takenaka 1975, 7, 13). Takenaka's research underscored the growing Western market. He noted that he found many of the artists featured in his survey through art on display "at the headquarters of mission boards and societies in the West," eventually locating them in their respective countries (Takenaka, 13). The situation Takenaka encountered suggests that Lehmann's call had been heeded.

### Role of ACAA

In 1978, shortly after the publication of *Christian Art in Asia*, the Asian Christian Art Association (ACAA) was founded to raise awareness of and support the work of the increasing number of artists working in the genre. Through periodic publications; conferences dedicated to the development of indigenous art throughout Asia; the regular publication of the magazine *Image: Christ and Art in Asia*; and an active web presence (www.asian-christianart.org), the ACAA has become a key part of the network encouraging artists throughout Asia.

### The Bible Through Asian Eyes

*The Bible Through Asian Eyes,* the companion volume to *Christian Art in Asia*, was published in 1991. Written by Takenaka and Ron O'Grady and copublished by the Asian Christian Art Association, the lavishly illustrated book documents the state of Asian Christian art trends in one hundred contemporary works. This volume is notable for its full-page color reproductions and the entries that accompany them. Takenaka and O'Grady made a concerted effort to offer a context beyond that of a presumed shared Christian faith for each work. Most significantly, the authors offered a more open definition of Asian Christian art, acknowledging that (like Christian art in general) much Asian Christian art has been and continues to be created by artists who are not Christian.

This shift marked a potential sea change; early literature emphasized the faith underpinning Asian Christian art. Fleming, for example, carefully noted several instances of how Christian artistic creation by local artists sometimes led to conversion, suggesting this to be the desired outcome.

In his recent historiography of the field, Wilson Yates notes how over the last fifty years Christian churches have become increasingly interested in the arts. Pertinent to our discussion are the institutions he identifies as encouraging the intersection of art and theology historically. Noting that three seminaries were at the forefront of the movement in 1950, he identifies Union Theological Seminar in New York to be one of them. It is no surprise then to realize that the seminal survey of the early field of Asian Christian art was written by a faculty member at Union: *Each With His Own Brush*, by Daniel Johnson Fleming.

TRICIA PONGRACZ

## Further Reading

Buck, P. (2005). *The good earth.* New York: Pocket Books. (Original work published 1931)

Butler, J. F. (1972). India and the Far East. In G. Frere-Cook (Ed.), *Art and architecture of Christianity.* Cleveland, OH: The Press of Case Western University.

Dryness, W. A. (1979). *Christian art in Asia.* Amsterdam: Editions Rodopi N.V.

Fleming, D. J. (1938). *Each with his own brush: Contemporary Christian art in Asia and Africa.* New York: Friendship Press.

Lehmann, A. (1969). *Christian art in Africa and Asia* (E. Hopka, J. E. Nopola, & O. E. Sohn, Trans.). St. Louis, MO: Concordia Publishing House. (Original work published 1966)

Morgan, D. (2005). *The sacred gaze: Religious visual culture in theory and practice.* Berkeley: University of California Press.

Poerwowidagdo, J. (2004, September). Editor's note. *Image Christ and Art in Asia, 100,* 2.

Takenaka, M. (1975). *Christian art in Asia.* Tokyo: Kyo Bun Kwan in association with Christian Conference of Asia.

Takenaka, M. & O'Grady, R. (1991). *The Bible through Asian eyes.* Auckland, New Zealand: Pace Publishing in association with the Asian Christian Art Association.

Yates, W. (2005). The theology and arts legacy. In K. Vrundy & W. Yates (Eds.), *Arts, theology, & the church: New intersections.* Cleveland, OH: Pilgrim Press.

# Asia, Central

The spread of Christianity across Central Asia began as early as the second century CE. Over the centuries, the Roman Catholic Church, the Orthodox Church, the Church of the East, and Protestant denominations have sought converts from among this vast region's largely Turkic Muslim population. The region's domination by the USSR during much of the twentieth century halted mission activities, but since 1991, the region has again become the focus of evangelization efforts.

Central Asia encompasses the republics of Turkmenistan, Uzbekistan, Azerbaijan, Tajikistan, Kazakhstan, Kyrghyzstan, Afghanistan, and western China's Xinjiang-Uighur Autonomous Region. This area is also referred to as Central Eurasia, a term that emphasizes its geographic location between the Middle East and East Asia. Mongolia, directly north of China and conventionally viewed as part of Asia, is included here because of its historic role in Central Asia and its close ties to the Turkic peoples who comprise the majority of Central Asia's population today.

## Early Christianity in Central Asia

The earliest reference to a Christian presence in Central Asia dates from 196 CE when Christian converts were reported among the Bactrians whose kingdom included present-day Afghanistan. Although there are no details about these earliest of Central Asian converts, it is probable that their conversion resulted from contact with members of Christian communities in what is now Iran. By the third century, Christian enclaves already had been established there: the city of Merv (in today's eastern Iran) and Herat (in western Afghanistan) both had Christian communities under bishops of the Iranian Christian church, which declared itself independent of the Western church in 424 CE.

## Nestorian Christianity

The earliest missionaries in Central Asia were Nestorian Christians, followers of Nestorius (381?–451 CE), the bishop of Constantinople who was condemned for heresy by the Council of Ephesus in 431 CE. As a result, Nestorians dispersed into Persian lands, where they received sanctuary, and Persian Nestorian priests thus became the first missionaries among the nomadic Turkic peoples of Central Asia. According to one source, by the sixth century, seven Nestorian priests lived among the Turks for seven years and baptized many. The priests learned to speak the language and rendered it into a written form for the first time, using the Syriac alphabet.

The success of the Persian Nestorians can be seen in the 628 CE establishment of a Nestorian archbishopric at Samarkand, then the premier city of the Sogdian empire, followed by others in the Silk Road cities of Bukhara and Kashgar. Altogether, over twenty Nestorian bishops had dioceses west of the Amu Darya (Oxus) River by the seventh century.

Sogdian became the principal language used in the spread of Christianity into Central Asia and western China, primarily because of frequent contact between Sogdian traders and the nomadic Turkic peoples of the region. Chinese sources also record the presence of Sogdian Nestorians in the Turkic empire centered directly north of China, in modern-day Mongolia during the early Tang dynasty (618–907 CE). Sogdians and Turks were often present at the Chinese court following their submission to Emperor Tang Taizong (reigned 626–649 CE) in 630 CE, and Chinese records make clear that followers of Nestorian Christianity, Judaism, and Manichaeanism all resided in Tang China.

## Mass Conversions among the Turkic Peoples

A series of mass conversions among the Central Asian Turkic peoples occurred beginning in the seventh century. The first of these was accomplished by Elias, the Metropol of Marv. He used a crucifix to stop a thunderstorm, a feat that so impressed a local Turkic ruler that he vowed to follow Christianity and abandon shamanism. An unknown number of his subjects followed his example.

A second mass conversion occurred in 781–782 CE, again among the Central Asian Turks. The numbers involved are not known, but they were sufficiently encouraging for the Nestorian Catholicos (or Patriarch) in Baghdad, Timotheos (780–823 CE), to establish a Central Asian metropolitan to oversee and encourage the spread of Christianity among the Turkic peoples of the Eurasian steppe.

A third conversion took place in 1007 when some 200,000 Turks and Mongols reportedly became Christians. Central Asian peoples who were said to have adopted Christianity by the eleventh century include the Turko-Mongol groups such as the Naiman, Kerait (or Kerayit), and Onggud (or Ongut), as well as some Tatars and Mongolian Merkits (or Markit). While the numbers of converts and the depth of such conversions cannot be known, Nestorian Christianity was clearly a well-established Central Asian religion on the eve of the Mongol conquests in the thirteenth century.

One element that may have contributed to these conversions was a perceived similarity between the powers that Central Asians ascribed to their shamans and the ability some Christian missionaries displayed to show their own powers over natural phenomenon. For example, as mentioned in the preceding paragraph, one mass conversion resulted from a Christian missionary's ability to quell a storm, a power that paralleled indigenous expectations of religious leaders. In another instance, a Turkic leader believed a saintly apparition had saved his life on the steppe and thus led his people to accept Christianity. The longevity of conversions affected by this method is uncertain, but some clearly only lasted for the lifetime of the converted ruler.

## Sogdian and Persian Nestorian Texts

Many Sogdian texts were discovered in western China's Tarim Basin during the early twentieth century, attesting to the role played by Sogdians in transmitting Christianity across Central Asia. Some of the unearthed documents were used at a Nestorian center near Turpan (also spelled Turfan), where Nestorian priests received religious training in the ninth and tenth centuries. Among the types of documents surviving in the arid Gobi sands are hymns, prayers, psalms, lectionaries from the New Testament, and commentaries. While some of the texts are translations from Syriac, the main liturgical language of Nestorian Christianity, other texts and documents contain previously unknown material. These have extended our understanding of Nestorian teachings as presented to Central Asian peoples a thousand years ago. The materials also illustrate the presence of Christianity among the Uighurs, a Turkic people who had settled in the region of Turpan after the destruction of their Mongolian-based kingdom in 840.

Nestorianism was thus well represented in the major Central Asian cities and towns of the old Silk Road when Islam began its spread eastward along the great Eurasian trade routes. As early as the eighth to ninth centuries, Islam began displacing other faiths. One perceived advantage for a local ruler who accepted Islam was a possible increase in commercial contacts with wealthy states further to the west. Nonetheless, Nestorian Christianity remained the faith of many devoted adherents. Around 1180, the Nestorian Church renewed its presence in Kashgar. At that time, the city was part of the Karakitai (or Kara-Khitai) state, which dominated easternmost Central Asia. The Nestorian Patriarch Elias III gave this metropolitan authority over present-day southern Kazakhstan.

## Mongolian Conquests and Christianity

A new wave of Christian interaction with Central Asia was inaugurated as a result of the campaigns led by Chinggis Khan (also Genghis Khan) (1162–1227) beginning in 1220. Mongol armies swept westward and took control of the major trading cities of the Central Asian Silk Road. From there, they began a virtually unimpeded march west that brought them to the edges of Europe. Their conquests resulted in a vast Mongolian empire covering northern Asia, Central Asia, much of the Middle East, Russia, and later, India, forming the largest land empire in world history.

In the Mongolian domains, religious policy can be described as one of noninterference. Despite their destruction of religious buildings and icons during the conquest period, they nonetheless inaugurated a period of tolerance based in the belief that all teachings were of equal merit. Christian captives of the Mongols as well as Christian allies of the Mongols continued to practice their faith. For example, the Alans, a people originally from the Caucasus, had converted to Eastern Orthodox Christianity in the tenth century and remained Christian even when moved further east into Central Asia to serve the Mongol Khan. Further evidence of Mongolian tolerance of Christianity and other faiths can be seen in Russia, where after the Mongol conquest, the Russian Orthodox Church not only survived but expanded its following in formerly pagan rural areas.

In Europe and Russia, initial Mongolian victories over Christian princes and their armies were viewed as a threat to Christianity itself. In response, the Vatican dispatched envoys to the Mongol Khan in hopes of forestalling future Mongol attacks and, if possible, bringing the Mongols to Christianity. Franciscan priests undertook several such missions beginning in 1245 when Pope Innocent IV sent John of Plano Carpini (or Giovanni de Plano Carpini) (1180–1252), who made the arduous trek across then little-known Central Asia to what is now Mongolia. To his dismay, he discovered Nestorian Christians present in the Mongolian capital of Karakoram and wielding influence at court. For example, the Khan's daughter-in-law, Sorgatani, was a Nestorian Christian, and as the mother of Kublai Khan (1215–1294), who conquered China in 1279, she contin-

ued to hold considerable power even after the death of her husband. Ultimately, John's mission failed to impress the Mongols, but he returned to Europe with a valuable store of information on the people Europeans incorrectly referred to as "Tatars" or "Tartars."

A second mission to the Mongols was led by William of Rubruck (c.1210–c.1270), a friar at the court of King Louis of France. William's goal was to serve as a missionary among the Mongols, but he was denied permission to do so. Nonetheless, his account of years among the Mongols also extended knowledge about the Mongol empire. William held a low opinion of the Nestorians he encountered, reporting that they practiced divination, for example. If true, this supports the possibility that Christianity had adapted to local practices and beliefs, as suggested earlier.

One outcome of these travels was the establishment of three mission fields, or vicariates, specifically for the Mongols (at the same time as others were being established for Russia, southeastern Europe, and North Africa). Pope Paul XXII also sent a Dominican to Samarkand (in today's Uzbekistan) in an effort to convert the city's Muslims to Christianity.

In the thirteenth century, a China-born Onggud Turk and follower of Nestorianism journeyed across Central Asia to Baghdad, the seat of the Nestorian Church. Rabban Sauma (1260–1313) made this remarkable journey with his student, Markos, who in 1281 was named the Patriarch, or Catholicos, of the Nestorian Church of Baghdad, serving as Mar Yaballaha. Rabban Sauma was later sent to Europe on a diplomatic mission, visiting both Paris and Rome in an unsuccessful effort to persuade the Pope and European kings to unite with the Mongol rulers of Persia against the Muslim Mamluks. No alliance resulted, although Bar Sauma was well received. He returned to Baghdad, where he and the Patriarch served as symbols of the expansive world of Nestorian Christianity.

In contrast to the relatively open exchanges of the thirteenth century, the next hundred years brought a decline for Central Asian Christianity. Despite attracting adherents from among the Mongols and Turkic peoples, it faltered as the heirs to the great Mongol empire were replaced by descendants who converted to Islam and saw little advantage in allowing Christianity to continue in their domains. Christians maintained a toe-hold in the westernmost areas of Central Asia, particularly southern Kazakhstan and Semirechie, but these communities were decimated by the plague in 1338 and 1339, as recorded on many tombstones discovered in the region. Over the years, the number of

## Extract from *In the Guardianship of God* by Flora Annie Steel

It was the night before the great Eclipse. A vast, vague expectancy brooded over the length and breadth of India. Of prophesying there had been no lack, for signs and wonders had been as blackberries in September.

So, far and near, east and west, south and north, the people of Hindustan—many-hued, many-raced, many faithed were watching for they knew not what, watching with grave, silent, yet curious composure.

But there was no outward sign of this inward expectation on either side. The millions of dark faces behind which it lay were as inscrutable as the telegraph wires through which the mere fraction of white faces responsible for the safety of those millions of dark ones were flashing silent messages of warning and preparation.

And here, in the Sacred City, beside the Sacred River, in which multitudes of those millions hoped to bathe on the morrow during the fateful moments of the sun's eclipse, the dim curves of the world had never been outlined against a calmer, more restful sky—a sky almost black in its intensity of shadow. Yet the night was clear, full of starlight that could be seen, which showed the bend of the broad river, angled on one side by the straight lines of its curved sequence of bathing steps that swept away to the horizon on either side...

Behind this long length of bathing steps—irregular in height, in slope, in everything save an inevitable crowning by the tall temple spires–lay Benares... Benares, with its sunless alleys, full of the perfume of dead flowers and spent incense—alleys which thread their way past shrine after shrine, holy place after holy place; mere niches in a worn stone, perhaps, or less even than that; only the bare imprint of a bloody hand on the tall, blank walls of the crowded tenement houses which seem to narrow God's sky as they rise up towards it. Benares, where the alien master steps into the gutter to let a swinging corpse pass on its way to the Sacred River, but where the priest behind it—his dark forehead barred with white, or smeared with a bold patch of ochre—steps into the opposite gutter, and clings to the shrine-set wall like a limpet, lest he be defiled by a touch, a shadow. Benares, which is, briefly, the strangest, saddest city on God's earth.

Source: Steel, F. A. (1903). *In the guardianship of God.* Leipzig, Germany: B. Tauchnitz.

---

Christians rapidly declined as Central Asia became predominantly Muslim.

In the middle of the sixteenth century, Nestorian Christians became part of the Church of the East (also called the Assyrian Church), and the word *Nestorian* was used primarily to refer to the period before 1552. Central Asia was dominated by Muslim khanates that controlled access and trade into the nineteenth century.

## Russian Empire and Christian Influence

The expansion of the Russian empire brought the next wave, albeit a lesser one, of Christianity to the Eurasian steppes. By 1868, the Tsarist conquest of Central Asia was virtually complete, placing the region's Muslim population under officials loyal to an Orthodox Christian ruler. In general, however, Russian policy was to abstain from any interference in religious matters and to allow the conquered population to continue their Muslim faith. However, a small number of Russian administrators sought to encourage and support Christian missions, particularly among the Kazakhs. By the middle of the nineteenth century, small numbers of Kazakhs reportedly had been baptized as a result. In the 1860s, the Steppe Commission considered the possibility of encouraging the spread of Christianity as a means to draw the Kazakh regions closer to Russia and prevent the introduction of more conservative Muslim practices, but this effort was soon abandoned. Nonetheless, in Semirechie, a cathedral was built in Vernyi (today's Almaty, Kazakhstan), and in 1881, a monastery opened on the shores of Lake Issyk-Kul, followed by establishment of a new diocese at Omsk to forward work among Kazakhs. For a time, the Omsk diocese claimed some success. At Orenburg, forty to fifty Kazakhs received baptism each year in the early twentieth century but in 1905 these efforts ended. Many converted Kazakhs reportedly returned to Islam. In 1916, the Orthodox monastery built on the banks of Lake Issyk-Kul was destroyed and the monks killed.

## Central Asia under Soviet Domination

The Russian revolution of 1917 brought most of Central Asia, as well as Mongolia, under Soviet rule. Initially, the new government avowed that all citizens would enjoy freedom of religion, but in 1928 an aggressive campaign against religion began. Both Orthodox Russians and the Muslim peoples of Central Asia were targeted as churches and mosques closed and religious education ceased. In Mongolia, severe repression of religion led to the destruction of Buddhist relics as well as entire temple complexes. World War II saw a decrease in efforts to eliminate religion, and by the 1950s a limited number of churches and mosques reopened. While perestroika and glasnost emerged more slowly in Soviet Central Asia, by the 1980s a small number of Christian missionaries began working in Central Asia. For example, German Mennonites focused their efforts on the Naryn area of Kyrghyzstan, and these provided a base for expansion after the fall of the USSR in 1991.

## Western China's Turkic Muslims

In western China at the turn of the twentieth century, the Muslim population included several million Turkic Uyghurs (also spelled Uighur or Uygur) and smaller numbers of Kazakhs, Uzbeks, Kirghiz, and Tajiks, all of whom remained free to follow their beliefs. The region had been conquered by the Qing dynasty (1644–1912) in 1759, but religious practice was not affected, and few Chinese migrated to the region. Protestant missions opened as early as 1884, followed by Catholic priests, starting with Father Hendricks at Kashgar in 1890. The longest enduring Protestant mission was founded by the Stockholm-based Swedish Mission Church, later allied with the China Inland Mission. Their mission station was at Kashgar, with branches in Yarkand and Yengi Hissar. Mission workers eventually reported a congregation of 200, most of whom were former Muslims. In 1905, George Hunter (d. 1946) of the China Inland Mission began working in the northern part of the region, joined in 1918 by Percy Mather (d. 1933), and, for a time in the 1930s, four British and one American volunteer. Itinerant evangelists Alice Mildred Cable (d. 1952), the sisters Evangeline (d. 1960), and Francesca French (d. 1960), all of the China Inland Mission, began outreach to Muslim women in northwestern China in

the 1920s, following the Silk Road in China and crossing into what is now Kazakhstan. However, in 1938, the local warlord, Sheng Shicai, ordered all Western missionaries expelled. When World War II ended, the missions were not allowed to reopen.

After China's 1949 revolution and the inauguration of communist rule, religious practice was initially tolerated, but Western missionaries were expelled. Public religious observance disappeared during the tumultuous Cultural Revolution (1966–1976). Following the death of communist leader Mao Zedong in 1976, China began dramatic economic and political reforms. The "opening up" of China allowed the return of Western businesses and, gradually, of Christian missionaries.

Protestant groups took the lead in sending missionaries to China's Muslim northwest. Christians of various denominations and nationalities (e.g. Japan, South Korea, Singapore, and the United States) accepted positions teaching English or enrolled as students in local universities in order to establish links among the local population as part of their unofficial outreach. By the turn of the twenty-first century, individual missionaries reported converts from among the traditionally Muslim Uyghurs, but the total number of such conversions is not known.

## Central Asian States since 1991

With the fall of the USSR in 1991 and the independence of the Central Asian republics, Islam reemerged as the predominant faith of Central Eurasia. At the same time, the door was opened for Christianity, and missionaries, predominantly Protestant, began to arrive in growing numbers, principally from Europe, South Korea, and the United States. The years of secular rule and suppression of religion were viewed by some as making Central Asia's population more amenable to the Christian message than at any other time in history. By 2000, the largest number of missionaries worked in Kyrghyzstan, where some 1,000 are officially registered, including 700 who represent conservative Evangelical Protestant groups. In addition, many Christian workers from Western countries spend short periods, for example, summers, in the country. Several nongovernmental organizations (NGOs) employ workers also actively seeking converts. Numbers between 10,000 and 50,000 are cited in various sources for the number of converts since the 1990s.

Continuing strife in early twenty-first century Afghanistan made evangelism especially difficult and dangerous but did not prevent Christian organizations from establishing bases there. The 2001 detention of

Christian workers in Kabul by the Taliban highlighted the dangers inherent in some parts of Muslim Central Asia for those who do not understand fully the culture or the language.

In contrast, Mongolia began admitting Western mission groups since 1987, the year in which formal diplomatic relations with the United States began. The withdrawal of the USSR led to the rapid revival of Tibetan Buddhism, as seen in the many restored temples and proliferation of *ovos*—shrines for the worship of gods and spirits. At the same time, Protestant churches and charities began work in the country, some addressing urgent needs of the country's poorest members, especially women and children. The Mormon Church began sending missionaries in 1992 and, as in China, teaching English provided a means to establish connections with young Mongolians. Two Protestant groups, the interdenominational Church of Mongolia and an umbrella organization called the Mongolian Evangelical Churches Association offer Christian instruction. The Joint Christian Services (JCS) provides a variety of social services, as do other NGOs. Although no official statistics are available, a figure of 4,000–5,000 converts (out of a total population of only 2.5 million) was reported in the 1990s. While Mongolia may be more conducive to the Christian message than the Muslim states of Central Asia, reports of customs officials confiscating Bibles and Christian videos indicate that despite an officially open policy, resentment and/or opposition to Christian evangelism also exists.

## Future of Christianity in Central Asia

To some Western evangelical Christians, the Muslim regions of the world constitute the single most important mission field for the twenty-first century. Parts of Central Asia are within the "10/40 window," a phrase that refers to those countries located between 10 and 40 degrees north latitude, where "unreached" peoples are the majority of the population. However, Western intervention in Afghanistan and the Middle East in the early twenty-first century has renewed the old association of Christianity with militarily dominant and aggressive Western states, and this can be expected to have an impact on Christian efforts at evangelization in all the Central Asian republics. Further, except for the Buddhist Mongolians, Central Asians' identity is intrinsically linked to Islam, so much so that there is little distinction between being a member of a particular ethnic group or nationality, for example, Uzbek, Kazakh, and being a Muslim. When the Central Asian states move beyond the current group of Soviet-trained

leaders—who, in many respects, have continued Soviet-style administration with only a patina of change—nationalism and Islam may combine to make further efforts of Christian missionaries difficult, despite hopes to the contrary.

LINDA K. BENSON

### Further Reading

Barthold, W. (1966). *Turkestan down to the Mongol invasion.* Taipei, Taiwan: (Original work published 1928)

Cable, M. (1942). *The Gobi Desert.* London: Hodder and Stoughton Limited.

Dowley, T. (1995). *Introduction to the history of Christianity.* Minneapolis, MN: Fortress Press.

Foltz, R. C. (1999). *Religions of the Silk Road: Overland trade and cultural exchange from antiquity to the fifteenth century.* New York: St. Martin's Press.

Frye, R. N. (1998). *The heritage of Central Asia: From antiquity to the Turkish expansion.* Princeton, NJ: Markus Weiner Publishers.

Hultvall, J. (1987). *Mission and change in eastern Turkestan.* Erskine, UK: Heart of Asia Ministries.

Latourette, K. (1929). *A history of Christian mission in China.* London: Society for the Promotion of Christian Knowledge.

Murzakhalilov, K. (2004). Proselytism in Kyrgystan, Central Asia and the Caucasus. *Journal of Social and Political Studies, 1,* 83–87.

Sinor, D. (Ed.). (1990). *The Cambridge history of early Inner Asia.* New York: Cambridge University Press.

Skrine, C. P. (1986). *Chinese Central Asia.* Hong Kong, China: Oxford University Press. (Original work published 1926)

Whitfield, S. (2004). *The Silk Road: Trade, travel, war and faith.* Chicago: Serindia Publications.

## Asia, East

Situated in the northeastern part of the Pacific Rim, East Asia is believed to be the area deserving undivided attention in every aspect, in particular in terms of the Christian mission. While having a church history longer than that of Europe, East Asia still remains the most inhospitable region to Christianity except for South Korea, mainly owing to strong religions, high cultures, and anticolonialism. The most densely populated area and the home of a quarter of world's population, East Asia expects the church to develop its ministry from self-expansion to service to the multicultural, multireligious, multiethnic, and even multiideological communities.

While closely interconnected as a regional unit, East Asia is an area of contrast and confrontation *par excellence:* It is the last battlefield of the outmoded Cold War between China and Taiwan, as well as between two Koreas; it houses Japan, the second richest capitalist country, and China, the largest communist country; it witnesses the transformation of Mongolia, escaping the communist legacy and groping for a new way of socialism. In this context, the East Asian churches recently tackled the issue of globalization, alongside existing problems such as development, political and economic liberation, human rights, reconciliation, and the integrity of creation, on the one hand, and developed fellowship and solidarity among themselves and beyond, on the other hand. Then, how is the East Asian Church, which faces these enormous tasks, formed? Historically, whereas it had been outreached by the Eastern church along the land route in the earliest centuries, East Asia was reevangelized by the Western church by sea in the wake of Vasco Da Gama's exploration. The waves of mission are interrelated, and missionary efforts in different countries are intermixed to the extent that a synoptic history of mission is demanded.

## Mongolia

Missionaries of the Eastern church, in particular Nestorian missionaries, fanned out to almost every part of Asia from the beginning of Christianity. Located at the heart of Asia and as the gateway to East Asia, Mongolia has benefited from several waves of the spread of civilization, including the Gospel, and thus perhaps became evangelized earlier than any other East Asian countries. The existence of Mongolian Christianity, however, can be historically confirmed from the time when some of the Christianized tribes were incorporated into the emerging Mongolian Empire. Chinggis Khan (also Genghis Khan) and his successors held a religious policy that adopted religious tolerance and yet demanded prime loyalty to the king.

### Beginning of Roman Catholicism (1246–1764)

In 1246 John of Plano Carpini, the first Catholic missionary to Mongolia, arrived in Mongolia with a mixed agenda, religious as well as diplomatic. When the new empire was searching for a new state religion matching its changed status, it reportedly invited the Catholic

Church to send one hundred gifted missionaries. As the Catholic Church hesitated to take the chance, Tibetan Buddhism superseded Shamanism, the existing state religion. Christianity instead became an officially recognized religion such as Daoism, Confucianism, and Islam, while "Jews and Manicheans were tolerated" individually (Kemp 2000, 115). As Nestorian and Catholic missions were satisfied with the status quo as international churches mainly for the expatriate, they failed to plant indigenous Mongolian churches, fighting for hegemony between them. After the fall of the Yuan Dynasty, the then-Mongolian empire, in 1368, the xenophobia of the Han-Chinese Ming Dynasty wiped out all the remaining vestiges of Mongolian imperialism including Christianity, and thus mission to East Asia by land was no longer available.

### Beginning of Protestantism (1764–1989)

Taking the land route, Protestant missions reached out to some Mongolian ethnic groups within the Russian border such as the Kalmucks (1764) and the Buriats (1817), in the face of competition from the Orthodox Church. Only after the First Opium War (1839) was missionary access to Mongolia possible from China, which was opened from the coast. While varied efforts were made by Catholic, Protestant, and Orthodox missions, all failed to leave a lasting legacy other than the Mongolian Bible.

### Resumption of Missions (1989–present)

The sudden demise of Communism in 1989 enabled missions to recommence ministry in the context of spiritual vacuum. After a number of false starts, both by missionaries and nationals, and challenges from the government, the church has been established well and yet leaves much to be desired. At a conservative estimate, 1–2 percent of the total population, thirty to sixty thousand, is claimed to be Christians.

## China/Taiwan

Church history in China may be traced back to the ministry of St. Thomas, as the legend has it that he visited China as well as India in the first century. However, the first church that can be dated by evidence, in particular the famous Nestorian Tablet unearthed in 1623 at Hsianfu, owes its existence to Alopen, a Nestorian missionary who arrived in China in 635. Although the church in the T'ang Dynasty enjoyed a temporary prosperity thanks to tolerance policy and royal favor, it could never succeed in taking roots in Chinese soil. The church that had faithfully followed the Syrian Church tradition was hardly indigenized and largely remained foreign until it was uprooted by subsequent persecutions. As noted in the section on Mongolia, in the Yuan Dynasty (an alien dynasty) the church history and mission history of Mongolia and those of China overlapped. During this period the Nestorian Church was revived but could not successfully convert the Han-Chinese, not to mention the Mongols. After having been swept away by the Ming Dynasty, it never substantially resuscitated.

### Beginning of Roman Catholicism (1246–1807)

The Catholics in the Yuan Dynasty were destined to share the same fate as the Nestorians. In the Ming Dynasty Matteo Ricci, the first Jesuit missionary, arrived in Beijing in 1601 and adopted the mission policy of accommodation, enjoying royal favor. When the Nestorian Tablet was found, Catholic missionaries attempted to exploit this as a historical defense for mission. In the Qing Dynasty conflict among Catholic missions developed into the Rites Controversy and triggered the proscription of Christianity in 1724. It is interesting to note that in the wake of this catastrophe, missionaries could stay in China only as representatives of Western civilization, not Western faith. Ancestor worship, the main issue in the controversy, had similar implications for missionary work in other countries with Confucian backgrounds, in particular Korea, where it occasioned cold-blooded persecutions. On the other hand, during this chaos, the Russian Orthodox Church opened a mission in China in 1721. Prior to the revolution in October 1910, Russian missions worked in four overseas areas: China, Japan (1860), Korea (1900), and North America (1793). Although, "in consequence of the intrigues of the Jesuits," the Metropolitan Philotheus of Tobolsk, the Apostle of Siberia, could not provide the Beijing mission "a regular and perfected" organization, the mission developed slowly. (Smirnoff 1903, 75)

### Beginning of Protestantism (1807–1949)

Since China was reopened to missions by unequal treaties with colonial powers, Christianity was closely associated with colonialism. Robert Morrison, from the London Missionary Society, the first Protestant missionary to China, arrived at Macao in 1807 and translated the Bible in 1823. Once China was opened, missionaries flocked to treaty ports. With the establishment of the China Inland Mission by Hudson Taylor in 1865, the hinterland of China was also open to missionary infiltration. In spite of enormous missionary reinforcement, in terms of money, and men, the missions largely failed to establish strong national churches and instead muddled through antiforeign and anti-Christian challenges from the Chinese.

### Beginning of the Church under the Communist Rule (1949–present)

The rise of the Chinese Communist Party and its victory in 1949 fundamentally changed the fate of the church. A new sociopolitical context forced the church to transform itself into being totally independent of foreign influences and thoroughly national. Such a change resulted in the organization of the Protestant Christian Three-Self Patriotic Movement and the Catholic Three Autonomies, the precedent of the Chinese Catholic Patriotic Association, in 1951. This new church raises the question as to the church in postdenominationalism and theology in the "post-liberation stage of history" (Whitehead 1989, 96). It, however, also raises the issue of division among Christians, for instance, "orthodox" and "patriotic" Catholics. Recently, alongside overall social change owing to the return of Deng Xiaoping to power, the church draws worldwide attention to its remarkable growth or revival, the renaissance of Christian studies by Christian and non-Christian scholars, and the interest of the public in Christianity.

### Christianity in Taiwan (1624–present)

Although the national identity of Taiwan has been a disputed point in international politics, its ecclesiastical identity leaves no room for doubt. The history of Christianity in Taiwan can be divided by three missionary waves, and yet "all three waves arrived in the Island at times when Taiwan was caught up in the international turmoil in East Asia" (Thomas 1979, 93): the first wave by the Dutch Reformed Mission (1624) and the Spanish Dominican Mission (1626), the second by the British and Canadian Presbyterian Missions (1847 and 1871, respectively) and the Dominican Mission (1859), and the third in the aftermath of World War II by various denominational and interdenominational missions. Previous missionary efforts only left a minority church within a multiethnic society that was dominated by an exile government. Recently, church life has been closely related to this sociopolitical disorder, one ecclesiastical response to which was the epoch-making Public

## A Missionary in Korea

**In this piece of autobiographical text based on ten years of mission work in Korea around the turn of the twentieth century, Robert Moose describes the role of the missionary.**

In many of these markets there is still another man with his wares spread on a mat, while he stands and talks to the people about him as if he had something to say and knew how to say it. He is not a merchant who is there for the sake of gain. It is true that he has something to sell, but not for the sake of profit. He is a colporteur or a missionary with his stock of Scriptures and tracts, which he offers for sale at such a low price that the people are astonished at him. Then, too, he is saying such strange things about people loving one another—yes, even their enemies. And, even more, he is telling them of a wonderful Person who died to save all men from sin and is now willing to save all who will believe on him. This all sounds very strange in the market place where every man's hand is against that of his fellow, hoping if possible to seize the long end of the rope in every pull. It is in these markets that many thousands of people have heard the gospel for the first time.

Source: Moose, J. R. (1911). *Village life in Korea.* Nashville, TN: M.E. Church.

Statement on our National Fate made by the Presbyterian Church in Taiwan in 1971. The political confusion fuelled by ethnic discrimination resulted in the contextualized theology called Homeland Theology, mainly by exile theologians such as C.S. Song and Shoki Coe.

## Japan

Although some traces of Nestorianism having entered Japan earlier than Catholicism have been found, the paucity of evidence barely allows reliable historical reconstruction.

### Beginning of Roman Catholicism (1549–1858)

Under the Padroado system, a mixture of colonization and propagation of the gospel, Spanish and Portuguese missions competed to approach the Japanese coast in the sixteenth century. Francis Xavier, the famed Jesuit, arrived in Japan in 1549 and was also instrumental in opening missionary work in China. Much indebted to warlike feudal lords who wished to make the most of foreign influence, the church was established and even claimed rapid growth in its early days. The changes of political situations such as the unification of the nation under the military government and the arrival of traders from Protestant countries such as the Netherlands that deliberately dissociated themselves from mission led to the inauguration of bloody persecutions and the hibernation of Christianity in the early seventeenth century.

### Beginning of Protestantism (1858–1945)

In terms of Protestantism, the cross followed the flag. Perry's visit to Japan in 1853 and the ensuing American-Japanese treaty in 1858 brought the end of isolationist policy and paved the way to mission. The arrival of Protestant missions, predominantly American, was accompanied by the idea of modernization, which helped establish the Protestant Church in the beginning but soon proved detrimental to the missionary cause, as the Japanese government vigorously pushed forward with the process of modernization without Christianization. Moreover, facing the spirit of nationalism and the militarization of the nation, the church struggled with the baffling question of identity as to whether it was fundamentally a foreign or nationalistic institution. In those days Mukyokai (nonchurch movement), the most famous Japanese indigenous form, which unashamedly claimed to be free from Euro-Americanism as well as denominationalism, symbolically emerged. On the other hand, the Roman Catholic Church was largely satisfied with the recovery of the church, and the Japanese Catholics who survived the persecutions were divided into two groups: While the underground Christians joined the returned Catholic Church, the hidden Christians (Okure Kirishitan) chose to hold fast to their ancestors' faith. However, the latter has now steeply declined in importance because of its sharp decrease.

### Beginning of the Postwar Church (1945–present)

A religious minority amounting to 1 percent of the total population, the postwar Japanese church played an important role as a conscientious objector in pacifism, human rights, etc. Its contribution was also found in ecumenism and theology, in particular the contextualized theology called *burakumin* (Japanese outcaste) theology. Recently, the landscape of the church became more kaleidoscopic, owing to the rise of indigenous and Pentecostal groups. However, there is evidence that its influence is widely felt beyond its religious affiliation: For instance, while in 1982 "most weddings (90 percent) were still conducted by Shinto priests," by 1998 "the percentage of Christian weddings had increased to over 53 percent" (Mullins 2003, viii).

### Christianity in Okinawa (1844-present)

Whereas it was officially annexed to Japan in 1879, Okinawa, the former Ryukyu (or Loochoo), had had close links with Japan as well as surrounding countries. Isolationist policy began to be eased in Okinawa earlier than in Japan proper, when missionaries started their work in anticipation of mission to Japan: the Catholic Société des Missions Etrangères in 1844 and the Protestant Loochoo Naval Mission in 1846. However, no foreign religions including Christianity have successfully taken root in Okinawa, which is the "only known place where [Shamanistic] women lead the official religion" (Sered 1999, v). In the wake of World War II, the tiny church in Okinawa, an epitome of every possible problem the church faces in Japan, has struggled with numerous questions such as foreign occupation, human rights, ethnic identity, and integration into Japan.

## South and North Korea

Whereas it is admitted that Nestorianism might have entered Korea in the Shilla Dynasty, and even a Catholic war chaplain visited Korea accompanying Japanese Christian invaders in 1593, the history of Korean Christianity with supporting evidence began in a more miraculous way.

### Beginning of Roman Catholicism (1774–1884)

Several Catholics self-evangelized through the study of Western sciences and Catholicism established an indigenous church and then sent a member to China to be baptized by missionaries in 1774. The church soon developed in great measure by the entering of expatriate priests, Western and Asian, into Korea. The early years of the church were interspersed with consecutive persecutions, which resulted in the delay of Protestant missionary work in Korea in comparison with China and Japan.

### Beginning of Protestantism (1884–1895)

In 1884 Dr. H. N. Allen, the first Protestant resident missionary, entered Korea under the guise of the medical doctor to the American legation. Prior to this historic year, however, several missionary attempts had already been made outside of the Korean border, in particular the translation of the Korean Bible by missionaries and nationals. Some Koreans who were evangelized outside Korea voluntarily participated in evangelistic outreach, founded the churches in Manchuria and Japan, and brought Christianity into the Korean peninsula at the risk of their own lives before the arrival of missionaries. For the first decade, however, the missions were at a standstill and had to wait for their remarkable growth, mainly doing educational and medical work.

### Settlement of the Protestant Church (1895–1910)

From the beginning, Presbyterian missions comprised the majority of missions, and as a result, the Presbyterian churches came to be predominant in Korea. However, the first two missions, Presbyterian and Methodist, were soon joined by others. The missions enjoyed their success in church planting and ecumenical endeavor, and the Korean churches rapidly grew in quantity and quality, in particular through revival in 1907.

### Colonial Rule (1910–1945)

The colonial rule in the first half of the twentieth century dramatically transformed the church: the nationalistic elite striving for independence gradually detached themselves from the church, while the church underwent the process of depoliticization and retained other-worldly religiosity. Having been humiliated by conflict over Shinto Shrine worship, the church, coupled with ecumenical organizations, was forced to be merged into Japanese Christianity toward the end of the colonial rule.

### Liberated Korea, South Korea (1945–present)

In the aftermath of the chaos of the liberation and the subsequent Korean War, the church emerged as one of the most rapidly growing churches and an important mission force. While accomplishing church growth and world mission, the church has been greatly challenged for problems such as division and materialism. Since the 1970s the church has struggled with the pending issues of democratization, unification, and globalization and, as a result, has developed a number of contextualized theologies such as Minjung theology, jubilee theology, and immigration theology, together with traditional conservative theology. One fifth of the total population, ten million, is claimed to be Christians, with many world-ranking mega churches including the Yeouido Assembly of God Church.

### Christianity in North Korea (1945–present)

With the establishment of a communist government in North Korea, the church found itself in a new hostile situation. The Christian churches and organizations were closed or integrated into a government-controlled organization and finally vanished after the Korean War. Since the 1970s, alongside ideological thaw between two Koreas, the church has begun to reemerge, and Christian organizations such as the Protestant Korean Christian Federation (1972) and its Catholic counterpart (1988) were formed. This new indigenized church resembles the Chinese Three-Self Church in many ways and aims to develop ecumenical ties with the South Korean and international churches and organizations. Nowadays, there are three official churches, two Protestant and one Catholic, and house churches, with the constituency of about ten thousands.

## Looking Ahead

Mission history in East Asia raises a number of missiological questions, besides typical missionary problems such as competition, foreignness, and colonialism. Politically, the church continued to face the issue of church and state, which more often than not resulted in persecutions and reemerged in different contexts such as Asiatic despotic monarchy, colonial rule, and Communism. Culturally, the attitude of missions and the church toward traditional cultures and religions also occasionally caused persecutions and predisposed the trajectory of indigenization. Socially, as a religious minority, the church endeavored to maintain its identity rather than playing an influential public role. The point is whether the church can complete unfinished missionary agendas and grow into a genuinely national, indigenous, and responsible church.

KYO SEONG AHN

## Further Reading

Ahn, K. S. (2003). Christian mission and Mongolian identity: The religious, cultural, and political context. *Studies in World Christianity, 9*(1), 103–24.

Athal, S. (Ed.). (1996). *Church in Asia today: Challenge and opportunities.* Singapore: Asia Lausanne Committee for World Evangelism.

Bawden, C. R. (1985*). Shamans, lamas, and evangelicals: The English missionaries in Siberia.* London: Routledge & Kegan Paul.

Brown, G. T. (1983). *Christianity in the People's Republic of China.* Atlanta, GA: John Knox Press.

Camps, A. (2000). *Studies in Asian mission history, 1956–1998.* Leiden, Netherlands: Brill.

Clark, A. D. (1971). *A history of the church in Korea.* Seoul, Korea: Christian Literature Society of Korea.

Dawson, C. (Ed.). (1966). *Mongol mission: Narratives and letters of the Franciscan missionaries in Mongolia and China in the thirteenth and fourteenth centuries.* London: Sheed and Ward. (Original work published 1955)

Fairbank, J. K. (Ed.). (1974). *The missionary enterprise in China and America.* Cambridge, MA: Harvard University Press.

Hanson, E. O. (1980). *Catholic politics in China and Korea.* Maryknoll, NY: Orbis.

Hoke, D. E. (Ed.). (1975*). The Church in Asia.* Chicago: Moody Bible Institute.

Hunt, E. N., Jr. (1980). *Protestant pioneers in Korea.* Maryknoll, NY: Orbis.

Ion, H. A. (1990; 1993). *The cross and the rising sun: The British Protestant missionary movement in Japan, Korea, and Taiwan, 1865–1945.* Waterloo, Canada. Wilfrid Laurier University Press.

Kang, W. J. (1997). *Christ and Caesar in modern Korea: A history of Christianity and politics.* Albany: State University of New York.

Kemp, H. P. (2000). *Steppe by step: Mongolia's Christians, from ancient roots to vibrant young church.* London: Monarch Books.

Keum, J. (2000). Church, Minjung, and state: The revival of Protestant Christianity in North Korea. *Studies in World Christianity, 8*(2), 264–284.

Kim, J. C., & Chung, J. J. (Eds.). (1964). *Catholic Korea: Yesterday and today.* Seoul, Korea: Catholic Korea Publishing Co.

Lancaster, L. R., & Payne, R. K. (Eds.). (1997). *Religion and society in contemporary Korea.* Berkeley: University of California Press.

Latourette, K. S. (1929). *A history of Christian mission in China.* London: SPCK.

Moffett, S. H. (1992; 2005). *A history of Christianity in Asia* (Vols. 1–2). Maryknoll, NY: Orbis.

Mullins, M. R. (2003). *Handbook of Christianity in Japan.* Leiden, Netherlands: Brill.

Overmyer, D. L. (Ed.). (2003). *Religion in China today.* Cambridge, UK: Cambridge University Press.

Paik, L. G. (1971). *The history of Protestant missions in Korea, 1832–1910.* Seoul: Korea Yonsei University Press. (Original work published 1927)

Paton, D. M. (1953). *Christian missions and the judgment of God.* London: SCM.

Phillips, J. M. (1981). *From the rising of the sun: Christians and society in contemporary Japan.* Maryknoll, NY: Orbis.

Sered, S. (1999). *Women of the sacred groves: Divine priestess of Okinawa.* Oxford: Oxford University Press.

Smirnoff, E. (1986). *A short account of the historical development and present position of Russian Orthodox missions.* Powys, UK: Stylite Publishing Ltd. (Original work published 1903)

Suggate, A. (1995). *Japanese Christians and Society.* Bern, Switzerland: Peter Lang.

Thomas, T. K. (Ed.). (1979). *Christianity in Asia: North-East Asia.* Singapore: CCA.

Tong, H. K. (1961). *Christianity in Taiwan: A history.* Taipei, Taiwan :China Post.

Whitehead, R. L. (Ed.). (1989). *No longer strangers: Selected writings of K.H. Ting.* Maryknoll, NY: Orbis.

Yap, H. K. (1995). *From Prapat to Colombo: History of the Christian Conference of Asia, 1957–1995.* Hong Kong: CCA.

# Asia, Southeast

Alongside migrants, merchants, civil servants, chaplains, soldiers, and wandering adventurers, Christian missions and missionaries have long contributed to the spread of Christianity in the countries of East Timor, Indonesia, Kampuchea, Laos, Malaysia, Myanmar, the Philippines, Singapore, Thailand, and Vietnam. Although a minority faith, Christianity in Southeast Asia developed as an Asian religion. From 1900 to 2000 the percentage of Christians increased from around 10 percent to over 20 percent, and now ranges from over 90 percent of the population in East Timor and the Philippines to 1 to 2 percent in Cambodia, Laos, and Thailand, and from 8 to 13 percent in other countries.

Despite denominational diversities and ethnic differences, Christianity provides shared values, common core beliefs, and a number of Asian and Southeast Asian institutional expressions of regional identity. The peoples now represented within the Association of Southeast Asian Nations (ASEAN) connect not only through geographical proximity, but also through shared historical experiences, similar material cultures, and widespread social traits. These include an underlying primal spirituality, the influence of Indian and Chinese cultures and religions, the spread of Islam, long periods of colonial rule and influence, the effects of war, struggles to achieve or maintain independence, and the challenges of cultural and economic integrity in an age of globalization. Malay peoples are widespread, as are Chinese who have migrated over the centuries. Islam is the majority faith in Indonesia, Malaysia, and the southern Philippines. Hinduism has had a wide political, cultural, and religious influence, particularly in the South and West, as has Buddhism in its major variants across the region. Interactions with Christianity have helped define some of these identities at the same time as it has been shaped by the contexts they provide.

## Early Contacts

There is evidence of Christian communities in Southeast Asia from the sixth century, and in medieval times Christian travelers from Europe passed through the region en route to and from China. By the late fifteenth century Christian traders from West and South Asia had been reported in south Myanmar, west Sumatra, and Melaka on the Malay Peninsular.

In 1511 the Portuguese conquered Melaka, and their presence in Ternate and Ambon facilitated mission in the east of the region. Francis Xavier (1506–1552) reached Melaka in 1545 and his missionary journeys, teaching the creed and basic prayers in local languages, took him and other Jesuits to the Moluccas, as well as to Japan.

The Spanish reached the Philippines in 1521 but their zealous evangelization didn't begin until 1565, and intensified only after the arrival of Franciscans in 1578, Jesuits in 1581, and Dominicans in 1587. About half of those under Spanish rule had been baptized by 1620, although Islam remained strong in the south, as it continues to do.

The port of Thanlyin on the Myanmar coast, for a period under Portuguese rule, developed a Christian community until it was captured in 1613. Christians were employed at court and in 1721 a Barnabite mission began, which produced in 1776 the first printed books in the vernacular.

Around 1550 the Dominican Gaspar de Santa Cruz sought to enter Cambodia and Vietnam. The French Jesuit Alexandre de Rhodes (1591–1660) reached central

Vietnam in 1624 and worked there and in the north until he was forced to leave in 1630. After a decade in Macao he returned in 1640 and was finally expelled in 1645. He had to face conflicts between rival dynasties, and with the Portuguese over his use of French missionaries under the Propaganda Fidé (1622). The Chinese rites controversy over ancestor rituals also had repercussions in Vietnam. Christians and missionaries escaping persecution in Japan aided the mission, and success in establishing a Vietnamese church was aided by Rhodes's language skills, catechism, organization of catechists, and his establishment of a Catholic hierarchy.

## Nineteenth-century Missions

Protestant Christianity reached Southeast Asia with the Dutch East India Company (VOC, 1602–1799), which took Ambon from the Portuguese in 1605 and Melaka in 1641. It based itself at Batavia in 1619. The Dutch forced

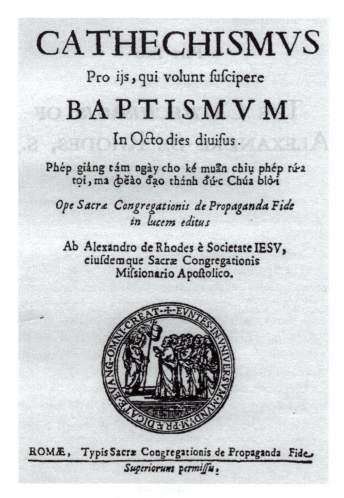

The frontispiece of Alexandro de Rhodes's 1651 Latin *Catechesis*, a volume used in de Rhodes's mission work in Vietnam. *Courtesy of Peter Phan and Orbis Books.*

Catholics to become Reformed, but many kept their faith despite the absence of priests. Although mission was limited, and there was no sustained move to develop local leadership, the New Testament was translated into Malay by 1668 and the complete Bible by 1733. After 1799 the Dutch government set up the Protestant Church in the Nederlands Indie (Netherlands East Indies) as a state church and Catholic priests were allowed to return.

Independent missions and missionaries were sporadic before the mid-nineteenth century. The Dutch evangelist Joseph Kam (1769 1833) trained with the London Missionary Society (LMS, 1795) and reached Batavia in 1814 and the Moluccas the following year. Possibly the only minister in East Indonesia at the time, he preached, organized prayer and revival meetings, administered the sacraments, and began schools. Ludwig Nommensen (1834–1918) of the Rheinische Missionsgesellschaft (RMG, 1799) arrived in Sumatra in 1862 and served the Batak people until his death. He lived through early years of frustration and the persecution of converts to see mass conversions and the building of schools and hospitals as well as self-reliant churches. In the Poso region of central Celebes, Alburtus Kruyt (1869–1949) emphasized anthropological research and language study as the basis of a "sociological missionary method" and a contextualized faith. Patience and informed respect laid the foundation for baptisms of groups rather than individuals. In remote central Java the Dutch Jesuit Franz Van Lith (1863–1926) founded schools, a training college, and a minor seminary. He taught Christians to defend their rights and take leadership roles in church and government.

Adoniram Judson (1788–1850), who reached Yangoon in 1813, pioneered American Baptist missions in Myanmar. British interest in Southeast Asia expanded from India to Myanmar and also included the Straits Settlements of Penang (1786), Melaka (1795), and Singapore (1819). They provided a stable environment for East India Company churches and chaplaincies, the Roman Catholic Seminary in Penang (previously in Thailand), and the London Missionary Society. The Anglo-Chinese College and printing press in Melaka under the leadership of the LMS missionary William Milne (1785–1822) laid a foundation for intercultural understanding as well as Christian mission until the LMS left for China after 1842. In 1874 the Treaty of Pangkor allowed for the expansion of British influence in the Malay peninsula and limited mission to non-Malay peoples.

Thailand engaged with the increasing presence of European trading and colonial powers, but succeeded in maintaining its independence. Missionaries visited, and Christians from elsewhere in the region, particularly

## Arrival of the Belgian Missionaries

The following account describes the early wok of Belgian catholic missionaries among the indigenous Ifugao people of the northern Philippines.

One of the most important factors in "civilizing" the Ifugaos was the effective missionary work of the Belgian Fathers. These missionaries, however, were not the first to implant the seed of Christianity among the Ifugaos.
[…]

The arrival of the Congregation of the Immaculate Conception Missionaries (CICM) in the Mountain Province in 1907 marked a new era in the propagation of the Catholic faith among the mountaineers. Reinforced by a second group in 1908, the missionaries opened their first permanent center in Baguio City. Other mission settlements soon sprouted in the different subprovinces.

Among the missionaries who arrived in 1908 was energetic 26-year-old Father Jerome Moerman, the son of a Dutch manufacturing magnate. This young CICM missionary was sent alone to Ifugao where he quickly went into action. From the remnants of the Spanish convent in Kiangan, Father Moerman built the first CICM mission chapel in Ifugao, completing it on June 10, 1910. In contrast with the Dominican system of converting the natives, he adapted himself to the Ifugao way of life. He learned the dialect and studied everything Ifugao so thoroughly that after some years he could have passed for an Ifugao except for his physical features. Aside from his religious activities, he exerted great effort for the education of his parishioners. He established the Sacred Heart School, which was later named St. Joseph's School of Kiangan. Father Moerman was later assisted in his missionary work by Fathers Francisco Desnick and Francis Lambrecht, who established mission centers in Burnay and Banaue respectively.

As the years went by, more CICM missionaries came to the Mountain Province. Several Belgian sisters, who came to Ifugaoland during the 1930's, assisted Father Moerman in Kiangan. The sisters who particularly devoted their efforts to the education of the Ifugao youth were Sisters Dominic, Balbina, Vincent, Renata, and Godliva. Near the end of World War II, in 1945, fierce fighting destroyed the church and the mission school in Kiangan. Still active, the redoubtable Father Moerman directed the building of a modern church as well as the present St. Joseph's School. He also gave financial support to deserving Ifugao students. Until today, his annual scholarships are offered to all worthy high school graduates in Ifugao.

Truly, Father Moerman deserves his title of "Father of the Ifugaos" for he has fulfilled his promise to the Ifugaos: "I will stay here and die here. I have given my life to the Ifugao people and they are the best people in the world."

The hardships endured by these indomitable pioneer missionaries in Ifugao bore fruit at last: the conversion of numbers of Ifugaos to Christianity. In 1915, after five years of missionary work among the natives, Father Moerman was contented with barely 47 Christian converts among the 17,000 Ifugaos. In the matter of education the mission primary school supplemented the government schools. In 1914, there were 359 pupils in the mission schools and in the following year the number was almost doubled.

Source: Dumia, M. A. (1979). *The Ifugao world* (pp. 39–40). Quezon City, Philippines: New Day Publishers.

---

Vietnam, were often in Bangkok. Dan Beach Bradley (1804–1873) of the American Board of Commissioners for Foreign Missions (ABCFM) arrived in 1835 and was among those who established good relations at the royal court. His son in law, Daniel McGilvary (1828–1911), pioneered Presbyterian missions in Chiang Mai and helped negotiate an edict of toleration in 1878.

Methodism in Southeast Asia was initiated by American rather than British Methodism. James Thoburn (1836–1932), an evangelist in India, was designated a missionary bishop in 1888. He was in Yangon in 1878, and appointed William Oldham (1854–1937) to Singapore in 1885. From Singapore, Methodism spread rapidly to Malaya, Sarawak, Sumatra, and the Philippines. Commitment to education and the development of publishing ventures was part of a strategic sense of the importance of migrant Chinese communities from South China and of the need for mission to be locally supported. An entrepreneurial business style ethos was also connected to a rising demand for education in English, even if the synergy of American culture and Asian need could not always be sustained.

The success of Catholic missions in Vietnam was challenged by severe persecutions, yet there was growth as well as bloodshed. Between 1820 and 1885, some 130,000 people lost their lives, including bishops, priests, catechists, and members of Les Manates de la Croix, an order for women founded in 1640. During this time France became increasingly involved, capturing the south of Vietnam in 1859, and treating the Center and the North as a protectorate from 1883. Despite the many martyrs and difficulties the church grew rapidly, and by 1915 there were eight dioceses in French Indo China covering Laos, Vietnam, and Cambodia.

In the Philippines, Christianity helped frame movements for Filipino equality, identity, and then independence in the nineteenth century, as opposition to Spanish rule increased.

## After World War I

By 1914 Christianity had become the majority faith in the Philippines, where Spanish rule had been replaced by that of the Americans in 1898, a significant religion in Vietnam, ruled by the French, and in parts of Indonesia under the Dutch. Thailand maintained its independence and permitted missionaries in the North, though there was not a great deal to show for their efforts. Christians in Myanmar were associated with tribal groups and, less so, with Burmese Buddhists. In Sarawak and Sabah, Anglican and Catholic missionaries were having a small but steady impact.

In Vietnam, Protestants were excluded until the British and Foreign Bible Society (BFBS, 1805) established a base in Tourane (Da Nang) in 1903. Robert Jaffray (1873–1945) of the Christian and Missionary Alliance visited Vietnam in 1911 and was allowed to remain. The CMA Bible School (1921) and an emphasis on self-supporting congregations laid the foundations of the Evangelical Church of Vietnam.

The Chinese revivalist John Sung (1901–1944) had a profound effect in a series of visits to Indonesia, Malaya, Sarawak, the Philippines, Vietnam, Thailand, and Singapore between 1935 and 1939. Some evangelism bands formed at his meetings were still active over fifty years later.

## Mission to the West

Japanese occupation from 1942 to 1945 brought renewed suffering to the churches and people of Southeast Asia, but also accelerated the forces gathering for political and ecclesiastical independence and an emerging sense of regional identity. The Communist revolution in China saw the relocation of missionaries to the region in the 1950s as conflicts with Communists developed in Malaya and Vietnam. Ecumenical cooperation fought losing battles with increasing denominational diversity, but achieved some significant successes in theological education as the need for local trained leadership became urgent.

As newly independent nations moved beyond nation building and churches in Southeast Asia took control of their own destiny, the roles of the expatriate mission and missionary were transformed into partnerships. Vietnamese, Filipino, Malaysian, Singaporean, and Indonesian Christians are now influential missionaries and migrants in other parts of the world.

JOHN ROXBOROGH

*See also* Asia, Central; Asia, East; Asian Theology; Buddhism; China; Commerce; Conquest; Islam; Protestant Churches; Roman Catholic Church

### Further Reading

Barrett, D. B. (2001). *World Christian encyclopedia* (2nd ed.). New York: Oxford University Press.

Francisco, J. M. C. (2006). Christianity as church and story and the birth of the Filipino nation in the nineteenth century. In S. Gilley and B. Stanley (Eds.), *World Christianities* (pp. 528–541). Cambridge, UK: Cambridge University Press.

Goh, R. B. H. (2005). *Christianity in Southeast Asia.* Singapore: Institute of Southeast Asian Studies.

Moffett, S. H. A. (2005). *History of Christianity in Asia* (Vols. 1–2). New York: Orbis.

Phan, P. C. (1998). *Mission and catechesi: Alexandre de Rhodes and inculturation in seventeenth-century Vietnam.* Maryknoll, NY: Orbis.

Phan, P. C. (2006). Christianity in Indochina. In Sheridan Gilley and Brian Stanley (Eds.), *World Christianities* (pp. 513–527). Cambridge, UK: Cambridge University Press.

Roxborogh, J. (1995). Contextualisation and re-contextualisation: Regional patterns in the history of Southeast Asian Christianity. *Asia Journal of Theology, 9*(1), 30-46.

Roxborogh, J. (2006). Christianity in South-East Asia, 1914–2000. In Hugh McLeod (Ed.), *The Cambridge history of Christianity* (pp. 436-49). Cambridge, UK: Cambridge University Press.

Sunquist, S. (2001). *A dictionary of Asian Christianity*. Grand Rapids, MI: Eerdmans

# Asian Theology

There are many ways of approaching Asian theology. One recent three-volume, 2,131-page bibliography takes the geographical route and structures its exposition according to three regions: South and Austral Asia, Southeast Asia, and Northeast Asia (England 2002). Asian theology can also be examined chronologically, tracing its historical twists and turns. These tacks have the advantage of comprehensiveness and thoroughness, but risk missing the forest for the trees. Rather than taking a geographical or chronological approach, this article will present a systematic analysis of the major themes of Asian theology.

## Historical Context

Historians have recently grown more aware that Christianity is an Eastern rather than a Western religion. Geographically speaking, it is an Asian religion, since its founder was born in the Middle East (Southwest Asia). Furthermore, from its very beginnings, Christianity spread not only to the western parts of the Roman empire but also deeper into Asia—in particular, to Syria, Mesopotamia, Persia, Armenia, and India. What was brought to these lands by missionaries as well as by merchants along the Silk Road was not a monolithic Christianity but rather a variety of Christianities with different languages, liturgies, spiritualities, theologies, organizational structures, and cultures. This dizzying diversity was compounded by the many and various ways in which the Christian faith was received and transformed in these countries. As a consequence, from its very birth, Asian Christian theology was marked by multiplicity and diversity, characteristics still prevalent in its contemporary trends and forms.

Historically, Asian Christianity may be divided in three periods, each with different ecclesiastical and secular forces shaping its theology. In the pre-colonial era, from the first to the fifteenth century, the main form of Christianity and Christian theology was Syrian. There is an ancient tradition, maintained by the Thomas Christians, that Christianity was brought to South India (Malabar) by the apostle Thomas (and, according to another source, also by the apostle Bartholomew). A different tradition holds that it was brought by merchants and missionaries of the East Syrian or Persian Church. This early Indian Christianity is said to be "Hindu in culture, Christian in faith, and oriental in worship" (England 2002, vol. 1, 195).

According to the inscription on the famous Xi'an stele (781 CE), the Nestorian/East Syrian monk Alopen went to Changan, China, in 635 CE. Nestorian Christianity, which made use of Buddhist, Confucianist, and Daoist concepts and terminology to formulate its theology, flourished until the fall of the Tang dynasty in 907 CE. Roman Catholic missionaries came to China under the reign of Khubilai (1260–1294) but did not have any long-lasting influence.

The second era of Asian Christianity, from the sixteenth to the beginning of the twentieth century, coincides with the Western colonization of many Asian countries and the establishment of massive missions, first Catholic and then Protestant. The ecclesiastical structures, the theologies, and the pieties of the Western churches were unavoidably exported to Asia, though there were notable attempts at inculturating them, especially by the Jesuits.

The third era, from the middle of the twentieth century to our time, has been marked by liturgical and church reforms and by theological creativity. In the Roman Catholic Church, this renewal was the fruit of the Second Vatican Council (1962–1965) and its main agency has been the Federation of Asian Bishops' Conferences (FABC), founded in 1972.

## Theological Elaborations

All theologies are necessarily contextual; they have to make use of local languages and thought forms to make the Christian faith accessible to people in new sociopolitical, cultural, and religious environments. The Asian context is often represented as characterized by extreme poverty, cultural diversity, and religious pluralism, and Asian theologies can be viewed as self-conscious attempts to respond to these three features: liberation (to poverty), inculturation (to cultural diversity), and interreligious dialogue (to religious pluralism). Chronologically, the introduction of Asian Christian theologies began with inculturation, followed with liberation, and ended with interreligious dialogue.

### Dialogue with Culture

The first to attempt a systematic expression of the Christian faith in indigenous cultural terms belongs to the Nestorian/East Syrian missionaries during the T'ang dynasty. As can be seen from the inscription on the Xi'an stele, its author, Jing-jing, made a creative use of Buddhist, Confucianist, and Daoist concepts and terms to expound the Trinity, creation, the original fall, Satan's rule, the Incarnation, salvation, the Bible, baptism, evangelization, ministry, morality, fasting, the liturgy of the hours, and the Eucharist. Similar borrowings can be found in the so-called Duahuang Cave Documents, such as the *Book of Jesus-Messiah, Discourse on Monotheism,* and *Book of Mysterious Rest and Joy.*

In the seventeenth century, under the influence of Alessandro Valignano (1539–1606), the Jesuits carried out an extensive work of inculturation, particularly in China, Japan, Vietnam, and India. In China, Matteo Ricci's (1552–1610) use of Confucianism, for example, in his famous *Tianzhu shiyi* (The True Meaning of the Lord of Heaven) and his adoption of the controversial practice of ancestor veneration, and the work of Giulio Aleni (1582–1649) and the *figurists* (who believed that Christian doctrines were "prefigured" in Chinese philosophy and culture) were path-breaking in formulating an Asian theology. In India, Roberto de Nobili lived as a sannyasi and taught the Christian faith using the philosophical and religious categories of Hinduism. In Vietnam, Alexandre de Rhodes (1593–1660) wrote a catechism in Vietnamese.

In more recent times, the focus has been, especially in the Catholic Church, on liturgical inculturation, with the adoption of indigenous rituals, vestments, music, dance, and architecture. Another extremely important achievement is the translation of the Bible into local languages, which is in itself a work of inculturation, to which Protestant missionaries have made an enormous contribution.

### Dialogue with the Poor

Even though Asian Christian theology had not ignored the sociopolitical and economic dimensions of their new constituents, it was only in the 1970s, under the influence of Latin-American liberation theology, that Asian theologians began developing indigenous forms of liberation theology. The sources of Asian liberation theology are drawn less from Marxist theories than from the experiences of those who were oppressed by colonialism and military dictatorships. In Korea, *minjung* theology was elaborated to defend the people (*minjung*) against human rights abuses, especially under President Pak Jung Hee's regime and to seek release from the collective bottled-up anger due to oppression (*han*). The *minjung* is identified with the crowd (*ochlos*) of the gospels and Jesus is presented as a member of the *minjung*.

In the Philippines, the "theology of struggle" was developed during the years of martial law imposed by President Ferdinand Marcos; it reclaimed the tradition of Filipino nationalist movements and emphasized the process and spirituality of the struggle rather than its outcome of liberation. In India, *dalit* (broken) theology was developed to combat discriminations perpetrated by the caste system, and tribal theologies were developed to draw attention to abuses of tribal rights, especially land rights, by colonialism and the central governments that followed. In Taiwan, "homeland theology" and *Chhut Thau Thin* theology supported the right of the Taiwanese people to self-determination.

One important recent development in Asian liberation theologies is Asian feminist theology, which combats the patriarchy and androcentrism prevalent in many Asian cultures and seeks to foster the full flourishing of Asian women.

## Interreligious Dialogue

Asia is the cradle of most of the world's major religions, and Christians have been very active in dialogue with the followers of these other faiths, even in the earliest centuries, particularly in China and India. Today, such dialogues, according to the FABC, should include four aspects: life, action, theological reflection, and spiritual experience. In the recent past, these fourfold dialogues were carried out especially by Western monks and clerics, including Jules Monchanin, Henri Le Saux, Francis Mahieu, Bede Griffiths, and Thomas Merton, many of whom lived as sannyasis in ashrams. In the theological aspect, the focus has been on the doctrines of God, the Trinity, Christology, and spirituality. Also relevant are the works of Raimundo Panikkar (with Hinduism), Aloysius Pieris (with Buddhism), William Johnston (with Zen Buddhism), Peter Phan (with Confucianism), and Joseph Wong (with Daoism).

## Ongoing Challenges

In the ongoing dialogue of Christianity with Asian religions, the Christian God is interpreted using Emptiness,

Brahman, and Dao; the Trinity is interpreted in terms of the Trimurti and Heaven-Earth-Humanity; Christ is interpreted in terms of monk, guru, avatar, buddha, and teacher; and spirituality in terms of contemplation, monasticism, yoga, *wu-wei, ren,* and yin-yang. Asian theology is on a fruitful course as it responds to the triple challenges of inculturation, liberation, and inter-religious dialogue.

PETER C. PHAN

## Further Reading

Amaladoss, M. (1997). *Life in freedom: Liberation theologies from Asia.* Maryknoll, NY: Orbis Books.

England, J. C., et al. (Eds.). (2002). *Asian Christian theologies: A research guide to authors, movements, sources* (3 vols.). Maryknoll, NY: Orbis Books.

Phan, P. C. (2004). *Being religious interreligiously: Asian perspectives on interfaith dialogue.* Maryknoll, NY: Orbis Books.

## Bible

When William Carey published his *Enquiry into the Obligations of Christians, to Use Means for the Conversion of the Heathens,* in 1792, he was doing what Christians traditionally do (but in Carey's day had been badly neglected), namely demonstrating from the Bible that cross-cultural missionary work was an essential part of the calling of the church.

### Biblical Texts as Authority for Mission

The text Carey chose to expound as his primary justification was Matthew 28:18–20, in which the risen Jesus, on the basis of his claim to authority as Lord of heaven and earth, mandated his own disciples to go and make disciples of all nations—a text that has come to be known in missionary circles as "the Great Commission."

The Bible has always been the source of the authority on which Christians believe they can legitimately engage in the broad sweep of mission activities all over the world.

However, that authority does not rest on a single text. Even Jesus himself did not imagine that he was launching a new idea in the mission of the church. Rather, in the equivalent passage in Luke 24:46–47 Jesus told his disciples, "This is what is written: The Christ will suffer and rise from the dead on the third day, and repentance and forgiveness of sins will be preached in his name to all nations, beginning at Jerusalem."

The phrase "this is what is written" refers to the Scriptures we now call the Old Testament. Jesus claims that the Scriptures as a whole not only point toward his own identity as the messiah who would suffer and rise again (the center point of the whole Christian faith), but also point beyond that to what must inevitably follow—namely, mission to the nations in the name of Christ. Putting both Matthew and Luke together, then, it is clear that Christian mission sees its authority and legitimization both in the Lordship of Christ and in the whole message of the Bible as endorsed by Christ.

Mission flows, then, not just from one or two "missionary texts," but from the total Christian worldview that is built upon the Bible's own grand narrative. The Bible presents to us an understanding of reality within which mission finds its own validation and understanding. The Bible is the story of the mission of the one true living God. In creation, God acted with purposefulness culminating in the creation of humanity with the mission of caring for the earth. In response to the devastating effects of human rebellion and sin (in the Fall and its sequel, see Genesis 3–11), God initiated a mission of redemption that will ultimately include all nations and the whole creation. It began with God's covenant promise to Abraham, to bless all nations through him. The people of Abraham, therefore, had a mission—not, in Old Testament times, to "go and be missionaries," but to live as the distinctive people of Yahweh God, as a light to the nations, and ultimately as the vehicle of redemptive blessing going to the nations through the saving work of the Messiah.

With the coming of the Messiah Jesus, God's mission of salvation was accomplished in his cross and resurrection. The outpouring of God's Spirit, at Pentecost, then launched the era of centrifugal mission to the nations. The final vision of the Bible is of a redeemed and renewed creation, the ultimate "mission accomplished."

The over-arching story of the whole Bible (from Creation through the Fall, redemption within history, and the hope of the New Creation) thus provides the Christian worldview, which sees the mission of God for the redemption of creation as the key to history, "life, the universe, and everything."

## Bible as the Focus of Mission

Given such an understanding of the significance of their Scriptures as the revelation of the mind and mission of God for the world, it is not surprising that both Jews and Christians have engaged in the translation of these Scriptures from earliest times. Nehemiah 8 records an occasion in the fifth century BCE when the Hebrew scrolls of the Torah were orally translated and explained during its public reading to people who were already probably speaking early Aramaic. Between the third and first century BCE, the Hebrew Scriptures were translated into Greek, mainly by and for Greek-speaking Jews in Alexandria. These Greek texts (the Septuagint) provided a scriptural platform for the dissemination of the Christian message in the early Gentile mission of the church to the Greco-Roman world. In these early centuries, the Hebrew and Greek texts of the Bible were translated also into Latin and Syriac, as the church in mission moved west and east.

The Reformation saw a massive upsurge in the translation of the Bible into many of the vernacular languages of Europe because of the renewed emphasis on the importance of God's word being available to ordinary people. This is a powerful missiological principle, even if for many years it was confined to Europe (at least in the Protestant world). John Wycliffe, who lived 200 years before the Reformation had translated the Bible from Latin into English around 1380, while William Tyndale (1494–1536) produced a translation from the original texts that has had profound influence on the English language, just as Luther's translation did for the German language. The missiological drive behind these efforts was captured by Tyndale, who said his goal was to make even the common ploughboy to know more of the Scriptures than most of the clergy of his day.

With the dawn of the modern era of Protestant missions, however, there was an explosion of effort in Bible translation that has increased decade after decade. Some of the earliest European missionaries were remarkable linguists, mastering several indigenous languages, studying the associated cultures and religions, and translating the Bible indefatigably (e.g., William Carey, Hudson Taylor, Henry Martyn, Adoniram Judson). The work of agencies such as the United Bible Societies and Wycliffe Bible Translators has resulted in parts or all of the Bible being translated into thousands of languages all over the globe, including some of the most remote regions with languages spoken by relatively small populations. At the other end of the scale, the Chinese church in recent years has printed some 40 million Bibles in Chinese.

The missiological motive behind this remarkable volume of translation work is clear. In Christian understanding, the Creator God reaches out in self-communicating revelation to his human creation. This revelation is expressed in his word. The living word of God became human in Jesus of Nazareth, a man born in a particular culture, speaking a particular language, but the significance of his life, teaching, death and Resurrection is relevant for all people and cultures. Similarly, the written word of God came by human means, in the languages of the ancient Israelites (Hebrew and some Aramaic in the Old Testament) and of the early

A page from an old Chinese-language Bible. The text is Ezekial 16: 25–26.

first-century Christians (Greek in the New Testament). The particularity of this scriptural revelation has always served its universality. The God who loves the whole world also wills to be known throughout the world, in all human cultures and languages. The purpose of Bible translation is thus to bring the life-giving and life-transforming word of God into the hearts of all by providing it in the language of the heart for all.

The cultural impact of Christian missional commitment to Bible translation has been profound, though insufficiently recognized. Contrary to the myth that missionaries destroy cultures, the reverse has most often been the case, especially through Bible translation and all the essential work that precedes it. Language is the most vital tool and expression of any human culture. Lose or destroy a language, and you suffocate its culture. Many languages throughout history and still today exist in prewritten forms. Christian mission has been at the forefront of reducing oral languages to writing; providing the technical support of orthography, grammars, dictionaries, etc.; initiating and extending literacy projects; setting up publishing houses; training indigenous writers, editors, and so on. All of this has been critical to the survival of some remote cultures and in the development of their sense of identity, dignity, and rightful status in the human multicultural family (See Sanneh 1989 and Walls 1996).

## Bible and the Scope of Mission

As the rest of this volume makes clear, Christian mission incorporates a very wide variety of activity, of which Bible translation is but one. The phrase "holistic mission" is often used to describe this, and it also has deep roots in the Bible itself, for the Bible, as we saw above, presents the mission of God as the foundation on which all human missionary efforts must be built. Each part of the canon of the Bible contributes to this foundation. The Pentateuch tells the story of creation, fall, and God's plan of redemption through Abraham. The exodus provides the classic model of God in action as Redeemer. The laws of ancient Israel sought to model a society committed to holiness, compassion, and justice. The prophets called Israel to account for their constant failure to fulfill their mission of being an ethical light to the nations and pointed to a different future. The worship and wisdom of Israel echo with notes of universality, pointing us to the nations as the scope of God's saving interest. The gospels narrate the climax and core of the whole Bible story in the incarnation, death, and Resurrection of Jesus. Acts and the epistles record the initial missionary expansion of the church beyond the boundaries of historic Israel in a process that has continued for 2,000 years and reached the very ends of the earth.

Mission is broad and holistic because God's concern is as wide as his whole creation, at every level of its brokenness and need. It is because the Bible shows God to be concerned about the poor and oppressed that Christian mission tackles the issues of poverty and all forms of injustice. Because God is the healer who, through the example of Jesus, cares for the sick, Christian mission has had a compassionate and medical dimension throughout its long history. Because God longs to bring people to repentance, forgiveness, and eternal life, Christian mission includes evangelistic proclamation of the good news of the atoning death of Jesus and the victory of his Resurrection. Because God loves his creation, commanded us to care for it, and will ultimately redeem it, Christian mission includes ecological concern and action. Because God calls human beings to account in every context of their working lives, biblically informed Christian mission refuses to dichotomize the sacred and the secular, giving priority and attention only to the former. Rather, biblical mission seeks to apply the radical challenge and the extraordinary good news of the Gospel of Jesus Christ to every area of life on our planet that has been affected by sin and evil and then calls the whole church to utilize all the gifts and resources that have been entrusted to it by God to address them in Christ's name. Or, to use the slogan of the Lausanne movement, the kind of mission that the Bible envisages involves "the whole church taking the whole Gospel to the whole world."

CHRISTOPHER J. H. WRIGHT

## Further Reading

Bauckham, R. (2003). *Bible and mission: Christian witness in a postmodern world*. Grand Rapids, MI: Baker Publishing

Chukwuma Okoye, J. (2006). *Israel and the nations: A mission theology of the Old Testament*. Maryknoll, NY: Orbis

Nissen, J. (1999). *New Testament and mission: Historical and hermeneutical perspectives*. New York: Peter Lang

Rowley, H. H. (1944). *The missionary message of the Old Testament*. London: Carey Press

Sanneh, L. (1989). *Transforming the message: Missionary impact on culture*. Maryknoll, NY: Orbis Books.

Walls, A. F. (1996). *The missionary movement in Christian history: Studies in the transmission of the faith*. Maryknoll, NY: Orbis.Books.

Walls, A. F. (2002). *The cross-cultural process in Christian history.* New York: Continuum.

Wright, C. J. H. (2006). The mission of God: Unlocking the Bible's grand narrative. Downers Grove, IL: IVP.

## Bible Translation

The Old Testament was originally written in Hebrew and the New Testament in Greek. Today we are dependent on translations of the Bible in order to be able to read and understand it. This article will provide an overview of Bible translation through the past two centuries.

## First Three Centuries

About forty years after Jesus was crucified the city of Jerusalem was completely destroyed by the Roman government. At this time Christians were scattered all over the known world. And wherever they went Christian communities were started, and the Scriptures were translated from the Greek and Hebrew into the languages of the many new believers. So in this period translation of the Scriptures flourished. They were known simply as "the writings," from the Greek *hai graphai*.

## Fourth Century

Rome was ruler of the world; Latin was the international language. Several Latin translations, often inaccurate, leaked into circulation; the church needed an official translation. Pope Damasus assigned the job to Jerome, the great classical scholar, and he spent twenty-five years in Bethlehem translating the Bible from the Greek and Hebrew into the common, ordinary Latin spoken by the people, the "vulgar" Latin. This translation became known as the Latin Vulgate. Jerome's Vulgate was the basis of the first translations into English.

### Standard for the Western World

This Latin Bible is important because through the Roman Catholic Church it became the standard version for the entire Western world until the Reformation. It remains the official version of Catholicism, although since Vatican II in 1962 Catholic translations have been sanctioned from Hebrew and Greek into other languages. The Vulgate was revised in 1592 and is called the Sixto-Clementine Vulgate. Later other revisions

were undertaken but not completed. The Latin Vulgate as well as the Latin language in general has had a lot of influence on English and the English Bible. Words such as "justify" and "sanctify," for example, are derived from Latin.

## Fifth to Thirteenth Centuries

For the next one thousand years the Scriptures were limited to only Latin by the church and government authorities. They refused to allow them to be translated into the languages of the people for fear the people would misrepresent them.

There were exceptions. Armenia, located north of Syria, was evangelized by the Syrian church. Early Armenian versions were done in Syriac. The now-standard Armenian version dates from the fifth century. In the late eighth century Charlemagne commissioned a translation of parts of the Bible for the use of his missionaries in the drive to convert pagan Germans. And in the ninth century two Greek brothers, Cyril and Methodius, were sent from Constantinople to Moravia to translate the Gospels and parts of the Old Testament into Slavonic.

A translation was also completed in Ethiopia in the early centuries, one version of which was made from the Syriac. The New Testament was translated into Arabic from Syriac, Coptic, and Greek after the time of Muhammad (570–632). The Arabic Old Testament was translated from the Hebrew in the tenth century.

## Fourteenth Century

As centuries passed, common people could no longer understand the Latin Scripture. The church hierarchy, instead of promoting new translations, clung to the Vulgate because it forced people to rely on the church's teaching.

### First English Bible

John Wycliffe, often called the Morning Star of the Reformation, defied the clergy. His life was changed through reading the Scriptures in Latin, and he determined to translate Latin Scriptures into English. He was the first to translate the Bible into English and recruited traveling preachers, called Lollards, to spread God's Word in English. The Lollards would copy the Scripture by hand and in secret, and these "poor preachers" (as they were known among the people) went up and down the land of England reading the Scriptures to the people in their own language. People working in the fields, people gathered at a well or at a

Wartburg Castle, where
Martin Luther translated
the Bible into German.
*Courtesy of istockphoto.com.*

market, people walking down the roads or sitting in their homes—for the first time these people were hearing God's word in their own languages. Many who read and many who listened were punished, and some were burned at the stake. Though Wycliffe's Bibles, and later his bones, were burned, he had sparked a Reformation.

John Wycliffe died of old age in 1384; thirty years later (1415) the church authorities ordered his body to be exhumed, his bones burned, and his ashes thrown into the river Swift. With that taken care of, the land of England was once more considered by the church to be free from "pollution." It was at this time that Wycliffe's followers were imprisoned, and a great many of them were killed. Nevertheless, the book that John Wycliffe had translated and his followers had read and taught to the people influenced England for the next 150 years and did much to shape its history.

## Fifteenth Century

This was the century of Johan Gutenberg of Germany, the man who invented the printing press and changed the world. The first book to be printed was the Latin Bible in 1464.

## Sixteenth Century

In Germany a monk name Martin Luther found that his life had been changed through reading the Scriptures in Hebrew and Greek. Defying the church and state, he declared that his conscience was governed only by the Word of God, that the authority of the Scriptures took precedence over the authority of the church.

In order to protect him, his friends hid him in the Castle of Wartburg. It was there that he translated the New Testament from the Greek into the German language. He published about 100,000 copies of his German translation, and soon translators across Europe made God's Word available in every major language.

### First English Printing

During this same time period William Tyndale translated the New Testament into English from the Greek rather than from the Latin text. His was also the first English New Testament to be printed, despite the continued popularity of the handwritten Wycliffe version. He was determined to make the Scripture available for all. The authorities in England denied his attempt to translate the New Testament, so he was forced to flee to the continent, where his New Testament was printed in 1525–1526. When copies arrived in England the Bishop of London confiscated as many as he could and burned them. Others attacked it as heresy because Tyndale abandoned ecclesiastical terms such as "church," "priest," "penance," and "charity" for more common words such as, respectively, "congregation," "senior," "repentance," and "love."

His translation was bold and free, good flowing English. He revised it in 1534 and again in 1535, but it is the 1534 edition that is considered his best. He also undertook to translate the Old Testament and finished the Pentateuch, Jonah, Genesis, and the historical books to 2 Chronicles; he was cut short of completion by his arrest in Antwerp, Belgium, and imprisonment near Brussels. He was strangled and burned at the stake at Vilvorde on October 6, 1536. His final words were, "Lord, open the King of England's eyes."

While Tyndale was in prison, an associate named Miles Coverdale completed, on his own, an entire English Bible that was made up of all Tyndale's work plus the rest of the Old Testament. In a great twist of irony, the King of England in 1537—just one year after Tyndale's martyrdom—gave his official approval to Coverdale's version, even though it was substantially Tyndale's, which he had so recently vigorously opposed.

## Seventeenth and Eighteenth Centuries

The translation that has become central to English culture, as Luther's is to German, is the King James Bible (also called the Authorized Version). Edited by forty-seven scholars between 1604 and 1611, it aims to take the best from all earlier translations. By far its major source is Tyndale.

### Missionary Use

The Bible was virtually a European book, since the majority of Scripture translations were done in languages spoken only in Europe. Missionaries changed that. Matthew's gospel in Malay, which appeared in 1629, began a movement to see Scriptures in more non-European languages. In America, John Eliot translated the Bible into the language of the Massachusetts Indians. His translation appeared in 1662 and became the first Bible for missionary use in America.

By 1800 there were sixty-six languages with some portion of Scripture, forty with the whole Bible. An English cobbler named William Carey forwarded translation in India and Asia. Believing that the Bible was the most effective way to advance Christianity, Carey translated or helped translate Scripture in over twenty Indian languages. With his colleagues he translated and printed Scripture in forty-five languages and dialects in Asia, thirty-five for the first time. This work was done between 1793 and 1834.

## Twentieth Century

Beginning in 1804 Bible societies were formed for the translation, publication, and distribution of the Scrip-

tures, and translation became a worldwide effort to reach people who had never heard the Good News.

In 1917, a young missionary named William Cameron Townsend found it difficult to evangelize the Cakchiquel people with a Spanish Bible. While working on a Cakchiquel New Testament, Townsend caught a new vision for Bible translation—every people group, no matter how small or remote, should have a Bible they could read.

Townsend founded Wycliffe Bible Translators and its sister organization, the Summer Institute of Linguistics, to fulfill his vision. For over fifty years, these organizations have worked with others, united in the belief that God wants people to read His Word.

## The Future

The current figures from the *Ethnologue* list 7,299 languages in the world today. More than half of these languages do not have a translation of the Bible available in that language. It is encouraging to see the progress in Bible translation during this past century. At the start of the twentieth century there were just over five hundred translations, but by the end of the century there were well over 2,200 translations. However, the current estimate by Wycliffe Bible Translators when work will be started in all languages still needing translations is 150 years.

ANDREW GALLMAN

### Further Reading

Bruce, F. F. (1953). *The Books and the parchments.* London: Pickering & Inglis, Ltd.

Carmack, M. M. (1938). *John Wyclif and the English Bible.* New York: American Tract Society.

Comfort, Philip W. (1991). *The complete guide to Bible versions.* Wheaton, IL. Tyndale House.

*The English Bible.* (1961). New York: Oxford University Press.

Goodrick, E. W. (1988). *Is my Bible the inspired word of God?* Portland, OR: Multnomah.

Gordon, R. G., Jr. (Ed.). (2005). *Ethnologue: Languages of the world* (15th ed.) Dallas, TX: SIL.

Larson, M. L. (1984). *Meaning-based translation: A guide to cross-language equivalence.* Lanham, MD: University Press of America.

Nida, E. (1952). *God's word in man's language.* New York: Harper.

Smalley, W. A. (1991). *Translation as mission.* Macon, GA: Mercer University Press.

# Bibliography

For much of the past century, mission scholars had to travel to major libraries, often internationally, for thorough research. Undergraduate students were limited to books and periodicals in local libraries. Today mission bibliographies, and often full text, are available online for undergraduates as well as seasoned scholars. The purpose of this article is to outline available resources through a brief history of mission bibliographies.

## Library Collections

Cataloguers at major research libraries provided the first bibliographies of missions and missionaries. Initially they included only published books in the field, but today they may also include unpublished archival sources in their collections. Mission scholars in 1950 accessed sources primarily through three printed multivolume catalogues—those of the Library of Congress in Washington, D.C.; the British Museum in London; and the Missionary Research Library in New York. The latter, printed in seventeen volumes by G. K. Hall in 1968, was remarkable for its inclusion of more than thirty thousand pamphlets and extensive subject indexing of the collection. Today the collection can be accessed online through the catalogue of the Burke Library of Columbia University. It includes archival papers.

Catalogues of most research libraries are now accessible by online searches using Google or another search engine. Learn to use Boolean operators to narrow subject searches. Combine keywords with "and," "or," and "not" between them to make your search more focused.

## Mission Bibliographies

Although published books remain invaluable sources, journal articles often are more current or detailed in coverage. Before computers, printed bibliographies of these sources were made available through the commitment and dedication of a small number of mission bibliographers, many of whom gave a lifetime of dedication to this task. Some are now accessible online.

### Europe

Robert Streit pioneered in Roman Catholic development of mission bibliographies. His greatest contribution was the founding of *Bibliotheca Missionum* and his editing of volumes 1–5 (1916–1929). It is a topical bibliography in chronological order of Roman Catholic missions in America, Asia, and Africa. Upon Streit's death Johannes Dindinger and Johannes Rommerskirchen took up the project and by 1974 had extended the work to thirty volumes. The quarterly journal *Zeitschrift für Missionswissenschaft,* published by the University of Münster since 1911, contains mission bibliographies.

In 1925 Willem Marinus Cardinal Van Rossum, prefect of Propaganda Fide, the Vatican's missionary arm, called Streit to Rome to develop a new collection that was to form the nucleus of a new Pontifical Missionary Library. Inspired by this growing collection, Streit's successor, Dindinger, founded *Bibliografia Missionaria* (*BM*) in 1935. This annual bibliography of scholarly literature on mission studies initially included both books and periodical articles from Catholic sources, with indexes in Italian. After the Second Vatican Council (1962–1965) the material in *BM* broadened to include works in the major European languages and ecumenical sources. Willi Henkel of the Oblate Order, edited *BM* from 1972 to 2000. He changed its name in 1986 to *Bibliographia Missionaria* and provided yearly indexes in English and a broader subject coverage.

The Interuniversity Institute for Missiological and Ecumenical Research (IIMO) leads in work on mission bibliographies in the Netherlands. Since 1972 it has published *Exchange: Journal of Missiological and Ecumenical Research.* A quarterly publication now available online, *Exchange* includes topical bibliographies on issues of Christian mission and culture, as well as updates on the contents of the more than 450 theological journals received from non-Western countries.

Le Centre de Documentation et d'Information Missionnaire (CEDIM) was founded in Paris, France, in 1979. It provides access to a computerized database of publications of the churches in francophone Africa, Asia, and the Americas.

Missionswissenschaftliches Institut (mission-scientific institute or MISSIO), founded in Aachen, Germany, in 1971, contains over 120,000 volumes. It specializes in supplying information on the current situation of church and theology in Africa, Asia, Oceania, and Latin America. Using VThK, the metacatalogue for German-speaking theological and special libraries, which provides English translation, the researcher has access to over 5 million sources, including those of MIKADO, the mission library and catholic documentation place of MISSIO.

The Nordic Institute for Missiological and Ecumenical Research (NIME) is an interdisciplinary network for the scholarly study of Christian missions and ecumenism worldwide. Its website gives access to the *Missio Nordica* (MISSNORD) database of missiological material from the Nordic region from 1989 to 1996.

Servizio di Documentazione e Studi (SEDOS), based in Rome, Italy, has provided documentation of mission concerns, including those of the relation between church and society since Vatican II. Its website provides full text of articles in English, French, Italian, and Spanish.

The Centre for the Study of Christianity in the Non-Western World (CSCNWW), now affiliated with the University of Edinburgh, provides access not only to its own collections but also to those in other countries. African Christian Bibliography is a searchable database that includes books, pamphlets, journal articles, dissertations, and seminar papers from several African countries.

### Ecumenical

Following the World Missionary Conference (Edinburgh 1910), its organizer, Joseph H. Oldham founded the *International Review of Missions* in 1912. Published quarterly and indexed annually, it included from its first issue a classified and annotated bibliography of the most important missionary books and periodical articles in various European languages. It included subjects related closely to missionary work, such as the non-Christian religions and linguistic study. With Oldham as its editor until 1927, the *IRM* established itself as the most prominent missionary periodical in the world.

In 1969 the *IRM* dropped the "S" in its title to become the *International Review of* Mission. Mission was no longer a one-way outreach from the north to the south but rather the primary business of all Christians in every country. Andrew F. Walls (b. 1928), founder of the CSCNWW in Scotland, began in 1972 his long and present editorship of the journal's quarterly bibliography. He changed its scope to include the burgeoning literature on churches engaged in mission in Africa, Asia, Latin America, and Oceania and on mission related to culture, society, economic life, and politics. The cumulative bibliography of the *IRM* is published online by CSCNWW.

Most mission bibliographies have limited annotation describing the content of the works cited. One exception is the *International Mission Bibliography, 1960–2000,* edited by Norman E. Thomas. Sponsored by the American Society of Missiology and the International Association for Mission Studies, it contains entries by an international team of thirty-seven scholars of about twelve thousand books published in European languages.

### North America

In 1891 Rev. Samuel Macaulay Jackson compiled an international bibliography of five thousand books published in the nineteenth century on foreign missions. His sources were library collections in the United States and Europe. It was published both as Appendix A of the *Encyclopedia of Missions* (1891) and independently.

One century later a sea change had occurred. Unlike in Europe, where mission institutes had led in developing access to mission sources, in America the American Theological Library Association (ATLA) took the lead. Founded in 1946 as a scholarly, ecumenical, and non-profit organization, ATLA by 1991 provided the leading international database on religion, including mission studies. It indexed articles in periodicals from 1949 and books from 1975. Increasingly, it provides linkages to the full text of articles, including those in *Missiology* and the *International Bulletin of Missionary Research.*

## Other Resources

*Missionalia,* published since 1973 by the Southern African Missiological Society, covers more than publications in southern Africa. In three issues per year it also abstracts about a thousand articles on missions and missiology.

In Latin America the *Bibliografia Teológica Comentada del Area Iberoamericana,* has been the major resource on Latin American, Spanish, and Portuguese Christianity. Published annually from 1973 to 1996 by ISEDET, the ecumenical center of higher theological education in Buenos Aires, Argentina, it contains many annotated works.

## The Electronic Revolution

Space does not permit enumeration of resources accessible on six continents. The best portal for accessing documents, archives, and media is provided by the Yale Divinity School at www.library.yale.edu/div/MissionsResources.htm. Increasingly, full text of documents will be available online, bringing abundant resources on missions and missionaries to every home and school.

Norman E. Thomas

*See also* Archives; Biography; Internet; Journals; Libraries

## Further Reading

Anderson, G. H. (1994). *Mission legacies: Biographical studies of leaders of the modern missionary movement.* Maryknoll, NY: Orbis Books.

Henkel, W. (1982). The legacy of Robert Streit, Johannes Dindinger, and Johannes Rommerskirchen. *International Bulletin of Missionary Research, 6*(1), 16–21.

Jackson, S. M. (1891). *A bibliography of foreign missions.* New York: Funk & Wagnalls.

Thomas, N. E. (Ed.). (2003). *International mission bibliography, 1960–2000.* Lanham, MD: Scarecrow Press.

Whiteman, D. (Ed.). (1999). Tools of the trade. *Missiology, 27*(1), 5–122.

## Biography

Missionary biographies and autobiographies tell the stories of men and women who have felt called and sent by God into the world to witness in word and deed to the gospel of Jesus Christ. Their stories have inspired countless others to follow in their footsteps and have encouraged many more at home to support the missions with prayers and gifts.

### Pioneers

Biographies of some pioneers have become classics. Among these are accounts of Francis Xavier in Asia, Alessandro Valignano in China and Japan, Matteo Ricci in China, Roberto de Nobili in India, Bartolome de Las Casas in Spanish America, Father Damien and Mother Marianne of Molokai (Hawaii), William Carey in India, Adoniram and Ann Judson in Burma, David and Mary Livingstone in Africa, J. Hudson Taylor in China, Mary Slessor of Calabar (Nigeria), Lott Carey, the first black missionary to Africa, Lottie Moon in China, and Dr. Ida Scudder in India.

### Tool for Teaching

Biographies are used by scholars for teaching, to learn from the past, and to develop new theories, policies, and strategies for future mission initiatives. *Missiology,* the journal of the American Society of Missiology, devoted its October 1999 issue to "Missionary Biography as Missiology," and featured articles that explored the ways in which missionary biographies contribute to mission studies. A popular feature that appears regularly in the *International Bulletin of Missionary Research,* called the "Mission Legacy" series, profiles outstanding missionaries. Alan Neely's *Christian Mission: A Case Study Approach* (1995) is a prime example of the use of missionary case studies as a creative tool for teaching. Ruth Tucker skillfully uses biography to study the history of missions in *From Jerusalem to Irian Jaya: A Biographical History of Christian Missions* (2004).

Biographies of missionary martyrs tell of those who made the ultimate sacrifice, as in Elisabeth Elliot's *Through Gates of Splendor* (1957). Her compelling account of five young American missionaries who lost their lives in the jungles of Ecuador in 1956 when they were speared by the Waorani (Auca) Indians they were trying to reach with the gospel was dramatized in the films *Beyond the Gates of Splendor* (2005) and *End of the Spear* (2006). Ana Carrigan's *Salvador Witness* (1984) describes four American Catholic women who were murdered in El Salvador in 1980. In *Jean de Brebeuf, 1593–1649* (1975) Joseph P. Donnelly profiles one of the numerous Jesuit missionaries who were martyred in North America.

### Sources

The largest comprehensive reference work for the study of missionary biography is G. H. Anderson's *Biographical Dictionary of Christian Missions* (1998, 1999). It includes articles on 2,400 outstanding persons in the history of Christian missions, who represent Anglican, Orthodox, Pentecostal, Protestant, Roman Catholic, independent, and indigenous churches. As described in the preface, "Persons included in this work were chosen because they made a significant contribution—often a pioneering role—to the advancement of Christian missions. Nearly one hundred were martyrs. Not all those included were missionaries. Some were involved at the home base in promotion, recruitment, administration, missiology, teaching, writing, prayer, funding, 'the diffusion of intelligence,' and other forms of missions advocacy" (Anderson 1999, vii).

Another type of resource is the *Biographical Dictionary of Methodist Missionaries to Japan: 1873–1993* (1995), edited by John W. Krummel, a definitive bilingual source for the missionaries of one denomination in one country. The *New International Dictionary of Pentecostal and Charismatic Movements* (2004), edited by Stanley Burgess and his colleagues, includes the major missionary figures of one tradition to all parts of the world. Other reference works that include missionary biographies are *Encyclopedia of Missions* (1904), edited by Edwin Munsell Bliss; *Concise Dictionary of the Christian World Mission* (1970), edited by Stephen Neill and his colleagues; *Dictionary of Asian Christianity* (2001), edited by Scott W. Sunquist; *Evangelical Dictionary of World Missions* (2000), edited by A. Scott Moreau; and *Dictionary of Scottish Church History and Theology* (1993), edited by Nigel de S. Cameron.

A portrait of John Eliot, seventeenth-century missionary to New England and the first to translate the Bible into a Native-American language.

## Neglected Subjects

Women have played a significant role in missionary work, especially in the nineteenth and twentieth centuries, but their contributions have not always been recognized. Protestants generally did not send single women missionaries until after the mid-nineteenth century, and often married women were not listed by name or even counted, since they were considered spouses and not missionaries unless their husbands died and they carried on alone. Fortunately, there is a growing number of notable studies with rich biographical data that describe women in mission. These include Jane Hunter, *The Gospel of Gentility: American Women Missionaries in Turn-of-the-Century China* (1984); Patricia R. Hill, *The World Their Household: The American Woman's Foreign Mission Movement and Cultural Transformation, 1870–1920* (1985); Ruth A. Tucker, *Guardians of the Great Commission: The Story of Women in Modern Missions* (1988); Patricia Grimshaw, *Paths of Duty: American Missionary Wives in Nineteenth-Century Hawaii* (1989); Mary Zwiep, *Pilgrim Path: The First Company of Women Missionaries to Hawaii* (1991); Penny Lernoux, *Hearts on Fire: The Story of*

the Maryknoll Sisters (1993); Dana L. Robert, *American Women in Mission: A Social History of Their Thought and Practice* (1996); Angelyn Dries, *The Missionary Movement in American Catholic History* (1998) and Anne C. Kwantes, *She has Done a Beautiful Thing for Me: Portraits of Christian Women in Asia* (2005).

Another much neglected area of missionary biography concerns workers from Asia, Africa, Latin America, and the South Pacific. Their contributions have not been well documented, but they will be more fully recognized in years to come, as scholars discover accounts of their work. Some initial efforts to meet this need include David A. Shank's book on William Wade Harris, *Prophet Harris: The "Black Elijah" of West Africa* (1994); Susan Billington Harper's study of Bishop V. S. Azariah, *In the Shadow of the Mahatma* (1999); and the autobiography of the Tongan Methodist missionary, Semisi Nau, *The Story of My Life,* edited by Allan K. Davidson (1996).

## New Initiatives

A new effort to meet the need for biographies of Christian workers in the non-Western world has been initiated by Jonathan Bonk with the *Dictionary of African Christian Biography* (DACB). This non-proprietary electronic database, which is steadily added to, contains biographical facts on 1,150 African Christian leaders, evangelists, and lay workers. The entire database is available in a CD-ROM version and on the DACB website, www.dacb. org. Future plans include language versions in Arabic, French, and Kiswahili. The DACB project model has encouraged scholars in other regions of the world to undertake similar initiatives. The *Biographical Dictionary of Chinese Christianity,* for instance, is developing an electronic database that will be available in a CD-ROM version and on the website, www.bdcconline.net.

GERALD H. ANDERSON

*See also* History; Internet

## Further Reading

Allen, C. B. (1980). *The new Lottie Moon story.* Nashville, TN: Broadman.

Anderson, C. (1956). *To the golden shore: A life of Adoniram Judson.* Boston: Little, Brown.

Anderson, G. H. (1999). Missionary biography: A select annotated bibliography. *Missiology* 27(4), 459–465.

Anderson, G. H. (Ed.). (1999). *Biographical dictionary of Christian missions.* Grand Rapids, MI: Eerdmans.

Anderson, G. H. et al. (Eds.). (1994). *Mission legacies.* Maryknoll, NY: Orbis.

Beaver, R. P. (1980). *American Protestant women in world mission*. Grand Rapids, MI: Eerdmans.

*Dictionary of African christian biography*. (2002). Retrieved May 11, 2005, from http://www.dacb.org.

Eddy, S. (1945). *Pathfinders of the world missionary crusade*. Nashville, TN: Abingdon.

Kwantes, A.C. (2005). *She has done a beautiful thing for me: Portraits of Christian women in Asia*. Manila, Philippines: OMF.

Neely, A. (1995). *Christian mission: A case study approach*. Maryknoll, NY: Orbis.

Seamands, J. T. (1967). *Pioneers of the younger churches*. Nashville, TN: Abingdon.

Swift, C. M. (1984). *Gladys Aylward: The courageous English missionary*. Basingstoke, UK: Marshall Pickering.

Tucker, R. (1988). *Guardians of the Great Commission: The Story of women in modern missions*. Grand Rapids, MI: Zondervan.

Tucker, R. (2004). *From Jerusalem to Irian Jaya: A Biographical History of Christian Missions* (Rev. ed.). Grand Rapids, MI: Zondervan.

# Buddhism

Predating Christianity and Islam, the two most notable missionary religions, Buddhism evinced a similar dynamic right from its very inception in the fifth century BCE. After converting several ascetics in Magadha (North India), the Buddha instructed his monastic companions, "Go forth, and walk...out of compassion for the world" (Lamotte 1988, 297). Over time, Buddhism developed into a pluriform religion (Theravada, Mahayana, Vajrayana) and was widely diffused throughout Asia and, more recently, the Western world. Monks of the various monastic fraternities, globetrotting heralds of the Dharma, have always been the primary carriers of the Buddha's teachings. Encounters with Christian missionaries—sporadic until the mid-sixteenth century, some two millennia after converts first entered the Buddhist fold—were hardly ever irenic and almost always fraught with far-reaching political consequences. Interactions between the two, however, have proven transformative; through a process called "protestantization," new variants of Buddhism have emerged, and along with them, modern forms of mission.

## Pre-Christian Buddhist Missions

In the Pali literature of Buddhist antiquity, the word most closely approximating "missionary" is *dharmab-* *hanaka* (Dharma reciter)—that is, one who makes the Four Noble Truths and Eight-Fold Noble Path understandable to those who have not heard them before. Other terms, however, have gained currency; in South and Southeast Asia, for instance, one who propagates Buddhism (as opposed to Christianity or Islam) is nowadays referred to as a *dharmadhuta* (Dharma messenger). Though the difference may seem negligible, behind it lie important changes in Buddhist understandings of Dharma, from doctrine and practice to religion, changes that occurred as non-Indic missionary movements (Christian and Islamic) introduced new varieties of religious orientation into societies that had become almost monolithically Buddhist.

Still, to the *dharmabhanaka* of the past and the *dharmadhuta* of the present, non-Buddhists were and are to be converted (*prasadita*, "made acquiescent") compassionately, not coercively. Formally, a person or population is considered Buddhist upon taking refuge in the Triple Gem (Buddha, Dharma, Sangha)—that is, by publicly professing the primacy of Buddhism—and by pledging to practice the Buddhist moral precepts. Though processes of gradual Buddhicization have occurred, conversion has been notably individualistic because of Buddhism's monastic character, which is coeval with the first Buddha. Induction into the Sangha (fraternity of monks) is only of persons, not populations. While the laity was always essential to the infrastructure of organized Buddhism, the ideal of an indigenous monastic community was, by all accounts, vigorously pursued from the earliest times.

Although Buddhism's expansion was, as it were, Sangha-centric, it was also notably vernacular. All languages, not only the Pali of the earliest Canon in which the monastic community was mostly literate, were considered capable of conveying the Dharma. In fact, early texts portray the Buddha as averse to all forms of linguistic elitism, particularly to the Sanskrit used by Hindu Brahmans, against whose beliefs he had worked out his own radically un-Brahmanical interpretation of Dharma. Which language the Buddha actually spoke is a matter of considerable controversy; still, his opposition to "fine speech"—most probably a reference to Sanskrit—as the preferred medium for preserving the Dharma is mentioned by the texts of antiquity; in one (*Cullavagga*, 5.33), he is even represented as endorsing linguistic diversity: "I authorize you, monks, to learn the Buddha's words each in his own dialect" (Lamotte 1988, 552). Accordingly, the sacred texts are available in a variety of languages, each considered the equal of the others; Pali may have a certain classical cachet, but the Dharma is believed to be infinitely translatable.

Most emblematic of the Buddhist missionary endeavor, of course, is the Buddha himself, an indefatigable itinerant who traversed Magadha converting kings and commoners. All such accounts, canonical and noncanonical, are problematic as factual histories; overlooked in the larger picture, for instance, is the important role of merchants—vernacularists par excellence—and other nonmonastic travelers in the diffusion of Buddhism along the trade routes into Central, Southeast, and East Asia. While the process continued into the thirteenth century, until the last major population blocs converted (the Thai and Khmer), Buddhist historians—including those writing in Pali—invariably represent those missions as vernacular enterprises.

The classic instance is the earliest, the Ashokan mission to (Sri) Lanka around the middle of the third century BCE. One of nine missions, Emperor Ashoka of the Maurya Dynasty, is said to have dispatched the Lanka mission, led by the monk Mahinda (his son) and the nun Sanghamitta (his daughter), and used the vernacular language from the outset: We are told that Devanampiya Tissa, King of Anuradhapura, acquiesces to the Dharma within moments of their arrival when he is catechized in Sinhalese, his native language, instead of in Pali.

## Christian Missions

So much a part of Asia had Buddhism become, except in certain interstitial areas where traditional (tribal) societies survived, that Buddhist missions were virtually defunct by the mid-sixteenth century when Christian missions commenced in tandem with Europe's overseas expansion. Still, Buddhists (unlike Hindus, who had no mission legacy) found it relatively easy to recognize Christian missionaries as individuals motivated by familiar religious compulsions. The eminent Bible translator Adoniram Judson (1788–1850), for instance, was dubbed *shasanapyusaya* (teacher who propagates religion) by Burmese Buddhists who evidently thought of him as a Western corollary of the indigenous *dharmabhanaka*. Initially welcomed, warmly if warily, Christian missionaries rarely understood the epistemological

**A statue of the Buddha in Polonnaruwa, Sri Lanka.**
*Courtesy of Emma Holmwood/istockphoto.com.*

relativity underlying Buddhist inclusivism; their own theocentric truculence and soteriological exclusivism, moreover, made cordial exchange all but impossible. More open perspectives emerged slowly, mainly in the twentieth century.

In Sri Lanka, one of the most thoroughly documented cases, by the mid-sixteenth century interreligious tensions had been aggravated by colonial encroachment; Emmanuel Morais, a Franciscan, reported in 1552 that *bhikkhus* (monks) hid themselves whenever he sought them out. The second half of the nineteenth century—Sri Lanka was then experiencing its third century of European domination—saw the Sangha revived and militantly anti-missionary. From 1865 to 1873, monks and missionaries met each other in public debate; the final encounter, on the seaside at Panadure (south of Colombo), ended in humiliation for the Christian party represented by David de Silva (1817–1874), a Sinhalese Wesleyan. Though a celebrated event, from the angle of religious change, Panadure also signified Buddhism's protestantization (which Sri Lanka exemplifies but hardly exhausts). It is to these encounters with Christian missions throughout Asia that aspects of modern Buddhism, such as scripturalization and laicization, can be traced.

## Buddhist Missions Today

While traditional processes of Buddhicization, sometimes actively promoted by government-appointed *dharmadhutas*, still occur in Asia's interstitial regions (Myanmar being a prime example), modern Buddhist missions are increasingly focused on the West, particularly on the United States, which is nowadays home to remarkably diverse Buddhist populations. Whether to Europe or to the Americas, immigrants bring a Sangha-centric faith orientation; this, in turn, has been a spur to missions from the Buddhist world to communities whose associations with monastic fraternities had been severed. Being preadapted for the West by protestantization, Buddhist missions are geared toward a textualized, creedalized Buddhism that has vast appeal among mainstream population cohorts who welcome cognitive Buddhism while remaining reserved toward cultural Buddhism. Still, even in the West, Buddhist missions seek to induct indigenes into the Sangha; in this, they have been resoundingly effective, and the West itself now sends missionaries back to Asia, where Buddhism began.

RICHARD FOX YOUNG

## Further Reading

Gombrich, R. F. (1988). *Theravada Buddhism: A social history from ancient Benares to modern Colombo.* London and New York: Routledge and Kegan Paul.

Gombrich, R. F., & Obeyesekere, G. (1988). *Buddhism transformed: Religious change in Sri Lanka.* Princeton, NJ: Princeton University Press.

Keyes, C. F. (1993). Why the Thais are not Christians: Buddhist and Christian conversion in Thailand. In R. W. Hefner (Ed.), *Conversion to Christianity: Historical and anthropological perspectives on a great transformation* (pp. 259–84). Berkeley and Los Angeles: University of California Press.

Kiblinger, K. B. (2005). *Buddhist inclusivism: Attitudes towards religious others.* Aldershot, UK, and Burlington, VT: Ashgate.

Lamotte, É. (1988). *History of Indian Buddhism from the origins to the Saka Era.* Louvain, France: Université catholique de Louvain, Institut orientaliste.

Lai, W., & Brück, M. von (2001). *Christianity and Buddhism: A multi-cultural history of their dialogue.* Maryknoll, NY: Orbis.

Learman, L. (Ed.). (2005). *Buddhist missionaries in the era of globalization.* Honolulu: University of Hawai'i Press.

Thelle, N. R. (1987). *Buddhism and Christianity in Japan: From conflict to dialogue, 1854–1899.* Honolulu: University of Hawai'i Press.

Walters, J. S. (1998). *Finding Buddhists in global history.* Washington, DC: American Historical Association.

Young, R. F. (1989). Deus unus or dei plures sunt? The function of inclusivism in the Buddhist defense of Mongol folk religion against William of Rubruck (1254). *Journal of Ecumenical Studies, 26*(1), 100–137.

Young, R. F., & Somaratna, G. P. V. (1996). *Vain debates: The Buddhist-Christian controversies of nineteenth-century Ceylon.* Vienna: Sammlung de Nobili (Indological Institute, University of Vienna).

# C

## Caribbean

The Caribbean is a microcosm in which cultural diversity, religious crossroads, language formation, music creativity, poetic imagination, and new social fabric have expressed the richness of a people who have tried to fulfill their future and destiny.

Christopher Columbus landed in Guanahaní (part of the Bahamas) in 1492 and changed its name to San Salvador (Holy Savior), a clear reference both of his conquering project and the conviction that naming was a fundamental principle in expanding Christendom in the Caribbean. The region was a laboratory at the beginning of the sixteenth century for all kinds of colonial experiments, including the *encomienda* (trusteeship), a system introduced by the Spaniards for the first time in the Caribbean, which was used as a socioeconomic religious instrument of exploitation and oppression. In theory, the colonizers were to teach the Indians the Christian faith and provide for the sharing of Christian values and way of life. This trusteeship (*encomienda*) required that Indians who were entrusted to the colonizers for labor be evangelized. The other experiment was the *Requerimiento* (requirement), a document based on theological principles that was read by the colonizers as a requirement to the Indian chiefs. Through this document the conquerors stated that Christ was now Lord over the whole world and invited them to accept and submit themselves to the authority of the Pope and to the Spanish crown.

The conquest and colonization of the Caribbean was established as an ideological-religious structure of domination. In 1513 Martín Fernández de Enciso espoused the theory that divine providence favored the Spaniards, promising a new land and the dominion and expansion in the new conquered territories. The main emphasis was on a Christian civilization that was expanding and extending the blessings of the Christian faith to this people who were living outside of the church and the faith. The Church was established early in the sixteenth century in the Caribbean. The first dioceses were organized in Santo Domingo, Concepción de la Vega in Hispaniola (Dominican Republic), and Puerto Rico between 1511 and 1512.

By the late fifteenth century the Caribbean Sea was already a region populated by a diversity of people and ethnic groups. The Arawaks migrated from the Orinoco basin in South America to the Caribbean. The Caribs came from the Amazon River in Brazil and occupied Trinidad and later settled in the Lesser Antilles. The Guanajatebeys and the Ciboneys lived in Cuba and the Taínos in Guanahaní and Puerto Rico. The coming of the Spaniards and the British introduced new factors of confrontation and conflict and initiated a clash between two ways of life. The colonizers and the soon-to-be colonized started a complex process of forming new racial, social, ethnic, and economic entities. What is considered today as the Caribbean is the by-product of a colonial enterprise in which slavery and plantation economy (primarily sugar), as well as race and class within Creole culture and institutions, forged a Caribbean identity. The slave system was introduced in the seventeenth century to bring an African labor force to the new sugar plantations. The Portuguese established a slave trading system to bring slaves from Guinea in Africa to Hispaniola in the Caribbean. The slave trade and the slave system lasted for two centuries, deepening both the political and economic domination in a colonial society.

The first signs of resistance to this colonial system started within the Roman Catholic Church. On the fourth Sunday in Advent 1511, Antonio de Montesinos, a Dominican friar, preached the first sermon crying for justice for the indigenous people of the Caribbean and claiming that Spain needed to repent from its cruelty and exploitation of these human beings. Father Bartolomé de Las Casas, an *encomendero* living in Cuba (1515) transformed his theological and political convictions from a colonizing enterprise to a prophetic and pastoral commitment in favor of the indigenous people, becoming the defender of the Indians in the Spanish royal court.

The Caribbean region became a mosaic of colorful contrasts, combinations, and shades. The geography itself demonstrates this diversity. What is called the Caribbean today includes Cuba, Haiti and the Dominican Republic, Jamaica, Puerto Rico, Guadaloupe, St. Kitts-Nevis, Grenada, Aruba, Bonaire, Curacao, St. Marteen, the Bahamas, Bermuda, the Turk and Caicos Islands, Guyana, Suriname, Belize in Central America, and the northern part of Colombia and Venezuela.

The history of the Caribbean is a complex texture with many layers. Its mosaic of languages includes new formations of Creole (French and English) and new combinations of European languages in Papiamento, Patois, and other languages. For more than five hundred years the people of the Caribbean have lived, struggled, constructed, survived, dreamed, and created a new cultural form.

These societies have recreated and transformed the initial colonial fabric into a new social, cultural, and anthropological texture. One of the most important components of this culture is the faith of a people expressed in a popular religiosity that is as complex and diverse as colonial domination itself. On each Caribbean island, religion plays a dominant role. The number of distinctive religious movements in the Caribbean is impressive. The most dominant Afro-Caribbean religious movements are Santería, a Yoruba religion, mixed with Roman Catholic practices and doctrines, that the slaves brought with them to Cuba; Voodoo in Haiti, an African religion from Western Africa; and Rastafarianism, a twentieth-century religious movement founded in Jamaica (1930). All of these religious movements show a strong element of syncretism (both cultural and religious), a distinctive worldview from African religion, and a resistance to colonial domination.

A unique experiment in mission took place in Barbados at the Condrington plantation owned by the Anglican Church, which included trying to convert and transform the slaves in a clear Christian and humanitarian effort, and becoming supporters of mission in other parts of the world through the Society for the propagation of the Gospel. Many planters supported this initiative by churchmen and others criticized it as hypocrisy. Condrington College became a center for higher education, including theological education.

The Protestant churches arrived in the Caribbean as part of the British colonial expansion in the seventeenth century and the United States expansion and influence in the region starting in 1898. The Protestant churches that established their mission in the Caribbean were Anglicans, Baptists, Congregationalists, Disciples of Christ, Moravians, and Presbyterians. The Pentecostal movement arrived in the Caribbean between 1916 and 1930, with the missionary presence of U.S. Pentecostal denominations: Assemblies of God; The Church of God, Cleveland, Tennessee; and The Four Square Gospel, among others. During the past 20 years a new wave of both Indigenous Charismatic churches and Charismatic groups from the United States have changed the religious landscape in which televangelism, the electronic church worship model, and mega churches with prosperity theology have become major religious forces.

The churches in the Caribbean were able to share in mission. James Henry Emmanuel Hemans and his wife Maria Cecilia Clementina Gale from Manchester County, Jamaica, served as missionaries for many years in Lake Tanganyika in central Africa. Pentecostal missionaries from Puerto Rico went to Dominican Republic in 1917 and to Cuba in 1933 to help plant Pentecostal congregations in those countries. Other initiatives in cooperation and interregional collaboration have taken place among Ministerial Associations and Councils of Churches in Cuba, Jamaica, Barbados and Puerto Rico.

One of the issues that the churches need to face in the Caribbean is the role of non-Christian religions and their relationships with Christian traditions: How can the church develop the necessary interreligious dialogue and broaden its scope of ecumenical commitments both in terms of doctrine and mission? This is a crucial question.

The issue of identity needs to be addressed in the context of mixed races, diverse cultures, and religious plurality. Religious diversity and religious fragmentation are present all over the region. A solid and deep analysis of the missiological and theological implications of interreligious dialogue is becoming increasingly important. The churches need to take seriously this challenge in a region that every day is more reli-

## The Church—Then and Now

**The following ethnographic description tells how Carib devotion to Roman Catholicism on the island of Dominica has changed over the years**

Catholic missionaries beginning in the 17th century made concerted attempts to Christianize the Caribs, but most of these evangelists candidly confessed to being singularly unsuccessful in their attempts at conversion. These, the first Europeans to live peacefully with the Caribs, encountered constant frustration because of what they referred to in their memoirs as Carib obstinacy. A French priest working among the Caribs early in the 18th century complained with unabashed ethnocentrism that "these people are so lazy and conceited that infinite tact is required to manage them at all. They will obey no order, and if they do anything wrong you must be most careful how you reprove them, or even appear annoyed, for their vanity is inconceivable. They do what they please and only when they please. The best thing to do is to have nothing to do with them, or at any rate never depend on them for anything" (Labat 1970, 83). However, by the middle of the nineteenth century, most of the Caribs considered themselves to be Catholics. At this time, with no priest on their side of the island, infants were carried by canoe to neighboring French Islands to be baptised. Early in the 20th century, a priest stationed in the north came to the Reserve on horseback periodically to conduct mass and baptisms; many of the older residents can remember walking in groups for six or seven hours to attend distant Christmas Eve midnight masses or Easter services. These older Caribs claim that there was more interest in the Church in those days and that the priests felt more concern for the Caribs. In discussing the relative lack of religious commitment today, one old woman in Bataka offered the following explanation:

"Was an old French priest my grandmother told us about, from Vieille Case. Was the only one to reach Calvary: he got all the nails and that. He could stop rivers and did, more than once. He came this way one day during Holy Week where some men was working a sugar mill. He told them to stop, to tell the white man and stop. They didn't when he leave, and the mill said to them 'Oh, I is so tired, so tired.' They certain scared and went and told the white man, and the syrup boil all over everywhere. This priest never ask for money. He went barefoot everywhere. When he need money, he have a black marble and place it on the bed, on a white sheet, and money come when his hand over the marble; it just there. Today, priests only want money, for mass, for wedding, for everything; always ask for money. Today, priests are different; so people only have the name [Catholic], not the faith!"

Source: Layng, A. (1983) *The Carib Reserve: Identity and security in the West Indies* (p. 78). Washington, DC: University Press of America.

gious, more sectarian, and having the potential to canalize all the religious forces as positive liberating forces toward Caribbean emancipation.

All Christian traditions in the Caribbean are facing some pressing issues in the beginning of the twenty-first century. For the past four decades the ecumenical movement, expressed particularly in the Caribbean Conference of Churches, founded in 1973 and including mainline Protestant denominations, Pentecostal churches, and the Roman Catholic Church, has promoted Caribbean integration at different levels: First, the call to social change is an integral, holistic concept of transformation and development. Second, solidarity with the poor as a concrete manifestation of the communion of the Holy Spirit and the commitment to discern God's mission and the role of the churches in the region is an ethical and theological imperative. Third, the decolonizing process continues to be a crucial issue in the Caribbean. Many countries still have a colonial status, for example, Martinique and Puerto Rico. Fourth, cultural identity and the challenges of globalization require a diligent and attentive attitude, balancing the tension between the local and the global in an increasingly interdependent world. Fifth, to fight underdevelopment and economic injustice the region needs integration while affirming diversity and pluralism.

The Caribbean has come a long way in the past four decades. The struggle for freedom in the Caribbean is the saga of a colonized, acculturated people, racially mixed, oppressed, and marginalized, but always affirming their dignity. To understand the cry for justice in the Caribbean, it is important to see the interconnection of social, economic, cultural, religious, and anthropological dimensions of the formation of Caribbean society and life. The cry for freedom, political sovereignty, and emancipation can be seen in the Cuban Revolution (1959) and the independence movement that liberated most of the Caribbean islands under British domain in the 1960s.

The theological implications of these struggles and aspirations toward emancipation are expressed in a twofold principle: "decolonizing theology" (Noel Erskine, Howard Gregory) and "emancipation theology" (Kortright Davis). The attempt is to examine the roots of oppression while affirming the sources of hope and freedom for the future.

As the Caribbean region faces the challenges of the twenty-first century, it continues to claim its historical roots, its cultural and religious diversity, its poetic imagination, and the rhythm of a vibrant music while promoting unity and integration and envisioning a better future for its people.

CARMELO ÁLVAREZ

## Further Reading

Bisnauth, D. A. (1989). *A history of religions in the Caribbean.* Kingston, Jamaica: Kingston Publishers.

Bolioli, O. (Ed.). (1993). *The Caribbean: Culture of resistance, spirit of hope.* New York: Friendship Press.

Davis, K. (1990). *Emancipation still comin': Explorations in Caribbean emancipatory theology.* Maryknoll, NY: Orbis Books.

Dayfoot, A. C. (1999). *The shaping of the West Indian church 1492–1962.* Gainesville: University Press of Florida.

Gregory, H. (Ed.). (1995). *Caribbean theology: Preparing for the challenges ahead.* Kingston, Jamaica: Canoe Press.

Lewis, G. K. (1983). *Main currents in Caribbean thought: The historical evolution of Caribbean society in its ideological aspects, 1492–1900.* Baltimore: The John Hopkins University Press.

Williams, E. (1970). *From Columbus to Castro: The history of the Caribbean, 1492–1969.* New York: Vintage Books.

# Celtic Missions

The mission of Celtic Christianity stands as arguably the greatest sustained cross-cultural mission in Christianity's history. The period preceding the movement frames its achievement.

In the years following Pentecost, the early Christian movement exploded across the Judean hills, and moved (roughly as mandated in Acts 1:8) from Jerusalem, to Judea, to Samaria, to much of the known world. Following the paradigm of Jesus' ministry with lepers, and blind, deaf, and possessed people, and other groups excluded from the temple and assumed to be hopeless, many of the apostles later reached "barbarian" and other "hopeless" populations, even cannibal groups.

However, by the second century, the range of this vision was forgotten. The faith continued to spread through the Roman Empire's cities for two more centuries, but it had become establishment Christianity—it assumed that being "civilized" (that is, Latin speaking, literate, and culturally Roman) was a prerequisite to being "Christianized." Rural peoples were seen as subhuman, little different from the beasts they herded; it appears that postapostolic Christianity launched no mission to rural peoples until the mission of St. Martin to the rural population of Tours in 371 CE.

Furthermore, establishment Roman Christianity assumed that the Goths, the Visigoths, the Franks, the Vandals, the Vikings, the many Celtic peoples, and the other "barbarian" peoples in the empire's hinterlands were even less fit for Christianization. There was no mission to "barbarians" because, by definition, they were not civilized enough to become Christians. In the fifth century, however, Pope Celestine appears to have harbored private doubts about his church's assumption; when he heard that an English priest named Patrick believed himself called to reach the Irish, Celestine proposed to ordain Patrick as apostolic bishop to the Irish.

Patrick, with an apostolic band of perhaps a dozen people, is thought to have sailed for Ireland about 432 CE. As a young man, he had spent six years in Ireland as a slave; he had now taught his band the Irish language and culture. They befriended the people of a settlement at present-day Saul, and there they planted the first church of the Irish Christian movement. By Patrick's death in 460 CE, Patrick's team and other teams had reached perhaps forty of Ireland's 150 tribes; their successors reached the other tribes within two generations.

In 563 CE, the Irish Church sent a team with Columba, an Irishman of royal descent, to establish a community on the island of Iona, and from there to reach the Picts of Scotland. In 633 CE, Aidan, an Irish monk, left Iona for Lindisfarne to reach the Anglo-Saxon peoples who had streamed into England, largely displacing the Britons. Meanwhile, the Irish sent the monk Columbanus with a team to Western Europe. They in turn raised up other apostolic bands, which established other monastic communities, from which they planted churches far and wide. Within two centuries, western Europe had become substantially Christian for a second time; the Celtic Christian movement had brought Europe out of the Dark Ages and ushered in the Holy Roman Empire—and *that,* in the words of Thomas Cahill, is how "the Irish saved civilization."

## How They Succeeded

What accounts for their astonishing achievement? First, they *organized* for mission. The monastic communities they established did not function as retreats from the world, like Eastern monasteries, but as mission stations from which to reach the world. People spent months in the community, sharing its group life and worship life, learning the Scriptures and learning to pray, learning how to be involved in ministry with people—including the ministry of witness with the stream of seekers who also found their way to these communities. They learned how to obey God and to love lost people. They were then sent out in apostolic teams which would camp next to an unreached settlement, befriend and minister to the people, teach the faith, plant a church, and then move on to another unreached settlement.

Second, their achievement is substantially explained by the classic mission principle of *indigenous Christianity.* Patrick must have understood that the Latin language and Roman cultural forms were alien to the Irish people, because he ministered to the people in Gaelic, and raised up a culturally unique Irish form of local Christianity that featured Irish music and art. As the movement spread, it adapted to each local dialect and culture. The Celtic Christian movement, in contrast to the politically dominant Roman branch of the Church, dismissed the idea of imposing ecclesiastical uniformity everywhere. They believed that culture was the best medium for God's revelation to each group of people. However, in the Synod of Whitby (664 CE), the Roman branch of Christianity began reining in the creative Celts and imposing the Roman way of "doing church." The enforcement of conformity took more than a century, but by that time the Celtic movement had won Europe for a second time—while Rome's spokesmen carped at them for not doing it "the Roman way."

Third, the perspective of *rhetorical theory* also helps explain their apostolic success. For instance, the ethos of the Celtic Christian advocates made their message seem believable; they understood their message and knew what they believed, and they seemed to embody it. The "barbarian" peoples experienced them as people of character and transparent goodness and goodwill. (Even their best-known ecclesiastical detractor, the Venerable Bede, celebrated the devoted character of every Celtic Christian leader he wrote about.) They identified with the people and were experienced enough

An arch at the ruins of a monastery on the island of Lindisfarne, off the Northumberland coast. *Courtesy of Bjarne Henning Kvaale/istockphoto.com.*

to understand the people, and to believe in what the people could become by the grace of God. They welcomed many people into the fellowship of their camps, churches, and monastic communities *before* they believed; the experience helped many to experience faith. Spending time in the community made a great difference because nonbelievers experienced the Celtic Christian leaders and believers as completely credible—men who lived by what they believed. No one embodies this as dramatically as Patrick, who returned to the Irish (who assumed they still owned him) at great personal risk, to bring the gospel to them.

Again, the *logos* of their message played its role in this movement—as in all valid Christian movements. Their approach was distinctive, however. They adapted to the imaginative culture of the Celtic peoples, and often communicated the meaning of their message through music, analogy, poetry, dance, narrative, and the visual arts—such as the great standing crosses and the Celtic knot—as well as through traditional preaching and teaching.

The Celtic leaders seem to have known that human beings are basically emotional creatures who are sometimes capable of thinking. So what the rhetoricians called the *pathos* of the audience and what Jonathan Edwards saw as the self-authenticating power of "religious affections" played a powerful role in engaging the people of Ireland.

## Applying Their Strategies

Ancient Celtic Christianity offers more than an inspiring history lesson. If Christianity is to reach "the new barbarians" (a term for people who have a wild streak, who are looking for life in all the wrong places) that now populate our cities, it will need to rediscover Celtic strategic perspectives—like preparing Christians in a community and deploying them in teams, engaging people's imaginations and passions, and helping people to belong so they can believe.

GEORGE G. HUNTER III

### Further Reading

Bede. (1994). *Ecclesiastical history of the English people.* New York: Oxford University Press. (Original work published 731 CE)

Bradley, I. (1993*). The Celtic way.* London: Darton, Longman, and Todd.

Bradley, I. (1996*). Columba: Pilgrim and penitent.* Glasgow, UK: Wild Goose Publications.

De Poar, L. (1993). *Saint Patrick's world: The Christian culture of Ireland's apostolic age.* Notre Dame, IN: University of Notre Dame Press.

De Poar, M. B. (1998). *Patrick: The pilgrim apostle of Ireland.* New York: HarperCollins.

Finney, J. (1996*). Recovering the past: Celtic and Roman mission.* London: Darton, Longman and Todd.

Gougaud, L. (1992). *Christianity in Celtic lands: A history of the churches of the Celts, their origin, their development, influence and mutual relations.* Dublin, Ireland: Four Courts Press. (Original work published 1932)

Hunter, G. G. III. (2000). *The Celtic way of Evangelism: How Christianity can reach the West . . . again.* Nashville, TN: Abingdon.

Hunter, G. G. III. (2003). *Radical outreach: The recovery of apostolic ministry and evangelism.* Nashville, TN: Abingdon.

Lehand, B. (1968). *The quest of three abbots: The golden age of Celtic Christianity.* New York: Viking.

Mackey, J. P. (1989) *An introduction to Celtic Christianity.* Edinburgh, UK: T & T Clark.

# Central America

The term *Central America* normally refers to the nations stretching between Mexico in the north, and Colombia in the south: Belize, Guatemala, El Salvador, Honduras, Nicaragua, Costa Rica, and Panama. Excerpt for Belize, they were colonized and "Christianized" by Spain in the sixteenth century along with of the rest of Spanish America.

## Spanish Colonialism

In 1493 papal bulls placed the lands and inhabitants of the Americas under the authority of the Spanish Crown. The system of *Patronato* meant that the Crown and its representatives exercised authority in religious, economic, administrative, political, and military matters related to the colonies. Its representatives, the viceroys and governors, had the authority to nominate bishops, establish dioceses, and send priests, monks, and nuns to the territories. Thus the Roman Catholic Church was established in Central America by representatives of the Spanish government and made subservient to it. Some missionary priests were heroic, walking from village to village, preaching through interpreters and in the native languages, baptizing the people. There were mass baptisms of the inhabitants with little attempt to understand their culture. The result was religious syncretism in which traditional beliefs and practices were maintained underneath a thin overlay of Catholicism. But very little religious instruction or pastoral care took place. Bishops were appointed in Panama (1513), Guatemala (1543), and Honduras (1541). However, from the beginning there was a great shortage of priests, and nearly three centuries would pass before anyone without European blood was ordained.

The greatest advocate for the indigenous peoples, Bartolome de las Casas, accused the colonizers of imposing "on the indigenous peoples the most arduous, horrible, and bitter slavery." He was referring to the system in which they were forced to live in settlements called *encomiendas,* under the total control of the colonists. In the middle of the sixteenth century, las Casas and the bishops of Nicaragua, Guatemala, and Honduras spoke out against the cruelty of the practice and committed themselves to the welfare of the "Indians," risking expulsion, imprisonment, and even death. Las Casas was appointed Bishop of Chiapas in southern Mexico but was opposed by the colonists and many of his priests. When he visited Guatemala, he was rejected, nearly seized by colonists, and forced to return to Chiapas and then to Spain. Antonio de Valdivieso, Bishop of Nicaragua, entered the struggle on behalf of the "Indians," attempted to inform the king of the injustices, and as a result was assassinated in 1850.

Thus, from the beginning, the pattern was established in which a social and economic gulf existed or a gulf was created between those with Spanish blood and the indigenous peoples. The *criollos,* of Spanish blood, were the ruling class, the *mestizos,* of mixed blood, were found mainly in the cities, while the indigenous peoples, approximately 50 percent of the population, were located in the rural areas. The economic and social differences varied from country to country and were probably the greatest in Guatemala and the least in Costa Rica. Costa Rica avoided the almost constant conflict and established a relatively stable democracy, but that was not the norm. The colonial role of the Roman Catholic Church continued. In general it supported the political, economic, and military status quo and served the religious needs of the Spanish population. It also helped incorporate the indigenous people into the political and religious system, but at times a minority of priests and bishops advocated radical political and economic reforms.

## Independence from Spain

Early in the nineteenth century Spanish America broke with Spain in a series of struggles. While the bishops were opposed, many of the priests were in favor of the movement. When Central America, as part of Mex-

ico, declared its independence in 1821, thirteen of the twenty-nine persons who signed the document were priests. In 1823 Central America declared independence from Mexico, and by 1840 had splintered into the five nations that make up the present Central America, with the exception of Panama, still part of Colombia, and Belize, which was an English colony. In all except Belize, Roman Catholicism was the religion of the state, and political independence did not include religious liberty. The *criollos* continued to hold political and economic power.

The British brought African slaves to work in plantations on the Caribbean coast, but by the end of the nineteenth century the United States became dominant in the area. American commercial interests began to grow bananas, harvest hardwoods, and mine gold. American intervention took various forms. In 1903, with the collusion of the United States, Panama declared its independence from Colombia. The Panama Canal was constructed, and the American-dominated Canal Zone was established. When the nationalist movement in Nicaragua, led by Augusto Sandino, forced the Ameicans to withdraw in 1932, the United States sponsored the Somoza family, which soon installed a military dictatorship, and Sandino was assassinated. In 1950 Jacobo Arbenz was elected President of Guatemala and began a program of reform aimed at correcting some of the abuses in the nation and redistributing the land. As Arbenz moved further left, Carlos Armas led a U.S.-backed invasion of the country and Arbenz was forced to resign and flee.

Thus, until late in the twentieth century, little had changed in Central America. The overwhelming majority of the people, especially the indigenous peoples, were desperately poor and illiterate. For example, in 1871 it was estimated that 97 percent of the population of Guatemala was illiterate. Political, economic, and military power were firmly in the hands of a small, wealthy elite class. Attempts at change were met with violent repression, especially in Guatemala, Nicaragua, and El Salvador. Military dictatorship was the most common form of government. At times liberal movements arose, but the Roman Catholic hierarchy supported the conservative governments.

## Twentieth-century Movements

Then three new movements entered the region. The first was Protestantism, beginning at the end of the nineteenth century. The second was Marxism, seen by many young intellectuals as the only viable alternative to the status quo, especially after Castro's revolution in Cuba. The third was Roman Catholic liberation theology. It

## Protestantism and Catholicism in Chan Kom

One of the classic ethnographic works in anthropology is Robert Redfield's study of the village of Chan Kom (a pseudonym) in Yucatan Mexico in 1931–1933 and 1948. In the following account he describes the evangelization of the nominally Catholic village in the early 1930s.

During 1931 and part of 1932 the evangelizing effort was energetic and frequently repeated. The missionaries strove to convert to the new faith this rising village, deep in the bush but obviously a progressive community prepared to lead the people of its region. Two missionaries made extended visits. A portable organ was brought, and hymns were taught. Later, for periods of more than a week, groups of six or eight town-educated Protestants, including several women, stayed in Chan Kom to preach and to conduct prayer meetings. A local congregation was formally organized in 1932, with a board of directors consisting of three men of Chan Kom.

By the summer of 1932 the community was apparently converted to Protestantism. Except for half-a-dozen families, all the people of Chan Kom were attending Protestant services. These had now been transferred to the civic building ("Municipal Palace") so that all the people might be present. Thus an official approval, by the local government, was given to the new movement.

The *comisario,* the head of this government, was at this time Don Eus Ceme. This man, the most energetic and influential of the village leaders, labored to help the missionaries. He took into his charge arrangements for the meeting and for the comfort and convenience of the missionaries. The little thatched church was closed; no services took place there. The effigy of San Diego, the village patron, was removed to the house of the Tamay family, one of the few that would have nothing to do with the new religion; and the day of the saint came and went without any public celebration.

Most of the people of Chan Kom were talking of the new cult, attending its meetings, and studying its tenets through the words of the missionaries and discussion among themselves. It was said in neighboring settlements that Chan Kom had turned Evangelista.

Only in appearance, however, was this transformation a further expression of the unity and social solidarity of the village. The conversion itself, in so far as it was real and permanent, rested upon a factional division that had long existed within the community and was soon to accentuate that division.

Source: Redfield, Robert. (1962). A village that chose progress: Chan Kom revisited (pp. 91–92). Chicago: University of Chicago Press.

began with adoption of the slogan "the preferential option for the poor" by the Latin American bishops in 1968. The latter two opened the door for many Catholics and some Protestants to overcome their fear of Communism and support leftist movements. In desperation after centuries of poverty and hopelessness, many saw no other alternative.

Early in the nineteenth century Protestants began work in the British-dominated areas along the Caribbean coast, and by mid-century Bible societies distributed the Scriptures in Spanish Central America. In 1882 the liberal President of Guatemala, believing Protestantism to be a liberalizing force, asked the Presbyterian mission board in New York to send a missionary. He initiated work among the poor and started a church and school, the Colegio Americano. Other Protestant missions soon entered the region. Their primary emphasis was on evangelization, that is, seeking to win people to evangelical Christianity with its focus on personal faith and a lifestyle that rejected such behaviors as drunkenness and adultery. The Protestant emphasis on education led to the establishment of schools. In Guatemala Presbyterians began to teach some indigenous peoples in their own languages, even though it was prohibited by law. Eventually Bible institutes and theological seminaries were established to prepare pastors for the growing churches. Hospitals were built in Costa Rica, Guatemala, and elsewhere.

The strength of Protestantism lay in its ability to appeal directly to the poor with a more personal message of hope than was the case with the more formal institutionalized Catholicism. While Protestants trained and ordained their converts as pastors, the Catholic Church suffered from a severe shortage of priests, and even so, over half were foreign. The Protestant focus on literacy often led to upward social mobility, but there were Protestant weaknesses. Fragmentation among many groups led to undue competition. At times they were seen as bearers of North American values and politics, and many of the more fundamentalist groups taught that their adherents should avoid social, political, and economic issues, focusing only on spiritual questions.

The second phase of Protestant missions began when various Pentecostal groups came shortly after 1910. Pentecostalism began in Los Angeles in 1906 and emphasized the power of God to heal and bring ecstatic experiences to believers. With a world view similar to that of folk Catholicism, it eventually became the largest Protestant movement in Latin America.

Three countries suffered years of violence in the last half of the century. Thirty-six years of civil war in Guatemala that ended in 1996 led to atrocities against indigenous peoples. Hundreds of thousands died. The Sandinista movement in Nicaragua overthrew the corrupt Somoza government in 1979, but the U.S.-backed "Contras" and the failure of the Sandinistas' Marxist policies brought great turmoil. They were defeated at the polls in 1990, and the country is still mired in poverty, with 40 percent unemployment. A revolution in El Salvador lasted from 1981 to 1993, again with the intervention of the United States against the rebels. In both Guatemala and El Salvador the estimate is that 80 percent currently live below the poverty line.

In all three countries many Christians, both Catholic and Protestant, advocated change and suffered for it. Archbishop Romero, assassinated in San Salvador in March, 1980, and the four American Catholic women killed a few months later, received wide attention, but there were many others, priests, pastors, and laymen, who died in the conflicts. A number of church councils, ecumenical, Baptist, Episcopal, and Moravian, protested the actions of the United States. Other Protestants and Catholics feared Marxism more than the current poverty and opposed the revolutions. Many Protestants, reflecting on past experience, saw no reason for hope in any political solutions.

## Outlook for the Future

The religious landscape of Central America has changed. Protestantism has grown dramatically and now includes anywhere from 10 percent of the population in Costa Rica to 20 to 25 percent in El Salvador, Nicaragua, and Guatemala. In some areas Roman Catholics have organized grassroots base communities among the poor. Many movements, Catholic and Protestant, seek to help the poor take greater control of their lives and bring hope. Protestants are providing greater access to education for the poor. For example, the Assemblies of God have initiated an educational system that seeks not only to help children who are victims of poverty, but to begin to change the society that creates such poverty. Churches are working with street children and community development in rural areas.

It will take decades to overcome the heritage of four centuries of neglect and oppression. Stable democratic governments, educational and social reform, outside investment, and vital religious communities are all necessary for the process to succeed, but there seems to be more hope at this point in history than any time in the past.

PAUL E. PIERSON

## Further Reading

Deiros, P. (1992). *Historia del Cristianismo en America Latina.* (*History of the Church in Latin America*). Buenos Aires, Argentina: Fraternedad Teologica Latinoamericana.

Dussel, E. (Ed.). (1992). *A History of the Church in Latin America: 1492–1992*. London: Burns & Oates.

Haslam, D. (1987). *Faith in struggle: The Protestant churches in Nicaragua and their response to the revolution*. London: Epworth Press.

Nelson, W. (1984). *Protestantism in Central America*. Grand Rapids, MI: Eerdmans.

Garrard-Burnett, V. (1998). *Protestantism in Guatemala: Living in the New Jerusalem*. Austin: University of Texas Press.

## Children, Youth, and Missions

The story of Jesus responding to his disciples by calling a child to stand in the midst of them (Matthew 18:2) reflects well the relationship between children, youth, and missions. Children appear to be ever present in the history of missions, but until the end of the twentieth century, they were seldom the primary focus. The care and discipleship of children have been a major concern, which grew more intense when the social and physical risks were greater. Missionaries have engaged in ministry to children and youth as part of their fulfillment of the great commission, primarily through spiritual nurture, education, healthcare, and vocational preparation.

## Responding to Physical, Political, and Social Conditions

The care of children and youth in the early centuries followed the same pattern as the rest of society. Christian nurture came in the local congregation and household of the parents. As the Gospel penetrated society, concern for children became evident. Two major changes illustrate the impact in the fouth and sixth centuries. The successive efforts of Emperors Valentinain, Valens, and Gratian outlawed the common practice of infanticide, making it punishable by death in 374 CE. Under Justinian (529–553 CE), houses were established to care for abandoned infants and churches became refuges for the poor, especially children.

Cycles of war and natural disasters deeply impacted children, the most vulnerable of society. In response to the devastating conditions, missions were often on the frontline of care for children. One example in the wake of the Thirty Years War in seventeenth-century Germany was the missions of the German Pietists. Among the most notable were the schools for poor children, followed by the orphanage at Halle established in 1696 by August Hermann Francke.

Similarly, in times of economic development or decline, children and youth were exploited for their labor under intolerable working conditions. The role of dedicated Christians in the political arena combined with missionary efforts by individuals to address the social issues. Anthony Ashley-Cooper, Lord Shaftesbury (1801–1885), provides a good illustration from the nineteenth century. Shaftesbury advocated for the Mines Act of 1842, which protected women and children from the horrors of coal mining, and the Factory Act (Ten Hour Bill), which passed in 1847, reducing the hours a child could work in a factory to ten per day. Shaftesbury was also instrumental in promoting the efforts of many individuals, predominantly Christians, to establish schools. In 1844 he became the first president of the Ragged Schools Union for children in the poorest urban slums.

Among all the missionary efforts to address social conditions, those dedicated to caring for the infirm have deeply impacted the lives of countless individuals, particularly orphans and vulnerable children. The stories of Amy Carmichael and Mother Teresa illustrate the impact of those dedicated to children and the poor. Missionary Amy Carmichael founded the Dohnavur Fellowship in 1901 to care for children living in danger from deplorable conditions of poverty in South India. For the next fifty years, Carmichael dedicated her life to establishing a mission committed to the care and nurture of children. Another missionary to India, Mother Teresa, founded the Missionaries of Charity in 1952 to reach the poor of Calcutta, particularly children. The Missionaries of Charity established over 160 homes in India in addition to orphanages and schools for poor children around the world. So notable were her tireless efforts, that Mother Teresa was awarded the Nobel Peace Prize in 1979.

## Education as Mission

Christian schools have been the most prolific of all missionary efforts. Responding to the threat to Christian families as early as the fourth century, monasticism led the mission movement of Christian schools. Monastic schools were established as a means of propagating the faith and providing religious education with a strong focus on moral training. These schools, with their emphasis on teaching catechism, helped spread the Christian faith globally.

Among the earliest efforts were those of the disciples of St. Benedict, launched in the sixth century. A hallmark of the Benedictine Rule was a commitment to the work of education. The Benedictine monasteries established schools to educate children, primarily to prepare them for the monastic order. Subsequent monastic orders also embraced education, most notably the Jesuits beginning in the early sixteenth century.

A second type of school emerged in the eighth century associated with Cathedrals. Cathedral schools, both primary and secondary, became centers for learning and for maturing the congregations. As Protestant churches formed larger congregations with their own central parish or cathedral, they also established schools.

The Protestant missionary movement established mission schools in a similar manner. During the nineteenth and twentieth centuries, schools were built as part of the expansion of missionary efforts, particularly in rural areas. In many cases the schools were sanctioned by colonial governments as part of their efforts at social development. For example, in Papua New Guinea during the post–World War II era, missionar-

A large congregation of Kenyan men and women at a baptisim service presided over by a black pastor and a white missionary. *Courtesy of istockphoto.com.*

ies were recruited to teach in denominational community schools associated with the establishment of local and regional government centers. As a result, many of the first-generation leaders in what would become the newly independent nation in 1975 were trained in mission schools.

## Missionary Societies and Nongovernment Organizations

Another educational approach to mission among children began in the late eighteenth century. Initially an outreach to urban children of the working class, the Sunday School Movement associated with Robert Raikes (1780) in England was adapted to fit local churches. As Sunday Schools grew in popularity, they tended to be primarily a means of nurturing children in the Christian faith within the churches. By the late nineteenth and early twentieth centuries, other movements arose to reach children and youth outside the churches. One of the earliest Evangelical movements was Scripture Union (SU) founded in 1867 as Children's Special Service Mission. Scripture Union engaged in schools, camps, and local meetings along with the distribution of daily reading materials. The efforts of SU to teach the Bible raised a clear standard for nurturing children in their faith. So effective is their ministry in Ghana, for example, that a leader of SU observed that often when a young person wants to say he or she is a Christian, they will say, "I'm SU." Other groups followed with a focus on mission to

children and youth such as the Boys' Brigade (1883) and the Girls' Brigade (1893).

During the middle of the twentieth century, missions and organizations were launched with a specific focus on the needs of children and youth. The Child Evangelism Fellowship begun in 1937 by Jesse Irvin Overholtzer was specifically organized to evangelize children and disciple them in local churches. Two of the largest mission societies were both founded to mobilize youth for the cause of world mission. Youth with a Mission began in 1960 as a movement founded by Loren Cunningham. Similarly, founder George Verwer launched Operation Mobilisation after graduating from college in 1960.

The tragedy facing orphans during the Korean War so deeply impacted church and mission leaders in North American that two major missional responses to children and youth emerged. World Vision, now the largest Christian organization, was founded by Bob Pierce in 1950 as an outreach to orphans in Asia. Another outreach to Korean children began as a ministry of evangelist Everett Swanson in 1956, changing its name in 1963 to Compassion. Missions and organizations among children proliferated between 1950 and 2000.

The exponential growth in the world population between 1965 (3 billion) and 2000 (6.1 billion) created an unprecedented urgency for mission to children and youth. In 1994 Patrick McDonald, a young Danish missionary, raised the alarm among Evangelicals worldwide and launched a new kind of response in the form of the Viva Network. From its humble beginnings by four dedicated young people in a flat in Oxford, England, Viva Network has become a global movement of Christian workers from 48 countries serving more than a million children in 2006.

## The Future

The continued growth of the population, estimated to be 7.5 billion by 2020, centered primarily among the world's poorest populations, mandates a growing focus on children and youth. The range of responses will doubtless grow as a natural shift in mission focus. The greater challenge appears to be the role of local churches as an expression of God's care for the young. The current efforts among the churches in areas devastated by the HIV/AIDS pandemic have moved beyond the educational models into more holistic ministries, even to the point of becoming family for orphans and vulnerable children. This expression of the family of God may in fact be the most significant missional response. Bringing together missionary outreach and congregational nurture provides a healthy change in the expression of our mission theology. In the end, children may not be the center of mission but rather an inextricable part of the intergenerational mission of God to humankind.

DOUGLAS MCCONNELL

## Further Reading

Ariès, P. (1962). *Centuries of childhood: A social history of family life* (R. Baldick, Trans.). New York: Knopf.

Brewster, D. (2005). *Child, church, and mission.* Colorado Springs, CO: Compassion International.

Bunge, M. J. (Ed.). (2001). *The child in Christian thought.* Grand Rapids, MI: Eerdmans.

Butcher, A. (1996). *Street children.* Milton Keynes, UK: Authentic Lifestyle.

Couture, P. D. (2000). *Seeing children, seeing God: A practical theology of children and poverty.* Nashville, TN: Abingdon Press.

DeMause, L. (Ed.). (1974). *History of childhood.* London: Souvenir Press.

Kilbourn, P. (Ed.). (1996). *Children in crisis: A new commitment.* Monrovia, CA: MARC books.

Miller-McLemore, B. J. (2003). *Let the children come: Reimagining childhood from a Christian perspective.* San Francisco: Jossey-Bass.

Miles, G. M., & Wright, J. J. (Eds.). (2003). *Celebrating children.* Carlisle, UK: Paternoster Press.

Strange, W. A. (1996). *Children in the early church: Children in the ancient world, the New Testament and the early church.* Carlisle, UK: Paternoster Press.

# China

The church in China has gone through four periods when it seemed as if the church no longer existed. Following the Nestorian period in 845 CE, the early Roman Catholic period at the end of the Yuan dynasty in 1368, the later Jesuit period in 1724, and the coming of the Peoples' Republic of China in 1949, it appeared that Christianity had either disappeared or was "lost" and no longer of significance in Chinese society. Compared with these early efforts, the growth of Christian churches in the past five decades has been spectacular, far exceeding the speed and extent of growth seen anywhere in all of Christian history.

## The Nestorians in China

The first Christian missionaries to come to China were Nestorians who traveled overland following trade routes from Persia and Mesopotamia. They were led by Bishop Alopen and came to Changan (Xian) in 635 CE, early in the Tang dynasty (618–907 CE). Coming without any powerful political or military backing from their home countries, these early missionaries were warmly welcomed and backed by the patronage of Tai Zung, a liberal-minded emperor, with the result that the faith spread widely. Despite its seeming success, it was persecuted severely by the government in 845 CE, along with Buddhism and other religions, and ceased to exist in China. Its demise has been traced to too much political favor under some emperors and possibly being over accommodating in language and thought to Buddhism in their preaching of the Christian faith. Some Nestorian descendants who fled to the north influenced many minority groups and the Mongols with the Christian faith.

## Early Roman Catholics in China

The next missionary advance into China came with a Franciscan, John of MonteCorvino, who arrived in the then capital, Cambaluc, in 1294 during the Yuan (Mongol) dynasty. The New Testament and Psalms were translated at this time, but the language used was probably not Chinese. The Franciscans zealously spread the Gospel in many areas of China, and by 1328 had as many as 100,000 converts. When the Mongols were replaced by the Chinese Ming dynasty in 1368, the Chinese church again passed from the scene.

## The Jesuits in China (1540–1724)

In 1540, as one result of the Protestant Reformation, Roman Catholics in Europe organized the society of Jesus. One of its first missionaries, Matteo Ricci, came to China with a colleague, Nichole Rugierri, in 1582 and resided in south China. Initially as they attempted to identify with Chinese culture, they adopted both the dress and attitudes of Buddhist monks, the religious leaders. Very quickly they realized this was a mistake and then took the role of Confucian scholars in order to reach the elite at the top of the Confucian value hierarchy. This led them to have long discourses with Chinese scholars on many aspects of Chinese life. After living for several years in various southern Chinese cities, Ricci moved to Beijing. Here he had the opportunity to influence the imperial court on many matters—astronomy, calendar reform, clock repair, and cartography.

His greatest influence came in writing related to the Christian faith. His major work was a book, *Tianzhu Shihyi* (*The True Idea of God*). Here he argued that theological and moral truth could be found in ancient Chinese classics if rightly interpreted. When clarified or corrected by Biblical truth, this could be the Gospel for China.

Other Catholics, particularly the Dominicans and Franciscans, who came later to China did not agree with Ricci. Their disagreements waxed and waned among later arriving missionaries, Chinese emperors, and the Vatican for 150 years to the end of the Ming dynasty in 1644 and into the new Qing dynasty. The final outcome was that the Christian faith was prohibited in China by the emperor in 1724, and the Jesuits were disbanded as a missionary society by the Pope in 1774. At this time Catholics in China may have numbered as many as 300,000, but they had very little leadership, and the future of their faith in China was uncertain.

## Protestant Missionaries Come to China

Robert Morrison was the first Protestant missionary to come to China. He was appointed by the London Missionary Society in 1807. When he arrived in China, he could not act directly as a missionary but served as an interpreter for the British East India Company. Other missionaries from a variety of boards (American Board of Commissioners for Foreign Missions, American Presbyterians, Protestant Episcopal Church of the United States, and American Methodists) soon followed. These early missionaries could not enter China properly, but built a "wall of light around China," settling in Canton, Macao, Singapore, Penang, Malacca, Bangkok, and Batavia. In these centers they engaged in Bible translation, produced Christian literature, printed Christian magazines, ran medical clinics, and established schools for children. In some instances they ministered in various ways to non-Chinese living in these cities.

Dissatisfied by these efforts outside of China, some bolder missionaries engaged in missionary voyages: in chartered ships, going up the coast and into the rivers of China. In these trips they distributed literature, met Chinese officials, preached as they were able, and learned more about Chinese society. This gave to them their first serious contact with Chinese folk religion, Daoism, and with Buddhism, which was introduced into China from central Asia in the first century CE. This also was their first in-depth contact with Confucianism, which is less a religion than an ethical system that influences all aspects of Chinese life. American church and mission magazines reported these trips as a sign that China was "open." Chinese officials, however, accused the missionaries of "lawless activities."

## The Opium War

In the 1830s and 1840s Great Britain sought to import opium, raised on its plantations in India, into China. When China resisted this effort, a conflict developed in 1842, with a continuation related to it in 1858, between China and Great Britain. In the ensuing treaties (with Great Britain and also with France, Russia, and the United States) five ports (Canton, Shanghi, Amoy, Foochow, and Ningpo) and eventually China's interior were opened to foreigners and to the Christian faith. These "unequal treaties," as they came to be called, enabled missionaries to enter all of China to engage in preaching, literature distribution, and all types of educational and humanitarian ministries. There was a cost. Even though the missionaries made clear to the Chinese and to their home constituencies their opposition to opium, non-Christian Chinese over the years have accused them, saying, "You brought us opium and Christianity, neither one of which we wanted."

As missionaries pressed into the interior of China, many disputes arose between them and the local populace and its leaders. These problems were usually settled by an appeal to treaty regulations, often followed by military intervention referred to as a "gunboat diplomacy." With this ill-gained freedom, both Roman Catholics and Protestants were able to carry on their work in all of China. By 1949 the Catholics had 3,251,347 baptized believers and many schools, hospitals, orphanages, and seminaries. Chinese priests numbered 2,542 and foreign priests 3,046. Protestants experienced similar growth and at their height there were 160 mission societies and 8,000 missionaries. Their involvement with local churches, universities, hospitals, and humanitarian activities equaled that of the Catholics, although their converts were fewer. These numbers include not only the major denominations from Western countries, but also many grassroots movements, such as the True Jesus Church (1917), the Little Flock or Christian Assemblies (1926), and the Jesus Family (1921). The indigenous character of these groups gave them much more staying power in the post-1949 period. Unfortunately the total Christian growth did not diminish strong anti-Christian and antiforeign attitudes and activities spurred by ongoing reaction to the unequal treaties.

The biggest example of the antiforeign agitation came with the Boxer (League of Righteous Fists) rebellion of 1900, which resulted in the death of 189 Protestant missionaries and their families and many Chinese Christians in various places around the country.

## Bible Translation

A continuing task for Protestant missionaries was to produce an adequate translation of Scripture. Robert Morrison succeeded in translating the entire Bible into Chinese and also made the first Chinese-English dictionary. Subsequent revisions and new translations, both by individuals and committees over the next several decades, concluding with the Union Bible (He He Ben) in 1917, ran constantly into the "term" question. Should the term for God be *shen* or *shang di,* two terms found in the Chinese classics and seeming to refer at times either to one "God" or to local idols. Some Protestants even wondered about using the Catholic term for God. (*Tian Zhu* or Heavenly Lord). Protestant missionaries divided sharply on this terminology, and most versions of the Bible, then and now, have separate editions with different terms for God.

## The Taiping Heavenly Kingdom (*Taiping Tian Guo*)

An indigenous brand of Christianity developed in China from 1850 to 1864. Several years previous to this time, south China was in a state of economic, social, and political turmoil. The time was ripe among the majority Hakka populations for a new religion. At that time a young man, Hung Xiuquan, disappointed by his failure to pass the civil service examination, had a vision in which he claimed he was transported to heaven and saw God, Jesus, and Confucious. He was given a mandate as a brother of Jesus to eliminate all idols. Strengthened by contacts in Hong Kong with a Baptist missionary, Issachar Roberts, he organized a society called the God-Worshippers. Eventually this group proclaimed itself as the Heavenly Kingdom of Great Peace. Its initial purpose of worshipping God and destroying idols was broadened to oppose the ruling Manchu dynasty. It established a capital in Nanjing and hoped to enforce its semi-Christian ideology on all of China. Although Hung opposed opium smoking, he urged his followers to keep the Sabbath, conducted worship services, and wished to circulate the Bible, his concept of the Christian life was limited. He believed in one God, the Ten Commandments, sin, a type of salvation, and the future life, but his views were largely formed by the Old Testament. His concept of God the Father's supremacy led him to deny the deity of Jesus.

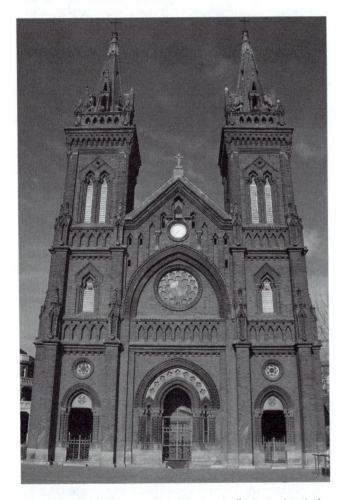

Shenyang Cathedral, rebuilt in 1912, was first constructed by French missionaries in 1898. *Courtesy of istockphoto.com.*

Many Protestant missionaries initially hoped to work out a relationship with the Taipings that would enable them to both encourage and correct Hung. Ultimately they realized this was hopeless and regretted that this type of movement, which had seemed to have the potential for Christianizing China, was doomed to failure. With the help of foreign armies, the Manchu government recaptured Nanjing and destroyed the Taipings in 1864.

## Minority Nationalities in China

The Chinese Constitution of 1954 defines the country as a "unitary multinational state in which all the nationalities are equal." After many years, during which ethnographers, sociologists, and historians sorted out evidence presented by more than 400 groups that wished to be counted as minorities, fifty-six were identified. The principal nationality was the Han people, numbering more than 1 billion. The other fifty-five nationalities (thought by some independent researchers to be as many as 500) total more than 100 million, 8 percent of China's total population.

The populations of each nationality range from 15 million to several hundred. In general, all of the nationalities in northern China are Muslims, with the exception of the Mongols. The Mongols and Tibetans follow Lamaism, a form of Buddhism. Nearly every nationality in southwest China is dominated by a belief in animism, a traditional folk religion.

Christian missionaries have sought for more than 1200 years to bring the Gospel to the minority nationalities of China. Beginning with the Tang dynasty (618–907 CE), emissaries of the Gospel have tried to penetrate Mongolia, Tibet, and areas now in Xinjiang in northwest China. Only in the late nineteenth century was missionary work commenced among the many nationalities in southwest China.

Under the regime of the present government, as contrasted with the Guomindang government, these nationalities were encouraged to live in autonomous regions, prefectures, and counties and allowed to have equal rights with the Chinese. They had freedom to use their own language and culture. In general, China was not to be a melting pot, with forced assimilation of people with different language and culture, but more like a tossed salad. The response to the Gospel among the groups adhering to folk religion has been positive. This is the case among the Miao, Lisu, Lahu, Wa, Jingpo, Hani, and the Black Yi of Yunnan. In one group, the Lisu, the response to the Gospel has been so great that government officials refer to them as the "Christian Nationality." Not all of the southwest nationalities have been as responsive. The Zhuang, Naxi, Tujia, Yao, Dong, Bouyie, Yi of Southern Sichuan, and Li of Hainan Island have not responded in large numbers to the Christian faith.

Why have the minority nationalities responded so well to the Christian faith? One factor is their lack of systematic, classic religion. These people tend to be poor, nomadic, and pastoral, often isolated in mountainous areas, and frequently oppressed in a system of virtual serfdom or slavery. They have received Jesus as the liberator from political and social bondage. Jesus has given them hope and a vision of a better life, both now and in a heavenly future. The messengers of the Gospel have often been charismatic individuals, such as James Fraser with the Lisu and Samuel Pollard the Miao. With compassion and boldness these missionaries stood with them and for them against all forms of political, religious, and cultural oppression. As subordinate groups within a dominant society that could bring about their fall, the Christian faith was a renewing and revitalizing force.

## The Churches in China

Form 1949 to 1956 the Protestant churches needed to align gradually with government policy. The constitution (revised in 1982) granted freedom of religion, which basically meant freedom to believe as long as religion was necessary. Following their assumption of power, government leaders worked with a nucleus of more compliant church leaders to form what was called the Three Self-Patriotic Movement (for the church to be self-supporting, self-governing, and self-propagating). Under the control of the government's Religious Affairs Bureau and the United Front Work, the Three Self Movement began to work out relationships and procedures between the government and church bodies. One such effort was the Christian Manifesto, eventually signed by 400,000 Protestant Christians. This document required the signers and their churches to support the government's policies, to accept no funds or personnel from abroad, to oppose American imperialism, and to cease all services except on Sunday during the upcoming period of land reform.

Some conservative church leaders, such as Wang Mingdao and Watchman Nee, resisted all of these government efforts to control the churches. As a result, they and many other church leaders were accused in public meetings and sentenced to long prison terms. By this time, nearly all foreign missionaries had left China. They initially had desired to stay in China for a longer period, but the outbreak of the Korean War made this impossible.

## Period of Forced Unity 1956–1966

During this period the Religious Affairs Bureau put pressures on churches to merge, so that in Shanghai, as one example, twenty-five churches were reduced to four. Rules were issued for permissible preaching topics, and churches were required to some degree to promote government agendas.

## The Cultural Revolution 1966–1976

The third phase through which the church passed in the post-1949 period was the Cultural Revolution, when a leftist clique within the new government sought to destroy all religion as a hotbed of superstition. The Christian church no longer existed in its overt institutional form, and Christians were dispersed throughout society as worshipping house communities.

The experience of Catholics under the new regime was similar to that of Protestants. Catholics, loyal to the new government, founded the Patriotic Association of Chinese Catholics in 1957. Many, however, could not identify with this association because it refused to have any relationship with the Vatican.

## Since the Death of Mao 1976–1985

Under the leadership of Deng Xiaoping, following the death of Mao in 1976, China began to rejoin the family of world nations. Protestant and Catholic church structures, dismantled during the Cultural Revolution, were restored, and other religions—Daoists, Buddhists, and Muslims—were allowed to establish comparable organizations.

With such general government sanction, all religions in China experienced a great resurgence. With the revival of Protestant Christianity came the organization of the China Christian Council, responsible for matters of ministry, leadership, training, and church life. Church leaders, along with societal leaders, formed the Amity Foundation, which has engaged in many educational and humanitarian activities, as well as publishing, in cooperation with the United Bible Society, 30 million Bibles (the China Union Bible and translations into ten minority languages) by late 2005.

## Churches in China 1985–2006

The Protestant church in China today is composed of four church groups. First are the registered churches related to the China Christian Council, which are overseen by the State Administration of Religious Affairs.

With few exceptions, these churches are evangelical. They are largely urban with trained professional clergy, both men and women, and have adequate church buildings. In general, these 55,000 churches conduct a full week of various church services, including Sunday School classes. There are eighteen seminaries, numerous Bible schools, and lay training classes.

The second type of church is meeting point churches. Often extensions of the China Christian Council churches, these are registered and meet in homes. They are usually led by elders rather than professionally trained clergy.

The third type is unregistered house churches meeting in homes and apartments. They are largely urban and led by Christian leaders, who, for the most part, do not wish to have relations with the registered churches. In various parts of China, these three types of churches have close relations with one another. Many of these house churches also run training schools to prepare leaders. In some areas of China, depending on relationships with local government officials, they have faced periods of severe persecution. China is a huge country, and the relationships of these house churches with the government can vary greatly.

The fourth type of church is the rural churches that are located deep in isolated countryside areas far from organized churches in large cities and towns. Their meetings are known to the government, and issues of registration or nonregistration are not crucial issues for them. Their leaders are usually untrained, and their members are susceptible to false teaching and heresy.

Within the Catholic Church the Patriotic Association of Chinese Catholics has been supplemented by the services of the Catholic National Administration Commissions, which supervises pastoral concerns, such as marriages, baptisms, funerals, confessions, pilgrimages, and Bible stories. Seven Catholic seminaries for leadership training have been opened.

Many estimates have been made of the number of Protestant Christians in China, ranging from 20 million to 100 million. Figures for Catholics also vary widely, but are considerably less than for Protestants. The Orthodox Church, once Russian-led, also exists in China as an autonomous Chinese church, but with only 20,000 members and two bishops.

In the past decade a great migration has occurred in China, bringing tens of millions to the cities in order to find jobs and a better life. Both Protestant and Catholic churches have developed new departments of social work, often in cooperation with the government and nongovernmental organizations, in and outside of China, to help in job searching, education for children, and medical needs. Expatriates from many countries have many opportunities to cooperate with local China churches and agencies to meet many of these needs.

China's entrance into the World Trade Organization (WTO) and her successful bid for the 2008 Summer Olympics have given it a new relationship with the world community, with both social and economic benefits. People now have a new sense of rights as citizens. The government sees people as having legitimate human interests as, for example, in the ownership of land and property. Broadcasting outside of China, wide use of video tapes, the Internet, and television programs are all being used by outside groups as new methods of introducing the Christian faith to all of China.

RALPH R. COVELL

## Further Reading

Barrett, D., Kurian, G., & Johnson, T. (2001). *World Christian Encyclopedia* (2nd ed.). London: Oxford University Press.

Burklin, W. (2005). *Jesus never left China: The rest of the story.* Enumclaw, WA: Pleasant Word.

Covell, R. (1986). *Confucius, the Buddha, and Christ.* Maryknoll, NY: Orbis.

Hunter, A., & Chan, K. (1993). *Protestantism in contemporary China.* Cambridge, England: Cambridge University Press.

Macinnes, D. (1989). *Religion in China today: Practice and policy.* Maryknoll, NY: Orbis.

Uhalley, S., & Wu, X. (Eds.) (2001). *China and Christianity burdened past hopeful future.* Armonk, NY: M.E. Sharpe.

# Christendom

*Christendom* is a term that scholars use in many ways. One use is *linguistic: Christendom* was the term which Christians in Western Europe used from the seventh century onward to describe their civilization, in which all inhabitants of the area except the Jews shared a common religious observance (Van Engen 1986, 546). In late medieval English *cristendom* could mean infant baptism (Nichols 1994, 193). A second use is *cultural:* missiologist Andrew Walls (2002, 35) sees Christendom as "territorial Christianity...the Christian nation, with a single body of custom." Christendom began when Christianity expanded from the Greco-Roman Mediterranean world to the primal societies of northern Europe, in which kinship was the basic denominator and communities made decisions about faith corporately. A third use is *theological:* theologian Oliver O'Donovan views Christendom as an "idea" of a society in which the kings of the earth have bowed to the Lordship of Christ and have established a "confessionally Christian government" (O'Donovan 1996, 195).

This article will be based on a fourth use, which is *descriptive.* Historian Hugh McLeod (2003, 1) describes Christendom as "a society where there were close ties between leaders of the church and those in positions of secular power, where the laws purported to be based on Christian principles, and where, apart from clearly defined outsider communities, every member of the society, was assumed to be a Christian." To this description of Christendom we will add two things: the use of powerful incentives (inducement, compulsion, and at times lethal violence) to Christianize society and a vision of the Lordship of Christ as the basis of the unitary society. Both of these were evident in 388 when Bishop Ambrose of Milan justified the action of Christians who plundered a synagogue "that there might not be a place where Christ was denied" (Ambrose, Epistle 40.8, in De Romestin, 1989, 441). These elements of Christendom were well in place by the fifth century—well before the accession of Christianity in tribal northern Europe. Note that, according to all of these definitions, Christendom is not the same as Christianity, whose message and embodiment can take many forms.

## Origins of Christendom

In its early centuries, Christianity was an illegal religion in the Roman Empire. It was a *superstitio*, subject to periodic waves of persecution. Nevertheless it was growing rapidly. Its mission was carried by ordinary believers, not by specialists. (See article "Ancient Church.") When the emperor Constantine (who ruled from 306 to 337) converted to Christianity in the early fourth century, there was a shift in Christianity's configuration. Constantine tolerated all religions but gave advantages to Christianity. After 380 his successors issued a succession of imperial laws that suppressed non-Christian options. A law of 380 proscribed worship of heretical Christians; a law of 392 made it illegal for pagan religions to engage in public worship; finally, a law of 529 required the baptism of all inhabitants of the Roman Empire. All of these laws were backed up by the threat, if not the actuality, of "extreme punishments." This "Christendom shift" (Murray 2004, 74) altered Christianity and its mission, which now employed three methods that the pre-Christendom church had eschewed.

The first new method that emerged as Christendom was established was the use of *incentives*. From the fourth century the church grew because its association with the emperors attracted ambitious people. Aristocratic males, who had hitherto been most resistant to conversion, now began to join the church and to become its natural leaders. The relationship between political and ecclesiastical leaders became intertwined and intense. Christian mission came to be associated with political power, social prestige, and the conferring of advantages.

The second new method was to "lower the hurdles" (Bradshaw 2002, 218). To accommodate new members, the church altered its requirements for those who presented themselves for baptism; it speeded up catechesis and changed the content of conversion by emphasizing doctrinal assent rather than behavioral transformation. Observers now began to deride the converts as "hypocrites." Mission under Christendom came to be associated with shallow catechesis and quick baptism.

The third new method was compulsion. The early Christians had confessed that "compulsion is not God's way of working" (Epistle to Diognetus 7, in Richardson 1953, 219), but as Christendom emerged, from the late fourth century onward, Christian rulers, supported by bishops and theologians, passed laws that discriminated against adherents of non-Christian religions and justified the use of force. At times conversion was inspired by "fear of the imperial laws" (Augustine, Epistle 93, in Parsons 1953, 73) or by actual violence; in 395, in the pagan city of Gaza in Palestine, soldiers beat people with "clubs and staves" while some Christians chanted psalms and shouted, "Christ has conquered" (Hill 1913, 27.52, 63). As Christendom took shape, Christian mission came to be associated with violence. Christian lords pressured their peasants to be baptized, and a many-faceted exchange took place in which ordinary Europeans engaged in passive resistance and secretive paganism while Christian practices were inculturated and, in various ways, paganized (MacMullen 1997).

These changes furthered the expansion of Christianity within the Roman Empire. In the Persian empire and beyond, the Christian Church spread without Christendom's advantages, carried by nonconformist communities, merchants, and monks (Hunter 1996). In northern Europe heroic mission efforts by Irish and English monks carried Christianity into new territories. Equally important in the expansion of Christianity was the conversion of monarchs. "Christian missionary work could not succeed without the support of the king" (Mayr-Harting 1991, 98). Many people invoked the precedent of Constantine I, and missionary work typically followed a top-down strategy. A notable example was the conversion around 500 of Clovis, king of the Franks, which was followed by the baptism of more than three thousand of his troops. Later monarchs used heavier-handed methods. Charlemagne, the Frankish king who in 800 was declared "Holy Roman Emperor," had earlier conquered the Saxons. He required them, on pain of death, to be baptized and to promise "that they would be Christians and [bind] themselves to the lordship of King Charles" (Fletcher 1997, 214–215). Where mission efforts aiming at voluntary conversion fell short, and where tribal solidarity was incomplete, monarchs employed force to complete the Christian uniformity of their people.

Charlemagne's world called itself "Christendom," which was the dominant form of society in the West from the fifth to the late twentieth centuries. Christendom societies manifested a constellation of characteristics. Some of these characteristics emerged gradually over the centuries; others began to fragment in the sixteenth century, beginning with the Protestant Reformation. However, this constellation of Christendom organizational patterns and assumptions was dominant, not only in the Roman Catholic Church but also in the territorial churches that originated in the Protestant Reformation.

## Characteristics of Christendom

Religious unity: In Christendom societies, the Christian Church was one and had universal pretensions. Everyone in society (except the Jews) belonged to the church, into which they were baptized as soon as possible after birth. Often they received minimal catechesis.

Territorialized Christianity: Although Christendom was "universal," in every political entity the churches' territorial units paralleled secular units. Ecclesiastical dioceses were often based on civil administrative areas. From the sixteenth century onward, the national Protestant churches also reflected political boundaries. Throughout Christendom, the "parish" was the basic building block of both civil and religious life. Whereas the ancient Christians called themselves *paroikoi* (resident aliens), under Christendom Christians were known as *parochiani* (residents). In every parish there was a priest or incumbent who was charged with the "cure of souls" of the parishioners of that geographical area.

Church and state in symbiosis: From the parish to the national and transnational levels, ecclesiastical and secular authorities ideally supported each other, protecting the church in its spiritual ministries and justifying the position and actions of civil authorities. Church leaders could call on civil authorities to do things that it were deemed inappropriate for churchmen to do; for example, church authorities tried heretics, but they "delated them to the secular arm" for execution.

Participation in religious observances: This was considerable but spotty, even when church attendance was officially obligatory. Christians enthusiastically attended Masses, festivals, and pilgrimages (Duffy 1992), but religious observance was far from complete. Throughout the Christendom centuries there were countless examples of irreverence, misbehavior, ignorance, and unbelief. The Christian Church of Christendom, whose formation had involved a missionary policy of compulsion, continued to be associated with many-tiered coercion—required attendance, statutory financial exactions (tithes), and the persecution of religious nonconformists.

Conventional "Christian" values: In Christendom societies, clerics exhorted the laity to be observant, orderly, and to give alms, but not to live by Jesus' teaching on wealth or violence. They urged those who wished to live by heroic values—"counsels of perfection"—to join the clerical orders, which society admired, or, in the late period of Protestant Christendom, to become foreign missionaries. Up to the seventeenth century, church leaders viewed people who left the church to follow Jesus and joined illicit nonconformist groups as shatterers of the unity of Christendom who deserved persecution and, at times, execution for heresy.

The priority of worship and "the cure of souls": In Christendom, the Christian Church existed to provide for the spiritual needs by word and sacrament, thereby ensuring the eternal salvation of Christian people. Mission existed in Christendom, but in comparison to worship it was marginal.

## Mission under Christendom

Mission within Christendom territories: Since the inhabitants by definition were formally Christian, local mission was a marginal activity. Nevertheless, on occasion there were authorized missional activities within Christendom societies. In the Middle Ages the Church at times sought to evangelize and revive the faith of ordinary Christians (laity) through preaching campaigns; in eighteenth-century France well-known Catholic preachers engaged in "parish missions" to renew the parishioners' sacramental participation. Unauthorized missionary activities also occurred. In the sixteenth century, in both Catholic and Protestant territories, Anabaptist missionaries spontaneously crossed parish and diocesan boundaries in their missional activities. On a much larger scale, the preaching missions of John Wesley and his associates in eighteenth-century England and the Salvation Army campaigns of the nineteenth century disregarded territorial boundaries. Leaders of the Christendom churches, both parochial and diocesan, disapproved of these campaigns and at times invoked state power to impede them.

Mission beyond Christendom: The word mission was first used by Ignatius of Loyola for efforts to propagate the faith beyond the confines of Christendom territories (Bosch 1991, 228). These "missionaries" found themselves in a long tradition, which at times employed force abroad as it did at home. Precedents included the Crusades in the eastern Mediterranean, but also in Spain and northeastern Europe, which were attempts to extend Christian hegemony by military means. Other missionary efforts in the Christendom era were vulnerable and costly. Catholic missionary efforts were carried out primarily by religious orders. In the Middle Ages, Franciscan and Dominican missionaries, unsupported by state power, gave sacrificial witness in North Africa, among the Mongols, and in China. In the sixteenth and seventeenth centuries, Catholics engaged in missionary activities in China, Japan, India, Africa, and Latin America (Bevans and Schroeder 2004). Protestant missionary efforts began late in the Christendom era, but like Catholic missions they were the products of voluntary specialists rather than central ecclesial organizations. Out of pietist renewal came the Moravian missionary efforts of the eighteenth century. These were followed, in the 1790s in England, by Baptists, Anglicans, and Reformed Christians who founded missionary societies. In the nineteenth and twentieth centuries these missionary societies sprang up in other countries and attained considerable momentum; they gave vision to Protestants, who sent enthusiastic volunteers as missionaries to many places. Meanwhile, the Catholic Church sent missionaries to many countries. The central bodies of churches in Christendom countries viewed these missionary efforts as laudable but peripheral to the primary concerns of Christians. When Anglicans began the Church Missionary Society in 1799, they jump-started the church into missionary action "without waiting for opinion to change in the Church's hierarchy" (Nazir-Ali 1995, 53).

## Role of Mission in Christendom

In Christendom, mission was not central to the churches' life or imagination. The Christendom traditions' classic statements of ecclesiology mention the fostering of truth, the enabling of right worship, and the provision of proper authority, but mission is missing (Shenk 1993, 22). A representative Roman Catholic theology of mission, written in late Christendom, maintained that mission ends when the Church has been established in a society; mission is only a temporary function of the church (Charles 1956, 26f). Owen Chadwick's *The Victorian Church* (1966) is an indicator of mission's peripheral place in Christendom's self-awareness; in two volumes, which treat a period in which British churches were sending missionaries to many countries, Chadwick does not once mention the British missionary movement (Walls 1991, 146).

Nor was mission central to theology in the Christendom world. Missionary concerns had been important to the fathers of the Christendom theological traditions such as Augustine and Gregory the Great, but as Christendom institutions became generalized in Europe and North America, mission withered. In the classical theological education, if mission appeared at all, it was a supplement to the least prestigious discipline, practical theology. "Mission was something completely on the periphery of the church and did not evoke any theological interest worth mentioning" (Bosch 1991, 490). In Christendom, theologians spent little time reflecting on the interaction of the gospel with their own cultures; they did not monitor the inculturation, unconscious and therefore over-confident, that was happening in their own societies. An "illegitimate alliance with false elements in culture" was inevitable (Newbigin 1986, 147).

As a result, when missionary initiatives began to proliferate in the nineteenth and twentieth centuries, they were often associated with dominant Christendom values. Western missionaries at their best were sensitive servants, but they were not always at their best. Programmed by Christendom assumptions, missionaries were prey to alliances with merchants and colonial administrators. As in Christendom's origins, so also in its foreign mission efforts—advantage and compulsion went hand in hand, as did the alliance of church and state. General Douglas MacArthur represented this tradition when he, as the head of the American occupation of Japan, called for American churches to send "thousands of missionaries" to the recently conquered country (Woodard 1972, 281).

In late Christendom, a new distinction began to emerge—between missions and evangelism. German theologian Johannes Warneck, the father of the discipline of missiology, introduced this distinction. Evangelism was directed toward Christendom; it was an attempt to restore, renew, and revive an implicit faith that had become cool or distant (Shenk 1995, 50).

Evangelism did not involve a critique of the worldview, structures, and mores of society in light of the gospel, but elicited conversion that entailed a "strengthened commitment to shared social norms" (Murray 2004, 225). Mission, in contrast, was directed toward heathendom. Central to mission was the Matthean Great Commission's imperative to "go." Missions took place beyond the bounds of Christendom, where missionaries sought to establish the church where it had not been before; evangelism took place within Christendom to reinvigorate the faith of nominal Christians.

## Mission after Christendom

Mission, always a marginal movement within Christendom, led to the transformation of global Christianity. Especially in the latter half of the twentieth century, Christians in the global South appropriated the faith and spread it with joy and sacrificial zeal. This led to a massive growth of Christianity in Africa, Asia, and Latin America at the same time that Christian observance in Christendom's heartlands was waning.

The decline of the Christendom world began with the effects of the Protestant Reformation. National churches, breaking with their Roman Catholic mother, attempted to realize the Christendom vision in their own territories. The Wars of Religion leading to the Enlightenment also played a fracturing role, as did the emergence of Christian denominations and the crumbling of coercive Christendom institutions, such as religious requirements for admission to educational institutions or the assuming of political office.

Post-Christendom's beginnings vary by country and region. In the de-Christianized atmosphere of Paris in the 1940s, the city's Cardinal Archbishop, Emmanuel Suhard, inspired Godin and Daniel's *France, A Country of Mission?*, which called the Church to a vigorous missionary engagement with French society (Ward 1949). This was controversial. But by the 1990s there was a general sense that Europe, in the 1960s if not before, had taken leave of its Christendom assumptions. Christian thinkers were aware that many people had come to think that Christianity was intrinsically violent, compulsory, and conventional; as a result, people wanted to discard it as old, boring, and hypocritical. In 1999, the Cardinal Archbishop of Vienna, Franz König, wrote, "The Christian community in Europe, which from the Emperor Constantine's conversion in the fourth century onwards had the respect and support of public opinion, has today been thrown back on itself by a non-believing, indifferent, often even hostile environment ... A second turning-point as fundamental as the Constantinian one confronts us. Faced with a cold wind of resistance, the . . . Christian community is once again becoming the salt of the earth and the light on the mountains (König 1999).

In the post-Christendom world, the means by which Christianity spread in early Christendom—incentives and compulsion—no longer work. In a setting in which Christianity has low prestige, a lowering of the hurdles makes no sense. Christianity will survive insofar as its thinking, behavior, and common life are interesting and noteworthy. This quality of life will come about as Christians "engage in a radical re-formation," repositioning themselves penitently in light of the challenges of a changed world (Smith 2003, 11).

In post-Christendom, debates about Christendom will continue. In the global South, where Christianity is at times numerically preponderant, some Christians reflexively resort to the violent strategies of Christendom (Jenkins 2002, 190). In Europe, where in many countries the parochial system is collapsing and church attendance is low, neo-Christendom stances are less common than in America. But even in America, where approximately one-fifth of the populace attends church weekly (Hadaway and Marler 2005), thinkers are now reexamining Christendom assumptions. Two signs of this are the Gospel and Our Culture movement, inspired by Lesslie Newbigin, and the Missional Church Network (Guder 1998). Also significant is the coincidence of the emergence of *missio dei* theologies with the collapse of Christendom. All of these are signs that the church, in post-Christendom as in pre-Christendom, can thrive without legal advantages and social privileges.

ALAN KREIDER

## Further Reading

Bevans, S. B., & Schroeder, R. P. (2004). *Constants in context: A theology of mission for today.* Maryknoll, NY: Orbis Books.

Bosch, D. J. (1991). *Transforming mission: Paradigm shifts in theology of mission.* Maryknoll, NY: Orbis Books.

Bradshaw, P. F. (2002). *The search for the origins of Christian worship* (2nd ed.). New York: Oxford University Press.

Brown, P. (2003). *The rise of Western Christendom* (2nd ed.). Oxford, UK: Blackwell.

Charles, P. S. J. (1956). *Etudes missiologiques.* Louvain, France: Desclee De Brouwer.

De Romestin, H. (Ed.). (1989). *St. Ambrose, select works and letters. Nicene and post-Nicene fathers.* Edinburgh, UK: T&T Clark.

Duffy, E. (1992). *The stripping of the altars: Traditional religion in England, 1400–1580.* New Haven, CT: Yale University Press.

Fletcher, R. (1997). *The conversion of Europe: From paganism to Christianity, 371–1386 AD.* London: HarperCollins.

Guder, D. L. (Ed.). (1998). *Missional Church: A vision for the sending of the Church in North America.* Grand Rapids: Eerdmans.

Hadaway, C. K., & Marler, P.L. (2005). How many Americans attend church each week? An alternative approach to measurement. *Journal for the Scientific Study of Religion, 44*(1), 307-322.

Hill, G.F. (Ed.). (1913). *Mark the Deacon: The life of Porphyry, Bishop of Gaza.* Oxford: Clarendon Press.

Hunter, E. C. D. (1996). The Church of the East in Central Asia. *Bulletin of the John Rylands Library, 78,* 129–142.

Jenkins, P. (2002). *The next Christendom: The coming of global Christianity.* New York: Oxford University Press.

König, F. C. (1999, November). The pull of God in a godless age. *The Tablet.*

Kreider, A. (1999). *The change of conversion and the origin of Christendom, Christian mission and modern culture.* Harrisburg, PA: Trinity Press International.

Kreider, A. (2005). Beyond Bosch: the early Church and the Christendom shift. *International Bulletin of Missionary Research, 29*(2), 59–68.

MacMullen, R. (1997). *Christianity and paganism in the fourth to eighth centuries.* New Haven, CT: Yale University Press.

Mayr-Harting, H. (1991). *The coming of Christianity to Anglo-Saxon England* (3rd ed.). University Park: Pennsylvania State University Press.

McLeod, H., & Ustorf, W. (Eds.). (2003). *The decline of Christendom in Western Europe, 1750–2000.* Cambridge, UK: Cambridge University Press.

Murray, S. (2004). *Post-Christendom: Church and mission in a strange new world.* Carlisle. UK: Paternoster Press.

Nazir-Ali, M. (1995). *Mission and dialogue.* London: SPCK.

Newbigin, L. (1986). *Foolishness to the Greeks: The Gospel and Western culture.* Geneva, Switzerland: World Council of Churches.

Nichols, A. E. (1994). *Seeable signs: The iconography of the Seven Sacraments, 1350–1544.* Woodbridge, UK: Boydell Press.

O'Donovan, O. (1996). *The desire of the nations: Rediscovering the roots of political theology.* Cambridge, UK: Cambridge University Press.

Parsons, W. (Ed.). (1953). *Saint Augustine, Letters, 2. Fathers of the Church, 18.* Washington, DC: Catholic University of America Press.

Richardson, C. C. (Ed.). (1953). *Early Christian Fathers. Library of Christian Classics 1.* Philadelphia: Westminster Press.

Shenk, W. R. (Ed.). (1993). *The transfiguration of mission: Biblical, theological and historical foundations.* Scottdale, PA: Herald Press.

Shenk, W. R. (1995). *Write the vision: The Church renewed.* Harrisburg, PA: Trinity Press International.

Smith, D. (2003). *Mission after Christendom.* London: Darton Longman & Todd.

Van Engen, J. (1986). The Christian Middle Ages as an historiographical problem. *American Historical Review, 91,* 519–552.

Walls, A. F. (1991). Structural problems in mission studies. *International Bulletin of Missionary Research, 15*(4), 146–155.

Walls, A. F. (2002). *The cross-cultural process in Christian history.* Maryknoll, NY: Orbis Books.

Ward, M. (1949). *France pagan? The mission of Abbé Godin.* London: Sheed and Ward.

Woodard, W. B. (1972). *The Allied occupation of Japan, 1945–1952, and Japanese Religions* (pp. 281–283). Leiden, Netherlands: Brill.

# Church Growth Movement

The term *church growth* is inseparably linked with the name of Donald Anderson McGavran (1897–1990), a third-generation missionary to India. At the heart of the concept is the making of disciples (followers-in-training) of Jesus Christ, the forming of new faith communities (churches), and the revitalizing of existing congregations through their recommitment to the Great Commission as given by Christ just prior to his Ascension (Matthew 28:18–20). McGavran developed his key concepts from the 1950s to the 1970s as a critical response to the broader understanding of mission that became popular at that time. Many nations were gaining their independence from colonialism and Western missionary-sending agencies were going through a time of soul searching and recognition of the need for independent churches to establish their authentic identity. McGavran's foundational texts are *The Bridges of God* (1955) and *Understanding Church Growth* (1970).

McGavran was concerned lest the broader concerns of mission in terms of social service, political liberation, and social justice should prove to be diversions from the primary task of disciple making. Although this focus is not the whole of mission, in his view it is the heart of it. But his concern also arose initially from his personal experience in India, where he served under the auspices of the United Christian Missionary Society. He was in-

volved in a wide variety of tasks including hospital administration and education, in addition to rural church planting. It was this church-planting experience that led him to question why some churches grew while others did not, which the Mid-India Provincial Council asked him to investigate. His findings were published in 1936 under the title *Christian Mission in Mid-India,* which was republished in 1956 under a new title, *Church Growth and Group Conversion.* After a period of further research and teaching, he founded the Institute of Church Growth at Northwestern Christian College in Eugene, Oregon, in 1961. From there he transferred to Fuller Theological Seminary in 1966 to become the founding dean of the School of World Mission and Institute of Church Growth. He continued to teach until he was 83.

## Church Growth: Basic Concepts

The cluster of concepts that represent the church-growth paradigm consist of the following: reproducible, indigenous churches (as against the "mission station" approach that McGavran criticized in *Church Growth and Group Conversion* as well as in *The Bridges of God*); people-movement conversion (as against an extractionist, one-by-one approach); statistical research (clearing away the fog of vague and often misleading promotional language); learning from the insights provided by the social sciences of sociology and anthropology (the gospel may be rejected not so much because it is considered false as it sounds foreign and irrelevant); the Homogeneous Unit Principle (the most controversial of McGavran's insights), which was later translated into a more acceptable, Unreached Peoples strategy; Resistance/Receptivity (recognizing that at certain times and under special conditions people may become more receptive to the gospel).

### Early Influence

From the late 1970s until the early 1990s church-growth concepts exerted a considerable influence among church leaders in the West as a response to the serious decline experienced by almost all denominations in North America, northern Europe, and Australasia. Thousands of church leaders, both pastors and denominational executives representing home missions departments, attended church-growth seminars developed by the Fuller Institute of Church Growth and other agencies. Prominent among the teachers were C. Peter Wagner, Elmer Towns, George Hunter III, Mike McIntosh, and a number of pastors of the megachurches that emerged at that time. These courses provided insight into vision casting, goal setting, mobilizing of the membership in ministry according to their spiritual gifting, leadership development, and the importance of prayer and signs and wonders to empower evangelism.

## Growing Pains

Many of the practical insights that were shared at those seminars proved helpful to pastors, whose seminary training had been deficient in providing practical ministry insights. However, the undue focus on lessons to be learned from growing megachurches proved frustrating for many pastors in long-established, small, and struggling traditional churches. They envied the freedom and entrepreneurial spirit of the founding pastors of megachurches, most of which were located in newer, affluent, growing suburbs. Urban ministry presented a different set of challenges that were rarely addressed.

Furthermore, as pastors had not been trained in missional insights, church growth became translated into marketing principles. Consequently, McGavran's original concerns tended to be overlooked, especially in the spate of popular church-growth books that appeared at that time. Emphasis was placed on growing a church without giving due attention to where the growth was coming from. With a highly mobile population, most church growth turned out to be transfer growth, at the expense of other churches, rather than new growth resulting from the conversion of previously unchurched persons or from the restoration and spiritual renewal of the lapsed or "nominal" dechurched former members and attendees.

## Reconnection and Reassessment

The emergence of the missional church discussions, arising out of the insights of Lesslie Newbigin and the Gospel and Our Culture Network and the emerging church phenomenon, have reconnected ecclesiology and missiology, recognizing that the church is both the outcome of mission as well as the agent of mission. This missional emphasis leads back to the early work of Donald McGavran, applying it to the current challenges facing the churches in the West. Missional church leaders need to be able to exegete the cultures they are seeking to engage incarnationally. Furthermore, they must abandon a "mission station approach" of inviting those outside the community of faith to come to them on their terms, replacing it with a church that meets people in their social contexts. The church is not just an occasional gathering of people but a community that is dispersed to bear its witness on a day-to-day basis.

### Critical Voices

The church growth movement has had its detractors over the years. Some have criticized it for its narrow ecclesiocentric focus, accusing it of losing sight of a broader kingdom of God faithfulness. Others have objected to its statistical approach, insisting on priority being given to quality criteria. Still others consider it the child of modernity, with its emphasis on strategic goal setting and pragmatic assessments, while others have questioned a more recent emphasis highlighted by some advocates on signs and wonders and "spiritual warfare" intercession.

While church growth no longer enjoys the popular interest of former decades, it is now entering a time of reassessment as the church in the West engages with the rapidly growing and spiritually vibrant churches of the non-Western, majority world, many of which instinctively embody the key insights of church growth.

EDDIE GIBBS

*See also* Church Planting; Mission Methods and Strategy; Theory—Catholic, Protestant, Evangelical

### Further Reading

Engle, P. E., & McIntosh, G. L. (Eds.). (2004). *Evaluating the Church growth movement.* Grand Rapids, MI: Zondervan.

Gibbs, E. (1990). *I believe in Church growth.* Grand Rapids, MI: Eerdmans/Hodder & Stoughton.

McGavran, D. (1955). *The bridges of God.* London: World Dominion Press.

McGavran, D. (1970). *Understanding church growth.* Grand Rapids, MI: Eerdmans.

McIntosh, G. (2003). *Biblical church growth.* Dartmouth, MA: Baker Books.

Rainer, T. S. (1993). *The book of church growth.* Nashville, TN: Broadman Press.

Wagner, C. Peter. (1976). *Your church can grow.* Ventura, CA: Regal Books.

## Church Planting

The words "church planting" are not in the Bible. However, the Apostle Paul used the same metaphor: "I planted the seed, Apollos watered it, but God made it grow" (1 Cor. 3:6). This verse suggests that establishing a church is a corporate work between human beings and God—that is, it is both divine and human. Paul goes on to explain, "So neither he who plants nor he who waters is anything, but only God who makes it grow. The man who plants and the man who waters have one purpose, and each will be rewarded according to his own labor. For we are fellow workers; you are God's field, God's building" (1 Cor. 3:7–9).

A successful church planting requires four essentials: God, church planters, seeds, and target people. Successful church planters understand that a church-planting ministry is a divine work and they acknowledge the leadership and ownership of the Holy Spirit (Acts 1:4–8; John 21: 15–18; 1 Chron. 16:9; 2 Tim. 2:20–21). Upon hearing Simon Peter's confession of faith, "You are the Christ, the Son of the living God" (John 16:16), Jesus said that he will build his church on earth: "On this rock I will build my church" (Matt. 16:18). His disciples, who best understood his will, planted churches whenever and wherever converts were made. The primary concern of church planters is similar, that is, to find an unreached group of people in a strategic location.

The Apostle Paul describes the importance of the Church as follows: "And God placed all things under his feet and appointed him to be head over everything for the Church, which is his body, the fullness of him who fills everything in every way" (Eph. 1:22–23, NIV). Christians therefore believe that their churches are the agents of the kingdom of God on earth. They believe that when this kingdom comes, the Church will be born, and when the Church proclaims the gospel, the kingdom will come. They think it is their responsibility to proclaim the kingdom of God until He comes again.

Theologian George Eldon Ladd explains the relationship between the Kingdom and the Church as follows: "The church is the community of the Kingdom but never the Kingdom itself. Jesus' disciples belong to the Kingdom as the Kingdom belongs to them; but they are not the Kingdom. The Kingdom is the rule of God; the church is a society of men.... the Kingdom creates the church. The dynamic rule of God, present in the mission of Jesus, challenged men to response, bringing them into a new fellowship" (1964, 258–265). Theologian J. David Hesselgrave also acknowledges the importance of fellowship: "The primary mission of the Church and, therefore, churches is to proclaim the gospel of Christ and gather believers into local churches where they can be built up in the faith and made effective in service, thereby planting new congregations throughout the world." (1980, 20)

Although experts believe that church planting is the most effective way to evangelize the world, many gospel workers are currently engaged in a church-planting ministry without a proper understanding of the purpose of their undertaking. Missionaries tend to transplant their home churches into other cultures, even though such churches are generally weak and not reproducible because they depend on paid agents and are not indigenized and contextualized. When churches are not planted after the New Testament methods they do not become healthy, dynamic, and reproducible.

The church in Thessalonia is one of the most successful cases of church planting. It was born after only three weeks of Paul's ministry, and he believed that it grew and became a dynamic church by the power of the Holy Spirit. As Paul and his missionary team preached the gospel, they became a model to all believers in Macedonia and Achaia, and their faith in God became known everywhere (1 Thess. 1:4–8). The aim of the church planters should therefore be to plant churches like the one in Thessalonia. In doing this, however, it is important that planters remember what Paul meant when he said, "You know how we lived among you for your sake." (1 Thess. 1:5). In the same way, church planters should strive to adopt Paul's attitude of living an exemplary life.

TIMOTHY PARK

*See also* Mission Methods and Strategy; Theory—Catholic, Protestant, Evangelical

### Further reading

Cho, D. C. (1991). *People and religion.* Seoul, South Korea: Byul.

Hesselgrave, J. D. (1980). *Planting churches cross-culturally.* Grand Rapids,MI: Bakers.

Ladd, G. E. (1964). *Jesus and the kingdom: The eschatology of biblical realism.* New York: Harper & Row.

McGavran, D. A. (1990). *Understanding church growth* (3rd ed.). Grand Rapids, MI: Eerdmans.

Wagner, C. P. (1990). *Church planting for a greater harvest.* Ventura, CA: Regal Books.

# Civilization

What does the widely used, but rarely well-defined, concept of "civilization" mean? Is every human society (an aggregate of persons with values, beliefs, and practices located within a given geographical area) "civilized"? Most social scientists would probably say no, arguing that to be a "civilization," a human society needs to have a relatively high level of cultural and technological development as well as complex social, economic, and civic institutions.

This definition implies that an isolated society whose people live in caves, have no metal tools, are only able to hunt and fish, have only subsistence clothing and shelter, and are not able to ignite a fire, is not a civilization and that a society whose people no longer live in caves, have metal tools and weapons, are able to light fires, possess wheeled vehicles, and trade goods with people outside of their society's geographic boundaries is a civilization. But what if this civilization permits slavery, abortion, infanticide, child abandonment, and cannibalism? Is it still a civilization? In short, what role do moral values and practices play in defining the concept of civilization?

Unfortunately, many definitions of civilization fail to include moral values and practices. However, if morality is an essential part of being civilized, then what kind of moral values must a society have? What is the source of its moral values? Are they derived from the principle of might makes right or are they derived from what the Greco-Roman philosophers like Cicero (106–43 BCE) called "natural law"? To Cicero, "True [moral] law is right reason in agreement with nature; it is of universal application, unchanging and everlasting; it summons to duty by its commands, and averts from wrongdoing by its prohibitions." (Cicero 1928, 211)

St. Paul in the first century equated natural moral law with the Bible's Ten Commandments. He argued that the Gentiles (pagans and non-Jews) who did not have the Ten Commandments nevertheless heeded them, for they had the natural moral law "written in their hearts" (Rom. 2:15). Martin Luther argued in the sixteenth century that the Ten Commandments were the natural moral law stated clearly. He asked, "Why does one then keep and teach the Ten Commandments? Answer: Because the natural laws were never so orderly and well written as by Moses" (Jan Pelikan 1958, 98). Luther, like Cicero, contended that "all [human] reason is filled [with] natural law" (Brandt 1962, 128).

But not all societies obey the natural moral law—some practice cannibalism, some, like the Greeks and Romans, accept slavery, infanticide, child abandonment, abortion, and pederasty, and some participate in genocides, like the Germans under the Nazis. Historians, ignoring the question of moral values, have consistently referred to Greece and Rome and Germany as civilizations, leading others to wonder what component a civilization must lose in order to no longer qualify as a civilization? Is the loss of some moral practices more

**A statue of the Ten Commandment tablets in Kielce, Poland.** *Courtesy of Luke Daniek/istockphoto.com.*

pertinent than the loss of others? If a society becomes more civilized when it adopts more humane moral values and practices, then Christian teachings have elevated Western civilization to a higher level than it had in the Greco-Roman era. Christianity opposed abortion, infanticide, child abandonment, pederasty, and suicide, and elevated the status of women. Over time it converted many important leaders who outlawed these practices, thereby transforming Western civilization.

Christianity also enhanced other aspects of Western civilization. For example, it introduced works of charity and hospitals soon after it received legal status in the Roman Empire in the fourth century. It introduced the principle that no man was above the law when Bishop Ambrose demanded that Emperor Theodosius repent for slaughtering thousands of innocent people in a riot at Thessalonica in 390. In 1215 this principle was further underscored in the Magna Charta, formulated by individuals influenced by Christian values, including Archbishop Stephen Langton. Christian values helped introduce and institutionalize property rights, derived from one of the Ten Commandments that assumes the possession of property: "You shall not steal." Christianity has also inspired countless individuals who have significantly enhanced Western civilization's science, art, architecture, music, and literature. This is clearly evident when one considers the brilliant contributions of only a few individuals, for instance, the scientific work of Roger Bacon, Francis Bacon, Johannes Kepler, and Robert Boyle; the art work of Leonardo da Vinci, Raphael, Rembrandt, and Tintoretto; the architecture of majestic Gothic cathedrals; the musical compositions of Bach, Beethoven, Mozart, and Handel; and the literary works of St. Augustine, Chaucer, Dante, Milton, and Shakespeare. Western civilization is admired by many non-Westerners. Recently a Chinese observer noted what he believed accounted for the West's high achievements. After examining a number of possible reasons, he and his colleagues concluded, "[In] the past twenty years, we have realized that the heart of your culture is your religion: Christianity. That is why the West is so powerful. The Christian moral foundation of social and cultural life was what made possible the emergence of capitalism and then the successful transition to democratic politics." (Aikman 2003, 5) This non-Western assessment suggests that Western civilization has reached its highly developed state largely because of Christianity's powerful influences.

ALVIN J. SCHMIDT

*See also* Art; Christendom; Enlightenment; Europe; Materiality; Modernity; Technology

### Further Reading

Aikman, D. (2003). *Jesus in Beijing: How Christianity is transforming China and changing th global balance of power.* Washington, DC: Regnery Publishing

Brandt, W. (Ed.). (1962). *Luther's works, 45.* St. Louis, MO: Concordia Publishing House.

Cicero, M. T. (1928). *De re publica* [On the republic] (C. W. Keyes,Trans.). Cambridge, MA: Harvard University Press.

Jan Pelikan, J. (Ed.). (1958). *Luther's works, 40.* St. Louis, MO: Concordia Publishing House.

## Commerce

One of the iconic images of modern Protestant missions is that of William Carey, cobbler and Baptist pastor, sailing from England to India in 1793 on a Danish ship in defiance of the East India Company which forbade the presence of missionaries because their preaching might disrupt trade and profits. Forced to live and missionize in a Danish colonial enclave outside Calcutta, Carey persisted, slowly winning converts and translating the Bible into a number of languages. He was appointed professor of Sanskrit and Bengali at the East India Company's own Fort William College in 1801 and in 1813 saw the Company's antimissionary policy overthrown. David triumphs over Goliath; steadfast faith routs intransigent commerce; and, obstacles removed, the field is now clear for missionary advance, never mind that there were missionaries in India before Carey and that he himself was, among other things, an astute entrepreneur.

In fact, from its earliest days the fortunes of the missionary movement from the West have been intertwined with business and commerce. This was true of the Jesuit "reductions" in Paraguay in the 1600s and 1700s. It was true of Samuel Marsden's ventures in the South Pacific in the early 1800s and of William Duncan's theocratic communities in British Columbia in the late 1800s. It is true of Christian evangelicals today who establish businesses as means of access to locales and among peoples where they otherwise would not be permitted to reside. The relationship between mission and commerce has, however, worn many different faces and taken many different forms (Baker 2006).

## Mission in Distinction from Commerce

At times mission organizations have engaged in business activities so as to earn a profit from which they could fund activities and personnel more directly conceived as being missional. The New England Company for Propagation of the Gospel in New England and the Parts Adjacent in America provides an example. Chartered in England in 1649 and still in existence today, the New England Company raised money by subscription. It then invested the money in land which it rented out. The yearly rental income was used to support missionaries such as John Eliot among the Native Americans in the 1600s and publication of his translation of the Bible into Algonquin.

At the beginning of the 1800s, Samuel Marsden became a forceful advocate for imparting the "arts" of civilization before attempting to evangelize, expecting commerce to draw the Maoris of New Zealand away from warfare and cannibalism. Commerce and the benefits of civilization were to act as a step up that would prepare them for the higher truths of the Gospel.

On a more personal level, not infrequently nineteenth-century missionaries, far from mission headquarters and receiving irregular and inadequate support allowances, engaged as individuals in smaller- or larger-scale commercial enterprises so as to provide for themselves and their families. Some were expected and encouraged by their sending mission societies to do so.

Missionaries have often been charged by their foes or credited by friends (such as James Barton in the early 1900s) with being trailblazers for Western commercial expansion. In the same period, sociologist James Dennis thought that he could track expansions and contractions of commerce in mission lands in proportion to the rise or decline of the missionary presence.

## Mission Opposition to Commerce

Commercial drummers may have followed missionaries, but the missionaries were far from being front persons for commerce. They were in fact likely to be the indigene's sole advocate and bulwark against commercial exploitation, speaking out against extortion, rape, confiscation, outright robbery, and enslavement—one thinks of Bartolomé Las Casas's defense of Native Americans in the 1500s, the hue and cry raised by missionaries against "blackbirding" in the South Pacific in the 1800s (Young 1922), and Alice Seely Harris's photographic exposé of the brutality of King Leopold's minions in the Congo at the beginning of the 1900s (Thompson 2002).

Missionaries were sharply antagonistic to the liquor traffic, opium trade, and slave trade. Their tactics were similar in each case. Through the wide readership of mission magazines, they sought to arouse popular moral indignation, petitions, and votes in Western missionary sending countries. They pressured colonial administrators to enforce existing prohibitions. At times they opened commercial houses directly or as parallel enterprises so as to undercut commercial firms that participated in liquor trafficking or to obviate the in-country economic motive for slave trafficking.

The best known missionary of the 1800s, David Livingstone, worked tirelessly in impassioned articles and stirring speeches to bring traffic in human beings to an end. It is in this light that his words in 1857 at Cambridge ("I go back to Africa to try to make an open path for commerce and Christianity") are to be understood. Following Thomas Fowell Buxton (1840) he saw legitimate commerce as an engine that could be harnessed in service of a Christian purpose, the extirpation of the slave traffic.

## Mission Engaging in Commerce

Viewed from a different perspective—that of mission organizations seeking to accomplish missional objectives—mission agencies always and everywhere have entered into innumerable commercial ventures, many as outright businesses, others with a strong commercial component. As instruments to convey their message or as services to convert communities, mission organizations have set up printing plants; published books, magazines, and booklets; taped radio broadcasts, filmed TV programs, and recorded music. They have built hospitals, orphanages, hospices, and study and conference centers, and have established schools of all levels and types, including industrial and agricultural schools.

Out of a desire to meet basic human needs and to alleviate suffering, missionaries engage in community development and foster economic growth—for example, by opening cooperatives and providing microcredit opportunities. They establish well-drilling operations in remote areas that others consider too dangerous or financially unrewarding. They operate transportation and communication systems in areas where such service is not otherwise available.

Each of these activities draws on financial, organizational, and managerial skills and knowledge that parallel the expertise to be found in the for-profit world. Whether buying TV air time or seeking to realize a gain on disposable property, mission administrators are performing operations familiar to any business manager.

## Mission Undone by Commerce

Mission enterprise has an inevitable business component, and some shifts in mission governance echo passing fads in corporate management. The early 1900s in the United States saw denominational departments of mission eagerly announcing that they had shifted to scientific fund-raising and were applying scientific business principles to office procedures and personnel oversight (Patton 1924). Nevertheless, mission itself and mission agencies are not simply an unfolding of commercial enterprise cloaked in another name. Though there are areas of overlap, mission and commerce differ in goals, values, objectives, and methods.

John Stone (1839) denounced the damage unrestrained and unprincipled commerce did to the people to whom missionaries ministered. At the same time it must be acknowledged that some missionaries and mission agencies misused their position of trust for personal or institutional aggrandizement, giving substance to the accusation that they went out to do good, but ended up doing well—at the expense of those they came to serve. In 1898 some missionaries, turned by the opportunity for quick gain, threw their denomination into two decades of turmoil and nearly wrecked its flourishing Alaskan mission when they went prospecting for gold and struck it rich (Carlson 1951).

## Mission Blending with Commerce

Beyond the level of agricultural missions, industrial missions, and schools established by missions specifically to train a cadre of white-collar workers to meet the personnel needs of colonial administrative offices and expatriate commercial firms and farms, some missions at particular times and places have set up businesses that were intended themselves to carry out missional purposes. For example, in the 1800s the Basel Mission's operations in India, including tile manufacturing and weaving, were intended to accomplish several purposes, each of which fit within the mission's overall purpose. They provided employment and, therefore, support for converts, as well as for others as long as they did not actively oppose Christianity. In so doing they provided an economic base for the new churches. Importantly, they placed missionaries and nationals in close contact over extended periods. This extended contact enabled the Basel missionaries to give practical demonstration of honesty and high ethical conduct in business, becoming living examples of the message they preached (Danker 1971).

The final quarter of the 1900s saw renewed interest in creation of enterprises intended to blend business with missional purposes. With colonialism swept aside, a number of countries had become reluctant to grant visas to persons identified as missionaries. Business, along with teaching appointments and medical work, together often spoken of as tentmaking, became means for gaining residency permits. More recently, under the label of business as mission, interest has grown in establishment of businesses that are seen as being missional in themselves, being both the locus and instrument of mission. Individuals and entities within the business as mission movement are heterogeneous, representing a number of business configurations, motivations, and expectations. In scale and approach they range from the very smallest of face-to-face shops to large-scale manufacturing plants to venture capital firms (Yamamori and Eldred 2003).

Too frequently "tentmakers" were charged with creating sham businesses as fronts for missionizing but not carrying out much commercial activity. To address the ethical issues raised and to gain depth on the business side of its dual identity, the movement has created a number of forums, leading to a broadening flow of literature, courses, conferences, and supportive networks.

## Mission Surrounded by Commerce

Many ancillary businesses have grown up around the mission movement to be of service to missionaries, to aid their work, or to serve the needs of the longer-term missionary lifecycle: e.g., furlough and retirement housing complexes; travel agencies, logistics handlers, purchasing services, and shipping expediters; insurance providers; communications services, including services to print and mail missionary prayer letters; and boarding schools for missionary children. These businesses and the services they provide frequently are not thought of as being directly missional, but as existing to support and assist missionaries.

A number of these ancillary businesses come together in servicing the burgeoning movement of mission tourism, itself ancillary to the mission movement. Often referred to as short-term missions and lasting from several days to several months in duration, mission tourism is flourishing and has become an increasingly dominant feature of U.S. Protestant and Roman Catholic mission involvement in the late 1900s and early 2000s.

## Disciplinary Linkage

Mission and commerce constitutes a subdivision of immense significance within the wider field of the study of the business aspects of religious organizations and the religious aspects of business organizations (Hall 1998).

Dwight P. Baker

*See also* Civilization; Development; Economics; Empire; Globalization; Materiality; Money; Opium; Slavery

### Further Reading

Baker, D. P. (2006). Missional geometry: Plotting the coordinates of business as mission. In T. Steffen & M. Barnett (Eds.), *Business as mission: From impoverishment to empowerment* (pp. 37–64). Pasadena, CA: William Carey Library.

Barton, J. L. (c. 1912). *Human progress through missions.* New York: Fleming H. Revell.

Buxton, T. F. (1840). *The African Slave Trade and Its Remedy.* London: John Murray.

Carlson, L. (1951). *An Alaskan gold mine: The story of No. 9 Above.* Evanston. IL: Northwestern University Press.

Commerce and missions. (1891). In E. M. Bliss (Ed.), *The Encyclopedia of missions: Descriptive, historical, biographical, statistical* (Vol. 1, pp. 308–312). New York: Funk & Wagnalls.

Danker, W. (1971). *Profit for the Lord: Economic activities in Moravian missions and the Basel Mission Trading Company.* Grand Rapids, MI: Eerdmans.

Dennis, J. S. (n.d.). *Commerce and missions.* New York: Laymen's Missionary Movement.

Hall, P. D. (1998). Religion and the organizational revolution in the United States. In N. J. Demerath III, P. D. Hall, T. Schmitt, & R. H. Williams (Eds), *Sacred companies: organizational aspects of religion and religious aspects of organizations* (pp. 99–115). New York: Oxford University Press.

Kellaway, W. (1961). *The New England Company, 1649–1776: Missionary society to the American Indians.* London: Longmans.

Patton, C. H. (1924). *The business of missions.* New York: Macmillan.

Porter, A. (2004). *Religion versus empire? British Protestant missionaries and overseas expansion, 1700–1914.* New York: Manchester University Press.

Stone, J. S. (1839). *The bearings of modern commerce on the progress of modern missions.* New York: William Osborn.

Thompson, J. (2002). Light on the "dark continent": The photography of Alice Seely Harris and the Congo atrocities of the early twentieth century. *International Bulletin of Missionary Research, 26,* 146(149.

Usher, J. (1974). *William Duncan of Metlakatla: A Victorian missionary in British Columbia.* Ottawa, Canada: National Museums of Canada.

Yamamori, T., & Eldred, K. A. (Eds). (2003). *On Kingdom business: Transforming missions through entrepreneurial strategies.* Wheaton, IL: Crossway Books.

Yarwood, A. T. (1996). *Samuel Marsden: The great survivor.* Carlton, Australia: Melbourne University Press.

Young, W. A. (1922) .*Christianity in the South Pacific: The influence of missionaries upon European expansion in the Pacific during the nineteenth century.* London: Oxford University Press.

## Conciliar Missions

By "conciliar missions" we refer to the missiological understandings or positions taken by a council or councils of church/es. In the second-half of the twentieth century, the term came to refer more specifically to the ecumenical theology and practice of mission associated with the World Council of Churches, its regional, national, and allied councils, and member churches. Although church council or councils rarely occupy themselves in the practice of missions directly, they do provide principles and theological basis for the practice and understanding of mission. Church councils played an important role in Christian history. Most creeds and doctrinal statements of churches are created or validated by councils. In history, conciliarity in general and theories of conciliarity in particular developed in response to circumstances such as schisms, controversies, and conflicts in churches. Similarly, new challenges and diverging opinions as to what constitutes Christian mission and how mission should be carried out forged new thoughts and ideas on mission. Such thoughts converged into conciliar missionary theories through church or missionary councils.

Like its related term "ecumenical," the term conciliar has also followed a history of its own assuming different references and meanings at different times. The term is derived from the Latin verb *conciliare* ("to call together"). The noun *concilium* ("gathering" or "assembly") is closely associated with the church in the early period of Christianity. Its Greek synonyms *synagesthai* and *synerchesthai* are used commonly to describe the church and its activity in the New Testament. The gathering or assembly of the people of God is an important biblical image of the church. Therefore, the term conciliar is essentially ecclesial and has been used to describe the nature and activity of the church. From such an inclusive use of the term, it has also come to acquire more specific references in the history of the church. While the idea of council has always been closely associated with the church, the question of "whose council" came to acquire practical importance. In fact, the concept of conciliar or conciliarity came to prominence in the Middle Ages especially during the Great Schism in the west as an alternative to papal authority. The Conciliar Party came into existence during the so-called Great Schism which held a position that papal power could be curtailed and regulated by periodical assemblies of bishops. Although the party broke up later and papal authority was restored, the idea of conciliarity continued to remain side by side with papal authority in the Western church. While the idea of conciliarity came about in the Western churches as an alternative model to papal authority, what may be identified as a form of conciliar authority has been in effect among the Orthodox churches. Patriarchs of churches developed close working relations, and the synod of bishops has always been given high authority in matters of faith. In the West, division of the church after the Reformation and the birth of numerous Protestant churches and denominations came to demand new conciliarity. Although most Protestant denominations have councils of their own in which lay members are also actively involved, the concept of conciliarity as a basis of unity across denominations did not surface until the missionary movement gave birth to ecumenism in the late nineteenth and early twentieth centuries. It was through the missionary practices of the churches that conciliar relations and ecumenism are realized by Protestant churches. The developing conciliar relation had taken its early and most visible organized form in the World Council of Churches (WCC). The conciliar impression of the WCC was strengthened when the majority of the Eastern and Oriental Orthodox churches joined the council. In the ecumenical discussion on the theories and goals of ecumenism within the WCC, conciliar fellowship as a form of church unity continues to occupy a significant place.

In the twentieth century, the formation and the works of the World Council of Churches and its constituent regional and national councils became the most conspicuous conciliar model representing Orthodox churches and the vast array of mainline Protestant churches. For many, "ecumenical" or "conciliar" refer to the life, work and thought of the WCC, especially those ideas and practices which are in contradistinction to the conservative-evangelicals. In the Catholic Church, Vatican II was the most conspicuous conciliar event in recent times. Both in terms of its ecumenical achievement and process, it truly was a conciliar missional event. While the WCC assumed an organizational stature representing the vast majority of non-Roman Catholic churches, the latter was a major conciliar event within the Catholic Church.

Ironically, "conciliar mission" and "conciliar missiology" are terms introduced and popularized first by opponents of the conciliar missions. As a clear reference to the missiological thought or thoughts developed in the ecumenical movement in contradistinction from those developed by the conservative-evangelicals, Donald A. McGavran used the term in his book *The Conciliar-Evangelical Debate: The Crucial Documents 1964-1976.* McGravran's lead has been followed by a few others in narrowly defining the theology of conciliar mission as a contradistinctive theology of mission from conservative-evangelical theology of mission. While this has helpfulness to identify polarity between (and perhaps among) the theologies of mission, it must not hide plurality within each of the two theologies and the existence of theological positions between the two. Just as there is no one conciliar theology of mission, there is no one evangelical theology of mission. Furthermore, there are theologians who are both ecumenical and evangelical, and those who intentionally hold the two thoughts in creative tension. The history of the conciliar missiological thought, with its many twists and turns, can be traced back at least to the World Missionary Conference of Edinburgh in 1910. As a major conciliar missiological event, the conference gave birth to an ecumenical missiological development spearheaded by the International Missionary Council and, from 1961, the Commission on World Mission and Evangelism of the WCC. The movement became the most dominant force in the twentieth century. Whereas the earlier period of the development was characterized by the quest for unity in mission, conciliar missiology turned to radical humanism and social activism in the early 1960s and drew much criticism. It was in reaction to the radical missiology of the conciliar ecumenical group that brought convervative-Evangelicals together. From radical humanization and social activism, conciliar mission has also made efforts toward holistic mission.

One of the best summary of holistic conciliar missiology is to be found in the document "Mission and Evangelism: An Ecumenical Affirmation" issued by the Commission on World Mission and Evangelism of the WCC in 1982. Much has changed since 1982 in the social and political order of the world, but the fruit of the broadness of the affirmation is seen in its continued relevance even after two decades. While its refusal to be definitive in its affirmations has often been seen as its weakness, it has also been its strength. To meet the changed "world's realities," the CWME issued another statement on mission and evangelism in 2000 entitled "Mission and Evangelism in Unity Today." The new document tends to be more definite its points and takes up several new issues such as globalization and the changing face of world Christianity. The clearer and more definitive perspective can be seen to be less embracing and to have tilted toward the left in some points. It failed to draw the attention of practitioners and theorists of mission. The ecumenism and conciliar mission led by the WCC seem to have lost the popularity and esteem it once held both to its supporters and opponents. The new century and millennium seem to have brought a new form of conciliarity in mission thinking which brought together different confessional, regional and denominational bodies into missiological dialogue. The less formal and fluid nature of the new conciliarity is replacing the older and monolithic conciliarity.

LALSANGKIMA PACHUAU

## Further Reading

Commission on Faith and Order of the National Council of the Churches Christ in the USA. (1982). *Conciliar fellowship: A study of the Commission on Faith and Order of the National Council of the Churches Christ in the USA.* New York: National Council of the Churches Christ in the USA.

Commission on World Mission and Evangelism. (1982). *Mission and evangelism—an ecumenical affirmation.* Geneva: World Council of Churches.

Commission on World Mission and Evangelism. (2000.) *Mission and evangelism in unity today.* Geneva: World Council of Churches.

Glasser, A. F., &. McGavran, D. A. (1983). *Contemporary theologies of mission.* Grand Rapids: Baker Books.

Hogg, W. R. (1952). *Ecumenical foundations: A history of the International Missionary Council and its nineteenth century background.* New York: Harper & Brothers, Publishers.

McGavran, D. (Ed.). (1977). *The conciliar-evangelical debate: The crucial documents, 1964–1976.* Pasadena, CA: William Carey Library.

Newbigin, J. E. L. (1982, October): Crosscurrents in ecumenical and evangelical understandings of mission. *International Bulletin of Missionary Researc,* 6(4), 146–151.

Pachuau, L. (Ed). (2002). *Ecumenical missiology: Contemporary trends, issues, and themes.* Bangalore, India: United Theological College.

Phillips, J. M., & Coote, R. T. (Eds). (1992). *Toward the 21st century in Christian mission: Essays in honor of Gerald H. Anderson.* Grand Rapids, MI: Wm. B. Erdmans.

Rouse, R., & Neill, S. C. (Eds.). (1968). *A history of the ecumenical movement, 1517–1948* (2nd ed). Philadelphia: The Westminster Press.

## Conquest

The long and convoluted relationship between Christianity and conquest is most often approached through contrasting Christian teachings or persons who advocated peaceful persuasion over and against conquest or coercion as the appropriate means for spreading the Christian gospel. In that way Christianity has at times been compared or contrasted to other religions—especially Islam—that have also been marked by histories of religious conquest. However, the history of Christian thought and practice on that relationship is (as with other religions) considerably more complex than such a bifurcation would suggest. It is rather in the tensions of Christian belief and practice that the relationship between Christianity and conquest is to be found rather than in specific dogmatic or ideological positions. That history is also inseparable from the history of the European empires.

The problem of military conquest in Christian experience has always been bound up with evangelization. There is no Christian teaching available that provides for the forced conversion of unbelievers, and yet there has been considerable debate over what kinds of coercive force—military, legal, institutional—may or may not be appropriate means of providing the space within which persuasion was likely to be more successful. Hence, the primary rubric through which Christianity has sought to understand the place of conquest has not been in the service of forced conversion, but in what was thought necessary, expedient, permissible, and warranted to ensure the "free" and "unrestricted" preaching of the gospel. That framework has historically included considerations over how to obtain access to lands whose rulers may be hostile to Christianity, how to ensure the survival of nascent Christian communities in areas thought inhospitable to Christianity, and how to establish political, social, and institutional forms that were thought to best facilitate the establishment and spread of Christianity. Those political and institutional considerations have been the very ground upon which centuries of Christian thought have developed and which has shaped substantial portions of the relationship between Christianity and various political orders.

## Late Antiquity and the Roman Empire

Whatever social forces Christianity was able to marshal in its formative years, Christians did not have at their disposal the instruments of legal or state-sanctioned coercion, much less those of military conquest and colonization. Christianity existed rather in the complex world of the Roman Empire, tolerated or persecuted depending on the exigencies of forces quite outside of its own control. Debates raged on whether Christians could serve in the Roman armed forces or hold legal offices in the empire, but those were most often refracted through the problems of idolatry and what was considered the moral degeneracy of most Roman soldiers and politicians rather than principled positions on violence, conquest, or state-sponsored coercion. The Roman Empire thus held an ambiguous moral status for many, yet the rise of Christianity from sect to predominance in late antiquity was in no small way facilitated by that same empire as Christianity spread throughout the Jewish diaspora and was established in Gentile communities throughout Asia Minor. Roman trade networks, facility of travel, and the dominance of the Greek and Latin languages were all cited by early Church fathers as instrumental in the rise of Christianity. However, the tenuous relationship between Christianity and the Roman Empire was permanently altered with the conversion to Christianity of the Emperor Constantine in the fourth century and the eventual replacement of Roman civil theology as the guiding religion of the empire with Christianity.

The fourth century transformation of a new Christianity now formally empowered by the Roman Empire cannot be underestimated—and new problems between Christianity and the practices of military conquest quickly emerged as Christians now had at their disposal the military forces and territorial ambitions of Rome. Among the earliest of the Church fathers to exult in those new possibilities was Eusebius of Caesarea, who eulogized Constantine as the one sent from God, from whom the "twin blessings" of Christianity and the Roman Empire would now be bestowed upon the world. Paramount to Eusebius' considerations was Rome's claim to have established peace and harmony throughout the world by ending civil wars, petty strife, and the territorial ambitions of others. That the *pax Romana* would be the precondition for the *pax Christiana* would be a remarkably potent pattern of understanding for the next millennium. Although at times less enthusiastic a champion of that empire than Eusebius, Augustine of Hippo further reflected upon this shift in his monumental *The City of God,* where in the fourth book he described how God "gave empire to the Romans when he willed and to the extent that he willed." Yet the establishment and expansion of that empire through territorial conquest was a bloody affair whose effects Augustine often lamented. That very tension of sustaining a providential view of how God works in the world, both granting empires to whom He wished yet quite often in spite of what even Augustine described as imperial motives of greed and avarice, would become among the most powerful rationales available for an emergent *imperium Christianum.*

## Middle Ages and Early Modernity

The conversion of Europe to Christianity was a complex and multifaceted process. Yet the predominance of canon law in the Middle Ages also recognized that central to that process in many places was the conversion of rulers to Christianity, who in turn were to establish political structures, laws, and other institutional forms that "reward those who do good" and "punish those who do evil" along specifically Christian axes.

Simultaneous to that, both theological and civil reflection emerged on the status of non-Christian territories and jurisdictions. In cases where a non-Christian ruler established policies or practices that served to impede the establishment, growth, and survival of Christianity in territories under their control, a case could be made for the use of military coercion to remove that ruler and establish another if other methods of influence failed. Also emergent were transformations in the older Roman categories of natural law (*ius naturale*) and the accepted range of human customs (*ius gentium*), violations of which may constitute grounds for a "just war" (*iustum bellum*) and allegedly end such practices while protecting innocents. The relationship of Christian thought and practice to practices of military conquest under such conditions facilitated both the expansion of Christianity throughout Europe and—perhaps the most paradigmatic example of conquest—the Crusades.

The Crusades both were and were not examples of conquests whose purported end was the spread of Christianity. On the one hand—although competing rationales for the Crusades were offered at different times and in accordance with the specifics of the various military incursions into the Middle East over three centuries—the recovery of territories lost to Christians by an expanding Islam or the establishment of Christian sovereignty over new territories mostly remained the primary proposed consideration. Conversion to Christianity was most often thought to follow once the appropriate political, legal, and institutional preconditions were established. Debates certainly existed during the Middle Ages and the Crusades over the question of forced conversion, but these nearly always took place in the context of the rights and responsibilities of Christian princes or rulers over their own subjects rather than in the context of what conquering armies would themselves do. Hence, the primary category at stake in conquests by Christians was almost always one of proper or improper jurisdiction, within which debates over how to best evangelize were then carried out among missionaries, secular priests, and the religious orders. The consequence of such conquests would be the spread of Christianity, but accomplished primarily through the expansion of jurisdiction of Christian rulers and the concomitant political, legal, and institutional transformations that would follow.

The second most paradigmatic example of Christianity and conquest—the Spanish conquests of the Americas in the sixteenth century—contained many of the same tensions as before. Although quite different historical processes were in place in the sixteenth century than during the Crusades, the conquest of the

Americas was primarily intended to establish Christian jurisdiction, under which successful evangelization by "persuasive preaching" could be carried out. Spanish jurists and theologians had two primary explanatory frameworks for the conquests: that God had "donated" jurisdiction over these newly discovered territories to Christian rulers and that the conquests were "just wars" in the classic Roman sense. In the first instance the success of Columbus' voyages and of the Portuguese establishment of commercial colonies in Asia occasioned what was to become the defining structure of Catholic relationships with early modern colonial projects: the so-called *patronato real* (royal patronage), which legally obliged missionaries and other Church representatives to work under the jurisdiction of the Catholic monarchs of Spain and Portugal. Thus, the dependence of Christian missionary work on commercial interests occasioned by new discoveries and sea travel was furthered by legally obliging the Spanish and Portuguese monarchs to oversee the missionary endeavors of the Church in their own jurisdictions.

The occasion for this new arrangement was what would become a highly contested "donation" made in 1493 by Pope Alexander VI of "temporal and spiritual dominion" over newly discovered territories in the East to the Portuguese and in the West to the Spanish monarchs. Second, concerned with establishing legally protected Christian communities and purportedly concerned with Aztec practices of human sacrifice and other "crimes against nature," the Spanish wars of conquest were carried out under the rubric of the "just war" (although such claims were very contentious and just-war arguments were used both by advocates and critics of the conquest). Yet in both cases the centrality of evangelization remained—both as among the chief rationale for Alexander's donation of jurisdiction over the Americas to the Spanish monarchs (as God has granted Roman dominion "to the extent that he willed" in Augustine's classic formulation) and as grounds for a just war should missionaries be harassed, expelled, or killed.

Thus, a leading advocate of the Spanish conquests argued that "barbarians" should not be converted by force, since "the will . . . without which there is no room for faith, cannot be forced." He argued rather that "as far as it rests with us they [should] be brought back from the edge of the precipice and be shown the way of truth by means of pious teachings and evangelical preachings," and that "this does not seem possible to accomplish by any other way than first subjecting them to our rule." "How can one preach if they are not sent, as St. Paul says," he asked, and "how are they to be sent

if these barbarians are not conquered first?" Successful evangelization, according to this view, required prior pacification—and hence the force of the Spanish pattern of "pacification, colonization, evangelization" that marked early Christian experience in Spanish America. Yet the theological and jurisprudential history of those debates, as well as Spanish practices in Mexico and Peru, created conditions that led one Spanish critic of the conquest of the Americas to complain that such disparate and incommensurate activities as "announcing the gospel of peace" and "extending the sword of war" had become legally and necessarily interdependent in ways that ultimately proved destructive to the gospel itself. Both the unchecked greed of the colonial project and the imposition of jurisdiction by conquest, he continued to argue, often created conditions of resentment that made people "more perverted than converted" by that experience.

## Modernity and the Colonial Enterprise

Christianity entered the modern era largely without the territorial and jurisdictional claims that sustained its earlier conquests. From the fourth century until the collapse of Christendom in the aftermath of the European internecine religious wars of the sixteenth and seventeenth century territorial conquests were often shaped by debates over evangelization and the hand of God in granting empires for that purpose. By the seventeenth century the power of the Spanish and Portuguese empires began to decline, and those of England, France, and Holland began to ascend. As the religious experience of both the English and Dutch colonial enterprises were quite different from those formed by Catholicism, marked shifts in the relationship of specific forms of Christianity to those colonial projects also followed. Yet those European colonial projects that reached their apex in the nineteenth century continued to inform the direction of Christian reflection over the relationship between conquest, jurisdiction, empire, and evangelism.

The relationship between Christianity and later European wars of conquest—especially in Africa and South Asia—continued to be complex and enigmatic. A strong similarity with past Christian experience was the "civilizing mission" of the European colonial projects. It was possible for Spanish Catholics and British Protestants alike to see certain kinds of civilization as conditions of possibility for successful evangelization and for sustaining a Christian presence in the rapidly expanding New World—and although the specific understandings of jurisdiction, sovereignty, and rights had shifted tremendously from the sixteenth century to the nineteenth, wars of conquest and impositions of new forms of political order remained the predominant form for ensuring those preconditions thought necessary to Christianity. Hence, Christianity continued to act in some form as a legitimating institution for various colonial projects and at other times as its critic. It often acted to buttress colonial regimes in the face of internal and external criticism and in many parts of the world remained in measurable ways antagonistic toward independence movements. Yet Christianity also worked to impose strict laws regulating treatment of indigenous peoples, protected indigenous languages, joined with others to outlaw certain forms of exploitation and slavery, deeply criticized the violence of European wars of conquest, and purported itself to be the conscience of Europe around the globe. Hence Christianity served as both legitimator of the colonial enterprise and critic of what it perceived to be its excesses.

Throughout its history Christianity has possessed multiple resources for legitimating the use of force to impose social, cultural, and political conditions through which conversion by "persuasion" was more likely to be successful. Hence, the difficulty of the history of Christian thought and practice on the problem of conquest is that it ultimately impinges less on the problem of forced conversion than on the question of social and political order itself and what may be the complex relationship of Christianity to certain kinds of structures through which it sees itself most compatible. Christianity contains sufficient historical and theological reflection on this problem for those who have argued for the legitimacy and necessity of European wars of conquest elsewhere in the world—and it certainly contains enough resources to find such conquests morally and theologically reprehensible. Hence, it is precisely the tensions and edges of the colonial experience from late antiquity to modernity that have shaped the complex relationship between Christianity and conquest rather than its own doctrinal positions.

PATRICK PROVOST-SMITH

*See also* Ancient Church; Christendom; Civilization; Conversion; Crusades; Empire; Islam; Militarism; Pacifism; Peace Churches; Politics; Roman Catholic Church

### Further Reading

Fletcher, R. (1997). *The conversion of Europe: From paganism to Christianity, 371–1386 AD.* London: HarperCollins.
MacMullen, R. (1997). *Christianity and paganism in the fourth to eighth centuries.* New Haven, CT: Yale University Press.
Mayr-Harting, H. (1991). *The coming of Christianity to Anglo-Saxon England* (3rd ed.). University Park: Pennsylvania State University Press.
Van Engen, J. (1986). The Christian Middle Ages as an historiographical problem. *American Historical Review, 91,* 519–552.
Woodard, W. B. (1972). *The Allied occupation of Japan, 1945–1952, and Japanese religions.* Leiden, Netherlands: Brill.

# Contextualization, Models of

Missiological anthropology as a discipline and contextualization as a method are important in Christian mission to combat ethnocentrism in missionaries and cultural imperialism in the missionary enterprise. Without an adequate cross-cultural understanding of how the Gospel relates to culture, it is easy for missionaries to assume that those who respond to their message and convert to Christianity should become like the missionary in the way they think, worship, and organize their churches. Contextualization helps us understand the importance of cultural relevance in how the Gospel is communicated, how new Christians respond, and how they order their new life in Christ. This essay traces the development of the field of missiological anthropology, notes the significant contributions missionaries have made to the field of anthropology, enumerates the contributions of contemporary missiological anthropologists, and discusses the concept of contextualization.

## Anthropology as a Discipline

The field of anthropology emerged in the mid-nineteenth century as armchair social philosophers speculated on the origins of human beings, their religion, and their culture. Edward B. Tylor (1832–1917), recognized today as the founding father of anthropology, partly because he occupied the first chair of anthropology at Oxford University, developed elaborate evolutionary schemes to demonstrate how "primitive" people evolved into "civilized" cultures. He, like most anthropologists, had little use for Christianity and Christian mission activity. These early anthropologists did not conduct firsthand fieldwork but rather drew their data for their speculative theories initially from explorers and travelers and later from missionaries. Not until the 1920s and 1930s did fieldwork became important in the discipline. Tylor and Lewis Henry Morgan, among others, corresponded with missionaries, inquiring about the people among whom they lived and outlining areas of research for missionaries to pursue.

It is noteworthy that anthropologists have been loath to recognize the great debt they owe to missionaries, not only in the early stages of anthropology's development but even today, as missionaries provide hospitality, vocabulary lists, and other aids to fledging anthropologists in the field. It is arguable that the discipline of anthropology would not have emerged without its heavy reliance on ethnographic data provided by missionaries. Despite the fact that there was little appreciation of how anthropology could contribute to mission during this period, it is ironic that much of the ethnographic data used by anthropologists to spin their theoretical designs came from missionaries.

## Missionary Contributions to Anthropology

This nineteenth-century anthropological use of missionary writing began a long stream of missionary ethnographic contributions, which was anticipated several centuries earlier by Catholic missionary ethnographers such as Bartolomé de Las Casas (1484–1566) and Bernardino de Sahagun (1499–1590) in Latin America; Joseph-Francois Lafitau (1681–1746) and Gabriel Sagard (c. 1590–c. 1650) in North America; Matteo Ricci (1552–1610) in China; and Roberto de Nobili (1577–1656) in India. Many Protestant missionaries in Melanesia, such as Lorimer Fison (1832–1907), an Australian Wesleyan missionary in Fiji who wrote *Tales from Old Fiji* (1907), made important ethnographic contributions. Another was Robert H. Codrington (1830–1922), an Anglican missionary with the Melanesian Mission in the Solomon Islands and New Hebrides, who after writing a book on Melanesian languages produced his landmark book, *The Melanesians: Studies in Their Anthropology and Folklore* (1891).

Additional missionary contributions to anthropology were those made by John Batchelor (1854–1944), an Anglican missionary among the Ainu of Japan for twenty years, who reduced their language to writing, translated the entire Bible, and planted a church. He wrote *Ainu Life and Lore* (1927). Maurice Leenhardt (1878–1954), the French Protestant missionary to New Caledonia (1902–1927), wrote the classic *Do Kamo: Person and Myth in the Melanesian World* (1947). "The author of one of the finest anthropological monographs yet written," according to E. E. Evans-Pritchard (1964, 114), was Henri Alexandre Junod (1863–1934) of the Swiss Romande Mission, who published *The Life of a South African Tribe* in 1912. *Behind Mud Walls* (1930), a pioneer work in Indian anthropology, was written by William

Wiser (1890-1961) and Charlotte Wiser (1892-1981), Presbyterian missionaries in India.

We cannot leave this topic of missionary contributions to anthropology without mentioning the substantial contribution made by Wilhelm Schmidt (1868–1954). Although never a field missionary himself, as a trainer of missionaries he nevertheless encouraged and organized members of his own Society of the Divine Word and others to produce carefully researched ethnographies of the people among whom they worked. He himself produced more than 650 publications. In 1906 he founded the ethnological journal *Anthropos* as a venue for publishing the many ethnographic reports he received from missionaries, and in 1932 he established the Anthropos Institute as a center for anthropological research.

## Emergence of Missiological Anthropology

The earliest call for applying anthropology to mission work was made in 1868 in an address by George Harris to the Manchester Anthropological Society, in which he encouraged anthropologists and missionaries to work together instead of opposing each other. Unfortunately, his admonition went unheeded for more than fifty years, and it was not until the 1920s, following the devastation of World War I and the expansion of colonialism, that anthropologists began to think about applying their theories to solve human problems. In 1921 proposals were made for the establishment of a school of applied anthropology in Great Britain, suggesting that "the anthropological point of view should permeate the whole body of the people" and that the lack of this "was the cause of our present troubles" (Peake 1921, 174).

A significant landmark on the road of anthropology's becoming an applied science was Bronislaw Malinowski's 1929 article entitled "Practical Anthropology," in which he noted the huge gap that existed between the theoretical concerns of anthropology and the practical interest of colonial administrators and missionaries. Applied anthropology emerged in the 1930s in Great Britain and the United States, but most anthropologists at the time were quite hostile to the missionary enterprise and distanced themselves from missionaries and their concerns. Nevertheless, during this same period missionaries with an anthropological perspective began calling for developing a missionary anthropology. The term "missiological anthropology" would not emerge until 1988, with the publication of Louis Luzbetak's (1914–2005) *The Church and Cultures: New Perspectives in Missiological Anthropology.*

## Beginnings of Missionary Anthropology

Missionaries at the beginning of the twentieth century were beginning to get in touch with the value of anthropology for their work. Ecumenical mission conferences were held in New York in 1854 and in Liverpool in 1860, and in 1888 the Centenary Conference on Protestant Missions was held at Exeter Hall in London, with sixteen hundred representatives from fifty-three mission societies. Over this thirty-year period the missionary movement had grown statistically in a remarkable way, but it had also become more paternalistic, with more vested interests. There is little evidence of either awareness of or need for anthropological insight coming out of these conferences.

But the World Missionary Conference in Edinburgh in 1910 was a different story. The report of the commission was a large series of nine volumes, with volume five devoted completely to the preparation of missionaries. The importance of understanding the cultures and customs of the people to whom missionaries go was stressed from this time onward. Edinburgh is important because it shows that missionaries were struggling with all the points of criticism that anthropologists would make, long before they ever started to speak on the matter. One of the features of this conference was the recognition of the fact of sociocultural change, as well as the need to move beyond ethnocentric evaluations of cultural differences. The call for anthropological training of missionaries was clearly sounded at Edinburgh. The report says,

> It is, therefore, clear that the missionary needs to know far more than the mere manners and customs of the race to which he is sent; he ought to be versed in the genius of the people, that which has made them the people they are; and to sympathise so truly with the good which they have evolved, that he may be able to aid the national leaders reverently to build up a Christian civilisation after their own kind, not after the European kind. (World Missionary Conference, 1910, Vol. 5, 170)

The earliest leading advocate for applying anthropological insights to mission was Edwin W. Smith (1876–1957). Smith, born of missionary parents of the Primitive Methodist Mission in South Africa, served as a missionary in Zambia among the Baila-Batonga people from 1902 to 1915. Although he often thought of himself as an amateur anthropologist, he nevertheless was held in high esteem by contemporary anthropologists of his day. He was a member of the Royal Anthropological In-

stitute of Great Britain from 1909 until his death in 1957 and served as president from 1933 to 1935, the first and only missionary to do so. He contributed substantially to anthropology (Smith 1907; Smith and Dale 1920) and wrote frequently in the *International Review of Missions*. In 1924 in an article entitled "Social Anthropology and Missionary Work," Smith argues that "the science of social anthropology [should be] recognized as an essential discipline in the training of missionaries." He goes on to note that we need to understand people from their point of view, not just our own, if mission work is to be effective (E. W. Smith 1924, 519) He notes in language characteristic of his time that:

> A study of social anthropology will lead the young missionary to look at things always from the native's point of view, and this will save him from making serious blunders. Tact is not enough; nor is love.... Tact needs to be based on knowledge; love there can hardly be without understanding. (Smith 1924, 522–523)

Another early advocate for connecting anthropology and mission was Henri Philippe Junod, a missionary in South Africa and son of the missionary ethnographer Henri A. Junod mentioned above. Writing in 1935, he bemoans the fact that "Mission policy, however, has had too little to do with anthropology..." (Junod 1935, 217). He goes on to say, "I believe that anthropology can help us greatly. It can widen our views, it can open our eyes, it can teach us to understand, it can improve our educational policy and point out to us the dangers of the way" (Junod 1935, 228). Missionary anthropologists like Edwin W. Smith and Henri A. Junod had more impact on European missionaries from mainline denominations than on American evangelical missionaries. The first post–World War II era book on anthropology and mission in the United States, written in 1945 by Gordon Hedderly Smith, was *The Missionary and Anthropology: An Introduction to the Study of Primitive Man for Missionaries.* This is a quite inadequate book, drawing too much on E. B. Tylor and John Lubbock, nineteenth-century evolutionary anthropologists. Smith argues for the importance of anthropological training as part and parcel of missionary preparation, but given the shortcomings of this book, it is not surprising that it had limited influence.

A high-water mark in the history of missiological anthropology came in 1954 with the publication of Eugene Nida's *Customs and Cultures: Anthropology for Christian Missions.* Although Nida's Ph.D. is in linguistics more than in anthropology, as a translation consultant for the American Bible Society, Nida traveled widely, working in some two hundred languages in seventy-five countries. From this vast experience Nida saw firsthand the problems and challenges faced by missionaries and translators, and his anthropological perspective enabled him to make keen observations and write copious notes, from which *Customs and Cultures* was written.

## Founding of Practical Anthropology

One index that an academic field is reaching maturity is when a journal in that field is published. This was the case with the field of missionary anthropology and the publication of *Practical Anthropology,* begun in 1953. *Practical Anthropology* developed into a journal primarily for missionaries and Bible translators needing the insights offered by anthropology and wanting a forum where they could share their ideas and their anthropologically informed experiences of mission in the field. *Practical Anthropology,* published six times a year, ran for nineteen years, continuing as an outlet for anthropologically minded missiologists like Jacob Loewen, Eugene Nida, William Reyburn, William Smalley, Charles Taber, and William Wonderly, all of whom were committed to cross-cultural mission and Bible translation. The pages of the early editions of this journal are full of stories and examples of how anthropology can illuminate the cross-cultural complexities of effective mission work. William Smalley captured the best of *Practical Anthropology* in two books, entitled *Readings in Missionary Anthropology* (1967) and *Readings in Missionary Anthropology II* (1978).

In 1973 *Practical Anthropology* merged into *Missiology,* the journal of the American Society of Missiology. At this time there were over three thousand subscribers to *Practical Anthropology,* indicating the tremendous growth this journal underwent in a relatively short span of time. The anthropological focus continued with missiological anthropologist Alan Tippett (1911–1988) as the first editor of *Missiology* (January 1973–April 1976), followed by anthropologist Darrell Whiteman's long tenure as editor (1989–2002).

## Contemporary Missiological Anthropologists

Important contributions have been made to missiological anthropology by both Roman Catholic and Evangelical Protestant anthropologists. Among Roman Catholics, Louis J. Luzbetak, SVD (1918–2005), has written the classic text, initially published in 1963 as *The Church and Culture: An Applied Anthropology for the Religious Worker* and completely revised in his magnum opus *The Church and Cultures: New Perspectives in Missiological Anthropology* (1988). Gerald Arbuckle, a Marist priest from New Zealand, has written and lectured widely. His popular books *Earthing the Gospel: An Inculturation Handbook for Pastoral Workers* (1990) and *Refounding the Church: Dissent for Leadership* (1993) capture much of his anthropological insights for mission.

Another significant Catholic missiologist is British missionary anthropologist Aylward Shorter, a White Father who studied under E. E. Evans-Pritchard at Oxford. Drawing on his extensive mission work in East Africa, Shorter has brought anthropological insights to bear on the church in Africa, notably his *African Culture and the Christian Church: An Introduction to Social and Pastoral Anthropology* (1974); *Jesus and the Witchdoctor* (1985); and *The Church in the African City* (1991). Shorter's more theological works, which have contributed significantly to the field of contextualization, include *African Christian Theology* (1977) and *Toward a Theology of Inculturation* (1988).

Anthony Gittins, C.S.Sp., who has had mission experience in West Africa, is a third Catholic missiological anthropologist. His book *Mende Religion* (1987) is an in-depth anthropological study of the belief system of the Mende in Sierra Leone. Some of his other works, which draw on his anthropological perspective, include *Gifts and Strangers* (1989); *Bread for the Journey* (1993); *Life and Death Matters: The Practice of Inculturation in Africa* (2000); and *Ministry at the Margins* (2002).

The most influential and most prolific evangelical missiological anthropologist was Paul Hiebert (1932–2007), whose *Anthropological Insights for Missionaries* (1985) is one of the most widely read missiological anthropology books in print today. His work on epistemology and mission (Hiebert 1999) has broken new ground for missiology, and his contribution to the discussion of contextualization (1987) has been significant.

Alan Tippett, an Australian Methodist missionary anthropologist to Fiji for two decades, helped bring anthropology into the stream of missiological training as one of the founding professors of the School of World Mission at Fuller Theological Seminary in 1965. Tippett's *Solomon Islands Christianity* (1967) demonstrated the value of an anthropological perspective in analyzing how Christianity connects to or misses the mark in a specific culture. This led to Darrell Whiteman's anthropological study of the impact of Anglican Christianity in the Solomon Islands in a book entitled *Melanesians and Missionaries* (1983).

Charles Kraft's groundbreaking book *Christianity in Culture* (1979, 2005) is an important contribution to missiological anthropology, and his textbook *Anthropology for Christian Witness* (1996) captures the essence of his popular course, taught at Fuller Theological Seminary since 1969. Other important contributions have been made by Marvin Mayers' *Christianity Confronts Culture: A Strategy for Cross-Cultural Evangelism* (1974). Charles Taber has written a history of the concept of culture in missionary work in *The World Is Too Much with Us: "Culture" in Modern Protestant Mission* (1991) and has synthesized the relationship between anthropology and mission in *To Understand the World, to Save the World: The Interface between Missiology and Social Science* (2000).

## Avoiding Cross-Cultural Misunderstanding

Many of the mistakes missionaries have made in translating the Bible and in communicating the Gospel to people different from themselves could have been avoided if they had taken an anthropological approach to understanding the people among whom they served by knowing their language and culture at a deep level. An illustration will suffice. In Paraguay one hears the phrase, "Paraguayans speak in Spanish but think in Guarani," the indigenous language spoken before the Spanish conquest. One would hope, therefore, that they read the Bible and worship in Guarani, but no, they use Spanish. In other words, Christianity is expressed through the medium of Spanish, rather than in the heart language of Guarani.

Moreover, when the Jesuits came to this area in the seventeenth century, they asked for the local name of the highest god in the Guarani cosmology and were given a name for God that they used instead of the Spanish *Dios*. Only recently has an anthropologist researching the Guarani cosmology learned that the Guarani had a god that was higher than the god whose name they gave to the Jesuits, but that god was so high in the sky that no name was given to it. In other words, here was the Unknown God, alive and well in the Guarani cosmology, but because the missionaries did not adequately research and understand the Guarani cosmology, the Christian God they introduced was confined to a subordinate position to the Unknown God of the Guarani.

The missionaries also searched for a word that they could use to convey the meaning of baptism and finally came up with a term they thought captured the essence of baptism for the Guarani. Anthropological investigation, however, hundreds of years later, discovered that the term used for baptism actually meant "becoming Spanish." Mistakes like this could be avoided if missionaries were properly trained in anthropological methods of research and if they had an anthropological perspective to help them cope with and understand cultural differences.

## Anthropological Connection to Contextualization

It is not surprising that many of the contributions to developing the concept of contextualization have been made by missiological anthropologists, such as Charles Kraft (1979), Paul Hiebert (1987), and Darrell Whiteman (1997) among Evangelicals and Gerald Arbuckle (1990), Louis Luzbetak (1988), and Aylward Shorter (1988) among Roman Catholic anthropologists. Anthropology gives missionaries the tools and insights to connect the Gospel to people embedded in a different culture in ways that are culturally relevant. Contextualization captures in method and perspective the challenge of relating the Gospel to culture.

In this sense the concern of contextualization is ancient—going back to the early church as it struggled to break loose from its Jewish cultural trappings and enter the Greco-Roman world of the Gentiles (Acts 15). On the other hand, contextualization is something new. Ever since the word emerged in the early 1970s, there has been almost an explosion of writing, thinking, and talking about contextualization, although there still remains in many parts of the world a huge gap between the theory of contextualization and the practice of mission.

Contextualization is part of an evolving stream of thought that relates the Gospel and church to a local context. In the past, words such as *adaptation, accommodation,* and *indigenization* have been used to describe this relationship between Gospel, church, and culture. The term *contextualization,* introduced in 1971, and *inculturation,* a companion term in Roman Catholic missiology that emerged in the literature in 1974, are deeper, more dynamic, and more adequate terms that describe the challenge of connecting the Gospel to all of life today. The concept is still evolving, as evidenced by a recent book edited by Charles Kraft entitled *Appropriate Christianity* (2005) in which many forms of contextualization are explored.

The Gospel is contextualized so that it will be heard and understood. Contextualization attempts to communicate the Gospel in word and deed and to establish the church in ways that make sense to people within their local cultural context, presenting Christianity in such a way that it meets people's deepest needs and penetrates their worldview, thus allowing them to follow Christ and remain within their own culture. Contextualization is a fine balancing act between necessary involvement in the culture, being in the situation, and maintaining an outside, critical perspective that is also needed. In anthropology this is known as holding in tension emic and etic perspectives—the insider's deep understanding with the outsider's critique.

The Gospel is contextualized so that it will be felt. The biblical critique of culture is often "offensive" to people. Mission practice needs to make sure it is offending people for the right reasons and not the wrong ones. When the Gospel is presented in word and deed, and the fellowship of believers we call the church is organized along appropriate cultural patterns, then people will more likely be confronted with the offense of the Gospel, exposing their own sinfulness and the tendency toward evil oppressive structures and behavior patterns within their culture. This is contextualization at its best.

The Gospel is also contextualized so that it will be internalized within individuals and their society will be transformed. When the Gospel is contextualized, it will be understood in ways the universal church has neither experienced nor understood before. The challenge is trying to create a community that is both Christian and true to its own cultural heritage and identity.

## Future of Missiological Anthropology and Contextualization

This essay has briefly traced the development of the discipline of anthropology and shown how it slowly developed the field of applied anthropology and eventually the area of missiological anthropology. There are specific areas where anthropology can contribute to various aspects of Christian mission, but unfortunately there are still many people involved in Christian mission who have yet to understand and appreciate the value of anthropological insights for cross-cultural ministry. Nevertheless, we can anticipate that as Christianity enters more diverse cultural contexts, missiological anthropology and contextualization will become even more important to effective Christian mission.

DARRELL WHITEMAN

### Further Reading

Arbuckle, G. A. (1990). *Earthing the Gospel: An inculturation handbook for pastoral workers.* London: Geoffrey Chapman.

Arbuckle, G. A. (1993). *Refounding the Church: Dissent for leadership.* Maryknoll, NY: Orbis Books.

Batchelor, J. (1927/1971). *Ainu life and lore: Echoes of a departing race.* Tokyo, Kyobunkwan, New York: Johnson Reprint Corp.

Bonsen, R., Marks, H., and Miedema, J. (Eds.). (1990). *The ambiguity of rapprochement: Reflections of anthropologists on their controversial relationship with missionaries.* Nijmegen, the Netherlands: Focaal.

Brandewie, E. (1990). *When giants walked the earth: The life and times of Wilhelm Schmidt, SVD.* Fribourg, Switzerland: University Press.

Burridge, K. (1991). *In the way: A study of Christian missionary endeavours.* Vancouver, Canada: University of British Colombia Press.

Codrington, R. H. (1891). *The Melanesians: Studies in their anthropology and folklore.* Oxford, UK: The Clarendon Press.

Conn, H. (1984). *Eternal Word and changing worlds: Theology, anthropology and mission in trialogue.* Grand Rapids, MI: Zondervan

Evans-Pritchard, E. E. (1964). *Social anthropology and other essays.* New York: The Free Press.

Fison, L. (1907). *Tales from old Fiji.* London: Alexander Moring.

Franklin, K. (Ed.). (1987). *Current concerns of anthropologists and missionaries.* International Museum of Cultures, No. 22. Dallas, TX: The International Museum of Cultures, Summer Institute of Linguistics.

Gittins, A. J. (1987). *Mende religion: Aspects of belief and thought in Sierra Leone. Studia Instituti Anthropos, 41.* Nettetal, Germany: Steyler Verlag-Wort und Werk.

Gittins, A. J. (1989). *Gifts and strangers: Meeting the challenge of inculturation.* New York: Paulist Press.

Gittins, A. J. (1993). *Bread for the journey: The mission of transformation and the transformation of mission. American Society of Missiology Series, No. 17.* Maryknoll, NY: Orbis Books.

Gittins, A. J. (2000). *Life and death matters: The practice of inculturation in Africa.* Nettetal, Germany: Steyler Verlag.

Gittins, A. J. (2002). *Ministry at the margins: Strategy and spirituality for mission.* Maryknoll, NY: Orbis Books.

Harris, G. (1868). *On foreign missions in connection with civilization and anthropology.* London: Bell and Daldy.

Hiebert, P. G. (1978). Missions and anthropology: A love/hate relationship. *Missiology, 6,* 165–180.

Hiebert, P. G. (1985). *Anthropological insights for missionaries.* Grand Rapids, MI: Baker Books.

Hiebert, P. G. (1987). Critical contextualization. *International Bulletin of Missionary Research, 11*(3), 104–112.

Hiebert, P. G. (1994). *Anthropological reflections on missiological issues.* Grand Rapids, MI: Baker Books.

Hiebert, P. G. (1999). *Missiological implications of epistemological shifts: Affirming truth in a modern/postmodern world. Christian Mission and Modern Culture* series. Harrisburg, PA: Trinity Press Int.

Junod, H. A. (1912/1962). *The life of a South African tribe* (Vols. 1 & 2). New Hyde Park, NY: University Books Inc.

Junod, H. P. (1935). Anthropology and missionary education. *International Review of Missions, 24*(94), 213–228.

Kirby, J. P. (1995). Language and culture learning IS conversion...IS ministry: Toward a theological rationale for language and culture learning as part of missionary formation in a cross-cultural context. *Missiology, 23*(2), 131–143.

Kraft, C. H. (1979). *Christianity in culture: A study in dynamic biblical theologizing in cross-cultural perspective.* Maryknoll, NY: Orbis Books. Revised edition with Marguerite Kraft, 2005.

Kraft, C. H. (1996). *Anthropology for Christian witness.* Maryknoll, NY: Orbis Books.

Kraft, C. H. (Ed.) (2005). *Appropriate Christianity.* Pasadena, CA: William Carey Library.

Leenhardt, M. (1947/1979). *Do kamo: Person and myth in the Melanesian world* (Basia Miller Gulati, Trans.). Chicago: The University of Chicago Press.

Lingenfelter, S. (1996). *Agents of transformation: A guide for effective cross-cultural ministry.* Grand Rapids, MI: Baker Books.

Luzbetak, L. J. (1963). *The church and cultures: An applied anthropology for the religious worker.* Techny, IL: Divine Word Publications.

Luzbetak, L. J. (1985). Prospects for a better understanding and closer cooperation between anthropologists and missionaries. In D. L. Whiteman (Ed.), *Missionaries, anthropologists, and cultural change: Studies in Third World Societies, No. 25* (pp. 1–53). Williamsburg, VA: College of William and Mary.

Luzbetak, L. J. (1988). *The church and cultures: New perspectives in missiological anthropology.* Maryknoll, NY: Orbis Books.

Malinowski, B. (1929). Practical anthropology. *Africa, 2,* 23–38. (Reprinted in *Applied anthropology: Readings in the uses of the science of man,* pp. 12–25, by J. A. Clifton, Ed., 1970, Boston: Houghton Mifflin Company)

Mayers, M. K. (1974). *Christianity confronts culture: A strategy for cross-cultural evangelism.* Grand Rapids, MI: Zondervan.

Nida, E. A. (1954). *Customs and cultures: Anthropology for Christian missions.* New York: Harper & Row Publishers.

Ott, C., & Netland, H. A. (Eds.). (2006). *Globalizing theology: Belief and practice in an era of world Christianity.* Grand Rapids, MI: Baker Academic.

Peake, N. J. E. (1921). Discussion. *Man, 21*(103), 174.

Priest, R. J. (2001). Missionary positions: Christian, modernist, postmodernist. *Current Anthropology, 42*(1), 29–70.

Rynkiewich, M. A. (2002). The world in my parish: Rethinking the standard missiological model. *Missiology, 30*(3), 301–321.

Salamone, F. A. (1986). Missionaries and anthropologists: An inquiry into the ambivalent relationship. *Missiology, 14,* 55–70.

Sanneh, L. (1989). *Translating the message: The missionary impact on culture.* Maryknoll, NY: Orbis Books.

Shorter, A. (1974). *African culture and the Christian church: An introduction to social and pastoral anthropology.* Maryknoll, NY: Orbis Books.

Smalley, W. A. (Ed.). (1967). *Readings in missionary anthropology.* Tarrytown, NY: Practical Anthropology.

Smalley, W. A. (1978). *Readings in missionary anthropology II.* Pasadena, CA: William Carey Library.

Smith, E. W. (1907). *Handbook of the Ila language.* London: Oxford University Press.

Smith, E. W. (1924). Social anthropology and missionary work. *International Review of Missions, 13*(52), 518–531.

Smith, E. W. & Dale, A. W. (1920/1968). *The Ila-speaking peoples of northern Rhodesia* (2nd ed., Vols. 1 & 2). New Hyde Park, NY: University Books.

Smith, G. H. (1945). *The missionary and anthropology: An introduction to the study of primitive man for missionaries.* Chicago: Moody Press.

Stipe, C. (1980). Anthropologists versus missionaries. *Current Anthropology 21,* 165–168.

Sutlive, V. H. Jr. (1985). Anthropologists and missionaries: Eternal enemies or colleagues in disguise? In D. L. Whiteman (Ed.), *Missionaries, anthropologists, and cultural change,* Studies in Third World Societies, No. 25 (pp. 55–90). Williamsburg, VA: College of William and Mary.

Taber, C. (1991). *The world is too much with us: "Culture" in modern Protestant mission.* Macon, GA: Mercer University Press.

Taber, C. (2000). *To understand the world, to save the world: The interface between missiology and social science.* Harrisburg, PA: Trinity.

Tippett, A. R. (1967). *Solomon Islands Christianity.* New York: Friendship Press.

Whiteman, D. L. (1983). *Melanesians and missionaries: An ethnohistorical study of socio-religious change in the southwest Pacific.* Pasadena, CA: William Carey Library.

Wiser, W., & Wiser, C. (1930). *Behind mud walls.* New York: R. R. Smith. Revised edition, Berkeley, CA: University of California Press, 1971.

World Missionary Conference, Edinburgh. (1910). The preparation of missionaries. *Report of Commission V.* Edinburgh, UK: Oliphant, Anderson & Ferrier.

# Conversion

As Christianity has become a global religion, differing patterns of conversion have appeared, often at variance with the expectations of Western missionaries. These patterns have elicited studies that examine the definition of conversion, the process of conversion, and the means and methods employed. Because communication inevitably takes place through persons and in a specific locale and time, pure transmission of ideas or doctrines is impossible. Conversion patterns, it becomes evident, are a function of the culture in which they evolve and are also influenced by the personalities and values of the transmitters and by the local historical and economic environment. Conversion is, furthermore, both a personal experience and a public statement that affects the convert's social standing and relationships. Conversion and perceptions of Christianity thus vary according to individual personalities and the convert's needs. Over the centuries, both Christianity and the historical context have been in a state of flux. Conversion is not a static concept.

Many early converts accepted baptism for economic reasons, such as employment or support by Western missionaries. Others sought new values and spiritual guidance amidst the social breakdown and economic hardship associated with population pressures, political instability, and the disruptions of imperialism. A correlation is to be found between conversion patterns and a high incidence of violence in a region. The fusion of culture and religion that characterized many traditional societies, however, meant that acceptance of foreign teachings and practices could be traumatic; the social and cultural costs were high. Missionaries insisted on the exclusivism of monotheistic Christianity. They had the power of definition, and for them, Christianity meant Christianity as defined in Western Europe during their era. Often their converts were required to give up practices and beliefs that the missionaries deemed superstitious. Reconciling national identity and Christian identity could be difficult. Not surprisingly, many converts to Christianity came from marginal people and minority groups. Residents in rural villages often proved to be more receptive to the Gospel message than urban inhabitants. Converts who became evangelists were frequently more successful than foreign missionaries in tailoring appeals to local audiences.

As the pioneer missionaries faced the challenges of a foreign society and ethic, numerous questions arose. For example, which should receive priority, spreading the Good News to as many heathens as quickly as possible, replicating Western denominational churches, or founding Christian communities? For those who believed that all heathens stood on the brink of damnation, choosing between extensive and intensive evangelizing could be stressful. What was necessary to merit baptism and who had the authority to baptize? Only institutionally ordained ministers or designated assistants as well? What was acceptable proof of conversion? What degree of adaptation was permissible? Should one build on the traditional religious teachings or was a confrontational approach required?

Protestant missionaries customarily hoped that converts would acknowledge a conviction of sin, a yearning for redemption, and a personal spiritual awakening followed by belief in the one Almighty God and in Christ as the means to salvation. They expected converts to lead a moral life, and to affiliate themselves publicly with the church. For missionaries, this emotional rebirth constituted conversion, and could be dated from a moment in time. However, such a conversionary experience was more typical of Christian societies than of non-Christian societies. In the former, conversion often referred to a revival experience by a nominal Christian and might be called rebirth. This is not to say that instant conversion did not occur in non-Christian cultures. Charismatic preachers in Africa rejoiced when dozens or even hundreds testified to their faith during a revival. In those cases, instruction in Christian doctrines and rituals followed conversion. Pentecostal missionaries conducting revival meetings in South America have drawn thousands of Roman Catholics to faith churches.

According to many scholars, however, the conversionary process rather than the conversionary event was typical in non-Christian societies. Conversion involved several stages, often beginning with a quest for meaning in life and an encounter with a religious teacher. These experiences could occur in either order and sometimes they were preceded by a personal crisis. Interaction ensued as the inquirer learned of new doctrines, participated in rituals, and formed new relationships. Commitment might follow, with rituals of incorporation such as baptism, but even this was sometimes only the first step toward a personal transformation. Rejection or temporary reversion was always possible.

For early converts, socialization into Christianity was not a possibility, and there was no nominal Christianity to act as a reference group. Converts were often subjected to ostracism or persecution by kinfolk. Only later do we find instances of socialization into Christianity within Christian families, and even today Christianity is a minority religion in much of the world. When societies lack support mechanisms for new converts, assistance has to be provided by the religious community itself. Thus, Christian communities frequently assume a variety of functions beyond religious worship and instruction—for instance, social support at weddings and funerals; aid to aged and indigent members, parochial schools, hospitals and medical clinics; celebration of alternative holidays and festivals; a joint burial place; and a center for social activities as well as worship.

Missionaries and local evangelists employed a variety of tactics as they sought an audience for the Gospel message. Since healing was frequently associated with spiritual power, medicine served as an access point to Christianity. When an evil spirit possessed an individual and caused illness, the demon had to be exorcized or conquered by a more powerful deity. Local evangelists and foreign missionaries offered demonstrations of the superior power of the Christian God and the ineffectiveness of folk deities. Pentecostals and other faith churches continue to practice divine healing. Medical missionaries, with their more advanced knowledge and techniques, helped overcome fear or antagonism toward the foreign religion, while evangelists handed out Christian tracts and preached among the waiting patients. More than one nonbeliever acknowledged the Christian God after he or she or a relative had been cured by a missionary. Medicine became a popular profession among converts, some of them employing a combination of traditional and modern approaches. In China opium addicts turned to Christian evangelists in search of a cure, or they entered rehabilitation havens founded by Christians. One of the most successful evangelizing agencies in Hong Kong today is a substance abuse center. As always, the relapse rate is high, but recovered addicts are among their most dedicated workers.

Education enabled missionaries to draw a stable audience that could be socialized into Christianity. Along with Bible courses and required participation in worship services, the schools provided courses in the local language and Western learning and languages. When parents realized that literacy could open doors to social and economic mobility, they enrolled their children in the parochial institutions even if they had no desire for them to become Christians. The conversion rate among pupils never rose as high as the missionaries hoped, but many Christian teachers, doctors and nurses, social service workers, and evangelists came from the ranks of the graduates.

The importance of kinship in conversion patterns can hardly be overemphasized. This was the approach taken by the majority of local evangelists. They began with their immediate family and branched out to close relatives and fellow lineage or tribal members. In view of the common perception that affine ties eroded soon after marriage in India and China, it is interesting how often contacts via the wife's relatives played a role. There were good reasons for converts to begin evangelism at home since social contacts depended heavily on kinship, and they needed the support of family. Conversion set the convert apart in a society that valued community and consensus, and it could lead to ostracism. It was difficult for a husband to maintain a Christian atmosphere in the home if the wife continued non-Christian rituals. Because women were largely responsible for the socialization of young children, Christian mothers were considered essential to building Christian families.

Legal protection sometimes came into play. Westerners in colonial territories had access to power, and even in China Westerners enjoyed extraterritorial rights, which, in effect, removed them from national jurisdiction. Individuals, tribal branches, and whole sect groups, in trouble with the law, might profess conversion to Christianity. Missionaries, despite uneasiness about these sudden conversions, often accepted the "converts" into the fold, particularly during the nineteenth century. Sometimes the missionaries believed the claims of persecution because they lacked sufficient information about the current situation. Sometimes they baptized the professed converts in the expectation that they could provide instruction that would lead to true believers. Roman Catholic missionaries were perhaps more willing to offer legal protection since the revivalist tradition was not strong in Catholicism. The norm was baptism followed by instruction in the catechism and ritual practices, which culminated in confirmation and full membership in the church.

Pioneer Protestant missionaries devoted much time to translating the Bible and producing religious tracts. Because Protestants considered the Bible the inerrant Word of God, they wanted it made accessible to all converts and interested inquirers. Missionaries and colporteurs distributed hundreds of thousands of Bibles, New Testaments, and Christian tracts under the assumption that readers of these "silent messengers" could not but be convinced of the Christian truth. As the tracts multiplied, however, it became all too evident that the imperfect and awkward style of the Christian works and the foreignness of the teachings repelled rather than attracted many recipients. The Scriptures, product of a different culture than the Chinese, required elucidation. Concepts, terminology, and metaphors needed human explication. Only a relatively few instances of conversion based solely on reading Christian writings can be cited. Nevertheless, a Christian terminology was developed, improved versions of the Bible issued, better type fonts and printing invented, and a written vocabulary devised where only an oral literature had been available. Some of the religious tracts continued in use for decades, and standardized versions of the Bible in many languages and dialects gained acceptance.

In many countries a significant proportion of the early converts were in the employ of the missionaries. Many, in fact, had initially professed Christianity for economic purposes. Only gradually did they internalize their Christianity and develop a deeper understanding of Christian teachings. As they fulfilled the role of evangelists, they found a new identity and a new self-esteem. They restructured their lifestyle. They were not simply passive recipients of the missionary's message; they translated Christian teachings and they developed an evangelistic methodology that spoke to their fellow nationals. In China, for example, they favored moralistic storytelling in the Buddhist tradition; in Africa, singing and dancing were an important ingredient in Christian worship and festivities. Conversion for these Christians had been a gradual process. Apostasy was always a real possibility, but some who entered the faith through the economic route became effective and devoted evangelists, even enduring persecution in the defense of Christianity.

With the establishment of Christian families and the conversion of second and third generation Christians, socialization in Christian rituals and practices became possible. These Christian families became the source of ministers, church workers, evangelists and parochial school teachers. They assumed control of Christianity on their own. As Christianity became rooted in local society, the sharp dichotomy that Western Christians saw between Christianity and local beliefs became blurred. In many cultures the conflict between national identity and Christian identity dissolved even if Christianity remained a minority religion. A translation process occurred as nationals developed their own understanding of Christianity, often emphasizing those teachings and values that were most meaningful to them. When local evangelists presented Christianity to their fellow compatriots, they selected aspects that would appeal to their audience and would also be understandable: the healing power of God, God the Father of all peoples, the love of Jesus which was available to everyone, God as all-powerful, superior to all other forces and spirits, the Holy Spirit as an ever present guide, and the promise of reward in heaven. Many of these teachings resonated with folk religion, though doctrines such as monotheism and the Trinity could be stumbling blocks. The issue of imperialism was an ever-present deter-

rent. Indigenization of Christianity nevertheless proceeded. In the process, the definition of conversion was stretched and broadened.

JESSIE G. LUTZ

*See also* Contexualism; Culture; Education—Religious, Theological; Medicine; Protestant Churches; Roman Catholic Church; Theology; Translation

## Further Reading

Lamb, C. & Darrel, M. (Eds.). (1999). *Religious conversion, contemporary practices and controversies.* London: Cassell.

Lutz, J. G., & Lutz, R. R. (1998). *Hakka Chinese confront Protestant Christianity, 1850–1900.* Armonk, NY: M. E. Sharpe.

Morrison, K. (1992). *Understanding conversion.* Charlottesville, VA: University of Virginia Press.

Nehemia Levtzion, (Ed.). (1979). *Conversion to Islam.* New York: Holmes & Meier.

Rambo, L. (1993). *Understanding religious conversion.* New Haven, CT: Yale University Press.

Ranger, T. & Weller, J. (Eds.). (1975). *Themes in the heritage of Central Africa.* London: Heinemann Educational Press.

Sanneh, L. (1989). *Translating the message: The missionary impact on culture.* Maryknoll, NY: Orbis Books.

Tiedemann, R. G. (2001). Conversion patterns in North China: Sociological profiles of Chinese Christians, 1860–1912. In K. Wei-ying & K. De Ridder (Eds.), *Authentic Chinese Christianity: Preludes to its development.* Leuven, Belgium: Leuven University Press.

Tse-Hei Lee, J. (2003). *The Bible and the gun, Christianity in South China, 1860–1900.* New York: Routledge.

Walls, A. F. (1996). *The missionary movement in Christian history: Studies in the transmission of faith.* Maryknoll, NY: Orbis Books.

# Coptic Church

This article seeks to uncover the missionary roots of the Coptic Orthodox Church, as well as its self-identity as a missionary church, and to provide information regarding the Coptic revival of the twentieth century that has led to an unprecedented growth of the Coptic Orthodox Church through its missionary endeavors.

## Origins of the Apostolic Coptic Church

The church in Egypt is one of the oldest in the world, deriving its identity directly from the day of Pentecost.

Acts 2:10 states that there were "Egyptian" Jews present in Jerusalem who heard the disciples preaching. These Egyptians returned to their homeland, presumably Alexandria (the largest Jewish community in the Diaspora), with the message of the Gospel. It is from these witnesses that Apollos would have been instructed in the Gospel (Acts 18:24) and begun his ministry in Ephesus.

The organization of the church in Egypt, however, takes its roots from the tradition of St. Mark. Eusebius states that Mark came to Alexandria in 43 CE, although other early and medieval sources have slightly different dates (Davis 2004, 6–7). The late fourth- or early fifth-century *Acts of Mark* ascribes to Mark the organization of the Coptic church and the founding of the patriarchate of Alexandria, to which the contemporary "pope" of the Coptic Orthodox Church owes his direct apostolic succession.

In addition to the evangelism of Mark, the visit of the Holy Family to Egypt (Matthew 2:13–15), has provided another pillar of identity for the Coptic Church. The traditions of the Holy Family in much of the New Testament Apocryphal literature have provided a basis of identity for Copts. Holy sites have developed around events portrayed in the traditions that have become the focus of an evangelical witness of the Gospel (see, for example, the Pseudo-Gospel of Matthew and the Arabic Infancy Gospel). These sites have become proof for Copts of the power of Jesus and Mary to produce miracles that continue to affect the daily lives of Egyptians.

## Early Mission

The Coptic Church sees itself as developing the first apologies for the Gospel in the post-apostolic age. The church in Alexandria generated theologians and apologists and organized the first monastic communities that became the shock troops of evangelical witness to the world. In addition, early Coptic missionaries carried the Gospel to both sub-Saharan Africa and Europe.

The Catechetical School of Alexandria, beginning with Pantanaeus (d. 190), was one of the earliest public witnesses for the Gospel in Alexandria, the second-largest city in the Roman Empire. Eusebius records that Pantanaeus was "a herald of the Gospel of Christ to the nations in the East, and was sent as far as India" (Schaff 1890, Church History 5X). Clement (d. 215), Pantanaeus's successor, was an ardent apologist of the Christian faith in the face of Greek culture and philosophy (Roberts 1885, Stromateis, Exhortation to the Heathen). Origen (d. 253), the third director of the school, was sent by Patriarch Demetrius to the Province of Arabia to correct heterodox teachings of Bishop Beryllus of Bostra (Schaff,

1890, Church History 6.XIX.15; 6.XXXIII; 6.XXXVII). St. Athanasius (296–373), patriarch of Alexandria, is also well noted for his evangelical teaching, especially during his first two exiles from his Holy See to Trier and Rome, respectively (336–337, 339–346). It is said that he introduced the *vita* of St. Anthony and the Coptic form of monasticism to the West at this time. Lastly, an important Coptic missionary of the sixth century who traveled widely was Cosmas Indicopleustes. Once a merchant, Cosmas became a monk and traveled as far as India preaching the faith. His record of his travels can be found in *Christian Topography*.

## Monasticism and Its Role in Mission

The Copts see monasticism as one of the basic elements of Christian mission and witness. The monasteries of Egypt are a barometer for the life of the Coptic Church. When the monasteries thrive with faithful servants, the church grows. Throughout history, the monasteries of Wadi Natrun and the Red Sea Monasteries of St. Anthony and Paul, as well as others throughout Egypt, have attracted seekers looking to imitate the ways of monks. The widespread knowledge of the way of the Desert Fathers drew such Western church fathers as Jerome, Rufinus, and John Cassius, the Abbot of Lerins Monastery in France. According to tradition, St. Patrick himself learned the Coptic monastic way of life after his conversion in the monastery at Lerins and spread its tenets among the Irish.

In the late twentieth century, a revival in the Coptic Church has led to the unprecedented growth of the monasteries. Well-educated and mature monks fill most of the monasteries and provide a great deal of leadership to Copts, pilgrims, and tourists who flock there. In the Coptic tradition, it is the monastery that provides a public witness to the faith and is "the gift of Egypt to Christendom" (Atiya 1968, 59). Since the 1980s, publications by Pope Shenouda III (a former monk) and the Abbott of St. Mecarius Monastery, Matthew the Poor, as well as the *Sayings of the Desert Fathers* and *Sayings of the Desert Mothers* have been made available in English and other Western languages. These publications have been very important in the revival of the Coptic Orthodox Church throughout the world and are understood as a public witness of faith in Christ.

## Mission to Africa

Coptic mission to sub-Saharan Africa has strong historical roots. The Nile and its headwaters made for the easy transportation of the Gospel south.

## Nubia

It is possible that the persecutions of the fourth century in Egypt gave rise to the flight of Christians both into the deserts and south beyond the cataracts into Nubia. In addition, the growth of monasticism during this same century gave rise to monks who looked further and further abroad for wildernesses in which to engage in their pious undertakings. By the fifth century, monks of the order of St. Shenute were already engaged with the tribes up the Nile.

The seventh-century historian, John of Ephesus, records the mission efforts of both the Byzantine emperor Justinian (527–565 CE) and his staunchly Monophysite wife, Theodora. While Justinian sent missionaries up the Nile to evangelize Nubians in the kingdom of Meroë under the Orthodox teaching of the Council of Chalcedon, Theodora dispatched a monk by the name of Julian who "instructed and baptized the king and his noblemen and a lot of people with them" in the non-Chalcedonian formula. Julian's successor, Longinus, was then consecrated as the Nubian non-Chalcedonian bishop. By 580 CE the kingdoms of Nubia, Nobatia, and Alodia were officially Christian under the direction of the Coptic Church, while Makuria held to the authority of Constantinople.

## Ethiopia

Ethiopia exhibits the greatest feat of Coptic mission. Although Acts 8 records the conversion of the "Ethiopian" eunuch of the court of "Candace" by Philip (8:26–40), it is more likely that the official was from Nubia. "Aethiopia" had been utilized as a general term for "land of the blacks," and "Kandaka" was a specific term for the royalty of Meroë in Nubia (de Saram 1992, 18).

Thorough evangelization of Ethiopia took place in the fourth century, when an Alexandrian living in Tyre and his two sons, Frumentius and Aedesius, were shipwrecked in Ethiopia on their way to India. Rufinus of Aquileia (b. 344 CE), in his *Church History* (Amidon 1997), records how Frumentius became the tutor of the crown prince Aeizanas. When Aeizanas became king, he declared Christianity the official religion of the empire. Frumentius traveled back to Alexandria and was consecrated Bishop of Aksum by St. Athanasius, becoming the first patriarch of the Ethiopian Church (sometime between 341 and 346 CE) (Meinardus 1999, 132).

In the Arabic translations of the Canons of the Council of Nicea, the patriarch of Alexandria is given authority over the Ethiopian Church (Schaff 1890, vol. XIV). This privilege continues to exist, although it has been the source of much tension. With Eritrean independence from Ethiopia at the beginning of the twenty-first century, Shenouda III consecrated Philipus as the first patriarch of the Eritrean Orthodox Church in 1998. The Ethiopian Church, however, continues to consider the territory of Eritrea as part of its own internal ecclesiastical jurisdiction.

## Mission to Europe

Two important areas of expansion for the Coptic mission were the Theban League, where there is evidence of Christian activity as early as the third century, and Ireland, where historical references point to Egyptian missionaries there during the eighth or ninth century.

### Theban League

One of the most prominent traditions of Coptic missions is that of the Theban League. The Roman Theban legion (from present day Luxor) was stationed in Switzerland. On the eve of battle in 285 CE, the general Maximian gathered the troops to pray to the gods for victory. A group of soldiers, led by Maurice, publicly declared their Christian faith and refused to worship the Roman gods. Hoping to frighten the Christians into submission, Maximian had every tenth man of the legion killed (i.e., decimated) but to no avail. Other traditions report that up to 6,600 of the legion were ultimately beheaded.

Three Christians who survived this massacre, the legionnaire Felix and his sister Regula, as well as another named Exuperantius, went on to preach the Gospel and baptize converts in the area of Lake Zurich until they were ultimately caught and martyred by Decius, the Roman governor. The origin of this tradition issues from a fifth-century letter that has come under great scrutiny in recent years. Further traditions add the story of Verena, a nurse of the legion who witnessed the massacre. She, too, spent the remainder of her life in Switzerland preaching the Gospel and providing basic medical care to the local people.

### Ireland

The British traveler Stanley Lane-Poole introduced the modern debate regarding the relationship between Coptic and Celtic Christianity. "It is more than probable," he wrote, "that to them [the Copts] we are indebted for the first preaching of the Gospel in England.... But more important is the belief that Irish Christianity ... was the child of the Egyptian Church" (Lane-Poole 1898, 203). The origins of Coptic missions to Ireland became an important area of research at the end of the nineteenth century and the beginning of the twentieth century. Several publications noted the similarities between Coptic and Celtic architecture, art, and worship practices (including John Stirton's *The Celtic Church and the Influence of the East* [1923], and De Lacy O'Leary's "The Coptic Church and Egyptian Monasticism," in S. R. K. Glanville [Ed.], *The Legacy of Egypt* [1942]).

Two important historical markers signifying the Egyptian influence in Ireland are worth noting here. The first is a gravestone in County Cork that reads, "Pray for Olan the Egyptian" (King 1947). The second comes from the *Martyrology of Oengus,* written by Oengus (a ninth-century bishop at Tallaght), and found in the twelfth-century *Book of Leinster.* A phrase of the *Martyrology* reads, "Seven monks of Egypt in Disert Ulilaig, I invoke unto my aid, through Jesus Christ." These markers have been understood as verifying the presence of Egyptian missionary monks in Ireland.

Although the Coptic influence in Ireland is clear, its origins are less certain. While it is probable that Coptic influence arrived in Ireland in the late eighth century with the Arab incursions into Europe, it is more likely that Western pilgrims who came to Egypt, such as John Cassian, abbot of the monastery at Lerins, returned to Europe with a great deal of admiration for the Coptic monastic tradition. (The reference to Egyptian merchants traveling to Britain in the ninth-century *Life of St. John the Almsgiver* should not be taken as a specific incident here but as a general movement of Mediterranean trade to Europe, as noted by Blanc-Ortolan and du Bourguet.) By the ninth century the Coptic tradition had filtered down through the monastic communities in Ireland, as monastic centers on the continent sent out their own missionaries. It is through this connection that Patrick would have been introduced to the Egyptian monastic system during his time in Europe.

## Living under Muslim Rule

The coming of the Arabs in 642 CE brought about a new era in the life of the Coptic Church. From the seventh until the nineteenth century, the Copts spent most of their energy simply surviving as an institution. Originally, the Copts saw the Arabs as freeing them from the "Roman [Byzantine] oppression." The Arabs implemented a common Near-Eastern practice of the Sassanian Empire, with the Edict of Yazdegard in 410, by recognizing indigenous religious communities, canon law, and ecclesiastical authority as the legal governmental representatives. This system, later known as the *millet* system under the Ottomans, provided for both the survival and the restriction of the Coptic Church. As a religious minority under Islamic rule, Copts were considered *dhimmīs* (Cahen, "al-Dhimma," *EI²*). Under this system they were "protected minorities" of the Islamic rulers but faced numerous restrictions and prohibitions, including the ability to build new churches, publicly preach the faith, or convert Muslims.

After the Arab conquest, although there was communication within the region with other Oriental churches, such as the Armenian, Ethiopic, and Syriac Churches, the Coptic Church developed quite separately from the rest of the Western Christendom (i.e., Constantinople and Rome). Monks from other Oriental churches frequented the monasteries of Wadi Natrun and the Red Sea Monasteries and insured a continued relationship within the non-Chalcedonian Orthodox churches. However, further activity of the church was limited by the dominant Muslim faith. The church was allowed to exist and to carry out its communal functions, but it was occasionally subject to persecution— churches were burned or Coptic officials were forced to convert to Islam in order to maintain their positions in the government, especially during the reigns of 'Abd al-Malik (692–705 CE), Umar ibn 'Abd al-Aziz (717–720 CE), al-Mutawakkil (847–861 CE), and al-Hakim (996–1021) and throughout much of the troubled fourteenth century. Thus, for nearly one thousand two hundred years the Coptic Church existed as an insular community, seeking to maintain itself under Islamic rule.

### Advent of Catholic and Protestant Missionaries

When Catholic and Protestant missionaries came to Egypt, they found a rather isolated church. Early Latin Catholic missions, first through the Franciscans and Dominicans, arrived on the shores of Egypt in the medieval period for the purpose of converting the Muslims. The tradition of St. Francis's preaching to Sultan al-Kamil during the Fifth Crusade stands as the classic tradition of Western Christian mission in Egypt. The Mendicant orders, however, had little effect on the religious landscape. By 1630 the Capuchins shifted their focus from the Muslim community to the Coptic Orthodox Church. Their work resulted in the creation of an independent church in 1741, the Coptic Catholic Church, which takes its authority from the Bishop of Rome.

When Western Presbyterian missionaries first came to Egypt in 1854, it was their desire to revive what they saw as a "dead" or "mummified" church. John Hogg, one of the most important Presbyterian missionaries, saw the state of the Coptic Orthodox Church as a problem to the overall goal of evangelizing Muslims.

# The Coptic Church and Christian Mission

**The church in Egypt, the Coptic Church, is one of the oldest in the Christian era and one of the earliest involved in mission work.**

The visit of the Holy Family to the African soil of Egypt was the first mission in the Christian era. The picture of the Virgin Mary riding an ass with the child Jesus in her arms and Joseph walking by her side continues to remind Christians everywhere, and indeed the whole world., that the mission of God incarnate, on whose birthday the angels came to earth around his manger, has been extended to the whole world. The Son of God has taken refuge from the persecution that took place in his homeland among his own people into the peaceful land of Egypt.

The African apostle St. Mark the Evangelist, a citizen of Cyrenaica of Pentapolis, now Libya, came on his first mission to Egypt... Through the power of the Word, he founded the first Egyptian church in the house of Anianus, whom he baptized with his family, and later ordained as Bishop of Alexandria... According to Coptic tradition, St. Mark was the first patriarch in the Coptic Orthodox Church and Anianus was the second.

For twenty centuries, the Coptic Church has been an expression of a continuing Christian witness that has embodied mission in different circumstances as the continuing act of God in Egypt and through the Egyptian people. They have continued to bear witness to the truth of the gospel that was carried to them on a shining hot day by the young apostle Mark.

Source: Assad, M. (1991). Mission in the Coptic Orthodox Church—Perspective, doctrine and practice. *International Review of Mission, 81*, 251–252.

---

In 1914, he wrote, "The great stumbling-block in the way of doing much for them [Muslims] is the Coptic church. Mohammedans have not the means at present of knowing what true Christianity is." Although the church in Egypt experienced difficult times during the Mamluk Period (1250–1517) and the early Ottoman Era (1517–1805), the early twentieth century saw a revival in the mission of the church that is unprecedented.

## Modern Missions

The revival of the Coptic Orthodox Church in the twentieth century, which is attributed to the rise of the "Sunday School Movement," has provided the personnel needed for responding to the mission of the church in the twentieth and twenty-first centuries.

### Missions "in the lands of immigration"

Two waves of immigration of Egyptians to Europe and North America—during the Nasser regime (1952–1970) and during Sadat's *infitah* (1970–1981)—have dramatically transformed the landscape of the Coptic Church (Stene 1997). Coptic emigration was motivated by several factors but primarily poor economic opportunities and the disenchantment with a growing Egyptian Islamic identity. In addition, throughout the 1980s, Copts, along with other Muslim Egyptians, sought employment opportunities throughout the Arab world, including the Gulf, Iraq, Lebanon, and Libya. The number of Copts in the diaspora is difficult to ascertain. The *Coptic Encyclopedia* estimated 300,000 in 1991; certainly that number has grown considerably in the twenty-first century.

Growing communities of Copts in the "lands of immigration" prompted a new avenue of mission work. The patriarch Cyril VI began planting the seeds of this overseas mission by authorizing Bishop Samuel, bishop of social and public affairs, to establish churches outside Egypt. Coptic communities required and requested the church to send priests who would minister to the immigrant communities. "Without a priest, children cannot be baptized, confessions cannot be heard and Holy Communion cannot be received" (Stene 1997, 261). Throughout the 1960s and 1970s, priests were sent to California, New Jersey, Australia, Canada, and England. In 1973 when Shenouda III became patriarch, there were seven churches abroad. By 2005 there were more than

150 Coptic churches outside Egypt, including monasteries in Australia, Germany, Italy, and the United States.

The 1990s, especially, has been called the "decade of expansion." Churches were opened throughout Europe (Austria, England, France, Germany, the Netherlands, and Switzerland) as well as in South America and the Caribbean. In 1993 the British Orthodox Church requested that it be brought under the See of Alexandria (Meinardus 1999, 131), and in 1995 a Bishop for Mission was consecrated on the Festival of Pentecost.

Most Coptic churches in "the lands of immigration" have been active cultural centers, providing a sense of Egyptian Christian communal identity that revolves around a bishop, who maintains a visible tie to the apostolic tradition of St. Mark. The diaspora communities have also been successful in producing publications about the Coptic Orthodox Church, its origins and traditions. The growth and establishment of Coptic communities abroad has led to the evangelization among some Europeans and North Americans who have married into Coptic families or those who have been drawn to the ancient identity of the Coptic church. The largest community of diaspora Copts includes the Diocese of Los Angeles, Southern California, and Hawaii; the Archdiocese of North America; and the Diocese of the Southern United States, which was established in 1993. In 2002 Pope Shenouda ordained a new bishop, Bishop Daniel, to provide for the care of the Coptic community in the Diocese of Sydney and affiliated regions, including the Coptic communities in East Asia.

Coptic English periodicals and websites have provided a further method of mission. The journal *Keraza* has been in publication since the 1960s and has provided an official outreach not only to Coptic immigrants around the world but to non-Copts in the West as well. Numerous Coptic civic organizations, including *Copts.com* and *The American Coptic Association*, have begun posting websites not only as a method of mission, but also to speak out against what they argue is the persecution of Egyptian Christians by the Muslim majority and the Egyptian government's complicity with such actions. Often these outspoken immigrant organizations, who are vital supporters of Coptic ministries inside Egypt, find themselves at odds with the official statements of the hierarchy in Egypt.

### Bishopric of African Missions

Modern missions to sub-Saharan Africa began in 1962, when Pope Cyril VI established a Department of African Studies within the Institute of Coptic Studies in Cairo. By 1965 the patriarch of Alexandria officially added the title "Pope of Alexandria and of all Africa" to his title (Meinardus 1999, 135). This additional title reflected the Coptic Orthodox Church's view of itself. According to Coptic tradition, Mark was from the Pentapolis (in modern-day Libya), and therefore the Coptic church is the first true African church. In addition, the early development of monastic communities up the Nile into Nubia and the continued tradition of the patriarch of Alexandria being given spiritual authority over the Ethiopian Orthodox Church have solidified the church's view of itself as African.

Although by 1948 there had been attempts to work in sub-Saharan Africa, it was not until Antonius Markos was consecrated as bishop for African affairs in 1976 that the mission became truly effective. Since that date the church has been exceedingly energetic in founding churches in Ghana, Kenya, Namibia, South Africa, Tanzania, Zaire, Zambia, and Zimbabwe (including a monastery in Harare). In 2002 two Coptic priests were ordained from within the Southu and Khosa tribes of South Africa. These priests were then sent to Abidjan, Ivory Coast, to begin a church there.

In addition to the active work done by Coptic personnel, there have two major movements from other Orthodox churches seeking union with Alexandria. In 1993 the African Orthodox Church (which broke from the Anglican Church in 1924) sought permission to be brought under the authority of the patriarch of Alexandria. (For the history of the AOC, see Platt 1989.) The Eritrean Orthodox Church came into being under the authority of the Copts in 1998. (However, four years earlier, in 1994, the Ethiopian Orthodox Tewahido Church sought independence and was granted an autocephalous standing from Alexandria.)

### Methods of Mission

Two important methods of evangelism have worked well for the Copts in Africa. The first is the translation of the liturgy, rites, and synaxarium (the commemoration of saint days) of the church. Because the Bible had already been translated into most languages by Catholic and Protestant mission organizations there was only a need to translate church traditions for the local people. The liturgy has been translated into Bemba, Dioula, English, Freth, Herero, Kikamba, Kikongo, Kikuyu, Lingala, Luhya, Luo, Ndebele, Oshivambo, Sotho, Swahili, Shona, Xhosa, and Zulu (Markos 2001, 47). These translations have gone a long way to explain the purpose of Orthodox worship. Incense, icons, and liturgical music have all been used as catechetical devices to teach people the symbolism of the Orthodox faith. In this way, worship itself has been an evangelistic tool that engages all of the senses and creates a desire for the whole person to learn more about faith in Christ.

The second method of evangelism has been the building of church structures. Because of the Orthodox focus on the celebration of the Eucharist as an essential part of the *ecclesia,* there has been the need to procure a "fixed altar" and a sanctuary. This has prompted Bishop Markos to insist upon proceeding to purchase land legally in any foreign country and patiently wait for the necessary building permits. Although this method is founded upon liturgical and theological practices (i.e., the necessity of having a consecrated altar in order for the church to "be"), it has provided practical results. Coptic Orthodox churches have thrived because they have taken the time to follow legal measures. The church building, along with adjoining educational buildings, has allowed indigenous Africans to attend the liturgy, enter the catechumate, then be sent to Egypt for further theological education. This has created a new generation of sub-Saharan African priests and deacons to be ordained under the authority of the Alexandrian See.

## Coptic Orthodox Theology of Missions

Historically, Catholic and Protestant Missions in the Middle East have seen the Oriental churches as a stumbling block to effective Christian witness to Muslims. Their traditions, structures, and liturgies have been seen as lifeless and without true faith in Christ. To truly understand and appreciate twentieth- and twenty-first-century Coptic Orthodox missions, one needs to become familiar with Oriental Orthodox identity and praxis.

### Identity as "Apostolic"

The Coptic Orthodox Church sees itself as one of the oldest churches in the world. As an "apostolic" church, the Coptic church derives its authority from those individuals who had a direct link to the living Jesus of Nazareth. Mark, closest companion of Peter, was one of the earliest apostles to communicate the words of Christ to the world. Mark's first disciple, Anianas, became the second bishop of Alexandria. Thus, the traditional link between Mark and the patriarchs of Alexandria provides "an expression of a continuing Christian witness that has embodied mission in different circumstances as the continuing act of God in Egypt and through the Egyptian people" (Assad 1991, 252). This witness has provided teachers, preachers, and martyrs who have extolled the apostolic faith from the first century. Founded

by the first missionaries, the Coptic Orthodox Church sees itself as missionary by nature. The activity and role of the patriarch of Alexandria and the other bishops, priests, and deacons is seen as the ongoing work of the apostolic fathers.

### Participation in Apostolic Community

Whereas Western Protestant Evangelical missions have focused upon individual salvation, primarily through an active conversion experience, the Coptic Orthodox Church, as do other Orthodox churches, sees the salvation of the individual taking place within the established Orthodox community of faith and its activities. Conversion is sought in the liturgical sharing of the Word; the experience of conversion and repentance are found concretely in the moment when the celebrants and the faithful, the whole of the people of God, declare with one voice their repentance and earnestly seek "the grace, mercy and *philanthropia* (love towards humanity) of the One Son....Only a community of converts can bear a sincere missionary testimony, and one that is effective" (Markos 1989, 251).

Thus, the salvation of the individual comes through participation in the apostolic community and its sacramental life, by entering its life through baptism and participating in its sacraments, primarily the Eucharist, in which believers take in the actual body and blood of Christ, thereby taking Christ with them into the world. This participation is Trinitarian in nature—the unity of the Father, Son, and Holy Spirit is the same unity that holds together the Orthodox church, the body of Christ. The Father sends the Son, and through the Spirit sends the church. Participation in the Triune Mission of God, then, for the Orthodox faith is impossible unless it is done through the *koinonia* of the Church.

### Public Markers (Holy Sites and Saints) as a Witness

In the Coptic view of mission, the physical presence of a church structure is a public witness to the world. The altar and surrounding dome are a "manifestation of a living church" (Assad 1972, 125). This is why the building of churches and altars becomes the primary means of mission for the Coptic Orthodox Church. It is through the altar, where the living Christ is transmitted, that the community is able to participate in its primary calling and, at the same time, serves as a "light to the nations," inviting all to come and see. It is in the sanctuary that one comes into contact with the witness of the church universal as it gives praise to the living Lord.

Furthermore, the tradition of monasticism is seen as a vital public evangelical witness to the faith. Just as Christ retreated to the desert to fight the demons of the world, Anthony, Paul and Pachomius laid the foundations of a monastic tradition that serves the Christian faith by providing a beacon toward "the godly life." The revitalization of the monastic tradition in the twentieth century and the establishment of Coptic monasteries around the world is seen as an essential marker of the faith.

## Future Role

The Coptic Orthodox Church now sees itself as fulfilling its role as an apostolic witness and a faithful missionary-minded church. The theology of mission in the Coptic Orthodox Church has a different focus from that of its Protestant counterparts. Rather than centering upon the preaching of the Word to individuals, the Coptic church understands the celebration of the divine liturgy (and the Eucharist) among a gathered community and the taking of Christ into the body, and thus into the world, as the primary witness of the Christian faith.

DAVID D. GRAFTON

*See also* Africa; Ancient Church; Middle East

### Further Reading

Amidon, P. R. (1997). *The church history of Rufinus of Aquileia: Books 10 and 11.* Cambridge, UK: Oxford University Press.

Assad, M. (1972). The Coptic Church and social change in Egypt. *International Review of Mission (61),* 117–129.

Assad, M. (1991). Mission in the Coptic Orthodox Church—Perspective, doctrine and practice. *International Review of Mission (80),* 251–261.

Atiya, A. S. (1968). *A History of Eastern Christianity.* London: Methuen and Co.

Atiya, A. S. (1979). *The Copts and Christian Civilization.* Salt Lake City: University of Utah Press.

Atiya, A. S., Ed. (1991). *The Coptic Encyclopedia.* New York: McMillan.

Cahen, Cl. (1986). al-Dhimma. In C.E. Bosworth (Ed.), *Encyclopedia of Islam, 2nd ed.* Leiden, the Netherlands: Brill.

Capunani, M. (2002). *Chritian Egypt.* Cairo: American University in Cairo Press.

Carter, B. L. (1986). *The Copts in Egyptian politics.* London: Croon Helm.

Davis, S. (2004). *The early Coptic Papacy.* Cairo, Egypt: AUC Press.

Gabra, G., (2001). (Ed.). *Be thou there: The holy family's journey in Egypt.* Cairo, Egypt: AUC Press.

Gabra, G. (2002). *Coptic monasteries.* Cairo, Egypt: AUC Press.

Glanville, S. R. K. (1977). *The Legacy of Egypt.* Westport, CT: Greenville Press.

Griggs, C. W. (1991). *Early Egyptian Christianity, from its origins to 451 CE.* Leiden, the Netherlands. Brill.

Hasan, S. (2003). *Christians versus Muslims in modern Egypt.* New York: Oxford University Press.

Ibrahim, S. (1996). *The Copts of Egypt.* London: Minority Rights Group.

Kamil, J. (2002). *Christianity in the land of the pharaohs.* Cairo, Egypt: AUC Press.

King, A. (1947). *The Rites of Eastern Christendom.* N.p.: Catholic Book Agency.

Lane-Poole, E. (1898). *Cairo: Sketches of its history, monuments and social life.* London: J. S. Virtue & Co.

Markos, A. (1989). Orthodoxy in mission: Reflections and perspectives from an African experience. In G. Lemopoulos (Ed.), *Your Will Be Done: Orthodoxy in Mission* (pp. 214–259). Geneva, Switzerland: WCC.

Markos, A. (2001). *An Introduction into theology of mission.* Johannesburg, South Africa: The Coptic Orthodox Church, Bishopric of African Affairs.

Marshall, D. N. (1994). *The Celtic Connection.* Grantham, UK: Standborough Press.

Masri, I. H. (1982). *The Story of the Copts.* Cairo, Egypt: St. Anthony Coptic Orthodox Monastery.

Meinardus, O. F. A. (1999). *Two thousand years of Coptic Christianity.* Cairo, Egypt: AUC Press.

Meinardus, O. F. A. (2002). *Coptic saints and pilgrimages.* Cairo, Egypt: AUC Press.

Pearson, B. A. (1986). *The roots of Egyptian Christianity.* Philadelphia: Fortress Press.

Platt, W. (1989). The African Orthodox Church. *Church History 58*(4), 474–488.

Roberts, A. (1885). *Anti-Nicene fathers,* Series II, Vol. I–X. Grand Rapids, Michigan: Eerdmans Press.

Schaff, P. (1890). *Nicene and post Nicene fathers,* Series II, Vol. I–XIV. Grand Rapids, Michigan: Eerdmans Press.

Stene, N. (1997). Into the lands of immigration. In N. Doom-Harder & K. Vogt, Eds., *Between desert and city: The Coptic Orthodox Church today* (pp. 225–265). Eugene, OR: Wipf & Stock.

Stirton, J. (1988). *The Celtic Church and the influence of the East.* Carine, WV: Scotpress.

Swan, L. (2001). *The forgotten desert mothers.* New York: Paulist Press.

Tritton, A. S. (1930). *The Caliphs and their non-Muslim subjects.* London: Oxford University Press.

Van Doorn-Harder, N., & Vogt, K. (1997). *Between desert and city: The Coptic Orthodox Church today.* Oslo, Norway: Institute for Comparative Research in Human Culture.

Wakin, E. (2000). *The lonely minority: The modern story of Egypt's Copts.* Lincoln, NE: Backinprint.com.

Ward, B. (1987). *Sayings of the desert fathers* (Rev. ed.). Collegeville, MN: Cistercian Publications.

Ward, B. (2003). *In the heart of the desert: The forgotten sayings of the desert fathers and mothers.* Bloomington, IN: World Wisdom.

Winstedt, E. O. (1909). *Christian topography of cosmas indicopleustes.* Cambridge, UK: The University Press.

Woods, D. (1994). The origin of the legend of Maurice and the Theban Legion. *Journal of Ecclesiastical History 45,* 385–95.

# Counter Reformation

The Counter, or Catholic, Reformation/Restoration represented a movement aiming at the renewal of the Catholic Church in response to the Protestant Reformation. These different names indicate how wide-ranging explanations of the process have been given in relation to the varying confessional and secular factors involved. During the era of the Counter Reformation the Catholic Church sought not only renewal and the restoration of Rome-based Christendom, but also the evangelization of newly explored continents where "heathens" lived without the knowledge of the gospel. The latter gave rise to new Catholic orders taking on the task of mission to the peoples of the Americas, Asia, and Africa.

## Cause of Problems and Urging to Reform the Catholic Church

The extravagance and excesses of the medieval church were peculiar traits of a spiritual power unable to resist the lure of political and economical advantages. This was especially true under Pope Alexander VI (1492–1503). The Reformation broke out under the rule of Leo X (1513–1522), who intended to rebuild St. Peter's Basilica in Rome through the selling of indulgences. This issue became unbearable for a growing number of people in the German electorates.

The exploitation of spiritual monopoly for economic ends would provide a crucial impetus for Martin Luther's protest. His proclamation, that salvation is attained by faith alone (*sola fide*), was a protest against buying one's eternal life with deeds. Yet his constructive criticism of his church was far more complex. He threw light on abuses of the Catholic Church and from Wittemberg called for renewal from within on 31 October 1517. His teachings were rejected in the end and he was sentenced to death. However, he received political support from Frederick the Wise, a powerful elect-prince of Saxony. Also, the political situation allowed for the possibility of the German elect-princes to balance the power of a foreign ruler, Charles V and Charles I, who sought an absolutist control over the Holy Roman Empire. Luther's reform provided the German princes with a religious worldview to which many aligned themselves for political reasons.

## Bridging the Gap between Protestants and Moderate Catholics

In contrast to Luther's teaching, the dogma of salvation appropriated by works and faith was reaffirmed by the conservative and moderate–liberal high priests of the Catholic Church. These trends signaled that there was a movement from the Papal court yearning for reforms. However, they refused Luther, Calvin, and Zwingli's view that only two (Baptism and the Lord's Supper) of the seven sacraments are acceptable. Cardinal Contarini, a moderate reformer, tried to appease Protestant voices by negotiating with the similarly moderate Protestant reformers such as Melanchton and Bucer. The Colloquium of Ratisbon represented some success on this front in 1541. Although the leading Protestant reformers' theological views varied from one another, they all refused the Catholic teaching of transubstantiation, which stated that the consecrated bread and wine were held to become substantially the body and blood of Christ. In addition, there were strong views in both Protestant and Catholic religious camps which argued that the differences were nonnegotiable. Finally, the political powers expressed their concern. France, for instance, had little desire for a united, powerful Holy Roman Empire under the Habsburg Charles, who also ruled Spain. The liberal Catholic reformers lost their leading figure upon Contarini's death in 1542.

## Council of Trent

Conservative reformers gradually began to govern the course of events. While Luther represented a grassroots-level initiative to reform the Catholic Church from within, the response to the emergence of Protestantism was from the top. Thus, an official counter reform movement within the Catholic Church was initiated by Pope Paul III (1534–1549) when he summoned the Council of Trent. This general council, which met in three sessions, (1545–1547, 1551–1552, 1562–1563), served as the central event of the Counter Reformation. It came to be regarded as the source of the acceptable Catholic reforming movement, which was under the influence of conservative Catholic reformers.

The Council of Trent first tried to respond to the Protestants' critique addressing the issues of indulgence, veneration of relics and saints, pilgrimages, and financial abuse prevailing in the church. It also attempted to meet doctrinal challenges. The council declared Church tradition to be of equal authority as the Bible in guiding the believers' lives, whereas the reformers emphasis rested on the Scripture alone (*sola scriptura*). The Catholic Church also claimed the exclusive right to explain and communicate the Bible to the people. Protestants, however, challenged Rome's monopoly over the interpretation of the Bible, and this led to a various trends within the new movements. Protestants also argued that preaching had to be done in the vernacular languages of the people, whereas all Catholic liturgies were in Latin, a language largely incomprehensible to the masses, until Vatican II. Although the false selling of counterfeit indulgences was forbidden, the council expressed indulgences to be an acceptable expression of faith.

During its second session the Council sought to draw the opposing Protestant and Catholic stances closer together, but by November 1551 the attempt had failed. Four years later Cardinal Caraffa, the greatest opponent of moderate reforms, was elected as Pope Paul IV. During his reign conservative Catholic reformers were dedicated to improving the administrative sphere and discipline of the Church. Well before Luther's action Caraffa belonged to a society of priests and lay people named the *Oratory of Divine Love,* founded in 1497 at Genoa. This small reform party gradually achieved influence, but not before the Reformation in Germany was out of papal control.

The new conservative pope introduced reforms including an Index that prohibited the printing and distribution of many books. The list included authors such as Abelardus, Erasmus, Henry VIII, Boccaccio, and all Protestant writers. When the last session of the council convened, it was decided to combat the influence of Protestantism by using the same means Protestants had utilized such as printing, establishing schools and colleges, as well as actively asserting the influence of powerful nobles and rulers loyal to their cause.

It was the Jesuits (Society of Jesus) who began to follow the same pattern as the Protestants. They pressed for establishing new seminaries to educate rural priests who did not know Latin and lacked proper training. This provided the church with a model. The Council of Trent was a benchmark for spreading devotional and popular books that described how to be good priests and confessors. Bishops residing outside of their dioceses were sent back to their administrative spheres.

Parallel to the trends developing under the sway of Protestants, the Catholics Church saw a boom in newly established societies, such as the Theatines (1524) and the Capuchins (1525), intent on evangelizing the common people. These religious orders reformed the spiritual life of the church and reached out to the poor, prostitutes, orphans, and the sick. However, it was the Jesuits who carried the banner of Counter Reformation. Like other orders, they were missionary minded, but they differentiated themselves through their ability to accommodate the gospel to the changing society more effectively. The order was tightly centralized, and its top leaders made an oath of unconditional obedience to the Pope. Step by step, they became advisers to the ruling class and made themselves indispensable. Adjusting better to culture than the old monastic orders, Ignatius Loyola eliminated many monastic obligations such as meditation that could have been done individually.

## Mission as Converting Protestants and Heathens

The Jesuits became the extended arm of the papacy in areas where Protestantism took a very strong hold such as Germany, Austria, Hungary, and Poland. By the end of the sixteenth century, the entire Hungarian Kingdom, as well as Poland, was Protestant. Protestantism was a success. Nonetheless, Poland returned to Roman Catholicism with the assistance of Jesuits during the seventeenth century. France also experienced bloody wars of religious faith until the end of the seventeenth century, by which time the Huguenots were wiped out. In Germany the demarcation lines between Catholic southern Bavaria and the Lutheran principalities and electorates in the north and southwest consolidated. In the Netherlands, England, and Scotland Calvinism won its cause fully during the course of 1600s, while the persecution of Calvinists and Lutherans in Hungary continued under the dominant Catholic Habsburg rulers until 1790. This represented the longest struggle in Europe between Catholics and Protestants. Despite of the fact Jesuits often used the force of inquisition if persuasion did not succeed, the missionary zeal took on a different robe when moving into the New World.

Francis Xavier (1506–1552), part of the nucleus establishing the society, was one of the greatest missionary figures of the order to Hindus, Confucians, and Zen Buddhists. Similarly, Roberto de Nobili (1577–1656), a missionary to India, and Matteo Ricci (1552–1610), an outstanding Jesuit missionary to China, used entirely different methods than those implemented in Europe as they accommodated the gospel to the different faiths of Asia.

ÁBRAHÁM KOVÁCS

See also Christendom; Protestant Churches; Protestant Reformation; Radical Reformation; Roman Catholic Church

## Further Reading

Bireley, R. (1999). *The refashioning of Catholicism, 1450–1700: A reassessment of the Counter Reformation*, Washinton, DC: Catholic University Press.

Bucsay, M. (1959). *Geschichte des Protestantismus in Ungarn*, Stuttgart, Germany: Evangelisches Verlagswerk.

Evans, R. J. W. (1985). *Calvinism in east central Europe: Hungary and her neighbours*. In M. Prestwich (Ed.) *International Calvinism 1541–1715* (pp. 167–196). Oxford, UK: Clarendon.

Jones, M. D. W. (1995). *The Counter Reformation: religion and society in early modern Europe*, New York: Cambridge University Press.

Hulme, E. M. (2004). *The Renaissance, the Protestant Revolution and the Catholic Reformation in continental Europe*, Blackwood, NJ: Kessinger Publishing.

Luebke, D. M. (Ed.). (1999). *The Counter-Reformation: The essential readings*. Oxford, UK: Blackwell.

MacCulloch, D. (2003). *Reformation: Europe's house divided, 1490–1700.*, London: Allen Lane.

Mullett, M. A. (1999). *The Catholic Reformation: council, churchmen, controversies*. New York: Routledge.

O'Connell, M. R. (1974). *The Counter Reformation 1559–1610*. New York: Harper & Row.

Olin, J. C. (1969). *The Catholic Reformation: Savonarola to Ignatius Loyola (Reform in the Church 1495-1540)*. New York: Harper & Row.

Péter, K. (1991). The struggle for Protestant religious liberty at the 1646/47 diet in Hungary. In R. J. W. Evans & T. V. Thomas (Eds.), *Crown, church and estates: central European politics in the sixteenth and seventeenth centuries* (pp. 261–268). Houndsmills, Basingstoke, UK: Macmillan.

Péter, K. (1996). Tolerance and intolerance in sixteenth-century Hungary. In O. P. Grell & B. Scriber (Eds.), *Tolerance and intolerance in the European Reformation* (pp. 249–261) Cambridge: Cambridge University Press.

Po-chia Hsia, R. (2005). *The world of Catholic renewal, 1540–1770* (2nd ed.). Cambridge, UK: Cambridge University Press.

Pörtner, R. (2001). *The Counter-Reformation in central Europe: Styria 1580–1630*, Oxford, UK: Clarendon Press; New York: Oxford University Press.

Stasiewski, B. (1960). *Reformation und Gegenreformation in Polen: neue Forschungsergebnisse*. Münster, Germany: Aschendorff.

Wright, A. D. (2005). *The Counter-Reformation: Catholic Europe and the non-Christian World*. Burlington, VT: Ashgate.

# Criticism

Missions work has provoked criticism throughout Christian history, forcing missionaries to rally support for their efforts rather than simply tapping into abiding reservoirs of promissions sentiment. Studying criticism of missionaries exposes the failures of foreign missions from an indigenous perspective. It also uncovers the tensions between competing factions of sending cultures, undermining the widespread assumption that modern missions work has been nothing more than the religious arm of Western racism, imperialism, and commercial expansion.

## Theological and Ecclesiastical Criticism

Denominational competition and theological beliefs have long produced criticism of missions work from within the church. Most Protestants, for example, have viewed Roman Catholic missionaries with deep suspicion, and vice versa.

Gender roles have provided another source of theological criticism. Only after many decades did nineteenth century American women's missionary societies win acceptance from Christian men resistant (on biblical grounds) to female leadership within the church.

Certain strains of predestinarian theology led some to believe that missions work was unnecessary since God had already chosen whom he would save. The story is told that when William Carey, the English missionary to India in 1793, proposed that a gathering of ministers discuss foreign missions, one thundered, "Young man, sit down; when God pleases to convert the heathen, he will do it without your aid, or mine" (Anderson 1869, 20).

During the nineteenth century, antimission Baptists in the United States argued that mission boards arrogated power best reserved for local congregations; some also claimed that most people were nonelect and could not be converted through missionary outreach.

## Telescopic Philanthropy

A more common criticism has been that foreign missions work consumes resources and personnel needed at home. The first missionaries to leave America in 1812 were discouraged from going by many people, including a minister who argued that there was more than enough work to do in the United States. John Paton, who began working in the South Pacific in 1858, was criticized for leaving his fruitful urban ministry in Scotland.

Charles Dickens advanced a more barbed version of this criticism, condemning British Christians who professed concern for the foreign poor while turning a blind eye to the needy in their own backyards. His 1853 novel *Bleak House* featured a woman named Mrs. Jellyby who could "see nothing nearer than Africa." Jellyby practiced "telescopic philanthropy," obsessing over poor Africans while neglecting her own children.

## Racist Criticism

Such arguments could, and in the nineteenth century often did, move quickly into racist claims that missions work was wasted on biologically inferior peoples. Belief in the superiority of whites over nonwhites could fuel missionary efforts to "uplift" foreign populations, but it also led some to question missionary labor. As one critic wrote of work in the Pacific in 1868, "All the efforts of the missionaries have proved utterly useless or unavailing; the moment they are left without restraint [the natives] lapse into idolatry and savageism" (Smith 1993a, 128). Another racist detractor argued that "under the direction of the Saviour and His disciples, the gospel was confined to a fractional part of the inhabitants of the earth; and this fractional part was in exact proportion to its population of pure whites" (Smith 1993b, 792). Somewhat milder versions of racist criticism allowed that nonwhites benefited from missions but claimed that amelioration of their degraded condition consumed too much time and money.

## Colonialist Criticism

While the Christianization of foreign peoples was one of the major arguments used by European powers to justify their brutal and exploitative colonial regimes, colonial officials and merchants were among the fiercest critics of missionary work. The antagonism between Jesuit missionaries and Spanish and Portuguese colonial and commercial officials in South America portrayed in the 1986 film *The Mission* (set in the mid-1700s) is one good example.

Another is the rift between missionaries and officials of the British East India Company during the nineteenth century. Colonial authorities ordered English and American missionaries to leave India, while officials in England blamed Indian mutinies on missionary influence and claimed in 1813 that any attempt to evangelize India would cost England its empire there. One official stated that he would rather see a band of devils in India than a band of missionaries.

Further examples of colonial criticism of missions include King Leopold II of Belgium, who brought suit in 1909 against an American missionary who exposed aspects of his genocidal misrule in the Congo, and nineteenth century traders and seamen in Hawaii and throughout the Pacific who found that missionaries hindered their economic exploitation of local peoples.

## Indigenous Criticism

Sometimes rightly, sometimes wrongly, indigenous peoples often saw missionaries as agents of colonization and treated them accordingly. One such case was the Boxer Rebellion (1899–1901) in China, intended to eradicate foreign influence. The rebellion saw the murder of scores of missionaries and thousands of Chinese Christians. Similarly, in 1898 tribal groups in Sierra Leone reacting against a tax by the British colonial administration massacred missionaries during the Hut Tax Rebellion. Liberian tribesmen who murdered a missionary and his followers around 1901 explained that they had no fight with white men but knew that the missionary would bring his country to war against them unless they killed him first. In this view (shared by many Westerners), missionaries blazed a trail for merchants, armies, and colonial officials.

Missionaries were also criticized by local people for interfering with traditional beliefs, customs, and power structures. Christian influence in Japan was nearly eradicated in the early seventeenth century as rulers seeking to consolidate political power expelled Jesuit missionaries and persecuted Japanese converts. Hindu and Muslim elites in India printed popular religious books during the 1840s in a bid to thwart the efforts of Protestant missionaries by reviving their own religious traditions. Opposition to missionaries in China stemmed in part from the fact that many Chinese attributed the ills of widespread opium addiction to Christian influence.

Indigenous peoples have criticized missionaries for failing to master native languages, respect local customs, and adopt indigenous standards of living, criticisms that may multiply as Western churches sponsor growing numbers of short-term foreign missions trips.

## Cultural Relativist Criticism

The accusation that missions work destroyed valuable indigenous cultures first appeared during the colonial era and grew into a dominant form of criticism by the late twentieth century. In his early novels *Typee* (1846) and *Omoo* (1847), American author Herman Melville criticized missions work in the Pacific, claiming that missionaries eradicated useful and innocent customs and traditions. Such criticisms were elaborated during the 1950s and subsequently by Western and non-Western writers associated with postcolonial cultural studies. By the late twentieth century, the standard depiction of missionaries in the West was the stereotype of the culturally insensitive fundamentalist found in Barbara Kingsolver's *The Poisonwood Bible* (1998).

The prestige of cultural anthropology beginning in the early twentieth century increased Western appreciation of other cultures and lent authority to anthropological claims that missions work too often disrupted indigenous cultures. Additionally, the growth of cultural and religious relativism in the West produced criticism of missions work on the grounds that Christianity was only one among many equally legitimate world religions.

Perhaps in response to the criticism of outsiders, some missions theorists have begun to call for Western missionaries to withdraw from the developing world, claiming that the best role for the West is offering financial support to indigenous missionaries.

While the future of such arguments is uncertain, the study of this and other criticisms reveals much about the ways that missionaries relate to the cultures in which they serve and the cultures from which they have been sent.

ANDREW WITMER

### Further Reading

Anderson, R. (1869). *Foreign missions: Their relations and claims.* New York: Charles Scribner and Company.

Barton, J. L. (1906). *The missionary and his critics.* New York: Fleming H. Revell.

Frear, W. F. (1935). *Anti-missionary criticism, with reference to Hawaii.* Honolulu: Advertiser Publishing.

Kingsolver, B. (1998). *The poisonwood Bible.* New York: HarperCollins.

Porter, A. (Ed.). (2003). *The imperial horizons of British Protestant missions, 1880–1914.* Grand Rapids, MI: Eerdman's Publishing.

Porter, A. (2004). *Religion versus empire? British Protestant missionaries and overseas expansion, 1700–1914.* Manchester, UK: Manchester University Press.

Robert, D. L. (2002). The influence of American missionary women on the world back home. *Religion and American Culture, 12*(1), 59–89.

Smith, J. D. (Ed.). (1993a). *Anti-black thought: The "Ariel" controversy.* New York: Garland Publishing.

Smith, J. D. (Ed.). (1993b). *Anti-black thought: The biblical and "scientific" defense of slavery.* New York: Garland Publishing.

Stipe, C. E. (1980). Anthropologists versus missionaries: The influence of presuppositions. *Current Anthropology, 21*(2), 165–168.

## Crusades, The

Jonathan Riley-Smith's little book *What Were the Crusades?* (1977, 74) defines the Crusades as follows: "A crusade was a manifestation of the Christian Holy War, fought against infidels in the East, in Spain and in Germany." In later editions Riley-Smith modified this definition, but it will do to begin with. He calls it *a* manifestation of Christian Holy War. It could be argued that there had been an earlier one. In the 620s the Emperor Heraclius (575–641 CE) went to war against the Persians who had captured Jerusalem and seized the relic believed to be the cross upon which Jesus was crucified. To encourage his soldiers he claimed that those killed in battle would be martyrs, because they were fighting in a Christian cause. In 630 CE the victorious Heraclius entered Jerusalem, on foot, carrying the recovered relic. In this instance the "infidels" were Persian Zoroastrians. In what is generally understood to be the crusades the "infidels" Riley-Smith mentions were, except in Germany, Muslims.

The followers of Muhammad (c. 570–632 CE) had come out of Arabia in October 630. They returned two years later under Muhammad's successor, and this time they stayed, invading Mesopotamia, the Eastern coast of the Mediterranean, and then all along the Mediterranean's southern coastline. Damascus fell in 635 CE, and Jerusalem in 638 CE. In 711 CE they found their way to Spain. By 732 CE they had reached—and were defeated at—Poitiers in central France. These were more

**The city wall of Jerusalem.** *Courtesy of Claudia Dewald/istockphoto.com.*

or less Christian lands, but the invaders were not out to convert, certainly not to convert Christians and Jews. Nonetheless, by 850 CE in the Near East Islam was the majority faith.

The reasons the Muslim armies had come are many, but there is one of particular significance for understanding the Crusades. Muhammad had united the tribes of the Arabian peninsula around a single God. They could no longer fight each other, as had been more or less their way of life. If fighting was to be done, it had to be exported; if there was plunder to be gained, it had to come from non-Muslim lands.

Despite the fall of the Holy Land, Christian pilgrimage was still possible, all the more so after the conversion of Hungary in the late tenth century opened up a land route, but there were times in the eleventh century when the journey was especially dangerous. Moreover, the Christian Emperor in Constantinople—modern Istanbul—had been thoroughly defeated in 1071 at the battle of Manzikert, near Lake Van in Armenia. Not only were more Christian lands about to fall into Muslim hands, but the way appeared to lie open to the capture of Constantinople itself. It happened just at the time when Pope Gregory VII (c. 1020–1085) was considering raising an army to go to the defense of the Emperor, perhaps not just to regain Christian lands but also to heal the breach between the Church of Rome and that of Constantinople, which had occurred in 1054. It seems the Pope was prepared to lead the Christian army himself.

Church law was full of injunctions against the shedding of blood. In 1078 Gregory himself had ap-proved one such, insisting that the career of a knight, precisely because it involved shedding blood, was sinful. The knights needed forgiveness, specifically for shedding Christian blood. The Church had made a number of efforts to reduce the level of violence within western Europe. There were sets of rules regulating warfare that, for instance, forbade fighting on certain days and insisted on the noncombatant status of certain classes in society. When Pope Urban II (c. 1035–1099) in 1095 preached the first of what came to be called the Crusades, he may well have been intent, as Muhammad had been in Arabia, on moving violence out of Europe. He was himself a Frenchman. He knew the damage that had been done by constant skirmishes on French soil.

## The Crusade Is Launched

What persuaded the men to go? First and probably most importantly, the knights were promised a remission of their sins. This was to be a penitential pilgrimage to the Holy Land in reparation for shedding Christian blood. Instead, they were to shed Muslim blood, and anyone who died on the way, or was killed in battle, was promised by the pope full remission of sin. (Later on this became formalized as the "crusading indulgence"). Second, this was being done in imitation of Christ who commanded "take up your cross and follow me": crusaders wore a red cross on their tunics to mark them out. Third, in a slightly later development, they vowed to go. As Urban seems to have pointed out in his sermon (only reports of it have been preserved) they could go knowing that peace would be preserved while they were away, guaranteed by the Church.

The first to depart, however, were not the knights. In 1096 peasants went, a host, it has been estimated, of between 50,000 and 70,000, led by the charismatic Peter the Hermit (c. 1050–c. 1115). Though setting off to fight Muslims, en route they massacred any non-Christians—Jews—in their midst. They were a rabble, and after causing havoc across Europe, they were wiped out in their first encounter with Muslim troops at Nicaea, modern Iznik. The following year what is known as the First Crusade set off from various points in Europe. They fought their way across Asia Minor. At Antioch on the Orontes they were first the besiegers and then, when another Muslim army approached, the besieged. They were there from October 1097 to January 1099, the troops encouraged by the reported finding in the city of the lance with which, it was supposed, Christ's side had been pierced.

It was a much depleted army that arrived outside the walls of Jerusalem on 7 June 1099, about a third of the size it had been at the start of the campaign. Nonetheless the city fell on 15 July. A massacre followed. One chronicler—not an eye witness—claimed there were 10,000 dead, Muslims and Jews, as the Christians celebrated their triumph. The struggle was not yet over. The crusaders had still to capture the other towns in the Holy Land: the last significant one, Tyre, fell in 1124. They had also to set up a structure of government: the Latin Kingdom of Jerusalem, with a French king, was established. For the most part the crusaders lived more or less in harmony with the Jewish and Muslim inhabitants of Palestine, but the massacre in Jerusalem was not forgotten or forgiven.

The hold on Palestine was precarious. On Christmas Eve 1144 the first of the crusader states to be established, that of Edessa, fell to a Muslim army. It prompted Pope Eugenius III (d. 1153) to issue, a year later, a call to another Crusade. His appeal was heard by the French king and the German king, and the latter set out for the Holy Land in May 1147, the former a month earlier. This expedition was a disaster, and an attempt to attack the Muslim stronghold of Damascus was doubly so. The two kings went home with nothing accomplished, leaving the Latin Kingdom to fend for itself. It was aided by groups of knights who had formed themselves into religious orders with the dual purpose of defending pilgrims and looking after the sick. There were, in time, several of these orders, but the two earliest, and best known, were the Knights of St. John of Jerusalem, surviving today as the Sovereign Military Order of Malta, and the Knights Templar,

whose rather mysterious suppression at the beginning of the fourteenth century has given rise to many myths. These orders controlled the Holy Land through a string of castles along its length.

The knights, however, met their match in the Muslim leader Saladin (1137–1193). On 3 July 1187 the Christian army of which they formed a part suffered a crushing defeat at the Horns of Hattin. The battle left the way open to Jerusalem, which fell to Saladin on 2 October. Only the city of Tyre remained in Christian hands. A new Crusade was called: the German emperor Frederick Barbarossa (c. 1123–1190) set out in May 1189, and Richard I (1157–1199) of England and Philip Augustus (1165–1223) of France left more than a year later. Frederick was accidentally drowned, Philip went home after Acre was captured, but Richard managed to restore a coastal strip to Christian control: Acre became the new capital of the Latin Kingdom.

Another crusade was proclaimed in 1198. A substantial army gathered in Venice: the Republic had undertaken to provide ships. The army moved on to Constantinople, the ancient Christian capital of the East. Power struggles within had made it vulnerable. Instead of coming to the aid of the Eastern Emperor, on 17 July 1204 the crusaders and the Venetians captured Constantinople and ransacked it. They went no further.

There were other crusades. In 1228 the Emperor Frederick (1194–1250) managed to recover Jerusalem. He was advised that the terms he agreed were too unstable, but he refused to listen. In 1248 King (St.) Louis IX of France (1215–1270) set out, with a mostly French army but with contingents from England, Scotland, and Italy. His plan was to attack Egypt, which he did, but disastrously, was captured and had to hand over a huge ransom. He stayed on in the Holy Land, however, until 1254. Little by little the towns, and the knights' castles, fell to Muslim forces until only Acre was left. That, too, fell on 18 May 1291, and although popes occasionally called for a new Crusade, the attempt to recover the Holy Places was effectively over.

## Other Crusades

Outside Palestine the situation was somewhat different. The reconquest of Spain for Christianity was largely undertaken by Spaniards themselves. When the last Muslim city, Granada, fell on 2 January 1492, Muslims—and Jews—were offered baptism or exile.

In the Baltic States the situation was different again. Here another religious order, the Teutonic Knights, fought their way along the Baltic, through what are now the countries of Lithuania, Latvia, and Estonia, converting as they went. They even pressed into Russia until halted at the Battle of Lake Peipus on 5 April 1242 by (St.) Alexander Nevsky (1218–1263), Prince of Novgorod. They had been hoping to bring some at least of the Orthodox back into communion with Rome.

The Crusades to the Holy Land, however, had not been launched to convert Muslims or Jews. Just as Christians in Muslim territories, so Muslims and Jews in the Latin Kingdom lived more or less peacefully. When in 1290 some Christians newly arrived to defend Acre and, unaccustomed to the practice in the Kingdom, massacred Muslims, it was regarded on all sides as a scandal.

MICHAEL J. WALSH

### Further reading

Barber, R. (1995). *The knight and chivalry.* Woodbridge, UK: Boydell Press.

Bull, M. (1993). *Knightly piety and the response to the first Crusade.* Oxford, UK: Oxford University Press.

Christiansen, E. (1980). *The northern Crusades: The Baltic and the Catholic frontier 1100–1525* London: Macmillan.

Flori, J. (1990). Guerre sainte et rétribution spirituelles dans la 2e moité du Xi siècle [Holy war and spiritual retribution in the second half of the eleventh century]. *Revue d'Histoire Ecclésiastique, LXXXV* (2), 617–49.

Forey, A. (1994). *Military orders and the Crusades.* Aldershot, UK: Variorum.

Johnson, J. T. (1981). *Just war tradition and the restraint of war.* Princeton, NJ: Princeton University Press.

Kedar, B. Z. (1984). *Crusade and mission: European approaches toward the Muslims.* Princeton, NJ: Princeton University Press.

Maier, C. T. (1994). *Preaching the Crusades: Mendicant friars and the cross in the thirteenth century.* Cambridge, UK: Cambridge University Press.

Mastnak, T. (2002). *Crusading peace: Christendom, the Muslim world, and Western political order.* Berkeley: University of California Press.

Peters, F. E. (1985). *Jerusalem.* Princeton, NJ: Princeton University Press.

Riley-Smith, J. (Ed.) (1990). *The atlas of the Crusades.* London: Times Books.

Riley-Smith J. (1986). *The first Crusade and the idea of crusading.* London: Athlone Books.

Riley-Smith, J. (1977, 2002). *What were the Crusades?* Basingstoke, UK: Palgrave Macmillan.

Walsh, M. (2003). *Warriors of the Lord.* Alresford, UK: John Hunt; Grand Rapids, MI: Wm. B. Eerdmans.

# Culture

"Culture" is a highly contested notion among social scientists, who often skirmish over its meaning, applicability, and value. For nonspecialists, however, "culture" is a useful concept that helps them talk about themselves or others in general terms as groups or as members of groups.

## History

During the Enlightenment, culture was something possessed by an individual or a group and understood in terms of its presence or absence: Either one "had" culture or one did not, and those who had culture were seen as different from those who lacked culture. Culture was seen as synonymous with sophistication or civilization; it was identified with refinement, a taste for the arts (opera, drama, music), and a degree of material comfort. Culture could be accumulated, which meant that people or groups might have more or less of it, and could therefore be considered more or less "cultured." By the middle of the nineteenth century, "cultures" (plural) was used to characterize different social groups according to their attributes or habits; cultures themselves could be contrasted as better or worse, higher or lower.

Not surprisingly, those who expatiated on the concept of culture in the eighteenth, nineteenth, and twentieth centuries—Westerners, mainly Europeans—saw themselves as embodiments of the highest culture. Occasionally, like a comet, someone born and raised far from Western civilization and sophistication would burst on the scene and be lionized in the salons of the West as a person of "culture." It was always assumed that such persons had "learned" or "caught" their culture from someone who already possessed it: a Westerner. However, this patronizing and exclusive notion of culture ("us" versus "them") gradually collapsed before a new and more empirically based understanding of humanity and human society, promoted, in the main, by the fledgling social science of anthropology, which developed during the twentieth century.

Simply put, the contemporary view of culture is that it is what people do with and to the world in which they live. It is the [hu]man-made part of the environment, the form of social life, and a meaning-making system. As a defining characteristic of humanness, culture is universal, rather than particular: It applies universally to people in society—a critically important qualification, for culture is a social rather than a purely private matter. An individual may love Beethoven or the Beetles, but "culture" is more about *common* understandings or ways of acting than about personal preferences.

## Social Institutions

Every social group must have enough in common to assure its well-being and survival. Without a common focus and purpose, a degree of collaboration, effective sanctions to underpin such a collaboration, and communication and understanding, a community will simply not survive. Every culture, then, requires social institutions and common symbols, particularly language. Social institutions ("standardized modes of co-activity") constitute the skeleton or matrix around which a living culture grows its particular form. Though no two cultures are identical and no single culture is uniform or homogeneous, every culture is built around four social institutions: politics, economics, kinship, and religion.

The institution of politics covers everything to do with law and order, the control of sanctions, and the distribution of authority (legitimated power) within a social group. Politics in this sense is not concerned primarily with political parties but with the governance of the *polis*, the city (or its more dispersed cultural equivalent, which may range from a relatively small band to a large clan or a nation).

Economics handles all matters dealing with the distribution or allocation of goods and services within and between communities. Economic rules (and supporting sanctions) are sometimes intended to secure the free flow of goods and services, and other times to legitimate or ensure the very opposite: that certain people, but not all, have access to some goods and services. Economic rules and practices determine where a society lies on a line between egalitarian and highly stratified.

Kinship systems identify and regulate the members of a community in terms of their relationships (primarily biological but also, critically, socially acknowledged or determined). Rules clarify who belongs to which group, how ancestors and descendants are constituted, who may and may not marry, and who (the man, the woman, both, or their respective kin-groups) determines membership for each individual within the group, whether by birth, marriage, or fostering (and, by extension, enslavement or capture). Kinship regulations stipulate principles of descent and filiation (from which group one derives, and for which group one reproduces), inheritance rules, and duties to forebears.

The fourth social institution (sometimes called "belief and thought") is religion: It deals with matters relating to God or gods, the creation and significance of the empirical universe (cosmogony and cosmology), and the addressing of imponderable questions (Why did this happen? Who caused it? Where do we come from? What happens after we die? What is the meaning of life?).

### Institutionalized and Embedded

It is helpful to distinguish "institutionalized" from "embedded" social institutions. The former describes the way some cultures and societies attempt to separate the four institutions. In the United States, the church (religion) is viewed as separate from the state (politics). A funeral is seen as a religious institution, a market as an economic institution, a local election as a political institution, and marriage as a kinship institution. But many societies bring all four institutions into proximity by embedding them: Institutions are not separated from each other but deeply interrelated. In cultures with embedded institutions, it is neither possible nor desirable to separate aspects of social life. For example, where institutions are embedded, people believe that marriage is both religious and political, and that it is intimately connected with kinship and politics.

### Material and Symbolic

Social institutions are necessary but not sufficient to describe a culture. The various other aspects of a culture can conveniently be divided into "material" and "symbolic." Material components of a culture are identifiable in artifacts like buildings, furnishings, and other human creations that use physical materials in a natural or manufactured state: stone or wood, cement or steel, pottery or plastic, fabric or pharmaceuticals. But some materials are particularly perishable, and many cultures (societies) use a minimum of materials. People who live in tropical rain forests, for instance, may leave little trace of themselves even a few decades after their passage through a particular area.

The symbolic aspects of a culture include everything generated by human agency or adapted for human use that is not simply practical or in which something stands for something else—for example, music, dance, poetry, ritual, and language. Symbolic aspects also include what might be called "moral culture." For example, language (and philosophy, theology, logic, and other pursuits associated with meaning making, meaning maintaining, and values or virtues) is both symbolic and interpretative or value-laden.

**115**

## Making Meaning

Every culture is a meaning-making system. Because social groups need, create, and maintain meaning and values, an adequate understanding of a culture must include whatever becomes part of a people's shared identity or aspirations. Not every culture produces philosophy or poetry or cathedrals, but every culture addresses questions of meaning, maintenance of standards, and articulations of moral values. Socialization is the process whereby a child learns the meanings and values of the broader society. A person who is not incorporated into a cultural meaning-making system is considered unsocialized or insane, and a person who repudiates it is called a rebel or an anarchist.

A culture is a living, moving, volatile entity, a social process rather than a static thing, in-the-making rather than complete. It encompasses the whole of social reality—the way people understand and use time, space, incarnation or embodiment itself, and other people (strangers). Humanity is capable not only of great achievement but of despicable acts, and in every culture there is (in theological language) both grace *and* sin: poetry *and* pollution, opera *and* oppression, generosity *and* genocide.

Culture is not only learned but also contested and constantly refashioned; it is a result of both exigency and choice. Human beings are all the same and all different, a single species occupying widely varied environments. Culture—like skin—does not absolutely define people, but people would not survive for long without it, imperfect though it may be. Since culture is part of humanness, faith can only be expressed in and through culture. Faith may indeed challenge every culture, but it cannot do without it. Faith is always expressed culturally.

Anthony J. Gittins

### Further Reading

Geertz, C. (1973). *The interpretation of cultures.* New York: Basic Books.

Gorringe, T. J. (2004). *Furthering humanity: A theology of culture.* Burlington, VT: Ashgate.

Schreiter, R. (1997). *The new catholicity.* New York: Orbis.

Tanner, K. (1997). *Theories of culture.* Minneapolis, MN: Fortress Press.

# D

## Development

The term *development* in missionary activity has normally referred to the process by which the physical and social needs of persons and groups are given attention along with their spiritual needs. The goals have been to raise people from poverty, alleviate suffering, and improve the social situation of the oppressed. The motive has been twofold. First was the desire to follow the mandate of the Old Testament prophets, who called on Israel to care for the poor, the widow, and the orphan, and to follow Jesus Christ, who healed the sick and reached out to the marginalized. Second came the hope that such activities would make the Christian message more credible. Development refers to the long-term effort to bring about change, while the term *relief*, often used along with development, refers to the immediate response to a crisis such as famine, flood, or war.

Christian missionaries assumed that by accepting their message people would improve their social and economic conditions; they believed that Christian teachings could improve human relationships and increase cooperation. Their first step was to encourage literacy. As early as the fourth century Christian missionaries created alphabets for spoken languages in order to translate the Bible, teaching people to read in the process. The Armenian and Cyrillic alphabets are examples of this. Nestorians spread literacy across central Asia from the fifth to the twelfth centuries. The Celtic movement, initiated by St. Patrick, encouraged literacy and learning in Ireland, England, Scotland, and on the Continent, and many scholars have described the strong link between Irish missionary activity and the growth of learning in Ireland. The monastery of Fulda, founded by St. Boniface in the eighth century, became the main center of learning for much of Germany. Through the Western missionary movement, educational institutions were eventually established at every level in Asia, Africa, and Latin America.

The second step taken by Christian missionaries was to encourage agriculture. Although monasticism focused primarily on prayer and worship, it valued work, in the field as well as the library. As monks formed their communities, often in deserted areas, they had the patience, skill, and time to clear the land, reclaim neglected fields, and experiment with innovations in agriculture. Their example helped the surrounding communities to increase food production. For example, the Cistercians in the twelfth century worked out new methods of agricultural administration and became the greatest wool producers in Europe, furnishing raw material for the textile industry.

The Roman Catholic missionary movement from Europe to Asia and Latin America began at the end of the fifteenth century. During the sixteenth and seventeenth centuries in Latin America, its major contribution, beyond Christianizing people, was to establish universities. However, they were only for the elites, who were destined to serve either church or state, and did little to improve the economic life of most people. The most striking examples of Roman Catholic community development were the Jesuit communities for tribal peoples in southern Brazil and Paraguay; the Jesuits improved agriculture and education while protecting people from the exploitation of other European colonists. However, the Roman Catholic missionary movement disintegrated after the dissolution of the Jesuit Order in the eighteenth century.

## Missionary Work in South Texas

**The following account of Mexican-American life in South Texas in the early twentieth century shows how missionaries were aware of many issues facing the immigrant community and the efforts they made beyond conversion.**

Despite the scarcity of resources available to the Church, some members of the Catholic hierarchy in Texas succeeded in going beyond strictly pastoral care. Thus, between 1914 and 1941 Bishop Anthony J. Schuler of El Paso established hospitals, clinics, orphanages, and day nurseries, largely with help received from the Catholic Extension Society. However, these efforts were not intended to effect far-reaching changes in the levels of living of the Mexican-American population. The climate of public opinion in the region was not conducive to social reform, and a Church just beginning to grow and sponsor allied institutions for the benefit of the community was not likely to challenge the status quo.

[...]

But the conditions of Mexican Americans did not go unnoticed by the priest-missionaries struggling with their pastoral labors. In the pages of *Mary Immaculate*, a small monthly published by the Oblate Fathers of Mary Immaculate (who, until recently, provided the majority of priests in the Corpus Christi diocese), detailed diary-like accounts were published in almost every issue. Six articles appearing between 1928 and 1934 indicated a remarkable awareness of the Mexican Americans' problems.

One missionary commented on the changes brought about by irrigation. Where only Mexican settlers existed before, now a "prosperous American community, largely Protestant...devote their energies and their money to the development of the country." The Mexicans are laborers "who carry out the industrial part of the work." The result is that "we have, in fact, two absolutely distinct people, two classes of society as widely apart as the castes of India." Another priest wrote of "the sordid huts, set back in intricate obscure lanes." Mexicans "work for a pittance," suffer and endure "their sufferings as only Mexicans can, with barely enough to eke out a miserable existence." A third, writing of Crystal City, Texas, noted that the winter harvests there brought in, annually, "thousands of Mexicans from elsewhere, to divide or take away entirely, at lower prices, the work from the home population. Occupation and a fair wage for 8,000 people hardly means more than tortillas and coffee for 16,000."

A later writer told his readers that Mexican immigrants are "often subject to very unfair discrimination and contempt." Because they know no English and belong "to the very humble class of the cheapest day laborers, they are regarded with scorn." The "middle-class Mexicans," especially, "deeply resent the fact that they are treated as an inferior race." They suffer "bitterly as a result of social and racial prejudices of which they are the victims."

Source: Grebler, L. (1970). *The Mexican-American people, the nation's second largest minority* (p. 455–456). New York: Free Press.

Protestant missionary efforts began with John Eliot, an English Puritan, who arrived in New England in 1631. In his life developmental activities were entwined with the struggle for justice. Eliot worked extensively with Native Americans near Boston, transcribing their language and translating the Bible. He also brought cases to court to prevent defrauding of their land, fought the selling of people into slavery, established schools for children and adults, and sought to secure streams and lands for Native American use.

When the German Pietist Barthomeu Ziegenbalg arrived in the Danish colony of Tranquebar, India, in 1706, he followed the examples of his colleagues in Germany. He established schools for the poor, including girls, and opened an industrial school designed to improve economic life. He also began to prepare the way for the arrival of the first medical missionary to India, who arrived after his death.

William Carey, often called the father of the Protestant missionary movement, arrived in Serampore, near Calcutta, in 1793. His primary goal was to evangelize and establish a church. He translated the Bible into a number of Indian languages, and is equally well-known for his struggle to end infanticide, to abolish the custom of suttee, in which widows were cremated on the funeral pyres of their husbands, to establish Serampore College, and to initiate horticultural research.

The early Congregationalist missionaries to Hawaii have often been unfairly maligned. The missionaries were hated by some because they attempted to protect the Hawaiians from sexual and economic exploitation by outsiders. Their main goal was to convert the Hawaiian people to Christian faith, but they also worked to educate them and to protect them from sexual and economic exploitation by the sailors and traders who came to the islands. After a few decades the islands were dotted with churches and with schools staffed by Hawaiian teachers. An alphabet was created for the local language, and by 1873, 153 books and 13 magazines had been published in it.

Nearly all Western-style universities in Africa during the colonial period were established by missionaries. These schools opened their doors to women, and the common people. Up until that point, traditional education was reserved for the elite. Korea and China also benefited. Ehwa, in Seoul, Korea, was started by Mary Scranton, a Methodist missionary. She arrived in 1885 and the following year started the school that became the largest women's university in the world. It was the first school for girls in the nation. Reporting on the educational work of the Basel Mission in Ghana in 1921, a commission stated that it had "produced one of the most interesting and effective systems of schools observed in Africa . . . First of all, their mechanical shops trained and employed a large number of natives as journeymen . . . Secondly the commercial activities reached the economic life of the people, influencing their agricultural activities and their expenditures for food and clothing . . . The Basel Mission in Ghana established an effective educational system that included mechanical work, commerce, and agriculture. In 1993 the Latin American Childcare program of the Assemblies of God [created] two hundred sixty-one schools at the primary and secondary levels in 18 countries with 67,487 children enrolled. The goal was not simply to aid the children but to raise the educational and economic level of their societies" (Peterson 1997, 152–153).

Along with education and agriculture, medical work was an important means of development. Its goal was not only to treat the sick but to improve the health of the population as a whole. Women missionaries from the United States initiated the first medical work for women in India and China, established the first girls schools, and founded nursing and medical schools for women. That had a powerful impact on medical care for women and helped to improve their social status. Today medicine is among the most prestigious professions open to women in India. Christian institutions took the lead in treating victims of leprosy and tuberculosis, often training those who worked among them. At the turn of the twentieth century, two American Presbyterians called attention to the scandal of forced labor in the Belgian Congo.

Until the middle of the twentieth century the term *development* was rarely used in mission circles. When Westerner missionaries spoke of changing, and as they understood it, improving, the lives of people in Asia, Africa, and Latin America, they often used the term *civilizing*. They assumed that Western institutions and concepts, along with the Christian message, would be readily accepted by those of other cultures and lead to positive change. That was often true, but only at one level. Educational and medical institutions were readily accepted in many areas, but because the Christian agenda was imposed from above by outsiders, it was often resisted by people who were proud of their own ancient religious and cultural traditions. There was the further problem that when Western technology was accepted, it often created dependency, and when Westerners left, projects collapsed. Because of this new understanding, by the middle of the twentieth century Westerners began to take a more positive attitude toward other cultures, and Christian missionaries and development agencies such as World Vision began to reassess their approach.

This led to the concept of *transformational development,* and reflects the desire to seek positive change in the whole of human life, especially of the poor. It includes material, social, and spiritual dimensions; it also assumes a positive view of the values of the receptor people and their culture and attempts to discover their concerns instead of imposing agendas from outside. The process is not easy; it is a constant journey, involving the poor, the non-poor, and the development staff. Ultimately, for Christians, the goals of transformation are to enable people to discover their true identity as human beings created in the image of God, and to find their vocation as productive stewards, caring for the world and its people.

Transformational development will often include practical contributions, like improving water resources for drinking and agriculture, improving health care at the village level, and improving preventive medicine and agricultural methods. But at a more basic level it will seek profound changes in the world view of the poor, including the way they view themselves. In many cases they have been told that they are powerless, that nothing can ever change their condition. Sometimes that message has religious sanctions and other times it is imposed by social and political systems. A recent movement in Uttar Pradesh state in India has seen about one million 'Bhangis' or untouchables become Christian. The movement has put a strong stress on education of all children and on economic development. The basic message is "You are Banghis [Bhangis] and Jesus can transform you spiritually, economically, and socially. The work of God and Jesus is to bring salvation in two parts: a life of dignity here and eternal life on the other side (Pierson 2004, 38).

The leading theorists of development today focus on "expanding the political and social power of poor families by supporting grassroots democratic practices and building civil society." Another approach sees development as "responsible well-being, building on the principles of equity and sustainability and pursued by increasing the livelihood, security, and capabilities of the poor." A third approach, by an Indian Christian, sees "development as a kingdom response to the powerlessness of the poor that exposes the web of lies about the identity and worth of the poor and the god-complexes of the non-poor, to the transforming truth and demands of the Kingdom of God" (Myers 1999).

Throughout the Christian missionary movement there has been a consistent desire to contribute to the material and social well-being of people. Of necessity the methods of doing so have varied according to their historical contexts. But the missionary movement has always been motivated by the conviction that such activities are an essential aspect of the Christian faith.

Paul E. Pierson

*See also* Environment; Medicine; Mission Methods and Strategy; Missionary Vocation and Service

### Further Reading

Beaver, R. P. (1980). *American Protestant women in world mission*. Grand Rapids, MI: Eerdmans Press.

Elliston, E. J. (Ed.). (1989). *Christian relief and development*. Nashville, TN: W. Publishing Group.

Myers, B. (1999). *Walking with the poor: Principals and practices of transformational development*. Maryknoll, NY: Orbis Books.

Peterson, D. (1997). *Not by might nor by power*. Carlisle, UK: Send the Light.

Pierson, P. E. (2004). *Transformation from the periphery: Emerging streams of church and mission*. Pattaya, Thailand: Lausanna Committee for World Evangelization.

# Dialogue

The word *dialogue* has its roots in the Greek word *dialogestai* ("to converse"), which in turn is derived from the preposition *dia* ("across") and the verb *legein* ("to speak"). In its original sense the word is epitomized in the so-called *Dialogues of Plato* (c. 428–348 BCE), in which Socrates held conversations designed to probe deeply into such things as the nature of the soul, good government, and virtue. In recent times, the term has been used in theological language to designate various kinds of conversations that take place between Christians in various denominations or branches of the church ("ecumenical dialogue") and followers of various religious traditions; for example, between Buddhists and Christians ("interfaith dialogue"). While "conversation" is its synonym, dialogue connotes a serious, formal conversation, structured to clarify difficult and disputed matters.

## Roots of Ecumenical Dialogue in the Modern Period

The need for ecumenical dialogue was first recognized in the late nineteenth century, as rivalries, competition, and disagreements in missionary situations were seen as a strong counterwitness to the Gospel. In fact, the "ecumenical movement" that led to the formation of the World Council of Churches in 1948 to promote Christian unity can be traced to the World Missionary Conference held in Edinburgh in 1910. Roman Catholicism did not enter into bilateral or multilateral dialogues until after the Second Vatican Council (1965).

Ecumenical dialogues today move forward on bilateral tracks between such groups as Roman Catholics and Anglicans and Lutherans and Presbyterians, producing important milestones in understandings on areas such as Marian doctrines and ministry. They proceed also on multilateral tracks under WCC Faith and Order auspices that have produced such important milestones as the Lima document *Baptism, Eucharist, and Ministry.*

## Roots of Interfaith Dialogue

Understanding of non-Christian religions on their own terms made great strides in the West, generally in university environments, where fields such as history of religion and comparative religion began in the nineteenth century. Followers of other religious ways, such as African traditional religions, Islam, and Daoism, had been learning about Christianity but mainly in missionary-contact situations in which Christians sought to convert them. Serious studies of world religions achieved critical mass in the mid-twentieth century, though mainly in the West. Followers of other traditions continued to feel they were placed in a one-down situation because the methods and languages used in such studies followed Western models.

Interfaith dialogue—understood as conversations among representatives of the world religions treating each other as equals—did not become common or officially recognized as legitimate until the meeting of the World Council of Churches in Delhi in 1961 for Protestants and at Vatican Council II in 1965 for Catholics. Acknowledgement by Christians that interfaith dialogue was necessary, in other words, occurred as the West withdrew from colonial possessions and revivals of Asian religions made it clear not only that Christian mission had not made substantial numbers of converts among followers of faiths such as Islam, Buddhism, and Indian religions but also that it was likely not to in the foreseeable future. Thus for many leaders of such traditions suspicions arose that dialogue was a code word for surreptitious proselytizing.

Among Christians who became active in dialogue, basic questions were frequently raised about the validity of doctrines expressed in scriptural phrases (such as Acts 4:12) that indicated there was no salvation aside from faith in Christ. Hearing such questions expressed by its advocates, interfaith dialogue became highly suspect among traditionalist-minded Christians. Intra-Christian debates became and remain contentious, and attitudes among those favoring interreligious dialogue fall roughly along lines demarcated by persons identified as progressives on the one hand and with the Evangelical movement on the other. The term "interreligious interchange" began being used increasingly in the early 1990s by those seeking to outflank ideological barriers that have grown up around the word "dialogue."

## Basic Approaches to Interfaith Dialogue

The origins of interfaith dialogue can be found, as the previous section indicates, in two different social locations. From the one side came persons convinced by comparative and historical studies that the world's religions stand in rough parity and that dialogue is necessary to articulate both their distinctive and common features and teachings. That goal would be framed as one of overcoming exclusivist claims that are often accused of causing war and prejudice. This form of dialogue tended to be initiated by Christian academics who had unearthed many points of contact between traditions and also tended to find favor among Westerners who sought out interlocutors among fellow academics, chiefly in Asia. Such dialogues have produced many interfaith friendships, study groups, and jointly edited journals that have introduced the tenets of the various traditions to people in other religions. In the distinction noted by Mircea Eliade and Joseph Kitagawa, however, such perspectives are "outsider" views that aim to help nonbelievers attain what are taken to be "objective" understandings of the religious "other."

Starting from the perspective of faith, another large cadre of scholars and religious leaders—usually persons well informed by historical and comparative studies—concluded that such outsider studies were not faithful to what religion looked like from the "inside." Insider perspectives, they believed, were the only ones that could articulate adequately the religious experience and worldview of a given tradition and lead to dialogue as conversation among equals. When insider perspectives were brought into conversation, claims of common denominators, it was alleged, were often exaggerated, when the reality is that world religions embody deep and apparently incompatible worldviews, revelations, and perhaps even experiences.

### Five Kinds of Dialogue

Within the WCC, interreligious dialogue came under the purview of a Sub-unit on Dialogue with People of Living Faiths and Ideologies in 1971, and in 1979 at Chiang Mai (Thailand) the WCC formulated its *Guidelines for Dialogue.* In 1984 the Roman Catholic Church's Secretariat for Non-Christians, in its *Reflections and Orientations on Dialogue and Mission,* stated that sincere and patient dialogue was essential for followers of Christ in the contemporary era. It also suggested that there are at least five different kinds of dialogue, each important for the mission of the church and interreligious understanding: (1) the *dialogue* of *life*, which is a manner of living that exemplifies attitudes and conduct and that radiates concern and respect for followers of other traditions; (2) the *dialogue* in *daily life*, which enjoins Christians to bring the Gospel wherever they live; (3) the *dialogue of works* that leads to deeds of collaboration to alleviate suffering and create a more humane world; (4) the *dialogue of experts* that is carried on among partners well versed in their respective traditions' teaching and doctrine; and (5) the *dialogue of religious experience*, in which persons "rooted in their own religious traditions can share their experiences of prayer, contemplation, faith... as well as their expressions and ways of searching for the Absolute" (Gioia, 1997).

## The Ambiguity of Dialogue and the Way Forward

While the concept of dialogue appears at first blush to be unambiguously positive, in reality it is not, for both historical and practical reasons. *Historically*, calls for dialogue arose among Christians. Such calls can appear to Buddhists, Daoists, Muslims, Confucianists, and followers of the many Indian religious traditions as little more than attempts by Christians to gain by stealth what they could not accomplish by overt means in the sixteenth- through the twentieth-century colonial era.

Among followers of "local" (sometimes called "primal") religious traditions, there is sometimes expressed a feeling of suspicion that now the Western Christians who destroyed "our way of life" are engaged in paternalistic attempts to learn its secrets. And among local Christians, especially in Asia where they live in minority situations, it seems strange to see Westerners wanting to dialogue with, for example, Hindus or Muslims, whose relegation of Christians to second-class status is felt as oppressive. Such "dialogues," they fear, run the risk of upsetting patterns of interaction developed over generations by people who do not have to live with the consequences.

In addition, the "scientific" methods used by theologians who advocate formal dialogue are often viewed as relativistic and potentially corrupting both by conservative Christians and by teachers and the leaders in other traditions with whom they seek to dialogue. *Practically*, it is alleged, dialogue is carried on according to Western rules and according to systems of logic and standards of evidence that disadvantage believers and undermine tradition. The Buddhist or Hindu teacher or the Muslim imam who enters into such conversations can often find himself distrusted by his coreligionists.

Given the ambiguities that attach to interfaith dialogue, it has become increasingly common to suggest that conversations that promote practical cooperation in important areas on an interfaith basis may be more apropos. This approach is frequently termed "intercultural dialogue" and may produce practical norms for understanding how and why gender roles and sexual ethics function as they do in various cultures. From such forms of interreligious interchange, it is hoped that better understanding and practical action can alleviate suffering, stop the importation of culturally inappropriate entertainment, or improve cooperation in such areas as overcoming environmental pollution, promoting more just economic systems, and providing better healthcare and nutrition. It is clear to those who engage in such intercultural dialogues that—as difficult as conversations among religions, cultures, and civilizations are—globalization makes them necessary in the twenty-first century.

WILLIAM R. BURROWS

## Further Readings

Brück, M. von, & Lai, W. (2001). *Christianity and Buddhism: A multicultural history of their dialogue.* Maryknoll, NY: Orbis Books.

Burrows, W. R. (Ed.). (1993). *Reading* Redemptoris missio *and* Dialogue and proclamation. Maryknoll, NY: Orbis Books.

Fitzgerald, M. L., & Borelli, J. (2006). *Interfaith dialogue: A Catholic view.* Maryknoll, NY: Orbis Books.

Gioia, F. (Ed.). (1997). *Interreligious dialogue: The official teachings of the Catholic Church (1963–1995).* Boston: Pauline Books and Media.

Kitagawa, J. W. (1990). *The quest for human unity: A religious history.* Minneapolis, MN: Fortress.

Lossky, N. et al. (Eds.). (1991). *Dictionary of the ecumenical movement.* Geneva, Switzerland: WCC Publications; Grand Rapids, MI: Eerdmans.

Muslim-Christian Research Group. (1989). *The challenge of the Scriptures: The Bible and the Qur'an.* Maryknoll, NY: Orbis Books.

World Council of Churches. (1979). *Guidelines on dialogue with people of living faiths and ideologies.* Geneva, Switzerland: WCC Publications.

E

## Economics

Missionaries have always had to deal with economic issues whether they wanted to or not—partly because they needed to finance their religious and humanitarian projects, partly out of concern for the economic condition of the people they served, and partly to induce local rulers to allow missionary access and local people to voluntarily expose themselves to missionary teaching.

### Creative Financing

Out of necessity, missionaries and their organizations found ways to finance their overseas operations. Some of these methods were successful, a few were not, and most had some negative aspects that made them problematic.

#### Financing with Trade

One approach missionaries used to finance themselves was business or trade. For example, early Catholic missionaries transported goods on Spanish galleons and set up agricultural communities. An early Protestant missionary to India, William Carey, worked as an indigo planter and later as a language professor for the British East India Company. Two early Protestant missionaries to China, Robert Morrison and Karl Gützlaff, worked as translators, sometimes for companies involved in the opium trade. However, to avoid conflicts of interest and negative associations, mission boards increasingly banned missionaries from involvement in business (although in the late twentieth century there was a revival

of "tentmaking" to enable missionaries to enter "creative access countries").

#### Financing through State or Company

A second approach missionaries used was state or company financing. Most Catholic colonizers (Spain, Portugal, France, Italy) negotiated or forced agreements with the pope that allowed them to appoint or approve missionaries in exchange for paying missionary salaries and restricting Protestant access. The Dutch East India Company also chose and paid the salaries of missionaries (in this case mostly Protestant) and initially restricted Catholics. This approach meant that missionaries were vulnerable to manipulation by the state or company.

#### Development of Organizations

A third approach missionaries used to fund their operations was to develop organizations to collect finances and transfer money to the missionaries in the field. Although this has become the dominant pattern, it was not always possible. This approach left missionaries more free to follow their own interests and to critique colonial abuses.

### Concern for Those Served

Missionaries were also concerned about the economic condition of the people they served. Most of the major Protestant missionary conferences gave attention to economic issues, and some published books exclusively on the topic; for example, the Jerusalem meeting of the

International Missionary Council in 1926 published *The Christian Mission in Relation to Industrial Problems.*

Interestingly, all extant statistical research suggests that missionary work actually did have long-lasting positive economic effects (unfortunately, most of it was unpublished when this article went to press). Woodberry (2004) demonstrates that countries and regions with more Protestant missionaries per capita and longer exposures to Protestant missions currently have more education and more "economically friendly" institutions. Research by William Roberts Clark, John A. Doces, and Robert D. Woodberry use the same data to show that countries with more exposure to Protestant missions currently have higher GDPs. James Feyrer and Bruce Sacerdote confirm this in an analysis of most island countries around the world, as do Ying Fang and Yang Zhou in an analysis of Chinese cities. These results are large and robust to a substantial array of statistical controls and quasi-experiments—including attempts to measure colonial mortality rates and to repeat analyses in areas with similar disease climates and precolonial conditions.

## Use of Education to Boost the Economy

One way missionaries influenced the economy was through education. A large branch of economic literature suggests that education transmits skills to people (called "human capital") that fosters later economic growth. Yet different countries end up with vastly different amounts of education and quality of educational institutions. Some of this variation is a result of the historic prevalence of missionaries, particularly Protestant missionaries. Protestants wanted people to read the Bible in their own language, so they began schools and printed texts almost immediately after entering each new linguistic area. Catholic missionaries and other religious groups also invested in mass education, but especially when competing with Protestants.

Colonial officials and white settlers typically resisted mass education of nonwhites. They wanted a small, educated elite that they could control. Even in countries that were not formally colonized, missionaries were early advocates and providers of formal education; for example, in China, Japan, Thailand, Persia, the Ottoman Empire, and Ethiopia.

Missionary education fostered later educational expansion by (1) demonstrating the economic benefit of Western education, (2) spurring reaction among non-Christians who pressured governments and non-Christian religious groups to expand education so their children would not be exposed to proselytism, and (3) providing books and trained teachers that allowed others to expand nonmissionary educational systems.

Thus, areas that had earlier and broader exposure to Protestant missionary activity continue to have higher levels of education. This is true both between countries and between provinces of every country this author has analyzed (i.e., India, Nigeria, and Kenya). This is also reflected at the individual level. In India, Christian converts came primarily from the lower castes and from tribal peoples (most of whom had no written language prior to missionary contact). Yet throughout the twentieth century Indian censuses suggest that Christians had higher literacy rates than Hindus, Muslims, Buddhists, or "tribals." In Taiwan also, Protestants are disproportionately educated and have higher educational expectations for their children. Thus, this educational emphasis seems to have had long-term influence.

## Protecting Land Rights

A second way missionaries influenced the economy was by protecting indigenous land rights and fighting for the rule of law in European colonies. Missionaries were not as activist as many contemporary scholars would wish, but prior to the twentieth century, protests on behalf of indigenous land rights and for legal protection of nonwhites came almost exclusively from missionaries. Early Catholic examples are Bartolome de Las Casas and the Jesuits in Paraguay. Protestant examples include James Philip and John McKenzie's attempts to protect indigenous land in South Africa and Botswana; Evan and John B. Jones's attempts to protect Cherokee land in the Carolinas and Georgia; various missionaries helping aborigines in Australia; CMS missionaries and the Maori in New Zealand; James Long and the movement to protect landless peasants from exploitation in India—to name just a few (Woodberry 2004, Etherington 2005).

## Abolition of Slavery

Nonconformist missionaries were also important in trying to protect slaves from arbitrary punishment in the British Caribbean and eventually in spurring the movement for the immediate abolition of slavery (Woodberry 2006). Thomas Fowell Buxton (vice president of the Church Missionary Society) led the campaign for immediate abolition in British colonies and after abolition commissioned a survey of missionaries in an attempt to reform British colonial policy. The committee he formed to evaluate British colonialism eventually evolved into the Aborigines Protection Society.

# Extract from David Livingstone's Cambridge Speech of 1857

**David Livingstone (1813–1873) was a Scottish missionary and explorer of Africa. Between 1840 and 1873, Livingstone covered nearly a third of Africa, spreading Christianity, opposing the slave trade, recording the geography and customs of African peoples, and opening up Africa to commerce.**

My object in going into the country south of the desert was to instruct the natives in a knowledge of Christianity, but many circumstances prevented my living amongst them more than seven years, amongst which were considerations arising out of the slave system carried on by the Dutch Boers. I resolved to go into the country beyond, and soon found that, for the purposes of commerce, it was necessary to have a path to the sea. I might have gone on instructing the natives in religion, but as civilization and Christianity must go on together, I was obliged to find a path to the sea, in order that I should not sink to the level of the natives. The chief was overjoyed at the suggestion, and furnished me with twenty-seven men, and canoes, and provisions, and presents for the tribes through whose country we had to pass.

In a commercial point of view communication with this country is desirable. Angola is wonderfully fertile, producing every kind of tropical plant in rank luxuriance. Passing on to the valley of Quango, the stalk of the grass was as thick as a quill, and towered above my head, although I was mounted on my ox; cotton is produced in great abundance, though merely woven into common cloth; bananas and pine-apples grow in great luxuriance; but the people having no maritime communication, these advantages are almost lost. The country on the other side is not quite so fertile, but in addition to indigo, cotton, and sugarcane, produces a fibrous substance, which I am assured is stronger than flax.

The Zambesi has not been thought much of as a river by Europeans, not appearing very large at its mouth; but on going up it for about seventy miles, it is enormous. The first three hundred miles might be navigated without obstacle: then there is a rapid, and near it a coal-field of large extent. The elevated sides of the basin, which form the most important feature of the country, are far different in climate to the country nearer the sea, or even the centre. Here the grass is short, and the Angola goat, which could not live in the centre, had been seen on the east highland by Mr Moffat.

My desire is to open a path to this district, that civilization, commerce, and Christianity might find their way there. I consider that we made a great mistake, when we carried commerce into India, in being ashamed of our Christianity; as a matter of common sense and good policy, it is always best to appear in one's true character. In travelling through Africa, I might have imitated certain Portuguese, and have passed for a chief; but I never attempted anything of the sort, although endeavouring always to keep to the lessons of cleanliness rigidly instilled by my mother long ago; the consequence was that the natives respected me for that quality, though remaining dirty themselves.

Source: Livingstone, D. (1857). Cambridge speech of 1857. Retrieved July 12, 2007, from http:/www.cooper.edu/humanities/core/hss3/d_livingstone.htmlwww.cooper.edu/humanities/core/hss3/d_livingstone.html

## Effect of Reporting of Abuses

Missionaries also appealed to Evangelicals in the colonial office, such as James Stephen and Lord Glenelg, to report abuses by white-settler-controlled legislatures, courts, and police systems. At times the colonial office removed magistrates and even governors who distorted British law in favor of white-settler interests and who had been reported by missionaries (Woodberry 2006).

Although the legal system was far from perfect in British colonies, these checks helped restrict abuses of power by white settlers in ways they were not restricted in other colonies and initiated a pattern that influenced postcolonial legal systems. Cross-national statistical research suggests that the legal system in former British colonies has functioned more effectively than that in non-British former colonies. It seems plausible that nonstate missionaries helped develop these patterns.

A major branch of economics argues that economic-friendly institutions—particularly protection of property rights and relatively impartial application of law—are important factors in long-term economic growth. Statistical research suggests that societies that had greater exposure to nonstate Protestant missionaries do better on both of these outcomes, and the missionary variable removes the impact of dominant predictors economists use (British colonization and settler mortality rates).

## Role of Competition

A third way missionaries influenced the economy was by fostering economic competition. During the nineteenth century, Anglo-Protestant Nonconformists allied themselves with "free-market" economists (called "political economists" at the time). A coalition of missionary supporters and political economists blocked the British East India Company's charter in 1813 and again in 1833, forcing the BEIC to allow both missionaries and noncompany traders to enter their territory. Over time the coalition between free-market economists and free-market religionists has declined, but it had important influences on British colonialism (Levy and Peart 2003).

In Africa many missionaries hoped that "Christianity and commerce" would give African rulers new values and income sources and thus undermine the slave trade. Nonconformist missionaries were also consistent opponents of forced labor: slavery, abuses of the apprentice system for former slaves, "blackbirding" in the Pacific, the violent abuses of the rubber companies in the Belgian Congo, and the continued practice of slavery in Portuguese cocoa plantations. It is unlikely the movements would have gained widespread popular support without their inside information and advocacy (Woodberry 2004; Grant 2005; Etherington 2005).

## Agricultural Innovations

A fourth way missionaries influenced the economy was by introducing new crops, products, and expertise. For example, missionaries were the first to bring cocoa to Ghana and apples, pears, and dairy cattle to China. They introduced experimental garden plots in countries from India to South Africa and academic agricultural

training in countries like China. They also created "industrial schools" to train people in practical skills such as carpentry, masonry, and embroidery. In some places, such as South Africa, they even introduced currency to train people how to function in a market economy.

## Providing Resources

Of course, missionaries were not entirely motivated by humanitarian goals. Without the power to coerce, nonstate religious groups must often provide resources to convince rulers to allow them to enter a particular territory and to convince people to expose themselves (or their children) to the missionaries' messages. Education and medical care are resources missionaries could offer. In addition, once one religious group provided particular services, other groups felt pressure to imitate for fear of losing converts.

However, schools and hospitals are expensive, and missionaries usually did not provide substantially higher resources than necessary to gain access to elites. Asian societies already had formal education systems and text-based medical systems. Thus, missionaries disproportionately created universities, hospitals, and medical schools in Asia. In the preliterate societies of Africa and Oceania, missionaries focused primarily on elementary schools and clinics; hospitals and universities were not necessary to entice the elite. It was not until the mid-twentieth century that missionaries began transferring more expensive medical and educational institutions to Africa.

Moreover, not everything missionaries did increased the lifespans and livelihoods of indigenous peoples. Often missionaries congregated formerly nomadic peoples into settled agricultural communities. Increased contact with Europeans and dense living situations often contributed to the spread of disease and decimated local populations, particularly in the Americas. However, in areas where white settlers encountered indigenous people prior to nonstate missionary contact, indigenous people typically faired far worse. Overall, statistical evidence suggests that where missionaries were more prevalent and more independent from state control, colonialism had less deleterious effects, and postcolonial societies have been more prosperous.

ROBERT D. WOODBERRY

## Further Reading

Etherington, N. (2005). *Missions and empire.* New York: Oxford University Press.

Grant, K. (2005). *A civilised savagery: Britain and the new slaveries in Africa, 1884–1926.* New York: Routledge.

International Missionary Council. (1928). *The Christian mission in relations to industrial problems.* New York: International Missionary Council.

Levy, D. M., and Peart, S. J. (2003). Who are the canters? The coalition of evangelical-economic egalitarians. *History of Political Economy*, 35(4), 731–757.

Woodberry, R. D. (2004). *The shadow of empire: Christian missions, colonial policy, and democracy in post-colonial societies.* Unpublished doctoral dissertation. University of North Carolina–Chapel Hill.

Woodberry, R. D. (2006). Reclaiming the M-word: The consequences of missions for nonwestern societies. *The Review of Faith and International Affairs*, 4(1), 3–12.

# Ecumenism

The word *ecumenism* derives from the Greek, οἰκουμένη (*oikoumene*), which itself derives from two words, οικος (house, household or family) and μένη (one). It has three common usages in New Testament and early Christian literature. It can mean "the world" in the sense of the inhabited earth (Psalm 24:1 [REB]) or "all the inhabitants of the earth;" that is, the whole of humankind (Acts 17:31) or "the whole Roman Empire" (Acts 24:5).

This article will focus on the twentieth century and will trace the origins of the modern ecumenical movement within the missionary enterprise, the development in the ecumenical understanding of missions and mission during the century, and the key themes that have emerged in the ecumenical debates about mission, especially through the International Missionary Council (IMC) and the World Council of Churches (WCC). It will also examine some of the key issues of convergence and challenge that face Christians in relation to mission at the beginning of the twenty-first century.

## The Beginnings

Two main streams of influence brought the modern ecumenical movement into being at the beginning of the twentieth century. The first included the Young Men's Christian Association (YMCA), the Young Women's Christian Association (YWCA), and the Student Christian Movements (SCM), with the latter meeting together in the World Student Christian Federation (WSCF). From the beginning these organizations felt a strong impetus toward closer relationships and deeper unity with one another and among their churches.

### Edinburgh 1910

The second stream began at the World Missionary Conference in Edinburgh in 1910. This conference brought together representatives of a broad range of Protestant missionary societies based largely in Europe, North America, South Africa, and Australia that sent missionaries to "young" churches in what came to be called the Third World. There were no official representatives from churches as such and no Orthodox or Roman Catholic representatives, and only seventeen of the fourteen hundred delegates came from Third World countries. But their voices were nevertheless heard. Of particular significance was a call from V. S. Azariah from India to rethink the relationships between the missionary societies and local Christians and leaders: "Give us friends. The favourite phrases, 'our money, our control' must go … We shall learn to walk only by walking—perchance only by falling and learning from our mistakes, but never by being kept in leading strings until we arrive at maturity" (Koshy 2004, 17).

The missionary task was at the heart of this conference, and its emerging thrust was "the evangelization of the world in this generation" (Potter 1991) and how to bring the Gospel of Jesus Christ to the unreached peoples of the world, a theme taken up with renewed vigour by the Lausanne Covenant churches in 1974.

The formative insight of the conference as far as the ecumenical movement is concerned was that its evangelistic and missionary goal could only be achieved if churches and missionary societies worked in greater partnership with one another. As a result, an International Continuation Committee was appointed, in the words of John Mott, the conference chairman, to look "steadily at the world as a whole, confronting the world as a unity by the Christian church as a unity" (Potter 1991, 690). As a consequence of this insight and decision, Edinburgh 1910 is generally seen, despite the limited nature of its representation, as the beginning of the modern ecumenical movement.

### Three Key Streams

The origins of three key streams of the modern ecumenical movement may be traced back to Edinburgh 1910. The Faith and Order movement that developed largely under the influence of Bishop Charles Brent (1862–1929) engages primarily in ecumenical studies of the faith, tradition, and nature of the church, its ministry, its

# A First-Hand Account of the World Missionary Conference in Edinburgh 1910

**The following extract of text is from a longer account by Charles Clayton Morrison, the editor of the *Christian Century*.**

### Edinburgh, June 20, 1910

"About the biggest thing that ever struck Scotland," said my Edinburgh host as we sat together in his drawing room talking over the conference which had brought me to his city, and on account of which a thousand Edinburgh homes have been thrown open to entertain delegates from all parts of the earth.

[…]

It is a great assemblage of the church's greatest men. But all are on the same level. Germans, French, Americans, Englishmen, Scandinavians, Japanese, Chinese, Hindus, Africans—all are here and mingle together in an easy equality. Missionaries, preachers, teachers, editors, statesmen, business men—all come into the hall and sit where they happen to find a place, with no scale of precedence arranged for. It is an unparalleled confluence of the big men of the kingdom of God.

The most admirable feature of the conference is the thoroughness of the preparation that has been made by its leaders. A vast deal of thinking was done before the delegates assembled. You will note that many of the members hold in their hands a rather unwieldy document as the president rises to announce the work of the day. That document is the proof sheet report of a commission of experts who have been at work for two years gathering materials on the problem which is to be the subject of discussion today.

There are eight of these commissions. To each of them the conference devotes one day, taking as the basis for its discussions the report prepared by the commission, the proof sheets of which were put into the hands of some of the delegates some time before they left their homes for Edinburgh. Note the subjects with which the commissions deal: "Carrying the Gospel to All the Non-Christian World"; "The Church in the Mission Field"; "Education in Religion to the Christianization of National Life"; "The Missionary Message in Relation to Non-Christian Religions"; "The Preparation of Missionaries"; "The Home Base of Missions"; "Missions and Governments"; "Co-operation and the Promotion of Unity."

Source: *Christian Century* (1910, July 7). Retrieved July 12, 2007, from http:/www.christiancentury.org

---

sacraments, and its unity. It held its first World Conference in Lausanne, Switzerland, in 1927.

The Life and Work movement owed a great deal to the leadership of Archbishop Nathan Söderblom (1866–1931) of the Lutheran Church of Sweden. Söderblom's concern was to bring Christian influences to bear on the international social, political, and economic issues of the postwar period. The first Universal Conference of Life and Work was convened in Stockholm in 1925.

## The International Missionary Council

But for the purposes of this article, the most significant consequence was the recognition of the need for greater collaboration and joint reflection on God's mission and the missionary enterprise. The First World War (1914–1918) intervened in this follow-up process. It was in 1921 that the International Missionary Council was formed: "it united Protestant national missionary councils and councils of churches in Africa, Asia and Latin America in a federation with Protestant councils of missionary agencies in Europe and North America" (Stransky 1991, 527).

### Effects of World Events

The Council met in a series of world conferences over the next forty years. The emerging themes of these conferences map out the developing ecumenical perspectives on mission, missions, and the missionary enterprise during that time. The Jerusalem conference in 1928 was deeply influenced by the way in which the world war had challenged the ideal of Western civilization and its perceived roots in the Christian Gospel. Similarly, the Communist revolution had shattered the idealistic dreams of world evangelization that were the driving force of Edinburgh 1910. Mission had to be rethought and redefined, not least in the context of a growing awareness of other world religions.

The Tambaram (India) conference in 1938 was shaped by the threat of Fascism and the need for the church (particularly the local churches), rather than the missionary societies, to be at the heart of mission. Representatives from younger churches, in a small minority at Edinburgh, were now in the majority.

### A New Language

"Partnership in Obedience" became the slogan of the first IMC conference to be convened after World War II in Whitby (Canada) in 1947. The language referring to "Christian" and "non-Christian" countries was abandoned, and a new language of collaborative relationships in mission began to emerge.

It was at the next conference in Willingen (Germany) in 1952 that the key concept of the *missio dei* (the mission of God) began to emerge. The Christian mission was not ours but God's. This new approach to ecumenical mission theology meant that the church was no longer the main focus of mission, but rather the church was part of God's universal mission in the world. The task of the church was to engage in those activities demanded of it in obedience to God's mission.

## The World Council of Churches

At this point, our account needs to be interrupted. Following an invitation from the Church of Constantinople (the Orthodox Ecumenical Patriarchate) in 1920, discussions began toward a worldwide "league of churches," supported by J. H. Oldham (1874–1969, secretary to Edinburgh 1910) and Söderblom. In July 1937 representatives of Life and Work and Faith and Order met in London and agreed to set up a representative world assembly of churches. Both conferences (in Oxford and Edinburgh respectively) agreed to the proposal, and a provisional committee of "the World Council of Churches in process of formation" was subsequently appointed, with William Temple (1881–1944, Church of England archbishop of York and subsequently of Canterbury) as chairman, and W. A. Visser t'Hooft (1900–1985, of the Netherlands) as general secretary. The first assembly met in August 1948 in Amsterdam, when the WCC was duly constituted and established, with Faith and Order and Life and Work integrated within it. At this first Assembly, a crucial call for an integrated understanding of the Gospel imperative came from G. T. K. Wu of China: "What is needed is the *whole* Christ and the *whole* Gospel for the *total* need of the *total* world" (Koshy 2004, 31).

However, at this stage the IMC did not become integrated with the WCC, partly because of the reluctance of some of the missionary societies that constituted the IMC to come under the control of the churches and denominations and partly because of a fear that the younger churches, which were playing an increasingly significant role in the IMC, would be in danger of being dominated by the churches of Europe and North America.

### Toward Integration

At its meeting in Accra, Ghana, in 1958, however, the IMC agreed to unite with the WCC, with which it now shared a number of programs. The final step was taken at the third assembly of the WCC in New Delhi in 1961, and the IMC became the Division on World Mission and Evangelism of the WCC. This symbolized a new integrated understanding of church and mission and a commitment to practice the "partnership in obedience" that had become the missiological paradigm within the IMC.

The world mission conferences that had been formative events in shaping the understanding of mission and missionary relationships would continue. But from now on they would become more fully ecumenical, since they would draw together Protestant and Orthodox churches that were in the membership of the WCC. After the Second Vatican Council (1962–1965) with its emphasis, among other matters, on a renewed understanding of unity and the church's witness, there would also be Roman Catholic involvement in these conferences (though not full membership until 2005).

## The Outworking of Integration

The first conference after integration was held in Mexico City in 1963. Its notable theme was "Mission in Six Continents." No longer was mission to be understood as "the North" sending to "the South." Mission encompassed every continent and nation. A holistic approach to mission was developed at the world mission conference in Bangkok in 1973, under the theme "Salvation Today." Salvation could no longer be seen only in individual and personal terms but had to be understood also in socioeconomic, political, and cultural terms. The Bangkok conference will probably be remembered chiefly for the proposal for a moratorium on sending missionaries to the countries of Africa, Asia, and Latin America, in order to reduce the dangers of dominance by the North and to enable the churches in the South to develop their own priorities and resources in Christian witness and mission.

This series of world conferences, from Tambaram (1938) to Bangkok (1973), was formative in reshaping ecumenical mission theology, structures, and relationships. While future conferences did not have the same crucial influences, they did explore key missiological themes. Melbourne (1980) placed particular emphasis on "Good News for the Poor" (a theme that was central to the liberation theology of Latin and Central America) and contributed to an understanding of the key relationship between Christian witness and the justice that was inherent to the kingdom (or rule) of God. San Antonio (1989) brought into greater prominence the relationship between Christian mission and witness and the other world religions. "The consensus found can be summarized in three sentences: We cannot point to any other way of salvation than Jesus Christ; at the same time we cannot put any limit to God's saving power. There is a tension between these affirmations which we acknowledge and cannot resolve" (World Council of Churches 2005).

The relationship between Gospel and culture was the focus of the Salvador da Bahia conference in Brazil in 1996. Cultural and ethnic diversity were to be celebrated as gifts of God, but cultures were also under the judgment of God. The Athens conference in 2005 was the first to be held in a predominantly Orthodox context, and for the first time nonmember churches of the WCC (the Roman Catholic Church and Evangelical and Pentecostal churches) participated as full members of the conference—another sign of changing mission relationships. One of the key themes to emerge from Athens 2005 was "the need for reconciliation between East and West, North and South, and between Christians and people of other faiths" and that "the call to non-violence and reconciliation stands at the heart of the Christian message" (*The Letter from Athens to the Christian Churches*, World Council of Churches 2005).

## Convergence in Mission and Evangelism

In 1974 an International Congress on World Evangelization met in Lausanne, partly in response to concerns among many Evangelical Christian leaders that the ecumenical understanding of mission had lost the evangelical focus on the priority of evangelism. Its theme was "The Unfinished Task of World Evangelization," and its focus was evangelism to those who had not been reached by the Gospel. The *Lausanne Covenant*, which was adopted by the Congress, was an expression of its commitment "to obey Christ's commission to proclaim [the Gospel] to all mankind and to make disciples of all nations" (1974, Introduction). The paragraph on "The Urgency of the Evangelistic Task" stated that 'More than 2,700 million people, which is more than two-thirds of all humanity, have yet to be evangelised. . . . We are convinced that this is the time for churches and para-church agencies . . . to launch new efforts to achieve world evangelization" (para. 9). The *Lausanne Covenant* also recognized the centrality of social responsibility for the Christian churches: "We . . . should share [God's] concern for justice and reconciliation throughout human society and for the liberation of men and women from every kind of oppression. . . . Although reconciliation with other people is not reconciliation with God, nor is social action evangelism, nor is political liberation salvation, nevertheless we affirm that evangelism and socio-political involvement are both part of our Christian duty" (para. 5).

The WCC had also been reflecting—not least at the Melbourne world conference in 1980—on the nature of evangelism. In 1982 the WCC Central Committee adopted "Mission and Evangelism: An Ecumenical Affirmation." Its emphasis was on the holistic nature of Christian mission: "Liberation, development, humanization and explicit evangelism are all integral parts of mission" (Castro 2002, 448). In the words of the Affirmation: "A proclamation that does not hold forth the promises of the justice of the kingdom to the poor on earth is a caricature of the gospel; but Christian participation in the struggles for justice which does not point towards the promises of the kingdom also makes a caricature of a Christian understanding of justice" (1982, para. 34).

In 1974 a special synod of Roman Catholic bishops was convened by Pope Paul VI to consider evangelization in the modern world. Its results were published as a papal encyclical, *Evangelii Nuntiandi*. It affirmed evangelization as "the essential mission of the Church" (Castro 1991, 397) but recognized also that it could not ignore "justice, liberation, development and peace in the world. . . . She even states that her contribution to liberation is incomplete if she neglects to proclaim salvation in Jesus Christ."

A notable ecumenical convergence was emerging in relation to the understanding of salvation, evangelism, and justice in the *Lausanne Covenant,* the WCC *Ecumenical Affirmation* and the papal encyclical.

## Proselytism and Common Witness

During the 1990s one of the most challenging issues had been proselytism, which may be defined, in this context, as evangelism that does not only proclaim the Gospel to the unreached but seeks to draw people away from traditional churches into new Christian fellowships, communities, and churches. This was often as a result of the missionary enterprise of "foreign" missionaries. This issue had been on the WCC's agenda since the New Delhi Assembly in 1961 but was brought into sharpest focus following the enormous political changes in Europe after the collapse of the Soviet Union, especially in predominantly Orthodox countries with a long tradition of Christian faithfulness. One important response to this situation was to encourage "common witness," which envisioned a shared understanding of the Gospel, a growing partnership in mission and evangelism between different Christian traditions, and a recognition that Christian witness and evangelism must be rooted in the life of the local churches.

## Ecumenical Approaches to Other World Religions

The relationship between Christianity and other major world religions was a major ecumenical issue during the twentieth century. In Edinburgh 1910 and during the decades immediately following, the ecumenical emphasis was on the proclamation of the Gospel to the unreached, especially in the non-Christian world. But this had to be done "with sympathy and respect ... [and] in appreciation and love" and in the light of deeper understanding of the theologies of other religions (Selvanayagam 2004, 151).

At the WCC Assembly in Nairobi (1975) there was a controversial call for "a community of communities" of faith. This call revealed a tension between "adherents of Christian uniqueness and religious plurality" (Selvanayagam 2004, 155). There was a fear among some that openness could lead to "a wider inter-religious ecumenism," while others emphasized "the significance of dialogue for the authentic existence and spiritual maturity of the church."

During the years immediately following, "Guidelines for Relations with People of Living Faiths and Ideologies" were developed, which were adopted by the WCC Central Committee in 1979. Dialogue emphasized relationships of mutual commitment and openness and employed the paradigm of "mutual witness" rather than mission and evangelism.

These debates still continue, not least in the context of relationships between the *Lausanne Covenant* churches and the World Council of Churches.

## Challenges in a New Century

The themes that have been explored in this article will continue to challenge the churches of the world. The priority of evangelism and its relationship with proclamation and action toward the justice and liberation of the kingdom, the growing centrality of global ecumenical partnership in mission, the need for structures and relationships of mission that reflect this ecumenical perspective, proselytism and common witness, and the missiological understanding of other faiths have been key issues for ecumenism. The ecumenical movement globally, nationally, and locally, continues to address these issues.

As the ecumenical family faces the future, however, perhaps the greatest challenge to its understanding of mission and evangelism is the dramatic shift in the numerical strength of Christian churches around the globe during the last century. The greatest growth within Christianity is clearly in Africa, Asia, and Latin America, often within Evangelical and Pentecostal churches, whereas those churches in the West and North, that were the sending churches at the beginning of the twentieth century, are often in dramatic decline. This shift will not only have important resource and programmatic implications for the ecumenical family; it will also raise sharp ecumenical challenges to the issues of power, partnership, and common witness that have been explored in this article. The future of global ecumenical relationships in mission, within a religiously plural world, will depend crucially on the churches' responses to these fundamental challenges.

NOEL A. DAVIES

## Further Reading

Castro, E. (1985). *Sent free: Mission and unity in the perspective of the Kingdom.* Geneva, Switzerland: WCC.

Castro, E. (1991). *Evangelism.* In N. Lossky, et al. (Eds.), *Dictionary of the ecumenical movement.* Grand Rapids, MI: Eerdmans.

Castro, E. (2002). *Evangelism.* In N. Lossky, et al. (Eds.), *Dictionary of the ecumenical movement* (2nd ed.). Geneva, Switzerland: WCC.

*Common witness: A study document of the Joint Working Group of the Roman Catholic Church and the World Council of Churches.* (1982). Geneva, Switzerland: WCC.

*Evangelii Nuntiandi,* Encyclical of Paul VI. (1975). Retrieved on May 1, 2006, from http://www.vatican.va/roman_curia/congregations/cevang/pont_soc/pospa/documents/rc_pospa_doc_20011027_home_en.html

Fey, H. E. (Ed.). *A history of the ecumenical movement, 1948–1968.* Geneva, Switzerland: WCC.

Flannery, A. (1983). *Vatican Council II.* Dublin, Ireland: Dominican Publications.

Goosen, G. (2001). *Bringing churches together: A popular introduction to ecumenism.* Geneva, Switzerland: WCC.

*Guidelines of dialogue with people of other faiths and ideologies.* (1979). Geneva, Switzerland: WCC.

*International Review of Mission.* (1912 to date). Geneva, Switzerland: WCC.

Kinnamon, M., & Cope, B. E. (Eds.). (1997). *The ecumenical movement: An anthology of key texts and voices.* Geneva, Switzerland: WCC.

Koshy, N. (2004). *A history of the ecumenical movement in Asia.* Hong Kong SAR, China: WSCF Asia-Pacific, YMCA Asia and Pacific, CCA.

*The Lausanne Covenant.* (1974). Retrieved on May 1, 2006, from http://www.lausanne.org

Limouris, G. (Ed.). (1994). *Orthodox visions of ecumenism: Statements, messages and reports on the ecumenical movement, 1902–1992.* Geneva, Switzerland: WCC.

Mission and evangelism: An ecumenical affirmation. (1982). *International Review of Mission, 71,* 1982, 427–451.

Potter, P. (1991). Mission. In N. Lossky & J. M. Bonino (Eds.), *Dictionary of the ecumenical movement* (p. 690). Geneva, Switzerland: WCC.

Rouse, R., & Neill, S. C. (Eds.). (1986). *A history of the ecumenical movement, 1517–1948.* Geneva, Switzerland: WCC.

Selvanayagam, I. (2004). Interfaith dialogue. In J. Briggs, M. A. Oduyoye, & G. Tsetsis (Eds). *A history of the ecumenical movement, 1968–2000.* (pp. 149ff.) Geneva, Switzerland: WCC.

Stransky, T. (1991). International missionary council. In N. Lossky & J. M. Bonino (Eds.), *Dictionary of the ecumenical movement* (p. 527). Geneva, Switzerland: WCC.

Thorogood, B. (Ed.). *Gales of change: Responding to a changing missionary context: The story of the London Missionary Society, 1945–1977.* Geneva, Switzerland: WCC.

van Elderen, M., & Conway, M. (2001). *Introducing the World Council of Churches.* Geneva, Switzerland: WCC.

World Council of Churches. Retrieved May 6, 2006, from http://www.wcc-coe.org/wcc/what/mission

Yates, T. (1994). *Christian mission in the twentieth century.* Cambridge, UK: Cambridge University Press.

# Education—Religious, Theological

During the nineteenth century missionaries did not go to foreign fields to found schools or foster education. They envisioned preaching the Gospel to heathens on the brink of damnation and bringing them into the Christian fold, and the majority of nineteenth-century missionaries did actually engage in direct evangelism. Yet significant numbers were soon engaged in teaching and in administering schools. Within three months after arrival in Tengchow (Dengzhou), Shandong, China, Julia and Calvin Mateer had organized a boarding school for eight boys in the Buddhist temple where they resided. By the twentieth century more China missionaries were engaged in education and social service work than in evangelism. In those African territories controlled by the British there were 6,000 church schools and only 100 government schools, a small effort for so large a population. Roman Catholic orders also entered the educational field; for example, their Catholic Normal School in Nigeria in the 1920s was graduating over 220 teachers a year for their parochial schools. Of India's 279,309 educational institutions in 1949–1950, 100 thousand were administered by Christian churches. Why did home mission boards devote so much manpower and money to education? What role did the local populace have in this expansion of parochial schools?

## Consequences of Mission Education

Along with these issues is the question of the consequence of the educational work, both for the mission field and for the home supporters. Some have argued that the most important legacy of Christian missions has been secular education and its contribution to modernization of the non-Western world. Others have called the church schools cultural imperialists and have criticized them for alienating their students from their traditional heritage and denationalizing them. It is said that the national leaders they produced tried to impose Western institutions and values ill suited to the society and culture of their country. The schools, with their Western curriculum and structure, contributed to a growing gap between the rural populace and the urban centers, where Western pressures and influences were concentrated.

Then, there is the fact that both empire building and Christian missions in the nineteenth century became a global phenomenon. What were the differences in the roles of the church schools in colonial countries and

## The Delaware Baptist Mission School

**This description of a mission school in the mid-nineteenth century was provided by upstate New York attorney Lewis Henry Morgan, best-known for his ethnographic descriptions of the Iroquois.**

This school, under the supervision of Rev. John G. Pratt, a matron, Mrs. Muse, and a teacher, Miss Morse, is in a very flourishing condition and superior to any I have seen in the territory. It has accommodations for 78 Indian scholars as boarders and lodgers. The number last term was 64, the number the present term is about 50, as they have held back for the payment, and will soon come in now.

The buildings consist of a two and a half story farm house large on the ground, designed for the sleeping and clothing rooms of the school; another of the same size with a wing for a kitchen, designed for the residence of the superintendent and teachers, and is the eating and cooking place for all. Also a large school house with folding doors in the center so as to separate the boys and girls, although they are as yet all together. There are numerous outbuildings, as a farm is carried on in connection with the school of about two hundred acres. The buildings were erected a few years ago with school money belonging to the Delawares, and is supported with funds in the hands of the government reserved for that purpose.

The children are clothed, boarded and taught by the Mission, and the government allows $75 per annum per scholar. They have two terms of five months each, and the children are kept in school about seven hours per day. They study reading, writing, and spelling, geography, arithmetic, with blackboard exercises. The scholars are mostly young, those now at school ranging from 6 to 18 years. They look well and healthy and free from sore eyes, and are decently and comfortably clad. This is the true system of Indian education, beyond a doubt, and this school is by far in the best condition of any I have seen. We see here New England cleanliness, system and good management. I did not visit the Mission School of the Methodist Southern Board among the Shawnees. It is a large and flourishing school, I believe, but complaints are made of the principal of unfairness, of avarice, etc. He has made himself rich and also the Mission, they having secured by treaty between about 2000 acres of land, and at the same time he was active to prevent Friend Harvey from selling his Mission farm of 200 acres, evidently desiring to break up the Friends Mission.

Mr. Pratt commenced his missionary life 22 years ago with his present wife then 20 years of age. He was accepted as a missionary to Burma, but was requested to fill temporarily an Indian mission then vacant among the Stockbridges near Fort Leaven-worth, and went from there to the Shawnee Baptist Mission now closed, and from there to this Mission about 12 years ago. His wife is still young looking [she was forty-five at the time, ed.] and must have been beautiful as a girl. They are very worthy, refined and agreeable, and my short stay with them has been very pleasant indeed. Mr. Pratt is a well educated and superior man.

Source: Morgan, L. H. (1959). *The Indian journals, 1859–62* (pp. 53–54). Ann Arbor: University of Michigan Press.

---

those in autonomous states like China, which was not occupied but whose sovereignty was seriously compromised by unequal treaties? Were there also similarities? Answers to all these questions have altered in recent decades, for the context has shifted dramatically. After World War II, colonial empires disintegrated as nation after nation gained its independence. New educational issues arose in the postindependence mission fields. New mission theories and methodology emerged during the early twentieth century, and later the "faith" missions came to the fore. The explosive growth of African Christianity, the surprising popularity of Christian teachings in the post-Mao era of China, and the rise of fundamentalist Hinduism brought new perspectives.

## Motivation for Founding Schools

The goal of Catholic educators was to provide a Christian setting in which the children of Christian converts could be instructed in church doctrines. They therefore concentrated on catechumen and primary schools during the nineteenth century. Only during the twentieth century did they turn their attention to middle schools and institutions of higher education. Protestant missionaries initially viewed schools as an aid to evangelism. Instead of a shifting audience for the Gospel message, they would work with a continuing group of students insulated from heathen society. Since most nineteenth-century Protestants accepted the Bible as the inerrant Word of God and the ultimate source of all truth, it was essential that all converts should have direct access to the Bible. They should be literate so that they could read the divine message themselves. Western evangelists also quickly realized that conversion of the world was a daunting task for the limited number of foreigners available; they would need local assistants, and these would require training, that is, schools. But why a curriculum that included mathematics, science, Western history, geography, and literature in addition to Biblical studies and instruction in the native language and literature? Partly because the missionaries had great faith in the ability of Western science to corrode superstition. Partly because the missionaries assumed the superiority of Western learning, which for them was the source of Western political and military power, industrial expansion, and cultural achievements, and partly because the curriculum and structure of Western schools represented the norm for them; this was what they had experienced.

Of growing importance was the perception of the local populace that a Western education was the avenue to economic and political mobility. Especially in colonies, facility in the language of the ruling power was an asset. Christian congregations and even non-Christians desired schools of Western learning, and they wanted schools where the language of the ruler was the medium of instruction. They anticipated that their sons would find positions in the colonial establishment, in the foreign commercial companies, in a foreigner's home as servant or tutor, or best of all a chance to study abroad.

## Present and Future

Steadily, church schools grew in number and expanded in academic level. By the twentieth century, parochial institutions ranged all the way from primary and catechumen schools to universities with graduate offerings. Contributing to the expansion of parochial institutions was the British policy of grants in aid to private institutions. Instead of assuming direct responsibility for most education in its colonies, Britain adopted a policy of funding parochial schools that met certain academic standards and content and of leaving the teaching and administration up to the church. Increasing numbers of sisters and single Protestant women volunteered for foreign missions, and since the majority of them concentrated on education and social service, this trend facilitated the expansion of Christian schools. Mission concentration on education was justified by the Social Gospel, which stressed demonstration of Christian love in good works and the Christianization of society more than direct evangelism. Accompanying the growth of foreign missions, therefore, was a burgeoning educational program. Almost without plan, parochial schools became a worldwide phenomenon. In China church schools still educated only a minority of the student population, but as indicated above, a high proportion of the schools in India and Africa were under Christian auspices.

As for the significance of such a massive effort, it must be admitted that schools as instruments of conversion were generally a disappointment to the missionaries. This was especially true of China and India where many youths enrolled with no intention of converting to Christianity but with the vocational goal of learning English and studying Western learning. Schools in Africa claimed a higher rate of conversion, but even there growing numbers perceived the institutions as a means to social and economic mobility. Yet a significant number of graduates did find employment in Christian institutions and serve them well. Schools, hospitals, churches, YMCAs and YWCAs, and other social service agencies depended heavily on mission school graduates for their staff. Church schools introduced professional medical and nursing training and initiated formal education in agriculture, journalism, law, education, and library science. Missionaries founded some of the first schools for women in societies where women were not generally considered worthy or capable of education. Not only did missions take this first step toward the liberation of women, but the church institutions consistently enrolled a higher proportion of women than did the government schools.

In China a high proportion of the intellectual elite who graduated from Christian institutions entered business and industry or the professions; others found government positions in fields specifically requiring Western learning such as diplomacy, transportation and communication, and the customs service. The alumni never dominated the political scene, however, and shortly after the establishment of the People's Republic in 1949, both Christian missions and Christian education were brought to an end. The schools had, nevertheless, formed church leaders, some of whom survived the Anti-Rightist Campaigns and the Cultural Revolution to guide the Christian revival of the post-Mao era. In independent India many church school alumni staffed the bureaucracy and held high political positions. Most were not practicing Christians, and in recent years fundamentalist Hindus in several states have passed laws forbidding Christian evangelism. The practice of government grants in aid has declined but has not been abandoned. Despite some lapses, India is considered a democracy, and its economic growth in recent decades has been impressive. It may not be possible to demonstrate the precise influence of the Christian schools, but many of their alumnae participate in the political and economic life of contemporary India.

Africa, where parochial education was much less accessible, is a different story. Both Islamic and Christian communities have grown dramatically, and the southern half of Africa now accounts for more Christians than the continent of Europe. Much of this expansion has been the work of African, not Western evangelists, and many Christians belong to African sectarian groups. After traumatic and even tragic experiences following independence and the departure of the colonial rulers, a few states such as South Africa have achieved a degree of political and economic stability. Grants in aid to church schools continue to be widespread, and a larger proportion of the school-age population is enrolled in educational institutions. Christian schools are still a source of many economic and political leaders.

Continuing ethnic and political conflict characterizes many of the independent African countries. They have been called "collapsed states" under the rule of competing warlords. Except for copper, precious metals, and, in certain regions, oil, Africa is a poorly endowed continent. Parochial education, which was the major form of schooling, never penetrated deeply enough to lift most of the populace out of illiteracy, poverty, and disease. The political leadership with its Western training has been accused of isolation from the rural masses, while the latter lack the political clout to check the personal ambitions of the warlords. Perhaps only time and the spread of education will eventually bring peace and prosperity.

JESSIE G. LUTZ

## Further Reading

Fowler, S. (1995). *Oppression and liberation of modern Africa. Examining the powers shaping Africa today.* Potchefstroom, South Africa: Potchefstroomse Universiteit.

Gregg, A. (1941). *China and educational autonomy: The changing role of the Protestant missionary in China, 1807–1937.* New York: Syracuse University Press.

Hayhoe, R. (Ed.). (1996). *Education and modernisation: The Chinese experience.* Oxford, UK: Pergamon Press.

Holmes, B. (Ed.). (1963). *Christian education in Africa.* London: Oxford University Press.

Holmes, B. (Ed.). (1967). *Educational policy and the mission schools. Case studies from the British empire.* London: Routledge & Kegan Paul.

Hrangkhuma, F. (Ed.). (1998). *Christianity in India: Search for liberation and identity.* Dehli, India: CMS/ISPCK.

John, B. (2001). *A study on Christian contribution to the nation building.* Dehli, India: ISPCK.

Kimpianga Mahaniah, J. (1981). *Église et education: Histoire de l'Enseignement Protestant au Zaire, 1878–1978.* Kinshasa, Zaire: Centre de Vulgarisation Agricole.

Lutz, J. G. (1988, December). *Christian education in China: a retrospective. Tripod,* 28–48.

Lutz, J. G. (1971). *China and the Christian colleges, 1850–1950.* Ithaca, NY: Cornell University Press.

Perumalil, H. C., & Hambye, E. R. (Eds.). (1972). *Christianity in India. A history in ecumenical perspective.* Alleppey, India: Prakasam Publishers.

# Empire

Because Christian expansion coincided with the spread of European economic and political hegemony, it was initially understood as a consequence of imperialism. But recent revisionist history and anthropology of empire have uncoupled many of the assumed linkages between Christianity and empire. Christian expansion occurred both before and after empire. It also occurred outside and in spite of empire. There was often little attempt to found a state church abroad, and indigenous believers were usually the primary agents of evangelism. As Imperial Historian Andrew Porter observes,

"Religion and empire frequently mingled, but were as likely to undermine each other as they were to provide mutual support" (1999, 245). The British Empire is a preeminent example of how the sheer diversity of mission organizations, divided by denomination, theology, nationality, class, and historical context, meant that relations between church and state were never straightforward. In local hands, Christianity quickly escaped missionary control.

## Missions and Commerce

Missionaries have been accused of being the handmaidens of capitalist imperialism, creating the preconditions for the spread of colonialism and commerce. This was partly because most eighteenth-century British missionaries, who were products of the alliance between evangelical revivalism and the antislavery movement, insisted that good trade was essential for driving out bad trade in slaves. They saw Christianity as intimately linked to legitimate commerce and the introduction of Western ways of life to indigenous societies. They believed that if the Gospel touched people's social condition its abstract message would become more accessible. They thought that missionary planter's fields and carpenter's shops would make Jesus intelligible to man.

But the missionary faith in industrialization subsided when its social effects became apparent. Many of the graduates who joined the Universities Mission to Central Africa (UMCA) at the end of the nineteenth century had worked in Britain's slums, and they went to Africa to save people from industrialization. German

German pastor Louis Harms, with missionaries he recruited and trained for work in South Africa in the 1850s. Harms established churches among indigenous Africans and fought to end the slave trade.

Lutherans, British Anglicans, and Roman Catholics increasingly came to view the city as a place of evil where the church had far less influence than in the countryside. By the 1930s, Leonard Beecher had defined the goal of the Church Missionary Society in Kenya as being to produce "a contented, educated Christian peasant community" (Strayer 1978, 90).

## Missions and Colonialism

Missionaries such as David Livingstone in Central Africa and James Chalmers in the Pacific indirectly opened up vast tracts of territory for exploitation by imperial powers through their travels, publications, and speaking tours. But these missionaries had different objectives from the colonialists with whom they cooperated. They wanted to spread the Gospel and to eliminate abuses such as slavery, witchcraft, the pledging of young girls, and female circumcision. Often missionaries had no option but to choose between colonial powers. John MacKensie of the London Missionary Society (LMS) supported the occupation of Zimbabwe by Cecil Rhodes because he thought it would be preferable to its occupation by the Boers. On a local level, missionaries often cooperated with traders and relied on them for transport and resources. But they could also come to blows with traders and settlers over the liquor trade, gambling, and the treatment of indigenous workers.

The most blatant linkages between missions and imperial protection happened in China where the unequal treaties of 1842 and 1858 allowed missions to operate in certain port cities and to buy land. Foreign missionaries in China, capitalizing on the notion of extraterritoriality, were not subject to Chinese laws. In Colonial Africa some missions benefited from the land grab just like ordinary settlers. In colonies such as South Africa, Southern Rhodesia, and Kenya, there at times appeared little distinction between missionaries and white settlers. Missionaries acted as chaplains and padres to soldiers and school children and were regular guests at settler clubs and dinner tables. In such contexts some of them came to accept the color bar. Here too Anglicans attempted to make themselves into the quasi-establishment church, but the sheer diversity of empire and the plurality of missions thwarted their schemes.

The British government, having long ruled a multicultural and multireligious Empire whose most important territory was Hindu and Muslim India, but which also included Catholic countries such as Malta and Quebec, kept a distance from the Church of England. In India, where Britain ruled with the Hindu-dominated Raj, or Northern Nigeria, where it governed indirectly with the help of Muslim emirs, Protestant evangelism was positively discouraged for fear of antagonizing important allies. Indeed, in India Christianity advanced most where imperial authority was least—on its margins. In the Pacific, mission ran ahead of empire. Missionaries initially worked as guests of indigenous rulers, not as colonial agents, and quickly grasped the importance of training a host of islander evangelists who founded a network of village Christianities in Samoa and New Zealand.

Relations between missionaries and colonial states were most congenial in the context of modernizing projects of education and health care. In a post-Versailles age, epitomized by Frederick John Dealtry Lugard's Dual Mandate (1922) and the Phelps-Stokes Commissions on African education, missionaries provided a crucial legitimating ideology of development to the colonial state, receiving in return much-needed subsidies. But while missionaries dominated British education in Africa, they never had the same access to educational provision in China and India. Even in Africa, mission education could incur the wrath of white settlers who believed that the "trousered black" products of missionary tutelage had been given ideas above their station.

Finally, many missionaries within the British Empire were not British. In Kenya an Italian Consolata Father might be left standing outside a settler back door like an African visitor. In Southern Rhodesia, German Trappists were interned during World War I. Throughout the twentieth century there was a steady increase in the number of American Protestant missionaries whose religious heritage left them with a deep-seated mistrust of the British colonial establishment. Unfettered by a colonial nexus, American and Scandinavian missionaries were at liberty to uphold an international humanitarian tradition. Historians of India are only now beginning to grasp the significance of German Pietist missionary work among tribal people.

## Cultural Imperialism

Missionaries have often been accused of cultural imperialism, but the sheer diversity of the missionary response to indigenous cultures makes this assertion difficult to sustain. There was an enormous difference between the earliest Catholic mission enterprises and those of the first Nonconformist missionaries. The first wave of Catholic missionaries to sixteenth-century Congo happened under the aegis of the Portuguese State. Mission took the form of a single religious enterprise conceived of in terms of territory. Co-opting state machinery in a union of faith and politics, Portuguese Catholics sought to create Christian kingdoms through the conversion of elites. The early nineteenth-century Nonconformist missions were an extension of the culture of voluntary association and private enterprise that underpinned British industrialization. Nonconformists in the LMS in southern Africa were not especially interested in converting kings and aristocrats, but rather in turning ordinary Africans into sober and industrious Christians.

Missionaries also differed over the meaning of conversion. High Church Anglicans from the UMCA, German Lutherans, and Catholics believed that salvation was received through the sacraments and the liturgy, and sought to Christianize entire communities. By contrast, Protestants, influenced by revivalism, placed a greater emphasis on personal salvation, and their emphasis on moral conduct and lifestyle led to a greater separation of converts from their former community. While many missionaries were ethnocentric and culturally arrogant, others did make a sincere and concerted attempt to come to terms with African culture and religion. As early as 1855 Bishop Colenso of Natal wrote a cogent argument for the toleration of polygamy in his *Remarks on the Proper Treatment of Polygamy*. By the twentieth century, a whole spectrum of missionary responses to local settings had emerged. The most common response was to attempt to adapt traditional rituals of initiation—for example, the well-known endeavors of the UMCA Bishop to Tanzania, Vincent Lucas of Masasi, to Christianize the traditional rite of passage.

Indeed, while many missionaries to Africa have been criticized for their cultural imperialism, others have been taken to task for their conservatism. The German missionary and anthropologist Bruno Gutmann believed that the growth of African personality and morality was connected to the essential forms of community life: clan, neighborhood, and age grade. He developed an "indirect rule" approach to mission, highly attractive to the Tanzanian colonial state, which sought to create Christian communities through traditional institutions and leadership. When the radical black American educationalist W. E. B. Du Bois visited West Africa in 1923, he criticized the fashionable emphasis on the preservation of traditional culture. Du Bois thought this missionary conservatism formed part of a white man's plot to maintain the African as a willing and useful servant of the imperial cause.

Perhaps unexpectedly, the twentieth-century Pentecostal movement, which followed earlier Catholic and Nonconformist waves of missionization, has been the most adversarial toward traditional culture and religion. While taking indigenous belief systems seriously, Pentecostalism nevertheless saw them as inherently evil. Traditional spirits, whether good or bad in local cosmological terms, were collapsed into the category of the demonic, and charms and fetishes were destroyed as polluted objects. Nevertheless, Pentecostalism has appealed to Africans seeking to escape the constraints of traditional culture. Pentecostalism's Adventist theology and its emphasis on divine healing and evangelism also brought its missionaries into conflict with colonial states because they spurred modernizing development and concentrated on the work of personal conversion.

## Indigenous Agents

Finally, and most importantly, within empire, indigenous carriers were the primary agents of Christianization, with missionaries in facilitating roles. Few and far between, pioneer missionaries were often responsible for vast tracts of territory; their priority was translation work and then the construction of mission infrastructure. Many simply struggled to survive disease and learn the local language. The work of conversion was left to local agents such as catechists, evangelists, schoolteachers, and *Bible women* (zealous members of church women's associations and fellowships). The shift from mission to church in both Asia and Africa began long before the movements of decolonization.

In remote Asian regions where Hinduism, Buddhism, or Islam had never arrived and among some people in India, Indonesia, and Papua New Guinea, there were Christian movements miles from missionary supervision. The movements began as early as the late eighteenth century but were more numerous in the late nineteenth century. In Africa, the first major conversion movement happened in Buganda in the last fifteen years of the nineteenth century. It spread to the neighboring people of the Great Lakes in the first decades of the twentieth century, culminating in the mass conversion of Rwanda and Buganda in the 1930s.

## Conclusion

Mission was neither an adjunct nor an analogue of empire. It preceded the flag and continued after it. Empire helped create conditions favorable to evangelism by imposing *pax Britanica* and a lingua franca, chiefly through structures of transport and communications, and also by increasing the circulation of labor. Indeed, movements of mass conversion coincided with these great moments of social and economic transformation, but as the Pacific case illustrates, such moments were not contingent upon empire. And empire could also impede evangelism, as in the cases of India and Northern Nigeria. Finally, missionaries were not essential for the work of proselytism, although their absence or decline could speed up rates of conversion. Once the indigenous people of empire grasped the enormous intellectual and instrumental possibilities of the faith through its traditions and scriptures, the southward shift of Christianity began.

DAVID MAXWELL

## Further Reading

Comaroff, J., & Comaroff, J. L. (1991, 1997). *Of revelation and revolution. Christianity, colonialism and consciousness in South Africa* (Vols. 1–2). Chicago: University of Chicago Press.

Etherington, N. (Ed.). (2005). *Oxford history of the British Empire companion series. Missions and empire.* Oxford: Oxford University Press.

Gray, R. (1990). *Black Christians and white missionaries.* New Haven, CT: Yale University Press.

Hastings, A. (1994). *The church in Africa 1450–1950.* Oxford, UK: Clarendon.

Kaplan, S. (Ed.). (1995). *Indigenous responses to Western Christianity.* New York: New York University Press.

Maxwell, D. (1999). *Christians and chiefs in Zimbabwe: A social history of the Hwesa people c. 1870s–1990s.* Edinburgh, UK: Edinburgh University Press.

Maxwell, D. (2006). *African gifts of the spirit. Pentecostalism and the rise of a Zimbabwean transnational religious movement.* Oxford, UK: James Currey.

Porter, A. (1999). Religion, missionary enthusiasm and empire. In A. Porter (Ed.), *Oxford history of the British Empire* (Vol. 3). Oxford, UK: Oxford University Press.

Porter, A. (2004). *Religion versus empire? British Protestant missionaries and overseas expansion, 1700–1914.* Manchester, UK: Manchester University Press.

Ranger, T. (1972). Missionary adaptation of African religious institutions: The Masasi case. In T. Ranger & I. Kimambo (Eds.), *The historical study of African religion.* London: Heinemann.

Robert, D. (2000). *Shifting southward: Global Christianity since 1945. International Bulletin of Missionary Research 24, 2.*

Strayer, R. (1978). *The making of mission communities in East Africa. Anglicans and Africans in colonial Kenya.* London: Heinemann.

Yates, T. (1994). *Christian mission in the twentieth century.* Cambridge, UK: Cambridge University Press.

# Enlightenment, The

The Enlightenment was the dominant intellectual movement in Europe and North America throughout the eighteenth century. It was a major stage of the modern period, or modernity. The Age of Reason of the seventeenth century associated with the rationalist epistemology of René Descartes (1596–1650) established the modern program. Prior to Descartes it was assumed that theology was the starting point for intellectual inquiry. Now Descartes made human reasoning the starting point. Based on the principle of methodological skepticism, Descartes asserted he could arrive at indubitable knowledge by carefully subjecting all possible propositions to doubt. Those that withstood this test then formed a system of organically related true propositions. A generation later in his *Philosophiae Naturalis Principia Mathematica* (1687) Sir Isaac Newton (1642–1727) presented his comprehensive theories of the laws of motion and gravitation that revolutionized physics and cosmology. The universe could now be explained in terms of immutable laws that regulated the entire system.

Because the Enlightenment accepted and built on the main themes and tendencies of the previous era, it is not easy to distinguish between the main features of the Age of Reason in the seventeenth century and the Enlightenment that followed. The Enlightenment is best understood as a further stage in the program of modernity.

## Main Features

The Age of Reason took shape in the period of the Thirty Years War (1618–1648) that had left Europe devastated. Descartes' generation was desperate to find an alternative to what could only be regarded as senseless destruction and irrational behavior. Several characteristics defined the emerging modern period. (1) Modernity is *anthropocentric*. Descartes made the "thinking self" the basis for his epistemology. (2) Modernity is *universalizing*. Reacting to the irrationalism of early seventeenth-century Europe, modern thinkers attempted to find universal principles on which to base society. They rejected the particularities of context in order to free themselves to discover universals. (3) Modernity is *reductionist*. The developing scientific method emphasized that the path to knowledge was to isolate, identify, and analyze the essential component parts of any object. (4) Modernity is *foundationalist*. Descartes held indubitable knowledge to be the foundation of all knowing.

The Enlightenment embraced these characteristics. According to Peter Gay (1966–1969), "In the century of the Enlightenment, educated Europeans awoke to a new sense of life. They experienced an expansive sense of power over nature and themselves." These new perspectives energized Western culture and gave it new direction, promising escape from the turmoil, poverty, and hardships of the past. Now the watchword was *innovation;* the human enterprise was freed from tradition and oriented toward the future. The Enlightenment itself was understood to be as much an open-ended process as a finished state. As the eighteenth century progressed, tension between Enlightenment thinkers and religion grew. Several of the leading Enlightenment philosophers were agnostic toward all religion.

A group of influential European intellectuals shaped the Enlightenment. The French *Encyclopédie* edited by Voltaire and d'Alembert, the first volume of which appeared in 1751, became an important means of disseminating the new knowledge stimulated by the Enlightenment. Although the meaning of *Enlightenment* remained a matter of debate, a cluster of ideas and assumptions defined the intellectual outlook in the eighteenth century and permeated the quest for new knowledge.

With unbounded confidence in the potential of modern rationality, the Enlightenment fostered optimism with regard to the possibility of finding solutions to all the problems confronting humankind. Education was the key to perfecting the human being. Convinced that Enlightenment ideals were universal, the West was obliged to bring their benefits to other peoples. Increasingly, this notion was cast in terms of an evolutionary process. "Civilization" based on Enlightenment ideals contrasted with "uncivilized" people and their traditional folkways. Inculcating civilization became a moral cause.

The concept of the autonomous individual implied inherent rights—enshrined, for example, in the United States Declaration of Independence as "life, liberty and the pursuit of happiness." Enlightenment thinkers grounded these basic rights directly in human dignity, not privileged social status. The Enlightenment seemed to promote a progressive agenda with regard to issues such as slavery. Forms of slavery are found in most cultures throughout history. The Enlightenment espoused an anthropology that required that all humans be treated as rational thinking beings. Yet Enlightenment philosophy lacked a moral center. From the perspective of the emerging eighteenth-century evolutionary perspective, "primitive" peoples had to be helped to advance. But other forces were at work. Under the impact of the growing capitalist economy, the demand for cheap labor on plantations, especially in the Americas, spawned a new form of slavery based on enslaving people, especially from Africa, for this purpose.

## Enlightenment and Christian Missions

Modern Christian missions emerged in an intellectual climate shaped by modern ideals: The possibilities for human development based on rationality were unlimited; modern knowledge was destined to benefit all peoples, and it was an act of benevolence that the strong assist the weak.

The Puritan missions to Native-Americans established in New England after 1640 became the prototype for Protestant missions in the modern period. From the outset it was assumed that the missionary task was twofold: people could only be "Christianized" if they were also "civilized." Thus, the missionary approach had to include a comprehensive program for "civilizing" converts. The only question was the order of priority: Christianization or civilization? This debate continued well into the nineteenth century.

The missionary model pioneered by John Eliot (1604–1690) in Massachusetts—i.e., building "praying towns," complete with church and school for Christian Native-Americans—would be foundational for the modern mission movement. "Civilization" was inseparable from "Christianization." Education was essential both to civilization and Christianization. As Western civilization evolved the model was elaborated to include medical, agricultural, industrial and other missions. After 1840 a third "C" was added. The banner of modern missions was now "Christianity, Civilization, and Commerce." Legitimate commerce would finally drive out the illegitimate slave trade.

WILBERT R. SHENK

### Further reading

Bosch, D. J. (1991). *Transforming mission.* Maryknoll, NY: Orbis Books

Gay, P. (1966–1969). *The Enlightenment: An interpretation* (2 vols.). New York: Alfred A. Knopf.

Outram, D. (1995). *The Enlightenment.* Cambridge, UK: University Press.

Toulmin, S. (1990). *Cosmopolis: The hidden agenda of modernity.* Chicago: University Press.

# Environment

Christian environmentalism is action based on the belief that all humans made in God's image are obligated to care diligently for God's created world. For Christians this stewardship is undertaken out of obedience to God and love for their neighbor, and ultimately as an act of devotion to the Creator. Though the Bible overflows with both praise of God's creation and instructions on its care by His people, Christian involvement with environmental issues has been spotty throughout history and deemed suspect by many secular environmentalists. Some Christians challenge the connection between environmental care and the mission of the church or are merely suspicious of secular or mystical New Age agendas in environmentalism. But at the beginning of the twenty-first century, Christian environmental activism is gaining momentum.

## Theological Grounds

Overwhelming biblical evidence makes the case for creation stewardship. The Bible opens with God's activity of creation and of assigning the task of caring for the earth to humans (Gen. 1–2). Israel's laws included rules for the care of land and animals (Deut. 25). The Old Testament poets and prophets declared many truths about the creation: The earth belongs to God (Ps. 24; Isa. 66:1–2); it declares His glory as a grand instrument of praise (Ps. 19, 96, 104, and 148; Isa. 40:26); it is made for the good of mankind (Ps. 65 and 104); and its calamities are a consequence of the Fall of man into sin (Isa. 24:5–6; Hosea 4:1–3).

The New Testament links creation to Christ the co-creator and sustainer of all things (Colossians 1:15–20; Heb. 1:2–3). Jesus illustrated many of his spiritual truths using images from the world of nature (Matt. 10:29; Luke 12:27). He likewise made justice and compassion for the inhabitants of this world part of his ministry and a crucial obligation for his followers (Luke 4:18–19; Luke 6:31; Matt. 22:37–40). Paramount to "incarnational" mission in this world is Jesus' own example of coming in human flesh and ministering to the physical and spiritual needs of mankind (John 1; Phil. 2). The cross of Christ, the heart of the gospel the church proclaims, ultimately puts all things in the universe back in order (Colossians 1). The eventual restoration of the created order is part of God's redemptive plan (Rom. 8:19–23; Rev. 21–22). At the heart of stewardship is doing the will of the Father *on Earth,* in the created realm, as it is done in heaven (Matt. 6:10).

## Environment and Mission

Countering the importance of environmentalism is the view of some missiologists that God's main concern is spiritual salvation. Legitimate missions proclaim the Word of God and the hope of eternal salvation, not the establishment of earthly *shalom.* But theologian John Stott sees ecological involvement as part of missions:

> Mission embraces everything Christ sends his people into the world to do, service as well as evangelism. And we cannot truly love and serve our neighbors if at the same time we are destroying environment, or acquiescing in its destruction, or even ignoring the environmentally depleted circumstances in which so many people are condemned to live." (Harris 1993, x)

Many contemporary strategies in mission—for example, teaching the English language, sports, and tentmaking methods—stand on the platform of earning the right to be heard, on being salt and light in the world (Matt. 5). Proclamation follows established legitimacy.

## Models in Mission

Through the centuries notable church pioneers like St. Clement and St. Francis, church leaders like Martin Luther and John Wesley, missionaries like William Carey and Robert Moffat, and countless movements have lauded the marvels of God's creation and praised human involvement with nature. Christian environmentalists today are making an impact and being heard. In Portugal in 1983 Peter and Miranda Harris embarked on Christian conservation by establishing *A Rocha* [The Rock] *Trust,* now with active projects in Canada, the Czech Republic, France, Kenya, Lebanon, and the United Kingdom. Mainline and Evangelical networks partnering in projects, providing resources and publications, offering education, and generally promoting Christian environmental action include groups such as the Ausable Institute (a network of Christian universities with multiple training sites), the American Scientific Affiliation (a group of science professionals), Target Earth (an activist network in fifteen countries), the Christian Environmental Association, the Evangelical Environmental Network, and Interfaith Network for Earth Concerns.

Mission and compassion organizations are increasingly initiating projects that address land usage and protection, reforestation, agricultural processes, animal health and husbandry, water protection, and other environmentally sensitive issues. Some very active organizations include World Vision, World Relief, MAP International, Missions Society for United Methodists, Christian Camping International, and Youth with a Mission. Family Life Outreach, a small mission in Haiti, models holistic ministry by complementing its indigenous church development, discipleship, stewardship, and family ministries with a major tree nursery project for reforestation.

## Looking Ahead

Challenges of deforestation, climate change, and dwindling resources for the poor are increasing across the world. The growing global church must heed the needs of humanity. A 2006 public stance of eighty-six noted Evangelical leaders in the United States for action to abate global warming, which was not without opposition from some groups, illustrates how united Christian efforts can impact more than just the religious world. Individual Christians, single churches, larger communities and networks, and mission organizations will become increasingly involved in protecting natural resources, fighting against pollution, addressing environmental ethics, advocating for ecologically sensitive policies, and generally going about the task of loving their neighbors as Christ commanded.

PAUL SHEA

## Further Reading

Berry, R. J. (Ed.). (2000). *The care of creation: Focusing concern and action.* Leicester, UK: Inter-Varsity Press.

Bouma-Prediger, S. (2001). *For the beauty of the earth: A Christian vision for creation care.* Grand Rapids, MI: Baker.

Brandt, D. (Ed.). (2002). *God's stewards: The role of Christians in creation care.* Monrovia, CA: World Vision.

DeWitt, C. B. (Ed.). (1991). *The environment and the Christian.* Grand Rapids, MI: Baker.

DeWitt, C. B. (Ed.). (1998). *Caring for creation: Responsible stewardship of God's handiwork.* Grand Rapids, MI: Baker.

Harris, P. (1993). *Under the bright wings.* Vancouver, Camada: Regent.

Hessel, D. T., & Ruether, R. R. (Eds.). (2000). *Christianity and ecology: Seeking the well-being of earth and humans.* Cambridge, MA: Harvard University Press.

Hesslegrave, D. J. (2005). *Paradigms in conflict.* Grand Rapids, MI: Kregel.

Mark, C. J. (Ed.). (2004). *Healing God's creation.* New York: Morehouse.

Northcott, M. S. (1996). *The environment and Christian ethics.* Cambridge, UK: Cambridge University Press.

Oelschlaeger, M. (1996). *Caring for creation: An ecumenical approach to the environment.* New Haven, CT: Yale University Press.

## Ethics

On the biblical understanding, mission starts with God. That is, the Bible presents the living creator God as "on mission" to bring about the salvation of humanity and redemption of the whole creation. Whatever mission or missions Christians engage in at the level of human initiative and activity have their origin and their validation in the mission of God. And God's mission is in response to the wickedness and brokenness that human rebellion has inflicted upon the earth. There is, therefore, an inescapably ethical dimension to mission, simply because it is driven by the agenda of the biblical God, who is moral, holy, and personal, and to whom ethical living is a more pleasing dimension of human response than religious devotion.

God entrusts his mission to the people whom he called into existence for the purpose of being the vehicle of his redemptive blessing to others. In the Old Testament this begins with the call of Abraham, through whose descendants God promised that all nations on Earth will ultimately find blessing (Genesis 12:1–3). The ethical dimension of this national mission comes quickly into view when God says, regarding Abraham, "I have chosen him, that he may charge his children and his household after him to keep the way of the LORD by doing righteousness and justice; so that the LORD may bring about for Abraham what he has promised him" (Genesis 18:19, NRSV). This is said in the context of God's judgment on Sodom and Gomorrah, so the implication is that God's mission to bless the nations ("what he has promised him") is dependent on Abraham's future community being distinctive. They were to be committed to the "way of the LORD" (a strongly ethical phrase in the Old Testament for behavior that reflects the character of Yahweh)—not the way of Sodom. They were to do "righteousness and justice," not the oppression, perversion, violence, and neglect of the poor that characterized Sodom (cf. Ezekiel 16:49). In Genesis 18:19, ethics is the central fulcrum between election and mission.

When Israel had become a nation through the exodus (the great Old Testament model of God's redemptive mission in action), God conferred upon them a missional identity—to be his priesthood in the midst of the rest of the nations (Exodus 19:3–6). Priests taught the knowledge of God to the people and brought the people's sacrifices to God. Thus, the metaphor of priesthood for the people of God in the midst of the nations is a way of saying that, through Israel, God would become known to the nations (in revelation), and through Israel the nations would be drawn into a covenant relationship with God (through redemption). The matching requirement, however, was that they must be a "holy nation"—that is, morally distinctive from the nations in social, economic, political, and personal life. Such a distinctive ethic, shaped by obedience to God's law, according to Deuteronomy 4:6–8, would indeed make Israel a visible model to the nations, arousing questions about the God they worshiped and the social justice of their national life. That was the missional motivation for ethical obedience—even if it was sadly neglected in the centuries ahead. Such texts, however, still lay the foundation for the essential link between the mission of God's people and the ethical quality of their lives.

In the New Testament one finds the same strongly ethical exhortation as a prerequisite for effective mission. Jesus urges his disciples to standards of ethical living that would shine as light in the darkness and stem corruption like salt on raw meat (Matthew 5:13–16). The missional thrust of his metaphors is very clear in his famous saying at the end of the passage: "Let your light shine before others, so that they may see your good works and give glory to your Father in heaven" (Matthew 5:16, NRSV). Peter, probably recalling that saying, combines it with the concept of Christians, as the Israel of God, functioning as God's priesthood in the midst of the nations, and immediately draws the ethical implication. If that is the missional status that Christians have, then their missional ethic is clear: "Live such good lives among the pagans that, though they accuse you of doing wrong, they may see your good deeds and glorify God on the day he visits us" (1 Peter 2:9–12, NIV). Such a commitment to positive and Christlike behavior, he says to Christian wives of unbelieving husbands, can be evangelistically effective even when verbal witness is stifled (1 Peter 3:1–2). By such "doing good" (one of Paul's favorite expressions), even slaves, by honesty and trustworthiness, can "make the teaching about God our Savior attractive" (Titus 2:10, NIV).

The ethical quality of life of the people of God is an essential prerequisite for any mission they believe themselves called to do in the name of Jesus Christ. There is no biblical mission without biblical ethics.

## Ethical Issues and the Agenda of Mission

Given that the mission of God addresses the wickedness of humanity, it is not surprising that Christian mission in God's name does the same. Accordingly, Christian mission through the centuries has not confined itself to the goal of populating the new creation by "saving souls" but has engaged with the pressing issues of this life, wherever the best purposes of God for human life and for his creation are thwarted, perverted, or ignored. This is not by any means meant to overlook the moral blind spots that Christian churches and their missionaries have suffered from in every generation. There are many wrongs that Christians have failed to put right and some others that they have perpetrated or made worse. It nevertheless remains true that there has always been, and still is, a pervasive ethical core and thrust within the worldwide Christian missionary movement.

Even in Old Testament times, the mission of Israel to be distinctive from the nations led them to oppose the Canaanite combination of sacralized sex (with its abuse of women through ritual prostitution) and sacrificed babies. Christian mission has faced comparable evils in other cultures. The list of ethical issues tackled in the history of Christian mission would include:

- Refusing to participate in warfare in the early, pre-Constantine centuries of the church
- Peace-making and conflict-resolution efforts
- Tackling threats to human equality and dignity in response to inequalities such as the caste system in India or slavery
- Opposing the system of widow-suicide on the death of a husband
- Championing the justice rights of the poor, the illiterate, the sick, the ethnically vulnerable, prisoners, etc.
- Seeking to raise the standards of sexual ethics in many cultural contexts
- Addressing the prevalence of female genital mutilation in some parts of the world
- Raising the perceived value of human work and addressing ethical issues of working relationships, conditions, treatment, payment, etc.

In today's world, Christian mission includes within its scope such pressing ethical issues as ecology, conservation, and climate change; poverty; HIV/AIDS; global trade justice, etc.

All such ethical concerns are valid dimensions of Christian mission since they all flow from Christian commitment to the kingdom of God, whose values of love and justice we are commanded to seek first. Mission is not just a means of escape to some other world of tomorrow. It is a prophetic challenge, in the name of Christ, to all the effects of sin and evil in the world today.

## Ethical Integrity and the Methods of Mission

Finally, if biblical mission flows from the will of God, it must be characterized by the ethical values and priorities that make up the character of God. Jesus himself, God in mission incarnate, is the supreme model, inasmuch as he carried out his mission in self-giving love; noncoercive, nonviolent appeal; humility; compassion; integrity of speech; and life. Those who claim the name of Christ must follow his example in mission. Mission on Christ's authority must also be mission in Christ's way.

- Because mission flows from the God of truth and integrity, we agree with Paul that the gospel cannot be commended through trickery or deceit and reject all that smacks of bribery or manipulation (2 Corinthians 4:2).
- Because God made all persons in his image, there is no place for contempt or denigration of other human beings—of whatever faith or race.
- Because God gave humanity freedom and seeks our free response of faith and love, Christian mission cannot include the tools of violence, torture, or coercion, and all episodes of such monstrous denials of the gospel must be exposed and disavowed by Christians as having nothing to do with the mission of the biblical Christ.
- Because love and justice are central to the character of God, we reject any form of missionary methodology that results in exclusion or discrimination or that colludes with injustices that are ethically repugnant to God.

Thus, while we may not question the biblical authorization and legitimacy of mission per se, we may certainly question the ethical legitimacy of any and all methods of mission. However noble the end, we are not at liberty to be unscrupulous about the means. Behavior that is unethical in the sight of God cannot be justified on the grounds that it had a missionary motivation. If anything, that renders the sin all the more obnoxious.

CHRISTOPHER J. H. WRIGHT

### Further Reading

Boers, A. P. (1991). *On earth as in heaven: Justice rooted in spirituality*. Scottsdale, PA: Herald Press.

Davies, B. & Walsh, M. (1984). *Proclaiming justice and peace: Documents from John XXIII–John Paul II*. New London, CT: Twenty-Third Publications.

DeBerri, E. P, and Hug, J. (2003). *Catholic social teaching: Our best kept secret* (4th ed.). Maryknoll, NY: Orbis Books.

Nicholls, B. (Ed.). (1985). *In word and deed: Evangelism and social responsibility* Grand Rapids, MI: Eerdmans.

Thompson, J. M. (2003). *Justice and peace: A Christian primer* (2nd ed.). Maryknoll, NY: Orbis.

Wright, C. J. H. (2004). *Old Testament ethics for the people of God*. Downers Grove, IL: IVP.

Wright, C. J. H. (2006). *The mission of God: Unlocking the Bible's grand narrative*. Downers Grove, IL: IVP.

# Ethiopianism

The term *Ethiopianism* is the name given to a series of movements among African Christians, or people of African descent outside Africa, based on Psalm 68:31: "Princes shall come out of Egypt; Ethiopia shall soon stretch out her hands unto God."

## Beginnings

This verse was often quoted by Richard Allen (1760–1831), the first bishop of the African Methodist Episcopal Church in the United States, and also by Mangena Mokone (1851–1931), the founder of the Ethiopian Church in South Africa. Mokone, who had broken away from the Wesleyan Methodist Church in Pretoria in 1892, founded the Ethiopian Church, which soon made contact with the African Methodist Episcopal Church (AMEC) in the United States and amalgamated with it in 1896. Thus, Ethiopianism in North America and southern Africa influenced each other.

The movement was given a significant boost when an invading Italian army was defeated by Ethiopian forces at Adwa in 1896 and Italy recognized the independence of Ethiopia in the treaty of Addis Ababa.

## Growth of the Ethiopian Movement

Not all members of the Ethiopian Church in southern Africa were happy with the union with the American group, however; some broke away to found independent bodies, and some, led by James Mata Dwane, affiliated with the Anglican Church of the Province of South Africa (CPSA) as the Order of Ethiopia, where they retained some of their Methodist polity.

The Ethiopian Catholic Church in Zion, founded in 1904 by Samuel Brander (1851–1928), brought together several Ethiopian leaders who had been involved in different denominations. Among these were Kanyane Napo, a former Anglican who had founded the African Church in 1888, joined the Ethiopian Church in 1893, but finally broke away to reestablish the African Church in 1908. Another of the early leaders was Daniel William Alexander, who left to join the African Church in 1920 and then broke away to form the African Orthodox Church in 1924.

The ecclesiastical tradition of the Ethiopian Catholic Church in Zion was a mixture of Anglican and Methodist, but Brander emphasized the Anglo-Catholic heritage.

Several other denominations formed part of the Ethiopian movement in southern Africa, mostly formed by schism from those already mentioned. According to some accounts, Mokone had made contact with the leaders of an earlier movement in Thembuland, begun by Nehemiah Tile (d. 1891). Tile had formed a Thembu National Church and had been influenced by James Mata Dwane. One of his successors, Jonas Goduka (1846–1914) joined the Ethiopian Church but left after it united with the AMEC in 1895 and continued with his African Native Mission Church. Another of Tile's successors, Jantje Gqamana, was involved in the establishment of the Ethiopian Catholic Church.

Some of the Ethiopian denominations attempted to trace a kind of apostolic succession from Tile, who was referred to by some as Saint Tile. Others, such as Goduka's group, tried to play down the association with Tile. While the relations between particular groups are often unclear at any particular time, what is clear is that in the period 1890–1920 there was a group of denominations linked by the Ethiopian movement and an Anglican-Methodist heritage. Some of the better-known leaders may be found in different groups at different times, but in spite of their fissiparousness, the Ethiopian Churches and leaders remained in touch with one another.

These groups were also of concern to the secular authorities, who regarded Ethiopianism as a potential threat to white rule. The Ethiopian rejoicing at the defeat of the would-be Italian imperialists at the Battle of Adwa was disturbing: the European powers might be rivals in the scramble for Africa but were united in their fear of African resistance.

In 1904 Zionist missionaries from the United States established a base in South Africa, and Pentecostal missionaries did likewise in 1908, when the Zionist missionaries left. The Zionist cause, with some Pentecostal additions, was carried forward, however, by local black Zionists, who also formed numerous independent churches. After about 1920 the Zionist growth eclipsed that of the Ethiopians, and their emphasis on healing seemed far more attractive to many.

## Later Development of Ethiopianism in Southern Africa

As time passed and the first generation of Ethiopian leaders died off, the vision of the founders began to grow dim. The new generation often did not understand the things they had inherited. Theological training was minimal; for most, it was (at best) a short course at a Bible college run by a generic Protestant Evangelical group or a Bible correspondence course run by such a group. These courses were often of a Baptist tradition rather than the Anglican-Methodist traditions of the Ethiopian founders.

The Order of Ethiopia, in association with the Anglican Church, was an exception, as its clergy were trained in Anglican theological colleges, but when, in 1979, it was decided that the Order of Ethiopia could have its own bishop, it disintegrated rapidly. One group formed an independent denomination, the Ethiopian Episcopal Church, under Bishop Sigqibo Dwane, the grandson of James Mata Dwane, the founder of the order. Another, led by Canon E. L. M. Hopa, who had been Provincial of the Order, united with the Ethiopian Orthodox Tewahedo Church and so could perhaps be said to have at last fulfilled its Ethiopian destiny.

## Movement or Ideology?

Though some have spoken of Ethiopianism as an ideology, it was rather too diffuse for that. In more recent times it has developed ideological characteristics in Rastafarian circles, where conceptions of Ethiopia and its government have played a far more prominent role in the minds of its adherents than they did in the Ethiopian churches of southern Africa.

In southern Africa there was little real interest, knowledge, or understanding of the history of Christianity in Ethiopia. Ethiopia was a symbol of an African Christianity that was older than that of most of Europe, and therefore a counter to the smug superiority of European missionaries in the time of the New Imperialism and the scramble for Africa. Only with the disintegration of the Order of Ethiopia did some of the South African "Ethiopians" discover what Ethiopian Christianity was really like.

STEPHEN HAYES

## Further Reading

Campbell, J. T. (1995). *Songs of Zion: The African Methodist Episcopal Church in the United States and South Africa*. New York: Oxford University Press.

Campbell, J. (1987). *Conceiving of the Ethiopian movement*. Johannesburg, South Africa: University of the Witwatersrand, African Studies Institute.

Chanaiwa, D. (Ed.). (1976). *Profiles of self-determination*. Northridge: California State University.

Chirenje, J. M. (1987). *Ethiopianism and Afro-Americans in Southern Africa, 1893–1916*. Baton Rouge: Louisiana State University Press.

Cuthbertson, G., Pretorius, H., & Robert, D. (Eds.). (2003). *Frontiers of African Christianity: Essays in honour of Inus Daneel*. Pretoria: University of South Africa.

Dwane, S. (1999). *Ethiopianism and the Order of Ethiopia*. Glosderry, South Africa: Ethiopian Episcopal Church.

Kamphausen, E. (1976). *Anfänge der kirchlichen unabhängigkeitsbewegung in Südafrika: Geschichte und theologie der Äthiopischen bewegung 1872–1912* [Beginning of the church independence movement in South Africa: the Ethiopian movement 1872–1912]. Bern, Switzerland: Herbert Lang.

Lewis, W. F. (1993). *Soul rebels: The Rastafari*. Long Grove, IL: Waveland.

Pretorius, H. L. (1993). *Ethiopia stretches out her hands to God: Aspects of Transkeian Indigenous Churches*. Pretoria, South Africa: Institute for Missiological Research.

Sundkler, B. G. M. (1961). *Bantu prophets in South Africa*. Oxford, UK: Oxford University Press.

Verryn, T. D. (1972). *A history of the Order of Ethiopia*. Pretoria, South Africa: Ecumenical Research Unit.

# Europe

Paul was the first apostle of Jesus Christ to preach the Gospel in Europe. He visited Greece, Italy, and Spain and wrote letters to the Christians in Rome and in Corinth. He made the Christian message known among Jews and Gentiles in the Roman Empire.

The first period in the history of the evangelization of Europe, from the New Testament to Constantine the Great (r. 306–337), is characterized by two major shifts: from Jewish Christianity to Gentile Christianity in and outside the Roman Empire; and from a Jewish-Gentile Christian minority position to a Gentile Christian majority status in the Roman Empire (severe persecutions and martyrdom before Emperor Constantine did not stop church growth).

The second period, from Constantine the Great to the French Revolution (1789), is known as the period of Christendom (*corpus christianum*). It can be subdivided into periods before and after the birth of Islam (622 CE), and before and after the discovery of the New World and new sea routes (1492, 1498). The birth and growth of Islam caused Christians considerable losses of territory, not only in the Middle East but also in Europe. This decline of Christianity caused a shock and compelled an answer: the Crusades (1096–1291). Inaugurated by Pope Urban II, the Crusades did more harm than good to the cause of the Gospel and the church. Finally, the Hagia Sophia in Constantinople was lost (1453).

Before the appearance of Muhammad, Christianity had expanded beyond the European borders of the Roman Empire: Ulfilas (c. 311–383 CE) evangelized the Goths, and Patrick (c. 389–461) labored in Ireland. Eventually nearly the whole of Europe, from Ireland and Iceland in the West to Russia under Vladimir (c. 980–1015) in the East, was Christianized (the Lithuanians, in 1386, were the last to adopt Christianity). From 1246 onward, in the wake of the Crusades, the first European missionaries (mainly Franciscans and Dominicans) were sent outside their own continent to do missionary work in China.

Between 1492 and 1789 Europe was renewed. Humanism, the Renaissance, the Reformation, and the Enlightenment helped Christianity to mature. Although the Deists and the Enlightenment philosophers moved away from established Christianity, the vast majority of Europeans remained baptized church members. Columbus, Vasco da Gama, and other discoverers, who were all committed members of the Roman Catholic Church, paved the way not only for emigration to the newly discovered continents, but also for world trade, colonialism, and overseas missions. European Jesuits such as Francis Xavier (1506–52) in China and Robert de Nobili (1577–1656) in India took the lead. In 1622 Pope Gregory XV established the Sacred Congregation for the Propagation of the Faith to coordinate missions. Protestant missions came into being more than one century later. At the very beginning they were bound to colonial borders: Dutch missions in overseas Dutch dominions, English missions in overseas British dominions, and so on. The Moravians, at the instigation of Nikolaus L. von Zinzendorf (1709–1760), were the first to establish Protestant missions without regard to borders.

The French Revolution separated church and state in France and subsequently in other European nations. In that way it ended the period of Christendom (*corpus christianum*) inaugurated by Constantine the Great and started a new post-Christian era. The churches lost, once and for all, their religious monopoly. Jews, Deists, and atheists received the same rights as Christians. Since that time, secularization has been the main problem of European Christianity: In the nineteenth century the exodus of members was small, but in the course of the twentieth century it grew large.

However, nineteenth century European Christians increased their home and foreign missions. Following in the footsteps of William Carey (1761–1834), various orthodox Protestant foreign mission societies were established, each with its own overseas mission field and missionaries. Liberal Protestants, especially in Germany, believed that spreading European culture was the same as spreading Christianity. But the Roman Catholic author Anton Huonder (1921) regarded such Europeanism as a serious obstacle to proper missions. On the Protestant side, Hendrik Kraemer (1938) was even more radical in objecting to Eurocentrism in missions.

During World War II, European Christians admitted for the first time that the world could no longer be divided into a Christian West and a non-Christian East and South: The non-Western world gave birth to many native churches and Europe became a mission field. World War II ended not only European colonialism and imperialism but also the hegemony of Christian missions in the non-Western world. Hindu missions, Buddhist missions, and Muslim missions became as self-conscious and active as Christian missions, at home and abroad. They viewed Europe, demoralized by two world wars, as an excellent mission field. Europe, which had about 14 percent of the world population at the end of the second millennium, now experiences the immigration of thousands of Hindus, Buddhists, and Muslims, as well as the arrival of thousands of non-Western Christians. These Christians either became members of established European churches or planted their own churches. Some of these migrant Christians and churches are active in doing mission among their own countrymen in Europe or among Europeans.

The secularization process paved the way for pluralization: Although about 70 percent of Europe is still Christian, Europe is now secular in its public life. This profound and massive shift since the French Revolution implies the need to rethink missions in the European context, which includes growing agnosticism and atheism (c. 20 percent of Europe's population), growing multireligiosity (c. 5 percent of Europe's population), and growing multiculturality. Many churches, theologians, and missiologists try to cope with the new challenges both theoretically (apologetic, dialogical, and other reflections) and practically (new types of missionary work). The Roman Catholic Council of European Bishops Conferences (CCEE) and the ecumenical Conference of European Churches (CEC) set up and coordinate missionary and other programs for Christian churches inside and outside the European Union. At a conference in Stavanger, Norway, in 1998, European members of the International Association of Mission Studies (IAMS) started their own continental network.

JAN A. B. JONGENEEL

## Further Reading

Barrett, D. B. (Ed.). (2001). *World Christian encyclopedia: A comparative survey of churches and religions in the modern world* (2nd ed., Vols. 1–2). Oxford, UK: University Press.

Gay, P. (1968). *The Enlightenment: An interpretation: The rise of modern paganism.* New York: Vintage Books.

Godin, H.–D.l Y. (1943). *La France, Pays de mission?* [France, mission country?] Paris: Cerf.

Huonder, A. (1921). *Der Europäismus im Missionsbetrieb.* [Europeanism in the missionary enterprise]. Aachen, Germany: Xaverius-Verlag.

Jongeneel, J. A. B. (2002). The challenge of a multicultural and multireligious Europe. In: F. W.-P. Nissen (Ed.), *"Mission is a must": Intercultural theology and the mission of the church* (pp. 178–191). New York: Rodopi.

Kraemer, H. (1938). *The Christian message in a non-Christian world.* London: Edinburgh House Press.

Latourette, K. S. (1971). *A history of the expansion of Christianity.* Exeter, UK: Pater Noster Press. (Original work published 1937–1945)

Ter Haar, G. (1998). *Halfway to paradise: African Christians in Europe.* Cardiff, UK: Cardiff Academic Press.

Ter Haar, G. (Ed.). (2001). *Religious communities in the diaspora.* Nairobi, Kenya: Acton Publishers.

## Evangelicalism

The Evangelical missionary enterprise is one of the most dynamic expressions of the Christian missionary impulse. While there is no single, definitive Evangelical approach to missions and scholars disagree about how to define evangelicalism, British historian David Bebbington has identified four common beliefs and attitudes that characterize the movement as a whole. These include commitment to the necessity of personal conversion, recognition of the importance of Jesus Christ's atonement, acknowledgement of Biblical authority, and devotion to the active propagation of the Christian gospel.

Cross-cultural missions express the Evangelical commitment to active service for Christ and his kingdom. The history of Evangelical missions, including its origins in the eighteenth century, its rapid expansion in the nineteenth and twentieth centuries, and its future prospects, is an important part of the global history of Christianity.

## Eighteenth-century Origins

Evangelical missions are as old as the evangelical movement itself, which dates from the eighteenth century and emerged out of the European Pietist movement and the trans-Atlantic religious revivals. Modifications to Calvinist theology by figures such as Jonathan Edwards (1703–1758) and Andrew Fuller (1754–1815), and adjustments to Arminian theology by John (1703–1791) and Charles Wesley (1707–1788), placed evangelistic outreach on firm theological foundations. However, Anglo-American Evangelical leaders did not channel this evangelistic enthusiasm into cross-cultural mission automatically.

Though several important efforts at cross-cultural evangelism by English Puritans and Dutch Pietists in the seventeenth and eighteenth centuries attracted some attention, the Moravians, revivalists exiled from their home in Bohemia, exercised direct and decisive influence. Their evangelistic work around the world proved a direct inspiration to evangelicals in Britain who established a flurry of voluntary societies dedicated to the support of overseas missions such as the Baptist Missionary Society (1792), the interdenominational London Missionary Society (1795), the Anglican Church Missionary Society (1799), and the British and Foreign Bible Society (1804).

## Nineteenth-century Expansion

At the beginning of the nineteenth century there were only 100 Protestant missionaries at work. By the century's end, Britain alone sent over 9,000 missionaries overseas. Though Britain remained the leader in Evangelical missions throughout the nineteenth century, enthusiasm for voluntary missionary societies spread to America and Europe as the founding of the American Board of Commissioners for Foreign Missions (1810), the German Missionary Society (1816), and the Paris Evangelical Missionary Society (1822) demonstrate.

While theological developments and contact with Moravians shaped the early contours of Evangelical missions, cultural, social, and political factors also played their part. The expansion of the British Empire into India, Africa, and Asia opened new geographical horizons for many and in some cases made those societies more accessible to the missionary-minded. Charles Grant (1746–1823), an employee of the British East India Company, experienced Evangelical conversion and used his commercial and political connections to help open India to Christian missions.

The trans-Atlantic campaign against slavery served as an additional spur to Evangelical missionary endeavor. British abolitionists founded Sierra Leone, a colony for freed slaves that they intended to serve as beachhead for the evangelization of Africa, and a freed slave, Olaudah Equiano (1747–1797), effectively promoted antislavery and missionary activity to Africa throughout the Anglo-Saxon world in such writings as *The Interesting Narrative of Olaudah Equiano*, published in 1789.

In some cases, ideas concerning cultural and racial superiority also promoted missionary endeavor. Josiah Strong (1847–1916), a leading figure in the Evangelical Alliance in America, spoke about missions in terms of the triumphant spread of Anglo-Saxon culture. While imperial politics, antislavery agitation, cultural arrogance, and racial pride all contributed to the growth of Evangelical missions in the nineteenth century, none of these factors alone were determinative, nor were they essential features of the enterprise.

Evangelical missions have typically emphasized evangelism and church planting. Three of the most important Evangelical missionary theorists of the nineteenth century, Henry Venn (1796–1873), Rufus Anderson (1796–1880), and Gustav Warneck (1834–1910), developed complementary strategies that emphasized the creation of independent indigenous churches as the goal of Christian mission. Despite such principles, Evangelicals could be paternalistic and stifle indigenous agency. Furthermore, this emphasis on church planting did not preclude involvement in education, economic development, humanitarian relief, or political activism. For example, because of the complexity of the evangelistic task, pioneering missionaries like William Carey (1761–1834) could become involved in nearly all these spheres of activity.

## Twentieth-century Developments

If the British were the leading promoters of Evangelical missions in the nineteenth century, America assumed that role in the twentieth. In 1953, America sent out over 9,300 Evangelical missionaries. By 1985, that number had grown to over 35,300.

## A Former Slave's Conversion

**Below is a passage from Olaudah Equiano about his conversion to Christianity. Put into slavery as a child, Equiano later purchased his freedom, and went on to live a very spiritual life devoted to abolition.**

I saw the Lord Jesus Christ in his humiliation loaded and bearing my reproach, sin, and shame . . . It was given me at that time to know what it was to be born again, John iii. 5. I saw the eighth chapter to the Romans, and the doctrines of God's decrees verified, agreeable to his eternal, everlasting and unchangeable purposes. The word of God was sweet to my taste, yea sweeter than honey and the honey comb. Christ was revealed to my soul as the chiefest among ten thousand. These heavenly moments were really as life to the dead, and what John calls an earnest of the Spirit. This was indeed unspeakable, and, I firmly believe, undeniable by many. Now every leading providential circumstance that happened to me, from the day I was taken from my parents to that hour, was then, in my view, as if it had but just then occurred. I was sensible of the invisible hand of God, which guided and protected me, when in truth I knew it not: still the Lord pursued me although I slighted and disregarded it; this mercy melted me down. When I considered my poor wretched state, I wept, seeing what a great debtor I was to sovereign free grace. Now the Ethiopian was willing to be saved by Jesus Christ, the sinners only surety, and also to rely on none other person or thing for salvation. Self was obnoxious, and good works he had none; for it is God that worketh in us both to will and do. Oh! the amazing things of that hour can never be told—it was joy in the Holy Ghost! I felt an astonishing change; the burden of sin, the gaping jaws of hell, and the fears of death, that weighed me down before, now lost their horror; indeed I thought death would now be the best earthly friend I ever had. Such were my grief and joy, as, I believe, are seldom experienced. I was bathed in tears, and said, What am I, that God should thus look on me, the vilest of sinners? I felt a deep concern for my mother and friends, which occasioned me to pray with fresh ardour; and, in the abyss of thought, I viewed the unconverted people of the world in a very awful state, being without God and without hope.

Source: Carretta, V. (Ed.). (1995). *The interesting narrative and other writing of Olaudah Equian*o (pp. 190–191). New York: Penguin Books.

Though new trends in Protestant missions in the early twentieth century highlighted humanitarian and development projects, Evangelicals remained committed to church planting. Small, independent Evangelical faith missions, such as the Sudan Interior Mission (1893), which took its inspiration from the China Inland Mission (1867) of J. Hudson Taylor (1832–1905), gradually distanced themselves from the older missionary organizations and grew into leading missionary-sending agencies in their own right.

Fundamentalists also founded independent Evangelical missions and, for a time, redefined Evangelical missionary strategy in ways that precluded social activism. This reemphasis on personal conversion took place against the backdrop of a rapidly changing political environment after World War II, including the demise of the British Empire and the rise of American cultural and economic influence throughout the world. In this new environment, missionaries sometimes conflated the proclamation of the gospel with the exportation of American culture. However, though this remained a constant temptation, it was not a constant feature of evangelical practice.

After World War II, American Evangelicals developed more sophisticated strategies to address traditional concerns. William Cameron Townsend (1896–1982) established Wycliffe Bible Translators (1942) and SIL (1934) to finish the global task of Bible translation, and Bob Pierce (1914–1978) institutionalized Evangelical concern for the social and economic needs of others through World Vision (1950) and Samaritan's Purse (1970). Evangelicals also promoted the academic study of missions through the creation of centers for practical training and scholarly reflection like Fuller Theological Seminary's School of World Mission (1965), led by Donald McGavran (1897–1990), who would become one of the century's leading missionary strategists through his exposition of the principles of church growth.

Other leading Evangelical missionary statesmen, including Max Warren (1904–1977), Lesslie Newbigin (1909–1998), John Stott (b. 1921), and Billy Graham (b. 1918), reevaluated traditional Evangelical assumptions and built bridges to the non-Western world. Warren reemphasized holistic mission and Newbigin highlighted the West as a missionary field in its own right, while Graham and Stott helped organize gatherings like the International Congress on World Evangelization in Lausanne, Switzerland (1974), which provided 2,300 evangelical leaders from 150 different countries with a forum for critical reflection and constructive planning. Lausanne also highlighted the emerging importance of non-Western evangelicals.

## Future Prospects

The twentieth century witnessed a surprising development: the rapid growth of non-Western Christianity and non-Western missions. In 1973, there were approximately 3,400 non-Western missionaries working worldwide. By 2006, this number had skyrocketed to over 100,000. Though it is very difficult to determine what percentage of these missionaries consider themselves Evangelical, it is likely that evangelical influences have shaped the outlook of a significant portion of this emerging force.

Though Christian missionaries transported the faith abroad, indigenous agents in Latin America, Africa, and Asia played the key role in spreading Christianity. These indigenous evangelistic efforts have served to stimulate new endeavors in cross-cultural mission. In the near future, it is likely that non-Western missionaries will outnumber Western ones. Developments in Korea provide an excellent illustration of this global shift. Korean Evangelicals have helped to make Korea the leading non-Western missionary-sending country in the world. The Korean missionary force has grown rapidly, from approximately 1,200 in 1991 to over 13,000 in 2006. As non-Western missions continue to grow and non-Western theologians assume a greater role in the development of evangelical missionary theory, Evangelical missions will continue to thrive and explore new frontiers in cross-cultural outreach.

TODD M. THOMPSON

*See also* Bible Translation; Church Growth Movement; Church Planting; Empire; Faith Missions; Fundamentalism; Moravians; North America; Pietism; Protestant Churches; Slavery

### Further Reading

Anderson, G. H. (Ed.). (1998). *Biographical dictionary of Christian missions.* Grand Rapids, MI: Eerdmans.

Barrett, D. B., Kurian, G. T., & Johnson, T. M. (Eds.). (2001). *World Christian encyclopedia* (2nd ed., Vols. 1–2). New York: Oxford University Press.

Bebbington, D. W. (1992). *Evangelicalism in modern Britain: A history from the 1730s to the 1980s.* Grand Rapids, MI: Baker.

Bonk, J. (Ed.). (2003). *Between past and future: Evangelical mission entering the twenty-first century.* Pasadena, CA: William Carey.

Carpenter, J., & Shenk, W. (Eds.). (1990). *Earthen vessels: American evangelicals and foreign missions, 1880–1980.* Grand Rapids, MI: Eerdmans.

Hutchinson, M., & Kalu, O. (Eds.). (1998). *A global faith: Essays on evangelicalism and globalization.* Sydney, Australia: Centre for the Study of Australian Christianity.

Lewis, D. M. (Ed.). (2004). *Christianity reborn: The global expansion of evangelicalism in the twentieth century.* Grand Rapids, MI: Eerdmans.

Moll, R. (2006, March). Missions incredible. *Christianity Today,* 28.

Noll, M. (2003). *The rise of evangelicalism: The age of Edwards, Whitefield and the Wesleys.* Downers Grove, IL: InterVarsity Press.

Porter, A. (2004). *Religion versus empire? British Protestant missionaries and overseas expansion, 1700–1914.* Manchester, UK: Manchester University Press.

# Exploration

Christian missionaries have played a leading role in exploring the world, in part because their creed claims relevance for all peoples and recognizes no borders. The first missionaries were Near Easterners, though most subsequent missionary exploration has been conducted by Europeans or people of European descent, usually Roman Catholics. The relationship between missionary exploration and European imperial expansion has been intimate but complicated. Missionaries explored alongside traders, soldiers, and settlers, sometimes in close harmony with them, sometimes in open conflict. Missionary explorers have been driven by many motivations, including religious conversion, political and commercial expansion, and the "civilizing mission" to spread the European way of life. They have been unusually attentive to local languages and customs, and their reports have been influential among home audiences.

## The Early Centuries

Beginning with Paul's first-century journeys into Asia and Greece, Christianity expanded rapidly from its birthplace in Palestine. Some missionaries traveled eastward, reaching India in the first century and China no later than the seventh century. Others journeyed to North Africa and Europe, reaching Ireland during the fifth century. Irish monks soon evangelized England and explored the British Isles and Iceland. Roman missionary Augustine arrived in England in 597 CE and was followed by Theodore, from Asia Minor, and Hadrian, from North Africa.

As the centers of Christianity shifted westward, missionaries reported back to Europeans about distant lands. But Western knowledge of the world did not progress without interruption, declining significantly after the collapse of the Roman Empire and the Islamic conquests of the seventh and eighth centuries. Subsequent exploration often merely rediscovered what had been known by the Greeks, Romans, and Byzantines and was still known in the Arab world.

## Eastern Missions

Medieval European ties to Palestine were sustained by pilgrimages, which continued even after Arabs conquered the Holy Land during the 630s, and crusades, which sought to take back Palestine for Christendom. The Letter of Prester John circulated in Europe from the late 1100s onward, spurring eastern travel. It fraudulently purported to have come from a Christian ruler in the East whom Europeans hoped would help them defeat Islam and recapture Palestine.

The founding of the Dominican and Franciscan orders of the Catholic Church during the early 1200s was an important development for missionary exploration. When Mongol conquests opened Asia to the West, Catholic popes sent Dominican and Franciscan explorers into the new lands to convert Asian rulers and search for Prester John. These explorers included Giovanni Da Pian Del Carpini, a Franciscan who traveled to the court of the Mongol Khans during the 1240s and wrote the first full European account of Mongol society, and Guillame de Rubrouck, who traveled to the Mongolian court during the 1250s. Carpini and Rubrouck described Mongolia well before Marco Polo visited Mongol-dominated China during the 1270s and 1280s.

Other important early travelers included Franciscans Giovanni di Monte Corvino, who authored the first general European account of India after traveling there on a 1289 missionary journey, and Odoric di Pordenone, whose narrative of Eastern travels during the 1320s was a source for the fabricated but popular *Travels of Sir John Mandeville* (studied by Christopher Columbus, among others).

Some of the leading figures in the expansion of Europe's geographical horizons during the 1500s were members of the Society of Jesus (known as Jesuits), a Catholic missionary order founded in 1534. One of its founders, Francis Xavier, planted churches in India, Malaysia, and Japan. Jesuits gave Europeans most of their knowledge of the East during the 1500s and 1600s. Antonio de Andrade disguised himself as a Buddhist pilgrim in 1624 in order to become the first European to visit Tibet, and Jesuits pioneered a route through the Himalayas during the 1660s.

Missionary exploration of the East continued into the nineteenth and twentieth centuries, as Armand David discovered the giant panda in China during the 1860s and 1870s, and Mildred Cable, Francesca French, and Eva French explored the Gobi Desert during the 1920s and 1930s.

## The New World

Catholic missionaries were some of the most important explorers of the Americas during the sixteenth and seventeenth centuries, often accompanying Spanish and French adventurers.

The first Jesuit in the New World, Manuel da Nobrega, began work in Brazil in 1549. Missionaries were the leading early informants on Indian life in Brazil; their reports were read eagerly by Europeans. Dominican Gaspar de Carvajal was among the first Europeans to descend the Amazon River. Jesuit Samuel Fritz explored the Amazon during the late 1600s, and Thomas Falkner's *A Description of Patagonia* (1774) was an important work on South America.

Roman Catholic missionaries were integrally involved with Spanish expansion into North America during the sixteenth century. Friars accompanied conquistador Francisco Coronado on a 1540 expedition that failed to discover the legendary Seven Cities of Cibola but explored parts of Pueblo territory, the Great Plains, and the Colorado River. Jesuits advanced as far north as the Chesapeake Bay in 1570, and Franciscans led the way in establishing New Mexico.

Salinas Pueblo Missions National Monument in the U.S. state of New Mexico. *Courtesy of Endi Dewata/istockphoto.com.*

Further north, the Jesuit Claude Allouez explored the Great Lakes region, and Jacques Marquette, also a Jesuit, traveled in 1673 with Louis Jolliet to the Mississippi's confluence with the Arkansas. Other French Catholic missionaries lived with American Indian tribes and explored the North American interior. The seventy-three-volume *Jesuit Relations and Allied Documents* compiled their fascinating reports from the seventeenth and eighteenth centuries.

## The Heart of Africa

Beginning in the 1500s, missionaries helped expand European understanding of Africa. Francisco Alvares published an account of his visit to Ethiopia during the 1520s, and Pedro Paez worked with other Jesuits during the early 1600s to map Ethiopia and describe the sources of the Blue Nile. The eighteenth-century explorer James Bruce only rediscovered for the West what Paez had already established about Ethiopia and the Blue Nile.

Protestant missionaries were among the most important nineteenth-century explorers of the African interior. John Campbell was a Scottish missionary whose 1822 account of travels in South Africa included information about unknown territories. Samuel Crowther accompanied the Niger River expedition of 1841. Johannes Rebmann and Johann Krapf fascinated Europe with their descriptions of snow-topped Mount Kenya and Mount Kilimanjaro in the 1840s.

Perhaps the most famous missionary explorer was David Livingstone, who was the first Westerner to dis-

cover the Zambezi River and Victoria Falls, and was the first European to complete a coast-to-coast crossing of Africa. Livingstone authored *Missionary Travels and Researches in South Africa* (1857) and was greeted by Henry Stanley in 1871 with, "Dr. Livingstone, I presume?"

## The Missionary Contribution

The degree to which missionaries differed from other explorers is unresolved. Thomas Laurie argued that missionaries were more reliable: "educated missionaries describe their own homes, and are masters of the vernacular . . . They do not hurry through a land, intent on the next railroad connection, but make it their permanent abode" (Laurie 1885, 2). At the least, as Laurie observed, missionaries often lived among indigenous peoples and studied their languages.

Missionaries sometimes challenged colonial abuses, but in many cases their presence and writings offered religious sanction for Western exploitation of other peoples. European scholars frequently mined missionary accounts. Roger Bacon drew on Jesuit descriptions of Asia, and two of the greatest scholars of exploration, Giovanni Battista Ramusio and Richard Hakluyt, used Jesuit reports for their sixteenth-century travel collections. Gottfried Leibniz recognized the scientific importance of missions work. Karl Ritter, a founder of modern geography, claimed that he could not have written his nineteen-volume tome without missionaries.

Nineteenth-century missionaries circulated news about their discoveries to millions of ordinary Westerners through lectures, books, and newspaper and magazine articles.

Through their travels and reports, missionaries, particularly Roman Catholics, established themselves as some of the leading explorers of the world.

ANDREW WITMER

*See also* Ancient Church; Celtic Missions; Conquest; Monasticism

## Further Reading

Hanbury-Tenison, R. (2005). *The Oxford book of exploration.* New York: Oxford University Press.

Laurie, T. (1885). *The Ely volume; or, the contributions of our foreign missions to science and human well-being.* Boston: American Board of Commissioners for Foreign Missions.

Marshall, P. J., & Williams, G. (1982). *The great map of mankind: Perceptions of New Worlds in the age of Enlightenment.* Cambridge, MA: Harvard University Press.

Pagden, A. (2003). *Peoples and empires.* New York: The Modern Library.

Palmer, S. H., & Reinhartz, D. (Eds.). (1988). *Essays on the history of North American discovery and exploration.* College Station: Published for the University of Texas at Arlington by Texas A&M University Press.

Phillips, J. R. S. (1988). *The medieval expansion of Europe.* New York: Oxford University Press.

Speake, J., ed. (2003). *Literature of travel and exploration: An encyclopedia* (3 vols.). New York: Fitzroy Dearborn.

Sykes, P. (1934). *A history of exploration.* London: George Routledge & Sons, Ltd.

# F

## Faith Missions

Many Evangelical Protestant missions, including many of the largest and most influential, have their roots in the faith-mission tradition. Examples of such missions include the China Inland Mission (now the Overseas Missionary Fellowship), Africa Inland Mission, Christian and Missionary Alliance, Wycliffe Bible Translators, and New Tribes. The founding principle, which remained the most distinctive characteristic of faith missions, was that they permitted no overt fundraising but relied on quiet faith in God to meet financial needs.

Designed initially as complements to the denominational mission boards that dominated the missionary enterprise in the nineteenth century, faith missions were offering a competing ideal for missionary service by the end of the century. Motivated by premillennial theology, many Evangelicals were anxious to hasten the process of world evangelization and eager to launch missionary endeavor into areas untended by the denominations.

This haste to evangelize the world led to the second distinctive characteristic of faith missions, the commitment to expand greatly the missionary force by employing poorly educated but highly committed missionaries. While the denominational boards required college and seminary, making their candidates some of the most educated people in the world, the vast majority of early faith mission candidates had not even completed high school. This was fine with faith mission leaders, because, as the Africa Inland Mission Manual stated, "Members of the Mission are accepted because of their desire and ability to win souls above all other requisites, and all else is secondary" (No. 81, 16). With their zeal and biblical knowledge fortified by a few months to a year or two at one of the many Bible institutes springing up around the United States and Canada, candidates hurried to the foreign field as soon as they had "prayed in" their passage money.

Candidates were inspired to hurry because of the third essential characteristic of faith missions, a commitment, at least at the board level, to a single-minded focus on evangelism. Here the faith missions drew the distinction between themselves and the denominational boards most sharply. The founders of the faith missions felt that the boards wasted valuable time and money building schools, hospitals, and orphanages, time better spent on direct evangelism. Believing that the return of Christ was just around the corner and that countless millions were descending yearly to "Christless graves," they insisted that there was no time for anything save evangelism. As the controversies between Fundamentalists and liberals heated up in the denominations after the turn of the century, faith mission leaders drew this distinction even more sharply as a way of distinguishing themselves from the liberal-tending denominational boards, even as faith missionaries on the field often found themselves building schools and hospitals when faced with the overwhelming need.

## First Faith Missions

The roots of the faith basis in Christian work go all the way back to the New Testament. Christ once sent out missionary teams, telling them not to take any money with them. They were to trust that they would be aided by those to whom they ministered. The specific

**155**

tradition of faith missions within evangelical Protestantism, however, can be traced directly to George Müller and J. Hudson Taylor, the two men most responsible for popularizing faith methods.

George Müller (1805–1898) was profoundly influenced by Anthony Norris Groves, a founder of the Plymouth Brethren, who after an intensive study of the Bible decided that Christ was speaking literal truth when he said "Sell what you have" (Luke 12:33, KJV) and "Do not lay up for yourselves treasures on earth" (Matthew 6:19, KJV). Influenced by Groves, Müller left the London Society for Promoting Christianity Among the Jews because he felt he should be guided by God alone in his activities rather than by men. He gave up his regular salary as a minister because it was based on pew rents and lived on free-will offerings alone, refusing to discuss his needs with anyone. Eventually Müller became justly famous for his large orphanages, which he ran on the faith basis. He refused to ask for financial support, relying on God to prompt Christians to give to his ministry. The stories of miraculous deliveries of food as the hungry orphans sat around an empty dinner table are still recounted in the evangelical community.

The decision of J. Hudson Taylor (1832–1905) to conduct Christian ministry on the faith basis seems to have been a very personal one that stemmed from a literal interpretation of Scripture. Christ's sending out of the teams of unprovisioned evangelists inspired Taylor to believe that Christian ministry ought to operate the same today. A premillennialist, he decided to live as if Christ might return tomorrow. He gave away unneeded possessions and lived frugally. Determined to become a missionary who lived by faith, Taylor began his now famous "exercises" to strengthen his faith. He refused to remind his forgetful employer to pay his salary, enduring whatever hardship ensued with no complaint, simply praying and trusting God to jog the elderly doctor's memory. For Taylor, difficult circumstances led to more frequent prayer, which in turn resulted in a more profound relationship with God.

When Taylor founded his enormously influential China Inland Mission (CIM) in 1865, he chose to operate it on the same basis. Mission policy stated that support would come only through the "freewill offerings of God's people. The needs of the work are laid before God in prayer, and no member of the Fellowship is authorized to solicit funds on his own behalf or that of the Fellowship, and no announcement of material needs is authorized." (Bacon 1983, 29) The mission also refused to go into debt, as to do so indicated a lack of faith in God's eventual supply. Taylor continued to appeal for new missionaries whether or not funds were on hand

for their support. Missionaries simply traveled to China trusting that God would supply their needs. Despite this seemingly impractical policy, the CIM grew at a tremendous rate and had become one of the most influential missions in the world by the end of the nineteenth century.

## Faith Mission Practice

Virtually all the independent Evangelical Protestant missions founded after the CIM followed the faith pattern established by these two men and their organizations. By 1890, faith mission "rules" were pretty well fixed. Faith missionaries learned that one of the primary means of determining God's will was through what might be called the "Divine financial weather vane." If a missionary was truly called to go overseas, or if a project was in the will of God, God would supply the funds. The missions hoped, of course, that the missionary's friends and home church would undertake their support. Few missionaries, however, went out with anything remotely resembling even the promise of full support. They nevertheless departed in high spirits, relying explicitly on God and implicitly on the mission council to raise funds for their support. Few were prepared for the sort of privation that awaited them in the field, even as many learned to bear up under it, if not endure it proudly, as a sign of God's special testing.

Taylor and other faith mission pioneers saw the faith method as a way of ceding complete control of the enterprise to God himself, thus ensuring that God, not man, received the praise for any accomplishment. The faith basis of operation increased the spirituality of Christian workers who were forced to spend long hours on their knees looking to God alone for their provision. Because of the drift of denominational boards away from a singular focus on evangelism, their reliance on the gifts of possibly unregenerate church members, their willingness to go into debt if need be to support missionaries, and their unwillingness to enter new fields unless they were financially viable, faith mission pioneers were able to argue that their missions "made more efficient use of funds, cultivated greater spirituality among their missionaries, and were more aggressively evangelistic than the denominational mission societies" (Carpenter and Shenk 1990, 55).

## Professionalization of Faith Missions

The impetus for the modification of faith mission practice came from the smaller missions competing for attention with the CIM. By the mid-1920s leaders from less well-known missions such as the Central American Mission and the Africa Inland Mission, after undergoing years of privation, were willing to acknowledge in more explicit ways that aggressive publicity did not necessarily undermine faith. It would take another generation, however, before new and more businesslike mission leaders, such as William Cameron Townsend (1896–1982) of the Wycliffe Bible Translators (WBT), began to expand the definition of faith work to include more professional promotional practices. Townsend believed that building a large constituency was an integral part of the fiscal process even for a mission operating on the faith basis. By mid-century WBT missionaries were raising at least a year's support before going overseas, and the mention of financial needs in WBT publications, while still resisted by some, was becoming much more explicit.

The WBT, with its commitment to Bible translation, also deeply impacted missionary training. Learning indigenous, often unwritten, languages and then translating the Bible into those languages required the kind of training supplied by secular academies and doctoral programs, and almost from its inception, WBT pushed for higher standards in missionary education. At the same time, many of the Bible institutes, which had sent so many graduates to the faith missions, were becoming Bible colleges and universities, and missionary training was becoming more thorough and academic. The discipline of anthropology, which had made inroads into Evangelical colleges by the 1960s, changed missionary education dramatically.

## Landscape Today

Many, if not most, of the large Protestant mission societies have come from the faith mission tradition. Faith missions have been remarkably successful because of their ability to adapt to changing times and needs. Today the independent Evangelical missions have very professional fund-raising operations, and few missionaries go overseas without their entire yearly quota committed in perpetuity through promises from friends, family, and churches. "Partnership development" is the new euphemism for fund-raising, and missionary partners know they can count on regular reports on the needs of their favorite missionary, and in truth, few would probably wish it otherwise. Evangelical missionaries today are highly educated, and they use their education in a variety of ways beyond strict evangelism. Probably the only way today's independent missions still resemble the faith missions of the nineteenth and early twentieth centuries is that they continue to seek innovative ways

to fulfill the command of Christ to "go into all the world and make disciples."

WILLIAM L. SVELMOE

*See also* Bible Translation; Evangelicalism; Fundamentalism; Linguistics; Mission Methods and Strategy; Parachurch; Partnership; Protestant Churches; Theology; Translation

### Further Reading

Anderson, D. (1994). *We felt like grasshoppers: The story of Africa inland mission.* Nottingham, UK: Crossway Books.

Bacon, D. W. (1983). The influence of Hudson Taylor on the Faith Mission Movement. Unpublished doctoral dissertation, Trinity Evangelical Divinity School, Deerfield, IL.

Brereton, V. (1990). *Training God's army: The American Bible schools, 1880–1940.* Bloomington: Indiana University Press.

Carpenter, J. A., & Shenk, W. R. (Eds.). (1990). *Earthen vessels: American evangelicals and foreign missions, 1880–1980.* Grand Rapids, MI: Eerdmans.

Eskridge, L., & Noll, M. A. (Eds.). (2000). *More money, more ministry: Money and Evangelicals in recent North American history.* Grand Rapids, MI: Eerdmans.

Fiedler, K. (1994). *The story of faith missions: From Hudson Taylor to present day Africa.* Oxford: Regnum Books.

Hutchison, W. R. (1987). *Errand to the world: American protestant thought and foreign missions.* Chicago: University of Chicago Press.

Rupert, M. (1974). *The emergence of the independent missionary agency as an American institution, 1860–1917.* Unpublished doctoral dissertation, Yale University, New Haven, CT.

Steer, R. (1981). *George Muller: Delighted in God.* Wheaton, IL: Harold Shaw.

Svelmoe, W. L. (2001). A new vision for missions: William Cameron Townsend in Guatemala and Mexico, 1917–1945. Unpublished doctoral dissertation, University of Notre Dame, Notre Dame, IN.

Taylor, J. H. (1987). *Hudson Taylor.* Minneapolis, MN: Bethany House.

## Family

Family has recently become a mission issue and a topic for discussion and there is now a growing body of literature on the subject. Although in reports of apostles sent out by the early church there is no mention of family, this is not true in reports of women, who show a wide range of involvement in Christian ministry in the

A photograph of a mission family
from the early 1900s in China.

Gospels. While Priscilla had an itinerant ministry along with Aquila, Mary and Martha, for instance, were apparently at home with their families, and some early women martyrs, such as Perpetua and Felicitas, were mothers before they were martyred for their faith.

However, most of the missionaries in these early reports were men, mainly single and celibate and part of early monastic orders. Among these orders were the Benedictines (sixth century), who focused on keeping the Christian faith alive, the Dominicans (thirteenth century), who concentrated on teaching and studying the faith, and the two great missionary orders, the Franciscans (thirteenth century) and the Jesuits (sixteenth century), who were concerned with spreading the faith.

Women were also involved in monastic orders, but by the ninth century, monastic women were almost reduced to invisibility by the imposition of the cloister. Women mystics, such as Hildegard of Bingen (twelfth century), Catherine of Siena (fourteenth century), and Julian of Norwich (fourteenth century), were all single. In fact, for the first eighteen centuries of Christian

missions in the West, most missionaries, both men and women, were either single or had taken a vow of chastity. It was not until the founding of the Protestant mission societies at the end of the eighteenth and the beginning of the nineteenth centuries, when married men were sent overseas as missionaries, that families became an issue.

## Home and Family as a Missionary Strategy

At the beginning of the nineteenth century mission societies burgeoned. The Baptist Missionary Society, the London Missionary Society (Congregationalist), the Church Missionary Society (Anglican), and other societies in the United States and Europe were all founded around this time. These Protestant societies were committed to sending out married men. They refused to send single women because they believed that missionary service was too dangerous for them, but they found that wives could serve several very useful purposes. First, the existence of a wife generally signified that a missionary had a peaceful intent; second, she reduced her husband's temptation to sexual philandering; and finally, she provided an excellent model of feminine behavior and was able to teach domestic skills.

The missionary wife was vital to the creation of the "civilized" Christian home, which became a conscious missionary strategy—in fact, an object lesson. These homes, in turn, provided a rationale for the involvement of married women in mission work. Missionary wives were expected to model pious domesticity and a Christian family life, and it was believed that this would transform societies not yet influenced by the Gospel. Until the second half of the nineteenth century, marriage was the only way for many women to become missionaries.

## Contemporary Situation

By the mid-twentieth century, family issues were often discussed in mission circles. The mushrooming literature on family issues reflected the desire of contemporary missionaries to create the best possible lives for their families. Among the most important issues were education, health care, culture shock, entry and reentry into the "home" culture, transition, language, retirement, rootlessness, and identity. For example, while in the nineteenth century it was common for missionary parents to send their children to boarding schools, many other options are available now, including home schooling, local schools, international schools, mission schools, and visiting home tutors.

Missionary children are now categorised as *tcks* (third culture kids). These are children who, having spent a significant part of their developmental years in a culture other than that of their parents, have developed a relationship to both cultures and hence almost belong to a third culture. Many studies have been done on what it means to be a *tck,* and *tck* networks are available through the Internet.

Member care, an attempt to provide holistic pastoral care for missionaries and their families, has also inspired a growing body of literature. Because it involves caring for every aspect of life, member care networks represent perspectives from both the West and the non-Western world. A related issue is how both parents exercise their roles in mission. Many women expect to be fully engaged in mission service, and this will impact family life in new and unexpected ways. More research also needs to be done on the impact of single-parent and blended families involved in mission.

An increasing number of missionaries are now from the majority world and may have different expectations from Western missionaries on what it means to be a family engaged in mission. Majority-world cultures also have a different understanding of family from Western culture. For instance, in the former, extended families are the norm, while the latter usually assumes a nuclear family. It will take time to see how majority-world families work out issues of family life in a mission context.

## Future Directions

Family issues are on the agenda for mission and will stay there. There is a growing literature on all aspects of Western and non-Western family life. Future studies will be needed to better understand the changing configurations of families—particularly single-parent and blended families and the families of majority-world missionaries—and their changing impact on Christian mission.

Cathy Ross

### Further Reading:

Kirkwood, D. (1993). Protestant missionary women: Wives and spinsters. In F. Bowie, D. Kirkwood, & S. Ardener (Eds.), *Women and missions: Past and present anthropological perspectives* (pp. 23–42). Oxford, UK: Berg.

Knell, M. (2003). *Families on the move.* London: Monarch.

Langmore, D. (1989). The object lesson of a civilised Christian home. In M. Jolly & M. Macintyre (Eds.), *Family and gender in the Pacific, domestic contradictions and the colonial impact* (pp. 84–94). Cambridge, UK: Cambridge University Press.

O'Donnell, K. (Ed.). (2002). *Doing member care well, perspectives and practices from around the world.* Pasadena, CA: William Carey Library.

Pollock, D., & van Reken, R. (2001). *Third culture kids, the experience of growing up among worlds.* Yarmouth, ME: Intercultural Press.

Robert, D. (1996). *American women in mission: A social history of their thought and practice.* Macon, GA: Mercer University Press.

Taylor, W. (Ed.). (1997). *Too valuable to lose, exploring the causes and cures of missionary attrition.* Pasadena, CA: William Carey Library.

## Fiction

Over the centuries, writers have reworked Biblical portraits of the apostles and other early proselytizers, from hagiographies like Jacob de Voragine's *Golden Legend* (c. 1260) to contemporary novels like Walter Wangerin Jr.'s historical drama *Paul* (2000) and Dan Brown's *The Da Vinci Code* (2003). Generally, however, two flourishes of mission have inspired modern fiction writers: the Portuguese, Spanish, and French Roman Catholic missions of the sixteenth and seventeenth centuries, which revived in the nineteenth century, and the British and North American Protestant missions of the nineteenth and twentieth centuries. Both periods saw Christian missions established round the world as spiritual outposts of Western expansion. Images in fiction portraying missions from these periods range from the heroic to the hypocritical.

### Depictions of Roman Catholic Missions

Among the earliest depictions of Catholic missions is Sydney Owenson's *The Missionary: An Indian Tale* (1811), set in seventeenth-century Kashmir. The book dramatizes an unconsummated romance between the Portuguese Franciscan missionary Hilarion and the Hindu priestess Luxima, a liaison resulting in her death and his disillusionment. Decades later, James Hilton's *Lost Horizon* (1933) depicts another strange Catholic venture in South Asia: the Tibetan lamasery of Shangri-la, run by Father Perrault, a two-hundred-year-old Belgian Capuchin missionary.

Other writers have portrayed Catholic missionaries in the New World. In Brian Moore's *Black Robe* (1985), Father Laforgue learns compassion for the doomed Hurons of the Jesuit mission of Saint Marie in seventeenth-century New France. In Willa Cather's *Death Comes for the Archbishop* (1927), a cathedral in the desert symbolizes Father Jean Marie Latour's nearly forty years of Jesuit service after the Mexican War (1846–48). While Bernice Scott's fictionalized biography *Junipero Serra, Pioneer of the Cross* (1976) portrays the eighteenth-century founder of California missions in hagiographical terms, Native-American Leslie Marmon Silko's *Almanac of the Dead* (1991) includes missionaries in a critique of nonnative exploitation of North and South American indigenous peoples. Poignantly, *Kiss of the Fur Queen* (1998), by Native-Canadian Tomson Highway, exposes Father Roland Lafleur, Oblate of Mary Immaculate, sexually abusing Cree Indian boys in a mission school.

Catholic clerics in Africa have received mixed reviews in fiction, as well. In Graham Greene's *A Burnt-out Case* (1961), at a missionary leprosarium in the Belgian Congo, the celebrated French ecclesiastical architect Querry is at first consumed by apathy but later realizes, "I suffer, therefore I am." Indigenous African writers are often censorious of missions. Catholic clerics disrupt African birthright traditions by removing sons to the mission school in *Blade among the Boys* (1962) and *The Only Son* (1966), by Nigerians Onuora Nzekwu and John Munonye respectively, and in *Jingala* (1969), by Malawian Legson Kayira. In *A Fighter for Freedom* (1983), by Zimbabwean Edmund Chipamaunga, the mission school is controlled by Father Truss, who belongs to Ian Smith's racist Rhodesia Front. Also set in Zimbabwe, Tsitsi Dangarembga's *Nervous Conditions* (1988) dramatizes the ambiguous effects of the Catholic mission's Young Ladies' College of the Sacred Heart upon the traditional roles of Shona women. More ambivalently, Kenjo Jumbam's *The White Man of God* (1980) suggests a common humanity between European and African by portraying Father Cosmas as a compassionate young priest who succumbs to the disease from which he has protected his congregation.

## Evangelical Revivals as Source

Numerous writers turned for material to the Evangelical revivals that spawned waves of British and North American Protestant missions after the late seventeenth century. In Charlotte Bronte's *Jane Eyre* (1847), St. John Rivers chooses "the wild field of mission warfare" over "the parlours and the peace" of English country life. More ironically, in Charles Dickens's *Bleak House* (1853) Mrs. Jellyby lets her children starve while she raises money for missions to Africa. Charlotte Yonge's *The Daisy Chain, or Aspirations* (1856) is notable for endorsing

the proselytizing efforts both of Samoan converts in the South Pacific and of missionary women in overseas and domestic English fields. Sir William Wilson Hunter's *The Old Missionary* (1890) is similarly enthusiastic about early nineteenth-century mission life in Bengal. By contrast, Herman Melville's autobiographical novels *Typee: A Peep at Polynesian Life* (1846) and *Omoo* (1847) recognize that missionaries improved morality, produced vernacular Bibles, and established churches and schools in the South Pacific, but the novels lament their racial prejudice and insensitivity to local traditions.

All the same, by the late nineteenth century Protestant publishing houses were producing numerous popular tales featuring heroic missionaries carrying the white man's Gospel to benighted heathens. Canadian-frontier adventures like Ralph Connor's *Black Rock: A Tale of the Selkirks* (1898) and *The Sky Pilot: A Tale of the Foothills* (1899) typify this trend. Such novels portray the evangelist as a man muscular in flesh and spirit, unfazed by natural calamities and wild-animal attacks, frontier bar brawls and Catholic perfidy. Similar missionary romances were set in Africa, and to a lesser extent India and Australia, New Zealand and the South Pacific.

## Skepticism and Ambiguity

The beginning of the twentieth century saw less certainty about Protestant Christian partnership with Western expansionism. In *Siri Ram, Revolutionist* (1912) and *Abdication* (1922), Edmund Candler identifies the missionary presence in India with imperial power, exercised to the benefit of hypocritical self-interest. Between World Wars I and II, three short stories epitomize this increasing skepticism. Edith Wharton's "The Seed of the Faith" (1919) tells of Mr. Blandhorn, a desperate American Baptist missionary in Eloued, Morocco, who contrives his own martyrdom by publicly desecrating the Qur'an and declaring "Christ crucified!" W. Somerset Maugham's "Rain" (1921) finds Alfred Davidson quarantined in American Samoa, where the missionary commits suicide after sleeping with the prostitute Sadie Thompson. The third story, E. M. Forster's "The Life to Come" (1922), posits interracial homosexual relations. Vithobai, a tribal chieftain in central India, identifies Christ's love with the young English missionary Paul Pinmay, then murders him for denying their passion, and commits suicide.

Several interwar novels further explore missionary ambiguities. In Sylvia Townsend Warner's *Mr. Fortune's Maggot* (1927), the volcanic South Pacific island of Fanua erupts, killing Timothy Fortune's only convert, the angelic boy Lueli, and with him the Church of England missionary's faith. Decapitating her infant son Abba to the rainmaking chant, "All de tings I lak de mos / I sacrifice dem to His blood," a convert at the Shibi Mission conflates Nigerian *ju-ju* traditions of sacrificial appeasement with Mr. Carr the evangelist's teachings about Christ's self-sacrifice in Joyce Cary's *Aissa Saved* (1932). Less violent, Rumer Godden's *Black Narcissus* (1939) dramatizes Sister Clodagh's difficulties establishing an Anglican mission in the former pleasure palace of a Himalayan potentate. And in Australia, Xavier Herbert's *Capricornia* (1938) describes how the Gospel Mission profits from coconut plantations worked for free by the Reverend Theodore Hollower's Aborigine converts, who receive Christian indoctrination for free in return.

## Other Regional Settings

Several postwar North American writers set their stories in China. Cornelia Spencer's *The Missionary* (1947) explores tensions among American evangelists whose mission shelters the wounded in China's civil conflict, while John Bechtel's *The Year of the Tiger* (1946) depicts missionaries as beacons of hope when World War II threatens to overwhelm a Chinese family. In John Hersey's *The Call: An American Missionary in China* (1985), the evangelical David Treadup realizes that educational and agricultural reform have more to do with improving life on earth than with saving souls. Other North American novelists turn to other geographies. Charles E. Mercer's *Rachel Cade* (1956) portrays an American nurse cursed by local shamans for climbing the sacred Mountains of the Moon in the Belgian Congo. Alice Walker's *The Color Purple* (1982) reverses the Middle Passage, as letters about the Reverend Samuel's missionary work in West Africa enable the protagonist, Celie, to recover her spiritual health. In *First and Vital Candle* (1963), Canadian Mennonite writer Rudy Wiebe suggests that both Catholic and Protestant magisterial missions were interested only in imposing ecclesiastical disciplines upon Arctic Inuit peoples, whereas later nonconformist evangelists converted by example. And in Australia, Randolph Stow's *To the Islands* (1958) portrays an Anglican missionary who believes he has murdered an Aborigine and flees into the outback, not to avoid justice but to explore the frontiers of his tormented soul, while Herbert's *Poor Fellow My Country* (1975) satirizes denominational rivalries between the Protestant Mission Society's teetotaling Reverend James Tasker and Father Glascock, who greets visitors to the Catholic Leopold Islands Mission with a beer.

## Late Twentieth Century and Beyond

Either side of the new millennium, a flurry of novels have depicted Protestant missions and missionaries in Africa. In *Crossing the River* (1993), by black British writer Caryl Philips, Nash Williams, an emancipated slave sent as a missionary to early nineteenth-century Liberia, suffers an identity crisis, disappears, and dies. In Hilary Mantel's *A Change of Climate* (1994), South African apartheid and the kidnapping of their infant son for body parts by a spirit healer in Bechuanaland leave English lay missionaries Ralph and Anna Eldred convinced that radical evil transcends race. Less pessimistic, *Swimming in the Congo* (1995), a collection of short stories by Margaret Meyers, explores the interplay between Protestant and Congolese tribal beliefs from the perspective of a missionary's seven-year-old daughter in the 1960s. Also set in the Belgian Congo, Barbara Kingsolver's *Poisonwood Bible* (1998) portrays the American Baptist missionary Nathan Price, whose zealousness so infuriates the villagers of Kilanga that they burn him, still preaching from his perch atop a coffee plantation *tour de maître,* to be dragged to his death by animals. More hopeful, *Joshua's Bible* (2003), by the African-American writer Shelly Leanne, tells the story of Joshua Clay, who abandons his interwar mission board's instructions to preach in English and adopts Xhosa translations and the struggle against racism in South Africa.

Various locations provide settings for other recent novels. In Julia Blackburn's *The Book of Colour* (1995), a nineteenth-century English missionary's efforts to "civilize" the natives on an Indian Ocean island engender a legacy of madness for his descendants. *Tapu* (1997) and *Slow Water* (2003), by New Zealanders Judy Corbalis and Annamarie Jagose respectively, draw upon historical events: Beginning in 1814, the first portrays evangelists Thomas and Jane Kendall, who violate the *tapu* world of the Maoris they hope to convert; and the second fictionalizes the shipboard affair between William Yates and a sailor while traveling from London to Sydney in 1836 and the scandal following fellow Anglican Richard Taylor's outing of the homosexual cleric.

Contemporary American authors take us to other mission fields. In Nora Okja-Keller's *Comfort Woman* (1998) and *Fox Girl* (2002), Protestant missionaries in Korea demean the victims of Japanese violence in World War II and preach the superiority of the United States to the "throwaway children" of American servicemen from the Korean War. John Dalton's *Heaven Lake* (2004) follows Vincent Saunders from Red Bud, Illinois, to Toulio, Taiwan, where his affair with a student costs him a job teaching English in a Presbyterian Bible school.

And in Philip Caputo's *Acts of Faith* (2005), American evangelical Quinette Hardin helps to ransom Christian blacks enslaved by Arab raiders in the 1990s, marries a leader of the Sudanese People's Liberation Army, and campaigns for armed rebellion against Khartoum's Islamist government.

## Indigenous Writers' Contributions

Such postcolonial tensions between Western and non-Western cultures have long preoccupied indigenous writers, too. The British legacy in Africa, for example, inspired Akiki K. Nyabongo's *Africa Answers Back* (1936), in which Mujungu finds more meanings in biblical stories than evangelists intend, including scriptural backing for polygamy. *Things Fall Apart* (1958), by Nigerian Chinua Achebe, portrays the missionaries Mr. Brown and Mr. Smith as two faces of colonial Christianity, one benevolent, the other autocratic. In Achebe's *Arrow of God* (1964), John Goodcountry, a native Christian missionary, and Ezeulu, a priest of the traditional god Ulu, embody the clash between tribal Igbo and European mores. Kenya's Ngugi wa Thiong'o also highlights the ambiguities of the missionary presence. In *Weep Not, Child* (1962), Ngugi writes of evangelists who "never talked down to Africans," but in *The River Between* (1965), the Reverend Mr. Livingston's ban on female circumcision sets the traditionalist Kameno against the Christian Makuyu. Missionary teaching likewise disrupts tribal traditions in Francis Selormy's *The Narrow Path* (1967), where Christian notions of family undermine Ghanaian patrilineality.

Along different lines, Ndatshan, the missions school's native teacher in Stanlake John Thompson Samkange's *The Mourned One* (1975), is falsely accused of rape and sentenced to death on testimony from the missionary, "his brother in Christ, but not his brother in law . . . a white man first and a Christian second." Conniving with Ian Smith's racist Rhodesian regime compromises the ethical authority of the Anglican missionary church in Zimbabwean Dambudzo Marechera's *The House of Hunger* (1978), while André Brink's *Praying Mantis* (2005) fictionalizes events at Bethelsdorp, Cape Colony, where the London Missionary Society's J. T. van der Kemp and James Read abandon the Khoi convert Kupido Kakkerlak just after 1800.

Two final examples illustrate how postcolonial issues have captivated writers from other formerly British domains, too. In Mulk Raj Anand's *The Untouchable* (1935), Bakha the toilet cleaner believes flush technology to be a more likely relief from the ills of untouchability than the Christian teachings of Colonel Hutchinson, while Philip McLaren's *Sweet Water—Stolen Land* (1993) has German Lutheran Karl Maresch murdering Australian settlers who herd scapegoated Aborigines into the Neuberg Mission, thus justifying the killings in the evangelist's crazed mind.

## Fiction in Other Languages

Among fictional depictions of missions and missionaries in languages other than English, the Japanese novel *Silence* (1966) stands out. In Shusaku Endo's story, the Portuguese Catholic priest Sebastian Rodrigues travels from Macao to Japan in the 1630s to atone for the apostasy of his mentor, Christovao Ferreira, then as God remains silent, succumbs to apostasy himself in order to save tortured Christian peasants.

### Brazil

More frequently, though, missions and missionaries appear in the growing national literatures of Europe's former colonial and imperial domains, notably in Latin America and Africa. In the early Brazilian novel *Simá* (1857), by Lourenço da Silva Araújo Amazonas, Carmelite priests help natives displaced by Portuguese colonizers to transform jungle into an agricultural settlement, while Herculano Inglêz de Souza's *O missionário* [*The Missionary*] (1891) has Father Antonio de Morais abandoning noble intentions to convert the native Mundurucus, taking a mistress, and pursuing personal ambitions in the ecclesiastical hierarchy.

Several Brazilian novelists have dramatized the Guaranítica War (1752–56), which saw the Jesuits expelled from Portuguese and Spanish possessions. Érico Verissimo's *O continente* (1943), Manelito de Ornellas's *Tiaraju* (1945), Alcy Cheuiche's *Sepé Tiaraju* (1978), and Rui Nedel's *Esta terra teve dono* [*This Land Has an Owner*] (1983), explore the relationship between the Jesuits and the guerrilla Sepé Tiaraju, who served as prefect of the Mission of San Miguel before becoming a native defender of mission settlements against Portuguese and Spanish forces. Religion and politics intermingle in other Brazilian fiction, too. In Antonio Callado's *Quarup* (1978), time amongst the Xingu natives inspires the young priest Nando to denounce the military coup of 1964, while Darcy Ribeiro's *Maira* (1976) portrays Italian Jesuits competing to transform the lives of Mairum natives with apocalyptic American evangelicals whose mission station is shaped like a flying saucer. Similar themes permeate other Latin American fiction, as well. Mario Vargas Llosa's *El Hablador* [*The Storyteller*] (1987) laments the way in which Catholic missionary efforts to convert the Machiguengas along the Urumba River in Peru's Amazon rainforest have contributed to the loss of tribal culture.

### African Fiction

In African vernacular fiction, numerous short pieces celebrate the triumph of Christianity over native superstition, among them Malawian S. A. Paliani's Nyanja narrative, *In 1930 Came a Witchdoctor* (1930); Zairean Stephen A. Mpashi's *The Catholic Priests Arrive among the Bemba* (1956); and Zimbabwean works like David Ndoda's Ndebele tale, *In Days Gone By* (1958), and Patrick Chakaipa's Shona story, *Love Is Blind* (1966). By contrast, A. C. Mzolisa Jordan's Xhosa story, *The Wrath of the Ancestors* (1940), suggests that African pride awakened by Anglican missionizing is really a masked revival of precolonial tribal identity.

Many Francophone and Lusophone African writings portray Catholic missions unflatteringly. *Le pauvre Christ de Bomba* (The Poor Christ of Bomba) (1956), by Cameroon's Mongo Beti, satirizes Father Drumont's efforts to frustrate premarital sex. Catechists rape native girls confined in the *sixa,* sowing seeds of syphilis among future generations of Africans. In *Une vie de boy* (Life of a Boy) (1956), by another Cameroonian, Ferdinand Léopold Oyono, Father Gilbert uses conversion to bring French civilization to Africa, but gonorrheal catechists reflect European Christianity's true decadence. Zairean Thomas Mpoyi-Buatu also frames missionary corruption in sexual terms. Ranging from mid-nineteenth-century to contemporary Kinshasa, *La re-production* (1986) attacks Catholic missions for being partners in the colonial exploitation of Africa. In *La mort faité homme* (1986), another Zairean, Ngandu Nkashama, identifies the mission school's Father Director as an abusive hypocrite. Similarly, José Luandino's Lusophone Angolan collection, *Vidas novas* (New Lives) (1976), includes the short story "Dina," which implicates missionaries in colonial cruelties, as the title character, a prostitute, recalls how Portuguese troops killed her parents even as they sought sanction in the Mission of Sao Paulo. Once again, the missionary here fares ill in the hands of the secular skeptic.

### Twenty-first-century Evolvement

As the interplay of cultures continues apace worldwide, the panorama of missions and missionaries portrayed in vernacular and in English-language and other national literatures will doubtless continue to grow more various and more colorful.

Mindful of the frequently mixed motives of their former mentors, for example, indigenous churches now send missionaries to preach the gospel in former colonial and imperial centres in Europe and North America, and we may expect to see these figures featuring in future short stories and novels. At the same time, ironically, lecturers in Western seminaries and theological colleges, equally aware of the checkered record of colonial and imperial missionizing, today include mission fiction in their syllabuses in an effort to add a degree of human ambiguity to the idealistic image of the missionary enterprise so often portrayed in less self-reflective mission histories and missiological treatises.

JAMIE S. SCOTT

### Further Reading

Blodgett, J. (1997). *Protestant evangelical literary culture and contemporary society.* Westport, CT: Greenwood Press.

Chapman, R. (2002). *Godly and righteous, peevish and perverse: Clergy and religious in literature and letters.* Grand Rapids, MI: Eerdmans Publishing

Johnston, A. (2003). *Missionary writing and empire, 1800–1860.* Cambridge, UK: Cambridge University Press.

Scott, J. S. (Ed.). (2001). *"And the birds began to sing": Religion and literature in postcolonial cultures.* Atlanta, GA: Rodopi Bv Editions.

## Film

Sometimes adapted from literature, sometimes from life, and sometimes original in conception, different kinds of film have portrayed missions and missionaries. Silent movies feature various forms of evangelism, usually Protestant. The trope continues in big-screen and later made-for-television "talkies," including musicals. Third, biographical pictures and documentaries have depicted evangelists in feature films and television productions. Fourth, recent years have seen the burgeoning of Christian cinema as a distinct genre, and in a related development various denominations make use of film in proselytizing. Missions and missionaries also figure in educational videos.

### Missions in Silent Movies

Although many silent pictures are lost, storylines and stills survive, depicting missions and missionaries in various domestic and foreign fields. On the home front,

Evangelicals battle urban poverty and frontier savagery. The Edison Company one-reeler *Land beyond the Sunset* (1912) portrays the Fresh Air Fund, a mission created in 1877 by the Reverend Willard Parsons to provide summer holidays for inner-city children. In Easy Street (1917; director, Charles Chaplin), the Hope Mission's beautiful organist inspires a down-and-out Charlie Chaplin to join the police to bring order to South London's slums. The New Mission dominates the film's closing sequence, as church bells accompany the on-screen apothegm: "Love backed by force, forgiveness sweet, / Brings hope and peace to Easy Street." Such sentiments infuse numerous other silent films, including *Susan Rocks the Boat* (1916; dir., Paul Powell), *The Day of Faith* (1923; dir., Tod Browning), and *Good Morning, Judge* (1928; dir., William A. Seiter). Likewise, in the comedy *For Heaven's Sake* (1926; dir., Sam Taylor), a wealthy playboy defies family and friends, finances a storefront mission, and marries the evangelist's aptly named daughter, Hope.

Pictures portraying American frontier missions usually end happily as well, such as the shorts *The Mission Waif, The Mission Father,* and *The Mission in the Desert,* all produced in 1911. In *Sky Pilot* (1921; dir., King Vidor), a muscular Protestant evangelist finds love taming adventurers and civilizing Indians in the Canadian Northwest, while an Indian rebel and his mission orphan wife accede to the governor's mansion in *The Diamond Bandit* (1924; dir., Francis Ford). A Roman Catholic priest dies helping these native South American freedom fighters, though, so not all ends well.

Numerous silent pictures represent missions in "exotic" locales like Africa, China, the South Pacific, and India. In *The Mystery of the Poison Pool* (1914; dir., James Gordon), sub-Saharan cannibals, a giant python, and a poison pool fail to quell the passion between a missionary and a diamond prospector wrongly accused of murder. In *The Arab* (1924; dir., Rex Ingram), a North African Bedouin falls in love with an American missionary and prevents the massacre of a Christian community in Turkey, while *A Daughter of the Congo* (1930; dir., Oscar Micheaux) suggests mission education will redeem a beautiful mulatto girl rescued from Arab slave traders by African-American soldiers keeping the peace in Liberia. Elsewhere, a mission-educated Eurasian girl styles herself as a Chinese goddess in *Red Lantern* (1919; dir., Albert Capellani), then commits suicide when her prophecies supporting the Boxer Rebellion fail. Equally sobering, *Where the Pavement Ends* (1923; dir., Rex Ingram) closes with a missionary and his daughter returning home, after his proselytizing leads to a bar owner's death and his daughter's flirtations end in a

South Pacific chieftain's suicide. An Indian prince becomes an Anglican missionary in *The Rip-Tide* (1923; dir., Jack Pratt), then abandons Christianity to marry an Indian princess.

## Missions in "Talkies": The Bad, the Good, and the Ambiguous

In the late 1920s "talkies" developed the more nuanced attitudes towards missions and missionaries foreshadowed in silent pictures.

### The Bad

One example of this foreshadowing of later attitudes was *Just Like a Woman* (1923; dir., Scott R. Beal and Hugh McClung), in which the heroine leads a double life as aspiring evangelist by day and frolicsome flapper by night, and the more unforgiving *Sadie Thompson* (1928; dir., William Cameron Menzies and Raoul Walsh), soon remade as the talkie *Rain* (1932; dir., Lewis Milestone), in which a hypocritical South Pacific missionary preaches morality to a prostitute servicing American servicemen, then rapes her himself. Other less-than-sympathetic portrayals follow.

On the domestic front, small-town America is the backdrop for confidence tricksters posing as evangelists in the comedy *Tillie and Gus* (1933; dir., Francis Martin), while *Elmer Gantry* (1960; dir., Richard Brooks) pillories the Evangelical marketing of Christianity in the American Bible Belt. Missions in foreign fields receive severe treatment, too. In *East of Borneo* (1931; dir., George Melford), a medical missionary serves as drunken physician to an African despot, while a puritanical evangelist browbeats Pacific islanders in *Return to Paradise* (1953; dir., Mark Robson), a theme reiterated in *Hawaii* (1966; dir., George Roy Hill). Set in the Peruvian Amazon, the Swedish *Djungelaeventyret Campa-Campa* (Jungle Adventure Campa Campa) (1976; dir., Torgny Anderberg) dramatizes tensions between Campa natives and a priest who abducts children to raise them as Christians.

Paralleling the aspirations of a zealous missionary and an obsessed inventor, *The Mosquito Coast* (1986; dir., Peter Weir) confirms the futility of fanaticism, a tragic theme humorously rehearsed in *Eversmile, New Jersey* (1989; dir., Carlos Sorin), in which an Eversmile Foundation of New Jersey dentist resolves to preach "dental consciousness" to Argentinian Patagonia's darkened souls. *At Play in the Fields of the Lord* (1991; dir., Hector Babenco) depicts tensions between fundamentalist

Protestant and Roman Catholic missions competing to convert Brazil's Niaruna Indians.

## The Good

Numerous talkies maintain the good repute of missions and missionaries, however. Domestic evangelism remained a popular film vehicle in the 1930s. *Madonna of the Streets* (1930; dir., John S. Robertson) involves mission intrigue on San Francisco's Barbary Coast, while *The Miracle Woman* (1931; dir., Frank Capra) sees a blind man's trust transform a disillusioned minister's daughter from sham revivalist into genuine evangelist. In *Soul of the Slums* (1931; dir., Frank Strayer), a framed convict falls in love with an inner-city mission worker, forgoes revenge upon his accusers, and dedicates his life to her cause.

Other pictures portray overseas missions favorably, especially in Africa, China, and the South Pacific. In *Trader Horn* (1931; dir., W. S. Van Dyke), a dedicated evangelist's death inspires adventurers to good deeds in Africa, while a British missionary's demise in German East Africa prompts romanticized World War I action in *The African Queen* (1951; dir., John Huston). Several films ennoble medical missionaries: in *A Distant Trumpet* (1952; dir., Terence Fisher) , brothers in London and Africa swap doctoring duties; in *Men against the Sun* (1953; dir., Brendan J. Stafford), a medical missionary sweetens a surveyor building a railway from Mombassa, Kenya, to the Ugandan interior; and in *White Witch Doctor* (1953; dir., Henry Hathaway), kindly Christian medics criticize colonial speculators for pressuring Congolese tribesmen into revealing remote gold deposits.

Missionaries also question Western mineral exploitation in *Jungle Drums of Africa* (1953; dir., Fred C. Brannon), a 12-part serial feature reedited for television as *U-238 and the Witch Doctor* (1966); and African-American evangelists return to their Ghanaian tribal roots in *The Color Purple* (1985; dir., Steven Spielberg).

Some films feature Roman Catholic missionaries. In *The Keys of the Kingdom* (1944; dir., John M. Stahl), a priest hones his pastoral skills in China before returning to Scotland to minister to troubled youth, and in *The Left Hand of God* (1955; dir., Edward Dmytryk), nuns shelter a downed American pilot posing as a priest to avoid capture by Communists.

South Asia provides settings for a few good missionaries, as do Haiti, Indonesia, and South America. Steamy relations among India's colonial élites include a mission runaway in *The Rains Came* (1939; dir., Clarence Brown). *Black Narcissus* (1947; dir., Michael Powell) depicts Saint Faith Order nuns turning a Himalayan potentate's former pleasure palace into an Anglican mission. After India's independence, an evangelist's blind daughter distracts a mercenary from running guns to Ghandahari rebels in *Thunder in the East* (1953; dir., Charles Vidor). In Haiti a missionary helps to save a young woman from living death among zombies in *White Zombie* (1932; dir., Victor Halperin).

Eighteenth-century rivalries between Spain and Portugal over Latin American colonies becomes an allegory for contemporary tensions in *The Mission* (1986; dir., Roland Joffé), which contrasts two Jesuit priests, one an idealist preaching peaceful native resistance, the other a reformed slaver and fratricide, who abandons his vows to lead armed opposition to European aggression. In *Paradise Road* (1997; dir., Bruce Beresford), a British missionary forms an a cappella ensemble to occupy European women interned in Sumatra after the Japanese conquest of Singapore in World War II.

## The Ambiguous

Lastly, several talkies offer decidedly ambiguous depictions of missionaries. In *Laughing Sinners* (1931; dir., Harry Beaumont), a Salvation Army captain exchanges his ministry for a suicidal nightclub singer, while a missionary's widow kills for her shipboard lover in *So Evil My Love* (1948; dir., Lewis Allen), repenting only when he betrays her. In *Black Robe* (1991; dir., Bruce Beresford), a Jesuit priest's efforts to convert Huron Indians in seventeenth-century Québec eventuate in his spiritual humbling and their falling victims to long-time enemies, the Iroquois. In *The Apostle* (1997; dir., Robert Duvall), a Pentecostal evangelist among Lousiana's rural poor goes to jail for murdering his wife's lover, a curate at his former church in Texas.

Overseas, the Congo serves as setting for several pictures: in *The Sins of Rachel Cade* (1961; dir., Gordon Douglas), a downed World War II flyer impregnates a medical missionary, who seeks solace with a spurned colleague when the flyer leaves; in the Italian-Spanish *Encrucijada para una monja* (*Crossroads for a Nun*, 1967; dir., Lucio Fulci), natives rape a nun, who must then give up her baby to remain in the order or abandon her calling to become a single mother. A sister forsakes the veil in *The Nun's Story* (1969; dir., Fred Zinnemann) after her superiors wastefully redirect her medical skills from Congolese natives to European colonials.

Elsewhere, in *The Bitter Tea of General Yen* (1933; dir., Frank Capra), a Chinese general prefers suicide to dishonoring an American missionary's fiancée who captures his heart, and in *Ethan* (1964; dir., Michael DuPont), an alcoholic priest dies defending the Filipino woman he loves. An evangelist's nymphomaniac daughter adds spice to the lives of Europeans seeking enlightenment in *Bali* (1970; dir., Ugo Liberatore), while an Anglican priest falls in love with a nineteenth-century Australian businesswoman in *Oscar and Lucinda* (1997; dir., Gillian Armstrong), then wagers that he can safely transport her glass church into the interior. Gone native after twenty-five years in a Ugandan leper colony, a priest returns in 1936 to remind rural Roman Catholics of their pagan Irish roots in *Dancing at Lughnasa* (1998; dir., Pat O'Connor).

Some musicals and made-for-television movies ring changes on these images, including a remake of the silent pictures *The Belle of New York* (1952; dir., Charles Walters) and *Miss Sadie Thompson* (1953; dir., Curtis Bernhardt), a bowdlerized version of *Rain* (1932; dir., Lewis Milestone), itself a reworking of the silent film *Sadie Thompson*. In *Down among the Sheltering Palms* (1953; dir., Edmund Goulding), a missionary and an American army captain would prevent the troops from fraternizing with South Pacific island girls, while a New York gambler takes a Salvation Army worker to Havana on a bet in *Guys and Dolls* (1955; dir., Joseph L. Mankiewicz), returns in love, then risks losing her by using the mission as a casino.

**Made for TV**

Made-for-television films include *U-238 and the Witch Doctor* (1966; dir., Fred C. Brannon), a reediting of the serial *Jungle Drums of Africa* (1953), in which a missionary's daughter teams with uranium explorers against spies, lions, and African tribes. A missionary finds his vocation among Northwest Canadian Indians in *I Heard the Owl Call My Name* (1973; dir., Daryl Duke), while South American Indians prevent a crazed missionary from sacrificing airplane-crash survivors in *Valley of Mystery* (1967; dir., Joseph Lejtes). South American jungles shelter another mad missionary in *The Lost World* (2001; dir., Stuart Orme).

## Christian Missionizing through Films and Videos

Christians proselytize through pictures, too. The silent *In the Land of the Setting Sun; or, Martyrs of Yesterday* (1919; dir., Raymond Wells) tells of Marcus and Narcissa Whitman, American Missionary Board evangelists who in 1836 brought the Gospel to Washington State's Walla Walla River region. Other silent pictures include the Belgian *Missionaires italiens aux Indes* (*Ital-

ian Missionaries in the Indies,* 1932; dir., Raphaël Algoet) and *The Call* (1938; dir., Léon Poirier), about Charles de Foucauld (1858–1916), Trappist priest to the Saharan Touareg. *Abuna Messias* (1939; dir., Geoffredo Alessandrini) glorifies Capuchin Franciscan Guglielmo Massaia (1809–1889), who tried to convert Ethiopia's Galla Copts to Roman Catholicism, while films like *L'Élite noire de demain* (*The Black Elite of Tomorrow,* 1950) document European missions in other foreign fields.

The 1950s also saw the biopics *Battle Hymn* (1956; dir., Douglas Sirk), about Dean E. Hess, who bombed German orphans in World War II, then saved Korean ones in the Korean War; *Inn of the Sixth Happiness* (1958; dir., Mark Robson), about Gladys Aylward, an English missionary in Japanese-occupied China; and *Molokai, la isla maldita* (1959; dir., Luis Lucia), about Damian de Veuster (1840–1889), the Belgian Holy Heart priest who ministered to lepers on Molokai, Hawaii's "island of the damned," a life revisited in *Molokai: The Story of Father Damien* (1999; dir., Paul Cox).

*Chariots of Fire* (1981; dir., Hugh Hudson) features Eric Liddell, a Scottish missionary running for God in the 1924 Paris Olympics. Other examples include *Light in the Jungle* (1990; dir., Gray Hofmeyr), about Albert Schweitzer; Zamperini; *Still Carrying the Torch* (1992; dir., Michael O. Sajbel), about an American sports and war hero converted to Christian service at Billy Graham's First Crusade, San Francisco, 1949; and *Obstacle to Comfort: The Life of George Mueller* (1997; dir., Ken Connolly), about the founder of the independent Baptist Scriptural Knowledge Institute for Home and Abroad.

*The Other Side of Heaven* (2002; dir., Mitch Davis) lionizes John H. Groberg, an American Mormon missionary to the South Pacific's Tongans. Particularly poignant is *Beyond the Gates of Splendor* (2002; dir., Jim Hanon), which documents the murder of five missionaries by Waodani Indians in Ecuador in 1956, a story of conversion and reconciliation recreated in *End of the Spear* (2005; dir., Jim Hanon). In made-for-television films, *Mother Theresa* (2003; dir., Fabrizio Costa) celebrates the Albanian Roman Catholic founder of Missionaries of Charity, while *Black Bearded Barbarian: Mackay of Taiwan* (2006; dir., Susan Papp) pays tribute to George Leslie Mackay, a Canadian missionary in Taiwan during the second half of the nineteenth century.

### Films That Celebrate

Finally, Christian organizations produce and distribute films and videos celebrating missionary accomplishments, like the Wycliffe Bible Translators' *The Good Seed* (1986), which portrays the missionizing of the Tzeltals in Southern Mexico and the Payas in the mountains of Colombia, or the New Tribes Mission's *The Taliabo Story: The Search for the River of Eternal Life* (1997), which details the conversion of the inhabitants of a remote Indonesian island. The Inter-Varsity Christian Fellowship markets videos of the plenary addresses at their triennial student-mission conventions.

### Christian Cinema as an Industry

As well, Christian cinema has blossomed as a distinct industry. Depicting everyday life for an American missionary family in France, *Yes and Goodbye* and *A Dream Begun* typify the extensive list of Harvest Productions, "the film ministry" of the Evangelical Baptist Missions, which focuses on the Bible's role in conversion. *Road to Redemption* (2001; dir. Richard Vernon), by the Billy Graham Evangelistic Association's World Wide Pictures (WWP), adopts the conventions of the road movie for Christian outreach. Other releases dramatize evangelizing, like *Last Flight Out* (2003; dir. Jerry Jameson), which pits a medical missionary against Columbian drug runners.

The Church of Jesus Christ of Latter Day Saints has backed shorts, like the early *Worthy to Stand* (1969; dir., Judge Whitaker), as well as features, like *Suits on the Loose* (2005; dir. Rodney Henson), in which posing as Mormon missionaries leads juvenile delinquents to confront their past. Events like the San Antonio Independent Christian Film Festival and the itinerant Christian Film Festivals of America provide venues for proselytizing films. Christian educational institutions promote missionary visual material, too; see, for example, the website *Missions Films, Videos and Movies: Missiological Video Resources at the Southern Nazarene University Media Center* (http://home.snu.edu/~HCULBERT/videos.htm). Secular videos often portray missions, too; for example, *Christianity: The First Two Thousand Years* (2001) or *The Pacific Century* (1992), the ninth episode of which counts missionaries among American "sentimental imperialists" in Asia.

JAMIE S. SCOTT

### Further Reading

Baugh, L. (1998). *Imaging the divine: Jesus and Christ figures in film.* Lanham, MD: Sheed & Ward.

Bergeson, A., and Greeley, A. (2000). *God in the movies.* New Brunswick, NJ: Transaction Publishers.

Bernstein, M., and Studlar, G. (1997). *Visions of the East: Orientalism in film.* New Brunswick, NJ: Rutgers University Press.

Fraser, P. (1998). *Images of the Passion: The sacramental mode in film.* Westport, CT: Praeger.

Jewett, R. (1993). *Saint Paul at the movies: The apostle's dialogue with American culture.* Louisville, KY: Westminster/John Knox Press.

Johnston, R. K. (2000). *Reel spirituality: Theology and film in dialogue.* Grand Rapids, MI: Baker Book House.

Reinhartz, A. (2007). *Jesus of Hollywood.* New York: Oxford University Press.

# Fundamentalism

Protestant Fundamentalism, particularly in North America, has played a role in missions for about one hundred years, and at the same time missions has intensified the controversies surrounding Fundamentalism. The dispute in North America in the early twentieth century between the Fundamentalists and the modernists was considered especially acute because, many church leaders believed, the survival of the young indigenous churches in the missions fields was at stake. As theologians debated at home, missionaries also battled one another on the field and passionately instructed the indigenous Christians under their care. These local believers, in some cases, picked up the debate with the same fury as the missionaries. Thus, spread by partisan missionaries, Fundamentalism by the 1920s and 1930s had become a global phenomenon.

The development of Fundamentalism along with its relationship to missions will be discussed in three time periods. Popular contemporary connotations of the term "fundamentalism" need to be distinguished from the historic development of Fundamentalism. In contemporary parlance "fundamentalism" might be considered synonymous with bigotry or intolerance, but historically the term refers to Protestants that affirmed historic Orthodox interpretations of Christianity even in the face of modern secular scholarship. Fundamentalism grew out of the specific context of eighteenth- and nineteenth-century evangelicalism, became prominent as it spread around the world through missions, and in the twenty-first century now may be losing its explanatory power.

## Split of Nineteenth-century Evangelicalism in America, 1870–1919

Through the eighteenth and nineteenth centuries in America, distinctive denominational characteristics diminished to some degree and churches of various denominations began to identify with the revivals and the growing Evangelical movement. Evangelicalism had emerged in Britain in the context of the Enlightenment and the revolutionary era of the seventeenth and eighteenth centuries. Although hard to define, church historian David Bebbington proposes all Evangelicals tend to share four characteristics: conversionism, crucicentrism, biblicism, and activism.

As Great Britain burst onto the scene as an imperial superpower in the nineteenth century, Protestant English-speaking missions also expanded around the globe. British and, later, American missionaries spread Protestant Evangelical Christianity to all parts of the world. As Evangelicals, they stressed personal conversion and belief, the single-significance of the work of Christ on the cross, and the centrality of the Bible.

By 1870, therefore, there was a general Evangelical consensus across numerous denominations in America. On the missions fields, missionaries were even more keen to cooperate interdenominationally in order to avoid, as much as possible, introducing all of the Western denominations and divisions. In the Evangelical tradition of "activism," missionaries were involved in pioneer evangelism and church planting, as well as in efforts of social uplift, including the building of schools and hospitals.

"Inland" and "faith" missions would also play a role after 1870 in the development of both the missions movement and Fundamentalism. Based on the model of the China Inland Mission founded by J. Hudson Taylor in 1865, new missions were initiated with the express desire to push inland beyond the port cities in Africa and Asia, and they mobilized missionaries from outside of the traditional denomination and support structures who served as missionaries "by faith."

Starting around 1870, however, evangelicalism began to split. Darwinism and biblical criticism were challenging the traditional roots of Christianity, and Evangelicals divided over how to respond to the modern secular challenges. Although the theological debates were increasingly strident, on the missions fields both sides of the debate initially continued to cooperate in both pioneer evangelism and building institutions.

## Modernism and Fundamentalism, 1920–1940

The deepening theological divide in the American churches prompted the publication from 1909–1912 of "The Fundamentals," a series of tracts defending what the authors believed was historic orthodoxy. Funded by oil tycoon Lyman Stewart, these tracts were sent to numerous church leaders defending five fundamental points: the virgin birth, substitutionary atonement, the physical resurrection of Jesus, the second coming, and the infallibility of the Bible.

After festering for several decades, the controversy between the modernists and the Fundamentalists exploded around 1920 after the conclusion of World War I. As the dispute became more strident, Fundamentalists began to withdraw into their own churches and denominations in the 1920s and 1930s. As the Fundamentalists settled into their own institutions, both the Fundamentalists and the modernists seem to have adopted increasingly extreme positions. Public perception of the Fundamentalists disintegrated and they were marginalized and sometimes disdained within the broader culture.

The implications of the modernist-Fundamentalist split for missions were profound. Significantly, the missionaries' concern for the indigenous Christians contributed to the fierceness of the debate in North America. Some Fundamentalists established their own denominational missions structures, but they also went outside denominational structures and helped build the growing faith missions movement into a dominant force in missions. The Fundamentalists militantly defended what they believed was historic orthodoxy, and they also zealously pursued evangelism and church planting on the missions field. As the modernists shied away from evangelism, they redoubled efforts at providing social uplift and promoting the social gospel. Certainly there were moderates on the missions field, and many missionaries continued to be involved in both pioneer evangelism and in, for example, education, but the line between the Fundamentalists and modernists theologically and in missionary practice became more entrenched.

Faith missions, which seem to have started with a less partisan purpose, became the stronghold of many of the more conservative missionaries. Some observers suggest there might be a discernable class element in the division between modernist and fundamentalist missionaries. The higher educated and ordained modernists tended to serve in the YMCAs, the universities and the hospitals, while the less educated, sometimes not ordained, faith missionaries often served in the inland areas carrying out pioneer evangelism under harsher conditions.

The indigenous churches that were developing on the missions fields were courted by both modernists and Fundamentalists. Modernists tended to hold that the Christian message must be accommodated to contemporary intellectual standards for the Christian faith to survive in the globalizing modern world. Fundamentalists were equally convinced that only the historic faith could maintain relevance in an increasingly secular and sinful world. Modernist Christianity on the missions fields tended to center in the urban centers around universities and publishing houses, while Fundamentalist Christianity tended to spread into the rural areas and maintained its anti-intellectual reputation.

By the 1940s the chasm between the modernists and Fundamentalists was deep, both theologically and in the practice of ministry and missions. Fundamentalism, from the 1920s to the 1940s, was comprised of a broad spectrum of theological conservatives, including, for instance, such disparate theologians as the Presbyterian J. Gresham Machen (1881–1937) and the dispensationalist C. I. Scofield (1843–1921). This broad movement from the 1920s and 1930s, then, must be distinguished from the more narrow Fundamentalism that arose after the 1940s.

## Liberalism, Fundamentalism, and Evangelicalism, 1940–present

During the 1940s a group within the Fundamentalist movement became increasingly uncomfortable with what they perceived as the Fundamentalists' anti-intellectualism and lack of cultural engagement. While certain factions were determined to remain separate from the modernists, others desired a return to the broader mainstream of nineteenth century evangelicalism. Thus, some theologically conservative leaders, such as theologian Carl Henry (1913–2003) and evangelist Billy Graham (b. 1918), originated neo-evangelicalism in the 1940s and 1950s. This new movement, often referred to as "evangelicalism," believed they could forge a middle path between the Fundamentalists and the liberals, remaining theologically conservative but also engaging in scholarship and society. Fundamentalists have taken more extreme positions, avoiding cooperation with liberals and drawing clear theological distinctions.

In missionary practice, Evangelicals also tried to regain a middle position, emphasizing both cultural engagement and evangelism. Thus, for example, in the early twenty-first century, the prominent Evangelical Rick Warren (b. 1954), author of *The Purpose Driven Life*, has established a well-publicized antipoverty and AIDS initiative in Africa. Liberals from the early twentieth century have tended to emphasize social and political engagement, but the missions movement growing out of the mainline American denominations has been in

numerical decline for several decades. At the same time, the number of missionaries from the more conservative end of spectrum has continued to grow.

Looking toward the future, the fate of Fundamentalism may be tied with Pentecostalism. The growth of Pentecostalism in the twentieth century is also part of the story. Pentecostal history might be comparable to that of the Fundamentalists, and the Charismatic movement, in some ways, parallels the neo-Evangelical movement. While this simple categorization is problematic, both of these movements generally share the conservative theology of the Fundamentalists and Evangelicals, but with a distinctive interpretation of spiritual gifts.

The story of fundamentalism and Pentecostalism in missions, in some ways, is only just the beginning. As Protestant Christianity explodes in Asia, Africa, and Latin America, it is often conservative forms that thrive. Indigenous churches in Asia, Africa, and Latin America will establish their identity and they will evaluate their ties to the Western churches and some of the theological debates that have framed Christianity over the past decades and centuries. An earlier generation of these majority-world Christians did embrace the modernist-Fundamentalist controversy, but today they may debate more indigenous questions, such as the role of ancestor practices during funerals or the relation of the church to a secular Marxist or Muslim state. Thus, Fundamentalist missions can claim some success, as the churches are largely conservative, but the distinction between Fundamentalist and liberal may be breaking down and it is not clear if the labels will continue to apply. The future direction of these churches will now proceed independently from Western missions.

As these majority-world churches mature, they are themselves entering into foreign missions. Led by vibrant missions movements from countries like Korea and Brazil, missionaries from Asia, Africa, and Latin America are being sent to all parts of the world. Missions has become, "from everywhere, to everywhere." As these missions movements grow, they will need to navigate challenges such as the relationship of evangelism and social action as they write the next chapter in the history of the expansion of Christianity.

RICHARD R. COOK

## Further Reading:

Bebbington, D. W. (1989). *Evangelicalism in modern Britain: A history from the 1730s to the 1980s*. New York: Routledge.

Marsden, G. M. (2006). *Fundamentalism and American culture* (2nd ed.). New York: Oxford University Press.

Carpenter, J. A. (1997). *Revive us again: The reawakening of American Fundamentalism.* New York: Oxford University Press.

Sweeney, D. A. (2005). *The American evangelical story: A history of the movement.* Grand Rapids, Michigan: Baker Academic.

Jenkins, P. (2002). *The next Christendom: The coming of global Christianity.* New York: Oxford University Press.

Jenkins, P. (2006). *The new faces of Christianity: Believing the Bible in the global South.* New York: Oxford University Press.

# G

## Gender

The largest organized women's movement in North America in the early twentieth century was the women's missionary movement, whose expansive involvement reached across the globe into Asia, Africa, Latin America, and the Middle East. Women missionaries constituted an indispensable workforce in the foreign missionary enterprise, representing almost 60 percent of the entire mission personnel by 1890. Despite the significant role of women in the foreign missionary enterprise, it is only since the 1980s have women missionaries and their subjects of conversion begun to draw scholarly attention. Since then, much research has shown that, although women were precluded from clerical rights because of highly patriarchal church organizations, the unique experiences of women missionaries in the separate sphere called "woman's work for woman" made a significant impact on mission methods and strategies. It also reveals the complex intersections of gender with race and class in transcultural encounters between missionaries and the members of non-Christian societies.

American women's engagement in the foreign missionary enterprise was largely governed by two prevailing ideologies. One was the nineteenth century's singular notion of civilization, primarily informed by a worldview based in Christian and Enlightenment ethics. The other was the Victorian concept of True Womanhood, which privileged religious piety and domesticity. In line with these dominant ideologies, women were called upon to undertake "woman's work for woman"—to rescue "heathen sisters." Women missionaries ventured into the unknown world, regarding it as their "household," where they would practice the feminine virtues of care, sacrifice, and devotion. The mission field in turn provided them with unprecedented opportunities to exercise power and authority in their own separate female sphere, in which women were empowered but at the same time constrained while they struggled to find their enhanced role and status within the male-centered church organizations.

## Separate Female Sphere

In the nineteenth century, the status of women became an important criterion in measuring the level of civilization a society had achieved. Numerous missionary writings reported the oppressed life of women in "heathen" lands who were confined to the inner chambers, received no formal education, and were bound by long-standing customs, such as foot binding, early marriage, concubinage, and slavery. Set against the idealized position of women in the Christian West, who presumably enjoyed freedom, honor, and dignity, the exaggerated image of downtrodden women in "heathen" societies compelled many American Christian women to feel obliged to engage in rescuing their unfortunate sisters and to spread the gospel as a sure sign of liberation.

Where the custom of the separation of genders prevailed in the Middle East and Asia, male missionaries could not have access to women. Therefore, as Dana Robert points out, the "strongest public justification for including women in the foreign mission enterprise at all was not to be companions and helpmates to their husbands, but rather to reach the otherwise unreachable women and children" (Robert 1996, 36). Given the role of women as mothers to future generations, the conversion of women was considered of special importance to ensure the success of the foreign mission. The creation of the Woman's Foreign Missionary Societies (WFMS) in various denominations from the 1860s further spurred a greater involvement of women, providing better educated women of the time with an outlet to discover and use their talents and leadership. Especially for single women, who were prevented from becoming missionaries earlier, the WFMS served as a means to legitimize their religious and professional commitment.

### Developing Sense of Professionalism

In line with the prevailing gender ideology based on the Victorian notion of "separate spheres," women missionaries were channeled into the "feminine" domestic arena as teachers and doctors for women and children, while men missionaries assumed leadership roles in the religious, evangelical domain through preaching and organizational supervision. Although most women missionaries readily accepted their status as the subordinate sex, the separate "woman's work for woman" proved to be a fertile ground for many of them to learn and exercise leadership, organizational skills, independence, and professionalism. They organized their own women's conferences with significant autonomy. Women's mission journals, such as *Heathen Woman's Friend* (later *Woman's Missionary Friend*), *Woman's Work for Woman,* and *Woman's Missionary Advocate,* were crucial media for them to propagate their unique contribution to the foreign mission as well as to develop a growing sense of professionalism. Along with the significant changes in political and cultural milieu, especially after World

A school for girls founded by British missionaries in East Africa in the mid-1800s. A separate school was established for boys.

War I, a greater number of women missionaries were able to pursue personal and professional ambitions that went beyond the traditional gender boundaries (Brouwer 2002).

## Gender and Race in Transcultural Encounters

The experience of women missionaries as the subordinate gender in the American cultural context can be contrasted with their status as the presumably "superior" race in relation to "the Other," and this tension reveals a more complicated picture of the legacy of women missionaries. There are various interpretations of the role of women missionaries in shaping new womanhood in "heathen" lands, ranging from their functioning as liberators on one end to acting as cultural imperialists on the other. Missionary-led social and cultural reforms, such as educational and occupational opportunities for women and the prevention of early marriage and concubinage, point to the liberator role that women missionaries played. On the other hand, their Eurocentric colonialist views of the Other and their sense of racial and religious superiority render them as cultural imperialists.

However, the wide range of activities and experiences of women missionaries in the culturally diverse foreign-mission fields cannot be understood in a clear-cut, binary fashion. While they were significantly influenced by the prevailing religious doctrines and West-centered worldview of the time, they were in a position to confront much more complex cultural dynamics with indigenous people, who were far from passive recipients of a foreign religion and culture.

### Adapting to Foreign Cultures

While rarely compromising the fundamental tenets of Christian teachings, missionaries nevertheless tried to adapt to the particular local situations that demanded more flexible and innovative ways of distributing the gospel. For example, American missionaries were shocked by the extreme degree of separation of genders in Korea, where boys and girls began to be segregated after age seven. Respecting the custom, missionaries came up with the idea of putting a paper screen in the middle of the church so men and women could attend together but would not see each other.

Kwok Pui-lan points out how Christian symbolism was feminized in the Chinese cultural context. Missionaries saw Chinese women not only as the victims of the Chinese patriarchal system but also as the catalyst for sociocultural changes in China, and thus gave more emphasis to the close relationship between Jesus and women, especially oppressed women (Kwok 1992, 29–57).

### Agents of Change

While spreading the gospel was the ultimate goal of all missionaries, the gender-specific division of labor drove women missionaries toward more cultural and secular activities. Leslie Flemming notes that "because of their exclusion from public evangelical activities, and because of their identification with domestic, educational and health-related activities in north American culture, most women missionaries responded more strongly to the call to be civilizers, characterizing themselves as agents of change and emphasizing the 'uplifting' nature of their activities" (Flemming 1989, 2–3).

In fact, the "civilizing" or "modernizing" aspect of mission activities often drew more positive response from people these missionaries tried to convert than strictly a religious aspect did. In her analysis of American women missionaries in China, Jane Hunter points out that what the Chinese wanted most was not a Western religion but modern knowledge and technology, and thus "the key to the impact of missionary women on Chinese women's history lies less in their religious program than in the secular message transmitted by their lives" (Hunter 1984, 26).

While women missionaries contributed to "modernizing" women in the mission field, there was a tension between evangelical goals and the modernizing forces at the time. Since missionaries viewed some modern characteristics to be antireligious and culturally corrupt, their perception of true modern womanhood was not the same as what was prevailing in 1920s American society. Nonetheless, American women missionaries are often remembered by the people they served as pioneers in constructing modern womanhood, largely because the most prominent accomplishments of women missionaries are found in their work in educational, medical, and social work–related areas.

## Further Research

Research studies have often based their analysis on the missionaries' writings, such as annual reports, correspondences, diaries, and mission fictions. However, a fuller understanding of the activities and influence of women missionaries can be achieved only after we incorporate the perceptions of the converted. Unfortunately, it is not easy to find records that detail their reaction in their own words because women, in particular, were illiterate

at the time of the religious and cultural encounters and did not leave much writing of their own. Nonetheless, the local church records, memoirs, and (auto)biographies of related people offer some rare information on how women missionaries absorbed, resisted, or appropriated the new religion and cultural views and how their lives were affected by their encounter with the missionaries. Only after these perspectives are included can we assess more thoroughly the scope and nature of the activities of women missionaries that left an imprint not only on the converted but also on missionary women themselves.

HYAEWEOL CHOI

### Further Reading

Brouwer, R (2002). *Modern women modernizing men: The changing missions of three professional women in Asia and Africa, 1902–69.* Vancouver, Canada: University of British Columbia Press.

Flemming, L. (1989). *Women's work for women: Missionaries and social change in Asia.* Boulder, CO: Westview.

Hill, P. (1985). *The world their household: The American woman's foreign mission movement and cultural transformation, 1870–1920.* Ann Arbor: University of Michigan Press.

Huber, T., & Lutkehaus, N. (1999). *Gendered missions: Women and men in missionary discourse and practice.* Ann Arbor: University of Michigan Press.

Hunter, J. (1984). *The gospel of gentility: American women missionaries in turn-of-the century China.* New Haven: Yale University Press.

Kwok, P. (1992). *Chinese women and Christianity, 1860–1927.* Atlanta, GA: Scholars Press.

Robert, D. (1996). *American women in mission: A social history of their thought and practice.* Macon, GA: Mercer University Press.

Ruether, R. R., & Keller, R. S. (Eds.). (1981). *Women and religion in America. Vol. 1: The nineteenth century.* San Francisco: Harper & Row Publishers.

Thomas, H. F., & Keller, R. S. (Eds.). (1981). *Women in new worlds.* Nashville, TN: Abingdon.

## Globalization

The term "globalization" has gained currency and many meanings since sociologist Roland Robertson introduced it into the English language as a matter for scholarly inquiry in the 1950s. It refers to a worldwide set of dynamic social and cultural developments that are influencing every local context, all people, all nations, and the ecology of the earth itself. The way in which the missionaries and the people receiving them interpret these developments will profoundly shape the missiological response.

Specialists treat the changes in terms of their disciplines and tend to attribute the dynamics to the factors that most interest them. Thus, economists, business leaders, and critics suspicious of business treat globalization as an economic dynamic (Duchrow 1994, Hardt 2001). They focus on capitalist practices and institutions that can leap over the borders of nations to escape legal limitations, establish new markets, and find cheap labor. Some of these practices and institutions, critics hold, need more restraint (Wolf 2004, Bhagwati 2005). Political scientists, politicians, and public-policy critics study globalization in terms of the emerging realignment of power relations after the collapse of the Soviet Union and the rise of the United States as the sole superpower (Held 1999). They praise some policies for building new alliances and blame others for causing disruption and conflict, while contrasting partisans point out the need for temporary conflict to preserve or establish prospects of peace and prosperity. At the margins of political opinion are advocates of benevolent imperialism and opponents of any hegemony.

Technologically-oriented communications specialists speak of the spread of information technology and media availability that allows people to discover new commonalities, while cultural critics speak of a postmodern fragmentation of meaning as earlier dominant cultural assumptions are shattered by their exposures to a host of alternatives (Appadurai 1996). Other specialists quote demographers who speak of massive migration flows from the South and East to the North and West; anthropological romantics celebrate the values of traditional cultures and mourn the global forces that disrupt indigenous societies.

More general definitions seek to integrate these partial perspectives. Thus, some argue that all the factors mentioned above contribute to the formation of a social and technological infrastructure that, while still fragile, could well result in a new worldwide civilization (Friedman 2005). A contrasting school of social scientists stresses the profound pluralism in these developments and the prospects of a "clash of civilizations," between civilizations with distinctive traditions shaped by the great world religions (Huntington 1991). A more modest form of this view stresses the pluralistic ways in which the forces of globalization are adopted and adapted into each context in ways that allow interactions between contexts (Berger 2003).

It is likely that contemporary globalization is essentially a civilizational shift, signaling a change similar to the shift from tribal societies to agricultural societies, urban societies, and then industrialized nation states. Each shift is shaped by both material and power factors, and by dominant ethical and religious transformations. Similar forces are now forming the infrastructure of what could become a new, federated civil society, and may never become a global civilization. The world is currently dynamic, complex, increasingly inclusive, but inequitable in its benefits. However, more people benefit than lose, for globalization creates new middle classes at geometric rates. More people see material and moral benefits than liabilities, a fact that continues to drive the globalizing forces (Friedman 2005).

Notably, this partially formed global civil society, as messy, pluralistic, and conflicted as it is, is developing without being under the control of any state. More-developed countries, especially the United States, Great Britain, the European Union, Japan, and increasingly, China and India, are rapidly adapting to the changes demanded, taking advantage of the opportunities afforded, and thus reinforcing the developments and the emerging legal arrangements that legitimate them. In this context, the United States, as the only superpower, shows signs of imperialism (Hardt 2001); many countries expect it to intervene in any trouble spot in the world, from Haiti to Darfur, from North Ireland to the Balkans, from the drug trade in Latin America to the AIDS crises of Central Africa, to nuclear disputes with North Korea and Iran.

Indeed, some argue that the United States is already functioning as a hegemonic power, influencing political, military, cultural, economic, educational, technological, and social patterns around the globe, while leaving little space for other centers of authority and governance to operate on their own terms. Of course, the scope of this influence and the power to intervene directly or indirectly through international agencies are resented by many countries, and many people see the impact of American popular culture by music, videos, and movies as homogenizing and immoral, even though such cultural borrowings are more often invited than imposed. In any case, assessments of real or hoped-for gains, or of the sense of loss, involve calculations not only of material and social benefits but also of sensibilities about moral and spiritual values.

Today's globalization seems to be a trans-state dynamic that is reaching the whole known world. After humans spread to most parts of the earth and developed distinctive local religions and civilizations, some began to develop links among them. Driven by cultural curiosity, a desire for adventure, religious zeal, hopes to learn from others, a quest for profitable trade, a lust for power, and a love for the exotic, people created routes of travel between West and East, North and South.

Combinations of material and ideal interests drove merchants and adventurers, monks and literati to develop a variety of paths collectively called the old Silk Road that joined Turkey with China, and connected routes in the West to Europe, Arabia, and Africa, and in the East to India, Korea, and Japan. For centuries, goods, ideas, gold, and pieties were exchanged, and civilizations were enriched. Many died en route while some gained handsomely; imperial conquerors and local war lords used these roads to their own advantage, sometimes raiding trading posts and demolishing monasteries in search of gold or to punish those disloyal to this or that emperor or false god.

Centuries later, new technologies fostered by the view that nature was fallen and needed repair and the transformations that could more nearly approximate the promised New Jerusalem, camel caravans were replaced by clipper ships and then steamships. These new technologies accelerated the exploration of new continents and the colonization of new portions of the globe. They enabled the expansion of slavery, which was already widely practiced, but they also enabled missionary activity in unprecedented numbers. Christians from the West took particular advantage of these conditions. Priests and preachers, educators and doctors, soldiers and administrators brought new perspectives on God and humanity, new interpretations of the universe and the Earth, new means of nurturing the young and curing the sick, and new modes of organizing the common life and protecting law and order. The missionary impulse to bring development to the peoples left out of current globalization dynamics is a legacy of profound theological and social traditions.

Cooperation between colonizers and missionaries at times obscured the missionary message and almost overwhelmed indigenous societies. These societies adopted only portions of what was offered, and selectively modulated their preexisting beliefs and practices. New cultural syntheses were generated and visions of humanity widened. New worldviews made it possible to speak of a common humanity that increasingly valued human rights, emancipation, nation-building, development, and the modernization of the economy, medicine, and social life.

Today's globalization may be another such wave of development, marked by new means of communication from jumbo jets to the Internet, new prospects of genetic and ecological engineering, and new interchanges between cultures and religions. The increased ability to control the bio-physical world, including the capacity to blow it up, forces all people to consider what values, principles, and purposes should drive our responses to globalization's promises and perils. Everyone knows, for example, that special attention must be paid to those left behind. But equally striking is the dramatic resurgence of world religions, which suggests that there is a quest for a guiding ethical and spiritual worldview. People are seeking a comprehensive vision of morals and meaning that realize countervailing views and resolve the complexities of myriad cultures and differentiated societies. This new worldview will also need to be simple enough to capture the loyalties of people from a wide range of cultures and religions.

Max L. Stackhouse

## Further Reading

Appadurai, A. (1996). Modernity at large: Cultural dimensions of globalization. Minneapolis: University of Minnesota Press.

Bhagwati, J. (2003). *In defense of globalization.* New York: Oxford University Press.

Berger, P., *et al.,* (2003). *Many globalizations.* New York: Oxford University Press.

Duchrow, U. (1994). *Alternatives to global capitalism.* Utrecht, The Netherlands: International Books.

Friedman, M. (2005). *The moral consequences of economic growth.* New York: Alfred Knopf.

Held, D., et al. (1999). *Global transformations: Politics, economics and culture.* Standford, CA: Stanford University Press.

Hardt, M., et al. (2001). *Empire.* Cambridge, MA: Harvard University Press.

Huntington, S. (1991). *The clash of civilizations.* New York: Simon & Schuster

Mandelbaum, M. (2005). *The case for Goliath.* Washington, DC: World Affairs.

Robertson, R. (1992). *Globalization: Social theory and global culture.* London: Sage.

Stackhouse, M. L., et al. (2000, 2001, 2003). *God and globalization* (3 vols.). Harrisburgh, PA: Trinity Press International.

Wolf, M. (2004). *Why globalization works.* New Haven, CT: Yale University Press.

# History

Over the course of the twentieth century, mission history became an object of concern to a growing legion of scholars. Besides missiologists and religious historians, the history of mission now draws the interest of specialists in politics and economics, Marxists, feminists, historical anthropologists, and many other kinds of social historians. In this article, the study of mission history from within the discipline of missiology will be highlighted.

## Common Problems and Objectives

Missiologists who study the history of mission share many overlapping concerns with their colleagues in other disciplines, not the least of which is the requirement to practice good historical technique. Some common aims likewise drive much historical work on missions today, such that missiologists find themselves working alongside other scholars who are also seeking to understand the dynamics of cultural and religious change, the emergence and diffusion of modern ideas, the art of apologetics, and the conduct of interfaith dialogue, plus the nature of the church and its place in the world.

With respect to methods, missiologists have no special set of procedures to apply to the problems of history. They have to follow the same rules of evidence that pertain to everyone else who studies the history of mission or any other kind of history, for that matter. If widely recognized scholarly standards of verification in history are ignored, then accuracy suffers and what purports to be description or analysis slides instead into the category of mere speculation about the past. Therefore, missiologists, like other historians, have to be concerned about what (if anything) constitutes an objective fact, about how material evidence can be used to buttress or disprove the claims of texts, about the problems of agency and causation in history, plus the need to differentiate between perceptions of an event and the historical event itself.

No scholar has all the evidence that he or she would like to possess to solve the conundrums of mission history. The data are always fragmentary. The memories still preserved are faulty and sometimes contradictory. The archives are not only incomplete but heavily skewed in the direction of the foreign missionary agent. This imbalance in the record is a serious methodological problem to be overcome, which explains why investigators of every kind (including missiologists) are so eager to recover lost voices and to lift up the contributions of lesser-known actors in the history of mission. Material evidence of indigenous missionary activity, oral histories, and other forms of nonliterary self-representation are among the means available to scholars to recover more of what may otherwise be missing from what is already known about the history of mission.

Filling in the gaps is not the whole story, however. Equally important is the fact that such techniques can enable the living legacies of earlier missionary effort—the new communities of faith that came into being as a result of Christian mission—to participate more directly in the writing of what is their history, too.

Another area where the requirements of competent historical practice are bound to apply equally to missiologists and their counterparts in related fields has to do with the way in which the environment of mission is studied. More and more, missiologists are striving to assemble complex descriptions of interfaith encounter and Christian witness, rather than simply transcribing stories of heroic missionary action. This means taking into account large-scale patterns of social change of which the missionaries themselves may have been only vaguely aware. Or asking about the ways in which factors like geography, economics, organizational theory, politics and the exercise of social power not only influenced missionary choices but also, perhaps, shaped evangelistic outcomes.

### Influence of Missionary Experience

At first glance, missiologists do seem to face at least one special problem of interpretation when functioning as historians of mission. Many more of them will have previous or current missionary service in their résumés than would likely be the case for the rest of the history profession. This circumstance does not necessarily make it impossible for missiologists to attain a critical distance from the object of their research. In fact, their problem is a slightly different permutation of a persistent scholarly dilemma. Historians have long argued over whether participants or more detached observers are better placed to write their accounts of the past. Participants have the advantage of direct personal experience, which could be a means to access otherwise poorly documented aspects of the events in question or to gain a "feel" for the time and situations one is attempting to describe. But detachment can serve a purpose, too, especially if it enables researchers to avoid telling their stories in ways that inflate their own importance.

The larger question at issue here concerns the different ways scholars more generally relate to their subjects. Missiologists are by no means the only ones obliged to examine their motives for writing history. Biases and partisan concerns threaten to intrude every time historical questions are posed and answered, since no researcher can begin to work without them. Complete objectivity is certainly beyond any researcher's grasp, but a measure of transparency regarding intentions and interests can be achieved. Only so may the work of contemporary historians hope to earn a degree of lasting respect from present and future generations.

### Results That Matter

A final common expectation that missiologists necessarily share with other students of mission history concerns the written results of their research. As Robert Frykenberg (1996, 253–260) has demonstrated, the

discipline of history is exceedingly complex. History is not only a science with a distinctive methodology and largely agreed-upon rules with which to evaluate evidence but is also practiced as a form of philosophy, insofar as it prompts deliberation over questions of language, perception, human experience, and the nature of social change over time. In addition, history is an art. That is to say, it has a creative element, which leaps to the fore as soon as it becomes time to present to the public or the profession what one has learned about the past.

In this latter respect, the requirements of good historiography are at least three. First, one's written account has to be coherent, in the sense that a logical interpretive argument is constructed on the basis of plausible data, supported by reputable sources of authority. It should also be persuasive, which means putting forward a case that is not just credible but one that can move readers to agree with the author's conclusions, even when alternative explanations are given a fair hearing. Perhaps the most daunting test of history's contemporary narratives is posed by the question of significance. At the end of the day, will anybody care? Probably not, if the product of one's labors is presented in dull, unappealing discourse. Missiologists, no less than any other historian of mission, are obliged to reach for prose that sings, if they would hope to create and hold an audience for their work.

## Hazards to Be Avoided

Even for missiologists, the ultimate goal of mission history cannot be to celebrate missionary heroes, despite the many stories of courageous triumph and self-sacrifice that fill the record. Nor should it be reduced to a kind of cheerleading for one side in the global competition of religions. If mission history is made to serve an apologetic purpose, its integrity as a science is undoubtedly put at risk. Put more positively, a mature field of study will reward the investigation of both success and failure, because each of these aspects of missionary experience can shed light on the deepest questions of meaning that inevitably arise in connection with this subject.

It follows that missiology is not primarily about producing "insider" histories for the purpose of stimulating enthusiasm for contemporary missionary challenges. Neither should practical considerations (for example, a desire to know what "works" in mission) be allowed to dictate how missiologists approach the history of mission. The improvement of missionary technique is one possible use of mission history, but the historical dimension of missiology can hardly be contained within the bounds of practical theology.

Another limitation to be avoided would have missiologists conceive of mission history as an unvarying story of missionary initiative, followed by indigenous response. Such an assumption—that foreign missionaries acted but natives could only react—grounded much of the work done on the modern Protestant missionary movement until quite recently, which led to no end of West-centric treatments of mission in the post-Reformation era. A missiological perspective on the history of mission will be broader than this. The movements and decisions of foreign actors are certainly important, especially at the beginning of any new effort to preach Christ where that name is virtually unknown. But no missionary undertaking can be sustained unless indigenous enterprise asserts itself as more than just a reaction to what other, more fully self-aware subjects are doing first. As a rule, the earlier foreign control is shouldered aside, the more successful and deeply rooted any new expression of Christian faith in community is likely to become.

A missiological reading of mission history also has to resist the temptation to affect an omniscient point of view with respect to the processes of world evangelization. In other words, missiologists have to admit their inability to attain a God's-eye perspective on the history of mission. Methodologically, this means giving up the use of providential frameworks for interpreting the past, which is not always an easy thing to do, especially if one affirms a biblical mandate for Christian mission. The danger here lies not in having such convictions, but in letting them overrule the requirements of sound historiographical practice by subordinating one's account of mission history to a theological point of view. What Andrew Walls (2002, 18) has to say about church history may apply equally well to missiologists who hope to write the history of mission: "The church historian cannot present bad history under the plea that it is good theology."

## The Missiological Angle on Mission History

As already indicated, competent missiologists have no choice but to emulate the best practices of other historians. To do otherwise is to run the risk of producing substandard historiographical work that deserves to be ignored. Likewise, the historical work of missiologists should not be made subordinate to its practical value for the broader cause of Christian mission today, its apologetic function or usefulness to the theology of mission. A thoroughly missiological approach to the study of mission history is grounded instead on several important investigative habits that this group of scholars brings to its task.

### Multivariable Analysis

Given the history of mission over the past two centuries especially, it is now normal for the church to find itself in conversation with the broadest possible array of religious traditions and living cultures. At once, these engagements take place across the full spectrum of human experience, ranging from the cognitive to the material, with the result that the theoretical aspects and practices of mission are not easily separated. Adding to this complexity is the fact of Christian diversity. Multiple approaches to outreach are to be expected from a worldwide Christian community that has no organizing center or universally shared philosophical framework.

On the whole, missiologists are not different from other historians when it comes to reckoning with the multifaceted character of Christian mission, except in one vital respect. The interdisciplinary demands of history weigh equally on all who would hope to study the record of missionary action, such that, as the scholar of comparative religion Eric Sharpe (1989, 76) has phrased it, "the ideal missionary historian will be to some extent a social, political, and economic historian; a geographer, ethnologist, and historian of religions, as well as a Christian historian in the more usual sense." The difference comes in the way matters of faith are typically treated by missiologists when compared to the work of other scholars of mission history.

Simply put, the ethos of missiology encourages its practitioners to take spiritual realities very seriously, even when the researcher does not share the same worldview as those whose history is being studied. Thus, it is not the custom of missiologists to bracket out of their analyses factors of religious conviction. This is the extra variable that often distinguishes the historical work of missiologists from that produced by many secular historians and most social scientists.

A look at two studies of mission will serve to illustrate the point. The first is a pioneering work of historical anthropology, produced in the 1990s by a pair of distinguished ethnologists, John and Jean Comaroff. Their massive study of Nonconformist British missions among the southern Tswana in the nineteenth century, *Of Revelation and Revolution*, interprets these activities within a larger effort to colonize much of southern Africa in the name of Great Britain. The professed aim of the authors is to show how agents of the London Missionary Society and Wesleyan Methodist Missionary

Society functioned as "harbingers of a more invasive European presence" that eventually sought to dominate the Tswana in every possible way (Comaroff and Comaroff 1997, xvi). According to the Comaroffs, the missionaries' special role was to shape the collective consciousness of the natives in advance of direct imperial rule, to colonize their minds, as it were, by contriving a new conceptual reality for them that would pave the way for their mastery by foreign powers. In this way the missionaries not only became "vanguards of imperialism" but also "human vehicles of a hegemonic worldview," whose civilizing axioms "they purveyed . . . in everything they said and did" (Comaroff and Comaroff 1991, 36, 310).

For purposes of comparison, some recent work by Mrinalini Sebastian (2003, 2004) on nineteenth-century missions in India is instructive. As an Indian feminist scholar of religion and culture, with a particular interest in postcolonial literary criticism and subaltern studies, Sebastian wants to read old missionary texts in new ways, just as the Comaroffs have done. Like them, she also wants to understand the corruptive influence of colonialism on European missionary action in the modern era, but she does not stop there, preferring instead to go on to ask what past evangelistic encounters may have meant to the natives whose stories were captured and represented in missionary narratives. In particular her article on how to read missionary archives from a postcolonial feminist perspective nicely illustrates the kind of methodology that could support or complement a fully missiological approach to the history of mission.

In this essay Sebastian (2003) focuses on the native Bible women who worked for the Basel Mission in India. She shows how their work was obviously shaped, if not distorted, by Victorian-era missionary ideas about "the Christian home" that only partly rested on Gospel values. A commitment to feminist concerns pushes Sebastian to explore the liberative potential of missionary education for women in India, which connects to her primary topic insofar as these native missionaries promoted literacy through their activities. She also considers the possibility that the Bible women were among the earliest examples of professional women in India, such that their work had emancipatory significance. Up to this point in her essay, about three-quarters of the way through, Sebastian is tracking very closely with the approach of the Comaroffs, albeit not at the same level of detail. But then a turn in her investigative strategy comes, which Sebastian describes as follows:

> In my engagement with the histories of the Bible women so far, I have tried to present a secularized view of their work. I deliberately have not dwelled too much on their faith or their attempts to convert other women to Christianity. Yet the primary motive for their becoming Bible women, for their inadvertent transgression [across caste boundaries] was their faith. And the primary purpose of their visits to other women's houses was to communicate the message of the gospel. (Sebastian 2003, 22)

A very personal reason lay behind the decision to introduce the factor of faith into Sebastian's scholarly discussion of mission. As she explains, her own grandmother was a Bible woman in India long before this article was conceived and written. For that reason she wants to ask: What moved my grandmother and so many other native Christian women to share the story of Jesus with their neighbors in the day-to-day context of Indian village life, sometimes over the course of a lifetime? By raising such a question, Sebastian has chosen to pitch her researcher's tent squarely on missiological ground. Without resorting to a providential framework to explain the workings of history, she has nevertheless allowed the realm of faith to begin to receive a measure of the same consideration so freely given by countless academics to the realm of sight.

As the historian Mark Noll (1998, 112) has observed, this is what missiologists do. They operate somewhere between the "functional atheism of the academy" and the "functional gnosticism of sending churches" that sometimes blinds those churches or agencies to historical realities. Thus, to think missiologically about the history of mission means, in part, to practice a form of critical empathy with one's subject. A degree of empathy makes it possible to resist the strong modern urge to brush aside religious convictions as unimportant. At the same time, a willingness to be critical commits one to a methodology that is suitably rigorous and scientific.

### The Dynamic Aspect of Mission History

Related to the persistently multivariable disposition of missiology is its particular interest in the dynamic character of Christian history. That is to say, there is an inbuilt bias in missiology to concentrate on those points in Christian history where the community acts less like a custodian of tradition or repository of settled answers to familiar questions than a source of energy for fresh engagements of the world with the gospel. One way to understand what is at stake here is to consider the difference between church history as it is often practiced and a missiological perspective on the history of Christianity. If church history is largely about describing established but partially hidden patterns of denominational life and understanding how ecclesiastical institutions have gone about their usual business, then missiology is drawn especially to circumstances of change within Christian history. Efforts to plant the church where it has not previously existed obviously qualify, as would any struggle to understand the gospel story in new cultural terms. Missiologists also have a special affinity for those parts of the Christian story where conversions into the community, growth, development and critical self-examination are considered normal aspects of church life, rather than the exception.

The effect of these biases on a missiological approach to mission history can be far-reaching. Missiologists have learned, for example, that mission history is not simply a matter of extension and expansion from metropolitan centers to distant peripheries. Thus, they do not expect missionaries to function as mere chutes through which liquid concrete from abroad is poured into forms fashioned out of local materials. Truly missionary encounters in history are intense moments, full of unpredictability but also promise. Old certainties about what is essential to Christianity may be tested and found wanting in these engagements. New understandings of gospel truth sometimes emerge out of intercultural and interreligious exchange. In any event, when contemporary missiologists reflect on mission history they are more likely to look for evidence of Christianity as a movement rather than a set of institutions or a collection of fixed doctrines to be disseminated far and wide.

### Local and Global

There is a strong tendency within missiology to think about mission history in both local and global terms. The local side of this equation receives attention whenever issues of contextualization are brought into focus. As Werner Ustorf (2002, 210) has observed, the Christian faith, by nature, is *"fides semper inculturanda,"* and nowhere is this more apparent than in the history of mission when multiple contemporary contexts are studied side by side. The idea of translation is another means by which missiologists explore the local dimensions of Christian outreach. Translation in this sense means not only rendering Scripture into new languages but also the creation of vernacular Christianities that make sense in their own cultural settings even as they challenge some of what their communities had come to regard as received wisdom from the past.

The global dimension of missiology is expressed in a variety of ways. Here, one thinks of the geographic development of Christianity into a truly global religion, of course, and also about the birth of the ecumenical movement in the heyday of modern Protestant missions. Less often appreciated, perhaps, is the way in which the history of mission itself is stamped with the indelible mark of global interconnectivity. Many churchgoers in the West in the eighteenth century, for example, eagerly awaited the latest news of their own missionaries but also began to pray fervently for the spread of the Gospel by others. Acting on the same impulse, the missionary societies founded just before the turn of the nineteenth century sought new ways to share intelligence gained from around the world among themselves and to inform the public of their activities; hence the invention of the missionary magazine at about the same time.

Most intriguingly, one finds far-flung modern-era missionaries trying to learn from each other despite the challenges of geography, while also thinking about their work in increasingly global terms. Jennifer Selwyn (2004) has provided a wonderful example of this in a study of early modern Jesuit missions in Naples. As she shows, the kingdom and city of Naples became a kind of proving ground within the Jesuit system for would-be missionary candidates to the New World. Coincidentally, theorists in the Society of Jesus considered how certain techniques and ideas learned in one place could be adapted for use elsewhere. In a striking conceptual move, Jesuits assigned to Naples in the sixteenth and seventeenth centuries came to refer to their mission field in southern Italy as "our Indies" or the "Indies down here." This is language that clearly points to a globalized project of evangelization.

The multivariable character of Christian mission, its dynamic aspect, and the balancing of local and global concerns will likely continue to shape the study of mission history in the future. This research may well have implications for other topics of particular interest to missiologists at the start of the twenty-first century, including the interface of theology with culture, the problem of religious pluralism, the need to evaluate current methods of Christian outreach, and the special vocation of mission service. In these and other related areas of missiological concern, insights gleaned from the history of mission can be expected to stimulate further thought and research.

STANLEY H. SKRESLET

### Further Reading

Bosch, D. J. (1991). *Transforming mission: Paradigm shifts in theology of mission.* Maryknoll, NY: Orbis.

Comaroff, J. L., & Comaroff, J. (1991). *Of revelation and revolution: Christianity, colonialism, and consciousness in South Africa*. Chicago: University of Chicago.

Comaroff, J. L., & Comaroff, J. (1997). *Of revelation and revolution: The dialectics of modernity on a South African frontier*. Chicago: University of Chicago.

Elphick, R. (1995). Writing religion into history: The case of South African Christianity. *Studia Historiae Ecclesiasticae, 21*(1), 1–21.

Evans, R. J. (1999). *In defense of history*. New York: Norton.

Frykenberg, R. E. (1996). *Faith and belief: The foundations of historical understanding*. Grand Rapids, MI: Eerdmans.

Hutchison, W. R. (1987). *Errand to the world: American Protestant thought and foreign missions*. Chicago: University of Chicago.

Kalu, O. U. (2003). Clio in sacred garb: Telling the story of Gospel-people encounters in our time. *Fides et Historia, 35*(1), 27–39.

Megill, A. (1989). Recounting the past: "Description," explanation, and narrative in historiography. *American Historical Review, 94*(3), 627–653.

Noll, M. A. (1998). The potential of missiology for the crises of history. In R. A. Wells (Ed.), *History and the Christian historian*. Grand Rapids, MI: Eerdmans.

Peel, J. D. Y. (1995). For who hath despised the day of small things? Missionary narratives and historical anthropology. *Comparative Studies of Society and History, 37*(3), 581–607.

Porter, A. (2002). Church history, history of Christianity, religious history: Some reflections on British missionary enterprise since the late eighteenth century. *Church History, 71*(3), 555–584.

Rakotonirina, R. A. (1999). Power and knowledge in mission historiography: A postcolonial approach to martyrological texts on Madagascar 1837–1937. *Studies in World Christianity, 5*(2), 156–176.

Robert, D. L. (1997). From missions to mission to beyond missions: The historiography of American Protestant foreign missions since World War II. In H. S. Stout & D. G. Hart (Eds.), *New directions in American religious history*. New York: Oxford University Press.

Sebastian, M. (2003). Reading archives from a postcolonial feminist perspective: "Native" Bible women and the missionary ideal. *Journal of Feminist Studies in Religion, 19*(1), 5–25.

Sebastian, M. (2004). Mission without history? Some ideas for decolonizing mission. *International Review of Mission, 93*(368), 75–96.

Selwyn, J. D. (2004). *A paradise inhabited by devils: The Jesuits' civilizing mission in early modern Naples*. Aldershot, UK: Ashgate.

Sharpe, E. J. (1989). Reflections on missionary historiography. *International Bulletin of Missionary Research, 13*(2), 76–81.

Shenk, W. R. (Ed.). (2002). *Enlarging the story: Perspectives on writing world Christian history*. Maryknoll, NY: Orbis.

Ustorf, W. (2002). Mission and missionary historiography in intercultural perspective: Ten preliminary statements. *Exchange, 31*(3), 210–218.

Walls, A. F. (1996). *The missionary movement in Christian history*. Maryknoll, NY: Orbis.

Walls, A. F. (2002). *The cross-cultural process in Christian history*. Maryknoll, NY: Orbis.

# Human Rights

The idea that all persons, regardless of race, sex, nationality, religion, cultural background, legal status, or physical condition, have a right to be treated with dignity and as moral agents has a long history, and today human rights are often seen as central to a basic understanding of justice. The importance of the idea is that human rights stand as a set of universally valid moral principles to which all can appeal if they are treated badly or if they believe that a legal system or governmental policy is unjust. Some things, as constitutional scholar Michael Perry argued in 1998, ought not to be done to anyone, and some things ought to be done for everyone.

The origin of the idea is disputed. Some point to the first book of the Bible, where an account of the peculiar dignity of humanity, compared to all other creatures, is given. Humans, says the text, were created in the "image and likeness" of God. Thus, to violate that conferred dignity is to defile that which is most divine in humanity. Others see the idea as a moral norm developed out of long social experience: Life seems more fair and goes more smoothly if each person and group is given respect. Still others attribute human rights to the evolution of a constitutional theory that was developed in the West and is now widely adopted by many people around the world. These theories are not necessarily incompatible. Indeed, the awareness of human rights may well have emerged at different times among different people in different ways, and only later been recognized as universally valid. Religious, philosophical, practical, and legal issues often overlap in this area of ethical thought and action.

## History

Language that defines notions similar to modern notions of human rights can be found in ancient legal codes. It is found in the laws of Solon in Greece (c. 594 BCE), the edicts of Cyrus of Babylon (c. 539 BCE), the laws of Ashok in India (c. 365 BCE), and the philosophy of Cicero of Rome (c. 46 BCE) as well as in the Bible. Rights were also granted to subjects in other classical civilizations. However, these rights are usually seen to be "concessions" or acts of generosity by the reigning political authorities, who could, and sometimes did, revoke them by edict. Nor were they applied to all humans; they were applied only to those over whom a particular regime ruled. In this regard, they anticipated modern notions of civil rights and liberties, which apply only to those who are citizens of a nation-state, rather than foreshadowing the idea of universal human rights to which rulers and states are also supposed to be subject.

In the High Middle Ages in Europe a clearer theory of rights began to emerge. Philosophical and legal theories of "natural right" and "natural law" became deeply intertwined with Biblical and theological insights regarding human nature and divine law. In this context, a theory of rights was developed as a set of universal principles. The historian Brian Tierney argued in 1997 that the idea of God-given natural rights was presumed by the philosophical theology that generated the canon law, the first written constitutional law in history that claimed to be valid for all people. Tierney asks whether this development of human rights principles is an invention of a particular tradition that actually applies only to those shaped by this tradition or if those who developed the principles of rights discovered something genuinely universal in content and implication. He supports the view that ideas of human rights were neither an invention nor a discovery of modern, secular Enlightenment thinkers, as is widely believed by legal theorists. Instead, he argues that Enlightenment developments were more dependent on previous traditions than their advocates admitted.

Many rights that are today taken as decisive were not seen as central in the earlier stages of the idea of human rights, and are not seen as valid in some parts of the world today. The right to convert to a new religion, for instance, had to be fought for by Protestants in the West, and was not (and is not) widely recognized in those parts of the world that had an established religion or an official state ideology. Even in places where Protestants won the right to convert to a new religion, some who tried to establish a new religion denied that freedom to others. Nevertheless, battles for freedom of association, of the press, of speech, and of assembly were eventually won. These freedoms, which were rooted in debates about religion at that time, were defended on religious and philosophical grounds by such figures as Johannes Althusius in Holland and John Locke in England. They spilled over the edge of religious convictions and institutions and, once gained, covered a host of nonreligious actions, attitudes, and organizations that are now associated with the rise of democracy.

Such rights were claimed in the British Bill of Rights of 1689 following the much earlier Magna Carta, in the constitutions of several colonies of North America, and in the American Declaration of Independence of 1776; they were central in the Bill of Rights of the United States Constitution, adopted in 1789. A related, but distinct perspective was set forth in the French Declaration of the Rights of Man and Citizen, also in 1789, and in the Prussian General Code in 1794. The Anglo-American view accented God-given individual and associational liberties that put limits on intrusions by the state into the institutions of civil society, while the Franco-Prussian view emphasized the humanly established state as the guarantor of national solidarity and allowed more civil intrusions by the state to advance the social and economic equality of all citizens.

The rights of women and minorities were not fully recognized in these documents, but were advanced around the world by missionary movements in the nineteenth century. These movements founded schools and colleges for the disadvantaged, and became advocates for them with colonial rulers, home governments, and industrial employers. They sought to guarantee rights for all people to make their own decisions about their roles in family and economic life and to have access to educational, social, and political opportunities. Emancipation, suffrage, and anticolonial movements grew from these missionary roots. Substantially due to missionaries, human rights ideas became global in reach, and many people seeking political independence became advocates of movements that fostered guarantees of human rights.

## Modern Developments

New concerns for human rights arose in the twentieth century when Hitler came to dominate European politics. The inhumanity and barbarism of his National Socialist (Nazi) policies put the world on notice that human rights could not be allowed to lapse. As human rights lawyer Mary Ann Glendon, Christian historian John Nurser, and others have documented, an alliance of political, philosophical, and religious leaders foresaw the necessity of recasting the historic legacy of human rights for new conditions. During and immediately after World War II, far-sighted leaders from around the world came together to form the United Nations and to draft the Universal Declaration of Human Rights, which was passed on December 10, 1948. In order to prevent a religious debate, all references to the particular religious or philosophical roots of human rights ideas were struck out of the document at the last minute. It thus appears that the authority of human rights provisions derives solely from the consent of those who passed the Declaration. The rights identified in this Declaration are statements of principles and aspirations that can be used to guide or assess laws, practices, and national or international policies.

Subsequently, further specifications of rights were articulated in various international "Covenants" and "Conventions," which have been ratified by some, but not all, nations in the United Nations. In 1976, for example, the UN adopted the Covenants on Civil and Political Rights and on Economic, Social and Cultural Rights. The first follows the Anglo-American, and the second the Franco-German traditions. More specific are the "Conventions" against genocide (1951), racial discrimination (1969), sexual discrimination (1981), torture (1984), and child exploitation or abuse (1989). In addition, the Helsinki Accords of 1974 sought to mitigate some of the conflicting ideas of rights between the Soviet Union and the Western allies in the Cold War, and the Vienna Declaration of 1993 sought to resolve debates about Asian values and Western ideas of human rights.

## Contemporary Challenges

The first decade of the twenty-first century saw the growth of international institutions, and the globalization of the medical, educational, media, and especially, economic sectors. These trends include not only international regulatory institutions such as the World Bank, the International Monetary Fund, and the World Trade Organization, but also nongovernmental institutions that foster aid, development, and advocacy, such as World Vision, Amnesty International, and Human Rights Watch, and multinational, transnational corporations and regional economic agreements. These developments challenge the sovereignty of every nation-state and sometimes bring with them the clash of cultures and religions that invite gross violations of human rights. They also entail increased wealth for the most developed nations, such as those of the North Atlantic and Japan, the massive growth of new middle classes in rapidly developing nations such as China, India, Korea, and Malaysia, and the very slow economic growth, and occasional decline, in some parts of Africa and South America.

Whether the principles of human rights can be preserved and made more operational in this expanded context is an open but urgent question. An equally open and urgent question is whether the people of the world can find a common basis for affirming and defending human rights without appealing to transcultural or religious principles.

MAX L. STACKHOUSE

## Further Reading

An-Na'im, A. (Ed.). (1992). *Human rights in cross-cultural perspectives*. Philadelphia: University of Pennsylvania Press.

Bucar, E. M., & Barnett, B. (2005). *Does human rights need God?* Grand Rapids, MI: Eerdmans.

Donnelly, J. (1989). *Universal human rights in theory & practice*. New York: Cornell University Press.

Glendon, M. A. (2001). *A world made new: Eleanor Roosevelt and the Universal Declaration of Human Rights*. New York: Random House.

Gustafson, C., & Juviler, P. (1999). *Religion and human rights: Competing claims?* New York: M.E. Sharp

Martin, R. C. & Witte, J. (Eds.). (1999). *Sharing the book: Religious perspectives on the rights and wrongs of proselytism*. Maryknoll, NY: Orbis Books.

Nurser, J. (2004). *For the peoples; For the nations*. Washington, DC: Georgetown University Press.

Perry, M. (1998). *The idea of human rights*. New York: Oxford University Press.

Porter, J.(1999). *Natural & divine law: Retrieving the tradition for Christian ethics*. Grand Rapids, MI: Eerdmans.

Rouner, L. S. (Ed.). (1988). *Human rights and the world's religions*. Notre Dame, IN: Notre Dame University Press.

Stackhouse, M. L. (1997). *Creeds, society & human rights: A study in three societies*. Grand Rapids, MI: Eerdmans. (Original work published 1984)

Tierney, B. (1997). *The idea of natural rights: Studies on natural rights, natural law and church law, 1150–1625*. Grand Rapids, MI: Eerdmans.

Witte, J., & van der Vyver, J. (Eds.). (1996). *Religious human rights in global perspective*. The Hague, Netherlands: Martinus Nijhoff.

# Inculturation

The term "inculturation" or "enculturation" was originally coined by sociocultural anthropologists to refer to the process by which individuals acquire their culture as members of a human society. Subsequently, "inculturation" was appropriated by mission theologians to refer to the evangelization of culture, the process by which the Gospel illuminates and transforms culture, while culture reexpresses and even—to a certain extent—reinterprets the Gospel. Joseph Masson, SJ, first used the term in this way in 1962, but it came into current usage in the 1970s, after the earlier terms "adaptation" and "incarnation" were deemed missiologically unsatisfactory. The most important influence on the development of the term in this sense was the letter on inculturation addressed to the whole Society of Jesus by Pedro Arrupe in 1978.

## Culture and Mission

Culture is a system of meaningful forms that provides human beings with a shared design for living. It is a set of images, collectively inherited and experienced, that enable people to relate to one another and to the world in which they live, intellectually, emotionally and behaviorally. Culture gives to human groups a collective identity and controls their perception of reality. It is thus a historical tradition into which human beings enter. Culture, in effect, is the prism through which the human individual perceives and confronts every aspect of experience—a fundamental characteristic of the human phenomenon.

Mission is the historical process by which Christians of a particular culture seek to evangelize people of another culture. It should not offer violence to culture; still less should it attempt to deprive people of the right to their own culture. Because Christianity does not identify exclusively with any particular culture, and because Christians believe that their faith resonates with the inherent truth of every culture, evangelization shares in the creative dialogue between cultures. Faith must become culture, if it is to be fully received and lived.

## Inculturation Explored

Although the terminology developed more slowly, the idea of inculturation was already being explored among Catholics at the Second Vatican Council and the subsequent Roman Synods and in the Reformation churches at general assemblies of the World Council, and interchurch federations. Although inculturation has always taken place throughout the history of Christianity, it was not a self-conscious process. Today it is necessarily a deliberate and conscious undertaking. This is partly because culture is a modern discovery but also because it is necessary to react against the monocultural assumptions of classicist theology and colonialism. Christians cannot subscribe to assumptions of cultural superiority that claim the right to dominate the cultures of others.

A minor controversy exists between those who make use of the terms "culture" and "inculturation" and those who prefer the discourse of "context" and "contextualization." Anthropologists prefer the term "culture" as being more inclusive and more precise than "context." In general, Catholic theologians have also adopted this usage. "Context" and "contextualization" are more common in the Reformation churches and in places where traditional culture has been used by minority regimes to hold back education and social development.

## Inculturation and Globalization

Globalization is basically the one-sided unification of the globe by the so-called first world through sophisticated technology and financial, industrial, and military power. Western economic forces manipulate markets and promote economic rationalism and consumer materialism. Western television and visual media promote these forces and bombard the cultures of the less-developed world. However, human cultures are not ultimately subject to technological determinism, and the global process is not homogeneous. Moreover, the real locus of popular culture is found at the level of small-scale activities in everyday life. Popular culture draws from many sources and frequently operates on its own terms. People reinvent or reconstruct their culture selectively, preserving continuities with the tradition that gives them identity.

What emerges, therefore, is not a universal culture but a creolization of traditional culture. Cultural diversity is not doomed to extinction. It remains a fact of life. Inculturation implies the acceptance of people in their difference and in their local creativity. Christianity offers them the faith ingredients for making their own cultural synthesis and for transforming their culture as it changes.

Inculturation, therefore, has an ecclesiological impact. It demands the recognition of cultural diversity by Christians and the development of a culturally pluriform church. Christianity should not be harnessed to globalization. It should not be identified with the rich and powerful but rather with the poor. Inculturation comes from below and depends on local initiatives. By definition, it cannot be imposed from above or from outside.

## Inculturation and the Bible

It is true that the subject of inculturation is Jesus Christ himself. He takes the riches of all cultures to himself, acquiring successive cultural identities through evangelization. Culturally diverse peoples identify with Jesus and enter into union with him. Through his Resurrection salvation becomes available to people of all cultures. Knowing, loving, and serving Jesus—adopting the values of the Kingdom he inaugurated—are indispensable outcomes of evangelization. But to know Jesus we must go to the Bible. The Bible is culturally privileged, because Jesus is human and was historically conditioned by culture. However, there is no single culture of the Bible. God revealed himself through an interaction of cultures, and Jesus himself was born into a culturally complex situation. Moreover, he opposed the exaltation of culture over religious faith. We need to read the Bible culturally in order to understand Jesus, but we also accept his challenge to cultures to die and rise with him.

## Liturgical Inculturation and Encounter with Whole Cultures

Liturgical inculturation is not merely a piecemeal process of inserting exotic elements from another culture into a Western ritual framework. It must make the celebration into an authentic cultural event. It can do this less by the creation of texts than by nonverbal means: music, gesture, dance, and other liturgical arts. This was the reason for the success of the Ndzon Melen Mass in Cameroon and later of the Zaire Mass in Congo, both of which offered an audiovisual package that was immensely popular. The functional substitution of a Christian for a traditional rite is another means to the same end, the Catholic Zimbabwe rite for the reinstatement of the deceased, or "Second Funeral," being an excellent example. Such approaches lean more toward an encounter between Gospel and culture than mere textual creativity.

Inculturation at its best consists in the encounter of the Gospel with whole cultures, and this is especially the preserve of theological formulation, homiletics, and catechetics. Christensen's brilliant account of how the Gbaya (Cameroon) have transformed their organic universe through a Biblical reinterpretation of its root symbols touches all the life contexts of this rural African people. Something similar is happening spontaneously among the Pogoro of Tanzania, in Catholic Marian devotion, celebrating the Blessed Virgin Mary as the compassionate and bereaved Mother of Jesus. Shorter's homiletic experiment among the Kimbu of Tanzania belongs to the same genre. Applying the choric story format to the Sunday sermon, it was possible to carry out a dialogue between Biblical themes and aspects of the Kimbu organic universe. This form of inculturation is what Monica Hellwig calls "ascending Christology" (1997). The physical setting of human life speaks to people about God and the redemption wrought by Christ. A similar experience of ascending Christology has taken place in the urban environment. The city is an "organization of diversity," (Hannerz 1992). a multiethnic phenomenon, in which Bible-sharing base communities understand the humanity of Jesus through their own experience of being human and rise to an intuition of his divinity.

## The Future

The future of inculturation is likely to rest less with formal texts—liturgical or theological—and more with spontaneous creativity at the grassroots. It is only there that authentic cultural redefinition and doctrinal reexpression can take place.

AYLWARD SHORTER

### Further Reading

Christensen, T. (1990). *An African tree of life.* Maryknoll, NY: Orbis Books.

Green, M. (2003). *Priests, witches and power. popular Christianity after mission in southern Tanzania.* Cambridge, UK: Cambridge University Press.

Hannerz, U. (1992). *Cultural complexity: Studies in the social organization of meaning.* New York: Columbia University Press.

Hellwig, M. (1997). Christologies emerging from small Christian communities. In R. S. Pelton (Ed.), *Small Christian communities: Imagining future church* (pp. 27–34). Notre Dame, IN: University of Notre Dame Press.

Luzbetak, L. J. (1988). *The church and cultures.* Maryknoll, NY: Orbis Books.

Maloney, R. (1988). The Zairean Mass and inculturation. *Worship, 62*(5), 433–442.

Paul VI, Pope. (1976). *Apostolic exhortation on Evangelization in the modern world (Evangelii Nuntiandi).* Washington, DC: United States Catholic Conference.

Pelikan, Y. (1985). *Jesus through the centuries: His place in the history of culture.* New Haven, CT: Yale University Press.

Shorter, A. (1969). Form and content in the African sermon: An experiment. *African Ecclesiastical Review, 11(3),* 265–279.

Shorter, A. (1988). *Toward a theology of inculturation.* Maryknoll, NY: Orbis Books.

Shorter, A. (2003). *Inculturation in Africa: The way forward.* Chicago: Catholic Theological Union.

## India

India, with its diverse peoples, languages, and cultures, comprised for millennia what is presently much of South Asia. At the present time, the country consists of thirty-five different political units, called states or union territories, each with considerable political autonomy. Many units have their own language and culture, and several of them also have an ethnic identity and a specific religious tradition. With a population of over 1 billion, everything about India is big. While 80.5 percent of the population are Hindus, the Muslims, though a minority, number 120 million. Christianity is the majority religion in three states of the country, and is present in significant numbers, though not large percentages, in several other states. Sikhism, Buddhism, and Jainism are also found in the country.

According to tradition, Thomas, one of the apostles of Christ, proclaimed the Gospel in India in the first century in the present southern state of Kerala. Today a flourishing community of some 4 million people attribute the origin of their Christian faith to Thomas. He is believed to have been martyred in 72 CE near the city of Madras.

There is a long gap between this early mission in the fourth century and the next phase of evangelization, which took place towards the end of the fifteenth century. Vasco da Gama discovered the new sea route to India in 1498. This was followed not only by explorers and traders but also by missionaries. The name that stands out most prominently during this period is that of St. Francis Xavier. He reached Goa in 1542. The state at the time was important and rich. He preached with great effectiveness on the Fishery Coast, Travancore, and Cochin. His method was to go in search of people rather than wait for them to come to him. He went to territories outside the sphere of colonial influence. Though he kept pushing to the East, he returned briefly to India in 1548 and 1552. His entire missionary career lasted only ten years, but he left an imprint on mission history. Theologically a child of his time, he brought remarkable youthfulness and enthusiasm into mission. He baptized children at once, but insisted on instruction for adults before baptism. Through children he reached out to families. He used the dialogue method in teaching and made good use of music. He got help from lay persons in his work. Several Christian communities in the western part of India trace their origin to him.

Another great Jesuit missionary at this time is Roberto de Nobili. He reached Madura in South India in 1606. He learned the local language and distanced himself from the colonial power. He greatly valued people's customs and culture. He presented himself as a Christian Brahmin, an ascetic, and a guru. He lived in the Brahmin quarter of the village. He advised his superiors to appoint different missionaries to lower castes and higher castes. He studied Hindu literature and used

Sanskrit in the liturgy. He ate only vegetarian food and socialized only with Brahmins, who accepted him. He used Tamil terms of religion instead of Latin ones. He was accused of syncretism and met with opposition. However, he was allowed by Church authorities to continue his work. He died at Mylapore in 1656. Several decades after his death, the controversy surfaced again. Many practices that he and like-minded missionaries had introduced were eventually rejected by Church authorities, the final order banning them coming from Pope Benedict XIV in 1744.

In the north of India, it was a different story. The Jesuit Aquaviva was invited to visit the court of the great and tolerant Mughal emperor Akbar in 1578, but Akbar's successors were not as broadminded. Shah Jahan, who built the famous Taj Mahal, destroyed the mission of Hooghly in Bengal. The fanatic emperor Aurangazeb imposed restrictions on the missionaries. Jesuits, Carmelites, Agustinians, Capuchins, and Franciscans carried out missionary service in the Mughal Empire, but their Christian communities were small. In 1666, there were about 33,000 Christians in Bengal. In 1775, Calcutta had about 25,000 Catholics.

In the eighteenth century, Christians in India numbered between 1 and 2 million, but tragedy was brewing in the South. Tippu Sultan (1750–1799), the ruler of Mysore, unleashed a severe persecution against the Church. The 80,000 Catholics of Mangalore were reduced to 10,000, and all their churches were destroyed. However, revival followed soon after.

The missionaries, in their zeal to serve society, also undertook literary activities. Costanzo Beschi, a Jesuit from Italy, who wrote a long composition on St. Joseph, *Tambavani*, also wrote a Tamil grammar and compiled a Tamil dictionary. Thomas Stephen Buston, Jesuit from England, wrote *Christian Purana*, the life of Christ, in Marathi, and a summary of Christian doctrine in Sanskrit. Joseph Tieffentaller, Jesuit from Bozen in the Tyrol, wrote a book on the geography of India. Paulinus Bartholomaeo, a Carmelite from Austria, wrote a Sanskrit grammar in 1790.

By the end of the eighteenth century, with the rise of the British and Dutch trading companies in India, the Portuguese and Spanish influence faded. Since the new colonial powers were Protestant, Protestant churches came into direct contact with the non-Christian population of India. The reading of the Bible fired individual Protestants with missionary zeal, which led to ardent missionary activity. They were inspired by the word of God, in the changing context of the day, characterized by substantial contacts with non-Christians. Thus, for example, William Carey's enormous interest in geography, coupled with his deep religious sentiments, fed by the scriptures, stimulated him to undertake foreign missionary service.

Frederick IV, king of Denmark, sent missionaries to Tranquebar in 1706: Bartholomaeus Ziegenbalg, and Heinrich Plütschau, from Germany, were two of those sent. They worked hard and were successful, but died young. In 1750 Christian Frederick Schwartz, a German, came to India and worked with great commitment. By 1800 the mission counted about 20,000 converts in Tranquebar, Tanjavur, Tiruchinappally, Madras, Cuddalore, and Tirunelvely. Converts were mainly from the lower castes. Moravian missionaries arrived in Tranquebar in 1760, but withdrew in 1803. Chaplains attached to the East India Company began to show concern for mission. David Brown, who was in Calcutta between 1787 and 1812, set up a boarding school for Hindu children. The Church Missionary Society was established in 1799 as an evangelical missionary organization.

The arrival of William Carey (1761–1834), an Englishman, in Calcutta in 1793 was a landmark in the mission history of India. His 1792 book *An Enquiry into the Obligation of Christians to Use Means for the Conversion of the Heathen* and his zealous motto, "Expect great things from God; attempt great things for God," formed the basis of his intense missionary commitment. Carey was met with opposition from the East India Company to his staying in India, who objected to his missionary work in India thinking the introduction of a new religion would offend local people, mostly Hindus and Muislims, and adversely affect the company's commercial interest. To counter this, he became the manager of an indigo plantation, where he worked for five years and learned Bengali perfectly and started translating the Scripture. Then he withdrew to the Danish settlement of Serampore, where he enjoyed greater freedom of activity. He was joined by two remarkable men: Joshua Marshman, a Chinese language scholar, and William Ward, a printer and preacher of note.

The guidelines of their missionary activity were the following: (a) study Indian languages, the Hindu religion, and the customs of the people; (b) preach the Gospel in all towns and villages; (c) translate and print the Bible in the languages of India; (d) found a church on Baptist principles; (e) start a college to form preachers and ministers. Being a professor of Sanskrit and Bengali, he drew a pay from the new college and used this to help support the mission. He was a botanist of great repute and his garden was admired throughout Asia. He campaigned against suttee, the custom of a Hindu widow willingly being cremated on the funeral pyre of her husband to show her devotion to him.

THE SALVATION ARMY IN INDIA.

This series of drawings depicts the Salvation Army at work in India in the 1800s.

Alexander Duff (1806–1878), educator, preacher, and statesman, was a missionary of the Church of Scotland to India. He found many young Hindus eager to study Western literature and science. He opened a school in Calcutta in 1830, based on Christian principles. This was a new method of missionary activity. It was imitated by others and eventually became the most widespread method of mission in India. Catholic religious orders like the Jesuits were to make a name in this regard. Duff favored the introduction of modern medical education, opened classes for adults, and started a school for girls and a hostel for Christian students. He favored the establishment of the first Indian universities. He edited the Calcutta *Review*. He firmly believed that the missions were the primary end of the Church, and was deeply convinced of the great missionary responsibility of the Church.

The East India Company, which was truly secular, was not favorable to missionaries. However, it did certain things that turned out to be very useful to the country, which in turn aided the growth of missions. It helped to unify India by building railways, improving post and telegraph communications, providing security, and introducing English as a common language. But Indians looked upon Christianity as the religion of their colonial oppressors. The matter became highly sensitive in the context of the independence movement. The foreign tag still remains, despite the passage of time and the end of colonialism.

By the middle of the nineteenth century, the missions were flourishing. Most missionaries and funds came from Europe. Protestant churches enjoyed considerable prestige, given the fact that most British rulers were

Protestants. The Catholic Church had the services of religious sisters. These sisters were members of Catholic religious orders, who dedicated themselves to voluntary service in the missions. Church authorities recognized their service. Their sacrificing work benefited particularly women and children. In fact, the role of religious women, though a comparatively recent phenomenon in mission history, was especially effective in India.

The first baptisms in Chota Nagpur, in eastern India, took place in 1873, and twelve years later, in 1885, the great apostle of Chota Nagpur, Fr. Constant Lievens (1856–1893), a Belgian, arrived. There followed a mass movement toward Catholicism. He defended the poor tribals of the area with great effectiveness and had recourse to legal remedies against oppression by land owners and moneylenders. In four years, he received more than 65,000 people into the Church. Ill health forced him to return to his home country, where he died at the age of thirty-nine in 1895. In their methods and organization, Jesuit missionaries like Fr. Lievens, seemed to have imitated the Lutherans, who also helped people save their land through legal action.

In spite of caste, child marriage, and suttee, Hindus took to English education. Freed from Muslim rule by the British, an Indian renaissance followed, accompanied by patriotism and the independence movement. However, the Muslim community was less open to progressive forces. There were also huge numbers of people in a third group, namely the tribals and *dalits* (socially oppressed groups). These were the most open to the Gospel message. Although the fear of caste ostracism put a brake on conversions, by about 1878 in the Telugu area of southeast India, a million people were led into the Church by Anglican, Baptist, Methodist, and Lutheran missionaries.

The most remarkable mission success, beginning in the latter half of the nineteenth century, was the result of Christian missionary work, both Catholic and Protestant, in northeast India (earlier called Assam). The region emerged as the most Christian area in the country. The predominantly Christian hill tribal areas of the northeast have their own states, and thus enjoy considerable political power within the country. The northeastern part of India differs greatly from the rest of the country. While most of India is Aryan or Dravidian in origin, this area has a powerful Mongoloid component. Large groups of people belong to tribal societies and have taken to Christianity with ease. The numerical growth of the Christian community was prodigious and may be called a modern mass movement. Christianity enabled these tribes to preserve their identity. Sometimes this also led to conflicts, which resulted in aspersions being cast on the patriotism of local Christians.

Although there are indications of Catholic presence in the region in the seventeenth century, it was the Protestants who initiated planned missionary activity. The Baptists and Welsh Presbyterians led the way. The New Testament was published in the Assamese language in 1819 and the entire Bible in 1833. The New Testament in Khasi was printed at the Serampore Baptist Press in 1824. The Serampore mission of William Carey opened a mission and school at Gauhati in 1829. The American Baptist Mission started work in Assam in 1836. They opened several village schools, began translation of books into local languages, and proclaimed the Gospel with great dedication and witness of life. The first Welsh Calvinistic Methodist missionary, Thomas Jones, reached Cherrapunjee in the Khasi Hills in 1841. With his arrival, Christianity began to take firm roots in the area. The most effective means used by the missionaries were village visits and educational activities. By 1870 the local Christian community had begun to grow rapidly. The helpful attitude of the government here, unlike elsewhere in the country, was also a positive factor.

Small numbers of Catholic missionaries had passed through the region in the seventeenth century on their way to Tibet, but organized Catholic mission didn't start until 1890. The pioneers were the German Divine Saviour Society, who were replaced by the Salesians of Don Bosco in 1922. The first local converts were received into the Church in 1891. The first bishop of Shillong, Louis Mathias, was a man of great ability. Missionaries like Constantine Vendrame, Leo Piasecki, and Bishop Marengo, with their remarkable zeal and dedication, were able to reach out to numerous people, especially the tribals, with the good news of Jesus Christ. The people in turn responded enthusiastically. Now the Catholic church in northeast India counts 1.1 million people in fifteen dioceses. Worthy of special mention is the contribution of the church to health care and education on all levels, including technical education. The Christian majority states of Mizoram, Nagaland, and Meghalaya are all in northeast India.

Christianity gathered momentum in several parts of India during the twentieth century. However, its progress should not be measured only in terms of numerical growth. The Christian faith influenced all of Indian thought and culture. The leader of the Indian independence movement, Mohandas Gandhi, had a great appreciation of Jesus Christ and his teachings.

In 1947 India gained freedom from British rule. Despite the fact that the people were intensely religious, India chose to be a secular country. Secularism in India is understood as respect for all religions, not as an antireligious ideology; this tolerant attitude, which is integral to Hinduism, was also influenced by the centuries-old Christian mission in this vast country. Another interesting development of 1947 was the formation of the Church of South India (CSI) by the union of several Protestant churches. Similarly, seven Protestant denominations united to form the Church of North India (CNI) in 1970.

There was some opposition to mission after independence, sometimes in an organized way, and foreign missionaries were eventually banned. However, there were large numbers of Indian missionaries by the time, and leadership in most churches had passed into local hands. In fact, mission in reverse was beginning, with missionaries from India undertaking mission abroad, and in the fields of education and social service, Christian churches continued to serve the nation. Schools, professional training centers, colleges, hostels, hospitals, orphanages, centers for the care of the less privileged and the young at-risk, and numerous other services continued to multiply. Millions of people, predominantly non-Christians, profited from them. Governments and public opinion remained appreciative. The crowning moment was when the saintly missionary, Mother Teresa of Calcutta, died in 1997 and the government honored her with a state funeral.

However, contrary to expectations, the turn of the twenty-first century witnessed a change toward Christian mission in the country. There were several examples of violence against Christian religious personnel. The most heinous atrocities were the burning alive of the Australian missionary Rev. Graham Staines and his two little children in the state of Orissa in 1999 and the murder of Sr. Rani Maria in the state of Madhya Pradesh in 1995. In spite of these attacks, there were strong indications that anti-Christian feelings were not widespread but were fueled by fundamentalist elements who hoped to capture the majority Hindu vote by playing communities against each other. However, the general elections of 2004 were a clear indication that the people of India were mature enough to prevent any polarization based on sectarian grounds.

Thanks to two thousand years of missionary service in this vast country by many Christian churches, Christian witness is beyond doubt well established. To make this witness even more effective, it will need to pay greater attention than ever before to the pressing demands of the Gospel's encounter with the complexities of Indian culture. To put down roots in this land, the good news of Christ will need to become part of the evolving culture. The challenge Christian mission faces today is to communicate effectively to the people of India that Jesus Christ came not to destroy but to fulfill and perfect, that in him, "the way, the truth and the life," they will find lasting fulfillment of all their genuine aspirations.

PAUL VADAKUMPADAN

*See also* Asian Theology; Buddhism; Contextualization; Education; Hinduism; Inculturation; Protestant Churches; Roman Catholic Church

### Further Reading

Becker, C. (1980). *History of the Catholic missions in northeast India.* Shillong, India: Vendrame Missioloigcal Institute.

Karotemprel, S. (Ed.). (1995). *Following Christ in mission.* Bombay, India: Pauline.

Latourette, K. S. (1976). *A history of the expansion of Christianity* (Vols. 1–7). Grand Rapids, MI: Zondervan.

Maliekal, G. (2005). *History of the Catholic church among the Khasis.* Shillong, India: DBCIC.

Mundadan, A. M., et al. (1982–1992). *History of Christianity in India* (Vols. I, II, V). Bangalore, India: The Church History Association of India.

## Indigenous Religions

Indigenous religions are primarily defined by their orality, their cosmological orientation, and their ritual practices in specific geocultural landscapes. In indigenous religions, beliefs and practices are transmitted from one generation to another through myths, legends, paintings, sculpture, songs, and dances. "Indigenous" is a generalized reference to thousands of small- to large-scale societies with distinct languages, kinship systems, mythologies, ancestral traditions, and homelands. Although precise demographic estimates are not available, these societies, which have diverse cultures and languages, comprise between 300 and 350 million people on all continents. They form about 6 percent of the total world population with over 5,000 distinct peoples in at least seventy-two countries. "Indigenous" refers to societies recognized as such either by other groups (scholars, the United Nations, and the World Bank) or by themselves.

Africa, the world's second largest continent, is home to a huge diversity of ethnic and linguistic groups. Indigenous peoples may be found among the larger sub-Saharan groups such as the Yoruba, Igbo, Bambara, Akan, Ewe, Mandinka, Zulu, Shona, and Xhosa peoples, and it has become common to trace indigenous peoples to even smaller groups such as the Gwari, Tuareg, Ogoni, and Wodaabe in the West; the Chaga, Makonde, Nyakyusa, and Maasai in the East; the Khoisan, Khoikhoi, Herero, and Kalahari Bushmen in the South; and the Baka, Twa Pygmies, Mbuti, and Bakongo in Central Africa.

American Indians who lived on the Northern Plains encompassed over six hundred traditions, eight major language families, and probably three distinct racial strains, which have now run together. Their territory included what are now the states of Montana, North and South Dakota, and Wyoming, and the northern portions of Nebraska. Euroasia, the geographical landmass composed of Europe and Asia, is home to several indigenous peoples including the Komi, Sorbs, Mordvins, Tatars, Vespians, Mari, Buryat, Kashubians, Circassian, Eskimos, and Celts. Indigenous people in Australasia include the Australian Aborigines, the New Zealand Maoris, Native Hawaiians, the Chamorros, and several different Papua Melanesian groups such as the Dani and Korowai.

The religions of these indigenous peoples do not have a monolithic structure. They vary, from traditions of remote societies, hunter-gatherers, mountain and cave dwellers, settled agricultural communities, and nomadic peoples, to large, complex societies, empires, and kingdoms. Thus, North America has the religions of the Naskapi, Kwakiutl, Powhatan, Cherokees, Zuni, Iroquois, Apache, Dakota, Lakota, Navajo, and Pawnee peoples, and Mesoamerica and South America have the religions of the Guarani, Tupi, Nukak, Aztecs, and Incas. In Euroasia, there are the Komi, Sami, Ingrains, and Celtic religions, and the Maori, Torres Strait Islanders, and Aboriginal religions are popular in Australasia. African indigenous religions include the Yoruba, Zulu, Azande, Akan, Nuer, Xhosa, Shona, Massai, and Chewa, and the religions of the Kalahari Bushmen. Numerically, they are significant in the demographical context of world religions. In actual fact, indigenous religions are the majority of the world's religions.

Indigenous religions pose an interesting, complex problem of description and interpretation. Because indigenous languages have no word for "religion," the appropriation of that word to describe a worldview or a set of behaviors can be seen as an invention or a Western academic construct. However, the absence of that specific term does not imply that indigenous peoples are not religious. Their social structures and cultural traditions are infused with a spirituality that cannot be easily separated from the rest of their community's life. To analyze religion as a separate system of beliefs and practices apart from subsistence, kinship, language, politics, and the landscape is to misunderstand indigenous religions. In fact, these phenomena have been misunderstood, romanticized, and misappropriated through labels such as primitive, animism, syncretistic groups, superstition, and savage systems. Other, related terms include Native peoples, Aborigines, First Peoples, autochthonous, and fourth world. Because these essentially pejorative labels have been employed by nonindigenous peoples to represent indigenous peoples and their religious worlds, their acceptance and rejection have important political and strategic implications.

## Common Concerns

Because indigenous peoples and their religious collectivities are characterized by a complex diversity, it is impossible to see African, Native American, Australasian, and Euroasian religions as a single whole. However, their historical specificities, cosmological systems, and ritual dimensions do suggest that there is some unity in all that diversity. For example, while indigenous societies range from those that were significantly exposed to the colonizing activities of other societies, mostly European and American, to those that remain in comparative isolation, almost all indigenous societies have had some sort of encounter with colonization and been exposed to religions such as Christianity, Islam, Buddhism, and Hinduism. In the nineteenth and early twentieth centuries, most of Africa came under colonial rule.

The history of European contact with the Aborigines, Africans, American Indians, and other indigenous peoples is characterized by the expropriation and the destruction of their cultural patterns, sacred sites, and objects. Only a few isolated groups remain in which there has not been a substantial European influence of one form or another. As a reflection of their claims to precolonial antecedents and legitimation, localized forms of religious expression are often distinguished as "traditional" or "indigenous"' to distinguish them from "world religions." The encounter with Europeans led, on the one hand, to the denigration of indigenous religions, culminating in their rejection and abandonment by some indigenous peoples. On the other hand, the encounter also led to mutual influence and transformation and to innovation and creativity.

Indigenous peoples have existed for centuries, and their histories are encoded in myths, art, music, songs, and dances. However, the earliest written sources about them are derived from Christian missionaries and other colonial observers in the late nineteenth and early twentieth centuries. This initial phase was followed in the thirties and forties by a new phase of scholarly engagement with indigenous peoples, one marked by empathy, relative objectivity, and a variety of approaches. Because of this evolution, the historiography of indigenous religions may be characterized as a perceptual shift from viewing indigenous peoples as objects to understanding them as subjects. Indigenous peoples are increasingly becoming involved in the study of their own cultures and religions, which can be seen in the demography of scholars and the proliferation of academic research areas such as African Studies, Native American Studies, Australian Aboriginal Studies, and Maori Studies. In spite of these various attempts, however, there is still a relative dearth of written sources on indigenous religions.

Indigenous religions engage in activities of a collective nature in which individuals often have considerable freedom. One distinctive aspect is the large extent to which activities are community-based and have no real meaning outside the context in which the ritual acts are regularly performed, stories told, songs sung, and ceremonies enacted. Another shared characteristic is the reliance of the practitioners upon subsistence-based production in predominantly nonurbanized societies. In this context, they confront diverse issues and concerns, ranging from status and identity negotiations, to interactions with other cultural groups and responses to changes in their environment. Challenges, which may be specific to a particular group or commonly experienced, include linguistic preservation, land rights, environmental degradation, exploitation of natural resources, political autonomy, and the preservation of religiocultural identities.

The systemic pressures of colonial experience, which have worked to eradicate, suppress, or erode indigenous religious traditions, continue in the legal and economic activities of corporate and government interests in places with traditional spiritual values. During the late nineteenth and early twentieth centuries, enormous social pressures were placed on indigenous peoples in North America, and at the end of the twentieth century, deeply held traditional beliefs were politicized, partly by academics and activists. The economic and political autonomy of Native-American peoples, which were seriously undermined through conquest and destruction, resulted in their confinement to reservations established by treaties with the U.S government, where many Native-American peoples still live. While land rights of indigenous peoples such as the Austra-lian Aborigines are gradually being recognized, with restitution of stolen lands occurring in some cases, in other places governments are still appropriating land. For example, land belonging to the Twa, Mbuti, and Kalahari Bushmen has been appropriated for National Parks and Game Reserves without adequate compensation made to the land owners.

## Cosmologies and Belief Systems

Indigenous societies demonstrate common affinities in their religious worldviews, their belief in spiritual entities, their use of concepts to represent them, and their ritual attitudes toward their manipulation and control. Oral narratives, which describe the web of human activities within the spiritual cosmos, represent a vital source for understanding religious cosmologies, the creation of the universe, the origin of man, and societal norms. A Navajo origin myth explains the emergence of humans onto the earth from a series of underworlds; in the myth, the natural and supernatural intertwine. The Iroquois origin myth begins with the Sky people who inhabit a disk world above the earth, and describes a pregnant woman who made the descent from the Sky people, propagating the earth.

Indigenous religions, which are concerned with identifying underlying life forces, vital forces, energies, or other mysterious powers, commonly include a belief in a transcendental reality, a supreme being and lesser divinities, as well as in spirits, ancestors, magic, sorcery, and witchcraft. The names, functions, rankings in hierarchy, and emphasis on each aspect vary according to the context—for instance, while animals, forces of nature, natural objects, and unseen forces always qualify as spirits, different indigenous religions assign the same objects to different ranks in their hierarchies. The Apache religion centers on the conception of a supernatural power that manifests itself in almost every facet of the Apache world. The Dakota believe in Wakan Tanka as a sacred power and creative force revealed in humans, nature, and the spirit world. The Kewa of Melanasia talk of a benevolent Sky Deity, Ya-kili, to whom appeal is made in times of hardship. Their relationship with their ancestors is also significant.

Mediation plays an important role in indigenous religious systems because the source of power from the Supreme Deity cannot be received directly. Thus, the religious world is characterized by a multiplicity of divinities, spirits, and ancestors, and beliefs and practices concerning them are a dominant element. While the divinities and spirits are proxy to the affairs of the living, they mediate between the earth and the sky.

# Religious and Political Change in South India

**The following extract of ethnographic text describes transformations in the religious life of Badaga community, a small, indigenous group in southwest India.**

Since 1913 important developments have occurred in the Badaga Christian community. From the earliest years of the present century, according to the missionary reports, the Christian community has been recognized by the Badagas as a distinct caste inferior to Hindu Badagas but superior to Kotas, and rigid patterns for interaction between the Christians and Hindus have been formalized. During the period 1913–1947 the Hindu Badagas, like the Christians before them, became increasingly dependent on the economy and the labor market which was ultimately controlled by the British. As a result of this the former acts of violence toward Badaga Christians ceased: as many Hindu Badagas now found it desirable to maintain outwardly friendly attitudes towards the British, they could not simultaneously be openly antagonistic toward the religion of the British.

After the Christians had become a separate social group, Roman Catholic priests became active—mainly in converting Protestant Badagas—and thereby split the Christians into two culturally very similar but structurally opposed groups, each maintaining a self-righteous and antagonistic attitude not only toward the other Christian group but also toward the Hindus (Périe 1932, 1–8).

This situation continued with little change until after 1947, by which time the Catholics were almost as numerous as the Protestants. Independence brought new factors into play, however. Conversion of Hindus to either Christian sect virtually ceased with national Independence, as did most conversion of Protestants to Catholicism. While there are still some points of disagreement between members of the two churches (preëminently in ecclesiastical matters), as there are between Christians and Hindus, these are being obfuscated as other cultural orientations become more relevant to the changing conditions of life in the Nilgiris. There are now some indications in casual conversation that the cultural orientations of the Badagas are being adapted to a newly emerging pattern of social solidarity; one which links all Badagas, whether Christian or Hindu, in the face of competition with all other Indians. Some Hindu Badagas, for example, were willing to tell me that "The Christians set us a good example"; by these words they were alluding to the standards of honesty, hard work, education, and "progressive" treatment of their women for which the Christians are noted (*cf. Ranga 1934, 5–6). The Badaga community is now always called a "caste," and its members are more strongly aware of their identity as "Badagas," a community which the Government shows particular concern and beneficence for by treating as a "Backward Class." The chances of material benefit through better employment opportunities which, a century ago, prompted a few Badagas to change their attitudes sufficiently to become Christians, now prompt their descendants to alter other orientations not closely related to religious values but rather to a government and its new classification of employment priorities. Such a change in orientation holds out the chance of upward mobility; but in that process conversion to Christianity is now an anachronistic mechanism.*

Source: Hockings, P. (1965). *Cultural change among the Badagas: A community in southern India* (pp. 132–133). Ann Arbor, MI: University Microfilms International.

These spiritual forces can be approached through ritual action or through ancestors, who play an intermediary role between the mundane and the supersensible realms; ancestors are the guardians and custodians of the moral and religious values of society. The beliefs and rituals associated with spiritual forces constitute a distinctively indigenous pattern of religious thought and action. Indigenous culture is thus a complex web of religion, attitudes, behavior, morality, politics, and the economy.

Aboriginal cosmology centers upon what has been translated as the "dreaming" or "dreamtime," which refers to a creative period and a continual, temporal metaphysical reality. Yoruba cosmology is a coherent thought system codified in the *Ifa* literary corpus. The Yoruba worldview divides the cosmos into earth and sky. The cosmos is believed to be the creation of Olodumare (the Supreme Being). His several names and attributes reveal his nature. Olodumare created and assigned the *orisas* (divinities) as functionaries in the orderly maintenance of the universe. Human beings also occupy a significant position in indigenous cosmology. Each human being has a dual makeup: the physical and the spiritual mien. The spiritual aspect of humans serves as a nexus between them and the ethereal world. The Zulu make a distinction between three aspects of being: the physical body, which perishes or decomposes after death; vital force or breath, which keeps people alive; and personality or force of character.

## Ritual Cosmos

Rituals are geared toward ensuring and sustaining cosmic harmony at individual and collective levels, particularly in the pursuit of health and fertility, and in maintaining a balance between humans and nature. The well-being of individuals, the community, or social groupings is attained through explanation, prediction, and control. Rites of passage are a common feature of religious life, and their ritual structures draw largely upon a philosophy of relationships. An individual's passage through life is monitored, marked, and celebrated from before birth to parturition, childhood, transition to adulthood, adulthood, marriage, old age, death, and the living-dead. The rituals associated with these life-stages are significant in the indigenous cultural matrix.

Ritual action, which typically includes a ritual object, enhances the relationship of indigenous peoples to the powers of life. The Lakota religious system is dominated by ritual enactments to the deities in order to ensure successful buffalo hunts. The sacred rites which form the basis of Lakota religion include the Sweat Lodge, the Vision Quest, Ghost Keeping, Sun Dance, Making Relatives, Puberty Ceremony, and Throwing the Ball. Northern Plains peoples believe that "bundles," which are composed of a variety of objects such as pipes, special plants, animal and bird skins, animal bones, and pebbles, have potency and that their power can be released into the world through ritual action. Various Sun Dances parade one or more bundles at the core of their rituals. The Blackfoot Natoas bundle is a significant ritual object in the Sun Dance ceremony.

Some of the many special roles in indigenous religious practice include the headman or priest, clan head, diviner, medicine man, heaven-herd, chiefs, sorcerers, and witches. In these contexts, political, social, and religious functions overlap and interact. Sacral kingship represents one of the most distinctive features of indigenous political organization. Divination is an important activity and the role of the diviner is widespread. The diviner or medicine man is a pivotal force for order and rapprochement between man and the spirit world. The Yoruba people divine to discover the behest of supernatural beings, and to inquire about their destiny. Diviners are consulted whenever illness, misfortune, or unusual events occur. *Ifa* is the most widespread means of Yoruba divination. Other systems include the casting of kolanuts, sixteen cowries, and *Opele*.

Spirit possession and spirit mediumship are integral to the indigenous religious world. They are the chief means of communicating between the spirit and the physical world. Spirit mediums, spirit possession cults, diviners, and medicine men form a large section of the indigenous health care system. There is a strong link between gender, spirit possession, and mediumship in many indigenous religions, with an overwhelming majority of mediums being women. Women's role and status are regarded as wholesome to the welfare of the entire community, and women carry out crucial ritual functions.

## Globalization of Indigenous Religions

Indigenous religions have been introduced to new contexts through migration. The African diaspora resulting from the trans-Atlantic slave trade profoundly influenced the cultures of Brazil, Cuba, Haiti, and the rest of the New World, partly leading to the development of African-derived religions such as the Santeria (Lukumi, Macumba) in Cuba, the Candomble Nago in Brazil, and voodoo, Yoruba-Orisha traditions, and other West African-rooted traditions across the Americas. These religious forms are proliferating in the diaspora and both practitioners and clientele have been widened ethnically and racially. Yoruba funerals reincorporate the dead as "ancestors" in their London-centered community. Mama Lola, a voodoo priestess in Brooklyn, New York, is an interesting example of immigrant voodoo that emphasizes a personal relationship with the spirit world.

With growing revitalization and internationalization of indigenous religions, many people are beginning to appreciate their traditional religions or to engage in both indigenous and other, newer religions. Indigenous peoples have experienced something of a religious revival and have become concerned with the preservation of their cultural and religious heritage. Aboriginal Australian *didjeridu* players or First Nation Canadian drum groups play their religious music to a wider audience at the World of Music, Arts and Dance (WOMAD) and other festivals. Maori *tolunga* purify auditoriums before Maori opera singers perform there. Festivals in commemoration of local divinities have become internationalized. The annual festival for the Yoruba Osun deity now attracts devotees and tourists from all parts of the world. This ritual event has thus been transformed from an ethnic-based one to one with an international audience and participation.

The spread of Islam and Christianity saw the introduction of new religious ideas and practices into indigenous religions. The encounter transformed indigenous religious thought and practice but did not supplant it; indigenous religions preserved some of their beliefs and practices but also adjusted to the new sociocultural milieu. The interaction also produced indigenized forms of Islam and Christianity. The contact produced new religious movements, with some appropriating indigenous symbols and giving them a new twist. Indigenous religions have deeply influenced world art, sculpture, and painting. The commodification of indigenous art and religious objects is on the increase, and indigenous cultural artifacts can be found in museums, galleries, libraries, and art exhibitions.

European language was also enriched by its contact with indigenous religions; borrowed words such as "shaman," "taboo," and "voodoo" are now part of the English vocabulary. Western horticultural, culinary, and medical knowledge has also had significant input from indigenous peoples and their epistemology. On the other hand, indigenous religions are increasingly appropriating new communication technologies such as the Internet, which they now use to transmit their religious ideologies. Their Web sites have assumed a conscious strategy of self-insertion and identification within a global religious landscape, and are used as an alternative medium to recruit new clientele. The character of indigenous religions in the new global environment will continue to be shaped by how and to what extent indigenous peoples negotiate continuity, identity, and change.

AFE ADOGAME

*See also* Africa; Art; Asia, Central; Asia, East; Asia, Southeast; Central America; Islam; Latin America; North America; Orality

## Further Reading

Alpers, A. (1964). *Maori myths and tribal legends.* Auckland, New Zealand: Longman Paul.

Benjamin C. R. (2000). *African religions: Symbol, ritual and community* (2nd ed.). Upper Saddle River, NJ: Prentice-Hall.

Berndt, R. M., & Berndt, C. H. (1989). The speaking land: Myth and story in Aboriginal Australia. Camberwell, Australia: Penguin.

Best, E. (1924). *Maori religion and mythology: Being an accountant of the cosmogony anthropology, religious beliefs and rites, magic, and folklore of the Maori folk of New Zealand* (Part 1). Wellington, New Zealand: Government Printer.

Blakely, T. D., et al. (Eds.). (1994). *Religion in Africa: Experience and expression.* London: James Curry.

Brokensha, D., Warren, D., & Werner, O. (Eds.). (1980). *Indigenous knowledge systems and development.* Washington, DC: University Press of America.

Brosted, J., et al. (1985). *Native power: The quest for autonomy and nationhood of indigenous peoples.* New York: Columbia University Press.

Brown, K. M. (1991). *Mama Lola: A Vodou priestess in Brooklyn.* Berkeley: University of California Press.

Collins, J. J. (1991). *Native American religions: A geographical survey.* Lewiston, ME: The Edwin Mellen Press.

Edwards, W. H. (1989). *An introduction to Aboriginal societies.* Wentworth Falls, Australia: Social Science Press.

Elkin, A. P. (1986). *The Australian Aborigines.* North Ryde, Australia: Angus & Robertson.

Flood, J. (1989). *Archaeology of the dreamtime: The story of prehistoric Australia and its people.* Sydney, Australia: Collins.

Geertz, C. (1976). *Religion of Java.* Chicago: University of Chicago Press.

Harris, J. (1990). *One blood: 200 years of aboriginal encounter with Christianity—A story of hope.* Sutherland, Australia: Albatross Books.

Harvey, G. (Ed.). (2000). *Indigenous religions. A companion.* London and New York: Cassell.

Hultkrantz, A. (1987). *Native religions of North America.* San Francisco: Harper and Row.

Olupona, J. K. (Ed.). (2000). *African spirituality, forms, meanings and expressions.* New York: Crossroad Publishing.

Olupona, J. K. (Ed.). (2004). *Beyond primitivism. Indigenous religious traditions and modernity.* New York and London: Routledge.

Rowse, T. (1994). *After Mabo—interpreting indigenous traditions.* Melbourne, Australia: University Press.

Sullivan, L. E. (Ed.). (1989). *Native American religions: North America.* New York: Macmillan.

Sullivan, L.E. (Ed.). (2000). *Native religions and cultures of North America: Anthropology of the sacred.* New York: Continuum.

# Internationalism

The mission of the Christian church has been international since the day of Pentecost. The issues facing Christian mission in every era and place have been shaped and reshaped by prevailing patterns of internationalism and cross-cultural interaction. Examining the mission of the church without placing it in the broader context of key developments in internationalism and foreign policy is to misunderstand the universal impulses at the heart of the Gospel.

The fruits of the Protestant missionary movement provided an expanded view of the world to the leading American internationalist and foreign policy leaders of the last century. Powerful internationalist establishment leaders such as the Rockefeller family, Woodrow Wilson, Henry Luce, John R. Mott, John Foster Dulles, and Dean Rusk were all either sons of clergy or missionaries, or strong supporters of Christian mission. American mission experiences had deep ties to the expansion of the Eastern Protestant business and political Establishment, ties that helped shape American foreign policy throughout the twentieth century.

## Wilson, Mott, and J. D. Rockefeller Jr.

In response to America's heightened industrial production through World War I and the need for international markets at the height of colonial imperialism, Woodrow Wilson developed an internationalist foreign policy. It was a worldview that mixed the interests of expanding big business with the need to project American values of special providence toward other nations. Wilsonian internationalism sought policies to keep the world safe for democracy and protect the remnant of Western culture's better values. The son of a Presbyterian minister, Wilson constructed an enlightened theological rationale: to baptize the twin interests of promoting American business and using Christian values to stabilize and rebuild the broken global system in the post–World War I era. This took form in Wilson's Fourteen Points for Peace.

These ideas, which hoped to provide postwar financial and political stability, gave rise to the League of Nations. Ironically, Wilson's ideas failed to find institutional form when Congress voted against involvement in the League of Nations. However, Wilson's ideals of Christian values serving in partnership with the business, political, and religious needs of the global community continued to impact American foreign policy in attenuated forms.

Links abound between the foreign policy elite, American internationalist business interests, and the expansion of the church. The three most important links prior to World War II were the relationships between Wilson, Mott, and the Rockefeller families. The common denominator of these powerful men and ideas was the most uncommon John R. Mott. Raised a devout Methodist, Mott had a clear experience of a "reasonable and vital faith" while listening to the renowned cricketer-cum-missionary C. T. Studd speak at Cornell University in 1886. Mott became the college secretary for the YMCA and helped organize the Student Volunteer Movement for missions. Through the expanding work of the YMCA and YWCA, which he came to lead, Mott leveraged the enthusiasm of young people while soliciting the support of wealthy businessmen to finance a massive network of global Christian connections. With seemingly endless energy and enthusiasm, Mott created a worldwide network in the World Christian Student Fellowship. He employed youth leadership to promote education, health care, evangelism, and economic prospects in countries in which U.S. churches and government were often unable to work effectively. Mott's travels—the most extensive of any lay evangelist in Christian history—made him the strongest U.S. voice for mission and ecumenism before World War I. He organized and led the World Missionary Conference in Edinburgh in 1910, and out of this work came continuing committees that led to the formation of the World Council of Churches in 1949.

As America entered World War I, John Mott offered the services of the worldwide YMCA to President Woodrow Wilson, and they grew close through this work. Mott was offered an appointment as U.S. Ambassador to China in 1916, but he turned down the post to concentrate on his international religious networks. Wilson later sent Mott as a diplomat to the 1916 Mexican Commission, and then as a delegate to the Special Diplomatic Mission to Russia in 1917. On the home front, Wilson appointed Mott to head the U.S. National War Work Council, whose mission was to promote awareness among the population to serve the interests of America in the war. Through the YMCA, Mott led relief work in Europe after the war, and for his wartime leadership he won the Distinguished Service Medal. Similar relief work through the YMCA in the aftermath of World War II earned Mott the Nobel Peace Prize in 1946.

Mott also drew the attention of the Rockefellers—particularly of J. D. Rockefeller Jr., who saw in Mott's work a way to promote social changes worldwide consistent with his family's ideals and financial interests. For his part, Mott realized that he needed Rockefeller support and organizational acumen to evangelize the world in one generation. He found in the values of the Rockefeller Foundation a way to cut through the Fundamentalist-modernist debate—which in Mott's view only threatened to divide the church and delay the "Millennial Kingdom of God." Mott also saw the organizational model of Standard Oil, with its myriad global subsidiaries, as an effective model for the worldwide church.

The Rockefeller family poured millions into Mott's organizations. Mott and J. D. Rockefeller Jr. concentrated on organizing education and health services, which they believed could prevent angry nationalistic or indigenous uprisings from disturbing the unity of the churches and, of course, the flow of oil to America. After popular revolutions swept Mexico and China in 1910, Rockefeller sent Mott to China to set up the China Medical Board, which blended medicine, science, and religious impulses to create the Peking Union Medical College. Mott was keen to train the first generation of indigenous Christian medical doctors after the formation of the Chinese Republic in 1911, and Rockefeller wanted a secure China to keep an open flow of resources to and from the Chinese market. Indeed, Standard Oil kerosene had lit most of the lamps of China since the 1890s—so much so that Standard Oil used a biblical motif as their slogan: "Standard Oil: The Light of the World." By the late 1920s, Standard Oil had subsidiaries with strong holdings in Venezuela, Mexico, the Balkans, the Middle East, South Africa, India, Indochina, the Philippines, and at the time, the Dutch East Indies. Its area of greatest expansion and opportunity was across Latin America: Bolivia, Columbia, and Guatemala. This expansion made the Rockefeller Foundation flush with money and able to further underwrite the kind of modernist ecumenical missionary work Mott led.

The Rockefeller Foundation and Trusts contributed generously to a number of important internationalist Christian causes and institutions: They helped mount the Laymen's Foreign Missions inquiry by financing research teams and the publication of a book by William Ernest that explored ways to improve modernist missions. They provided an atmosphere for creative and prophetic American theological education through the Union Theological Seminary in New York. They donated seed money for the ultimately unsuccessful Interchurch World Movement (1919–1921)—a unified, aggressive interdenominational mission agency dedicated to promoting the social Gospel. They funded the Federal Council of Churches, which later became the National Council of Churches. And, finally, they supported the World Council of Churches and the International Missionary Council, which had begun with Mott's committee work at Edinburgh's World Missionary Conference. Thus, the Rockefellers in conjunction with Mott left a lasting imprint on both international relations and world ecumenism.

## Luce, Dulles, and Rusk

Henry Luce, born to missionary parents in China, became the founder of *Time* and *Life* magazines. In the middle third of the twentieth century, Luce was perhaps the foremost proponent of exporting American values and faith around the world in order to thwart Communism. His publishing work, based on his international experience in China, called for America to take its rightful place as an international power in order to save China for democracy. He used his magazines and media empire to preach this message to the public as well as to policy makers. After the Harry S. Truman administration delayed sending help to President Chiang Kai-Shek and his nationalist army and government retreated to exile in Formosa (Taiwan), Chairman Mao emerged victorious and free to pursue the Communist Cultural Revolution in 1949. Luce used his media apparatus to mount a campaign against Truman and the Democrats, criticizing them for "losing China." He pressed hard for American intervention in the world, particularly in Asian countries he saw as vulnerable to Communism. His advocacy influenced the Democrats through the Korean War, and rose to its apex in shaping the policy of containment that emerged in the policies of Eisenhower's Secretary of State, John Foster Dulles.

Dulles, the son of a Presbyterian clergyman and a brother of the first Central Intelligence Agency director, had first gained notoriety as a delegate to the committee that negotiated the Treaty of Versailles after World War II. He went on to become a prominent international Wall Street banker, financing deals with global political implications. Having lived as a nominal Christian in his adult years, Dulles had a spiritual revival in 1937. He attained what he described as his "great enlightenment" at the Universal Christian Council for Life and Work conference in Oxford, where he met Mott, Niebuhr, and many other giants of the prewar ecumenical movement. These men helped him to realize how the church and its principles could be used to resolve global problems of competition. He was converted to the view that the mainstream modernist churches—working in concert across the global church—could leverage their resources to protect the values of individual liberty.

After this conversion at Oxford, Dulles threw himself into work as a leader in the Federal Council of Churches (later NCC). After World War II, he worked on drafting the constitution of the United Nations, which included Christian principles of tolerance, charity, mutual interdependence, and protection of human rights; he was a leading representative at the San Francisco conference that convened the newly created United Nations in 1949. He became secretary of state in 1952 as his maternal grandfather had been before him. Influenced by both his family background in diplomacy and the mission movement, Dulles sought to exercise a moral leadership consistent with Wilsonian ideas. However, in the aftermath of the fall of China and North Korea to Communism, Dulles came to believe that American foreign policy should be directed by a tougher containment policy toward the Soviet Union and China. He argued that the United States should reserve the right to act unilaterally—ironically, without permission from the very United Nations he helped create.

Dulles's thinking launched America on a collision course with Communism in Vietnam. His brand of neo-Wilsonian containment committed Dean Rusk—Secretary of State to presidents John F. Kennedy and Lyndon B. Johnson, and the son of a clergyman—to policies in the early 1960s that made the national and international tragedy of the Vietnam War both inevitable and intractable. Rusk's first principles were instinctively Wilsonian: deeply Christian and committed to implementing an international rule of law. Having learned as an intelligence officer in China, India, and Burma during World War II that missionaries were important sources of information, Rusk turned to them in the sixties and was impressed by their efforts to dismantle colonialism and promote self-determination for indigenous peoples. These discoveries helped shape his policies as Secretary of State. He tried to reposition containment theory from a purely defensive posture to a way to protect free societies; he saw in this policy a chance to promote liberation for indigenous peoples in the non-Western world.

Trying to move past Dulles's realpolitik and pure containment, Rusk sought an opening for neo-Wilsonian morality and international justice. But the Bay of Pigs threat and the Cuban missile crisis, as well as the escalation of bombing in Vietnam, Cambodia, and Laos, defeated his desire for quiet, determined diplomacy. By the time he was Secretary of State in the Johnson administration, his high ideals had given way to a hard pragmatic realism more reminiscent of Dulles: Rusk pursued open demonstrations of raw power so that direct war upon America would prove "a disaster for the enemy." There is a sad irony that American foreign policy during the height of the Cold War was in the hands of clergy sons Dulles and Rusk—two openly Christian neo-Wilsonians. The ambiguous results of their careers suggest both the potency and the potential for abuse when religion and realpolitik converge.

The lines of influence running from Wilson to Rusk demonstrate a continuous, evolving relationship between the mission of American foreign policy and the mission of the church in the world. Deep immersion in the national and global life of Christian churches offered these leaders a view of the world that enhanced their ability to reshape the world—for both good and ill. They shaped, individually and together, a century in which America rose to world dominance and the global church flowered. However, their stories are, finally, a cautionary tale about the limitations and unintended consequences of conflating the mission of the church with the mission of America. Yet America, the American church, and even the global church owe much to these leaders who were inspired by missionary and ministerial service.

W. Harrison Daniel

## Further Reading

Colby, G., with Dennett, C. (1995). *Thy will be done: The conquest of the Amazon, Nelson Rockefeller and evangelism in the age of oil.* New York: Harper Collins.

Halberstam, D. (1993). *The fifties.* New York: Fawcett Columbine.

Herzstein, R. E. (2006). *Henry R. Luce,* Time *and the American crusade in Asia.* Cambridge, UK: Cambridge University Press.

Immerman, R. H. (1999). *John Foster Dulles: Piety, pragmatism, and power in U.S. foreign policy.* Wilmington, DE: Scholarly Resources.

Zeiler, T. W. (2000). *Dean Rusk: Defending the American mission abroad.* Wilmington, DE: Scholarly Resources.

# Internet

Originally conceived in the United States as a fail-safe means of computer-based communication in the event of nuclear war, what we think of as the Internet today is a worldwide communication network that is having a dramatic impact on economies, politics, religious faiths, and—for the purposes of this article—missions.

The statistical growth of the Internet is by every account impressive. According to Internet World Stats (www.internetworldstats.com), as of 2007 the estimated number of users was just over 1.1 billion, or some 16 percent of the total world population. This represents a growth of more than 6200 percent over the past decade—though from 2000 on the growth rate was a more modest 182 percent. A major change during that decade is that English, while still having the most users (30.6 percent), no longer dominates the Internet. How, then, is the Internet impacting missions? The following is intended only as an overview list of selected areas (see Pocock, VanRheenen and McConnell 2005, 299–320, for more extensive discussion).

## Internet Communication Modes

The ability to connect in real time with people virtually anywhere in the world has resulted in dramatic changes in mission. Churches, supporters, families, supervisors, and friends all demand immediate two-way access to the contemporary missionary. On the positive side this enables a sense of connectedness with loved ones who are physically far away, the possibility of quick resolution of issues and problems, reporting for purposes of prayer and advice, and so on. However, with this connectivity can come attendant distractions. Missionaries who remain closely connected to those at home will have a harder time connecting with those among whom they work. Churches that financially support missionaries may have higher expectations for reporting and expect priority handling of their requests. People who are prone to dash off a letter in anger or frustration may find themselves losing time in repairing distant relationships rather than building local ones.

## Distance Education, Training, and E-learning

Agencies are starting to take advantage of the Internet to provide in-service education or other training for their workers. There is less need to gather missionaries in international groups for training conferences when they can all stay at home and learn together via the Internet. While such learning experiences do provide their own type of socialization for those involved, they still are not as effective in developing relationships as face-to-face gatherings. In addition, doing them well via the Internet takes extensive developmental time and associated costs.

## Mobilization and Recruiting

Agencies were quick to realize that they could access far more people than ever before if they developed viable websites that explained them to those who are interested and browsing. Institutions that developed to support agencies—such as Arbeitsgemeinschaft Evangelikaler Missionen (German; www.aem.de), Association Missionnaire Européenne (TEMA) (www.temanet.org/fr/homefr.html), Evangelical Fellowship of Mission Agencies (http://community.gospelcom.net/Brix?pageID=7115), India Missions Association (www.imaindia.org), and International Fellowship of Missionary Agencies (www.ifmamissions.org)—also realized the value of the Internet, not only to their own constituents but to the associations themselves.

Today any web-savvy person looking for an agency will expect to be able to read all about that agency from its website. Those people will instantly remove from consideration any agency that does not have a website or whose website is disorganized, incoherent, hard to navigate, or otherwise unhelpful (Moreau and O'Rear 2005).

## Access to Knowledge

Another helpful potential of the Internet for missions is the access it can provide to timely and helpful knowledge. The fact that "Google"—the name of the most widely used search engine on the Internet—has become a verb among contemporary Internet users is but one indication of what people expect. Google's project to "create a comprehensive, searchable, virtual card catalog of all books in all languages" (http://books.google.com/googlebooks/library.html) is an example of the visionary possibilities for those organizations with deep pockets and corresponding financial commitment.

In mission circles, numerous organizations are working hard to provide access to an incredible array of information previously accessible only to those with access to well-endowed missions libraries in Western settings. DeepSight Trust (www.deepsight.org) provides articles and extensive annotated bibliographies focused on gospel and culture. The Dictionary of African Christian Biography (www.dacb.org) contains thousands of articles not available in print. The Henry

Martyn Centre for the Study of Mission and World Christianity (www.martynmission.cam.ac.uk) offers articles, library access, and other resources. Missionary E-Texts Archive (www.missionaryetexts.org) has writings by and about a limited number of missionaries from Paul to Samuel Zwemer. The Network for Strategic Missions KnowledgeBase (www.strategicnetwork.org/index.php?loc=kb) has amassed more than 16,000 articles from several hundred sources on missions in a single searchable database. World Christian Database (http://worldchristiandatabase.org/wcd) offers searchable statistical information from *The World Christian Encyclopedia*.

### Journal Archives

Almost every major missions journal provides at the very least a home page and often subscription-based access to archived articles—including *Evangelical Missions Quarterly* (www.emqonline.com), *International Bulletin of Missionary Research* (www.omsc.org/ibmr.html), *International Review of Mission* (www.wcc-coe.org/wcc/what/mission/irm.html), *Journal of Asian Missions* (www.apts.edu/jam.htm), *Lausanne World Pulse* (www.lausanneworldpulse.com), *Missiology* (www.asmweb.org/missiology.htm), *Mission Frontiers* (www.missionfrontiers.org), *Mission Studies* (www.missionstudies.org), *Svensk Missiological Themes* (www.teol.uu.se/homepage/SIM/SMT_en.htm), and *Transformation* (www.ocms.ac.uk/transformation/index.php) (for a more complete list go to www.mislinks.org/research/periodicals.html).

Missions archives are also important sources that are available on the Internet. The Billy Graham Center Archives (www.wheaton.edu/bgc/archives/archhp1.html) provides an extensive collection of materials from organizations such as the Billy Graham Evangelistic Association and the Lausanne Committee for World Evangelization, as well as papers and interviews of hundreds of missionaries. The Centre for the Study of Christianity in the Non-Western World (www.div.ed.ac.uk/worldchristi_16.html) provides several searchable databases of bibliographies, including a cumulative bibliography of *The International Review of Mission* (http://webdb.ucs.ed.ac.uk/divinity/cmb) and the African Christianity Bibliography (http://webdb.ucs.ed.ac.uk/divinity/africa/index.cfm). The Lausanne Committee for World Evangelization makes a large portion of their documents available online (www.lausanne.org/Brix?pageID=12890), including the Lausanne Occasional Papers and documents from Lausanne 1974, Pattaya 1980, Manila 1989 and the 2004 Forum. Mundus (www.mundus.ac.uk) provides access to over four hundred collections of archival materials from agencies and missionaries housed in the United Kingdom.

### Services and Resources

Missiological associations are also taking advantage of the Internet to offer services and resources to their constituents. The American Society of Missiology (www.asmweb.org), Aotearoa New Zealand Association for Mission Studies (www.missionstudies.org/anzams), Association of Professors of Mission (www.asmweb.org/apm), British and Irish Association for Mission Studies (BIAMS) (www.martynmission.cam.ac.uk/BIAMS.htm), Evangelical Missiological Society (www.emsweb.org), International Association for Missions Studies (www.missionstudies.org), Southern African Missiological Society (www.geocities.com/Athens/Parthenon/8409), and World Evangelical Alliance Missions Commission (www.worldevangelical.org/commissions/missions.htm) all provide home pages with resources ranging from papers and books to syllabi and organizational newsletters.

Finally, dedicated missions directory sites provide valuable links to a host of missions-related materials. For example, EveryPeople.net (www.everypeople.net/home.html) was created to "develop means to bridge the gap between Christian Web sites and Web sites designed for Christians who are already actively involved in missions." GlobalConnections (www.globalconnections.co.uk) focuses on resourcing and connecting missions from the UK. MisLinks (www.mislinks.org) provides over 2,000 links arranged in six major categories and numerous subcategories. The World Evangelical Alliance (www.globalmission.org) provides help, tools, databases, and books.

## Implications for the Future

The publicly accessible version of the Internet is still in its infancy. The fact that almost one-sixth of the human population already has access is astonishing. The rapid mutations and permutations over the past decade, both in what is offered and what people can do, make it impossible to project what the impact will be ten years from now, let alone fifty. Whatever that may be, it can be stated with certainty that finding appropriate and helpful ways to use the Internet will be an ongoing challenge for missionaries, missiologists, and mission-related organizations for the foreseeable future.

SCOTT MOREAU

**201**

*See also* Archives; Education; Journals; Libraries; Media and Mass Communications; Professional Associations; Reference Tools

## Further Reading

Baker, J. D. (1997). *Christian cyberspace companion: A guide to the Internet and Christian online resources.* Grand Rapids, MI: Baker Books.

Barrett, D. B., Kurian, G. T., & Johnson, T. M. (2001). *World Christian encyclopedia: A comparative survey of churches and religions of the world.* Oxford, UK: Oxford University Press.

Brasher, B. E. (2004). *Give me that online religion.* New Brunswick, NJ: Rutgers University Press.

Groothuis, D. (1997). *The soul in cyberspace.* Grand Rapids, MI: Baker Books.

Levine, J. R., Young, M. L., & Baroudi, C. (2005). *The Internet for dummies.* Indianapolis, IN: Wiley Publishing.

Moreau, A. S., & O'Rear, M. (2005). Missions resources on the web: improving missions websites. *Evangelical Missions Quarterly, 41*(3), 378–383.

Pocock, M., VanRheenen, G., & McConnell, D. (2005). *The changing face of world missions: Engaging contemporary issues and trends.* Grand Rapids, MI: Baker Books.

Postman, N. (1992). *Technopoly: The surrender of culture to technology.* New York: Alfred A. Knopf.

Schultze, Q. J. (2003). *Habits of the high-tech heart: Living virtuously in the Information Age.* Grand Rapids, MI: Baker Books.

# Islam

Islam arose in the early seventh century and largely supplanted Christianity in the Middle East and North Africa and is now the largest non-Christian religious community in the world. Although the Arab world has remained the heartland of the faith, a majority of Muslims now live in South, Southeast, and Central Asia.

## Origins

The prophet of Islam, Muhammad (570–632 CE), was born in Mecca, a commercial and religious town in western Arabia. Distressed by the polytheism and injustice around him, he felt called by God to recite God's message to humankind, and it was subsequently recorded in the Qu'ran. He saw himself as the last link in a chain of biblical prophets: He cleansed the Kaaba sanctuary in Mecca of its idols but left a picture of Jesus and Mary. He called all to worship the one God, "Allah," the name that Arab Christians used for God. When his enemies plotted to kill him, he fled with his followers to Medina, where he began to build a Muslim community. This date (632 CE) marks the start of the Muslim lunar calendar.

The pillars of worship came to include, first, the confession that "There is no god but God, and Muhammad is the apostle of God." Second was ritual prayer five times a day. Except for references to Muhammad, its content is characteristic of Jewish and Christian prayer. Originally worshippers faced Jerusalem, but the direction of prayer was changed toward Mecca when many of the Jews of Medina opposed him.

The third, almsgiving, is called *zakat*, an Aramaic word used by rabbis for charitable gifts. The fourth, fasting, is designated by another Judeo-Aramaic word, *sawm*, and follows a Jewish practice of fasting only during the day. Though originally observed with Jews before the Day of Atonement, it was changed to the pre-Islamic Arab sacred month of Ramadan.

The last pillar, a yearly pilgrimage to Mecca which all Muslims should observe at least once in their lifetime, incorporated elements of an annual pagan pilgrimage but reinterpreted them as worship of the one God, Allah. Some of the practices parallel Old Testament ones—for example, circumambulation of the sanctuary (Ps. 26:6), the wearing of special garments, and not cutting one's hair while in a consecrated state (Lev. 16:4, Num. 6:5).

## Varieties

Muslims developed a sense of community regulated by divine Law (*shariah*), which resembles much of rabbinic law and applies to all areas of life. The major division arose over the successor to Muhammad. The Sunnis (currently about 85 percent of all Muslims), following the Arab tribal practice in which elders chose the most capable or powerful among them as a leader, chose Abu Bakr as caliph (a political and military successor of Muhammad). The Shias (currently about 15 percent), following a pattern closer to that of the empires of West Asia in which divine kingship was passed from father to son, chose Ali, Muhammad's nearest male relative, as Imam (a political and military successor of Muhammad who could also speak ex cathedra). The Shias subsequently divided into Ithna Asharis (Imamis), Isma'ilis, and Zaidis because of disagreements over the choice of subsequent imams.

The Sunnis divided into four orthodox schools (or traditions) of Law—Hanifi, Maliki, Shafi'i, and Hanbali. The Shia developed their own schools. While Law guided the outer duties of Muslims, Sufi mysticism developed to guide inner piety. The latter was expressed through different orders, which often were named after those who inspired them. Some Sufis wrote beautiful poetry or developed philosophy. On the other hand, at the popular or folk level, animistic beliefs and practices were often mixed with formal Islam.

Various trends may be discerned in the Muslim community. One group, the adaptionists, advocate Islamic acculturation. This group includes modernists who advocate religious, social, and legal reforms. Another group, the conservatives, believe that the boundaries of legitimate religious interpretation were fixed in the ninth century after the four orthodox schools of Sunni Law were established.

A third group is made up of fundamentalist reformers who seek to find guidance in the modern world by returning to the fundamentals of the Qur'an and the practice (sunna) of Muhammad and his companions, unbound by subsequent legal decisions. Contemporary Islamists are drawn from the fundamentalist reformers and conservatives who share the conviction that Muslims should be governed by a divine system of laws rather than a human system such as democracy or socialism. Advocates of any of these perspectives can be militant or peaceful—their attitudes are influenced by their social and political contexts.

## Spread

Islam is a missionary religion because Muhammad came to understand that the faith he proclaimed was for all people (Qur'an 34:28). The witness should warn and dispute in the best way (16:125), but polytheists and hypocrites—such as Jews and Christians—should be fought (9:5; 38–52) until they submitted and paid tribute (9:29), after which they were to be protected.

Islam was spread by both peaceful and military means. Where political control was established militarily, conversion, if it took place, was usually more gradual; motives for the adoption of Islam ranged from genuine spiritual conversion to a temporary allegiance for expediency. After Muhammad's death, Arab Muslim armies conquered the Middle East and North Africa, a task facilitated by the exhaustion of the Byzantines and Persians from years of conflict and the fact that the Arabs were perceived as more tolerant of Christians considered heretical than the Byzantines had been. In North Africa the Christians had already been ravaged by the Vandals, and their Christianity was more a Roman import than an indigenous faith. Subsequently the churches declined.

From North Africa, Muslim armies advanced through Spain, where they developed a spectacular culture of art and education before they were conquered in the fifteenth century. Islam spread into sub-Saharan Africa largely through trade and Sufi preaching, though there were also military conquests.

When the central Arab lands declined they were invaded by non-Muslim Turks and Mongols from central Asia who were converted to the Muslim faith of their subjects. Meanwhile Islam spread into Eastern Europe, and from Central Asia, Muslim armies conquered Northern India, where an artistic Mogul culture developed; peaceful trade and preaching spread the faith into the South. Muslim traders entered ports of China in the East while Muslim tribes of Central Asia entered it from the west. By the twelfth and thirteenth centuries, merchants and Sufis had brought Islam to the Malay-Indonesian archipelago, and from there it spread to the southern Philippines and Thailand.

During the twentieth century large numbers of Muslims have migrated to Western Europe, England, and North America, where African-Americans have been particularly receptive to their message. On the international level, the Muslim World League was formed in Mecca in 1962 to address Muslim concerns, including missionary outreach, which were further delineated in 1974.

## Historic Muslim-Christian Encounter

From the seventh to the tenth century, the theological interaction of Muslims and Christians was frequently apologetic or polemic. In 639 CE, just seven years after Muhammad's death, John I, the Jacobite Patriarch of Antioch, was summoned to defend Christian doctrine before 'Amr ibn al-'As, the Muslim conqueror of Egypt. This set the subsequent pattern in which Christians dealt with the topics that Muslims chose. The most influential apologist during this period was John of Damascus (c. 676–749 CE), who described Islam as "the youngest Christian heresy" in the tract *A Dialogue between a Christian and a Saracen*. However, he used references to Jesus in the Qur'an and the Bible, such as "Word" and "Spirit," as bridges. Others, like Timotheos, the Nestorian Patriarch from 780 to 823 CE, and the Nestorian al-Kindi in 830 CE, added arguments for the superiority of Christ to Muhammad to their theological discussions.

The period of the Crusades and the immediately following centuries produced both polemic and ironic writings. Even Pope Urban II, who called for the First Crusade, recommended care and respect for Muslims with the hope that "they would be converted." In Spain in 1141 Peter the Venerable, Abbot of Cluny, and his associates started to develop literature to explain and refute Islam and to call Muslims to salvation. St Francis of Assisi accompanied the Fifth Crusade in 1219 and tried unsuccessfully to persuade the Sultan of Egypt to convert. William of Tripoli, in his work *On the Condition of the Saracens*, points out areas of commonness between the Muslim and Christian faiths. Likewise, Ricoldus de Monte Crucis (d. c. 1309) includes the traditional areas of polemic but also recognizes Muslim virtues in his *Confutatio Alcorani*. Most noteworthy was Raymon Lull (1232–1314), who wrote evangelistic literature, helped to establish centers of Arabic and Islam, and engaged in direct proclamation in northern Africa, which resulted in his death by stoning.

During the Reformation and European expansion from the sixteenth to the eighteenth centuries, the same forces of the Renaissance that led to the Reformation led also to an improved understanding of and respect for Islam. The reformers were preoccupied with Roman Catholicism and the development of the clergy in Europe, but the seeds of later missionary activity were formed in their teaching. In 1522 Martin Luther (1483–1546) said that the Pope should send evangelists rather than soldiers to the Turks. He also wrote the preface to a Latin translation of the Qur'an and the German edition of Ricoldus's *Confutatio Alcorani*.

The major impetus for Protestant missions arose with the discoveries, commercial ventures, and colonizations of the period. Employees of the Dutch East India Company were involved in evangelizing the people of Indonesia, where the Muslims had preceded them. A seminary in Leyden trained ministers for Indonesia between 1620 and 1633, and the New Testament was translated into Malay in 1688. The British East India Company was also established among Muslims but placed greater restrictions on its chaplains regarding mission activities. Volunteer mission agencies also entered into Muslim areas. These included the Anglican Society for the Promotion of Christian Knowledge (1699) and the Moravians, who entered the Near East in 1740. During this period more reliable information on Islam became available and Chairs of Arabic were established at Cambridge (1632) and Oxford (1636).

Roman Catholics had been even more actively involved in proselytism and missions. Granada, the last Muslim stronghold of Islam in western Europe, was defeated in 1492, after which thousands of Muslims were converted through preaching and education. In India, Akbar, who ruled the Muslim Mogul Empire from 1556 to 1605, invited the Portuguese Jesuits of Goa to his court to explain Christianity. Fr. Rudolph Aquaviva and his companions arrived at the court in 1580, but Akbar, although he was disturbed by the divisive effects of existing religions, was not ready to substitute Christianity for them, and developed his own eclectic monotheism, *Din illahi* ("the divine religion"). Pope Gregory XV founded the *Congregatio de propaganda fide* in 1622. Many of its missionaries exhibited a positive approach to Islam—for example, the French Jesuit Pere Nau in Syria encouraged Christians to "deal with Muslims with a humble air full of gentleness as the Gospel commands."

Various Eastern Orthodox churches had been in contact with Muslims since the earliest days of the rise

**Great Mosque at Djenne, Mali, the largest mud building in the world.** *Courtesy of Alan Tobey/istockphoto.com.*

of Islam. Although these Christians influenced their Muslim rulers, direct evangelism was restricted. The Russian Orthodox Church had experienced the invasion of the Tartars, who subsequently adopted Islam. Ivan IV, the Terrible, campaigned against the Tartar Khanate of Khazan and forced the inhabitants to be baptized or expelled. In 1700 Peter the Great called for the proclamation of the Christian faith. The mission on the upper Volga had many converts, especially when they received exemption from military service. Though the Muslim Tartars were more resistant than the pagans, 8,310 of them were baptized.

Modern missions of the nineteenth and twentieth centuries started with missions and colonialism coming together, even in places where the colonial powers opposed the missionaries. This period ended when the colonized countries became independent and, in some cases, initiated their own missionary activity.

Sizable Christian minorities remained in most of the Middle Eastern lands conquered by Islam, but centuries of restrictions had left them largely defensive. Both Roman Catholic and Protestant missions sought to reinvigorate these indigenous churches so that they in turn might evangelize Muslims. Roman Catholic missionaries tried to bring the ancient churches into communion with Rome, which resulted in Uniate communities of the traditional oriental rites. The Protestant attempts to revitalize the ancient churches sometimes resulted in "revived" members being excommunicated from their churches and evangelical ones being organized as a result. The missionary witness to Muslims was largely through the establishment of schools, hospitals, and other forms of service.

Between 1815 and 1850 the Mediterranean Mission of the Church of England sought to establish work among the ancient churches of Constantinople and Egypt but discontinued their attempt when it was unfruitful. The American Board of Commissioners (Congregational and originally Presbyterian and Dutch Reformed) served in Turkey from 1831, focusing on literature and education, with Roberts College in Istanbul being the best-known result. They started in Syria, including present-day Lebanon, in 1923, supervised the translation of the Bible into Arabic, organized churches, and formed the Syrian Protestant College (now the American University of Beirut). The French Jesuits organized St. Joseph University and the Catholic Press in Beirut. The American Board opened work in Persia in 1934 among the Nestorians with whom the Roman Catholic missionaries had worked since the seventeenth century.

The American Presbyterians took over the work of the American Board in Syria and Persia in 1870. The United Presbyterians began work in Egypt in 1854 but were more successful with the Coptic Orthodox than with the Muslims. The Anglican Church Missionary Society started in Palestine with educational and medical work in 1851, in Constantinople in 1858, and in Egypt in 1861. The debating style that Karl Pfander brought from India to his work in the Middle East led to great opposition, unlike the increasingly irenic approach that Temple Gairdner later brought to Egypt. In Yemen the Free Church of Scotland commenced medical work in 1885. The Arabian Mission was started in 1889 by Samuel Zwemer and others from the Reformed Church of America, which subsequently adopted the mission. They established schools, hospitals, and clinics along the Persian Gulf. Recently mission work has been established in the Middle East by other denominational groups and a number of interdenominational organizations. These in turn have been supplemented by Christian "tentmakers," missionaries who witness through their occupations.

Unlike the Middle East, where there were large remnants of ancient churches, in North Africa most churches had disappeared. French, Spanish, and Italian colonial expansion reintroduced Roman Catholic Christianity in the nineteenth century. In Algeria the White Fathers (starting in 1873) and the White Sisters worked with Muslims. The British and Foreign Bible Society, the North Africa Mission (1888, now Arab World Ministries), and the Algiers Mission Band (1888) were among the first missions, and were later joined by many others. Especially in the 1990s and thereafter, significant numbers of Kabyle Berbers in Algeria and Morocco have become Christians. Conversions to the Christian faith in other groups and regions have been more modest, though a number of North African Muslims in France and Spain have converted.

In sub-Saharan Africa both Islam and Christianity are growing rapidly at the expense of African traditional religions; the growth of Christianity was especially large in the postcolonial period. While Muslims currently predominate in the North and Christians and traditional religionists in the South, the belt of countries just south of the Sahara is more equally divided between Muslims and Christians, and some of these countries, like Sudan and Nigeria, experienced religious conflicts that became entangled with ethnic, economic, and political tensions. Christian relief and development agencies have been active in ministries in these areas of conflict and drought.

By the middle of the sixth century Nestorian Christianity had spread through Central Asia to China but it was decimated by the Mongol invasions and the coming

**205**

of Islam. By the end of the nineteenth century only an abandoned Armenian church remained in Kabul, Afghanistan. When expatriate Christians started to work in Afghanistan in 1947, they began meeting for worship in homes. In 1966 the International Afghan Mission (now the International Assistance Mission) was formed as an umbrella organization for Christian development programs, though proselytism was forbidden. Following the Soviet invasion of 1979 and the subsequent fighting among mujahideen groups and the Taliban, many Afghans fled to neighboring countries where some of them, who have now returned to Afghanistan, became Christians.

In the Central Asian republics, which were included in the Soviet Union, little missionary work took place after Tartars in the Middle Volga region were bribed to convert in the mid-eighteenth century. The Basel Mission did work in Transcaucasia from 1822 to 1835, but during the Soviet period the Russian and German Christians attempted little outreach to the Muslims. Since the breakup of the Soviet Union, some Muslims from the Central Asian republics have become Christians and either formed their own churches or joined with Russian Christians.

The Jesuits who had been invited to the court of Akbar in 1580 served there until the middle of the eighteenth century. However, the Anglican Henry Martyn (1781–1812) was the first modern missionary to the Muslims of the Indo-Pakistan subcontinent which, with Pakistan, Bangladesh, and India, has the largest concentration of Muslims in the world. Because the majority of Christians in these countries are the result of conversions from Hindu scheduled castes, they have made little outreach to the Muslims. Yet in all these countries some Muslims are following Christ, especially in Bangladesh, where many are meeting in homes for worship and Bible study while retaining, to the extent possible, Muslim social and legal identity.

In Southeast Asia the greatest concentrations of Muslims are in the Philippines, Malaysia, and Indonesia, though there are also smaller clusters in Thailand and Burma. In the Philippines most are in the southern island of Mindenao, where they feel suppressed by the Roman Catholic majority in the country. In Malaysia, Muslims are only slightly more than half the population but the Malay Muslims are favored politically over Chinese Christians and others who have more economic power. Indonesia, the largest Muslim nation in the world, has made belief in God (rather than the practice of Islam) one of its five unifying principles. This has allowed greater freedom for the Christian church, with the result that after the failure of an attempted Communist coup in the 1960s, over 2,000,000 Muslims became Christians, and more are currently becoming Christians through the national church.

J. Dudley Woodberry

*See also* Africa; Asia, Central; Asia, Southeast; China; Christendom; Conquest; Coptic Church; Crusades; Middle East; Nestorians; Orientalism; Orthodox/Coptic Missions; Protestant Churches; Reformation; Roman Catholic Church

## Further Reading

Arnold, T. W. (1961). *The preaching of Islam.* Lahore, Pakistan: Ashraf.

Barrett, D. B. (Ed.). (1982). *World Christian encyclopedia.* Nairobi, Kenya: Oxford University Press.

Johnstone, P. (Ed.). (2001). *Operation world* (6th ed). Waynesboro, GA: Paternoster Lifestyle.

Kateregga, B. D., & Shenk, D. (1997). *Islam and Christianity.* Scottdale, PA: Herald Press. (Original work published 1981)

Lapidus, I. M. (2002). *A history of Islamic societies* (2nd ed). Cambridge, UK: Cambridge University Press.

Latourette, K. S. (1937–1945). *A history of the expansion of Christianity* (Vols 1–7). New York: Harper & Bros.

Musk, B. (1989). *The unseen face of Islam.* Oxford, UK: Monarch Books.

Shimmel, A.(1977). *Mystical dimensions of Islam.* Chapel Hill: University of North Carolina Press.

VanderWerff, L. (1977). *Christian mission to Muslims.* Pasadena, CA: William Carey Library.

Voll, J. O. (1994). *Islam: Continuity and change in the modern world.* Syracuse, NY: Syracuse University Press.

Weekes, R. V. (1984). *Muslim peoples: A world ethnographic survey* (2nd ed.). Westport, CT: Greenwood Press.

# Jehovah's Witnesses

Considered an insignificant American sect with around 500,000 followers in 1955, the Jehovah's Witnesses, or The Watchtower Bible and Tract Society of New York Inc. to give them their official name, have experienced exponential growth for the past fifty years, making them a minor world religion with around 6,613,829 core members, 98,269 congregations, and 16,383,333 followers in 2005. Of these only 1,035,802 are in the United States and 127,206 in the United Kingdom; the rest are scattered across the globe.

As late as the 1970s sociologists like James Beckford were able to characterize the Jehovah's Witnesses as a working-class phenomenon that they interpreted in terms of deprivation theory. Today, as Jim Penton points out from the rich United States to poor countries like Zambia, where there are only 127,151 members, they are clearly a predominantly upwardly mobile middle-class group interested in education and trade.

## Origins and Spinoffs

The movement originated in 1870 with Charles Taze Russell (1852–1916), who organized an independent Bible-study group opposed to such things as the doctrine of hell and Calvinist predestination. Russell soon became the group's pastor, and his organization became the Zion's Watch Tower Tract Society in 1884. In 1909 he moved its headquarters to Brooklyn, New York, where it has remained, taking its present name in 1956. He began publication of *Zion's Watchtower* in 1876. Eventually it became today's *Watchtower*. The original theology of the movement was articulated by Russell in his seven-volume *Studies in the Scriptures* (1886–1917). The appearance of the final volume, a year after Russell's death, led to a schism in the organization.

Most of Russell's core followers joined J. F. Rutherford (1869–1942) to form the Millennial Dawnists, who changed their name to Jehovah's Witnesses in 1931. Following Rutherford's death, the movement was led by Nathan H. Knorr (1905–1977), who was succeeded by Frederick W. Franz (1893–1992). Milton Henschel (1920–2003) became president in 1992, and when he retired in 2000, he was replaced by Donald A. Adams (1925– ).

A smaller group that rejected Rutherford's leadership also developed to become the Dawn Bible Student's Association. Today their membership is unknown, although people associated with Russell's original teachings maintain an increasingly visible presence on the Internet.

## Theological Development

As the group's theology developed, the Witnesses increasingly denied traditional Christian teachings about the person and work of Christ, arguing that Jesus was "a god" who died on a "torture stake" as a ransom to the devil. Thus a pseudo-Arian Christology emerged that emphasized Jesus as the "Second Adam" or perfect man. The idea that baptism and the Lord's Supper are sacraments was rejected and baptism by total immersion advocated as a "witness" to God.

### Three Key Doctrines

Three other key doctrines developed to form an essential part of the movement's beliefs. First, eschatology, or the imminent return of Christ, is largely borrowed from the Plymouth Brethren but differs from the Brethren's beliefs by the repeated attempts of the Witnesses to predict the exact date of Christ's return. At first this was said to be 1914. Since then several other dates have come and gone without apparently affecting the faith of the movement's core membership in the movement's ability to correctly interpret both Scripture and current events.

A second and far more controversial belief is the group's refusal to imbibe blood in any form, which has led to a rejection of both military service and blood transfusions. Third, the preaching work, whereby Witnesses are expected to proclaim their Gospel, was incorporated into their beliefs about the means of salvation. This means evangelistic activities become a means of obtaining salvation through works.

In addition to baptism as a sign of membership of the organization, Witnesses also accept what the organization calls "baptism into Christ," which consecrates the 144,000 (cf. Revelation 7 and 14) elect Believers who will attain heavenly glory. The Lord's Supper then becomes an annual feast that can only be fully participated in by those Witnesses who "know" that they are among the 144,000 "consecrated believers." These elect members represent the totality of Christians that will go to be with Christ in heaven following His return and the end of this world. Other Witnesses have to content themselves with eternal life on earth.

## Role of Tradition and Leadership

Resembling traditional Roman Catholics rather than Protestants, because of their emphasis on tradition and the power of leadership, the Jehovah's Witnesses hold an ever-evolving theological position that has changed significantly over the years. From at least 1895 onward "Pastor Russell," as he is known, functioned more as a prophet than a pastor. His prophetic office was given official recognition as a result of challenges to his authority by dissident members in 1895. At that time his wife, Maria Russell, answered her husband's critics by arguing that he was the "faithful and wise servant" of Matthew 24:45. This notion was later applied to Russell's successors and the collective leadership of the Witnesses, who give the group a doctrinal stance almost identical to the magisterium of the popes.

Thus tradition, ascribed first to Russell and then his successors, became the medium through which Scripture was to be interpreted, indicating the development of a form of apostolic succession. Similarly, the spiritual obedience demanded by the leadership of the Wit-

nesses is like the Roman Catholic understanding of the pope's ability to speak ex cathedra. Complicating the matter is the fact that the authority of the leadership is bound together by an understanding of progressive revelation, whereby the leadership receives both direct revelation from God and an authoritative understanding of Scripture through their function as the "faithful and discreet slave," which is a prophetic class within the organization.

### Key to the Theology

This understanding of doctrinal and ecclesiastical authority is the key to the Witnesses' theology because it allows the leadership to develop responses to changing situations, thus enabling them to reinterpret apparent failures in their statements about the future and the timing of the end of the world. The confusion of outsiders is increased because of their lack of a clearly defined systematic theology and tendency to publish major statements of faith in their magazines. The best-organized book on their theology produced by the movement is *Let God Be True.*

## Emerging World Religion

Although they originated as a Christian sect, today's Jehovah's Witnesses are clearly an emerging world religion comparable to the Baha'i, the Mormons, or the Sikhs. This development is a tribute to the skill of their leadership in promoting their beliefs and the dedication of their members, who tirelessly proclaim what they believe to be God's truth.

IRVING HEXHAM

### Further Reading

Beckford, J. (1975). *The trumpet of prophecy: a sociological study of Jehovah's Witnesses.* Hoboken, NJ: John Wiley & Sons.

Botting, H. & G. (1984). *The Orwellian world of Jehovah's Witnesses.* Toronto, Canada: University of Toronto Press.

*Let God Be True.* (1944). Brooklyn, NY: Watch Tower Bible and Tract Society.

Penton, M. J. (1985). *Apocalypse delayed: the story of Jehovah's Witnesses.* Toronto, Canada: University of Toronto Press.

Rogerson, A. (1969). *Millions now living will never die: a study of Jehovah's Witnesses.* London: Constable.

Russle, C. T. (1886–1917). *Studies in the Scriptures.* Brooklyn, NY: International Bible Students Association.

*2005 report of Jehovah's Witnesses worldwide.* Retrieved July 4, 2006, from http://www.watchtower.org/statistics/worldwide_report.htm

# Journals

From its beginnings in the late eighteenth century, the modern missionary movement made great use of periodical publications to inform supporters and to mobilize financial support, prayer, and recruits. Missionary societies and presses were quick to adopt new technology and business techniques, both at home and on the mission field, where printing presses were often established. As the nineteenth century wore on, the number of titles and specialisms by field, audience, denomination, and mission type increased. This trend continued in the twentieth century despite wartime disruptions and financial constraints. Periodicals devoted to the scholarly discussion of mission were also established.

## Beginnings

William Carey's *Enquiry into the Obligations of Christians to Use Means for the Conversion of the Heavens* (1792) and the beginning of the missionary movement coincided with a boom in periodical publishing of all kinds including the religious and church press. This can be linked to cheaper production methods and a better-educated reading public. This was especially the case in the British Isles where journals of religious opinion flourished, with an estimated 3,000 titles published between 1760 and 1900. At first, missionary intelligence was included in or was a supplement to general religious and denominational magazines, but missionary societies were soon publishing their own periodicals.

The *Evangelical Magazine*, published from 1793 to 1904, is particularly noteworthy. It was launched monthly at a price of sixpence and in its early years claimed a circulation of 18,000 to 20,000. The London Missionary Society published extracts from letters and journals of missionaries in the *Evangelical Magazine* until 1813, when these extracts were brought together and given their own title page as the *Missionary Chronicle* (the magazine then became the *Evangelical Magazine and Missionary Chronicle*). This arrangement continued after 1836, although in that year the *Missionary Magazine and Chronicle* began to be separately circulated.

The Moravians were pioneers of the missionary movement and the first to publish their own periodical with *Periodical Accounts relating to Foreign Missions of the Church of the United Brethren* published in London from 1790. Six *Periodical Accounts relative to the Baptist Missionary Society* were published between 1800 and 1817, preceding a substantial series of Annual Reports from 1819. The *General Baptist Repository* (1802–1822) published a regular column of missionary intelligence before transmuting to the *General Baptist Repository and Missionary Observer* (1822–1853).

The Church Missionary Society published annual proceedings from 1805. It published, for the benefit of its humbler and poorer supporters, quarterly *Missionary Papers for the Use of Weekly and Monthly Contributors* from 1815 and claimed that over half a million copies circulated in 1822. The *Church Missionary Record* (1830–1890), *Church Missionary Gleaner* (1841–1870, 1874–1921), and *Church Missionary Intelligencer* (1849–1906) later joined the CMS stable. All ran for well over half a century.

The Methodist Conference published *Wesleyan Missionary Notes* monthly from 1816, at a price of one penny, free to supporters subscribing a minimum of one shilling per week. Welsh-speaking Methodists were publishing even before this. *Yr Eurgrawn Weleyaidd* ran from 1809–1960. The *Missionary Herald at Home and Abroad*, which became the organ of the American Board of Commissioners for Foreign Missions, was launched in Boston in 1805. It ran continuously until 1951.

Early periodicals from continental Europe included: *Evangelisches Mission-Magazin*, Basel Evangelical Missionary Society (1816–[now merged in *Zeitschrift für Mission*]) and *Journal des missions évangéliques*, Société des Missions Evangéliques chez les Peuples non-Chrétiens á Paris (1826–1940).

These journals borrowed material and reprinted material from each other, and a sense of common purpose was more evident than denominational rivalry. By the 1850s most of the major missionary societies had monthly magazines. Although there were denominational differences, similar patterns were established. Each society had basic magazines with titles such as *Missionary Record*. Contents typically included accounts of indigenous cultures from a Christian viewpoint, lists of subscribers, news of home-based fund-raising efforts, sermons, cycles of prayer, statistics and accounts, missionary biographies, and obituaries.

## Missionary Periodicals for Children

By the mid-nineteenth century missionary societies were also investing heavily in children's literature and organizing networks of juvenile collectors. The

*Baptist Children's Magazine and Sabbath Scholars' Reward*, launched in 1827, gave a leading place to missionary articles and biographies. The Coral Missionary Fund published a monthly *Children's Missionary Magazine*, priced at one penny from 1838. John Snow of Paternoster Row (publisher to the London Missionary Society) produced *The Missionary Repository for Youth* in 1839 and eight issues of *Children's Bible and Missionary Box: An Illustrated Magazine for Little Collectors and Contributors* in 1854, offering 100 copies for 2 shillings/6 pence. Anglicans, Wesleyans, the Church of Scotland and the Free Church of Scotland, and the London Society for

Promoting Christianity amongst the Jews all followed. Deathbed scenes and spiritual horror tales predominated, as did urgent calls to conversion.

By the beginning of the twentieth century, the tone had softened, although there was still a heavy emphasis on collecting schemes and missionary boxes. More fiction was introduced. Competitions became popular—quizzes and puzzles as well as tests of scriptural and missionary knowledge. Many of the periodicals for adults included a "Children's Corner" or model Sunday School lessons.

## Developments and Diversification

By mid-century certain commercial publishers and printers like Nisbet in London and Funk & Wagnalls of New York had come to occupy an important position in the religious publishing field. Missionary publishers continued to be quick to exploit new technology and techniques. *China's Millions*, published from 1875 by the China Inland Mission, with J. Hudson Taylor himself as first editor, was groundbreaking. Hudson Taylor laid great stress on the importance of visual material, and from the outset the journal was characterized by numerous and high-quality illustrations and maps, in the manner of secular magazines such as the *Illustrated London News* and *The Graphic*. Many missionaries and missionary magazines were quick to take up the camera and the dissemination of photographic images.

### Increase in Diversity

The diversity of missionary periodicals increased as the century wore on. Interdenominational and Faith Missions published their own magazines. Roman Catholic missions turned to periodicals rather later than Protestants. *Illustrated Catholic Missions: A monthly illustrated record in connection with the Society for the Propagation of the Faith* appeared monthly from 1886 and was followed by periodicals from the Catholic missionary orders: the African Mission Society, the Holy Ghost Fathers, the Franciscans, the White Fathers, and the St. Joseph's Society for Foreign Missions (Mill Hill Fathers).

Growing interest in Zenana missions and "women's work for women" gave rise to such periodicals as the Wesleyan *Ladies' Papers: Occasional Papers of the Ladies' Committee for Ameliorating the Condition of Women in Heathen Countries* (1859–1903, later entitled *Woman's Work on the Mission Field*, 1904–1932), *Our Sisters in Other Lands* (1879–1937), *India's Women* (1881–1895, later entitled *India's Women and China's Daughters*, 1896–1939, and then *Looking East*, 1940–1957). *Medical Missions at Home and*

AN

ENQUIRY

INTO THE

OBLIGATIONS OF CHRISTIANS,

TO USE MEANS FOR THE

CONVERSION

OF THE

HEATHENS.

IN WHICH THE

RELIGIOUS STATE OF THE DIFFERENT NATIONS OF THE WORLD, THE SUCCESS OF FORMER UNDERTAKINGS, AND THE PRACTICABILITY OF FURTHER UNDERTAKINGS, ARE CONSIDERED,

BY WILLIAM CAREY.

For there is no Difference between the Jew and the Greek: for the same Lord over all, is rich unto all that call upon him. For whosoever shall call upon the name of the Lord shall be saved. How then shall they call on him, in whom they have not believed? and how shall they believe in him of whom they have not heard? and how shall they hear without a Preacher? and how shall they preach, except they be sent?

PAUL.

LEICESTER:

Printed and sold by ANN IRELAND, and the other Booksellers in *Leicester*; J. JOHNSON, St. Paul's Church yard; T. KNOTT, Lombard Street; R. DILLY, in the Poultry; *London*; and SMITH, at Sheffield.
[Price One Shilling and Six-pence.]

MDCCXCII.

The title page to William Carey's journals on conversion and missions.

*Abroad* (1878–1924) was the precursor of a number of titles devoted to medical missions. At least six titles (including juvenile magazines) were devoted exclusively to missions to the Jews.

Periodicals might be targeted at certain social classes or educational levels. Prices ranged from a halfpenny with bulk discounts for distribution to Sunday School children and the poor to expensive "parlour editions" and annuals costing several guineas.

## Publishing and Periodicals on the Mission Field

Outside Europe and Northern America, missionaries played a significant role in establishing printing presses and developing publishing and periodicals in both metropolitan and vernacular languages, a role still insufficiently researched and appreciated. William Carey and his colleagues at Serampore founded a printing press in 1799 and produced periodicals, including the *Samachar Darpan* or *Mirror of Intelligence* and the *Calcutta Christian Observer* (1832–1841), which not only reported missionary news and views but played an important role in publishing Indian literary works in translation.

American missionaries in Hawaii produced a weekly quarto of four pages, *Lama Hawaii*. In Australia the first magazine published was edited by Methodist missionaries. Missionaries and church groupings were largely responsible for the beginnings of the periodical press in New Zealand with, for example, the *Maori Messenger* in 1840 and the *New Zealand Evangelist* in 1848. Rev. John Ross of the Glasgow Missionary Society established a printing press at Lovedale in South Africa in 1823 that trained Africans in printing and bookbinding, provided a vehicle for black South Africans to publish their work, and pioneered the printing of vernacular literature.

## Twentieth Century and Today

Today missionary periodicals still flourish, as mission agencies continue to place a high priority on communication—but in a world where new media, first broadcasting and then the Internet, have played an increasing role. The *World Christian Encyclopedia* gives a global statistic of 24,000 Christian periodicals.

Scholarly periodicals devoted to the theory and practice of mission should also be noted. Foremost is *International Review of Mission* (*Missions* until 1969), published since 1912 first by the World Missionary Conference Continuation Committee, then the International Missionary Council, and later by the Division of World Mission and Evangelism of the World Council of Churches, and noted for its scholarship, ecumenical scope, and valuable bibliographies. As missiology was established as a separate discipline, and as secular historians and social scientists took a new interest in missions, a number of journals were established providing analysis and critiques and, often, the dissemination of reflections and scholarship from the two-thirds world. Particularly noteworthy are *Exchange: Journal of Missiology and Ecumenical Research*, *International Bulletin of Missionary Research*, *Le Fait Missionaire*, *Missiology* (American Society of Missiology), *Missionalia* (Southern African Missiological Society) and *Neue Seitschrift für Missionswissenschaft*.

## Future Research

Much remains to be learned about missionary periodicals. Nineteenth-century publications have received more attention than those of the twentieth, and British periodicals have been studied more than those from North America and continental Europe. More work is needed to analyze readership, document the role and careers of influential editors, uncover often anonymous authors and their working methods, and discuss the economics of publishing and the histories of printing and publishing firms. Meanwhile, missionary periodicals provide a wealth of material for the study of the theology and practice of Christian missions; of how support for mission was mobilized, molded and manipulated; of how the non-Western and non-Christian world was presented to and perceived in Europe and North America; and of how ideas and images changed over time. They provide fascinating case studies in the history of gender, childhood, and popular piety.

TERRY BARRINGER

### Further Reading

Barrett, D. B. (2001). *World Christian encyclopedia*. New York: Oxford University Press.

Barringer, T. (2004). From beyond alpine snows to homes of the East—a journey through missionary periodicals: The missionary periodicals database project. *International Bulletin of Missionary Research, 26*(4), 169–173.

Barringer, T. (2004). What Mrs. Jellyby might have read. Missionary periodicals: A neglected source. *Victorian Periodicals Review, 37*(4), 46–74.

Billington, L. (1986). The religious periodical and newspaper press, 1770–1870. In M. Harris & A. Lee (Eds.), *The press in English society from the seventeenth to nineteenth centuries.* Rutherford, NJ: Fairleigh Dickinson University Press.

Johnston, A. (2003). *Missionary writing and empire, 1800–1860.* Cambridge, UK: Cambridge University Press.

Johnston, A. (2005). British missionary publishing, missionary celebrity and empire. *Nineteenth Century Prose, 13*(2), 20–47.

Missionary Periodicals Database. (n.d.) Retrieved June 10, 2006, from http://research.yale.edu:8084/missionperiodicals/index.jsp

Padwick, C. E. (1917). Children and missionary societies in Great Britain. *International Review of Missions, 6,* 561–575.

Rowbotham, J. (1998). "Hear an Indian sister's plea": Reporting the work of the nineteenth century British female missionaries. *Women's Studies International Forum, 21*(3), 247–261.

Sivasundaram, S. (2005). *Nature and the godly empire: Science and evangelical mission in the Pacific, 1795–1850.* Cambridge, UK: Cambridge University Press.

Vann, J. D., & VanArsdel, R. (1996). *Periodicals of Queen Victoria's empire.* Toronto, Canada: University of Toronto Press.

## Latin America

From the late fifteenth century to the present, Latin America has been the recipient of continuous missionary activity. Sometimes myopic and sometimes farsighted, this activity has played a major role in shaping the culture of the southern half of the Western Hemisphere.

## Catholic Missionaries in the Colonial Period

In 1493 Christopher Columbus made his second voyage to America. Included with his colonists were members of religious orders, but only three of these attempted to evangelize the native population. They were lay brothers Ramón Pané, a Jeronymite who in 1498 wrote a short account of his mission work, and Juan Deledeule and Juan Tisin, both Franciscans about whose labors we know nothing. These were the first Christian missionaries in the Americas.

Due to an arrangement with the papacy known as the *patronato real,* the Spanish and Portuguese Crowns were granted full authority to "maintain the Church and propagate the faith" in the Americas. The Spanish monarchs, far more so than the Portuguese, took this responsibility seriously, assigning Franciscans to the "New World" in 1502, Dominicans in 1509, Mercedarians in 1514, Augustinians in 1533, Jesuits in 1565, and Capuchins in 1657. Secular clergy were also sent to America, but missionary work was the exclusive domain of religious orders.

## Encomienda *System*

Military power was employed in the initial attempts to evangelize the indigenous population, and by the early sixteenth century large numbers of subjugated Indians were forced to participate in the *encomienda* system. This was an arrangement in which certain Spanish colonials (*encomenderos*) were granted jurisdiction over native peoples, who were forced to manufacture wealth for them through manual labor. In return, *encomenderos* were expected to feed and protect their charges while also instructing them in the Catholic faith. From the beginning the *encomienda* system was abused; Indians were overworked, often to the point of death, and little was done to provide religious instruction.

The first to challenge this harsh system was the Dominican Antonio de Montesinos, who in 1511 delivered a blistering homily in which he accused the *encomenderos* of Hispaniola of murder because of their mistreatment of Indians. He announced that the Dominicans on the island would henceforth deny the colonists absolution for their sins.

Montesinos's sermon had enormous consequences for Spanish America. It helped win Bartolomé de Las Casas to the Indian cause, and this priest, after renouncing his participation in the *encomienda* system, dedicated his life to the pursuit of justice for native peoples. He was the first to propose peaceful evangelization and was eventually able to convince Spanish authorities to allow him to put his plan into effect in northern Guatemala. His project was successful and later served as a model for Franciscan and Jesuit *reducciones* (Christian Indian communes).

In 1516, Las Casas was appointed "priest protector of the Indies." Using his new authority, he had a remarkable group of missionaries appointed to America who courageously defended the natives against Spanish oppression. Many suffered imprisonment, expulsion from their dioceses, and deportation for their efforts. One, Antonio de Valdivieso, was murdered by colonial authorities in Nicaragua in 1550.

### Importance of Working within Indian Culture

Although this first generation of missionaries vigorously fought to curtail European mistreatment of the native population, they were less successful in their attempts to directly evangelize the indigenous masses because they did not realize the importance of understanding Indian culture and mastering indigenous languages. Only with the second generation of missionaries did some come to recognize the limitations of a Eurocentric mission methodology. One of the first to do so was Bernardino de Sahagú, a Franciscan who spent years learning the Aztec language and culture in order to better deliver the Gospel message to the Indians of Mexico. The culmination of his work was his *Historia General,* a brilliant study in ethnohistory and a major advance in understanding the Indian mindset. The Jesuit missionary to Peru, José de Acosta, following the lead of Sahagú, produced in 1590 his *Historia Natural y Moral de las Indias,* a masterpiece in explaining Indian religion, government, and culture.

Another notable missionary was Toribio de Mogrovejo. Named archbishop of Lima in 1580, the future saint immediately began studying the local Indian language. Instead of administering his diocese from the capital, he spent most of his twenty-five years as archbishop traveling from village to village directly evangelizing the native population. Like Las Casas, he was in constant conflict with oppressive civil and religious authorities. Other sixteenth-century missionaries produced indigenous grammars and dictionaries, as well as written sermons and catechisms in the Indian tongue.

Although the Portuguese Crown was less vigilant than its Spanish counterpart in its evangelization efforts, one of its missionaries merits special mention. In the seventeenth century, the Jesuit Antonio Vieira spent much of his life fighting against the European exploitation of both Indians and Africans in Brazil.

### Decline of Catholic Missionary Efforts

The eighteenth and nineteenth centuries proved disastrous for American Catholic missionary efforts. The Jesuits were expelled from Brazil in 1759 and from the Spanish colonies in 1767. By then the most able missionaries in the Americas, the Jesuits had set up about fifty *reducciones* in what is today Brazil, Paraguay, and Argentina. Although based on a paternalistic methodology, these missions sheltered about 100,000 Indians and protected them from European exploitation. After the expulsion of the Jesuits, land-hungry colonists successfully conspired to acquire the mission lands and consequently the *reducciones* slowly declined and disappeared.

## Post-independence Period

Following independence in the early nineteenth century, the Latin American Catholic Church became isolated from its European counterpart. It lost most of its foreign clergy, thereby creating a severe shortage of priests that has hindered its effectiveness down to the present day. In many mission areas secular clergy replaced religious-order priests, but since they were inferior in education and moral rectitude, the church's missionary efforts suffered greatly.

With the rise of the anticlerical Liberals in the second half of the nineteenth century, the church was further decimated. In many countries religious orders were suppressed and foreign clergy deported. Consequently, only about a third of the population was able to participate on a regular basis in the sacramental life of the church. Rural areas were hit especially hard. Without priests, the indigenous population developed a folk Catholicism that blended veneration of the saints with elements of pre-Christian legend and shamanism. There was little understanding of Catholic doctrine and liturgical rites.

By the end of the nineteenth century, however, Rome began to take measures to remedy the situation. Franciscan, Jesuit, Capuchin, Redemptorist, Salesian, Pallottine, Spiritan, Divine Word, and other missionaries were sent from the various countries of Catholic Europe, as were sisters from several religious congregations. Many Indian missions that had shut down were reopened, and new ones were established. Improvement was made, but it was too little too late.

## Catholic Focus on Latin America

With the advent of World War II, the missionary situation in Latin America changed dramatically. The war made it too dangerous for European missionaries to cross the Atlantic. Since it was likewise unsafe for American missionaries to travel to Asia, U.S. Catholic mission congregations shifted their overseas efforts southward. The Catholic Foreign Missionary Society of America (Maryknoll), for instance, first shifted missionaries to Latin America in 1942 and by 1990 had 282 of its members serving in ten Latin countries. By 1950

# Letters from Missionaries

**The extracts below are from letters written by missionaries in Latin America shortly before they were killed in the early 1980s.**

Brother James Miller, a missionary in Guatemala who was murdered by a death squad on 13 February 1982 wrote: "I am personally weary of violence, but I continue to feel a strong commitment to the suffering poor of Central America. "God's ways are not man's ways," says the Bible. God knows why He continued to call me to Guatemala when some friends and relatives encouraged me to pull out for my own comfort and safety, but I have been a Christian Brother for nearly 20 years now, and my commitment to my vocation grows steadily stronger in the context of my work in Central America. I pray to God for the grace and strength to serve Him faithfully by my presence among the poor and oppressed of Guatemala. I place my life in His Providence; I place my trust in Him."

Two weeks before lay missionary Jean Donovan was raped and murdered on December 2, 1980 by Salvadoran soldiers, she wrote: "...and so the Peace Corps left [El Salvador] today, and my heart sank low. The danger is extreme and they are right to leave, but it seems that the more help is needed, the less help is available. Now I must assess my own position, because I am not up for suicide. Several times I have decided to leave—I almost could except for the children, the poor bruised victims of adult lunacy. Who would care for them? Those heart would be so staunch as to favor the reasonable thing in a sea of their tears and loneliness? Not mine, dear friend, not mine."

Source: Brett, D. W., &. Brett, E. T. (1988) *Murdered in Central America: The stories of eleven U.S. missionaries (pp. 158, 252). Maryknoll, NY: Orbis Books.*

Latin America had become the major focus of most U.S. Catholic congregations involved in mission work. Nevertheless, even when coupled with the return of European missionaries following the war, it was not enough, especially since the population of Latin America had grown by 50 million in the 1950s.

## The Mission Call of Pope John XXIII

On 17 August 1961 Pope John XXIII sent Monsignor Agostino Casaroli to the University of Notre Dame to address a meeting of major superiors of U.S. women's and men's religious congregations. The Vatican was concerned with the growth of Protestantism and Marxism in Latin America and felt that more clergy were needed in the region for the church to effectively meet the challenge. Thus, speaking for the pope, Casaroli asked the North American church to send 10 percent of its clergy and religious sisters and brothers as missionaries to Latin America.

Although the 10 percent goal was never reached, several thousand U.S. priests, religious, and lay Catholics responded to the call over the next thirty-five years.

Most were sent to areas where the priest shortage was most acute. Some U.S. religious congregations actually took control of whole departments in countries like Bolivia, Guatemala, and Honduras. Amply supplied with large sums of money from the home front, American priests created new parishes that often included schools and clinics run by U.S. religious sisters and brothers. The missionaries also created development projects aimed at alleviating the poverty of the masses. Lay mission organizations were formed and language schools were set up for mission volunteers in Mexico, Peru, and Brazil.

## Theology of Liberation

These new U.S. mission efforts coincided with major developments in the global and Latin American Catholic Church, most notably the Second Vatican Council (1963–1965) and the Latin American Bishops Conferences at Medellín, Colombia (1968), and Puebla, Mexico (1979), where the church incorporated a radical new theology of liberation and declared its "preferential option for the poor." Social justice issues now received more attention than in the pre-Vatican II period, and many missionaries began to employ consciousness-raising techniques, especially through Bible discussion groups called Christian base communities (*comunidades de base*).

But all did not go smoothly. The new emphasis on social concerns produced a split in the Latin American Catholic Church between traditionalists, who thought that the church had become too radical, and progressives, who disagreed. Most missionaries identified with the progressives, and over time several were killed because their work with the poor was considered by some to be subversive. Due to Pope John Paul II's suspicion of liberation theology, coupled with the spread of democracy in most Latin countries in the 1980s and 1990s, missionaries began to place less emphasis on political matters. Nevertheless, social justice remained a major concern of their apostolate.

## Early Protestant Efforts

For much of its history, Latin America was an almost exclusively Catholic region, albeit with large numbers of its population only nominally Catholic. After independence in the 1820s, most Latin American nations kept Catholicism as the official state religion, and at least until the 1860s almost all Protestants in Latin America were foreigners.

During the first half of the nineteenth century, however, an enthusiasm developed in Britain and the United States for Protestant foreign missionary endeavors. Consequently, the British and Foreign Bible Society was established and soon sent colporteurs to Latin America, who were somewhat similar to circuit riders in North America. They traveled by foot or horseback from town to town, selling Bibles and preaching wherever possible. James Thomson was the head agent for the society. Arriving in Argentina in 1818, he traveled to Chile and up the western coast of Latin America, selling Bibles and creating Bible schools. Another notable colporteur was Allen Gardiner, who organized a mission in Patagonia, Argentina. After enduring much hardship, he and his associates died in 1851 from starvation and exposure to cold weather.

In 1859 local Indians killed eight additional missionaries who arrived in the region under the auspices of the Patagonian Missionary Society. Inspired by the heroic efforts of these pioneers, the Church of England took over that organization and changed its name to the South American Missionary Society. Its agents labored among the indigenous population of Argentina, Chile, and Bolivia. They created written languages for Indian dialects; grammars and dictionaries were produced,

and the Scriptures were translated into various local dialects. Toward the end of the century, however, alliances that missionaries had forged with liberal politicians broke down, and consequently, their evangelizing efforts bore little fruit. Bible translation and distribution, however, remained a widely used method of Protestant proselytizing.

### Jungle Foothold

In the small jungle regions where European Protestant nations retained power throughout the nineteenth century, Protestantism was able to gain a permanent foothold. This was the case in Dutch Guiana and also along the Miskito Coast of Central America, where Moravian (United Brethren) missionaries converted large numbers. Surprisingly, Protestants were less successful in British Honduras. Due to the efforts of mostly European Jesuits, by the end of the nineteenth century about two-thirds of the mixed Indian and black population was Catholic. Anglican, Methodist, and Baptist missionaries, however, did gain the allegiance of the other third.

## Protestant Immigration

In the early nineteenth century but especially after 1860, when they came to power in most of Latin America, Liberal governments encouraged European and U.S. Protestants to migrate to the region. This was not done because these governments were sympathetic to Protestantism but because they wanted to counter the power of the Catholic hierarchy, which was critical of liberal reform policies, and because they thought that Protestants would bring the work skills and liberal traditions of their homelands to the Latin world.

By the end of the century there were small Protestant congregations in almost all of Latin America. Protestants of various traditional denominations came from the U.S. and Britain but also from other European countries and from South Africa. At first these immigrant Protestants were reluctant to proselytize the native population, but by the last half of the century, they felt secure enough to distribute Bibles to their neighbors. They also encouraged their U.S. and British denominational counterparts to give priority to sending missionaries to Latin America.

## Protestant Efforts Fail

Soon mission organizations, such as the British-based South American Mission Society and the U.S.-based United Foreign Missionary Society and American

Board of Commissioners for Foreign Missions, were involved in launching the first large-scale effort to "convert" Latin America. Those who came were mostly from the larger, more traditional denominations—Methodist, Presbyterian, Episcopalian, Baptist, Congregationalist, and Disciples of Christ.

These missionaries put much of their efforts into building schools, opening religious bookstores, and distributing Bibles. Soon their schools developed a reputation for being the best in Latin America. They also set up hospitals and health clinics. Yet in spite of these Herculean efforts, Protestantism attracted only a small number of native converts. Indeed, by 1930 less than one percent of Latin Americans were Protestant and as late as 1960 only 3.8 percent. This lack of success was in large part due to the chauvinism of missionaries who saw Hispanics and Latin American culture as inferior to that of northern Europe and North America.

This becomes evident when one looks at the conduct of the Foreign Missions Conference of North America. Formed in 1913 to foster cooperation among the various Protestant denominations involved in Latin American missionary work, it held its first Congress in Panama in 1916. The fact that all business proceedings were conducted in English, rather than Spanish, is telling. Seven regional meetings followed, along with two more Congresses, one in Uruguay in 1925 and a second in Cuba in 1929, in which Spanish or Portuguese was employed. Nevertheless, native Latin Protestants were left out of all decision-making.

## Pentecostal Success

Large-scale Protestant success in Latin America did not come about until the second half of the twentieth century, when it resulted from an explosive growth of Pentecostalism. This movement, decentralized and hard to categorize, originated in Latin America almost simultaneously with its development in the United States. It was first introduced into Chile in 1909, when W. C. Hoover, a Methodist missionary, broke from his denomination and formed the Methodist Pentecostal Church, a unique combination of Pentecostalism and Calvinism that differs from Pentecostalism elsewhere in Latin America. Two Swedes and an Italian, Gunnar Vingren, Daniel Berg, and Luigi Francescon, introduced Pentecostalism into Brazil in 1910. All three went to Brazil as missionaries after first immigrating to the United States. where they were "baptized in the Spirit."

Other North Americans and Europeans brought Pentecostalism to Argentina (1910), Peru (1911), Nicaragua (1912), Mexico (1914), and Guatemala (1916). From these

countries it soon spread throughout the continent. Thus, Latin Pentecostalism can trace its roots to both U.S. and European sources. Nevertheless, it is not an institutional extension of either, because from its origin it developed indigenous leadership and was financially self-sufficient. Moreover, Latin-American Pentecostalism, individualistic and inclined to schismatic fragmentation, adapted itself to the local and national culture as it spread.

### Many Forms Today

Today there are many different forms of Pentecostalism in Latin America. The largest groups are the Assemblies of God, the Church of God in Christ, the International Church of the Foursquare Gospel, and the United Pentecostal Church International. There are also numerous smaller independent churches and groups.

In the 1960s and 1970s several Neo-Pentecostal churches emerged. They trace their roots to missionaries from conservative U.S. churches and embrace a U.S. anticommunist mind-set that pits them against progressive Catholicism and Protestantism. Older Pentecostal churches do not view them as associates.

## The Future

Barring a drastic change in global Catholicism that would allow married priests, Latin America will continue to have an ever-increasing shortage of native clergy, especially since the continent's population is expected to grow at a rapid rate. For this reason, the Latin Catholic Church will need an ever-increasing influx of foreign missionaries, many of whom will be laypeople. Moreover, due to the sacramental nature of Catholicism and the continually decreasing pool of potential missionary priests from the United States and Europe, it seems safe to predict that in the future the Latin American Catholic Church will have to rely more on African and Asian priests to help fill its sacerdotal needs.

Pentecostal missionaries from the United States will continue to descend on Latin America, but as in the past they will play only an ancillary role in the evolution of these forms of Latin-American Protestantism, since there will continue to be an ample supply of Latin-born pastors. Traditional Protestant churches will continue to rely at least to some degree on U.S. and European missionaries to staff and finance their social projects. At any rate, it seems safe to assume that at least throughout the twenty-first century Latin-American Christianity will continue to be heavily influenced by missionaries.

EDWARD T. BRETT

## Further Reading

Burgess, S. M. (Ed.). (2002). *The international dictionary of Pentecostal and Charismatic movements*. Grand Rapids, MI: Zondervan Publishing.

Cleary, E. L., & Stewart-Gambino, H. W. (Eds.). (1997). *Power, politics, and Pentecostals in Latin America*. Boulder, CO: Westview Press.

Dussel, E. (1981). *A history of the Church in Latin America: Colonialism to liberation*. Grand Rapids, MI: William B. Eerdmans Publishing Company.

Escobar, S. (2002). *Changing tides: Latin America & world mission today*. Maryknoll, NY: Orbis Books.

Goodpasture, H. M. (Ed.). (1989). *Cross and sword: An eyewitness history of Christianity in Latin America*. Maryknoll, NY: Orbis Books.

Klaiber, J. (1998). *The church, dictatorships, and democracy in Latin America*. Maryknoll, NY: Orbis Books.

Latourette, K. S. (1975). *A history of Christianity* (Vol. II). New York: Harper and Row.

Rivera, L. N. (1992). *A violent evangelism: the political and religious conquest of the Americas*. Louisville, KY: Westminster/John Knox Press.

Sigmund, P. E. (Ed.). (1999). *Religious freedom and evangelization in Latin America*. Maryknoll, NY: Orbis Books.

# Liberalism

The unifying idea at the core of theological Liberalism is not so much a set of beliefs or doctrinal views as an intellectual vision informed by the idea that "the claims of truth are ultimately higher than those of revelation, whether those known from Scripture or through the church" (Houlden 1993, 321). This idea, which came to fruition during the Enlightenment, was later shaped by a reaction to Evangelicalism. Liberalism in its various forms affected, in turn, the academy, the pulpit, and the program of the Church in succeeding centuries, both locally and internationally.

Recurring themes in Liberalism have included a wariness toward dogma (sometimes reflecting an openness toward new developments and insights), a greater emphasis on the humanity of Jesus, a degree of skepticism toward the miraculous, an attraction to the idea of the immanence of God in creation, a heightened interest in the ethical and moral dimensions of Christianity (and some degree of detachment from traditional doctrinal formulations), and a great deal of optimism toward finding common ground between Christianity and other religions.

It is not surprising that the recasting of Christianity along these lines has had substantive, though in some ways gradual, effects on the understanding of the mission of the church among those who espouse liberal theological views. This is so for several reasons: Liberalism has tended quite consistently to hold its strongest appeal among the highly educated; its "lifestyle expressions" have often appeared to be arid, rather than fervent; the intellectual traditions that shaped Liberalism may not be meaningful (or even comprehensible) in cultures that don't share common intellectual traditions; the extent to which Liberalism offers an attractive new message might be limited to the West.

It seems clear that some of these traits could weaken the potential for, and possibly even the logic of, a sense of mission. For example, the more hopeful and fervent is one's sense of commonality between religions, the less sense it makes to send missionaries to persuade adherents of non-Christian faiths to change religions. Nevertheless, Liberalism was not intrinsically incompatible with the notion of mission but rather with traditional ideas of mission. Historically, in its various forms (for example, Christian socialism and social gospel), Liberalism had its share of remarkably zealous workers and reformers: Washington Gladden, Walter Rauschenbusch, Francis Willard, and others. The nature of their work differed from traditional missions in that it took aim at social and structural reform rather than at individual salvation. Causes—poverty, housing, fair wages, and the rights of women—took precedence over "the passion for souls," which had been prevalent in traditional conceptions of Christian mission.

An earnest, luminous, and still-influential endeavor in this line is represented by the work of Shirley Jackson Case, Shailer Mathews, and George Birney Smith, who created a new message of salvation by combining brilliant scholarship in religion with a serious impulse toward political and social reform. In the broader sphere of overseas cross-cultural missions, a comprehensive rethinking of the essence of Christianity on the continent, in Great Britain, and in America also had an effect on both the motivation for missionary work and the message itself.

As William Hutchison of the Harvard Divinity School pointed out, late nineteenth-century Protestant missions didn't carry out their endeavors under labels such as "orthodox" or "conservative" or "liberal." Their tendencies, however, were clear enough, and mission agencies as well as individual missions could be recognized as aligned with "civilizing" missions (those whose interests included bringing Western cultural advantages to foreign fields) or with a "pure gospel" tradition. As Hutchison put it, "The theologically revisionist or negative elements in the liberal gospel were probably just as important, over the long run, in supporting a civilizing or social-service emphasis in missions. Liberals...simply lacked enthusiasm for direct evangelism, whether at home or overseas" (1987, 103).

There is at least some perception that it was the Evangelicals (with their pure gospel tradition) rather than the liberals whose mission work was particularly prone to charges of cultural imperialism. But as Hutchison points out, "disparagement of doctrine helped open the way for enterprises of social salvation" (1987, 104). This casts light on a highly important distinction between liberal and conservative philosophies of mission: The former saw the gospel message as one part of a gradual work of God, while the latter viewed the gospel and its presentation as central, absolutely unique, and of the greatest possible urgency.

These divergent priorities can be understood at least partly in terms of eschatology. Within a postmillennial framework (the default setting for most liberals), it was to be expected that the "Kingdom" would be take shape slowly; Evangelicals, by contrast, were impelled by watchfulness for a "Master" who could return at any moment. This broad difference in interpretation had other nuances as well: It influenced ideas about the nature of the Kingdom, the impulse for mission, and the uniqueness and supremacy of the Christian message.

Every retelling of the Christian message requires a degree of reinterpretation, only some of which is conscious and deliberate. Liberalism's hold on the theological imagination of some sectors of Western Christianity is not what it once was. In the final analysis, the dwindling momentum of mission in the liberal tradition cannot be explained without reference to developments within the sending churches or agencies. These include, among other factors, a significant decline in membership among theologically liberal denominations in America and a wholesale rethinking and revaluing of the very idea of mission.

DAVID STEWART

See also Enlightenment; Ethics; Evangelicalism; Fundamentalism; Social Gospel; Theology

## Further Reading:

Bishop, D. L. (2005). Mission and the dis-established church. *Wisconsin Conference of the United Church of Christ.* Retrieved September, 15, 2006, from http://www.wcucc.org

Houlden, L. (1993). Liberalism: Britain. In A. E. McGrath (Ed.), *The Blackwell companion to modern Christian thought.* Oxford, UK: Blackwell, 320–25.

Hutchison, W. R. (1976). *The modernist impulse in American Protestantism.* Oxford, UK: Oxford University Press.

Hutchison, W. R. (1986, January 1–8). Past imperfect: History and the prospect for Liberalism (Vol. 1). *Christian Century,* 11.

Hutchison, W. R. (1986, January 15). Past imperfect: History and the prospect for Liberalism (Vol. 2). *Christian Century,* 42.

Hutchison, W. R. (1987). *Errand to the world: American Protestant thought and foreign missions.* Chicago: University of Chicago Press.

Sanneh, L. (1987, April 8). Christian missions and the Western guilt complex. *Christian Century,* 331–334.

Wacker, G. (2000). *Religious Liberalism and the modern crisis of faith.* National Humanities Center, TeacherServe. Retrieved September 16, 2006, from www.nhc.rtp.nc.us/tserve/twenty/tkeyinfo/liberal.htm

Walls, A. F. (1996). *The missionary movement in Christian history: Studies in the transmission of faith.* Edinburgh, UK: Clark.

# Liberation Theology

Liberation Theology (LT) is beyond doubt one of the most significant theological movements of the twentieth century. It started in Latin America in the early 1960s. Within a few years it had influenced the development of similar theologies in other continents, especially in Asia and Africa. Its historical roots may be traced back to Iglesia y Sociedad en America Latina (ISAL), whose launching platform was the First Latin American Consultation on Church and Society (from 23 to 27 July 1961), held in Lima, Peru. This meeting, sponsored by the World Council of Churches (WCC), coincided with the beginning of intensive political activism on the part of Christians in the midst of increasing social unrest in a revolutionary situation. ISAL was initially a think tank made up mainly of Protestant theologians such as Julio de Santa Ana and Julio Barreiro of Uruguay, Jose Míguez-Bonino of Argentina, and Rubem Alves of Brazil. Eventually, however, ISAL produced its greatest impact in Roman Catholic circles, to such an extent that LT became known largely as progressive Roman Catholic theology, represented by outstanding theologians such as Gustavo Gutierrez of Peru, Juan Luis Segundo of Uruguay, Pablo Richard of Chile, Enrique Dussell of Argentina, Jose Miranda of Mexico, Leonardo Boff and Clodovis Boff of Brazil, and Jon Sobrino of Spain and El Salvador.

## Early Works

The first major LT work, *A Theology of Human Hope* (1969), was written by Rubem Alves, based on his Ph.D. thesis at Princeton Theological Seminary. Another early fruit of LT, much more widely known than Alves's, was Gustavo Gutierrez's *A Theology of Liberation* (1973), originally published in 1971 in Spanish and soon translated into several languages, including English. As a result of this work, Gutierrez came to be known as "the father of liberation theology."

An important factor that favored the development of LT in Roman Catholic circles in Latin America was the Second Vatican Council (1962–1965) and the social encyclicals issued by John XXIII and Paul VI, especially *Populorum Progressio* (1967). The insights that emerged from this *aggiornamento* of the church provided the basis for the document produced by the Second Latin American Episcopal Conference (CELAM) held in Medellin, Colombia, in 1968. This document, signed by the 130 prelates present, was critical of the Latin American situation as a "situation of sin," condemned "institutionalized violence," advocated the promotion of the *comunidades eclesiales de base* (grassroots ecclesial communities), and ratified "God's preferential option for the poor." The basis was thus laid for social and political activism and for "a new way of doing theology" (Gutierrez 1973) on behalf of the liberation of the poor from all kinds of oppression, including that related to socioeconomic dependence.

## Decade of Captivity

Many priests and nuns who wanted to identify with the poor in order to implement the Medellin conclusions went to live among them in the slums, rural areas, and jungles. Their aim was to achieve liberation in terms of socioeconomic justice, if necessary through class struggle and confrontation, instead of waiting for the rich ruling elite to give handouts to the poor. Their approach to change provoked a double reaction. On the one hand, the conservative constituency of the church accused them of promoting a theology of violence and endangering the unity of the church. On the other hand, many were murdered by the anti-Marxist, fascist, and national security governments that had been established in several Latin American countries during the 1970s. According to some estimates, during this decade of captivity approximately 1,500 priests, nuns, and active laypersons were arrested, imprisoned, tortured, exiled, or assassinated. The cost of prophecy paid by people committed to LT was indeed very high.

A memorable example of their willingness to pay that price was that of Archbishop Oscar Romero of El Salvador, who said, "Martyrdom is a grace of God that I do not feel worthy of, but if God accepts the sacrifice of my life, my hope is that my blood will be like a seed of liberty and a sign that our hopes will soon become reality" (Dennis, Golden, and Wright 2000, 87). One month later, in 1980, he was shot dead while celebrating Mass.

## Activism for the Poor

In sharp contrast with much of Western Christian theology, which is primarily concerned with doctrine, LT was focused on action for the sake of the poor. From this perspective, it made a significant contribution mainly in three fields:

1. **Hermeneutics**. LT insists that if theology is to fulfill its task it should take as its starting point the present historical situation, which in Latin America, as in the rest of the two-thirds world, is marked by the overwhelming presence of the poor. The practice of truth ("historical praxis") always has the priority over theology, which is always a "second act"—a critical reflection on historical praxis. For the sake of relevant praxis, however, the historical situation needs to be analyzed; consequently, theology must be interdisciplinary. It is at this point, at least for some of the liberation theologians, that Marxism becomes important, mainly as a tool of socioeconomic analysis.

2. **Christology**. LT is not particularly interested in the doctrine of Christ or in the search for the historical Jesus of Nazareth to which Western theology has devoted so much attention. Instead, it concentrates on Jesus's liberating praxis among the poor of his time. It centers on Christ the liberator and the practical implications of his life and ministry for the life and ministry of the church.

3. **Ecclesiology.** LT takes very seriously the view of the church as primarily a community rather than an institution. Accordingly, it interprets the emergence of thousands of grass-roots ecclesial communities in Latin America as a "new genesis" or a "reinvention" of the church. In these communities the Bible is read in the context of poverty and oppression, a critical understanding of the situation of the poor is promoted, possible courses of action to change

the situation are explored, every aspect of life is placed under the influence of the Gospel, and the practical exercise of the priesthood of all believers is encouraged.

## LT for the Future

Undoubtedly, the political activism of the liberation theologians, whose critique of the ruling elite was sometimes accompanied by Marxist overtones of class struggle, contributed to a large extent to the heated internal debate that LT unleashed in the church. More than that, however, their ecclesiology was perceived as a real threat to the ecclesiastical hierarchical structure centered in Rome. As a result, in the 1980s Joseph Cardinal Ratzinger (now Pope Benedict XVI), at that time Prefect of the Congregation for the Doctrine of the Faith, issued two cautionary documents regarding LT, the *Instruction on Certain Aspects of the Theology of Liberation* (1984) and the *Instruction on Christian Freedom and Liberation* (1986). This opposition on the part of the Vatican, to which was added the fall of the Marxist regimes in the Soviet Union and Eastern Europe at the end of that decade, brought LT to a standstill. The fact remains, however, that the problems that motivated LT in the 1960s and 1970s have not been solved but aggravated, with the rich getting richer and the poor getting poorer. A new LT for a world that lies under the spell of globalization is urgently needed.

C. René Padilla

### Further Reading

Alves, R. (1969). *A theology of human hope.* New York: Corpus Books.

Bussmann, C. (1985). *Who do your say? Jesus Christian Latin American theology* (R. R. Barr, Trans.). Maryknoll, NY: Orbis Books. (Original work published in German in 1980)

Colonnese, L. M. (1973). *The Church in the present-day transformation of Latin America in light of the council: Second general conference of Latin American bishops, Bogota, 24 August, Medellin, 26 August–6 September, 1968.* Bogota, Columbia: General Secretariat of CELAM.

Dennis, M., Golden, R., & Wright, S. (2000). *Oscar Romero: Reflections on his life and writings.* Maryknoll, NY: Orbis Books.

Ferm, D. W. (1986). *Third world liberation theologies: A reader.* Maryknoll, NY: Orbis Books

Gutierrez, G. (1973). *A theology of liberation: History, politics and salvation* (Sister C. Inda & J. Eagleson, Trans.).

Maryknoll, NY: Orbis Books. (Original work published 1971)

Paul VI, Pope. (1967). *Populorum progressio.* Costa Mesa, CA: Paulist Press.

Ratzinger, J., Cardinal. (1984). *Instruction on certain aspects of the theology of liberation.* Boston: St. Paul Editions.

Ratzinger, J., Cardinal. (1986). *Instruction on Christian freedom and liberation.* Boston. St. Paul Editions.

Sobrino, J. (1978). *Christology at the crossroads* (J. Drury, Trans.). Maryknoll, NY: Orbis Books.

Tombo, D. (2002). *Latin American liberation theology.* Boston: Brill Academic Publishers, Inc.

## Libraries

The purpose of this entry is to help the nonspecialist identify library resources for the study of Christian missions and world Christianity, both historical and contemporary. The resources available for this study include the following types of documentation:

- Secondary literature, including monographs and serials, scholarly and popular.
- Official publications of mission agencies, denominations, and other ecclesial agencies, including annual reports, directories, periodicals, and newsletters.
- "Grey" literature, including printed material with limited distribution (for example, literature sent out by mission agencies to congregations and clergy) and ephemeral material (for example, brochures, flyers, and pamphlets).
- Archives of mission agencies, denominations, church-related agencies, ecumenical agencies, and congregations.
- Personal papers of missionaries and church leaders.
- Oral histories.

The division of labor between libraries and archives is not always clear-cut. Many libraries collect secondary literature. Research libraries may also collect official publications and "grey" literature, as well. Archival repositories may contain documentation from all six categories. A seventh category, that of electronic resources, especially those that are born digital, is emerging.

The Internet is making access to bibliographical information increasingly easy. WorldCat, from the Online Computer Library Center (OCLC), and Eureka, from the Research Libraries Group (RLG), are databases that provide access to millions of bibliographic records in thousands of libraries around the world. Library catalogs are increasingly available on the World Wide Web, so that researchers can search a catalog before visiting a library or requesting an item on interlibrary loan. Another resource is Mundus, a gateway to missionary collections in the United Kingdom. While the primary focus of Mundus is on archival resources, it also directs the researcher to library collections in the UK and has links to repositories around the world.

Many types of libraries collect materials on missions, often for reasons other than documenting missionary activity. *Christianity in China* (Crouch et al. 1989) attempts a comprehensive listing of resources in libraries and archives in the United States. It lists holdings of repositories ranging from Harvard and Yale, which have extensive library and archival collections, to the Adorers of the Blood of Christ provincial house in Red Bud, Illinois, which has one box of archival material documenting its work in China. National libraries and those that serve as copyright depositories are rich sources for mission documentation. The Library of Congress serves this function for the United States, as do the British Library, the Bodleian at Oxford, and Cambridge University Library for the UK. Many national libraries outside the West, such as the Singapore National Library, attempt to collect material about their country as well as publications produced in their country.

The Center for Research Libraries (CRL) in Chicago coordinates area-studies preservation microfilming projects for Africa, Latin America, the Middle East, Eastern Europe, South Asia, and Southeast Asia. The libraries participating in these programs have collections documenting these regions, especially material published there. While mission history is not a primary focus, since they often collect comprehensively in a given region, their collections include the history of missions and documentation on the life and thought of Christianity in the region. Lists of participating institutions can be found at the CRL website (http://www.crl.edu/content.asp).

Libraries around the world have area studies collections. The library of the School of Oriental and African Studies at London University has extensive library and archival holdings for Asia, the Middle East, and Africa. The Toyo Bunko is the largest library and research center for Asian studies in Japan. The University of South Africa is a center for the study of Africana. The Mitchell Library in Sydney, Australia, gathers documentation on Melanesia (as well as missions to Australia's aboriginal people), and the Alexander Turnbull Library of the New Zealand National Library collects material documenting Polynesia. The Deutsche Forschungsgemeinschaft has assigned responsibility for building research collections to the major German libraries, including responsibility for area studies collections; so, for example, South Asia is covered by Heidelberg, Ibero-America, East and Southeast Asia by Berlin, and Africa south of the Sahara and Oceania by Frankfurt. Tübingen is assigned general responsibility for theology, including missions.

Many seminaries and divinity schools collect material on missions and world Christianity. They are mandated to do so in North America by the accreditation standards adopted by the Association of Theological Schools. Nevertheless, coverage is spotty. Generally speaking, university-related divinity schools in North America have the strongest collections.

Historically the two strongest mission collections in the United States are the Day Missions Library (founded in 1892) and the Missionary Research Library (founded in 1911). The Missionary Research Library began as a collection supported by Protestant mission boards with initial funding from the Rockefeller Foundation. In 1967 it was deposited at Union Theological Seminary in New York, but without adequate funding, its collections did not continue to grow as they had previously. In 2005 Union's Burke Library became part of the Columbia University Library. As one of Columbia's special collections, its funding is likely to be more stable.

The Day Missions Library was integrated into the Yale Divinity Library in 1932. It has an aggressive acquisitions program for both print and nonprint documentation of the history of Christian missions and the life and thought of world Christianity. Its strongest collection concerns United States mainline Protestant missions in the nineteenth and early twentieth centuries, but it also collects exhaustively all published material dealing with missions (Protestant, Catholic, and Orthodox) and world Christianity; it also has extensive archival collections, both as original documents and in microform. In 2002 it launched the Kenneth Scott Latourette Initiative for the Documentation of World Christianity, a proactive program to preserve print and nonprint resources that compliment the Day Library held by other institutions.

In addition to these two distinctive collections, the Pitts Theological Library at Emory University, which obtained the bulk of the Hartford Seminary mission collection, has particular strength in African Christianity, and the Speer Library at the Princeton Theological Seminary has strength in Latin American Christianity. The most important library for mission research in Canada is at Victoria University on the University of Toronto campus.

The Billy Graham Center library and archives were founded in 1973, in part to gather documentation of

American nondenominational missions. In 2004 the library was integrated into the Wheaton College Library where (as of this writing) plans are underway to establish it as a part of the library's special collections as the Billy Graham Missions and Evangelism Collection. The primary focus of the collection will be on worldwide evangelism and American Evangelical missions.

The Maryknoll Library, which was once considered a significant collection documenting Roman Catholic missions, has now been dispersed. Today the major collection for Roman Catholic missions in North America is the Catholic Theological Union Library in Chicago.

In Europe mission agencies once housed extensive libraries supporting their work. Today many of these libraries have been incorporated into academic institutions, as is the case with the Dutch Reformed missions library, now housed at the University of Utrecht and the Church Missionary Society collection, now housed at the University of Birmingham. Other European universities with significant Protestant collections are at Århus, Oslo, Uppsala, Hamburg, Marburg, and Edinburgh.

For Roman Catholic missions, the Urbaniana and the Gregoriana libraries in Rome have the most significant collections. The Bibliothèque Asiatique des Missions Étrangères in Paris documents French Catholic missions in Asia. Roman Catholic universities with significant missions collections include Münster, Louvain, Lisbon, and Madrid.

A small but growing number of institutions in the non-Western world are developing library resources. Payap University has an excellent collection documenting Christianity in Thailand. Trinity Theological College in Singapore has established a Center for the Study of Christianity in Asia that has as part of its mission improving the documentation of Christianity in Singapore, Malaysia, and Indonesia. Libraries such as those at the United Theological College of the West Indies in Kingston, Jamaica, and the Pacific Theological College in Suva, Fiji, make documenting Christianity in their regions a priority.

PAUL F. STUEHRENBERG

### Further Reading

Crouch, A., et al. (1989). *Christianity in China: A scholars' guide to resources in the libraries and archives of the United States.* Armonk, NY: Sharpe.

Gill, K. D. (2000). Mission libraries. In A. S. Moreau (Ed.), *Evangelical dictionary of world missions* (pp. 639–640). Grand Rapids, MI: Baker Books.

Neill, S., et al. (1971). Mission libraries. In S. Neill, G. H. Anderson, & J. Goodwin (Eds.), *Concise dictionary of the Christian world mission* (p. 407). Nashville, TN: Abingdon Press.

Smalley, M. L. (1993). *The Day Missions Library centennial volume.* New Haven, CT: Yale Divinity School Library.

Peterson, S. L. (1991). North American library resources for mission research. *International Bulletin of Missionary Research, 15,* 155–164.

Price, F. W. (1960). Specialized research libraries in missions. *Library Trends, 9,* 175–185.

Shuster, R. (1981). Library and archival resources of the Billy Graham Center. *International Bulletin of Missionary Research, 5,* 124–126.

# Linguistics

Linguistics is the scientific study of both *language* (shared mental constructs) and the *languages* (specific sounds and patterns characteristic of a group of speakers) that humans use in the course of their everyday activities. Linguists examine the rich repertoire of symbols humans use to communicate as well as properties of symbolic communication, for it is through the creation, apprehension, and manipulation of symbols that all human speech, writing, and other forms of communication are manifested.

## History of Linguistics

The Western tradition of studying language can be traced back to Plato and Aristotle in the fourth and fifth centuries BCE; it continued with influential figures like the Roman rhetorician Cicero (106–43 BCE) and Erasmus (1469–1536 CE). By the early years of the Enlightenment, the tradition was deeply rooted in the study of the Indo-European language family—that is, most languages were simply assumed to be similar to the patterns of Sanskrit, Greek, Latin, and the languages of greater Europe.

As the European explorers encountered cultures very different from their own, language scholars found that newly discovered languages could not be described and classified using the presumed categories and existing models of the European language systems. That realization, together with the post-Enlightenment shift to studying humans "objectively" and "scientifically" produced the nineteenth- and early-twentieth-century climate in which language specialists began to focus on other language patterns, contrasts, and structures.

The late-nineteenth-century Swiss scholar Ferdinand de Saussure (1857–1913) is widely credited as the father of modern linguistics, also known as descriptive linguistics, a discipline associated with the influential school of structuralism, which permeated the social sciences.

## Modern Linguistics

Modern linguistics theory posits that every language in the world has its own unique, and relatively limited, set of contrasting phonemes, sounds that function in relation to each other to make meaningful distinctions (like the difference between /t/ and /d/ in English). Phonemes are clusters of descriptive sound features that are linguistically significant for speakers; although different speakers articulate the phonemes idiosyncratically and in different contexts, such variations are nevertheless perceived by native speakers as the same sound. (The variations themselves are called allophones.) Descriptive features for consonants include voicing (whether or not the vocal chords vibrate when the sound is produced), manner of articulation (how the sound is produced in the mouth), and point of articulation (where the sound is produced in the mouth). For vowels, distinctive features include voicing, tongue height (high, mid, or low), tongue position in the mouth (front, central, or back), and degree of lip rounding. To use one phoneme instead of another in an otherwise identical context can change the meaning (for example, in English "tie" is very different from "die"; the two contrasting sounds, /t/ and /d/, are different phonemes and function as a minimal pair).

Phonemes are combined into meaning-bearing units called morphemes (like "cat," or "-s," the suffix which means "more than one"). Speakers combine the morphemes into words, phrases, and sentences which linguists analyze as the syntax, or the syntactic patterns (the ways those words, phrases, and sentences are ordered), of the language. In addition, stress, pitch, and timing in speech are also important aspects of language. The lexicon, or dictionary, of a language is an inventory of all the words of the language, while semantics is the study of how meaning is conveyed from one speaker to another via the syntactic patterns as well as the words.

The grammar, an abstract, unconscious mental model that describes basic, simple sentences with concepts like "subject," "action," and "direct object"—who does what and to whom—originates effortlessly in young children. Native speakers learn their mother tongues in their earliest years; by the time children are five or six years old, they have essentially mastered the language. As children mature, they learn to produce variations of these basic structures—that is, to generate questions and commands; to construct more elaborate, detailed sentences for scholarly papers or public speeches; to build narrative structures for good storytelling; or to deliver the punch lines of jokes. But all the variations, or *transformations*, are simply rule-governed shifts and elaborations of the grammar's basic, simple sentences where the most essential components of meaning lie.

## Areas of Specialization in Linguistics

Many sub-specialties of linguistics have emerged: Articulatory, or acoustic, phonetics is the careful study of all the sounds in a language in order to discern the phonemes, the specific set of contrasting sounds. Linguists utilize the symbols of the International Phonetic Alphabet (IPA) as diagnostic tools in order to determine the contrasting sounds in each language. In addition to studies in phonetics and phonemics, linguistics includes morphology and morphological analysis (the study of how the morphemes of a language are arranged); syntactic analysis; lexicology; semantic analysis; historical, or comparative, linguistics; textual analysis; psycholinguistics; sociolinguistics; anthropological linguistics; computational linguistics; and other combined disciplines. Furthermore, linguists and good translators are always conscious of how aspects of their labors are informed by other social sciences—anthropology, communication theory, psychology, sociology—and, to some extent, literary theory.

## Linguistics, the Bible, and the Church

As the Church sought from its earliest days to be obedient to Jesus's command to "go and make disciples of all nations," Christians translated the Scriptures wherever they traveled and made their homes. Early Christians seem to have assumed that God's word could, and should, be translated into the vernacular languages of their surroundings since they themselves lived in contexts where Greek-speaking Jews used the Septuagint (the translation of the Jewish texts from Hebrew into Greek) and where Aramaic-speaking Jews used the Targums (the various translations of the Jewish books from Hebrew into Aramaic).

The histories of the Church and of Bible translation are complementary and mutually illuminating. In the early centuries of the Church, the text was translated into Latin, Syriac, Coptic, Armenian, Georgian, Old Church Slavonic, and Ethiopic. Later, Arabic and

Persian translations appeared, followed by versions in Dutch, German, Hungarian, Norwegian, Spanish, and other languages of the European peoples.

Jerome translated the Bible into Latin in the fourth century (c. 390–405 CE), though it was not selected as the authorized Latin version and named the Vulgate until the Council of Trent (1545–1563). Martin Luther produced his German translation of the Scriptures in the early decades of the 1500s; those years also marked the introduction of an English translation by William Tyndale, which was superseded in 1611 by the publication of the King James Version.

In the Protestant Reformation, and the development of the modern missionary movement beginning with men like William Carey and Adoniram Judson, translation of Scripture into the world's vernacular languages reemerged with a sense of urgency that remains today. Johann Gutenberg's fifteenth-century introduction of the printing press to Western culture exponentially expanded the potential for Scripture distribution and personal study and laid the groundwork for much of the literacy training that was to follow.

Although Roman Catholics elevated and prioritized Latin for many centuries, it had become clear to their missionaries long before the twentieth century that effective mission, witness, and ministry needed the fluency of missionaries as well as Scriptures in the local language. Not until Vatican II (1962–1965), when use of the indigenous languages in the Mass was accepted, did Latin's dominance begin to decline; nevertheless, Latin remains a pervasive influence in Roman Catholic circles.

## Linguistics and Bible Translation

Through the centuries, the quality of translations of Scripture has varied widely; the translators—some superb, others unskilled—simply worked according to the prevailing standards of their own eras. But by the middle of the twentieth century, two outstanding linguists associated with the Summer Institute of Linguistics (Wycliffe Bible Translators)—Kenneth L. Pike and Eugene A. Nida—had organized language-learning training for missionaries. The training was intended to prepare the missionaries for two primary tasks before their departure for the field: to learn the local language and to translate the Bible into it. The translation methodologies, approaches, and theories developed and implemented by Pike and Nida have continued to be modified and expanded, but they all incorporate key linguistics themes.

First is the knowledge that the relationship between meaning and form is arbitrary and, except for occasional onomatopoeia, completely unpredictable. Second is the recognition that anything that can be said in Language A can be said in Language B. Third is that every language is unique and creative and thus must be respected for its inherent integrity. Fourth, meaning in language is always more important than literal form. Fifth, and correspondingly, the forms of Language A cannot be rigidly, artificially imposed onto Language B. Sixth, accurate, clear, and faithful translation of the text is the goal, so good translators must be aware of their own biases and preferences in order to avoid them as much as possible. Seventh, when checking the meanings of the translated text, the judgment of discerning native speakers is superior to the judgment of nonindigenous translators; for that reason, the best translators are the mother-tongue speakers themselves, who work in their own committees under the guidance and supervision of linguistics consultants skilled in helping translators work through awkward passages, structural forms with which the translators are unfamiliar, obscure Scripture verses, and other potential difficulties. Lastly, language and culture are so closely intertwined that neither one can be properly interpreted or understood without the other.

Thus, the ideal goal in effective translation is often called "dynamic equivalence," "functional equivalence," or "meaning-based translation." The goal of a dynamic equivalence translation is to produce in the lives, hearts, and minds of the hearers the impact of the original text on its hearers.

## Linguistics and Translations Teams

In any act of translation, there is always meaning in Language A that needs to be conveyed in Language B. This formidable challenge is even more complex when the original text to be translated is written in Hebrew or Greek; often members of translations teams have limited or no knowledge of the original languages and will consequently use a variety of "translations helps" as they work—that is, they will use a translation that already exists among a neighboring language group; a translation that was completed at an earlier historical point but is now deemed unsuitable for whatever reason; commentaries on the biblical passages; or conversations with colleagues at regularly scheduled workshops held by groups like the United Bible Societies (UBS) and others who publish Scriptures. Effective translators are always aware of their limitations, yet also confident of the guidance of the Holy Spirit, committed to the fact that God speaks to human beings in their own

## Martin Luther on Translation

**Part of the challenge of Christian mission work has always been conveying the message from the missionary to those being visited. The extract that follows is an examination of Martin Luther's views on translating the Bible.**

Luther was insistent that his translations should 'sing the Lord's song in a strange land.' To do this was no easy task, for there are so many things in the Bible which were not known in the Germany of Luther's day. Luther was not content to pass over hard words and difficult phrases by simply transliterating them into German. He knew that they would mean no more than they would in Hebrew letters, except that the German alphabet might make them appear more deceptively familiar. He sought out Jewish scholars to gain information about Old Testament weights and measures. He visited slaughterhouses to get the terms which could be used to describe various processes and objects of Old Testament sacrifice. He studied the court jewels in order to make certain that he had the proper names for the gems of the book of Revelation. He listened to children in their play and to artisans in their work. From all of them he gleaned a rich harvest of words to be used in the translation of the Bible, which he insisted should be in the language of the people and not in the pedantic, high-sounding German of the university classroom and the law courts.

Luther's translation became the cornerstone of the new Protestant faith—'protestant,' from the original meaning of this word, namely, 'to witness,' for these men witnessed to the redeeming grace of God in Christ. This witness spurred an Englishman, William Tyndale, to do for his native land what Luther was doing for his.

Source: Nida, E.A. (1952). *God's word in man's language* (p. 89). *New York: Harper & Row.*

language, and willing to discipline themselves to the sometimes tedious, meticulous, agonizing groundwork that accompanies translation. They know that their rewards will come when other members of their language group hear a newly translated portion of Scriptures in their mother tongue for the first time and say, "Aha! So *that's* **what it means!"**

## Future of Linguistics in Mission

The work of translation endures for two important reasons. First, older translations eventually lose their timeliness and suitability, and newer translations are required. Second, although the Scriptures do exist in the major languages of the world, there remain groups whose only access to God's word is secondary, often via the resources in a trade language or an area's dominant language. In early 2006, the United Bible Societies (UBS) reported having over 600 Scripture translations projects underway in 495 unique languages. At the same time, the SIL online *Ethnologue* stated that there were 6,912 living languages in the world; SIL personnel noted 1,640 translations projects in progress worldwide and

Wycliffe involvement in 1,294 of those. Generally speaking, the UBS translations projects target larger populations, while SIL focuses on translations projects among groups of relatively small populations of speakers. Among these smaller, more remote groups of people, teams of missionaries and translators are still at work in often challenging living conditions—struggling to learn the local languages, stumbling over new sounds in their initial attempts to hear and speak an unfamiliar vernacular language, and patiently subjecting themselves to the humbling experiences that are always necessary when adults learn a previously unknown language.

Literacy training increasingly accompanies the work of translation, especially among smaller groups with little previous exposure to books and other written materials. Developing appropriate texts for adults who are newly literate differs significantly from developing age-appropriate texts for children. In addition, linguists who have previously used computers and computer programs for typesetting and basic preproduction tasks while in the field are now able to utilize increasingly sophisticated computer programs in translations projects to help with painstaking tasks like word checks and general consistency in spelling, or to help ascertain commonalities among languages in language groups, or to analyze dialect variations. In recent years, linguists have been members of teams that have explored how to convey God's word through various forms of emerging contemporary media. Thus, as human communities experience change, the need for God's word in the vernacular remains, and linguists will continue to make valuable contributions to the Church's mission in the world.

SUSAN G. HIGGINS

*See also* Bible; Bible Translation; Contextualization; Culture; Inculturation, Mission Methods and Strategy; Protestant Churches; Reformation; Roman Catholic Church; Translation

## Further Reading

Castro, E., & Fick, U. (Eds.). (1981). The Bible in mission. *International Review of Mission, 70*(279), 113–188.

Clark, V. P., Eschholz, P. A., & Rosa, A. F. (1994). *Language: Introductory readings* (5th ed.). New York: Bedford/St. Martin's Press.

Escobar, S. (2006). The United Bible Societies and world mission. *International Bulletin of Missionary Research, 30*(2), 77–78, 80–81.

Gordon, R. G., Jr. (Ed.). (2005). Ethnologue: Languages of the world (15th ed.). Dallas, TX: SIL International.

Hill, H. (2006). The vernacular treasure: A century of mother-tongue Bible translation. *International Bulletin of Missionary Research, 30*(2), 82–88.

Hogg, W. R. (1984). The Scriptures in the Christian world mission: Three historical considerations. *Missiology, 12*(4), 389–404.

Larson, M. L. (1984). *Meaning-based translation: A guide to cross-language equivalence*. Lanham, MD: University Press of America.

Metzger, B. M. (1993). Theories of the translation process. *Bibliotheca Sacra, 150*(598), 140–150.

Neill, S. (1964). *A history of Christian missions*. New York: Penguin Books.

Nida, E. A. (1952). *God's word in man's language*. New York: Harper & Row.

Nida, E. A. (1960). *Message and mission: The communication of the Christian faith*. New York: Harper & Row.

Nida, E. A. (1961). *Bible translating* (Rev. ed.). London: United Bible Societies.

Nida, E. A., & Reyburn, W. D. (1981). *Meaning across cultures*. Maryknoll, NY: Orbis Books.

Nida, E. A., & Taber, C. R. (1969). *The theory and practice of translation*. Leiden, Holland: E. J. Brill.

O'Grady, W., Archibald, J., Aronoff, M., & Rees-Miller, J. (2005). *Contemporary linguistics: An introduction* (5th ed.). New York: Bedford/St. Martin's Press.

Orlinsky, H. M., & Bratcher, R. G. (1991). *A history of Bible translation and the North American contribution*. Atlanta, GA: Scholars Press.

Smalley, W. A. (1963). *Manual of articulatory phonetics* (Rev. ed.). Tarrytown, NY: Practical Anthropology.

Smalley, W. A. (1991). *Translation as mission: Bible translation in the modern missionary movement*. Macon, GA: Mercer University Press.

Smalley, W. A. (1995). Language and culture in the development of Bible society translation theory and practice. *International Bulletin of Missionary Research, 19*(2), 61–64, 66–71.

## Liturgy

The term *liturgy* is currently used in the Orthodox, Roman Catholic, Anglo-Catholic, and many Protestant traditions to describe the official, public worship of the church. The original Greek word *leitourgia* is a compound expression composed of *leit* (from *laos*: people or public) and *ergon* (from *ergazomai*: to act, to work). This term signified a public duty or the work of the people in classical usage. It was used to describe any public works project such as the construction of an aqueduct or the subsidizing of athletic competitions on behalf of one's town or city-state. By the time of the Septuagint it had come to be applied particularly to religious functions and the services of the temple. The term has evolved over the centuries. The public character of worship and liturgy has, nevertheless, remained. The conflicts in Corinth during Paul's ministry are particularly instructive for emphasizing this public dimension of Christian worship (Keifert, 1992). The Eucharistic meal and its liturgical form, for example, was a way of creating the bridge between the private and the public in the early church. This bridge protected access for the stranger and the marginalized to the new community centered in Christ. The word *liturgy* in English is most commonly used in two senses: (1) It refers to all the prescribed public services of the Church, that is, the canonical hours, as contrasted with private devotions; and (2) specifically, liturgy serves as a title of the Eucharist as the chief part of public worship.

In the New Testament, *leitourgia* is used in three different ways: (1) it describes good works done on behalf of others (Rom. 15: 27; 2 Cor. 9:12); (2) it designates the Levitical ritual of the Old Testament and, by extension,

Christ's atoning death as linked to these rituals on the Day of Atonement (Hebrews, chapters 7–10); and (3) it describes spiritual worship (Rom. 15:16). Although *leitourgia* was used in early centuries to refer to both the ministry of church officials and any act of divine worship, its later focus narrowed only to Eucharistic worship. The church's liturgy is not normally used in the broad sense today in referring to the entire activity of the church. Evangelism, catechesis, social action, and other ways of ministering the gospel are indeed forms of Christian worship but not liturgy. Nor is liturgy the only occasion where Christians pray.

Although the word *liturgy* became popularized in the nineteenth century, its use in Roman Catholic circles became especially important in the twentieth century. One of the most influential liturgical documents of the twentieth century is *Sacrosanctum Concilium* (SC), the first document of Vatican II (1963). This statement has served as the foundation for the subsequent liturgical reform in the Roman Catholic Church. This reform has also influenced the revision of the worship traditions of other churches around the world.

In recent years one of the most fascinating aspects of liturgical renewal across the world has been the linking of liturgy and mission. Emil Brunner said, "The Church exists by mission as fire exists by burning." This insight lies at the heart of the apostolic call by God to God's people for their service and witness in the world. Christian theology and practice have often succumbed to describing church and mission as connoting distinct and sometimes conflicting ideas; even two different kinds of societies. The understanding of *mission* (*Missio Dei:* God's activity in the world) can be confused by reducing it to *missions* (the activities of the church). It is precisely the interconnection between God's activity in the world and the church that has been emphasized since at least the 1930s in both the ecumenical missionary movement and in Roman Catholic theology. What is intriguing is the remarkable level of convergence that emerged by the 1980s around the Trinitarian foundation for mission among Ecumenical, Evangelical, Orthodox, and Roman Catholic missiologists and theologians and its implications for worship and liturgy. Thus, the former distinctions between church and mission are no longer deemed helpful for grasping the fullness of the missionary dynamic of the Christian community in the world. This dynamic is expressed most fully in the church's worship and liturgies. Participation in Christ and in the life of the Trinity means simply participating in God's mission to the world. It is this fundamental connection between church and mission that lifts up the fascinating connection between the church's liturgy and mission. Liturgy cannot be understood without grasping the mission of God.

J. G. Davies, in his book *Worship and Mission,* nevertheless noted the lack of contemporary reflection on the relationship between the church's worship and its mission. Indeed, an examination of the work of liturgiologists and missiologists, according to Davies, might raise questions about the "complete dichotomy and even incompatibility" of worship and mission. In contrast, much recent reflection about liturgy and mission has been motivated by questions about inculturation or contextualization in those parts of the world that have received patterns of worship from European and North American missionaries. The advent of a post–Christian era in the West has encouraged significant reflection about the forms of worship appropriate to this missional situation.

Thomas Schattauer (1999) uses three paradigms for describing the various approaches to mission and liturgy: "Inside and out" (conventional), "outside in" (contemporary), and "inside out" (radical traditional). These paradigms outline much of the movement over much of church history in the relationship between mission and liturgy. Schattauer's goal is to underline the missional character of inside-out worship.

- Inside and Out: This paradigm starts by clearly demarcating mission and liturgy as separate spheres of the church's life. Worship takes place inside the Christian community preparing God's people for their mission of love, justice, and witness to the neighbor out in the world. Worship thus nurtures, sustains, and informs how mission is to be accomplished outside of the community. This description of the relationship between mission and liturgy has informed much of the fields of both missiological and liturgical practices at home and abroad.
- Outside In: A response to the "inside and out" paradigm throughout Christian history has been the outside-in approach. The goal of this model is to bring the "outside" mission activities directly into the context of worship. Whenever worship becomes increasingly irrelevant to everyday life, these "worldly" agendas are integrated back into the worship experience (e.g., liberation themes, entertainment evangelism, rock music, feminism, etc.).
- Inside Out: This approach locates the liturgical assembly itself within the arena of the *missio Dei*. The focus is on God's mission toward the world, to which the church witnesses and into which it is drawn, rather than on specific activities of the church un-

dertaken in response to the divine saving initiative. The *misso Dei* is God's own movement outward in relationship to the world. Here there is no separation between liturgy and mission.

As the forms of Christian liturgy adapt and change to meet the changing needs of various cultures and contexts, it will be critical to remember that the liturgy is the place where God's mission takes place by the people of God for the world. Worship is a public locus of mission. The liturgy sung, spoken, and lived out in the world by the people God is the church in mission.

RICHARD H. BLIESE

## Further Reading

Davies, J. G. (1966). *Worship and mission.* New York: Association Press.

Keifert, P. R. (1992). Welcoming the stranger: A public theology of worship and evangelism. Minneapolis, MN: Fortress.

Schattauer, T. (1999). *Inside out: Worship in an age of mission.* Minneapolis, MN: Augsburg Fortress Press.

Senn, F. (1993). *The witness of the worshipping community: Liturgy and the practice of evangelism.* New York: Paulist Press.

White, J. (1980). *Introduction to Christian worship.* Nashville, TN: Abingdon Press.

# M

## Martyrdom

A martyr is defined as "one who voluntarily suffers death as the penalty of witness to and refusing to renounce his religion" (*Webster's Third New International Dictionary of the English Language*). For purposes of quantification, Christian martyrs are "believers in Christ who have lost their lives prematurely, in situations of witness, as a result of human hostility." This definition can be expounded as follows: "Believers in Christ" are individuals from the entire Christian community of Roman Catholics, Orthodox, Protestants, Anglicans, Marginal Christians, and Independents. "'Lost their lives" restricts it to Christians actually put to death, for whatever reason. "Prematurely" means martyrdom is unexpected and unwanted. "In situations of witness" refers to the entire lifestyle and way of life of the Christian believer, whether or not he or she is actively proclaiming at the time of being killed. "As a result of human hostility" excludes deaths through accidents, earthquakes and other "acts of God," illnesses, or other causes of death however tragic.

The English word *martyr* is derived from the Greek *martys,* which carries the meaning "witness." In New Testament Christian usage, it meant "a witness to the Resurrection of Christ." This witness resulted so frequently in death that by the end of the first century *martys* had come to mean a Christian who witnessed to Christ *by his or her death.* Martyrdom came about because of persecution and resulted in a death that was in itself a witness for Christ. According to Latin American theologian Leonardo Boff, martyrs exist for two reasons: (1) Christians prefer to sacrifice their lives rather than to be unfaithful to their convictions, and (2) those who reject proclamation persecute, torture, and

kill. This latter antagonism, combined with Christian devotion, is at the root of martyrdom.

Martyrs are not simply individuals who courageously refuse to recant their faith in front of a firing squad. In fact, most Christian martyrs have been murdered in groups, for example, entire Christian villages targeted by Idi Amin in Uganda in the 1970s. These groups become the basis for estimates of martyrs killed in "situations." Table 1 provides a list of the ten martyrdom situations (out of over 600 listed in *World Christian Trends*) with the greatest number of martyrs. Note that over 20 million Christians were martyred in Soviet prison camps between 1921 and 1980 and that well over half of the 70 million Christian martyrs were killed in the twentieth century alone. Even though state-ruling powers (atheists and others) are responsible for most martyrs, closer examination of the entire list of martyrdom situations reveals that Christians themselves have been the persecutors responsible for martyring 5.5 million other Christians. Table 2 reveals that over half of all martyrs have been Orthodox Christians. One partial explanation for this is the vast anti-Christian empires throughout history centered in eastern Europe and central Asia. Nonetheless, all Christian traditions have suffered martyrdom. (Note: All statistics below are documented in Part 4 of "Martyrology" in Barrett and Johnson, *World Christian Trends*).

Josef Ton, persecuted as a Christian in Romania, developed a theology of martyrdom centered on God's purpose for human history. Ton outlines two major purposes of martyrdom as instruments (1) by which God achieves His purposes in history and (2) by which God shapes and forms the character of Christians who suffer and die. Under the first purpose three things are

**Table 1.** Martyrdom Situations in Christian History Ranked by Size

| | |
|---|---|
| 1. 1921–1950, Christians die in Soviet prison camps | 15,000,000 |
| 2. 1950–1980, Christians die in Soviet prison camps | 5,000,000 |
| 3. 1214, Genghis [Chinngis] Khan massacres Christians | 4,000,000 |
| 4. 1358, Tamerlane destroys Church of the East | 4,000,000 |
| 5. 1929–1937, Orthodox Christians killed by Stalin | 2,700,000 |
| 6. 1560, Conquistadors kill Amerindians, many of whom were baptized Christians | 2,000,000 |
| 7. 1925, Soviets attempt to wipe out Roman Catholics | 1,200,000 |
| 8. 1258, Baghdad captured in massacre by Hulagu Khan | 1,100,000 |
| 9. 1214, Diocese of Herat sacked by Genghis [Chinngis] Khan | 1,000,000 |
| 10. 1939, Nazis execute thousands in death camps | 1,000,000 |

achieved: (1) the triumph of God's truth: unbelievers' eyes opened by the manner of death (Mark 15:39); (2) the defeat of Satan: those formerly in bondage are brought to light (Revelations 15:2–4); and (3) the glory of God: voluntary suffering reflects God's love and power (2 Corinthians 4:7–12). Under the second purpose Christians are made perfect as Christ was made perfect through suffering and even death (Hebrews 2:10).

"The blood of the martyrs is the seed of the church" (Metz and Schillebeeck, 16) was famously stated by Tertullian, a third century lawyer who in his investigation of Christian martyrdom was converted to Christianity. In assessing the impact of martyrdom situations in Christian history, it is not possible to make a definitive statement about the relationship between martyrdom and the growth of Christianity. One can point to the massacres of Christians in central Asia under the Mongols and later under Tamerlane. This did not lead to further

church growth but rather to the disappearance of one of Christianity's most vibrant missionary traditions—the Church of the East. On the other hand, hundreds of years later, the purges of Stalin did not result in the extinction of Christianity in the Soviet Union. In fact, the church there today is enjoying a renaissance. Another contemporary example is the church in China. In 1949 there were only 1 million Christians in China. Fifty years of antireligious Communist rule produced some 1.2 million martyrs. The result was explosive church growth to today's nearly 100 million Christians. Major martyrdom situations continue today in Sudan, Indonesia, Nigeria, and other hot spots around the globe.

Christian martyrs, perhaps hastily consigned to the first two or three centuries of Christian history, have been a regular feature of Christianity throughout its entire history. The number of martyrs continues to grow as, on average, over 400 new martyrs are killed every day. The rate of martyrdom across the world throughout the ages has been a remarkably constant 0.8 percent. One out of every 120 Christians in the past has been martyred or in the future is likely to so be. We might be tempted to believe that mankind will gradually grow out of its violent nature and that, perhaps one hundred years in the future, will no longer be killing others, for whatever reason. However, this is not likely to be the case. The future almost certainly holds more martyrdom situations, and the names of individual martyrs are likely to continue mounting year after year at the same rate of over 160,000 a year.

T. M. JOHNSON

**Table 2.** Confessions of Martyrs, Totals from 33 to 2000 CE

| | |
|---|---|
| Orthodox | 43,000,000 |
| Russian Orthodox | 25,000,000 |
| East Syrians (Nestorians) | 12,800,000 |
| Ukrainian Orthodox | 4,000,000 |
| Gregorians (Armenian Apostolic) | 1,200,000 |
| Roman Catholic | 12,200,000 |
| Catholics (before 1000 CE) | 900,000 |
| Independents | 3,500,000 |
| Protestants | 3,200,000 |
| Anglicans | 1,100,000 |
| Marginal Christians | 7,000 |
| Other martyrs (undocumented or unknown) | 7,000,000 |
| Total all martyrs | 70,000,000 |

## Further Reading

Barrett, D., & Johnson, T. (2001). *World Christian trends*. Pasadena, CA: William Carey Library.

The massacre of Madagascar Christians in 1849 ordered by the rulers who saw Christianity as a threat to indigenous beliefs.

Baumeister, T. (1972). *Martyr invictus*. Münster: Regesnsburg.

Chenu, B., et al. (1988). *Livre des martyrs chrétiens*. Paris: Éditions du Centurion.

Metz, J., & Schillebeeck, E. (1983). *Martyrdom today*. Edinburgh: T. & T. Clark.

Wood, D. (1993). *Martyrs and martyrologies*. Oxford, UK: Blackwell.

Ton, J. (1997). *Suffering, martyrdom, and rewards in heaven*. Lanham, MD: Rowman & Littlefield.

# Materiality

A message-driven religion may appear to some of its adherents to be moving through the world with only the shape of an idea, an intellectual content ideally delivered in the privileged medium of speech or sacred writ. In fact, of course, missionaries carry an entire world with them and perform their messages in the material dress of bodies, clothing, medicines, food, images, print, architecture, and technology. A critical understanding of the materiality of missions and their reception among host societies sheds considerable light on the cultural interactions of peoples and on the variety of practices that constitute lived religion in the mission field. Moreover, it is in the form of material things that a religion takes root, or fails to do so, in a new world. The materiality of missions should be seen as a telling register of the processes of indigenization.

## Missions in India

The relevance of the body could not be more concrete in the situation encountered by German Pietist missionaries working for the Society for the Promotion of Christian Knowledge (SPCK) in British territories in South India during the eighteenth century, where they struggled with the tenacious problem posed by castes among Hindus. Mission diaries frequently mention the obstacles formed by the social dynamics of tensions among castes. When an unknown Indian man of high caste attended a Tamil worship service in Tiruchchirappalli

**233**

in 1802, missionary Christian Pohle assumed that he was Christian because he stood with his hands upraised during worship and because in conversation afterward he heaped special scorn on the Brahmins "and spurned the difference between meals, and ate what we ate" (Pohle 1806, 216).

But it was all apparently a ruse or a brief conversion, for a few weeks later the man was expelled from the mission after he had "showed his impure thoughts in manifold ways and appeared no longer to accept Christianity." The man's defection was a surprise to Pohle, who said that "his pretense at first was convincing, particularly since he ate our food, because people of the upper castes would rather fall dead or go hungry before they would do that" (Pohle 1806, 216). Conversions among Brahmins and higher castes were much less common than among the lowest, in part because those occupying the bottom of the social hierarchy had less to lose and more to gain by converting to Christianity, even though conversion removed them from their caste and made them untouchable. Family members scorned and often disowned those who converted, and converts frequently recanted.

### Effects of Climate

The body made other demands as well. In his annual report of 1799 regarding the SPCK's mission in Veperey, India, the German missionary Carl Wilhelm Päzold pointed out the physical stress of preaching in three languages. It was no longer as difficult as it first was, he wrote, but he felt it necessary to explain to his patrons in London that "the business of the mind and the body do not work so well or so quickly in this hot climate as they do in Europe," where the preacher might bring to the intellectual preparation of his sermon the good health that a moderate climate occasioned (Päzold 1801, 776). It is not surprising then to learn that the Europeans selected a shady spot under a tree as the place to sit and deliver a sermon in the villages or along the roads of India. This was of course where the natives gathered to avoid the sun, and it was where village elders might assemble. Placing themselves there not only avoided the extremes of the heat but put the missionaries in close contact with those they sought to evangelize.

### Depraved or Defunct Spirituality

On other occasions the bodies of Hindu faithful served as an unambiguous signifier of depraved or defunct spirituality for British missionaries. The annual ritual celebrating Jugannatha (Juggernaut), a title of Krishna, drew thousands of devotees to Orissa along the eastern coast and was infamous among Europeans for the reported suicides of frenzied pilgrims who threw themselves beneath the colossal car carrying the cult statue. British mission publications carried illustrations of the horrific scene. One account by a British traveler who visited the festival in 1806 was quoted at length several years later in the *Missionary Register* as British Evan-

**Vintage and antique religious items, including a cross and a bible, used by missionaries.** *Courtesy of Michael Flippo/istockphoto.com.*

gelicals joined Anglicans in pressuring Parliament to forbid any government subsidy of the temple at Orissa, where the annual event took place. The travel narrative compared the scene of Jugannatha to the slaughter of children sacrificed to the Canaanite deity Moloch in Leviticus 18: 21 (Juggernaut 1817, 304).

Accounts like these aimed at mobilizing domestic support for missionary efforts. And just as British Protestants were scandalized by the thought of such "abuses" of the body under the auspices of the Empire, they also lobbied for the elimination of suttee, the ritual burning of widows with their deceased husbands in India, and the painful binding of feet among Chinese women. In these cases, and many more, Christian missionaries in the field and Christians back home supporting missions focused on actual or exaggerated portrayals of bodily practices that bound non-Christians to their beliefs through ritual violence and pain.

It is not uncommon for Protestantism to be criticized as opposed to the body. But the charge misses the strong interest among Protestant missionaries in medical care and hygiene, the development of healthcare infrastructure, town planning, farming, and dietary and health initiatives. Rather than simply subverting or denying the body, nineteenth-century Protestant missions exerted a degree of control over the bodies of indigenous peoples by supplanting one cultural regime of embodiment for another, urging the modification of the local culture with Western conceptions of health and hygiene. One fascinating study of Catholic and Protestant missions in China over the course of the nineteenth century focused on the ways in which eating, food, diet, bodily odor, gesture, bowing, kneeling, hair, and clothing structured the missionaries' cultural encounter and (mis)interpretation of the Chinese (Reinders 2004).

## Different Methods of Engagement

Protestants historically have made the invisibility or bodilessness of the divine the salient feature of Christianity's difference from its rivals. For example, Christian Pohle related an encounter with Hindus to whom he read from a tract, telling them that Jesus was their only hope of reaching heaven. This resulted in the following exchange, which began when his listeners replied: "Everything you said and read is very good, but show us God. I answered: You ask something very strange. Can you see your souls? No, they said. I [replied]: Nor can you see the eternal God, who has no body; you must worship him in spirit and in truth" (Pohle 1790, 1352). In place of a statue of his deity, Pohle offered the tract

from which he read, making a gift of it, pitting print against statuary.

The psychology of missions has by no means always turned on such a confrontational manner of engagement. Catholics and Protestants have exhibited far more nuanced appreciations of cultural relations. Jesuit Matteo Ricci is famous for his deft use of indigenous dress and language as a genuine way of bridging East and West. Jesuit artists also found subtle ways for Catholic piety to map itself over indigenous visual practice, such as the alignment of the Virgin and Child with the Chinese goddess Guan Yin, who had long served as the entrée for Buddhism into China as the indigenous manifestation of the Indian Bodhisattva, Avalokiteśvara (Bailey 1999).

But the ambivalence of identity is something that some religions accommodate and others abhor. When the Indian painter and Christian Alfred Thomas produced a body of work showing the life of Christ in a visual idiom drawn from Hindu art, in which Jesus appeared in an ethereal manner and in clothing and pose that recalled Buddha, some Christian Indians expressed concern that his images might fail to draw a meaningful distinction between Christianity and Buddhism. John Butler, a British missionary in India, likewise indicated that, in his view, Thomas's paintings were too indebted to Buddhist art and to "the most sensuous side of popular Hinduism" (Butler 1956, 157). The partially nude body of Christ hovers or sits delicately among other seminude male figures, swathed in an aura that dissolves the contours of his form. The result struck some observers as less than masculine. But another missionary and authority on Indian art, Richard Taylor, replied that critics failed to grasp that "in classical Indian art softness and smoothness are one thing, femaleness another" (Taylor 1975, 121).

Indian critics were alarmed by the similarity of Thomas's work to Hindu and Buddhist art because it failed to posit a clear distinction that was important to recent generations of converts. Theologians interested in the issue of art and the new Christian churches in Asia and Africa in the twentieth century noted that this difference was far more important to indigenous Christians than it appeared to many in the West, who were fond of insisting, as John Butler himself did, that "Christianity will never be properly rooted in [non-Western] lands till faith and art are properly integrated in them" (Butler 1956, 160). First-generation converts were more likely to ask for the pictures that the "whites" have, then watch the next generation seek to recover what their elders had abandoned, particularly in the postcolonial search for sources of national identity (Lehman 1969, 45; Morgan 2005, 170–187).

DAVID MORGAN

## Further Reading

Bailey, G. A. (1999). *Art on the Jesuit missions in Asia and Latin America, 1542–1773.* Toronto, Ontario: University of Toronto Press.

Butler, J. F. (1956, April). Christian art overseas. *Congregational Quarterly 34,* No. 2, 154–161.

Juggernaut. (1817, July). *Missionary Register,* pp. 300–309.

Lehman, A. (1969). *Christian art in Africa and Asia* (E. Hopka et al., Trans.). Saint Louis, MO: Concordia Publishing House.

Morgan, D. (2005). *The sacred gaze: Religious visual culture in theory and practice.* Berkeley: University of California Press.

Päzold, W. (1801). Auszug aus einem Berichte des herrn Missionarius Päzold an den Herrn Doctor Gaskin in London, Wepery, den 17 May, 1799. In *Neuere Geschichte der evangelischen Missions-Anstalten,* no. 57 (pp. 771–779). Halle, Germany: Verlag des Waisenhauses.

Pohle, C. (1790). Herrn Pohle Tageregister von Jahr 1786 und 1787. In J. L. Schulze (Ed.), *Neuere Geschichte der evangelischen Missions-Anstalten,* no. 36 (pp. 1342–1388). Halle, Germany: Verlag des Waisenhauses.

Pohle, C. (1806). Auszug aus Herrn Pohle Tagebuch vom Jahr 1802. In G. C. Knapp (Ed.), *Neuere Geschichte der Evangelischen Missions-Anstalten zu Bekehrung der Heiden in Ostindien,* no. 62 (pp. 205–233). Halle, Germany: Verlag des Waisenhauses.

Reinders, E. (2004). *Borrowed gods and foreign bodies: Christian missionaries imagine Chinese religion.* Berkeley: University of California Press.

Taylor, R. W. (1975). *Jesus in Indian painting.* Madras, India: Christian Literature Society.

# Media/Mass Communication

Communication is not something accidental and supplementary for human beings. We communicate because we are communicators by nature. The average person spends most of his or her active time communicating: listening, speaking, reading, writing, or watching television and movies. The interest in communication is also increasing, and almost every discipline concerned with human society and human behavior has during the last few years concerned itself with communication.

The word *communication* has, like a number of other familiar words, developed from the Latin word *communis,* which means to share, to have in common. These words point to relationships. It is thus impossible to separate the word *communication* from implications of mutual involvement and relationship, the development of commonality between peoples.

Marshall McLuhan called media "human extensions." They can extend us and our work in various ways. The microphone becomes an extension of the voice, the pencil an extension of the hand, and the camera an extension of the eye. In Christian communication, we use media to extend ourselves and our message to others. Each medium has its own possibilities and limitations and such possibilities depend on whether it functions alone or in conjunction with other media.

The important question is one of media mix, or rather, of using the right medium at the right time, and according to the inherent and obvious advantages of that particular medium or method in that particular situation. A realistic view of a medium's capabilities will, therefore, need an intercultural analysis and an appreciation of the external factors that influence its use and application in a given context.

A program created for one medium will not have the same effect when communicated through another medium. For example, a tape recording of a church service will never be able to capture the total visual communication and atmosphere evident during the service. Only the sound will be captured. If a church service is to be communicated through an audio medium, certain effects will have to be added to compensate for the loss of visual communication signals. Similarly, a so-called straight reading of the Scriptures on tape will usually not give an accurate translation. We are then faced with the challenge of a medium that, by its very nature, communicates more than the printed page indicates. On the other hand, if the printed page includes pictures or illustrations, then explanations or effects will have to be added to the audio program to compensate for such illustrations. We can never go directly from one medium to another.

## Media Definitions

It is easier to describe the media than to define media. In popular usage "the media" refers to the whole complex of broadcasting, particularly television, and its many uses. One way of classifying a medium would be to look at its use. We can then differentiate between personal media, group media, and mass media. Personal media are the media used by a single person.

Group media signify media that are used to enhance or stimulate interaction with or among a group of people. Mass media is understood as media that aim at communicating with multiple audiences at the same time. A given audience may be small, in fact it may consist of just one person, as is the case of the reader of a newspaper or the lone radio listener in his or her car on the freeway, so the receptor may not necessarily feel a mass situation. The typical mass media are radio, television, and newspapers, but we also need to include other printed matter, either addressed to individuals or distributed to all, as well as audio cassettes, CDs, videos, DVDs, and so on, which are created for mass distribution.

The primary difference between interpersonal and mass communication is, then, that the latter involves multiple audiences. Programs may be fiction or drama, or they may be live performances that communicate with audiences in real time. Each situation and use of media is relevant to Christian communication, but each kind of use also demands a different approach and provides its own unique opportunities.

Mass communication is more complicated than interpersonal communication. An organization is usually inserted into the communication chain. This organization operates around a "machine," which makes the choice of content difficult due to a lack of immediate feedback. Social demands and social controls on the mass media are louder and stronger than on an individual, since a society usually has rather definite ideas of what it wants its mass media to be and to do.

## Radio as an Example

Like other media, radio can be used for good and it can be used for evil. Radio is truly a mass medium. Everywhere people listen to radio. It is also one of the most widely used mass media in Christian work. Its advantages are many, and in the hands of those with knowledge, means, and courage, radio is a powerful and effective tool. Some of the major difficulties with the use of radio have been vaguely defined goals and purposes, and the relative lack of training of those who have used it. But radio is a flexible tool with many uses. Radio can do certain things no other medium can. For example, as long as people have a receiver, radio can reach them everywhere—even while they are engaged in doing something else. There is no screen to watch, no reading to do, no records to turn, and no other people to rely on. Radio will easily adjust to changing social and cultural conditions.

But we need to understand the nature and unique-

ness of the medium if it is to be used effectively. Radio is not like a church where listeners are sitting in rows or pews. The listener cannot read along in his or her own Bible when driving a car. Other listeners may not even know what a Bible looks like. The voice of a pulpit speaker will be dramatically different from the voice you like to listen to in your earphones or from your high-quality speakers in a cozy living room. Radio works in the mind of the listener, and he or she provides the context through his or her own imagination. This gives radio many more possibilities than most other media.

But, like all mass media, radio also has limitations. The broadcaster cannot see the audience and the immediate response of the listener, so there are difficulties with feedback. Radio comes on at a specific time, and the listener has no control over this timing.

The first missionary radio station was "The Voice of the Andes," which began broadcasting in 1931 from Ecuador. The Far East Broadcasting Company was founded in 1946, and was followed by Trans World Radio, which presently operates stations around the world. Most of the early stations broadcasted on shortwave. Today the use of shortwave is very limited. Local FM stations are used, and in countries like Indonesia local Christian organizations like YASKI are setting up FM stations. A further development is the opening of local community stations, and organizations around the world, like the Voice of Peace in Thailand, are involved in such developments. Recently, broadcasting through the Internet provides global access for even small organizations and languages.

## Television Usage

Television is all-pervasive and it brings the world into our living rooms. For most people today, television is the primary time-consumer, and in some countries the average household spends more than seven hours a day watching it. So, apart from working and sleeping, more hours are spent in front of the TV with its heroes, villains, and news stars than in school, in church, or at other organized activities.

It is obvious that the basic values communicated by television will have an effect on such an audience. It is important for all Christian leaders to be aware of the possibilities of using the medium for Christian communication, and also of the implications of using such a medium. Some notable writers, like Malcolm Muggeridge, have stated that it is next to impossible to communicate truth through television, but others have seen it as a major medium for Christian communication.

The primary limitation is one of finances, as television broadcasting is expensive.

The electronic church was basically an American phenomenon, but today we see others adopting this American format. For example, churches in Ghana, in particular Pentecostal groups, are using television extensively. A different use of television is the SAT-7 network that reaches the whole of the Middle East through satellite broadcasting, and in various Asian countries, Christian agencies are putting special programs on national television networks. Such programs are often more like documentaries and basic teaching of Christian values—for example, the Campus Crusade film *Jesus*, which is a reenactment of the life of Jesus, has been shown around the world.

Print is the oldest mass medium and has been one of the major activities of Christian organizations. The Bible is in print, and much Christian literature and training material is also in print. The big challenge today is one of declining reading habits, and the large nonreading sections of the world. Print is therefore a medium that by its very nature reaches only a section of the population, that is, those who can and do read. By and large the poor sectors of the population are outside its reach.

## Media and Local Churches

Mass media make communication possible over great distances as well as over great spans of time. Messages of the past still communicate, as we experience with a book, a cathedral, or a symphony. Two-way communication hardly seems possible here, but that is not easy with the local newspaper, either. Yet, given the right situation, such distant communications may have very powerful results. One striking example is the Bible itself.

A real challenge is to integrate the use of media with local churches. Because communication is basically relational in nature and the Christian message is one of community building, the integration of media with local churches is of the utmost importance; however, this is unfortunately not always the case, in particular for international agencies. When contact addresses are in far-away cities, it does not inspire local community and relationships. Mass communication agencies will therefore do well to develop local contacts and local involvement in both strategy design and program development.

## Media Associations

Various attempts have been made at forming global media fellowships, but this has been difficult to sustain for Evangelical groups. The ecumenical World Association of Christian Communication (WACC) is providing contact between many media groups through publications, conferences, and training programs.

Viggo B. Søgaard

## Further Reading

Fore, W. F. (1987). *Television and religion: The shaping of faith, values, and culture*. Minneapolis, MN: Augsburg.

Fuglesang, A. (1973). *Applied communications in developing countries*. Uppsala, Sweden: Dag Hammarskjold Foundation.

Jorgensen, K. (1981). The role and function of the media in the mission of the church. Unpublished doctoral dissertation, Fuller Theological Seminary, School of World Mission, Pasadena, CA.

Kraft, C. H. (1991). *Communication theory for Christian witness* (Rev. ed.). Maryknoll, NY: Orbis.

McLuhan, M. (1964). *Understanding media: The extensions of man*. New York: McGraw-Hill.

Muggeridge, M. (1977). *Christ and the media*. London: Hodder and Stoughton.

Schramm, W. (1971). *The process and effects of mass communication*. Urbana: University of Illinois Press.

Schramm, W. (1975). *Mass communications*. Urbana: University of Illinois Press.

Søgaard, V. B. (1993). *Media in church and mission*. Pasadena, CA: William Carey.

Søgaard, V. B. (2001). *Communicating scriptures: The Bible in audio and video formats*. Reading, UK: United Bible Societies.

## Medicine

Medicine has not been a topic of concern for Christian missions until the advent of medical missions. This is surprising, since the disciples were mandated to preach *and* to heal (Matthew 10:8; Luke 9:2, 10:9 NRSV) and given the fact that healing was one of the dominant features of spreading the Good News during the first centuries of the church's existence (Mark 16:20; Amundsen & Ferngren 1986, 47–52). The reason for such neglect is twofold. First, the disciples were explicitly charged not to make their living by healing (Matthew 10:8), and second, medicine had not yet become a powerful science. Instead, it was suffused with religion and virtually indistinguishable from either the cult of Asclepius or the Greco-Egyptian Serapis, which in Hellenistic times (i.e.,

300 BCE–300 CE) were extremely popular. The sick, including those beyond one's own kin, could be cared for without compromising the faith, thereby witnessing to God's unconditional love for all humankind something impressively epitomized in the parable of the Good Samaritan (Luke 10:25–34).

## Missionaries as Caregivers

Caring for the sick eventually became the hallmark of Christianity, fundamentally changing the overall societal attitude toward the sick (Sigerist 1943, 69–70), while active involvement in medicine was not on the agenda.

The fourth Lateran Council (1215) ruled that no cleric should practice medicine, especially surgery, for fear of committing unintentional homicide; later, the study of medicine was prohibited, too. However, in cases of necessity in the absence of medical help, clergy and religious leaders moved by pity and charity did whatever they could under the constraints of the limited means and skills at their disposal—as is known to have occurred among Franciscan and Jesuit missionaries in the sixteenth and seventeenth centuries.

In the age of patronage missions (1492–1622), "hospitals" were built in areas under Spanish rule, notably in Mexico, Uruguay, the Philippines, and Japan, while in the territories under Portuguese patronage charitable organizations, called *Misericórdia* societies, were established whose members vowed to care for the needy. In the eighteenth century the early Protestant mission societies such as the Danish-Halle Mission and the Herrnhut Brethren sent out professionally trained physicians to attend to the health-care needs of the missionaries suffering from tropical diseases, especially malaria, and also to treat indigenous people in case of illness.

Still, the impact of such initiatives, which remained only marginal in this period, was severely hampered by the kind of medical help that could actually be rendered. It was hardly any different from or superior to the established approaches toward healing already in place in the respective cultures (Grundmann 2005, 22–37).

## Impact of Medical Advances

This changed dramatically during the nineteenth century when medicine turned decisively away from its focus on the teachings of classical authorities like Hippocrates, Galen, and Avicenna and began to study uncompromisingly the nature of the human body and its physiology. Such an approach had begun long before, as is indicated by the anatomical drawings of Leonardo da Vinci (1452–1519) and the *Seven Books on the Structure of the Human Body* by Vesalius (1514–1564), as well as the discovery of the circulation of the blood in 1628 by William Harvey (1578–1657).

But this approach reached its climax only in the nineteenth century, when it gained significant momentum through three developments: the discovery of anesthesia (1846) and antisepsis (1847/1867), leading to the previously unimaginable rise of surgery; the detection of the importance of public hygiene and sanitation—providing safe drinking water and proper disposal of sewage—for the prevention of epidemics (1854/1859); and, last but not least, laboratory-based cellular pathology.

### Prevention and Treatment of Disease

This brought about the age of bacteriology (Rudolf Virchow, 1821–1902; Robert Koch, 1843–1910; Ronald Ross, 1857–1932) and with it the discovery of all the disease-causing pathogens of the epidemics known to date at the level of their causation—including those common in tropical countries, leading consequently and in rapid succession to the development of appropriate measures of prevention and effective treatment (Ackerknecht 1982, 145–174). Physicians were now enabled truly to heal diseases considered fatal until then.

## Medicine's Integration into Mission by Medical Missions

Coinciding with medicine's transformation from an old-fashioned, authority-bound *scientia* into a modern science, the concept of medical missions emerged. After several failed attempts it finally took definitive shape on 21 February 1836, with the foundation of the Medical Missionary Society in China at Canton (Guangzhou). This was a joint philanthropic venture by missionaries, medics, and businesspeople of different nationalities, denominations, and religions for the provision of institutional backing of hospital-based missionary physicians trained in rational-scientific medicine, enabling the gratuitous treatment of those kinds of diseases that traditional Chinese medicine was unable to handle. They hoped thereby to befriend a xenophobic people and to establish genuine mutuality (Grundmann 2005, 65–71). The enterprise thus became a means to various ends, the proclamation of the Gospel being one among others, rendering it highly suspicious in the eyes of those who were solely interested in the pursuit of straightforwardly religious goals.

**239**

An undeveloped water source. Mission work has come to involve public health and sanitation practices as well. *Courtesy of istockphoto.com.*

As medicine became more and more powerful, an ever-increasing number of pious physicians were determined to serve as missionaries. They yearned for "the evangelization of the World in this generation" in the wake of the Evangelical revival inspired by Dwight L. Moody (1837–1899), and medical missions became "the heavy artillery of the missionary army" (Walls 1982, 290). It was deemed so essential that by the end of the nineteenth century it was held that no mission could "be considered fully equipped that has not its medical branch" (*Report* 1900, Vol. II, 199).

### Medical Missions Not Universal

While these statements suggest that medical missions were being universally recognized, the reality was different. Only a fraction of the Protestant missionary societies (26 percent) were engaged in medical missions, and medical missionaries, both male and female, foreign and indigenous, represented just 5 percent of the missionary personnel overall (Dennis 1902, 264; Grundmann 2005, 150, 159). The figures have continued to dwindle ever since they reached their zenith in 1923 (Beach and Fahs 1925).

What can reasonably be said, however, is that by the turn of the twentieth century, medicine had become a topic of real concern for Protestant missions, albeit a controversial one, while—with the exception of a remarkable initiative by Cardinal Lavigerie on the island of Malta from 1881 to 1896 (Grundmann 2005, 121–124)—Roman Catholicism, bound by canon law,

was remarkably hesitant to embrace it. This, however, changed dramatically once the Society of Catholic Medical Missionaries (Medical Mission Sisters, SCMM) was founded by Anna Dengel, MD, in 1925 in Washington DC, and the official church altered its approach to the study and practice of medicine by religious in 1936 (Dengel 1945, 8–29).

## Toward Primary Health Care (PHC)

The latter half of the twentieth century saw significant changes in the once-so-innocent attitude toward medicine within the circles of medical missions. This was mainly caused by further advancements in medical science (expensive high-tech and intensive-care medicine necessitating more adequate facilities and establishing a corresponding medical model), by developments on the national and international level (World Health Organization, WHO, 1948; formation of national departments/ministries of health), and by the emergence of indigenous "young churches" with minimal financial resources.

All of this prompted a reevaluation of the church's ministry of healing and led to the creation of the Christian Medical Commission (CMC) by the World Council of Churches in 1968, an "outspoken ecumenical" venture having Roman Catholic representation on its staff (van der Bent 1986, 303) and charged "with responsibility to promote the national coordination of church-related medical programs and to engage in study and research into the most appropriate ways by which the churches might express their concern for ... health care" (McGilvray 1981, 41).

### Need to Reset Priorities

Medicine and the task of medical missionaries were now seen in a much broader context than before. Christian medical work could no longer remain content with just benefiting individuals and running costly hospitals. In the emergent competition with private and government hospitals, priorities had to be set for investing the scarce resources at hand, priorities that were to be critically informed by the Gospel. These were identified as bringing about life in abundance (John 10:10) and justice (shalom) by focusing on the commonly neglected diseases of the poor; i.e., the masses suffering from preventable diseases. This meant, practically speaking, providing sanitation and safe drinking water; caring for pregnant women; training traditional midwives in safe methods of delivery; and securing sufficient, nutritious foods and a basic generic drug supply for the most common diseases.

In concentrating on primary health care (PHC) with a focus on enabling the health-care potential of local communities, medical missions turned away from the hospital-centered medical work and became engaged in a program so effective that the WHO adopted it as official policy in 1978 (Declaration of Alma Ata; McGilvray 1981, 70–80). PHC also holds great potential for successfully coping with the HIV/AIDS pandemic.

## Pertinent Challenges

Medical missions pose vital challenges, both to missiology and to medicine, challenges that call for an ongoing conversation, thereby keeping the quest for authentic Christian mission alive.

First, medical missions remind the church that her own recovery of the ministry of healing cannot be pursued to the exclusion of medicine but that medicine has to be gratefully acknowledged as a gift to humankind.

Second, medical missions challenge the long-held conviction that the soul is more precious than the body, a conviction chastised by one deeply immersed in the Evangelical revival of the nineteenth century, himself a physician: "To merely talk piously and tell suffering people of a future state, while neglecting to relieve their present needs, when in our power to do so, must be nauseating both to God and man, and certainly is a libel upon the Christianity Christ both taught and practiced, in which He combined care for the whole being of man, body and soul" (Dowkontt 1897, 24). At the root of too

spiritual a concept of mission and too material a concept of health lies a misconceived biblical anthropology, one profoundly distorting the church's witness to God incarnate in Christ.

Third, through the skillful use of medicine for the sake of bringing about life and preventing untimely death, medical missions are witnesses to the corporeality of salvation and to the proper use of knowledge, skills, and funds for the benefit of all, thereby critiquing other ways of doing medicine.

CHRISTOFFER H. GRUNDMANN

### Further Reading

Ackerknecht, E. H. (1982). *A short history of medicine* (2nd ed.). Baltimore: Johns Hopkins University Press.

Amundsen, D. W. & Ferngren, G. B. (1986). The early Christian tradition. In D. W. Amundsen & R. L. Numbers (Eds.), *Caring and curing—Health and medicine in the Western religious traditions* (pp. 40–64). New York and London: Macmillan Publishing Company.

Balme, H. (1921). *China and modern medicine—A study in medical missionary development.* London: United Council for Missionary Education.

Beach, H. P., & Fahs, C. H. (Eds.). (1925). *World missionary atlas—Containing a directory of missionary societies, classified summaries of statistics, maps showing the location of mission stations throughout the world, a descriptive account of the principal mission lands, and comprehensive indices.* Edinburgh, UK: Edinburgh House Press.

Browne, S. G. (Ed.). (1985). *Heralds of health—The saga of Christian medical initiatives.* London: Christian Medical Fellowship.

Dengel, A., MD. (1945). *Mission for samaritans.* Milwaukee, WI: Bruce Publishing Company.

Dennis, J. S. (1902). *Centennial survey of foreign missions—A statistical supplement to "Christian missions and social progress," being a conspectus of the achievements and results of Evangelical missions in all lands at the close of the nineteenth century.* New York, Chicago, and Toronto: Fleming H. Revell.

Dowkontt, G. D. (1897). *Murdered millions* (5th ed.). New York: Medical Missionary Record.

Ewert, D. M. (1990). *A new agenda for medical missions.* Brunswick, GA: MAP International.

Grundmann, C. H. (1991). The contribution of medical missions: The intercultural transfer of standards and values. *Academic Medicine, 66,* 12, 731–733.

Grundmann, C. H. (2005). *Sent to heal!—Emergence and development of medical missions.* Lanham, MD: University Press of America.

McGilvray, J. C. (1981). *The quest for health and wholeness.* Tübingen: German Institute for Medical Missions.

*Report of the ecumenical missionary conference on foreign missions, held in Carnegie Hall and neighboring churches, April 21 to May 1, 1900* (Vols. 1–2). (1900). New York: American Tract Society.

Sigerist, H. E. (1943). *Civilization and disease.* College Park, MD: McGrath Pub. Co.

van der Bent, J. (1986). *Vital ecumenical concerns.* Geneva, Switzerland: World Council of Churches.

Walls, A. F. (1982). "The heavy artillery of the missionary army": The domestic importance of the nineteenth-century medical missionary. In W. J. Sheils (Ed.), *The church and healing* (pp. 287–297). Oxford, UK: Blackwell.

# Middle East

Reflecting on mission in relation to the Middle East requires understanding missions both *from* as well as *to* the Middle East. The Middle East is understood here to be the region bordered by Turkey and Armenia in the north, Yemen in the south, Iran in the east, and Morocco in the west. The eastern Mediterranean is usually referred to as the Mashriq, while North Africa is known as the Maghreb.

## Missions from the Middle East

Global Christian mission originated in the Middle East and was at first directed primarily to the Middle East: At the first Pentecost, described in Acts 2: 9–11, it is notable that apart from Romans and Cretans all the other peoples mentioned are from the Middle East. Although Christianity is perceived to have moved northwards and westwards (Rome/Constantinople, Kiev/Moscow, Wittenberg/Geneva) before in contemporary times spreading globally, Christianity never left the Middle East, and the church there has continually engaged in mission in various forms over the last two thousand years.

In the early centuries of the church, Christianity grew into the Roman Empire's heartlands via Anatolia (and beyond: Armenia made Christianity its official religion at the end of the third century), but even by the time of Constantine's conversion, four of the five Patriarchs were still in the Middle East itself (Jerusalem, Antioch, Alexandria, Constantinople), with the remaining fifth Patriarch being in Rome. This is of significance in relation to missions and the Middle East in that the subsequent ecumenical councils that tried to resolve divergent theological understandings of the divine and human natures of Jesus Christ—Ephesus 431, Chalcedon 451, and Constantinople 533—led to the creation of a number of Middle Eastern churches, especially the Assyrian Church (or Church of the East, or East Syrian, sometimes incorrectly called "Nestorians") with its center at Seleucia–Ctesiphon in Persia, and the Syrian Orthodox and Coptic churches. This furthered the divide between the Western Rome–oriented church and the Eastern Byzantium–oriented church, a divide cemented in 1054 with Rome's papal bull directed at the Constantinople Patriarch, reciprocated shortly thereafter by an equivalent excommunication directed at Rome. Attempts at reconciliation, such as the Council of Florence 1438–1439, did not meet with success.

Mission work deriving from the Eastern churches is perhaps most notable in terms of the efforts of the Assyrian Church, which from the sixth century onwards engaged in missionary work well beyond Persia, into India and by the seventh century had reached China. Western churches were largely unaware of this until Jesuits arrived in China in the sixteenth and seventeenth centuries to engage in mission work and discovered Christianity had been brought there before them. The foundation of this mission was trade: Persian Christian traders would establish a trading post, and the monks followed as missionaries and established an ecclesial hierarchy among the converts. A pillar almost three meters tall in Xian (Shaanxi province, in the heart of China) from 781 CE has both Chinese and Syriac inscriptions, clearly indicating a Middle Eastern presence; in 638 CE the Emperor Tai–Tsung had even recommended the Chinese adopt Christianity in the form in which it had been communicated to the Chinese by the Assyrian missionaries. This openness to missionary activity from the Assyrians continued until 845 CE when imperial religious policy changed and strict adherence to Confucianism was demanded, and by the eleventh and twelfth centuries Christianity had all but died out in China. The spread of the Eastern churches occurred not only by direct missionary work: it was often determined by the religious affiliation of rulers (for example, in 989 CE Vladimir of Kiev was baptized, thereby bringing what was later to become Russia into the Byzantine rite).

Whilst the Syrian Orthodox and Coptic churches did not engage in missionary activity of such geographical reach as the Assyrian Church, there was also expansion: By the twelfth century the Syrian Orthodox Patriarch oversaw twenty Metropolitans with about one-hundred bishops in Syria, Asia Minor, and Cyprus in the west, and in the east, a vice-patriarch oversaw a further eighteen bishops; there were also a number of monasteries in Egypt. Two of the greatest Orthodox missionaries of this era are perhaps the brothers Methodius (815–885 CE) and Cyril (826–869 CE), who initiated the Christianization of the Balkans, primarily through the provision of biblical and liturgical material in Slavic languages (the Cyrillic script is named after Cyril, an indicator of his influence). It is worth noting that this flourishing was under the jurisdiction and protection of Muslim rulers.

Although Islam frequently provided a safe context for the churches, it is also undoubtedly the case that the advent of a strong religious contestant in the form of Islam represented the most significant religious competition for the Eastern churches. From the hijra in 622 CE to the fall of the Mamluks in 1517, Islam gradually advanced throughout the Middle East, North Africa and parts of southern Europe (Spain in the west, the Balkans in the east), primarily through conversion (the theological disputes and divided nature of the churches proved fertile ground for the transfer of religious allegiances) and marriage (children with a Muslim parent had to be Muslim). North Africa abandoned Christianity altogether, with the Muslim conquest of parts of Latin Spain heralding the conversion of the last of the Christian communities of the Maghreb. This expansion of Islam meant that the position of the churches with regard to mission changed. Islam as practiced by the Prophet Muhammad's successors codified confessional affiliations, and although opportunistic conversions to Islam did take place, the core groupings of diverse religious communities were mostly able to survive in relative security in this context. Christians (and other minorities, including Jews and Zoroastrians) suffered a certain level of discrimination and sometimes outright persecution (the Crusades represented a particularly problematic time for local Christians, as they were at times closely associated with the Western Christian invaders; for example, in Baghdad, Christians were for a while compelled to wear distinctive clothing). However, in many areas Christians were the most highly educated of the local population, and this often helped them integrate to a certain extent into the new power structures. Because proselytism of Muslims was not permitted, the primary focus of the churches became their own preservation in a context in which the majority faith was Islam; such attempts at disputing faith positions as there were tended to be at an academic level, and foundered on the basic principles of the doctrine of the Trinity and the unity of the divine, or on the understanding of the place of Muhammad (some

Muslim theologians saw Muhammad as the Paraclete announced by Jesus, whereas Christians tended to regard him more as the AntiChrist who would lead people astray). Conversions to Christianity were few and far between, and with the churches' energies being directed more towards maintaining and consolidating their status than in seeking widespread conversion, their relationship to the new Western missionaries of the nineteenth century were marked by complications and misunderstandings, as the Eastern churches were accused of having "lost" their central missionary purpose.

The accusation by Western missionaries that the Eastern churches had lost their missionary purpose stems most obviously from a different use of language and variant understandings of the purpose of the church. In general, it can be said that the purpose or mission of the church in, for example, the Orthodox tradition, is not centered on individualistic and spiritualistic soteriology, but rather on the Eucharistic liturgy and the church itself. The church has its home in heaven but is sent out into the world as its salvation. Rather than being primarily a "religious organization" offering "religion" to humanity, the church seeks to redeem the whole life of individuals and thereby the life of the world, giving meaning to Jesus' concept of the kingdom of heaven being near and yet also being already present. This goes some way towards explaining the church's active participation in and identification with national and cultural entities: the church is seeking to sanctify the material world, thereby bringing it under God. Personal and individual salvation as understood by Western missionaries, particularly Protestants, bears little relation to such an approach, which is one of the main reasons why nineteenth-century Western missionaries had such difficulty relating to the churches they encountered in the Middle East. Missions to the Middle East have, however, led the Eastern churches to define more closely their understanding of mission.

## Missions to the Middle East

Western missions to the Middle East have taken various forms. Helena, the mother of Constantine, established pilgrimages to sites supposedly connected to the biblical narrative, and this led to a continuing movement of individuals from west to east. There have been repeated attempts to bring the Eastern churches under the influence of the Catholic Church based in Rome—for example, in 1181 there were concerted efforts to bring the

Maronites into the Catholic fold, and following a visit of Francis of Assisi to Palestine in 1219, the first Franciscan order in the Middle East was created in 1332. Although in 1523 the Franciscans had to vacate their premises and sought refuge with Georgian monks, they maintained and gradually strengthened their position in Palestine, with various elements of Assyrian and other communities accepting the direction of the Roman church. This was clearly mission, albeit directed towards other Christian communities.

In terms of individuals engaged in mission, the most prominent individual of this era was undoubtedly Raymond (or Ramon) Llull (or Lull) (c. 1235–1315), a philosopher and scholar who learned Arabic in order to engage in missionary work in the Maghreb. In 1265 he experienced a religious awakening and eventually became a Franciscan. Particularly in his later work (he wrote over 260 books and pamphlets in Latin, Catalan and Arabic, including works on philosophy, theology, literature, novels and more), he was concerned to address the reform of the church in order to refocus its attention on the conversion of "infidels" (to use his language). He traveled to Tunis to pursue missionary work amongst Muslims, Jews. and other non-Christians. Two further trips to North Africa took place, the latter partly on behalf of the Pope, who wanted him to explore the possibility of a new crusade; Llull's recommendation on his return in 1408 was that prayer should be the means of conquest. Llull spent considerable time studying Islam, and his extensive writings represent one of the first detailed theological reflections on the Christian encounter with Islam. His work has influenced many missionaries over the centuries, including Samuel Zwemer, who wrote a biography of Llull.

Beyond this, the aftermath of the Crusades saw very little involvement from the West. Franciscans maintained their presence in Palestine, but it was to be the seventeenth century before Catholic missions returned to the Middle East: Capuchins arrived in Syria in 1625 and later went on to Lebanon and Iraq, while around the same time Jesuits went to Istanbul, Syria, Beirut and Cairo, and Carmelites arrived in Aleppo. In 1750 Dominicans created a mission in Mosul and once the Jesuits' order had been dissolved, the Lazarists took over their mission (1773). The primary tool was education: schools were created and influence sought. Local reactions varied: for example, Maronites in Lebanon gradually moved closer to the Catholics (eventually joining the Catholic church in 1736), while the Coptic Church sought to make use of the influence of the local Muslim rulers in its attempts to stifle foreign missionary work,

before creating its own network of schools to counteract Western influence more directly.

### Ottoman Empire

The Ottoman Empire dominated much of the context for missions in the Middle East in this period. The growth of the Ottoman Empire stemmed not just from a desire for material gain, but in part from the tradition of *ghaza*, war against non-Muslims in order to increase the reach of Islam. The empire can be traced to a thirteenth-century Anatolian tribal warrior, Osman, and his son Orhon; by the fourteenth century the area controlled by Osman's successors had grown to the Sea of Marmara—Europe's southeastern boundary. Within two more centuries, a huge expanse of territory belonged to the Empire, from southeastern Europe in the north, and the Arab heartlands in the south. The year 1453 saw the taking of Constantinople by Sultan Mehmet II and the end of Byzantium as the symbolic centre of Eastern Christianity. With the creation of a modern navy and regular army, the Ottoman Empire became the most powerful force in the eastern Mediterranean and the Black Sea, easily displacing the hitherto dominant Venetians. Ottoman rule of its territories was decentralized: regions were obliged to pay taxes and supply the resources, military and other needs of the state, but existing societal structures remained largely intact. The codification of religious communities was further defined (they were known as millets, or nations), with movement from one millet to another virtually impossible (naturally, proselytism of Muslims remained forbidden). This then, represented the context for Western engagement in the Middle East from about the sixteenth to the early twentieth century.

### The Role of Western Churches

Western churches' efforts in the Middle East had to relate to this situation. In part this happened through national geopolitical interests: the Republic of Venice agreed a treaty with the empire which included the so-called protection of Franciscans in the empire's domains; this and similar treaties were known as the Capitulations (named after the capita or chapters by which they were structured). France followed with a similar treaty in 1535, seeking to "protect" Catholics in general in the empire, and followed this with several further agreements, so that by the middle of the eighteenth century France was regarded by Rome and most of the European powers as the protector of Ottoman Christians in general, and Catholics in particular. These treaties became ever more directed to trade and political intervention, so that "protection" rapidly became a somewhat loaded term. Russian attempts to secure capitulation agreements overseeing the Empire's Orthodox citizens were hampered by Western intervention (Western powers were concerned to limit Russian political influence in the region), until agreement was finally reached in 1878 for Russia to be granted limited rights. These agreements facilitated the efforts of Western missionaries. The British had no Christian communities they could relate to and, therefore, in a move determined as much by geostrategic concern as religious motivation, claimed the right to "protect" Jews in the Empire. This ensured a political foothold, but also helped foster widespread missionary activity among Jews, particularly in the Mashriq. Although the capitulatory agreements greatly facilitated missionary work in the Middle East, it is important to remember that the European states blatantly used the minority communities of the region in their attempts to secure control over the eastern Mediterranean and the crumbling Ottoman Empire.

Protestant missionaries from the U.S. Congregational Church's American Board for Foreign Missions arrived in the region in 1821; others rapidly followed. Within the Ottoman Empire, Turkey, Syria, Beirut, Palestine, and Egypt in particular received a great deal of attention; beyond this, missionaries were also active in Armenia, Persia, and in the Maghreb. Missionaries came from most of the Protestant denominations and from many countries, though Germany, Britain, and the United States featured particularly strongly. They tended to concentrate primarily on schools and medical work, since direct proselytism was either forbidden (Muslims) or almost completely unsuccessful (Jews)—in fact, most of the Protestant communities recruited their membership from amongst the Christian churches already in the region, a fact that has marred relationships between some of the Eastern and Western churches to this day. In the course of providing education and medicine, Western models of modernization were also communicated, and significant numbers of Christians, especially in the Mashriq, became prominent international traders and cultural intermediaries. Perhaps the most significant missionary of this era was Samuel Marinus Zwemer (1867–1952), not because of the number of converts from Islam that his work resulted in—there were very few—but because of his lifelong study of Islam and his theological reflections about how Christianity and Islam should relate to one another. Working in Egypt and Arabia from 1890 to 1929, Zwemer systematized thinking around the finality of Christianity over against Islam (sometimes described as "fulfilment theology"), but did so with a deep understanding and respect for Islam that many of his fellow missionaries failed to develop. He wrote numerous books about the need for Christianity to relate appropriately to Islam (perhaps most famously *The Reproach of Islam*—the reproach being to Christians who did not engage appropriately with Muslims), and fostered the study of Islam in the West: He taught in the United States for many years after retiring from the mission field, but also traveled widely and was a driving force behind several major conferences on missions to Muslims.

Although there were (and are) relatively few Jews in the Middle East, missions to the Jews in the region deserve a particular mention. Many Western Christians, especially from the nineteenth century onward, accorded Jews a special role in their understanding of the world and the divine, and this led to concerted efforts at conversion, particularly in Palestine, which many saw as the ancient home of Jews. Although some missionaries were aware of the gross injustices that the implementation of Zionism would entail, this theological understanding made many missionaries and their supporters keen advocates of Zionism. Even after it became clear to most missionaries in Palestine that Zionism was clearly detrimental to many of the Christian communities that they were involved with, Western churches and missionary organizations often spoke out in support of Zionist aims. After World War II, the creation of the State of Israel, and reflection on the context and background to the Holocaust, efforts were made to respect and relate to Jews as Jews rather than as targets for conversion. Now such mission work is scorned by virtually all of the mainstream Western churches, though there is reason to be concerned at some of the more Fundamentalist communities, particularly in the United States., that appear to be advocating and even engaging in such work. In Israel, attempts to convert Jews are not welcomed, though the unquestioning political support offered to Israel by some of these groups means that they are generally allowed to remain in the country.

Elsewhere in the Middle East, the independence of many former colonial or dependent territories after World Wars I and II has reduced the possibilities for missionary activity. Turkey under Kemal Ataturk took on an avowedly secular nature, while Islam remained the dominant faith; Western missionaries seeking to proselytize were not welcome. In Lebanon, the only Middle Eastern state with a sizeable, though shrinking, Christian population, the primary focus of the churches is the maintenance of their considerable political and social status; conversion of others is not a priority, and indeed, engaging in proselytism would destabilize the fragile sectarian arrangements that dominate the country. All other states in the Middle East either identify themselves as Muslim or view Islam as the dominant religious tradition. Mission work, particularly from Western missionaries to whom suspicions of political motivation are all too easily attached, is generally frowned upon if not expressly forbidden. The 2003 U.S. invasion of Iraq was accompanied by news reports that some Fundamentalist groups in the United States were seeking to engage in proselytism of Muslims in newly conquered Iraq; given the difficulties that already exist between the constituent communities of Iraq, it is undoubtedly a positive sign that such work appears to have been stifled by the U.S. government.

Mission in the Middle East is now understood to be less about conversion and more about "presence and witness," as the Middle East Council of Churches—a regional grouping of the World Council of Churches to which most of the Eastern churches belong—has put it. The number of Christians in the region is diminishing due to widespread emigration as job prospects (and in some instances safety) appear better overseas. This means that the churches are focused on what they see as their mission of keeping the Christian faith alive in the region of its birth that is now dominated by Islam (or in Israel by Judaism). That there are often difficult political ramifications to maintaining their "presence and witness" makes the situation more complex, and support from the global church is therefore often appreciated, provided it respects the desire of the local churches to interpret their mission in their own terms.

MICHAEL MARTEN

### Further Reading

Marten, M. (2005). Anglican and Presbyterian presence and theology in the Holy Land. *The International Journal for the Study of the Christian Church, 5*(3) 182–199.

O'Mahony, A. (Ed.). (2007). *Christianity and Jerusalem: Theology and politics in the Holy Land.* London: Gracewing Publishers.

Wilson, J. C. (1952). *Apostle to Islam: A biography of Samuel M. Zwemer.* Grand Rapids, MI: Baker Book House.

Zwemer, S. (1902) *Raymond Lull: First missionary to the Moslems.* New York: Funk and Wagnall

# Militarism

All sovereign states have a military presence to defend their territory and their interests, but on the government of empires military personnel and ideals have a higher level of influence. When military ideals and priorities dominate national identity, "militarism" has gained ascendancy.

From its earliest days Christian mission has had an ambivalent relationship with militarism. Jesus was executed by the Roman military that occupied Palestine, yet the Gospels portray the Roman governor as a reluctant executioner. Paul and other early Christian missionaries relied on the infrastructure of the Roman Empire to travel throughout the Mediterranean region, and they appealed to Roman justice when they were persecuted by their opponents. Paul was rescued from a mob in Jerusalem by Roman troops and was escorted to safety in Caesarea by these soldiers when a plot against his life was discovered. Ultimately, however, Roman soldiers guarded him in prison until the empire executed him.

In the first three centuries the church was pacifist. The power of militarism was used against the church by the empire. When Paul and other Christian authors used military images in their writing they stressed that the battles they were describing were not of this world, and that the kingdom of God that they were proclaiming would not be established by "might or by power."

In the centuries in which the church and civil society became nearly coterminous in Europe, much missionary activity on the frontiers of that society did not rely on and was not supported directly by militarism. Yet missionaries and church leaders (such as, for example, Winfrid-St. Boniface in Germany and Friesland) gained access to new populations when Christian rulers expanded their areas of military supremacy.

There are three major eras of Christian history in which militarism was a significant factor in Christian mission.

## Crusades

The Crusades (1095–1270) were not a missionary enterprise. Their goal was to reclaim Christian "holy places" from the control of their Muslim rulers, not to convert Muslims to the Christian faith. Fortresses and temporary residential communities of Christians were established by the European Crusaders. They had ambivalent relationships with the existing Christian states and communities in the region, sometimes engaging them in warfare, sometimes supporting and strengthening them. Crusaders did not engage in evangelism or service among local non-Christian populations, but instead, attempted to destroy or subjugate them.

In the following centuries, in the Iberian Peninsula, Christian kingdoms in the north embodied the crusading spirit as they forced the Muslims south to Grenada. From the 1470s to the 1490s, under Isabella and Ferdinand, Muslims and Jews were expelled from their remaining enclaves in the south. A long-term unintended consequence of this extraordinary era of Christian militarism has been a strong antipathy between Christians and Muslims that has hindered Christian mission to this day. Another consequence was the use of the term "crusade" to designate Christian missionary and evangelistic mass campaigns until late in the twentieth century, when this terminology was recognized as problematic and largely abandoned.

## Colonial Era

The colonial era of Christian European expansion, from the end of the fifteenth century to the mid-twentieth century, combined mission and militarism. Kings, queens, bishops, popes, adventurers, traders, bankers, soldiers, and ship captains expressed their intention to find gold, spices, and Christians. In the western hemisphere the confrontations between Europeans and regional rulers was often framed as a battle of gods. The military conquests by Spain and Portugal were interpreted as a triumph of the Christian god. Lands and people were claimed and conquered in the name of God and king or queen. Franciscan or Dominican missionaries usually accompanied the soldiers. Mission and militarism were inseparable.

This relationship was complex. Christopher Columbus, for example, expressed the opinion that even though the newly conquered territories were justly subject to the Church and the Spanish sovereign, the Christian religion should be spread in a peaceful manner that did not cause harm to the indigenous people. He also, however, upheld the right of the Spaniards to intervene with force if local converts were induced to leave the Christian faith.

European domination of the Americas was usually first established by military power and then extended to all areas of life. In Spanish and Portuguese territories this domination soon became oppressive. The dissenting voices that expressed concern for the indigenous people and protested the actions of the conquerors came mostly from the missionary orders. Foremost among these voices was the Dominican, Bartolomé de Las Casas (1474–1566).

## Protestant Era

Protestant mission activity was prominent in the nineteenth and twentieth centuries, primarily in Africa and Asia. Critics of that movement have characterized it as "the Bible in one hand and a gun in the other." That is an oversimplification. The British East India Company, for example, refused to permit missionaries in most of its territories until forced to do so by an Act of Parliament in 1813. But as the missionary movement grew and British territorial authority expanded, missionary personnel and programs received substantial implicit and explicit support from the colonial authority. In the mid-twentieth century, when missionaries were endangered and expelled from some countries as colonial authority ended, they were often protected and escorted to safety by a foreign military power. However, it is important to recall that throughout the colonial era many missionaries carried out their ministries without the protection of military power, and a significant number experienced deprivation, persecution, and death.

The ambivalent relationship between Christian mission and militarism continues to the present. In most of the Muslim world the Christian cross is interpreted as a symbol of Crusader military intervention and domination. In other cultures Christian mission is portrayed as the imposition of a foreign way of life on indigenous patterns. The two World Wars, the Holocaust, and the use of the atomic bombs symbolize the moral failure of the Gospel of peace, reconciliation, and forgiveness. Within Christianity there has been widespread acceptance of the separation of church and state and a profound rethinking of just-war theory. The theology of liberation has identified the God of Jesus as the God of the victim and the oppressed. Much local and global mission in the early years of the twenty-first century is being conducted in relative powerlessness by Christians from poor communities without access to the privileges of military power.

JAMES N. PANKRATZ

*See also* Christendom; Colonialism; Conquest; Crusades; Islam; Revolution

## Further Reading

Goodpasture, H. M. (Ed.). (1989). *Cross and sword: An eyewitness history of Christianity in Latin America.* Maryknoll, NY: Orbis.

Gutierrez, G. (1993). *Las casas: In search of the poor of Jesus Christ.* (Robert R. Barr, Trans.). Maryknoll, NY: Orbis.

Johnstone, A. (2003). *Missionary writing and empire.* Cambridge, UK: Cambridge University Press.

Stanley, B. (1990). *Bible and the flag: Protestant missions and British imperialism in the nineteenth and twentieth centuries.* Leicester, UK: Apollos.

# Millennialism and Adventism

The eschatological vision of the return of Christ, resurrection of the saints, judgment and eternal life based upon the promises of Christ, and New Testament witness are incorporated in both the Apostles' and Nicene Creeds as a fundamental article of the Christian faith. When the prophecy of Revelation 20:1–10 was wedded by the early church to this prior belief in Christ's personal return, the concept of a millennial rule of Christ was a natural result.

## Types of Millennialism

Prophecies relating to the millennium have been interpreted in several different ways, with the result that the concept, which at base is straightforward, has become enormously complex. Three major understandings of the millennium have been advanced: premillennialism, postmillennialism, and amillennialism. Millennial views shaping concepts of eschatology, sublimated at times but repeatedly revived, have been a powerful influence in the life and mission of the church, especially so during the last two centuries in America.

### Premillennialism

Premillennialism signifies that Christ's return precedes the millennium. Nondispensational premillennialism is usually based upon a fairly literal historicist hermeneutic; i.e., the details of prophecy relate to events covering the broad course of human history. In this view it is generally held that signs such as the worldwide preaching of the Gospel, wars, famines, and calamitous days of apostasy and evil will precede the Second Coming. Believers will be resurrected at the Advent and will reign with Christ for a thousand years, during which evil will be suppressed. Events marking the close of the millennium include the release of the devil, the resurrection of the wicked, and a final rebellion. The judgment of the "great white throne" will then take place, and the devil and the wicked will be cast into the lake of fire. The saints will then be gathered together in the eternal happiness of the "new heaven and new earth" (Revelation 21:1–3 [NRSV]).

One of the distinguishing marks of historic premillennialism is its teaching regarding the above two resurrections—one at the beginning, the other at the close of the millennium.

### Postmillennialism

In this view the Second Coming will follow the millennium; no great eschatological events separate the present from the millennium. This is an eschatology shaped by a worldview in which the church prepares the way for the great last-day events. Evil will diminish as commitment to Christianity increases and the church exercises greater social and political influence, leading to a heightened morality. A broad spiritual revival is expected to usher in the "golden age" of the reign of Christ in world history. The millennium will be brought to an end by the Second Advent, accompanied by the resurrection, the judgment, and the final overthrow of evil.

In this view, which builds on the Great Awakenings and the optimism of the Enlightenment, there is a sense of continuity between the present age and the millennium. Jonathan Edwards is generally regarded as the father of postmillennialism in America, and this vision inspired the great American missionary outreach movements of the late eighteenth and early nineteenth centuries.

### Amillennialism

Strictly speaking, those endorsing this view are not millennialists, for they deny that there will be a literal thousand-year epoch of the rule of Christ. Revelation 20 is held to be a figurative description of the rule of Christ through the church and not a designated period before or after the Second Advent. The resurrection portrayed in Revelation 20:4–6 is interpreted as a spiritual awakening and the millennium as the age of the church. Augustine is generally regarded as the father of amillennialism. This interpretation largely informed the eschatology of the medieval church and lives on in various forms.

### Dispensationalism

Dispensationalism is a form of premillennialism based upon a *futurist* interpretation of prophecy that coalesces the predictions of prophecy into a relatively short period preceding the Second Advent. The underlying concept of dispensationalism is that God works with human beings in distinct ways in a series of eras or dispensations. Israel is given a special place in this scheme of salvation history, and it is expected that the church will be secretly raptured from earth seven years before the Advent.

## The Rise of Adventism

Several apocalyptic groups arose or were revitalized during the Second Great Awakening (1796–1840). Among these were the Shakers, the Oneida Community, the Mormons, the Adventists led by William Miller (1782–1849), and the Jehovah's Witnesses. With an interest aroused by the "millennial fever" of the time, Miller set out to study the prophecies for himself. He rejected the postmillennialism of the time and applied a literalistic historicist interpretation to the prophecies of Daniel and Revelation. He interpreted the twenty-three-hundred-day prophecy of Daniel 8:14, which formed the pinnacle of his exposition, as indicating the Second Advent would occur in 1843–1844. His calm expositions and graphic charts attracted a large following, including a number of prominent clergymen, and his interpretation became the most public millennial movement of the time. After the "Great Disappointment" of October 1844, the movement broke into several smaller groups still expectantly awaiting the Advent.

One of these groups developed into the Seventh-day Adventist Church. They affirmed belief in the imminent return of Christ, reinterpreted 1844 as an event that transpired in heaven rather than on earth, and accepted the seventh-day Sabbath introduced to them by Seventh Day Baptists.

## Seventh-day Adventist Missions

This new denomination endorsed a nondispensationalist premillennialism and was ardently evangelistic. As the church spread across the United States, it gained members among European immigrants, who in turn bore witness to family and friends back home. As a result, J. N. Andrews was sent to Switzerland in 1874. This marked the beginning of a worldwide work.

### Exploring Opportunities for Expansion

After the mid-1880s there was frequent discussion regarding missions at church conferences, accompanied by appeals for support. Church papers carried announcements of new openings and appointees and gave encouraging reports of progress. Not infrequently phrases such as "God's last mission of mercy to the world," which indicate the apocalyptic enthusiasm of the movement, appear in these messages. In 1889 S. N. Haskell embarked on a world expedition to explore missionary opportunities and published enthusiastic reports in the *Youth's Instructor*.

A broad missionary approach was employed using schools, which probably became the greatest instrument of mission; personal and public evangelism; medical missions; and the distribution of literature. Government grants-in-aid for schools and medical work were accepted in many colonial areas, and as a literate population evolved publishing houses were established. The development of the church in "homeland countries," which functioned as missionary bases for work in contiguous and/or colonially connected areas, was encouraged.

The rapid spread of the church and establishment of mission institutions around the world created the need for increasing numbers of missionary workers. This encouraged the development of a network of colleges and medical institutions in the "homelands." Battle Creek College was moved to Berrien Springs (1901) and renamed Emmanuel Missionary College (now Andrews University); the college in Washington DC was reorganized as the Washington Foreign Missionary Seminary (1905) (now Columbia Union College); and the College of Medical Evangelists (now Loma Linda University) was established at Loma Linda (1909). Missions were established in Argentina, Jamaica, India, Japan, and Egypt during the 1890s, and by 1910 there were Adventist missions in many countries. There has been a slow transition over the years from an urgently apocalyptic eschatology to a serious "work and wait" and "between the times" orientation that places emphasis on the unfinished task but leaves the timing to God.

The Adventist church, which counts membership on a "believers church" basis, had seventy-six-thousand members in 1900, the majority of whom were in North America. It has now grown into a world community of 15 million with a presence in 204 of the world's 230 countries. Accessions are about one million per annum.

RUSSELL STAPLES

## Further Reading

Clouse, R. G., Hosack, R. N., & Pierard, R. V. (1999). *The new millennium manual: A once and future guide*. Grand Rapids, MI: Baker Books.

Greenleaf, F. (2005). *In passion for the world: A history of Seventh-day Adventist education.* Nampa, ID: Pacific Press Publishing Association.

Knight, G. R. (1993). *Millennial fever and the end of the world: A comprehensive survey of Millerism and America's fascination with the millennium in the nineteenth century.* Nampa, ID: Pacific Press Publishing Association.

Land, G. (Ed.). (1986). *Adventism in America: A history.* Grand Rapids, MI: William B. Eerdmans Publishing Co.

Landes, R. A. (2000). *Encyclopedia of millennialism and millennial movements.* New York: Routledge Publishing Co.

McGinn, B., Collins, J. J., & Stein, S. J. (Eds.). (2003). *The continuum history of apocalypticism.* New York: Continuum International Publishing Group Inc.

Reid, G. W., & Dederen, R. (Eds.) (2000). *Handbook of Seventh-day Adventist theology.* Hagerstown, MD: Review and Herald Publishing Association.

Rowe, D. L. (1985). *Thunder and trumpets: Millerites and dissenting religion in upstate New York, 1800–1850.* Chico, CA: Scholars Press/American Academy of Religion.

Schwarz, R. W. & Greenleaf, F. (2000). *Light bearers: A history of the Seventh-day Adventist Church.* Nampa, ID: Pacific Press Publishing Association.

# Millenarianism

"Millennialism" is derived from the Latin word for a thousand and based on a passage in Revelation (20:1–10) in which the devil is bound and thrown into a bottomless pit for a thousand years. According to this doctrine, the removal of Satanic influence will be accompanied by the resurrection of the Christian martyrs, who will reign with Christ during the millennium, a period during which all of humankind's yearning for an ideal society characterized by peace, freedom, material prosperity, and the rule of righteousness will be realized. This doctrine, also known as millenarianism, claims that the vision of the Old Testament prophets, who foretold a period of earthly prosperity for the people of God, will find fulfillment during this era.

There are three major views of the millennium: (1) postmillennialism, (2) amillennialism, and (3) premillennialism. These categories are used despite the fact that in a sense they are misleading, for the distinction involves much more than merely whether Christ returns before or after the millennium. The kingdom expected by the postmillennialist is quite different from that anticipated by the premillennialist, not only with respect to the time and manner with which it will be established but also with regard to the nature of the kingdom and the way Christ will exercise his control over it.

The postmillenarian believes that the kingdom of God is extended through Christian preaching and teaching, as a result of which the world will be Christianized and will enjoy a long period of peace and righteousness. This new age will not be essentially different from the present and will emerge gradually as a larger share of the world's population is converted to Christianity. Evil will not be eliminated but will be reduced to a minimum as the moral and spiritual influence of Christianity is heightened. During this age the church assumes a greater importance, and social, economic, and educational problems are solved. The period closes with the second coming of Christ, the resurrection of the dead, and the final judgment.

In contrast to the view of postmillenarians, amillennialists believe that the Bible does not predict a period of universal peace and righteousness before the end of the world. Instead, they believe that both good and evil will continue until the second coming of Christ, when the dead will be raised and the last judgment held.

The third major millennialist interpretation, premillennialism, affirms that the Lord's return will be followed by a period of peace and righteousness before the end of the world, during which Christ will reign as king, either in person or through a select group of people. This kingdom will not be established by the conversion of individual souls over a long period of time, but suddenly and by overwhelming power. The new age will be characterized by the conversion of the Jews and the reign of harmony in nature to such an extent that the desert will blossom like a rose and even ferocious beasts will be tame. Evil is held in check during this period by Christ who rules with a rod of iron. Despite their idyllic condition, men are not satisfied and launch one last rebellion against God and his followers. This final exposure of evil is crushed by Christ and then the last judgment is held. Many premillennialists believe that during this golden age believers who have died will be reunited with glorified bodies to mingle freely with the rest of the inhabitants of earth. Usually, premillenarians have taught that the return of Christ will be preceded by certain signs, such as the preaching of the Gospel to all nations, a great apostasy, wars, famine, earthquakes, the appearance of the Antichrist, and a great tribulation.

Although these interpretations have never been without adherents in the history of the church, in certain ages one or another of them has predominated. During the first three centuries of the Christian era, premillennialism appears to have been the dominant eschatological interpretation. In the fourth century, when the Christian church was given a favored status under the emperor Constantine, the amillennial position was accepted, and the millennium was reinterpreted to refer to the church. The famous church father, Augustine, articulated this position, and it became the prevailing interpretation in medieval times.

The Protestant Reformers accepted Augustinian amillennialism. However, they did inaugurate changes in eschatological interpretation that set the stage for a great renewal of premillennial interest during the seventeenth century. Martin Luther (1483–1546), for example, advocated a more literal approach to the Scriptures, identified the papacy with the Antichrist, and called attention to biblical prophecies. Some later Lutheran scholars redirected this interest to focus on a premillennial interpretation, and the German Calvinist theologian Johann Heinrich Alsted (1588–1638) revived the teaching of premillennialism in the modern world. Alsted's 1627 book, *The Beloved City,* caused the learned Anglican scholar Joseph Mede (1586–1638) to become a premillennialist. The works of both men helped to inspire the desire for God's kingdom on earth, which accompanied the outbreak of the Puritan Revolution of the 1640s. It was only with the restoration of the Stuart rulers that this outlook was discredited.

As premillennialism waned, postmillennialism became the prevailing eschatological interpretation, receiving its most important formulation in the work of Daniel Whitby (1638–1726). According to Whitby, the world was to be converted to Christ, the Jews restored to their land, and the pope and Turks defeated, after which time the earth would enjoy universal peace, happiness, and righteousness for one thousand years. At the close of this period, Christ would return for the last judgment. Perhaps because of its agreement with the views of the eighteenth-century Enlightenment, postmillennialism was adopted by the leading Protestant theologians of the era.

During the nineteenth century, premillennialism again attracted widespread attention. This interest was fostered by the violent uprooting of European political and social institutions during the French Revolution. One of the more influential leaders at this time was Edward Irving (1792–1834), who published many works on prophecy and influenced the Albury Park prophecy conferences. These meetings set the pattern for millennial gatherings throughout the nineteenth and twentieth centuries. The prophetic enthusiasm of Irving spread to other groups and found support among the Plymouth Brethren.

J. N. Darby (1800–1882), an early Plymouth Brethren leader, articulated the dispensationalist understanding of premillennialism. His teaching, spread by such means as the Scofield Reference Bible, led to the popularity of dispensational premillennialism in the English-speaking world.

Missionaries have been motivated by each of these millennial outlooks. Perhaps the greatest influence has been that of postmillennialism, which was adopted by many of the founders of modern missions. New England Puritans, continental pietists, and Evangelical revivalists of the eighteenth century all encouraged the emphasis on millennialism. One of the most outstanding missionary spokespersons of this period, Jonathan Edwards (1703–1758), was a devoted postmillennialist.

Despite the development of dispensationalism, postmillennialism continued to be the dynamic for much of the missionary enthusiasm of the nineteenth century. America, many claimed, was the agent of God to bring in the last times. Timothy Dwight (1752–1817) anticipated the day when the Gospel would triumph. Other spokespersons merged the language of Manifest Destiny with millennialism and dreamed of the conquest of the world. It was this confidence that led John R. Mott to publish *The Evangelization of the World in This Generation* and inspired the World Missionary Conference in Edinburgh in 1910.

However, the new age did not come and a number of those involved in the missionary movement adopted a premillennial view. Rather than trying to bring God's kingdom to earth, they turned to winning individuals to Christ and preaching the Gospel as a witness to all nations so that Christ would return. Two world wars, genocide, economic depression, the rise of pluralism, the success of liberalism, and the privatization of religion in a secular society convinced them that only a supernatural return of Christ would help the world. Yet changes in dispensational doctrine, a renewed emphasis on the spirit of God by Charismatic groups, and the concept of reaching whole groups of people with the Gospel continue to foster the postmillennial view.

ROBERT G. CLOUSE

See also Christendom; Evangelicalism; Fundamentalism; Jehovah's Witnesses; Millennialism and Adventism; Reformation; Theology

## Further Reading

Clouse, R. G. (1977). *The meaning of millennium: Four views.* Downer Grove, IL: Intervarsity Press.
Clouse, R. G. (2006). *The end of days.* Woodstock, VT: Skylight Paths Publishing.

DeJong, J. A. (1970). *As the waters cover the sea: Millennial expectations in the rise of Anglo-American missions 1640–1810.* Kampen, Netherlands: J. H. Kok.

Kromminga, D. H. (1945) *The millennium in the church.* Grand Rapids, MI: Eeerdmans.

Toon, P. (1970). *Puritans, the millennium and the future of Israel.* Greenwood, SC: The Attic Press.

Travis, S. (1982). *I believe in the second coming of Jesus.* Grand Rapids, MI: Eerdmans.

Tuveson, E. L. (1964). *Millennium and utopia.* New York: Harper.

Tuveson, E.L. (1968) *Redeemer nation: The idea of America's millennial role.* Chicago: University of Chicago Press.

Weber, T. P. (1987) *Living in the shadow of the second coming.* Chicago: University of Chicago Press.

Weber, T.P. (2004) *On the road to Armageddon: How evangelicals become Israel's best friend.* Grand Rapids, MI: Baker Academic.

# Miracles

In the historical expansion of Christian missions, the scope of miraculous happenings broadly refers to events attributed to Providence, claims of paranormal phenomena, and manifestations of the charismatic gifts of the Holy Spirit (1 Cor. 12:8–10). Beginning with the Acts narrative, which states: "The apostles performed many miraculous signs and wonders among the people" (Acts 5:12a TNIV), miracles have accompanied the growth of Christianity, gaining particular attention in the late nineteenth and twentieth centuries. Records variously tell of visions, dreams, signs in the heavens, physical healings, resurrections of the dead, unexpected provision of needs, deliverances in times of danger, divine guidance, exorcism of demons, and other extraordinary occurrences.

## Early Accounts

Reports of miracles circulated in the postapostolic and medieval periods in the activities of Gregory the Wonderworker (Asia Minor), Nino (Georgia), Gregory the Illuminator (Armenia), Augustine of Canterbury (England), Takla-Haymanot (Ethiopia), and Nestorian missionaries (central Asia), along with many others. Information comes from sources such as *Ecclesiastical History* (c. 325 CE) written by Eusebius of Caesarea and *Ecclesiastical History of England* (c. 731 CE) by Bede. While the miracle stories they contain frequently have fantas-

tic proportions, others clearly parallel incidents in the first-century church.

## Controversies among Other Religions

During the sixteenth-century Reformation, Luther and Calvin disavowed the Catholic doctrine of the communion of saints. By so doing, they dismissed the traditional value set on the saints, holy relics, pilgrimages, and shrines and the miracle stories that developed around them, declaring that miracles largely had vanished with the apostolic church. Robert Bellarmine, like other Catholic theologians of the time, sharply contested this conclusion and saw the survival of miracles in Catholic missions as a mark of the apostolicity of the Roman Church. Among those noted for apostolic ministries with miracles, Catholic and Greek Orthodox Christians celebrated the marvels of the Jesuits (in Japan and Brazil) and Kosmas Aitolos (in the Balkans), respectively. For political reasons and gender prejudice, however, Portuguese Catholic authorities condemned the supernatural claims of Kimpa Vita (Dona Béatrice) who sought to Africanize Christianity in her own country (the Congo).

### Acts of "Special Providence"

In the centuries that followed, Protestants, though skeptical of Catholic claims, generally believed that if miraculous happenings did take place, they represented sovereign exceptions, categorized by some as acts of "special providence" (Mullin 1996, 14). This could then account for the results of Hans Egede when he prayed for the sick in Greenland, Ludwig Nommensen's survival of poisoned food in the Dutch East Indies (Indonesia), stories of divine protection of Seventh-Day Adventist missionaries, and even the belief of Johannes Warneck that God had allowed the temporary reoccurrence of supernatural phenomena to bring Batak people in Sumatra (Indonesia) to conversion. The Edinburgh World Missionary Conference in 1910 recognized the importance of special divine agency with the report, "Carrying the Gospel to All the Non-Christian World."

## Factors in Growing Popularity

At least two developments in the nineteenth century stirred the anticipation of miracles on a broader scale. First, the increasing popularity of premillennial eschatology led many to look for the imminent return of Jesus

## A Miracle in South Africa

At one time, when Rev. W. J. Davis was stationed [in the Transkei region of the Eastern Cape of South Africa], the country was dried up, the cattle were dying, and there was a general apprehension of famine. Chief Rili assembled a large body of "rain-makers" near to the mission premises, and with a great gathering of the people, they went on with their incantations and "vain repetitions" daily for a week. Brother Davis kept himself advised . . . of all their proceedings. Finally the rain-makers said they could not get any rain. . . . the missionaries were the cause . . . and there would be no rain while [they] were allowed to remain in the country. . . . When [Davis] heard of the grave charge brought against the missionaries, and specially against himself and [his] family . . . he rode into their camp . . . and demanded a hearing: "No stop all this nonsense, and come to chapel next Sabbath, and we will pray to God, who made the heavens and the earth, to give us rain, and we will see who is the true God."

At the hour for service the usual congregation assembled, and besides them the great chief and his mother [Nomsa], and many of the heathen people. . . . After some preliminaries, [Davis] asked the people to kneel down, and unite with him in prayer to the Lord God of Elijah. . . . while they remained on their knees in solemn awe, in the presence of God, they heard the big rain drops begin to patter on the zinc roof of the chapel, and lo, a copious rain, which continued all that afternoon and all night. The whole region was so saturated with water that the river nearby became so swollen that the chief and his mother could not cross it that night. . . . That seemed to produce a great impression on the minds of the chief, his mother, and the heathen party in favour of God and His missionaries, and Brother Davis got the name of a great rain-maker; but signs, wonders, and even miracles, will not change the hearts of sinners, for Nomsa lived and died a heathen, and her royal son remains an increasing dark and wicked heathen to this day.

Source: Taylor, W. (1867). *Christian adventures in South Africa*
(pp. 273–277). London: Jackson, Walford, and Hodd.

---

Christ and the closure of human history. Strategically prior to this, God would "pour out" the Spirit in the End Times (Joel 2:28 TNIV) to empower Christians to speedily evangelize the world. The contemporaneous influence of the Wesleyan and Keswick Holiness movements prompted many Protestant missionaries to pray for a postconversion baptism of the Holy Spirit for spiritual enablement.

Since the number of converts in the mission lands lagged behind expectations, radical Evangelicals, reflecting the influence of romanticism and restorationist ideals on evangelicalism, criticized the seemingly pedestrian methods of the conventional mission societies and called for a return to "New Testament methods." Influential publications appealing to the apostolic model of "faith missions," which emphasized dependence on divine provision over receiving salaries from mission agencies (viewed as simply human resources), included *Missionaries After the Apostolical School* (1825) by Edward Irving and *Christian Devotedness* (1825) by Anthony Norris Groves. Building on expectant faith as a prerequisite for miraculous signs to accompany the preaching of the gospel, A. J. Gordon in his *Ministry of Healing* (1881) and A. B. Simpson in *The Gospel of Healing* (1885) envisioned that the "prayer of faith" would be followed by physical healings and demonstrate God's power before non-Christians.

Arthur T. Pierson took a more cautious approach, one that appealed to a wider audience. His four-volume *Miracles of Missions: Modern Marvels in the History of Missionary Enterprise* (1891–1902) surveyed a broad range of divine activity in human affairs: unusual circumstances leading to conversions; astonishing answers to prayer for financial resources and other needs; deliverances from danger; new opportunities for ministry; the "miracles" of medical missions; new means of transportation; and occasionally physical healings. Interest in healing missions also emerged in the Anglican Communion, in part through the work of the Boston physician Charles Cullis, Australian lay evangelist James Moore Hickson, and Irish Anglican prelate Herbert Pakenham-Walsh (India).

### Charismatic Movements

The second development surfaced in the majority world from Christians who read about the healings and exorcisms performed by Jesus and the apostles in Bible translations. Though missionaries usually doubted the possibility of miracles, the biblical narratives had immediate relevance in the worldviews of these believers. Indigenous movements arose around charismatic figures with a range of prophetic and healing gifts and skills at exorcism, including Justus Joseph (India), Hsi Shengmo (China), and early in the twentieth century, William Wadé Harris (West Africa), Simon Kimbangu (Congo), and John Sung (China).

In the twentieth century, the Pentecostal movement and Charismatic renewals in the mainline Protestant, Roman Catholic, and Eastern Orthodox churches, as well as new interest in the Holy Spirit among conservative Evangelicals, resulted in a major shift toward reassessing the role of the Holy Spirit in the mission of God. Accordingly, the reappearance of the charismatic gifts and miracles authenticate gospel proclamation by showing the continuation of Christ's ministry in the church through the work of the Holy Spirit. Notable leaders who have encouraged the miraculous dimension of Christian mission include, among Pentecostals and Protestant Charismatics, T. L. Osborn (U.S.), John Wimber (U.S.), Reinhard Bonnke (South Africa), Carlos Annacondia (Argentina), Sunday Adelaja (Ukraine), and David Yonggi Cho (Korea); Anglicans: Chui Ban It (Singapore) and Francis MacNutt (U.S.); Roman Catholics: Briege McKenna (Ireland), Mathew Naickomparambil (India), and Mariano Velarde (Philippines); Greek Orthodox: Eusebius Stephanou (U.S.).

In the past, historians and other observers, particularly in the West, have disputed the reliability and importance of paranormal claims due to philosophical and theological assumptions, questions about sources, and the ideological agendas of the authors that controlled the evaluation of evidence. Nevertheless, recent studies have pointed to the significance of miracle stories in the conversion of non-Christian peoples, the contextualization of their faith, and their views on Christian spirituality.

GARY B. MCGEE

### Further Reading

Goldingay, J. (1991). *Signs, wonders and healing.* Downers Grove, IL: InterVarsity Press.

Gordon, A. J. (1881). *Ministry of healing.* Harrisburg, PA: Christian Publications.

Groves, A. N. (1825). *Christian devotedness.* London: James Nisbet.

Harrell, D. E., Jr. (1979). *All things are possible: the healing and charismatic revivals in modern America.* Bloomington: Indiana University Press.

Hiebert, P. G. (1994). *Anthropological reflections on missiological issues.* Grand Rapids, MI: Baker Academic.

Irving, E. (1825). *For missionaries after the Apostolical School: a series of orations: in four parts.* N.p.: Hamilton, Adams.

Kydd, R. A. N. (1998). *Healing through the centuries: Models for understanding.* Peabody, MA: Hendrickson Publishers.

MacNutt, F. (1974). *Healing.* Notre Dame, IN: Ave Maria Press.

McGee, G. B. (2001, October). Miracles and missions revisited. *IBMR 25,* 146–156.

Mullin, R. B. (1996). *Miracles and the modern religious imagination.* New Haven, CT: Yale University Press.

Pierson, A. T. (1891–1902). *The miracles of missions: or, the modern marvels in the history of missionary enterprise.* New York: Funk & Wagnalls.

Simpson, A. B. (1986). *The gospel of healing.* N.p.: Christian Alliance Publishing Co. (Original work published 1886)

Spicer, W. A. (1926). *Miracles of modern missions: Gathered out of the mission records.* Washington, DC: Review and Herald Pub. Association.

*Today's new international version* (Bible). (2005). Grand Rapids, MI: Zondervan.

Walker, D. P. (1988) The cessation of miracles. In I. Merkel & A. G. Debus (Eds.), *Hermeticism and the Renaissance: Intellectual history and the occult in early modern Europe.* Washington, DC: Folger Press.

World Missionary Conference. (1910). Carrying the Gospel to all the non-Christian world. *Reports of Commissions.* Edinburgh, UK: Oliphant, Anderson & Ferrier.

# Missiometrics

*Missiometrics* is a neologism that describes the systematic measurement and compilation of statistics describing the progress of the Christian missionary endeavor at clearly specified times and places across the world. Mission statistics have been collected, analyzed, published, and studied seriously throughout the twenty centuries of Christian history, from the writings of Augustine of

Hippo (426 CE) and Isidore of Seville (600 CE) to more recent yearbooks and encyclopedias. Whereas the wider discipline of missiology examines missions through the lenses of biblical exegesis, theology, philosophy, history, methodology, biography, and bibliography, missiometrics is "the science of mission with special reference to measurement, statistics, and analysis." Missiometrics is the art and science of counting, concerned with the numbers of religionists and growth rates, key trends related to Christian mission, and the collection of statistics; it occupies millions of Christian workers and costs over $1 billion annually.

The emergence of the term *missiometrics* parallels that of many new sciences that came into existence in the twentieth century. A look at the *Oxford English Dictionary Online* shows that some eighty new sciences with names ending in "-metrics" are now being practiced. In most cases they are part of larger disciplines but restrict themselves to purely empirical aspects. Thus, economics has created a branch called "econometrics," which handles mathematical applications, as illustrated in the 1994 book *A Dictionary of Econometrics*. Other mathematical applications to larger disciplines include bibliometrics, cliometrics, biometrics, and jurimetrics. In global mission, the larger discipline is widely understood today by the term "missiology." There are counterparts in other languages: in German *Weltmissionswissenschaft*, in Dutch *Wereldzendingswetenschap*, and in French *science missionnaire mondiale.*

The term coined here to cover the empirical aspects of missiology centers on measurement: *missiometrics.* Since churches and missions worldwide regularly measure each year well over a thousand different numerical indicators of their life and progress, missiometrics is thus presented with a gold mine of annual data waiting for analysis.

Starting with biblical criteria, missiometrics draws from the Old Testament a vast storehouse of censuses and statistical data and from the New Testament a surprising number of empirical mandates, such as "Count the worshipers!" and "Measure the temple!" (Rev. 11:1, ERV) or "Work out the number!" (Rev. 13:18, ERV). There are some twenty-three verbs found in the major English Bible versions, with another fifty-three close synonyms, which (together with the forty Greek biblical words associated with these synonyms) delineate the domain of the science of missiometrics. Because the twenty-three verbs enable us to measure the phenomena of mission, they are the basic dimensions (from the Latin *dimensio*, a measuring) of the science of missiometrics. These biblical imperatives suggest that Christians have a significant new method—metrical investigation—assisting them in a contemporary understanding of Christ's great commission.

Missiometrics measures everything relevant to mission and world evangelization. A sample of the 180 major subject areas measured each year by churches and missions includes church membership, church growth, places of worship, clergy, women workers, home missionaries, foreign missionaries, colporteurs, evangelists, audiences, catechumens, converts, baptisms, finances, scripture distribution, literature production, church administration, broadcasting, and computer usage. One remarkable example is *Annuario Pontificio*, an annual assessment of every Roman Catholic diocese in the world. Voluminous annual series of statistical data, if seriously investigated, can result in highly effective mission strategies and tactics. A major concern in this respect is that Christians involved in world mission be effective and imaginative in utilizing the vast new areas of data and communications now available over the Internet. Because the world is enormously complex entity—6.5 billion human beings grouped into 13,000 ethnolinguistic peoples speaking over 13,500 languages—navigating through these massive new data sources becomes a missiological priority.

The annual collecting of statistics on church membership and religion can be compared to the bookkeeping aspect of accounting—simply recording financial transactions. Missiometrics, on the other hand, is parallel to accounting in the financial world, defined as "the system of classifying, recording, and summarizing business and financial transactions in books of account and analyzing, verifying, and reporting the results" (*Webster's Third New International Dictionary*). The emphasis in accounting is on analyzing and reconciling large amounts of data that may or may not be comparable. Missiometrics serves this function in the assessment of the quantitative status of global Christianity.

Three significant trends in missiometrics indicate its growing role in global Christianity. First, new Christian research centers are sprouting up around the world. This reverses a recent trend when such centers were being closed down in rapid succession. In 1970 over 900 Christian research centers operated around the world, dropping precipitously to only 300 by mid-2000. The main reason for this decline appears to have been organizational fatigue over negative findings such as declining church membership. Today new research centers are emerging, not surprisingly, among Christians in the southern hemisphere, where Christianity is vibrant and growing rapidly.

Second, with the rise of the postdenominational churches (independents are now over 20 percent of all Christians), one might expect an aversion toward counting and, consequently, a dearth of reports of membership figures. Paradoxically, these movements have shown that they are intensely interested in keeping track of their members. African, Asian, and Latin American church leaders have continuously published their own stories, insisting that accountability (implying counting) is a central feature of their movements. Even for what would seem to be the most disorganized and diffuse movements, reports are available on the number of cells, their growth rates, and the location of new cells. Third, over half of the world's governments continue to ask a question about religion in their censuses. This provides another rich source of data in trying to assess the demographic status of Christianity and other religions.

Missiometrics, as a relatively new science, has a potentially bright future in describing the empirical state of Christianity in the twenty-first century. In the South, where Christianity is growing the fastest, research centers, detailed membership reports, and a concern for accuracy are proliferating. In the postmodern North, churches continue to produce both quantitative and qualitative assessments of their members. In both cases, understanding and interpreting numbers related to global Christianity and world evangelization are essential.

T. M. JOHNSON

### Further Reading

*Annuario Pontificio.* Annual. Citta del Vaticano: Tipografia Poliglotta Vaticana.

Barrett, D. B., & Johnson, T. M. (2001). *World Christian trends, AD 30–AD 2200: Interpreting the annual Christian megacensus.* Pasadena, CA: William Carey.

Barrett, D. B., Johnson, T. M., & Crossing, P. F. (2005). Missiometrics 2005: A global survey of world mission. *International Bulletin of Missionary Research, 29*(1), 27–30.

Barrett, D. B., Kurian, G. T., & Johnson, T. M. (2001). *World Christian encyclopedia: A comparative survey of churches and religions in the modern world* (2nd ed., Vols. 1–2). New York: Oxford University Press.

## Mission Conferences

Missionary conferences were a feature of the nineteenth and twentieth centuries following the missionary expansion of the late eighteenth century in the Protes-

tant world. They provide much instructive material for understanding the development of the Christian mission and its major preoccupations, especially after 1850. William Carey (1761–1834), the Baptist pioneer who reached India in 1793, had the vision of a missionary conference to be held at Cape Town in 1810, which his friend Andrew Fuller referred to as a "pleasing dream": it was to be "a general association of all denominations of Christians" (Carey 1792) to take counsel on missionary issues.

There were indeed to be missionary conferences in South Africa in 1904 and 1909, and perennial topics at such meetings were the relations of the missions to governments, the production and distribution of missionary literature, the approach to education, and the nurture of indigenous churches. But as the Baptist scholar Ernest Payne noted in his preface to Carey's *Enquiry* of 1961, the real fulfillment of Carey's vision had to wait a century, until the World Missionary Conference at Edinburgh in 1910.

### Conferences before Edinburgh 1910

India and China, where many missionaries were at work in the nineteenth century, had series of such conferences. In an early example in Madras in 1848, one important issue was that of caste and its effects on church life. This was a continuing concern at Bangalore in 1879 and the conference of 1900. The two Madras conferences of 1900 and 1902, especially the latter, provided a model from which Edinburgh 1910 benefited. Committees were appointed to handle large subjects, which could then be treated in depth in plenary sessions, and the system of having representative figures or delegates was adopted to make the 1902 meeting more representative of missionary opinion.

In China Shanghai was the center for three conferences. The first, in 1877, was notable as the birthplace of the missionary slogan "the evangelization of the world in this generation," according to American Robert Wilder (1863–1938), pioneer leader of the Student Volunteer Movement that produced many missionaries. It became known as "the Watchword" and was widely used in the early years of the twentieth century.

Two further conferences at Shanghai followed, one in 1890, when some 500 missionaries attended, and another in 1907, which was held in part to celebrate the arrival of the first Protestant missionary, Robert Morrison (1782–1834), in Canton in 1807. This was a multinational occasion, with twenty-five countries represented and over one thousand members, including many missionaries working in China.

Japan too had a series of conferences beginning in 1872, and in the years before Edinburgh 1910, a number of international gatherings were held in New York (1854), Liverpool (1860), and London (1878, 1888). The London conference of 1888 numbered over fifteen hundred members and included Asian Christian representatives. The culmination of this series of meetings in the nineteenth century was the so-called Ecumenical Missionary Conference in New York in 1900. The initial word referred to its worldwide nature, for no Roman Catholic or Orthodox Christians were participants. Some 200,000 took part in the conference, including the then president of the United States, William McKinley, and Theodore Roosevelt.

The meeting had an air of Anglo-American triumphalism about it, which the German professor of missions, Gustav Warneck from the University of Halle, addressed critically. He discerned the danger of confusing the spread of European and American culture and language with Christian mission. In one respect the New York conference was more remarkable than Edinburgh, as it was attended by large numbers of women, supporters of the missions, but in general it was more of a demonstration than a conference.

## Edinburgh 1910

The careful preparation for the Madras conferences in India of 1900 and 1902 and the use of delegates for greater representation were duly noted by those preparing for Edinburgh 1910. Here, too, commissions were charged with preparatory work on large subjects. By the time the meeting was held in the assembly hall of New College, Edinburgh, from 12 to 23 June 1910, there had been nearly two years of preparatory work for the twelve hundred delegates. J. H. ("Joe") Oldham (1874–1969), its secretary, had the administrative capability and thoroughness of a great government official. He had studied classics at Oxford and theology at Edinburgh, to which he added missionary study under Warneck at Halle.

After his formal appointment in 1908, eight commissions were formed, each charged to produce a report on its subject, which would be set before the conference and debated. Carefully chosen members of the commissions served under an equally carefully chosen chair; hence, Commission IV on "The Missionary Message and the non-Christian Religions" was chaired by the Scottish systematic theologian, D. S. Cairns. He was put in charge in 1908, which gave time for an extensive questionnaire to be sent to missionaries in the field serving among Muslims, Hindus, Buddhists, and Confucians.

Their replies supplied the background data for a written report and digest for the Edinburgh delegates. Oldham, and the whole conference when in session, owed much to the decisiveness of the chairman, John R. Mott (1865–1955). It was Mott who took steps to ensure that the conference became genuinely international after a shaky beginning in 1907–1908.

Meanwhile, Oldham managed to make the conference more genuinely ecumenical by the inclusion of such Anglo-Catholic leaders as Bishop Charles Gore (1853–1932), as well as the American bishop in the Philippines, Charles Brent (1862–1929). Edinburgh proved to be the birthplace of the modern ecumenical movement, and figures like V. S. Azariah (1874–1945) and C. Y. Cheng (1881–1829) became leaders of the younger churches, while stewards included the future Anglican archbishop, William Temple (1881–1944) and other future leaders.

The conference was much concerned about the spread of Islam in Africa, unable to foresee that the 10 million Christians of its own day would be 200 million or more by the end of the century. A hundred years later its tone seems overly optimistic, and Mott's final speech tended toward a view of Christian world conquest in the near future that was not borne out by experience in the twentieth century. Nevertheless, Edinburgh 1910 was a meeting of great importance, only rivaled by Vatican II later in the century.

## The Fruits of Edinburgh 1910

The most significant single result from the conference was the creation of a Continuation Committee, again under Mott's chairmanship. A missionary journal also resulted, the *International Review of Missions,* in 1912 under J. H. Oldham's editorship. The Continuation Committee turned into the International Missionary Council (IMC) in 1921, again with Mott as chairman, and Mott traveled the globe, bringing to birth various National Christian Councils that related to the IMC in China (1922), India (1923), Japan (1923), and Korea (1924), followed by others.

The IMC mounted further conferences at Jerusalem (1928), where 231 members attended, including 25 percent from the younger churches, and at Tambaram, Madras (1938), where 500 met. These included around 50 percent from Asia, Africa, and Latin America. The first was notable for its "Message," drafted by William Temple, Archbishop of York, which expressed the unanimous view of the conference that the Gospel was God's truth for all people. Tambaram, Madras, was remembered not least for its preparatory volume, written

## A World Sampling of Mission Conferences

### J.R. Mott, Commission I, World Missionary Conference (1910)

"It is a startling and solemnizing fact that even as late as the twentieth century the Great Command of Jesus Christ to carry the Gospel to all mankind is still so largely unfulfilled...There may have been times when in certain non-Christian lands the missionary forces of Christianity stood face to face with as pressing opportunities...but never before has there been such a conjunction of crises and opportunities and of opening doors in all parts of the world...as the present decade."

### Council Statement at IMC meeting, Jerusalem (1928)

"We call on the followers of non-Christian religions to join with us in the study of Jesus Christ as he stands before us in the Scriptures...to cooperate with us against the evils of secularism...we would insist that when the Gospel of the Love of God comes home with power to the human heart, it speaks to each man, not as Muslim or as Buddhist, or as an adherent of any system, but just as man."

### International Congress on World Evangelization in Lausanne (1975)

"We reject...every kind of syncretism and dialogue which implies that Christ speaks equally through all religions and ideologies...evangelism itself is the proclamation of the historical, biblical Christ as Savior and Lord, with a view to persuading people to come to him personally and so be reconciled to God...we affirm that evangelism and socio-political involvement are both part of our Christian dutythe gospel evaluates all cultures according to its own criteria of truth and righteousness and insists on moral absolutes in every culture."

by the Dutch lay missionary from Indonesia, Hendrik Kraemer (1868–1965), and called *The Christian Message in a Non-Christian World.* While adopting a controversial stance on the relationship of Christianity to alternative religious traditions, characterized as that of "discontinuity," the book also faced the ideological realities of the time—a world dominated by national socialism and Communism, which were regarded as modern "tribalisms" confronting the Gospel.

In the post-1945 world, the IMC family of conferences continued at Whitby, Ontario (1947), Willingen (1952), and, in Africa, Accra, Ghana (1958). This last conference met in the wake of the formation of the World Council of Churches (WCC) in 1948, and it was proposed that the WCC and the IMC should merge, against a background of some unease by IMC members. This was expressed by Canon Max Warren (1904–1977) at the Ghana meeting; the merger was advocated by Bishop Lesslie Newbigin (1909–1998) and duly took place at

the New Delhi meeting of the WCC in 1961. Thereafter, missionary issues were handled by the Department (later Commission) of World Mission and Evangelism (CWME), and further conferences followed, mounted now by CWME, at Mexico City (1963); Bangkok (1973); Melbourne (1980); San Antonio, Texas (1989); Salvador, Bahia, Brazil (1996); and Athens in 2005.

## New Approaches

Although it falls outside the strict scope of this article as not a missionary conference, Vatican II (1963–1965) was a historic meeting that produced important documents for wider missionary consumption in *Lumen Gentium* (the Church as the Light of the World), *Nostra Aetate* (which handled the question of relationship to other religions), and *Ad Gentes,* which emphasized the importance of proclamation in missionary activity and the needs of the 2 billion people who had not then heard the gospel. Evangelicals, who had been uneasy at Ghana 1958 (an unease intensified by the Uppsala meeting of the WCC in 1968) over the merger of the IMC with the WCC, mounted a Wheaton Congress on World Evangelization in 1966 and the Lausanne International Congress on World Evangelization in 1974. This meeting and its documentation bear comparison with Edinburgh 1910, Jerusalem 1928, and Tambaram 1938 for its weighty handling of missionary issues. Among other emphases was a strong note on the need for social involvement, insisted on not least by Latin American leaders such as Samuel Escobar, Rene Padilla, and Orlando Costas.

The Lausanne Covenant, drafted by John Stott (b.1921), was an important and influential statement, which judged that "evangelism and sociopolitical involvement are both part of our Christian duty." Lausanne, like Edinburgh 1910, resulted in conferences in a new family at Pattaya, Thailand (1980), and Manila, Philippines (1989), the first being termed a "Consultation on World Evangelization" and the second as Lausanne II, an "International Congress on World Evangelization." Lausanne has also created an ongoing committee, the Lausanne Committee for World Evangelization, and has promoted studies on missionary subjects by specialist groups, which have published papers on such subjects as Christian Witness to Jewish People.

## Implications for the Future

As the bibliography indicates, missionary conferences have provided a wealth of material for reflection on the importance of missionary activity, which can run the risk of being shallow and activist. Much missionary experience can be found in the various reports, which contain a depth of insight and perspective that twenty-first-century Christians need to learn on such subjects as the Gospel and culture, dialogue with other faiths, and appropriate forms of proclamation.

TIMOTHY YATES

### Further reading

Abbott, W. M. (1966). *Documents of Vatican II*. New York: US Catholic Publications.

Bosch, D. J. (1991). *Transforming mission: Paradigm shifts in the theology of mission*. New York: Orbis.

Carey, W. (1792). *An enquiry into the obligations of Christians to use means for the conversion of the heathens*. (Second edition with introduction by Ernest Payne 1961). London: Carey Kingsgate Press.

Clements, K. (1999). *Faith on the frontier: A life of J. H. Oldham*. Edinburgh, UK: T. & T. Clark.

Douglas, J. D. (Ed.). (1975). *Let the earth hear His voice: International Conference on World Evangelization in Lausanne*. Minneapolis, MN: World Wide Publications.

*Edinburgh World Missionary Conference report*. (1910). 9 Vols. Edinburgh, UK: Oliphant, Anderson & Ferrier.

Gairdner, W. H. T. (1910). *Edinburgh 1910: An account and interpretation of the World Missionary Conference*. Edinburgh, UK: Oliphant, Anderson & Ferrier.

Hogg, W. R. (1952). *Ecumenical foundations*. New York: Harper.

Hogg, W. R. (1970). Missionary conferences. In S. C. Neill, G. H. Anderson, & J. Goodwin (Eds.). *A concise dictionary of the Christian world mission*. London: Lutterworth Press.

Hopkins, C. H. (1979). *John Mott: A biography*. Grand Rapids, MI: Eerdmans.

*Jerusalem Meeting of the IMC of 1928: Report and addresses*. 8 Vols. London: Oxford University Press.

Neill, S. C., Anderson G. H., & Goodwin, J. (Eds.). (1970). *A concise dictionary of the Christian world mission*. London: Lutterworth Press.

Orchard, R. K. (Ed.). (1958). *The Ghana Assembly of the IMC*. London: Edinburgh Press.

*Tambaram Madras papers series*. (1939). 7 Vols. London: International Missionary Council.

Yates, T. (1994). *Christian mission in the twentieth century*. Cambridge, UK: Cambridge University Press.

## Mission Methods and Strategy

Starting in the seventeenth century, the notion of mission methods and strategy began to develop. Christian missions were entering a new stage of development, and this flowering of missions coincided with the growth of modern consciousness that emphasized rationality and the application of the scientific method to all areas of life. By contrast the earliest missionaries, including the apostle Paul, did not discuss strategies or methods of missionary work.

## Culture as a Bridge

The Jesuit missionary to China, Mateo Ricci (1552–1610), arrived in China in 1583. Previous attempts to establish missions in China, starting with the Nestorians in 635 CE, had failed due to intense Chinese opposition. But Ricci took with him samples of European culture—clocks, astronomical instruments, printed books, and a large map of the world. He sincerely appreciated Chinese culture while freely sharing Western scientific knowledge and culture and gained the approval of the Chinese emperor in 1601. He settled in Beijing as the court's official astronomer and mathematician. Ricci understood culture to be an important bridge for intercultural communication.

But the flowering of the Enlightenment toward the end of the seventeenth century caused Westerners to regard their culture as superior to all others. For example, increasingly it was assumed that the missionary should rely on the model of church life in the homeland in establishing new churches in other cultures. In his apology for missions published in 1792, *An Enquiry into the Obligations of Christians, to Use Means for the Conversion of the Heathens,* William Carey (1761–1834) emphasized that Christians should use practical "means" in order to carry out the missionary task throughout the world. Carey reflected the modern ethos and the confidence that any goal can be achieved by employing the proper resources. This modern perspective helped define the classical model of modern missions.

## Identifying a Strategy

Modernity fostered the notion that every physical or social process was governed by certain principles. By the early nineteenth century missionary thinkers emphasized the importance of identifying the correct strategy of missionary work and then pursuing that strategy using the most effective methods.

### Roman Catholic Strategy

In 1622 Pope Gregory XV created the Sacred Congregation for the Propagation of the Faith (SCPF), or Propaganda de Fide, with the mandate to provide overall guidance for Roman Catholic missions. Through its hierarchical system, the Vatican appointed apostolic delegates to each country where missionaries were at work. All the missionary orders working in a country automatically came under the jurisdiction of the apostolic delegate. The SCPF formulated the strategy for the entire Roman Catholic mission that was then implemented through the apostolic delegates all over the world.

In 1919 Pope Benedict XV instructed the SCPF to emphasize the development of indigenous clergy for the Roman Catholic churches in Asia, Africa, and Latin America so that leadership responsibility for these churches would be transferred as quickly as possible. In spite of the opposition of the missionary orders,

this important change in strategy was successfully implemented.

### Protestant Strategy

Protestants have never had a mechanism for centralized control and coordination. As a result, Protestant missions have followed varied strategies or have operated without any clear plan. That is not to say that the weaknesses of unsupervised Protestant missionary activity were not recognized. In the late nineteenth century a movement was launched to provide coordination of Protestant missions on a national basis, starting with India, where formal agreements were adopted in 1902 (Beaver 1962, chapter 3). The comity system was organized to define areas for each mission to work and guidelines for supervising intermission relations. The overriding concern was to avoid duplication of effort by encouraging missions to spread out and thus maximize impact in the particular country. Unfortunately, the comity system broke down after World War II.

A second means used by Protestants to foster unity of purpose and develop a more coherent strategy was the convening of world mission conferences, starting with the New York Missionary Conference in 1854. Subsequent conferences were held in Liverpool, England, in 1860; London in 1888; New York, 1900; and the World Missionary Conference in Edinburgh in 1910. The 1910 conference made two decisions that would shape future mission strategy: In 1912 *The International Review of Missions* was established and became the authoritative channel for the dissemination of current critical thinking about Christian missions throughout the Protestant world. Second, it was decided to establish the International Missionary Council (IMC), though World War I delayed the organization of the IMC until 1922. The IMC organized a series of world mission conferences that grappled with current issues: Jerusalem, 1928; Madras/Tambaram, 1938; Whitby, 1947; Willingen, 1953; and Accra, 1958. Each of these assemblies focused on a main issue of strategy in light of the present environment and the challenges being faced.

The IMC assembly at Jerusalem in 1928 introduced the concept of the *comprehensive approach.* Missions were urged to view the human being as a whole and ensure that mission strategy address the whole person—physical, mental, and social—and relate the spiritual to all other dimensions (IMC 1928, VI: 287). This was essentially a corrective measure, for throughout the nineteenth century the number of specialized missions—including educational, medical, leprosy, agricultural, child wel-

## Protestant Methods in South Texas

**The following account describes reactions to Protestant proselytizing in the Roman Catholic Mexican-American community in south Texas in the 1960s.**

Some Catholics feel so strongly about door-to-door proselytizing that their homes bear signs reading, "This is a Catholic home. Protestants are not welcomed." Other signs amend the last sentence to read, "Protestants and other salesmen are not welcomed."

The in-fighting among Protestant sects that are competing for Latin converts often amuses the Catholics. A Mexican-American Catholic said: "The only real difference between them and us is that we honor the saints. God is God wherever He is but each Protestant church seems to think He is someone else."

Although most Latin Catholics object only to the intolerance and missionary zeal of the Protestants, a few conservative members of the Latin community see a deeper threat. An old gentleman said: Our people have always worshipped God in our own way. Let the Protestants say what they will, our souls will be saved by Catholicism as easily as theirs will be by Protestantism. The way they see God is not what bothers me. It's the way they act. The Protestant way is the Anglo way. Have you ever watched them? Their kids speak out as if they were wise men and even contradict their elders. The Protestants have no respect even in worship. Those alleluias shout and stamp in church as though they were drunk. It's not dignified and it's a poor way to address the Lord. This may be the Anglo way. It's not our way and it never had been.

Some Protestant preachers openly attack Mexican-American loyalty to their religious tradition. A Protestant minister proclaimed that "our way is the way to Progress." A woman missionary also emphasized the value of change, "The Catholics are Catholics because their fathers were. If we change our mode of eating, dressing, and curing the sick, why shouldn't we also change our religious beliefs for the better?"

The differences between Protestantism and Catholicism are viewed by one educated Latin Catholic as different concepts of the nature of man, "The Protestants see only saints and sinners. The Catholics, however, have high esteem for the average person who is seen as neither all good nor all bad. I think the Catholic viewpoint is more realistic and more humanistic."

Source: Madsen, W. (1973). *Mexican-Americans of south Texas* (pp. 64–65). New York: Holt, Rinehart and Winston.

---

fare, service to women—had increased, and mission strategy had become fragmented.

It was widely recognized that World War II was a historical watershed. Approximately half of the world was still controlled by Western colonial powers, but the colonized peoples were demanding that they be granted their political independence. Christian missions were called upon to respond proactively in this environment (Davis 1946, 303–313).

## Conservative Protestants

A significant portion of Protestants either never participated in the IMC or withdrew from it as the IMC developed ever-closer relations with the emerging World Council of Churches. Starting in the 1960s conservative Protestants convened a series of international consultations that were devoted to mission strategy. These events included the Wheaton Congress on the Church's Worldwide Mission (1966), the Berlin World Congress on Evangelism (1966), and the International Congress on World Evangelization held at Lausanne, Switzerland, in 1974. The latter marked a high point in terms of the number of participants—approximately twenty-four-hundred delegates from 150 nations. The Lausanne movement stimulated a series of additional consultations, all concerned in some way with mission strategy.

Several people played important roles in stimulating and sustaining the Protestant Evangelical missionary movement in the post–World War II period. Evangelist Billy Graham was the visionary behind both the Berlin and Lausanne Congresses. John R. W. Stott, noted British pastor and pastoral theologian, helped unify Evangelicals around the Lausanne Covenant, and Donald A. McGavran, a major missions strategist in the twentieth century, provided crucial conceptual leadership.

### Church Growth as a Strategy

Convinced that the classical modern missions strategy had run its course, McGavran, a missionary to India from 1924 to 1954, proposed a major new strategy—based on research in India—in his book, *The Bridges of God: A Study in the Strategy of Missions* (1955). He advocated that mission strategy be focused on church growth as the primary goal with all other dimensions of missionary work being subsidiary. McGavran found a sympathetic hearing only among conservative Protestants (McGavran 1972, Part 3). His ideas stimulated a number of new developments, including the widely used concept of "Unreached" or "Hidden People Groups." Many conservative Protestants have used this strategic concept since McGavran introduced it at the Lausanne Congress in 1974.

## Mission Methods

A method is a procedure or process for implementing a strategy. This often takes the form of a program or activity that is organized around a particular theme or concern. When William Carey arrived in India in 1793 as an inexperienced missionary, he formulated his approach by drawing on his knowledge of Moravian missions acquired through reading their many reports and from his own common sense. Carey's supreme aim was to establish a church that was viable in Bengali culture. He adopted a fivefold methodology: (1) the preaching of the Gospel wherever and in whatever way possible; (2) produce and distribute the Christian scriptures in the vernacular languages as widely as possible; (3) organize a local church as soon as possible; (4) study carefully the culture and language of the host people; and (5) train an indigenous ministry as rapidly as possible.

Until the mid-nineteenth century mission methods generally were limited to preaching, teaching, and printing. Preaching was the essential to winning adherents to the Christian faith, and Protestant missionaries emphasized the importance of Biblical literacy if new believers were to be properly catechized and discipled. To foster biblical literacy the scriptures had to be translated, printed, and distributed. In many instances, the vernacular language had not been reduced to writing. From the beginning missionaries established elementary schools so that the Christian community would be literate.

## Adapting to New Needs

Mission methods continued to multiply as modern knowledge became more specialized and new professions were developed: medical, industrial, and agricultural occupations and services geared to women and children all emerged in the late nineteenth century. After World War II large-scale emergency relief and development programs were established. In the wake of the Korean War after 1952 specialized child welfare programs that included orphanages and adoption services were set up. The range of methods has continued to expand based on new needs—e.g., the HIV/AIDS pandemic—and new technologies.

Since the 1980s Catholics and mainline Protestants have had little to say about mission strategy, while conservative Protestants have sought to develop strategy that is attuned to current religious and political reality. On the other hand, there has been wide agreement that evangelization must address the whole person. As a result, the line between evangelistic methods and social ministry methods has become increasingly blurred.

WILBERT R. SHENK

### Further Reading

Beaver, R. P. (1962). *Ecumenical beginnings in Protestant world mission*. New York: Thomas Nelson and Sons.

Davis, J. M. (1946). Mission strategy in the new age. *International Review of Missions, 35*, 303–313.

Dayton, E. R. (Ed.). (1984). *The future of world evangelization: Unreached peoples '84*. Grand Rapids, MI: Wm. B. Eerdmans Co. One of several volumes published by the Strategy Working Group of the Lausanne Committee for World Evangelization.

Douglas, J. D. (1975). *Let the world hear His voice: International Congress on World Evangelization*. Minneapolis, MN: World Wide Publications.

Henry, C. F. H., & Mooneyham, S. W. (Eds.). (1967). *One race, one Gospel, one task: World Congress on Evangelism* (2 Vols.). Minneapolis, MN: World Wide Publications.

Horner, N. A. (1965). *Cross and crucifix in mission: A comparison of Protestant–Roman Catholic missionary strategy*. New York: Abingdon Press.

Horton, W. M. (1946). Missionary strategy yesterday and tomorrow. In W. K. Anderson, *Christian world mission* (pp. 174–182). Nashville, TN: Commission on Ministerial Training.

International Missionary Council. (1928). *The Christian mission in relation to industrial problems* (Vol. VI). London: IMC.

Lindsell, H. (Ed.). (1966). *The church's worldwide mission. Proceedings of the Congress on the Church's Worldwide Mission, April 9–16, 1965, Wheaton, IL.* Waco, TX: Word Books.

McGavran, D. A. (1955). *The bridges of God: A study in the strategy of missions.* London: World Dominion Press.

McGavran, D. A. (Ed.). (1972). *Eye of the storm: The great debate in mission* (Part 3). Waco, TX: Word Books.

Soper, E. D. (1943). *The strategy of the world mission: Part 4. The philosophy of the Christian world mission.* New York: Abingdon-Cokesbury.

## Missionary Vocation and Service

"Missionary vocation" and "service" are terms that describe essential elements of the Roman Catholic call to be a missionary. These elements of a missionary vocation, considered important by key mission writers, especially after the restoration of the Society of Jesus in 1814, can be divided into three periods: 1800 to 1920, 1920 to about 1969, and 1970 to the present.

### 1800 to 1920

Initially, a mission vocation was considered a specialized vocation, connected with but beyond one's baptism, to be found in a special state of life, especially for clergy and for women and men religious (Sisters and Brothers). As was true for all vocations, the call was to be discerned through personal prayer, attendance at Mass, and conversation with a spiritual director or parish pastor. Unlike the other vocations, however, the call of a missionary vocation was influenced by mission literature.

Some groups whose foundations were in Europe, such as the Jesuits, the Divine Word Missionaries, and the Oblates of Mary Immaculate, arrived as missionaries in North and South America, Australia, and elsewhere, and carried with them a missionary spirituality influenced by the spirit of their religious communities in Europe. The spirituality of French groups, many of which were formed or reestablished after the French Revolution, often emphasized heroism and a willingness to be a martyr. The view of missionaries as ascetic arose from their isolation and from the physical, cultural, and spiritual difficulties they were likely to encounter in a new country and among an unfamiliar people.

Italian Paolo Manna (1872–1952), a missionary to Burma and Superior General of the Pontifical Institute for Foreign Missions, promoted mission vocations among the clergy, with the idea that the clergy would then make the rest of the church mission-minded. The missionaries depicted in his books became the standard view. He described the missionary as an apostle with a commission, a man of action, "a voice crying in the wilderness." The missionary was called to be "another Christ" and to be broad in outlook and large of heart. With a love for Christ and souls, missionaries must desire to sacrifice themselves to God and to dedicate themselves to the extension of God's kingdom.

### 1920 to the 1960s

The Catholic Foreign Mission Society of America, popularly known as Maryknoll, in its publications and mission magazine, *The Field Afar,* created a portrait of the missionary vocation that embodied some of the characteristics noted by European authors but also emphasized virtues arising from the American experience. Maryknoll publications, especially those of China missionary James E. Walsh (1891–1981), identified characteristics like a desire to serve God, intelligence, good health, generosity, and faith, as well as the ability to learn another language, have common sense, and engage in manual work, which was the lot of most of the people living where the missionaries would be sent. Walsh noted eleven mission virtues: accessibility, adaptability, affability, charity, confidence, courage, hardness, humility, initiative, frankness, and loyalty.

While much of the literature emphasized the mission vocation for priests, a theology of the Mystical Body provided a foundation for the growth of lay mission activity, beginning in Europe about 1920 and spreading quickly to North America and elsewhere. The terms "apostolate" and "apostle" began to be applied to the laity. The Catholic Action movement of the 1940s and 1950s was evidenced in groups such as the Young Christian Workers and the Young Christian Students, founded by Belgium's Joseph Cardinal Cardijn (1882–1967). The movement used the method "observe, judge, and act" to shape lay missionaries within their own home environments, especially if they were working class. The Catholic Students Mission Crusade, founded in 1917, emphasized prayer, study, and reading about mission activity. Missionaries who addressed the national conventions held great appeal as models for young adults to consider a mission vocation.

A teen volunteer reads the Bible to a homeless person. *Courtesy of Lisa F. Young/istockphoto.com.*

While the decree on missionary activity issued by the Second Vatican Council (1962–1965) emphasized the continued need for specialized religious communities to carry out the task of mission and evangelization (*Ad gentes divinitus* IV, 23), the decree also reiterated that "Christ stirs up a missionary vocation in the hearts of the faithful" through the power of the Holy Spirit. In this spirit, English laywoman Edwina Gateley began the Volunteer Missionary Movement in 1969. The lay group, an independent Christian international and ecumenical mission community arising out of the Catholic faith tradition, is open to people of all Christian faiths. The members, who covenant with each other, witness in a unique way to Christ's love and work, especially among the poor and marginalized. They see Christ's mission as one of liberation, justice, and dignity for others.

## 1970s to the Present

While the mission vocation was consistently related to baptism, the revision of the Rites of Christian Initiation of Adults in 1972, which followed more closely the pattern of the early Church, provided a more developed and specific relationship between baptism and mission, and emphasized the responsibility of the entire Christian community to respond to the baptismal call to mission, i.e., immersion in Christ in the baptismal water provides the impetus to live His mission in service. Those seeking baptism were to participate in the prayer, life, and mission work of the local Christian community.

Pope John Paul II's 1988 Apostolic Exhortation, *Christifidelis laici,* placed incorporation into Christ as the basis of all vocation and mission. All in the church are called to holiness, which is intimately connected to mission. The role of the laity is to serve in the world, as well as in areas of catechetics, liturgy, and social justice. Pope John Paul II's 1990 *Redemptoris Missio* is the lengthiest and most complete statement of the Catholic Church's understanding of mission and the mission vocation in the twentieth century. Missionary call derives from the call to holiness and sanctity and manifests a mission spirituality whereby a person is led by the Spirit, lives the mystery of "the One who was sent," and loves the Church and humanity as Jesus did.

Anthony Bellagamba, an Italian Comboni missionary and director of the United States Catholic Mission Association, described the vocation of cross-cultural ministers as including contemplation (the ability to be present to God and others); an asceticism of faith, hope, and love; *metanoia* (self-sacrifice for the sake of mission); and poverty (living in solidarity with the poor). On a practical level, people preparing for cross-cultural mission also need skills to participate in interfaith dialogue and ecumenism, and in team ministry. In the 1990s, Catholic scholar Robert Schreiter identfied a focus on reconciliation as a key aspect of mission vocation.

While the contexts and theology of mission and approaches to mission have changed since the 1800s, mission vocation continues to call for some form of prayer, for a practical response to God's call to extend the mission and life of Christ in the world through service, for generosity, and for the ability to understand people and cultures beyond one's own.

ANGELYN DRIES

*See also* Christendom; Mission Methods and Strategy; Roman Catholic Church

### Further Reading

Bellagamba, A. (1992). *Mission & ministry in the global church.* Maryknoll, NY: Orbis Books.

John Paul II. (1988). *Christifideles Laici: The Vocation and the mission of the lay faithful in the church and in the world.* Washington, DC: United States Catholic Conference.

John Paul II. (1990). *Redemptoris missio: On the permanent validity of the church's missionary mandate.* Washington, DC: United States Catholic Conference.

Lyons, J. M. (1941). *Means of fostering the missionary vocation in the Catholic primary and secondary schools.* Washington, DC: The Catholic University of America Press.

Manna, P. (1911). *The workers are few: Reflections upon vocations to the foreign missions* (Joseph McGlinchey, Trans.). Boston, MA: The Society for the Propagation of the Faith.

Manna, P. (1954). *Forward with Christ: Thoughts and reflections upon vocations to the foreign missions* (Joseph McGlinchey, Trans.). Westminster, MD: Newman Press.

Schreiter, R. (1992). *Reconciliation: Mission and ministry in a changing social order.* Maryknoll, NY: Orbis Books.

Walsh, J. E. (1955). Description of a missioner. *Worldmission,* 6(4), 402–416.

# Modernity

"Modernity" can be a politically loaded term, especially when Europeans have used it to differentiate themselves from other societies. Increasingly, scholars argue that much of what is included under the term modernity is not neutral or universal. If countries outside Europe and North America were politically, economically, and militarily dominant, modernity might be defined differently. Moreover, when "modern" institutions are transplanted into different cultural contexts, they are often fundamentally transformed. Still, regardless of these complexities, missionaries were important carriers of many aspects typically associated with modernity; for example, mass education, mass access to printed material, Western medicine, political democracy, religious liberty, civil society, and greater rights for women.

## Advocating Civilization

Despite the role of missionaries in fostering modernity, there was considerable debate among missionaries about how much they should advocate "civilization"/ modernization in other societies. In 1622 *Propaganda Fide* instructed Catholic missionaries not to try to change the "manners, customs, and uses" of the people they served, except when these customs were "evidently contrary to religion and sound morals." Missionary leaders from Henry Venn (CMS), Rufus Anderson (ABCFM), and Francis Wayland (BMS) to Robert E. Speer (Student Volunteer Movement) all warned against trying to Westernize others' cultures. In fact, the Harvard historian William Hutchison argues that "[mission] executives and theorists...spent more time and ink on these controverted issues [about civilizing versus preaching Christ only] than on the straightforward advocacy and cheerleading for which they are best known" (1987, 12).

### Missionaries as Agents of Westernization

Yet by bridging between cultures and attempting to mitigate social problems missionaries were important agents of modernization and Westernization. For example, in the 1500s to 1700s Jesuit missionaries in Asia introduced world maps, more accurate astronomical instruments, Western geometry and science, new techniques in architecture and art (including polychrome enamels that allowed detailed colored painting on Chinese porcelain and perspective and realism that spurred Mogul miniatures).

Missionaries such as Young J. Allen, W. E. B. Martin, Gilbert Reid, and Timothy Richard openly advocated that the Chinese adopt Western science and reform their institutions in order to prevent famine, foster economic growth, and gain the strength to resist Japanese and European imperialism. Other missionaries introduced printing to most societies, as well as Western medicine, Western education, new crops and livestock, new agricultural techniques, and so on.

## Investments in Mass Education

Protestant missionaries were also the main advocates of mass education throughout the Global South during the nineteenth and early twentieth centuries. Colonial administrators typically wanted a small, educated, elite that they could control. When freed from Protestant missionary agitation, they invested little in formal education for nonwhites. White settlers tended to be extremely averse to education for nonwhites, and non-European elites also did not tend to advocate mass education prior to missionary contact. However, Protestant missionaries wanted people to be able to read the Bible in their own language; thus, they invested heavily in mass education. In order to compete with them, other groups invested in mass education as well; hence, the historic prevalence of Protestant missionaries is a strong predictor of literacy and educational enrollments in countries in both historic and current data. It is also a strong predictor of literacy and educational enrollments in provinces in sub-Saharan Africa and in states of India. Even in Japan, historic missionary activity is a strong predictor of the availability of private education (Woodberry 2004).

### Spread of Printing Technology

One of the technologies that allowed the rapid spread of the sciences and other aspects of modernity was the printing press. We often think printing spread with knowledge of printing technology, but this is not necessarily true. Throughout the Muslim, Hindu, and Theravada Buddhist worlds, people knew about printing for hundreds of years before using it (i.e., all of North Africa, the Middle East, South Asia, Southeast Asia, and islands in the Indian Ocean). Catholic and Protestant missionaries generally introduced the first presses and vernacular fonts, and local elites did not copy the technology until confronted with mass-produced tracts and Bibles.

For example, the printing press was first used in the Ottoman Empire in 1493—but only used by Jews and Christians. In India Jesuits introduced printing in 1556. In Persia Carmelite friars introduced a printing press in the 1600s. The *Propaganda Fide* began being published in Asian languages in the early 1600s—expanding into Arabic, Persian, and Turkish. Jesuit missionaries brought printed texts to the Ottoman, Persian, and Mogul courts, as well as to Hindu and Buddhist kingdoms in India, Sri Lanka, and Southeast Asia. Protestant missionaries followed, printing in Tamil in 1712, in Arabic in 1720, and in Sinhalese in 1737. Portuguese, Dutch, Danish, French, and British trading companies imported printed texts from the sixteenth through the nineteenth centuries. The British East India Company imported a press in 1778, printing official documents in Persian and Bengali.

However, none of these presses spurred imitation, perhaps because they all (1) produced small numbers of texts, mostly intended for elites; (2) closed after a short

period of time; or (3) produced official (noncontroversial) documents. Widespread printing did not begin in Muslim, Hindu, or Theravada Buddhist societies until the 1800s and seems to be linked to the advent of widespread Protestant missionary printing, although there were other causes as well.

After the 1790s Protestant missions began to grow rapidly. This new wave of missionaries used printed material as a primary evangelistic tool. They wanted everyone to be able to read the Bible in his or her own language, so they made the investments in presses, fonts, and mass literacy necessary for the profitability of mass printing, and they came in sufficient numbers to sustain these presses and literacy campaigns.

In Thailand and Burma, Protestant missionaries introduced the first printing press and newspapers. Printing was so closely associated with Christianity that many monks refused to read printed books. In the Middle East, graduates of mission schools and workers from mission presses started and edited the first Arab-owned newspapers, and missionary fonts were the standard for decades. In India, Protestant missionaries started the first Indian-language journal, *Digdarśana,* and the prototype Bengali newspaper *Samārcāra Darpana,* and their fonts were the standard throughout the nineteenth century. The first Indian-owned presses and newspapers were run by people who had worked at the mission presses, such as Ram Mohan Roy and those in his circle, and most of the early publications focused on reforming Hinduism and countering missionary propaganda.

### Beyond the Elite

Even in China and Korea, which already had printing technology, missionaries helped expand the availability of printed matter beyond the elite. For example, Koreans first invented metal movable-font type in 1403, and King Sejong developed a phonetic writing form to facilitate printing with this new technology and make reading easier for ordinary people (it is easier and cheaper to print with a couple of dozen interchangeable letters than with thousands of Chinese pictographic characters). But the Korean literati opposed the new writing system because it undermined their elite status, and so the alphabet and technology fell into disuse. However, both were revived in the nineteenth century with the advent of Protestant missions.

Thus, what seems more crucial for widespread printing than technical knowledge is a transformed idea about who books are for. Protestants wanted everyone to be able to read their message, so they invested in printing before it was profitable. Once missionaries had absorbed the start-up costs, demonstrated the usefulness and feasibility of the technique, and created incentives to respond to proselytizing messages, other groups adopted the technology for their own ends.

## Political Democracy

Missionaries, particularly Anglo-American Protestant missionaries, were early advocates of democracy in the Global South. This is clear from books they translated or wrote on political economy, legal institutions, and the histories of Western nations. However, most of missionaries' effect on democracy was indirect. Missionaries promoted mass education, which fostered new elites and expanded existing elites. Protestants spurred social movements and religious organizations outside state control. Under conditions of religious competition, various nonstate religious groups flourished and later became the foundation of anticolonial movements and political parties. Thus, most early nationalists and social reformers in Africa and Asia had close connections with Protestant missionaries or rose to prominence in "antimissionary" organizations.

When independent from direct state control, missionaries were also able to moderate colonial abuses and establish some legal protections for nonwhites. Cumulatively, these factors facilitated postcolonial democratization. Statistical evidence suggests that societies that had more Protestant missionaries per capita and longer exposures to Protestant missionaries have significantly higher levels of political democracy and rule of law. In fact, controlling for historical missionary activity removes the impact of who colonized each country and most other factors traditionally associated with democracy in empirical research (Woodberry 2004; also see articles on politics in this encyclopedia for more details).

## Western Medicine

Missionaries were also crucial to the early proliferation of Western medicine around the world. Colonial governments often imported doctors to treat Europeans and elite non-Europeans' employees. But until the twentieth century, these doctors had little impact on the non-European population. Missionaries generally brought the first Western doctors that treated nonwhites and created the first hospitals and medical education. Well into the twentieth century, missionaries and religious groups were the main sources of Western medicine for nonwhites in many countries of the Global South (Woodberry 2004, Grundmann 2005). Missionaries also improved health standards by teaching hygiene and public health; educating women about childbirth, nutrition, and infant health; and introducing new crops and livestock, thereby improving nutrition.

Because of these missionary investments, countries that had greater exposure to Protestant missionaries have lower infant mortality (even with a wide array of statistical controls). This pattern is repeated between regions of the same country. For example, the states of India that had more Protestant missionaries per capita have lower infant morality than those that had fewer missionaries, and states like Nagaland and Mizoram have exceptionally low infant mortalities, despite being mountainous jungle areas on the border with Burma/ Myanmar that were occupied by hunter-gatherer societies 150 years ago. Currently unpublished research by Juan Carlos Esparza and by Charles H. Wood, Philip Williams, and Kuniko Chijiwa suggests a similar pattern among the indigenous populations of Mexico and Brazil respectively.

## Women's Rights

Finally, missionaries had important influences on the rise of women's rights in the global South. Missionaries were probably the main promoters of female education outside Europe during the nineteenth and early twentieth centuries. Missionaries persisted in advocating female education, despite initial resistance in most societies. Moreover, many of the social reforms that missionaries fought for (and were willing to lose converts over) were also women's issues. For instance, missionaries tended to oppose polygamy and child marriage wherever it occurred. In India missionaries mobilized opposition to suttee (burning widows on the funeral pyres of their dead husbands) and promulgated a law against consummating marriage before age twelve. This law was so controversial that it helped spur Indian nationalism and was never enforced. In China missionaries opposed foot binding and selling girls into slavery. In East Africa missionaries fought clitorectomy/female genital mutilation. The opposition to this campaign helped spur the Mao-Mao uprising in Kenya. Because these women's movements tended to engender opposition, some missionaries proposed preaching "Christ only" and letting the Gospel slowly leaven society. But many of the reforms advocated by modern Western feminists were first publicly advocated by missionaries.

ROBERT D. WOODBERRY

## Further Reading

Grundman, C. H. (2005). *Sent to heal! Emergence and development of medical missions.* Lanham, MD: University Press of America.

Hutchison, W. R. (1987). *Errand to the world: American Protestant thought and foreign missions.* Chicago: Chicago University Press.

Woodberry, R. D. (2004). The shadow of empire: Christian missions, colonial policy, and democracy in post-colonial societies. Unpublished doctoral dissertation, University of North Carolina—Chapel Hill.

Woodberry, R. D. (2007). The social impact of missionary higher education. In P. Yuen Sang Leung & P. Tze Ming Ng (Eds.), *Christian responses to Asian challenges: A glocalization view on Christian higher education in East Asia.* Hong Kong: Centre for the Study of Religion and Chinese Society, Chung Chi College, Chinese University of Hong Kong.

# Monasticism

Monasticism has remained a very central ideal through the ages of Christian history. Human perfection, especially in the religious context, quite often takes the ideal of monasticism very seriously. Even in our times it is still practiced both in Roman Catholic and Orthodox circles and varieties of it is even present in some Protestant circles.

The phenomenon of Monasticism, or Monachism as it is sometimes referred to, is a very central factor and idea in Christian (and also Buddhist) religion. It brought a new dimension to Christian life and it must be seen as a reaction to the growing worldliness and institutionalization of the church. The term *Monasticism* is derived from Greek *monos* (alone), and *Monachism* from Greek *monachos* (monk, celibate, single). While the Semitic religions such as Islam and Judaism have mainly remained unsympathetic to the ideal of Monasticism, in religions like Christianity and Buddhism human perfection takes the form of the monastic ideal. In the case of the latter two religions the dominant form of the monastic life has come to be that of the community.

What is of great interest about Christianity is that Monasticism takes a central position both in Western Catholic and Eastern Orthodox Christianity. However, Protestants were sometimes not totally sympathetic toward Monasticism, because they believed that behind the theory and practice of Monasticism there probably lies concealed a denial of the doctrine of justification by faith. However, recently there have been some signs of a more accommodating attitude toward the monastic ideal. This can be illustrated by the foundation by the (Calvinistic) Reformed Church of the monastic community at Taize, France.

Because the history and practice of Monasticism do raise some questions for the Christian church and its theology, a historical perspective on its development will provide some insight, and a focus on theological aspects related to Monasticism will provide further perspectives.

The history and roots of Christian Monasticism go as far back as the late third century. The earliest form of Christian Monasticism can be found in the so-called eremitism. This ideal, the life of the solitary monk, was sometimes thought to depend on a preliminary phase in which the ascetic lived in the community. One of the earliest and most influential eremites (hermits or anchorites) was Antony of Egypt (d. 356 CE), who is known as the founder of anchoritic monasticism. His retreat in pursuit of perfection can partly be attributed to lay ambitions for the heroism of the martyr and the growing laxity in the church, which was imperially patronized and at peace Hellenized. The eremites in Egypt, mainly Coptic *fellahin,* mostly abandoned church and civilization, but in the course of time informal colonies developed in some of the deserts southwest of the Nile delta. In these colonies learning remained minimal and manual tasks were predominant. So-called common monastic life, or Cenobitic Monasticism, was started in Egypt by Pachomius (346 CE), who subjected the communities under his control to a basic common rule. In these types of monasteries and around centers such as Oxyrhynchus, monks multiplied. The spirituality of the Desert Fathers, which had its roots in Origen's teachings, was preserved in the "Sayings of the Fathers" (*Apophthegmata Patrum*). Antony's disciple, Hilarion (371 CE), propagated anchoritism near Gaza in Palestine, and nearby, Epiphanius, future bishop of Salamis, founded the first cenobitic monastery.

The monastic developments in Syria were independent of those models in the Egyptian context. Some of the important early anchorites were Jacob of Nisibis (338 CE) and Juliana Saba (366 CE). The importance of Syria in monastic development extends to the missionary Monasticism of the Persian Church and beginnings in eastern Asia Minor. Monasticism moved from the East to the West primarily with exiled travelers such as Athanasius and Jerome. From the beginning its influence was clearly seen in cultural and clerical circles as nowhere in the East. Jerome's ascetic inclination attracted a large following among the Roman aristocracy, but it also created ecclesiastical disfavor. Monastic ideals had the greatest influence in Gaul through some early efforts of Martin of Tours (397 CE) and John Cassian (435 CE), and also in Celtic Ireland, where virtually the whole Christian Church in the sixth century assumed a monastic mold.

Monastic rules and even rigors multiplied in the fifth and sixth centuries, also through the influence of Augustine of North Africa, Caesarius of Arles, and Columban. This was eventually overshadowed by the Rule of Benedict (550 CE), who was the greatest creative personality in Western monasticism. The pattern set out by Benedictine Christians largely overshadowed developments in medieval Europe. Accompanying an economic resurgence in medieval Europe came a spiritual renewal. Its early origins lay in the reform movement that began with the founding of the Cluny monastery in Burgundy, implying a return to the strict rules of Benedict. In the course of time various new orders appeared such as the Cistercians, the Augustinians, the Franciscans, and the Dominicans, and each played an important role in the furthering of monasticism.

The motives behind the earlier forms of Christian Monasticism are mostly complicated. Although the main motivation was theological, there definitely were social and political factors as well. Two questions at least can be raised in this respect: Has the monk a permanent significance for the Christian believer? Is there a necessity for such a movement of withdrawal? Early Christian ascetic writings show clearly the place given to the ideal of man as a *peregrinus* (pilgrim) on the way back to a lost paradise, gradually recovering the lost perfection and virtue of Adam. The idea of the imitation of Christ was very powerful, Christ being for the monk the model as the second Adam. The monk was being approximated to the image of the simplicity and unity of God. Another motivation is the ideal of perfection, being interpreted as detachment from the world, which is, for example, expressed in surrender of material possessions in poverty, personal will in obedience, and sexual life in celibacy. A basic question regarding Monasticism is whether it contains a latent Prometheanism. Finally, a relatively serious reservation about Monasticism is the emphasis on celibacy at the cost of the view that the married relationship is inferior and that the highest goal of discipleship is open only to those who are celibate. This is not of necessity the case, because a married relationship can have as one of its effects a liberation from self-gratification.

In itself Monasticism is a very interesting phenomenon and, especially in our times because of the new interest in spirituality and the like, is worthy of further study and research. All over the world and all over the ages it has been a living aspect of religious life and theology, influenced by theological, sociopolitical, and cultural factors.

J.W. Hofmeyr

The monastery overlooking Lake Sevan, Armenia. *Courtesy of Steve Humphreys/istockphoto.com.*

## Further Reading

Hart, T. A. (Ed.). (2000). *The dictionary of historical theology*. Grand Rapids, MI: Eerdmans.

Hofmeyr, J. W. & Pillay, G. J. (Eds.). (1991). *Perspectives on church history*. Pretoria, South Africa: HAUM Tetiary.

# Money

When Jesus sent out twelve and later seventy-two of his disciples—the first two recorded instances of Christian missionaries—he advised them against taking money or material provisions of any kind (Luke 9:1–6; 10:1–17). In the early church, similarly, although there were charlatans who "peddled the word of God for profit" (2 Cor. 2:17 NIV), St. Paul—the archetypal missionary—reminded the church in Ephesus that he was self-supporting: "You yourselves know that these hands of mine have supplied my own needs and the needs of my companions. In everything I did, I showed you that by this kind of hard work we must help the weak, remembering the words the Lord Jesus Christ himself said, 'It is more blessed to give than to receive'" (Acts 20:34–35).

Since the post-Constantine fusion of Christianity with political power that resulted in Christendom, mission finance has generally been sufficient to provide missionary personnel and institutions with the basic material entitlements of their home societies. The expansion of Western economic hegemony during the past five hundred years has issued in a corresponding boost in missionary finance. Over the past century, the income of global foreign missions has grown from an estimated $200 million in 1900 to $21 billion by mid-2006, according to estimates appearing in the January 2006 issue of the *International Bulletin of Missionary Research*. This money financed the activities of some 62,000 Christian foreign missionaries in 1900 and 448,000 in 2006—excluding the tens of thousands of North Americans taking short-term (two weeks or less) mission trips each year. Robert Wuthnow, director of the Center for the Study of Religion at Princeton University, estimates that 1.6 million Americans went on these mission trips in 2005.

Increasingly problematic for Western missionaries have been the relational, communicatory, and ethical dynamics of gross material inequity in close social proximity. When North Americans relocate to most other countries as missionaries, it is almost as though they had inherited a peerage. Not surprisingly, their religious vocation is seen as an extraordinary way to make a lucrative living (being paid to be religious somewhere else), providing not only an enviably comprehensive compensation package for the family, but a level of prestige and influence that are the natural concomitant of personal association with large sums of money.

As the World Bank's *World Development Report 2006* observes, inequities between nations or within communities are mirrored in disparate access to health, education, and employment opportunities (2006, 55–69). According to the same report, while absolute poverty rates have declined over the past twenty years, so that an estimated 400 million fewer people lived on less than $1 per day in 2001 than in 1981, during the same period "the number of poor people in sub-Saharan Africa al-

**Table 1.** Countries with More than Fifty U.S. Mission Agencies

| Country | Number of Agencies | Full-time U.S. Personnel | Country | Number of Agencies | Full-time U.S. Personnel | Country | Number of Agencies | Full-time U.S. Personnel |
|---|---|---|---|---|---|---|---|---|
| Mexico | 159 | 1,657 | South Africa | 73 | 447 | Asia–General | 63 | 2,330 |
| India | 155 | 305 | France | 72 | 584 | Colombia | 62 | 346 |
| Philippines | 133 | 1,278 | Thailand | 72 | NR | Uganda | 61 | 278 |
| Brazil | 112 | 1,403 | Haiti | 72 | 225 | Bolivia | 60 | 416 |
| Kenya | 106 | 1,032 | Indonesia | 71 | 727 | Ecuador | 57 | 568 |
| Russia | 96 | 589 | Guatemala | 70 | 350 | Nigeria | 57 | 229 |
| United Kingdom | 89 | 714 | Honduras | 69 | 273 | Costa Rica | 55 | 263 |
| Japan | 86 | 921 | Peru | 68 | 491 | Argentina | 55 | 281 |
| Ukraine | 77 | 336 | Romania | 64 | 291 | Australia | 52 | 352 |
| Germany | 76 | 601 | Ghana | 64 | 160 | Hungary | 51 | 283 |
| Spain | 73 | 497 | China | 64 | 350 | Taiwan | 51 | 289 |

Source: Welliver & Northcutt (2004, passim).

most doubled, from approximately 160 million to 313 million" (2006, 66).

Among the nearly 400,000 (346,270 short-term and 45,617 full-time) reported North American Protestant missionaries serving in 211 different countries, those who are based in wealthier nations find themselves at the other end of the inequity equation, as a comparison between Tables 1 and 2 below indicates. Nevertheless, it is generally the case that Western missionaries do well by doing good, when judged by the economic standards of most of the globe's population.

While per capita expenditure varies widely between agencies, financial figures provided by North American Protestant agencies simply serve to accentuate the economic power represented by North Americans—including missionaries.

Such figures do not, of course, translate directly into missionary salaries. Mission organizations are usually

**Table 2.** U.S. Mission Agencies Providing Over $10 Million Income for Overseas Ministries

| U.S. Mission Agency | Number of Overseas Personnel | Reported Income for Overseas (including gifts in kind) |
| --- | --- | --- |
| World Vision | NR | $447,313,000 |
| Southern Baptist Convention | 5,437 | 197,866,000 |
| Wycliffe Bible Translators | 3,907 | 86,551,480 |
| Assemblies of God | 1,708 | 177,262,833 |
| New Tribes Mission | 1,496 | 32,247,000 |
| Campus Crusade for Christ | 1,096 | 123,279,000 |
| Christian and Missionary Alliance | 722 | 24,743,649 |
| TEAM—The Evangelical Alliance Mission | 675 | 23,540,000 |
| Seventh Day Adventists General Conference | 573 | 62,973,862 |
| CBInternational (formerly Conservative Baptist Foreign Mission Society) | 558 | 19,155,068 |
| SIM USA | 557 | 26,670,750 |
| Baptist Mid-Missions | 495 | 19,200,000 |
| Africa Inland Mission International | 456 | 15,062,725 |
| Evangelical Free Church Mission | 352 | 17,120,282 |
| UFM International | 312 | NR |
| Avant Ministries (formerly Gospel Missionary Union) | 257 | 8,200,000 |
| SEND International | 222 | 11,458,957 |
| CAM International | 210 | 6,260,000 |
| OMF International | 187 | 5,000,000 |
| Eastern Mennonite Missions | 140 | 3,078,974 |
| WEC International | 135 | 3,044,824 |
| World Baptist Fellowship | 130 | 5,600,000 |
| Baptist General Conference | 127 | 8,572,110 |
| South America Mission | 94 | 3,277,763 |
| Child Evangelism Fellowship | 72 | 4,460,518 |
| Mennonite Mission Network | 72 | 5,686,027 |
| MBMS International—Mennonite Brethren Missions/Services | 53 | 1,088,272 |
| Brethren In Christ Mission | 36 | 1,117,069 |
| Samaritan's Purse | 19 | 111,797,883 |
| Africa Inter-Mennonite Mission | 16 | 696,591 |
| Reformed Baptist Mission Services | 16 | 301,517 |

Source: Welliver & Northcutt (2004, 29, 69–303, passim).

involved in a broad range of overseas programs, including medicine, education, community development, agricultural assistance, aid and relief, literature production, support of national churches, and technical assistance of various kinds. Nevertheless, such data do indicate the resources that—in the eyes of host peoples—missionaries represent, to some degree control, and benefit from personally.

In 2005, a typical support package for a North American missionary couple serving in South Africa was approximately $5,000 per month, exclusive of funds for travel and special projects. However reasonable $60,000 per annum might be for sustaining a North American family at levels of minimal social and material entitlement in a bicultural, intercontinental ministry, such compensation guarantees missionaries a place among the privileged in South Africa.

In North America, there seems to be no escaping from the one-way material entitlement escalator whereby one generation's luxuries mutate into another generation's needs. Peter C. Whybrow, chairman of psychiatry at the University of Pennsylvania, noted that "As America's commercial hegemony has increased and our social networks have eroded, we have lost any meaningful reference as to how rich we really are, especially in comparison to other nations." (2005, 38) Given the extent to which the Christian community is infused with the values of the dominant culture, it would be surprising indeed if Western missionaries were somehow exempt from these powerful influences. As David Hesselgrave, emeritus professor at the Trinity Evangelical Divinity School, recently observed, "In 1998 the total income reported by mission agencies in the United States came within a hair's breadth of . . . $3 billion. By 2003 this had increased to over $3.75 billion. Nevertheless, most missions and missionaries continue to report a serious need for support. What are we to make of this state of affairs?" (2005, 228). A good question.

JONATHAN BONK

*See also* Faith Missions; North America; Protestant Churches; Short-term Missions

### Further Reading:

Barrett, D. B., Johnson, T. M., & Crossing, P. F. (2006, January). Missiometrics 2006: Goals, resources, doctrines of the 350 Christian world communions. *International Bulletin of Missionary Research, 30*(1), 27–30.

Bonk, J. (2007). *Missions and money: Affluence as a Western missionary problem . . . revisited* (Rev. ed). New York: Orbis.

Hesselgrave, D. J. (2005). *Paradigms in conflict: 10 key questions in Christian missions today.* Grand Rapids, MI: Kregel.

Welliver, D., & Northcutt, M. (2004). *Mission handbook 2004–2006: U.S. and Canadian Protestant ministries overseas.* Wheaton, IL: Evangelism and Missions Information Service (EMIS).

Whybrow, P. C. (2005). *American mania: When more is not enough.* New York: Norton.

The World Bank. (2006). *World development report 2006: Equity and development.* Washington, DC: The International Bank for Reconstruction and Development/The World Bank & New York: Oxford University Press.

## Moratorium

During the first half of the decade of the 1970s, a lively discussion went on in world mission circles about a proposal to enact a "moratorium" on the activity of foreign missions. The proposal for a moratorium, if agreed to, would have resulted in the suspension by foreign mission agencies of the sending of missionaries and the granting of financial subsidies to Christian churches in the third world. By the same token, the moratorium would have obliged churches in the third world to forgo receiving missionaries from abroad and to decline the acceptance of monetary gifts or foreign subsidies for a specified period. The aim of the proposal was variously described as promoting more mature relationships between sending organizations and receiving churches, liberating givers and receivers from the unhealthy syndrome of dominance and dependence, or simply fostering the growing selfhood of emerging churches.

### History

The moratorium idea was not entirely new. During both World War I and World War II, the missionary movement had experienced the phenomenon of "orphaned missions," or mission work disrupted by wartime conditions. A rupture in communications and support between some German and Scandinavian mission societies and their overseas mission fields in China, Indonesia, India, East Africa, and elsewhere had left these fledgling churches isolated and virtually abandoned by their parent bodies, imposing severe hardships on indigenous evangelists and local congregations, schools, and clinics. The International Missionary Council (IMC) was able to negotiate trustee relationships between some of these orphaned missions and other mission agencies of the same denominational background, saving them from being seized as wartime booty. The lesson learned was that struggling and vulnerable Christian communities needed to be assisted in achieving autonomy and independence from parent mission agencies at the earliest possible moment.

Nineteenth-century Western missions generally paid lip service to the "three-self" principle of independence as enunciated by Henry Venn of the Church Missionary Society (CMS), and Rufus Anderson of the American Board of Commissioners of Foreign Missions (ABCFM): self-government, self-support, and self-propagation. But missionary paternalism delayed implementation of the goal. When Protestant churches and Roman Catholics in China were forced by their government after the revolution of 1949 to sever personnel and financial links with foreign mission agencies, they turned to the nineteenth-century three-self principle as the basis for their declaration of independence from foreign ties.

## African Initiative

During the 1960s most former European colonies in Africa underwent decolonization and became independent. Freedom from colonialism led to a general mood of optimism but also prompted deep reflection about the still-dependent state of African churches. In 1971 John Gatu, a leading East African Presbyterian Church leader, called for a moratorium on foreign-mission activity, arguing that continuation of the existing pattern of missionary relationships was a "hindrance to the selfhood of the church" and declaring that "the time has come for the withdrawal of foreign missionaries from many parts of the Third World." The moratorium should last not less than five years, Gatu stated, to allow "each side to rethink and formulate what is going to be their future relationship" (Anderson 1991, 702).

Some Asian and Latin American church leaders echoed this sentiment. The proposal gained momentum in many quarters. The 1974 Lusaka Assembly of the All Africa Conference of Churches (AACC) called on its member churches to embrace the proposal and to support the call for moratorium as a "strategy for self-reliance.... The moratorium would be a strategy to allow the churches of Africa to make sure of their own identity and integrity as responsible communions of Christians ... taking full responsibility for the work of the church in their own country and continent and a self-giving commitment to support it and its mission." Some advantages to be gained were discovery of an authentic African form of Christianity; the overcoming of dependent attitudes; establishment of African priorities, with churches becoming fully missionary in their own right; and the enabling of traditional missionary-sending bodies in the West to reexamine the nature of their own mission and their future partnership with other churches.

## Ecumenical Responses

Already in 1973 the Commission on World Mission and Evangelism of the Bangkok Assembly of the World Council of Churches (WCC) had taken note of the moratorium proposal in the context of a heated discussion on power sharing between churches and overcoming one-sided relationships of dominance and dependence. In its report, Section III, "Partnership in Mission," the Bangkok Conference pleaded for "a mature relationship between churches" based on "mutual commitment to participate in Christ's mission to the world" (Report 1973, 221). The widest possible discussion of the moratorium proposal was recommended as a possible strategy for mission in the future.

In 1974 the Lausanne International Congress on World Evangelization, sponsored by the Lausanne Committee for World Evangelization, obliquely referred to the moratorium proposal in one article of the Lausanne Covenant, giving it a qualified endorsement. "A reduction of foreign missionaries and money in an evangelized country may sometimes be necessary to facilitate the national church's growth in self-reliance and to release resources for unevangelized areas" (Lausanne Covenant 1975, 6).

At the Fifth Assembly of the World Council of Churches meeting in Nairobi (1975), the moratorium debate was not the center of discussion but was never far from the thinking of delegates. The Nairobi Report suggested that churches should study the reasons for the call for a moratorium and encourage development of a cross-cultural model for mission in six continents in which gifts, evangelistic models, and contributions might be pooled and shared. "World mission is a privilege and responsibility of the whole church," said Nairobi, and "it is inside this search for a better missionary service and a deeper unity that the debate on moratorium should proceed" (Paton 1976, 304).

By 1975 the terms of the debate had moved from the discussion of a possible moratorium *on* or *from* mission toward a moratorium *for* mission as the joint privilege and responsibility of churches in all six continents. All aspects of the moratorium issue were taken up and examined in minute detail at annual consultations of the Committee on Ecumenical Sharing of Personnel (ESP), a joint committee of the World Council of Churches dealing with both interchurch aid and mission. By 1975 angry denunciations by some Western missionary spokespersons of the moratorium as a betrayal of the Great Commission were no longer heard. There was now general agreement that the understanding of mission had changed and that the structures for carrying out mission must also change.

There is no evidence that the moratorium proposal as originally defined was ever carried out. But there is considerable evidence to suggest that it formed a kind of watershed in thinking about the nature of world mission at the end of the second millennium and the structures needed for carrying it out. This can be seen in the creation of new missionary structures that bridge the gap between North (traditional Western mission-sending agencies) and South (churches in the third world which have arisen from Western missionary activity) and offer new models for missionary decision making and joint missionary action.

JAMES A. SCHERER

### Further Reading

Anderson, G. H. (1974). A moratorium on missionaries? In G.H. Anderson & T.F. Stransky (Eds.), *Mission Trends No. 1*, 133–141. New York: Paulist.

Anderson, G. H. (1991). Moratorium. *Dictionary of ecumenical movement* (1st ed.). Geneva: WWC.

Lausanne Covenant. (1975). *Let the earth hear His voice: International congress on world Evangelization, Lausanne, Switzerland, 1974*. Minneapolis, MN: World Wide Publications.

Paton, D. M. (Ed.). (1976). Breaking barriers: Nairobi 1975. *Fifth Assembly of the World Council of Churches*. London: SPCK.

Report of Bangkok Conference Section III. (1973, April). *International Review of Mission (IRM)*, 52(246).

## Moravians

The Moravian Church is generally regarded as the first Protestant missionary church. Its history reaches back to the Czech Reformation in the fifteenth century, when attempts at church reform led to the founding of a small denomination known as the Unity of Brethren. By the sixteenth century, the Unity consisted of three branches in Bohemia, Moravia, and Poland, but subsequently, it was violently suppressed by the Catholic Counter-Reformation in the aftermath of the Thirty Years' War (1618–1648).

In 1722 several descendants of the "ancient" Unity from Moravia sought refuge on the estate of Count Nikolaus Ludwig von Zinzendorf (1700–1760) in the eastern part of Saxony/Germany. They established a small settlement named Herrnhut, which under Zinzendorf's leadership soon developed into the center of an international Evangelical renewal and missionary movement, calling itself *Brüdergemeine* (brethren's community). Although only a fraction of its membership came from Moravia, the community soon became known as the "Moravians" in the English-speaking world. Mission work was begun by the "renewed" Moravian community in 1732 and has been an integral part of its identity ever since. As a result, the present-day Moravian Unity is comprised of nineteen provinces representing more than twenty-five countries.

### Herrnhut and the First Mission to St. Thomas, 1732

The beginning of the Moravian missionary activity is inseparably linked to the spiritual development of the Herrnhut community under the leadership of Count Zinzendorf. Belonging to the Lutheran confession by birth, Zinzendorf was raised in the spirit of German Pietism and spent four years at the famous boarding school of August Hermann Francke at Halle. The missionary attempts by Ziegenbalk and Plütschau in India, which Francke supported, awakened Zinzendorf's interest in missionary activities. At age 16 he formed a covenant with several friends to commit himself to the task of evangelizing among peoples that had not been reached by the Gospel.

The arrival of Protestant refugees from Moravia on his estate in 1722 gave Zinzendorf the opportunity to organize a religious community according to Pietist principles. Herrnhut was intended to be a village composed of true believers, modeled after the example of the early church. It soon attracted a growing number of Pietists and spiritual seekers of various backgrounds. The experience of a transforming spiritual renewal in 1727 provided the community with a strong sense of unity and purpose. Zinzendorf and the Moravians eagerly reached out to other Evangelical believers and began building a network of friends and supporters throughout Germany and beyond.

A. *Der Priester welcher tauft.*    **TAUFE**    C. C. *Die Arbeiter von ihrer Nation.*
BBB. *Die Täuflinge.*    der Indianer    D. D. *Die Indianer-Gemeine.*
in America

This drawing shows the baptism of Native-Americans at the Moravian chapel in Bethlehem, Pennsylvania, around 1750. *Courtesy of Dr. Paul Peucker, Moravian Archives, Bethlehem, Pennsylvania.*

The sending of Leonard Dober (1706–1766) and David Nitschmann (1697–1772) to the black slaves on the Caribbean Island of St. Thomas in 1732 marks the beginning of Moravian missions. This venture was occasioned by the encounter with a former black slave, Anton, who visited Herrnhut in 1731 and reported about the desperate spiritual state of African slaves on the Caribbean plantations. Dober, a potter by trade, felt called by God to share the Gospel with these people, even if it would require him to become a slave himself.

After one year of deliberation and preparation, he and Nitschmann traveled by foot to Copenhagen where they secured passage across the Atlantic, arriving on St. Thomas 13 December 1732. Having received no other instruction than to follow the guidance of the spirit of Jesus Christ, they spent the first months to learn the language and establish contacts among the black population. Slowly they gained the slaves' trust, especially by providing medical assistance and offering some rudimentary schooling for children. In his preaching Dober emphasized that Jesus had come as a savior for all people, not only whites. The first convert, a young orphan by the name of Carmel Oly, traveled with Dober to Europe in 1734 and was baptized there in 1735. Dober's successors, Friedrich Martin and Matthäus Freundlich, were able to establish a congregation of some 600 converts by 1738 and extended the mission to St. Croix and St. Jan.

## Moravian Missions under Zinzendorf's Leadership, 1732–1760

The first mission to St. Thomas set the stage for a number of other missionary ventures that followed in quick succession. Three missionaries went to Greenland in 1733, baptizing their first converts in 1739 and establishing a congregation in 1747. In 1734 a group of eighteen Moravians went to St. Croix to establish a plantation and mission station; a second group was sent to Savannah, Georgia, to begin mission work among Cherokee Indians. Both attempts failed within a few years. Incidentally, it was in the context of the Georgia mission that John Wesley came into closer contact with the Moravians.

In 1735 first steps were undertaken for a mission in Dutch Guyana (Suriname), and in 1736 one missionary, Georg Schmidt, was send to the Cape of South Africa to work among the Khoikhoi. Between 1738 and 1743 an attempt was made to reach out to the Jewish community in Amsterdam. In 1740 Christian Heinrich Rauch began mission work among the Mohicans in New York State. His first converts were baptized in 1742 when Count Zinzendorf visited Pennsylvania. In the same year, the Moravians established Bethlehem, Pennsylvania, as an outpost for further outreach to the Delaware and Iroquois Indians. There were also short-lived attempts at

Guinea (1736–1741), Sri Lanka (1739–1741), and Labrador (1752).

It is important to note that by 1735 the initial Herrnhut community had begun to evolve into an interdenominational renewal movement, which attracted hundreds of followers throughout Europe. A number of additional congregations and societies were established in Germany, the Netherlands, and England. These communities provided the economic basis and the human resources to sustain the growing mission work. Between 1732 and 1760, 226 men and women were sent to the various mission fields, approximately 5 percent of the total membership. Few of them were ordained pastors; mostly they were lay people, trained in some trade or craft. The death toll was considerable, as many faced hazardous journeys, adverse climatic conditions, and violent hostility. The total number of baptized converts came to about three thousand persons by 1760.

The Moravian approach to mission evolved out of the practical experiences and needs in the mission fields, but it was also significantly shaped by the theology of Zinzendorf. The main objective of mission work was, in Zinzendorf's words, "to win souls for the Lamb." The Moravian community felt obliged to the biblical commission to preach Christ to all the nations, especially as they attributed to this task an important role in the economy of salvation. Zinzendorf believed that, as the second coming of Christ was drawing near, it was important to sow the seeds of the Gospel at the most remote and neglected places. His goal was not to convert the masses but to make a beginning among those whom the Holy Spirit had prepared as the "first fruits" of their people (cf. Rev. 14:10). Missionaries should avoid all forms of coercion and colonialism and respect the cultural particularities of the indigenous population. Rather than preaching abstract doctrines, they should focus on the message of Christ as the incarnate and crucified Savior. The most effective means in their effort was to be their own conduct and example.

## The "Classic" Era of Moravian Missions, 1760–1900

Zinzendorf's death in 1760 marked the transition of the Moravian community from an interdenominational movement toward becoming an independent church. The existing missions were continued, and a number of new initiatives took shape. Mission work among the North American Indians flourished under the leadership of David Zeisberger until the disruptions in the aftermath of the American Revolution. Political difficulties caused the end of this mission at the beginning of

the nineteenth century. The Moravians extended their outreach in the Danish and British West Indies and sent missionaries to India (1759–1803), South Russia (1768–1823), and Egypt (1768–1783). Successful attempts were made in Labrador (1772) and South Africa (1792).

Under the leadership of Zinzendorf's successor August Gottlieb Spangenberg (1703–1791), Moravian missions became effectively organized through the administration of a central governing board. A number of mission societies were established, and several detailed histories appeared in print, notably the history of the Moravian mission in Greenland by D. Cranz (1765), in the West Indies by C. G. A. Oldendorp (1777), and among the Indians in North America by H. Loskiel (1789). These publications contributed to the growing reputation of Moravian missions among other Protestant denominations. Indeed, the example of the Moravians arguably played an important role in the missionary awakening in England and Germany at the end of the eighteenth century.

By the middle of the nineteenth century the organization of the Moravian Unity was restructured, creating four provinces (Continental Europe, England, USA Northern Province, and USA Southern Province), to which the various mission areas were assigned. In the West Indies, the abolition of slavery in the 1830s marked a new stage in the life and organization of the Moravian communities. It was recognized that the time had come for these congregations to move toward greater autonomy. Alfred Lind, the first black Moravian minister, was ordained in 1854; later a training school for teachers and a theological seminary were established. Similar efforts toward the formation of indigenous churches were also made in Suriname and South Africa. New mission work was begun in Nicaragua (1849), South Australia (1849–1919), Tibet (1853), British Guyana (1878), Alaska (1885), and East Africa/Tanzania (1891). In 1900 the mission in Greenland was transferred from the Moravian Church to the Danish Lutheran Church for political and financial reasons. At that time, the Moravians were active in about 20 different areas around the globe, employing about 400 missionaries and counting almost 100,000 baptized members in the mission fields.

## The Modern Era, 1900 to Present

The political events of the twentieth century, especially World Wars I and II, severely undercut the established system of Moravian missions. Oversight for the mission work passed from the central governing board in Germany to several administrative agencies in England, the United States, and the Netherlands. The general

Synod of 1957 in Bethlehem, Pennsylvania, affirmed the global unity of the Moravian Church and prepared the way for the transformation of former mission fields into self-governing provinces. Accordingly, fourteen new provinces were organized between 1960 and 1988: Alaska, Costa Rica, the Eastern West Indies, Guyana, Honduras, Jamaica, Labrador, Nicaragua, South Africa, Suriname, Tanzania Rukwa, Tanzania South, Tanzania South-West, and Tanzania West. In addition, the Moravian Church maintains a Christian school and several congregations in North India, operates a home for handicapped children near Jerusalem, and has started new mission initiatives in central Africa, Siberia, and Albania.

Due to its long missionary history, the Moravian Church today is very diverse geographically, ethnically, and culturally. Most of its members now live in Africa (c. 510,000) and South and Central America (c. 194,000). Moravians in North America number about 50,000, in Europe about 30,000. All provinces are self-governing but recognize the authority of the Unity Synod, which meets every seven years with elected delegates from each province. While the Moravian Church is now less tightly organized than in the nineteenth century, the transformation of former missions into independent provinces has created a new sense of global cooperation and communion.

PETER VOGT

## Further Reading

Atwood, C. D. (2004). *Community of the cross: Moravian piety in colonial Bethlehem.* University Park: Pennsylvania State University Press.

Atwood, C. D., & Vogt, P. (2003). *The distinctiveness of Moravian culture: Essays and documents in Moravian history.* Nazareth, PA: Moravian Historical Society.

Baudert, S. (1932). Zinzendorf's thought on mission related to his views of the world. *International Review of Missions, 21,* 390–401.

Buijtenen, M. P., & Dekker, C. (1975). *Unitas Fratrum: Moravian studies—Herrnhuter Studien.* Utrecht, Netherlands: Rijksarchief.

Freeman, A. J. (1998). *An ecumenical theology of the heart: The theology of Count Nicholas Ludwig von Zinzendorf.* Bethlehem, PA: Moravian Church in America.

Hamilton, J. T., & Hamilton, K. G. (1967). *History of the Moravian Church: The renewed* Unitas Fratrum, *1722–1957.* Bethlehem, PA: Moravian Church in America.

Hutton, J. E. (1922). *A history of Moravian missions.* London: Moravian Publications Office.

Krüger, B. (1966). *The pear tree blossoms: The history of the Moravian Church in South Africa.* Genadendal: Moravian Church of South Africa.

Lewis, A. J. (1962). *Zinzendorf, the ecumenical pioneer: A study in the Moravian contribution to Christian mission and unity.* Philadelphia: Westminster Press.

Mason, J. C. S. *The Moravian Church and the missionary awakening in England.* Rochester, NY: Boydell & Brewer.

Olmstead, E. P. (1997). *David Zeisberger: A life among the Indians.* Kent, OH: Kent State University Press.

Podmore, C. (1998). *The Moravian Church in England, 1728–1760.* Oxford, UK: Clarendon Press.

Rollmann, H. (2002). *Labrador through Moravian eyes: 250 years of art, photographs and records.* St. John's, Newfoundland: Special Celebration Corporation of Newfoundland and Labrador.

Schattschneider, D. A. (1975). *Souls for the Lamb: A theology for the Christian mission according to Count Nicolaus Ludwig von Zinzendorf and Bishop Augustus Gottlieb Spangenberg.* Doctoral dissertation, University of Chicago Divinity School.

Sensbach, J. F. (1998). *A separate Canaan: The making of an Afro-Moravian world in North Carolina, 1763–1840.* Chapel Hill: University of North Carolina Press.

Sensbach, J. F. (2005). *Rebecca's revival: Creating black Christianity in the Atlantic world.* Cambridge, MA: Harvard University Press.

Smaby, B. P. (1988). *The transformation of Moravian Bethlehem: From communal mission to family economy.* Philadelphia: University of Pennsylvania Press.

Sommer, E. W. (2000). *Serving two masters: Moravian brethren in Germany and North Carolina.* Lexington: University Press of Kentucky.

Vogt, P. (2005). Nikolaus Ludwig von Zinzendorf, 1700–1760, in C. Lindberg (Ed.). *The Pietist theologians* (pp. 207–223). Oxford: Blackwell.

Weinlick, J. R. (1956). *Count Zinzendorf: The story of his life and leadership in the renewed Moravian Church.* New York: Abingdon Press.

## Mormonism

With a missionary force of over 55,000 full-time missionaries in 334 mission fields, the Church of Jesus Christ of Latter-day Saints, LDS, or Mormon Church has one of the largest missionary programs of any church. Mormon missionary activity began in April of 1830 when Samuel H. Smith (1808–1844) traveled the rural areas of New York selling the recently published *Book of Mormon*. In the fall of 1830 four missionaries traveled to the edges of western Missouri in an attempt to convert the Native-Americans settled there under Andrew Jackson's Indian policy. The Native-Americans were promised a prominent role in building the Millennial Kingdom of God if they would convert to Mormonism. For many in America Smith's *Book of Mormon* would seemingly answer their questions regarding baptism, the nature of God, and the role of a church in civil society. The missionary message declared that a new age of signs and wonders was upon them, the return of Jesus to the American Zion was imminent, and the Millennial Kingdom was about to be established.

Mormon missionary efforts in the nineteenth century are impossible to separate from their millenarian views. With a view that the world was on the eve of the apocalypse, the founding prophet, Joseph Smith (1805–1844), sent Mormon missionaries to gather the elect to a specified place, North America, to escape the judgments of God. This concept, known as the "gathering to Zion," was the central motive for missionary activity until the twentieth century. It is only with the failure of the expected Parousia of the early 1890s that the message shifted from gathering the elect, an earthly salvation from the apocalypse, to one of offering a heavenly hope exclusively through membership in the Mormon church.

Nineteenth-century Mormonism intertwined temporal and spiritual realms. The largest missionary force in the movement's first sixty years, 334 political missionaries, campaigned for Smith in his bid for the presidency of the United States in 1844. In Utah under Brigham Young (1801–1877), economic missions formed part of a complex colonization and economic system. Mission activity sought to transform the heavenly Kingdom into the physical Kingdom of God on the Earth.

## Social Origins of Mormon Converts

Early Mormon missionary activity was concentrated in the rural areas of New England and eastern Canada. Converts were rarely from the lowest or highest rungs of society and had often been members of several churches prior to joining the Mormons. Most individuals came from primitivist, seeker, and revivalist sects: Baptists, Methodists, Presbyterians, and Shakers. The nature of the Mormon message—a conversion experience and an inner witness of the truth—resonated with certain segments of American society. Today, conversion still entails an inner witness that the "church is true."

## Areas of Missionary Activity

As a direct result of success in Canada, the first overseas mission was established in Great Britain in 1837. Between 1837 and 1890 about 88,000 converts immigrated to America, with 55,000 coming from the Brit-

The old farmhouse of the Joseph Smith family in rural New York State. *Courtesy of Eldon Griffin/istockphoto.com.*

ish Isles. British converts came mostly from among the working classes of Preston and Manchester. Converts from Methodism (Primitive and United Brethren), Presbyterian, and nonconformist sects were drawn by the Mormon's millenarian message and the concentration on lay clergy. At the time of Smith's death in 1844, more Mormons resided in Great Britain than in the Americas. Orson Hyde (1805–1878) expanded Mormonism into Holland and Germany in 1842; success was relatively small, with only one congregation emerging in Germany in 1843. With Smith's death in 1844, the movement splintered. No new missionary endeavors outside Canada and Great Britain were undertaken between 1844 and 1850.

## Encounters with Protestantism

In 1850, with a new leadership established in Utah territory, the LDS opened missions in Italy, France, and Scandinavia. Missions to Chile, Germany, Hawaii, and Gibraltar would soon follow, and in 1852 missions were opened in China, India, and Thailand. Outside Great Britain and Scandinavia the Mormons had limited success abroad. Mormonism's millennial views, its battles with the U.S. government, its practice of polygamy, and its attempt at establishing a theocracy led foreign governments to see the Mormons as seditious until the early decades of the twentieth century.

Until the arrival of the transcontinental railroad, Mormons in Utah remained isolated. By 1869, though, several American Protestant churches had begun missionary efforts in Utah. Baptists, United Methodists, Presbyterians, and Lutherans all had missions to the Mormons from the late 1860s to the early 1920s. The Protestant missions to Utah focused on education and social improvement rather than any direct proselytizing. As Utah had no public schools prior to 1890, Protestant churches saw an opportunity to proselyte the Mormons by establishing free primary and secondary schools. The Presbyterian Women's Home Missionary also established a home for destitute and abandoned polygamous wives in 1886. The Protestants in Utah pooled resources in an ecumenical effort to evangelize among the Mormons.

## Modern Missions and Growth

Mormonism is often heralded as one of the fastest growing religions in the world. Recent religious surveys and census results from around the world paint another picture. The group claims over 12 million members worldwide, yet only a fraction of this total consists of active members. Growth has stagnated, with more individuals

leaving than joining. Low retention levels of 50 percent and low activity rates averaging 30 percent worldwide are a factor. Despite sustained efforts to proselyte abroad for 150 years, the LDS church remains a predominantly U.S.-based church with the large majority of its active membership residing within the United States.

Mormonism has had its greatest success by consistently targeting countries with a dominant Christian culture. The majority of converts historically has been, and continues to be, from traditional Christian churches. Successes in Islamic, Buddhist, or Hindu countries have been negligible. Only 5 percent of Mormon missionaries proselyte in non-Christian countries. China, with a mission since 1852, currently does not have any Mormon missionaries, with about 125 active LDS. India, with a mission since 1852, has about 857 active LDS. Mormon proselytizing in Islamic nations yields similar results. In Indonesia, the most populous Muslim country, there are 1,377 active members. The ban until 1978 on people of color holding the priesthood (priesthood is necessary for any minor church duty) left much of Africa untouched for close to 150 years.

## Reactions to Mormonism

Mormonism has historically been successful in limiting the information about itself. By controlling its public image it has been able to find some success in its missionary efforts. In the digital age the information about Mormonism has become uncontrollable. The rise of electronic media has compounded problems for the LDS as access to information is no longer restricted to, or obtained only from, specialized sources or groups. Mormonism's historic position of initial nonfull disclosure and a hierarchical set of teachings has also created mistrust among potential converts. Ex-Mormon groups, for years centered primarily in the United States, have emerged in many countries where Mormons proselyte. These ex-Mormons feel an obligation to share their experiences through publications, videos, websites and blogs. Their arguments center on the leadership's deliberate attempts to mislead the membership, the media, and society at large.

Mormonism has encountered difficulties in the last few decades, resulting in stagnated growth. The major cause for this may be the failure of the leadership to recognize that the once-successful missionary approaches are no longer working in the information age. Perhaps for the first time in its history Mormonism is losing more members than it is gaining, even in its home country, the United States.

Kurt Widmer

## Further Reading

Allen, J. B., Esplin, R. K., & Whittaker, D. J. (1991). *Men with a mission: The quorum of the twelve apostles in Great Britain, 1837–1841.* Salt Lake City, UT: Deseret Book Co.

Beckwith, F. J., & Mosser, C. (Eds.). (2002). *The new Mormon challenge: Responding to the latest defenses of a fast-growing movement.* Grand Rapids, MI: Zondervan Books.

Bloxham, V. B., Moss, J. R., & Porter, L. C. (Eds.). (1987). *Truth will prevail: The rise of the Church of Jesus Christ of Latter-day Saints in the British Isles, 1837–1987.* Solihull, UK: Church of Jesus Christ of Latter-day Saints.

Erickson, D. (1998). *As a thief in the night: The Mormon quest for millennial deliverance.* Salt Lake City, UT: Signature Books

Ludlow, D. (Ed.) (1995). *The church and society: Selections from the Encyclopedia of Mormonism.* Salt Lake City, UT: Deseret Book Co.

Lyon, T. E. (1967, Fall). Religious activities and development in Utah, 1847–1910. *Utah Historical Quarterly 35*, 292–306.

Ostling, R. N., & Ostling, J. K. (1999). *Mormon America: The power and the promise,* San Francisco: Harper Publishing.

Palmer, S. J. *The church encounters Asia.* (1970). Salt Lake City, UT: Deseret Book Co.

Quinn, D. M. (1994). *The Mormon hierarchy: Origins of power.* Salt Lake City, UT: Signature Books.

Rosten, C. L. (Ed.) (1975). *Religions of America: Ferment and faith in an age of crisis: A new guide and almanac.* New York: Simon and Schuster.

Underwood, G. (1993). *The millenarian view of early Mormonism.* Urbana: University of Illinois.

Whittaker, D. J., & Moss, J. R. (1992). Missions of the twelve to the British Isles. In D. H. Ludlow (Ed.), *Encyclopedia of Mormonism, Vol. 1.* New York: Macmillan Publishing Co.

Widmer, K. (2000). *Mormonism and the nature of God: A theological evolution, 1830–1915.* Jefferson, NC: McFarland & Company.

Winn, K. H. (1990). *Exiles in a land of liberty: Mormons in America, 1830–1846.* Chapel Hill: University of North Carolina Press.

# Music and Ethnomusicology

Music has always played a central role in the life of Christian faith communities. It is through the vehicle of music, most particularly through *psalms, hymns, and spiritual songs* (Col. 3:16; Eph. 5:19), that the Scriptures attest to the dynamic spiritual link between Yahweh and the people among whom he makes himself known. Songs emerge as profound theological expressions of the people's spiritual pilgrimage, from music's origins with Jubal, the father of the harp and flute (Gen. 4:21) to the songs of Moses (Ex. 15, Deut. 31–32) and the Prophets (the songs of Isaiah), the Psalms, a hymn at the close of the Lord's Supper (Mt. 26:30), Paul and Silas in prison (Acts 16:25), and John's Revelation (Rev. 4:8, 11; 5:9-10, 12–13).

The study of Western church music reveals the presence of music in every era of the church. New music that expressed spiritual revivals can be found in the hymns of Luther, Calvin's practice of psalm singing, Bach's cantatas, and the song-centered worship of the eighteenth-century Moravians. Spiritual awakening in the nineteenth century elicited new forms of doing mission in which evangelist and music director teamed together in proclaiming the Gospel through song. In the United States, Ira D. Sankey and Dwight L. Moody published a pamphlet of the songs associated with their missions, called *Sacred Songs and Solos,* which developed into a collection of 1,200 songs by 1903. The Salvation Army followed suit with General Booth using music "to set the tone for the Army—rousing melodies with a martial flavour" (Wilson-Dickson 1996, 139). They captured the emotional appeal of music and used it for mission purposes.

## Music in Mission

The blossoming of Western Christian music in Europe in the seventeenth and eighteenth centuries, and nineteenth-century revival songs in America and England, set the stage for the role of music in mission during the nineteenth and twentieth centuries. Along with the cultural imposition practiced during the colonial era had come the custom of introducing Western church music as the truly Christian music of the church universal. Missionaries offered their favorite hymnbooks and Bibles linked together in one package. They introduced the hymns of their Western faith, translating them for the people among whom they worked. To be Christian was to sing Western hymns. Hymnals such as *Hymns Ancient and Modern* and the Gospel songs of Moody and Sankey continue to this day to make up the bulk of translated hymns sung worldwide.

Responses to Western hymns varied. What was profoundly meaningful to Western missionaries did not readily translate in positive ways to the peoples of non-Western mission churches. In many cases, the practice of introducing translated hymns into the life of mission churches had unforseen consequences. Among the Sen-

## From Greenland's Icy Mountains

**The following is a hymn, taken from a missionary hymnal, and written in the early part of the 1800s.**

From Greenland's icy mountains, from India's coral strand;
where Afric's sunny fountains roll down their golden sand:
From many an ancient river, from many a palmy plain,
they call us to deliver their land from error's chain.

What though the spicy breezes blow soft o'er Java's isle;
though every prospect pleases, and only man is vile?
In vain with lavish kindness the gifts of God are strown;
the heathen in his blindness bows down to wood and stone!

Can we, whose souls are lighted with wisdom from on high,
can we to those benighted the lamp of life deny?
Salvation! O salvation! The joyful sound proclaim,
till earth's remotest nation has learned Messiah's Name.

Waft, waft, ye winds, his story, and you, ye waters, roll
till, like a sea of glory, it spreads from pole to pole:
till o'er our ransomed nature the Lamb for sinners slain,
Redeemer, King, Creator, in bliss returns to reign.

Source: Oremus.org. (n.d.). Retrieved May 22, 2007,
from http://www.oremus.org/hymnal/f/f271.html

---

ufo peoples of Côte d'Ivoire, West Africa, for example, the song services in the mid-twentieth century were so lifeless and deadening that missionaries and evangelists longed to preach before the singing.

Problems translating Western hymns were encountered by missionaries crossing cultures. First, the meaning of the text might be destroyed due to the tonal structures inherent in the new language. Among the Senufo, one translated hymn boldly declared, "In heaven all our houses are cursed" rather than blessed. Second, Western musical sounds were unpleasant and distasteful to many new believers' ears. Senufo believers, for example, perceived the Hallelujah chorus as "crying music." This contributed to an unpleasant and irrelevant worship atmosphere that often put attendees to sleep. Third, inappropriate metaphors that did not relate to the new cultural context resulted in irrelevant and meaningless hymns. Ultimately, translated hymns played a major role in presenting the Christian faith as foreign. As in the case of the Senufo, they were often neither appropriate nor meaningful in their new contexts.

The foreignness of translated Western hymns and music also presented barriers to the development of indigenous faith communities in Asia. In 1956, Phuntshog, a Tibetan Christian, wrote about the Moravian church community in Ladakh:

The way of worship was quite foreign to them. The construction of the Church, the sitting arrangements in the Church, the Liturgy, hymns, tunes, music, all of them were in the Western way, though they were conducted in the vernacular language. These are of great contrast to the Eastern way and especially the Tibetan way. (Oswald 2001, 14)

Phuntshog poignantly asks, "Why can't we worship God in our own indigenous way as long as it is not contrary to Christian belief and doctrine?"

Translation of the Scriptures and songs into vernacular languages did not adequately address the

A nineteenth-century Chautauqua hand organ used by traveling mission-aries. *Courtesy of Russell Shively/istockphoto.com.*

cultural aspects of music and worship praxis in mission churches, in part because missionaries were uninformed about the critical link between music and culture. In 1950, Jaap Kunst, the Dutch musicologist, coined a new term, *ethnomusicology,* to describe an emerging discipline that offered new ways to investigate the cultural aspects of music.

## Ethnomusicology

Ethnomusicology can be defined as the study of the relationship between music and culture. Recognizing the great diversity of music in the world, ethnomusicology acknowledges that while music is universal, meaning in music is intimately linked to culture. Both Bruno Nettl (2005) and Alan Merriam (1964), leading American ethnomusicologists, have argued that ethnomusicology is the study of music in culture. According to Nettl, music, must be understood as a part of culture and a product of human society. Mirriam, on the other hand, proposed a proposed a tripartite model of three equally valid areas of study—concept, behavior, and sound. More recently, Nettle defined the discipline as (1) the comparative study of the world's music *and* the study of each society's understandings about its own music, (2) based on research in the field that focuses on music ethnographies, and (3) the study of all the musical manifestations of society—that is, ethnomusicology considers every musical genre, whether folk or high art. Finally, ethnomusicology provides a critical approach to studying music-*in*-culture, offering methodologies for studying any music system, whether tribal, village, urban, pop, or classical, and its relationship to culture.

## Ethnomusicology in Mission

The contributions of ethnomusicology to mission are growing. Vida Chenoweth (SIL) drew upon linguistic methods as an ethnomusicologist to develop indigenous songs for worship (1972). James Krabill (Mennonite) studied the growth and theological development of an indigenous West African church, the Harrists of Côte d'Ivoire, via their song texts (1995). Roberta King (WorldVenture) focused on music for Christian communication and contextualization in which local believers were encouraged to set scripture to song in culturally relevant ways (1989); Jean Kidula studied religious popular music in Nairobi, Kenya (1998).

More recently, there has been a groundswell of interest in employing ethnomusicology in mission. In July of 2003, a historic event focusing on ethnomusicology in mission, the Global Consultation on Music and Mission (GCoMM), was held in Fort Worth, Texas, and the International Council of Ethnodoxologists was founded. Christian institutions of higher learning, including Azusa Pacific University, Bethel University, Wheaton, and Fuller Seminary's School of Intercultural Studies, have introduced ethnomusicology into their curricula.

Key values and goals for applying ethnomusicology to mission include (1) the contextualization of music for worship, witness, and spiritual formation, (2) encouraging dynamic and authentic expressions of Christian experience for each culture, (3) the development of culturally appropriate songs that speak meaningfully to a given people, and (4) communicating the Gospel in culturally appropriate ways that reveal Jesus Christ as Lord of all nations.

ROBERTA R. KING

## Further Reading

Bohlman, P. V. (2002). *World music: A very short introduction.* Oxford, UK: Oxford University Press.

Chenoweth, V. (1972). *Melodic perception and analysis: A manual on ethnic melody.* Ukarumpa, New Guinea: Summer Institute of Linguistics.

Corbitt, J. N. (1998). *The sound of the harvest: Music's mission in church and culture.* Grand Rapids, MI: Baker Books.

Foley, E. (1996). *Foundations of Christian music: The music of pre-Constantinian Christianity.* Collegeville, MN: Liturgical Press.

Hawn, M. C. (2003). *Gather into one: Praying and singing globally.* Grand Rapids, MI: Eerdmans.

Loh, I-to (Ed.). (2000). *Sound the bamboo: CCA Hymnal 2000.* Tainan, Taiwan: Taiwan Presbyterian Church Press.

Kidula, J. N. (1998). "Sing and shine": Religious popular music in Kenya (television, gospel music). Unpublished doctoral dissertation, University of California, Los Angeles.

King, R. R. (2004). Toward a discipline of Christian ethnomusicology: A missiological paradigm. *Missiology: An International Review,* XXXII, 294–307.

King, R. R. (1989). Pathways in Christian music communication: The case of the Senufo of Côte d'Ivoire. Unpublished doctoral dissertation, Fuller Theological Seminary, Pasadena, CA.

Krabill, J. R. (1995). *The hymnody of the Harrist Church among the Dida of South-central Ivory Coast (1913–1949): A historico-religious study* (Vol. 74). Frankfurt-am Main, Germany: Peter Lang.

Merriam, A. P. (1964). *The anthropology of music.* Chicago: Northwestern University.

Nettl, Bruno (2005). *The study of ethnomusicology: Thirty-one issues and concepts* (2nd ed.). Urbana: University of Illinois Press.

Oswald, J. (2001). *A new song rising in Tibetan hearts: Tibetan Christian worship in the early 21st century.* Kathmandu, Nepal: CAF

Titon, J. T. (Ed.). (2001). *Worlds of music: An introduction to the music of the world's peoples* (3rd ed.). New York: Schirmer Books.

Wilson-Dickson, A. (1996). *The story of Christian music: From Gregorian chant to black Gospel, an illustrated guide to all the major traditions of music in worship.* Minneapolis, MN: Fortress Press.

# Native Americans

Mission work among Native Americans, whether Catholic or Protestant, is marked by incongruities and inconsistencies. Missionaries, though fired by zeal for the Christian faith, love of God, and concern for humankind, often confused Christianity with their own Western cultures. Wittingly or unwittingly, they frequently worked hand in hand with national governments as the humanitarian arm in colonial conquests. They could show deep compassion for those they sought to "save," while exhibiting the attitudes of paternalistic superiority that were current in their day. It should be little wonder that after five hundred years of missionization the number of Native American adherents to Christianity falls far short of the national average. Despite this legacy, Native congregations gather each week across North America and consistently provide gifted leadership and inspiring witness to Christian faith.

Missionaries accompanied Spanish, French, and English explorers and colonists to the Americas. Their early efforts, while differing in degree, primarily entailed learning the Native languages, writing Biblical texts, tracts, and grammars, and gathering converts into local communities called "praying towns" (Protestant) or "reductions" (Catholic). To varying extents, evangelization included teaching the converted to read and write, to adopt Western cultural, social, political, and economic norms, and to evangelize their own peoples. Pathogens to which Native Americans had no immunity, and the clash of European armies and Indian nations on the continent, however, devastated Indian populations and all but destroyed much of the early work. The goal of the nascent United States became simply to assimilate as quickly as possible all remaining American Indians. With the support of Christian missionaries, the government's treaty provisions usually included programs and resources for teaching the Indian populations to farm, operate mills, and learn other "civilized" mechanical skills, such as blacksmithing and carpentry, to more quickly integrate Natives into the dominant culture.

The federal government turned to Indian schools and education of the young to assist in realizing this goal. Fueled by the Second Great Awakening, a growing number of Christian churches and mission organizations were called upon to provide teachers. The cozy relationship between government and church was cemented with the passage of the Indian Civilization Fund in 1819, which allocated $10,000 annually to churches for organizing and staffing Indian schools. The mission boarding and day schools taught the rudiments of a Western-style education alongside training in domestic skills and Western cultural values in preparation for heavenly and American citizenship. High incidents of absenteeism, sickness, and homesickness severely limited the achievement of these goals, and the damage to family life and children torn from their homes at a young age have given grist to diatribes against church and state ever since. By the early 1900s the overall expense and ineffectiveness of many of the schools, and the growing antipathy between Catholics and Protestants over funding, led the government to pull mission school funds entirely and encourage Indian youth to attend local public schools.

Even when the missionary goals of Christianization and acculturation were met, social integration was not guaranteed. By the 1930s the Cherokees, with the support of several mission boards, had established a tribal government patterned after the federal government, a tribal newspaper, schools, courts, churches, and large and prosperous farms with slave laborers. In spite of this, covetous neighbors, supported by President Jackson, who refused to enforce the Supreme Court's ruling in favor of the tribe's right to remain, forcibly removed all Five Civilized Tribes of the southeast (Cherokees, Choctaws, Chickasaws, Creeks, and Seminoles) to Indian Territory west of the Mississippi River. The "Trail of Tears," in which fully a quarter of Cherokees alone were lost, marked an era of forced emigration and dislocation of Indians ahead of burgeoning western settlement. While some missionaries accompanied them, the greatest service rendered by the church was its training of the few Native pastors who were able to provide some solace when it appeared that the white man's religion had only made the white man more cunning and conniving.

Growing numbers of European immigrants and American settlers turned many mission stations into church parishes for an increasing number of pioneers moving west. Those missionaries who remained among the dispossessed Indian tribes became primarily chroniclers of the "disappearing race" and sought to provide what comfort they could. The worsening plight of the American Indians did not go unnoticed by the churches. The end of the nineteenth century saw a resurgence of missionary fervor. As Native Americans were being ruthlessly settled on reservations, churchmen and women descended on Washington. "Friends of the Indian" were many, and for several decades they gathered both formally and informally to contend with the government and cajole it to reconsider its Indian policies. Organizations such as the National Indian Association, the Indian Rights Association, and the Lake Mohonk conference sought to influence legislation to protect Indians from the worst of the evils assaulting them. Their success was limited. While they gained a hearing in Washington, they failed to consult with the Indians for whom they advocated, and changes in American Indian policy were often more detrimental than helpful to Indian tribes.

The era of the Indian reformers produced some of the worst legislation imaginable for American Indians. Hoping to curb the abuses of corrupt Indian agents who were installed to oversee the reservations and distribute government annuities, reformers turned to President Grant at the end of the Civil War. The result was the Peace Policy (1869–1882), which redistributed the reservations among the various denominations and placed agents chosen from the churches over them. Unfortu-

nately, many had never seen an Indian, and the attempt to curb growing Native discontent and replace corrupt Indian agents did neither. Squabbles between denominations over who should receive which reservations heightened tensions. Catholics, whose Indian work had embraced many reservations, were largely overlooked in the assignments. This prompted the organization of the Bureau of Catholic Indian Missions, which ultimately provided greater voice and direction for all Catholic Indian missions and helped to stem the tide of anti-Catholicism that had plagued the work of the Indian missions.

In the wake of the Peace Policy, matters for the American Indians worsened on the reservations. Indian unrest, delayed and denied annuities, and inept and even corrupt administrators continued to plague Indian-white relations. In 1887, again at the behest of concerned churchmen, congress passed the Dawes Severalty Act, which broke the reservations into individual farm plots. Reformers hoped the legislation would help to assimilate Indian farmers into the larger economy more quickly and eventually do away with the reservation system (and the "Indian problem") entirely. In effect, it merely impoverished Native Americans even further because nearly 90 million acres of "excess" Indian lands ended up in non-Indian hands. Native Christians and missionaries on the reservations continued to struggle to give leadership and support to tribal nations wracked by even greater poverty, distrust, and alienation. The resurgence of Native messiah movements, such as the Ghost Dance of the plains tribes, only served to raise false hopes for Indians seeking a return to former glory days, and prompted agency officials and missionaries to crack down all the harder on noncompliant Indian leaders. It was the tragedy of Wounded Knee in 1890 that brutally put an end to such movements.

By the early twentieth century the situation among American Indians had become so acute that the government abandoned all previous policies and adopted an altogether different tactic. The new head of the Bureau of Indian Affairs, John Collier, discarded the goal of Indian assimilation almost entirely, based upon the results of the Meriam Report (1928), a privately funded, federally supported study of "The Problem of the Indian Administration." To the consternation of many missionaries, the Indian New Deal reversed the dominant role of churches on the reservations and promoted Indian self-determination and self-reliance. The Indian Reorganization Act (the Wheeler-Howard Act) of 1934 allowed the formation of tribal governments and councils, economic charters, and, of most concern to the missionaries, religious freedom. And, for the first time, these

## A Missionary Account of the Delaware

**Reports by missionaries were often among the earliest descriptions by Europeans of Native-American life. This account of Native-American preachers and prophets—an important subject for missionaries—was provided by Moravian missionary John Heckewelder, who spent thirty years with the Delaware and other nations.**

There was a time when the preachers and prophets of the Indians, by properly exerting the unbounded influence which the popular superstitions gave them, might have excited among those nations such a spirit of general resistance against the encroachments of the Europeans, as would have enabled them, at least, to make a noble stand against their invaders, and perhaps to recover the undisturbed possession of their country. Instead of following the obvious course which reason and nature pointed out; instead of uniting as one nation in defence of their natural rights, they gave ear to the artful insinuations of their enemies, who too well understood the art of sowing unnatural divisions among them. It was not until Canada, after repeated struggles, was finally conquered from the French by the united arms of Great Britain and her colonies, that they began to be sensible of their desperate situation—this whole northern continent being now in the possession of one great and powerful nation, against whom it was vain to attempt resistance. Yet it was at this moment that their prophets, impelled by ambitious motives, began to endeavour by their eloquence to bring them back to independent feelings, and create among them a genuine national spirit; but it was too late. The only rational resource that remained for them to prevent their total annihilation was to adopt the religion and manners of their conquerors, and abandon savage life for the comforts of civilised society; but of this but a few of them were sensible; in vain Missionaries were sent among them, who, through the greatest hardships and dangers exerted themselves to soften their misfortunes by the consolations of the Christian faith, and to point out to them the way of salvation in this world and the next; the banner of Christ was comparatively followed but by small numbers, and these were persecuted by their friends, or, at least, those who ought to have been such, as well as by their enemies. Among the obstacles which the Missionaries encountered, the strong opposition which was made to them by the prophets of the Indian nations was by no means the least.

Source: Heckewelder, J. G. E. (1819). *An account of the history, manners, and customs, of the Indian nations who once inhabited Pennsylvania and the neighboring states* (pp. 287–289). Transactions of the Historical and Literary Committee of the American Philosophical Society (Vol. 1). Philadelphia: Abraham Small.

---

changes were not imposed, but left for tribes to decide about implementation.

In one regard, the reformers' disquietude was justified. With church leadership in both Protestant and Catholic churches still largely in the hands of laity or non-Indian clergy and missionaries, it was difficult to withstand the resurgence of Native religions or the syncretistic movements permitted under the new legislation, such as the peyotists of the Native American Church. Indeed, by the mid-twentieth century there were fewer than two hundred Indian clergy serving all the Protestant churches, and the number of Native Catholic priests could be counted on one hand. When in the 1950s the federal government made an effort to ease

out of its responsibilities to the American Indians by encouraging Native resettlement in urban areas, nearly half of the Native population chose to leave their reservations, hoping for better opportunities elsewhere. Indian churches struggled to remain open on the reservations and urban ministries were unprepared to reach those immigrating to the cities.

By the latter part of the twentieth century most Protestant and Catholic churches recognized that even after centuries of missionary work among Native Americans, few Indian churches were self-sustaining and only a handful had their own ministers. Pentecostalism made inroads into many reservations. With fewer hierarchical and educational restraints than mainline or Catholic mission organizations and a more attractive worship style, these independent missions began to outnumber the mainline ones. All this conspired to lead many Catholic and Protestant missions to follow the lead of the federal government and to consult Indian Christians about their future in the church. Appointing Native American clergy and laity to positions on general boards, consulting committees, and task forces began to give Native Americans a voice in determining their place in the church and in assessing their needs and roles.

Extremes of poverty, unemployment, illness, and teen suicide, as well as conflicts over which cultural elements should be allowed in the church, are the continuing legacies of the assimilationist policies of church and state. However, despite a history that has tried to subjugate American Indians to the dominant society and often rendered Indian Christians to second-class citizenship within the church, capable and gifted Native American women and men, clergy and lay, continue to emerge. Today Native American theologians are also emerging to participate in the interpretation of the Gospel and the evangelization of both Native and non-Native peoples.

BONNIE SUE LEWIS

*See also* Civilization; Conquest; Empire; Human Rights; Moravians; North America; Protestant Churches; Roman Catholic Church

## Further Reading

Berkhofer, R. F., Jr. (1965). *Salvation and the savage: An analysis of Protestant missions and American Indian response, 1787–1862.* Lexington: University of Kentucky Press.

Bowden, H. W. (1981). *American Indians and Christian missions: Studies in cultural conflict.* Chicago: University of Chicago Press.

Dries, A. (1988). *The missionary movement in American Catholic history.* New York:Orbis.

Keller, R. H., Jr. (1983). *American Protestantism and United States Indian policy, 1869–82.* Lincoln: University of Nebraska Press.

Kidwell, C. S., Noley, H., & Tinker, G. (2001). *A Native American theology.* New York: Orbis.

Lewis, B. S. (2003). *Creating Christian Indians: Native clergy in the Presbyterian church.* Norman: University of Oklahoma Press.

Martin, J. W. (2001). *The land looks after us: a history of Native American religion.* New York: Oxford University Press.

Prucha, F. P. (1984). *The great father: the United States government and the American Indians* (Vols. 1–2). Lincoln: University of Nebraska Press.

Treat, J.(Ed.). (1996). *Native and Christian: Indigenous voices on religious identity in the United States and Canada.* New York: Routledge.

# Nestorians

Nestorians were the Christian followers of Nestorius (d. c. 451), Patriarch of Constantinople, condemned as a heretic at Rome (430), the Council of Ephesus (431), and the Council of Chalcedon (451). The Council of Constantinople (553) anathematized his predecessors and associates: Theodore of Mopsuestia (c. 350–428), Theodoret of Cyrus (393–c. 460), and Ibas of Edessa (d. c. 457).

Nestorius grew up in Syria. At Antioch, he entered a monastery and probably studied under Theodore, who emphasized both human and divine natures in Christ and a union of the two by grace. While in Antioch, Nestorius gained a formidable reputation for his preaching and was called to the see of Constantinople by Emperor Theodosius II in 428. There he not only insisted on his Christology but also publicly through his chaplain, Anastasius, warned that Mary should not be called *Theotokos,* "the mother of God," but the *Christotokos,* "mother of Christ." His was a consistent theological view but one that indicated his condescending approach to popular piety.

## Alexandrian Conflicts

Cyril of Alexandria (c. 375–444) was a contemporary critic of Nestorius. In terms of ecclesiastical politics, Alexandria was angered at the claim accepted during the 381 Council of Constantinople that Constantinople was the New Rome, second only to Rome, displacing Alexandria. That animosity, as well as his theological and personal conflicts with Nestorius, shaped Cyril's views. Alexandrian tradition had insisted that Athanasius (d. 373), former Patriarch of Alexandria, taught one divine nature after the union of two natures in Christ. But that position came from an Apollinarian forgery (Apollinaris [d. c. 390] was condemned for teaching that Christ had no human intellect or will) under Athanasius's name. That Mary was the mother of God had brought solace to many Christians across the empire.

Nestorius's understanding of the unity of Christ's person seemed weak or nonexistent to some, but the Synoptic Gospels contained his emphasis on Christ's humanity. For him a union by grace was sufficient. Cyril defended a strong union through the communion of aspects from both natures (*communio idomatum*) but slighted Jesus's human activity by taking his conceptual cue from John 1.14, "the Word became flesh." Some made Cyril's views extreme and have been called Monophysite (one nature alone), Miaphysite (one predominate divine nature), or anti-Chalcedonian.

## Expansion Eastward

Illegal since the *Theodosian Code* (438), Nestorians moved out of the Byzantine Empire and became a widely spread Eastern missionary church. They and their school were a force after 457 at Nisibis in northeastern Mesopotamia and in Persia. Among the Muslims they were particularly noted as physicians and administrators. By working their way along the Silk Road, they reached China by the late sixth century.

When the East Syrian (Nestorian) Alopen entered China's capital in 635, the Emperor T'ai-tsung (625–649) welcomed him and wanted his books copied for the royal library. T'ai-tsung helped Alopen build a monastery with his picture on a wall and gave Alopen precious silk. We have two fine sources for the East Syrians in China: one is the Dunhuang documents, and the other is the Chang'an (Xi'an) Stele.

## Dunhuang Documents

The first, in Chinese, are the work of a Christian missionary who had not learned the language well, the efforts of a non-Christian translator who sought to sabotage them, or a misunderstanding of significant terms. But they do indicate a real concern to make Christianity understandable to Chinese.

The documents were found within one Dunhuang Buddhist monastery library, perhaps kept there as writings from a different Buddhism. The *Jesus Messiah Sutra* is specifically interesting because it praises Chinese communities who live rather good lives, probably Daoists and Buddhists, and rehearses the life and teachings of Jesus. The final pages that would have covered his death and Resurrection were lost to ground rot.

## Chang'an (Xi'an) Stele

The Chang'an (Xi'an) Stele was written and put up in public view at the Chinese capital during 781 by a skilled East Syrian translator, Chin-Chin, who also translated volumes for missionaries of other religions. On one side of the stele was a description of East Syrian Christianity in Syriac and on the other side the same in Chinese. The stele mentions important East Syrian monasteries and leaders, including a general retired from the Chinese army who used his wealth to build their monasteries. The teaching of the stele follows in fine contextualized form the Niceano-Constantinopolitan Creed of 381 confessed in many Catholic, Orthodox, and Protestant churches today.

## Later Expansions

Timothy (Timotheos) I, the Catholicos (patriarch) of the East Syrian Church in Baghdad (780–823), had an interesting debate about Christianity with al-Mahdi, the Muslim ruler of Baghdad, in which he carefully praised Muhammad as a prophet. In his letters Timothy quoted Gregory of Nazianzen (d. 390), a well-accepted Orthodox writer, more often than he cited Nestorius. Gregory accepted Jesus's active humanity. Timothy educated monks for mission and sent them to Persia, Turkey, India, Tibet, and China. Because of Muslim, not Byzantine, control, Timothy's cohorts also planted churches in Syria, Palestine, Asia Minor, Cyprus, and Egypt. Thus he ruled over the East Syrians from Cyprus to China and represented the greatest missionary expansion of Christianity until Portugal and Spain went to the New World and Japan.

## China

The persecution of "foreign" religions in China wounded the Buddhists but almost annihilated East Syrians. Primarily centered in monasteries, they had neither the numbers nor the power to defend themselves and continue to grow.

From 1253–1255 William of Rubruck, a Franciscan from Europe, traveled to China. He was surprised to meet East Syrians in the Mongolian Khan's court and found them wanting. Dressed in robes like the Buddhists, celebrating the liturgy in Syriac, eating meat on Fridays, they shocked him. They were also polygamists, liars, and diviners who kept the bodies of some of their dead within their churches. His perspective was quite Western and his judgment based on Roman Catholic commitments. But it is not unlikely that some East Syrians had reverted to various aspects of their native religions.

William and Marco Polo (1271–1288 in the Khan's court) had met the Turkic Uighars, who lived as a minority among the Mongols, later in what is now East Turkistan. The Uighars had been able to win various Manichaeans as well as others, perhaps adjusting the Gospel by eliminating Christ's incarnation. William claimed that some did. They lasted until the Turkic Muslim Karakhanid people conquered them. Over time nearly all the Uighars became Muslims.

In 1287, however, when The Great Khan sent to the West two East Syrians—an Uighar monk, Sauma, and the Patriarch Mark, probably an Ongut—Sauma served as the Khan's envoy. During the journey, Mark was ordained in Baghdad as Catholicos of all East Syrians after the previous Catholicos died. At Rome Sauma defended their faith as an ancient Syrian one, and Pope Felix IV allowed him to celebrate a Syriac mass. Those who attended did not understand Syriac but thought everything looked much like their own worship.

Particularly during the nineteenth century various Western missionaries in the Middle East worked among East Syrians, whom they at times called Assyrians, Chaldaeans, Nestorians, or East Syrians.

## Present Day

Presently the Church of the East still exists in various first world cities but only in small groups within its early Middle Eastern and Silk Road home ground. Recent conversations with other ancient churches and scholarly research have suggested that had the political and personal animosity not been so great, the views of the East Syrians might have been accepted as an alternative but faithful church from the beginning.

FREDERICK W. NORRIS

### Further Reading

Anastos, M. (1962). Nestorius was Orthodox. *Dumbarton Oaks Papers*, 16, 119–140.

Baum, W. (2003). *The Church of the East: A concise history.* London: RoutledgeCourzon.

Budge, E. (Trans.). (1928). *The monks of Kûbla Khan, emperor of China: or, The history of the life and travels of Rabban Sâwmâ, envoy and plenipotaentiary of the Mongol Khân to the kings of Europe, and Markôs who as Mâr Yahbh-Allâhâ III became Patriarach of the Nestorian Church in Asia.* London: Religious Tract Society

Emharadt, W. and Lamsa, G. (1970). *The oldest Christian people: A brief account of the history and traditions of the Assyrian people and the fateful history of the Nestorian church.* New York: AMS Press.

Gillman, I. and Klimkeit, H. J. (1999). *Christians in Asia before 1500.* Ann Arbor: University of Michigan Press.

Grant, A. (2004). *The Nestorians: or, The Lost tribes; containing evidence of their identity; an account of their manners, customs, and ceremonies; together with sketches of travels in Ancient Assyria, Armenia, Media and Mesopotamua, and illustrations of Scripture prophecy.* Piscataway, NJ: Gorgias Press.

Hage, W. (1997). *Syriac Christianity in the East.* Kottayam, India: St. Ephrem Ecumenical Research Institute.

Hurst, T. (1986). *The Syriac letters of Timothy I (727–823): A study in Christian-Muslim controversy.* Doctoral dissertation, The Catholic University of America.

Joseph, J. (2000). *The Modern Assyrians of the Middle East: Encounters with Christian missions, archaeologists and colonial powers.* Leiden, Netherlands: Brill.

Norris, F. (2006). Muhammad walked in the path of the Prophets and trod in the track of the lovers of God: Timothy I of Baghdad. *Catholicos* of the East Syrian Church, 780–823. *International Bulletin of Missionary Researcbh 30,* (pp. 133–136).

Tang, L. (2002) *A study of the history of Nestorian Christianity in China and in its literature in Chinese.* Frankfurt am Main, Germany: Peter Lang.

Tang, L. (2005) A history of Uighar religious conversions (5th–16th centuries). *Asia Research Institute, Working Papers Series, No. 44.* Singapore: National University of Singapore. Retrieved April 14, 2006 http//www.ari.nus.edu.sg/pub.htm.

Whipple, A. (1967). *The role of the Nestorians and Muslims in the history of medicine.* Princeton, NJ: Princeton University Press.

## New Religious Movements

Scholars of religious studies use the term "New Religious Movement" (NRM) to describe a religious movement that departs significantly from the dominant religion or religions in a particular society. There is no precise definition of an NRM; in fact, some religions that fall under the purview of NRM studies, such as Mormonism, Jehovah's Witnesses, and Baha'í, are not particularly new. An NRM may have its roots in other, more established religions; its characterization as an NRM is drawn from the fact that it is on the fringe of the dominant religious and secular culture. The designation "New Religious Movements" is now more widely used than other neutral designations such as "alternative religions" and "emergent religions." Because it is free of the negative connotations of older terms such as "sects," "cults," "the occult," or "fringe religions," it helps students of religion maintain their objectivity.

### Cults

Several factors have led to the recent growth of interest in the study of NRMs. One such factor was the 1965 change in U.S. immigration law. By eliminating racially

## The Twilight of Atheism

**Alister McGrath's book *The Twilight of Atheism* deals with the failure of the "liberating" idea of atheism to take hold, particularly in dealing with varied cultures. The extract below is from an article by McGrath exploring these ideas.**

In his problematic but fascinating work, *The Decline of the West*, Oswald Spengler argued that history shows that cultures came into being for religious reasons. As they exhausted the potential of that spirituality, religion gave way to atheism, before a phase of religious renewal gave them a new sense of direction. Might atheism have run its course, and now give way to religious renewal? The tides of cultural shift have, for the time being, left atheism beached on the sands of modernity, while Westerners explore a new postmodern interest in the forbidden fruit of spirituality.

Source: McGrath, A. (2005, March). The twilight of atheism. *Christianity Today, 49*(3), 36.

and ethnically based quotas, it allowed a great number of new immigrants from around the world to enter the United States, and these immigrants brought their religions with them. Another factor was that the social upheavals of the time led many people to experiment with new alternative spiritualities, often mixing elements of several religions. Globalization, worldwide immigration patterns, ease of travel, and new communication technologies contributed to the spiritual options and religions available to people around the world.

The rise of movements labeled "cults" in the 1970s caused a great deal of concern on the part of established religious leaders, parents, and government authorities. It was thought that people were being incorporated into cult movements through techniques such as brainwashing and mind control. Parents sought the help of "deprogrammers" in order to rescue their children, even adult children, from charismatic leaders they saw as sociopaths. The mass suicide of some nine hundred adherents of the Peoples Temple movement in Jonestown, Guyana, in 1978, under the leadership of Jim Jones, served to heighten concern over the proliferation of NRMs.

While there were several mass suicides carried out by adherents of fringe religious movements, most NRM scholars have insisted that the great majority of NRMs do not practice brainwashing, are not made up of intellectually or emotionally weak or socially marginalized people, do not depend upon an unhealthy allegiance to a charismatic leader, and do not have a proclivity toward religiously justified violence. Much of the literature on NRMs vehemently rejects the concerns raised over their proliferation, insisting that fundamental human rights

are threatened when unfair, uninformed, or coercive techniques are used to combat NRMs. The seemingly supportive stance taken by those involved in the NRM studies movement has sometimes led to NRM scholars being labeled cult apologists.

## Causes

Due to the growth in number of NRMs worldwide, the study of this phenomenon has become a specialization in its own right. *The World Christian Encyclopedia*, for example, adds two to three new religions every day to its database; in the United States alone, there are about a thousand NRMs. Much of the study of NRMs focuses on the causes of conversion to the new movements. Scholars debate whether the growth of NRMs is due to something inherent in the new groups or to extrinsic factors. In some cases, the attractiveness of an NRM is found in its practice—for example, the discipline of meditation or a fellowship in which one feels welcomed and loved. Other scholars, who believe that the rise of NRMs reflects the condition of society, concentrate on extrinsic factors such as the spiritual neediness in today's world or the relationship between modernity and secularization.

Sociologists of religion such as Max Weber, Ernest Troeltch, and Peter Berger postulated that with the rise of modernity there would be an accompanying decline in religion because people would see themselves as masters of the world rather than as subjects of spiritual forces. However, other religious observers, especially Rodney Stark and William Bainbridge, noting the continued vitality of religion in the modern world, have argued that religion is such a fundament part of the human experience that it will never disappear, although it may take new and alternative forms.

## Classifications

The wide variety of beliefs and practices observed by scholars of NRMs are difficult to organize into neat categories; however, several attempts have been made to arrange and classify them. In 1984 Roy Wallis, a sociologist and fromer dean of the Faculty of Economics and Social Sciences at the Queen's University of Belfast, Ireland, following Richard Niebuhr's 1956 descriptions of the kinds of relationships that can exist between Christianity and culture, categorized NRMs according to how they viewed the world around them—that is, whether they (1) *reject* the world, (2) *embrace* the world, or (3) *accommodate* the world. The lines between these categories can be blurred, since an NRM may display a mix of characteristics from each of these approaches to the world, and it is not clear which of the three kinds of NRMs will prove to be most popular and enduring.

Another typology for understanding the varieties of NRMs has been suggested by W. Michael Ashcraft and Derek Daschke based on the ways NRMs appeal to people and which deep-seated needs they endeavor to address. In their study, *New Religious Movements: A Documentary Reader* (2005), Ashcraft and Dashke divide NRMs into five categories, and provide examples of groups that fall into each category. NRMs offer a *new understanding* of the world and how it works, which makes it possible for adherents to transcend the limitations and deceptions of human sensory perceptions. Christian Science would be an example of this type of movement. Other NRMs offer an opportunity to achieve a *new self,* where one is empowered to overcome his or her debilities and attain perfection and even godhood. Wicca falls into this category. Still other NRMs provide a *new family* for their adherents—leaders play the role of parents. These kinds of NRMs are often seen as the most threatening because they imply rejection of the established family structures. Examples of this type of NRM include the Unification Church and Santería.

A fourth kind of NRM includes *new society* groups, which seek a transformation of society. Their concern is social oppression and injustice, and they are often politically active. This category includes the Nation of Islam and Peoples Temple. Finally, some NRMs are apocalyptic in that they promise a *new world*—this may be a totally transformed earthly existence, a new heavenly existence, or a new planet or world. Seventh Day Adventists and Jehovah's Witnesses are among these groups. These five promises of newness are interrelated, and each NRM will deal with all five categories in some way.

## Christianity

The growth of NRMs demonstrates that religion will continue to be a significant factor in modern life. While Christian apologists are concerned about the growth of movements that deviate from orthodox Christian teachings, the increasing body of literature available on NRMs provides a wealth of information on the needs, desires, hopes, and dreams of human beings in the contemporary context.

DOUGLAS L. RUTT

*See also* African Independent Churches; Jehovah's Witnesses; Mormonism; Secularism

### Further Reading

Barrett, D. (2001). *The new believers: A survey of sects, cults and alternative religions.* London: Cassell.

Berger, P. (1967). *The sacred canopy.* Garden City, NY: Doubleday.

Clarke, P. (2006). *Encyclopedia of new religious movements.* London: Routledge.

Cowan, D. E., Moore, R., & Wessinger, C. (Eds.). *Nova religio: The journal of alternative and emergent religions.* Berkeley: University of California Press.

Daschke, D., & Ashcraft, W. M. (Eds.). (2005). *New religious movements: A documentary reader.* New York: New York University Press.

Dawson, L. L. (2006). New religious movements. In R. A. Segal (Ed.), *The Blackwell companion to the study of religion* (pp. 369–384). Malden, MA: Blackwell.

Enroth, R. (Ed.). (2005). *A guide to new religious movements.* Downers Grove, IL: Intervarsity Press.

Hunt, S. (2003). *Alternative religions: A sociological introduction.* Burlington, VT: Ashgate.

Kaplan, J., & Lööw, H. (Eds.), (2002). *The cultic milieu: Oppositional subcultures in an age of globalization.* New York: Alta Mira Press.

Lester, T. (2002, February). Oh gods! *Atlantic Monthly,* 289(2), 37–45.

Lewis, J. (2003). *Legitimating new religions.* New Brunswick, NJ: Rutgers University Press.

Lewis, J. (Ed.). (2004). *The Oxford handbook of new religious movements.* Oxford: Oxford University Press.

Nichols, L. A., Mather, G. A., & Schmidt, A. J. (2006). Encyclopedic dictionary of cults, sects, and world religions. Grand Rapids, MI: Intervarsity Press.

Niebuhr, R. (1956). *Christ and culture*. New York: Harper and Row.

Partridge, C. (Ed.). (2004). *New religions—a guide: New religious movements, sects and alternative spiritualities*. New York: Oxford University Press.

Segal, R. A. (Ed.). (2006). *The Blackwell companion to the study of religion*. Malden, MA: Blackwell.

Stark, R., & Bainbridge, W. (1985). *The future of religion*. Berkeley: University of California Press.

Troeltsch, E. (1958). *Protestantism and progress*. Boston, MA: Beacon Press.

Wallis, R. (1984). *The elementary forms of the new religious life*. Boston: Routledge & Kegan Paul.

Weber, M. (1930). *The Protestant ethic and the spirit of capitalism*. New York: Scribner.

Wilson, B. R., & Cresswell, J. (Eds.). (1999). *New religious movements: Challenge and response*. London: Routledge.

# North America

Historically, the term "North America" has usually included the countries of Canada and the United States, along with the various countries that make up Central America and the Caribbean. There are distinct cultural differences that significantly differentiate Canada and the United States, however, in comparison to the countries of Central America and the Caribbean. Most of the latter share much in common with South America by way of the influence of Spain and Portugal, while the former share their sociocultural histories primarily with England and several northern European countries. It is now increasingly common to refer to the countries of Central America and the Caribbean as "Middle America" and to refer to Canada and the United States as "Northern America." This article reflects this distinction and limits its discussion to Canada and the United States

## A Few Basic Facts

In some ways Canada and the United States might be described as "Anglo-America," with English being spoken as the primary language, although Canada's unique settlement patterns created a binational identity of being both French and English. Northern America historically has been socially and culturally quite well defined, with both countries sharing similar traditions that stem from

their legacy as British colonies. However, the increased immigration in recent decades from the majority two-thirds world is creating a more multicultural reality in both countries, with Canada being somewhat further along in this regard than the United States.

Politically, the forms of government in Canada and the United States reflect similar democratic principles pioneered by the English. There is a significant difference, however, in how this common tradition was played out. Many of the colonies in the United States were settled by communities and persons seeking religious or political freedom from the state, especially from England. Historically, this fostered a much stronger democratic political identity that called for activism and participation in all levels of life, which was usually operationalized through voluntary organizations.

Canada, by contrast, has a political identity that was shaped more by the state and that functioned in a more top-down way in practice. This means there has always been a more active role of the state in Canadian life, such as in social welfare and health care. The political ideology in the United States has always been to seek to serve such needs through the private sector, with intervention by the state being for the purpose of facilitating equality of opportunity.

## Northern America as Mission Field

The concept of "Northern America as mission field" is now recognized by most missiologists as the necessary designation for both the United States and Canada. The rise of the modern missions' movement of the nineteenth century saw these countries becoming substantially involved in the practice of creating special mission societies along with denominational boards for the purpose of sending missionaries to all other parts of the world. Most of these missionary personnel were sent to the southern hemisphere, what is now being referred to as the majority two-thirds world. This vast enterprise of mission organizations and missionaries was created by rapidly growing denominations in both of these countries. Embedded within this enterprise was the assumption that Canada and the United States, following the ethos of the pattern of European state churches within Christendom, were assumed to be Christian countries, at least functionally, within their practice of the separation of church and state.

The patterns of the development of the church in Canada and the United States vary in a number of ways, as will be discussed below, but these patterns share at least three things in common. First, both countries experienced immigration and settlement by many persons for religious reasons from the seventeenth century forward, which often involved Christian sectarian groups from European countries seeking opportunities to practice their faith without restrictions. Second, both countries experienced the rapid growth of diverse denominations within their territories as these nations received waves of new immigrants and the continued settlement of their territories westward across the continent. Third, the churches in both of these countries have gone through significant change over the past two-hundred-plus years, with the most dramatic changes taking place in the last half of the twentieth century. During this period, many of the historical denominations stopped growing, and the role of Christianity within the social order became increasingly marginalized from the public sector.

It is important to recognize that the social location of Canada and the United States now represents mission fields just as much as other mission fields conceived throughout the history of the church. The challenge now before the church is to recontextualize the Christian faith in these countries. This is necessary for bringing a faithful witness both to the vast numbers of the population that do not have any direct or active association with a particular Christian congregation, as well as to the significant influx of new immigrant communities, most of which are coming from the majority two-thirds world.

## The Church in the United States

The story of the formation and development of the church in the United States can be told in terms of three phases of its disestablishment. The basic ethos of the church in the United States was forged during the Colonial period, as numerous immigrant groups settled in the various colonies from a variety of European nations. Although English settlers initially were prominent within the Puritan settlements in the New England colonies and the Anglican settlements in the southern colonies, they were soon joined by diverse settlements from other European countries. While many of these immigrants came for economic opportunities, the role of religion ran deep within many of the communities that were formed. By the time of the Revolutionary War, the pattern of the formation of distinctive denominations was clearly in place, and with the separation of church and state in the newly written Constitution, the first disestablishment of the church was achieved. While churches would be given privileged access to the public sector, they would not be established by the state.

The modern denomination represented a new way of conceiving and organizing the church in the development of Christianity. The formation of the United States as a new nation soon led to the creation of national and regional organizational structures among many of the diversely spread out and often ethnically shaped denominations. An increase in the number of denominations and their continued growth was the pattern throughout the nineteenth century. This was fed by the Second Great Awakening at the turn of the century and the seemingly endless impulse to bring revival and reform to the populations that were migrating rapidly into the ever-expanding frontier. The emphasis in this milieu was on personal conversation of the individual as the basis of effecting social reform. Chastened by the divide over slavery at midcentury, these denominations quickly recovered in responding to the emerging growth of urban centers that began in the last decades of that century. However, a distinct shift in immigration from northern European countries to southern and eastern European countries during this time led to a dramatic increase in the numbers of Roman Catholics and Jews entering the United States, who more often than not settled in the rapidly growing urban centers.

### Common Judeo-Christian Heritage

A second disestablishment of the church occurred in the first decades of the twentieth century as the ideals of the Protestant empire of the nineteenth century, often shaped by small-town and rural Protestant congregations, had to give way to a reconception of the United States as having a common Judeo-Christian heritage. Protestants, Catholics, and Jews all became legitimized in owning and shaping the American story. This took place in the midst of the rise of the social gospel and the increased influence of historicism and higher criticism in biblical studies that were coming from Germany, and as a result a growing separation developed among those who were more liberal and those who were more conservative, both within and between denominations. The earlier Fundamentalist movement that emerged at the turn of the century would morph by midcentury into the renewal of the Evangelical movement, a movement that continues to evolve at the beginning of the twenty-first century.

The conception of a common Judeo-Christian heritage continued, however, well into the middle of the twentieth century, when what became known as "civil religion" became the norm for much of Christianity. It was a unique blending of God, country, and America that commingled the Puritan notion of divine favor with the political and military realities of world responsibility, especially in regard to the necessary stand of democracy against the perceived evils of Communism.

### Effects of the Counterculture Movement

The tumultuous 1960s challenged this worldview. Building on the civil rights movement of the 1950s, the movement of the counterculture coalesced with an antiwar movement that opposed the U.S. involvement in Vietnam. In this dynamic situation a number of other important social movements were also given birth, including feminism and the ecological movement.

In the midst of the antiestablishment milieu of that period and the general mistrust of institutions and positional authority, the church in the United States went through a third disestablishment. This was characterized by the discrediting of civil religion along with the increased marginalization of the presence and voice of the church in the public sector. The days of privileged position of the church in the social order were ending. This third disestablishment was the result, in many ways, of what has now come to be recognized as the postmodern turn. This turn was rooted in a sharp critique of Enlightenment rationality and its assumptions of objectivity and progress and drew insight from the hermeneutical turn that repositioned all human knowing as being situational and interpreted. The emerging postmodern condition, which is commingled within the continued realities of late modernity, represents the worldview that the church must now address the United States as mission field.

There have been significant developments in the church since the 1970s. Largely stimulated by the 1976 bicentennial movement, there was by the 1980s a substantial conservative, Evangelical movement that saw the coalescence of TV evangelists, growing megachurches, and political activism. While conservative churches were growing, the mainline churches were experiencing significant declines, especially in light of their failure to pass on the faith to the baby-boom generation.

At the turn of the present century, one finds the religious landscape in the United States dramatically changed. There are increasing numbers of persons with different religious traditions, especially in light of increased immigration. There is a significant increase in the number of megachurches—those with over two thousand worshippers on a weekly basis; most of these churches are evangelical in theology and independent or semi-independent in polity. There is also a continued decline of the mainline denominations, with significant downsizing of their national church structures. There is a new form of church becoming evident that is known as the "emerging church movement," a movement populated primarily by the younger generations. And there is another movement, known as the "missional church" conversation, that is trying to take serious the premise of Northern America as mission field in seeking to recontextualize the church in both Canada and the United States.

## The Church in Canada

The story of the church in Canada differs a bit from that of the United States in that Canada, as noted above, has always had a bicultural identity as English and French. This colony, first established by the Hudson's Bay Company, later became part of the English Commonwealth. As it experienced immigration, the church was established in both of its diverse communities—the Catholic Church in French Quebec and the Anglican Church throughout the rest of the Canadian territories. As a result of these beginnings, the church in Canada historically occupied a more official place in society and had a primary role in guiding the social order. This lasted until the 1960s, when significant shifts took place in redefining the role of church in society.

The Anglican Church, outside Quebec, played a prominent role in the early years of the development of the Canadian territories by being the established church. The rights of other Protestant groups were protected throughout the various provinces, although Catholics restricted such rights in Quebec, while Protestants restricted the rights of Catholics outside Quebec. These two church communes found themselves in direct conflict in the mid-eighteenth-century war between the English and the French. The English victory and subsequent Treaty of Paris in 1763 brought Quebec under English control. While Catholics still controlled the religious life of Quebec and the Protestants controlled the rest of the Canadian provinces, now principles had to be established to protect the rights of each, which were usually played out in the public schools and universities.

By the early nineteenth century a transition began to take place in the makeup of and relative influence among the Protestants. The Anglicans failed to supply sufficient clergy for their congregations and also failed to be aggressive in bringing the church to the expanding frontier. Other Protestant denominations, many of

The Spanish mission in Carmel-by-the-Sea, in the U.S. state of California. *Courtesy of Glenn Frank/istockphoto.com.*

which had strong roots in or connections with their U.S. counterparts, filled this void. By the time of confederation in 1867, the privileged role of the Anglican Church had given way to a more general reconfiguration of Protestant churches.

The Protestant denominations in Canada tended to follow their U.S. counterparts by building national and regional church structures. These structures were the vehicles for the churches to engage in the work of promoting civilization, both at home among the peoples of the First Nations and increasing numbers of immigrants and around the world through foreign mission activity. The Catholic Church in Quebec during this period continued to strengthen its role in exercising influence over every aspect of life.

### Into the Twentieth Century

As Canada entered the twentieth century, the churches were impacted by the increased industrialization and urbanization that was common as well in the United States. The Canadian churches developed their own version of the social gospel that sought to reconceive how the Gospel related to broader institutional realities but managed to do so without experiencing the fracturing that accompanied this movement in the United States. The formation in 1925 of the United Church of Canada from among Congregationalists, Methodists, and Presbyterians was uniquely Canadian in reflecting more their shared commitments to fostering a moral

social order than to seeking to maintain theological consistency.

Similar to developments in the United States in the 1960s, Canadian society also experienced the counterculture and the numerous social revolutions that accompanied it. This upheaval in society significantly contributed to the demise of the older form of a functional Christendom, with the church having primary responsibility for fostering a moral society. This shift was evident in Quebec during this time and became known as the Quiet Revolution. There, levels of church attendance among Catholics declined from the 80 percent range following World War II to less than 40 percent twenty years later. Comparable changes took place within the Protestant churches in the other provinces, with declines from the 60 percent range following World War II to less than 20 percent twenty years later.

### Emergence of Nominalism

These declines continued on the other side of the counterculture, and today nominalism is the norm for most Canadians with regard to the church. While some still expect the church to provide for the rights of passage—baptism, marriage, burial—the vast majority of the population has little involvement in the institutional church. Alongside this sea of nominal Christianity, there has been an active resurgence of Evangelicals, especially in the western provinces. But their numbers are small in comparison to their counterparts in the

United States. The revivalism and activism so evident in U.S. church life never found its way into the Canadian church, and the influence of church growth and church effectiveness, along with the methodologies of the megachurches, likewise never took root to any significant extent on Canadian soil.

## Challenges Today

Though their historical developments vary significantly, there are at least three common challenges facing the churches today in Canada and the United States in light of Northern America now being understood as its own mission field. First, the churches in both countries face a changing population, one that is increasingly being shaped through immigration from the majority two-thirds world. Some among these immigrant communities are Christians and are bringing their congregational identities with them, while many others are persons of other faiths. These developments invite the churches of Canada and the United States to rethink and recast their historical tendencies to see themselves as part of the dominant culture. They need to develop contextualized missiologies with approaches that emphasize being "with the other" rather than being sent "to the other."

Second, the emerging postmodern condition in the midst of the continued influence of late modernity continues to challenge the churches of Canada and the United States to reflect on how to present the Gospel as good news to emerging generations who appear to hold quite different worldviews and personal values. This presents the ever-constant challenge of rethinking the faith in order to be able to translate it to those who see the world differently. The churches are in need of developing contextualized missiologies that operate from a translation approach, rather than their historical diffusion approaches, with their expectations of assimilation. This translation work also has implications for the shared practices and organizational forms of the churches. The challenge is to make the truths of the historic Christian faith come alive within new and ever-changing worldviews.

Third, the continued influence of globalization, driven by rapid technological changes and the expansion of the information age, requires the churches to reconceive how they engage in forming their congregational life and how they shape their shared identities. The churches are in need of developing contextualized missiologies that help foster and nurture new forms of social organization that share deeply a Christian identity while also being responsive to the changing patterns of the larger society. While much of what has gone before will be informative for this work, much will also need to change if these churches are to rise to this challenge.

Craig van Gelder

*See also* Central America; Colonialism; Europe; Evangelicalism; Globalization; Latin America; Native Americans; Postmodernism; Protestant Churches; Roman Catholic Church

## Further Reading

Ahlstrom, S. E. (1972). *A religious history of the American people.* New Haven, CT: Yale University Press.

Best, S., & Kellner, D. (1997). *The postmodern turn.* New York: The Guilford Press.

Bibby, R. W. (1987). *Fragmented gods: The poverty and potential of religion in Canada.* Toronto, Canada: Irwin Publishing.

Bibby, R. W. (1990). *Mosaic madness.* Toronto, Canada: Stoddart.

Brown, C. (Ed.). (2003). *The illustrated history of Canada.* Toronto, Canada: Key Porter Books.

Corrigan, J. & Hudson, W. S. (2004). *Religion in America* (7th ed.). Upper Saddle River, NJ: Pearson.

Fink, R. & Stark, R. (2005). *The churching of America, 1776–2005: Winners and losers in our religious economy.* New Brunswick, NJ: Rutgers University Press.

Grant, J. W. (1972). *The church in the Canadian era: The first century of confederation.* Whitby, Canada: McGraw-Hill Ryerson.

Gwyn, R. (1995). *Nationalism without walls: The unbearable lightness of being Canadian.* Toronto, Canada: McClelland & Stewart.

Stiglitz, J. E. (2003). *Globalization and its discontents.* New York: W. W. Norton & Company.

Wuthnow, R. (1988). *The restructuring of American religion.* Princeton, NJ: Princeton University Press.

# O

## Oceania

Christian missionary work in the Pacific Islands and Australasia has been dominated by two main expressions of Christianity: Protestantism rooted in Britain and North America and Roman Catholicism from continental Europe. Christianity first entered the Pacific Islands through the Spanish colonial presence on the Pacific Rim. In the sixteenth and early seventeenth centuries Spanish navigators in the Pacific searched for peoples to bring under the rule of imperial Spain and to convert to Catholic Christianity. They took away a small number of islanders for instruction and baptism. In the 1660s the Spanish royal house sent Jesuits from the Philippines to start missionary work in the Mariana Islands in the North Pacific. The decaying Spanish Empire undertook no further permanent missionary work in the region.

## First Missions in the South Pacific

In Britain during the second half of the eighteenth century the Evangelical Revival coincided with a series of French and British voyages of exploration of the Pacific, culminating in the three voyages (1768–1779) of Captain James Cook. These placed many of the principal island groups on the map of the world and, through published accounts, aroused interest in their inhabitants. Evangelicals interpreted these contacts as a sign from God of their duty to rescue the "perishing heathen" in the "South Seas." Meanwhile, in 1788 Britain founded a convict colony at Botany Bay (Sydney) on the east coast of Australia, named New South Wales. Sydney later became a center for the diffusion of British influence through the South Pacific and a base for missionary activity. An early Anglican chaplain, Samuel Marsden (1765–1838), played a central role in guiding and coordinating this work.

Christianity entered the South Pacific as part of the first wave of Western contact that brought the islanders steel tools, trade goods and firearms, new animals and plants, new diseases, and new ideas. The first permanent mission was begun by the London Missionary Society (LMS), founded in 1795, whose first contingent of thirty missionaries reached eastern Polynesia in 1797. The LMS missionaries were products of the English Dissenting tradition and the Evangelical Revival. Their object was to teach Christianity within the context of Western civilization. The mission had a shaky start, but after 1815 on the island of Tahiti there was a widespread popular movement toward Christianity. The LMS missionaries proceeded to organize a church on congregational lines that was intertwined with the structures and patterns of village life. Believing that Christians should be able to read the Bible for themselves, they put indigenous languages into written form and taught their converts reading and writing. Everywhere in the Pacific, the diffusion of Protestant Christianity was accompanied by the founding of village schools, the teaching of literacy, and the translation of the Bible and other religious texts into vernacular languages.

The broad movement of Christianity was from east to west. It was spread through the combined missionary efforts of both Europeans and Pacific Islanders. From the 1820s, numerous Christian converts went from their homes to other island groups as teachers of Christianity. Almost everywhere, they preceded the European missionaries. Although Europeans supervised this expansion and examined candidates for baptism, the majority of Pacific Islanders heard of the new religion in their own villages from Pacific Island evangelists and teachers. The best known LMS missionary of the early period was John Williams (1796–1839), who began missions on Rarotonga in the Cook Islands (1823) and Samoa (1830) and wrote a popular account of his experiences, *A Narrative of Missionary Enterprises in the South Sea Islands* (1837). In 1839, while on a voyage to plant Christianity in the southwest Pacific in the region known as Melanesia, he was killed after landing on Erromanga in the New Hebrides (now Vanuatu). The LMS continued its pioneering work in Melanesia, using missionaries from Samoa and the Cook Islands. Converts from the Loyalty Islands in 1871 planted Christianity in the Torres Strait Islands, north of Australia. LMS work began in Papua, the southeastern part of the large island of New Guinea, in 1872. An influential pioneer was the Cook Islands missionary Ruatoka (1846–1906). Alongside him was James Chalmers (1841–1901), who did much to publicize the work of the New Guinea mission and met a violent death, with others, at Goaribari Island.

During the following decades several other missionary bodies began work in the Pacific Islands. In most island groups the mission that first introduced Christianity gained the support of the majority of the population and became a socially unifying force. To avoid wasteful competition, the Protestant societies agreed informally to work in separate island groups, and only rarely (as in Samoa) did they overlap. The (Anglican) Church Missionary Society (CMS) from England began a mission at the Bay of Islands in the North Island of New Zealand in 1814. The American Board of Commissioners for Foreign Missions (ABCFM), supported by Congregationalists and based in Boston, sent its first company of missionaries to Hawaii in 1820. It later extended its operations to the Caroline Islands (1852), the Gilbert Islands (Kiribati) (1857), and other island groups in the region known as Micronesia. The (British) Wesleyan Methodist Missionary Society founded missions in New Zealand (1822) and Tonga (1826). From there, Wesleyan Christianity spread to Samoa (1828) and Fiji (1835), where an outstanding pioneer missionary was the Tongan Joeli Bulu (c. 1810–1877).

During the nineteenth century the British colonies of Australia and New Zealand became important bases of missionary work in the South Pacific. In 1855 the newly founded Australasian Wesleyan Methodist Conference assumed responsibility for the British Methodist missions. At the initiative of George Brown (1835–1917), missionary and later general secretary of the mission board, the Australasian Conference founded its own missions in the south-west Pacific: New Britain (1875), Papua (1891), and the Solomon Islands (1902). A Presbyterian mission, supported initially from Nova Scotia and Scotland but later from New Zealand and Australia, was established in 1848 in southern Vanuatu. In 1849 Bishop G. A. Selwyn, first Anglican bishop in New Zealand, seeking a Pacific mission field for the Church of England, began the Melanesian Mission, which eventually created a strong presence in northern Vanuatu and the Solomon Islands. The first bishop of Melanesia, J. C. Patteson (1827–1871), killed at Nukapu in the Santa Cruz group, was venerated by Anglicans as a missionary hero and martyr. Another Anglican mission was founded from Australia in Papua in 1891.

During the latter decades of the nineteenth century thousands of Melanesian islanders were recruited to work as laborers on sugar plantations in the Australian colony of Queensland, and some of these were converted to evangelical Christianity. On returning to their home islands, they were instrumental in the beginnings, from 1902, of a mission in Vanuatu supported by the Australian Churches of Christ and the South Sea Evangelical Mission, an interdenominational "faith mission," in the Solomon Islands in 1904.

Roman Catholic missionary activity in the Pacific Islands during the nineteenth century was dominated by France. Among the many new religious orders founded in the aftermath of the French Revolution were the Congregation of the Sacred Hearts of Jesus and Mary (Picpus Fathers), the Society of Mary (Marists), and the Missionaries of the Sacred Heart. From the 1820s these missionary orders were responsible for planting Roman Catholicism throughout the Pacific. The Picpus Fathers, occasionally supported by the French navy, began missions in Hawaii and in eastern Polynesia. Father Damien (Joseph Damien de Veuster, 1840–1889), a Belgian missionary priest who devoted his life to ministering to lepers at Molokai in Hawaii, was beatified by the Pope in 1994 and in 1999 was the subject of an internationally distributed film, *Molokai*. The Marists established their initial base in 1837 on the small islands of Wallis and Futuna in the central Pacific and in the following year extended their work to New Zealand. Pierre Chanel (1803–1841), who pioneered the Futuna mission, met a violent death. Honored as a Catholic martyr, he was beatified in 1889 and canonized in 1954 as patron saint of Oceania. The Missionaries of the Sacred Heart founded their first Pacific missions in Papua, New Britain, and Kiribati in the 1880s. Initially, the Catholic missionaries, keen to combat Protestant heresy, did not restrict themselves to places where the islanders were

## A Mission Report on Hawaii in 1823

**The following text is from a report of a two-month visit to the island of Hawaii by a group of missionaries in 1823, a few years after the abolition of idols in 1819.**

But though the chiefs have renounced their ancient idolatry, and the priests no longer perform the mystic and bloody rites of the heiau, (Temple), and though on the ruins of their temples, altars are now erecting for the worship of the living God, yet the deep impressions made in childhood, by the songs, legends, and horrid rites connected with their long established superstitions, and the feelings and habits cherished by them in subsequent life, are not, by the simple proclamation of a king, or the resignation of a priest, to be removed at once from the mind of the unenlightened Hawaiian, who, in the sighing of the breeze, the gloom of night, the boding eclipse, the meteor's glance, the lightning's flash, the thunder's roar, the earthquake's shock, is accustomed to recognize the dreaded presence of some unpropitious deity. Nor must we be surprised, if the former views which the Hawaiian has been accustomed to entertain respecting Pele, the goddess he supposes to preside over volcanoes, should not at once be eradicated; as he is continually reminded of her power, by almost every object that meets his eye, from the rude cliffs of lava, against which the billows of the ocean dash, even to the lofty craters, her ancient seat amid perpetual snows.

Nor is it to be expected, that those who feel themselves to have been released from the oppressive demands of their former religion, will, until they are more enlightened, be in haste to adopt a substitute, which presents imperious claims in direct opposition to all their unhallowed affections; especially since, while thus ignorant of the nature of Christianity, their recollections of the past must awaken fears of evil, perhaps not less dreadful than those from which they have just escaped.

Source: Ellis, W. (1917). *Narrative of a tour through Hawaii, or Owhyhee: with observations on the natural history of the Sandwich Islands, and remarks on the manners, customs, traditions, history, and language of their inhabitants* (p. 11). Honolulu, Hawaii: Hawaiian Gazette Co. Ltd.

---

still "pagans." This led to an intense competition for souls, in which theological and cultural differences between missions were reinforced by British and French national patriotism and imperial rivalries. The Catholics did not succeed in their aim of dislodging Protestants from those island groups where they were well established, but in many island groups they gained a minority following.

From the 1840s the older missions faced new rivals: missionaries from bodies that regarded all established versions of Christianity as false and therefore to be supplanted. The Church of Jesus Christ of Latter Day Saints (Mormons), from the United States, sent its first missionaries to French Oceania in 1844 and Hawaii in 1850. During the twentieth century the Mormons launched a vigorous missionary program, motivated by the church's teaching that the Polynesians were descendants of "Lamanites," originally from ancient Israel, whose history was recounted in the Book of Mormon. They gained a substantial following, especially among the indigenous Hawaiians and the Maori of New Zealand. The Reorganized Church of Jesus Christ of Latter Day Saints, beginning work in Tahiti in 1873, gained a foothold in French Oceania. Seventh-Day Adventists, also from the United States, began missionary work in the South Pacific in 1885 with high expectations. During the next thirty years they founded missions in almost every island group and achieved wide geographical spread, but in most places they remained a small minority of the Christian population. During the latter decades of the twentieth century the Adventists became less isolationist in outlook and moved closer to the historic Protestant churches.

## Missions in the Colonial Period

The spread of Christianity had political implications. Although the early Protestant missionaries attempted to remain apart from indigenous politics, they also wanted to create Christian societies regulated by the laws of

God. Often they played an important role as advisers to chiefly leaders. To replace the sanctions provided by the traditional religion, Christian chiefs needed a new basis for their authority. From 1819, with missionary support, they issued written codes of law that laid down punishments both for behavior that the missionaries regarded as sinful and for some traditional offences. In several island groups, as in Tahiti, Tonga, and Hawaii, missionaries assisted in the creation of monarchies with a Western-style constitution and machinery of government. Initially they sought to maintain the independence of these island kingdoms. Later in the nineteenth century, when Western powers began competing in the Pacific for spheres of influence and colonies, the majority of missionaries preferred the protection of European rule to the growing instability of indigenous governments. In some island groups the missionaries advocated annexation by their own nation. In New Zealand CMS missionaries played an important role in persuading Maori chiefs to sign the Treaty of Waitangi (1840) in which they ceded sovereignty to the British Crown. New Zealand then became a predominantly white settler colony.

Between the 1840s and the 1890s almost every island group in the Pacific became a colony of one of the Western powers: Britain, France, Germany, and the United States. Missionaries did not oppose colonial rule in principle. Despite tensions over particular issues, they usually cooperated with the colonial governments and deferred to their representatives. Colonial rulers usually recognized the practical value of Christian missions as a civilizing presence and, until the 1950s, relied upon them to provide island villages with primary schooling and basic medical services. Occasionally there were tensions, as when missionaries criticized government policies that they believed were unjust to the islanders or that appeared to threaten their own influence. Colonial governments were more inclined to trust missionaries of their own national background. For this reason, in the French Pacific colonies the LMS handed over its work to the (mainly French Reformed) Paris Evangelical Missionary Society: in French Oceania (Tahiti) in the 1860s and in New Caledonia in the 1890s. In the German colonies the government encouraged German-speaking missions. Led by Johann Flierl (1858–1947), the first Lutheran missionaries, of the Neuendetteslau mission, entered German New Guinea in 1886. A German-based Catholic missionary order, the Society of the Divine Word, began work there in 1896. From this nucleus, the Lutheran and Roman Catholic missions eventually became the largest religious bodies in the independent state (proclaimed in 1975) of Papua New Guinea. During the first half of the twentieth century the number of foreign missionaries in the Pacific Islands grew rapidly, from 1,277 in 1900 to about 1,700 by 1930 and 4,500 in the 1960s. Most of this increase was due to the opening

The house of the Bailey family, a missionary family on the island of Maui. *Courtesy of Scott Leigh/istockphoto.com.*

up to Christian influence of the eastern half of the large island of New Guinea, under Australian colonial rule. During the 1950s and 1960s the populous New Guinea highlands became one of the world's most intensively cultivated mission fields.

Despite denominational differences, the organization of Christian missions in the Pacific Islands until the mid-twentieth century was similar. Each body was attached to mission boards and societies, based in their homelands, which raised funds and recruited staff. In a region covering vast tracts of ocean and many small islands, missions needed their own small ships to maintain contact with their far-flung agents. Mission stations were usually composed of the residence of an ordained European missionary, a boarding school, and an institution to train village pastor-teachers. During the nineteenth century many Protestant stations extended their activities to include the operation of plantations, "industrial" missions (to teach carpentry and other practical skills), and basic medical services. They also began to recruit single women missionaries for work as teachers and nurses and for specialized work among island women and children. Catholic mission stations normally included a community of religious sisters, members of various European missionary orders. Mission stations were outposts of Western culture, regulated and controlled by Europeans.

## Australia and New Zealand

In Australia and New Zealand missionary work among the indigenous inhabitants was organized separately from pastoral ministry to the European settlers. In colonial Australia the churches showed little interest in converting the Aborigines to Christianity. Europeans generally had a low view of Aboriginal society, for the Aborigines were a seminomadic people whose religion was hard for outsiders to understand. Most of the first missions, founded in the 1820s, aimed at detaching Aborigines from traditional tribal society and creating self-supporting Christian communities based upon agriculture. They produced few converts, and within a few decades all of them had collapsed. During the second half of the nineteenth century some devoted individuals and missionary societies from Europe (such as the Moravians) started missions to the Aborigines in rural areas of southeastern and southwestern Australia, but eventually they were submerged by the spread of white settlement. New missions were also founded in remote areas of central Australia, northwest Australia, and the Northern Territory. These were places of refuge from the violence of white settlers and fitted with the gov-

ernment's policy of Aboriginal protection. An Aboriginal church with its own leaders was slow to emerge. Aborigines were ordained to the Christian ministry in significant numbers only from the 1970s.

In New Zealand the missionaries of the CMS, Methodist, and Catholic missions had greater success. From the 1830s the Maori embraced Christianity with enthusiasm, in a movement that began in the far north and moved southward. Missionary work in the central North Island was almost destroyed by the wars of the 1860s between the colonial government and "rebel" supporters of the Maori king, in which many CMS and Methodist missionaries allied themselves with the government. Following the wars many Maori rejected missionary Christianity, joining independent religious movements that the settler churches regarded as unorthodox. The CMS withdrew from New Zealand in 1902, expecting that the emerging Maori church would be absorbed into the church of the dominant white settlers. Despite this drive for assimilation, Maori Anglicans and Methodists successfully retained a distinct identity and during the twentieth century gained greater autonomy in the churches.

## Independent Churches

The ultimate goal of every mission in the Pacific was the eventual creation of a self-sustaining island church with its own ministry. At the village level the church had been led from the beginning by local pastor-teachers and catechists, who conducted worship and taught schools. However, in almost every island group until the mid-twentieth century Europeans made the important decisions in the church and controlled its administration and theological education. In Protestant missions the Pacific Islanders who were ordained to the ministry were usually in subordinate positions, while the number of indigenous Catholic priests, celibate and Latin-educated, was very small. Much of the pressure to increase the level of self-government came from outside the region, from mission headquarters in the home countries which were more open to international thinking on the need for indigenization. Local missionaries had to be prodded into action. The supplanting of a European-led mission by a fully self-governing and self-supporting church occurred first in Tonga and Samoa. After the end of World War II in 1945 the pace speeded up. This process paralleled moves by Western colonial powers in the postwar years toward decolonization. Almost everywhere the major Protestant and Anglican missions had developed into self-governing national churches before the achievement of political independence in the 1960s and 1970s. In the Roman Catholic Church the process of indigenization was boosted by new thinking that emerged from the Second Vatican Council (1963–1965). In many places Rome appointed Pacific Islanders as bishops of dioceses in which the majority of clergy were overseas missionaries. From the 1990s the number of Pacific Island priests grew rapidly. The experience of church self-government at various levels provided islanders with political skills for national self-rule. Mission schools and theological colleges produced many of the first generation of Pacific Island political leaders.

Since the latter decades of the twentieth century new waves of missionaries have entered the Pacific Islands, mostly from Australia, New Zealand, and the United States, intending to convert members of existing churches. These include Jehovah's Witnesses, the Assemblies of God and other branches of Pentecostalism, and agents of parachurch Evangelical organizations. Pentecostals have attracted a large following in expanding urban areas. The religious composition of island populations is thus more diverse than previously. Meanwhile, Pacific Islanders from the older churches have gone as pastors and missionaries to other parts of the Pacific and to minister to islanders who have migrated to Australia, New Zealand, and the west coast of the United States. The religion brought to the Pacific by Christian missionaries has profoundly shaped the lives and culture of the indigenous peoples of the region. At the beginning of the twenty-first century it remains a significant force in Pacific Island societies.

DAVID HILLIARD

*See also* Colonialism, Education—Religious, Theological, Evangelicalism, Inculturation, Jehovah's Witnesses, Millenialism and Adventism, Moravians, Mormonism, Protestant Churches, Revival, Roman Catholic Church

## Further Reading

Boutilier, J. A., Hughes, D. T., & Tiffany, S. W. (Eds.). (1978). *Mission, church, and sect in Oceania.* Ann Arbor, MI: University of Michigan Press.

Breward, I. (2001). *A history of the churches in Australasia.* Oxford: Oxford University Press.

Davidson, A. K. (2004). *Christianity in Aotearoa: a history of church and society in New Zealand* (3rd ed.). Wellington, New Zealand: Education for Ministry.

Ernst, M. (1994). *Winds of change: Rapidly growing religious groups in the Pacific Islands.* Suva, Fiji: Pacific Conference of Churches.

Forman, C. W. (1982). *The island churches of the South Pacific: Emergence in the twentieth century.* Maryknoll, NY: Orbis Books.

Garrett, J. (1982). *To live among the stars: Christian origins in Oceania.* Geneva: World Council of Churches and Suva, Fiji: Institute of Pacific Studies, University of the South Pacific.

Garrett, J. (1992). *Footsteps in the sea: Christianity in Oceania to World War II.* Suva, Fiji: Institute of Pacific Studies, University of the South Pacific and Geneva: World Council of Churches, 1992.

Garrett, J. (1997). *Where nets were cast: Christianity in Oceania since World War II.* Suva, Fiji: Institute of Pacific Studies, University of the South Pacific and Geneva: World Council of Churches.

Glen, R. (Ed.). (1992). *Mission and moko: Aspects of the work of the Church Missionary Society in New Zealand, 1814-1882.* Christchurch: Latimer Fellowship of New Zealand.

Gunson, N. (1978). *Messengers of grace: Evangelical missionaries in the South Seas, 1797-1860.* Melbourne, Australia: Oxford University Press.

Harris, J. (1994). *One blood: 200 years of Aboriginal encounter with Christianity: A story of hope* (2nd ed.). Sydney: Albatross Books.

Herda, P., Reilly, M., & Hilliard, D. (Eds.). (2005). *Vision and reality in Pacific religion: Essays in honour of Niel Gunson.* Christchurch, New Zealand: Macmillan Brown Centre for Pacific Studies, University of Canterbury and Canberra: Pandanus Books, Australian National University.

Hezel, F. X. (1991). *The Catholic Church in Micronesia: Historical essays on the Catholic Church in the Caroline-Marshall Islands.* Chicago: Micronesian Seminar and Loyola University Press.

Hilliard, D. (1978). *God's gentlemen: A history of the Melanesian Mission, 1849-1942.* Brisbane, Australia: University of Queensland Press.

Hilliard, D. (1999). Australasia and the Pacific, In A. Hastings (Ed.), *A world history of Christianity* (pp. 508–535). London: Cassell.

King, M. (1997). *God's farthest outpost: A history of Catholics in New Zealand.* Auckland, New Zealand: Penguin.

Lange, R. T. (2005). *Island ministers: Indigenous leaders in nineteenth century Pacific Islands Christianity.* Canberra: Pandanus Books, Australian National University.

Laracy, H. (1976). *Marists and Melanesians: A history of Catholic missions in the Solomon Islands.* Canberra: Australian National University Press.

Miller, J. G. (1978–1990). *Live: A history of church planting in the New Hebrides/republic of Vanuatu.* Vols. 1–2, Sydney: Committees on Christian Education and Overseas Missions, General Assembly of the Presbyterian Church of

Australia; Vols. 3–7, Port Vila, Vanuatu: Presbyterian Church of Vanuatu.

Munro D., & Thornley, A. (1996). *The covenant makers: Islander missionaries in the Pacific*. Suva, Fiji: Pacific Theological College and Institute of Pacific Studies, University of the South Pacific.

Owens, J. M. R. (1974). *Prophets in the wilderness: The Wesleyan mission to New Zealand, 1819–27*. Auckland, New Zealand: Auckland University Press.

Swain, T., & Rose, D. B. (Eds.). (1988). *Aboriginal Australians and Christian missions: Ethnographic and historical studies*. Adelaide: Australian Association for the Study of Religions.

Wagner, H., & Reiner, H. (Eds.). (1986). *The Lutheran Church in Papua New Guinea: the first hundred years, 1886–1986*. Adelaide, Australia: Lutheran Publishing House.

Wetherell, D. (1977). *Reluctant mission: The Anglican Church in Papua New Guinea, 1891–1941*. Brisbane, Australia: University of Queensland Press.

Whiteman, D. L. (1983). *Melanesians and missionaries: an ethnohistorical study of social and religious change in the southwest Pacific*. Pasadena, CA: William Carey Library.

Williams, R. G. (1972). *The United Church in Papua, New Guinea, and the Solomon Islands*. Rabaul, Papua New Guinea: Trinity Press.

Wood, A. H. (1975–1987). *Overseas missions of the Australian Methodist Church*. Vols. 1–4, Melbourne: Aldersgate Press; Vol. 5, Sydney: Commission for Mission, Uniting Church in Australia.

# Opium

Opium was a major problem for Protestant missionaries in China in the nineteenth and early twentieth centuries as they were linked with the drug in the minds of many Chinese. This association came about because the first Protestant missionaries to China in the early 1800s arrived on opium ships, which were the only means of transportation to the Middle Kingdom at that time. (Only one China trader, the American firm Olyphant and Company, decided to have nothing to do with the opium trade, considering it immoral.)

## Missionaries' Connection to Opium

Further complicating the matter was the fact that missionaries were usually the only Westerners with any knowledge of Chinese and so were co-opted by their countrymen to assist in various treaty negotiations. At these negotiations opium was usually a matter for discussion, as was the missionaries' right to propagate Christianity, further associating the two in the minds of China's government officials. Indeed, it was the 1860 treaties between China and the Western countries that both legalized the opium trade and gave the missionaries the right to spread Christianity throughout China.

In 1839 Commissioner Lin Cixu issued his famous "Moral Advice to Queen Victoria" denouncing opium, and later in the century China's leading statesman, Li Hung-chang, stated that China and Britain would never see eye to eye on the subject of opium since Britain's interest was only fiscal while China's was moral. When asked why China did not simply stop the trade, Li responded that his country had tried that once and the result was war.

Missionaries did not respond well to having Li, whom they considered heathen, lecture their countrymen on morality. (Li would later associate himself with the antiopium advocates, resulting in the missionaries' having to acknowledge that one need not be Christian to oppose opium!)

## Growth of Opium Trade

The trade in opium grew dramatically after 1860, with the Chinese Imperial Maritime Customs Service, created by treaty provisions and staffed by foreigners, keeping track of legal imports. About the same time, the Chinese began growing their own opium, which many users considered inferior to the imported varieties.

Opium addicts were found in all classes of society, but those at the bottom of the social ladder were the most pathetic. Lacking funds to buy both food and opium, the addict frequently chose the latter. Poor nutrition and opium use caused increasingly complicated health problems that resulted in death for many addicts.

The China missionaries represented all shades of Western Christian opinion, but on the subject of opium they spoke with one voice. Indeed, it was the only subject on which they all agreed. Addicts were known to be such unreliable people that missionaries refused to admit them to church membership, except for deathbed conversions.

Many missionaries found opium a hindrance to their work of converting the Chinese to Christianity. There were reports of missionaries who had attempted to preach in the streets, only to have someone in the crowd shout, "Who brought opium to China?"

## Curing and Converting

As the number of missionary medical doctors serving in China increased, many were sought out by addicts to cure their habits. Not infrequently the foreign doctors were summoned to save women who had taken opium, known as "swallowing gold," to commit suicide. Even missionaries who were not medical doctors tried to cure addicts, and an opium refuge became as much a part of the mission compound in China as the missionaries' residences, the school, and the church.

The cure most commonly tried in the refuges was locking the addict up, feeding him or her good food and praying over and preaching to the patient. Many missionaries reported that within three days they had cured the addict of the yen for the drug. (*Yen* in Chinese means smoke or, specifically, the craving for opium smoke. It soon became a loan word in English.) Unfortunately, the missionaries discovered that once the addict went home the addiction returned.

Many missionary doctors tried to produce medicinal cures for opium addiction. They created and sold a wide variety of compounds they hoped would work. Many of these cures contained a vast array of ingredients ranging from cinnamon to quinine and cayenne pepper. These were much sought after both by addicts and by missionaries who were not medical doctors. Eventually, morphine became the cure of choice, and missionaries dispensed so much of it that it was known as "Jesus Opium." Of course, this "cure" only replaced the addition to opium with an addiction to morphine.

Gradually, missionary doctors began to recognize that opium was a pernicious drug. Although it was a commonly prescribed cure-all in the nineteenth century, some medical doctors, particularly those serving in China, came to realize that if it were prescribed for a malady the patient soon had not only the original illness still uncured but also the opium habit. Accordingly, some doctors refused to prescribe it.

## Antiopium Crusaders

As the medical doctors came to realize how dangerous opium was, they joined with allies at home, primarily in Great Britain, to campaign against the involvement of the British government in the opium trade between India and China. The British Society for the Suppression of the Opium Trade was founded in 1874, primarily by members of the Society of Friends and dissenting churches, for the purpose of ending the government's involvement in the trade. By 1891 they succeeded in getting a Parliamentary resolution passed declaring the trade "morally indefensible." Then in 1893 a Royal Commission on Opium was created in response to the demands of the antiopium crusaders.

Opium had been a prominent topic of discussion at the all-China, ecumenical Missionary Conference of 1890 that met in Shanghai. When the Royal Commission visited India but not China, outraged missionaries, led by William Park of the American Southern Methodist mission in Soochow, who had been active in the antiopium cause since the 1890 meeting, organized the Anti-Opium League, which solicited opinions from all Western-trained medical doctors in China about opium. The results, published in 1899, as *Opinions of Over 100 Physicians on the Use of Opium in China*, provided scientific evidence that opium was indeed a pernicious drug.

Adding to the antiopium arguments was the study of the U.S. Philippine Commission on Opium led by the American Episcopal bishop Charles H. Brent. The report of this three-man commission, published in 1905, stated that there were no moderate opium users and the drug was indeed harmful. It went on to criticize the Chinese for their use of the drug, noting there was "no Chinese nation, there is merely a Chinese race." That statement aroused patriotic Chinese, many of them returned students with Western university degrees, who were a factor both in the antiopium movement and in the political revolution to come.

## Governmental Reforms

In the waning days of the Qing empire (i.e., after the Boxer Uprising of 1900), various types of governmental reforms were tried. The most successful of these was the one against opium. In 1906 the Qing issued an edict calling for the suppression of the trade, domestic growth of the poppy, and opium use. Along with the edict were ten regulations aimed at eradicating the drug. Then in 1907 the Chinese signed a treaty with Britain that called for ending the opium trade from India over a ten-year period. Under the terms of the treaty, once an area of China was determined to be free from domestic poppy production, imported opium was prohibited there. Chinese nationalism was an important factor in the success of this crusade against opium, but the 1911 revolution interrupted it, and in the chaos that followed the collapse of the Qing, opium once again flourished.

KATHLEEN L. LODWICK

## Further Reading

Brown, J. B. (July 1973). Politics of the poppy: The Society for the Suppression of the Opium Trade, 1874–1916, *Journal of Contemporary History 8,* 97–111.

Foster, A. (1899). *Report of the Royal Commission on Opium compared with the evidence from China that was submitted* to the Commission: An examination and an appeal. London: Eyre and Spottiswoode.

Lodwick, K. L. (1996). Crusaders against opium: Protestant missionaries in China, 1874–1917. Lexington: University Press of Kentucky.

Park, W. H. (1899). Opinions of over 100 physicians on the use of opium in China, Shanghai, China: American Presbyterian Mission Press.

# Oral History

Oral history is a rather loose concept. Some define it as a collection of oral testimonies that play the role of an ancillary technique of historical study. The emphasis in the United States is on the creation of historical data. The material produced through oral history research is then called oral archives. Historians in other countries, in Britain, Spain, and Latin America in particular, adopt a more ambitious definition of oral history. For them it is another way of doing and conceiving history. In The Voice of the Past (2000), the most widely read introduction to oral history, Paul Thompson writes that he hopes "to provoke historians to ask themselves what they are doing, and why. On whose authority is their reconstruction of the past based? For whom is it intended?" The oral historians who follow this line of thought tend to see oral history as a "movement."

## The Purpose of Oral History

Oral history is practiced for different reasons. One can distinguish three main types of aims: academic, social, and educational. The outcome of oral history differs according to the purpose one has when doing it.

From an academic point of view, the purpose of oral history is to document the stories of social actors usually neglected in historical research. Oral history complements document-based history. It "fills the gaps." In this perspective, the preservation of the oral material is critically important. Oral historians may be sensitive to social issues, but these are not in the forefront. An interview transcript that is not available to researchers is virtually useless. In many cases oral history material is collected in the context of an oral history project, under the auspices of an academic institution, a non-governmental organization, a church, or other group of individuals. But oral history research is also conducted for private use—for a degree, for instance, or out of personal interest. Private researchers rarely make efforts to preserve the material they have gathered.

From a social point of view, the purpose of oral history is to empower interviewees and to help them deal with their past. Oral history can contribute to healing—being interviewed sometimes helps deal with unfinished business. Oral history is affirming: It contributes to the development of a sense of identity, particularly in marginalized groups. In this perspective, the process is more important than the result, even though the fact that the conversation is recorded and preserved may help the process. What happens during the interview is very important; oral historians need counseling skills so they are equipped to deal with traumatic situations.

From an educational perspective, the purpose of oral history is to transfer skills (e.g., listening, assessing evidence, developing a sense of chronology, using a tape recorder and a computer) to learners, students, activists, or community members. Most important is what the learners gain from the process. School projects can contribute to knowledge, but that is only incidental. Similarly, the interviewees may benefit from the interviews, although this is not the main objective.

## Is Oral History Reliable?

Oral history is based on reminiscences, hearsay, or eyewitnesses' accounts that occurred during the lifetime of the people who are interviewed. Oral historians typically interview participants who have been involved in recent or very recent events, when historical consciousness in the communities involved is still in flux. But what happens when stories are passed from mouth to mouth for a period of time beyond the lifetime of the people? Jan Vansina, the Belgian anthropologist, called these stories "oral traditions" to distinguish them from oral history. In Oral Tradition as History (1985), he questions their validity as historical sources. The distinction between oral tradition and oral history is now widely accepted, particularly in Africa.

History as an academic discipline tends to rely almost exclusively on written sources. Critical methodology, conventional historians say, primarily applies to archival material. Oral data appear as imprecise and unreliable. As a result, written sources are always given the preference. Oral sources only come as a second best, when no written evidence is available. Written and oral sources are to one another what the diva is to the understudy. When the star cannot sing, the understudy appears. When writing fails, tradition comes on stage.

Written documents have an undisputable advantage: They are immovable. One can submit a letter or a diary for critical examination at different periods of time. This helps reduce the bias that individual readers inevitably introduce. In history, independent confirmation is conclusive of proof. By contrast, the spoken word is ephemeral. *Verba volant, scripta manent:* Words fly away, writings stay. There is no guarantee, say the advocates of written documents, that the messages conveyed by oral tradition are transmitted faithfully.

In many contexts, however, the primacy given to written sources is questionable. Written sources only reflect the point of view of the people having access to literacy. What about the nonliterate or poorly literate people who constitute the majority of the population? What about women who, until recently, were excluded from mainstream history? What about African people? What about refugees? This also applies to the history of Christianity. A history of missions exclusively based on written documents faces several important limitations. First, it overemphasizes the institutional aspects of Christianity, to the detriment of the social and cultural dimensions of church life. Second, it reflects the outsider's rather than the insider's point of view. The contribution of the indigenous people to the life of the church is ignored or misunderstood. Third, the dynamics of hegemony and resistance are overlooked. History is often written in reference to the public discourse. The "hidden transcript" (Scott, 1990)—what happens offstage—tends to escape attention.

## A Human Encounter

A good oral history practitioner is an active listener. Many people do not share their memories because they think, rightly or wrongly, that nobody is interested in their stories. Good interviewers are sensitive and empathetic. They indicate—by nodding or by asking further questions—that the stories they hear are important to them. Oral history is more than an exchange of information. It is a human encounter. The sharing of memories has an impact on the two parties who are present: the person who speaks and the person who listens.

Good listening skills are particularly important when the person shares painful memories. Good listeners are not people who keep their own emotions at a distance and remain "objective." This, in fact, is impossible. When listening to the interviewee's story, the interviewer's own past comes to the surface and shapes his or her way of listening. A female interviewer who has experienced discrimination in her own family, for instance, will react differently to a story of gender oppression than a male who struggles to make sense of it. This does not mean that oral historians should be led by their emotions uncritically and passively. They should acknowledge that they, too, have a past and find a way of dealing with the emotions triggered by the story. By developing self-awareness they will increase their capacity to listen. The result will be a quality interview.

PHILIPPE DENIS

## Further Reading

Denis, P. (2003). Oral history in a wounded country. In J. A. Draper (Ed.), *Orality, literacy and colonialism in southern Africa* (pp. 205–216). Atlanta, GA: Society of Biblical Literature Semeia Studies.

Grele, R. (1991). *Envelopes of sound: The art of oral history* (2nd ed.). Westport, CT: Greenwood Publishing Group.

Perks, R., & Thomson, A. (Eds.). (1998). *The oral history reader.* London: Routledge.

Ritchie, D. (2003). *Doing oral history. A practical guide* (2nd ed.). New York: Oxford University Press.

Scott, J. (1990). *Domination and the arts of resistance.* New Haven, CT: Yale University Press.

Slim, H., & Thompson, P. (1993). *Listening for a change: Oral testimony and development.* London: Panos Publications.

Thompson, P. (2000). *The voice of the past: Oral history* (3rd ed.). Oxford, UK: Oxford University Press.

Vansina, J. (1985). *Oral tradition as history.* London: James Currey.

# Orality

Orality is essentially communication by means of the spoken word. It remains the predominant method of human discourse throughout the world. In recent years there has been a steady increase in reflections on how we can understand orality. From a brief look at these studies we explore two of these perspectives: orality as a communication strategy and as a type of mentality; that is, a way of understanding the world. These two perspectives offer insights into how orality has played an important role in the history of mission and how such a means of communication can shape the way mission happens in the future.

## Twentieth-century Research on Orality and Literacy

There has been a long-lasting debate on the relationship of literacy to orality (Finnegan 1988, Goody 2000). Whereas it is not our purpose to support a dichotomous view of this relationship, it does prove helpful in our focus on orality to demonstrate its characteristics and its impact on a society. These oral features resonate especially in societies that have not experienced widespread literacy. In the 1930s, studies in orality contributed to new understandings of literature from antiquity; e.g., Homer's *Odyssey* (Lord 1960, Havelock 1986). Support for these studies came from anthropological research in various contemporary oral societies. Later research explored how, even in societies heavily influenced by literacy, the spoken word demonstrates unique communication patterns in comparison with the written word (Foley 1988).

## Orality as a Strategy of Communication

The spoken word is linear and does not remain throughout time (Halliday 1989). This evanescence has repercussions as to how things are communicated. To assure comprehension, elements of speech are repeated, albeit with variance. Speech reverberates with emotion as a hearer is moved not only by what is said but by how it is said. Such oral communication uses concrete examples and images, shying away from abstract notions. The spoken word cannot always be replicated in writing; prosodic features of rhythm, stress, intonation, vocal quality, and volume and the silence in pauses cannot easily be communicated in writing.

## Orality as a Mentality

Beyond the linguistic characteristics, orality as a primary mode of communication has an impact upon society. This impact is such that orality can arguably be used to define a society. Such oral societies differ from societies that have been heavily influenced by literacy. Studies from antiquity and from modern-day societies demonstrate a varied view of life that can be described (or arguably explained) by its primary mode of communication (Ong 1982). Evidence for this comes from anthropological studies of contemporary societies in which literacy is nonexistent or minimally functional. One important characteristic is how spoken words are viewed as instrumental in changing the world. A word spoken by an appropriate person in the right context can transform reality.

## Orality and the History of Mission

Such discussions of the influence of orality (and literacy) upon societies have had ramifications for Christian mission throughout the past two thousand years. For the first fifteen centuries of the Common Era, societies can be described as primarily oral, with the minority of populations influenced by either a scribal or manuscript culture. Not until 1450 CE, with the Western invention of the printing press, do we see a growing influence of the written word into a print culture.

Beginning in the eighteenth century with what has become known as the beginning of the modern missionary era, we see that a primary motivation of missionaries and their sending agencies was to bring "civilization." Included in their notion of civilization was literacy. It was difficult for Europeans to understand how a society without any writing system could be civilized. As a result, literacy and education (often in a European language) became one of the activities of the missionary endeavor (Draper 2004).

Nevertheless, missionaries, as well as newly converted Christians, demonstrated the importance of the spoken word as the Gospel was proclaimed orally, through teaching and preaching (Graham 1987). Local theologies were proclaimed and discussed by means of the spoken word. These theologies may never have been printed, but their social impact cannot be questioned. The Bible, as predominantly a narrative genre, collaborated well by providing stories that could be passed on by word of mouth. The content of these biblical stories often corresponded to the local context. When Jesus says, "Your faith has healed you," or when Jesus calms a storm with the words "Peace, be still!" people from an oral society can appreciate the power of the spoken words of Jesus.

## Orality in the Twenty-first Century

By the end of the twentieth century, Christian mission became ever more conscious of the strategic advantage of using the spoken word in the proclamation of the Gospel. "Faith comes by hearing," the apostle Paul reminds us. Literacy is not a prerequisite for being a Christian. Although there are tremendous advantages to literacy, societies where literacy is still a minor means of communication have demonstrated the continued value of the spoken word. In a sense this brings the Christian message full circle to the first-century Christians, who predominantly heard and verbally proclaimed the Christian message (Kelber 1983).

## Still Primary

The spoken word continues to be a primary means of human communication. Its distinguishing features from literacy have been documented from antiquity through the Middle Ages to today's contemporary societies. Christian mission has demonstrated a variety of relationships with the spoken word and literacy.

Although Christian mission's intimate relationship with the Bible and literacy can be understood, throughout the history of mission, proclamation by spoken word remains a critical means of communication, with an impact on societies.

JAMES MAXEY

## Further Reading

Draper, J. A. (Ed.). (2004). *Orality, literacy, and colonialism in Southern Africa.* Leiden, Netherlands: Brill.

Finnegan, R. (1988). *Literacy and orality: Studies in the technology of communication.* New York: Blackwell.

Foley, J. M. (1988). *The theory of oral composition: History and methodology.* Bloomington and Indianapolis: Indiana University Press.

Goody, J. (2000). *The power of the written tradition.* Washington DC: Smithsonian Institution Press.

Graham, W. (1987). *Beyond the written word: Oral aspects of scripture in the history of religion.* Cambridge, UK: Cambridge University Press.

Halliday, M. A. K. (1989). *Spoken and written language.* Oxford, UK: Oxford University Press.

Havelock, E. A. (1986). *The muse learns to write: Reflections on orality and literacy from antiquity to the present.* New Haven, CT: Yale University Press.

Kelber, W. (1983). *The oral and the written Gospel: The hermeneutics of speaking and writing in the Synoptic tradition, Mark, Paul, and Q.* Philadelphia: Fortress Press.

Lord, A. B. (1960). *The singer of tales.* Cambridge, MA: Harvard University Press.

Ong, W. J. (1982). *Orality and literacy: The technologizing of the word.* New York: Routledge.

# Orientalism

Though a Western fascination with "the Orient" goes back to the Roman Empire, during the modern period "Orientalism" acquired a more specific meaning. It came to denote an exploration of the cultures of the East (the Middle East and Turkey as well as South Asia, China, and Japan) in a systematic and scholarly way; an "Orientalist" was someone who had made himself a recognized expert in one of the fields related to this study. It was a Western enterprise, conducted by Westerners and intended for a Western audience. Some Orientalists established themselves in Western universities studying ancient texts, while others were involved in field research and could claim authenticity because they had lived among "the natives." Orientalism included an amazing volume of very varied work: Geographical "discoveries," cultures and customs (a precursor to anthropology), flora and fauna, languages, fine arts, archaeology, history, ancient texts, and religions all came up for inspection. The last was of special interest to missions and missionaries.

Orientalists were often scholars who were fascinated by the exotic nature of the East (at least as conceived by Westerners). Orientalism was therefore an elitist discourse. It tended, where possible, to approach its subjects through the past. The history of a religion was often deemed more interesting than its current practice. Languages such as Sanskrit were studied rather than vernacular languages, and more time was spent on "high'" religion than on folk religion. History dealt with captains and kings, and the past was always "splendid." This aspect of Orientalism infiltrated the missionary movement. World religions were taught in missionary training institutions from the top down rather than the bottom up, for example, with the result that folk religion—the reality that missionaries were likely, in fact, to encounter—was hardly touched on at all.

Less frequently, the motive behind Orientalist studies was utilitarian. There was an attempt to represent the Orient in a scientific way, by codifying and recording objectively. Imperial agents were expected to find this information useful, and to draw on it to do their jobs better, and the same expectation was sometimes applied to missionaries. In this mode, Orientalism had something of the Enlightenment delight in classification and rational order. It was a controlling mechanism. It applied the rational method in order to gather up the chaotic and elusive and to put it somewhere where it could be studied, and perhaps in the end exploited.

In addition to its utilitarian value, Orientalism proved popular because it fed the human desire for strange tales from afar. In this sense the missionary on furlough giving a lantern slide address was an Orientalist in a low-key way. Missionary biographies were hugely popular in Victorian and Edwardian Britain along with travel adventures of a less religious sort. Orientalists were essentially storytellers. Something they were also expected to convey, if they were to be successful in this mode, was glamour, preferably rather shocking glamour, such as vivid descriptions of a Sultan's harem, or a widow dying voluntarily on her husband's pyre. Orientalists such as Richard Burton owed much of their popularity to a mixture of supposed scholarly authority and an expertise in exotic and scandalous information. Artists also traded in these wares. Some of the paintings by Delacroix and Ingres portraying scenes of Eastern life were hugely popular for exactly these reasons.

Scholarly missionary Orientalism contributed widely to the discipline as a whole. Both Roman Catholic and Protestant scholars were at work during the Western missionary movement. Abe Dubois, for example, wrote a monumental study, *Hindu Manners, Customs and Ceremonies* (published first in French in 1807), which was republished as recently as 1999, a mark of its intrinsic worth. The Scottish missionary John Wilson, who worked in Bombay from 1829, provides a Protestant example. He was an expert not only in the local vernaculars—Marathi and Gujarati—but in Hindustani, Persian, Hebrew, Arabic, and of course Sanskrit. He was the foremost contemporary expert on the Zand language, which enabled him to produce an influential and controversial book on the Parsi religion. He researched Indian religions widely, largely through original manuscripts and inscriptions. He was a recognized expert on various local cave temples, produced a popular history of early Aryan civilization, and served as president of the Bombay Asiatic Society. And all this is just a selection of his many scholarly activities. Wilson may have been exceptional, but he was not unique. In almost every field, missionary Orientalists could be found.

There was some doubt expressed about the value of Orientalist studies for missionaries. At one level there was a simple questioning as to whether this was a suitable way for missionaries to spend their time. At another there was some confusion as to whether non-Christian religions and cultures were being studied because they had value in themselves, or on the basis of a "know the enemy" approach. In fact, some practitioners did move to a more sympathetic and even pluralist position as a result of their fascination with the religious systems they were studying. In this they tended to come closer to the earlier (eighteenth century) Enlightenment Orientalists, such as William Jones (1746–94) and H. T. Colebrooke (1765–1837), who openly expressed their admiration for non-Christian oriental religions, believing that, at the very least, they had a splendid past. The purpose of scholarship, as they saw it, was to restore this past and then to initiate a period of exchange on the basis of mutual profitability.

The whole discourse of Orientalism was given a radical new twist by the writings of Edward Said. Up to this point, speaking generally, Orientalism was thought of positively as an impressive scholarly enterprise that had collected together many useful and fascinating details about little-known parts of the world. An educational institution such as the School of Oriental and African Studies, for example, was considered both repu-

table and admirable. Said's book *Orientalism* (with the subtitle *Western Conceptions of the Orient*), published in 1978 and republished in 1994 with a new afterward, changed the climate of opinion, however. In a series of brilliant studies of such political and literary luminaries as Lord Cromer, Arthur Balfour, Ernest Renan, Antoine-Isaac Sacy, Louis Massignon, Edward Lane, T. E. Lawrence, Richard Burton, and Gustave Flaubert, he examined the thinking of Orientalists. His main thesis was quite simple: Orientalism was a "discourse of power" (an idea derived from the French philosopher Foucault) constructed by Westerners who created a number of suppositions, images, and indeed fantasies, which enabled them to define the Orient as an "other" and thereby also to define themselves in flattering contrast. The conscious and unconscious purpose of this process was more effective self-assertion and control; in other words, it was a colonial enterprise.

From the first, Said's work proved both influential and controversial. He was by profession a literary critic, but his work opened up avenues in a whole range of discourses: history, anthropology, political science, art history, and sociology, and contributed to new developments in feminist and minority studies. Similarly, his chief interest was the Middle East, but not exclusively so, and Indologists and Africanists were also inspired by his work. It can fairly be said to have initiated the movement that we call *postcolonialism*.

While there were many who were inspired by his work there were also those who were hostile, and many more who felt that his central thesis needed some modification. Old-style Orientalists, believing that they had been given an overly sinister role, felt uncomfortable with Said's assertion that it was not possible to make a division between Orientalism as an innocent scholarly discipline, on the one hand, and as an accomplice to empire on the other. Others, more subtly, pointed out that Orientalism had been portrayed as a single monolithic discourse when it was nothing of the sort. There had been many sorts of Orientalism and the discourse had been used by many sorts of people, some of whom—the Indian nationalists, for example—were not imperialists, which therefore broke the connection between Orientalism and imperialism that Said had assumed.

Even more importantly, the recipient culture of the East was not uniform either, nor did it take on Western culture as some uniform bequest. In this view, Said had exaggerated the weakness and futility of the oriental response to Orientalism. The Orient was not a passive and silent "other" but was frequently engaged in answering back, even during the colonial period. Colonial culture refused to be defined by its rulers. Again, this response was different in different places. None of these critics, however, was attempting to deny Said's thesis that issues of knowledge and power were central to Orientalism. (Said maintained subsequently that he had been misrepresented, though the criticisms mentioned above have remained attached to him, whatever his original intention.)

Said's thesis and the development of it remain important for missions and missionaries. Missionaries have been, and still are, part of Orientalism in the Saidian sense. They have stereotyped and "othered" non-Western societies, and used this as a technique to impose their own cultural preferences and to maintain their own authority. Fortunately, indigenous Christians were not necessarily passive under this onslaught, finding the means to answer back to the missionaries out of the resources of their own cultures. In this area, at least, Said's critics seem to have been right.

Said's Orientalism is still with us. Lumping together Islam and terrorism, for example, is a modern form of this discourse. So are theories such as Samuel Huntingdon's "clash of civilisations" which allow us to perpetuate the "us" and "them" of so much colonial thinking. Said wrote Orientalism in an attempt to break down this sort of binary opposition. He believed that Orientalism drew a line between "us" and "them" as a foundational assumption, and that that was why it needed to be exposed.

Inasmuch as mission today is "from everywhere to everywhere" and not "the West to the rest," it is possible that in the future Orientalism as an "othering" discourse may fade away. On the other hand, the creation of stereotypes for reasons of power and control is a practice as old as the human race. When the time comes that mission scholars in the global South begin to compile detailed studies of Western culture in order to understand mission in the West better (will this be called "Occidentalism"?), they may need to avoid the dangers of Orientalism that Edward Said has identified. Meanwhile, the practice of Orientalism in the more general sense of detailed, committed studies of the cultures of non-Western societies remains an urgent requirement for missions and missionaries.

JONATHAN INGLEBY

### Further Reading

Macifie, A.L. (2000). *Orientalism, a reader.* Edinburgh, UK: Edinburgh University Press.

Said, E. (1993). *Culture and imperialism.* London: Chatto & Windus.

Said, E. (1994). *Orientalism: Western conceptions of the Orient.* New York: Random House

Stanley, B. (1990). *The Bible and the Flag.* Leicester, UK: Apollos

Walls, A. (1996). *The modern missionary movement in Christian history.* Edinburgh, UK: T & T Clark

# Orthodox/Coptic Missions

Any description of the missionary enterprise of the Eastern Orthodox Church must begin with agreement on the beginning of Orthodox missions. Since the Orthodox Church considers itself to be the original form of Christianity, from which all others have departed, the journeys of Paul and of the other apostles are considered to be Orthodox missionary work. With recognition that the Orthodox claim both the apostolic and postapostolic eras of the expansion of Christianity, most historians date Orthodox missions from the refounding of Constantinople by the Emperor Constantine in 330 CE.

## Characteristics of Orthodox Missions

Three characteristics distinguish Orthodox missions from Western (Latin) missions; the use of the vernacular for both the liturgy and Bible translation, promotion of indigenous clergy, and the selfhood of the national church. While not always present, this methodology is found in the most representative of Orthodox missions and serves as another marker to distinguish Orthodox missions from even some of the postapostolic expansion of the Gospel.

The use of vernacular languages in preaching and worship accounted for the spread as well as the transformation of cultures in the eastern half of the Roman Empire. Gregory the Illuminator (240–332 CE) brought the Gospel to Armenia and preached in Armenian. King Tiridates was converted, and what followed was a national conversion from the aristocracy on down; in 410 CE the New Testament was translated into Armenian. The transformation of all aspects of culture (including language, religion, and social organization) explains the influence of Orthodox Christianity on many ethnic groups.

## Coptic Christianity

The use of the vernacular allowed the development of Coptic Christianity after the Council of Chalcedon (451 CE) led to the schism over the understanding of the doctrine of the two natures of Christ. Labeled Monophysites because of their disagreement on the formula of two natures as defined at Chalcedon, the Coptic Church of Egypt maintained a separate existence. These differences have been the topic of discussion in late-twentieth-century dialogues with the Eastern Orthodox. The Copts, however, were responsible for a remarkable piece of missionary history, albeit unintentionally, in the founding of the Ethiopian Coptic Church.

The origin of the Ethiopian Church comes from the witness of two brothers from Tyre, who were shipwrecked on the coast of the Red Sea and taken as slaves to the court of King Ezana at Axum. Finding royal favor, Frumentius and Aedesius were able to win converts to the faith and, aided by Christians from Egypt, build a church. When Frumentius traveled to Alexandria to ask the Patriarch Athanasius to appoint a bishop for the church, Athanasius responded by elevating Frumentius to that office (341 CE).

## Slavic Missions

While the Gospel spread to the eastern regions by the use of the vernacular, the breakthrough that created the majority of Orthodox Christians came through the pioneering work of two brothers from Salonica, Constantine (826–869 CE), later called Cyril after his monastic name, and Methodius (c. 815–885 CE). Sent from Constantinople in response to a request from Prince Ratislav of Moravia (the present Slovak Republic), they are known as the "Apostles of the Slavs" and are so commemorated in the Orthodox liturgy. One of their qualifications for undertaking this imperial mission was their knowledge of the Slavic language. Before arriving in Moravia, Cyril constructed an alphabet, the Glagolitic (of which the Cyrillic is a later simplification) and translated the liturgical services and the Bible into the Slavonic language.

Facing opposition from Latin-speaking missionaries, who objected to the use of the vernacular, the brothers traveled to Rome, where they obtained the blessing of Pope Hadrian II to use Slavonic. Cyril died in Rome, and Methodius was hindered from returning to the bishopric to which the pope had appointed him. While Methodius was permitted at first to use the Slavonic language, the vernacular was later suppressed and the dream of a Slavonic church extinguished. Eventually their disciples were driven from Moravia but carried the Gospel to other Slavic peoples, including Bulgaria, Serbia, and Russia.

The Gospel had been preached in Bulgaria, but the Greek liturgical language was unintelligible to the common people. When Slavonic was introduced, the Gospel spread quickly. A Bulgarian church was created and in 926 CE a Bulgarian patriarchate established. As in Serbia, the use of Slavonic was a turning point in the establishment of a national church.

Photius had also sent a mission to Russia around 864, but the nascent church was snuffed out by Prince Oleg in 878 CE. There continued to be a Christian witness, however, and by 945 CE there was a church in Kiev. Even though Princess Olga became a Christian in 945 CE, it was not until her grandson, Vladimir, Prince of Kiev, was converted in 988 CE that Orthodoxy became established as the state religion and remained so until 1917. Vladimir's adherence to Orthodoxy and his forceful coercion of his subjects to accept the faith was total, destroying idols, ordering mass baptisms, founding monasteries, and building churches. His focus on the social and philanthropic aspects of the faith meant that under his rule the harsher punishments were abolished. Under Vladimir, Christianity spread to other areas of Russia, and by the time of his death there were three bishoprics. He is commemorated in the Russian Orthodox liturgy as "Istapostolos," "equal to the Apostles."

### Conversion of the North

Although the conversion of southern Russia appears to have been completed by Vladimir's death, the conversion of the northern regions proceeded more slowly. As in the west, the missionary expansion was through the witness of monks as they penetrated the northern forests. Establishing hermitages, they witnessed by their labor as well as their words. Their hermitages grew into monasteries, and around them towns developed. Through this gradual conversion both the Gospel and Russian culture spread. While the monks' social role is undeniable, their initial calling was to the monastic vocation.

The history of Russian missionary work is tied to the political fortunes of the country and the decisions of the rulers. Alternatively using evangelism as a means of Russification and at times forbidding evangelism to placate ethnic groups, the missionary enterprise moved across the vast regions of Russia. Some missionaries resorted to forcible conversions at the point of the sword, while others were content to administer baptism without any instruction in the faith, either before or after the sacrament was administered.

## The Revitalization of Russian Mission

There were missionaries who took seriously the catechetical task and endeavored to teach their converts

This Eklutna, Alaska, cemetery combines the native Athabascan culture (colorful spirit houses) with the Russian Orthodox Church. *Courtesy of Vera Bogaerts/istockphoto.com.*

both what to believe and how to live. Like the Western rebirth of missions from the time of William Carey, Orthodoxy also experienced a "Great Century" of missions in which earnest attempts at true conversion were undertaken.

Marcarius Gloukarev (1792–1847), a brilliant student who at the age of 29 became rector of the Kostroma Seminary, later withdrew to a hermitage in the remote Glinsk desert. Answering a call issued by the Holy Synod of Russia (the ruling body) for missionaries in 1828, he chose the Altai mountain ranges of central Asia. Learning the local languages of the various tribes, he preached to the nomads. Finding no response but unwilling to believe that God did not have a claim upon these tribes, he changed his methodology to include social services in the form of preventive medicine and hygiene, going so far as to clean the nomads' huts himself. In his fourteen years of missionary service, he founded more schools than churches. While his contemporaries in other areas were rushing converts through baptism (for which the state rewarded the missionaries), he baptized only 675 adults. Settling his converts in Christian villages similar to the Jesuit *reductions* in South America, he devoted considerable time to Christian education to ensure not only the spread of the Gospel but its comprehension.

Another notable figure in the effort to promote understanding of the faith is found in the work of Nicholas Ilminski, who was technically never a missionary but a lay academician. A brilliant linguist, Ilminski was chosen as part of a translation committee that was charged with translating the Bible and liturgical books into the Tartar language. The Tartars were falling away and returning to Islam, and it was thought that using the vernacular would arrest the apostasy. The translation was proceeding using the language of the Qur'an and Arabic script, since the Tartars had no script of their own.

Rather than loosening their ties with Islam, this method had the reverse effect of strengthening the connection. Ilminski proposed using the colloquial language of the people and substituting Russian characters for Arabic script. The breakthrough allowed the Tartars to worship God in their own language and produced a true Tartar church. Ilminski's recognition of the importance of the vernacular and the need for the Gospel to become incarnate in the living tongue of the Tartars allowed the expression of their deepest religious consciousness.

## Orthodox Alaska

Following the expansion of the Orthodox faith must include the venture into North America, in the Russian colony of what is now Alaska. Russian fur traders crossed the Bering Sea to exploit the riches of Russian America, and with the traders came priests to evangelize and pacify the natives. Most famous of these Russian missionaries is John Veniaminov (1797–1879), a parish priest from Irkutsk in central Russia.

Answering a call for missionaries to Alaska, Veniaminov moved his family in 1824 to Unalaska. A skilled craftsman, he built his own home as well as a church. He learned to navigate a kayak to visit his far-flung flock. His skill in linguistics is demonstrated by his mastery of the vernacular languages of the various tribes to whom he ministered. His book, written in Aleut, *Indication of the Way into the Kingdom of God,* was later translated into Russian and from 1839 to 1885 went out in forty-six editions. He was canonized as St. Innocent in 1977.

Mention must be made of another Alaskan missionary, Father Herman (died 1836), who labored for over forty years in Alaska. His spirituality, the monastic simplicity of his life, and his devoted service to the native peoples earned profound respect. He was canonized in 1970 as the first American saint of the Orthodox Church.

## Japan and China

One of the missionaries that St. Innocent impacted was Nicolas Kassatkin, the apostle to Japan. In two encounters with Nicolas, St. Innocent gave him direction for his work by encouraging him to study Japanese. Nicolas was chaplain to the Russian consulate in Hakodate when he came into contact with an extremely nationalistic samurai, Sawabe. Fearful of the damage that the priest's religion could do to his country, Sawabe determined to best Nicolas in debate and if he could not win, slay the priest. Instead, Sawabe himself was converted and in time led two of his friends to the Christian faith. Since conversion was still illegal for Japanese, they were baptized in secret by Nicolas.

As the political tide in Japan changed, Nicolas moved to Tokyo, where he was successful in establishing a church. His catechetical method was to require his students to share what they had learned with others before the next lesson. In this way, Nicolas used the principle that those who teach others learn more fully themselves. The mission never had more than four Russian priests, relying instead on indigenous workers. During the Russo-Japanese war, Nicolas remained in Japan but withdrew from public worship in the Cathedral of the Resurrection, which he had built on a prominent hill in Tokyo. At his death in 1912, he left behind a church numbering 33,000 with thirty-five Japanese priests serving 266 congregations.

The Orthodox Church in China owes its existence to some Russian soldiers captured by the Chinese along with their priest and taken into the service of the emperor. The Chinese allowed the Russians to keep their religion, and the church attracted a small number of Chinese adherents. Throughout the time of the Russian empire, the mission to Peking had a more diplomatic and strategic emphasis than it did a religious one.

## New Developments in Mission

The conquest of the Byzantine empire, conveniently encapsulated by the fall of Constantinople in 1453 with the death of the last Byzantine ruler, effectively put an end to Orthodox missions from the Greek Church, though the missionary effort had been hampered for years. The cessation of missionary work was mirrored in Russia in 1917 with the success of the Russian Revolution.

New fields continued to be opened for Orthodoxy as emigrants fled traditionally Orthodox lands, either from political oppression or to find financial opportunity. As Greeks, Russians, Ukrainians, and other Orthodox populations settled in western Europe, the United States, and Australia, they brought with them their Orthodox faith. This diaspora, however, was not one of outreach but of preservation. These were not missionary churches; rather they were social and religious centers that kept the traditions of the homeland alive. This explains why in the countries of the diaspora, there are ethnic and linguistic jurisdictions instead of one national Orthodox church.

### Africa and Greece

The revival of foreign Orthodox missionary work came in part through an unusual source. An African Initiated Church founded in East Africa by Africans adopted Eastern Orthodoxy as their expression of Christianity. Eventually recognized by the Patriarchate of Alexandria, these African churches in Uganda, Kenya, and Tanzania sparked a new interest in spreading the Gospel by the Orthodox. Porefthendes, the Inter-Orthodox Missionary Centre in Athens headed by Anastasios Yannoulatos, promoted missionary work through visits to Greece by Reuben Spartus, one of the African Orthodox Church founders. The Centre's missionary publication, also entitled *Porefthendes,* encouraged missionary thinking by intermingling reports on current missionary work with theological and historical studies of early Orthodox mission. The current missionary publication of the Centre, *Panta ta Ethni,* continues to report on Orthodox missionary work.

Yannoulatos himself published works in Greek on African religions, as well as writing the first nonpolemic work on Islam to appear in Greek. This pioneer of mission was for a time director of the Home Mission of the

Church of Greece and sought, by evangelistic tracts and other publications, to combat the secular mindset of his countrymen. He served as a missionary bishop in East Africa and led the mission to Albania to restore Eastern Orthodoxy to that country, which under Communism had been thoroughly atheistic. Drawing to himself a core of younger missionaries, including many from the United States, Yannoulatos has been successful in building churches and establishing a theological seminary for the training of indigenous clergy in Albania.

### North America

The missionary impetus in North America has been fueled largely by the Orthodox Mission Committee headed by Father Alexander Veronis, whose interest in missions began as a seminary student. The Mission Committee raised the consciousness of foreign missions among Orthodox congregations, especially those belonging to the Greek Orthodox Diocese of North America, and supported financially the theological training of priests from East Africa. In 1984 the Orthodox Christian Mission Center was established in Florida, and since that time missionaries and short-term mission teams have been sent out. Serving both as a training center and missionary-sending organization, the center conducts work in many countries, including India, Tanzania, Kenya, Uganda, Guatemala, Albania, and Romania.

### Christian Converts

In addition to foreign missions, the Orthodox churches have received a swell of converts from other Christian denominations. Some of these converts come as a result of overt evangelism, especially from mission parishes of the Antiochian Orthodox Christian Archdiocese of North America. The Antiochian Archdiocese absorbed the Evangelical Orthodox Church, a fellowship of formerly evangelical Protestant churches that adopted the practices of Eastern Orthodoxy. Even apart from these efforts at proselytism, a large number of non-Orthodox Christians have found their own way into the various Orthodox jurisdictions. At St. Vladimir's Theological Seminary of the Orthodox Church in America (formerly the Russian Orthodox Church), as many as 40 percent of the students are converts to the faith. The vitality of Orthodoxy is seen in both its missionary enterprises and its ability to attract converts from other traditions.

JAMES J. STAMOOLIS

## Further Reading

Bolshakoff, S. (1943). *The foreign missions of the Russian Orthodox Church.* London: SPCK.

Bratsiotis, P. I. (1950). The evangelistic work of the contemporary Greek Orthodox Church. *The Christian East, 1:21–32,* 38–41.

Bria, I. (Ed.). (1980). *Martyria /mission: The witness of the Orthodox churches today.* Geneva, Switzerland: World Council of Churches.

Cary, O. (1909). *Roman Catholic and Greek Orthodox missions: Vol. I. A history of Christianity in Japan.* New York: Fleming H. Revell Co.

Doulis, T. (1986). *Journeys to Orthodoxy: A collection of essays by converts to Orthodox Christianity.* Minneapolis, MN: Light and Life Publishers.

Drummond, R. H. (1971). *A history of Christianity in Japan.* Grand Rapids, MI: Eerdmans.

Dvornik, F. (1970). *Byzantine missions among the Slavs.* New Brunswick, NJ: Rutgers University Press.

Garrett, P. D. (1979). *St. Innocent: Apostle to America.* Crestwood, NY: St. Vladimir's Seminary Press.

Gillquist, P. E. (1992). *Coming home: Why Protestant clergy are becoming Orthodox.* Ben Lomond, CA: Conciliar Press.

Glazik, J., and Stamoolis, J. J. (2003). Missions, Orthodox. In *The new Catholic encyclopedia* (Rev. ed.). Farmington Hills, MI: Thomson Gale.

Harper, M. (1999). *A faith fulfilled: Why are Christians across Great Britain embracing Orthodoxy?* Ben Lomond, CA: Conciliar Press.

Lacko, M. (1963). *Saints Cyril and Methodius.* Rome: Slovak Editions.

Meyendorff, J. (n.d.). Orthodox missions in the Middle Ages. In *History's lessons for tomorrow's mission* (pp. 99–104). Geneva, Switzerland: World's Student Christian Federation.

Oleska, M. (1993). *Orthodox Alaska: A theology of mission.* Crestwood, NY: St. Vladimir's Seminary Press.

The Orthodox Church: A new dynamic in Australian church life. (1979). *International Review of Missions, 68,* 22–25.

Schmemann, A. (1961). The missionary imperative in the Orthodox tradition. In *The theology of Christian mission.* New York: McGraw-Hill.

Smirnoff, E. (1903). *A short account of the historical development and present position of Eastern Orthodox missions.* London: Rivingtons.

Spinka, M. (1968). *A history of Christianity in the Balkans.* Hamden, CT: Archon Books.

Stamoolis, J. J. (1986). *Eastern Orthodox mission theology today.* Maryknoll, NY: Orbis. (Reprint ed., Eugene, OR: Wipf and Stock.)

Struve, N. (1963). The Orthodox Church and mission. *St. Vladimir's Seminary Quarterly, 7,* 31–42.

Struve, N. (1965). Macaire Gloukharev: A prophet of Orthodox mission. *International Review of Missions, 54,* 308–314.

Ware, T. (1997). *The Orthodox Church.* London: Penguin.

Yannoulatos, A. (1964). Byzantium, evangelistic works. *The encyclopedia of religion and ethics* (in Greek) (Vol. 4, pp. 19–59). Athens, Greece: n.p.

Yannoulatos, A. (1969). Monks and mission in the Eastern church during the 4th century. *International Review of Missions, 58,* 208–226.

Yannoulatos, A. (1971) *Various Christian approaches to the other religions.* Athens, Greece: Porefthendes.

# P

## Pacifism

Pacifism is a philosophy whose adherents reject violence, particularly war. The root meaning of the word comes from the Latin *pax* (peace) and *facere* (to make); i.e., to make peace. Pacifism is found from ancient times to the present, among both secular and religious persons, in simple societies as well as in advanced technological states. Pacifism is not to be confused with passivity. Making peace is active—adherents are committed to building a peaceful world.

When pacifists refuse to serve in the military, they are known as conscientious objectors. Today a growing number of countries legally recognize conscientious objection, but many nation-states still exert harsh punishment on those who refuse to serve in the army for reasons of conscience.

### Pacifism in Eastern Religions

In the religions of Asia, pacifist thought and practice are widely found. Daoism says that the *Dao,* the divine principle of the universe, teaches the return of love for hatred. The concept of *ahimsa*—harmlessness or nonviolence—is adhered to by Jains, Buddhists, and Hindus. Jainism teaches its followers to be scrupulously nonviolent, wearing coverings over their mouths and sweeping the path in front of them so that they will not inadvertently kill even a tiny insect. The founder of Buddhism, Gautama Buddha (566?–c. 480 BCE), taught reverence for life and compassion toward all beings. The Hindu Mohandas Gandhi (1869–1948) said, "Nonviolence is not passivity in any shape or form. Nonviolence…is the most active

force in the world…Nonviolence is the supreme law." He successfully applied pacifist thought to nonviolent social change and liberation on a scale never imagined before.

The Muslim Badsah Khan (1890–1984), from the fierce Pathan tribe of India's Northwest Frontier, based his nonviolence on Islam, with its belief in *salaam,* which is similar to the Jewish *shalom.* Khan said that compassion is the hallmark of Muslim life, and in fighting British rule he organized the world's first nonviolent army.

## Judaism

Judaism has at its heart the belief in *shalom,* or harmony—peace with all people, with God, and with the earth. In the teachings of the eighth-century BCE prophets such as Isaiah and Micah, the way of peace is central: "They shall beat their swords into plowshares, their spears into pruning hooks. Nation shall not lift up sword against nation, neither shall they learn war any more" (Micah 4:3b, Revised Standard Version).

Although references to wars are found in Jewish thought, the vision of peace is always paramount. God is righteous and is on the side of the poor, the oppressed, the widow, and the orphan. "The effect of righteousness will be peace" (Isaiah 32:17).

Rabbinic thought allegorized biblical references to war, saying, for example, the sword refers to prayer and the bow refers to supplication. David is exalted for the psalms, not for his battles. Jewish heroes are the spiritually great, those who convert enemies into friends. The Jewish calendar does not commemorate war and conquest but the way of compassion, the love of neighbor as oneself. "Not by might, nor by power, but by my Spirit, says the Lord of hosts" (Zechariah 4:6).

## Christian Teaching

Jesus's teaching reflected the Jewish prophetic tradition, but he made "love of enemy"—a part of that tradition—central to his message. In the Sermon on the Mount, Jesus says, "Blessed are the peacemakers, for they shall be called the children of God" (Matthew 5:9). He says, "Love your enemies and pray for those who persecute you, so that you may be sons of your Father who is in heaven; for he makes his sun rise on the evil and on the good, and sends rain on the just and on the unjust. For if you love those who love you, what reward have you?" (Matt. 5:44–46). St. Paul, writing after Jesus's death and resurrection, says that "God, who through Christ reconciled us to himself ... gave us the ministry of reconciliation" (II Cor. 5:18–19). In Romans 12:21 Paul says, "Do not be overcome by evil, but overcome evil with good."

For the first three centuries the church was pacifist, following the way of nonviolence and forgiveness, even to the point of death. However, when the Roman emperor Constantine (c. 288–337 CE) became a Christian, events were set in motion that led in 380 CE to Christianity's becoming the empire's official religion. No longer were Christians forbidden to be in the army; now to serve in the army one had to be Christian!

The theological justification for this dramatic reversal was Augustine's (354–430 CE) concept of the "just war," wherein there is a just cause waged by legitimate authority. This Constantinian stance became the majority position of the church in succeeding centuries, and it remains persuasive for most Christians to the present day.

After Christianity accepted the just-war position, the pacifist witness remained but was now in the minority. Pacifism continued among the clergy and in monastic and similar communities, seen, for example, in the followers of Francis of Assisi (1182–1226 CE) and, with the Protestant Reformation, in communities that came to be known as the Historic Peace Churches—the Brethren, the Mennonites, and the Society of Friends (Quakers).

## The Future

As the destructiveness of modern warfare has increased, threatening the future of civilization itself, pacifist thought and practice have grown dramatically. Many churches—Catholic, Orthodox, and Protestant—that have followed the just-war tradition are grappling with the futility and sheer horror of modern war. This is seen

in the papacy of John XXIII (1881–1963), whose papal letter *Pacem in Terris* calls humanity to "the universal common good." The World Council of Churches has likewise been a strong advocate of overcoming violence and war.

Other signs of current commitment to peace and the rejection of violence are seen in the witness of the International Fellowship of Reconciliation, Pax Christi International, and the American Friends Service Committee; the annual Nobel Peace Prize; the United Nations' call for "a culture of peace and nonviolence"; and the growing interfaith efforts against war. Evidence is found in the influence of persons like Leo Tolstoy (1828–1910), Baroness Bertha von Suttner (1843–1914), Albert Luthuli (1898–1967), Dorothy Day (1897–1980), Martin Luther King, Jr. (1929–1968), Thich Nhat Hanh (b. 1926), and Muriel Lester (1884–1968).

RICHARD DEATS

## Further Reading

Bainton, R. (1960). *Christian attitudes toward war and peace: A historical survey and critical re-evaluation.* Nashville, TN: Abingdon Press.

Brown, D. W. (2003). *Biblical pacifism.* Nappanee, IN: Evangel Publishing House.

Easwaran, E. (1984). *A man to match his mountains: Badshah Khan, nonviolent soldier of Islam.* Tomales, CA: Nilgiri Press.

Egan, Eileen. (1999). *Peace be with you: Justified warfare or the way of nonviolence.* Maryknoll, NY: Orbis Books.

Fahey, J. J. (2005). *War and the Christian conscience: Where do you stand?* Maryknoll, NY: Orbis Books.

Fischer, L. (Ed.). (1962). *The essential Gandhi.* New York: Random House.

Gandhi, M.K. (1960) *All men are brothers.* Ahmedabad, India: Navajuivan Publishing

Polner, M., & Goodman, N. (Eds.). (1994). *The Jewish tradition of peace and justice.* Gabriola Island, Canada: New Society Publishers.

Schell, J. (2003). *The unconquerable world: Power, nonviolence, and the will of the people.* New York: Metropolitan Books.

Washington, J. M. (Ed.). (1991). *The testament of hope: The essential writings and speeches of Martin Luther King, Jr.* New York: HarperCollins.

Wink, W. (1992). *Engaging the powers: Discernment and resistance in a world of domination.* Phoenix, AZ: Fortress Press.

Yoder, J. H. (1994). *The politics of Jesus* (2nd ed.). Grand Rapids, MI: Eerdmans.

# Parachurch

In the period since 1945 Western Christianity has become increasingly characterized by a plethora of specialist organizations attempting to extend the life and ministry of the traditional denominations. In Protestant parlance these are often labeled "parachurch" organizations (Greek: *para*, beside or alongside), to denote their supposed complementary character. In the Roman Catholic context such organizations are more commonly referred to as "sodalities," denoting their symbiotic relationship with the church universal. Protestant theologian Thomas Finger argues that the church

> cannot be something that takes exactly the same form in every situation. It must be a dynamic reality which itself is hastening towards consummation. If so, theology will begin to identify it only by considering the church in action—by first attending to the church's mission. (Finger 1985, Vol. 2, 245)

While only one opinion among many, this statement highlights the culturally dynamic nature of Christianity and helps to explain the many historical variants of Christian expression that have emerged, including that of parachurch. At the same time it hints at a definitional tension over how "church" is theologically and structurally understood. Such tensions have both historical and contemporary dimensions. This article traces the historical contours of this voluntary aspect of Christianity and briefly indicates areas of significance.

## Medieval Sodalities

Activism and spiritual devotion have long been linked together in the Christian tradition, and it is in this relationship that the parachurch concept has its genesis. Its historical roots may extend as far back as the Old Testament and the intertestamental eras (finding expression in such groups as the prophetic brotherhoods and Jewish proselytizers) or to the New Testament era (particularly the missionary tours of St. Paul). Commentators are more agreed that the parachurch/sodality model was intrinsic to the alternative monastic communities that developed in the mid-fourth century CE, first in Egypt and then more particularly in both the eastern Mediterranean and western Europe. Between the fifth and twelfth centuries, for example, such orders as the Benedictines and the Cistercians enabled a broad cross-section of men and women to combine service, piety, and devotion within independent communities under diocesan jurisdiction.

Irish monasticism also developed from the fifth century, parallel to other monastic forms but initially with a more federated structure under the authority of abbots as opposed to bishops. Over the next two centuries bands of Irish monks (the *peregrini*) were responsible for the evangelization of Scotland and many parts of northern Europe. Portability and devotion were similarly combined by St. Cyril and St. Methodius in the mid-ninth century, by the mendicant orders from the early thirteenth century (exemplified by the Franciscan and Dominican orders), and by the Jesuit order from the mid-sixteenth century. Papal proscription of the Jesuits in 1773, however, indicated that such groups could also be seen as a threat. In the wake of the Counter Reformation, a large number of other sodalities emerged, parallel with the established orders, which focused the attention and energies of their members on pious devotion, acts of mercy, and mission.

## Sodalities and Parachurch Organizations in the Modern Era

While sodalities continued to be a vital force within Roman Catholicism, they were not a part of Protestant Christianity until at least the late seventeenth century. Within the Church of England, the Society for the Promotion of Christian Knowledge (SPCK, formed in 1698) and the Society for the Propagation of the Gospel in Foreign Parts (SPG, formed in 1701) were two of the earliest such groups to be formed. More particularly the Moravian Brethren (Germany, 1722) combined aspects of church and sodality, with their focus on community service and missionary endeavor. William Carey's thinking, and the missionary approach exemplified by the Baptist Missionary Society (1792), owed much to the Moravian model, as did the Wesleyan Methodist movement emerging in the same period. Therefore, contrary to populist thinking, Carey was not technically the "father" of the modern Protestant missionary movement.

The denominational missionary organizations that emerged from the 1790s onward were precursors of the great nineteenth-century explosion of "extra-church" organizations (both Protestant and Roman Catholic) that sought to exploit and harness the religious energies of the wider populace. They were also one expression of the increasing democratization of Christianity in this period and were ambiguously yet unavoidably related to the imperial and colonial expansion of Europe. Representative of such organizations were the British and Foreign Bible Society (1804), the Societies of Mary (1816) and St. Vincent de Paul (1833), George Müller's orphanage in England (1833), and Scripture Union (1879).

By the early twentieth century there was a growing distinction between denominational and interdenominational Protestant missionary and service groups, with denominations like the American Presbyterian Church attempting to centralize and incorporate such functions. The sodality model was kept alive in such missionary organizations as the China Inland Mission (1865) and the Bolivian Indian Mission (1908).

Denominational and theological divisiveness in the interwar period added further impetus to the growth and acceptance of (mainly) evangelical Protestant organizations. Missionary organizations and other sodalities or parachurch groups were given added impetus in the post-1945 era. This was fueled by such factors as the energy of returned servicemen, the emergence of a distinctive youth culture, the visible developmental gaps between older nations and those newly emerging postcolonial nations, and the reforms of Vatican II. The "revolutionary" decade of the 1960s, for example, witnessed the emergence of such organizations as World Vision, Youth for Christ, and Youth with a Mission—each organization focusing on a particular niche market of need and expertise. The *World Christian Encyclopedia* notes this explosive growth, grouping parachurch organizations into 74 categories, covering 62 pages (Barrett 1982, 912–974).

Internationally, these groups now fulfill a broad range of specialist functions including education, evangelism and evangelization, discipleship, media, political and social activism, aid and development, and relief work. At the same time, especially in American Protestant circles, there has been ongoing theological debate over how far such organizations can be tolerated or can be viewed as legitimate expressions of "church." Debate such as that raised by Ralph Winter's notion of a "two-structures" approach to ecclesiology seems to be as much a reflection of the culture-boundedness of Christianity as it is of theology per se. Such debate also reflects the decline in many Western denominations and the corresponding competition for increasingly scarce resources of finance and personnel.

## The Significance of Parachurch Organizations

This historical survey illustrates the ways in which sodalities or parachurch organizations embody the intrinsic desire of Christian people to be practically and strategically useful. They have characteristically arisen in periods of renewal, reformation, and revival, capturing and channeling the energies and imaginations of people reinvigorated in their faith. In the twentieth century, in particular, this tendency has been bracketed with the increasing professionalization and specialization of both society and church. They have therefore filled a set of specialist gaps not so easily filled by the historic denominations—such as children's and youth ministries; Bible production and translation; and larger-scale relief, aid, and development.

This division of labor between churches and parachurch groups has been more recently challenged by the megachurch movement, in its attempt to be as comprehensive as possible in its relationship to wider society. Roman Catholic and the Anglican/Episcopal communions appear more relaxed in their ability to incorporate a range of specialist functions within their wider definition of "church," and to allocate people and other resources to those ends.

Many larger parachurch organizations appear little different from multinational corporations both in the scale of their operations and their centralized authoritarian control. Yet they have also been an important vehicle for the liberation of people and gifts, both in the church and in relation to wider society. They have been particularly important for the public ministry of women, especially from the mid-nineteenth century, and an outlet for children's and young people's energies. Since 1945 many Protestant organizations have become truly international in that they have relinquished centralized control, made space for autonomous regional and national expression of their ministries, and created councils that are equally represented by all regions. Scripture Union International is one example, as is World Vision, of such organizations that continue to struggle to be more completely international and inclusive in both ministries and structure. World Vision also exemplifies the ways in which such groups have attempted to bridge the church-society divide, appealing to wider sentiments of human compassion and altruism in the attempt to address global inequalities and to respond to natural emergencies and disasters.

In conclusion, the church has been invigorated by the parachurch phenomenon, while struggling at times to understand the relationship between the pastoral and the missional elements of ecclesiology that such groups at times challenge. These groups or organizations have simultaneously extended the possibilities of the church in society and enriched the lives of its members.

HUGH MORRISON

## Further Reading

Barrett, D. B. (Ed.). (1982). *World Christian encyclopedia.* New York: Oxford University Press.

Camp, B. K. (1995). A theological examination of the two-structure theory. *Missiology, 23*(2), 197–209.

Finger, T. (1985). *Christian theology: An eschatological approach* (2 vols.). Scottdale, PA: Herald Press.

Hilgers, J. (2005). Sodality. *The Catholic encyclopedia.* Retrieved May 15, 2006, from http://www.newadvent.org/cathen,14120a.htm

Küng, H. (1968). *The church.* London: Burns & Oates.

Lineham, P. J. (1980). *No ordinary union: Centenary history of Scripture Union in New Zealand.* Wellington, New Zealand: Scripture Union in New Zealand Incorporated.

Mellis, C. J. (1976). *Committed communities: Fresh streams for world missions.* South Pasadena, CA: William Carey Library.

Robert, D. (Ed.). (2002). *Gospel bearers, gender bearers: Missionary women in the twentieth century.* Maryknoll, NY: Orbis Books.

Senter, M. (1992). *The coming revolution in youth ministry.* Wheaton, IL: Victor Books.

Sheils, W. J., & Wood, D. (Eds.). (1986). *Voluntary religion.* Oxford, UK: Ecclesiastical History Society, Basil Blackwell.

Sylvester, N. (1984). *God's Word in a young world: the story of Scripture Union.* London: Scripture Union.

Walls, A. (1996). *The missionary movement in Christian history: Studies in the transmission of faith.* Maryknoll, NY: Orbis Books.

White, J. (1983). *The church and the parachurch: An uneasy marriage.* Portland, OR: Multinomah Press.

Winter, R. (1974). The two structures of God's redemptive mission. *Missiology, 2*(1), 121–139.

# Partnership

"Partnership" has been a dominant theme in missionary organization and theology for more than fifty years. It owes its popularity to disparate sources: (1) its Biblical pedigree, (2) a contractual-pragmatic understanding borrowed from the corporate world, (3) the redefinition of cross-cultural relationships in a postcolonial world, and (4) the theology of the ecumenical movement. Today partnership continues to act as a mediating concept for churches, parachurches, nonprofits, and other organizations in cooperative mission, and is used in a variety of contexts (in discussions of gender, other religions, and so forth). "Mission unites, doctrine divides" is one of the slogans of the modern missionary movement, and a major reason for partnership's wide circulation is that it allows groups with very different beliefs to cooperate under a positive shared vision. The pragmatism of "partnership" is both its strength and its weakness, since the word has become not only ubiquitous but also often devoid of deep meaning.

## History

The Christian scriptures use "partner" in several senses. It may refer to a spouse or marital partner (Mal. 2:14; 1 Pet. 3:7), a coworker (2 Cor. 8:23; Philem. 1:17), or a more general association (Prov. 28:24; Eph. 5:7). These references reflect the marital, ecclesiastical, and generic uses of partnership in mission organizations. The idea of partnership has also given rise to important metaphors—the Church as the body of Christ, for example, in which members are united in the Spirit for a common purpose. Apostolic cooperation (Paul, Apollos, Barnabas, and Timothy) provides another example.

### Corporate Influence

At the start of the modern missionary movement, lay leaders and clerics adopted strategic goals that required partnering; for instance, in 1805 leaders in Philadelphia from different denominations agreed that they could financially share the task of scripture translation abroad because such work was theologically neutral. However, such cooperation was not named "partnership" until the twentieth century. The word itself had "its origins in the business world ('business partners') via the 1920s colonials discussion, when the British wanted to keep control while granting some autonomy, and coined the term 'partnership' to describe this new relationship" (Funkschmidt 2002, 558). Partnership as an implied contractual participation in a shared enterprise was soon incorporated into church and missionary work.

### Postcolonial Relationship

Partnership flourished as a concept in the mid-twentieth century because it criticized patriarchal and nationalist models while allowing for ongoing relationships. Earlier relationship models (mother/daughter, teacher/student, sending/receiving, and older/younger) had been explicitly hierarchical or paternalistic. Partnership reflected the spirit of V. S. Azariah, the first Indian bishop in India, when he called at the 1910 World Missionary Conference in Edinburgh for true friends rather than benevolent foreign leaders. The word "partnership" implied, if not equality, at least a sharing of resources, responsibilities, and values.

It is possible to detect deeper roots for partnership in the missionary movement. For instance, the three-self theology advocated in the nineteenth century by Rufus Anderson and Henry Venn urged the creation of churches that were self-governing, self-supporting, and self-propagating. Throughout the missionary movement, the agency of local peoples has always been the goal of at least some missionaries and church leaders. Partnership represents the extension of this theology in a postcolonial age, facilitating cooperation between churches from different national and socioeconomic backgrounds while attempting to protect the integrity of all involved.

### Ecumenical Movement

The ecumenical movement was a major incubator for partnership theology, especially in the decade after World War II, which saw four major ecumenical events: a Lambeth conference, the IMC's Whitby Conference, the formation of the Church of South India, and the creation of the World Council of Churches. Each of these conferences marked a significant advance in terms of the inclusion of world church leaders and efforts toward international conversation. For Stephen Neill and others, partnership expressed the new relationships that were being created. In the International Missionary Council, the 1947 Whitby Conference spoke of "partners in obedience," and by the 1952 Willingen Conference, leaders advocated "partnership in mission." Max Warren of the Church Missionary Society in London gave a series of addresses, published in 1956, that treated the theological implications of partnership; he focused on partnership as an aspect of the *perichoresis* of the Trinity and the incarnation of Christ, and spoke of partnership as important for redressing social problems. Because the ecumenical movement was a major site for the reconsideration of church relationships, partnership has continued to flourish in its theology.

## Today

Today, partnership is often the expressed ideal for mission. For example, the Presbyterian Church in the United States has adopted "partnership in mission" as its theology of mission, and the church officially sends "partners in mission" rather than missionaries. Those who object to this emphasis argue that it eclipses other worthy goals. However, there is consensus that "partnership is the form and not the content of Christian mission" (Kirkpatrick 1995, 104). The use of partnership allows for a modest shared agenda while deferring discussions of the stickier theological, sociological, and ideological questions. Partners may maintain their own identities, reserving difficult questions for later.

Another area where partnership plays a prominent role is in discussions of gender. The World Alliance of Reformed Churches advocated for partnership between men and women; it has had a Department of Partnership of Women and Men since 1997. Feminist theologian Letty Russell used the theme of partnership in most of her earlier works, and discussed partnership as occurring both with God and with people. She sees partnership as a means for shared *diakonia* (service) and as a reflection of Biblical models of union and relationship. Partnership has also been applied to discussions of dialogue with other religions and to cooperation with secular entities. Because partnership is most commonly constructed around a shared goal, it is easily applied to many different aspects of mission.

With its adaptability and rich pedigree, partnership is one of a handful of dominant images in contemporary missions. Although critics question its lack of content and advocates ask for greater theoretical depth, partnership shows no signs of losing its value for mission.

Jonathan A. Seitz

*See also* Development; Economics; Materiality; Mission Methods and Strategy; Money; Paternalism

## Further Reading

Funkschmidt, K. (2002). New models of mission relationship and partnership. *International Review of Mission, 91*(363), 558–76.

Kirkpatrick, C. (1995). Response to Stanley Skreslet. *International Bulletin of Missionary Research, 19*(3), 104–05.

Lagenwerf, L., Karel, S., & Verstraelen, F. (Eds.). (1995). *Changing partnership of missionary and ecumenical movements.* Leiden-Utrecht, Holland: Interuniversity Institute for Missiological and Ecumenical Research.

Marsh, C. (2003). Partnership in mission: To send or to share? *International Review of Mission, 92*(366), 370–381.

Neill, S. (1952). *Christian partnership.* London: SCM.

Russell, L. (1979). *The future of partnership.* Philadelphia: Westminster Press.

Russell, L. (1981). *Growth in partnership.* Philadelphia: Westminster Press.

Skreslet, S. (1995) The empty basket of Presbyterian mission: Limits and possibilities of partnership. *International Bulletin of Missionary Research, 19*(3), 98–104.

Warren, M. (1956). *Partnership: The study of an idea.* London: SCM Press.

# Paternalism

Paternalism is an important subject of applied mission ethics. It is the principle of guarding against what could contravene the conventional teachings of the church by a body of believers or congregations that are not within the same geographical or cultural territories of the missionaries or sending agencies. One of the central issues in paternalism is the maintenance of balance between order and freedom. A premature granting of independence to the missionary-controlled church or an unduly delayed freedom from missionary control has corresponding dangers. Order tends to impinge upon freedom, but order also fosters necessary efficiency.

## Unique Problems Posed by Paternalism

Paternalism can give the connotation of parental involvement (positive) or an impatient dictation (negative) when the "parent" body assuming authority is slow to observe the development unique to the "baby" church or is not quick or adequate to recognize her idiosyncratic needs. In the contemporary church, evidence of paternalism on the part of missionary leadership can be seen in three common reactions on the part of new churches: First, new churches established by the missionaries often see their church autonomy as consistent with the struggle for liberation from all unjust bondage. Second, they often reject European culture as a way of resurrecting their own cultures that missionaries have suppressed in the life of the church. Third, they see paternalism as plainly discriminatory because most church leaders are white even in nonwhite societies.

Paternalism presupposes that missionaries can make better decisions than the converts for whom they act. It presupposes the incompetence of the new converts to direct their spiritual destiny and that it is better for the missionaries to be the custodian or proxy of the new Christians.

Paternalism has made it difficult for new Christians to develop indigenous Christian lifestyles in some regions and has created psychic damage in others. The longevity of Western domination of Christian culture in the world has strengthened the debates between what is Christian nurturing and what is paternalistic. When missionaries acclimatize themselves to new societies, they naturally assume that what is traditionally done in Europe is the norm and provides a reliable standard for a local adaptation of Christianity elsewhere.

Contemporary missiologists have aptly described Christianity as "infinitely translatable," and there is no doubt that Christian flexibility provides assurance of its continuous ability to adapt to divergent societies. Christianity will not fail to assume the habits and thought forms of the people that practice it, and much of Christian teachings will build upon pre-Christian religious and moral categories. Churches in the two-thirds world see paternalism as an overreach of authority when European missionaries tell them how to be Christian in their own particular context.

## Shortages of Roman Catholic Clergy

Since Vatican II (1962–1965) the Roman Catholic Church has been more creative in adapting to nontraditional Christian cultures in the world, primarily to encourage minority participation in the priesthood. For example, the church relaxed the mandatory Latin language for Mass and promoted the vernacular. It also made exceptions in certain parts of Africa so that priests could have family lives. In Europe and North America, however, the issues of paternalism continue unabated.

Two decades after the Vatican Council, the church prevented Reverend George Stallings Jr., an African-American Catholic priest in Washington, D.C., from incorporating aspects of African-American cultures when conducting Mass. Stallings wanted to blend traditional Catholicism with African-American culture to address the specific needs of his congregation. He felt that the Roman Catholic hierarchy had been paternalistic in its dealings with African-American Roman Catholics, and he sought to establish the Imani Temple, which would incorporate traditional African-American Gospel expression. He argued that "a people who do not direct its spiritual destiny by the genius of its own culture never achieve full spiritual maturity, especially when the very ones who exercise the final judgment and decisions over what is to be institutionalized are persons of European-American white male ancestral background."

### Ordination of Minority Priests

But it is not only measuring what the minority Roman Catholic priests do and do not do in their parishes that causes consternation among their bishops. What is causing hard feelings is also the keeping of tabs on the ordination of minority priests.

Until recently, there was not a consistent policy to promote the ordination of indigenous people in South and Central America to the priesthood, and although there are now native Roman Catholic bishops in South and Central America, few are archbishops and many fewer are cardinals.

The reasons for the shortage of priests in South and

Central America are numerous and complex. They can be traced back to the reluctance of Europeans who dominated the church during the colonial era to ordain native South and Central Americans to the priesthood. In 1953 lay delegates gathered in Peru to discuss the shortage of clergy in different countries, and the painful consensus was that the vast majority of Catholics in twenty South and Central American countries were *Catolicos solo de nombre,* or Catholics in name only. Paternalism was a major factor responsible for the lack of indigenous clergy in South and Central America. In the decades of the 1960s and 1970s, however, the church began an aggressive program to develop a lay apostolate in virtually all the countries of South and Central America.

## Paternalism in the Protestant Tradition

One of the strengths of the Protestant denomination is its open-ended approach to the calling of the clergy. This, however, could also be conceived as a weakness. Although formal theological training is still required in traditional mainline Protestant denominations (Anglican, Baptist, Lutheran, Methodist, and Presbyterian), candidates for ordination are not as scrutinized in these denominations as in the traditional Roman Catholic Church.

The Pentecostal churches in the United States, for example, do not have a formal way of scrutinizing anyone who declares him- or herself called by God to preach. With a porous border for qualification, paternalistic tendencies are minimized at the expense of church order and doctrinal uniformity. Pentecostal churches, for example, have never insisted that clergy be seminary graduates.

The insistence of the Roman Catholic Church that the priest must be trained or educated in the Roman Catholic seminaries, on the other hand, has brought respectable uniformity to the tradition. Among the Pentecostal churches, where formal theological training is not required, is optional, or, in extreme cases, is denigrated, the result has been an uncontrolled proliferation of Christian communities with an unwillingness to enter into partnership with traditional Christian denominations for missions. The irony is that most pastors in the Pentecostal movement wield authority, and they often become patrons, controlling the younger churches they have assisted in forming.

## Conclusion

European and North American missionaries often determine who should and should not be ordained. When circumstances have made missionaries concede control of the congregations they have formed, the nationalization of their work is often achieved uneasily and is frequently due to the initiatives and persistence of the nationals. In some cases in Africa, indigenous protests with a "missionaries go home" mentality have left missionaries with hard feelings.

While missionaries often inadvertently advocate for paternalistic policies, claiming that an overarching doctrinal unity overrides freedom of the converts in certain circumstances, the nationals often claim that Christian freedom supersedes doctrinal safety and an overreach of the missionary's authority may stifle Christian creativity. Perhaps what missionaries should do on the field to be successful is to withdraw creatively from the scene and let the converts formulate their own polity and theologies.

Caleb O. Oladipo

### Further Reading

Boring, M. E., Berger, K., & Colpe, C. (Eds.). (1995). *Hellenistic commentary to the New Testament.* Nashville, TN: Abingdon Press.

De Gruchy, J. W. (2005). *The church struggle in South Africa.* Minneapolis, MN: Fortress Press.

Hollis, M. (1962). *Paternalism and the church: A study of South Indian church history.* London: Oxford University Press.

Mills, J. S. (1978). *On liberty.* Indianapolis, IN: Hackett Publishing Co. (Original work published in 1859)

Neely, A. (1995). *Christian mission: A case study approach.* New York: Orbis Books.

Oladipo, C. O. (2006). *The will to arise: Theological and political themes in African Christianity and the renewal of faith and identity.* New York: Peter Lang.

Sartorius, R. (Ed.). (1983). *Paternalism.* Minneapolis: University of Minnesota Press.

Van DeVeer, D. (1986). *Paternalistic intervention: The moral bounds on benevolence.* Princeton, NJ: Princeton University Press.

## Peace Churches

The term "peace churches" usually refers to three churches—Quaker, Brethren, and Mennonite—that formed a Historic Peace Church (HPC) committee in 1935. The peace churches began to apply a theology of peace to their missiology more self-consciously around 1970, but a peace and mission orientation had always been implicit. Peace church members are usually committed to pacifism, nonresistance, or, more recently, active nonviolence. In spite of their name, peace churches should not be contrasted with "war" churches but rather with churches that hold to just-war teaching.

The wars of the twentieth century demonstrated an unimaginable capacity for evil and destruction, and contributed to a growing sense that all churches should be peace churches. The Holocaust, the Gulag, and the serious threat of a nuclear holocaust put just-war theory under unbearable strain, and by 1981 the World Council of Churches (WCC) had affirmed nuclear pacifism as an important ethical value. Growing concerns for justice, peace, and the integrity of all creation, and increased agreement on the essential elements of the Gospel, forced the church to focus on how to make peace rather than on how to justify wars and the participation of Christ's followers in them.

HPC members began meeting in 1985 in Prague with representatives of the Hussite or First Reformation, seeking to bring classic social-ethics concerns into the ecumenical arena. There were seven Prague Consultations through 2003; the last three were multilateral ecumenical conversations. This long tradition of talks led to three important achievements: the successful introduction of the Decade to Overcome Violence by Brethren influence at the WCC in Geneva, Switzerland; its affirmation by the WCC at its 1998 Assembly in Harare, Zimbabwe, at the initiative of a German Mennonite delegate; and the inclusion of a Swiss Mennonite in WCC program staffing. An international conference of the HPC in 2001 demonstrated a more conscious attention to voices from developing nations.

## Early Peace Churches

A philosophical commitment to absolute pacifism was not initially central to the Anabaptist-Mennonites, the Society of Friends (Quakers), or the Brethren. Their central concern was, rather, a commitment to Jesus Christ. They took the sayings of Jesus as binding, notably the Sermon on the Mount. They sought to obey Christ's commands not to kill, and understood that Jesus' life and death revealed a more demanding ethic than mere adherence to the Ten Commandments: He urged his followers to love their enemies and to "do good to them that despitefully use you."

The peace church tradition was dynamic in two important ways: on the one hand, it experimented with various forms of modification of total nonresistance, such as paying for substitute soldiers, accepting noncombatant military service or medical corps service,

serving in the military and hoping to avoid killing another human being, or refusing military service of any sort yet paying military taxes; on the other hand, it searched out active ways of peacemaking. One study of American Mennonites noted their linguistic shifts from "biblical nonresistance" to "way of nonviolence" to "active peacemaking."

The primary tensions within the HPC over the past half century revolved around the search to integrate peace and mission. One tendency was to concentrate on the peace witness: Some argued that living counterculturally as absolute pacifists was the witness; others gradually made common cause with other pacifists. Another tendency was to think of mission as proclaiming God's offer of salvation, and to introduce a full-orbed discipleship according to the rule of Christ as found in the Gospels later; this view saw peace as an add-on doctrine, one to be very diplomatic about in foreign countries.

Although peace church theology presupposes a close integration of ecclesiology and missiology, the peace churches developed distinct characteristics. Quaker leadership and involvement with mission during the past two centuries has been characterized not so much by the community's views but rather by the role of intrepid individuals who were often key in establishing voluntary societies—from the British and Foreign Bible Society in 1806 to Oxfam, a modern nongovernmental organization. The Church of the Brethren shifted in the 1960s from separatist tendencies to subordinating their programs to joint ministries under the WCC. Mennonite mission, service, and peacemaking ministries were at first denominational but gradually became more open to partnerships with other denominations and organizations linked to the World Evangelical Fellowship community or the community of the WCC, although it did not join either community.

## Anabaptists

The rise of radical Christian communities is closely associated with periods of turmoil in Christian history, most noticeably since the Protestant Reformation. The Anabaptist movement was part of the Reformation and retained the protestantizing factor longer than did the better-known Lutherans. Emerging in at least three regions of Germanic Europe—Switzerland, south Germany, and the Low Countries—its leaders began to notice shared values and to call each other "Brethren."

Their need to respond of their own volition to God's offer of grace caused early Anabaptists to be intensely evangelistic. Because of this, it remains a widely held belief that the Anabaptists were missionary. However, as scholarship is now showing, all the Reformation movements spread through active evangelism by lay believers and traveling clergy. Even more influential was the availability of Scripture in the vernacular, disseminated by new printing presses, which made every reader a missionary.

Another important missionary influence in the first fifty years was the approximately five thousand martyrs for the faith, persons who paid the ultimate price of witness. Anabaptists, along with Catholics, Lutherans, and English Protestants, circulated martyrologies. Of these martyrs, a disproportionately high number (just over 50 percent) were Anabaptists. However, in terms of cross-cultural mission, it was only Roman Catholic missionaries, largely from the southern sections of Europe, that carried the Gospel witness around the globe (which they had only recently learned was round).

## Mennonites

The largest congregation of Anabaptists was in the Low Countries, where a local man named Menno Simons, who had risen to leadership, remained the target of "Anabaptist hunters" till his death in 1561. His opponents came to call his followers "Mennists," or followers of Menno. Eventually "Mennonite" became the most widespread self-designation for members of this movement. However, the original organized communities in Switzerland and Holland have been officially named "Taeufer" or "Doopsgezinde," because of their emphasis on adult baptism and voluntary personal confessions of faith.

Like other reformers, Menno Simons devoted most of his writings to calling for the renewal of the church. As several recent biographies have shown, Menno's mission focus was on the fallen church of Rome. Menno's calls for a purified church eventually became a struggle for a pure church as a minority church. The emphasis of other leaders varied, but generally speaking, the long-term legacy of Menno has been a historical tension within the Mennonite church between a separatist mission with a peacemaking emphasis and a mission to struggle for broad Christian conversion for the sake of broad ecclesial renewal and greater obedience to the demands of Scripture.

For example, the Amish movement in the 1690s challenged the readiness of Swiss Brethren to consort with Reformed Christians, and emphasized avoidance and banning. The Amish have retained their absolute rejection of war, but are not missionary. In the Netherlands,

the Mennonite churches lived alongside the official (but minority) state church, the Dutch Reformed, but as toleration grew, the ongoing theological controversies with their resultant group fragmentation also involved Mennonites. It was hardly surprising that this more extensive interaction with other Christian bodies led to the Dutch Mennonites beginning cross-cultural mission in Indonesian colonies.

As early as 1700 Mennonites settled into distinctly national bodies and lived as tolerated minorities in the Netherlands, and in parts of present-day Germany, France, and Switzerland. Because of this, they experienced the subsequent rise of nationalism as separate stories. Further fragmentation occurred with the growth of the Russian Mennonite community and immigrations to Canada and the United States of Mennonites from diverse European regions. Generally speaking, immigrant communities relied on cultural separatism as a survival technique and Mennonite immigrant groups became increasingly alienated from one another. Numerous renewal movements resulted in further denominational splitting, though never over slavery or between Fundamentalists and modernists. As a result, the conscious recovery by the peace churches of a peace and mission theology has included renewed efforts at internal peacemaking and reconciliation.

## Quakers

To speak of Quakers, Brethren, and Mennonites as the three historic peace churches is common and accurate, but there were important fragmentations within each of these traditions. Among Quakers, for example, it is easy to distinguish between British (or possibly European) Quakers, the Society of Friends in eastern parts of the United States, and the Evangelical Quakers, who have stronger centers in the western United States.

During the second phase of the Reformation, the era of confessionalization, the Quakers emerged as an alternative to the dominant British Reformation church. Leaders such as George Fox, an eloquent preacher whose message spread by word of mouth, emphasized a spiritual renewal and spoke of an inner light of revelation that guided their searching of the Scriptures. This high view of the value of each human life helped account for their abhorrence of the taking of life, and it also led to a radical egalitarianism that included a strong leadership role for women. Rejecting the heavy reliance on institutions and structures that characterized Catholicism, Quakers chose to be highly decentralized as "Societies of Friends," with minimal rites of initiation. Rejecting the rituals of baptism and Eucharist (around which so much Reformation rhetoric and acrimony had centered), they emphasized that all life is sacred, that daily living is communion and witness, that what mattered, as Jesus had explained to the Samaritan woman, was to worship God in spirit and truth. Some early Friends had been so intense in their spiritual worship that their bodies had quaked, and hence the term "Quaker."

The Quakers relied on a strong sense of networking, sustained by frequent visits between communities and written correspondence. Persecuted and harassed in Britain, they sought safer havens in the colonies. Best known was the project to settle in America, where Quaker aristocrat William Penn was granted a huge territory. The Pennsylvania experiment soon included other radical Christian communities. The first German settlers, who came from Krefeld in 1683 and settled in Germantown (now part of Philadelphia), were a mix of Mennonites and Quakers; by 1719 immigrants from the newly formed Brethren had joined them. Pennsylvania became a place of experiment in the possibilities and limits of living by the rule of love, which was especially valuable after the American Revolution, when nonpacifist Christian politicians and constituencies had gradually replaced the long-prominent peace church orientations.

## Brethren

The Brethren began in German Europe, specifically in the town of Schwarzenau, in 1708. Early activists came mostly out of a Reformed church background that had been influenced by radical German Pietism, and developed views consonant with sixteenth-century Anabaptism; they also had close contact with contemporary Mennonites. The Brethren movement came to think of itself as spiritually integrating Pietism and radical Reformation concerns. For the next eighty years the movement expanded from near Hamburg, Germany, to Bern, Switzerland. Starting in 1719, all the congregations moved to the American colonies, settling first in Germantown.

Alexander Mack was regarded as a leader among the founders, as were several other gifted leaders during subsequent eras, but the polity that emerged was a combination of congregational and denominational. The highest authority resided with the Annual Meeting of delegates from congregations, which relied on elected ministers and deacons, who were expected to travel widely, visiting churches and fostering unity. Very early in the movement, printing efforts served that visiting function as well.

The German linguistic influence remained through the early twentieth century, signified by the name German Baptist Brethren. Their common characteristics included the immersion baptism of adults, the rejection of military service, and a zeal for spreading the Gospel. By 1977 when the major reference work *The Brethren Encyclopedia* was started, five denominations of Brethren (Dunkards) cooperated.

However, the original Dunker, or German Baptist, movement had divided into a variety of Brethren denominations in America, divisions triggered by debates over cultural integration and the impact of Holiness renewal movements. Major divisions had come between 1881 and 1883, when one group of five thousand, thereafter called the Old German Baptist Brethren, resisted the inroads of modernity by establishing dress codes, rejecting the automobile, and other such patterns reminiscent of conservative groups among old-order Amish and Mennonite communities.

A more progressive wing (also with around five thousand members), who named themselves the Brethren Church, established headquarters in Ashland, Ohio. They emphasized Sunday schools, evangelistic outreach, and foreign missions. The Grace Brethren Church, which split away in 1939, was more strongly premillennial in eschatology and identified more closely with Fundamentalist influences. That split had left fifty thousand German Baptist Brethren, who renamed themselves the Church of the Brethren at their bicentennial in 1908. At that point, with a membership of seventy-five thousand, the Church of the Brethren had become more progressive than the Brethren Church.

## Historic Emergence

Many of the restorationist churches that started in America, as well as those arising out of the Holiness movement of the mid-nineteenth century, had in common a commitment to a plain reading of Scripture, usually reading Scripture christologically. That meant they were evangelistic and missionary, and they were pacifist. Yet in the process of growth and adaptation to American culture, many such churches surrendered their pacifism during the Civil War, or during the jingoist era at the end of the nineteenth century, or in the war euphoria of World War I. The story of the peace churches includes pressures to conform: Many of their members bought war bonds and sought to show their good citizenship by supporting foreign mission endeavors.

Nevertheless, leaders from the Quakers, the Brethren, and the Mennonites began more concerted efforts to recover a principled peace witness that included the dual dimensions of systematic teaching of the youth facing obligatory military service and of organizing an alternative to military service. After 1935 representatives met together as the "historic peace churches" and negotiated with American government officials. That resulted in the establishment of the Civilian Public Service (CPS) program for conscious objectors. Run by the military (a concession HPC representatives were forced to agree to), the program provided spiritual and moral leadership in work camps. After the war the HPC worked together in the National Interreligious Service Board for Conscientious Objectors in negotiations with the U. S. Selective Service Board. World War I also served as a point of reference for other initiatives in the areas of mission, service, and peace.

Some members of the Brethren and Mennonite communities volunteered for international relief efforts through the American Friends Service Committee (AFSC) and were placed abroad. That experience stimulated the formation of service committees among Brethren and Mennonites. The longer record of Quaker peace work and nonpartisan relief distribution directly influenced the Mennonite Central Committee. Mennonites, who had assisted fellow Mennonites with relief and immigration, were challenged to offer a nonpartisan relief program during the famine of 1919–21 in Russia and Ukraine.

American Mennonite denominations decided to cooperate under the Mennonite Central Committee (MCC) but were unable to get Soviet government permission to enter the country—that is, until Lenin's wife received a postcard from a Quaker friend urging action. She forwarded the note to the Council of Ministers with the remark that she remembered the genuine nonpartisanship of the Quakers from their days when Lenin wrote for a New York newspaper, and recommended approval. Within a few days the MCC was registered as a nongovernmental relief agency. When such approvals were reviewed in 1923, the Mennonite relief (now also development) program was one of only seven permitted to function till 1928 when all such foreign agencies were expelled.

It was the extent of destruction during World War II and the dangers of a Cold War between the USSR and the United States that stimulated the organized service agencies of the peace churches and directly impacted their mission work. The Brethren had organized the Brethren Service Committee (BSC) in 1939 and restructured it in 1941 to administer the CPS program for the Brethren. Mennonite administration of its CPS projects was through the MCC. In the postwar reconstruction in Europe, the ministry focus of all the peace churches turned to Europe. They participated in CRA-LOG, a new ecumenical consortium through which churches supplied relief (food and clothing) in occupied Germany, as well as in the war-ravaged victorious countries—the Netherlands, France, and Britain—and in parts of eastern Europe. From this they learned to cooperate ecumenically, with each other and with persons from church traditions whose just war thinking had failed to prevent the destruction of the Jews and other atrocities.

CRALOG marked the beginning of organized social service ministries by churches in many European countries. After 1948, the structures of the World Council of Churches facilitated cooperation by assisting the development of newly independent colonies. When the NATO alliance sponsored the rearmament of Germany and introduced compulsory military service in 1957, there was a strong resistance by German church leaders. The following year, the HPCs, through their service agencies, helped found EIRENE (Christian Service for Peace), a nongovernmental organization through which conscientious objectors could be approved for alternative service, in particular for development programs in North Africa. Within the next several decades, EIRENE branches were functioning in the Netherlands, Switzerland, and France. At the same time, BSC and MCC were sponsoring exchange programs across the Cold War divide.

## Current Global Dynamics

By the time of the twentieth-century independence movements, self-organized Mennonite and Brethren churches in the southern continents had appeared. The Brethren, for whom BSC had become the major international program, had opted to encourage its church in India, for example, to join the United Church of North India. Increasingly, too, its service programs were turned over to the new Church World Service of the National Council of Christian Churches (USA). Mennonites, in contrast. found themselves with churches in the third world that related to mother churches via a mission board. The habits of cooperation between Mennonite denominations in MCC provided the opportunity for such mission boards to begin meeting regularly with MCC leaders.

From this emerged the Council of Mission Board Secretaries, followed by the Council of International Ministries (CIM) as a more inclusive North American Mennonite and Brethren in Christ consultative and coordinating body. MCC was formally entrusted, at a consultation with European Mennonite leaders in 1950, with an ambassador role between the North American and European Mennonites, and in 1997, MCC became a facilitator for Mennonite World Conference activities.

By 1980 the trans-Atlantic Mennonite agenda extended to the facilitation of a variety of forms of cooperation between MCC (and CIM) and European Mennonite relief, service, mission, and peace organizations. In the next few years, the Euro-American guiding role began to shift to consultative structures under the Mennonite World Conference (MWC). MWC emerged, like other global confessional bodies, as a vehicle to facilitate fellowship around the world, and by 2000 membership in Mennonite World Conference had surpassed one million, and a slight majority now lived in the southern hemisphere. Those were the "new" Mennonites, the result of mission initiatives, of migration as refugees from persecutions in the USSR, and of finding fellowship due to theological kinship as modern Anabaptist Christians.

Nevertheless, the economic inequities within the Mennonite world were as great as in society in general. What did change after 1990 was that the once 100,000-strong Russian Mennonite church had disappeared—that is, it had migrated in the short space of six years (from 1987 to 1993) to Germany and had begun the process of re-formation (under at least a dozen distinct structures), bringing the energy of a suffering and resurrected church to young people eager to reassert peace and mission practices.

An American initiative resulted in a conference of HPC spokespersons from around the globe, who met in Basel, Switzerland, in 2001. Although it was dominated by American perspectives, the resultant publication set a modest tone: *Seeking Cultures of Peace*. What had persisted through the three to five centuries of peace church existence was the conviction that the church must work not only to save souls, but also for peace.

At the beginning of the twenty-first century, the agenda of the peace churches is a central theme in the WCC, which has committed itself to work toward a just peace and to accept reconciliation as a central image for mission. However, new global attention to the peace church model has caught peace churches struggling to adapt. That is, the peace churches have grown more modest by examining their own disjunctures between theory and praxis, and also more experienced in the complexities of living the faith in different and changing contexts. To walk in the way of peace is now a challenge to all churches.

WALTER SAWATSKY

*See also* Conquest; Jehovah's Witnesses; Pacifism; Pietism; Protestant Churches; Reformation; Roman Catholic Church

## Further Reading

Barbour, H., & Frost, W. (1988). *The Quakers.* Westport CN: Greenwood Press.

Bittinger, E. F. (Ed.). *Brethren in transition. 20th century directions and dilemmas.* Camden, ME: Penobscot Press.

Bowman, C. F. *The cultural transformation of a "peculiar people."* Elgin, IL: Brethren Press.

Driedger, L., & Kraybill, D. B. (1994). *Mennonite peacemaking: From quietism to activism.* Scottdale, PA: Herald Press.

Durnbaugh, D. F. (1978). *On earth peace: Discussions on war/ peace issues between Friends, Mennonites, Brethren, and European Churches, 1935–75.* Elgin, IL: Brethren Press.

Dyck, C. J. (1992). *Introduction to Mennonite history* (3rd ed.). Scottdale, PA: Herald Press.

Enns, F., Holland, S., & Riggs, A. (2004). *Seeking cultures of peace: A peace church conversation.* Scottdale, PA: Cascadia Pub. House.

George Fox's legacy, Friends for 350 years. (2004, spring). *Quaker History, 93*(1).

Gregory, B. (1999). *Salvation at stake: Christian martyrdom in early modern Europe.* Cambridge, MA: Harvard University Press.

Hamm, T. (1988). *The transformation of American Quakerism: Orthodox Friends, 1800–1907.* Bloomington: Indiana University Press.

Keim, A. N. (1990). *The CPS story: An illustrated history of civilian public service.* Intercourse, PA: Good Books.

Kreider, R. S., & Goossen, R. W. (1988). *The MCC experience. Hungry, thirsty, a stranger.* Scottdale, PA: Herald Press.

Massaro, T. J., & Shannon, T. A. (2003). *Catholic perspectives on peace and war.* Lanham MD: Rowman & Littlefield.

Schlabach, T.; & Hughes, R. T. (Eds.). (1997). *Proclaim peace: Christian pacifism from unexpected quarters.* Urbana: University of Illinois Press.

Sawatsky, W. (Ed.). (in press). *The Prague consultations— Prophetic and Renewal movements.*

Voolstra, S. (1992). Themes in the early theology of Menno Simons. In G. R. Brunk (Ed.), *Menno Simons—A reappraisal.* Harrisonburg, VA: Eastern Mennonite College.

# Pentecostal and Charismatic Movements

It is not easy to define what is meant by "Pentecostal and Charismatic" Christianity, but generally it refers to those movements of renewal that commenced at the beginning of the twentieth century, in which manifestations of spiritual gifts such as healing, prophecy, and speaking in tongues are practiced. In broad terms, they include (1) "classical" Pentecostal denominations, the largest of which have origins in the United States, such as the Assemblies of God, the Church of God in Christ, the Church of God (Cleveland), the United Pentecostal Church, and the International Church of the Foursquare Gospel; (2) the independent "Spirit" and "prophet-healing" churches in the majority world, some of the largest found in Africa and China; examples are the Christ Apostolic Church, the Zion Christian Church, and the True Jesus Church; (3) the Charismatic Renewal within the older churches, of which the Catholic Charismatic Renewal is the largest expression; and (4) the Neo-Pentecostal or Neo-Charismatic independent churches, some of which were a direct consequence of or secessions from the other movements. All of these are included in the terms "Pentecostal" and "Pentecostalism" as used here.

## Fastest Growing Section of Christianity

The Pentecostal and Charismatic movements in all this variety are in the forefront of Christian missions and have been the fastest growing section of Christianity in the twentieth century. By 2000 they embraced almost every country on earth and some five hundred million adherents in over twenty thousand denominations, none of which existed in 1900. This is now predominantly a non-Western and independent-church phenomenon. Of course, statistics of such magnitude are controversial and require very careful analysis. In all probability, no one actually knows with certainty how many there are globally, as the wide discrepancy in statistics illustrates. But there can be no doubt that Pentecostalism is proliferating and that it has contributed to the reconstruction of the nature of Christianity itself and become "globalized" in every sense of the word.

The southward swing of the global Christian center of gravity is probably more evident in Pentecostalism than in other forms of Christianity. Whereas older Protestant churches bemoan their ever-decreasing membership and possible demise in the West in the early twenty-first century, a most dramatic growth continues to take place in Pentecostal and independent Pentecostal-like churches, especially outside the Western world. Classical Pentecostal churches like the Assemblies of God, the world's biggest and most international Pentecostal denomination, have probably only some 8 percent of their world associate membership in North America, with at least 80 percent in the majority world.

The present proliferation of Pentecostalism and indeed its inherent character are fundamentally a missionary movement of the Spirit from its beginning in the first decade of the twentieth century. The common belief in Evangelical circles at that time was that a worldwide revival would result in increased missionary activities. Reports of revivals in India from 1905 to 1907, for example, were accompanied by the news of the establishment of missionary societies initiated completely by Indian Christians.

## Proliferation in Early Twentieth Century

Based on the whims of the Spirit and with few discernible forms of organization, early Pentecostal missionaries scattered themselves within a remarkably short space of time to spread their newfound message wherever they went. When human organizations attempted to quench the flames (as they often did), more often than not this resulted in new fires breaking out in other places and the further proliferation of new independent churches. The revivals at the beginning of the twentieth century had the effect of creating an air of expectancy that the whole world would be reached for Christ in as short a time as possible and that supernatural gifts of the Spirit were being restored to the church in order to facilitate this. This was the driving force behind the first Pentecostal missions.

### The Beginnings

The earliest Pentecostal revival movements from 1901 to 1906 began with Charles Fox Parham (1873–1929) and his Apostolic Faith in Topeka, Kansas, where Pentecostal phenomena happened in 1901 and a distinct, if rather bizarre, Pentecostal theology of mission emerged. Parham taught that the gift of tongues had been restored so that the Gospel could be preached all over the world without the arduous task of language learning.

But the driving force behind the first Pentecostal missions from the United States was the Azusa Street revival (1906–1908) in a Los Angeles inner-city church, led by Parham's one-time African-American disciple, William Joseph Seymour (1870–1922). The May 1908 issue of the Azusa Street periodical *Apostolic Faith* headlined that "FIRES ARE BEING KINDLED By the Holy Ghost throughout the World." It described the spread of Pentecostalism in Ireland, England, China, West Africa, Palestine, Sweden, India, Scotland, and Australia, all of which had happened within two years of the beginning of the revival. One of the prominent convictions of the early Pentecostals was that their experience of Spirit baptism would spread all over the world, a last-

An old neon sign on the roof of a church in Charlotte, North Carolina, where Pentecostal and Charismatic movements are still strong. *Courtesy of David Raboin/istockphoto.com.*

days universal revival to precede the soon-to-be Second Coming of Christ. The Azusa Street revival was instrumental in turning what was until then a fairly localized and insignificant new Christian sect into an international movement.

### Expansion from Azusa Street

This movement was not to fragment into denominations until the 1910s and 1920s. Early Pentecostals were convinced they would overcome all obstacles through the power of the Spirit and thereby defeat the enemy, Satan, and conquer his territory, the "world." The followers of this movement were convinced that they had a simple but effective Scriptural plan for evangelizing the world. The going out from Azusa Street was immediate, in ever-widening circles. People started new Pentecostal centers in the Los Angeles area, and hundreds of visitors from all over North America and other continents came to see what was happening and to be baptized in the Spirit. Many of these began Pentecostal centers in various North American cities and eventually further abroad. Missionaries soon were heading for India and China, Europe, Palestine, and Africa, and on their way to embarking from the eastern seaboard, they visited several cities and started new Pentecostal churches there.

Another revival movement important in the spread of Pentecostal ideas was that in Pandita Saraswati Ramabai's Mukti Mission, near Pune, India, from 1905 to 1907. The leaders at Azusa Street saw this revival as a precedent to their own, an earlier Pentecostal revival that they thought had become "full grown" in Los Angeles. It is more likely that these were simultaneous rather than consequential events in a general period of revival in the evangelical world at the turn of the century.

### Women's Role in the Revival

Women played a more prominent role in the Indian revival than in the American one, although women leaders did play significant roles in both the Azusa Street revival and the early missionary movement that issued from it. But Ramabai (1858–1922) was an Indian woman who resisted both patriarchal oppression in India and Western domination in Christianity. This revival was preeminently among and led by young Indian women, motivating and empowering those who had really been marginalized and cast out by society. The revival movement was to result in an unprecedented missionary outreach of Indian Christians into surrounding areas and further abroad.

One of Ramabai's workers, former American Methodist missionary Minnie Abrams, contacted her friend and former Bible-school classmate in Valparaiso, Chile, Mrs. Willis Hoover, with a report of the revival in Mukti, and as a result the Methodist churches in Valparaiso and Santiago were stirred to expect and pray for a similar revival, which began in 1909. Willis Hoover (1858–1936) became leader of the new Chilean Methodist Pentecostal Church, which eventually grew to be the largest Evangelical church in Chile. It is important to note that Chilean Pentecostalism has its roots in the Mukti revival rather than in the American one.

### Beginnings of Denominations

The revivals in Los Angeles and India resulted in the rapid growth of Pentecostal missions. The first Pentecostal, "Apostolic Faith" missionaries (many of them women and African-Americans) went out from Los Angeles and other Western centers to countries all over the world. At first these were nondenominational, independent missionaries with neither central organization nor distinct methods. During World War I, Pentecostal missionaries were remarkably unfazed by these tumultuous events, and their attitudes toward these world conflicts, including their pacifism, was seen as further evidence of their conviction that this was the end of the world. Pentecostalism spread globally, especially in the mission networks of radical Evangelicals, with the expanding globalization of the movement as a result of transnational contact. The beginnings and proliferation of Pentecostal denominations can be traced to the war years and immediately after. Increasing missionary paternalism affected Pentecostal missions and the emergence of independent national churches as it had done in other missions.

## The Present Scene

Pentecostal theologies of mission, with their emphasis on Spirit baptism and its central relationship to the movement of missionaries, are grounded foremost in the conviction that the Holy Spirit is the motivating power behind all this activity. The early belief in "missionary tongues" gave way to "unknown tongues" as a sign of Spirit baptism and impacted missionary service. Priority was given to evangelism motivated by an exclusivist Christology and preoccupied the writings and activities of Pentecostal missionaries and the belief that the coming of the Spirit brings an ability to do "signs and wonders" to accompany and authenticate the Gospel message, a feature prominent in Pentecostal mission praxis from the beginning.

The particular premillennial eschatology motivated Pentecostal missions with its emphasis on world evangelism before the Second Coming of Christ. Furthermore, because the primary qualification for being a missionary was the power of the Spirit, ordinary members of Pentecostal churches without special educational advantages could immediately begin to work in the new churches, and the transition from "foreign" to "indig-enous" church generally took place much quicker than in other missions.

### Rise of Independent Churches

After about 1970 Pentecostalism worldwide began to expand further with the proliferation of new independent churches. Some of these became single congregations by the thousands, especially in the Americas, West Africa, and the Asian Pacific rim. In the Western world the greatest expansion of Pentecostalism has taken place in so-called "migrant" communities, especially African, Hispanic, and Korean congregations. Some new churches have advocated a "prosperity gospel" that promised health and wealth to its adherents in return for faith and financial giving to the church. It would be wrong to generalize about this new Pentecostalism, however, as many Pentecostals provide effective and comprehensive support services for their generally impoverished members. It is probably true to say that Pentecostalism has helped rescue the church from decreasing membership in an age of secularization and has revitalized it for many years to come.

ALLAN H. ANDERSON

### Further Reading

Anderson, A. (2004). *An introduction to Pentecostalism: Global Charismatic Christianity.* Cambridge, UK: Cambridge University Press.

Anderson, A. (2007). *Spreading fires: The missionary nature of early Pentecostalism* (forthcoming). London: SCM Press.

Barrett, D. B., Johnson, T. M., & Crossing, P. F. (2006). Missiometrics 2005: Goals, resources, doctrines of the 350 Christian World Communions. *International Bulletin of Missionary Research, 30*(1), 27–30.

Burgess, S. M., & van der Maas, E. M. (Eds.). (2002). *New international dictionary of Pentecostal and Charismatic movements.* Grand Rapids, MI: Zondervan.

Coleman, S. (2000). *The globalisation of Charismatic Christianity: Spreading the gospel of prosperity.* Cambridge, UK: Cambridge University Press.

Cox, H. (1996). *Fire from heaven: The rise of Pentecostal spirituality and the reshaping of religion in the twenty-first century.* London: Cassell.

Faupel, D. W. (1996). *The everlasting Gospel: The significance of eschatology in the development of Pentecostal thought.* Sheffield, UK: Sheffield Academic Press.

Goff, J. R. (1988). *Fields white unto harvest: Charles F. Parham and the missionary origins of Pentecostalism.* Fayetteville: University of Arkansas Press.

Hollenweger, W. J. (1997). *Pentecostalism: Origins and developments worldwide.* Peabody, MA: Hendrickson.

Kosambi, M. (Ed. & Trans.) (2000). *Pandita Ramabai through her own words: Selected works.* New Delhi, India: Oxford University Press.

Martin, D. (2002). *Pentecostalism: The world their parish.* Oxford, UK: Blackwell.

McClung, G. (Ed.) (2006). *Azusa Street and beyond.* Gainsville, FL: Bridge-Logos.

Synan, V. (1997). *The holiness-Pentecostal tradition: Charismatic movements in the twentieth century.* Grand Rapids, MI, & Cambridge, UK: Eerdmans.

Wacker, G. (2001). *Heaven below: Early Pentecostals and American culture.* Cambridge, MA, & London: Harvard University Press.

Wilson, E. A. (1997). *Strategy of the spirit: J. Philip Hogan and the growth of the Assemblies of God Worldwide, 1960–1990.* Carlisle, UK: Regnum.

# Philosophy

Philosophy is often translated as "the love of wisdom" because it comes from two Greek words—*phileo* (love) and *sophia* (wisdom). Missionaries, however, have often perceived philosophy to mean a specific kind of wisdom—worldly wisdom. It was with this view in mind that one of the earliest defenders of the Christian faith, Quintus Septimius Florens Tertullianus (c. 160–c. 220 CE), asked a witty question: "What has Athens to do with Jerusalem?" Contemporary missionaries continue to echo this sentiment, drawing a sharp distinction between Hellenistic philosophy and God's revelation in Jesus Christ.

Most missionaries today view philosophy as an attempt to satisfy human intellectual curiosity. Philosophy survives within missionary practice because many Christian doctrines cannot be understood apart from the backdrop of Greek philosophy. It is unquestionable that the two main sources of Christian knowledge in the West remain the Scriptures and Hellenistic culture, particularly Greek philosophy.

## Missionary Attitudes

One of the major responsibilities of missionaries is to proclaim the Gospel with clarity and confidence, and philosophy as an academic discipline provides them with important tools. Early Christian Church fathers realized that the subjects that philosophers discussed were also important for missionary effectiveness. To defend Christianity against non-Christian practices, ancient apologists or defenders of faith often quoted the Bible and the corresponding teachings in Greek philosophy. First-century Christianity would not have been as intellectually robust without the culture of ancient Greece. In fact, the distinction between what missionaries and philosophers are concerned about still remains difficult to pin down.

Yet missionaries have never been completely at ease with "worldly wisdom." In the history of missionary movements in the West, there are at least three types of missionary attitude. The first attitude is taken by missionaries who identify themselves with Western intellectual traditions and embrace Greek philosophy as consistent with God's revelation. This active identification echoes the sentiment of Justin Martyr (c. 106–c. 167 CE) that the Greek philosopher Socrates was "a Christian before Christ." When missionaries identify with the goals and intentions of philosophy, they often invoke the blessings of God upon philosophical assertions.

The second type of attitude is expressed by Christians and Western missionaries who take the opposite view and refrain from any integration of God's revelation with the claims of philosophy. They often see philosophical assertions as audaciously speculative, or worse, antithetical to the Gospel they proclaim. Tertullian of Carthage said it best when he stated that Athens had nothing to do with Jerusalem.

The third type of missionary attitude is expressed by missionaries who engage in a critical evaluation of philosophy in the traditions of St. Augustine (354–430 CE) and St. Thomas Aquinas (1225–1274). Most contemporary Western missionaries see philosophy as making the way for God's revelation and contend that it is in the best interest of missionaries to come to terms with philosophical claims. They often see philosophy as the foundation upon which God's revelation has been built and believe that Christianity has perfected Greek philosophy. In the works of Thomas Aquinas, Aristotle was quoted more frequently than the Bible to justify Christian claims.

## Missionary Objections

The rise of Evangelical Christianity in the West has rekindled an urge among missionaries to abandon Greek philosophy. The objection is not only that philosophy is about "worldly wisdom," but also that it is unduly anthropomorphic. The real concern of Evangelical missionaries is not that philosophy is not useful, but that it is unspiritual. They do not deny that philosophy is capable of making contributions; their argument is that the contributions made by philosophers are exclusively in the realm of "worldly" knowledge. The ancient Israelites, for example, did not base their belief in God on philosophical arguments about the existence of God and the order of the universe. They believed in God because of God's self-disclosure. The knowledge of God, therefore, is gained through God's revelation rather than by philosophical reflections or any other such means.

From the missionary viewpoint, the basic human problem is not ignorance but sin, and human needs can be met by knowing God's forgiveness through Jesus Christ rather than by being well informed through philosophy. Missionaries in the West have quoted Jeremiah 9:23–24 and Ecclesiastics 12:12–13 to justify the claim of the superiority of God's self-disclosure.

Philosophy always raises issues of metaphysical significance, such as the existence of God and the immortality of the soul. Missionaries in Evangelical circles, however, affirm God's existence and immortality by drawing concrete examples from the life and resurrection of Jesus Christ. Philosophical descriptions are abstract, missionaries argue, whereas the proclamation of the Gospel is concrete.

In the last few decades, a number of Evangelical Christians in the United States have formed the Association of Christian Philosophers. Most of them are Protestants and the purpose of their organization is to allay the fears of philosophy of fellow Evangelical Christians, stating that philosophers do not claim that their arguments are based on abstract thought. They maintain that it is the role of philosophy to describe how missionaries arrive at their conclusions and what considerations they accept and what forms of reasoning they regard as decisive in the proclamation of the Gospel. They insist that the function of philosophy is descriptive and point out that philosophers investigate the causes and laws that govern reality.

## Philosophy and Mission

Many contemporary missionaries in the West view philosophy as a seedbed of heresy, but they also use philosophical arguments to defend the Christian faith and extend the boundaries of its proclamation in the non-Western world. That missionaries assume a disdainful attitude toward philosophy, even while using its methods to proclaim the Gospel, further illustrates the uneasy relationship between philosophy and Christian beliefs. However, few missionaries would disagree that there are many philosophical ideas in the formulation of the Christian faith in the New Testament. In I Corinthians 8:6, Paul employed methods of premise and inference common in Greek philosophy to formulate Christian doctrines.

## Concept of God

One of the greatest disparities between missionaries and philosophers is in their views of God. They both see a fundamental distinction between God and the world, and they often agree that God created the world. Where they disagree is in how to bridge the gap between an eternal God and a changing world. Philosophers see God as "being" and creation as contingent and "becoming." Missionaries across many generations have accepted this, but have insisted that God is the "supreme being." Although both missionaries and philosophers agree that creation is subject to corruption and decay, a serious problem arises between them because the "being" of the philosophers is transcendent and immutable and without any direct contact with the world, while missionaries see the relationship between God and the world more personally, like a relationship between a parent and a child.

Greek philosophers did not have serious difficulties with missionary understanding. But they insisted that God has no direct contact with Creation because God is infinite and the world is finite, and that a mediator was required to bridge the gulf between God and the world. This mediating principle or power that can bridge the gap between God and the world, according to Greek philosophers, is the Logos. "Logos" has often been translated as "word," but it can also mean "reason," or "mind," or "ideas," or even "principle." The similarity between this concept and the first chapter of John in the Greek New Testament is obvious, but interpreting the meaning of Logos has remained problematic.

One major difference of interpretation centers on the cause of the mediating principle between God and the world. While Greek philosophers saw the Logos as necessary because God cannot deal directly with the changing world, missionaries viewed the Logos as necessary because of human sin. They associated Jesus of Nazareth with the Logos and believed that he came to bridge the gap between God and humanity.

A typical line of defense of missionary argument is that humanity sinned against God, causing alienation. Thus, human beings owe a debt they cannot pay. However, God took the initiative through Jesus Christ (the Logos) to pay the debt he did not owe. While Greek philosophers see the Logos or reason as the bridge between God and the universe, missionaries see Jesus of Nazareth as the bridge between God and humanity.

## Complementarity

Philosophers and missionaries can survive their atavistic hatred if both accept that they complement each other in their search for God, and for what matters most in the world. Greek philosophy and the New Testament are closely related in their views of the world, and their intellectual environments were also very similar. Perhaps what one needs most is exactly what the other possesses, yet it would be foolhardy to expect contemporary missionaries to embrace philosophical claims. Christianity is the fulfillment of Greek philosophy, and missionaries will continue to call people of every age to repentance through Jesus Christ in much the same way that first-century missionaries did within their philosophical environment.

The New Testament environment and Hellenistic culture were once indistinguishable, and the Church in the West still finds it difficult to crawl out of its Hellenistic skin. Contemporary missionaries know that dealing with "worldly wisdom" involves a careful inhaling and exhaling, and that it would be perilous to cut themselves off from Greek philosophy because it provides much of the air the Church in the West continues to breathe.

CALEB O. OLADIPO

*See also* Christendom; Civilization; Enlightenment; Postmodernism; Secularism and Atheism

### Further Reading

Allen, D., A. (1985). *Philosophy for understanding theology*. Atlanta, GA: John Knox Press.

Bosch, D. (1991). *Transforming mission: Paradigm shifts in theology of mission*. Maryknoll, NY: Orbis.

Copleston, F. S. J. (1962). *A history of philosophy: Greece & Rome* (Vol. 1). Garden City, NY: Image Books.

Jongeneel, J. A. B. (1995–97). *Philosophy, science, and theology in the 19th and 20th centuries: A missiological encyclopedia*. New York: Peter Lang.

Kirk, J. A. (2000). *What is mission? Theological exploration*. Minneapolis, MN: Fortress Press.

Lane, T. (1984). *Harper's concise book of Christian faith*. New York: Harper & Row.

MacKintosh, H. R. (1915). *The doctrine of the person of Jesus Christ*. New York: Scribner's.

Thangaraj, M. T. (1999). *The common task: A theology of Christian mission*. Nashville, TN: Abingdon Press.

Yandell, K. E. (1984). *Christianity and philosophy*. Grand Rapids, MI: Eerdmans.

## Photography

Large and dynamic supporters' movements at home provided the classical nineteenth-century missionary societies with finances and a recruitment pool. These societies invested considerable amounts of money and intellect in communications with this "home base." In fact, their word publications have become printed sources that historians have used for many decades. But their use of visual communications has been largely forgotten and is still incompletely researched. Two basic points are clear, however. First, for many missionaries photography was an important part of their lives abroad. Second, the history of mission photography not only has to include the taking of photographs overseas but also the history of their publication for readers "at home."

### An Outline History

The history of visual communication in mission begins before the invention of photography. In London and Stuttgart specialized mission periodicals were published in the early nineteenth century whose cover page showed an engraving that was based on a missionary's drawing or taken from some outside source, such as paintings from Captain Cook's expeditions. The few pages of text usually included a commentary on the engraving.

Missionary societies then responded to the new possibilities for visual communication following the invention of photography in 1839. The earliest images from a missionary context known to the present writer are the calotypes made by the London Missionary Society representative William Ellis in Madagascar in 1852. Judging by archival investigations among German protestant missions and the Christoph Merian Foundation, photography became widely used in missionary communications over the next twenty years.

### *Wood Engravings and Lantern Slides as Media*

Looking back, the decades leading up to the 1890s were almost archaic in terms of technology. Until the industrial production of camera-ready glass-plate negatives, toward the end of the nineteenth century (and soon after of photographic film), missionary photographers had to prepare and process their own negatives on the spot. And the resulting photographs could not be transferred directly to the printed page. Until halftone plates were invented and put into use, again toward the end of the nineteenth century, photographs had to be "redrawn" as wood engravings if they were to be printed in missionary publications. All the indications are that the engravers were highly skilled and conscientious people. Missionary and other engravings from these decades are a historical source not only for Western attitudes to non-Western cultures but more importantly for the history of non-Western cultures themselves. Mission supporters mostly saw photographs directly only at magic-lantern lectures, for already in 1850 photographs could be transferred automatically to lantern slides.

### Advent of Professional Photography

In a second period, lasting from the 1890s to the recent development of digital photography, missionary societies were able to use the full range of the increasingly sophisticated photographic technology characteristic of the twentieth century. This probably resulted in a bifurcation between amateur photographers, who often used a snapshot camera for images of mainly personal significance, and colleagues working at a more professional level with advanced cameras who were commissioned to produce photographs for specific publication programs. After 1950, as air travel became easier and cheaper, organizations based in Europe (and probably North America) employed professional photographers, who made journeys to the non-Western world to provide pictorial material for planned series of publications, although the missionary taking good quality photographs "on the spot" was still an important source of images for publication. On the publication side, photographs printed in missionary publications increased steadily in number and quality through the twentieth century until, in the 1970s and 1980s, color pictures were being routinely printed at a very high quality.

Meanwhile, the tradition of missionary slide shows continued as a major form of communication both with adults and children (confirmation classes), with pictures now enhanced by accompanying tape-recorded commentaries. And already in the interwar period missionary societies (in Germany, they were putting their resources together for this purpose) also began using moving films for their publicity at home—a field in which the bifurcation between amateur filmmakers and professionals was also significant.

## Missionary Photographs as a Research Resource

The number of photographs resulting from this concern with visual communication is not to be underestimated. In the Mission House in Basel, Switzerland, 50,000 photographs were discovered from the period 1850 to 1945, *one-third of them from before 1914.*

But mission photographs are not only found in organized collections. Missionaries' descendants often retain albums and single photographs long after the active generation has passed on. Moreover, increasingly, regional and local archives are keen to take over collections of missionary photographs from private hands. The absence of an organized collection of historical photographs in a mission archive is not evidence that no photographs were taken or that none survive. Equally, although websites are being developed offering large numbers of historical photographs from mission archives, even the Basel Mission website is not final and comprehensive—more images are turning up from family collections even from the nineteenth century that will significantly influence the interpretation of the images already available online.

### Freedom of Expression

In assessing and applying missionary photography to historical discussion, the tendency of postcolonial theorists to restrict the interpretation of missionary photography to a narrow organizational or ideological point of view (e.g., fund-raising, assertion of the worthlessness of non-Western cultures and religions) must be resisted. Very little is known about missionary societies' editorial policy, but it looks as if their photographers overseas had much freedom to photograph what they found interesting (indeed, in the Basel Mission, missionaries paid for their photography from their own pockets and were then recompensed for each image deemed fit for the society's official collection of images).

There are strong signs, moreover, that in tightly organized missions missionaries felt more freedom in their photographs than in their written reports to express their fascination with the cultures surrounding them. Furthermore, photography as an activity in the world at large influenced mission photography, with missionaries' search for interesting images being influenced by the productions of other photographers, with some missionaries becoming professional photographers abroad and many missionaries' children making a profession of an activity which had played an important part in their parents' lives.

The application of photographs as sources to the historical analysis of the history of missions and their successor churches is only now beginning. But there are two major fields in which it can already be shown that photographs can make a transforming contribution to our view of missions and non-Western churches, provided they can be documented as having been taken in a particular region and within a reasonably close bracket of years.

### Evidence of Women's Contributions

In missionary traditions where women are underrepresented in text sources, they usually appear in photographs as frequently as men. Such photographs can be a powerful stimulus to the historical imagination. They offer concrete evidence of the combination of Western and indigenous lifestyles propagated in mission institutions—how pupils were fed and what traditional crafts were taught in mission boarding schools for girls are key counterindications to the old theory that missions were alienating people from their local roots.

Photographs are also a major source on dress and the importance of women's handwork classes for the development of a local tailoring industry (the view that the Ghanaian fashion industry started on mission-house verandas would have been much more difficult to articulate without the thousands of photographs documenting the history of Ghanaian women's dress in the Basel Mission archive). And they support investigations of the way missionary births and the lives of small missionary children provided profound and vibrant emotional links between missionary and indigenous women, again during decades where the existing academic literature tends to see missionaries primarily in terms of their propagation of an external authority and an uncompromising Western lifestyle.

A separate but related issue is the history of women *photographers* in mission. Many may be buried in registers under the names of their husbands (note how often the photographer in the Basel Mission registers *appears* in the photograph ascribed to *him*. . . . ). Among named women, the best photographer in Basel Mission history before 1945 was an unmarried woman, Anna Wuhrmann, whose woman's skills in personal relations undoubtedly helped her to take perhaps the best and most intimate portraits of indigenous people taken by any missionary anywhere before 1914.

### Early History of Indigenous Churches

The beginning of missionary photography in many regions of the third world is often so early that it can be counted as a visual source for the final period of local and regional precolonial history. (This particularly applies to the inland regions of Africa and the regions of Southeast Asia that were subject to intensive colonization from the mid-nineteenth century onward.)

Correspondingly, photographs often offer early insights into the history of relations between a mission church and its environing society which text documents, dominated by a missionary-colonial frame of reference, do not reveal. Thus, photographs of traditional officials in an African kingdom document relations of contact and cooperation which in missionary word reports are depicted in adversarial terms. Photographs of congregations and baptismal candidates offer indications of the social and cultural background of Christian groups. Photographs of economic activities set missionary inputs in agriculture and craftwork in a specific context.

Carefully reviewed photographs may help the reader understand the defining pressures put on Christian congregations and their missionaries by local groups and value systems. The best missionaries have always understood the equality of all cultures in the sight of God. Photographs are a historical source that offers much food for thought for researchers trying to situate the impact of mission in a regional context and to understand the active roles indigenous people played in shaping the coming local church.

PAUL JENKINS

### Further Reading

Frey, N. B., & Jenkins, P. (1999). *Arresting entropy, enabling new synthesis. Conservation, access and the photographic record of the Basel Mission 1850–1945.* Basel, Germany: Basel Mission.

Geary, C. (1988). *Images from Banum: German colonial photography at the court of King Njoya 1902–1915.* Washington, DC: Smithsonian Institution Press.

Jenkins, P. (1993). The earliest generation of missionary photographers in West Africa and the portrayal of indigenous people in culture. *History of Africa,* 89–118.

Jenkins, P. (2002). Everyday life encapsulated? Two photographs concerning women and the Basel Mission in West Africa c. 1900. *Journal of African Cultural Studies,* 45–50.

# Pietism

Pietism, a movement that began in the seventeenth century, sought to revitalize the church in Europe and beyond by drawing attention to holy living, heartfelt faith, and personal devotion to the study of Scripture. Pietism has been described as the most important and widespread movement in Protestantism to emerge after the Reformation. It is a movement with no clearly defined end date; much of contemporary evangelical Christianity around the world resonates strongly with the emphases of historic Pietism. Pietism's importance in inspiring and shaping the modern Protestant missionary movement would be difficult to overstate.

As a movement that stressed holy living and personal devotion to God, Pietism's tenets are well illustrated in the lives of some of its key leaders. Johann Arndt (1555–1621) was the author of the very popular book *True Christianity*, which went through hundreds of editions in the seventeenth century. Arndt stressed personal introspection and the worship of God "in spirit and truth" (John 4:23) and denounced those forms of worship that were "external in figural ceremonies, statutes, and obligations." (Arndt in Lindberg 2005, 7) Pietism is often described as a reaction to Protestant Orthodoxy that had become dry and lifeless 150 years after Martin Luther's death. This is not a wholly accurate picture. Devotional literature thrived during the period of Protestant Orthodoxy. Arndt's contribution was that he placed additional stress upon the importance of sanctification and the interior life.

Phillip Jakob Spener (1635–1705) is commonly known as the "father of Pietism." His book *Heartfelt Desires (Pia Desideria) for a God-pleasing Reform of the True Evangelical Church, together with Several Simple Christian Proposals Looking toward this End* was one of Pietism's most influential texts. It was first published as a foreword to a collection of Arndt's sermons. Spener continued Arndt's emphasis on the individual's devotion to God and further stressed the formation of small groups for the purpose of Bible study and to encourage the laity's growth in sanctification.

## Halle Pietism

August Hermann Francke (1663–1727) may be Pietism's greatest organizer. Francke created a network of charitable institutions in Halle, Germany, including a home for orphans, schools, a medical dispensary, and publishing activities, all of which helped to spread Pietism and raise money for its missionary efforts. Francke's orphanage would later be admired by John Wesley, who sought to reproduce it on a much smaller scale. Francke's Orphan House was one of the largest buildings of its day in all of Europe. Francke's publishing work produced Bibles and Christian tracts in many languages which were distributed throughout Central and Southern Europe.

Halle became an important training center for the modern Protestant missionary movement in the late eighteenth and early nineteenth centuries, supplying newly founded British missionary organizations with many of their missionary candidates. Renowned missiologist Professor Andrew Walls notes that more than two-thirds of the missionaries sent under the auspices of the Anglican Church Missionary Society between 1799 and 1815 were from continental Europe. This pattern had been set in place a century earlier with the Danish establishment of a mission in Tranquebar, in southern India. The first missionaries for this effort did not come from Denmark but were former students of Francke, Bartolomäus Ziegenbalg and Heinrich Plütschau. It is important to note this continental European origin of the Protestant missionary movement, since William Carey's 1792 publication of *An Enquiry* is often considered its starting point.

Halle Pietism was also instrumental in North American mission efforts. Twenty-four pastors were sent from Halle to America in the second half of the eighteenth century to minister to the Lutheran immigrants who had settled there. One of the more famous of the pastors trained at Halle was Henry Melchior Mühlenberg, the founder in 1742 of the Lutheran Church in America. In the mid-nineteenth century, German Pietists also renewed the role of deaconesses in the church, and deaconesses became an integral part of several denominations' foreign and urban mission efforts in Europe as well as in the United States.

In spite of the vital importance of Halle as a significant training center for missionaries and the vast institutional network Francke established, Pietism, especially in its early years, was a movement on the margins of a society devastated by the Thirty Year's War, which ended for some regions in 1648. (For other areas of Europe, the conflict between Catholic and Protestant rulers continued for many more decades.) Professor W. R. Ward, historian of Pietism and Methodism explains, the Pietist movement grew through revivals taking place in barns and farmers' fields, as no churches were permitted by the rulers in regions such as Silesia, to the east of Francke's Halle. When Charles XII of Sweden invaded Silesia in 1707, he gave the Protestants in the region a measure of freedom they had not had for many years. His soldiers held outdoor "field worship" meetings (foreshadowing Methodist camp meetings in North America), and after they left, the children of the region followed their example. The word of this "revolt of the children" was spread by Francke's publishing empire, which was pouring Christian books by the thousands into Bohemia and Moravia.

## Moravian Pietism

The second great center for Pietism—especially with regard to the Protestant missionary movement—was Herrnhut, located in the extreme east-central corner of modern Germany. The Herrnhutters were a gathering in 1722 of religious refugees, half of whom were Moravians. While their common plight as refugees drew them together, the group was nonetheless divided by social class and differing perspectives on true Christian discipleship. It was Count Nicholas Ludwig von Zinzendorf (1700–1760) who was instrumental in drawing the factions of the community together on his Herrnhut estate by writing up a covenant for the community that stressed the importance of Christian fellowship.

Five years after its founding, a revival occurred in Herrnhut that symbolized a passing of the torch of Pietism's leadership from Francke (who had died that year) to Moravian leader Zinzendorf. The revival in Herrnhut in 1727 also contained echoes of the earlier "revolt of the children." Episodes of intense prayer and singing by children soon spread to the entire community.

Zinzendorf had gone to Halle to study as a boy and was strongly influenced at an early age by Pietism's missionary focus. He wasted little time in organizing the Moravians as a missionary movement. By 1732 the first missionaries had been sent to the West Indies, and by 1760 the Moravians had sent 226 missionaries abroad to such places as Greenland, Surinam, South Africa, Pennsylvania, Labrador, and Jamaica (Vogt in Lindberg 2005, 219). By 1782, a total of 165 missionaries were active around the world, and that number remained relatively constant for the remainder of the century (Mason 2001, 23–24).

The Moravians' activism in sending foreign missionaries, though very impressive, does not begin to explain the profound impact they had in the 1780s and 1790s in England's missionary awakening. J. C. S. Mason, historian of the Moravian movement in England, documents the extent of the Moravian network of relationships with persons who would eventually found the Baptist Missionary Society and other missionary organizations in Britain. The Moravian influence on John Wesley, founder of the Methodist movement, is also well-known.

The history of the modern missionary movement is replete with examples of renewed missionary fervor occurring simultaneously with a renewed emphasis on holy living, personal devotion to the study of Scripture, and heartfelt faith. The global Pentecostal movement, now growing throughout the world, may be described as Pietism's most recent descendant.

BENJAMIN L. HARTLEY

### Further Reading

Lindberg, C. (1983). *The Third Reformation? Charismatic movements and the Lutheran tradition.* Macon, GA: Mercer University Press.

Lindberg, C. (Ed.). (2005). *The Pietist theologians: An Introduction to theology in the seventeenth and eighteenth centuries.* Oxford, UK: Blackwell.

Mason, J. C. S. (2001). *The Moravian church and the missionary awakening in England, 1760–1800.* Woodbridge, UK: The Royal Historical Society and The Boydell Press.

Olson, J. E. (1992). *One ministry many roles: Deacons and deaconesses through the centuries.* St. Louis, MO: Concordia Publishing House.

Walls, A. (2001). The eighteenth-century Protestant missionary awakening in its European context. In B. Stanley (Ed.), *Christian missions and the Enlightenment.* Grand Rapids, MI: Eerdmans.

Ward, W. R. (1992). *The Protestant Evangelical awakening.* Cambridge, UK: Cambridge University Press.

# Pluralism

"Pluralism" can refer to social or religious diversity, and discussions of it can focus on any dimension of that diversity. Discussion may focus on sociological factors—for instance, on a particular language group, cultural tradition, or identity. Or it can focus on divisions within a single religious tradition—for instance, on the Christian ecumenical movement's search for unity among many different churches. The term has come to be used most commonly to refer to religious diversity, either within a single society or globally.

## Context for Mission

Awareness of the fact of religious pluralism is a necessary, but not sufficient, condition for the practice of mission. A culture united in a single religious tradition and largely isolated from others is unlikely to feel a missionary imperative. Christianity rose in a context that offered many religious options, both within the Judaism of its time and in the wider Mediterranean world. It understood its mission to be to share its faith across that diversity. As the Gospel was translated and introduced into new linguistic, cultural, and religious contexts, this pluralism had an impact upon the shape and content of Christian tradition. The pluralism of the mission field engendered a pluralism in Christian expression itself.

Although these aspects of pluralism are as old as the church, in contemporary discussions the term often points to a relatively new situation in which the internal religious diversity of most societies and their awareness of global religious variety have increased dramatically. This development is itself the proximate result of the modern missionary movement. Trade and colonialism brought the predominantly Christian lands of the West in contact with the varied religious traditions of Asia, Africa, and the Americas. The organized study of those religions was pioneered in limited, practical terms by colonial officials, and it was pursued with great depth and breadth by Christian missionaries themselves. Both groups used Christian assumptions. In retrospect, it is clear that missionaries in direct contact with other living faith traditions raised questions and formulated theological perspectives that anticipate those that have become common in contemporary discussions. Scholars have also demonstrated that this was true of the missionaries surveyed prior to the 1928 Tambaram mission conference.

The period of increased global religious contact corresponded to the rise of Enlightenment perspectives on religion in Europe, and the newly appreciated specifics of religious pluralism found their way into philosophical arguments about religion. In some cases, opponents of the church's political power or intellectual claims relativized Christianity's uniqueness by appealing to the reality of other religions. The existence of other religions, with notable moral aspirations and achievements, became a crucial premise for arguments against absolutist understandings of Christianity. This led to a new field of study, a study of other religions that would be objective and rational, without any presumption of Christian confessional allegiance. This gave rise, in turn, to departments of religion and the discipline of religious studies. Thus, while the study of religious pluralism is largely a product of Christian mission, it developed a perspective on religion that challenged the validity of mission.

## Diverse Perspectives

Religious diversity may be studied from a number of different perspectives. One approach is sociological and empirical, and ranges from the gathering of demographical and statistical information, to the historical analysis of religious change, to the political challenges involved in governing a multireligious society (questions of church and state). This approach studies religions and religious people largely in categories drawn from disciplines as diverse as anthropology, economics, and psychology. Another approach, religious studies, attempts to study each tradition on its own terms, and to take seriously the worldview intrinsic to each one. This approach studies religious traditions (as opposed to purely historical or political ones), but without a confessional commitment (or without that commitment playing a determinative role).

Interreligious dialogue is not a distinct discipline, but it is both a response to religious pluralism and a prominent expression of its reality. It takes place in many different forms, including academic conferences, meetings among spiritual practitioners, sustained conversations between representatives of religious bodies, cooperative social action, and numberless local and regional initiatives. Yet another approach is theological. As an aspect of Christian theology (or an analogous undertaking in other traditions), the theology of religions assumes a confessional commitment and attempts to interpret the reality of other religions from that perspective.

## Theologies of Religion

All these approaches to the study of religious pluralism have figured in Christian mission. Demographic and sociological studies, for instance, have long been instruments for assessing mission strategies. However, the closest connection has been with theologies of religion. Indeed, for most of Christian history, the theology of religions existed almost entirely as a minor aspect of missiology. The call of the great commission to convert the world stood in capital letters, and insofar as theologies of religion existed at all they addressed secondary or instrumental questions. They focused on explaining the presence of moral virtue or partial knowledge of God within non-Christian religions mainly by reference to a general revelation given by God through human reason and the natural world. Such theologies frequently did not address the religions themselves as such.

Today people often use the word "pluralism" to denote one of the crucial issues for basic Christian theology—not an esoteric optional question for specialists but an addition to the traditional list of mandatory topics such as creation or Christology. How to account for human religious diversity has become a challenge as central to the coherence of Christian faith as the challenge of understanding the existence of evil or coming to terms with the scientific description of the world. As Wilfred Cantwell Smith (1916–2000), a leading scholar of Islam and of comparative relgions, put it, "We explain the fact that the Milky Way is there by the doctrine of creation, but how do we explain the fact that the Bhagavad Gita is there?" (1972, 133).

In the later twentieth century, scholars discussed theologies of religion in terms of a three-fold typology: exclusivist, inclusivist, and pluralist. This typology was developed to describe the spectrum of Christian theologies of religion, but it is also used to describe those in other traditions. Muslims and Buddhists, for example, may be exclusivist, inclusivist, or pluralist in outlook. Exclusivism is the view that only one religion is true and all others are false. Inclusivism is the view that one religion contains the highest truth, but that elements of that truth may be found in other traditions; these elements prepare adherents of those traditions to accept fuller revelation when they encounter it, and sincere devotion to those truths may prove saving for those in other religions, despite a lack of explicit Christian confession. Pluralism is the view that all major religions are independently and separately valid: No one depends on any other, and no one is more or less true than another.

Insofar as churches have taken explicit positions on these questions, they have historically endorsed either exclusivist or inclusivist views. In this typology, the word "pluralism" has acquired a new meaning. It now signifies not a descriptive account of the situation of religious diversity, but a normative theological interpretation of that situation. In this sense, Christian pluralists are those who hold that no religion, including Christianity, should be privileged as uniquely saving or revealed. Exclusivists and inclusivists differ among themselves. Exclusivists who agree that their religion alone is true may disagree strongly over whether those of other faiths may be "saved." Inclusivists who agree that other religions share elements with Christianity may differ sharply over what is unique to Christian faith. Pluralists, likewise, come in several varieties.

## Pluralistic Theology

In a volume that served as a kind of pluralist manifesto, the writers stated their shared conviction that it was essential to move decisively "away from insistence on the superiority or finality of Christ and Christianity toward a recognition of the independent validity of other ways" (Knitter and Hick 1987, viii). The move

was motivated by some common experiences. In many cases, these theologians had found that assumptions in their prior theologies proved untenable in the face of closer acquaintance with people of other faiths. They tended to agree in broad terms with interpretations of the Bible and of Christian tradition that questioned the validity of maximalist readings of Christ's divinity or uniqueness. They were all in significant measure influenced by a concern for historical injustices instigated or rationalized through assertions of Christian superiority, and tended to see Christian exclusivism as the flip side of Western imperialism. And they shared a concern to enlist other religions in a common work for human betterment.

In spite of these shared tendencies, there are distinctly different paths to the pluralist conviction. For some the path is primarily philosophical. It advances through two main arguments. First, no religious ideas can be demonstrated to be immune to historical conditioning, and so none are sufficiently trustworthy to serve as a standard by which to judge others. Second, any rational assessment of religion must impartially weigh the data to be found in the total sum of religious experiences and teachings across all traditions. Since that sum includes many contradictory and inconsistent elements, if one wants to affirm any objective, universal truth in religion at all, it will have to be defined in terms that transcend the specifics of any particular religion. John Hick (b. 1922), the most important pluralist thinker of the twentieth century, framed his pluralistic hypothesis in these terms, arguing that the major religions "constitute different ways of experiencing, conceiving and living in relation to an ultimate divine Reality which transcends all our varied visions of it" (1989, 235–236). Many religions are valid ways of responding to the divine Reality, and their particular beliefs are supplied by their cultural assumptions. The ultimate religious object is held in common by all faiths, but nothing can be said of it except that it is "the Real" and that humans who respond to it authentically in these varied ways are regularly transformed from self-centeredness toward other-centeredness. Religions are equally valid because they all have the same object. They are equally relative because the divine object transcends any of their particulars.

A second path toward pluralism is more historical than philosophical. It depends less on knowledge that the divine or the Real is beyond concrete religious characterization, and more on knowing the nature of subjective religious experience. Religion does not refer to a divine object so much as it describes a human condition, one that is repeated phenomenally in all great religious traditions. Wilfred Cantwell Smith is the outstanding advocate of this approach. He is famous for arguing that the idea of a "religion" and above all the pluralizing of the noun (religions) were modern intellectual mistakes. Historical study revealed no such things as separate religions but only one continuous human spiritual quest, in which the identical human existential reality of faith—a subjective sense of trust and confidence in reality—is expressed in varied outward forms. If the philosophical path suggests that the Real is one and that human construals of it differ, this path maintains that the human experience of faith is one and that only the terms in which it is outwardly described vary. The faith that all religious people believe *with* is the same, and this is the essential thing: The beliefs they have faith *in* are often at odds, and these are accidents of history.

A third path toward pluralism is an ethical one. Recognition of the validity of multiple religious paths is an ethical imperative, for several reasons. First, belief in religious superiority has itself been the motive force behind much human conflict and violence. A view with such pernicious results deserves to be rejected. Second, it would be legitimate to evaluate religions in moral terms: If one were demonstrably more successful in making humans more moral, more loving, and more just, then it would be reasonable to commend that religion in preference to others. But to date no definitive evidence exists to support such a conclusion. Therefore the reasonable implication is that religions are roughly equally good or equally inadequate in meeting this challenge. Third, moral challenges now face humanity on a global scale (challenges like environmental threats or world poverty). In a religiously diverse world, it is beyond the power of any one religion to successfully confront these crises. The cooperation and mutual respect necessary to make common cause in these efforts will be impossible without recognition of each religion's intrinsic worth. The parity of the religions is not so much a philosophical conclusion or a shared experience to be discovered so much as it is an urgent calling to be realized in the course of efforts to alleviate suffering and injustice. Paul Knitter, professor of theology at Xavier University, is one of the most articulate representatives of this approach to pluralism.

Another important tributary to the ferment around religious diversity has come from movements for the contextualization or indigenization of Christian faith in different parts of the world. Most notably in Asia, where Christianity is generally a small minority, this has raised the question of what it means to contextualize Christianity in a culture defined by a distinct religious tradition, to contextualize it, in effect, within another

religion. Roman Catholics have been in the forefront of this process, and the church in India has been a particularly fertile setting for this reflection. The traditional search for points of contact between Christian witness and other faiths, such as Hinduism, has been joined by theological reflection on the providential purpose and validity of those religions in themselves.

## Other Options

Pluralistic theologies have occasioned vigorous debate in the scholarly world as well as within some Christian communions. For instance, whereas the modern ecumenical movement to overcome Christian divisions was largely driven by a shared commitment to missionary outreach, disagreements over the validity of other faiths and the interpretation of pluralism have become primary points of disagreement among Christians. The Vatican document *Dominus Iesus,* issued in 2000, is in part a response to this debate, affirming that it is necessary for Christians to maintain both the constitutive uniqueness of Christ in relation to salvation and the instrumental necessity of the church as the body of Christ. Critics of pluralistic theologies see it as undermining both of these principles.

Such debates continue for the most part to presuppose the exclusivist-inclusivist-pluralist framework, but other approaches that question the adequacy of that framework have appeared. One of these is comparative theology. This is an emerging and fluid field, in which adherents of one religious faith integrate some of the authorities, texts, and even practices of other religions as sources for their own theological reflection. Many of these practitioners argue that our knowledge of each other's traditions is too immature to allow us to make global judgments, whether of a pluralist or a nonpluralist type. Only over a long period in which correlations and contrasts in faith are explored in specific instances can the foundation for anything like a theology of religions be set out. Others see the three-fold typology as based on an unwarranted assumption that there is or can be but a single type of religious fulfillment and propose that we can credit the specific witness of varied religious traditions more fully if we accept that they may represent exclusive paths to alternative aims. Still others stress an appropriate competition among religions in which those that prove most able to recognize and be reformed by what is valid in other faiths will enhance their own transformative power. Dialogue and respect become the prime means for renewal and mission.

Although there are great differences to be found

among these thinkers, they share several features. They are suspicious of the claim of pluralistic theologies that there can be a single normative account of the true nature of all religions, suspecting that such accounts have their own imperial (and even Western) particularity. They also reject the homogenizing character of such theories, and the way they relegate the distinctive features of any religion to the status of mere historical accidents. These approaches value the detailed study of religions and their subtraditions and share a commitment to honor the significance of the differences among them.

Pluralism, as the existential encounter with religious diversity, now stands as a primary challenge for the practice of mission and the work of theology. The coherence and intelligibility of Christian faith are tested by the challenge to make sense of pluralism as a fact and to find room for the recognition of all that is learned in increasingly detailed and participatory encounters with varied religious traditions.

MARK HEIM

*See also* Buddhism; Conversion; Dialogue; Globalization; Indigenous Religions; Islam; Shinto; Theology—Catholic, Protestant, Evangelistic

## Further Reading

Clooney; F. X. (1993). *Theology after Vedanta: An experiment in comparative theology.* Albany: State University of New York Press.

Cobb, J. B. (1982). *Beyond dialogue: Toward a mutual transformation of Christianity and Buddhism.* Philadelphia: Fortress Press.

Cobb, J. B. (1990). *Beyond "plualism": Christian uniqueness reconsidered.* Maryknoll, NY: Orbis.

Cracknell, K. (1995). *Justice, courtesy and love: Theologians and missionaries encountering world religions, 1846–1914.* London: Epworth Press.

D'Costa, G. (1990). *Christian uniqueness reconsidered: the myth of a pluralistic theology of religions.* Maryknoll, NY: Orbis.

DiNoia, J. A. (1992). *The diversity of religions: a Christian perspective.* Washington, DC: Catholic University of America Press.

Dupuis, J. (1997). *Toward a Christian theology of religious pluralism.* Maryknoll, NY: Orbis.

Eck, D. L. (2003). *Encountering God: a spiritual journey from Bozeman to Banaras.* Boston: Beacon Press.

Fredericks, J. L. (1999). *Faith among faiths: Christian theology and non-Christian religions.* New York: Paulist Press.

Griffin, D. R. (2005). *Deep religious pluralism.* Louisville, KY: Westminster John Knox Press.

Griffiths, P. J. (1991). *An apology for apologetics: A study in the logic of interreligious dialogue.* Maryknoll, NY: Orbis.

Heim, S. M. (1995). *Salvations: Truth and difference in religion.* Maryknoll, NY: Orbis.

Heim, S. M. (1998). *Grounds for understanding: Ecumenical resources for responses to religious pluralism.* Grand Rapids, MI: Eerdmans.

Hick, J. (1989). *An interpretation of religion: Human responses to the transcendent.* Basingstoke, UK: Macmillan.

Hick, J., Okholm, D. L., et al. (1995). *More than one way? Four views on salvation in a pluralistic world.* Grand Rapids, MI: Zondervan.

Knitter, P. F. (1985). *No other name? A critical survey of Christian attitudes toward the world religions.* Maryknoll, NY: Orbis.

Knitter, P. F. (1995). *One earth, many religions: Multifaith dialogue and global responsibility.* Maryknoll, NY: Orbis.

Knitter, P. F., & Hick, J. (1987). *The myth of Christian uniqueness: Toward a pluralistic theology of religions.* Maryknoll, NY: Orbis.

Panikkar, R. (1973). *The Trinity and the religious experience of man; icon-person-mystery.* Maryknoll, NY: Orbis.

Pieris, A. (1988). *Love meets wisdom: A Christian experience of Buddhism.* Maryknoll, NY: Orbis.

Pinnock, C. H. (1992). *A wideness in God's mercy: The finality of Jesus Christ in a world of religions.* Grand Rapids, MI: Zondervan.

Samartha, S. J. (1991). *One Christ, many religions: Toward a revised Christology.* Maryknoll, NY: Orbis.

Sanders, J. (1992). *No other name: An investigation into the destiny of the unevangelized.* Grand Rapids, MI: Eerdmans.

Smith, W. C. (1963). *The meaning and end of religion: A new approach to the religious traditions of mankind.* New York: Macmillan.

Smith, W. C. (1972). *The faith of other men.* New York: Harper & Row.

## Political Economy

Political economy comes from two Greek words referring to the stewardship, management, and ordering of human communities or broadly to the ordering of the political, economic, and social spaces. Within the discussion on Christian mission, the concept is used to explore the relationship between missions and public spaces, religions and states, whether of the home base or of host communities in the mission fields. The relationship between missionary bodies and their home communities determined the resources and ideological bases for missions. For instance, when the idea of Christendom reigned supreme, state rulers determined the religious allegiance of the people. This was enshrined in the Latin formulary, *cuius regio eius religio.* The religion of the ruler was the religion of the state; the state ruler became the *defensor fidei,* the defender of the faith, and God's regent on the earth with the divine right to govern and to be obeyed. Religion buttressed the basis of authority or legitimized power and the rationale for the political economy. From this sacramental pedestal, the ruler designed laws and administrative structures often imbued with religious values, and maintained social control models: the socialization processes taught people acceptable values, restrictive processes restrained them from flouting such values, and punitive instruments punished those who offended, while those who upheld the salient values were rewarded with honors and other forms of communal approval. The interplay between religion, socioeconomic, and political order is an enduring one.

## Background

Even when the social order became more democratic and authority was deemed to have been derived from the people, dominant religious values determined the character of the political economy and the nature of religious freedom. These values restrict, control, and regulate the relationship between religion and the state. For instance, in many Islamic states, the religious environment is strictly regulated by the state because Islamic political theorists assert that the state's power and resources are to be used in the service of religion. Christian missions must use subterfuge to devise strategies to evangelize in these regulated religious spaces. In Western communities liberal religious values could also contest Christian missions by asserting the separation of religion and state based on either the notion that religions are like the rainbow colors or that religious practice is a private matter beyond the purview of the state except when cults become murderous. For instance, in contemporary America culture wars have focused on the public display of Christian symbols such as the Christmas tree in front of the White House, the home of the President, who may at yuletide wish people a "happy holiday" and not a "merry Christmas." In many parts of the world the interplay between religion and political economy has become a dysfunctional force with a profound influence on political dialogue and on the stability of regions. For example, religion has been manipulated in the violent conflicts in Northern Ireland, the Middle East, Eastern Europe, and Africa.

Thus, the discussion of political economy and mission must be set within the wider framework of religion and public spaces and should not be restricted to the relationship between missionaries and the structures in the mission fields. The environment at the home bases of mission remain essential for understanding the attitudes and practices of missionaries in the field. Western interest and affluence shaped the contours of missions. To illustrate with the Iberian cross-cultural missions, when the Portuguese voyaged into the Atlantic and Indian oceans in the fifteenth century, their goal was to respond to the political and economic challenges presented by the Muslims, who occupied Iberia for a century and transformed its culture. The process of recovery from Muslim hegemony included the recapture of Ceuta in 1415. This provided the agricultural resources of the Maghrib and destroyed the lucrative Muslim trans-Saharan gold and salt trade. Moreover, the Muslims occupied the land route across the Levant from the East Indies, the sources of spices, and dominated the trade of the Mediterranean Sea. Portugal sought a sea route that could reach the East Indies by circumventing the Muslims. The importance of spices for food, preservation, and toiletries could not be overemphasized. They imagined that combining with the lost, rich, Christian empire of Prester John, in an unknown location, before the Orient could overawe the Muslims. The quest was christened with a Christian missionary motif to evangelize the heathens because the motivator of the enterprise, Prince Henry the Navigator, was the patron of a Christian knighthood order.

This combination of security, crusading spirit, commerce, and Christianity determined the weakness of the missionary enterprise. The lucrative empire built with little capital attracted competition from Spain and other nations, especially when slaves became the major commodity in the trade. Evangelization diminished. Each nation built trading forts; only a few supported chaplains in these security enclaves. Thus, from the fifteenth through the nineteenth century, the economic motif stifled the tensile strength of missionary enterprise. Missionary contacts centered on shallow court alliances replicating the Christendom ideal. The attitude of Iberians to potential converts remained racist and exploitive. The brutality of the Spaniards in the Americas became notorious.

## Changes in the Nineteenth and Twentieth Centuries

A number of transformations occurred in the nineteenth century when abolitionism emerged in the social conscience of Evangelicals and Quakers. A new age of missionary enterprise surged from the West. New theories emerged: Some sought to destroy the indigenous political economies of non-Western communities as being tainted with idolatry; others advocated a process of inculturation that used the salient aspects of folk culture to build folk churches. Once again, the combination of gold, glory, and God, or of civilization, commerce, and Christianity reemerged because this was an age imbued with intense and competitive nationalism. To replace slave trade with legitimate trade, nations sought to combine treaties with chiefs, commercial projects in cash crops, western administrative, and legal structures, with the deployment of missionaries to "civilize" the non-Western communities through schools and other charitable institutions. There was an increase in the number of missionaries (both male and female), missionary bodies, voluntarist organizations, and fund-raising methods that enabled a wider band of social classes to be involved. The enlarged scale combined with the abolition of the slave trade to open up wide areas of Christian presence.

In Western societies this was the age of Industrial Revolution that changed lifestyles and shortened distances, an age of machines that heralded modernity. Competing nationalism produced colonial empires built on mercantilist theory, Social Darwinism, and other "scientific" racist theories. The background ensured that the civilizing projects implicated missions as the mediators of Western mental and material cultures: language, ideas, tools, economic enterprises, political reordering, and attacks on indigenous cultures, worldviews, and lifestyles. Missions contested the everyday life of host communities and served as the strongest transformative force, but the relationship with the "intimate enemies," the colonial governments, remained complex, with disagreements over the morality of power, ideals and curricula of education, attitude toward indigenous cultures and structures, and the paths of community development.

The world wars disrupted the colonial hegemony and incited political independence. Missionaries did not realize that indigenous people perceived all external change agents as the same. The process of decolonization became traumatic and drawn out because few indigenous structures existed to aid political and religious independence. Since then, the dance between religion and the political economies has merely changed steps, demanding new theories of conflict transformation because religion is often manipulated in ethnic and political conflicts.

OGBU U. KALU

## Further Reading

Bonk, J. (2004). *Mission and money: Affluence as a Western missionary problem.* Maryknoll. NY: Orbis Books.

Boxer, C. R. (1966). *The Portuguese seaborne empire, 1415–1825.* London: Hutchison & Co.

Curtin, J. D. P. (1964). *The image of Africa: British ideas and actions, 1780–1850.* Madison: University of Wisconsin Press.

Ellwood, R.S. (1997). *The fifties spiritual marketplace: American religion in a decade of conflict.* New Jersey: Rutgers University Press.

Kalu O. U. (2006). *Power, poverty and prayer: The challenges of poverty and pluralism in African Christianity, 1960–1996.* Trenton, NJ: Africa World Press.

Kalyvas, S. (1996). *The rise of Christian democracy in Europe.* Ithaca, NY: Cornell University Press.

Porter, A. (2004). *Religion versus empire?: British Protestant missionaries and overseas expansion, 1700–1914.* Manchester, UK: Manchester University Press.

Pui-lan, K. (2005). *Postcolonial imagination and feminist theology.* Louisville, KY: Westminster John Knox Press.

McLeod, D. H. (Ed.). (2006). World Christianities, c 1914–2000. *Cambridge history of Christianities.* Vol. Ix. Cambridge: Cambridge University Press.

Sanneh, L. 1996). *Piety and power: Muslims and Christians in West Africa.* Maryknoll, NY: Orbis Books.

Sheridan, G. & Stanley, B. (Eds.). (2006). World Christianities, c 1800–1914. *Cambridge History of Christianity* (Vol. 8). Cambridge, UK: Cambridge University Press.

# Politics

Missionaries have often had strict instructions to stay out of politics, but politics influenced the ability of missionaries to fulfill their main goals—converting people and assisting the local church. Thus, many missionaries were drawn into politics.

## Colonialism

During the colonial period some Western missionaries were strongly anticolonial, but most were not. Where missionaries thought colonialism was inevitable and/or missionary work was prohibited, they sometimes encouraged colonization by governments that suited their interests. However, when missionaries did not think colonization was inevitable and had freedom to proselytize, *nonstate* missionaries often helped indigenous rulers resist colonization—as in Thailand, Ethiopia, Madagascar, and post–Opium Wars China.

Regardless, most missionaries wanted a moderate form of colonization. Colonial abuses angered local people against Christianity—which most associated with the West—and thus made conversions harder. Missionary writings are full of complaints about how abuses by Western powers undermined their best efforts to win converts.

Missionaries were also in a crucial bridging position. Indigenous people had little power in the colonizing state, and settlers, business people, and colonial officials had no incentive to expose their own abuses. Moreover, colonial governments generally used settlers to staff the police, courts, and colonial administration. Thus, local legal and judicial institutions seldom challenged settler interests. However, missionaries had (1) incentive to fight abuses, (2) personnel directly exposed to abuses, (3) a support base in many colonizing countries, and (4) a massive media network to mobilize pressure against policies that hampered mission interests.

Missionaries were more effective reformers when they were independent of direct state control—as in British colonies—and in areas where they were financially independent of local white settlers. In French, Spanish, Portuguese, and Italian colonies, the state made or forced agreements with the Catholic Church under which the state paid missionary salaries, chose or approved bishops, and restricted Protestants. This usually silenced overt criticism of colonial policy, although there are exceptions such as Bartolomé de Las Casas. In German and Dutch colonies the government also maintained substantial control over missionaries—which hampered protest.

The British originally banned or restricted missions in their colonies, but the missionary lobby forced the British to expand religious liberty—initially by blocking the British East India Company charter in 1813. Over time, this independence of religious groups transformed British colonialism—for example, by spurring abolitionism.

In the West Indies Anglican clergy worked primarily with whites and defended slavery, but nonconformist missionaries worked with slaves. They initially stayed apolitical because they needed slave owners' permission to do their work. However, missionaries gathered slaves for group meetings, trained church leaders, and taught congregants to read. Literate slaves interpreted the Bible for themselves, read newspaper accounts of political rights in Europe, and initiated a series of slave protests and uprisings that drew missionaries into political action.

In 1823 slaves rebelled in Demerara (now Guyana). Planters blamed John Smith, a missionary with the London Missionary Society, and sentenced him to death. Slave owners in other British colonies burned nonconformist churches, harassed missionaries, and restricted missionary access to slaves. This infuriated Evangelicals. Under Evangelical pressure, the Colonial Office recalled the governor of Demerara, and Parliament passed a slave code restricting abuses of slaves and mandating provision for slaves' religious instruction. Thus, missionaries gained legal grounds for meeting with slaves. However, Caribbean magistrates and officials were closely tied to planters and generally ignored the code. Thus, missionaries increasingly complained directly to the Colonial Office.

Two incidents spurred this transformation. In June 1829 a Methodist slave, Henry Williams, passively resisted a ban of all Methodist services in St. Ann's District, Jamaica. Similarly, in 1830 a Baptist slave, Sam Swiney, lead an extemporaneous prayer meeting on Easter Sunday. Both slaves were imprisoned and severely beaten. Missionaries intervened to save their lives. When local courts dismissed the cases, missionaries complained to allies in the Colonial Office, who dismissed three magistrates and eventually the governor. Thus, conflict over religious liberty engendered legal protections for slaves, freed missionaries from slave-owner control, and let slaves know they had rights that the government would occasionally defend.

The next year (1831) nonconformist slave church leaders organized an uprising in Jamaica. In response, planters torched nonconformist churches, attacked missionaries, and barred slaves from meeting for worship. For nonconformists this was the final straw. Not only was slavery abusive, but it threatened the eternal destiny of African souls. Exiled missionaries toured Great Britain making fiery speeches and distributing petitions for the immediate abolition of slavery. They had witnessed the brutality of slavery and could describe it vividly. Over 59 percent of adult nonconformists and over 95 percent of Wesleyan Methodists signed these petitions. The movement forced the British to ban slavery in 1834 against direct opposition by planters and traders at a time when slavery was highly profitable and practiced by England's competitors.

Spurred by this success, missionary supporters established The Parliamentary Select Committee on Aboriginal Tribes in 1835 lead by Thomas Fowell Buxton, vice president of the Church Missionary Society. This group commissioned a worldwide investigation of "what measures ought to be adopted with respect to the Native Inhabitants of Countries where British

Settlements are made, ... in order to secure them the due observation of justice and the protection of their rights, ... and to lead them to the peaceful and voluntary reception of the Christian Religion." Much of the testimony came from missionaries and was used to initiate colonial reforms.

Over time missionary influence on colonial policy waned as businesspeople and settlers created counter-lobbying organizations and journals and the rise of "scientific" racism hardened British attitudes about the racial inferiority of subject peoples. Still, missions continued to influence policy. Other examples of missionary-initiated reform include leading the fight against the opium trade, fighting forced labor in Melanesia and Kenya, Rev. James Long and the Calcutta Missionary Conventions' intervention on behalf of landless peasants in India, bringing colonial officials to trial for killing blacks after the Morant Bay Rising in Jamaica, and John Philip and John Mackenzie fighting race-based laws and settler expropriation of indigenous land in southern Africa.

Although contemporary scholars often ignore the roll of missionaries in colonial reform, this roll is clear when we compare places they were with places they were not—such as French and Belgian Congo. During the late nineteenth and early twentieth centuries demand for rubber exploded. Congo rubber companies extracted wild rubber by giving villages annual quotas. If a village did not meet its quota, soldiers retaliated by burning the village's houses and crops and slaughtering villagers. Soldiers also kidnapped women and threatened to rape or kill them if their men did not transport company goods. To avoid these abuses, Congolese fled to the jungle, where many starved or died of disease.

Although exact figures are impossible, scholars estimate that in the rubber-growing regions of both French and Belgian Congo the population declined by about 50 percent in twenty years. Yet, although these abuses happened at about the same time in neighboring colonies, Belgian abuses spurred a massive international protest that forced the Belgian government to intervene; identical French abuses spurred three belated articles in a French Marxist newspaper, *L'Humanité*, and no government intervention. Why the difference? In Belgian Congo, nonstate Protestant missionaries worked in the rubber-growing regions, photographed abuses, wrote letters to their supporters, helped rally an international outcry, and served as guides and translators for international inspectors. In the rubber-growing regions of French Congo Protestant missionaries were systematically excluded. Thus, the only people exposed to the abuses directly benefited from them.

## Postcolonial Period

After decolonization, missionaries are still sometimes involved in politics, but their centrality has diminished. Now, most people get their international news from secular sources, not missionary periodicals. Missionaries are no longer in a crucial bridging role. They generally do not have much influence with postcolonial governments and can be kicked out by these governments if they complain. They have had moderate influence on U.S. foreign policy—for example, encouraging a pro-Arab foreign policy in the mid-twentieth century, advocating anticommunism in the 1950s and 1960s, pressuring for guarantees of religious liberty in the U.N. Declaration of Human Rights, and serving as sources for Amnesty International and Human Rights Watch. However, their political influence is minor relative to the nineteenth century.

Prior to Vatican II (1962–1965) Catholic missionaries were more likely to advocate Western military intervention and less likely to protest human rights abuses than their nonstate Protestant counterparts—even in areas like Kenya and Belgian Congo, where both were exposed to identical abuses. However, since the mid-twentieth century, Catholic missionaries are probably more likely to protest abuses. The Church has adapted to separation of church and state, and its resources are no longer threatened by anticlerical Enlightenment elites. Now the Church's size, hierarchical organization, and identifiable leaders give it greater protection from persecution than atomized Protestant churches. Thus, Catholic clergy have been central to exposing abuses in Latin America—both by local dictators and the U.S. government—and have been central to democratization movements throughout the global South.

Many missionary activities also have had indirect political consequences—for example, mission-initiated mass education, vernacular printing, organizations outside state control, and religious liberty. Protestant missionaries wanted everyone to read the Bible in their own language. This required mass literacy and vernacular printing. Thus, Protestant missionaries generally initiated Western formal education, created the written form of oral languages, imported the first printing technology, developed the first vernacular fonts, and began mass printing of Bibles, tracts, textbooks, and newspapers. When competing with Protestants, other religious groups also invested in mass education and printing and pressured governments to expand state education without religious content.

This education created new elites who often challenged old elites in their home societies. Foreign language training also gave reformers access to writings on democracy, nationalism, Marxism, and the Enlightenment that reformers modified and used to critique Western colonialism and even Christian missions. Vernacular printing and literacy created the foundation for national public discourse.

Missionaries also introduced new organizational forms that reformers copied and adapted for their own uses. In India Protestant missionaries initiated campaigns against sati (burning widows on the funeral pyres of their dead husbands), to allow untouchables to use public roads and wells and wear clothing above the waist, to ban consummation of marriage prior to age twelve, and so on. Their reformist and conversionary activities spurred Hindu reaction—some for reforms, others against reforms, but most against conversion. These new organizations, such as Bramo Samaj, Aria Samaj, and Dharma Sabha, copied the organization forms and tactics of missionary reform organizations. The British allowed these new organizations because they were initially antimissionary, not anticolonial. However, over time these groups gained power and provided the basis for the political parties and civil society that gradually forced the British to devolve power. A similar pattern of missionary-sponsored reforms and local religious response is clear in such diverse places as Sri Lanka, Palestine, Lebanon, Egypt, Korea, Japan, and China.

The importance of missionary influence is highlighted by the disproportionate number of early nationalists, reformers, and journalists who studied at mission schools or worked at mission presses. Virtually all early African nationalist leaders graduated from mission schools. In the Middle East the first wave of Arab nationalists and journalists generally also graduated from mission-related schools (particularly the American Universities of Beirut and Cairo). In China, Korea, and India early nationalists and reformers were also disproportionately mission educated. For example, China's first president, Sun Yetsen and many of the initial Guomindang cabinet members and ministry heads were Christians and/or mission educated. Similarly, in Korea about half of those who signed the Korean Declaration of Independence in 1919 were Christians—although Christians were about 1 percent of the population. Nationalist movements often became increasingly anti-Western and anti-Christian, especially after the failure of The Versailles Treaty to apply national self-determination to non-Europeans (for example, giving German territories in China to the Japanese) and after the rise of Soviet ideology and funding, but this does not negate missions' role in nurturing early nationalist leaders.

Similarly, statistical evidence indicates that the historic prevalence of Protestant missionaries explains about half the variation in the democracy of non-Western societies and removes the impact of former colonizer, gross domestic product, percent European, percent Muslim, and many other factors traditionally associated with democracy in the social sciences. Clearly, the missionary movement has had profound political implications that are still measurable today.

Robert D. Woodberry

## Further Reading

Etherington, N. (2005). *Missions and empire.* New York: Oxford University Press.

Rivera, L.N. (1992). *A violent evangelism.* Louisville, KY: Westminster.

Shorter, A. (2006). *Cross and flag in Africa.* Maryknoll, NY: Orbis.

Smith, C. (1991) *The emergence of liberation theology.* Chicago: University of Chicago Press

Stanley, B. (1990) *The Bible and the flag.* Leicester, UK: Apollos.

Turner, M. (1998). *Slaves and missionaries.* Kingston, Jamaica: The Press University of the West Indies.

Woodberry, R. D. (2004). *The shadow of empire: Christian missions, colonial policy, and democracy in post-colonial societies:* Ph.D. dissertation. University of North Carolina, Chapel Hill.

# Postmodernism

To understand postmodernism one needs to be familiar with the development of the conception of the world as "modern." This view was promoted by the northern humanists of Europe as the Renaissance was peaking in the fifteenth century and the Reformation was beginning in the sixteenth century. "Before the end of the seventeenth century, the periodization of history became fixed in the divisions familiar to us: ancient, medieval, and modern" (Thompson 1996, 30–31). The Enlightenment solidified these divisions into an ideology, an ideology that privileged the notion of a "modern world."

The modern world was viewed as superior and more progressive because it was a world shaped by autonomous reason (Descartes), scientific experience and knowledge (Bacon and Newton), and social contract (Locke). The Enlightenment developed these ideas by centering authority in the self as a rational, central actor;

viewing truth as objective, universal, and capable of being discovered through science; and understanding society as socially constructed and amenable to development and progress. This Enlightenment tradition shaped the past four hundred years of Western culture, and through the colonial expansion of the West, also significantly impacted the rest of the world.

## Modernism

While the accomplishments of this modern world in the West were profound, many felt that the drive to make life rational and truth objective often suppressed the emotional and intuitive aspects of human existence. In addition, Christians recognized that placing authority inside the human mind or in the social order cancelled out the necessity of a God in this objective view, thus suppressing the spiritual side of life.

These impulses toward the emotive, intuitive, and spiritual coalesced in a movement in the nineteenth century labeled romanticism, and later in the twentieth century known as modernism. In many ways, modernism represents the underside of modernity—the tendency of modernity to collapse the human, particular, and unique within its univocal system of truth. By the latter part of the twentieth century, it became clear that the rise of postmodernism had deep connections with the impulses expressed within romanticism and Modernism.

## Hypermodernity

Twentieth century developments of the modern intensified and globalized its logic through the emergence of "late capitalism" (1950 to present), the successor of two earlier epochs of capitalist expansion: market capitalism (1700–1850) and monopoly capitalism (1850–1950). In late capitalism, multinational corporations function within an international banking system that lies outside national boundaries and political controls. Some scholars describe this period as "hypermodernity" or radicalized modernity.

The effects of this shift include a change from production-centered capitalism to consumer-centered capitalism, the commodification of all of life, an increased mobility of capital flows, an increased scope and pace of change, and the collapse of time and space restrictions on information flows and consumption patterns. This emerging world culture of hypermodernity parallels postmodernism but moves in the opposite direction. The postmodern tends to privilege the diverse, the local, and the particular. Hypermodernity privileges

a homogeneous global culture that is layered across local and particular cultures, as illustrated by being able to travel almost anywhere in the world today by jet, stay at Western-style motels, drink Coca-Cola, eat at McDonalds, and never seriously interact with a local culture.

## The Postmodern Turn

The 1960s and 1970s are regularly identified as the transition point for the postmodern turn. In the midst of the social upheavals during those decades, new ways of theorizing about theory itself began to take shape. During the 1940s and 1950s a movement known as the structuralists decentered the rational self of modernity but tried to maintain a unified social order of functional systems by finding the inner codes of meaning in language and behavior. In reaction, the poststructuralists worked to deconstruct such notions of functionality, demonstrating inconsistencies within such codes as well as their socially constructed character. As this shift began to unfold, two types of postmodernism emerged, one that was negative (hard) and one that was positive (soft). Each of these can be found in two different expressions—as a theoretical critique and in popular culture.

Negative popular-culture postmodernism is reflected in the cynicism, despair, and nihilism often found within the culture. This is especially evident in contemporary movies where storylines are developed around a nihilistic relativism that deconstructs all of life's humanly constructed meanings. This expression of postmodernism is also associated with an increase in teenage suicides and an expansion of the drug culture among young people.

Positive theoretical postmodernism is best represented in the theoretical development of social critical theory, with its emphasis on the relativity of human knowing. While rejecting the totalizing of modernity's assumptions of objectivity and universal truth, it proposes the possibility of knowing the world around us—that there is a reality that can be known, even though our knowledge is rooted in a particular perspective and represents only one interpretation of reality. This relativity of knowing recognizes the embeddedness of all human knowledge but seeks to avoid nihilistic relativism.

Positive popular-culture postmodernism is reflected in the playfulness, collage, and irony that can be found in much of contemporary life—for example, in the numerous television programs that present a parody of society and current events. A nihilism that often lurks just below the surface of such programs, but an encounter with this is usually avoided by a humorous focus on the foibles of formal society.

## Interwoven Layers

It is a complex world in which we are now situated, a world that is simultaneously modern, hypermodern, and postmodern. What is important to note is that modernity has not been replaced or superceded by the latter two but rather has included them as part of its on-going realities. This comingling of all three presents a unique challenge to the church. Which aspects of these diverse worldviews does the church represent? Which aspects should it represent? Which of these realities does the church seek to engage through mission? Which aspects should it seek to engage through mission?

CRAIG VAN GELDER

*See also* Civilization; Culture; Enlightenment; Europe; Philosophy

## Further Reading

Best, S., & Kellner, D. (1991) *Postmodern theory: Critical interrogations.* New York: Guilford Press.

Best, C., & Kenner, D. (2001) *The postmodern adventure: Science, technology, and cultural studies at the third millennium.* New York: Guilford Press.

Erickson, M. J. (1998). *Postmodernizing the faith: Evangelical responses to the challenge of postmodernism.* Grand Rapids, MI: Baker Books.

Giddens, A. (1990). *The consequences of modernity.* Stanford, CA: Stanford University Press.

Grenz, S. J. *A primer on postmodernism.* Grand Rapids, MI: Eerdmans.

Jameson, F. (1984). Postmodernism, or the cultural logic of late capitalism. *New Left Review, 146,* 53–92.

Middleton, J. R., & Walsh, B. J. *Truth is stranger than it used to be: Biblical faith in a postmodern age.* Downers Grove, IL: InterVarsity Press.

Thompson, B. (1996). *Humanists & reformers: A history of the Renaissance and Reformation.* Grand Rapids, MI: Eerdmans.

van Gelder, C. (Ed.). Mission in the emerging postmodern condition. In G. H. Hunsberger & C. van Gelder (Eds.), *The church between gospel and culture: The emerging mission in North America.* Grand Rapids, MI: Eerdmans.

Missional context: Understanding North America culture. (1998). In *Missional church: A vision for the sending of the church in North America.* Grand Rapids, MI: Eerdmans.

# Prayer

Prayer is expressed in a variety of ways: praise and adoration, listening, confession and repentance, communion with God, submission, seeking counsel, intercession and petition, spiritual warfare, receiving grace and Holy Spirit fullness, commitment, waiting upon the Lord, and worship. According to John (15:16), Jesus promised his followers that if they pray, "then the Father will give you whatever you ask in my name."

Jesus himself is the most authentic model of mission permeated with prayer. Some months after his ministry commenced, Jesus invested a night alone in prayer on a mountainside. The next day he called those who were following him and chose twelve to be apostles (Luke 6:12–13). Jesus commissioned these men to give leadership to the urgent mission of proclaiming the Kingdom of God. Later Jesus commissioned his disciples to follow his example in praying forth laborers for mission. He saw many who were "harassed and helpless, like sheep without a shepherd." Then he told his disciples, "The harvest is plentiful but the workers are few. Ask the Lord of the harvest, therefore, to send out workers into his harvest field" (Matt. 9:36–38).

When the disciples asked Jesus to teach them to pray, he told them to avoid a multiplicity of words or public displays of piety, but rather to approach God praying, "Our Father in heaven, hallowed be your name, your kingdom come, your will be done on earth as it is in heaven.... " (Matt. 6:9–10). This has become the essence of the missionary prayer—beseeching God that his kingdom, which will be fulfilled at the conclusion of history, begin now in the life and mission of the church. Jesus said that earthly fathers give their children the blessings they ask for, and "how much more will your Father in heaven give the Holy Spirit to those who ask him" (Luke 11:12).

After the crucifixion and Resurrection, in his last appearance before his ascension, Jesus told his disciples not to conjecture about the times and seasons of the Kingdom of God, but rather to wait in Jerusalem until the Holy Spirit came upon them. For ten days they waited in prayer; on Pentecost the Holy Spirit emboldened and empowered them for mission. The prayerful expectation that preceded Pentecost set the pattern for the mission of the apostolic church. For example, when church members in Antioch gathered to pray and fast, the Holy Spirit commanded, "Set apart for me Barnabas and Saul for the work to which I have called them" (Acts 13:2). After further fasting and praying, they laid hands on these brothers and commissioned them to go to the Gentiles with the Gospel.

A man praying alone in a church. Many feel solitude provides the best environment for prayer. *Courtesy of Christy Thompson/istockphoto.com.*

The New Testament records prayers that ask that church and persons be filled with the grace of Jesus Christ and emboldened for faithful mission. Jesus prayed specifically for Simon Peter that Satan would not deflect him from his apostolic calling (Luke 22:31). He also prayed for the apostles and all believers to live in unity, "to let the world know that you sent me and have loved them even as you have loved me" (John 17:23). Paul implored the Ephesians, "Pray that I may declare it [the Gospel] fearlessly as I should" (Eph. 6:20). The book of Revelation also reveals a variety of images of the efficacy of prayer. As people pray, God restrains his apocalyptic wrath and judgment. It also describes signs on earth of the acts of God in response to the prayers of saints (8:1–5). Old Testament prophets also saw God move in power as they prayed. For example, when the prophet Isaiah was in prayer in the temple, he was convinced of his sinfulness and the Lord cleansed him with burning coals.

Jesus and the apostolic church modeled mission as a prayer movement, and this model has served believers for centuries. One modern example is Blasio Kigozi, who taught in a Church Missionary Society school in Rwanda in 1935. He invested a week in his room in solitude and prayer. The Holy Spirit touched him with deep repentance and a passion for the lost. When he left his prayer room, he first went to his wife and put matters right with her. Then he gathered his students and proclaimed Christ. Conviction gripped the students,

who wept in repentance. Within several weeks, Blasio took ill and died. These newborn Christians were nicknamed *abaka* (persons on fire). They organized mission outreach teams to carry the message of salvation across Uganda, and then to neighboring countries. Across East Africa believers gathered for prayer, and the Holy Spirit moved through the region with hundreds of thousands converted and brought into the fellowship of the churches. The East Africa Revival Fellowship has continued as a transformational mission prayer movement ever since Blasio's week of prayer retreat.

DAVID W. SHENK

*See also* Miracles; Theology—Catholic, Protestant, Evangelistic

### Further Reading

Anderson, W. B. (1977). *The church in East Africa, 1840–1974.* Dodoma, Tanzania: Central Tanganyika Press.

## Professional Associations (Academic)

Scholars who teach and write about Christian missions have formed networks or associations to foster the advancement of their work. These associations hold conferences, support research and publications, and promote collaboration and joint projects, to assist and encourage their members. The following information is taken from the websites and literature of the various organizations.

The oldest continuing association is the *Deutsche Gesellschaft für Missionswissenschaft* (DGMW or German Society for Mission Studies), established in 1918. While German in origin, members from other countries were included from the beginning: Nathan Söderblom joined in 1919; J. H. Oldham and Samuel M. Zwemer (the first American) in 1926; D. T. Niles in 1954; Paul Devanandan in 1962; and Christian Baeta in 1962. In addition to an annual meeting in Germany, it provides grants to support research projects and the publication of scholarly studies and sponsors the publication of a book series and the journal *Zeitschrift für Mission*. Website: www.dgmw.org

The *International Association for Mission Studies* (IAMS), established in 1972, is an international, interconfessional, and interdisciplinary professional society. It holds an international assembly every four years, publishes the journal *Mission Studies,* and sponsors interest groups on Healing and Mission, Biblical Studies and Mission, Women and Mission, and Documentation, Archives, Bibliography, and Oral History (DABOH). The DABOH group held international consultations in Rome in 1980 and 2002, has published a manual on archives management (in English, French, Portuguese, Spanish, Swahili, Korean, and Chinese), and has supported regional consultations in Madagascar, Bangalore, India, Singapore, and New Zealand. Website: www.mission-studies.org

The *International Association of Catholic Missiologists* (IACM) had its inaugural assembly in Rome in October 2000, promotes missiological research, and seeks to encourage scholarly collaboration among Catholic missiologists. Website: www.missionstudies.org/IACM

*Association of Professors of Mission in North America* (APM), an ecumenical fellowship established in 1952, is successor to the Eastern Fellowship of Professors of Missions that was formally established in 1940. The APM seeks to foster the effective teaching of mission studies and holds an annual meeting in tandem with the ASM meeting each June. See weblink at: www.asmweb.org

The *American Society of Missiology* (ASM), established in 1973, publishes the quarterly journal *Missiology,* holds an annual meeting in June, and sponsors a series of scholarly studies published by Orbis Books, and a Dissertation Series. Website: www.asmweb.org

*Evangelical Missiological Society* (EMS), formed in 1990, is successor to the Association of Evangelical Professors of Missions in North America, which was estab-

lished in 1968. It exists to "advance the cause of world evangelization." In addition to an annual national conference and eight regional meetings in the United States and Canada, EMS publishes the *Occasional Bulletin* three times a year. Website: www.missiology.org/EMS

*Southern African Missiological Society* (SAMS), successor (in 1983) to the South African Missiological Society founded in 1968, is a society for those engaged in all aspects of missiological research, especially in Southern Africa. Its journal, *Missionalia,* published three times a year, is noted especially for its missiological abstracts from a wide range of journals. An annual congress for members is held in South Africa in January. Website: www.geocities.com/SAMS

The *Nordic Institute for Missiological and Ecumenical Research* (NIME), established at a meeting in Åbo (Turku), Finland, in 1974, is an interdisciplinary network for the scholarly study of Christian missions and ecumenism worldwide, for those who are engaged in teaching and research from all the Nordic countries (Finland, Sweden, Norway, Denmark, and Iceland). It hosts a biennial research conference in one of the Nordic countries, supports the activities of the IAMS, and produces an online newsletter. Website: www.missionsresearch.org

The *International Fellowship of Evangelical Mission Theologians* (INFEMIT), founded in 1980, is sponsored by the Fraternidad Teologica Latinoamericana (Latin American Theological Fraternity), the African Theological Fellowship, Partnership in Mission: Asia, and INFEMIT: Eastern and Central Europe. It acts as a facilitating organization to foster mutual support, the sharing of resources, and the enhancement of evangelical mission scholarship, and to encourage holistic mission practice. Website: www.ocms.ac.uk/about/infemit.php

*International Society for Frontier Missiology* (ISFM) began in 1986 as the *U.S. Society for Frontier Missiology* and incrementally became more international. Its focus is on the remaining unfinished task of world evangelization, the "unreached peoples of the world." It publishes the quarterly *International Journal of Frontier Missions (IJFM)*. Website: www.ijfm.org/isfm

*British and Irish Association for Mission Studies* (BIAMS), founded in 1989, promotes the study of the history, theology, and practice of mission; publishes a newsletter; and meets every second year at a residential conference and holds day conferences in other years. Website: www.biams.org.uk

The *Lutheran Society for Missiology* (LSFM), founded in 1991, promotes the discussion and study of mission from a Lutheran perspective, holds an annual meeting, and publishes the journal *Missio Apostolica* and a news-

letter *The Communicator.* Website: www.lsfmissiology.
org

*Fellowship of Indian Missiologists* (FOIM), established
in 1992, is an ecumenical association of missiologists in
India that holds a meeting every other year, with workshops and papers on a study theme presented for discussion. The proceedings are published by ISPCK, Delhi,
in the FOIM series. Website: www.missionstudies.org/
Calendar/FOIM.htm

*Korea Evangelical Missiological Society* (KEMS), established in 1972 for Evangelical professors and pastors for
missions, meets two or three times per semester. They
publish the journal *Pokumkwa Sunkyo* (Gospel and Missions) and plan to publish a book series. A website is
in preparation.

*Korean Society of Mission Studies* (KSOMS), an ecumenical Protestant association established in 1992, holds
public lectures on a quarterly basis. Its journal, *Theology
of Mission,* published twice a year in Korean, English,
and German, includes material from the quarterly lectures and academic papers collected both domestically
and internationally. Website: www.ksoms.org

*Association Francophone Oecuménique de Missiologie*
(AFOM), an ecumenical French-speaking association
for missiology created in 1994, holds a general assembly
every year (usually in Paris in May), sponsors a series
of monographs published by Le Cerf Editions in Paris,
supports other scholarly studies in missiology, and has
developed an electronic database of French-speaking
missiological institutions. Website: www.afom.org

*Rede Ecumênica Latino-Americana de Missiolog@s*
(RELAMI; Latin American Ecumenical Network of Missiologists), founded in 1997, developed out of the missiology department of the Theological Graduate School
in São Paulo, Brazil. This network of collaborators works
for an open dialogue on mission out of the tension between liberation, salvation, and inculturation. Website:
www.missiologia.org.br

*Central and Eastern European Association for Mission
Studies* (CEEAMS), an ecumenical fellowship, was created in 2002 at a meeting in Budapest, Hungary. An
inaugural conference was held in Budapest in 2004 with
participants from Poland, Slovakia, the Czech Republic,
Russia, Ukraine, Serbia, Bulgaria, Austria, Romania,
and Hungary. Members want to develop more extensive systems of cooperation and increase missiological
research activity. First steps have been taken toward
publication of a new journal that will reflect the interests
and needs of members within the region.

*Aotearoa New Zealand Association for Mission Studies*
(ANZAMS), an interconfessional group of "reflective
practitioners" founded in 2000, holds a conference every

year or two, to address questions about Christian mission: theological, biblical, historical, practical, and contextual. Website: www.missionstudies.org/anzams/

The Australian Association for Mission Studies
(AAMS) was formed in 2006 out of the South Pacific
Association for Mission Studies (SPAMS), which was
founded in 1986. A new *Australian Journal of Mission
Studies* is the successor to the *South Pacific Journal of
Mission Studies,* published since 1989. Website: www.
missionstudies.org/au

GERALD H. ANDERSON

*See also* Archives; Journals; Missiometrics; Training

## Further Reading

Anderson, G. H. (forthcoming). *A history of the international
association for mission studies.*

Bloch-Hoell, N. E. (1975). Nordisk institutt for misjonsfor-
skning og økuemnisk forskning (Norwegian institute
for missions and ecumenical research). *Norsk Tidsskrift
for Misjon,* 41–44.

Gensichen, Hans-Werner. (1993). *Invitatio ad Fraternitatem:
75 Jahre Deutsche Gesellschaft für Missionswissenschaft
(1918–1993)* (Invitatio ad Fraternitatem: 75 Years of the
German Society for Mission Studies (1918–1993)). Münster; Hamburg, Germany: Lit Verlag.

Horner, N. (1987). The association of professors of mission:
The first thirty-five years. *International Bulletin of Missionary Research,* 120–24.

Myklebust, O. G. (1986). On the origin of IAMS. *Mission
Studies,* 4–11.

Shenk, W. R., & Hunsberger, G. R. (1998). *The American Society of Missiology: The first quarter century.* Decatur, Georgia: American Society of Missiology.

Van Niekerk, A. S. (1987). The kingdom dimension in the
church's mission. *Missionalia,*123–33.

## Protestant Churches

The Protestant churches developed out of the Reformation movements of the Catholic Church that were
forced, or chose, to leave it. The name Protestant comes
from the second Imperial Diet of Speyer held in 1529.
Fredrick the Wise (1486–1525), elector of Saxony, and
five other prince-electors, together with fourteen imperial cities, protested against the decision instructing Luther's followers to stop introducing new changes
and keep themselves to the edicts of Worms (1521). At
first those people were labeled Protestants. Later all

branches of the Reformation were grouped under the term Protestant. It is essential to underline that there is no such thing as the Protestant Church, *versus* the Catholic Church, since the name does not represent a single institutional entity. Rather, one can only talk about Protestant churches or denominations.

## First Churches: Lutherans, Calvinists, Anabaptists, and Anglicans

Today's Protestant churches grew from the various movements aiming to renew the Catholic Church from a grass-roots level. Several branches of the Reformation movement came into being in Europe during the sixteenth century. Martin Luther (1483–1546) ignited contemporary ecclesiastical life by calling for reformation within the Catholic Church. He stressed the *sola fide*, that is, salvation by faith alone as opposed to the Roman Catholic teaching that a person could achieve salvation through faith and deeds. Luther's followers came to be known as Lutherans, or Evangelicals, not to be confused with the subsequent British development. The followers of the Lutheran tradition spread in Germany, Scandinavia, the Baltic states, Poland, Hungary, and Transylvania during the course of the sixteenth century. The second branch was initiated in Switzerland by Huldrych Zwingli of Zürich (1481–1531) and later this movement was incorporated into Calvinism, named after John Calvin (1509–1564), the significant Geneva reformer.

Calvinism received two more labels, Reformed and Presbyterian, each alluding to a special characteristic of the Reformation as it developed. *Reformed* referred to the *semper reformanda* principle that the church is subject to an ongoing reformation. *Presbyterian* referred to the democratic government of the congregations that enabled the members of the church to choose their ministers and governing body freely. Calvin's teachings, the most well-known of which was predestination, were disseminated by preachers, merchants, and students through various means in the same way as those of Luther. His teachings reached Calvin's motherland, France, where the Huguenots were the defenders of the new faith until they were expelled from the country through many decades of heavy persecution by the Catholic authorities. This form of faith took an incredibly strong hold in Hungary, the Netherlands, and Scotland from the 1540s and 1550s onward.

The third branch of the Reformation is the less well-known Anabaptist movement stretching across Europe from Switzerland, Austria, and Moravia to the northern German principalities, the area of today's Belgium and the Netherlands. The Anabaptists, the so-called radical reformers, were rejected by the other two movements, the magisterial reformation of Lutheranism and Calvinism. All three originally started off in continental Europe. The most conspicuous faith difference of the Anabaptists was their belief in adult baptism. Contrary to popular thinking, not all of them were militants like Thomas Münzer (1489–1525). The Hutterites and Mennonites were peaceful and closed communities sometimes persecuted not only by Catholics but also by their fellow Protestants. Finally, the English reformation movement came to be known as Anglicanism. It was initiated neither by people at grass-roots level nor by faith conviction but by mere imperial interest by Henry VIII (reigned 1509–1547). Owing to this, many Anglicans rejected the name Protestant since they were inclined to agree with Roman Catholicism on most doctrinal points, rejecting, however, the primacy of the pope.

## Reformers and Mission

The reformers' perception of mission was heavily influenced by their cultural setting. They lived in Christian Europe where all subjects were regarded as Christian, and they did not see things any differently. Because of Protestantism, a deep line of division began to run in European society where Catholics, and the new "religion," Protestantism, each saw themselves as the embodiment of the true church. Worldviews shaped by theological views of Christianity were being developed, and the world the reformers knew was rather limited in space. They had a vague idea of "heathens" who were yet to be converted to Christianity according to their faith. The emerging Protestant powers did not yet have contacts with the peoples of the world, whereas the Portuguese and the Spanish did. The internal fights among the Protestants also drained their energy, unintentionally impeding missionary outreach. Also, the reformers believed that it was the responsibility of the ruler to Christianize their subjects. They preached the gospel in a new coat, but to the masses of Christian Europe. Thus, mission, in the sense of reaching out to those who had never been exposed to the gospel, remained naturally in the hands of the Catholic world, while Protestantism struggled to survive and then to identify itself.

## East and West: Disappearing and Emerging Protestant Churches

Peculiar developments took place during the course of the seventeenth century. Lutherans and Calvinists were wiped out in Poland within a short period of time. Con-

## Presbyterians in the U.S. Southwest

In Texas, missionary work among the Mexicans by the three major denominations started well before the Civil War. Presbyterians were active in Texas as early as 1838 and in the lower Rio Grande Valley by 1850. Melinda Rankin, the principal Presbyterian missionary, reported meeting her Methodist counterpart in the 1850s—just after the war with Mexico. Almost all missionaries from the three denominations held beliefs and conducted activities that would now be considered theologically conservative. Sin and salvation were seen as matters touching the individual soul alone, for man is seen as born full of sin. This is not a "humanistic" or "social" view of man or of God's kingdom. The sacred and the secular are perceived as realms apart, and the only strategy appropriate for the attainment of salvation (or for spreading the blessings of salvation) is to instill religious sentiments in individual believers. Faith is the important central concept—a direct responsibility of man to God. This is a *Bible* faith, and those not in a "Bible religion" are felt not to be Christian. Indeed, Roman Catholicism is defined by such conservatives as a major perverter of Bible faith and therefore actually as "non-Christian."

Miss Rankin's interest in the Mexicans was typical of the missionary's preoccupation with his special potential flock. She was clearly aware of her deviation from the general Anglo attitude: "I did not feel, as many others have expressed, that the sight of a Mexican was enough to disgust one of the whole nation." Characteristically, her principal approach was evangelism—the conversion of individuals to the personal knowledge and use of the Bible as self-evident truth. The Mexicans were defined as pagans, and she justified her mission to other Protestants, and especially to her Eastern sponsors, as that of combating Catholicism. She emphasized the presence of newly-arrived French priests. Yet she faced strong prejudices in her efforts to rally financial and moral support among Anglo Protestants: The idea of establishing a Protestant institution upon that papal frontier was regarded as chimerical and absurd in the extreme.... Even ministers of the gospel said to me, "We had better send bullets and gunpowder to Mexico than Bibles." My zeal and efforts were regarded as a sort of insanity, and I more dreaded meeting a Protestant Christian in my round of Bible distribution than I did a Romish priest...Some went so far as to say, "The Mexicans have a religion good enough for them, and we had better let them alone."

Source: Grebler, L. (1970). *The Mexican-American people, the nation's second largest minority* (pp. 490–491). New York: Free Press.

---

trary to this, Poland's neighbor, the former significant central European power Hungary, which was under dual attack from the Muslim Ottomans and the Catholic Habsburgs of Austria, managed to protect the Calvinist and Lutheran faith in upper Hungary, (inner) Hungary, and Transylvania. Quite interestingly, this latter Hungarian land developed a unique feature where the first freedom of religious tolerance, the edict of Torda in 1568, included the Unitarians as Protestants and allowed place for the Roman Catholics. At the other periphery of the former European Latin Christendom stood Scotland. It was a former refugee, John Knox, (1514–1572) who skillfully maneuvered the Scottish nation into the boat of Calvinism by the second part of the sixteenth century.

This development produced a state church called (the) Church of Scotland. Her southern neighbor, England, was slowly permeated by Calvin's teaching landing on the island through the channels of Geneva and the Dutch or French Reformed Churches. Here, unlike in Scotland, the seventeenth-century power struggle of the Protestant Anglican Church (Church of England), keeping episcopacy and many elements of Catholicism, stood side by side with the proliferation of Calvinist-based churches and movements that received the name Puritan.

English Protestantism became one of the most significant branches of the former Reformation. The emerging political-economic power, which saw itself as the defender of the true faith against the pope, often regarded as the Antichrist, carried a measurable weight to its voice. It also signals the second phase of Protestantism, in which new churches took root mainly in England and new trends such as Pietism gained ground in countries such as the northern principalities of Lutheran Germany, Moravia, and Scandinavia as well as the Calvinist Netherlands. The Protestant churches of this stage differ from their predecessors since religious fervor coupled with the expansion of English, Dutch, and Danish political power created a place for the possibility of mission outside Europe. In England the reformation of the church was desired by various people, but it took a much longer time for debates among Protestants to settle. The English developed unique movements such as the Baptists, Congregationalists, and Quakers, later forming churches, and many other dissenter groups along with the Church of England and the recurring Roman Catholics. Many of the Protestant believers changed allegiance within the English churches, and a so-called fairly broad label, Puritanism, was employed for them.

## Expansion of Protestant Churches in the New World

A peculiar trait of English Puritanism is that it transplanted itself to the New World and became the most decisive form for North American identity. It is held that the Puritan fathers established America. There one sees a development that is in constant contact with its prede-

cessors: England, Scotland, the Netherlands, Germany, and Switzerland. Perhaps the most intriguing feature of the American Protestant churches of the same period is that the Anabaptists were less persecuted there, unlike in Protestant lands in Germany, Scandinavia, and Switzerland. To have a balanced picture, it must be pointed out that the radical reformers were tolerated also in the Netherlands and Hungary under the rule of the Hungarian princes of Transylvania.

## Mission and Seventeenth-century Protestant Churches

Mission in the sense of converting the "pagans" was out of the question in Christian Europe since everybody was regarded as Christian. The only difference, from the Protestant point of view, was that the Roman Catholics held onto an inappropriate form of Christianity. Protestant confessions (of faith), such as that of Westminster, or the Debrecen-Egervölgy from Hungary, all declared the pope as evil, saw the Turks as heretic and the Calvinists as the elected people. Political and economic developments together with geographical settings proved to be decisive factors in shaping missionary thinking. Hungarian and French Protestants struggled for survival throughout the 1600s. After the revocation of the Edict of Nantes in 1685 the Huguenots were forced to flee to Prussia, Holland, England, Ireland, and the English colonies in America. Hungarian Protestantism had the bloodiest and longest struggle for survival. A string of wars aimed at religious free-

The Keawalai Congregational Church, founded in 1832 on the island of Maui. *Courtesy of Jordan Ayan/istockphoto.com.*

dom started off with István Bocskai (1557–1606), prince of Transylvania in 1606, with the counter-reformation lasting until 1791.

Parallel to these events, the Dutch and the English lands became powerful Calvinist countries. The Danish Lutheran state was also a stronghold as well as an expanding kingdom. As the Calvinists and Lutherans extended their political sphere, new roads opened up for mission to the non-Christians. By the second half of the seventeenth century the political-social climate was settled, which allowed for the expansion of Protestant faith in the form of various church or movement structures. The Halle pietists such as Herman Francke (1663–1727) and Hernnhut leader Nicolaus von Zinzendorf (1700–1760) managed to convey the gospel to the natives of Greenland. The Dutch Calvinists began to reach out to the people of the West Indies, and the English Puritans to the North American Indians.

## Protestant Churches: Pietism and the Methodist Holiness Movement

The third phase of the Protestant churches came with the emergence of Methodism in Britain. While the religious map of countries in Western and Central Europe remained static, the British Isles saw another reforming movement within its own borders. Some decades after the establishment of the United Kingdom in 1707, John Wesley (1703–1791) started a new movement in the Church of England. His theological ideas were permeated by German Pietism and shaped by the prevailing Calvinist Puritan tradition, yet he developed a new religious stance based on a former rejected teaching stemming out of Calvinism, called Arminianism. Wesley believed that all people could be saved. Although, like Luther, Wesley did not intend to leave the church to which he originally belonged, his followers formed churches giving rise to a new branch of Protestantism. The Methodist revival in the Church of England, the Pietist renewals in the Lutheran German states, and the Moravian Brotherhood in the Austrian-controlled Czech and Hungarian kingdoms impacted on nearly all Protestant churches across Europe and North America. Calling for renewal and adherence to the original ideas of the first reformers, these movements managed to stir orthodoxy in each branch of Protestantism and urged for mission at home as well as abroad. Besides Wesley, George Whitfield (1714–1770) played a crucial role, with his preaching sparking the flame of revival everywhere he went. In New England a Pietist revival, the Great Awakening (1726–1760), took place, cutting across denominational adherence. One of the key figures was Jonathan Edwards (1703–1758). Besides his pastoral duty as a Congregationalist minister, he began to work among the Mohawk Indians.

## Mission Under the Influence of the New Movements

The concepts of mission and evangelization were in the making, but it may be said that the eighteenth century marked a watershed since it challenged the very structure and doctrines of the Protestant churches in Western Christendom. Wesley accepted Jacobus Arminius's view that all people can be saved, whereas his friend Whitfield maintained the Calvinist stance. Both charismatic figures introduced new methods, such as itinerant preaching and open-air services and called for public confession of sin. They also urged people to reach out to "those not knowing Christ," that is to people outside any Christian denominational structure as well as caring for the alienated people of the lower classes. This Pietist renewal movement, in Britain slowly receiving the name Evangelicalism, laid a great emphasis on individual conversion, personal piety, and Bible study. It set a rule of public morality often including temperance and abolitionism. Evangelicalism, following the Puritan tradition of the seventeenth century, reproached sports, plays, shows, May Day games, hunting, feasts, and wakes. It also broadened the role of the laity by highlighting the principle of universal priesthood, which the Anabaptists kept dear from the origins of the Reformation. Millennialism, the expectation of Christ's return, had been an undercurrent theological view in Calvinism since Cromwell's Puritan Commonwealth, encouraging every believer to evangelize and teach the gospel.

Unlike the Catholic Church, the Protestant churches, lacking central authorities and having free autonomous congregations, were naturally hotbeds of new movements, resulting in the establishment of a series of churches. This freely floating aspect of Protestantism became incredibly multifaceted within North American Protestantism, producing an endless string of new churches and new religious movements and cults originating in Christianity. Owing to the revival of inner movements within the established Protestant denominations, mission came to the forefront of the church. Terms such as *home mission*, (*Innere Mission*) or *foreign mission* had not yet been coined, but like-minded people across Protestant denominational lines set off to evangelize people within, or outside, Christendom. Since it became the conscious propaganda of the new movements, this was a major shift.

Similarly, it was not only the Anabaptists, but an exponentially increasing number of lay people of various Calvinist and Lutheran churches who took on the task of preaching the gospel. Calvinism always maintained the theological view of universal priesthood, but it was only three centuries later when the laity surfaced as a strong and irresistible force of mission. Indeed, it was a lay person, William Carey (1761–1834), who was one of the prime movers of the first missionary society (Baptist Missionary Society). This process was peculiar to the British development. It is undeniable that one may see a strong interrelatedness in the impressive democratization of society and religion.

## Heyday of Expansion of the Protestant Churches

The next phase, by and large, overlaps with the nineteenth century. By then, the general scene of Protestantism was set, and the challenge of Enlightenment, and later that of romanticism, lurked as a "danger" that was undermining the doctrines and structures of both major areas of Christianity: the Roman Catholic Church and the Protestant denominations. Although the antagonism between both large camps remained alive, their common enemy forced them into a similar stance. They had to defend themselves not only from each other but also against the challenge of Enlightenment. However, humanist ideas stemming from the time of the Reformation were amplified by the ever-increasing secular form of humanism reaching its pinnacle in the French Revolution and challenging traditional Protestant beliefs such as verbal inspiration, the validity of prophecy, the person of Christ, Trinity, resurrection, and the like.

There were significant differences from region to region. France had a very small Protestant population by the nineteenth century. Switzerland, which was on the fringe of western European Protestant developments, had began to see the Réveil movement of Cézar Malan (1787–1864). The Baltic countries were under Orthodox Russian control. The Lutheran churches had to adapt to the situation. Mission was not a possibility for them. Similarly, Hungarian Protestants were under foreign control. The Austrian Catholics maintained political hegemony but gradually allowed space for Protestants in the political-administrative life of the monarchy. During the Reform Era (1820–1848) Protestants gained similar status in society to that so far given only to Catholics. Clearly, the political climate of the region set out the lines of ecclesiastical development. Hungarian Protestantism had to be united under such a heavy Catholic pressure over the centuries, so no new Protestant churches emerged here. On the contrary, the political-economic development of Britain gave rise to numerous Protestant churches until the nineteenth century. The constant flow of secessionist churches also became the hallmark of Scotland and the Netherlands.

The challenges of their rapidly changing societies, colonization, and Enlightenment all stimulated a reversed direction, namely the desire to have a unified stance among the Protestant churches. Though secession did not cease to happen, the foundation of new interdenominational organizations expressed the desire to work together on common ground. First mission societies and Bible and tract societies began to mushroom, and then voluntary organizations became widespread such as the YMCA, Student Volunteer Mission, Sunday school, and the like. Charity organizations also took part in responding to the needs of a changing society.

Not only Britain, but also the United States, saw similar developments. The religious-cultural link provided a channel for the trafficking of ideas appearing in both countries. Each had an impact on the other, but the American process was different to some degree. Perhaps the major difference between the two countries was that the United States saw less or no state control and did not have the conserving cultural baggage of an old Christian establishment. No wonder that from the latter part of nineteenth century the United States replaced Britain in producing a new flow of Christian-based religious movements such as the Jehovah's Witnesses, Mormons, Christian Science, and the like. U.S. church development mirrored the internal fractions of European Protantism because each dissenting Protestant group in Europe could gain equal status in the New World. The large space and relatively tolerant—better than any European country—religious climate allowed for a development unseen in Protestantism before. Various Calvinist, Lutheran, and Anabaptist churches from the Netherlands, Britain, Switzerland, Scandinavia, and Russia came to live side by side. They also often merged and influenced one another. An entirely different phenomenon can be spotted in the same land. Undoubtedly the German-Swiss Anabaptists' stories of Russia accentuate how much a little group managed to maintain its own religious identity.

## Protestant Churches and the Mission of Colonization

Britain and the United States took the leading role in mission. Besides them, the German, Dutch, and

Swiss societies were most significant. The century was characterized by mission societies and interdenominational organizations such as the foundation of the Evangelical Alliance in 1846 and the further proliferation of movements ending up in the foundation of new churches. In this century the fully developed structures of home and foreign mission can be discerned. Africa, Asia, and Latin America became prime mission fields. An endless stream of societies, denominational and interdenominational, managed to convert millions of people adhering to other religions. Indisputably, Evangelical and Pietist tradition played a crucial role in this, and their multifaceted actions led to the birth of the modern ecumenical movements of the twentieth century. Pentecostalism of the twentieth century had seen the axis of Christianity moving to the United States. The new waves of emerging churches owe their birth to the events following the Azusa Street revival. The role of the Holy Spirit in Christian worship had been there in the tradition but never before in history had it reached a status like in the United States. First, the Pentecostal churches such as Assemblies of God and Church of God became influential, followed in the 1950s by the Charismatic ones (Vineyard Movement, Sovereign Grace Ministries, New Frontiers).

Finally, it has to be mentioned that all these trends of unification materializing in the nineteenth century led to the foundation of two major organizations, Life and Work and Faith and Order, setting the scene for the first official unification of almost all official Protestant churches. The World Council of Churches was established in 1948. Another highly interesting issue is the development of Protestant churches of Africa, Asia, and Latin America, where the formation of churches after the final collapse of the colonizing powers led to a boom in Protestant churches unseen before in Christian history. This turn of events set the scene for the twenty-first century, when the majority, formerly third world, is likely to have a far stronger voice and influence within the Protestant camp.

ÁBRAHÁM KOVÁCS

## Further Reading

Ahlstrom, E. S. (1972). *A religious history of the American people*. New Haven, CT: Yale University Press.

Algermissen, K. (1953). *Christian denominations* (J. W. Grundner, Trans.). St. Louis, MO: B. Herder Book Co.

Balmer, R., & Winner, L. F. (2002). *Protestantism in America*. New York: Columbia University Press.

Cameron, E. (1991). European Reformation. Oxford, UK: Oxford University Press.

Day, P. (Ed.). (2003). *A dictionary of Christian denomination*. London: Continuum

Deryck, L. (Ed.). (2002). *The rise of the laity in Evangelical Protestantism*. London: Routledge.

Dillenberger, J., & Welch, C. (Eds.). (1998). *Protestant Christianity: Interpreted through its development*. New York: Prentice Hall.

Hardon, J. A. (1969). *The Protestant churches of America* (Rev. ed.). Garden City, NY: Image Books.

Hillerbrand, H. J. (2004). *The encyclopedia of Protestantism*. New York/London: Routledge.

Kent, J. (2002). *Wesley and the Wesleyans: Religion in eighteenth-century Britain*. Cambridge, UK: Cambridge University Press.

Marshall, P., & Ryrie, A. (2002). *The beginnings of English Protestantism*. Cambridge, UK: Cambridge University Press.

Noll, A. M. (2002). *America's God: From Jonathan Edwards to Abraham Lincoln*. Oxford, UK: Oxford University Press.

Noll, M. A. (2004). *The rise of Evangelicalism: The age of Edwards, Whitefield, and the Wesleys*. Westmont, IL: Intervarsity Press.

Maag, K. (Ed.). (1997). *The Reformation in eastern and central Europe*. Aldershot, UK: Scolar.

Prestwich, M. (Ed.). (1985). *Calvinism in east central Europe: Hungary and her neighbours in international Calvinism 1541–1715*. Oxford, UK: Clarendon.

Rhodes, R. (2005). *The complete guide to Christian denominations*. Eugene, OR: Harvest House Publishers.

Tyacke, N. (2001). *Aspects of English* Protestantism, *c. 1530–1700*. Manchester, UK: Manchester University Press.

Polish Research Centre (Ed.). (1944). *The Protestant churches in Poland*. London: Polish Research Centre.

# R

## Racism

It is difficult to make blanket statements about missionaries and their ideas concerning race because such ideas have differed dramatically over time. Moreover, racial attitudes have differed according to denomination, among sponsoring groups, from mission field to mission field (e. g., the attitudes of missionaries to Africa differed from those of missionaries to Asia), from mission station to mission station, and even among individual missionaries working in the same area and for the same organization.

### Perception of Other Civilizations

During the age of exploration, Europeans struggled to "make sense" of previously unknown parts of the world. European ideas about Africans and Asians differed markedly. Many Europeans thought of Africa as a continent where civilization had made the fewest inroads. Africa was the land of savages (Baker 1998). Asia—on the contrary—was seen as a place where civilization had already made inroads. The first protracted contact between Europeans and the Chinese, for example, was through merchants and missionaries in the late 1700s. Following a brief period during the Boxer Rebellion when missionaries and their Chinese Christian converts were exterminated, missionaries and merchants lived in harmony with one another and with the Chinese. However, the Chinese considered anyone who was not Chinese to be a barbarian, and missionaries—for their part—believed that because the Chinese did not worship the Christian God, they were heathens who needed to be saved (Reinders 2004).

In the United States an ideological justification for the policy of removing Native-Americans from their ancestral lands was based on racism and the underlying idea that the United States had a providential mission to tame and "Christianize" the continent (Berkhofer 1965). North American Indians were portrayed as religiously and morally incomplete. They were not considered fully human. Although some European settlers saw it as their duty to convert Native-Americans to Christianity, others sought to remove them or eliminate them from the continent altogether.

### Racism as a Concept

Racism is a comparatively new concept, largely unknown in ancient times. As Sue Peabody (2004, 113) asserts, "It is a truism that the modern or scientific racism that emerged in the late eighteenth century and flourished throughout Europe, the United States, and much of Latin America in the nineteenth and twentieth centuries was new and different from the collection of prejudices, myths, and attitudes that circulated during earlier periods." Peabody points out that modern racism formed a totalizing worldview, a system of concepts—judicial, political, and social categories that were implicated in the entire range of social relations.

#### Two Assumptions

Modern racism is predicated on two assumptions. First, it is assumed that all humans can be accurately and effectively ranked as superior or inferior according to physical differences. Racist theories claim (contrary to all biological evidence) that physical and mental characteristics are identical within each race. Such is not the case. A founder of American anthropology, Franz Boas, spent much of his career documenting that physical traits, language, and culture are separate entities (Boas 1940; Baker 1998). Second, it is assumed that physical differences can be correlated with differences in intellect, moral character, personality, and cultural attainments. Racial categories are thought to be natural, "in the blood," genetic, and/or God-given, and—in most cases—are believed to be immutable.

Modern conceptions of race are predicated on the idea that the white race is superior to all others. As noted, racism as an ideology provided a rationale for systems of social, political, and economic stratification as well as for longstanding patterns of domination and oppression (Banton 1987). As anthropologist Ashley Montagu (1942, 118) points out, "differences in physical appearance provided the convenient peg upon which to hang the argument that this represented the external sign of the ineradicable mental and moral inferiorities. It was an easily-grasped mode of reasoning and in this way the obvious differences in social status, in caste status, was equated with the obvious difference in physical appearance, which in turn was taken to indicate a fundamental biological difference."

### Classification of Humans

The first European to systematically classify all humans according to a single criterion—skin color—was Johann Friedrich Blumenbach (1752–1840). He divided all of humanity into five races: white, black, yellow, red, and beige. While Blumenbach acknowledged that classifications based on skin color were arbitrary and misleading, he defended his classification as useful.

Racism as a concept developed at about the same time as colonial expansion. How should Europeans deal with indigenous peoples? In the colonial era most Europeans assumed that the white race was superior to all other races. Nonwhites were seen as "savages" whose skin color indicated a preponderance of evil; dark-skinned people and devil worship were often equated (Baker, 1998). Europeans considered the civilization of white Europe as the one true civilization, and other civilizations—even of venerable ancient cultures like India and China—were deemed barbaric. These same assessments fueled (and continue to fuel) contemporary racist ideas.

### Churches Divided

From the nineteenth century onward, religion was perceived as being opposed to racism. The Abolitionist Movement, often rooted in Protestant churches, became a focal point for opposition to slavery. Some Abolitionists believed in the innate inferiority of blacks, but they understood presumed inferiority, not by recourse to religious discourse about the children of light and the children of darkness but to biology and later to cultural explanations that were not infused with theological arguments.

In the twentieth century, mainstream Christian churches remained divided. Many liberal Protestant denominations and liberal Catholics—the clergy often before the laity—embraced the civil rights movement. While some conservative religious bodies expressed vocal opposition to the movement, many churches simply remained silent on the issue. But by 1970 racism had been repudiated by religious bodies across the political spectrum. By the beginning of the twenty-first century, mainstream churches had become centers of antiracist discourse. Only at the periphery can one find religion being used to legitimate racism.

### Racism and Ethnocentrism

Prior to the sixteenth century, most rankings of humans were based on alleged cultural—not physical—differences (Malefijt, 1974). All human groups are highly ethnocentric; they believe that their particular culture is superior to all others. But in ancient times alleged superiority and inferiority were seldom linked to physical traits. Culture took precedence over biology, and it was assumed that individuals could change. Malefijt (1974, 257) characterized the ancient Greeks as extremely ethnocentric. They believed that their language, customs, and values were superior to all others. They labeled all non-Greeks "barbarians" (literally, people who did not speak the Greek language, so their words sounded like "bar-bar-bar"). Nevertheless, barbarians who learned Greek and adopted Greek culture could become Greeks irrespective of their physical traits.

The ancient Romans held similar ethnocentric views. Romans believed that Roman civilization was superior to all others but nevertheless selectively conferred Roman citizenship on those they had conquered—regardless of physical appearance. The most famous example is St. Paul, a Jew who was granted Roman citizenship as a consequence of his father's service to Rome. Paul was instrumental in separating Christianity and Judaism and cleared the way for Christian missionary activity among non-Jews. Following Paul, St. Augustine (an African) distinguished between "pagans" and "Christians." He did not assert

## Management of "Savages"

First published in 1855, three years after Sir Francis Galton's return from a short stint in South-West Africa, *The Art of Travel; or, Shifts and Contrivances Available in Wild Countries* earned Galton the Royal Geographical Society's Founder's Medal for 1854. Immensely popular for the next fifty years, the book appeared in eight successive expanded editions between 1855 and 1893. Like many other books written by scientific notables of the day, it provides a background against which to assess missionary attitudes and behavior of the time.

General Remarks—A frank, joking, but determined matter, joined with an air of showing more confidence in the good faith of the natives than you really feel, is the best . . . If a savage does mischief, look on him as you would on a kicking mule, or a wild animal whose nature is to be unruly and vicious, and keep your temper quite unruffled. . . .

Bush Law—It is impossible but that a traveler must often take the law into his own hands. Some countries, no doubt, are governed with a strong arm by a savage despot; to whom or to whose subordinates appeals must of course be mane; but, for the most part, the system of life among savages is—

> "The simple rule, the good old plan,—
> That they should take, who have the power;
> And they should keep, who can."

Where there is no civil law, or any kind of substitute for it, each man is, as it were, a nation in himself; and then the traveler ought to be guided in his actions by the motives that influence nations, whether to make war or to abstain from it, rather than by the criminal code of civilised countries. The traveler must settle in his own mind what his scale of punishments should be; and it will be found a convenient principle that a culprit should be punished in proportion to the quantity of harm that he has done, rather than according to the presumed wickedness of the offence. . . .

Seizing Food—On arriving at an encampment, the natives commonly run away in fright. If you are hungry, or in serious need of anything that they have, go boldly into their huts, take just what you want, and leave fully adequate payment. It is absurd to be over-scrupulous in these cases.

Source: Galton, F. (1872). *The art of travel; or, shifts and contrivances available in wild countries* (pp. 308–310). London: John Murray.

that pagans and Christians were equal, yet prayed fervently that eventually all pagans would be converted to Christianity.

## Monogenesis and Polygenesis

The theory of polygenesis attempts to account for human differences by positing a separate origin for each racial group. Polygenesis has had some highly respected advocates within the scientific community. In the 1735 edition of *Systema natura,* Linnaeus designated all humans as belonging to a single species: *Homo sapiens.* In later editions (after 1738) of his work, however,

Linnaeus modified his position, suggesting that *Homo sapiens* should be divided into four separate "varieties": *Homo sapiens americanus, Homo sapiens europaeus, Homo sapiens asiaticus,* and *Homo sapiens afer.* It is unclear whether Linnaeus considered these "varieties" to be separate species (in which case they could not interbreed and produce fertile offspring). In subsequent writings, he emphasized that most differences among *Homo sapiens* are due to climate and diet rather than heredity. Strictly speaking, Linnaeus was not a racist in the contemporary sense because he considered multiple criteria in his classifications and made ample provision for changes within a species.

Advocates of scientific racism often found themselves at odds with theologians. In the eighteenth and nineteenth centuries, scientists and theologians debated the doctrines of monogenesis and polygenesis. The biblical account clearly favored a single origin for all humankind. Scientists, on the other hand, found evidence supporting multiple origins and multiple species of humankind. Reverend Samuel Stanhope Smith (1750–1819), who served as professor of moral theology at Princeton, offered what many Christians saw as a convincing argument against the doctrine of polygenesis. Smith's central thesis was that God would not have created separate species that could successfully interbreed. According to Smith, this would make humans diverge from the laws that apply to the rest of nature. Thus, Smith interpreted scientific doctrines of polygenesis as an impious attack on God's work as Creator. Reverend Smith suggested that dark skin color was caused by environmental factors such as sunlight.

Another leading scientific proponent of monogenesis was Sir James Pritchard (1786–1884). Pritchard posited that environment alone could not account for the observed differences among humans and correctly asserted that physical distinctions such as skin color remain constant over many generations despite differences in climate, diet, and so on. Pritchard suggested that all humans were endowed with an innate sense of aesthetics that caused them to favor lighter skin over dark. Thus, earlier and darker races were said to be inferior to the lighter ones. Pritchard speculated that Adam and Eve were black.

In the mid-nineteenth century, Count Arthur de Gobineau proposed a highly influential racial theory in a three-volume study entitled *The Inequality of Human Races* (1855–1859). Gobineau was among the first to offer a pseudo-scientific—as opposed to theological— justification for racism. Gobineau postulated that there were once three "pure" races: white, yellow, and black. Each race possessed both positive and negative qualities; for example, yellows (Mongoloids) were intelligent and industrious, and blacks (Negroids) possessed athletic abilities. Gobineau incorrectly asserted that whenever members of different races interbreed, only the negative attributes manifest in their offspring. Thus, miscegenation (interbreeding) leads to a decline of the positive qualities in each of the three great races and, ultimately, to the decline of European (white) civilization. Gobineau argued that the effects of miscegenation were irreversible. Thus, his thesis provided an explanation for the cultural degeneration of Europe but did not provide a remedy.

STEPHEN D. GLAZIER

## Further Reading

Baker, L. D. (1998). *From savage to Negro: Anthropology and the construction of race, 1896–1954.* Berkeley: University of California Press.

Banton, M. (1987). *Racial theories.* Cambridge, UK: Cambridge University Press.

Berkhofer, R. F. (1965). *Salvation and the savage.* Lexington: University Press of Kentucky.

Boas, F. (1940). *Race, language, and culture.* New York: Macmillan.

Bonk, J. J. (1991). *Missions and money: Affluence as a Western missionary problem.* Maryknoll, NY: Orbis Books.

Burridge, K. (1973). *Encountering aborigines.* New York: Pergamon Press.

Chireau, Y. (2002). *Black magic.* Berkeley: University of California Press .

Coleman, M. C. (1986). *Presbyterian missionary attitudes toward American Indians, 1837–1893.* Jackson: University Press of Mississippi.

Davis, D. B. (1997). Constructing race: A reflection. *The William and Mary Quarterly* 54(1): 7–18.

Genovese, E. D. (1972). *Roll, Jordan, roll.* New York: Pantheon.

Glazier, S. D. (1999). Anthropology and theology: The legacies of a link. In F. A. Salamone & W. R. Adams (Eds.), *Anthropology and theology: Gods, icons, and God-talk* (2nd ed., pp. 209–223). Lanham. MD: University Press of America.

Gobineau, Count A. de. (1915). *The inequality of human races.* London: Heinemann.

Hanke, L. (1970). *Aristotle and the American Indians.* Bloomington: University of Indiana Press.

Johnston, A. (2003). *Missionary writing and empire, 1800–1860.* New York: Cambridge University Press.

Lincoln, C. E. & Mamiya, L. H. (1990). *The black church in the African American experience.* Durham, NC: Duke University Press.

Malefijt, A. de W. (1974). *Images of man: A history of anthropological thought.* New York: Alfred A. Knopf.

Montagu, A. (1942). *Man's most dangerous myth: The fallacies of race.* New York: Columbia University Press.

Pagden, A. (1982). *Fall of natural man.* New York: Cambridge University Press.

Peabody, S. (2004). A nation born of slavery: Missionaries and racial discourse in seventeenth century French Antilles. *Journal of Social History, 38(1),* 113–126.

Porter, A. (2004). *Religion versus empire: British Protestant missionaries and overseas expansion, 1700–1914.* Manchester, UK, and New York: Manchester University Press.

Porterfield, A. (1997). *Mary Lyon and the Mount Holyoke missionaries.* New York: Oxford University Press.

Raboteau, A. J. (1978). *Slave religion: The "invisible" institution in the antebellum South.* New York: Oxford.

Reinders, E. (2004). *Borrowed gods and foreign bodies: Christian missionaries imagine Chinese religion.* Berkeley: University of California Press.

Sobel, M. (1979). *Trabelin' on.* Westport, CT: Greenwood.

Turner, M. (1998). *Slaves and missionaries: The disintegration of Jamaican slave society, 1787–1834.* Mona, Jamaica: University of West Indies Press.

van der Geest, S. (1990). Anthropologists and missionaries: Brothers under the skin. *Man (n.s.) 25(4)*, 588–601.

Weber, M. (2002). *The Protestant ethic and the spirit of capitalism.* Los Angeles: Roxbury.

Willis, A. S. (2004). *All according to God's plan: Southern Baptist missions and race, 1945–1970.* Lexington: University Press of Kentucky.

# Reference Tools

Reference tools provide concise access to a variety of types of information. Atlases, dictionaries, encyclopedias, directories, and handbooks provide biographical information, information about mission-sending agencies, documentation of the locations and time line of mission work in particular geographical areas, and statistics regarding institutions and staffing. Reference tools also provide information about the existence and location of primary and secondary sources that document missions and missionaries. Online directories and databases now complement more traditional reference works in providing informational content about missions and missionaries, as well as information about sources of documentation.

One role of reference tools is to provide a broad overview of the history and context of an area of study. For missions and missionaries, this overview encompasses political and social factors at work both in the countries that sent missionaries and in the areas that received them. Factors like colonialism, evolving ideas of race and culture, and conflicts among divergent theologies are integral parts of the history of missions and missionaries. Though not designed specifically as reference tools, overview works such as Kenneth Scott Latourette's seven-volume *A History of the Expansion of Christianity* (Zondervan 1970) serve as important broad-based introductions to the field. Such classic overviews are now being updated by works that provide a more global perspective, such as the Cambridge University Press volumes *World Christianities 1815–1915,* and *World Christianities, c.1914–c.2000* (Cambridge University Press 2006). Other works that provide useful overviews include Andrew Walls' essays in *The Missionary Movement in Christian History* (Orbis 1996) and *The Cross-Cultural Process in Christian History* (Orbis 2002) and Timothy Yates's *Christian Mission in the 20th Century* (Cambridge University Press 1994). Two works by Norman E. Thomas provide important baseline information: *Classic Texts in Mission and World Christianity* (Orbis 1995), and the *International Mission Bibliography.* William R. Hutchison's *Errand to the World: American Protestant Thought and Foreign Missions* (University of Chicago Press 1987) remains a seminal work for understanding the background of American missions.

## Encyclopedias and Dictionaries

A number of encyclopedic works related to missions have been published since the mid-nineteenth century. These works include the *Cyclopedia of Missions* (Charles Scribner 1854) edited by Harvey Newcomb; the *Encyclopaedia of Missions* (Funk & Wagnalls 1891, revised 1904) edited by Edwin Bliss; the *Concise Dictionary of the Christian World Mission* (Abingdon 1970) edited by Stephen Neill, Gerald H. Anderson, and John Goodwin; the *Dictionary of Mission: Theology, History, Perspectives* (Orbis 1997) edited by Karl Müller (English translation of *Lexikon Missionstheologischer Grundbegriffe*); the *Evangelical Dictionary of World Missions* (Baker Books 2000) edited by A. Scott Moreau; and The *World Christian Encyclopedia: A Comparative Survey of Churches and Religions in the Modern World* (Oxford University Press 2001) edited by David B. Barrett, George T. Kurian, and Todd M. Johnson. As in the case of general monographic works, encyclopedias documenting missions and missionaries have shifted their focus over time from Western-based mission work toward world Christianity.

General encyclopedias and dictionaries are complemented by more specialized works. The *Biographical Dictionary of Christian Missions* (Eerdmans 1999) edited by Gerald H. Anderson is the most comprehensive source of biographical information. Though now somewhat out of date, the *Encyclopedia of Modern Christian Missions; the Agencies* (T. Nelson 1967) edited by Burton L. Goddard provides useful documentation related to the history and development of Protestant mission-sending agencies. An overview of Catholic missions is available in the *New Catholic Encyclopedia* (Thomson/Gale 2003). Documentation of the missionary activities of the Coptic and early churches is available in *The Coptic Encyclopedia* (Macmillan 1991).

Geographically specific works are also important tools, both those that focus on Christianity, such as

*A Dictionary of Asian Christianity* (Eerdmans 2001) edited by Scott Sunquist, and those of a more general nature, such as the African historical dictionaries series published by Scarecrow Press. Traditionally published encyclopedias and dictionaries are now often supplemented by Web-based resources such as the *Dictionary of African Christian Biography* (www.dacb.org/), *Biographical Dictionary of Chinese Christianity* (www.bdcconline.net), and the *Ricci 21st Century Roundtable Database on the History of Christianity in China* (ricci.rt.usfca.edu/).

## Atlases

Atlases, directories, and handbooks constitute another important type of reference tool for the study of mission and missionaries. These works provide a more granular level of information—specific locations, dates, staffing levels, and names. Mission atlases typically include maps showing the locations of mission stations and may also include information about the date when the station was established, numbers of missionaries, information about schools or medical works, and so forth. Some mission atlases focus on the work of particular denominational or church bodies while others incorporate information related to a variety of bodies.

Historical Catholic mission atlases include the *Atlas des Missions Catholiques* or *Katholischer Missions-Atlas* (Herder 1885, 1886) prepared by Oscar Werner, the *Catholic World Atlas* (Society for the Propagation of the Faith 1929) prepared by Karl Streit, and the *Atlas Missionum a Sacra Congregatione de Propaganda Fide Dependentium* (Ex Civitate Vaticana 1958). *The Twentieth Century Atlas of the Christian world; the Expansion of Christianity through the Centuries* (Hawthorne Books 1963) was prepared by Anton Freitag, S.V.D. Among the earliest works compiling information about Protestant missions were *A Geography and Atlas of Protestant Missions* (Student Volunteer Movement for Foreign Missions 1901–1903) prepared by Harlan P. Beach, the *Statistical Atlas of Christian Missions* prepared for the 1910 World Missionary Conference in Edinburgh, and the *World Atlas of Christian Missions* published by the Student Volunteer Movement for Foreign Missions in 1911.

Building on these earlier works, the *World Missionary Atlas* prepared by Harlan Beach and Charles Fahs was published in 1925 by the Institute of Social and Religious Research. These works provide listings of missionary societies, summaries of statistics, indices of mission stations, and maps of mission fields. They are valuable tools for determining which mission agencies were active in specific locations at specific times.

Of particular note for documenting Protestant

mission work in China is *The Christian Occupation of China* (1925), published by the International Missionary Council, which provides province-level maps and statistical information. Atlases produced by specific mission-sending agencies include the *Church Missionary Atlas* (first published 1859), documenting the missions of the Church Missionary Society, *The Churchman's Missionary Atlas* (1907–1922), documenting Anglican missions, the *Missionary Atlas Showing the Mission Fields of the American Baptist Missionary Union* (1907), and the *Moravian Missionary Atlas* (1908). Technological advances have led to a new generation of atlases related to missions and world Christianity, including publications of Global Mapping International, *World Missions Atlas Project* (WorldMAP), and the *Atlas of World Christianity: 2000 Years* (OM Publishing 1998) prepared by Peter Brierley and Heather Wright.

## Directories and Handbooks

Like missions atlases, some mission directories and handbooks compile information related to a number of church bodies while others are focused on a specific sending agency or geographical area. An early general directory is *The Blue Book of Missions* (Funk & Wagnalls 1905) edited by Henry Otis Dwight. The *Directory of Foreign Missions* (1933) and *Directory of World Missions* (1938), both published by the International Missionary Council, provide documentation regarding the fields of work of numerous sending agencies, the names of periodicals published by the agencies, and other useful information. More recent works focusing on Protestant missions include the *World Christian Handbook* (1945–1968), published by World Dominion Press, the *Mission Handbook,* a serial publication of the Missions Advanced Research and Communication Center, and the *World Churches Handbook* (Christian Research 1993), which is based on the Operation world database by Patrick Johnstone, WEC International, and edited by Peter Brierley. Directories of Catholic missions include *Le Missioni Cattoliche Dipendenti dalla Sacra Congregazione "De Propaganda fide"* (1950) and the *United States* Catholic *Mission Association Mission Handbook* (1973– ). *World Christian Trends, AD 30–AD 2200: Interpreting the Annual Christian Megacensus* (William Carey Library, 2001) edited by David B. Barrett and Todd M. Johnson is a statistical companion volume to the *World Christian Encyclopedia*. Statistical information is increasingly available in online databases such as the World Christian Database (worldchristiandatabase.org).

Handbooks and directories related to specific geographical areas include *The Christian Handbook of India*

(1902–1970), the *Indian Missionary Directory and Memorial Volume* (1886–1892) prepared by B. H. Badley, the *China Mission Year Book* (1910–1925) and *China Christian Year Book* (1926–1940), the *Directory of Protestant Missions in China* (1916–1950), and the *Catholic Directory of Eastern Africa,* now *AMECEA Catholic Directory* (1965–1993). Handbooks and directories are also available for specific sending agencies, such as the *Register of Missionaries (Clerical, Lay, & Female), and Native clergy, from 1804–1904* of the Church Missionary Society and *A Register of Missionaries, Deputations, etc., from 1796 to 1923* of the London Missionary Society, Southern Baptist *Foreign Missionaries* (1940), and unpublished volumes listing missionaries of the American Board of Commissioners for Foreign Missions prepared by John Vinton.

## Tools for Locating Primary and Secondary Sources

A second major category of reference tools includes bibliographies, directories, indices, and databases that identify primary and secondary sources of documentation related to missions and missionaries. Many online catalogs of libraries with strong collections in the area of missions are accessible to the general public, such as those of the Yale Divinity School Library, the Union Theological Seminary Library (including the Missionary Research Library collection), and the British Library. The *Cumulative Bibliography of The International Review of Mission* (webdb.ucs.ed.ac.uk/divinity/cmb/) and *African Christian Bibliography* (webdb.ucs.ed.ac.uk/divinity/africa/index.cfm), both published by the Centre for the Study of Christianity in the Non-Western World, are useful tools for identifying secondary literature, as is the *International Mission Bibliography, 1960–2000* edited by Norman E. Thomas (Scarecrow 2003). The *Bibliografia Missionaria* published from 1935 to 1986 (Soc. tip. A. Macioce and Pisani) is a basic tool for research on Catholic missions. The *Missionary Periodicals Database* (research.yale.edu:8084/missionperiodicals), hosted at the Yale Divinity School Library, aims to record and index all periodicals on foreign missions published in Britain between the eighteenth century and the 1960s.

Numerous tools exist for locating the personal papers of missionaries and the archival records of sending agencies. The Mundus Gateway (http://www.mundus.ac.uk/) is a freely accessible web-based guide to more than four hundred collections of overseas missionary materials held in the United Kingdom. Subscription databases in the United States such as ArchiveGrid and ArchivesUSA provide information about numerous mission-related archival holdings, and in some cases provide links to detailed online finding aids. The Ricci Roundtable (http://ricci.rt.usfca.edu/) provides detailed listings of archival and published resources on Christianity in China (including Taiwan, Hong Kong, and Macao); entries for archives and libraries in the United States are based on the book *Christianity in China: A Scholars' Guide to Resources in the Libraries and Archives of the United States* (1989), which was edited by Archie R. Crouch. Online finding aids and guides produced by many libraries and denominational archives are now freely available on the web and can be located using standard web search engines or library web research guides.

## Future of Reference Tools

Every good reference tool represents an enormous amount of painstaking work. Technological advances make the compilation and distribution of reference tools easier in the present era, but older tools will always remain of interest to historians for the valuable comparative data they provide and the light they shed on evolving theories and concepts.

## Additional Sources

The January 1999 issue of *Missiology,* titled "Tools of the Trade," contains a number of useful papers on reference tools, which were presented at the 1998 annual meeting of the American Society of Missiology. Of note among the various reference works mentioned in this article are the online, nonproprietary tools that will continue to develop and expand over time, including the *Dictionary of African Christian Biography* (www.dacb.org), the *Biographical Dictionary of Chinese Christianity* (www.bdcconline.net), the Ricci 21st Century Roundtable on the History of Christianity in China (ricci.rt.usfca.edu/), and the *Sources for Research: Missions and World Christianity* resource of the Yale Divinity School Library (www.library.yale.edu/div/MissionsResources.htm).

Martha Lund Smalley

## Reformation

The Protestant Reformation of the sixteenth century was a formative event that changed the character and redefined the identity of Western Christianity. It had far-reaching consequences for Western civilization, as well as important implications for the world mission and unity of the church.

## Antecedents

The late Middle Ages witnessed a variety of reform and protest movements and included two pre-Reformation church reformers. Monastic rules were being reformed to protect simplicity and guard against worldliness. Protests were lodged against clerical abuse and papal corruption. John Wycliffe (1330–1384), English philosopher and theologian, argued that church authority flowed from divine grace, maintained that the Bible was the sole authority for church doctrine, attacked the authority of the pope, and criticized monasticism as unbiblical. His writings influenced Jan Hus (1372–1415), a Bohemian reformer and preacher in Prague, who followed Wycliffe in attacking clergy morals and papal authority. Hus was excommunicated by the pope, tried as a heretic at the Council of Constance (1415), condemned, and executed by burning. His martyrdom sparked a movement for church reform in Bohemia, where his followers (Hussites) became advocates for clergy reform, vernacular liturgy, communion in both kinds, and free preaching of the Word of God. Martin Luther was later known as a "second Hus."

## Martin Luther and Lutheranism

Martin Luther (1483–1546) is regarded as the father of the Protestant Reformation. Born in Eisleben, Saxony, he was sent by his father to Erfurt to study law, but in 1505 a terrifying experience led to his dramatic conversion and decision to become a monk. Entering the Augustinian monastery at Erfurt, he obtained a degree in theology, was ordained a priest in 1507, and was sent to the new University of Wittenberg in 1508 to teach. While on a deputation to Rome (1510–1511), Luther was angered by the sight of pilgrimages, veneration of relics, and sale of indulgences. Obtaining his doctorate from the University of Erfurt, he was appointed professor of biblical exegesis at Wittenberg in 1511 and began a course of lectures on the Psalms and later on Paul's Epistle to the Romans.

On 31 October 1517 Luther drew up his famous "Ninety Five Theses" on indulgences and posted them with an invitation to an academic debate on the door of the Castle Church at Wittenberg. The reaction was unanticipated. A violent controversy ensued, intensified by the printing and wide distribution of the Theses. Luther called for an end to the sale of indulgences, defying the authority of Pope Leo X and the Archbishop of Mainz. Although denounced by Rome, Luther refused to recant and declined to go to Rome for a hearing. He was protected from extradition by the Elector of Saxony, Frederick the Wise, founder and patron of Luther's university. In 1520 Luther quickly wrote three popular treatises on the limits of papal authority, the rights of Christian laymen, and the captivity of the church, which were printed and widely distributed. In 1520 Luther received the papal bull threatening excommunication but proceeded to burn it publicly. His official excommunication by the pope followed, along with a summons to the Diet of Worms (1521) by the Holy Roman Emperor, Charles V. Appearing at Worms under safe-conduct, Luther refused to recant, insisting that he must be proved wrong on the basis of Holy Scripture. He was condemned and placed under the ban of the empire. The Elector of Saxony took Luther into protective custody, spiriting him away to the Wartburg Castle, where he completed the translation of the New Testament into German in eleven weeks.

Returning to Wittenberg in 1522, Luther resumed his preaching and teaching role. In 1525 he married a former nun, Catherina von Bora. He also dealt with major challenges to his leadership by radical followers, steering a middle course between Catholic tradition and more extreme views of the reformation. In 1529 he prepared the texts of the Large and Small Catechisms. Luther's most important reformatory work now came to an end with the emergence of Lutheranism as a heretical party within Catholicism.

From 1530 to 1555 the Lutheran faction continued a precarious existence as a defiant reforming movement within the still undivided Catholic Church. It survived thanks to the protection of the Elector of Saxony, and after 1531 was protected by a military alliance of pro-Lutheran princes, known as the Smalkaldic League. In January 1530 the Emperor Charles V summoned an imperial diet at Augsburg, with the ostensible aim of settling religious differences within the Holy Roman Empire. The emperor wished to present a united military front against the threatening Turks. Responding to this invitation, the Elector of Saxony asked the Wittenberg theologians to prepare an account of Lutheran beliefs and practices as a proposed basis for reconciliation at Augsburg. The Lutherans decided to prepare a common statement of Lutheran doctrines, based on existing documents (the Schwabach and Torgau Articles) and acceptable to all Lutheran theologians. The work was undertaken by Phillip Melanchthon (1497–1560), Luther's younger colleague. He drafted the final form of what is known as the *Augsburg Confession* in Latin and German versions. On 25 June 1530 the Latin version was publicly read before the Diet of Augsburg. Twenty-one articles dealt with essential evangelical doctrines (including Article IV on justification by faith and Article VII on the church), and seven more with abuses that had been corrected (marriage of priests, form of the mass, power of bishops, customs, foods and ceremonies, etc.). The preface to the confession claimed that it contained no new teachings—only those taught by the Bible and the early church—and that Lutherans had no desire to divide the church but only wished to restore it to its original foundation on the basis of Holy Scripture.

Roman Catholic theologians refuted the *Augsburg Confession* along with several other Protestant confessions, leading Emperor Charles V to declare that the Protestant cause was defeated. This led to the formation of the Smalkaldic League, a defensive alliance of Lutheran princes. Wherever Lutheranism was dominant, Lutherans organized themselves as a separate "confessional church," with territorial rulers acting as "emergency bishops" to provide for church government, parish regulations, and the calling and ordination of evangelical ministers. Lutheranism spread from its base in Wittenberg to countries in eastern Europe, the Baltic region, and Scandinavia. Religious wars broke out, but efforts toward compromise were unsuccessful. Finally, a compromise settlement was agreed on at the Imperial Diet of Augsburg in 1555. Catholic and Lutheran Diet representatives, weary of prolonged religious warfare, gave the Lutheran Confession official recognition within the Empire under the Peace of Augsburg. Under the principle of *cuius regio, eius religio*, territorial princes were given the right to determine the religious allegiance of their subjects and to enforce religious uniformity within their lands. They had the right to banish dissidents, and there was no religious freedom in the modern sense. Calvinists could also avail themselves of religious protection under the banner of the *Augsburg Confession*. In 1580 the Lutheran Reformation reached its highest point of doctrinal development when approximately 100 Lutheran electors, princes, and representatives of free cities subscribed the *Book of Concord* as a true exposition of the *Augsburg Confession*. This book incorporated three ecumenical creeds and seven Lutheran confessional statements and purported to resolve all outstanding intra-Lutheran doctrinal disputes and controversies with Catholics, Calvinists, and Zwinglians. It remains the doctrinal norm for most Lutheran churches today.

## Ulrich Zwingli, Swiss Reformer

Ulrich Zwingli (1484–1531), a contemporary of Luther, became the leading figure in the reformation in Zurich, a leading Swiss city. Educated in scholastic theology and humanism at Bern, Vienna, and Basel, Zwingli was ordained to the Catholic priesthood in 1506 and served two smaller parishes before being elected in 1518 as the "people's preacher" at the Old Minster (cathedral) in Zurich. Here he developed a platform for his exclusively biblical sermons and attacks on indulgences, abuse of pilgrimages, purgatory, the invocation of saints, and monasticism. Rejecting the advice of a Roman Catholic emissary Johann Faber, Zwingli in 1523 publicly defended the Sixty-Seven Theses from an earlier tract in which he challenged papal authority, the sacrifice of the mass, fasting regulations, and clerical celibacy. He maintained that the sole basis of truth was the Gospel. These theses led to the consolidation of the reformation in Zurich. In 1524, with the support of the Zurich council, he removed images from churches and in 1525 abolished the Roman Mass. Zwingli distanced himself from Luther on the nature of the "real presence" in the Eucharist. When Luther and Zwingli met for the only time at Marburg in 1529, Zwingli espoused a purely symbolic view of Christ's presence in the Lord's Supper, which led to a falling out between the two reformers. Zwingli dealt harshly with Anabaptist groups that split off from his mainstream Protestant movement around 1525, hunting them down mercilessly. Zwingli was killed in 1531 when several Catholic Swiss cantons made an attack on Zurich, but his reforms lived on after him.

## John Calvin and the Reformed Tradition

John Calvin (1509–1564), a French Protestant reformer, spent most of his life as an exile in Geneva, where he assumed leadership of the church and decisively influenced the shape of the Calvinist reformed tradition. Educated at the University of Paris in classical languages and French humanism, he began the study of law at Orleans and gradually developed an interest in theology, Scripture study in original languages, and the church fathers. When he began preaching reformed doctrines, he was forced to flee France to escape persecution. He went first to Basel in 1535, where he published the first Latin edition of his monumental *Institutes of the Christian Religion* (1536), and then passed through Geneva, where he was persuaded by Guillaume Farel (1489–1565), a local reformer, to stay on and help organize the incipient reformation in that city. The two reformers proclaimed a Protestant Confession of Faith and sought to impose "godly living" upon the local populace through ecclesiastical discipline. They were opposed by the Geneva council, and Calvin was ordered to leave. Taking refuge in Strasbourg, Calvin became pastor of a French congregation, married, and produced an enlarged edition of his *Institutes*. In September 1541 he received a renewed invitation from the Geneva city council to resume his work as a religious reformer. Calvin's Ecclesiastical Ordinances were adopted by the city council in November 1541. The reformer spent the next fourteen years laying down a theocratic model of government in that city.

As pastor of the Geneva congregation, Calvin preached three times each week and often conducted weddings, baptisms, and communion services. From 1541 to 1564 he lectured regularly in Latin on the Bible to scholarly audiences, extending and revising his *Institutes*, which appeared in a fifth and final edition in 1559. The *Institutes*, which dealt with God's work as creator and redeemer, the grace of Christ, the Holy Spirit, and the external means of grace, would become the first systematic exposition of the Protestant faith. Calvin's Geneva Ordinances (1547) embodied his attempt to regulate all aspects of the Christian's personal life according to "God's law" by imposing legal penalties on breaches of Christian behavior. Fines were imposed for disorderly behavior and for nonattendance at obligatory sermons and catechetical lessons. These attempts to Christianize behavior met with considerable resistance. In 1559 Calvin founded the Geneva Academy, later to become the University of Geneva, for the promotion of reformed teaching and the education of international scholars. Refugee preachers who studied at the academy would become the first generation of Reformed Church leaders in England, Scotland, France, Germany, The Netherlands, Hungary, and Romania.

John Calvin's lasting theological legacy is found in the Second Helvetic Confession of 1566 and in the "five points of Calvinism" affirmed by the Dutch Reformed Synod of Dort (1618–1619). The Westminster Confession of the Church of Scotland (1648) is the definitive statement of faith for English-speaking Presbyterian churches. Churches in the Reformed tradition that arose under Calvin's influence have emphasized justification by faith alone, Scripture as the sole rule of faith and life, God's omnipotence and sovereignty, the depravity and lostness of human beings, and the doctrine of predestination. Reformed churches advocate a polity based on the Word of God, with parity of all ministers, and participation by both ordained ministers and lay elders in church government. Calvinism's historic differences from Lutheranism are found in its understanding of Eucharistic theology, the relationship of church and state, discipline as a mark of the church, and the doctrine of predestination. These differences have been recently narrowed through international dialogues between Lutheran and Reformed churches.

## Reformation in England

The Reformation in England, which gave rise to the Church of England as the official state church, was not the result of a religious crisis but arose from church-political circumstances. The Tudor monarch Henry VIII (1491–1547) had himself declared "the supreme head on earth of the English Church" by Parliament and the religious Convocations of Canterbury and York when it became necessary to have his marriage to Catherine of Aragon annulled. The pope excommunicated Henry, who responded with the parliamentary Act of Supremacy (1534) legally repudiating papal authority. The king, who had written a tract condemning Martin Luther, was no Protestant sympathizer but wanted to remain faithful to Catholic tradition. He did, however, dissolve the monasteries in order to gain control of their lands and wealth.

When Henry's son Edward VI (1537–1553) ascended the throne in 1547 as a child of nine, reforms of doctrine and liturgy came about with the approval of a new *Book of Common Prayer* in 1549, followed by a revised edition in 1552 incorporating distinctly Protestant features. Priests were allowed to marry. A reversal set in when the faithful Catholic Mary, daughter of Catherine of Aragon, briefly succeeded to the throne (1553–1558). She repealed the religious laws enacted under Edward VI and Henry VIII's Act of Supremacy. Mary, however, alienated public opinion by burning at the stake Protestant martyrs (Cranmer, Ridley, and Latimer), thereby preparing the way for a restoration of Protestantism.

Protestantism was restored when Elizabeth I (1533–1603) came to the throne in 1558 as a Protestant sovereign. Under Elizabeth I parliament repealed the religious laws made under Mary and passed a new Act of Supremacy (1559) that designated the monarch as supreme governor of the realm in all spiritual and ecclesiastical matters. The Act of Uniformity (1559) reinstated the *Book of Common Prayer* and mandated its use in all churches. With the adoption of the doctrinal statements of the Thirty-Nine Articles (1563), the characteristic features of Anglicanism were now all in place. Theological influences from both Lutheranism and Calvinism can be found. Tensions between Protestant and Catholic tendencies have long persisted in the Church of England.

## The Radical Reformation

Accompanying and competing with the continental reformations in Wittenberg, Zurich, and Geneva were more radical groups and movements known collectively as "the radical reformation." These were in no sense a united movement, but they formed a powerful counter-current to the dominant Protestant confessional groups granted recognition under the Religious Peace of Augsburg (1555) and later the Peace of Westphalia (1648). They were radical in the sense of going directly back to the New Testament for inspiration. Their common elements were a belief in adult believers' baptism, strict church discipline, separation of church and state (voluntary church principle), freedom of conscience against all coercion, and the practice of discipleship in distinction from mere church membership. Many but not all were pacifist. Collectively they are known as Anabaptists ("rebaptizers"), although the term is not strictly accurate in view of their belief that infant baptism is no true baptism. Anabaptists spread their faith as they fled from persecution and sent out missionaries to many parts of Europe. They were considered subversive and were uniformly denounced by Luther, Zwingli, and Calvin. Both Roman Catholics and Protestants hunted them down and persecuted them. Today they form the left wing of the Protestant Reformation .They are treated in more detail elsewhere in this encyclopedia.

## Catholic Counter-Reformation

The Counter-Reformation, also known as the Catholic Reformation, was a general movement of ecclesiastical and doctrinal reform with a strong emphasis on the renewal of missionary activity. In part it was a response to the challenge presented by the Protestant Reformation, but it also expressed aspirations toward self-reform latent within medieval Catholicism. The Council of Trent, meeting in three sessions between 1545 and 1563, clarified the formulation of official Catholic teachings and repudiated the heresies of Luther, Calvin, and Zwingli. Trent passed decrees on religious orders, regulated the powers of bishops, and established seminaries. The Society of Jesus, founded by Ignatius Loyola (1491–1556) in 1540, worked to promote the propagation of the faith and the spread of Catholic piety by opening humanistic schools around the world. Though not founded to combat Protestantism, the Jesuit Order became deeply involved in reclaiming territories lost earlier to Protestantism (so-called re-catholicization) and in extending the Catholic faith to Asia and the Americas. One of its missionary goals was to compensate by conversion or reconversion to Catholicism for losses to Protestantism in Europe. The renewed Inquisition, or Holy Office, was charged with eradicating incipient Protestantism in Italy, and in Spain it turned its attention to nominally converted Muslims and Protestants. The Catholic Counter-Reformation is credited with giving Catholicism its characteristic postmedieval profile, which continued with minor changes right up to the convening of Ecumenical Council Vatican II (1962–1965).

## Reformation and Mission

The implications and consequences of the Protestant Reformation for world mission are significant but highly controversial. The Protestant Reformation disrupted the unity of Christendom and undermined the missionary monopoly of Catholicism. While ostensibly having little to do with the church's world mission, the reformers might have claimed that they rendered an indirect service to world mission by rescuing the church's mission from distortions and abuses such as papal crusades, forced conversions, and unevangelical methods. The Reformation thus prepared a solid foundation for future evangelical missions. In fact, however, the first generation of Protestants produced few missionary fruits, apart from spreading the gospel to regions that would newly convert to Protestantism. Roman Catholics, by contrast, became much more active in world mission during the Counter-Reformation. The Jesuits sent missionaries to India, Indonesia, Japan, China, and North and South America. The older Catholic mission orders intensified their work. Some Catholics even accused Protestants of being "unapostolic" and "antimissionary." Later descendants of first generation Protestants—notably the Pietists, Moravians, and Puritans—would decisively reverse this picture by committing themselves whole-heartedly to the Great Commission, but it would take nearly two centuries for this Protestant missionary outreach to occur.

In the period after the Reformation, mission work became a battleground for polemical exchanges between Catholic theologians and their Protestant opponents. Catholics such as Jesuit Robert Bellarmine (1542–1621) maintained that Lutherans had abandoned their claim to the marks of the true church, especially *apostolicity* and *catholicity,* by sending out no missionaries and failing to plant their church in all parts of the earth. He hinted that Protestants were too timid and cowardly to undertake foreign missions. In reply, the controversial Lutheran theologian Johann Gerhard (1582–1637) asserted that Catholics could not claim to be truly *apostolic* but were merely *pseudo-apostolic,* since their missionary work was not based on the true apostolic gospel as taught in the Scriptures. Further bolstering their own weak case, Lutheran scholastic theologians argued that evangelicals could lay claim to being *apostolic* without actually doing missionary work. This was the case because the Great Commission had expired with the original apostles, who had no true successors. The papacy, with its fraudulent doctrine of the apostolic succession of bishops, they said, was no guarantee of the truth of the gospel or the validity of the church. There was no longer a mandate to obey the Great Commission in any universal sense; only the command to baptize remained valid. At most, these theologians stated, evangelical rulers were obligated to provide for the religious instruction of non-Christian subjects in their overseas colonies, according to the territorial principle of *cuius regio, eius religio*. By adopting a position that was theologically dubious and self-serving, Lutheran Orthodoxy erected a major barrier that had to be overcome before missionary work could be undertaken. In certain reformed circles, a "hyper-Calvinist" view of predestination influenced the view that human missions constituted an affront to God's sovereignty and were for that reason not to be encouraged.

## A Protestant Missionary Breakthrough

The Reformation of the sixteenth century, it is said, reformed the church's doctrines and institutions, but the renewal movements that followed transformed human hearts, released the power of the Holy Spirit, and inaugurated the priesthood of all believers. In the eighteenth century Pietism, Moravianism, Puritanism, and later Methodism demolished the arguments that Protestant scholasticism had erected against Protestant missionary activity. In 1706 two German Lutheran Pietists, Ziegenbalg and Pluetschau, were sent by King Frederick IV of Denmark to the Danish crown colony of Tranquebar in South India to begin the first Protestant foreign mission in Asia. Begun as a limited Lutheran territorial mission to the king's colonial subjects, the Tranquebar Mission overleaped its geographical boundaries, gained the enthusiastic support of the Anglican Society for Promoting Christian Knowledge (SPCK), and evolved into a widening ecumenical mission to South India. In 1732 two Moravians from Herrnhut, Dobler and Nitschmann, disciples of Count Zinzendorf, left Europe for the Danish West Indies to evangelize the slaves. They were the first of some 226 Moravians who followed, choosing the most difficult places and settling in more than sixteen fields in North America, the Caribbean, Asia, Africa, and Europe by 1760. The Great Commission was now affirmed as universally valid. Small groups of believers, moved by the Holy Spirit but not yet supported by their churches, committed themselves to preaching the gospel to the unevangelized

everywhere. Puritans in North America undertook the evangelization of Native-Americans, and their work was continued by Moravians.

By the 1790s, voluntary mission societies were springing up in Great Britain, on the European Continent, and in North America. Theological opposition to mission based on conservative Reformation viewpoints vanished and gave way to enthusiastic affirmation of the claims of the Great Commission. Attention now turned to major unresolved issues that emerged when Protestants attempted to carry out Christ's mission through fractured and competing denominational efforts.

## Missionary Ecumenism

The major reformers had not wanted to divide the "one holy catholic and apostolic church" but to cleanse and purify it. Had they been able to envisage the nineteenth century world missionary movement, they would hardly have approved of its fragmentation. It is to the credit of the modern missionary movement that it took the lead in initiating the twentieth century movement for Christian unity, the "ecumenical movement." Contradictions in missionary work became apparent on the "mission field" much sooner than in the sending churches or mission agencies, where confessional pluralism was readily accepted as a way of life. How was it possible to proclaim "one Lord, one faith and one baptism" while at the same time inviting converts to become members of a particular Western denominational church? Was it ethical to tout the virtues of one's own group while stressing the alleged defects of another competing group?

In the second half of the nineteenth century these questions led to the holding of mission conferences in many regions, but especially in Asia. These called for mission comity agreements, closer cooperation, united institutions, united Bible societies, and even united churches. At the great World Missionary Conference in Edinburgh (1910) it was recommended that the missionary goal should be to plant a single national church in each nation or region. Given that a plurality of denominational churches already existed, this recommendation proved difficult to implement. It did point to an inescapable dilemma facing world missions and set the direction for future developments. Out of the Edinburgh Conference came two critically important developments: first, formation of the International Missionary Council in 1921 (IMC), an agency promoting ecumenical missionary cooperation, headed for many years by missionary statesman John R. Mott (1865–1955), and second, the call by Bishop Charles Brent (1862–1929) for the holding of a World Conference on Faith and Order (Lausanne 1927) to deal with theological and structural obstacles to church unity. The IMC was a longtime partner of the World Council of Churches (Amsterdam, 1948), and later became an integral part of it (New Delhi 1961). Faith and Order was from the beginning a key component of the World Council of Churches and included Roman Catholics in its membership. In this way, divisions precipitated by the Reformation, which were responsible for the "scandal of disunity" in world missions, were gradually on their way to a solution. In the world Evangelical missionary movement (Lausanne Congress 1974) there has been a similar recognition that evangelism is a summons to unity and united witness, calling for a pledge "to seek a deeper unity in truth, worship, holiness and mission" (Lausanne Covenant 1974, 7).

JAMES A. SCHERER

## Further Reading

Bainton, R. H. (1952). *The Reformation of the sixteenth century.* Boston: Beacon Press.

Douglas, J. D. (Ed.) (1975). Let the earth hear His voice. *The Lausanne Covenant,* 1–9. Minneapolis: World Wide Publication.

Hogg, W. R. (1952). *Ecumenical foundations: A history of the International Missionary Council and its nineteenth century background.* New York: Harper.

Janz, D. R. (Ed.). (1999). *A Reformation reader: Primary texts with introductions.* Minneapolis, MN: Augsburg Fortress.

MacCulloch, D. (2004). *The Reformation: A history.* New York & London: Viking.

Rouse, R., & Neill, S. C. (Eds.). (1954). *A history of the Ecumenical movement 1517–1948* (2nd ed.). Philadelphia: Westminster.

Scherer, J. A. (1987). *Gospel, church and mission: Comparative studies in world mission theology.* Minneapolis, MN: Augsburg Fortress.

Scherer, J. A., & Bevans, S. B. (Eds.). (1992). *New directions in missions and evangelization: Vol. 1. Basic Statements.* Maryknoll, NY: Orbis.

## Religious Communities

Religious communities are a particular form of living the gospel in the Roman Catholic tradition, generally characterized by a communal life and profession of the vows of poverty, celibacy, and obedience. The term *religious communities* is sometimes popularly applied to another type of specialized form of Christian life identified by groups of clergy who band together specifically for missionary activity. While church law defines religious communities and religious societies differently, they are both particular ways of living the missionary dimension of Christianity in a lifelong commitment. This article will treat both. Some form of religious community has been the setting from which Roman Catholics have undertaken the majority of formal missionary activity.

### Monastic Missions

Historically, Roman Catholics have used the term *mission* in several ways. Mission has been seen as the conversion of individuals and groups with the subsequent formation of new Christian communities, but mission has also been understood as the renewal or reinvigoration of Catholic communities. Religious communities were founded to respond to both senses of mission and have played significant roles in mission leadership, service, and theory.

The church of the first and second century CE was characterized by the local Christian community and eventually the bishop as the primary locus of mission. By the 400s, monasteries of men and women monks were established in Italy and Palestine. The well-known St. Patrick, born in Scotland and captured as a slave and taken to Ireland, began mission work in Ireland after living in monastic communities in Gaul. A great impetus for mission came with Benedict of Nursia (480–547 CE) and his twin sister, Scholastica (480–543), who founded monasteries, beginning with the men's community at Monte Cassino in what is now Italy. They were encouraged by the mission emphasis given the community by one of its members, Pope Gregory the Great. Columban (sixth-century mission from Ireland to France) and Augustine of Canterbury (sixth-century mission to England) were Benedictine monks who built monasteries in their new locations. The Benedictine motto, *"ora et labor"* (pray and work), became a foundation for the promotion of knowledge and learning, preaching, liturgy, and the "civilizing" arts of agriculture, music, and architecture. Monasteries thus became a stabilizing influence at a time when Europe was overrun with warring tribes. In the nineteenth century, Charles de Montalembert, a French layman, synthesized these "civilizing" functions of religious communities in his classic six-volume *The Monks of the West* (1860–1877).

When monasteries were the main locus for mission, women also provided strong mission leadership. Frideswide (680–727 CE) founded a men and women's monastery at Oxford under the leadership of an Abbess. Walburga (710–799 CE), an Anglo-Saxon princess and niece of the apostle Boniface, joined a monastery and became noted for her healing powers. Through the writings of Hugeberc, Abbess of Hildesheim, we learn of the mission activity of Anglo-Saxon men traveling among Muslim countries.

## Mission Religious Communities in the Thirteenth Century

By the 1100s CE, as feudalism was in its first stages of decline and the Crusades became an accepted way of dealing with "the infidel" Muslim, Francis of Assisi (c. 1181–1226), in his desire to lead a life according to the Gospel, to follow the "poor Christ," and to preach Christ crucified, became the leader of a band of men, called friars or brothers, who were itinerant preachers. When Franciscans traveled throughout Christian lands, they preached to laity and encouraged them to lead a life of peace and penance. Francis was the first leader of a religious community to include a mission clause in the Rule of Life (*Regulata non Bullata*, 1216) he wrote for the brothers and specifically identified a mission approach to the Muslims: "As for the brothers who go, they can live spiritually among [the Saracens and nonbelievers] in two ways. One way is not to engage in arguments or disputes, but to be subject to every human creature for God's sake and to acknowledge they are Christians. Another way is to proclaim the word of God when they that it pleases the Lord...." Francis himself went on several trips among the Muslims in the Holy Land in Dalmatia.

Dominic of Caleruega (c. 1170–1221), in the region of Castille, was a member of a Cathedral group of clergy called the Canons Regular. He traveled with his bishop on diplomatic trips to France. There he encountered the Cathars, or Albigensians, who held heretical doctrinal teachings, including dualist, mutually exclusive principles of good and evil. Dominic discussed doctrine with one of the Cathars late into the night and by early morning had convinced the man of the errors of his ways. Shortly after this, Dominic and Diego, the Canons Regular Prior, decided to engage in itinerant preaching. After several difficulties, Dominic founded an order of preachers in Toulouse, so that fruitful preaching and instruction could be available to Christians, especially the clergy, and that the Albigensians could be approached to reform their thinking.

## Modern Mission Communities

At the time of Pope Leo X, who ruled from 1513–1521, Martin Luther (1483–1546), and the eventual break up of Western Christianity, various areas of Latin Christianity were in great need of renewal. One of Luther's concerns was that the scriptures were not made available to people, nor were the people experiencing good preaching in their parishes. This was also the time when mendicant friars were sent as missionaries to the lands Europe discovered in North and South America. New types of religious communities called "apostolic societies," which were founded during the Reformation, also went as missionaries to indigenous peoples. Though initially hampered by the church from going abroad as missionaries, in 1535 Angela Merici (1474–1540) founded the Company of St. Ursula in Brescia, Italy, to educate young girls and women, thus becoming the first women's teaching order in the Catholic Church. Several groups of Ursulines were established in Italy and France, and in 1639 three of them sailed from Dieppe to Canada to found a mission to teach Native American girls. The letters of Ursuline Marie of the Incarnation to her son in France portray her mission method of looking at the similarities between the Amerindians and the French to highlight the capacity of the Native Americans for accepting Christianity. Marie wrote dictionaries in Algonquin and Iroquois and translated the catechism into the latter language. Nineteenth-century Ursulines from Ohio worked among the Native Americans of the Rocky Mountains and by the 1960s they served in Central America.

Five years after the foundation of the Ursulines, St. Ignatius of Loyola (1491–1556), a Basque and a former army officer, began the Company of Jesus, later known as the Society of Jesus, or Jesuits, after his conversion to a deeper imitation of Christ in 1521. The Company of Jesus was to be available to the Pope to be sent anywhere in the world, "among the faithful or the infidels, where [the Pope] would judge that Jesus Christ would be served best," as the mission clause of the Society's rule expressed it. The Jesuits were one of many "apostolic" groups over the next centuries defined as a religious "society," that is, a body of priests organized for apostolic work, following a particular rule of life, and relying on alms for financial support.

Several Jesuits stand out for their mission approaches in the 1500s and 1600s: Francis Xavier (Japan), Matteo Ricci (China), Roberto de Nobili (India), and Alexandre de Rhodes (Vietnam), all of whom made great efforts to inculturate Catholicism within local customs and language. Among the well-known Jesuit missionaries sent to the Americas were Isaac Jogues and his companions, martyred in New York, the Jesuit *reductions* of Paraguay in the 1600s and 1700s, Pierre-Jean de Smet among the Native Americans in the Midwestern part of the United States, and Eusebio Kino, who worked with the Pima Indians of northern Mexico and southern Arizona. Jesuits frequently combined the natural sciences, cartography, linguistics, and mathematics as part of their evangelization work.

In the 1600s several religious communities were founded to serve the poor and those with little knowledge of Catholicism. Some of these groups soon sent their members overseas in mission, as well. Among these are the Daughters of Charity, founded by Vincent de Paul under the leadership of Louise de Marillac in 1617, and de Paul's Congregation of the Mission (the Vincentians), begun in 1625; the Congregation of the Holy Ghost (Spiritans) founded in 1703; and the Congregation of the Most Holy Redeemer (Redemptorists) started by Alphonsus Ligouri in 1732.

## Missionary Religious Societies Since the Nineteenth Century

Religious communities were typically the mission "specialists" of Roman Catholicism, whether as monks, beginning in the seventh century; Franciscans, Dominicans, and other mendicant communities beginning in the twelfth century; or Jesuits and other mission societies of clergy and women of the post-Reformation period. Once settled in new countries, religious communities often established indigenous religious communities of men or women. The new communities continued the work of mission, by seeking to revive or develop the faith of local Catholics or by traveling as missionaries to another country. Some examples of the religious societies and communities formed in the nineteenth century are the Society of Mill Hill Fathers (London, 1866– ) and the Divine Word Fathers and Brothers (Steyl, Holland, 1875– ), followed in the twentieth century by the Catholic Foreign Mission Society of America (Maryknoll, New York, 1911– ), along with the Maryknoll Sisters, the Catholic Foreign Mission Society of Korea (1975– ), and the Missionary Society of St. Paul (Nigeria, 1977– ). Though some religious communities or societies have lay missionaries affiliated with them, by the mid-twentieth century, laity also formed their own groups for missionary activity.

With offices in Rome, an international organization of women's and men's religious communities has organized SEDOS, a service of documentation and study on global mission. The group holds annual conferences to develop issues related to mission and disseminates information about mission issues, encourages mission research, and publishes the *SEDOS Bulletin*.

## Importance of Religious Communities

Though each religious community has its own spirit, or "flavor," several themes have surfaced in their mission spirituality over the centuries: pilgrim, imitation of Christ, martyrdom, and evangelical spirit. The "civilization" theme, which has been critiqued as an imposition of Western culture, emphasized the value of the human person, "raising" the status of women in society, education, and the arts. These values, along with preaching, preparation for sacraments, health care, and relieving the needs of the poor were important activities of religious communities and formed the foundation of a holistic approach to mission. Because the majority of Roman Catholic mission activity has been accomplished primarily through religious communities or societies over the centuries, the development of the lay vocation to mission did not gain serious attention until the mid-twentieth century. At the Second Vatican Council (1962–1965), missionary religious communities played a key role writing of the document on missionary activity, *Missio ad gentes* (1965).

ANGELYN DRIES

## Further Reading

Abair, A. L. (1984). A mustard seed in Montana. Recollections of the first Indian mission in Montana. *Montana. The Magazine of Western History, 34*(2), 16–31.

Amaladoss, M. (2004). The mission institutes in the new millennium. *SEDOS Bulletin 36*(7/8), 205–211.

Bevans, S. B., & Schroeder, R. P. (2004). *Constants in context. A theology of mission for today.* Maryknoll, NY: Orbis Books.

Daniel, E. R. (1975). *The Franciscan concept of mission in the High Middle Ages.* Lexington: University Press of Kentucky.

Davis, N. Z. (1995). *Women on the margins: Three seventeenth-century lives.* Cambridge, MA: Harvard University Press.

Kollman, P. V. (2005). *The evangelization of slaves and Catholic origins in eastern Africa.* Maryknoll, NY: Orbis Books.

Motte, M., & Lang, J. R. (Eds.). (1982). *Mission in dialogue: The SEDOS research seminar on the future of mission.* Maryknoll, NY: Orbis Books.

Malone, M. T. (2001). *Women & Christianity. Vol 1.* Maryknoll, NY: Orbis Books.

Vicaire, M. H. (1964). *Saint Dominic and his times* (Kathleen Pond, Trans.). New York: McGraw-Hill.

# Religious Studies

At the University of Berlin in 1901, Adolf Harnack (1851–1930) vigorously rejected establishing what today we call a "department of religious studies." Arguing that religions could not be properly understood if they were divorced from the languages and cultures that give them birth, he rejected the equivalent of undergraduate courses devoted to broad overviews of religion and religions in favor of specialized institutes where Buddhism, Christianity, Hinduism, Islam, Judaism, and other religious traditions could be studied through original texts in their total cultural context. In his view, any other approach to the study of religion would lead to dilettantism and a decline in scholarly standards.

The study of religion can be traced back to the Greek historian Xenophanes in the sixth century BCE who observed that Thracians and Ethiopians depicted their gods after their own image. However, although writers like Saint Augustine made some acute observations on the differences between religions, it was not until the late nineteenth century, after the theory of evolution gained popularity, that the academic study of religion truly began. Under the influence of Darwin, various scholars discovered what they believed to be evolutionary links between different religions. F. Max Müller (1805–1898), Edward Burnett Tayor (1832–1917), and Sir James Frazer (1854–1941) were among the founders of the "science" of comparative religion. This approach rapidly gained respectability through the immense linguistic abilities of people like Müller and soon chairs were established in several institutions, particularly in the new universities of North America.

As Louis Henry Jordan (1855–1923) showed in his *Comparative Religion* (1905), in-depth studies based on a thorough command of the appropriate languages prevailed throughout the nineteenth century. According to Eric Sharpe (b. 1933) in *Comparative Religion: A History* (1975), this approach changed in North America following World War II when Joachim Wach (1898–1955) and Mercea Eliade (1907–1988) popularized the history of religions. Wach and Eliade contributed to the development of religious studies by promoting the notion that religious studies is an autonomous discipline separate from other disciplines such as theology, history, or sociology. For them and their followers religion was a universal experience rooted in the sacred. Rejecting standard disciplinary methods for the study of religion, such as history and sociology, they proposed an approach that to critics appears more like mystification than serious scholarship.

Various North American universities claim to have founded the first religious studies department during the 1950s. Most of these departments, in particular the ones at Western Michigan University, Oberlin College, and Stanford University, taught a broad nondenominational version of Christianity. However, in the late sixties a number of these departments transformed themselves into genuine religious studies departments by embracing a wide range of world religions. The motive behind the teaching of world religions under the title of religious studies appears, as Oberlin professor and religious studies scholar James C. Dobbins has pointed out, to be closer to the vision of liberal Christianity, or Unitarianism in the case of Stanford, than the older nineteenth-century approach to comparative religion. Under the influence of the University of Chicago, religious studies became an important element in the prevailing liberal consensus and a means of promoting cultural pluralism in the United States.

Behind such a development was a genuine idealism about the need to understand the spiritual longing of all people. Because this idealism coincided with a widespread decline of interest in theology, many universities and denominational colleges transformed their theology departments into religious studies departments as a way of keeping up student enrollment. Despite this clearly secular motive, a good case can be made that the first true religious studies department was established in the 1930s at Brigham Young University to train Mormon missionaries.

In Britain the situation was somewhat different. Rather than being driven by liberal Christianity and declining enrollments in theology departments, the study of non-Christian religions grew out of the needs of the British Empire; for example, the British approach to religious studies included the study of Asian languages and the history of colonial countries. With the transformation of the Empire into the British Commonwealth and the rapid growth of Asian immigration into Britain beginning in the early 1960s, the understanding of other religious traditions as ways of life became a pressing social need. Ninian Smart (1927–2001) founded Britain's first religious studies department at the new University of Lancaster in 1967. Soon afterwards, as a result of semigovernment bodies like the Schools Council, the teaching of religious studies replaced more traditional

Biblical education in British schools, where religious instruction is a compulsory subject.

The American Academy of Religion was incorporated in 1964 and its *Journal* began publication in 1965. A year earlier the journal *Religious Studies* was founded. Various other academic journals, such as *The Journal of Religion in Africa* (1967), *Religion* (1971), and *Studies in Religion* (1971), followed, as did academic societies like the Canadian Corporation for Studies in Religion (1971). Together, these journals and societies helped establish the study of religion as a legitimate enterprise deserving departmental status in universities.

One fundamental problem for more popular forms of religious studies is the simple observation that all religions are not equal or good and that in fact, upon closer study, the major world religions are at least as different as they are similar. As Fred Welbourn (1912–1986) argued, to point out that Ugandan women regularly use umbrellas as do British housewives tells us very little about the realities of female society in Uganda and Britain. Similarly, prayer in Christianity is very different from meditation in Buddhism, and the Christian belief in the individual person cannot be equated with Buddhist claims that no person exists.

Equally important are sociological realities. It is easy to talk about pluralism in an essentially secular country, but as soon as any form of classical or traditional religious society is considered, the problem of religious toleration and assumptions about the separation of church and state become acute. For example, many religions, like Islam, do not separate religion and politics; indeed, it is often impossible to make such a separation without doing serious violence to the integrity of the religion concerned.

Another problem is the implicit racism in most formulations of religious studies. For an earlier generation of writers like Max Müller, the study of African and other "primitive" religions played a key role in developing theories of religion—for example, *The Religious System of the Ama-Zulu* (1870) by the missionary Henry Callaway (1817–1890) was considered to have made an important contribution to the field. However, during the late nineteenth and early twentieth centuries, the religions of India assumed the central place in the development of religious studies. Thus, while hundreds of North American universities offer thousands of courses on "Hinduism" and "Buddhism," only half a dozen colleges in North America offer a dozen or so courses on African religions. The neglect of African religion is a serious gap in the current state of religious studies and is hard to explain except in terms of an unrecognized racism that biases scholarship away from Africa.

Few religious studies scholars are as honest as Edward Conze (1904–1979) was when he admitted that he had never visited India or any Buddhist country for fear that the reality of life would diminish his appreciation of Buddhism. Yet even when such scholars do visit other countries, many only stay in the best hotels and consort with the Westernized elite. Perhaps this lack of solid fieldwork explains the comments of popular writer and gay activist Bruce Bawer. Bawer's 2006 *While Europe Slept*, observes that one of America's leading "experts" on Islam, Professor John L. Esposito, presents an idealized description of Islam that was in stark contrast to the Islam he experienced in daily life.

The prophetic nature of Harnack's fears can be seen by examining many popular religious studies texts. For example, most introductory textbooks are clones of John B. Noss's pioneering work, *Man's Religions,* which was published almost sixty years ago. These books have become larger by adding additional pieces of information, but they are basically descriptive accounts of religions that, like Noss's book, ignore controversial issues such as sati in Hinduism, jihad in Islam, and the social implications of Buddhist theories of identity. The only critical sections are those dealing with the Crusades in Christianity.

If introductory religious studies texts are compared with similar textbooks in established disciplines, their weaknesses become even more apparent. In other fields and disciplines students are immediately introduced to conflicting theories and distinct methods that are applied to particular problems in specific settings. Religious studies texts, on the other hand, avoid the kind of dispute that makes other areas of study interesting. Instead, there is an almost universal blandness and a generalized niceness that never raises serious issues about historical conflicts or theoretical perspectives. Such a lack of intellectual ferment, apart from some heated discussions about feminist issues and postmodernism, shows that religious studies is intellectually stagnant.

Behind the growing trivialization of the study of religion is the perception of religious studies as an interdisciplinary field. Thus, instead of mastering specific disciplines, religious studies students are introduced to fragments of many disciplines, none of which they ever really understand. As a result, far too many people become jacks of all trades and masters of none. Among Indologists, such people claim to be students of Islam, but among scholars of Islam they claim to be Indologists. In reality, they simply dabble in both areas. At the undergraduate level this may not do much harm, but when these students become academics, serious problems, such as above-average instances of plagiarism, emerge that turn religious studies into dilettantism, as Haranck feared.

Given this dreary situation, perhaps the only solution is to replace existing religious studies departments with well-organized religious studies programs in which scholars are located in specific disciplinary departments, such as anthropology, history, sociology, and philosophy, where they have to compete with other scholars who are masters of their trade. Instead of encouraging the present state of intellectual apartheid, religious studies ought to be replaced with the study of religion within distinct disciplines. If this is done, we may escape the dilettantism Harnack feared and begin to produce works that really address religious issues in our rapidly changing world.

IRVING HEXHAM

See also Buddhism; Culture; Indigenous Religions; Islam; Journals; Mormonism; Philosophy; Racism; Sociology

## Further Reading

Hexham, I. (1988). *Text on Zulu Religion.* Lewiston, NY: Edwin Mellen Press.

Hexham, I. (1991). African religions and the nature of religious studies. In K. K. Klostermaier & L. W. Hurtado (Eds.), *Religious studies: Issues, prospects and proposals* (pp. 361–379). Atlanta, GA: Scholars Press.

Jordan, L. H. (1905). *Comparative religion.* Edinburgh, UK: T & T Clark.

Kippenberg, H. G. (2002). *Discovering religious history in the modern age.* Princeton, NJ: Princeton University Press.

Kraemer, H. (1960). *World cultures and world religions.* London: Lutterworth Press.

Ratzinger, J. (2003). *Truth and tolerance.* San Francisco, Ignatius Press.

Rudolph, K. (1985). *Historical fundamentals and the study of religion.* London: Collier MacMillan.

Sharpe, E. J. (1975). *Comparative religion: A history.* London: Duckworth.

Smart, N. (1958). *Reasons and faiths.* London: Routledge & Kegan Paul.

Wiebe, D. (1999). *The politics of religious studies.* New York: St. Martin's Press.

## Reverse Mission

"Reverse mission" refers to the sending of missionaries to Europe and North America by churches and Christians from the non-Western world, particularly Africa, Asia, and Latin America, which were at the receiving end of Catholic and Protestant missions as mission fields from the sixteenth to the late twentieth century. The enterprise is aimed at re-evangelizing regions that were once the heartlands of Christianity and the vanguards of missionary movements. It is a significant phenomenon with many social, political, and missiological implications.

Non-Western churches have begun to dictate the pace of growth and the essential features of world Christianity. Equally important, despite lower economic development and more recent contact with Christianity, the growth of missionary endeavors from the non-Western world, which rapidly gained momentum in the 1990s, has brought substantial geographical and demographic changes in world Christianity. This has contributed to a shift of the center of allegiance to Christianity from the Western to the non-Western world. The traditional missions fields have now become the mission bases of renewed efforts to re-evangelize the secularized societies of Europe and North America.

## Historical Background

Until the late twentieth century, Catholic missionary endeavors, which intensified greatly after the loss of a large part of Europe to sixteenth-century Protestantism, and Protestant missions, which began operating in 1792, defined the nature, scope, and history of Christian missions. When William Carey, an English Baptist minister, wrote his 1791 tract, *An Enquiry into the Obligations of Christians to Use Means for the Conversion of the Heathens,* a treatise that laid the foundation of Protestant missions, the people he believed needed the "civilizing" missions of Europe were in China, India, Japan, Australia, and the African continent.

With the control of financial and human resources and the unidirectional flow of these resources from north to south, the Western churches dominated and shaped the direction of the missionary movement. Accounts of European explorers, voyagers, and missionaries seemed to them to justify the need for redemptive missions from the West toward the societies of Asia, Africa, and South America. Eventually, in mission studies and practice, a distinction was created between the economically advanced Western world and the developing world, and between what Christian missionaries saw as complex Western societies and simple non-Western societies.

The emergence of indigenous Christian movements in the non-Western world in the late nineteenth century provided the background for the reverse direction of missions. For example, the Ethiopian churches in western and southern Africa translated the Scriptures and biblical symbols into their distinctive cultural paradigms. This new Christianity rejected Western-style missions, especially liturgies produced in Western languages and religious symbols fashioned from Western cultural norms. With the emergence of more educated leadership in the 1960s, non-Western Christians began to reflect on their own experience of the Gospel and to struggle against Western prejudices.

In 1971, the Western missions circle was stunned when Rev. John Gatu, a leader of the Presbyterian Church in East Africa, called for a moratorium on Christian missions from the Western world. Other third world Christian leaders supported this suggestion because they believed that it would break the circle of dependency on the Western church and create room for self-development. This process of empowerment of the third-world church brought changes in Western mission practices. Consequently, cooperation and partnership were promoted as new mission strategies at the International Congress on World Evangelization in Lausanne, Switzerland, in July 1974, and in subsequent congresses. Third-world Christians participated in these congresses and held other continental and regional conferences, which defined their own challenges and global opportunities.

## Causes

By the late 1970s, substantial demographic and social changes had resulted in homogenous churches among Koreans, Chinese, Africans, and other ethnic groups in Europe and North America. These churches used indigenous languages and ministered to the specific cultural needs of their immigrant members. By the 1990s, many of these churches had begun to define their missions as witnessing communities to the Western church, which was waning numerically and spiritually. In the closing decade of the twentieth century, reverse missions gradually gained ascendancy. Several factors were responsible for this.

First, economic decline and political conflicts intensified the migrations of Africans, Asians, and Latin Americans to the developed economies of the Western world in the late twentieth century. For example, in Germany at the turn of the twenty-first century, there were over 1,000 churches of migrant communities, over 200 of them founded by Africans. In England, there was a rapid rise from fewer than 100 churches in the 1970s to over 1,000 churches of migrants by the late 1990s. The number of Filipino immigrants in the United States,

most of whom were Christians, rose from 343,060 in 1970 to 1,406,770 in 1990, and 2,503,417 in 2001. Confronted by the secularization of Western society and the decline of church attendance and public piety, these migrants took up a revivalist agenda and defined themselves as historic Bible-based Christians. They believed that there was a divine task in their migration, namely, to bring the Gospel back to the former mission-sending countries of Europe and North America.

Second, the founding of the Third World Missions Association (TWMA) in Portland, Oregon, in 1989 enhanced the capacity of mission-sending agencies in Africa, Asia, and Latin America and transformed non-Western world missions into a global force in world Christianity. For example, while some Arab countries refused to admit Western missionaries, they remained open to African and Asian missionaries. Additional networking for evangelization and cross-cultural missions was provided by the AD 2000 and Beyond Movement, a global effort of world evangelization directed by third-world Christian leaders.

## Third-world Missions

By the mid-1990s the non-Western world was sending missionaries, most of them non-professional, to re-evangelize Europe. A notable example is the Overseas Filipino Workers (OFW), which represented the Filipino diaspora, one of the most successful diaspora Evangelical missionary movements in the Middle East, Europe, and North America. Other effective institutional diaspora movements exist among the Chinese and the Koreans, and Evangelical Christians have utilized such platforms for missionary enlistment.

The Universal Church of the Kingdom of God, a Brazilian church, had established 221 branches by 1995, 87 of which were in Europe and North America. The Korean missionary movement has also been very successful. By 2000, a total of 471 missionaries were serving in the United States and Germany, representing 11.7 percent of the Korean foreign missionary workforce. Likewise, a Nigeria-based church, Deeper Life Bible Church, has been evangelizing effectively among whites and migrants since the mid-1980s.

## Implications

By the late twentieth century, as Western churches were declining in number and in missionary significance, the impact of non-Western missions to Europe and North America became significant. Reverse missions brought a major shift in mission understanding to the Western church and helped members to appreciate the multicultural nature of Christianity in the twentieth century. Missions changed to become multilateral rather than unilateral, the number of apostolic itinerant missionaries grew, and missions moved from cultural transplantation to contextualization. Reverse missions offer the old heartlands of Christianity a model for renewal and demonstrate the need for a structural reform of the Western church to grapple with the challenges of migration.

MATTHEWS A. OJO

*See also* Christendom; Empire; Europe; Mission Methods and Strategy; North America; Paternalism; Protestant Churches; Roman Catholic Church

## Further Reading

Adogame, A., & Weisskoppel, C. (Eds.). (2005). *Religion in the context of African migration.* Bayreuth, Germany: Bayreuth African Studies Series, No 75.

Dempster, M. W., Klaus, B. D., & Petersen, D. (Eds.). (1999). *The globalization of Pentecostalism.* Oxford, UK: Regnum Books International.

Freston, P. (2001). The transnationalisation of the Universal Church of God. In A. Corten & R. Marshall-Fratani (Eds.), *Between Babel and Pentecost: Transnational Pentecostalism in Africa and Latin America.* Bloomington: Indiana University Press.

Hanciles, J. J. (2003). Migration and mission: Some implications for the twenty-first-century church. *International Bulletin of Missionary Research, 27*(4), 146–153.

Jaffarian, M. (2004). Are there more non-Western missionaries than Western missionaries? *International Bulletin of Missionary Research, 28*(3), 131–132.

Jaffarian, M. (2002). The statistical state of the missionary enterprise. *Missiology, 30*(1), 15–32.

Jenkins, P. (2002). *The next Christendom: The coming of global Christianity.* New York: Oxford University Press.

Johnstone, P., & Mandryk, J. (2001). *Operation world.* Carlisle, UK: Paternoster Lifestyle.

Moon, S. S. C. (2003). Recent Korean missionary movement; a record of growth, and more growth needed. *International Bulletin of Missionary Research, 27*(1), 11–16.

Nelson, M. L. (1976). *Readings in Third World missions: A collection of essential documents.* South Pasadena, CA: William Carey Library.

Ojo, M. A. (1997). The dynamics of indigenous charismatic missionary enterprises in West Africa. *Missionalia, 25*(4), 537–561.

Pantoja, L. Jr, Tira, S. J., & Wan, E. (2004). *Scattered; The Filipino global presence.* Manila, Philippines: LifeChange Publishing.

Ter Haar, G. (1995). Strangers in the Promised Land: African Christians in Europe. *Exchange, 24*(1), 1–33.

Ter Haar, G. (1998). *Halfway to paradise: African Christians in Europe.* Cardiff, UK: Cardiff Academic Press.

Van Dijk, R. (1997). From camp to encompassment: Discourses of transsubjectivity in the Ghanaian Pentecostal diaspora. *Journal of Religion in Africa, 27,* 135–160.

Walls, A. F. (2002). Mission and migration: The diaspora factor in Christian history. *Journal of African Christian Thought, 5*(2), 3–11.

Warner, S. R., & Wittner, J. G. (Eds.). (1998). *Gatherings in diaspora: Religious communities and the new immigration.* Philadelphia, PA: Temple University Press.

## Revival

The birth of the Protestant missionary movement was closely connected with the Evangelical Revival of the eighteenth century. An emphasis on revival within Protestantism was associated with disenchantment with a doctrinal conflict between confessional groups that engendered conflict over status and power in society. Revival emphasized the religion of the heart, the need for every person to acknowledge his or her sinful state and to seek salvation through repentance and faith in Christ, a transformation that was made possible through the outpouring of the Holy Spirit.

Although this work of the Spirit occurred within individuals, it could move through whole communities, converting large groups of people for whom religion had previously been a matter of external observance. New doubts about civilization, culture, and civility as necessary prerequisites for Christian faith created a new sense of missionary responsibility. Conversion to Christ was no longer seen as essentially a slow educational process in which a whole society became institutionally Christian. It could occur wherever men and women were born again by the Spirit. This allowed, at least in theory, for a new egalitarianism in which all societies were seen as alien from the Gospel, but in which people of all cultures and races could equally respond to the Gospel. It engendered a concern for mission to the "heathen," who, however benighted they may seem, were capable, simply on the basis of their humanity, of responding to the Gospel.

Pietist groups such as the Moravians were the first Protestants to become actively interested in converting non-Christians, and they established work in South India, among slave groups in the Caribbean, and among both settlers and Native Americans in the British colonies of North America. The Moravians also had an impact on the Evangelical awakening in Britain and North America, which stimulated the establishment of missionary societies and church boards of foreign mission and a concern for worldwide evangelism. The Evangelical and humanitarian campaign to abolish the slave trade and slavery was animated by the sense of a common identity of all human beings and an understanding of "freedom in Christ" as both spiritual and physical liberation.

Revival was thus important in the creation of a modern missionary movement, voluntary in nature and independent of state support or money. Revival was also important for recruiting missionaries, men and women often of relatively humble backgrounds whose lives had been renewed and transformed, and who had a burden to preach the good news to others, both in their own countries and abroad. As well as providing a general philosophy of mission, revivals (in the restricted sense of specific campaigns aimed at converting large numbers of people to religion) also continued to be important for missionary recruitment: The Moody and Sankey campaigns in the second half of the nineteenth century in the United States and the United Kingdom, as well as Holiness movements such as the Keswick movement in England, served to alert reawakened Christians, including university graduates, to the need for missionary work. Some of the great missionary figures of the late nineteenth and early twentieth centuries—John Mott in the United States, William Temple Gairdner of Egypt, George Pilkington of Uganda, and Amy Carmichael of Dohnavur in South India—were people whose lives had been touched by revival and whose commitment to mission service stemmed from that experience.

A concern for revival was also deeply inscribed in the formation of the churches that emerged from the missionary endeavor. Revival became an important technique in preaching and evangelizing "pagan" communities. Its emphasis on the transformation of the heart and the empowerment of the Spirit to enable that transformation was a factor in the primary evangelism of many Protestant missions, though it tended to supplement rather than replace the importance of catechetical training and baptismal preparation, which involved literacy and education. In Africa, the revival campaigns of William Waddy Harris, a Grebo (Liberian) evangelist, emphasized not education but a conversion that included the rejection of the traditional religion and its idolatrous symbols.

Such revivals were the culmination of Evangelical mission teaching over a hundred years. But missionaries, even those from a revivalist tradition, were also afraid of the subversive nature of revival as they experienced it in the mission field, where it could challenge missionary power and authority. It could create tensions between missionaries and their converts, especially when they challenged the faith and vocation of the missionary. Nevertheless, missionaries continued to pray for revival, at least in theory. Because they were often particularly concerned that the church of the second generation would settle into a comfortable orthodoxy and outward conformity, their revival preaching in these circumstances emphasized that the material gains of missionary adherence (such as education, the status of receiving a Christian name in baptism, and the opening up of job prospects) were not the essence of Christian conversion. As in Europe and America, when a revival did occur in an African mission church, it often served to recruit volunteers for Christian service and evangelism, both in the local community and in missionary endeavor.

An important movement, which demonstrates many of these classic features, is known as the "'East African Revival," the "Revival fellowship," or the "Balokole" (the Saved people). This revival occurred first within the Rwanda Mission, an autonomous mission of the Church Missionary Society, which worked from the early 1920s in the Belgian colony of Rwanda-Urundi (now the independent states of Rwanda and Burundi) and in southwest Uganda. The Rwanda Mission was a conservative Evangelical society with a strong emphasis on biblical authority and an insistence on the experience of conversion among its missionaries. It saw itself as upholding the ideals of evangelicalism against the assaults of liberalism and modernism in Western Christianity. The mission was critical of the (Anglican) Church of Uganda in whose diocese its missions were situated. The Church of Uganda had been in existence for some fifty years, born of martyrdom and a revival spirit created in the 1890s by George Pilkington, a lay missionary. But many Rwanda missionaries (and indeed others within the CMS Uganda mission) felt that the pioneering spirit of the church in Uganda had been slowly undermined by its position as a quasi-established church within colonial Ugandan society. In particular, what was seen as the poor spiritual life of the growing number of African clergy, lay catechists, and nominally Protestant political leaders presented a depressing scene.

Revival as a solution to this situation began in the late 1920s. An alliance between a missionary of the Rwanda Mission, Joe Church, based at Gahini in Rwanda, and a prominent lay figure in Uganda, Simeoni Nsibambi, created an eager expectation of a Spirit-filled renewal of Christian life. Nsibambi recruited Ugandans to assist Dr. Church in his hospital work at Gahini. It was here, in 1935, that an outpouring of revival was experienced, first among the hospital staff and then among the local population, manifest in confessions of sin, all-night prayer meetings, and enthusiastic praise and worship. Joe Church, rather like John Wesley, proved to a gifted organizer who was able to channel the enthusiasm of revival into teams of preachers who went far and wide throughout Rwanda, Burundi, and Uganda, calling people to repentance and salvation. In a racially stratified society, the collaboration of white missionaries with black converts in these revival teams was a great witness.

Revival inevitably provoked controversy, not least within the Rwanda Mission itself. All wanted revival; not all were convinced that this loosening of racial and hierarchical distinctions was to be welcomed. In Uganda itself, the Ugandan church was deeply skeptical of the arrogance and incivility (as they saw it) of some of the revivalists. Revivalists were uncompromising in their denunciation of "sin" wherever they saw it, whatever the status of the sinner. They offended many by their insensitivity to traditional cultural values and their open condemnation of polygamists and of those who made compromises with traditional religious values (for example, by having a shrine dedicated to one of the traditional divinities in their garden). The fact that revival encouraged African initiative and attracted many people with high educational qualifications and leadership qualities enabled it to have an impact far and wide in East Africa, among Presbyterians, Methodists, and Lutherans, as well as among Anglicans.

Although eschewing direct political involvement, the East African Revival became a major force in the late colonial period. It helped to define the spirituality of Protestant Christianity in the early years of independence in the 1960s. The Revival denounced the Mau Mau movement in colonial Kenya as a neo-pagan movement, but was equally critical of the violence of the colonial soldiers. It has been equally critical of authoritarian and corrupt independence regimes. Archbishop Janani Luwum of Uganda (murdered during the Amin regime in 1977), Bishop Henry Okullu and Archbishop David Gitari of Kenya, and Bishop Josiah Kibira of the Lutheran Church of Tanzania are all important church figures whose lives were steeped in the ethos of the East African Revival. Revival was also important in giving women an opportunity for public Christian ministry and for encouraging their more general participation in public life, though still within the structure of what was generally a patriarchal society.

It is remarkable that the East African Revival has strengthened rather than undermined the mission-established churches, and has generally opposed the creation of separatist churches. On the other hand, the revival in East Africa has had a tendency to divide into rival sects that contend for the purity of the revivalist ideal. At the heart of the East African Revival is the local fellowship, in which the 'ab'oluganda' (brothers and sisters) are strengthened and supported in their faith and life. The fellowships are remarkable for their strong discipline and ethical rigor. One of the persistent criticisms that the older Balokole Revivalists make of the newer charismatic groups, which have proliferated in East Africa since the 1960s, is that they lack discipline and make too many compromises with the secular world.

The modern Pentecostal or Charismatic movement is now the dominant (or at least the most active) form of Christianity in many parts of the global South. It has adopted many of the forms of older revivalism in its styles of worship, its demands of personal transformation, and its conformity to strict ethical standards. But it has also often found ways that eluded older styles of missionary work of adapting local cultures and speaking to the needs and aspirations of both traditional culture and of the globalizing aspirations of modern youth. In this way revival continues to be a major component of the contemporary global missionary movement.

KEVIN WARD

*See also* Africa; Conversion; Evangelicalism; Fundamentalism; Moravians; Pentecostal and Charismatic Movements; Pietism; Prayer; Protestant Churches; Slavery; Theology

## Further reading:

Bell, J. S. (Ed.). (1998). *The D. L. Moody collection: The highlights of his writings, sermons, anecdotes, and life story.* Chicago: Moody Press

Keswick Ministries. (2007). Welcome to Keswick Ministries. Retrieved May 29, 2007, from http://www.keswickministries.org/pages/home.asp

Lloyd, A. B. (1921). Dayspring in Uganda, Retrieved May 29, 2007 from http://anglicanhistory.org/africa/dayspring.html

Shank, D. A. (1994). *Prophet of modern times: Thought of William Wade Harris.* Leiden, Netherlands: Brill.

# Revolution

The global reach of Christian missionary activity accelerated during the twentieth century, a time in which unprecedented historical developments, some of which could be described as revolutionary, evoked a variety of responses from missionary organizations. Mission studies approached the issue of revolution in two very different ways. On the one hand, there was an effort to understand what happens to Christian mission within situations of rapid social change that could be described as revolutionary. On the other hand, there was a renewed interest in the socially transformative nature of the Christian message itself. Both approaches contribute to an understanding of Christian mission as a social process and of the Christian message as a transformative force.

## Opposing Definitions

Within the paradigm of modernity, the term "revolution" is generally associated with movements to overthrow existing governments through social pressure that finally takes the form of armed action by a significant number of people. The classic use of the term describes social processes as varied as the American and French revolutions in the eighteenth century and the Russian revolution in the twentieth century. For thinkers like Karl Marx (1818–1883), history itself moves forward through revolutions. However, many European Christian leaders and thinkers opposed revolution, in part because the French and Russian revolutions were critical of and even hostile toward established Christianity.

During the second part of the twentieth century, "revolution" came to be used as a description of transformative processes that deeply affect cultural and social structures at their base and that are not necessarily the result of an intentional short-term political move. For example, the term is used to describe both the Industrial Revolution in Europe at the end of the eighteenth century and the social consequences of the application of technology in communication or transportation. In the same way, the effects of urbanization and industrialization on non-Western societies were perceived as revolutionary. French sociologist Jacques Ellul (1912–1994) considered it important to keep the distinction between social processes that were the logical development of the application of science and technology on a massive scale and social processes in which a human decision and an intentional effort of the will were applied to achieve power and produce social change in the search for a more just society. In relation to Marxist revolutions that were considered radical, Ellul pointed out that they simply followed the logic of modernity: "Instead of a revolution which reverses the logical course of history, we have a revolution which is the climax of this process of logical development." (Ellul 1989, 24–25)

The use of the term "revolution" was also influenced by the revolt of peoples, nations, and races against the advance and domination of the West, especially in the struggles against European colonialism in Asia and Africa which developed after the World War I. During the Cold War the world became divided between the Western capitalist societies of Europe and North America and the Eastern socialist societies led by the USSR. The emerging countries that formed a block that came to be called the third world had a positive attitude toward the idea of revolution. The new countries formed in Africa and Asia were the result of revolutionary anticolonial struggles, and Latin American countries were also facing a time of rapid social change for which traditional social structures proved to be obsolete.

Because colonialism had formed the background of missionary activity during the nineteenth century and the first part of the twentieth, missiologists had the task of interpreting the new situation. They had to navigate between the conservative European Christian tradition, which was usually weary of revolutions, and Christians in the young emerging churches of the third world for whom revolution was necessary, and which therefore prompted individual Christians as well as churches to take part in it. Among the missiologists who explored this complex subject were Max Warren, Lesslie Newbigin, Stephen Neill, and Roger Mehl. One of their approaches was to examine the Christian message in the period of early Christianity before Christendom to determine its social significance.

## Early Christian Mission

The record of the initial stage of Christian mission within the first century, as it is found in the Gospels and the Book of Acts in the New Testament, points to the transformative nature of the Christian message and way of life. For instance, when Paul and Silas, two of the earliest Christian missionaries, arrived in the Greco-Roman city of Thessalonica, some people felt disturbed by their presence and denounced them to the local authorities with this commentary: "These people who have been turning the world upside down have come here also" (Acts 17:6).

The Book of Acts provides two other examples of the potential of the Christian message for creating social disturbance—the stories of its introduction in the important cities of Philippi and Ephesus. In both cases the record offers details of how some social groups were affected by the presence of the missionaries and reacted by organizing riots. In the case of Philippi (Acts 16:11–40) it was the reaction of the owners of a slave girl who, as a result of an exorcism, stopped her diviner activity: "But when her owners saw that their hope of making money was gone, they seized Paul and Silas and dragged them into the marketplace before the authorities" (16:19). The accusation was that the missionaries were Jews and were "disturbing our city...advocating customs that are not lawful for us as Romans to adopt and observe" (16:20–21). A riot starts against the missionaries and the authorities intervene and put them in prison; only later do the authorities recognize that their procedure has not been according to law.

In Ephesus (Acts 19:23–41), the acceptance of the Christian message prompts people to abandon the use of silver images of the goddess Artemis. A silversmith named Demetrius warns workers of the same trade that if the activity of the missionary Paul continues, "there is danger not only that this trade of ours may come into disrepute but also that the temple of the great goddess Artemis will be scorned and she will be deprived of her majesty" (19:27); a riot starts and the authorities have to intervene. Then, as well as in the following twenty centuries of history, as missiologist Max Warren (1904–77) pointed out, it has been impossible to disentangle the Christian message from the cultural and social vehicles that carry it across cultures; because of this, mission has a social impact that may become revolutionary (Warren 1955, 1967).

## Colonial Mission

The transformation of the Roman Empire due to the missionary expansion of the Christian Church was the subject of intense research during the final two decades of the twentieth century. The evangelization of the empire allowed the church to spread its influence, which accounted for a slow but significant transformation during the three centuries that preceded the conversion of Emperor Constantine. Through his Edict of Milan in 313, he introduced an attitude of tolerance that contrasted with the persecutions with which previous emperors had tried to stop the Church's growth and influence.

With the establishment of the Church as the imperial official religion, a new era started in which there was an increasing use of military action and conquest for the missionary purpose of converting people to the Christian faith. The apex of this fusion of mission and empire came in the sixteenth century through the Iberian conquest and the evangelization of the Americas. The colonial church that developed as a result provided an ideological legitimation of the conquest and of the dominion of Spanish and Portuguese conquerors over native populations. The Church became a symbol of the colonial establishment and exercised social control through the Inquisition. During the revolutionary independence movements of the late eighteenth and early nineteenth centuries, with very few exceptions, the official position of the Church was to oppose and condemn revolution.

The Iberian expansion in the Americas marked the beginning of a western European expansion that continued when Great Britain became the dominant global empire. Mission and empire were not so closely united in the Protestant missions of the nineteenth century, but missionaries still tended to support the imperial advance of their nation and worked within that frame. It is therefore understandable that theoreticians and leaders of revolutions such as Marx, Engels, and Lenin would tend to see revolutionary movements as hostile to Christian mission.

During the twentieth century the revolt of Asian, African, and Latin American peoples against the European colonial powers and the imperial role of the United States sparked a wave of self-criticism among missions. Max Warren said, "Mission has to be conducted in a world of feverish nationalism, of revolt against one kind of imperialism, of the threats of new kinds of imperialism. And the Church is inextricably bound up in the historical processes which have produced the day in which we live" (Warren 1955, 39).

Christian mission, although it was imposed through the colonial advance from Europe during the nineteenth and twentieth centuries, played an undeniable role in the sweeping modernization of some Asian and African societies. Leaders of these revolutions were frequently inspired by Christian ideas on human dignity learned in missionary schools, even though they adopted anti-Christian ideologies as vehicles for political action. African missiologist Lamin Sanneh, who examined in depth the cultural impact of Bible translations into African vernacular languages, describes a paradoxical effect: "the paradox of missionary agency in promoting the vernacular and thus inspiring indigenous confidence at a time when colonialism was demanding paternal overlordship" (Sanneh 1989, 128).

## Liberation Theologies

The issue of revolution was an important component of the theologies of liberation. In fact, a theology of revolution was the antecedent of the theologies that during the 1970s and 1980s proposed a new role for Christians

The Cathedral Asuncion in Paraguay, South America. *Courtesy of istockphoto.com.*

in revolutionary situations. Two currents of thought and action within Christianity were influential in the development of these theologies. On the Protestant side, the role of the World Council of Churches (WCC), which was formed in Amsterdam in 1948, was decisive. In its Second Assembly in 1954 the idea of a "responsible society" was central, and the final document affirmed that such a society included the freedom of all peoples "to control, to criticize and to change their governments" and that there should be an equitable distribution of power throughout society (Neely 1977, 117).

In 1955, the WCC sponsored a ten-year series of conferences under the title "Christian Responsibility Toward Areas of Social Change," to which theologian Richard Shaull (1919–2002) was invited. A Presbyterian missionary in Brazil, Shaull proposed that in the Latin American situation of contrasts between extreme poverty and abusive wealth, only structural changes could bring an end to misery and create a more just society and that the role of Christians was to work for those changes. The rising expectations of the poor were met by the resistance of the dominant elites, which used military force and social repression to perpetuate their privileges.

Development was the strategy recommended by the United States and adopted by most Latin American governments. However, development required structural changes that only a radical revolution could bring. The social tensions in the region were accentuated by the triumph of the Cuban revolution in 1959 and its adop-

tion of radical structural changes following a socialist pattern. In the writings of Shaull and a new generation of Latin American Protestant theologians, "revolution" was eventually replaced by "liberation."

On the Roman Catholic side a decisive factor was the Vatican II Council and the effort of Pope John XXIII to "update" the Church (*aggiornamento*). This was especially important for Latin America where half the Catholics of the world live. The return to biblical sources of the faith and the more ecumenical spirit fostered by the Council created an atmosphere in which bishops and theologians, concerned with the need to respond to rapid social change in Latin America, emphasized a missionary presence among the poor that was to bring what the Conference of Bishops of Medellín in Colombia in 1968 called "a preferential option for the poor." Pope John XXIII also recalled and renewed the social teachings of the Catholic Church in his encyclicals *Mater et Magistra* (1961) and *Pacem in Terris* (1963). The second one opened the way to acknowledging that a distinction could be made between "false philosophies," such as Marxism, and historical movements inspired by those philosophies that could evolve and be influenced by Christians (Smith 1991, 111).

Theologians of liberation proposed that a scientific aspect of Marxist analysis could be used to interpret the social conditions, but that the struggle of Christians for a radical revolution could be inspired by the imperatives of the Gospel, the Christian teachings on justice, peace, equality, and liberation. The dilemma faced by

**387**

Christians was not between underdevelopment and development but between economic dependence of the capitalist economies and liberation through revolution. Gustavo Gutiérrez (b. 1928), a Peruvian priest and theologian, wrote, "To support the social revolution means to abolish the present status quo and to attempt to replace it with a qualitatively different one; it means to build a just society based on new relationships of production; it means to attempt to put an end to the domination of some countries by others. The liberation of these countries, social classes and people undermines the very foundation of the present order" (Gutiérrez 1988, 48).

The most radical forms of this theology, struggling to overcome the scruples of a Christian conscience regarding the violent aspect of revolutions, attempted to develop a theory of "just revolution" by adopting medieval scholastic arguments in support of a "just war." Argentinian Methodist José Míguez Bonino (b. 1924) pointed out that the history of social change throughout the world "offers instances of both objectivistic procrastination and voluntaristic adventurism." In the face of these dilemmas he proposes an ethical thesis: "In carrying out needed structural changes we encounter an inevitable tension between the human cost of their realization and the human cost of their postponement. The basic ethical criterion is the maximizing of universal human possibilities and the minimizing of human costs" (Miguez Bonino 1983, 107). In the decades of the 1970s and 1980s, many Roman Catholic missionaries to Latin America and a few Protestant ones immersed themselves among the poor, took part in social revolutions, and in some cases became martyrs in the social struggle.

## Mission from Below

In the twenty-first century a shift in the demographic presence of Christians in the world has affected the direction of Christian missionary action. In terms of engagement in Christian mission, the initiative is now in the hands of Asian, African, and Latin-American churches; they are spiritually vigorous and numerically strong, while the presence and influence of Christian churches in Europe is declining. On the other hand, although a revolutionary view of history failed to achieve its aims, the result of the fall of Marxism, symbolized by the fall of the Berlin wall in 1989, globalization has accelerated some of the trends that were described as rapid social change in the 1960s.

The agenda for Christian mission proposed by liberation theologies needs a drastic revision. In its impulse and its patterns Christian mission today is increasingly becoming "mission from below," as it was in the first century. Any transforming or revolutionary impact will be the result not of political, military, or technological strength but of conviction about the power of the Gospel to change human beings and make them servants of others like their Master Jesus Christ.

SAMUEL ESCOBAR

## Further Reading

Castro, E. (1975). *Amidst revolution.* Belfast, Ireland: Christian Journals Limited.

Ellul, J. (1971*). Autopsy of revolution.* New York: Knopf.

Ellul, J. (1989). *The presence of the kingdom.* Colorado Springs, CO: Helmers & Howard.

Gutiérrez, G. (1988). *A theology of liberation.* Maryknoll, NY: Orbis.

Jenkins, P. (2002). *The next Christendom. The coming of global Christianity.* Oxford, UK: Oxford University Press.

Klaiber, J. S. J. (1998). *The church, dictatorships and democracy in Latin America.* Maryknoll, NY: Orbis.

Mehl, R. (1970). *The sociology of Protestantism.* London: SCM Press.

Míguez Bonino, J. (1983). *Toward a Christian political ethics.* London: SCM Press.

Neely, A. P. (1977). Protestant antecedents of the Latin American theology of liberation. Unpublished doctoral dissertation, American University, Washington, DC.

Neill, S. (1966). *Colonialism and Christian mission.* New York, NY: McGraw-Hill.

Newbigin, L. (1986). *Foolishness to the Greeks. The Gospel and Western culture.* Grand Rapids, MI: Eerdmans.

Sanneh, L. (1989). *Translating the message. The missionary impact on culture.* Maryknoll, NY: Orbis.

Smith, C. (1991). *The emergence of liberation theology. Radical religion and social movement theory.* Chicago: The University of Chicago Press.

Stark, R. (1996). *The rise of Christianity. a sociologist reconsiders history.* Princeton, NJ: Princeton University Press.

Walls, A. (1996). *The missionary movement in Christian history: Studies in the transmission of faith.* Maryknoll, NY: Orbis.

Warren, M. A. C. (1955). *Caesar the beloved enemy. Three studies in the relation of church and state.* London: SCM Press.

Warren, M. (1967). *Social history and Christian mission,* London: SCM Press.

Yates, T. (1994). *Christian mission in the twentieth century.* Cambridge, UK: Cambridge University Press.

# Roman Catholic Church

The etymology of the name "Roman Catholic Church" is anomalous in that the two adjectives are in contradiction with one another. *Roman* refers to a particular place. *Catholic* denotes something universal. When one goes deeper, the tension between them is important if one is to understand how the church that claims half the world's Christians as members understands itself.

*Catholic,* we are usually told, comes from the Greek word *katholikos* (universal) and connotes its "extensive" or "geographic" meaning. Broken down further are the words *kata* (according to) *holon* (whence the English word "whole"). *Kata* is most familiar to readers of the New Testament as the preposition used to name a gospel, as in the phrase, "the Gospel 'according to' Luke" (*kata loukon*). The elided version of the two words *kath holon* also has a theological or intensive meaning, "according to the whole [gospel or Christ]." In the extensive sense of the word, *the Catholic Church* is the term favored for speaking of the universal church spread from Lyons to Bagdad, from Jerusalem and Alexandria to Rome. The intensive sense of the word denoted a local church recognized by other churches in the nascent communion of churches as one that preserved the whole gospel as the message *of* Jesus and *about* Jesus as the Christ, the universal savior. The overseers (*episkopoi,* bishops) of the principal churches did this by judging that catholicity and three key characteristics of a genuine church were present ("unity" [with the universal church], "holiness," and "apostolicity").

In this context the "Roman" Catholic Church claimed: (1) it was founded by the apostles Peter and Paul, (2) that Peter was its first bishop, (3) that Peter had been given primacy over "the Twelve" by Christ, and (4) that his successors continued to enjoy that primacy. Over time, this primacy came to be understood as entailing the Bishop of Rome's divinely conferred ministry to symbolize and affect the unity of the universal church (*ekklesia katholika*).

In making this claim in ongoing centuries, the church of Rome invoked words such as the following from Irenaeus of Lyons (c. 130–200 CE), in his work *Against Heresies* (Book III, Chapter 3), where he argues that anyone can see the evidence for the lineage from Peter to the present Bishop of Rome. Moreover, he says, the tradition that the church of Rome is "universally known" to have been "founded and organized at Rome by the two most glorious apostles, Peter and Paul" and he maintains that "it is a matter of necessity that every

church should agree with this church on account of its pre-eminent authority."

As the Roman Empire declined and fell in the fifth and sixth centuries and as pressure from the Germanic nations brought about an entirely new social-political reality, bishops of Rome assumed the mantle of guarantors of both civil and ecclesial order. While *Roman* evoked a specific locality in the semantic world of the age, it also connoted a crumbling world's memory of universal order. As the empire was split between the Latin West and the Greek East, the division of European and West Asian catholic Christianity into complimentary and mutually recognizing forms of Catholicism was solidified. The Greek and Latin Catholic Churches went their distinct but cousinly ways until 1054, when they split at just about the time Slavic Catholic orthodoxy was growing in significance as a result of the missionary labors of Cyril, Methodius, and their successors.

## Roman Catholicism Develops in the West

It is hard to know whether it is more accurate to see the growth of Christianity in the West as the result of a missionary movement or as a form of religio-cultural diffusion. It suffices here to recognize that the growth of Celtic Christianity in Brittany, Wales, and Ireland and its expansion into northern Britain and eventually into northern Europe through the work of such legendary figures as Patrick (mid- to late fifth century), Columba (c. 521–597 CE), and monks sent by Pope Gregory I ("the Great," c. 540–604 CE) began a process wherein Roman liturgy, canons, and usages eventually became ascendant. Owing in large part to the use of monks following the rule of the Italian Saint Benedict of Nursia (c. 480–550 CE), the Catholicism of the church north of the Alps would be Roman in flavor and look to Rome for guidance when theological and ecclesial matters were in dispute. In addition to spurring the diffusion of Christianity northward, Gregory took a strong hand in ruling the church of Italy, upholding and broadening the recognition and power of the See of Rome, but he did so in ways that often alienated churches that took their signals from the Patriarch of Constantinople, whose claim to be the "Ecumenical Patriarch" Gregory refused to recognize. In the East, accordingly, recognition of Roman primacy was limited to granting Rome a primacy of honor, not authority to decide matters in dispute in other churches.

The next phase in the development of what becomes the Roman Catholic Church came in a centuries-long process too seldom identified. In it, migrating Teutonic

## Treaty of Tordesillas

The Treaty of Tordesillas (7 June 1494, extracted below, divided the as-yet largely unexplored New World into two territories, each under Spanish or Portuguese control. The division had an enormous influence on subsequent exploration and colonization.

[I.] That, whereas a certain controversy exists between the said lords, their constituents, as to what lands, of all those discovered in the ocean sea up to the present day, the date of this treaty, pertain to each one of the said parts respectively; therefore, for the sake of peace and concord, and for the preservation of the relationship and love of the said King of Portugal for the said King and Queen of Castile, Aragon, etc., it being the pleasure of their Highnesses, they, their said representatives, acting in their name and by virtue of their powers herein described, covenanted and agreed that a boundary or straight line be determined and drawn north and south, from pole to pole, on the said ocean sea, from the Arctic to the Antarctic pole. This boundary or line shall be drawn straight, as aforesaid, at a distance of three hundred and seventy leagues west of the Cape Verde Islands, being calculated by degrees, or by any other manner as may be considered the best and readiest, provided the distance shall be no greater than abovesaid. And all lands, both islands and mainlands, found and discovered already, or to be found and discovered hereafter, by the said King of Portugal and by his vessels on this side of the said line and bound determined as above, toward the east, in either north or south latitude, on the eastern side of the said bound provided the said bound is not crossed, shall belong to, and remain in the possession of, and pertain forever to, the said King of Portugal and his successors. And all other lands, both islands and mainlands, found or to be found hereafter, discovered or to be discovered hereafter, which have been discovered or shall be discovered by the said King and Queen of Castile, Aragon, etc., and by their vessels, on the western side of the said bound, determined as above, after having passed the said bound toward the west, in either its north or south latitude, shall belong to, and remain in the possession of, and pertain forever to, the said King and Queen of Castile, Leon, etc., and to their successors.

Source: Davenport, F. G. (1917). *European treaties bearing on the history of the United States to 1648.* Washington, DC: The Carnegie Institution of Washington.

---

tribes began to "Germanize" Latin Catholicism (according to James C. Russell in *The Germanization of Early Medieval Catholicism: A Socio-Historical Approach to Religious Transformation*). The societies into which Latin Christianity was grafted were ones in which religion and politics were closely aligned. Religion was predominantly magical, in contradistinction, as Russell (1994) says, "to being a pre-dominantly doctrinal and ethical" reality. In addition, the German view of politics was marked by a form of "sacral kingship," a worldview that will loom large in coming battles over the relative powers of princes and bishops.

In the end, the Roman form of Catholicism symbolized by St. Wilfrid, bishop of York (634–709 CE) was triumphant in Britain at the Synod of Whitby (664) became normative north of the Alps, but the process was not straightforward, and the ratio of Germanic to Mediterranean-Roman elements was negotiated over several centuries. As the Holy Roman Empire took shape in the north with the coronation of Otto I in 962 CE and conquered the northern two-thirds of Italy by 1100, one can fairly speak of the Germanization of Roman Catholicism. This takes place precisely in the age when canon lawyers are systematizing church law and bringing forth theories that the pope has, by divine will, universal jurisdiction (the power to emanate laws that must be obeyed by all a ruler's subjects). This sets the scene for the medieval struggle among bishops, princes, kings, emperors, and popes over where the jurisdiction of bishops and popes begins and ends.

The epitome of the emerging Roman self-understanding is revealed in the 1302 decree *Unam Sanctam* of Pope Boniface VIII, in which he sees "Peter's successor" as the one head of the church and says finally, "We declare, state and define that it is absolutely necessary for the salvation of all men that they submit to the Roman Pontiff." From the High Middle Ages to the Protestant Reformation, this was the *Roman* view of how the Catholic church was structured.

## Reformation and Roman Catholicism

The principles called into question by the Reformation were (1) whether the Roman form of ecclesial life and episcopal and papal authority was justified by the Gospel and (2) whether the body of devotions, pious beliefs, pilgrimages, and practices such as indulgences and prayers to and for the dead could survive the explosion of historical knowledge and the return to ancient sources that began in the late-medieval period. The Reformers were heirs to a new learning that sought to find purity by recovering ancient traditions and was suspicious of the warrants for later traditions. For Catholics, however, to attack such traditions was to discredit the authority of the church under which they had developed. Ultimately, both Luther and Calvin were men formed in the new methods and embarrassed by the sheer multitude of Catholic practices that made it hard to discern the core of Biblical teaching of and about Jesus the Christ. They also began movements that shattered church unity and led to church subordination to the national identities that were beginning to replace the patchwork of feudal relationships that had grown up in the Middle Ages.

Viewed in the perspective of the contemporary emergence of "world Christianity," the start of the missionary movement, not the Reformation, was the most important event of the late fifteenth and early sixteenth centuries. In seeking to understand the Roman Catholic Church today, the most important challenge is to understand its traditions in the context of the emergence and demands of world Christianity, not in the Counter-Reformation paradigm that has monopolized Eurocentric interpretations of Catholicism for too long.

## Roman Catholic Church within Emergent World Christianity

Jesuit historian John O'Malley makes the point that early modern Catholicism is not accurately described when it is characterized principally as a "Counter-Reformation." That label, in effect, misleads one into thinking that the Protestant Reformation defines Catholicism from the sixteenth century onward. On the contrary, what was beginning to emerge in the fifteenth century was an "early modern Catholicism" following trajectories that

encounter Protestantism in certain concrete ways, while for the most part developing and extending itself under its own spiritual, ecclesial, intellectual, and cultural impulses. Taking one's key on early modern (fifteenth through eighteenth century) and modern (nineteenth and twentieth century) Catholicism from O'Malley's insight allows one to understand the complexity and richness of Roman Catholicism on its own terms rather than taking one's bearings from Protestant perspectives.

From this perspective, the term *Counter-Reformation Catholicism* should be used only when Catholicism (1) pushes back against Protestant encroachment and seeks to regain lost ground or (2) seeks to purge itself of abuses that the Reformation brings attention to and that Catholics themselves agree need correction. Even though the Council of Trent (1545–1563) was well informed about Reformation doctrines and intent on opposing them, to a great extent Trent's reforms stemmed from inner-Catholic dynamism. In this reading, Trent is less an anti-Protestant council than a council called in recognition that discipline needed to be exerted, that the clergy needed better training, and that the diocese and parish must radiate Catholic life and teaching.

The life and career of Cardinal Francisco Ximénes de Cisneros (1436–1517), for example, shows how reforms begun in Spain before the Reformation set Spanish Catholicism on an indigenous path to reform and paved the way for the immense exertions of Spain in the early modern missionary movement. Seen in this way, other Catholic reforms, such as those sponsored by the Jesuits, took on the new learning and developed more or less independently on tracks both parallel and antithetical to the Reformation. Positively, church promoted the arts and devotional life and spiritualities suited to the emerging literate culture. Above all, when Pope Gregory XVI formed the Congregation for the Propagation of the Faith in 1622, it was in response to the need to bring order to efforts of those who had risen to the challenge of new missionary opportunities opened up by Portuguese and Spanish explorations.

Key to this interpretation of Catholicism is insight into the great saints of that period and the movements they inspired. They are epitomized by St. Ignatius of Loyola (1491–1556), St. Francis Xavier (1506–1552), St. Teresa of Avila (1515–1582), St. Vincent DePaul (1581–1660), St. Louise de Marillac (1591–1660), and St. Charles Borromeo (1538–1584). They inspired works such as overseas missionary efforts and renewals in both general and seminary education, parish animation through missions, delivery of charitable services, and, perhaps most important of all, the emergence of women in both charitable and educational ministries. Diocesan clergy coming from the new seminaries joined members of religious communities to provide a cadre of dedicated apostolic workers unlike anything Catholicism had ever known.

As one looks at the Catholicism that developed in the nineteenth and twentieth centuries, these saints are pioneers in whose footsteps dozens and ultimately hundreds of male and female orders arose. Among them are the Salesian orders of men and women founded by St. John Bosco (1815–1888) and its concern for ministry to youth as industrialization sweeps Europe; St. Elizabeth Ann Seton (1774–1821), the first saint born in the United States and founder of the Sisters of Charity; Mother Catherine McAuley (1778–1841), founder of the Mercy Sister movement; St. Daniel Comboni (1831–1881), a missionary pioneer and founder of the male and female Comboni Missionaries; and Cardinal Charles-Martial Lavigerie, founder of the male and female branches of the Missionaries of Africa (formerly known as the White Fathers and Sisters). Dozens more such figures could be listed, but these five can stand for the movements that energized religious life and began paying more attention to lay formation in the modern period.

At another level, centralization of power in the hands of the pope was made possible by new means of communication and necessary—in Rome's judgment—by unhealthy modern developments that needed to be opposed. The First Vatican Council's Dogmatic Constitution on the Church, *Pastor Aeternus* (1870), taught that the hierarchical nature of the church was divinely willed. It went on to teach and declare the "primacy of jurisdiction" of the pope as Peter's successor. It also stated as dogma that when "he defines . . . a doctrine concerning faith or morals to be held by the universal church," the pope possesses "the infallibility with which the divine Redeemer willed his church to be endowed." From the perspective of Rome, the council and popes were shoring up the church to fight what it considered the excesses (1) of the nation-state and (2) subjectivism in theology that had the effect of eviscerating Christianity's role in judging what was and was not progress in the social order and in morality. The universal/catholic church would not cede this ground to secular states.

When Pope John XXIII called the Second Vatican Council in 1962, there was a widespread feeling that the church needed to overcome its defensive posture toward the rest of Christianity and the world. Two of the major documents of Vatican II—*Lumen Gentium* (1964) on the nature of the church and *Gaudium et Spes* (1965) on the relationship of the church to the modern world—attempted to redress the imbalance by returning to ancient Biblical and patristic terminology, by recognizing the rise of democracy and human rights as good, and by affirming the ecclesial nature of other Christian churches and the positive value of non-Christian religious traditions. It is often forgotten, however, that Chapter 3 of *Lumen Gentium* reaffirms Vatican I's teaching on the hierarchical nature of the church. Nor did Vatican II put into place—in unambiguous juridical language—instruments and bodies that would encourage greater participation by laity, and ordinary priests in church governance. Lacking such implementing legislation, the meaning of the council

**Old Bohemia Church in Maryland, established by Jesuit priests around 1790.** *Courtesy of Karl Kehm/istockphoto.com.*

and the nature and scope of the updating of the church for which the council called have been left for the pope and the Roman Curia to decide.

None of the above denies sincere efforts to advance ecumenism and interfaith exchange on the part of the church in most regions of the world, including Rome. It is clear, too, that the Vatican II decree on divine revelation, *Dei Verbum* (1965), gave church teaching authority a role subordinate to the Word of God. Nevertheless, tradition, scripture, and magisterium are envisaged as "so connected and associated that one of them cannot stand without the others. Working together, each in its own way under the action of the one Holy Spirit, they all contribute effectively to the salvation of souls" (*Dei Verbum*, Article 10).

The skirmish lines that have characterized the battle to shape and define the Roman Catholic Church since Vatican II coalesce around five areas: (1) the nature and extent of church involvement in social reform and human liberation, (2) implementing "mediating" institutions and structures between the central organs of the church and local churches, (3) questions of sexual ethics and gender roles within the church, (4) mission and Christian relations with other religious traditions, and (5) the degree to which (a) local churches can adapt Roman traditions and norms to local cultures and (b) such adaptations are judged to weaken the unity of the church and obscure the divinity and universal and final mission and work of Christ.

At the beginning of the twentieth century, Roman Catholics numbered approximately 266 million in a world population of 1.6 billion (17 percent of the total). At the end of the century, they were 1.05 billion in a world population of 6.07 billion (still 17 percent). During that same period they were, respectively, 47.5 percent and 53 percent of the total number of Christians in the world. While Protestant, Anglican, and Orthodox churches declined from 45 percent of the total Christian population in 1900 to 31 percent in 2000, independent Evangelical and Pentecostal churches, which were a mere 1.4 percent of the world's Christians in 1900, had become 19 percent in 2000. Moreover, the percentage of members in Reformation-rooted Protestant and Anglican churches in the third world who agree with the independents on matters such as the authority of scripture, sexual ethics, and gender roles is high. If the sometimes dramatic process of alienation of Southern Christians from Northern churches continues in the twenty-first century, the percentage of mainline Protestant conservatives will grow in the South. Meanwhile, the percentage of Catholics living in today's socially liberal Europe, as a percentage of the global Catholic total, has declined from 67 percent in 1900 to 26 percent in 2000. Catholics in the United States are about 6 percent of the church's worldwide total. Catholicism has had an enormous numerical growth in Oceania, Africa, North and Latin America, and Africa. In Asia, its percentage growth has been 104 percent between 1975 and 2000, a period in which the general population has grown 61 percent (from 2.3 to 3.7 billion).

Another factor bearing on the likely character of emergent world Catholicism bears mention. First, a large proportion of Catholics in the South tend to be traditionalists in doctrinal, ethical, and gender-role discussions. Second, like recent popes, they tend to be progressive on social justice, war and peace, and economic issues. Thus, papal decisions not to accede to Northern Catholic progressives in gender-role and sexual ethical concerns means that Catholicism seems likely to move with global currents hostile to many aspects of the modern agenda.

The darkest cloud on the Roman Catholic horizon is that success at maintaining doctrinal orthodoxy is not accompanied by success in recruiting the numbers of diocesan priests, members of new movements (such as Opus Dei), or traditional religious orders who are key to Catholic liturgical and spiritual life as it has developed since the sixteenth century. In Africa, for instance, the number of Catholics per priest has risen from one priest for 2,907 in 1975 to one for 4,291 in 2000. In Latin America it has risen from one priest for 6,000 to one for 7,081 in the same period. In both Latin America and Africa, moreover, independent Pentecostal and Evangelical churches are growing by leaps and bounds, and in Latin America leakage of Catholics to Evangelical and Pentecostal churches will continue. It is, indeed, likely that in Brazil and Central America there are already more practicing Evangelicals and Pentecostals than Catholics. Either Catholicism is heading for a major decline or a new form of Catholicism—which is not yet apparent and does not seem to be envisaged by the three postconciliar popes (Paul VI, John Paul II, and Benedict XVI)—must develop.

## Future of the Roman Catholic Church

A splintered world Christian movement belies the prayer of Jesus in John 17:20–24 that his disciples would be one like himself and the Father, so that the world would know that he was sent by the Father. A truly catholic world church whose members *mutually* recognize the validity of diverse ways of manifesting Christ seems far off. When one reads the writings of John Paul II, especially his encyclical on Christian unity, *Ut Unum Sint,* one detects awareness that his own office may be an obstacle to unity (Article 88). The challenge to the Roman Catholic Church, seen from this perspective, is to become attractively catholic enough that a form of vital unity with it will be considered essential to the identity of churches not yet in communion with Rome. How Roman Catholicism adapts its particular traditions and becomes attractive to other Christian bodies will be the key to any such development. It may be significant that Joseph Ratzinger (Pope Benedict XVI ) has written the English preface to the most important book in modern times on the nature of Catholicism and the catholic principle. Like Henri de Lubac, the author of that book, *Catholicism,* Joseph Ratzinger knows the importance of getting beyond legalism to the mystical core of the Catholic principle, and it will be interesting to see how he puts such insights into practice.

WILLIAM R. BURROWS

## Further Reading

Alberigo, G., & Komonchak, J. A. (Eds.). (1995–2006). *Vatican Council II* (5 vols.). Maryknoll, NY: Orbis Books.

Alberigo, G. (2006). *A brief history of Vatican II.* Maryknoll, NY: Orbis Books.

Congar, Y. M. J. (1965). *Lay people in the church: A study for a theology of the laity.* Westminster, MD: Newman.

Conzelmann, H. (1973). *History of primitive Christianity.* New York: Abingdon.

De Lubac, H. (1988). *Catholicism: Christ and the common destiny of man.* San Francisco: Ignatius Press. (French original, 1947)

Flannery, A. (Ed.). (1996–1998). *Vatican Council II: The conciliar and post-conciliar documents,* 2 vols. Northport, NY: Costello.

Fletcher, R. (1997). *The barbarian conversion: From paganism to Christianity.* New York: Henry Holt.

Froehle, B. T., & Gauthier, M. L. (2003). *Global Catholicism: Portrait of a world church.* Maryknoll, NY: Orbis Books.

Irvin, D. T., & Sunquist, S. W. (2001). *A history of the world Christian movement: Vol 1. Earliest Christianity to 1453.* Maryknoll, NY: Orbis Books.

McBrien, R. P. (1994). *Catholicism.* San Francisco: HarperSan Francisco.

Neuner, J., & Dupuis, J. (2001). *The Christian faith: Doctrinal documents of the Catholic Church.* Staten Island, NY: Alba House.

O'Malley, J. W. (1993). *The first Jesuits.* Cambridge, MA: Harvard University Press.

O'Malley, J. W. (2000). *Trent and all that: Renaming Catholicism in the early modern era.* Cambridge, MA: Harvard University Press.

Rassam, S. (2005). *Christianity in Iraq: Its origin and development to the present day.* Leominster, UK: Gracewing.

Russell, J. C. (1994). *The Germanization of early medieval Catholicism: A socio-historical approach to religious transformation.* New York: Oxford University Press.

Stark, R. (1997). *The rise of Christianity: How the obscure, marginal Jesus movement became the dominant religious force in the Western world in a few centuries.* San Francisco: HarperSanFrancisco.

Tracy, D., & Happel, S. (1984). *A Catholic vision.* Philadelphia: Fortress.

Von Campenhausen, H. (1969). *Ecclesiastical authority in the church in the first three centuries.* Stanford, CA: Stanford University Press.

# Russia

Global attention to the Byzantine Slavic missions of Sts. Cyril and Methodius (863–885 CE) came eleven hundred years late, when in 1985 the Slavic pope, John Paul II, celebrated the occasion in the Czechoslovak Republic. That widely filmed event gave a further stimulus to the return of Christianity to social prominence in socialist Eastern Europe. It was closely followed in 1988 by celebrations of the millennium of Christianity in Rus. Majestic ceremonies in Moscow and Kiev were shown on television in Gorbachev's Russia, and local ceremonies continued for longer than a year, extending to the farthest towns and villages. Russia was recovering its spirituality (*dukhovnost*). By 1991 the Soviet Union had ended, and its control of Eastern Europe had already ended nonviolently in 1989, during that magic year of velvet revolutions.

In all of these changes, individual believers and the churches in general were now looked to as messengers of the promise of authentic living, for finding the way to the good civil society. Statues to Cyril and Methodius stood prominently not far from Moscow's Kremlin, and church bells calling people to worship began ringing everywhere. The thousand-year legacy of Slavic Christianity was claimed not only by those asserting direct links to the beginnings, namely the Russian Orthodox Church, but also by Roman Catholics, who were increasingly appropriating the iconography and spirituality of the East in major public worship, and by Russian Baptists. As the celebrations by Orthodox and Baptists continued into 1989, such widely attended ceremonies frequently became occasions for evangelism. Put simply, it was the year of the Bible, when everyone finally had one.

## Cyril-Methodian Mission

The conversion of Rus started with Prince Vladimir's ordering all the people into the Dnepr River for a mass baptism in 988 CE, but the conversion had many precedents. There was the claim that St. Andrew had crossed the Black Sea to raise the cross on what later became Russian lands. In 325 CE a bishop of the Bosporus sent missionaries to the Hunnic-Turkic migrants in the area between the Danube and the Caucasus. There was a request in 860 CE that a Byzantine delegation to the Khazar Kingdom (northeast of the Black Sea) include a Christian theologian. That triggered the sending by Patriarch Photius of the two brothers, who knew some Slavic dialects they had learned growing up on the Dalmatian coast, to start what has become known as the Cyril-Methodian mission.

They followed standard Orthodox mission methodology, whose key elements were "discovered" independently by Protestant missionaries in the 1860s. That Orthodox methodology sought to translate the Gospel in context, and its theological tones should not be seen merely as methodology. As Archbishop Anastasios (Yannolatis) formulated it more recently, at the forefront of the mission work was a desire to create a local eucharistic community. The key elements to that end were (1) the use of the vernacular, (2) the use of indigenous clergy, and (3) an indigenization emphasis fostering responsible selfhood of the church (autocephaly) (Stamoolis 1986, 22–23).

The Methodian mission resulted in the formation (and later modification) of an alphabet now known as the Cyrillic in honor of Cyril the linguist, once the patriarch's librarian and friend, who was sent as a missioner in 863 CE. That alphabet also served as the basis later for translations of the liturgy and key biblical texts into Russian or "church Slavonic," as it has long been known. Vladimir's decision to make an official commitment to Byzantine Christianity, because of the beauty of the worship experience his emissaries had experienced at St. Sophia Cathedral in Constantinople, did have a more developed background, since his mother, Princess Olga, was already Christian.

## Role of Monks

More to the point, the subsequent deep permeation of Christianity over the next five hundred years to an extent commented on by all foreign visitors, was due above all to the missionary role of the monks. It was not the story of a systematically organized mission, so much as the common witness of persons of deep piety to whom the people were attracted. Monks had settled as hermits in caves on the banks of the Dnepr near Kiev, but soon it was a monastic community providing *caritas* for the needy and shaping patterns of worship in the churches.

The model even accounted for the moralistic preaching reported centuries later. We now know of a trail of monk hermits who set out to seek solitude in the wide emptiness of the Russian steppe and forests. Frequently, after years of prayer, a community formed, followed by the churches and public Christian practice. Some, such as the missionary bishops St. Abraham of Smolensk and St. Cyril of Turov, set out more directly to confront tribal paganism with the Gospel, and the vita of St. Stephen of Perm (1340–96) still serves as a teaching model, to show how he immersed himself in the Zyrian (non-Slavic) culture, with a Zyrian national church resulting.

## Religious Diversity

If by 1589 there was a Russian Orthodox Church, now autocephalous with its own patriarch, the new Russian empire as it developed from about 1650 through 1917 had become ever more religiously diverse. Russia did not experience the drama of the sixteenth-century reformations directly; nevertheless, soon after, to meet the needs of diplomats and traders, both Protestant and Catholic places of worship had been established in Moscow. By the time of Alexander I in 1801, the Russian Empire included large sections of the former Lithuanian Commonwealth and Poland. Although the Russian Empire of the nineteenth century was officially Orthodox, there was freedom of worship for Catholic and Protestant confessions, negotiated by tsarist *privilegia* and overseen by a government department for "foreign" confessions. Nevertheless, although such regulations invariably prohibited mission among Orthodox faithful, it did not prohibit proselytizing among other peoples. The exposure to Catholics—particularly the Jesuits and the high quality of their education work and after their expulsion from all of Europe except Russia—resulted in some prominent conversions to Catholicism, as well as many other conversions.

There had also been an aggressive policy since the time of Catherine to foster agricultural settlements in the lands newly gained from the Ottomans. This brought in Catholic, Lutheran, Reformed, Mennonite, and Moravian Brethren settlements, at first to "new

Russia" (southeastern Ukraine); settlements then extended eastward as the frontier kept shifting, reaching western Siberia by the 1890s. Around most settlements, local peasants became familiar with the Bible and with alternate forms of Christian piety.

## Rise of Voluntary Societies

The era of Alexander I was particularly notable for the rise of numerous voluntary societies for the uplift of the people, almost all of which were the fruit of Pietism from Western Europe that was connecting with similar currents inside Russian Orthodoxy. Most important was the formation of the Russian Bible Society (1813), which sponsored the translation of the New Testament into modern Russian (by 1821). Its president, Alexander Golitsyn, close confidante of the tsar, controlled the entire state administration of education and religion (1816–1824). Key leaders of all the confessions sat on the national Bible Society committee, while local chapters were invariably ecumenical. Bible Society meetings were a mix of spiritual fellowship and reports on funding for translation and distribution.

Other societies that sprang up focused on teaching reading (Lancaster Schools Societies), visiting prisons, or providing relief for the poor in cities. British Quakers played a disproportionately strong role in these societies, but there were also traveling Pietist preachers (Catholic and Protestant) who were listened to in the salons of Petersburg and Moscow and in numerous worship gatherings throughout south Russia. By 1867 an organized Slavic evangelical movement had started, and by 1884 unions of such indigenous Protestant evangelical believers had formed, By 1905 these *baptisty* or *sektanty*, as they were referred to in the press, came to be seen as a grassroots force for reformation, a democratic, well-organized Christian movement demonstrating a high quality of civil society.

## Reacting to State "Reforms"

There was an uneven quality to this mission story. If tolerance was the theme during Alexander I's reign (1801–1825), it was followed by the reactionary years of Nicholas I (1825–1861), often characterized by the words autocracy, orthodoxy, and nationality. Then came a second round of state reforms that included administrative reforms within the Russian Orthodox Church to improve the quality of the clergy and an attempt to integrate the non-Orthodox communities into the empire through common education structures. These reforms had the effect of increasing Baltic Protestant influence in governmental bureaucracy. Again there followed a pro-Orthodox cultural reaction (during the reigns of Alexander III and Nicholas II), with new pressures for reform coming to a head with the abortive revolution of 1905.

Through each phase, the non-Orthodox communities sought greater religious influence, and reformist elements within Orthodoxy struggled for internal reforms and also experienced an energized missionary movement. The tsar's ministers, who struggled to contain developments, were most troubled by the indigenous *sektanty*. These had become increasingly more Protestant in character as the grassroots Bible movement was encouraged from abroad, and their status in particular took new legal form with the edict on religious toleration in 1905.

### Evangelical Christians and Russian Baptists Unite

In short order, a union of Evangelical Christians and a union of Russian Baptists had submitted legal registration applications with appropriate constitutions. The reality of their legality was of short duration, as the third and fourth Duma attempted stricter restraint policies again. The most striking fact about these indigenous sectarians turned out to be the way in which they could demonstrate modernizing qualities. That is, they were able to gain financial and moral support from adherents and quickly spread across the Russian Empire's vast expanse (from the Baltic to eastern Siberia).

Consequently, by around 1908–1910, there was a missionary vision and program already articulated by Evangelical Christians and Baptists, which guided the decade of greatest activism, namely 1918–1929, when they set out to win "Russia for Christ," as Ivan Prokhanov put it. Joining with the newly formed Baptist World Alliance (1905), they incorporated the slogan "every Baptist a missionary." They sought to carry out the vision by organizing groups of congregations in a region to finance the full-time ministry of a traveling evangelist (in John Wesley style). When a nucleus of believers had formed, it became a congregation soon affiliated with one of the participating unions. In short order, activists from the new congregation were expected to take a similar initiative in a nearby town or village to plant another congregation.

In the cities there were special gatherings for young people, women met together regularly in fellowship groups that included organizing assistance to the needy, and a printing press (Raduga Press) was formed. These were joint projects involving the Evangelical Christians and Baptists together with Mennonites, German Bap-

## The Russian Orthodox Church Enters Siberia

**The following account describes the first efforts in the mid-1800s by the Russian Orthodox Church to convert the Chukchee, an indigenous, reindeer-herding people of eastern Siberia.**

In 1848, at the instance of Archbishop Nil, a small church was built on the Arctic shore at the mouth of Big River (Large Baranikha River), two hundred miles from Nishne-Kolymsk, and A. Argentov was appointed the first missionary. It seems that before that he had been an ordinary priest on the Lower Kolyma for more than four years. He says in his diary that the place was selected not very happily, because the Chukchee do not live there continually, but only come from time to time. This, of course, is quite true.

Nevertheless Argentov went to his church along the seacoast with five boats of the usual Kolyma type. These boats are so clumsy and fragile that it is a matter of wonder that the expedition did not meet with some catastrophe. The people who came in the boats built a block-house for Argentov, and then went back, leaving him with his wife and a maid-servant. A few months after that Argentov was obliged to flee from his mission, because the Chukchee neighbors wanted to compel him to enter with them into a bond of group-marriage. The story is well remembered on the Kolyma among the Russians as well as among the Chukchee. Argentov, who travelled much among the Chukchee, and visited Chaun River and Cape Erri, was tempted to conclude friendship with one Chukchee, Ata'to, and also with his wife. Probably at that time he did not know the rules of the Chukchee group-marriage; but after a short time Ata'to returned the visit, and asked for reciprocity. He had some companions with him, and so refusal was of no avail. At the critical moment, however, the maid-servant consented to take the place of the mistress. The Chukchee probably did not know the difference; and, moreover, according to Chukchee ideas, the family has a right, in marriage complications, to substitute one woman for another. Some of these details I have from Ata'to himself, who in 1895 was still living. Shortly after that, Argentov left his lonely church. This was the first and the last attempt of the Chukchee missionary to live among the Chukchee in the desert.

Maydell, in 1870, undertook to build a church on the Yelombal River, an affluent of the Large Anui River. This church was to be the centre of the Christian propaganda among the Reindeer Chukchee. Amra'wkurgln donated to the church four hundred reindeer for slaughter. These were eaten by the Russian creoles; and the church, and the house for the priest, were built, but nobody ever lived there.

The next missionaries—probably owing to the unhappy episode told above—were selected among the monks. Their number gradually increased. At the close of the nineteenth century three of them were already on the Kolyma,—one as head of the mission in Nishne-Kolymsk; another in the village Piatistennoye, on the Large Anui River; and the third in the Yakut settlement Sen-quel, on the outskirts of the western tundra.

Source: Bogoraz-Tan, V. G. (1904–1909). *The Chukchee* (3 vols, pp. 722–726). New York: E. J. Brill, Ltd.

---

tists, and sometimes with Pietist Lutheran communities in southern and eastern Russia. Raduga Press (with offices in Molochansk, Ukraine, and St. Petersburg) not only helped print and circulate denominational papers and missionary leaflets, but through it came the efforts to obtain more Russian-language Bibles. There were also efforts to establish Bible schools whose emphasis was to foster the basics of Bible knowledge and doctrine and who used training courses and practicums to enable students to be evangelists and missionaries, the latter to ethnic or tribal communities in eastern Russia, Siberia, and central Asia.

## Liberating Society from Religious Vestiges

This aggressive missionary expansion ended with the Soviet Law on Cults of 1929 that initiated a rather violent war on all religion. The Orthodox leadership had already been almost totally decimated by 1927, when acting Patriarch Sergei capitulated, making a statement fully endorsing Soviet power without reservation. Thereafter, those of the peasantry and proletariat with religious commitments were also included in the sweep to liberate society from religious vestiges, to cite a popular phrase. The methods of evangelism ascribed above to the indigenous Protestant sectarians were listed in article 17 of the 1929 law and explicitly prohibited.

There were at least two major outcomes. On the one hand, in spite of archival research since 1990 to trace what happened to religious people who were arrested and disappeared, we still do not know the exact number who were martyred. We do know that Orthodox faithful and sectarians (including adherents of Catholic and Protestant traditions of long standing) in total constituted many millions of martyrs.

Just as martyrdom was the seed of the church during the early years of Christianity, so too it was during the Soviet era. It is a mistake to claim that between 1929 and 1990 mission had disappeared within the Soviet Union, but churches from the USSR were certainly prevented from cross-cultural mission outside its borders. In addition to the witness of the martyrs, sustained persecution, especially the harsh Stalinist persecution, did engender fear and drove religious practice underground. Some of the missions in north-central Siberia were not forcibly terminated till 1934, or even 1937 in one case, thanks to the slow spread of Soviet administration to the hinterlands. Religious practice resumed in the aftermath of World War II and was squelched again, only to appear more cautiously after Stalin's death in 1953.

Relying on the ever-improving quality of theological training in Orthodox seminaries and the theological academies (advanced study for the best seminarians), by 1854 the fourth theological academy in Kazan, established with a particular mandate to foster language and culture studies of the "east," also had a two-year missionary-training college. By the end of the nineteenth century, there was language study for what became Orthodox mission churches in China, Japan, and Korea. Although these activities were shut down between 1929 and 1990, translation projects were resumed later, and periodically we learn of some de facto missions that persisted far from centers like Petersburg and Moscow.

## Emergence of Indigenous Mission Societies

As the turn to religious values became more explicit just before the millennium mark of 1988, several in-

digenous mission societies emerged. One was the Latvian mission, in which Lutherans, Baptists, and some Pentecostals cooperated in charity work and joint or coordinated evangelism initiatives with youth. Light of the Gospel mission started in Rovno, Ukraine, as a vision of several individuals to bring the Gospel to isolated tribal communities along the Lena River in northern Siberia, their former places of exile. By 1991 that mission had numerous full-time missionaries in Siberia and the Far East and was engaged in organized witness in many Ukrainian cities or nearby regions of Russia. They started shelters for street children, lending libraries of religious literature with discussion circles in rented public facilities (that is, not churches) in a deliberate attempt to communicate with people lacking any religious exposure.

By 1997 it was possible to speak of a network of organized congregations of this style as Light of the Gospel churches. Having started with a missionary-training institute in 1991, by the late 1990s it had become Donetsk Christian University, offering a variety of Bible-college and seminary degrees. Similar indigenous initiatives accounted for over forty theological schools (by Evangelicals alone) by 1994, although increasingly mission societies and individual sponsors from abroad (especially the United States) became the financial lifeline. With the economic collapse of 1994–1997 and the stagnating economy in most post-Soviet countries, those mission-driven schools and even the new church associations remain in a state of financial dependency that is a widespread cause for concern.

The new Russian Orthodox Church of the 1990s nearly tripled the number of functioning parishes, ordaining priests and bishops who lacked theological training, though some were converted intellectuals. A synod of bishops meeting in 1994, reflecting conservative reaction to the foreign influence, while nearly voting to withdraw from the WCC, for example, also approved a declaration that it sought to become a missional church and instructed the seminaries to produce courses in missiology. Little came of this until the center for mission and ecumenism in Petersburg (Interchurch Partnership) printed a textbook on *Missiologia*. It consisted of speeches from prominent Orthodox hierarchs containing a theology of mission, including those of Greek and Russian-American Orthodox leaders, and the translation of Stamoolis's *Eastern Orthodox Mission Theology Today* (1986).

Although another Orthodox Mission Study Center opened in Moscow, and the patriarchate established a department of mission, few other publications have become known. Most important were three statements approved by the Jubilee Bishops Council (August 2000). The longest was the first systematic statement ever of a "social concept," another was a policy statement on ecumenism and an Orthodox approach to interfaith dialogue, and the third was a report on the work of the mission department. Together, they revealed a desire to apply the Christian Gospel to all spheres of life, to clarify what Orthodox teaching and practice must be, but also to make room for dialogue with other Christians.

WALTER SAWATSKY

## Further Reading

Basic principles for the relationship of the Orthodox Church to other faiths. (n.d.). Retrieved March 29, 2007, from http://www.russian-orthodox-church.org.ru/s2000r13.htm

Batalden, S. K., Cann, K., Dean, J. (Eds.). (2006). *Sowing the Word: The cultural impact of the British and foreign Bible Society 1804–2004*. Sheffield, UK: Sheffield Phoenix Press.

Bourdeaux, M. (1975). *Patriarch and prophets: Persecution of the Russian Orthodox Church today*. London: Mowbrays.

Coleman, H. J. (2005). *Russian Baptists and spiritual revolution, 1905–1929*. Indiana-Michigan Series in Russian and East European Studies. Bloomington: Indiana University Press.

Fedorov, V. (Ed.). (1999). *Pravoslavnaia missiia sevodnia* [Orthodox Mission Today]. St. Petersburg, Russia: Apostolskii Gorod.

Ioann, Archbishop (Belgorodski). (2001, July). Ecclesiological and canonical foundations of Orthodox mission. *International Review of Mission, 90*, 270–279.

Kharlampovych, K. V. (2001). *Archimandrite Makarii Glukharev: Founder of the Altai Mission: Vol. 6* (J. L. Haney, Trans.). Studies in Russian History. Lewiston, NY: The Edwin Mellon Press.

Maiyer, V. (1997). Russian Orthodox missions to the East. *Religion, State & Society, 25*(4), 369–380.

Noble, T. & I., Brinkman, M., Hilberath, J. (Eds.). (2006). *Charting churches in a changing Europe:* Charta Oecumenica *and the process of ecumenical encounter*. Amsterdam, Netherlands: Rodopi B. V.

Oleksa, M. (1993). *Orthodox Alaska: A theology of mission*. Crestwood, NY: St. Vladimir's Seminary Press.

Sawatsky, W. (1981). *Soviet evangelicals since World War II*. Scottdale, PA: Herald Press.

Sawatsky, W. (2005). Educators for mission and the Western missionaries. In P. F. Penner (Ed.), *Mission as theological education* (pp. 215–246). Schwarzenfeld, Germany: Neufeld Verlag.

Sawatsky, W. W., & Penner, P. F. (Eds.). (2005). *Mission in the former Soviet Union*. Schwarzenfeld, Germany: Neufeld Verlag.

Stamoolis, J. J. (1986). *Eastern Orthodox mission theology today*. American Society of Missiology Series; No. 10. Maryknoll, NY: Orbis Books.

Wanner, C. (2004, Winter). Missionaries of faith and culture: Evangelical encounters in Ukraine. *Slavic Review, 63*(3), 732–755.

Znamenski, A. A. (1999). *Shamanism and Christianity: Native encounters with Russian Orthodox missions in Siberia and Alaska, 1820–1917*. Contributions to the Study of World History, No. 70. Westport, CT: Greenwood Press.

Znamenski, A. A. (2003). *Through Orthodox eyes: Russian missionary narratives of travels to the Denaâina and Ahtna, 1850s–1930s*. Rasmuson Library Translation Series, V. 13. Fairbanks: University of Alaska Press.

# S

## Secularism and Atheism

"Secularism" is a philosophy that holds that the affairs and organization of society should be arranged according to principles and rules derived from experience and human insight without reference to customs, revelations, or sacred books whose authority is derived from God or the gods or ancestors. It is distinct from the process of "secularization" whereby the state, professions such as medicine and law, and academic fields such as archeology gradually take over areas of human life once governed by religion and the church. Both words derive from the Latin word *saeculum* ([this] world).

"Atheism" is a philosophical position that holds that there is no god or transcendent entity responsible for the origin of the universe or for the rules governing it or saving it from sin or whatever fate may be in store for it. The word derives from the Greek prefix *a* (not) and noun *theos* (god).

To understand the significance of secularism it is useful to recall a fundamental insight of the French sociologist and philosopher Emile Durkheim (1858–1917). He noted that every primary society is an expression of a "collective conscience" and that society-as-such functions as a "sacred" whole for its members. Seen from this perspective, Western societies were clearly ones that both kings and the church believed were ordered as they were by divine right. Ernst Troeltsch's work on the social teaching and life of the church reveals that premodern Roman Catholicism, in particular, believed that the church headed by bishops and popes, on the one hand, and emperors, kings, and subordinate lords, on the other hand, ruled the world in a way ordained by God. Moreover, in this organic view of society, when matters were in their proper order, human society on Earth—guided by the church—mirrored in a limited but real way the pattern of the heavenly realm that would be revealed when all was brought under the lordship of God at the Parousia (Second Coming).

In the West the church emphasized the belief that there were two realms: the sacred under the dominion of the church and the secular under the dominion of kings, with the church enjoying the right to tell kings what God demanded of them. From the ninth century on, conflicts on the boundaries between the sacred and profane realms abounded as the papacy grew in power and sought independence for itself and the church's bishops, monasteries, and orders to regulate their (ever-expanding) property, to determine what was right doctrine and worship, and—above all—to appoint popes, bishops, abbots, and parochial vicars. In the East, on the other hand, emperors were viewed as having the ultimate authority over both church and state as God's anointed ones.

After the Reformation and eighty years of wars fought over the Netherlands and thirty years of German religious wars, the Treaty of Westphalia brought relative calm to Western Europe. But among intellectuals, to a degree hard to ascertain among ordinary people, the legitimacy of the church's claim to have a major voice in how life was carried out in the secular realm had been seriously undermined. At the same time, professions such as medicine and law were coming out from under ecclesiastical direction. By the time modern nation states had been set up along geographical, cultural, and economic lines, a given Christian church might predominate in one nation, but evolution was pushing the world toward adopting secularization principles

## Emile Durkheim on the Sacred and Profane

All know religious beliefs, whether simple or complex, present one common characteristic: they presuppose a classification of all things, real and ideal, of which men think, into two classes or opposed groups, generally designated by two distinct terms which are translated well enough by the words profane and sacred. This division of the world into two domains, the one containing all that is sacred, the other all that is profane, is the distinctive trait of religious thought...

Source: Durkheim, E. (n.d.). *The elementary forms of the the religious life* (J. W. Swain, Trans., p. 12). London: George Allen and Unwin. (Original work published 1912)

concerning who and what would shape the new nations. Meanwhile, Protestantism had evolved in many of the new nations toward a state-church system.

In this context, although secularization was underway, secularism as such was not a fully developed philosophical or practical political position before the French Revolution in 1789. Still, by the time the Napoleonic wars ended in 1815, the scene had been set for major battles between *laïcite* (the doctrine that laity, not clergy would hold power) and *clericalisme,* which attempted to maintain the Catholic Church's position, especially in France and Italy, in the years from 1848 onward.

During this period, atheism was becoming an option for intellectuals who, for both practical and theoretical reasons, were finding implausible the idea of a personal God with whom they could enjoy an intimate relationship while on Earth and by whom salvation from eternal punishment due to sins could be granted. Prior to the French Revolution, it had been illegal to publish works that advanced the case for atheism. Even Plato's *Laws* had advocated the punishment of atheists, however, so one need not imagine that strictures against it are solely Christian in origin. Nor should one imagine that belief in some sort of "divine origin" of the universe by a metaphysical absolute that a philosopher might call "God" refers to the same reality that Muslims, Christians, or Jews intend when they use the same word about God as creator.

In the faith traditions mentioned in the previous paragraph, "God" refers to a reality transcending the visible universe, a "reality" with personal characteristics such as knowledge, will, love, and the ability to communicate and to interact with human beings to the extent of entering into a covenant with them. Thus God reveals the path on which humans are to walk to attain their proper destiny. For practical purposes, then, atheists deny that *this* kind of God exists. However, as Henri de Lubac shows masterfully, the drama of atheistic humanism, as propounded by figures such as Nietzsche, Freud, and Marx, has many profound lessons for humanity.

Logically speaking all atheists are at least functional secularists, for they have nowhere but this world from which to derive the principles by which nations, cultures, and societies are to be ordered. Not all secularists, however, are atheists. A deeply committed theist can hold a positive view of secularization and still believe that revelation may be helpful in providing insights into the ordering of the public realm. But theists can also believe that dialogue on such matters is quite different from letting organized religious bodies have a privileged place in deciding how pluralistic societies are to be ordered.

The distinction between secularization and secularism can be helpful. Persons convinced of the truth of divine revelation mediated by sacred texts and religious traditions can also believe that one of the characteristics of historical development is the differentiation of knowledge. On this principle, branches of human knowledge that were once enveloped in something like Durkheim's theory as a "social fact" develop out of what was once a total "religious" worldview. Secularization is the process whereby insights derived from experience, experiments, and reason—but not directly from revelation—are recognized as authoritative in their own right. Thus, one goes to an economist not a bishop for advice on how much debt a developing nation should incur in trying to alleviate poverty.

For Christians in a secularizing and globalizing world, then, the question is: How is one to concede the validity of secularization in many areas while not surrendering to secularism and atheism as ideologies that mock faith and seek to exclude the insights of religion?

WILLIAM R. BURROWS

*See also* Enlightenment; Europe; Reformation

## Further Reading

Berger, P. L. (1969). *The sacred canopy: Elements of a sociological theory of religion.* Garden City, NY: Doubleday Anchor.

Davie, G. (2000). *Religion in modern Europe: A memory mutates.* Oxford, UK: Oxford University Press.

De Lubac, H. (1967). *The drama of atheistic humanism.* Cleveland, OH: Meridian. (Original work published 1944)

Durkheim, E. (1995). *The elementary forms of religious life.* New York: Free Press. (Original work published 1912)

Illich, I. (2005). *The rivers north of the future: The testament of Ivan Illich as told to David Cayley.* Toronto, Canada: House of Anansi.

Mac Intyre, A., & Ricoeur, P. (1986). *The religious significance of atheism.* New York: Columbia.

Martin, D. (1978). *A general theory of secularization.* New York: Harper.

Shils, E. (1981). *Tradition.* Chicago: University of Chicago Press.

Troeltsch, E. (1976). *The social teaching of the Christian churches* (Vols. 1–2). Chicago: University of Chicago Press. (Original work published 1911)

## Sex Trade

The sex trade is a multibillion dollar business, which feeds on human trafficking with estimates internationally between 800,000 and 1.2 million persons per year and millions more domestically. Particularly grievous is the commercial sexual exploitation of children (CSEC), which is estimated to enslave 1 million additional children every year. CSEC, like any business, is based on supply and demand. From local markets for prostitution, often sanctioned by cultural and social norms, to global sex tourism increasingly targeting children in developing countries, the sex trade is a global scourge. Missionary efforts to confront the sex trade remain largely localized, yet emerging collaborative networks of missions and nongovernmental organizations, such as the Asha Forum and the International Justice Mission, are hopeful signs of expanding missional engagement.

## Conditions Supporting the Sex Trade

One of the most viral of all supporting conditions is the male-dominant societies that provide both the supply and the demand. The socialization of males fosters attitudes of entitlement that divide women into classes or castes that determine their relative worth. One outcome is that these divisions provide the categories for respect and disrespect leading to a relative standard for sexual exploitation. Another outcome is the understanding of what determines masculinity, often leading to positive attitudes toward sexual conquest. Thus, in times of military intervention or war, sexual gratification, rape, and other forms of sexual exploitation are rampant to the point to being used as a tactic of aggression.

Toleration of the exploitation of human beings is nearly a universal social phenomenon. Although some laws exist to fight the sex trade, a combination of corruption, ineffective law enforcement, and weak punishment combine to make it difficult to sustain significant opposition. Attempts to regulate the sex trade in many cases further enslave the victims by forcing a migratory approach by those who control the supply of sex workers.

Economics plays a major role in the sex trade globally. Poverty creates intolerable conditions, which force families to seek all possible sources of income for their basic survival. Such extreme need opens the door for all kinds of exploitation such as forced marriages and indentured servitude. For example, in Southeast Asia many destitute parents are promised that their daughters will work in restaurants or factories, when in reality they are forced into prostitution in the brothels of major cities. Labor migration, particularly for domestic help and manual labor, also create vulnerable populations for sexual exploitation. Additionally the growing accessibility and demand for pornography, prostitution, and sex tourism create conditions leading to a booming business for those who exploit the poor for the sex markets of the world.

Driven by media and marketing, globalization has raised expectations of material gain and consumerism. Owing to the lack of education and marketable skills, many enter and remain in prostitution as the only means of income generation. Money accessible through the sex trade not only profits those who control the industry but also provides income for sex workers to engage in the consumerist society. Other factors such as family breakdown, prior sexual abuse, substance abuse, and severe behavior problems are conditions that increase the vulnerability of youth to the domestic sex trade.

Among the many other conditions surrounding the global sex trade is the spread of the HIV/AIDS pandemic and its impact on the commercial sexual exploitation of children. This is a particularly despicable factor in that it combines the ignorance of the causal conditions of the disease with cultural norms that denigrate the value of children. As the disease has spread, the average age of those who are sexually exploited has dropped. The reasoning is often that they have yet to contract the disease and are therefore safer. In reality this is a false assumption since children and youth have less knowledge and power to protect themselves, which appears to lead to higher rates of infection. Another despicable yet widespread myth is that sleeping with a virgin will cure a person with HIV.

## Missional Responses

Many biblical narratives address sexual exploitation in some form (e.g. Deuteronomy 21:10–14; Judges 5:30; 2 Samuel 11:1–5; 2 Kings 4:1; Hosea; Jonah 7:53–8:11). One of the most widely used as a guide for ministry to sex workers is the story of the prostitute who anointed Jesus (Luke 7:36–50). Therefore, the missional focus is primarily on prostitutes. Missional efforts have sought to rescue those caught in the trap of the sex trade, rightly pointing to the power of the gospel to transform lives. Among the many examples of ministries to prostitutes, the Mary Magdalene Project in Van Nuys, California, launched in 1979 by the West Hollywood Presbyterian Church is an example of effective mission outreach. While it remains a daunting task to establish sustainable ministries, the many examples of both missions to prostitutes and church ministries with a particular focus on sex workers tend to be localized efforts.

Because of the complexities of the sex trade, increasingly missional responses go beyond the sex workers to the people and systems that generate and support the industry. The grievous sins of sexual exploitation require a more transformational view of the Gospel not only in the confrontation of the individuals, but also in concentrated efforts to seek justice on behalf of the exploited.

An outstanding example is the work of the Salvation Army. Although a logical element of their earliest efforts to reach the poor and downtrodden, it was in the 1880s that Mrs. Josephine Butler and her friend Mrs. Bramwell Booth launched a major initiative to help young women caught in the brothels of England and beyond. Their efforts went far beyond the practical local care for women to a broader-based advocacy incorporating influential friends of the Salvation Army in one of the earliest and most effective advocacy ministries. This work has grown internationally along with the missional efforts of the Salvation Army, making it one of the largest global efforts against sexual trafficking and exploitation.

Larger scale efforts to engage in mission both as restorative care for sex workers and advocacy for systemic justice appear to be gaining momentum. Along with the need for active engagement, there is a broad need to raise awareness to support significant change illustrated by the International Justice Mission (IJM) and the ASHA Forum. IJM began in 1997 as an agency dedicated to rescuing victims of sexual exploitation, slavery, oppression, and violence. IJM combines the skills of research, advocacy, intervention, and legal expertise in confronting the sex trade. The ASHA Forum, which is part of the Viva Network, is a global movement of Christians who are committed to the care of children suffering from all forms of sexual abuse. The individual members of the network work collaboratively to exchange both information and resources that serve to expand the impact on both children and those who exploit them.

## Greater Collaboration as a Global Response

The scale of the sex trade continues to escalate globally, far beyond the meager efforts of missions and nongovernmental organizations, yet the combined resources of missions and churches have the potential to make a significant impact on both the demand and the supply of this major industry. The mission mandate requires a serious reconsideration of the focus beyond that of individual victims and perpetrators, to a broader view of the issues of justice and the conditions of the persons affected. A broader view should translate into concerted efforts of networks to address the issues of poverty feeding the supply, collaborative efforts of advocacy and legal action against the perpetrators and users, education for churches, and a renewed commitment to the long-term care of the vulnerable caught in the sex trade, particularly children.

Douglas McConnell

## Further Reading

ASHA Forum. (2003). *The ASHA Forum resource CD*. Oxford, UK: Viva Network.

Brock, R. N., & Thistlethwaite, S. B. (1996). *Casting stones: Prostitution and liberation in Asia and the United States*. Minneapolis, MN: Fortress Press.

Crawford, C. F., & Crawford, M. (2005, Fall). Human trafficking: Children and the sex trade. In *Theology, News &*

*Notes*. Retrieved July 24, 2007, from http://www.fuller.edu/news/pubs/tnn

ECPAT International. (2001*). Child sex tourism action survey*. Retrieved July 24, 2007, from http://www.ecpat.net/eng/Ecpat_inter/Publication/Other/English/Pdf_page/Child_sex_tourism_action.pdf

Farr, K. (2004). *Sex trafficking: The global market in women and children*. New York: Worth Publishers.

Haugen, G. A., & Hunter, G. (2005). *Terrify no more*. Nashville, TN: W Publishing Group.

Johns Hopkins University School of Advanced International Studies. (2007). The Protection Project. Retrieved July 24, 2007, from http://www.protectionproject.org

Kilbourn, P., & McDermid, M. (Eds.). (1998). *Sexually exploited children: Working to heal and protect*. Monrovia, CA: MARC.

Miles, G. M., & Wright, J. J. (Eds.). (2003). *Celebrating children*. Carlisle, UK: Paternoster Press.

UNICEF. (2001). *Profiting from abuse: An investigation into the sexual exploitation of our children*. New York: UNICEF.

United Nations. (2003). *Combating human trafficking in Asia: A resource guide to international and regional legal instruments, political commitments and recommended practices*. New York: United Nations.

# Shinto

Shinto is a Japanese religion distinguished by a network of sacred sites called *jinja* (shrines), at which priests perform rites before the myriad *kami* (deities). The most sacred site is Ise, dedicated to the great *kami* Amaterasu, who is both Sun goddess and ancestress of Japan's imperial line. Shinto doctrine focuses on belief in a vast *kami* pantheon, of which Amaterasu is the greatest.

Shinto is a construct of the modern Japanese state, born of the Meiji revolution in 1868. In earlier times, Shinto had no autonomous existence. The fabric of premodern Japanese religion was thoroughly Buddhist, and Shinto was a nativist motif woven into the Buddhist fabric. In premodern Japan, this Shinto motif sometimes became prominent. The arrival of Christian missionaries in the late sixteenth century was one such occasion. The state's construction of Shinto after the 1868 revolution also took place against the backdrop of a mission-prompted crisis.

## Early Christian Mission

Shinto in late sixteenth and early seventeenth century Japan was the variety promoted by the Yoshida court family. The Yoshida, seeking to extend its influence across ever-greater stretches of Japan, owed their authority to sponsorship by the great military rulers of the day. History records no clashes between Yoshida Shintoists, still very few in number, and Catholic missionaries, but when Japan's military rulers articulated their fears of Christianity, they did so in Yoshida Shinto idiom. When the warlord Toyotomi Hideyoshi (1537–1598) sought to expel Jesuit missionaries in 1587, and when later he addressed the Governor of Goa about his Christian concerns, he spoke of Japan as "the land of the kami;" Christianity and the *kami* were incompatible. On no other occasions did Hideyoshi deploy the Shinto idiom.

His successor, Tokugawa Ieyasu (1542–1616), who founded the military dynasty that ruled Japan until 1867, made a state religion of Buddhism, but he too located Japan as the sacred Shinto realm in his anti-Christian edicts. Having expelled the missionaries, Ieyasu ordered the dissemination throughout Japan of prayers to the Sun goddess; regional lords were ordered to dispatch offerings to Ise, too. The dynamic is of a nativist order: The Christian menace generates a new and keen awareness of Japan as the land of Shinto *kami*, which in turn legitimates Christianity's persecution and expulsion.

Catholics were expelled from Japan in the 1630s and Japan cut itself off entirely from Catholic Europe, but the horrific memory of this episode endured. It did so on anti-Christian notice boards erected in every village in Japan, and in various widely disseminated anti-Christian chapbooks. This memory was complicated in the nineteenth century by new knowledge of Protestant Christianity as the source of the West's strength and stability. Dutch and Chinese books entered Japan beneath the censors' gaze, and circulated this new knowledge among intellectuals. In early nineteenth century, when the powers of Britain and Russia returned to Asian waters, this knowledge prompted in Japanese intellectuals new fears of Christianity as a dreadful foe; they too invariably deployed the nativist Shinto idiom.

*New Thesis* by Aizawa Seishisai (1781–1863), the most important tract of prerevolutionary Japan, is a classic example of this approach. Aizawa argued that Christianity was more to be feared than Western gunboats since it would bewitch the masses; Japan's only hope of survival lay in a complete restructuring of the polity. The emperor, his performance of state rites before the Sun goddess, and the revitalization of local shrine worship alone would guarantee Japan's ability to resist Christian temptations when foreigners forced their way into Japan, as certainly they would.

## Shinto Constructs

Japan's modern period opened with a revolution in 1868, which took the form of a restoration of political power to the emperor. The new leadership dramatized the myth of the emperor's direct descent from the Sun goddess to legitimate the new government which he headed and they ran. This involved appropriating the Sun goddess's shrine at Ise; "discovering" and claiming imperial mausoleums to display the longevity of the imperial line; and inventing new state rites that celebrated the descent of the emperor and his ancestors from the Sun goddess. The leadership declared shrines across Japan "sites for the performance of state rites" and instituted a program of shrine ritual to disseminate the imperial myth; a missionary program was also launched. This, then, was the essence of the new Shinto construct: imperial rites at center and periphery, nationalization of shrines and priesthood, and a missionary program.

Violence against Buddhism was integral to the process. Shinto *kami*, always deemed Japanese manifestations of Buddhist truth, were now accorded new Japanese identities, and Shinto shrines, usually located in Buddhist temple compounds, now acquired their own privileged space. Buddhism was not banned, but it was disestablished, and many temples were destroyed and priests defrocked.

In 1868, the leaders of the new Meiji government reissued the Tokugawa proscription against Christianity and used it to take radical action against native Christians. The Christians in question were the "hidden Christians" from Nagasaki, whose ancestors had gone underground over two centuries before and who were "discovered" by French missionaries in Nagasaki in the early 1860s. The new government now deported these Christians, since their very existence challenged the proscription, and banished them to domains across Japan. This they did despite the protests of foreign diplomats who had been stationed in Japan since the "unequal treaties" of 1858. Christianity thus became the major diplomatic issue for the new government until the Christians were released from exile in 1873. It was precisely at this time that the state set about constructing Shinto.

Some historians argue that the modern state's enthusiasm for Shinto explains the Christian proscription and the persecution of adherents. Others insist that the leaderships' entirely reasonable fear of missionaries backed by gunboats itself accounts, to some degree at least, for the state's enthusiasm for Shinto. Despite the complexity of cause and effect, a nativist dynamic is once again apparent here. As early Meiji leaders dis-cussed the imperial myth, state rites, shrines, and the missionary program, they regularly cited the threat of Christianity as a justification for taking action. The leadership argued, much like Aizawa in his *New Thesis*, that only the establishment of Shinto, both structures and doctrines, would protect Japan from Christian evil.

## Shinto Doctrine

The Meiji government, taxed by issues of Shinto doctrine, created a succession of bodies to compose a coherent doctrine for modern Japan that would be at once attractive to the masses *and* capable of countering the inevitable spread of Christianity. Such a doctrine, it was agreed, would have to address issues of the soul, heaven, hell, and creation, since these were the essence of Christianity and the secret of its popular appeal. One early formulation, penned by Shintoist interrogators of the Nagasaki Christians, cast the Sun goddess as "creator deity who rules heaven and earth and gives to humans their souls which, when they die, return to heaven." This prompted ridicule from other Shintoists in government. The creator *kami*, they insisted, was Ame no minaka nushi; he it was who gave humans their souls which, depending on their conduct in this life, would after death go to heaven or hell. The *kami* Okuni nushi judged human conduct and determined the fate of their souls.

These men were adducing the Shinto theories of Hirata Atsutane (1776–1843). In the 1830s, Hirata had studied the Christian theological writings of Jesuit missionaries in China, and inspired by them he reinterpreted Japan's eighth-century myths and discovered in them Japanese versions of much of Catholic doctrine. This Hirata Shinto now found favor with the religions ministry, established in 1872 with a specific counter-Christian brief. The religions ministry commandeered all Japanese religionists, shrine priests as well as Buddhist monks, as "state missionaries" whose role was to disseminate the doctrine across Japan. This government-sponsored mission quickly failed because Buddhists, deploying Western arguments on the separation of state and religion, resisted government pressure to preach Hirata Shinto theories of creation and the afterlife. The government relented, abolished the religions ministry, and freed Buddhists to preach and counter Christianity in their own way, as long as they respected the imperial myth.

Doctrine remained an issue of contention, however, within the Shinto community, represented now in a semiofficial body called the Shinto bureau. The bureau, under the control of Ise priests, endeavored to cast itself as the national Shinto center, and to this end built a new shrine at its Tokyo headquarters. The shrine accommodated the Sun goddess and the creator Ame no minakanushi, but this provoked outrage from other priests who insisted that the *kami* Okuni nushi must also be venerated. Okuni nushi was the *kami* enshrined at the ancient Izumo shrine, and the Shinto bureau's refusal to accommodate Okuni nushi led to a major rupture in the Shinto community between pro-Ise and pro-Izumo factions. So bitter was the dispute that the government intervened, fearful lest the Sun goddess be dragged into unseemly debates. The government determined that religious *kami,* be they creators or judges, had no place in the Shinto bureau. Only the *kami* who embodied the imperial myth, the Sun goddess and the imperial ancestors, should be venerated there.

The government initiated other steps, too, to make clear that it was uniquely concerned for the preservation and dissemination of the imperial myth, through the performance of shrine rites. It banned shrine priests' involvement in any form of religious propaganda. If priests wished to propagate theories about creation, heaven, and hell, they had to leave their shrines and found their own Shinto sects. This led, in the 1880s, to a split between "shrine Shinto" ("state Shinto"), which was myth-focused and "non-religious," and "religious Shinto," a split that was manifest in a flurry of new Shinto sects, whose founders and followers now engaged in proselytizing across Japan.

The Christian mission remained a matter of the gravest concern to these new Shinto sects. Some of the best known to emerge in the 1880s and 1890s owed their very existence to the founders' fears of Christian perniciousness. Among these new sects were Shinto shuseiha, founded by Nitta Kuniteru (1829–1902), Shinto taiseikyo, founded by Hirayama Seisai (1815–1890), and Shinrikyo, founded by Sano Tsunehiko (1834–1906). These three men were especially concerned by the successes in the 1870s and 1880s of the Russian missionary Nikolai. In a fascinating debate between Sano and Nikolai on the relative merits of Shinto and Christianity, he men argued over the formation of the two creeds, with Sano insisting Christianity was man-made in comparison to Shinto's natural quality. In discussing creation, Nikolai accused Sano of plagiarizing Christianity. They clashed over the soul, too, with Sano insisting that Shinto was no less sophisticated than Christianity. Finally, Sano asked whether Christian converts could ever be patriotic since they adhered to a creed that was foreign.

The government remained suspicious of Christianity and missionary motives, but it knew that Japan could never revise the humiliating treaties of 1858 and achieve parity with the Western powers unless it granted freedom of religion. This was one achievement of the Meiji Constitution of 1890.

## Shinto in Constitutional Japan

In its very first articles, the Constitution proclaimed the imperial line as "unbroken for ages eternal" and referred to the emperor himself as "sacred and inviolable." The essentially Shinto worldview articulated here was reproduced in the same year in the imperial rescript on education. It cited the heavenly ancestress and

Heian Jingu temple, one of the most famous attractions in Kyoto, Japan.
*Courtesy of Chai Kian Shin/istockphoto.com.*

the first emperor Jinmu, before proclaiming loyalty and filial piety as the "glory of the fundamental character of our Empire." These two documents constituted the ideological frame within which Christianity would be accommodated in prewar Japan. What were the implications for missionaries and their Japanese converts?

The first thing to note is that the Constitution granted to all Japanese freedom of religious practice "within limits not prejudicial to peace and order and not antagonistic to their duties as subjects." Later, in the 1920s, 1930s, and 1940s, the state came to regard attendance at (nonreligious) shrine rites as one of a subject's several duties, and Christians found themselves compelled to attend. More immediate in its impact was the education rescript. Indeed, in New Year 1891, the Christian convert Uchimura Kanzo (1861–1930) was dismissed from his post at a Tokyo high school for heeding his "Christian conscience" and refusing to bow before the rescript. Uchimura's actions led to a wave of anti-Christian invective from nationalist intellectuals and the right wing press. Christians went on the defensive for the next couple of decades, and their typical response was to disown Uchimura, insisting that the rescript was quite compatible with their beliefs and that there was no patriot like the Christian patriot.

From the second decade of the twentieth century, in response partly to the national trauma of the Meiji emperor's death, the enthronement of his successor, and the outbreak of the World War I, the government began to encourage teachers to take pupils to Shinto shrines and, before long, excursions to Ise became de rigueur. The content of state education began to change, too, as the imperial myth infiltrated history and ethics curricula. The whole scope of education was eventually dominated by "instruction in a politico-religious ancestralism centering on the Sun goddess." At first, schools and universities in the state sector were affected but not private institutions such as those run by Protestant or Catholic missions. In the 1930s, however, the Japanese government was embroiled in a bloody war with China and struggled to cope with acts of ultra-right-wing terror at home; it began to demand that all Christians display patriotic credentials. Shrine attendance and *kami* veneration became the litmus test of patriotism in these years. Three incidents suggest how these new pressures were applied to Japanese Christians.

In 1932, the Japanese army seized Manchuria, which prompted the government to demand that students from colleges all over Japan visit one shrine in particular. This was the new Yasukuni shrine in Tokyo, dedicated to the spirits of the imperial Japanese war dead. A number of students from Sophia, the Catholic university in Tokyo, refused to attend Yasukuni on the grounds that veneration was incompatible with their own religious beliefs, and that pressure to do so infringed their religious freedom. The press responded with invectives against Catholics and other Christians. When the Catholic archbishop of Tokyo was assured by the government that acts of veneration at Yasukuni were simply "manifestations of patriotism and loyalty," the archbishop relented and encouraged Catholics to participate.

The Protestant University of Doshisha in Kyoto put up stiffer resistance to the demands of state Shinto. In one incident, a right-wing student removed from the martial arts hall the photograph of the university's founder, Christian convert Niijima Jo (1843–1890), and replaced it with a *kami* altar. The university reprimanded the student and restored Niijima's portrait, but news got out and the university was attacked for its lack of patriotism. The army became involved, overcame the university president's resistance, and got its way. The president was subsequently pilloried for dismissing a lecturer who extolled the imperial myth, for misreciting the education rescript, and for removing protestors who occupied the university chapel to protest his lack of patriotism.

The target of the most brutal clampdown, though, was the Protestant Holiness church. When the pastor of the Hakodate branch refused to attend the local shrine, he was arrested and thrown in prison where he died. Hundreds of Holiness believers were rounded up on charges of lese-majesté, for they rejected the imperial myth and taught that the emperor was no less sinful than the rest of God's creation. The church was subsequently banned.

In the 1940s, as Japan embarked on total war, Christians of all hues came under ever greater pressure to demonstrate patriotism by conforming to Shinto dictates. All Protestant ministers, for example, were required to undergo Shinto training at Tokyo's Meiji shrine. In 1944, Catholic and Protestant churches were marshaled into the Great Japan religious patriotic society. Compliance with the state's ideological demands and the emergence in these years of a new form of patriotic Christian apologetic ensured the escape of the majority of Christians from the fate of the Holiness church.

## Shinto Missions Overseas

Shinto missionaries were rarely dispatched overseas. Buddhist missionaries typically accompanied the imperial army as it extended its influence over Asia. This was on account of the Buddhists' historical responsibility for funeral rites. Nonetheless, the Japanese imperial army built shrines, a majority dedicated to the Sun goddess, in most of its Asian colonies—in Korea, Taiwan, and Manchuria, to name the major sites—in order to "edify" colonial populations.

The religious Shinto sects that sprang up in the 1880s constitute an important exception to the rule about Shinto overseas missions. Of these sects, the Shinto shuseiha mission to Korea in the 1880s is the oldest; Tenrikyo followed suit in the 1890s with missions to Korea, Taiwan, and then the United States. Konkokyo, Omotokyo, and Seicho all launched missions in Korea and North and South American before the Pacific war broke out in 1941. Many of these Shinto-based sects are active overseas to this day in the Americas and Europe, as well as in former Japanese colonies.

JOHN BREEN

*See also* Asia, East; Buddhism; Militarism; Protestant Churches; Roman Catholic Church

### Further Reading

Breen, J. & Teeuwen, M. (Eds.). (2000). *Shinto in history: Ways of the* kami. Honolulu: Hawaii University Press.

Hardacre, H. (1989). *Shinto and the state, 1868–1988.* Princeton, NJ: Princeton University Press.

Holtom, D. C. (1938). *The national faith of Japan.* London: Kegan Paul and Tubner.

Nobutaka, I. (Ed.). (2002). *Shinto: A short history.* Oxford, UK: RoutledgeCurzon.

Mullins, M. (Ed.) (2003). *Handbook of Christianity in Japan.* Leiden, Netherlands: Brill.

## Short-term Missions

Within the past generation the Western Protestant church has experienced the explosive growth of short-term missions. The most recent version of the *Mission Handbook* (2004–2006) claims that the number of people going on short-term mission trips reported by United States agencies listed in the handbook grew from 97,272 in 1998 to 346,270 in 2001 (Welliver and Northcutt 2004, 13). That is an amazing 256 percent increase in three years. When combined with declining numbers of long-term missions personnel, some have called this change the most significant in modern missions history (Allen 2001; Barnes 1992). Considerable disposable wealth, inexpensive and efficient air travel, and excellent commu-

nication resources have aided short-term missionaries living in the West. In addition to the thousands of churches sending teams, there are now hundreds of specialized short-term-missions organizations that facilitate every aspect of the mission experience.

### Long-term Value

While most acknowledge that the short-term-mission phenomenon is here to stay, the movement has attracted considerable scrutiny and concern within the broader missions community. Concerns have been raised about the ethnocentrism, relational shallowness, self-serving impact, and overall cost of short-term missions (Slimbach 2000; Van Engen 2000; Atkins 1991). With the groundswell of interest in short-term missions has come many poorly organized and missiologically weak cross-cultural assignments that often do more harm than good.

What is the long-term value of the growing short-term-missions phenomena? While some proponents of short-term missions acknowledge the potential pitfalls inherent in sending young adults into cross-cultural settings for intense service and learning experiences, they also point to the life-changing discipleship opportunities these trips afford for all involved (Barnes 2001, 1992; McDonough and Peterson 1999; Borthwick 1996). The best models of short-term mission have anticipated the various missiological land mines inherent in this effort and have sought to avoid them through in-depth discipleship preparation, careful and appropriate service or mission under the leadership of hosting churches, and a thorough hosting ministry and participant debrief.

### Short-term Missions Defined

Short-term missions are a subset of the larger missionary effort. The term "missionary" comes from the Latin word *mitto*, which means "to send." Christian missionaries are those who have been sent out to share the Gospel of Christ, a Gospel that declares that creation can be reconciled to its Creator God through the substitutionary and completed work of Christ on the cross (Peterson, Aeschliman, and Sneed 2003, 43).

The MARC Missions Handbook describes long-term missionaries as those serving more than four years in a foreign field (Siewert and Valde 1997, 74). Short-term-mission work is divided among those serving from two weeks to a year, one to two years, and two to four years (Siewert and Valdez 1997, 74). The challenge with both defining and describing short-term missions is found in the variety of ways in which short-term mission is expressed. "Short-term mission" in North America has described everything from poorly planned local church youth group forays into Mexico for a week to well-planned programs incorporating hundreds and sometimes thousands of young adults, all divided into well-trained smaller teams and sent around the world.

STEM Director and short-term-mission researcher Roger Peterson notes that "time" or length of service is only one of eight primary defining variables of short-term mission. The eight variables include time, activity, size, on-field location, participant demographics, sending institution, ministry philosophy, and leadership/training. As a result, Peterson's definition of short-term mission is "the God–commanded, repetitive deployment of swift, temporary non-professional missionaries" (McDonough and Peterson 1999, 4).

## Response to New Generation

The growth in short-term missions, while difficult to categorize, has continued through the past thirty years and now includes the church from every continent. A significant portion of the short-term-mission movement is now coming from Korea, South Africa, and Brazil.

North American short-term-missions organizations that are responding to the unique challenges of a self-absorbed, experientially driven generation point to the life-changing impact of the mission experience on the participants themselves. Robert Bland, director of Teen Mission International states,

> We tell our people who are leading our teams that we're building kids, not buildings. The purpose isn't just what we'll do for these people, but what these people will do for us . . . there is not a single purpose in missionary work . . . but to us this is the first purpose (Allen 2001, 46).

However, this discipleship-focused approach of using missions trips to teach the short-term missionary is viewed by some as a significant divergence from past mission paradigms. Missiologist Sherwood Lingenfelter views this self-focus as an expression of our therapeutic culture. It is a direction that Lingenfelter feels could contribute to the church's distraction away from the path of the cross (Allen 2001, 12). Others respond that this concern is valid only if a self-focused motivation for service is foremost in the minds of those who are serving. If, however, the servant is blessed in the context of serving—as a by-product and not as the primary

motivation—then the self-benefit is neither unethical nor unbiblical (Barnes 1992, 381). Rather than being intentionally self-focused, short-term mission presents an opportunity to disciple an experientially driven generation toward a biblically Christian worldview.

To generalize about the motivation of participants in the short-term-mission movement as a whole is simply not possible. The activities of mission and ongoing growth as a disciple cannot be separated. Leaders of short-term-mission programs point out that mission experiences are not an end in themselves but merely another step in a life of mission and discipleship.

Missiologist Richard Slimbach claims that these same ethnocentric attitudes are systemic in the Western short-term-mission movement. His critique, while based on the worst cases of short-term-mission preparation, planning, and delivery, must be understood. Slimbach argues that short-term missions and the two-thirds world settings within which most assignments take place have become a commodity that spiritually disillusioned, experientially driven young people consume. This packaged spirituality "can actually feed the existential alienation many youth feel in an increasingly McDonaldized society" (Slimbach 2000, 430).

## "Edifice Complex"

The limited time frame and Western need to accomplish something adds further pressure to the meeting of cultures and leads to what some have called the "edifice complex," in which buildings and projects, not people, become the focus (Jeffery 2001, 6). The recipients of mission, who Slimbach calls "culture brokers," interact with their short-term-mission guests in a "staged tourist space" marked by disparities of power and levels of stereotyping that would not exist between neighbors or peers (Slimbach 2000, 431). These recipients of mission can also be treated as unfortunate objects to be rescued, rather than equals to learn from and walk alongside (Van Engen 2000, 22). Unequal relationships like these can lead to "benevolent colonialism" (Allen 2001, 44) or, even worse, "disabling help" or "malevolent generosity" (Slimbach 2000, 431).

The challenge in overcoming ethnocentrism within the short-term-mission experience is that the limited time frame prevents what missiologists call a paradigm shift. Without a paradigm shift, cross-cultural situations are always interpreted through the missionary's own cultural grid. Lingenfelter points out that this process of change requires language learning and living with people, "the fact of short-term missions is that, however long you're there, you never have to change the way you do your work" (Allen 2000, 42). Given these unavoidable ethnocentric realities, Lingenfelter recommends increasing the quality of pretrip preparation and raising the entry requirements for short-term mission participation. He cites his own experience in taking a team to Chad as an example (Allen 2000, 45).

Slimbach and others also call for better preparation of short-term-mission participants, including a deeper understanding of the whole Gospel and the climate of globalization within which the Gospel is lived. Attitudes such as humility, teaching ability, and a willingness to focus more cross-cultural mission at home are also encouraged. Others point to the need for joint discipleship assignments, in which participants from the host country are involved in planning and serving in the team assignment (Adeney 1996; Allen 2001; Slimbach 2000; Van Engen 2000).

There is nothing short-term about Christ's call to join Him in mission. While the challenges of the short-term-mission phenomena that is transforming the world of mission are great, so is the potential to reenergize and mobilize the mission vision of the church.

RANDY FRIESEN

## Further Reading

Adeney, C. (1996). McMissions. *Christianity Today, 40*(13), 14–15.

Allen, M. (2001). International short-term missions—a divergence from the Great Commission? *Youthworker Journal,* (17), 40–45.

Atkins, A. (1991). Work teams? No, taste and see teams. *Evangelical Missions Quarterly, 27*(4), 384–387.

Barnes, S. (1992). The changing face of the missionary force. *Evangelical Missions Quarterly, 28*(4):376–381.

Barnes, S. (2001). Ten emerging trends in short-term missions. *Missions Frontiers, 1,* 13–15

Borthwick, P. (1996). Short-term youth teams: Are they really worth it? *Evangelical Missions Quarterly, 32,* 403–408.

Friesen, R. (2005). The long-term impact of short-term missions. *Evangelical Missions Quarterly, 41,* 448–454.

Jeffery, P. ( 2001). Short-term missions trips. *Christian Century, 118*(34), 5–7.

McDonough, D., & Peterson, R. (1999). *Can short-term mission really create long-term career missionaries?* Minneapolis, MN: Stem Ministries.

Moreau, S. A., & O'Rear, M. (2004, January). All you ever wanted on short-term missions. *Evangelical Missions Quarterly,* 100–105.

Pelt, L. (1992). What's behind the wave of short-termers? *Evangelical Missions Quarterly, 28*(4):384–388.

Peterson, R., Aeschliman, G., & Sneed, R. W. (2003). *Maximum impact short-term mission.* Minneapolis, MN: STEM Press.

Peterson, R. P., & Peterson, T. D. (1991). *Is short-term mission really worth the time and money?* Minneapolis, MN: STEM Ministries.

Siewert, J. A., & Valdez, E. G. (Eds.). (1997). *Missions handbook 1998–2000.* Monrovia, CA: MARC Publications.

Slimbach, R. (2000). First, do no harm. *Evangelical Missions Quarterly, 36,* 428–441.

Van Engen, J. A. (2000). The cost of short-term missions. *The Other Side, 36,* 20–23.

Welliver, D., & Northcutt, M. (Eds.). (2004). *Mission handbook 2004–2006: US and Canadian Ministries Overseas.* Wheaton, IL: EMIS.

# Sickness and Healing

Just as the experience of sickness is universal, so, too, is the experience of healing. Throughout time and in every culture, people have fallen ill and regained strength, experiencing in this a dependency upon a source of life beyond their own control. This is what accounts for the religious dimension of sickness and healing and its relevance for missiological reflection. The primary question this raises is not, as is asked today, how to stay healthy—a very modern question tainted by affluence. Rather, the primary question is how to stay alive at all, indicating the close affinity—though certainly not an identity—between healing and salvation.

Cultures interpret sickness and healing according to their own particular worldview. For example, a disease attributed to witches requires a witch doctor and may include the elimination of the witch as part of the healing; thus the attempt to undo and avoid further harm may spark hatred and fear. But if a disease is attributed to the malfunctioning of a gland, a doctor will prescribe a remedy, such as medication, that may not have a direct impact on the community. In both cases, the lasting success of any healing requires compliance with the directives of the healer-expert. Both the patient and the healer accept a particular rationale for the healing regimen. Whatever the regimen, it, too, reflects the plausibility structure of a particular culture.

Because such differences will be pointedly articulated when people describe their experiences of sickness and healing, they need to be a top priority for missiological concern. Unfortunately, however, this was not fully realized until 1988 when the International Association of Mission Studies (IAMS) put it on its research agenda.

## History of Healing

The disciples of Jesus were sent to heal, and healing was always an important element in the life of the early church and in its growth and expansion during the first centuries. Caring, which was also ingrained in the nascent church, of course, eventually replaced healing and went on to become the only one of these activities accepted by the official church of the Latin West, most notably after the Fourth Lateran Council in 1215. This was in part the result of a change in attitude toward the compatibility of religious duties with the exercise of medicine, especially by those who were consecrated priests and religious. But the neglect of healing was also born, in part, out of a dualistic, neo-Platonic anthropology that held that "the soul is much more precious than the body." (Canon 22 of the council, see also Schroeder 1937)

The intention of the 1215 ruling can be understood as a way of protecting the integrity of the priestly office by safeguarding it against the possible commission of unintentional homicide and by protecting it from responsibility for the physical well-being of neophytes. However, it also blinded the church and its missionaries to the vital religious connotations of experiences like illness and healing. Religion thereby became something merely spiritual, leading to an atrophied understanding both of the human being and of the goal of genuine Christian witness.

And while the missionary encounter constantly exposed people to plausibility structures other than their own, especially in the rationalistic nineteenth and twentieth centuries, missionaries were left to their own devices when they had to deal with explanations of life-threatening diseases as caused by evil spirits, demons, or bewitchment. Missionaries were also left somewhat adrift when they had to relate to diviners, witch doctors, shamans, and medicine men, who were—and remain—vitally important for many indigenous systems of healing.

Most missionaries saw indigenous healers as representatives of superstition and magic and targeted them accordingly as "the main bulwark of Satan" against which they felt called to mount a "campaign." They did so, however, without providing neophytes with an adequate replacement, since dealing with spirit worlds was not regarded as the proper business of missionar-ies. Because of this, they left their neophytes vulnerable to other explanations; they also jettisoned pneumatology from missiological studies. This attitude was challenged when the interdependence of health and salvation was realized. This happened first in the mid-nineteenth century with the rise of medical missions, itself "an epiphenomenon of the history of the medical profession" (Walls 1982, 287) and also of the history of rational-scientific medicine in general. It was later challenged from another angle by Pentecostal and Charismatic healing movements in the United States and Great Britain, in the rediscovery of the ministry of healing within the Church of England, and in the World Council of Churches.

Perhaps the most striking of these developments was the emergence of innumerable healing churches around the globe, especially in sub-Saharan Africa. However, this did not simply reflect a reawakening of a vital dimension of the church's ministry; it also indicated an awareness of local responses to societal and cultural changes, the responses of those who are desperately trying to counteract the debilitating effects—the emotional stress and the fear of loss of identity—of globalization.

## Missiological Challenges

The dyad "sickness and healing" refers to the highly complex missiological issues tied to differences in the basic perception of the world and life. To communicate meaningfully about these topics, there must first of all be a terminology that can competently handle the broad variety of phenomena to be addressed, from both medical and religious perspectives, within the unavoidable intercultural and interreligious context of any such discourse today.

Further, questions have to be posed from at least three different angles, all of which have been more or less ignored in missiology so far and deserve further study. First, what is the disease-causing agent? If sickness is caused by evil spirits or by witchcraft, efforts have to be made to come to terms with the power ascribed to these causes by those who have been raised within that particular framework.

Second, to whom or to what is the healing process attributed? Is it potent, magically infused medicine, a miracle drug, or a charismatic person healing with special authority? Whatever the answer might be, grave differences will surface and have to be dealt with, once again without jumping too quickly to conclusions as to the superiority of one system over the other. Discernment, not judgment, is called for.

Third, how are experiences of debility and regaining strength generally interpreted and made sense of in different cultures? In the end, all these questions address the basic issue of how life—that of the individual as well as that of the human community at large—is perceived. The missiological challenge lies precisely here.

CHRISTOFFER H. GRUNDMANN

*See also* Development; Medicine; Mission Methods and Strategy; Missionary Vocation and Service; Social Gospel

## Further Reading

*A time to heal—a contribution towards the ministry of healing: A report for the House of Bishops on the healing ministry.* (2000). London: Church House Publishing.

Caplan, A. L., Engelhardt, H. T., Jr., & McCartney, J. J. (Eds.). (1981). *Concepts of health and disease: Interdisciplinary perspectives.* Reading, MA: Addison-Wesley.

*Church's Ministry of Healing—Report of the Archbishop's Commission, The.* (1958). London: Church Information Board.

Ferngren, G. B. (1992). Early Christianity as a religion of healing. *Bulletin of the History of Medicine, 66,* 1–15.

Grundmann, C. H. (1989). Aspects of further research within the study project "Healing." *Mission Studies, VI(1),* 70–71.

Grundmann, C. H. (2001). Healing—a challenge to church and theology. *International Review of Missions, XC(356/357),* 26–40.

Grundmann, C. H. (2005). Inviting the Spirit to fight the Spirits? *International Review of Missions, 94(372),* 51–73.

Grundmann, C. H. (2005b). *Sent to heal!—emergence and development of medical missions.* Lanham, MD.: University Press of America.

Harrell, D. E., Jr. (1975). *All things are possible—the healing and charismatic revivals in modern America.* Bloomington, IN: University of Indiana Press.

Kleinman, A. (1981). *Patients and healers in the context of culture.* Berkeley: University of California Press.

Larty, E., Nwachuku, D., & Kasonga, K. W. (Eds.). (1994). *The Church and healing—echoes from Africa.* Frankfurt, Germany: Lang.

Oosthuizen, G. C. (1992). *The healer-prophet in Afro-Christian Churches.* Leiden, Netherlands: Brill.

Schiefenhövel, W., Schuler, J., & Pöschel, R. (Eds.). *Traditional healers, Iatric personalities in different cultures and medical systems.* Braunschweig, Germany: Vieweg.

Schroeder, H. J. (1937). *Fourth Lateran Council, 1215. Disciplinary decrees of the general councils: Text, translation and commentary.* St. Louis, MO: Herder.

Seybold, K., & Müller, U. (1978). *Sickness and healing.* Nashville, TN: Abingdon.

Walls, A. F. (1982). The heavy artillery of the missionary army: the domestic importance of the nineteenth-century medical missionary. In W. J. Sheils (Ed.), *The church and healing* (pp. 287–297). Oxford, UK: Blackwell.

# Slavery

Slavery has intersected with Christian mission in many ways. The metaphorical enslavement of unbelief or sinfulness has long inspired missionaries to pursue the conversion of others for their genuine liberation. Yet literal slavery has in three important ways also shaped and been shaped by mission. First, Christian missionaries have on occasion targeted slaves who demonstrated their eagerness for Christianity. Sometimes slaves were the only potential converts since political circumstances prevented the evangelization of free persons. Second, slaves have responded to the missionary message, reshaping Christianity by their enthusiasm. Third, abolition has overlapped with European Christian mission. Catholic missionaries in the Americas first challenged the treatment of slaves, but English Protestants forged a connection between missionaries and the antislavery movement. Beginning in the late eighteenth century, missionary-initiated campaigns to make known the horrors of slavery mobilized mission with profound results for individuals and entire peoples.

## Defining Slavery

*Slave* denotes one who exists in a perpetual property relation to another and whose life and labor thus belong to another. Scholars disagree whether to consider slave status an essential aspect of identity generated by political dependence—thus one is a slave or not—or one extreme in a continuum of relationships that can be more or less exploitative—in which case some, usually designated nonkin, are more enslaved than others. Regardless, since exploitation of unfree labor has featured in human societies for millennia, Christianity has nearly everywhere faced slavery.

## Slavery and Christian Belonging

Owing to the ubiquity of slavery, those bringing Christianity to others in mission have met mixed populations defined by degree of enslavement. Potential converts have included both those owned by and those owning others, those considered kin and those beyond kinship (and thus subject to enslavement), and those designated free and those considered not free. Missionaries have taken varying strategies in the face of such social differences.

Already in the New Testament period, the prototypical Christian missionary, Paul of Tarsus, faced slavery. He encouraged the mild treatment of slaves and even sought to persuade at least one slave owner, Philemon, to free his slave Onesimus. Paul also, however, counseled slaves to obey their masters. Slaves and owners shared one faith, yet Paul never condemned slavery despite the implicit egalitarian message he preached: "There is neither Jew nor Greek, there is neither slave nor free person, there is not male or female; for you are all one in Christ Jesus" (Galatians 3:28).

Economic and political changes in Europe led to the near disappearance of slavery by the early medieval period. Efforts to free Christian slaves held by Muslims, however, generated a missionary impulse in the period leading up to, during, and after the Crusades, and captured Muslims suffered enslavement. Slavery then expanded in Europe as the Portuguese rounded Africa in the fifteenth century, with papal approval of the enslavement of Muslims—and, by extension, other Africans—who resisted Christianization. The economic pressures of exploiting new lands led slavery to expand enormously after the European discovery of the Americas.

## Mission and the Treatment of Slaves

Prior to the eighteenth century, attacks on the institution of slavery were almost unknown. Christians defended slavery based on the Bible and natural law, as well as on pragmatic grounds. Though not pursuing abolition, Christians often urged compassion for slaves and sought their conversion. In the Americas such calls had important effects by the early sixteenth century. Missionaries such as Antonio de Montesinos and Bartolomé de Las Casas condemned the brutality of Iberian slave practices that victimized Amerindians. Though an eventual formal ban on enslaving Native-Americans fostered the vast and tragic importation of African slaves, the implicit critique of unjustified enslavement also generated reflection on human dignity that arguably created a foundation for contemporary notions of human rights.

Unfortunately, humanitarian concern among missionaries initially did nothing to avert one of history's great moral catastrophes, the Atlantic slave trade. Starting in the sixteenth century, Europeans brought mil-

lions of Africans to the Americas to work in mines and on plantations. Enslavement and shipment of Africans began as a pragmatic approach to a labor problem but eventually acquired a racist ideology for its defense, sometimes linked to the supposed curse of Ham, Noah's son, a stigma putatively inherited by Africans.

Certain missionaries, Protestant and Catholic, worked to convert African slaves in the Americas, many of whom over time were drawn to the Christian message. Missionaries also sought to ease their suffering. Still others emphasized the long-standing expectation that conversion to Christianity meant manumission. Consequently slave-owners in the Americas, like their medieval predecessors holding Muslim slaves, resisted efforts to evangelize their slaves out of a desire to protect their property. In the Americas (and medieval Europe) this facilitated the formal legal acceptance of the enslavement of Christians, a dubious compromise that protected slavery while allowing evangelization. Slaves who converted to Christianity often responded by themselves transforming the gospel into a message congruent with African cultural forms, generating a "slave religion" suitable for their captive circumstances.

## Mission and Abolition

Enlightenment theorists and devout Quakers first challenged the morality of slavery as an institution. Such questioning generated campaigns for abolition that grew in strength toward the end of the eighteenth and into the nineteenth centuries. Former slaves like Olaudah Equiano became prominent spokespersons for abolition in Great Britain. The French Revolution led to a short-lived decree of abolition, and ardent British Protestant abolitionists eventually achieved a formal decree of abolition in 1807, though slavery remained legal in British colonies until 1832. British abolitionists such as William Wilberforce also urged missionary activity in Africa, linking efforts at spiritual and legal emancipation. Abolitionism led to the 1787 founding of the freed slave colony in Sierra Leone and early nineteenth-century campaigns for free labor in the Caribbean and later in Africa. A few missionaries encouraged slave uprisings, such as the 1823 Demerara Revolt in British Guyana, but most focused on stopping the slave trade from Africa and abolishing slavery legally. Famous abolitionists such as the Scottish Protestant missionary David Livingstone and the Catholic Frenchman Cardinal Lavigerie, founder of the White Fathers (or Missionaries of Africa), made ending slavery the heart of their missionary appeals as they sought to inspire potential missionaries and gather material sup-

## Missionaries and Abolition

Linking abolition and mission was more difficult for Catholics than Protestants because abolitionists in Catholic countries were generally anti-clerical, associating freedom from slavery with other freedoms associated with the French Revolution. Both Protestant and Catholic mission-sponsoring agencies, however, emphasized slavery's cruelties to support their evangelists, especially in Africa. Missionaries wrote in *The Anti-Slavery Reporter* from its inception in 1825 and spurred the 1841 Niger River Anti-Slavery Expedition and its predecessors, while mid-century writings and speeches by David Livingstone decried the horrors of slavery. Similar descriptions, with ink drawings of atrocities, also appeared in Catholic writings such as the *Annales de la Propagation de la Foi* and the more popular *Les Missions Catholiques.*

Both Protestant and Catholic missionaries also produced works recounting slave experiences. These included breath-taking tales of high-sea adventure to free emaciated Africans packed into slave-ships; tragic biographical accounts of African family life undone by enslaving marauders, with those taken then bound and marched to the coast after watching family members slain before their eyes; and gory descriptions of slave markets where heartless buyers probed and prodded Africans enfeebled by fatigue and fear. The Zanzibar-centered Catholic Holy Ghost Fathers, or Spiritans, thus produced *Suema* in 1865, the purportedly true account of a young girl enslaved and then rescued by the mission, eventually becoming a nun. The Spiritan seminarian Alexandre Le Roy, later an archbishop, ethnographer of Africa's religions, and professor in Paris, wrote the musical drama *Andalouma,* which featured an African chief's Christian son piously facing enslavement and near-martyrdom. Both tales and many others like them stressed the providential role of the mission in delivering slaves from affliction through redemption and/or conversion.

Nineteenth-century representations of slavery had important consequences. Missionary descriptions of slavery's horrors brought in money and recruited new missionaries; they also likely legitimated European overrule by emphasizing Africa's weaknesses and the need for benevolent intervention. And the legacy of such representations continues. Thus the personal sponsorship of individual children (with names and descriptions) by personal benefactors located in onetime mission-sending countries—a common practice today by mostly secular agencies—derived from missionary attempts to obtain money for ransoming and converting slave-children through similar personal connections. Letters between European benefactors and the African Christians they ransomed from slavery and then named for baptism exist from the 1860s, if not before, anticipating the dark, pleading faces that today urge benefaction in European or North American periodicals.

*Paul V. Kollman*

### Further Reading
Alpers, E. (1983). The story of Swema: Female vulnerability in nineteenth-century East Africa. In C. Robertson & M. Klein (Eds.), *Women and slavery in Africa* (pp. 185–219). Madison: University of Wisconsin Press.
Buxton, Thomas Fowell. (1839). *The African slave trade and its remedy.* London: Murray.
Gaume, J. (1870). *Suéma: or the little African slave who was buried alive.* London: Burns, Oates, and Co.
Temperley, H. (1991). *White dreams, black Africa: the anti-slavery expedition to the River Niger 1841–1842.* New Haven: Yale University Press.
Wright, M. (1993). *Strategies of slaves and women:Life-stories from East/Central Africa.* London: J. Currey.

port for evangelization. Though in retrospect slavery's evils often justified colonial intervention, missionaries generally pursued abolition, not European overrule.

Meanwhile, sizeable numbers of early African Christians were former slaves who became prominent leaders in their churches, both in the Americas and in Africa. In many parts of Africa such former slaves lived in so-called freedom villages composed of new Christians.

Samuel Ajayi Crowther, the first Anglican bishop in western Africa, was one of many ex-slaves who became missionaries themselves. In western Africa such people had often been freed from slave ships by the British. In eastern Africa, nineteenth-century missionaries targeted slaves for evangelization because open preaching was disallowed by the Islamic regime centered at Zanzibar. The evangelization of slaves became a temporary missionary strategy as Catholics and Protestants sought to form African coworkers for the more fruitful evangelization among non-Muslims anticipated inland from the coast. As in western Africa, many early African Christian leaders in eastern Africa were thus also former slaves, though none achieved the prominence of Bishop Crowther.

## Mission and Slavery Today

Though slavery is illegal everywhere in world, Christian missionaries continue to work for complete abolition in places where enslavement persists, such as certain parts of Africa. In addition, greater awareness about human trafficking in the international sex trade and other captive labor practices generates missionary attention to ongoing injustices.

PAUL V. KOLLMAN

### Further Reading

Davis, D. B. (2001). *In the image of God: Religion, moral values, and our heritage of slavery.* New Haven, CT: Yale University Press.

Drescher, S., & Engerman, S. L. (Eds.). (1998). *A historical guide to world slavery.* Oxford, UK: Oxford University Press.

Earl, R. R. (1993). *Dark symbols, obscure signs: God, self, and community in the slave mind.* Maryknoll, NY: Orbis Books.

Finkelman, P., & Miller, J. C. (Eds.). (1998). *Macmillan encyclopedia of world slavery* (2 vols). New York: Simon and Schuster Macmillan.

Goldenberg, D. (2003). *The curse of Ham: Race and slavery in early Judaism, Christianity, and Islam.* Princeton, NJ: Princeton University Press.

Hochschild, A. (2005). *Bury the chains: Prophets and rebels in the fight to free an empire's slaves.* Boston: Houghton Mifflin.

Klein, M. A. (2002). *Historical dictionary of slavery and abolition.* Lanham, MD: Scarecrow Press.

Kollman, P. V. (2005). *The evangelization of slaves and Catholic origins in eastern Africa.* Maryknoll, NY: Orbis Books.

Meillassoux, C. (1991). *The anthropology of slavery: the womb of iron and gold.* Trans. A. Dasnois. Chicago: University of Chicago Press.

Miers, S. (2003). *Slavery in the twentieth century: the evolution of a problem.* Walnut Creek, CA: AltaMira Press.

Miers, S., & Kopytoff, I. (Eds.). (1977). *Slavery in Africa: Historical and anthropological perspectives.* Madison: University of Wisconsin Press.

Miers, S., & Roberts, R. (Eds.). (1988). *The end of slavery in Africa.* Madison: University of Wisconsin Press.

Miller, J. C. (1999). *Slavery and slaving in world history: a bibliography.* Armonk, NY: M. E. Sharpe.

Patterson, O. (1982). *Slavery and social death: a comparative study.* Cambridge, MA: Harvard University Press.

Raboteau, A. (1978). *Slave religion: the "invisible institution" in the antebellum South.* New York: Oxford University Press.

Reid, A., (Ed.). (1983). *Slavery, bondage, and dependency in Southeast Asia.* New York: St. Martin's Press.

Rodriguez, J. P. (Ed.). (1997). *The historical encyclopedia of world slavery* (2 vols). Santa Barbara, CA: ABC-Clio.

Sensbach, J. F. (2005). *Rebecca's revival: Creating black Christianity in the Atlantic world.* Cambridge, MA: Harvard University Press.

Viotti da Costa, E. (1994). *Crowns of glory, tears of blood: the Demerara slave rebellion of 1823.* New York: Oxford University Press.

## Social Gospel

The term *social gospel* came into use around 1900 to describe a style of theologically based, moderately progressive social reform and cultural criticism that was influential in turn-of-the-century Protestantism. The relationship of the social gospel to the antebellum home missions and social reform movements is a matter of some debate in recent scholarship.

### The Traditional View: Response to the Urban-industrial Crisis

For most of the twentieth century, scholars viewed the social gospel as a response to the social crises of the mass industrialization, concentrations of capital into monopolistic corporate trusts, immigration, and urbanization in the late nineteenth century. According to many proponents of the traditional view, American social Christianity fell into three main categories. Conservative reformers focused on the spiritual and moral reform of the individual without challenging fundamental social and economic structures. Christian socialists were radicals who believed socialism was the necessary consequence of Christian faith and practice. The social gospel was a middle way between the two.

The urgency of the urban-industrial crisis in the last quarter of the nineteenth century became clear when violent labor riots erupted. By the mid-1890s, Protestant church leaders were preoccupied with "the social question," and the social gospel had penetrated most Protestant denominations. Nevertheless, it was always a minority movement, limited mostly to clergy and pioneers in the emerging fields of social science and social work.

Most historians acknowledge the first two decades of the twentieth century as the golden age of the social gospel, when the movement made its greatest inroads into the consciousness of American Protestantism. The Federal Council of Churches in the United States, at its inaugural meeting (1908), endorsed the social gospel as essential to Christianity when it adopted a report on the Church and Modern Industry, which included a broad statement of economic and labor reforms for urban-industrial America. The statement became known as the "social creed of the churches." The "Men and Religion Forward Movement" (1911–1912) represented the zenith of the social gospel's popularity among the laity.

After World War I the postmillennial optimism and crusading spirit that had driven the social gospel was crushed. Several of its greatest champions passed away, and many reform causes became institutionalized in the growing welfare state. Under pressure from resurgent theological conservatism in the form of the fundamentalist movement, theological liberalism's faith in God's immanence and its optimistic assessment of human nature gave way to neo-orthodoxy's emphasis on God's radical transcendence and human depravity. The strength of the social gospel was dissipated by 1940.

## The Revisionist View: Continuation of Antebellum Reform

In the past three decades some scholars have proposed revisions to the traditional view. They believe the social gospel was an outgrowth and continuation of the antebellum home missions and social reform movements. The continuation theory permits a much broader theological and geographical scope and a greater variety of social issues to be included in the social gospel. From this perspective, the urban-industrial crisis was one significant aspect of a much broader struggle against the structural foundations of poverty and social injustice. The social gospel also included, for example, the work of Christian reformers who attacked the issues of race, education, and poverty in the agrarian South, as well as the gender-based reforms of "municipal housekeeping" and "woman's work for woman," such as those pursued by the women's home missionary societies and the Woman's Christian Temperance Union (established 1874). The social gospel was a style of thought that informed numerous movements rather than a single cohesive movement.

## Walter Rauschenbusch

While the social gospel, broadly conceived, lacked theological uniformity, Walter Rauschenbusch (1861–1918), its most important theologian, wrote from a liberal theological perspective. An American-born Baptist clergyman of German descent, he served a church in New York's Hell's Kitchen (1886–1897) and taught church history at Rochester Theological Seminary (1902–1918). Rauschenbusch believed that Protestant orthodoxy was unable to meet the challenges of modern society. He argued that the teachings of Jesus and the Christian message of salvation, when properly interpreted and applied, could transform corrupt economic, social, and political institutions, leading ultimately to the establishment of the kingdom of God on earth. In order to equip Christianity for its role in social salvation, Rauschenbusch attempted to integrate the achievements of science (especially social science) and historical-critical studies of the Bible into his theology. He argued for the perfectibility of human nature and he believed that sin was as much a sociological problem as it was an individual moral problem. He affirmed the immanence of God and human solidarity and he believed that the establishment of the Kingdom of God on earth was within humanity's reach. His theologically informed cultural criticism epitomized the optimistic, crusading spirit of the social gospel. His writings include: *Christianity and the Social Crisis* (1906), *Christianizing the Social Order* (1912), *The Social Principles of Jesus* (1916), and *A Theology for the Social Gospel* (1917).

## Other Notable Figures

Other notable figures include Washington Gladden (1836–1918), "the father of the social gospel;" Josiah Strong (1847–1916), forceful spokesman for home missions and American imperialism; Richard T. Ely (1854–1943), founder of the American Economic Association

(1885); Vida D. Scudder (1861–1954), a literature scholar and Christian socialist active in the settlement house and women's labor movements; Nannie Helen Burroughs (1879–1961), corresponding secretary (1900–1948) and president (1948–1961) of the Woman's Convention, Auxiliary to the National Baptist Convention, and founder of the National Training School for Women and Girls (1909); and Jane Addams (1860–1935) and her colleagues at Chicago's Hull-House.

## Unresolved Questions

The definition debate continues, as scholars continue to propose personalities and movements from outside the traditional boundaries for inclusion in the social gospel fold. Questions exist regarding the relationship between the social gospel and social reform in the American foreign missionary enterprise. Finally, scholars debate the uniqueness of the social gospel and the degree to which the European varieties of social Christianity, which were familiar to many social gospel leaders, influenced the development of the social gospel in America.

KENDAL P. MOBLEY

*See also* Conciliar Missions; Ecumenism; Human Rights; Liberation Theology; Theology; Theory— Catholic, Protestant, Evangelistic; Urban Mission

### Further Reading

Carter, P. A. (1954). *The decline and revival of the social gospel: Social and political liberalism in American Protestant churches, 1920–1940.* Ithaca, NY: Cornell University Press.

Edwards, W. J. D., & Gifford, C. D. (Eds.). (2003). *Gender and the social gospel.* Urbana: University of Illinois Press.

Evans, C. H. (Ed.) (2001). *The social gospel today.* Louisville, KY: Westminster John Knox Press.

Gorrell, D. K. (1988). *The age of social responsibility: The social gospel in the progressive era, 1900–1920.* Macon, GA: Mercer University Press.

Handy, R. T. (Ed.). (1966). *The social gospel in America, 1870–1920.* New York: Oxford University Press.

Hopkins, C. H. (1940). *The rise of the social gospel in American Protestantism, 1865–1915.* New Haven, CT: Yale University Press.

Luker, R. E. (1991). *The social gospel in black and white: American racial reform, 1885–1912.* Chapel Hill: The University of North Carolina Press.

May, H. F. (1963). *Protestant churches and industrial America.* New York: Octagon Books, Inc. (Original work published 1949)

McDowell, J. P. (1982). *The social gospel in the South: The woman's home mission movement in the Methodist Episcopal Church, South, 1886–1939.* Baton Rouge: Louisiana State University Press.

Phillips, P. T. (1996). *A Kingdom on Earth: Anglo-American social Christianity, 1880-1940.* University Park: The Pennsylvania State University Press.

White, R. C., Jr., & Hopkins, C. H. (1976). *Religion and reform in changing America.* Philadelphia: Temple University Press.

# Sociology

Sociology, the study of human groups and their behavior, has become an essential tool for the study of missions and missionaries since its inception in late nineteenth-century Europe. The work of August Comte (1798–1857), George Simmel (1858–1918), and the classic sociologists of religion Emile Durkheim (1858–1917) and Max Weber (1864–1920) established the activities and self-understandings of religious groups as fruitful areas of academic study.

Sociologists are not the only scholars interested in studies of Christian missions. Religious studies scholars and missiologists, interdisciplinary scholars who use the academic disciplines of history, anthropology, psychology, and sociology to study Christian missions, also utilize sociological studies. In addition, denominational and church leaders and mission agencies use the tools of sociology to further their advocacy objectives by gaining knowledge of society.

The complex relationship between sociology and Christian missions can be divided into four areas: (1) sociological methods; (2) approaches and theories; (3) controversies; and (4) goals of both sociological studies of missions and of missiological studies that use sociology.

## Sociological Methods

Since sociology is modeled after the natural sciences, both quantitative and qualitative methods are used to study missions and missionaries.

Quantitative studies using statistical data on demographics, political and social movements, economics, and religious affiliations, for example, help sociologists understand Christian missions. The mathematical analysis of populations in Europe by Thomas Robert Malthus (1766–1834) and Emile Durkheim's study of suicide in France showed how statistical analysis could be used to predict trends in society. *Understanding Church Growth* (McGavarn 1990) and *World Christian Trends* (Barrett and Johnson 2001) are contemporary examples of a quantitative analysis of data used in this way.

Qualitative studies such as case studies, interviews, biographies, ethnographic field studies, participant observation reports, and historical studies also contribute to the understanding of religions in general and missions in particular. *Varieties of Religious Experience* by William James (1842–1910) Durkheim's *Elementary Forms of Religious Life,* and Weber's *Sociology of Religion* are classic studies that model qualitative approaches to understanding religion and religious behavior. Recent studies using qualitative approaches are legion and include contextual studies of mission organizations, missionary biographies, studies of the impact of missions on cultures, analyses of the impact of Christian movements such as fundamentalisms, and studies of mission and ideologies—for example, gender, political ideologies, and ideologies of mission itself.

Studies that combine statistical analysis and qualitative investigations can provide helpful guidance for churches and mission associations. Studies of race, class, and gender, for example, illuminate cultural and structural factors that can influence the decisions of mission societies and churches. Research on social change, conversion, migration, and family life also combine quantitative and qualitative methodologies and are used in this way.

## Approaches and Theories

Social theory provides theoretical parameters to aid sociologists in their choice of research questions and methodologies. Critical theory, structuralism, grounded theory, and the sociology of knowledge are examples of theoretical frameworks that inform research. Missiologists may also use theological frameworks to inform their studies. Protestant Reformed theology, Catholic social teachings, Latin-American and African-American liberation theologies, womanist or feminist theologies influence research on Christian mission. Understanding religion as a social construction (Berger 1967) or using a theistic framework for knowledge (Montgomery 1999), for example, yields different topics and produces contrasting results. Yet both can be productive sources of sociological inquiry as the impact of theory is acknowledged.

The scientific study of religion began as part of a movement in the human sciences that built on a natural science model. Nineteenth-century scholars Karl Marx, Max Weber, and Emile Durkheim studied the origins

and manifestations of religion. They believed that the scientific model they worked with demanded an objective and value-free approach. At the same time, each of them wanted to study society with a goal of improving societal life.

The perspectives of each and their goals for a better society brought values into the picture as the human science of sociology of religion developed. Marx's study of religion led him to conclude that religion was a source of alienation, leading the working class to deny their own oppression. Durkheim envisioned a future religion that prized the individual, yet connected people through different tasks. Weber's efforts to remain value-free led to a strict division between objective study and personal commitments, even as he investigated the role of meaning in action formation. That goal itself represented a value of scientific rigor. For missiologists, the values of Christianity may influence their choice of research projects and methods, as H. Richard Neibuhr's 1932 study of denominationalism in the United States showed. Finally, the natural science method itself includes values as part of its methodology. Integrity in methodology, honesty in reporting findings, and respect for research subjects and colleagues are a few of the values documented by Peter Berger in 1963.

### Controversies

Controversy about approaches to the sociological study of mission revolve around those issues of objectivity and values. Sociologists disagree about the possibility of value-free studies. Jacques Waardenburg argues that most scholars of religion study mission from a critical standpoint, that is, through an "objective" lens (1999). Sociologists of religion and missiologists may take this approach, as exemplified by Nancy Ammerman's 1997 study of churches and change in the United States. Alternatively, they may begin their sociological work within the values and framework of Christianity, as Hwa Yung does in his 1997 study of Christian theology in an Asian context. Missiologists may be hesitant to formulate ideas from sociological research unless they conform to Christian ideas and biblical interpretations, as David J. Hesselgrave argues in *Missiology and the Social Sciences.*

Postmodern scholarship in the social sciences rejects the idea of value-free objective research. Building on the sociology of knowledge developed by Karl Mannheim and Peter Berger, sociologist of religion Robert Bellah asserts that social science should be restored as public philosophy. Anthropologists argue that the constant fluctuations of cultures and the centrality of values for constructing meanings make a valuing dimension of social science research and the impact of the researcher on studies unavoidable.

### Goals of Sociological Study

The scientific study of religion and the valuing aspects of research in the human sciences led to the development of a sociology of religion that informed missiologists. Although sociologists attempt to study religion empirically and missiologists attempt to study religion normatively, there is no clear line between those perspectives. Every researcher comes to his or her investigation with a historical location and a point of view. Sociology, an empirical field of study, and missiology, a normative field of study, find links in the arena of values.

Although disagreement about the uses of sociology and the perspectives of scientific research continues, the objectives of both sociologists studying mission and missiologists studying society revolve around three major goals: understanding, influencing, and critiquing. To address sociology in a volume on missions and missionaries, both points of view must be summarized.

## The Sociology of Christian Mission

Christian missions have been studied from sociological points of view for as long as sociologists have studied religions. For example, James S. Dennis (1842–1914) established the sociology of mission(s) with his work *Christian Missions and Social Progress,* a three-volume sociological study of "foreign missions," and Ernst Troeltsch (1866–1923) compiled *The Social Teaching of the Christian Churches.* Post–World War II studies in the field emphasized the sociological presuppositions of missionary activities and perspectives, the structure of mission organizations, and the cross-cultural aspects of mission work. More recent post-colonialist critiques and historical studies stress the political and social implications of importing Christianity to non-Western societies (Lagerwelf et al. 1995; Bell et al. 2001).

### Understanding

Understanding how Christian mission efforts operate and what effects they have on societies are major goals of the sociology of Christian mission. Tracking changes in religious affiliation, researching social movements spawned by Christianity, studying the role of religion in the social construction of reality and group identity formation, and investigating the ways missionaries and mission organizations support or challenge political and economic structures are some of the approaches that sociologists take.

### Influence

The study of Christian mission efforts can be used to influence public policy on local, national, and international levels. Sociological studies are used to foster cooperative efforts between churches and governmental health and welfare agencies at the Center for Religion and Civic Culture of the University of Southern California, for example. Economic disparities and health issues in local communities can be addressed through such cooperative efforts. Research on the effects of religiosity on families and the impact of religious affiliation on educational choices and political engagement are other areas of sociological research that can influence activities of Christian churches and public service agencies.

### Critique

Studies of social change and the influence of Christian missions, particularly in relation to Western colonialist expansion, have resulted in critiques of missionary activities. Some critiques stress missionary complicity with political and economic structures as causes of both economic and cultural imperialism, for example, the relationship between economic interests, slavery, and the expansion of Christianity in Africa. Other studies of mission link positive changes in economic, political, and social conditions to Christian influence as education, health care, and democratic forms brought from the West impact societies.

Feminist sociological studies provide another angle of critique, arguing that the inherent gender theory in classic sociology of religion and understandings of modernity have supported patriarchal values to the detriment of women. Bringing women's concerns from the margins to the center of social theory, creating a sociology for women, and recovering histories of women in mission bring new perspectives to the sociology of mission.

## Missiological Use of Sociology

Missiologists use sociological studies in three major ways. First, in order to better understand religion in general and Christian missions in particular. Second, to chart religious movements and influences in order to predict and control trends in religious affiliation. Third, to analyze the influence of Christianity in society with a view to critiquing and correcting oppressive structures and practices.

### Understanding

The sociologists that began to study religion in the late nineteenth and early twentieth centuries wanted to understand religion and its role in society. Max Weber, Karl Marx, and Emile Durkheim each developed theories about the role and influence of religion in society. Weber suggested that religion developed in order to explain and control natural phenomenon. Durkheim postulated that religions sprang from the meaning given to liminal communal events that were documented in symbols that later became powerful in their own right. Marx understood religion to be a human attempt to justify bourgeoise-caused economic suffering by suppressing perceptions of reality and projecting a future life of tranquility to the proletariate.

Contemporary sociological theories are used by missiologists to understand the pluralities of religious expression and their bases. Peter Berger's 1969 theory of the social construction of reality posits religion as a "sacred canopy" used to maintain order against possible chaos in society. Robert Bellah's 1991 theory of institutions as loci of social change shows how religious institutions can impact society. Juergen Habermas' 1981 description of the "lifeworld" focuses on communication to better understand religious discourse. Clifford Geertz's 1965 theory that religion arises from moods and motivations in communities brings the social interaction that surrounds religious commitment to the fore. Thomas Kuhn's (1970) theory of the structure of scientific revolutions has been applied to paradigm shifts in understandings of Christian mission through the centuries.

### Influence

Understanding how religion operates in society helps advocates of a particular religion foster religious change through mission work. Statistics have long been used for this purpose. However, with the advent of computers, the gathering and analysis of information about religions has expanded exponentially. David B. Barrett and Todd M. Johnson's *World Christian Trends AD 30–AD 2200* analyzes statistics about Christianity to ex-

plain and generate social change among Evangelicals. The World Council of Churches' *Handbook of Churches and Councils: Profiles of Ecumenical Relationships* provides data on global Christian bodies, member churches, and ecumenical organizations around the world to encourage the ecumenical movement.

Qualitative research studies are also used by missiologists to influence congregational development and church growth. Nancy Ammerman's *Studying Congregations* outlines approaches to using interviews, opinion polls, and historical studies to augment understanding of the tradition, the context, and the vision of Christian churches. Gerald Anderson's *Dictionary of Mission Biographies* points missiologists to an examination of the lives of missionaries to aid them in understanding both the theologies and the contexts of Christian mission endeavors. Social theories such as Everett Roger's diffusion of innovations theory also help missiologists and mission organizations to work towards effective and responsible advocacy.

### Social Critique

Missiologists also use sociological analysis to critique social and political structures and movements. Data about voting records in the South was used to spur on the civil rights movement as Christians addressed the justice issue of equality in the 1960s. Missiologists have addressed the silencing of women's voices in the church through the use of historical and sociological research. Trends in church growth across the globe have been used by missiologists and church leaders to address economic and social inequities in denominational and worldwide church structures. Data on worldwide poverty, environmental degradation, and the effects of war have been compiled in a study bible that addresses social and economic injustice.

## Increasing Engagement

The development of sociological theories and methods, both quantitative and qualitative, has helped focus the scientific study of religions in general and the study of Christian missions in particular. Since its inception, sociology has been used by missiologists to understand, influence, and critique religion, particularly Christianity. Sociologists have studied Christian mission efforts and analyzed their influence on societies. Studies from both directions are useful to scholars of religion and to communities interested in the impact of Christian missions in local and global contexts. The use of both qualitative and quantitative sociological information and theories will increasingly direct the actions of missiologists and the activities of mission organizations, churches, denominations, and global councils because sophisticated data collection and techniques of analysis continue to grow. Today it is difficult to imagine a sociology that does not study Christian missions or a missiology that does not engage sociology.

Frances S. Adeney

*See also* Apologetics; Contextualization, Models of; Culture; Inculturation; Linguistics; Research; Statistics

## Further Reading

Ammerman, N. T. (1997). *Congregation and community.* New Brunswick, NJ: Rutgers University Press.

Ammerman, N. T., Carrol, J. W., Dudley, C. S., & McKinney, W. (1998). *Studying congregations: A new handbook.* Nashville, TN: Abingdon Press.

Anderson, G. H. (Ed.). (1998). *Biographical dictionary of Christian missions.* New York: Simon & Schuster.

Barrett, D. B., & Johnson, T. M. (Eds.). (2001). *World Christian trends: AD 30–AD 2200.* Pasadena CA: William Carey.

Barrett, D. B., Kurian, G. T., & Johnson, T. M. (Eds.). (2001). *World Christian encyclopedia* (2nd ed., Vols. 1–2). Oxford, UK: Oxford University Press.

Bell, L. S., Nathan, A. J., & Peleg, I. (Eds.). (2001). *Negotiating culture and human rights.* New York: Columbia University Press.

Bellah,, R. N. (1985). Social science as public philosophy. In R. Madsen, W. M. Sullivan, A. Swidler, & S. M. Tipton, *Habits of the heart: Individualism and commitment in American life.* Berkeley: University of California Press.

Bellah, R. N., Madsen, R., Sullivan, W. M., Swidler, A., & Tipton, S. M. (1991). *The good society.* New York: Knopf.

Berger, P. (1963). *Invitation to sociology: A humanistic perspective.* New York: Doubleday.

Berger, P. (1967). *The sacred canopy: Elements of a sociological theory of religion.* New York: Doubleday.

Bosch, D. J. (1991). *Transforming mission: Paradigm shifts in theology of mission.* Maryknoll, NY: Orbis Books.

Dennis, J. S. (1897). *Christian mission and social progress: A sociological study of foreign missions* (3 vols.). New York: Revel.

Durkheim, E. (1964). *The division of labor in society* (G. Simpson, Trans.). New York: Free Press. (Original work published 1933)

Durkheim, E. (1912). *The elementary forms of religious life* (K. E. Fields, Trans.). New York: Free Press.

Erickson, K. (1993). *Where silence speaks: Feminism, social theory, and religion.* Grand Rapids MI: Fortress Press.

Fung, J. M. (2003). *Ripples on the water: Believers in the Orang Asli's struggle for a homeland of equal citizens.* Johor, Malaysia: Majodi Publications.

Geertz, C. (1965). Religion as a cultural system. In M. Banton (Ed.), *Anthropological approaches to religion.* London: Tavestock.

Habermas, J. (1981). *The theory of communicative action: Reason and the rationalization of society* (T. McCarthy, Trans.). Boston, MA: Beacon Press.

Hesselgrave, D. J. (1996). Preface. In E. Rommen & G. Corwin, G. (Eds.). *Missiology and the social sciences: Contributions, cautions and conclusions.* Pasadena, CA: William Carey.

hooks, b. (1984). *Feminist theory: From margin to center.* Boston, MA: South End Press.

James, W. (1902). *The varieties of religious experience.* New York: Simon & Schuster.

Jongeneel, J. A. B. (1995). *Philosophy, science, and theology of mission in the 19th and 20th centuries: A missiological encyclopedia: Part I, The philosophy and science of mission* (2nd rev. ed.). New York: Peter Lang.

Kanyoro, M. R. A., & Njoroge, N. J. (Eds.). (1996). *Groaning in faith: African women in the household of God.* Nairobi, Kenya: Acton Publishers.

King, U., & Beattie, T. (Eds.). (2004). *Gender, religion and diversity: Cross-cultural perspectives,* New York: Continuum.

Kuhn, T. S. (1970). *The structure of scientific revolutions* (2nd ed.). Chicago, IL: University of Chicago Press.

Lagerwerf, L., Steenbrink, K., & Verstraelen, F. (Eds.). (1995). *Changing partnership of missionary and ecumenical movements: Essays in honour of Marc Spindler.* Leiden-Utrecht, Netherlands: Interuniversity Institute for Missiological and Ecumenical Research.

Mannheim, K. (1936). *Ideology and utopia* (L. Wirth & E. Shils, Trans.). New York: Harcourt.

Marshall, B. L. (1994). *Engendering modernity: Feminism, social theory, and social change.* Boston, MA: Northeastern University Press.

Marx, K., & Engels, F. (1964). *On religion.* Chico, CA: Scholars Press.

McGavran, D. A., & Wagner, C. P. (Eds.). (1990). *Understanding church growth* (3rd ed.). Grand Rapids, MI: Eerdmans.

Montgomery, R. L. (1999). *An introduction to the sociology of missions.* Westport, CT: Praeger.

Muck, T. C. (Ed.). (2005). *Faith in action study Bible: Living God's Word in a changing world.* Grand Rapids, MI: Zondervan.

Niebuhr, H. R. (1932). *The social sources of denominationalism.* Cleveland, OH: World Publishing.

Oduyoye, M. A. (1995). *Daughters of Anowa: African women and patriarchy.* Maryknoll, NY: Orbis Books.

Orr, J. (2005). Church state guidelines: When faith-based human service programs are funded by California taxpayers. Retrieved July 26, 2007, from www.usc.edu/schools/college/crcc/private/docs/child_care/church_state.pdf

Rabinow, P. R. (1983). Humanism as nihilism: The bracketing of truth and seriousness in American cultural anthropology. In N. Haan, R. N. Bellah, P. Rainow, & W. M. Sullivan (Eds.), *Social science as moral inquiry.* New York: Columbia University Press.

Robert, D. (1997). *American women in mission: A social history of their thought and practice.* Macon GA: Mercer University Press.

Robert, D. (Ed.). (2002). *Gospel bearers gender barriers: Missionary women in the twentieth century.* Maryknoll, NY: Orbis.

Rogers, E. M. (2003). *Diffusion of innovations* (5th ed.). New York: Free Press.

Rommen, E., & Corwin, G. (Eds.). (1996). *Missiology and the social sciences: Contributions, cautions and conclusions.* Pasadena, CA: William Carey.

Smith, D. (1987). *The everyday world as problematic: A feminist sociology.* Boston, MA: Northeastern University Press.

Stark, R. (1996). *The rise of Christianity: A sociologist reconsiders history.* Princeton, NJ: Princeton University Press.

Semple, R. A. (2003). *Missionary women: Gender, professionalism and the Victorian idea of Christian mission.* Suffolk, UK: Boydell Press.

Troeltsch, E. (1960). *The social teaching of the Christian churches* (Vols. 1–2, O. Wyon, Trans.). Chicago: University of Chicago Press. (Original work published 1931)

Waardenburg, J. (1999). *Classical approaches to the study of religion: Aims, methods, and theories of research introduction and anthology.* New York: De Gruyter.

Weber, M. (1946). Science as a vocation. In *From Max Weber: Essays in sociology* (H. H. Gerth & C. W. Mills, Trans.). New York: Oxford University Press.

Weber, M. (1904). *The Protestant ethic and the spirit of capitalism.* New York: Scribner's.

Weber, M. (1968). Sociology of religion. In G. Roth & C. Wittich (Eds.), *Economy and society: An outline of interpretive sociology.* Berkeley: University of California Press.

White, M. L., & Manis, A. M. (Eds.). (2000). *Birmingham revolutionaries: The Reverend Fred Shuttlesworth and the Alabama Christian movement for human rights.* Macon, GA: Mercer University Press.

World Council of Churches. (2006). *Handbook of churches and councils: Profiles of ecumenical relationships.* Geneva, Switzerland: World Council of Churches Publications.

Yung, H. (1997). *Mangoes or bananas? The quest for an authentic Asian Christian theology.* Oxford, UK: Regnum Books International.

# Sports

Sports attract the attention of the whole world when nations compete for the World Cup in football (soccer) or for "gold" in the Olympics. In ordinary life as well, this universal phenomenon of sports offers an ideal platform for athletes and others to practice their faith and promote the gospel. At the beginning of the twenty-first century sports and ministry are becoming ever stronger partners in mission.

## Sports and Culture

Sport, spontaneous or regulated play with a goal or end purpose (Guttmann 2004, 1), is found in the games of stickball common among pre-Columbian Choctaws and Cherokees and in ancient tribal wrestling rivalries in Africa. From Confucius' lauded archers to sumo wrestlers in eighth-century Japan, from organized Greek athletic contests to Roman gladiatorial matches, societies have engaged in sport with personal, political, and even religious zeal. The multibillion dollar allegiance to the business of sport and the sometimes fanatical following it attracts confirms its hold on the human race today. Historian and former Yale University president A. Bartlett Giamatti is quoted as saying, "Sports represents a shared vision of how we continue, as individual, team, or community, to experience a happiness or absence of care so intense, so rare, and so fleeting that we associate the experience with experiences otherwise described as religious..." (Buchanan 2003, 3)

## Sports and Faith

Scripture affirms athleticism in both Old and New Testaments (e.g., Zechariah 8:5; I Timothy 4:7–8; I Corinthians 9:20–27). Though historical links between sport and faith predate the nineteenth century, it was then that a prominent role for sport emerged. By mid-century, Victorian novelists Charles Kingsley and Thomas Hughes popularized the term "muscular Christianity"—spiritual, moral, and physical development for the good of the individual and the nation. Virtues such as fitness, fairness, self-restraint,

## A Case Study in Ethiopian Sports Ministry

**Over a period of four years in Ethiopia an outreach called "Sports Friends" of SIM (Serving in Mission) modeled the concrete results that can come from sports ministries.**

Vision—In 2002 two missionaries, Brian Davidson and Tripp Johnston envisioned broadened youth evangelism and discipleship and even church planting through the use of sports outreach.

Early stages—Missionaries enlisted local churches to begin sports outreaches in rural and urban settings. Communities responded enthusiastically with children and youth enlisting in clinics and matches.

Training—Missionaries began training eager national and local church workers in sports outreach. Workers returned to stations and watched numbers grow. National sports officials took note of the work with youth, especially female athletes and encouraged the church and mission endeavors all the more.

Extra help—Missionaries enlisted North American Christian college teams to make short term visits. Teams played larger matches, encouraged national officials, held school and community sports clinics, visited hospitals, and ran camps even in remote areas. Some students caught a vision and returned for subsequent team trips and even long term commitments to Ethiopia.

Larger vision—Church visitors came from five or more other African nations to model what they saw in Ethiopia. Kenyan, Sudanize, Ugandan, Rwandan and Nigerian idigenous leaders initiated their own "sports friends" outreaches.

Results—Even in what leaders consider the early stages of a long term ministry over 1,000 Ethiopian evangelists and workers have been trained to use sports to build relationships with youth and their families. More than 500 churches have initiated sports ministry programs. Over 1000 people including those from oposition religious groups have placed their trust in Christ. Several new churches have been planted as a result of "sports friends."

Evaluation—Similar scenarios are actually on record in Latin America and other parts of the world. Sports ministry can play an important role in decisions for Christ, discipleship, church planting, leadership development, and national youth development.

Source: Johnston, T., & Imes, C. (2006) New open doors for Sports Friends. *SIM Magazine.* Retrieved July 24, 2007, from http://www.sim.org/magazine/mag114.pdf

responsibility, honor, and endurance could be nurtured through sports. The YMCA, founded in London in 1844, carried forward the banner of Christian muscle and moral character.

## Leading Pioneers: Yesterday and Today

Outstanding figures on both sides of the Atlantic popularized the movement. British athletes who sacrificed fame to spread the gospel overseas included first-rank cricketer C. T. Studd (1860–1931) and later Olympic sprinter Eric Liddell (1902–1945). In the United States the YMCA was promoted by evangelist Dwight L. Moody (1837–1899) and led by Christian statesman John R. Mott (1865–1955). YMCA instructor James Naismith's creation of basketball in 1891 was only one of several sports including volleyball (1895) and racquetball (1950) born out of Christian motivations and designed to build up body and character. Former NBA star A. C. Green's Youth Foundation emphasizes character development and promotes sexual-abstinence education. Dave Dravecky, former Major League Baseball player, has founded Outreach of Hope, serving suffering people, especially those with cancer and amputation. World renowned women athletes, such as Michelle Akers and Mary Lou Retton, utilize their respective notoriety through soccer and gymnastics, respectively, to proclaim Christ in both the spoken and written word.

## Emerging Paradigms

Noteworthy Christian athletes were not enough to hold back the negative reactions to the corruption and distraction of sports for some revivalists before World War II. The general rise of evangelical fervor after the war was reignited by stars such as world class miler Gil Dodds, who gave his testimony before a 1945 Memorial Day crowd of 65,000 gathered at Soldiers Field in Chicago. Evangelical organizations such as Youth for Christ and Campus Crusade for Christ promoted godly athletes and spawned dedicated sports outreaches including Ventures for Victory/Sports Ambassadors (1952) and Athletes in Action (1966).

Diverse aims motivate sports ministries: nurturance and discipleship of professional and amateur athletes, public evangelism and testimony, Christian club teams (both amateur and pro), traveling witness teams, instructional clubs and camps for children and youth, church-related weekday activities and ministries, overseas friendship and evangelism teams, church planting ministries in limited-access countries and more. A growing number of Christian liberal arts colleges, including Belhaven, Houghton, Indiana Wesleyan, Judson, and Malone, are today including sports ministry as academic program options.

## Global Sport Networks and Ministries

The growth of sports ministry organizations has mushroomed in Europe and North America and now around the globe. Local church leaders are partnering with mission and parachurch agencies to form national and international networks for sports evangelism. Examples include the Association of Church Sports and Recreation Ministers (North America and Europe), Sports Outreach Institute (Africa, Mexico, United States), the European Christian Sports Union, and the International Sports Coalition. Prominent sports-focused ministries include Christians in Sport (United Kingdom), Sportler Rust Sportler (Germany), Church Sports International, Ambassadors in Sport, Athletes in Action, Fellowship of Christian Athletes, Missionary Athletes International, Pro Athletes Outreach, Sports Ambassadors and World Sports. Whether working in the remote corners of a developing country or clustering together at global events such as the World Cup or Olympic games, hundreds of Christian organizations are mobilizing Gospel outreach through sport.

## Present and Future

Sports opens mission doors just as drama, education, and medicine have for years. In the early 1990s a veteran missionary in a particularly resistant European region noted that a week-long outreach with an international soccer team triggered more viable Bible study and follow-up contacts than ten years of previous mission activity. On the African continent two years of local sports clubs and camps for children contributed greatly to the planting of several dozen new churches by local believers partnering with expatriate advisors.

Sports venues are societal gathering sites the world over, and sports ministries are relationally engaging the world on their turf. Age, gender, and ethnic diversity enhance the impact. Church-based ministries in developed and developing countries are successfully producing churches and nurturing believers. Christian athletes are making inroads through appearances and publications. Partnering and networking between agencies and across international boundaries will continue. Strategies and approaches will diversify even more. In the twenty-first century the link of sport and mission appears to be growing alongside the worldwide fascination and enjoyment of sports.

PAUL W. SHEA AND DAVID B. LEWIS

### Further Reading

Baker, W. J. (1982) *Sports in the Western world.* Totowa, NJ: Rowman and Littlefield.

Buchanan, J M. (2003). More than a game. *Christian Century, 120*(22), 3.

Garner, J. (Ed.) (2003) *Recreation and sports ministry: Impacting postmodern culture.* Nashville, TN: Broadman and Holman

Guttmann, A. (2004). *Sports: the first five millennia.* Boston: University of Massachusetts Press.

Higgs, R. (1995). *God in the stadium: Sports and religion in America.* Lexington: University Press of Kentucky.

Hoffman, S. J. (Ed.). (1992). *Sport and religion.* Champaign, IL: Human Kinetics Books.

Ladd, T., & Mathisen, J. A. (1999). *Muscular Christianity: Evangelical protestants and the development of American sport.* Grand Rapids, MI: Baker Books.

Magdalinski, T., & Chandler, T. J. L. (Eds.). (2002). *With God on their side: Sport in the service of religion.* New York: Routledge.

Watson, N. J., Weir, S., & Friend, S. (2005). The development of muscular Christianity in Victorian Britain and beyond. *Journal of Religion and Society, 7.* Retrieved July 26, 2007, from http://moses.creighton.edu/JRS/2005/2005-2.html

## Statistics of Mission and Missionaries

Statistics play a large and increasingly vital role in the past, present, and future of the Christian movement. With a million new statistics on churches and missions being collected each year, then published and put to many practical uses, it becomes important to understand their significance.

### Origins of Statistics

Information presented in abstract numerical form is described as statistics. Originally, statistics had nothing to do with numbers. The word originated in German in the eighteenth century, when economist G. Achenwall first coined the term *Statistik* to refer to "the political science of the several countries"; that is, the study of practical politics. The English term first appeared in a 1770 translation from the German (Bauer 1966, 75). "Statistics" is derived etymologically from the Latin *ratio status* and could well be translated as "state of the nation." For several hundred years the primary concern of those who called themselves statisticians was to set up a system of social indicators by which to judge the performance of the society with respect to its norms, values, and goals (Bauer 1966). When they referred to information on the "state" of the nation, they meant those statistical measurements that revealed the current situation of the nation, its population, and its economy.

### Statistics Defined Today

Today the term has evolved somewhat; the subject of statistics is "the association and bringing together of those facts which are calculated to illustrate the conditions and prospects of society" (American Statistical Association 1962). The full definition of the term is: "1. a branch of mathematics dealing with the collection, analysis, interpretation, and presentation of masses of numerical data 2. a collection of quantitative data" (Merriam-Webster's Collegiate Dictionary 2003).

Statistics, then, is the science of making valid inferences about the characteristics of a group of persons or objects on the basis of numerical information obtained from a randomly selected sample of the group. There are two broad subdivisions of this subject: de-

scriptive statistics and theoretical statistics. The latter involves probability and other complex mathematical approaches and is rarely attempted by churches or missions, who concentrate on the former. This is the use of numbers to describe the whole world and the Christian world around us.

### Uses of Statistics for Past, Present, and Future

Church and mission statistics help in understanding the past (church history), analyzing and implementing the present (day-to-day activities), and anticipating and planning for the future (futuristics).

#### Value to Church and Mission

A major advantage of church and mission statistics is that any statistical number or figure or total, with its precise definition, can be understood immediately, quoted and requoted in different contexts by persons of all kinds unfamiliar with the rigorous discipline of statistics. Normally, however, users get more meaning and value out of statistics if their wider context in today's globe is known and used. Hence, paragraphs that now follow depict this global context. Comments on tables 1, 2, 3 and 4 then also follow.

#### The Background Context for Christian Workers

Presented below are enumerations of Christian workers in the context of global Christianity and its mission, with comparison with other large non-Christian religions, in 2005. The first paragraph below enumerates the global context; next, paragraphs A, B, C, and D enumerate a selection of the more significant varieties of Christian workers, with overall totals in A = B + C + D, followed by a sampling of lesser categories. Paragraph D as the major mission category is set in bold type. Lastly, paragraph E enumerates non-Christian workers.

*Global status of Christianity* in 2005 (65.8 generations after Christ): Of world population of 6,453 millions, 66.9 percent (4.3 billions) are non-Christians, 33.1 percent (2,136 millions) are Christians (47.5 percent of them being white, 52.5 percent nonwhite), of whom 31.4 percent (2,026 millions) are affiliated church members in 350 Christian World Communions, 28 percent (688,034,000) are Great Commission Christians committed to Christ's worldwide mission, including 250,776,000 Evangelicals and 588,502,000 Renewalists (Pentecostals, Charismatics, Neocharismatics); of the wider world, 72.1 percent (4,653 millions) are evangelized (aware of the Gospel), with Scriptures translated into 4,300 languages (500 with whole Bible, 1,200 with New Testament only, and 3,700 with a Gospel only).

Paragraph A. *Total all full-time Christian workers:* 11,515,000 (61 percent men 7,085,000, 39 percent women 4,440,000), consisting of 1.2 million ordained male clergy/priests/pastors/ministers/deacons/preachers, 500,000 ordained women, 3,450,000 religious personnel (in 2,500 religious orders, institutes and congregations), 300,000 ordained brothers, 6,385,000 lay workers, 348,000 lay missionaries (so designated), 500,000 monks, 50,000 friars, 1,490,000 nuns, 1.1 million sisters, 3,506,000 catechists, 35,000 bishops/presidents/moderators/metropolitans/patriarchs, 1,050,000 theologians, 32,000 missiologists, 1.0 million seminarians (in 5,000 seminaries); retired workers 116,000, of whom 81,000 are pensioned and 35,000 unpensioned.

Paragraph B. *Christian home pastoral workers* (those not usually regarded or termed as missionaries): 5,012,000 (47 percent men, 53 percent women), 1,090,000 clergy (290,000 being women), religious personnel 2,585,000 (26 percent men, 74 percent women), lay personnel 1,337,000, seminarians 650,000.

Paragraph C. *Christian home mission personnel* (home missionaries, defined as all workers who are citizens of the country they work in, and are usually recognized and termed as missionaries): 6,060,000 (74 percent men, 26 percent women); mostly related to the world's 37,000 denominations; 480,000 clergy/priests/pastors/ministers/deacons including preachers, lay preachers, radio/TV preachers, 100 mega-evangelists, evangelizers, chaplains, lay readers, missioners, mission partners, 3,500,000 catechists, 60,000 colporteurs, 590,000 local evangelists/teachers; 120,000 administrators, 130,000 accountants; most use e-mail online, in 2,000 languages; incapacitated or sick workers, 44,000; retired home missionaries 56,000, of whom 16,000 remain unpensioned; background supporters in mission (Great Commission Christians) 220 million.

Paragraph D. *Christian foreign mission personnel* (foreign missionaries, defined as all workers who are aliens (noncitizens) in the country they work in): 443,000 in 4,340 mission-sending agencies (55 percent men, 45 percent women; 80 percent abroad at any one time, 20 percent absent on home leave): 100,000 male clergy/ministers, 30,000 ordained women; 120,000 male lay workers, 98,000 women lay workers; 135,000 married men, 110,000 unmarried men (singles, widowers, celibates, monks, contemplatives, friars); 95,000 married women (homemakers, wives, widows), 103,000 unmarried women (23,000 singles, 60,000 nuns, 20,000 sisters); traditional categories of worker—pastoral, medical, educational, agricultural, also broadcasters, scripture translators and distributors; 130,000 are career missionaries (over 10 years of service abroad); missionaries using e-mail online 400,000 in 5,000 languages; 8,000 independent missionaries (unaffiliated to any agency); missionaries murdered, 130 a year; incapacitated or sick missionaries 4,000; missionaries' children (under 15s) 30,000; professional tentmakers 210,000, short-termers (under 1 year abroad) 410,000; ex foreign missionaries (prematurely resigning) in attrition rate of 12,000 per year; retired foreign missionaries 10,000, of whom 3,000 remain unpensioned; background supporters in mission (Great Commission Christians) 468 million.

Paragraph E. *Non-Christian foreign missionaries sent abroad:* Muslims (who number 20.4 percent of the world) send out 200,000 engaging in Dawah (missionary activity) in 60 countries; Hindus and Neo-Hindus (13.5 percent of the world) send out 20,000; Buddhists (5.9 percent of the world) send out 20,000; Baha'is, Chinese universists, Sikhs, Jews, and Neoreligionists all send out significant numbers; with a grand total for all non-Christians (who number 66.9 percent of the world) sending out some 300,000 workers to 210 foreign countries.

## Table 1: The Annual Megacensus, 2005

The first detailed overall church census for which records remain was organized in 1676 by Henry Compton, bishop of London in the Church of England. Although lengthy and expensive, his census asked only one question and produced these answers: 95.3 percent of England's 2.6 million adults were Conformists and their established clergy (Anglicans and Presbyterians), 4.2 percent were Nonconformists (Dissenters) and dissenting clergy, and 0.5 percent were Papists (Roman Catholics). In subsequent years, major denominations and communions have expanded the questions asked until by 2005 over 1 million new numbers worldwide each year were being produced, covering all varieties of clergy and church workers together with their activities. Table 1, Box 3 lists the 220 major subjects enumerated.

## Accuracy of Counting

A factor often overlooked in surveys, and even in government-sponsored censuses, is the widespread undercounting that exists. A full description and analysis of methods of counting peoples and of censuses throughout history is given in Alterman (1969). This study begins with the Babylonians, the Egyptians, and censuses in the Bible. Censuses usually count heads throughout the whole population, using large numbers of enumerators. Either they count everybody, or they

**Table 1.** Providing a Million New Statistics of Churches, Missions, and Their Personnel Every Year: the Annual Megacensus, 2005

The circle describes, under 10 headings, organized Christianity's annual decentralized censuses held by most of its 37,000 denominations, 25,000 service agencies, and 11 million workers. In aggregate, these are termed here: the annual megacensus. Subjects are listed in box 3 below. Resulting data may be located from *World Christian Encyclopedia* (WCE) and *World Christian Trends* (WCT).

3. **Major religious subjects measured annually**
The following 220 subjects are quantified by churches, agencies, and missions worldwide each year:
**religions, adherents,** members, practice, attenders, polls, beliefs, sects, cults, megablocs, **communions,** confessions, ecclesiastical traditions, **councils,** conferences, **denominations,** jurisdictions, dioceses, cathedrals, basilicas, abbeys, priories, parishes, chapels, **churches,** worship centers, **affiliated members,** adult members, their children, **full-time workers,** clergy, priests, deacons, pastors, ministers, chaplains, lay workers, friars, brothers, monks, contemplatives, bishops, archbishops, metropolitans, cardinals, patriarchs, popes, **women workers,** sisters, nuns, lay readers, musicians, choirs, **missions,** preachers, missioners, home missionaries, foreign missionaries, medical missionaries, missiologists, colporteurs, catechists, evangelists, **evangelism,** evangelistics, evangelization, urban-industrial mission, campaigns, crusades, audiences, **church growth,** catechisms, catechumens, home visits, converts, **baptisms,** confirmations, ordinations, consecrations, marriages, divorces, funerals, excommunications, **renewals,** revivals, persecution, martyrs, **service agencies,** religious orders, societies, institutes, institutions, youth ministries, **schools,** colleges, universities, study centers, students, **hospitals,** clinics, beds, outpatients, medicines, orphanages, **research,** scholarship, scholars, theologians, **libraries,** holdings, bibliographies, **administrators,** nuncios, seminaries, seminarians, monasteries, convents, sunday-schools, ss teachers, ss pupils, retreats, pilgrimages, logistics, **strategies,** tactics, global plans, **finances,** offerings, collections, budgets, incomes, expenditures, properties, endowments, assets, embezzlements, audits, **literature,** tracts, books, magazines, periodicals, journals, newspapers, yearbooks, directories, annual reports, publications, publishing houses, bookshops, **scriptures,** scripture distribution, scripture density, scripture use, scripture translations, translators, names for God, **transportation,** travel, itineration, aviation, ships, vehicles, **communications,** broadcasting, radio/TV stations, listeners, films, viewers, viewings, audiovisuals, correspondence courses, tapes, discs, videos, DVDs, **computers,** computer personnel, e-mail volume, webmasters, websites, hits, networks, **futuristics,** projections, trends, prospects, scenarios.

1. **Background**
Interpretation and analysis of the annual megacensus is grounded in the following 6 secular documents.
• *UN Demographic Database,* also WHO, UNDP, etc.
• *Universal Declaration of Human Rights* (1948)
• *New Encyclopaedia Britannica* on race, ethnography
• *Linguasphere register of the world's languages*
• *Long-range world population projections to AD 2200*
• *World Futures and the UN: 250 books*
To the above 6 seminal documents must be added today's easy electronic access to the 55 million distinct book titles on the shelves of the world's 50,000 largest libraries.

### The annual megacensus

1. BACKGROUND
2. SECULAR DATA
3. SUBJECTS
4. ENUMERATORS
5. QUESTIONNAIRES
6. INSTRUMENTS
7. ANALYZERS
8. DATABASES
9. FINDINGS
10. GCIP PANELS

10. **Great Commission Instrument Panel** (GCIP)
This selection of instruments composed of the top 6 instruments critical for the progress of Christ's Great Commission is designed to serve the world's 5,000 computerized GC networks. It enables comparison of any country with other countries, facilitating strategy, tactics, decision making. It aids collaboration to avoid every agency working from scratch, overlapping or duplicating. It then assists navigation, targeting, up to closure. WCT Part 15 has GCIPs of the 77 countries each with population over 10 million; and WCE Volume 1, Part 4, shows GCIPs of all 238 countries.

2. **Secular data**
See *WCT* Table 12-1, cols. 1-53 (pages 407-413).

4. **Enumerators**
Like other church leaders, all Roman Catholic bishops (pictured in Sistine Chapel) are each required to answer every year 141 statistical questions concerning their work.

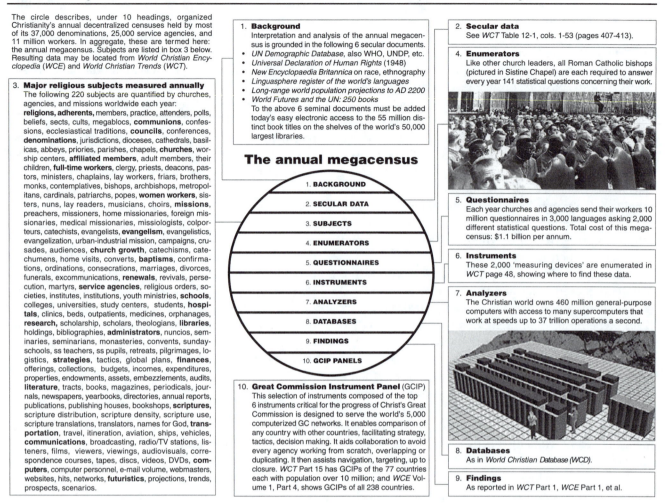

5. **Questionnaires**
Each year churches and agencies send their workers 10 million questionnaires in 3,000 languages asking 2,000 different statistical questions. Total cost of this megacensus: $1.1 billion per annum.

6. **Instruments**
These 2,000 'measuring devices' are enumerated in *WCT* page 48, showing where to find these data.

7. **Analyzers**
The Christian world owns 460 million general-purpose computers with access to many supercomputers that work at speeds up to 37 trillion operations a second.

8. **Databases**
As in *World Christian Database* (WCD).

9. **Findings**
As reported in *WCT* Part 1, *WCE* Part 1, et al.

enumerate a small random sample, usually 5 percent. Where such expensive methods are impossible, estimates are made.

There is an interesting parallel here with modern methods of counting large herds of wild animals, which aim to measure total numbers, size and structure of population, distribution, and migratory movements. These methods have revealed that counting error increases with counting rate, always in the direction of undercounting: "It must always be remembered that even highly experienced observers consistently undercount the numbers of animals in a group by as much as 40 percent" (Norton-Griffiths 1978, 46). The same error occurs in human demography too: "All evidence points to universal underenumeration" (Alterman 1969, 326). In Christian enumerations this usually occurs due to the exclusion of minorities such as Aborigines, illegal immigrants, gypsies and other nomadic peoples, prisoners, criminals, homeless persons, and the like.

### Table 2: Missionaries around the World

By 2005 foreign-mission personnel numbered 443,000 full-time employees of church and mission agencies. Table 2 lists each country's total personnel sent and received. Ten countries sent out more than 10,000 each: USA, 125,700; Italy, 33,300; Spain, 32,200; France, 32,200; Germany, 28,000; Brazil, 21,100; Britain, 19,500; Canada, 17,400; the Netherlands, 10,800; and Belgium, 10,800. Eleven countries received more than 10,000 each: USA, 35,100; Brazil, 26,400; Russia, 20,100; France, 16,900; Britain, 15,800; Congo-Zaire, 15,800; South Africa, 12,700; Italy, 12,700; Argentina, 12,700; Germany, 10,600; and the Philippines, 10,000. Overall, the numbers point to there being a very healthy international sharing of mission personnel. Of the world's seven continents, four receive more than they send: Africa, Asia, Latin America, and Oceania. Nevertheless, these four send out and support 97,192 of their own foreign missionaries.

**Table 2.** Foreign Mission Personnel Sent Out by and Received by 238 Countries around the World, 2005

The data on Christian foreign mission personnel shown below are arranged as one single large 5-variable column set out in 3 pieces consecutively across the page, listing the world's 238 countries in alphabetical order. The last 11 rows list totals by the 7 continents, and by the 3 missiological worlds (World A = unevangelized world, World B = evangelized but non-Christian world, and World C = Christian world, baptized, affiliated). The final righthand bottom row gives global totals. Within each of the 3 pieces, 5 variables are set out, giving total numbers of foreign mission personnel from all Christian churches and traditions, as follows.

1. Short name of country, or (last 11 lines) aggregate
2. Citizens of this country working abroad as mission personnel
3. Citizens working abroad per million of their home country's affiliated church members
4. Aliens from abroad working in this country as mission personnel
5. Aliens from abroad working in this country as mission personnel per million of this country's total population

| 1 Country | 2 MSent | 3 MSentPM | 4 MRecv | 5 MRecvPM |
|---|---|---|---|---|
| Afghanistan | 0 | 0 | 55 | 2 |
| Albania | 55 | 45 | 840 | 268 |
| Algeria | 20 | 364 | 530 | 16 |
| American Samoa | 65 | 1,262 | 210 | 3,237 |
| Andorra | 40 | 669 | 10 | 149 |
| Angola | 340 | 24 | 2,100 | 132 |
| Anguilla | 5 | 478 | 10 | 819 |
| Antarctica | 0 | 0 | 10 | 1,894 |
| Antigua | 2 | 31 | 75 | 920 |
| Argentina | 1,900 | 54 | 12,700 | 328 |
| Armenia | 110 | 44 | 55 | 18 |
| Aruba | 4 | 44 | 15 | 151 |
| Australia | 5,800 | 454 | 4,600 | 228 |
| Austria | 2,600 | 409 | 1,600 | 195 |
| Azerbaijan | 15 | 74 | 110 | 13 |
| Bahamas | 20 | 72 | 320 | 991 |
| Bahrain | 5 | 74 | 55 | 76 |
| Bangladesh | 30 | 28 | 1,100 | 8 |
| Barbados | 10 | 52 | 210 | 779 |
| Belgium | 10,800 | 1,312 | 2,700 | 259 |
| Belize | 10 | 45 | 420 | 1,557 |
| Belorussia | 110 | 17 | 530 | 54 |
| Benin | 55 | 23 | 630 | 75 |
| Bermuda | 10 | 195 | 110 | 1,714 |
| Bhutan | 2 | 117 | 210 | 97 |
| Bolivia | 3,000 | 353 | 4,400 | 479 |
| Bosnia-Herzegovina | 260 | 198 | 580 | 148 |
| Botswana | 85 | 94 | 420 | 238 |
| Bougainville | 10 | 51 | 110 | 515 |
| Brazil | 21,100 | 124 | 26,400 | 142 |
| Britain | 19,500 | 500 | 15,800 | 265 |
| British Indian Ocean | 5 | 5,669 | 10 | 5,000 |
| British Virgin Is | 4 | 266 | 10 | 454 |
| Brunei | 2 | 36 | 30 | 80 |
| Bulgaria | 110 | 17 | 210 | 27 |
| Burkina Faso | 40 | 16 | 1,100 | 83 |
| Burundi | 160 | 25 | 1,300 | 172 |
| Cambodia | 4 | 22 | 320 | 23 |
| Cameroon | 420 | 51 | 3,700 | 227 |
| Canada | 17,400 | 853 | 8,400 | 260 |
| Cape Verde | 85 | 176 | 110 | 217 |
| Cayman Islands | 2 | 65 | 20 | 444 |
| Central African Rep | 85 | 43 | 1,100 | 272 |
| Chad | 30 | 15 | 790 | 81 |
| Channel Islands | 15 | 154 | 10 | 67 |
| Chile | 1,800 | 128 | 8,400 | 515 |
| China | 5,300 | 48 | 4,200 | 3 |
| Christmas Island | 10 | 33,333 | 10 | 6,667 |
| Cocos (Keeling) Is | 5 | 37,037 | 5 | 7,813 |
| Colombia | 3,700 | 84 | 7,400 | 162 |
| Comoros | 2 | 589 | 40 | 59 |
| Congo-Brazzaville | 130 | 44 | 840 | 210 |
| Congo-Zaire | 1,100 | 21 | 15,800 | 275 |
| Cook Islands | 10 | 591 | 75 | 4,177 |
| Costa Rica | 740 | 178 | 1,500 | 347 |
| Croatia | 320 | 79 | 1,600 | 352 |
| Cuba | 20 | 3 | 260 | 23 |
| Cyprus | 55 | 94 | 210 | 326 |
| Czech Republic | 260 | 53 | 1,600 | 157 |
| Denmark | 630 | 136 | 1,500 | 276 |
| Djibouti | 5 | 373 | 80 | 101 |
| Dominica | 5 | 67 | 85 | 1,077 |
| Dominican Republic | 140 | 17 | 2,100 | 236 |
| Ecuador | 420 | 33 | 3,700 | 280 |
| Egypt | 320 | 30 | 1,600 | 22 |
| El Salvador | 210 | 31 | 1,500 | 218 |
| Equatorial Guinea | 55 | 125 | 320 | 636 |
| Eritrea | 130 | 63 | 210 | 48 |
| Estonia | 40 | 79 | 160 | 120 |
| Ethiopia | 260 | 6 | 2,600 | 34 |
| Faeroe Islands | 55 | 1,264 | 30 | 638 |
| Falkland Islands | 20 | 9,794 | 5 | 3,268 |
| Fiji | 110 | 230 | 630 | 743 |
| Finland | 1,500 | 332 | 530 | 101 |
| France | 32,200 | 781 | 16,900 | 279 |
| French Guiana | 20 | 127 | 210 | 1,123 |
| French Polynesia | 30 | 141 | 420 | 1,637 |
| Gabon | 20 | 18 | 420 | 304 |
| Gambia | 4 | 70 | 180 | 119 |
| Georgia | 65 | 23 | 110 | 25 |
| Germany | 28,000 | 480 | 10,600 | 128 |
| Ghana | 580 | 51 | 2,100 | 95 |
| Gibraltar | 10 | 428 | 40 | 1,433 |
| Greece | 420 | 41 | 530 | 48 |
| Greenland | 2 | 51 | 65 | 1,142 |
| Grenada | 10 | 101 | 130 | 1,263 |
| Guadeloupe | 150 | 352 | 420 | 936 |
| Guam | 25 | 164 | 480 | 2,830 |
| Guatemala | 480 | 41 | 3,700 | 294 |
| Guinea | 2 | 8 | 110 | 12 |
| Guinea-Bissau | 10 | 48 | 200 | 126 |
| Guyana | 10 | 26 | 320 | 426 |
| Haiti | 30 | 4 | 1,600 | 188 |
| Holy See | 120 | 156,454 | 210 | 268,199 |
| Honduras | 210 | 31 | 840 | 117 |
| Hungary | 260 | 29 | 1,300 | 129 |
| Iceland | 40 | 145 | 40 | 136 |
| India | 7,400 | 108 | 8,400 | 8 |
| Indonesia | 630 | 22 | 6,300 | 28 |
| Iran | 20 | 54 | 210 | 3 |
| Iraq | 40 | 54 | 85 | 3 |
| Ireland | 9,800 | 2,658 | 530 | 128 |
| Isle of Man | 20 | 389 | 4 | 52 |
| Israel | 55 | 287 | 1,100 | 164 |
| Italy | 33,300 | 700 | 12,700 | 219 |
| Ivory Coast | 320 | 56 | 1,800 | 99 |
| Jamaica | 43 | 38 | 740 | 279 |
| Japan | 840 | 254 | 7,900 | 62 |
| Jordan | 15 | 90 | 210 | 37 |
| Kazakhstan | 30 | 15 | 210 | 14 |
| Kenya | 840 | 31 | 6,300 | 184 |
| Kirgizstan | 30 | 93 | 55 | 10 |
| Kiribati | 10 | 109 | 55 | 554 |
| Kuwait | 10 | 39 | 110 | 41 |
| Laos | 5 | 30 | 85 | 14 |
| Latvia | 65 | 42 | 420 | 182 |
| Lebanon | 210 | 163 | 630 | 176 |
| Lesotho | 55 | 40 | 690 | 384 |
| Liberia | 75 | 76 | 530 | 161 |
| Libya | 5 | 30 | 110 | 19 |
| Liechtenstein | 25 | 838 | 20 | 579 |
| Lithuania | 230 | 81 | 420 | 122 |
| Luxembourg | 130 | 304 | 40 | 86 |
| Macedonia | 55 | 42 | 160 | 79 |
| Madagascar | 320 | 35 | 2,100 | 113 |
| Malawi | 420 | 50 | 1,600 | 124 |
| Malaysia | 95 | 42 | 1,100 | 43 |
| Maldives | 0 | 0 | 10 | 30 |
| Mali | 10 | 27 | 630 | 47 |
| Malta | 1,100 | 2,904 | 30 | 75 |
| Marshall Islands | 10 | 175 | 85 | 1,372 |
| Martinique | 85 | 228 | 210 | 530 |
| Mauritania | 0 | 0 | 55 | 18 |
| Mauritius | 40 | 101 | 320 | 258 |
| Mayotte | 0 | 0 | 30 | 261 |
| Mexico | 4,800 | 47 | 8,400 | 78 |
| Micronesia | 55 | 546 | 510 | 4,616 |
| Moldavia | 110 | 39 | 530 | 126 |
| Monaco | 20 | 669 | 160 | 4,539 |
| Mongolia | 5 | 131 | 420 | 159 |
| Montserrat | 2 | 469 | 10 | 2,228 |
| Morocco | 15 | 133 | 1,600 | 51 |
| Mozambique | 160 | 24 | 3,400 | 172 |
| Myanmar | 260 | 63 | 210 | 4 |
| Namibia | 55 | 33 | 1,300 | 640 |
| Nauru | 2 | 204 | 20 | 1,467 |
| Nepal | 110 | 116 | 950 | 35 |
| Netherlands | 10,800 | 1,162 | 2,200 | 135 |
| Netherlands Antilles | 20 | 129 | 630 | 3,449 |
| New Caledonia | 30 | 170 | 320 | 1,351 |
| New Zealand | 2,200 | 962 | 3,000 | 745 |
| Nicaragua | 260 | 50 | 2,100 | 383 |
| Niger | 10 | 159 | 480 | 34 |
| Nigeria | 2,600 | 42 | 5,600 | 43 |
| Niue | 10 | 7,536 | 5 | 3,460 |
| Norfolk Island | 10 | 7,289 | 5 | 2,322 |
| North Korea | 2 | 5 | 20 | 1 |
| Northern Cyprus | 2 | 727 | 40 | 210 |
| Northern Mariana Is | 5 | 70 | 130 | 1,609 |
| Norway | 1,900 | 436 | 1,100 | 238 |
| Oman | 2 | 28 | 40 | 16 |
| Pakistan | 55 | 14 | 1,600 | 10 |
| Palau | 10 | 535 | 20 | 1,003 |
| Palestine | 260 | 3,005 | 1,300 | 351 |
| Panama | 630 | 229 | 2,200 | 681 |
| Papua New Guinea | 110 | 24 | 3,800 | 670 |
| Paraguay | 480 | 83 | 1,300 | 211 |
| Peru | 840 | 31 | 7,200 | 257 |
| Philippines | 2,100 | 29 | 10,000 | 120 |
| Pitcairn Islands | 1 | 16,129 | 1 | 14,925 |
| Poland | 2,600 | 71 | 740 | 19 |
| Portugal | 5,300 | 551 | 790 | 75 |
| Puerto Rico | 970 | 259 | 2,600 | 657 |
| Qatar | 4 | 46 | 10 | 12 |
| Reunion | 10 | 15 | 250 | 318 |
| Romania | 210 | 10 | 1,100 | 51 |
| Russia | 1,100 | 13 | 20,100 | 140 |
| Rwanda | 130 | 19 | 1,300 | 144 |
| Sahara | 0 | 0 | 10 | 29 |
| Saint Helena | 5 | 1,217 | 20 | 4,067 |
| Saint Kitts & Nevis | 2 | 50 | 40 | 937 |
| Saint Lucia | 4 | 27 | 160 | 995 |
| Saint Pierre & Miquelon | 10 | 1,847 | 40 | 6,934 |
| Saint Vincent | 2 | 25 | 85 | 714 |
| Samoa | 320 | 1,847 | 840 | 4,541 |
| San Marino | 6 | 239 | 20 | 711 |
| São Tomé & Príncipe | 20 | 142 | 110 | 703 |
| Saudi Arabia | 10 | 8 | 110 | 4 |
| Senegal | 95 | 151 | 1,300 | 112 |
| Serbia & Montenegro | 530 | 80 | 1,100 | 105 |
| Seychelles | 15 | 202 | 160 | 1,984 |
| Sierra Leone | 10 | 17 | 740 | 134 |
| Singapore | 530 | 854 | 1,100 | 254 |
| Slovakia | 75 | 17 | 1,100 | 204 |
| Slovenia | 160 | 94 | 840 | 427 |
| Solomon Islands | 45 | 104 | 530 | 1,109 |
| Somalia | 4 | 68 | 55 | 12 |
| Somaliland | 0 | 0 | 10 | 3 |
| South Africa | 7,400 | 214 | 12,700 | 268 |
| South Korea | 5,800 | 301 | 3,000 | 63 |
| Spain | 32,200 | 820 | 2,600 | 60 |
| Spanish North Africa | 10 | 111 | 55 | 417 |
| Sri Lanka | 210 | 107 | 1,800 | 87 |
| Sudan | 110 | 19 | 740 | 20 |
| Suriname | 25 | 132 | 420 | 935 |
| Svalbard & Jan Mayen | 10 | 5,444 | 5 | 1,295 |
| Swaziland | 110 | 169 | 840 | 814 |
| Sweden | 2,100 | 350 | 1,100 | 122 |
| Switzerland | 3,600 | 593 | 2,300 | 317 |
| Syria | 160 | 162 | 110 | 6 |
| Taiwan | 420 | 335 | 3,200 | 140 |
| Tajikistan | 5 | 51 | 40 | 6 |
| Tanzania | 320 | 17 | 4,800 | 125 |
| Thailand | 30 | 28 | 2,100 | 33 |
| Timor | 40 | 50 | 110 | 116 |
| Togo | 85 | 33 | 630 | 103 |
| Tokelau Islands | 5 | 4,000 | 10 | 7,257 |
| Tonga | 55 | 593 | 420 | 4,105 |
| Trinidad & Tobago | 160 | 206 | 530 | 406 |
| Tunisia | 4 | 80 | 210 | 21 |
| Turkey | 30 | 121 | 530 | 7 |
| Turkmenistan | 2 | 27 | 55 | 11 |
| Turks & Caicos Is | 2 | 94 | 10 | 380 |
| Tuvalu | 2 | 231 | 10 | 958 |
| Uganda | 530 | 21 | 2,700 | 94 |
| Ukraine | 420 | 11 | 4,400 | 95 |
| United Arab Emirates | 10 | 23 | 130 | 29 |
| USA | 125,700 | 628 | 35,100 | 118 |
| Uruguay | 630 | 283 | 3,200 | 924 |
| Uzbekistan | 5 | 13 | 210 | 8 |
| Vanuatu | 10 | 53 | 320 | 1,514 |
| Venezuela | 970 | 39 | 7,400 | 277 |
| Viet Nam | 840 | 115 | 1,300 | 15 |
| Virgin Is of the US | 20 | 219 | 160 | 1,431 |
| Wallis & Futuna Is | 2 | 133 | 30 | 1,938 |
| Yemen | 2 | 55 | 160 | 8 |
| Zambia | 260 | 28 | 3,400 | 291 |
| Zimbabwe | 420 | 54 | 2,900 | 223 |
| | | | | |
| Africa | 18,406 | 46 | 95,765 | 106 |
| Antarctica | 0 | 0 | 10 | 1,894 |
| Asia | 25,862 | 75 | 61,405 | 16 |
| Europe | 203,211 | 381 | 111,829 | 154 |
| Latin America | 43,967 | 85 | 114,150 | 203 |
| Northern America | 143,122 | 649 | 43,715 | 132 |
| Oceania | 8,957 | 402 | 16,651 | 504 |
| | | | | |
| World A | 745 | 38 | 13,750 | 19 |
| World B | 44,511 | 79 | 112,020 | 28 |
| World C | 398,269 | 275 | 317,755 | 178 |
| **Global Total** | **443,525** | **218** | **443,525** | **69** |

# Statistics of Mission and Missionaries

**Table 3.** Foreign Mission Personnel Sent Out across the World via 350 Christian World Communions in 2005.

A Christian World Communion (CWC) is defined as an ongoing body uniting only churches and denominations with one similar ecclesiastical tradition or characteristic ('Adventist', 'Anglican', 'Baptist', 'Ecumenical', 'Evangelical', 'Lutheran', 'Mennonite', 'Methodist', 'Orthodox', 'Pentecostal', 'Reformed', 'Roman Catholic', etc.)

*Meaning of 5 columns*
1. Involvement of each CWC ranked by categories 1 to 10 (attitude to either ecumenical or non-ecumenical confessionalism as explained in the 10 first lines across each list of titles)
2. Each CWC's official title (in English, with vernacular titles added only where necessary to establish identity)
3. Each CWC's affiliated church members
4-5. Each CWC's personnel, in 2 descriptive letters

4. External strength: each CWC's foreign mission personnel sent out, coded A to E as follows:
   - A = Massive strength, over 100,000 personnel
   - B = Major strength, from 30,000 to 100,000 personnel
   - C = Moderate strength, form 10,000 to 30,000 personnel
   - D = Minor strength, from 1,000 to 10,000 personnel
   - E = Minimal strength, under 1,000 personnel
5. Internal influence on members: foreign mission personnel per million members, coded a to e as follows:
   - a = massive influence, over 250 personnel per million
   - b = major influence, from 100 to 250 personnel per million
   - c = moderate influence, from 50 to 100 personnel per million
   - d = minor influence, from 20 to 50 personnel per million
   - e = minimal influence, under 20 personnel per million

| 1 Involvement | 2 CWC Title | 3 Members | 4,5 Pers |
|---|---|---|---|
| **1. Conference of Secretaries of Christian World Communions (CSCWC), 1957-2006** | | | |
| Anglican Consultative Council (ACC)/Anglican Communion | | 79,739,000 | Cb |
| Baptist World Alliance (BWA) | | 101,000,000 | Dc |
| Church of the Brethren (German Pietists/Dunkers) | | 346,000 | Eb |
| Disciples Ecumenical Committee for Consultation (DECC) | | 1,500,000 | Ec |
| Ecumenical Patriarchate of Constantinople | | 17,594,000 | Ec |
| Friends World Committee for Consultation (FWCC) | | 507,000 | Eb |
| General Conference of Seventh-day Adventists (SDA) | | 25,000,000 | Ca |
| International Moravian Church in Unity of Brethren | | 1,042,000 | Ec |
| International Old Catholic Bishops Conference (IOCBC) | | 910,000 | Ec |
| Lutheran World Federation (LWF) | | 80,000,000 | Ca |
| Mennonite World Conference (MWC) | | 2,883,000 | Eb |
| Orthodox Patriarchate of Moscow | | 111,404,000 | Dd |
| Pentecostal World Fellowship (PWF) | | 29,821,000 | Db |
| Reformed Ecumenical Council (REC) | | 7,347,000 | Ee |
| Roman Catholic Church (RCC) (13 Patriarchates) | | 1,129,685,000 | Aa |
| Salvation Army (SA) | | 2,214,000 | Ea |
| World Alliance of Reformed Churches (WARC) | | 60,000,000 | Cb |
| World Convention of Churches of Christ (WCCC) | | 10,000,000 | Da |
| World Council of Churches (WCC/COE/ÖRK) | | 486,000,000 | Bb |
| World Evangelical Alliance (WEA) | | 335,000,000 | Aa |
| World Methodist Council (WMC) | | 70,226,000 | Db |
| **2. Not in CSCWC directly but related through a member participant** | | | |
| Bulgarian Orthodox Patriarchate of Sofia | | 11,769,000 | Ee |
| Catholic Charismatic Renewal (CCR, ICCRS) | | 120,000,000 | Ba |
| Council of Catholic Patriarchs in the East (10 Patriarchates) | | 5,400,000 | Ee |
| Global Forum of Christian Churches & Ecumenical Organizations | | 200,000,000 | Dd |
| Greek Orthodox Patriarchate of Alexandria | | 889,000 | Eb |
| Greek Orthodox Patriarchate of Antioch | | 1,026,000 | Eb |
| Greek Orthodox Patriarchate of Jerusalem | | 115,000 | Ed |
| International Pentecostal Holiness Church (IPHC) | | 1,052,000 | Eb |
| Orthodox Apostolic Catholicate of Georgia | | 2,536,000 | Ed |
| Romanian Orthodox Patriarchate of Bucharest | | 19,780,000 | Ee |
| Sacred Congregation for Bishops (3 Patriarchates) | | 884,875,000 | Cd |
| Sacred Congregation for the Evangelization of Peoples (SCEP) | | 220,304,000 | Aa |
| Sacred Congregation for the Oriental Churches (6 Patriarchal Synods) | | 15,312,000 | Ed |
| Serbian Orthodox Patriarchate of Belgrade | | 7,642,000 | Ed |
| Synod of Bishops (Synodus Episcoporum) | | 300,000,000 | Bb |
| Waldensian Evangelical Church | | 54,000 | Ea |
| **3. WCC-related bodies not members of CSCWC because never invited** | | | |
| Ancient Assyrian Patriarchate of the East | | 500,000 | Ec |
| Armenian Apostolic Catholicossate of Cilicia | | 852,000 | Ea |
| Armenian Apostolic Patriarchate of Constantinople | | 66,000 | Ea |
| Armenian Apostolic Patriarchate of Echmiadzin | | 5,593,000 | Ed |
| Armenian Apostolic Patriarchate of Jerusalem | | 18,100 | Ea |
| Brazil for Christ Evangelical Pentecostal Church (OBPC) | | 2,000,000 | Ee |
| Consultation on Uniting and United Churches (CUUC) | | 54,205,000 | Dc |
| Coptic Orthodox Patriarchate of Alexandria | | 10,354,000 | Ee |
| Czechoslovak Hussite Church (CCH/CHC) | | 221,000 | Eb |
| Eritrean Orthodox Patriarchate of Asmara | | 1,904,000 | Ed |
| Ethiopian Orthodox Patriarchate of Addis Ababa | | 26,093,000 | Ee |
| Great and Holy Council of the Orthodox Church (9 Patriarchs) | | 185,000,000 | Dc |
| International Charismatic Consultation on World Evangelization | | 5,100,000 | Ed |
| Mar Thoma Syrian Church of Malabar | | 1,115,000 | Ec |
| Organization of African Instituted Churches (OAIC) | | 33,002,000 | Db |
| Oriental Orthodox Churches Conference (10 Patriarchates) | | 49,974,000 | Dd |
| Orthodox Syrian Catholicate of the East (OSCE) | | 2,575,000 | Ed |
| Philippine Independent Church (IFI/PIC) | | 3,425,000 | Ed |
| Syriac Orthodox Catholicossate of India | | 1,300,000 | Ed |
| Universal Syriac Orthodox Patriarchate of Antioch | | 1,219,000 | Eb |
| **4. Monoconfessional Anglican minicommunions** | | | |
| Anglican Communion Network (ACN) | | 1,000,000 | Ec |
| International Communion of the Charismatic Episcopal Church (ICCEC) | | 950,000 | Ea |
| Traditional Anglican Communion (TAC) | | 400,000 | Eb |
| 16 other schismatic communions ex Anglicanism/Episcopalianism, including: Anglican Church International Communion, Anglican Orthodox Communion (AOC), Communion of the Evangelical Episcopal Church (CEEC), Reformed Episcopal Church (REC), et alia | | 7,600,000 | Ec |
| **5. African/Amerindian/Asian/Black/Latino/Oceanic minicommunions** | | | |
| Catholic Apostolic Church of Brazil.(ICAB) | | 3,000,000 | Ee |
| Celestial Church of Christ (CCC/ECC) | | 4,436,000 | Db |

| 1 Involvement | 2 CWC Title | 3 Members | 4,5 Pers |
|---|---|---|---|
| Christian Congregation of Brazil (Congregação Cristã do Brasil) | | 3,120,000 | Ea |
| Church of Christ/Iglesia ni Cristo (Manalista) | | 4,324,000 | Ec |
| Church of God in Christ (CoGiC) | | 10,000,000 | Da |
| Church of Jesus Christ through Simon Kimbangu (Eglise Kimbanguiste) | | 8,990,000 | Eb |
| Cornerstone Gospel Church (Igreja Pedra Fundamental, IPF) | | 3,200,000 | Eb |
| Deeper Life Bible Church (DLBC) | | 9,000,000 | Da |
| Indian Pentecostal Church of God (IPCG) | | 977,000 | Eb |
| International Evangelical Gypsy Social Association (ASNITE) | | 390,000 | Eb |
| Jesus is Lord Fellowship (JILF) | | 2,277,000 | Eb |
| Pentecostal Methodist Church of Chile (IMPC) | | 720,000 | Eb |
| Universal Church of the Kingdom of God (UCKG/IURD) | | 5,431,000 | Eb |
| Zion Christian Church (ZCC) | | 9,100,000 | Ec |
| 50 other Neocharismatic or Independent Non-White minicommunions each with under a million members worldwide who maintain or function as a separate communion: AACJM, AIPCA, CGMI, IFDA, IPDA, NMBCA, et alia | | 40,000,000 | Db |
| **6. European/North American monodenominational Protestant minicommunions** | | | |
| 70 major Protestant global denominations each linked with its worldwide daughter churches to form a separate communion: AEF, AIM, ARPC, AWM, CAM, CBI, Christian Brethren (CMML), EPC, LAM, OD, OM, OMF, OMS, SBC(IMB), SIM, TEAM, WEC, Worldwide Church of God (WCG), et alia | | 42,084,000 | Ca |
| **7. White-led Neocharismatic communions uninterested in CSCWC** | | | |
| Chaplaincy of Full Gospel Churches (CFGC) | | 8,385,000 | Ec |
| Coalition of Spirit-filled Churches (CSC) | | 500,000 | Ec |
| International Communion of Charismatic Churches (ICCC) | | 6,000,000 | Ec |
| International Fellowship of Charismatic Churches (IFCC) | | 2,000,000 | Ec |
| Manna Church International (Mana Igreja Crista) | | 200,000 | Ea |
| Morning Star International | | 1,100,000 | Da |
| Union of Messianic Jewish Congregations (UMJC) | | 142,000 | Ec |
| Willow Creek Association of Churches (WCAC) | | 804,000 | Ea |
| 30 other White-led Neo-Apostolic meganetworks each globally >50,000, plus a handful of smaller but significant bodies: AFMA, AIMS, EFICC, ICF, SACOC, UICC, YWAM, et alia | | 50,815,000 | Db |
| **8. Conservative communions opposed to ecumenism, to WCC, to CSCWC** | | | |
| Alliance World Fellowship (AWF) | | 4,366,000 | Da |
| Apostolic World Christian Fellowship (AWCF) | | 6,639,000 | Ed |
| Assembly Hall Churches (Local Churches, Little Flock) | | 2,323,000 | Da |
| Baptist Bible Fellowship International (BBFI) | | 2,500,000 | Ea |
| Christian Holiness Association (CHA) | | 5,000,000 | Ec |
| Global Network of Mission Structures (GNMS) | | 24,000,000 | Db |
| International Conference of Reformed Churches (ICRC) | | 132,000 | Ec |
| International Federation of Free Evangelical Churches (IFFEC) | | 846,000 | Ed |
| International Lutheran Council (ILC) | | 3,546,000 | Eb |
| International Spiritual Baptist Ministerial Council | | 20,000 | Ec |
| New Apostolic Church (Neuapostolische Kirche: NAC/NAK) | | 11,098,000 | Da |
| Old Ritualist Churches (Old Believers, Old Orthodox) | | 1,899,000 | Ed |
| True Jesus Church (TJC) | | 1,833,000 | Eb |
| Universal Fellowship of Metropolitan Community Churches (UFMCC) | | 171,000 | Ed |
| World Assemblies of God Fellowship (WAGF) | | 52,220,000 | Ca |
| World Council of Biblical Churches (WCBC) | | 8,400 | Eb |
| World Evangelical Congregational Fellowship (WECF) | | 53,900 | Ec |
| World Fellowship of Reformed Churches (WFRC) | | 1,109,000 | Ec |
| 40 other Conservative networks opposed to historic confessions: ABWE, BMM, EFMA, GMU, IARPC, IFMA, NTM, UFM, UPC, et alia | | 12,212,000 | Ee |
| **9. Worldwide communions with heterodox christologies** | | | |
| Church of Christ, Scientist | | 2,500,000 | Ec |
| Church of Jesus Christ of Latter-day Saints (CJCLdS) | | 12,291,000 | Db |
| International Alliance of Churches of the Truth | | 800,000 | Ed |
| International Council of Unitarians and Universalists (ICUU) | | 282,000 | Ed |
| Jehovah's Christian Witnesses (Watch Tower, IBRA, JWs) | | 16,541,000 | Da |
| Unification Church (Holy Spirit Association for World Christianity) | | 839,000 | Ed |
| 40 other non- or antitrinitarian heterodox communions: IACT, IARF, IGAS, INTA, et alia | | 2,000,000 | Ed |
| **10. Unattached denominations with no CWC, no minicommunion,** no claim to be one, no wider communion nor formal relations with other denominations of similar ecclesiastical tradition, sending out independent missionaries | | 206,353,000 | Dd |
| Total combined memberships in 350 CWCs | | 5,119,662,400 | Ab |
| Doubly-affiliated members (counted in 2 or more CWCs) | | -3,309,662,400 | |
| Total individual members in 350 CWCs throughout Christian world | | 1,810,000,000 | Ab |

**Table 4.** Worldwide Mission Activities in the Context of Global Christianity, 1800–2025

| Year: | 1800 | 1900 | 1970 | mid-2000 | Trend % p.a. | mid-2006 | 2025 |
|---|---|---|---|---|---|---|---|
| **GLOBAL POPULATION** | | | | | | | |
| 1. Total population | 903,650,000 | 1,619,625,000 | 3,692,495,000 | 6,070,581,000 | 1.22 | 6,529,426,000 | 7,851,455,000 |
| 2. Urban dwellers (urbanites) | 36,146,000 | 232,695,000 | 1,362,295,000 | 2,878,861,000 | 2.05 | 3,252,255,000 | 4,572,885,000 |
| 3. Rural dwellers | 867,504,000 | 1,386,930,000 | 2,330,200,000 | 3,191,720,000 | 0.44 | 3,277,171,000 | 3,278,570,000 |
| 4. Adult population (over 15s) | 619,000,000 | 1,073,621,000 | 2,313,053,000 | 4,241,871,000 | 1.66 | 4,682,974,000 | 5,950,587,000 |
| 5. Literates | 123,800,000 | 296,146,000 | 1,476,797,000 | 3,251,554,000 | 1.65 | 3,587,095,000 | 5,015,884,000 |
| 6. Nonliterates | 495,200,000 | 777,475,000 | 836,256,000 | 990,317,000 | 1.70 | 1,095,879,000 | 934,703,000 |
| **WORLDWIDE EXPANSION OF CITIES** | | | | | | | |
| 7. Metropolises (over 100,000 population) | 40 | 300 | 2,400 | 4,050 | 1.77 | 4,500 | 6,500 |
| 8. Megacities (over 1 million population) | 1 | 20 | 161 | 402 | 1.90 | 450 | 650 |
| 9. Urban poor | 18 million | 100 million | 650 million | 1,400 million | 3.09 | 1,680 million | 3,000 million |
| 10. Urban slum-dwellers | 3 million | 20 million | 260 million | 700 million | 3.29 | 850 million | 1,600 million |
| **GLOBAL POPULATION BY RELIGION** | | | | | | | |
| 11. Total of all distinct organized religions | 700 | 1,000 | 6,000 | 9,900 | 1.62 | 10,900 | 15,000 |
| 12. Christians (total all kinds) (=World C) | 204,980,000 | 558,131,000 | 1,234,339,000 | 2,000,909,000 | 1.25 | 2,156,350,000 | 2,630,559,000 |
| 13. Muslims | 90,500,000 | 199,914,000 | 549,226,000 | 1,196,451,000 | 1.90 | 1,339,392,000 | 1,861,360,000 |
| 14. Hindus | 108,000,000 | 203,003,000 | 462,379,000 | 808,175,000 | 1.38 | 877,552,000 | 1,031,168,000 |
| 15. Nonreligious | 300,000 | 3,024,000 | 532,339,000 | 762,099,000 | 0.23 | 772,497,000 | 817,091,000 |
| 16. Chinese universists | 310,000,000 | 380,006,000 | 231,866,000 | 390,850,000 | 0.65 | 406,233,000 | 431,956,000 |
| 17. Buddhists | 69,400,000 | 127,077,000 | 232,667,000 | 362,374,000 | 0.90 | 382,482,000 | 459,448,000 |
| 18. Ethnoreligionists | 92,000,000 | 117,558,000 | 163,477,000 | 239,103,000 | 1.21 | 257,009,000 | 270,210,000 |
| 19. Non-Christians (=Worlds A and B) | 698,670,000 | 1,061,494,000 | 2,458,156,000 | 4,069,672,000 | 1.21 | 4,373,076,000 | 5,220,896,000 |
| **GLOBAL CHRISTIANITY** | | | | | | | |
| 20. Total Christians as % of world (=World C) | 22.7 | 34.5 | 33.4 | 33.0 | 0.03 | 33.0 | 33.5 |
| 21. Affiliated Christians (church members) | 195,680,000 | 521,642,000 | 1,128,713,000 | 1,895,522,000 | 1.25 | 2,042,150,000 | 2,507,886,000 |
| 22. Church attenders | 180,100,000 | 469,303,000 | 885,777,000 | 1,359,420,000 | 1.04 | 1,446,457,000 | 1,760,568,000 |
| 23. Evangelicals | 25,000,000 | 71,726,000 | 98,358,000 | 224,791,000 | 2.11 | 254,797,000 | 348,648,000 |
| 24. Great Commission Christians | 21,000,000 | 77,931,000 | 277,153,000 | 650,094,000 | 1.13 | 695,229,000 | 853,179,000 |
| 25. Pentecostals/Charismatics/Neocharismatics | 0 | 981,000 | 72,223,000 | 526,916,000 | 2.08 | 596,096,000 | 798,320,000 |
| 26. Average Christian martyrs per year | 2,500 | 34,400 | 377,000 | 160,000 | 1.11 | 171,000 | 210,000 |
| **MEMBERSHIP BY 6 ECCLESIASTICAL MEGABLOCS** | | | | | | | |
| 27. Roman Catholics | 106,430,000 | 266,546,000 | 665,475,000 | 1,055,651,000 | 1.12 | 1,128,883,000 | 1,334,338,000 |
| 28. Independents | 400,000 | 7,931,000 | 96,926,000 | 379,085,000 | 2.23 | 432,832,000 | 607,670,000 |
| 29. Protestants | 30,980,000 | 103,024,000 | 211,052,000 | 347,764,000 | 1.52 | 380,799,000 | 489,084,000 |
| 30. Orthodox | 55,220,000 | 115,844,000 | 139,646,000 | 214,436,000 | 0.45 | 220,290,000 | 235,834,000 |
| 31. Anglicans | 11,910,000 | 30,571,000 | 47,409,000 | 75,164,000 | 1.24 | 80,922,000 | 107,557,000 |
| 32. Marginal Christians | 40,000 | 928,000 | 11,100,000 | 29,501,000 | 2.79 | 34,799,000 | 49,768,000 |
| **MEMBERSHIP BY 6 CONTINENTS, 21 UN REGIONS** | | | | | | | |
| 33. Africa (5 regions) | 4,330,000 | 8,756,000 | 117,227,000 | 346,415,000 | 2.33 | 397,676,000 | 595,821,000 |
| 34. Asia (4 regions) | 8,350,000 | 20,759,000 | 96,460,000 | 302,651,000 | 2.51 | 351,234,000 | 498,120,000 |
| 35. Europe (including Russia; 4 regions) | 171,700,000 | 368,209,000 | 467,935,000 | 532,107,000 | -0.06 | 530,090,000 | 513,706,000 |
| 36. Latin America (3 regions) | 14,900,000 | 60,027,000 | 263,561,000 | 477,149,000 | 1.35 | 516,974,000 | 623,355,000 |
| 37. Northern America (1 region) | 5,600,000 | 59,570,000 | 168,943,000 | 216,221,000 | 0.46 | 222,292,000 | 250,186,000 |
| 38. Oceania (4 regions) | 100,000 | 4,322,000 | 14,587,000 | 20,976,000 | 1.15 | 22,461,000 | 26,691,000 |
| **CHRISTIAN ORGANIZATIONS** | | | | | | | |
| 39. Denominations | 500 | 1,900 | 18,800 | 33,800 | 1.97 | 38,000 | 55,000 |
| 40. Congregations (worship centers) | 150,000 | 400,000 | 1,450,000 | 3,448,000 | 1.50 | 3,770,000 | 5,000,000 |
| 41. Service agencies | 600 | 1,500 | 14,100 | 23,000 | 2.06 | 26,000 | 36,000 |
| 42. Foreign-mission sending agencies | 200 | 600 | 2,200 | 4,000 | 1.64 | 4,410 | 6,000 |
| **CONCILIARISM: ONGOING COUNCILS OF CHURCHES** | | | | | | | |
| 43. Confessional councils (CWCs, at world level) | 20 | 40 | 150 | 310 | 2.04 | 350 | 600 |
| 44. International councils of churches | 0 | 10 | 36 | 59 | 1.10 | 63 | 80 |
| 45. National councils of churches | 0 | 19 | 283 | 598 | 1.50 | 650 | 870 |
| 46. Local councils of churches | 0 | 70 | 2,600 | 9,000 | 2.20 | 10,300 | 15,500 |
| **CHRISTIAN WORKERS (clergy, laypersons)** | | | | | | | |
| 47. Nationals (citizens; all denominations) | 900,000 | 2,100,000 | 4,600,000 | 10,000,000 | 1.00 | 11,072,000 | 14,000,000 |
| 48. Men | 800,000 | 1,900,000 | 3,100,000 | 6,800,000 | 0.90 | 6,830,000 | 8,000,000 |
| 49. Women | 100,000 | 200,000 | 1,500,000 | 3,200,000 | 1.10 | 4,242,000 | 6,000,000 |
| 50. Aliens (foreign mission personnel) | 25,000 | 62,000 | 240,000 | 420,000 | 1.10 | 443,000 | 550,000 |
| 51. Men | 21,000 | 47,000 | 160,000 | 240,000 | 1.00 | 245,000 | 270,000 |
| 52. Women | 4,000 | 15,000 | 80,000 | 180,000 | 1.20 | 198,000 | 280,000 |
| **CHRISTIAN FINANCE (in US$, per year)** | | | | | | | |
| 53. Personal income of church members, $ | 40 billion | 270 billion | 4,100 billion | 15,230 billion | 0.44 | 15,930 billion | 26,000 billion |
| 54. Giving to Christian causes, $ | 1 billion | 8 billion | 70 billion | 270 billion | 4.91 | 360 billion | 870 billion |
| 55. Churches' income, $ | 950 million | 7 billion | 50 billion | 108 billion | 4.42 | 140 billion | 300 billion |
| 56. Parachurch and institutional income, $ | 50 million | 1 billion | 20 billion | 162 billion | 5.23 | 220 billion | 570 billion |
| 57. Cost-effectiveness (cost per baptism, $) | 7,500 | 17,500 | 128,000 | 330,000 | 2.80 | 349,000 | 650,000 |
| 58. Ecclesiastical crime, $ | 100,000 | 300,000 | 5,000,000 | 16 billion | 5.77 | 22 billion | 65 billion |
| 59. Income of global foreign missions, $ | 25,000,000 | 200,000,000 | 3.0 billion | 15 billion | 5.70 | 21 billion | 60 billion |
| 60. Computers in Christian use (numbers) | 0 | 0 | 1,000 | 328 million | 5.80 | 460 million | 1,200 million |
| **CHRISTIAN LITERATURE (titles, not copies)** | | | | | | | |
| 61. Books about Christianity | 75,000 | 300,000 | 1,800,000 | 4,800,000 | 3.08 | 5,957,000 | 11,800,000 |
| 62. Christian periodicals | 800 | 3,500 | 23,000 | 35,000 | 4.28 | 45,000 | 100,000 |
| **SCRIPTURE DISTRIBUTION (all sources, per year/p.a.)** | | | | | | | |
| 63. Bibles, p.a. | 500,000 | 5,452,600 | 25,000,000 | 53,700,000 | 4.96 | 71,787,000 | 180,000,000 |
| 64. Scriptures including gospels, selections, p.a. | 1,500,000 | 20 million | 281 million | 4,600 million | 2.24 | 5,250 million | 8,000 million |
| 65. Bible density (copies in place) | 20 million | 108 million | 443 million | 1,400 million | 1.97 | 1,570 million | 2,280 million |
| **CHRISTIAN BROADCASTING** | | | | | | | |
| 66. Total monthly listeners/viewers | 0 | 0 | 750,000,000 | 2,150,000,000 | 2.30 | 2,465,000,000 | 3,800,000,000 |
| **CHRISTIAN URBAN MISSION** | | | | | | | |
| 67. Non-Christian megacities | 1 | 5 | 65 | 226 | 1.14 | 242 | 300 |
| 68. New non-Christian urban dwellers per day | 500 | 5,200 | 51,100 | 129,000 | 1.73 | 143,000 | 200,000 |
| 69. Urban Christians | 5,500,000 | 159,600,000 | 660,800,000 | 1,160,000,000 | 1.59 | 1,275,000,000 | 1,720,000,000 |
| **CHRISTIAN EVANGELISM** | | | | | | | |
| 70. Evangelism-hours per year | 600 million | 5 billion | 25 billion | 165 billion | 3.86 | 210 billion | 425 billion |
| 71. Hearer-hours (offers) per year | 900 million | 10 billion | 99 billion | 938 billion | 6.23 | 1,350 billion | 4,250 billion |
| 72. Disciple-opportunities (offers) per capita per year | 1 | 6 | 27 | 155 | 4.97 | 207 | 541 |
| **WORLD EVANGELIZATION** | | | | | | | |
| 73. Unevangelized population (=World A) | 674,300,000 | 879,672,000 | 1,641,300,000 | 1,718,072,000 | 0.84 | 1,806,065,000 | 2,039,813,000 |
| 74. Unevangelized as % of world | 74.6 | 54.3 | 44.4 | 28.3 | -0.38 | 27.7 | 26.0 |
| 75. World evangelization plans since AD 30 | 160 | 250 | 510 | 1,500 | 2.80 | 1,770 | 3,000 |

## *Table 3: Christian World Communions*

This table shows which ecclesiastical traditions are sending out these foreign-mission personnel. Only three communions send out over 100,000 each, and only two more from 30,000 to 100,0000. The great majority—310—each send less than 1,000 personnel abroad. Size is not of course a guarantor of influence; for this, readers should compare the figures of missionaries per million in table 3, columns 3 and 5, and also table 4, column 5.

## *Table 4: Worldwide Mission Activities*

Foreign-mission personnel are involved in all the sixteen major concerns and activities of Christianity shown in capital headings in this table. Missionaries are also involved in virtually every one of the seventy-five enumerated activities listed there, often as far back as the year 1800 (first column of statistics).

Total foreign-mission personnel have grown from 25,000 in 1800 to 443,000 by 2005. Of these today, 245,000 are men and 198,000 are women. But these figures refer to full-time workers, which means those employed full time by churches and missions. However, the rest of the population should not be labeled as part-timers. In fact, as detailed above, there are 688 million Great Commission Christians, defined primarily as persons believing in and committed to Christ's Great Commission and the worldwide mission of the church. Of these millions, this analysis divides this vast bloc into two: 468 million function as background supporters of worldwide foreign missions (paragraph D above and rows 42 and 50 in table 4). The remaining 220 million Great Commission Christians function primarily as supporters of home missions (Paragraph C above).

## Sources and Documentation

Most of the statistics listed in the preceding analysis come, in the first instance, from the multiple censuses and minicensuses that compose each year's megacensus. Due to differing definitions of the terms used by different denominations and Christian World Communions and to the overlapping categories at a number of points, the total picture presented here should be regarded as in the main an impressionistic portrait in oils rather than an exact photographic image with everything in focus. This situation, and its attendant problems, are described and discussed in detail in the presentation of data and methodology set out in Barrett and Johnson et al. (2001).

DAVID B. BARRETT

## Further Reading

Alterman, H, (1969). *Counting people: the census in history.* Orlando, FL: Harcourt.

American Statistical Association. (n.d.). Retrieved June 9, 2006, from http://www.amstat.org/index.cfm?fuse action=main

Barrett, D. B., Johnson, Todd, M., Guidry, C. (Ed.), & Crossing, P. (Ed.). (2001). *World Christian trends, AD 30–AD 2200: Interpreting the annual Christian megacensu*s. Pasadena, CA: William Carey Library Publishers.

Bauer, R. A. (Ed.). (1966). *Social indicators.* Cambridge, MA: MIT Press.

Norton-Griffiths, M. (1978). *Counting animals.* Nairobi, Kenya: African Wildlife Leadership Foundation.

# T

## Technology

Technology refers to the material elements of human culture—including artifacts, tools, machines, and computers—that help facilitate the pursuit of goals. Although technology predates science, today it commonly relates to applied science, including engineering, modes of transport, communication, medicine, warfare, print and visual media, electronics, and the digitization of information. Christian mission has learned to use technology to pursue its own goals.

Technology increases the capacity of people to achieve desired outcomes. It also creates its own cultural space with outcomes that may not have been anticipated. As a form of power, technology may contribute to oppression or to liberation, and lack of access to technology or to the skill to use it is a factor in inequality and poverty. Using technology constructively requires taking account of both culture and economy.

A missionary theology of technology might take as its text the biblical vision of beating swords into ploughshares (Isaiah 2:4). The cultures of engineering, technical education, and information technology are capable of being Gospel bearers, but like other dimensions of culture, they are also flawed. While intrinsically neither messianic nor demonic, some technologies present temptations that are difficult to resist and which may have devastating results. However, a theology that views creation as reflecting the glory of God but marred by sin and groaning for redemption (Romans 8:20–22) should also include the tools created by human beings.

The benefits and temptations of technology are components in the story of Christian mission. The use of the technology of woodworking to create an instrument of torture was a temptation which the Roman authorities gave in to. Jesus was a carpenter and the son of a carpenter, yet died on an instrument of torture and degradation. His disciples sailed boats, and caught fish with nets they made and mended. The temptations of fishing are that you go on fishing when you should be doing something else, yet the disciples resisted the temptation and followed Jesus. Paul could support himself making tents. Roman roads and Mediterranean shipping facilitated the travels of early missionaries as well as of armies. Writing, and the production of letters and books, recorded and distributed stories of Jesus and the responses of leaders to issues facing churches. The same tools distributed versions of the Gospel that needed to be corrected. Church buildings and Christian art gave material and visual expression to Christian faith, but also provided temptations to aggrandizement and idolatry. Military technology, instruments of navigation, and shipping skills expanded the empires of Christian rulers but also facilitated colonialism.

As Christian mission expanded, starting in the sixteenth century, the power of technology, including military technology and in the service of colonialism, to both facilitate and compromise Christian faith became serious. Clocks and astronomical instruments helped the Jesuits enter China. Artisan missionaries were part of the missionary societies' vision of Western civilization as a preparation for the Gospel, and missionaries brought agricultural and industrial training to their missions. They also brought printing presses, which both preserved vernacular cultures and challenged them. Medical techniques and instruments attracted people to the Christian message, and missionary education trained people to use them. Alexander Mackay in Uganda (1849–1860) was perhaps the first professional engineer employed by a missionary society. He built roads and maintained steamships as well as translated work, and became one many whose training and disposition provided a characteristic approach to problem solving, which still remains recognizable.

In the twentieth century, Catholic and Protestant missionaries began to use film, radio, computers, and the Internet to communicate their message. They quickly found that the culture of technology has a capacity to reach across generations in unexpected ways. However, they found no easy answer to the dilemma of technological inequality and the association of messengers of the Gospel with a power that may attract interest in its own right or undermine the beliefs and values they seek to represent. There are also no easy answers to concerns about industrialization, oil dependency, global warming, nuclear warfare, and pollution. The realization that not all human problems, including the missionary challenge of global evangelism, can be resolved by project management and mass-marketing techniques is important.

In a global society missionaries are not the only representatives of technological power, and the issue may not be whether they have access to a power that some others—even the majority—do not have, but rather whether that access is seen by people as appropriate to the role they wish the missionary to have. Christian radio, television, and other media have lost their novelty, but if the idea that the media is the message still holds some truth, then it is important that here, as in other areas of the application of technology to mission, technology remains the servant of Christian mission and not its master.

JOHN ROXBOROGH

*See also* Archives; Education—Religious, Theological; Internet; Media and Mass Communications; Medicine; Photography; Reference Tools

### Further Reading

Bonk, J. (1991). Missions and money: Affluence as a Western missionary problem. *American Society of Missiology Series, No. 15.* Maryknoll, NY: Orbis Books.

Hersey, J. (1985). *The call.* New York: Knopf.

Lochhead, D. (1997). Shifting realities: Information technology and the church. *Risk Book Series, No. 75.* Geneva, Switzerland: WCC Publications.

Roxborogh, J. (1999). The Information superhighway as a missiological tool of the trade. *Missiology, 27*(1), 117–122.

Conway, R. (1999). *Choices at the heart of technology: a Christian perspective, Christian mission and modern culture.* Harrisburg, PA: Trinity Press.

## Terminology

The terminology and vocabulary of Christian missions and Christian mission studies is mainly rooted in the Bible as a missionary book and in the history of Christianity as a missionary religion. The Hebrew term *shalach* in the Old Testament and the Greek terms *apostellein* and *pempein* in the New Testament mean "to send." In the Vulgate *mittere* is the translation of these verbs. The word *apostolate* originates from *apostellein,* and the word *missio,* from *mittere.* The terms *apostolate, propagation of the faith,* and *offering salvation to the heathen* were already widely used before in the sixteenth century *mission* became the leading technical term. Jesuits coined it for the designation of the journeys, destinations, and territories outside the Western world to which their missionaries were sent for the sake of the Gospel and the church. In the nineteenth century the expression "mission and evangelism" was invented by Protestants—evangelism as an accomplishment of mission to describe the missionary obligation and activities of Christianity in the Western world. In the early twentieth century the term *missiology* was coined by the Jesuits to replace older names of the discipline such as "the science of mission" (Ger.: *Missionswissenschaft*) and "mission history and mission theory." After World War II new terms of the discipline and its object were introduced; they either function as an addition to or as a replacement of the more or less classical terms: *witness, presence, encounter, dialogue,* etc. Moreover, *in academia* "intercultural theology" and "the theology of religions" circulate nowadays as additions and alternatives of "missiology."

The terminologies of the various Christian denominations differ to some extent. The Roman Catholic Church has a distinct vocabulary that is coined by, and used in, canon law, mission decrees such as *Ad gentes* (Second Vatican Council, 1962–1965), apostolic exhortations such as *Evangelii nuntiandi* (1975), and encyclical letters such as *Redemptoris missio* (1991): "canonical mission," "mission *ad gentes,*" "ecclesial basic communities" (especially in Latin America), etc. The vocabulary of Protestant denominations and missionary societies is more Bible-, and less church-centered (no canon law): "great commission," "conversion (of the heathen)," "proclamation (of the Gospel)," etc. The terminology of the Ecumenical Movement, the International Missionary

Council (1921–1961), and the World Council of Churches (1948 ff.) is less fixed and consequently more diverse and also more confusing, than Catholic terminology. The World Council's document *Mission and Evangelism: An Ecumenical Affirmation* (1982) referred to "the Gospel to all realms of life" and "Good news to the poor." The Evangelical Movement, known as the Lausanne Movement, developed a terminology that holds a middle position: less fixed than Catholic terminology and more precise than Ecumenical terminology. The Movement's documents *The Lausanne Covenant* (1974) and *The Manila Manifesto* (1989) paid attention to "the urgency of the evangelistic task" and "the uniqueness of Jesus Christ." The Church Growth Movement (Donald A. McGavran, Peter Wagner, et al.) inside the Evangelical Movement developed a distinct terminology of "(church) growth" and "multiplying churches." The terminology of David B. Barrett's *World Christian Encyclopedia* is also quite specific: "Great Commission Christians" (Christians devoting their time to Christ's Great Commission) and "First, Second, and Third Wavers" (Classical Pentecostals, Charismatics, and Neocharismatics, respectively). Outside the realm of the Evangelical Movement new terms were coined as well, for instance, "anonymous Christians" (i.e., non-Christians) as "Christians-without-a-name" (Karl Rahner) and "Christianness," (i.e., a personal religiousness), in addition to the terms *Christianity* (a religion) and *Christendom* (a civilization), expressing a confidence "that Christianity simply incarnates the primordial and original traditions of humankind" (Panikkar 1987, 104).

Since the birth and the growth of third-world churches and theological institutions, a clear paradigm shift has taken place: the third world is no longer the "mission field" of Western Christianity; the whole world became the mission field of the whole church, enabling and stimulating non-Western Christians to do missions and evangelism outside their own realm. Third-world church leaders and theologians transformed the terminology of colonial times: *context* instead of *indigenization* (of the Gospel), *liberation* instead of *development*, etc. They distinguished the "crucified mind" of the Gospel message from the "crusading mind" of Christendom since the Roman emperor Constantine the Great (Kosuke Koyama). They also renewed the theological vocabulary of the West, talking about Christ as "Ancestor" (Charles Nyamiti) and as "Liberator" (Latin-American liberation theologians). Third-world Christians who migrate to the Western world and establish their own churches and missions in this new environment develop a migrant view and a dispersion vocabulary.

The terminology of missions and mission studies is not only influenced by developments inside Christianity, but also by the Christians' encounters with adherents, or neighbors, of other religions, world-views, and ideologies. Bible translation work in six continents illustrates both the creation of new language and terminology (for instance the creation of a monotheistic vocabulary in polytheistic settings) and the use and transformation of the oral and written languages of other belief systems. In nineteenth-century China the proper translation of the key words *God* and *Holy Spirit* have provoked serious controversies among Western missionaries. In India the suitability of Hindu *advaita* terminology in Christian theology and worship is debated. In the context of secular worldviews and ideologies similar adaptations and creations are taking place: the "secular meaning of the Gospel" (van Buren 1963) can only be expressed in secular language. Religious language, rooted in human experiences of God, or the Ultimate, and investigated by analytical theologians and scholars of religious studies (cf. Ramsey 1957), continues to shape the minds and the hearts of countless adherents of the various religions and religious movements around the globe.

The terminology of missions and mission studies both influences and is influenced by the terminology of related academic disciplines such as linguistics, ethnology, and cultural anthropology. Missionaries produced not only many translations of the Bible, hymn books, and educational materials into the vernaculars of the non-Western world, but also many grammars and dictionaries. At the same time, grammars and dictionaries published by the adherents of other religions and worldviews were intensively used by Bible translators and other Christians in the field. Many missionaries were also pioneers in the field of ethnology and cultural anthropology and contributed to the vocabulary of these academic disciplines; at the same time, they learned a lot from secular scholars in the field. Today there is two-way traffic: to a large extent linguistic analysis and the renewal of anthropological terminology are a multidisciplinary and multicultural endeavor in which Bible translators, Christian theologians, mission scholars, and Western and non-Western missionaries around the globe take part.

Jan A. B. Jongeneel

## Further Reading

Barrett, D. B. (Ed.). (2001). *World Christian encyclopedia: A comparative survey of churches and religions in the modern world* (2nd ed., 2 vols.). Oxford, UK: University Press.

Glasser, A. F., & McGavran, D. A. (1985). *Contemporary theologies of mission*. Grand Rapids, MI: Baker House.

Jongeneel, J. A. B. (1995–1997). *Philosophy, science, and theology of mission in the 19th and 20th centuries: A missiological encyclopedia* (2 vols.). Frankfurt, Germany: Peter Lang.

Koyama, K. (1974). What makes a missionary? Toward crucified mind, not crusading mind. In G. H. Anderson & T. F. Stransky (Eds.), *Mission trends no. 1: Crucial issues in mission today* (pp. 117–132). New York/Grand Rapids: Paulist Press/Eerdmans.

Nyamiti, C. (1984). *Christ as our ancestor: Christology from an African perspective*. Gweru, Zimbabwe: Mambo Press.

Panikkar, R. (1987). Three kairological moments of Christic self-consciousness. In J. Hick & P. F. Knitter (Eds.), *The myth of Christian uniqueness: Toward a pluralistic theology of religions* (pp. 89–116). Maryknoll, NY: Orbis Books.

Ramsey, I. T. (1957). *Religious language: An empirical placing of theological phrases*. London: SCM Press.

Van Buren, P. M. (1963). *The secular meaning of the gospel based on an analysis of its language*. London: SCM Press.

Wagner, C. P. (Ed.). (1989). *Church growth: State of the art*. Wheaton, IL: Tyndale House.

# Theology

Any particular mission movement has a distinct understanding of the nature of its mission and the part it plays in the purposes of God, which may be implicit or explicit and may be called its theology of mission. The theology of an individual missionary or mission movement includes discussion of motivation, worldview, mission thinking, and vision. It attempts to enter into the missionary mind and the mission context to understand and describe the reasoning behind a particular mission enterprise and the influences that shape it. Theology of mission may also prescribe new modes of mission based on reflection on the Bible or other authoritative sources, on the history of mission, or on contemporary mission experience. Different theologies of mission operate as the rationales behind particular mission strategies, which can be used to justify mission activity and encourage participation.

Though the church has been engaged in mission since its inception, the theology of mission as a distinct discipline within the theological curriculum is a recent development from the late nineteenth century. Since the publication of David Bosch's *Transforming Mission* in 1991, mission theologians have generally followed his interdisciplinary approach, which describes a number of different theologies of mission that arose in different contexts. The sources of these theologies have been experience of God in Christ in the Christian community and reflection on Christian tradition, especially as written down in the Bible. The New Testament contains within it the seeds of later theologies of mission, but it does not present one unified theology. Each of the writers has a distinctive interpretation of the mission of Jesus and therefore of the mission of the disciples, which is derived from it, according to authorship and audience. Nor can we describe one Christian theology of mission in history but will identify several major yet distinct theologies, indicating how they have arisen with movements in particular times and places.

## Mission Theology in the Greco-Roman Empire

From the origin of the church at Pentecost, the Christian instinct was to reach out beyond its community and draw others in; that is, the church was missionary by its very nature. Christians regarded Jesus Christ as sent (the root meaning of "mission") from heaven to carry out God's purposes in Palestine by preaching, teaching, healing, and deliverance ministry. They came to regard his death by crucifixion at the hands of the religious authorities as also his glorification because, being vindicated by God, he rose from death and so opened a new way to God for all people. Believing that Jesus Christ was with them in power by the Holy Spirit and that they were also sent into the world, Christians declared his critical significance for the salvation of the whole world and lived out his teaching in community, expecting the imminent judgment of God on evil and the reign of Christ over all. Following the pattern of God who became man (incarnation) and believing God's Spirit was bestowed on all without partiality, the first Christians began to express the message in other cultures (inculturate it), particularly in the dominant Greek culture. A key figure in this process was Paul, a Hellenistic Jew who became Apostle to the Gentiles (non-Jews or Greeks). Paul was transformed by a spiritual encounter with the risen Christ, which led him to believe that the church, or Christian community, was the body of Christ and that this was most evident when Jews and Gentiles shared and ate together. By building up representative congregations in local centers, Paul believed he was gathering the first fruits of a harvest that would guarantee new and eternal life for the whole creation.

The early Christian confession that Jesus is Lord was a direct challenge to imperial power by a group that arose in an occupied corner of the empire, so Christian witness could attract persecution and occasionally martyrdom. Christians understood this theologically as identification with the suffering of their Master. Dying and rising with him, represented symbolically in baptism by immersion, was to participate in his mission of salvation for the world. However, after the conversion to Christianity of the Emperor Constantine (312–315 CE), Christianity became the official religion of empire and developed into a powerful institution. In this new climate the church became an arm of authority and was given responsibility for the spiritual welfare of all citizens. This change of situation radically altered the church's mission outlook and theological justification of it. Far from being a temporary in-gathering of believers awaiting the apocalypse, the church increasingly saw itself as the temporal expression of God's eternal kingdom. The mobile mission of apostles, prophets, and evangelists spreading the word and attracting converts gave way to the settled ministry of bishops and deacons, building up the church as the local expression of God's new society. Many churches, particularly in Asia, have never enjoyed the protection of the state and have often had to struggle for survival, but whether politically powerful or not, and despite continually rehearsing the gospel stories, the church has not always actively remembered its foundation as a servant community, in the world but not of it.

## Mission Theology of the Orthodox Churches

After the sixth century, the churches in the West and East began to diverge in their theological development along the fault line between Latin and Greek cultures, until by the schism of 1054 they had become distinct churches: Orthodox and Roman Catholic. In the Byzantine Empire of the East the church became closely allied with the state, endorsing its policies, and Christ was increasingly portrayed in images of the emperor cult. Furthermore, in their greater willingness to adapt themselves to local languages and cultures, the Orthodox churches became national churches. This affirmation of culture was expressed theologically in an emphasis on God's work in creation and on the incarnation of Christ: the preexistent Word becoming part of creation by taking human form. Salvation was understood as a gradual process of becoming like God, the divinization of a created order that, though flawed, was essentially good. This theology of the descent of God and the ascent of man owes much to scholarly engagement with Greek philosophy (especially Plato) by the Church Fathers, particularly Origen (185–254 CE) of Alexandria.

The church is central to Orthodox mission theology because it is understood to be the expression of heaven on Earth. Mission is centrifugal in drawing people into the church rather than going centripetally to take the gospel to people outside it. The church is the aim of mission because it is where the world is gathered and lifted up to heaven and where the Spirit of God is called down upon the earth. Therefore the liturgy (or worship) of the church is the chief missionary act, enlightening the darkness of the world, and the pattern for all other activity. This is not limited to the regeneration of humanity but renews the whole created order; it is a continuing expression of the love of the Father who sent Jesus Christ into the world (cosmos) as its light and life (John 3:16; 1:4).

## Mission Theology of the Roman Catholic Church

In the western part of the empire, the church adopted Latin as its universal language and developed a theology that, though it owed much to Greek thought, also reflected a distinct Western culture developed especially from the thinking of Augustine of Hippo (354–430). This theology was very aware of the problem of individual human sinfulness and emphasized the death by crucifixion of Jesus Christ more than his incarnation as the way in which human sin was atoned for. Interest in salvation was more to do with the individual soul rather than the whole creation and it was appropriated by penance, a punishment to which a person voluntarily submits to show sorrow for sin.

This moral discipline was enforced by the church, which saw itself the instrument of mission to bring about God's kingdom on Earth, or Christendom, such that there was no salvation outside the church. The Roman Catholic Church was the ally of states in spreading Latin culture across Europe (600–1000) and later overseas through colonization, particularly in the Americas in the age of discovery (1492–1773): the pope blessed and sanctioned rulers, and they, in turn, supported the church. In both Europe and America, the work of Christianization involved settling tribal peoples. This was carried out by the monastic orders and the maintenance of church authority by the priests and hierarchy. Among both the religious and the secular leaders there were figures whose witness through their lives was so outstanding and so closely reflected the suffering and glory of Jesus Christ that they became revered as saints of the church, to be emulated by believers (Hebrews 12:1). However, the institutional church also regarded its mission as going to those outside the church, whom they called pagans or heathen, to "compel them to come in" (Luke 14:23), and Christianizing them by a process of baptism and instruction. It also robustly defended its particular understanding of truth from heretics who criticized it, sometimes with excessive zeal and abuse of power. In the feudal climate of the Middle Ages, Christian mission even took the form of Holy Wars or Crusades to recapture the Holy Land (1095–1272), led by those who believed that the goal of the expansion of Christendom justified violent means to achieve it.

However, while the institution maintained into the twentieth century an uncompromising allegiance to the Latin tradition as the exclusive means of grace, in the mission field there was also an alternative Catholic theology at work. This became particularly apparent as Catholic missionaries encountered Asian cultures, which they were not able to dominate in the same way as they had done the native peoples of America. In keeping with the willingness of the Apostle Paul to "become all things to all people" (1 Corinthians 9:22), Matteo Ricci (1552–1610) in China and others were prepared to adapt the message, expressing it in local forms. This grass-roots approach led eventually to a theology of inculturation that contributed to the transformation of the official mission theology in the twentieth century. At the Second Vatican Council (1962–1965), which adopted a more conciliatory attitude to other Christians and believers in other faiths, the Roman Catholic Church redefined itself as "the people of God" and therefore as much a sign of salvation as the means of it. The contemporary Catholic theology of "evangelization" aims to bring about transformation of whole persons, societies, and cultures. Mission is an act of service after the way of Christ, that is, by word and deed, proclamation and service.

## Protestant Mission Theology

Protestant theology was forged in the struggles of mainly Northern Europeans in the fifteenth to seventeenth centuries to reform the Roman Catholic Church, which they experienced as oppressive and exploitative. It found expression in a number of different movements, which reflected the cultural conditions of this period of increasing knowledge and rapid social change. What Protestants shared was a desire to relate the Bible, newly translated into their local languages, directly to their faith and practice and circumvent the power exercised by the Roman Church, chiefly through the sacraments (rites to mediate grace). In the preaching that assumed a much enhanced role in worship and witness, Protestants such as Martin Luther (1483–1546) proclaimed that, for fallen human beings, salvation is only by the free gift of

God through the death and Resurrection of Jesus Christ. This is appropriated by personal faith (Romans 1:16–17), and therefore all believers are priests, to whom the grace of God comes directly. Radical groups dispensed with all the trappings of the traditional church altogether and took up a counter-cultural stance, while others forged a compromise and maintained a close link between the church and the local state.

The continued territorial understanding of Christendom meant that as Europeans settled in different parts of the globe, priests started to be sent to pastor congregations in the colonies (from about 1700). These missions soon expanded to meet the needs of the native peoples. However, in an age of overseas trade and exploration, some groups began to read the postresurrection command of Jesus, "Go and make disciples of all nations" (Matthew 28:18–20) as applying not just to the first apostles, who were assumed to have fulfilled it, but also to themselves. This "great commission" became the foundation of the centripetal movement from the late eighteenth century onward, in which missionaries—who were both ordained and lay, male and female—supported by voluntary societies were sent out from Protestant nations to regions that had not yet heard the Gospel. Making disciples was understood to involve not only preaching and founding new congregations (church planting), but also education and health care and otherwise meeting human needs.

However, as Christians reacted in different ways to the pressures of the Enlightenment and Darwinism on religion, the missionary movement divided into two. Some, who were optimistic about human progress, saw their role as mainly concerned with building the Kingdom of God, which they believed Christ had already established on Earth, by bringing about fullness of life (John 10:10), though often this was not clearly distinguished from Westernization. Others, often known as "evangelical," saw themselves as resisting the erosion by liberal and secular movements of the doctrine of the authority of the Bible and the lordship of Jesus Christ. They were less optimistic about human progress and had a tendency to think of their mission primarily as saving souls out of a doomed world. They developed a theology of mission, which they believed to be that of the earliest church, that centered on verbal proclamation about the death of Jesus Christ on the cross and its crucial significance for the eternal destiny of each person. Evangelists called for individual assent to the message, which was expressed by commitment to fellowship with other like-minded Christians, Bible study, adherence to certain moral codes, and evangelism of others. Evangelicals were motivated by gratitude for the salvation they received (cf. Galatians 2:20) to go to all parts of the world, sometimes at great personal cost, to bring the message of salvation. Today evangelicalism is strongest in North America, where the World Evangelical Alliance is based. This body has been creatively exploring the relationships between gospel and culture, evangelism and social responsibility, and biblical mandates and social sciences, but the rise of Fundamentalist Christianity, which by definition eschews a dialogical approach, makes agreement on such issues difficult.

## Ecumenical Mission Theology

In the colonial period Protestant mission was inevitably linked to imperial power, as were Roman Catholic and Orthodox mission movements. Though some missionaries opposed their own governments on behalf of the colonized people they served, most played an uncritical part in the process of colonization, although their motives may have differed significantly from those of other colonizers. In the twentieth century particularly, some of the colonized have strongly criticized missionary activity for attitudes of superiority, undermining local culture and leadership and dominating the new churches. In light of this, many European Christians and those in their former colonies, who now far outnumber them, have been rethinking the theology of mission. This has been done largely through the International Missionary Council and its successor in the World Council of Churches, which, since the middle of the twentieth century has been composed of Orthodox as well as Protestant churches and has also seen significant Roman Catholic involvement, though that church is not a member.

The theology that has emerged, known as "ecumenical," may be characterized by the "manifesto" statement of Jesus that he came, by the power of the Holy Spirit, to bring good news to the poor (Luke 4:18–19). This theology of liberation originally arose among Catholic priests in Latin America in the 1970s, who chose to oppose U.S.–backed military governments and the church hierarchy to struggle alongside the people for social justice. This has developed into a view that mission is focused on the well-being of all people and even the whole ecosystem is God's creation. It is not "for" people but "with" them in a postcolonial partnership to bring about justice by challenging oppressive social structures and forces of exploitation. Instead of condemning local spiritualities as superstition, it recognizes their contribution to a people's vision. Since it is inspired by the Spirit of God, who is the true agent of mission, mission is understood first and foremost as the mission of God (*missio Dei*) and not the possession of any church. As participants in God's life-giving mission, ecumenicals seek to address pressing problems of a globalizing world by rereading all scriptures using the interpretive key of liberation and by cooperative action with other religions and development agencies. Critics of the movement have drawn attention to lack of attention to evangelism in the sense of reexpressing the message of the gospel in today's world, which weakens the core of Christian mission.

## Pentecostal-Charismatic Mission Theology

The fastest growing Christian movement of the twenty-first century is the Pentecostal-Charismatic movement, which is represented both by particular new denominations and local congregations and also by movements within almost all the other bodies. These Christians, who are found across the world, but are strongest in Africa, share a style of worship that expects divine intervention to bring about healing, deliverance, and ecstatic experience. Their distinctive theology is derived from a particular reading of the story of Pentecost in which the Holy Spirit was poured out on the disciples (Acts 2). Since this incident is recorded as leading directly to the numerical growth of the church and giving testimony to Jesus Christ in an ever-widening circle, Pentecostal-Charismatic churches often have ambitious plans for expansion. They have (re-)introduced a theology of mission as an encounter with evil forces in which Jesus Christ's victory over death is demonstrated by believers with signs and wonders (cf. Mark 16:15–18). Their leaders, who are characteristically strong and visionary, are often accused of preaching a one-sided prosperity gospel that Jesus Christ will bless those who believe and solve their problems. However, their message also empowers many to change their lifestyle and encourages mutual support within the local congregation that enables individuals and communities to improve their lives and share with others.

## Mission Theologies According to Region

In view of the fact that the Christian populations of Africa, Asia, and Latin America now far outnumber those of other continents and increasingly take responsibility for mission not only in their regions but worldwide, it is not surprising that new theological developments increasingly emerge from these contexts. As churches in different regions of the world tend to share common environmental, socioeconomic and religio-cultural concerns, so it is increasingly possible to identify distinctive mission theologies by continent or subcontinent. We have already mentioned several theologies arising from European experience, North American evangelicalism, Latin American liberation theology, and the Pentecostal-Charismatic theologies of healing and blessing being articulated in Africa. While all the theologies so far mentioned are present in Asia, Christians there have particularly reflected on their experience as minorities in some of the most religious nations in the world. The theology of dialogue, largely developed by reflection on the Indian subcontinent, emphasizes not only proclamation but also listening to neighbors of other faiths. Where peace between religions is essential to social peace, Christians have reexamined Christian tradition and developed creation, cosmic, or spirit theologies that recognize that God is present and active in all people and societies. In this case religious plurality is appreciated as part of the diversity of creation, the Christian community is regarded as a partner with others in the community of communities, and God's revelation in Jesus Christ is seen as offering a distinctive contribution to human spirituality.

The recognition of the coexistence of different theologies of mission according to local context calls for a more realistic way of doing theology in an era of world Christianity that is also more true to the origins of the church as a reconciled and reconciling community of Jews and Gentiles. Rather than working in relativistic isolation or trying to synthesize all theologies into one over-arching theology of mission, the task is to affirm each, where it is a valid Christian response to a particular situation, and engage in an intra-Christian dialogue, bringing theologies into conversation with one another for the mutual enrichment of all.

KIRSTEEN KIM

*See also* Ancient Church; Celtic Missions; Christendom; Conciliar Missions; Coptic Church; Counter Reformation; Ecumenism; Enlightenment; Evangelicalism; Fundamentalism; Liberalism; Liberation Theology; Millennialism and Adventism; Modernity; Monasticism; Moravians; Nestorians; Orthodox/Coptic Missions; Peace Churches; Pentecostal and Charismatic Movements; Protestant Churches; Reformation; Roman Catholic Church; Social Gospel; Theory—Catholic, Protestant, Evangelistic

## Further Reading

Bevans, S. B., & Schroeder, R. (2004). *Constants in context: theology of mission for today.* Maryknoll, NY: Orbis Books.

Bosch, D. J. (1991). *Transforming mission: paradigm shifts in theology of mission.* Maryknoll, NY: Orbis Books.

Bria, I. (Ed.). (1986). *Go forth in peace: Orthodox perspectives on mission.* Geneva, Switzerland: WCC.

Burrows, W. R. (Ed.). (1993). *Redemption and dialogue: Reading* Redemptoris missio *and Dialogue and proclamation.* Maryknoll, NY: Orbis Books.

Hocken, P., & Hunter, H. D. (Eds.). (1993). *All together in one place: Theological papers from the Brighton Conference on World Evangelization.* Sheffield, U.K.: Sheffield Academic Press.

Karotemprel, S. (Ed.). (1996). *Following Christ in mission: A foundational course in missiology.* Boston, MA: Pauline Books & Media.

Kirk, J. A. (1999). *What is mission? Theological explorations.* London: Darton, Longman and Todd.

Köstenberger, A. J., & O'Brien, P. T. (2001). *Salvation to the ends of the earth: A biblical theology of mission.* Leicester, U.K.: Apollos.

Muzorewa, G. H. (1991). *An African theology of mission.* Studies in History of Missions 5. Lewiston, NY: Edwin Mellen Press.

Newbigin, L. (1995). *The open secret: an introduction to the theology of mission* (Rev. ed.). Grand Rapids, MI: Wm. B. Eerdmans Publishing Co.

Pachuau, L. (Ed.). (2002). *Ecumenical missiology: Contemporary trends, issues and themes.* Bangalore, India: United Theological College.

Samuel, V., & Sugden, C. (Eds.). (1999). *Mission as transformation: a theology of the whole gospel.* Oxford: Regnum.

Scherer, J. A., & Bevans, S. B. (Eds.) (1992). *New directions in mission and evangelization, Vol. 1, Basic statements.* Maryknoll, NY: Orbis Books.

Scherer, J. A., & Bevans, S. B. (Eds.). (1992). *New directions in mission and evangelization, Vol. 2, Theological foundations.* Maryknoll, NY: Orbis Books.

Scherer, J. A., & Bevans, S. B. (Eds.). (1992). *New directions in mission and evangelization, Vol. 3, Faith and culture.* Maryknoll, NY: Orbis Books.

Schreiter, R. (1997). *The new catholicity: Theology between the global and the local.* Maryknoll, NY: Orbis Books.

Taylor, W. D. (Ed.). (2000). *Global missiology for the 21st century: the Iguassu dialogue.* Grand Rapids, MI: Baker Academic.

Thangaraj, M. T. (1999). *The common task: a Christian theology of mission.* Nashville, TN: Abingdon Press.

Verstraelen, F. J., et al. (1995). *Missiology: an ecumenical introduction: Texts and contexts of global Christianity.* Grand Rapids, MI: Wm. B. Eerdmans Publishing Co.

Walls, A. F. (1996). *The missionary movement in Christian history: Studies in transmission of faith.* Maryknoll, NY: Orbis Books.

Walls, A. F. (2002). *The cross-cultural process in Christian history: Studies in the transmission and appropriation of faith.* Maryknoll, NY: Orbis Books.

Yates, T. (1994). *Christian mission in the twentieth century.* Cambridge, UK: Cambridge University Press.

# Theory–Catholic, Protestant, Evangelistic

Mission theory is essentially a modern idea that was developed in the nineteenth century. The term *theory of missions* first appeared in English in 1845. Rufus Anderson of the American Board of Commissioners for Foreign Missions (ABCFM), the leading American mission leader of his generation, introduced the term in a sermon title: "The Theory of Missions to the Heathen." The term soon gained currency.

## Mission Theory Defined

Although the term *mission theory* was used with some frequency after 1850, it has never been defined in a clear and consistent manner. However, from the ways in which the term is used in the literature, a working definition can be ascertained. First, mission theory seeks to establish a theoretical framework for the study of missionary work. This means emphasizing formal and critical reflection on the work that missionaries do rather than on their successes and the inspirational dimensions that are used to promote the cause of missions. Second, mission theory considers the total mission process, including (a) historical antecedents and development, (b) sociocultural environment of the sending church, (c) the social location of the missionaries deployed by a missionary society, (d) the sociopolitical environment to which missionaries are sent, (e) the theological foundation and operative assumptions of the mission, (f) the strategy guiding the mission, and (g) the main methods and operating principles. Third, mission theory guides the scholar in relating the study of missionary work to the cognate disciplines on which the missiologist depends. In other words, mission theory helps to maintain academic rigor in the study of missions.

## Early Developments

Roman Catholic missionary scholars produced a considerable body of writings in the sixteenth and seventeenth centuries. Among the earliest was missionary scholar José de Acosta (1540–1600). While serving in Latin America he wrote a pioneering work, *De Procuranda Indorum Salute* (1588), in which he explored how the Indians might be evangelized. In a second work, *Historia Natural y Moral de las Indias* (1589), he argued that God's hand could be discerned in the development of the great Indian civilizations that prepared the Indians to receive the Gospel. De Acosta reflected on the missionary work that he observed in Latin America and criticized his fellow missionaries for their lack of respect for indigenous cultures and their failure to learn local languages. His books influenced the way Catholic missionaries were trained for missionary service and stimulated other scholars to study this topic.

A Dutch Reformed pastor, Justus Heurnius (1587–1652), wrote an apology for missions, *De legatione evangelica ad Indos capessenda admonition* (1618) and was subsequently sent by the East India Campny to Jakarata in 1624 where he pastured a Dutch congregation and began evangelization among local peoples. A Dutch Protestant theologian, Gisbertus Voetius (1589–1676) influenced by Catholic missiological writings, wrote a comprehensive mission theology, *Selectae Disputationes Theologicae* (5 vols. 1648–1669) and in *Politica Ecclesiastica* (3 vols. 1663–1676). His remained largely unknown until Abraham Kuyper (1837–1920) and others discovered it in the late nineteenth century and drew directly on Voetius' main ideas in formulating a theology of mission. Enlightenment Influence

The eighteenth-century Enlightenment changed the Western intellectual landscape in two important ways. First, Newtonian cosmology led to a view of the universe as a remarkable machine that operated according to the "laws of nature." By extension, it was held that every area of human endeavor was governed by its own appropriate laws. In the eighteenth century theologians Bishop Joseph Butler and William Paley began recasting theology to show that Christian faith could be interpreted and defended using the modern rational scientific model. Apologists for the missionary enterprise understood it as an activity mandated by Jesus Christ in the Great Commission (Matthew 28: 18–20) that was to be conducted according to its own principles that could be discerned in Scripture and practical experience. Second, the scientific method set the standard for intellectual work in every field, including history, economics, and theology. Based on inductive reasoning—that is, using empirical evidence to discover underlying principles and laws, this new intellectual outlook directly shaped the mission movement that emerged at the turn of the nineteenth century. Mission theory would be developed by observing missionary work.

## Nineteenth Century

Between 1792 and 1830 several dozen new Protestant missionary societies were founded in Europe and North America. But there was no mission theory. No one had developed a manual of policies and principles to guide missionaries in their work. Pioneers such as William Carey (1761–1834) looked to the eighteenth-century Pietist and Moravian missionaries as role models.

In 1828 William Orme, a Scottish pastor and missions promoter, noted that after some thirty years of missionary work, there still was no adequate "philosophy of missions." He pointed out that a good deal of valuable experience had been accumulated and the time was ripe for someone to undertake the development of a proper philosophy of missions. Others joined Orme in calling for the formulation of such a philosophy—what would later be called mission theory.

What prompted the concern of William Orme and his contemporaries was that when they looked back on some thirty years of missionary work, they saw that the results did not bear out the initial claims made by the founders. One such claim was that the peoples of Asia and Africa would quickly embrace the Christian faith. Some indigenous peoples seemed responsive but others were not. The churches that had been established in West Africa and India seemed to lack vitality and were dependent on the missions.

From 1840 to 1841 the world economy was in crisis. Thoughtful mission leaders realized that a serious economic depression in Great Britain or the United States was putting at risk the work they were doing in other lands because their missions depended entirely on funds raised by the missionary societies of sponsoring churches. In the event of a collapse of the financial sector, there would be no alternative to simply closing down operations. The prospect was that fledgling churches in Africa and Asia would not survive. These practical concerns drove thoughtful missionary leaders to call for more careful reflection on the evangelization process. To do this well required a theoretical framework.

Henry Venn (1796–1873), leader of the Anglican Church Missionary Society, and Rufus Anderson (1796–1880) of ABCFM, largely independent of each other, were preoccupied with the same question during the 1840s. They concluded that the chief aim of the missionary enterprise was to establish churches that would be viable in their indigenous context. Between 1851 and 1862 Venn took the lead in crystallizing this insight into a theory of an indigenous church. Venn, with his lifelong interest in science and confidence in the scientific method, was convinced that by studying missions he could discover the proper principles and methods that surely were waiting to be discovered. Anderson and Venn agreed that a viable indigenous church would be marked by three characteristics: It would be self-financing, self-propagating, and self-governing. This definition of a viable indigenous church dominated Protestant mission studies for the next century.

However, both Venn and Anderson had difficulty convincing their missionary colleagues to follow their theory in the field, and over time it became clear that the theory and the practice of missions frequently diverged. In 1869 Anderson published the first comprehensive treatment of the theory and practice of modern missions, *Foreign Missions: Their Relations and Claims.* In the preface Anderson notes the problem: "Some may be ready to regard the theory of missions here described as being self-evident, seeing it is so simple. But such an impression would betray much ignorance of the history of modern missions. It is even now a controverted point with not a few friends of missions, to say nothing of others, whether civilization must not precede Christianity, or, at any rate, what is the precise relation of the two." He goes on to note other "controverted" points with respect to mission practice.

By 1870 a consensus had been reached among mission leaders: (1) there is a "science of missions" based on appropriate theory, (2) the task at hand is to establish and catalog the basic principles of mission, and (3) this should be regarded as an evolving process. During this period Anderson was the only person who attempted to develop a compendium of missionary principles and practice within a theoretical framework.

## Twentieth Century

The twentieth century marks the emergence of mission studies as an academic field. In 1897 Gustav Warneck, a German Lutheran pastor and a renowned expert in mission history and practice, was appointed to the first professorship in mission anywhere in the world; it was at the University of Halle. Between 1892 and 1903 Warneck had published an influential five-volume study called *Evangelische Missionslehre* (Evangelical Mission Theory). A few years later, in 1914, Joseph Schmidlin, another expert in the field, was appointed to the first Roman Catholic chair of missiology at the University of Münster, also in Germany. Schmidlin paid tribute to Warneck as an intellectual mentor, but in his book *Catholic Mission Theory,* he criticized Warneck's interpretation of Catholic missiology and developed an approach he believed was more consistent with Catholic doctrine and ecclesiology.

It is noteworthy that the first comprehensive and systematic expositions of mission theory were by Continental scholars. The Anglo-American approach was historical and pragmatic rather than theory-based. Mission studies in English-speaking countries focused on the growth and development of missions with special attention to the principles and methods of missionary practice. The term *missiology,* long used in Europe, was not accepted in the United States until the 1960s.

Following World War II, missions were preoccupied with issues raised by the ending of the colonial era. Discussions of indigenous churches were dominated by the demands for independence of the many mission-founded churches in Africa, Asia, Oceania, and Latin America. Around 1970 a new concept was introduced: contextualization. As its chief architect, Shoki Coe of Taiwan, explained, the intent was to retain all that was intended by indigenization but to highlight the importance of shifting the center of initiative to the local. Leaders of two-thirds of world churches promoted this shift in order to make clear that each church must be centered in its own historical, religious, socioeconomic, and political context.

WILBERT R. SHENK

*See also* Apologetics; Bible Translation; Church Growth Movement; Conciliar Missions; Mission Methods and Strategy; Orthodox/ Coptic Missions; Protestant Churches; Roman Catholic Church; Social Gospel; Theology

## Further Reading

Anderson, R. (1869). *Foreign missions: Their relations and claims.* New York: Scribner's.

Forman, C. W. (1977). A history of foreign mission theory. In R. P. Beaver (Ed.), *American missions in bicentennial perspective* (pp. 69–140). South Pasadena, CA: William Carey.

Hoffman, R. (1960). *Pioneer theories of missiology: A comparative study of the mission theories of Cardinal Brancati de Laurea with three of his contemporaries.* Washington, DC: Catholic University of America Press.

Schmidlin, J. (1931). *Catholic mission theory.* Techny, IL: Mission Press S.V.D. (Original work published 1919)

Shenk, W. R. (1996). The role of theory in mission studies. *Missiology, 24* (1), 31–45.

Shenk, W. R. (1999). *Changing frontiers of mission.* Maryknoll, NY: Orbis.

# Training

The term "training" refers to ministry preparation—in this case, cross-cultural equipping—through nonformal as well as formal educational systems. "Cross-cultural equipping" is training designed for those who will minister in a culture different from their own—whether geographically, linguistically, or ethnically. Missionaries are trained to speak to Muslims in Pakistan or Toronto; Buddhists in Sri Lanka or London; Hindus in Mumbai or Vancouver; Maya peoples in Guatemala or Los Angeles; or animists in Haiti or Miami. There are a diversity of missionary training programs, from doctoral-granting formal schools down to grassroots nonformal "schools of transformation" rooted in the life of a local church. Training is part of the preparation for cross-cultural mission ministry.

## History

Personal mentoring, transformational discipleship, and catechetical and cathedral schools characterized training until academic programs were established in Germany at the turn of the twentieth century. These new departments permanently changed the approach to ministry formation. They shaped the current three-tiered educational structure and eventually became the prime venue for all forms of training.

One negative reaction to formal educational training came from local churches, which claimed they could do it better and cheaper by focusing on issues of character and core skills for the ministry. However, because very few churches had the resources to effectively address the foundational issues that make for good training, many of them established strategic partnerships with formal schools and subcontracted out to them some of the critical content-loaded courses in cross-cultural mission.

Yet other churches and groups totally disdained all formal education, and the early years of the twentieth-century Pentecostal movement saw missionaries sent out with the assumption that all they needed was "the Spirit," who would give them the miraculous gift of speaking other languages. Time and reality changed this practice and now Pentecostal and Charismatic churches and church schools are seriously committed to full-spectrum equipping. Dedicated missionary training centers have grown up around the world, primarily in the global South, which is producing a growing number of graduates in long-term cross-cultural ministry.

## Training Options

Training options include local churches, denominational programs, individually run centers, and missionary training centers committed to community education. They also include formal and nonformal education, undergraduate Bible schools, and theological seminaries with missions majors. Effective training centers are based not only in the United States, but also in Korea, India, Nigeria, Malta, the United Kingdom, Brazil, and Argentina. The possibilities of distance education have also grown, from correspondence schools to a diversity of interactive Internet courses.

Over fifteen years of careful analysis of missionary training have led to a highly valuable tool that can evaluate what is needed in effective training. The template envisions six development phases:

1. Assessing needs: what is needed by whom, and where.
2. Identifying stakeholders: clients, resource providers, trainers, and policy makers.
3. Defining values and presuppositions: Biblical and theological, educational, and spiritual.
4. Defining product outcomes: the desired profile of a missionary.
5. Defining the program curriculum: resources and methods.

## New Realities

Globalization has permanently reshaped the Christian Church and its vision of mission. New programs are needed to equip people for different terms of service: shorter-term (up to two years), mid-term (three to five years) and longer-term (six years or more). They should include training for prefield preparation, mid-term changes, and life-long learning. They should also be trained to work in restricted-access contexts and with less-reached peoples. In the Philippines, for example, hundreds of thousands of Christian contract workers are equipped to work in restricted-access nations of the Islamic world. An adequate curriculum will include the areas of spirituality and instrumental knowledge.

New models are emerging, local churches are increasingly designing their own programs, and training options are more readily available on the Internet and in different languages. Yet there are still causes for concern. Many of the formal colleges and seminaries that offer degrees in missions are not interested in substantive self-evaluation or change. They prefer to follow accredited academic rules, although some educational bureaucracies are frozen in time and others are paralyzed by a false understanding of excellence. New mission leaders will not be bound by the strictures of formal academics and will be able to learn from others. Of particular importance to training efforts is that the North be able to learn from the South.

WILLIAM TAYLOR

*See also* Parachurch; Professional Associations (Academic); Religious Studies; Short-term Missions

## Further Reading

Brewer, M. (1992, November). Church-based missionary training. *Training for Cross Cultural Ministries, 92*(3), 1–2. Retrieved May 18, 2006, from http://www.wearesources.org/Publications.aspx

Brynjolfson, R., & Lewis, J. P. (forthcoming). *Integral ministry training design and development.* South Pasadena, CA: William Carey.

Chinchen, D. (1997). The return of the fourth "R" to education: Relationships. *Missiology: An international review, XXV*(3), 321–335.

Choi, H. K. (2000). Preparing Korean missionaries for cross-cultural effectiveness. Unpublished doctoral dissertation, E. Stanley Jones School of World Mission and Evangelism, Asbury Theological Seminary, Wilmore, KY.

*Curriculum models for missionary training.* (1996). Tamil Nadu, India: Indian Institute of Missiology.

Holistic training for cross-cultural ministry. (2005). *Connections: the Journal of the WEA Mission Commission, 4*(2), Rotterdam, Netherlands.

Escobar, S. (1992, January). The elements of style in crafting new international mission leaders. *Evangelical Missions Quarterly,* 6–15.

Ferris, R. W. (Ed.). (1995). *Establishing ministry training: a manual for programme developers.* South Pasadena, CA: William Carey.

Frayne, D. R. *Scribal Education in Ancient Babylonia.* (1999, Fall). Retrieved July 26, 2007, from http://www.sumerian.org/Frayne-ScribalEducation.htm

Harley, C. D. (1995). *Preparing to serve: Training for cross-cultural mission.* South Pasadena, CA: William Carey.

Kang, S. S. (1995). Development of non-Western missionaries: Characteristics of four contrasting programs. Unpublished doctoral dissertation, Trinity Evangelical Divinity School, Deerfield, IL.

Kelsey, D. H. (1993). *Between Athens and Berlin: The theological education debate.* Grand Rapids, MI: Eerdmans.

Lewis, J. (Ed.). (1990). Training for cross-cultural ministries. *World Evangelical Fellowship: Missions Commission Occasional Bulletin.*

López, B. (2005, April). The unfolding story of the Filipino tentmaking movement. *Connections: the Journal of the WEA Mission Commission, 5*(1), 15.

Stevens, R. P. (1992, June). Marketing the faith—a reflection on the importing and exporting of Western theological education. *Crux, 28*(2), 6–18.

Taylor, W. D. (Ed.). (1997). *Too valuable to lose: Exploring the causes and cures of missionary attrition.* South Pasadena, CA: William Carey.

Taylor, W. D. (Ed.). (1991). *Internationalising missionary training: A global perspective.* Grand Rapids, MI: Baker Book House.

Williams, T. (Ed.). (1983). *Together in mission.* Bangalore, India: World Evangelical Fellowship Missions Commission.

Windsor, R. (1995). *World directory of missionary training programmes: A catalogue of over 500 missionary training programmes from around the world.* South Pasadena, CA: William Carey.

Woodberry, J. D., Van Engen, C., & Elliston, E. J. (1997). *Missiological education for the 21st century: The book, the circle and the sandals.* Maryknoll, NY: Orbis.

# Translation

The missionary movement has highlighted the importance of vernacular translation for any understanding of Christianity. At the center of the Christian faith is the universality of the "good news." This idea has been expressed and received in different languages in various cultural contexts. John Wesley once described Jesus Christ as the general savior of humankind. This observation connects Jesus with people in all cultures, but it is important to add that Jesus meets them within the specificity of their culture, history, and language. This means that translation is always an essential part of the transmission of the Christian message of the Gospel—in fact, Andrew Walls, professor emeritus of the "Study of Christianity in the Non-Western World" at the University of Edinburgh, makes the claim that the story of the incarnation is actually the most compelling example of translation. When God became a human being, divinity was translated into humanity, and this means that the process took place in a particular context, within a particular ethnic group, and at a specific place and time.

## Affirmations

The New Testament provides many narratives that underscore the Gospel's sensitivity to cultural diversity. Christianity itself is based on the divine act of translation: "And the Word became flesh, and lived among us" (John 1:14, New Revised Standard Version). Translating the Bible into different languages rests on this *a priori* condition. The book of Acts talks about the Day of Pentecost when the Holy Spirit descended on the disciples and they started speaking in a multiplicity of tongues, enabling diverse people to "hear the great things that God has done" in Jesus Christ (Acts 2:12). Part of the audacity of the Gospel is that it makes it imperative to spread the Gospel to all nations and peoples. The story of the great multitude described in Revelation speaks of people from "every nation, from all tribes and peoples and languages, standing before the throne" (Rev. 7:9). The story accentuates the fact that Christianity must be experienced and expressed in different languages.

## The African Example

The African example presents a compelling case study for understanding translation as an integral part of the transmission of the Christian faith and as an engine of renewal and reform, because vernacular translation contributed immensely to the transformation of Christianity in Africa. It gave the impetus for the indigenous church movements that emerged all over Africa after colonial rule. In spite of Islam's longevity in Africa, Islam considered vernacular languages anathema, unfit for adoption as a scriptural medium. The vernacular was also considered unsuitable for devotion and piety, and Arabic remained the absolute standard for religious orthodoxy. The exclusive preeminence of sacred Arabic for the dissemination of religious instruction gave other languages a second class status, for they were, for all intents and purposes, relegated to the status of *'ajamī* (profane).

Christian missionaries and lay people, on the other hand, embarked on the indigenizing project of translating the Bible into many African languages. This process, according to Lamin Sanneh, the D. Willis professor of Missions at Yale Divinity School, is an indication that Christianity was not an imperialistic religion. The fact that Christian missionaries affirmed the importance of African languages is a telling testimony to the fact that they did not stigmatize African culture. This calls for a reexamination of the pervasive notion that the missionary movement and the religious institutions it established were unsympathetic to African culture. The view of missionary agents as self-serving, sanctimonious soul-seekers is contradicted by the grand policy of vernacular translation and appropriation all over Africa. While Islam maintained the pure character of the Arabic language, Christian missionary agents in

## The Perils of Translation

**The following story of an effort at translation into the language of the Copper Inuit of western Canada points to the difficulties of translation.**

It was hard going at first. There were only a couple of Eskimos at Baker who had any fluency in English, and they were away from the post out on the traplines, hunting or fishing much of the time. There was a small dictionary, a little red book put out by a Roman Catholic missionary, Father Thibert. Unfortunately the good Father had lived in several places and hadn't bothered to note which dialect a word might come from when he put it into his dictionary. There are many Eskimo dialects and the differences between them, in grammar as well as in vocabulary, can be enormous. An eastern Eskimo can only understand a western Eskimo with great difficulty and vice versa. Even between two settlements as near each other as Coppermine and Paulatuk, the differences could be startling. For example, if one wished to say 'A whiteman arrived yesterday' at Coppermine, the correct expression would be *qavlunaaq ikpaksaq tikittuq*, but at Paulatuk one would say *tanaaluk unnungmi tikittuaq.*

Source: Pryde, D. (1972). *Nunaga: my land, my country* (p. 31). Edmonton, Canada: M.G. Hurtig Ltd.

Africa were working to translate the word of God into different African languages. Success in translation correlated with sensitivity to traditional African cultures. In places where missionaries retained the indigenous African names for God, Christianity flourished and became dominant. God communicated to Africans in their local languages.

Ultimately the essential elements of Christian theology such as God, Jesus Christ, eschatology, creation, and salvation were reinterpreted through the idioms of local cultures. Translations gave Africans the opportunity to access and process the basic essentials of Christian revelation through African traditional religious categories and ideas. The idea of Jesus was acculturated within the African milieu and enabled Africans to embrace and celebrate the Christian faith through the idioms and precepts of their own culture. This pragmatic religious sensibility still provides the basis for theological reflection in Africa. Hearing the Word of God in one's own language engenders a passion for embracing the Gospel and for reshaping it without diluting its essential message.

Yorubaland offers an instructive example concerning the interrelation of Bible translation, evangelism, and indigenous self-determination that underscored the importance of indigenous agency in mission and evangelism. In Yorubaland, mission schools first trained students in the basic rudiments of the Yoruba language and then taught them to read the Bible in their mother tongue. Vernacular expression eventually became a *sine qua non* for liturgy, worship, mission, and theology.

Two influential missions were established, the Niger and the Yoruba Missions. Samuel Ajayi Crowther, a tireless missionary with a passionate penchant for preaching, and James Johnson, a dyed-in-the-wool nationalist, were actively involved in both of them. The Niger Mission was conceived by Thomas Fowell Buxton, a key figure in the Church Missionary Society (CMS), as a project of the CMS, and became one of the largest, most well-funded and dynamic missionary agency in Yorubaland in the nineteenth century. Crowther was co-opted into this venture through the prodding and encouragement of Henry Venn, secretary of CMS. Venn's vision of the "euthanasia of mission" led him to believe that the vernacular principle would enable the Christian church in Africa to become self-propagating, self-supporting, and self-governing, and free from Western hegemonic control. Crowther's book, *Vocabulary of the Yoruba Language,* became an important tool in the mission field as it was very useful in injecting an indigenous fervor into the missionary enterprise and ultimately enhanced Venn's vision. However, the patronizing and racist policies of the CMS led to his humiliation and eventual resignation from the Niger Mission.

The unsavory experience of Crowther added fuel to the embers of the movement for religious independence from foreign control and domination in Yorubaland. The indefatigable Bishop James Johnson, also an enthusiastic supporter of African agency in mission, advocated for literacy as an essential tool for evangelism and mission and encouraged his colleagues to be well-versed in three languages: Yoruba, English, and Arabic. He remarked in 1878 that the Bible in the native tongue was the most important accomplishment of the Yoruba Mission. As a passionate defender of effective African agency in mission, Johnson was able to escape the stain of CMS's racist policies. His nationalistic zeal gave him the much-needed armor against the inauspicious policies of the CMS.

## Universals

The theme of translation in the missionary project confirms the belief that Christianity is a universal religion. It is culturally translatable—that is, it can be at home in other cultural situations without being diminished. The Gospel belongs to everyone. Ultimately, it is imperative that "all of us hear . . . in our own languages . . . the wonders of God" (Acts 2:11).

AKINTUNDE E. AKINADE

*See also* Africa; Bible; Bible Translation; Contextualization, Models of; Culture; Inculturation; Language; Mission Methods and Strategy; Orality

### Further Reading

Bediako, K. (2004). *Jesus and the Gospel in Africa: History and experience.* Maryknoll, NY: Orbis.

Blyden, E. W. (1967). *Christianity, Islam and the Negro Race.* Edinburgh, Scotland: Edinburgh University Press.

Nida, E. A. (1952). *God's word in man's language.* New York: Harper and Brothers.

Sanneh, L. (1983). *West African Christianity: The religious impact.* Maryknoll, NY: Orbis.

Sanneh, L. (1989). *Translating the message: The missionary impact on culture.* Maryknoll, NY: Orbis.

Smalley, W. A. (1991). *Translation as mission: Bible translation and the modern missionary movement.* Macon, GA: Mercer.

Stine, P. C. (1992). *Bible translation and the spread of the Church: The last 200 years.* Leiden, the Netherlands: Brill.

Walls, A. (1996). *The missionary movement in Christian history.* Maryknoll, NY: Orbis.

## Urban Mission

World urbanization is one of the most significant developments facing the planet and the mission of the church. While at the beginning of the twentieth century less than ten percent of the world's population was urban, with the dawn of the twenty-first century more than half of Earth's population is/will be living in cities. Ahead is an urban millennium. As a result, urban mission is one of the primary expressions of the mission of the church in the world today.

Size and scale do not tell us everything about cities, and statistics are not always agreed upon or clear, but such information indicates significant trends. Africa is experiencing the fastest urban growth of any continent. Lagos, Nigeria, in the 1950s a city of under 300,000 residents, is now estimated to have in the range of 15 million residents, making it the sixth largest city in the world. By 2015 Lagos is expected to have 23 million residents. N'Djamena, the capital of Chad, had a population of 37,000 in 1950, but is expected to reach 2 million by 2015. Nairobi, Kenya, is approaching 4 million inhabitants. Asian megacities include Karachi, Pakistan, with nearly 12 million people, Mumbai, India, with over 18 million people, Manila, Philippines, with more than 10 million inhabitants, and Tokyo, Japan, which fits some 35 million into its metropolitan reach. China has more than 100 cities at over a million, and is undergoing arguably the most profound urbanization in history. In Latin America, Mexico City, Mexico, has a population near 20 million, as does Sao Paulo, Brazil. Among the major European cities are Budapest, Hungary, which approaches 2 million residents, the London, England, metropolitan area over 12 million, Berlin, Germany, over 3.5 million, and Moscow, Russia, more than 10 million. In the United States, New York City proper has more than 8 million residents.

Overall, it is essential to recognize that each city is unique, and should not be viewed through a Western lens. But overall, in the twenty-first century estimates suggest that that some 65 million people a year will be moving to cities, about 180,000 people per day. By 2015, it is expected that 4 billion people will live in cities, and 8 billion by 2050. Among the factors driving urban growth are the push away from rural areas because of a lack of jobs and the pull towards the city for new opportunities and experiences. Cities are spaces of creativity, diversity and opportunity, but also compress social and economic challenges.

Urban mission refers to Christian mission in, for, and with the city. The terms "urban mission" and "urban ministry" are commonly used interchangeably, and perhaps most people engaged in urban ministry do not even describe their work as "urban mission." They simply live and work in the city, and understand their faith to be highly relevant for their family, community, and city. Responding to the ever-changing city, mission must be improvisational. In practice, this involves church planting, evangelism, holistic ministry, and public activity. Dimensions of the emerging urban mission challenge include the AIDS pandemic, environmental degradation and global warming, religious pluralism, violence, and economic injustice. These are concerns of human dignity and life.

Arguably the single greatest challenge facing the city and the mission of the church today is growing urban poverty and in particular, "slum" settlements. According to the United Nations, in 2001 nearly one

## Urban Mission

Mission serving the Chinese in the East End of London in the 1880s. The mission was established by Methodist missionary George Piercy, who served for thirty years in Hong Kong and China.

billion people lived in slums, a number that is predicted to double in the next thirty years unless something is done to reverse course. The very existence of such massive slums suggests a growing worldwide experience of urban exclusion both in cities and between cities, a result many scholars have determined are due to the uneven effects of globalization.

Christian mission in the cities of Africa, Asia, and Latin America is taking place primarily through the churches of the city at the grassroots. In the shantytowns, slums and cities of the third world, Pentecostal churches are leading the way, forging dynamic models of urban mission. Ministries of healing, prayer, evangelism, and social concern enact a practical engagement

with the city. House-church movements in cities and tenement complexes emphasize the communal dynamic of mission. Catholic and Protestant mainline churches often take up public and prophetic ministries.

In North America, urban ministry faces an anti-urban and antipoor bias. Many Western mission agencies appear to still be adjusting to the rural-to-urban shift. Among a few church groups and denominations, establishing new center-city churches has become a mission trend. Important exceptions to the negative views of the city and poor in North America have been African-American and Latino churches, which have kept faith with the city through post-industrial decline. Gentrification is creating a new environment in many cities, challenging older models of community activism.

Historically Christianity has been an urban movement, evidencing a largely redemptive but not uncritical view of the city. Using the Roman road system for the spread of the Christian gospel, the Apostle Paul was an urban missionary. His mission strategy was building small communities of followers of Jesus in cities like Antioch and Corinth. Within the Catholic tradition, the Jesuit order emphasized the strategic value of establishing institutions in cities. And the European Reformation was robustly urban.

Today, Roman roads have been replaced by the new global architecture of Christian expansion, with cities as the nodes of globalization. Mission not only takes place in cities, but between cities of the world. Urban mission is now closely associated with the migration of people who are accompanied by their faith. Thus a new and large urban missionary movement is taking place that cannot be calculated by typical measurements. For example, it is now common to find African, Asian, and Latin American immigrants establishing new churches in Europe, North America, and other parts of the world. Urban mission in the twenty-first century is grassroots, transnational and global.

Constructing a theological framework for urban mission can draw on many resources in the biblical text. From beginning to end, the biblical story is filled with references to the city and cities. Indeed the culmination of the biblical narrative found in John's Revelation tells of a future city of peace. Urban missionaries and theologians frequently turn to Jeremiah 29, which mandates seeking the peace of the city through presence, prayer, and public concern. Similar emphases are continued in New Testament documents such as 1 Peter and Hebrews.

Luke's gospel and its companion volume the Acts of the Apostles give special attention to Christ's mission to the city. For example, making inter-textual connections to Isaiah, Jesus defined his ministry of good news for the poor as a jubilee for the cities. And in Acts, the development of the church depended on an urban diaspora. It was through the diaspora that the church experienced a cross-cultural diffusion that would prove so essential to its expansion. In both Luke and Acts, the Spirit is central to urban witness. Biblical themes concerning social justice, the poor, healing for the sick, and reconciliation are also important to urban mission.

One of the church's most important theological works remains Augustine's *City of God*, an apologetic for the Christian faith amidst the turbulence of a waning Roman Empire. In the *City of God*, Augustine narrates the world as an urban story that will end in a city of peace and God's people as a distinctive community of witness to this city. Augustine's theological approach, while subject to diverse interpretations, continues to resonate with many Christians in cities today. Overall, churches are building robust and often vernacular theologies based on a Trinitarian encounter with God.

With the growing importance of cities also come new requirements for the training and development of urban church leaders. However, few traditional seminaries emphasize mission in an urban context. As a result, much of the training of leadership for urban mission takes place through interpersonal relationships, in local churches, and alternative forms of ministerial education such as Bible Institutes.

It should be noted that many rural communities are becoming marginalized in an urban world. However, urban and rural communities should not be paired in opposition, but rather an integrated view of rural and urban areas should be forged for environmental and agricultural reasons. Yet by the numbers and on the ground, urban ministry is the future of the church's mission in the twenty-first century. Global urbanization suggests new mission thinking and practice will emerge along with theologies of mission to and for the shalom of the city. In an urban millennium, mission as good news to the city must be an absolute priority.

Mark R. Gornik

## Further Reading

Beltran, B. (2001). Searching for God in the Asphalt Jungles: Towards a Trinitarian theology of the city. In T. Malipurathu & L. Stanislaus (Eds.), *The Church in mission: Universal mandate and local concerns* (pp. 32–33). Anand, India: Gujarat Sahitya Prakash.

Berryman, P. (1996). *Religion in the megacity: Catholic and protestant portraits from Latin America.* Maryknoll, NY: Orbis Books

Conn, H. M. and Ortiz, M. (2001). *Urban ministry: The kingdom, the city, & the people of God.* Downers Grove, IL: Inter Varsity Press, 2001.

Davis, M. (2004). Planet of slums: Urban involution and the informal proletariat. *New Left Review, 26,* 5–34.

Gornik, M. R. (2002). *To live in peace: Biblical faith and the changing inner city.* Grand Rapids, MI: Eerdmans.

Gorringe, T. (2002). *A theology of the built environment: Justice, empowerment, redemption.* London: Cambridge University Press.

Meeks, W. (1983). *The first urban Christians.* New Haven, CT: Yale University Press.

Shorter, A. (1991). *The Church in the African city.* Maryknoll, NY: Orbis Books.

United Nations Human Settlements Programme. (2003). *The challenge of slums: Global report on human settlements 2003.* New York: Earthscan.

United Nations Human Settlements Programme. (2006). *State of the world's cities 2006–7: The millennium development goals and urban sustainability: 30 years of shaping the habitat agenda.* New York: Earthscan.

# W

## War

Whether viewed as the breakdown of civilization, as its ultimate and most ennobling expression, or as something in between, war has always been fraught with possibility and peril for religious leaders, activists, and people of faith. War amplifies passions and exposes societal rifts even as it generates calls for unity and narratives of common experience. War offers the hope of transforming hostile nations and peoples politically, culturally, and religiously, but also threatens to poison relations between victor and vanquished, liberator and liberated. War creates mission fields and troubles those very same fields.

After a brief historical review of Christian reflection on and engagement in war, this article will use two wars in which the United States was involved, the American Civil War (1861–1865) and World War I (1914–1918), as examples of the complex relationship among Christian faith, mission, and war. While these examples have dimensions specific to their historical moments, they also reflect the enduring conceptual and rhetorical entanglement of Christian missionary work and military campaigns: both are struggles; both seek "conversion" broadly understood; both have exalted self-sacrifice; both have debased men and women unable to move beyond the oppositional mindset that wars and missions often encourage. This article will conclude with a look at the broader lessons to be learned from examining missions through the lens of war and vice versa.

## Christians and "War"

War as military campaign for political ends and war as metaphor for the struggle between truth and error have long been on the mind of Christians in general and of evangelists and missionaries in particular. One way in which Christians in the Roman Empire set themselves apart was by their refusal to serve in the Roman military. They refused to take the required oath to the emperor and, in some cases, were put to death as a result. Early Christian resistance to military service was troubled and eventually trumped by the responsibilities that attended the acceptance of Christianity and of Christians in late ancient halls of power. This change prompted Augustine of Hippo, most famously, to think at length about the relationship among peace, war, justice, and Christianity. His conclusion was that an unjust peace was no peace at all and that Christians and their leaders had an obligation to defend the innocent and to work, in some cases to fight, for justice.

In his role as the bishop of the North African town of Hippo, Augustine was also confronted with another kind of "war." This was the struggle against religious error in which, regrettably, he also saw violence as acceptable. In his Epistle 185, *A Treatise Concerning the Correction of the Donatists* (c. 417 CE), Augustine used scriptural precedent, i.e., Paul being thrown down and blinded by Christ, the exhortation to "compel them to come in" in Luke 14:22–23, to justify the use of force to bring those living in error into the Church. If violence was done out of love, he reasoned, it was no different than a father rebuking a child or a doctor administering a distasteful remedy.

The deployment of putatively Christian armies in the service of governments and the use of force to achieve either, directly or obliquely, putatively Christian aims have generated a seemingly inexhaustible list of contradictions, manipulations, tragedies, and contorted moralities. From pre-Crusade pogroms in western and central Europe and the use of violence to stamp out the Albigensian heresy, to the bloody work of *conquistadors* and the less violent but no less destructive work of American Protestant missionaries to Native-Americans, Christianity and "war" have been tightly interwoven. At the same time (and often in these same sad circumstances) Christian voices have continued Augustine's attempts to define legitimate and illegitimate forms of violence (Thomas Aquinas, Grotius), to recognize non-Christian peoples as God's children and, therefore, worthy of respect (Bartolomé de Las Casas, Pundita Ramabai) and to challenge too-simple renderings of the relationship among Christianity, power, and violence.

## The United States and Its Mission

Within a wide and long tradition of Christian involvement in and critique of war, the United States plays a perplexing and currently crucial role. The United States' tendency to act the part of "redeemer nation" has wrought both good and ill in the United States. and on foreign soil. Wars fought for the material and spiritual conquest of indigenous peoples must be considered alongside wars to preserve the Union and dismantle slavery and wars to defeat fascist regimes in Europe and imperial Japan. Claims to Christian nationhood must be reconciled with the fact that men and women serving in the United States military have themselves been a mission field—subject to evangelistic and literary bombardments enjoining them to turn to Christ.

## Missions in War

War has traditionally accomplished a goal elusive to American churches, namely the in-gathering of young men. Churches, interdenominational organizations, religious aid agencies, and independent evangelists have treated the subsequent combination of large populations of young men and the possibility of sudden, violent death as an opportunity to evangelize and convert soldiers. War, they have argued, forces young men to ask questions of existence and meaning. For many reasons, not the least of them concern for eternal fates, religious leaders have tried to encourage soldiers to accept Christian answers to those questions. Oft "feminized" Christian ministers have also used the rugged life of the warrior as an occasion to model an ideal fusion of masculinity and religious devotion.

## The American Civil War: The Mission within the War

The American Civil War brought young men together to fight and die; it also forced them to live in camp communities where gambling, drinking, and swearing were common and positive moral influences were few. Union and Confederate churches took as their mission the evangelization of their respective armies both to counteract the negative moral and religious effects of separation from hearth and home and to prevent young men from dying before they were saved. Though frustrated chaplains complained early in the war that, "very few [soldiers] manifested any desire to become a Christian save the sick or wounded," and attendance at church services lagged, churches in the North and South persisted in their attempts to reach their young men.

## The Pen and the Sword

In support of this mission, denominational presses, tract and Bible societies on both sides ran their presses at unprecedented rates. The major churches of the South (Baptists, Methodists, Presbyterians) and their affiliated publishing concerns printed and distributed well over two hundred million pages of tracts, testaments, and other religious literature during the war. Tracts, usually pocket-sized booklets, were written, "to create abhorrence of evils common to Army life," and focused frequently on such common problems as swearing, gambling and drinking. A number also dealt with the eternal consequences of sin. Booklets bearing titles such as "Sufferings of the Lost," "Prepare for Battle," and "A Word of Warning to the Sick Soldier" used approaches ranging from the subtle—a discussion of the dangers of procrastination—to the heavy-handed—a description in excruciating detail of an unconverted sinner, "roasting over the lake of fire and brimstone,"—to focus the mind of a soldier on the importance of conversion before it was too late.

There is no reliable evidence as to how widely this literature was read on either side. The sheer volume of production and anecdotal accounts of enthusiastic receptions provided colporteurs give the impression, however, that this literary mission sowed the seeds of conversion and revival among the Confederates. "The record of their [colporteurs'] labors," wrote Confederate chaplain W. W. Bennett, "is the record of the army revival. They fanned its flames and spread it on every side."

## Mission Accomplished: Revivals in the Field

Preachers on both sides of the Civil War also worked among the troops hoping to win conversions. Before the opening of campaigns or individual battles, chaplains asked the young men to reflect on the state of their souls, "How know you but that ere tomorrow's sun rise the long roll may beat, and this brigade be called to meet the enemy? It may be that some of these brave men are hearing now their last message of salvation." Precombat altar calls attracted large numbers of converts in some army units and generated little interest in others.

The most famous example of a "successful" revival was not, however, the result of prebattle calls for conversion. Rather, it occurred in the wake of the war's pivotal battle at Gettysburg in 1863. The "Revival on the Rapidan" swept Robert E. Lee's Army of Northern Virginia in the fall and winter of 1863-64 in the wake of a horrific and depleting defeat. Chaplains' accounts of the revival tell of men racked with emotion, asking repeatedly for assurance of their salvation: "The young converts often come to us deeply affected, in many cases weeping and trembling, to ask for further instruction as to what constitutes conversion. They have an unspeakable dread of being deceived on this point." These were the "sheaves" brought in during what one chaplain described as "the rich, ripe harvest" of souls.

## Christian Soldiers?

The mission to Confederate soldiers had a moral and a soteriological dimension. It also had a military purpose. Federal covenant theology, articulated in many ways from Southern pulpits, held that a righteous

In this romanticized drawing, a missionary is shown stopping a war among the Maori of New Zealand.

society would be lifted up by its God. The more Christian the army, the better the chance that God would grant it victory. In addition, J. W. Jones, a Confederate chaplain and chronicler of the religious lives of Confederate soldiers, noted that the righteous made better soldiers than the unrighteous. He noted that on one occasion three regiments in which a revival had taken place "stood firm" under fire while two unregenerate regiments broke. Christian soldiers were a better bet to march onward.

A modern eye might see in these intrawar missions an uncomfortable commingling of military and religious goals. It is, indeed, difficult to separate genuine concern for conversion from the hope that conversion will make a soldier a better fighter. A modern eye might also detect in descriptions of converted soldiers' physical and emotional state evidence of posttraumatic-stress disorder. How, after all, can one distinguish between the physical "exercises" that have long attended revivalistic conversion and the symptoms of shell shock? Both of these concerns—the use of religion as a tool to achieve military ends and the exploitation the psychological toll of battle—point up potential problems with using war as a mission opportunity. The fog of war, it seems, covers matters of faith just as it covers military strategy and tactics.

A controversial twenty-first-century mission to the military is the Officers' Christian Fellowship, a lay-led organization founded during World War II. Since 1943 OCF has grown to include officers and enlisted men and women in all branches of the service. The OCF describes itself and its mission as "Christian Officers exercising Biblical leadership to raise up a godly military" and works not only with men and women in uniform but among their families as well. Supporters of OCF feel that a more Christian military will be a more effective military and laud the work of OCF's ambassadors for Jesus Christ in the military society. Critics express concern that military authority and federal facilities and funds are being used to promote a conservative Christianity that devalues the religious diversity of the United States and of its armed forces.

## War as Mission

Wars are missions. They are complex and multi-faceted attempts to convince a government and its people to change their behavior in the world. The larger mission of a war comprises many smaller missions: the taking and holding of ground, the destruction of certain elements of infrastructure, the killing of enemy soldiers, the widely discussed and notoriously precarious "battle

for hearts and minds." Many wars prosecuted by nations with large Christian populations have also been colored by a more explicitly religious mission: the conversion of a nation, a region, and, in the aspirations of some, the world to economic and political systems understood to be God-ordained.

## World War I

"Gott mit Uns" is perhaps the most appropriate phrase to emerge from the carnage of the Great War. Though engraved in the belt-buckles of countless officers and soldiers in the German army, the assumed divinity of "the cause" hung over all of the armies engaged in the fight. The war that popped the bubble of Christian progressive and Modernist thought in the United States and western Europe did so precisely because so many understood the war to be an expression of Christian duty. Noticeable by its absence from the upper echelons of political and military power was the humility expressed by Abraham Lincoln in his Second Inaugural Address: "Both [sides] read the same Bible and pray to the same God, and each invokes His aid against the other . . . The prayers of both could not be answered. That of neither has been answered fully. The Almighty has His own purposes." Small bands of Pentecostal missionaries circled the globe condemning the conflict and gathering souls in advance of the Apocalypse that it portended, but such Christian opposition to Great War was a rare commodity indeed.

Lincolnian humility and early Pentecostal abhorrence of war were, in some cases, blasted and shot and gassed into the bodies and minds of the soldiery. In other cases—cases that would shape the events and perceptions of nine subsequent decades—the war sowed the seeds of absolutism, dogmatism, and frequently rabid, racist nationalism. In Europe and in the United States, God-chosen-ness emerged from the war stronger and more vicious than it had been in 1914.

## America's Mission to Germany and the World

The American experience of World War I was characterized by myriad entanglements between church and state. For those who wrapped pulpits in the Stars and Stripes and those who wrote for the fledgling military newspaper, the *Stars and Stripes*, the Christianity of the American Expeditionary Force's spirit and cause, if not its manpower, were foregone conclusions. A righteous American army comprising volunteers and draftees was, according to the common narrative, fighting not for gain but for the good of humanity; their godly cause was the defense and promotion of democracy. Those who stood against either demonstrated their anti-Christian nature and their need for "conversion."

World War I thus became a "mission" to reconvert Germany and its people to "true" Christianity and, simultaneously, to sow in German soil and elsewhere in Europe the seeds of "true" government. There were conceptual problems with both missions. How could one convincingly paint Germany in an anti-Christian light given the long history of German contributions to Christian history, theology, and scriptural scholarship? How could one elevate democracy as God's favored form of government when it was so imperfectly practiced in the United States and when many allies embraced other forms of government?

To the first question, scholars, clergymen, and propagandists answered that Germany had fallen into worship of its own military might and that Kaiser Wilhelm—in league with the devil according to some depictions—was responsible for this change. Remove the satanic leader, the argument went, and a Christian, democratic nation will emerge. On the second question, America's Anglo leadership offered vague promises of equal opportunity for all willing to drop their "hyphenated" identity and fight for America. Religious and civic leaders in the African American community, skeptical at first, came to believe that fighting for democracy abroad would prove African Americans worthy of full participation in democracy at home.

To a surprising extent, this framing of the war as a mission to a religious and political heathen was reflected in the personal writings of American soldiers. Many saw their German foes as anti-Christian Huns, demonic in their desire for power and in their harsh treatment of civilians; many also described the prospect of a German victory as a direct threat to democratic forms of governance not only in Europe but in the Americas as well. Sometimes explicit and sometimes implied by soldiers was the need to correct and convert Germany and the Central powers to a more righteous path.

## A Military Mission to the Homefront

An interesting twist on the war-as-mission mentality in World War I was the development among American soldiers of a mission that was homeward-directed. The *Stars and Stripes* and its soldier-readership repeatedly expressed frustration with an American Christianity overly concerned with swearing, gambling, and drinking and unwilling to concede the special religious status of the combat-tested soldier. They shared the sense that soldiers could and should teach the nation something

about true, living, practical religion. The establishment and the activities of the American Legion represent one attempt by soldiers to contest the authority of American clergy and to draw young Americans, in particular young American men, into a truer "church."

## Missionary Wars Past and Present

Many of America's subsequent wars—both hot and cold—have been colored by the religious sense of mission seen in World War I. Though the Christianity of a people has not always been the issue that it was in that war, the compatibility of a governing philosophy (for example, communism) with Christianity has often been just beneath the surface of American opposition to the spread of an ideology or the growing influence of a nation. A recent and deeply problematic example of this kind of thinking came from General William Boykin, who in 2003 and 2004 appeared in churches in uniform to frame the current United States military engagements as battles between the true God and false gods. Military victory is thus at once an expression of divine favor and a proselytizing tool. Moreover, he seems to believe that if our current enemies were "Christian," there would be no conflict.

## Rethinking Wars and the Missions Within

The relationship between war and mission has at least two dimensions. Wars provide a nation's religious leaders an opportunity to do mission work among men; wars are often conceived as missions in support of a national ideology, if not a religion. These points of intersection provide interesting sets of questions for students, scholars, and concerned citizens in the twenty-first century. When considering the mission work that occurs in war, one might ask: How are intrawar, intra-military missions conducted? Do they respect the religious diversity of the modern American military and recognize the hazards of mission work in a federally-funded and hierarchical organization such as the military? Further, assuming that conversion to a vital and enduring religious life is the goal of mission work, to what extent do mission workers and evangelists in the military consider the environment to work in favor of or against such a goal?

When considering the missionary dimension of American wars, one might ask whether and to what extent the United States' vision of itself as a redeemer nation influences or interferes with foreign policy decision making. How do our understandings of the wars of the twentieth and twenty-first centuries change when we look at them as either democratic "missions" directed toward nondemocratic regimes or Christian missions to non- or anti-Christian societies? Given the fusion of new with old faith that inevitably attends religious conversion, how should those who would wage wars to transform (convert) a nation politically, temper their goals? Religious missions have rarely yielded the intended results and have done so in short order even more rarely. Why, then, should wars of political and cultural conversion yield anything other than syncretic and, to some, unsatisfying outcomes?

These are questions to ponder in the midst of a war that both sides have framed as religious. Answers to such question may help us to understand better the current wars in which the United States is engaged, and the wars that will surely come.

JONATHAN H. EBEL

## Further Reading

Abrams, R. H. (1969). *Preachers present arms: The role of American churches and clergy in World Wars I and II with some observations on the war in Vietnam.* Scottsdale, PA: Herald Press.

Bederman, G. (1995). *Manliness and civilization.* Chicago: University of Chicago Press.

Brown, P. (1967). *Augustine of Hippo: A biography.* Berkeley, CA: University of California Press.

Committee on the War and the Religious Outlook. (1920). *Religion among American men as revealed by a study of conditions in the arm.* New York: Associated Press.

Ebel, J. (2004). *Heroes in the cause of God: Faith, suffering, and American soldiers' experiences of the First World War.* Doctoral dissertation, University of Chicago, Chicago, IL.

Elshtain, J. B. (1992). *Just war theory: A reader.* New York: New York University Press.

Faust, D. G. (1992). *Southern stories: Slaveholders in peace and war.* Columbia, MO: University of Missouri Press.

Jones, J. W. (1887). *Christ in the camp or religion in Lee's army.* Richmond, VA: B.F. Johnson and Co.

Pencak, W. (1989). *For God and country: The American Legion, 1919–1941.* Boston: Northeastern University Press.

Piper, J. (1985). *The American churches in World War I.* Athens, OH: Ohio University Press.

Slotkin, R. (2005). *Lost battalions: The Great War and the crisis of American nationality.* New York: Henry Holt and Company.

Wiley, B. (1943). *The life of Johnny Reb, the common soldier of the Confederacy.* New York: Bobbs-Merril Company.

# Index

Note: Main encyclopedia entries are indicated by **bold** type

# Index

## Index

Commerce, **82–84**
  disciplinary linkage, 84
  mission, empire and, 136–137
  mission blending with, 84
  mission engaging in, 83
  mission in distinction from, 82–83
  mission in opposition to, 83
  mission undone by, 83–84
  *See also* Civilization; Development; Economics; Empire; Globalization; Materiality; Money; Opium; Slavery
Commission on World Mission and Evangelism, 86
Common witness, ecumenism and, 131
Communication, 236
  *See also* Media/mass communication; Oral history; Orality; Photography
Communism, 30, 31, 198, 199
Computers. *See* Internet
Comte, August, 418
Conciliar missions, **85–87**
Conferences. *See* Mission conferences
Confucianism, 242
Congo, 83, 110, 349
Conquest, **87–90**, 102
  *See also* Ancient Church; Christendom; Civilization; Crusades; Empire; Islam; Militarism; Pacifism; Peace churches; Politics; Roman Catholic Church
Conscientious objectors, 208, 319, 330
Constantine I (emperor)
  ancient church and, 13
  Christendom and, 73
  conquest and, 88
  Orthodox/Coptic missions and, 312
  revolution and, 386
Constantinople, 146
Contextualization, **90–96**
Conversion, 25, **97–99**, 138
  *See also* Contextualization; Culture; Education—religious, theological; Medicine; Roman Catholic Church; Theology; Translation
Conze, Edward, 379
Cook, Captain James, 299, 337
Coptic Church, **99–107**
  mission, early, 100
  mission, monasticism and, 100
  mission to, Catholic and Protestant, 102–103
  mission to Africa, 100–101, 104
  mission to Europe, 101–102
  missions, modern, 103–105
  Muslim rule and, 102
  origins, 99–100
  *See also* Africa; Ancient Church; Middle East; Orthodox/Coptic missions
Coronado, Francisco, 151
Costantini, Archbishop Celso, 22
Council of Trent, 107–108, 225
Counter Reformation, **107–109**, 321
  *See also* Christendom; Protestant churches; Reformation; Roman Catholic Church
Coverdale, Miles, 48
CRALOG, 330
Creoles, 2, 57, 58
Criticism, **109–111**
  colonialist, 110
  cultural relativist, 111
  ecclesiastical, 109–110
  indigenous, 110–111
  racist, 110
  telescopic philanthropy, 110
  theological, 109–110
Crowther, Samuel, 152, 416, 446
Crusades, the, **111–114**
  Christendom and, 75
  conquest, Christianity and, 88
  Europe and, 146
  Islam and, 203
  Middle East and, 243
  as militarism, 246–247
  religious communities and, 376
  slavery and, 414
Cuba, 62, 63, 199, 387
Cults, 290, 291, 397
Cultural Revolution, 28, 72, 135, 198
Culture, **114–116**
  history, 114–115

social institutions and, 115
  sports and, 423
  systems of, understanding, 116
  technology and, 433–434
  *See also* Inculturation; Music and ethnomusicology
Cunningham, Loren, 67
Cyril, Saint, 394

Damien, Father (Joseph Damien de Veuster), 51, 300
Dance, religious rituals and, 9, 22, 186
  *See also* Indigenous religions
Daoism, 69
Darby, J. N., 251
Darwinism, 168
Daschke, Derek, 292
David, Armand, 151
Davis, Rev. W. J., 253
Dawn Bible Student's Association, 207
Declaration of Human Rights (United Nations), 349
Declaration of Independence (United States), 140, 183
Declaration of the Rights of Man and Citizen (France), 183
"Decolonizing theology," 60
Delaware Baptist Mission School, 133
Deledeule, Juan, 213
Deng Xiaoping, 31, 72
Dengel, Anna, 240
"Deprogrammers," 291
Descartes, René, 139, 350
Development, **117–120**
  *See also* Environment; Medicine; Mission methods and strategy; Missionary vocation and service
*Dharmadhuta*, 53, 54
Dialogue, **120–122**
Dickens, Charles, 110, 160
Dictionaries, 367–368
Dindinger, Johannes, 49
Directories, 367, 368–369
Disease, treatment/prevention of, 239
  *See also* Medicine
Dispensationalism, 248–249, 251
Dober, Leonard, 275, 374
Dodds, Gil, 425
Dohnavur Fellowship, 66
Dominicans
  exploration and, 151
  family and, 158
  in Latin America, 213
  monasticism and, 269
  religious communities and, 377
Donnelly, Joseph P., 51
Dravecky, Dave, 424
"Dreamtime," 195
Du Bois, W. E. B., 138
Duff, Alexander, 188–189
Dulles, John Foster, 197, 198, 199
Duncan, William, 82
Durkheim, Emile
  secularism, atheism and, 401, 402
  sociology and, 418, 419, 421
Dutch East India Company
  economics and, 123
  India and, 188
  Islam and, 204
  Southeast Asia and, 36
Dutch Reformed Church, 2, 329
Dwane, Bishop Sigqibo, 145
Dwane, James Mata, 144, 145
Dwight, Timothy, 251

East Asia. *See* Asia, East
Eastern Orthodox Church. *See* Orthodox/Coptic missions
Ecclesiology, liberation theology and, 220–221
Economics, **123–127**
  agricultural innovations and, 126
  competition, role of, 126
  concern for those served, 123–124
  education and, 124
  globalization and, 174–175
  internationalism and, 197
  land rights, protecting, 124
  mission, ethics and, 143
  resources, providing, 126
  sex trade and, 403

# Index